TEXTBOOK ON

TORTS

Sixth Edition

Michael A. Jones

Assistant Editor
Alan Sprince

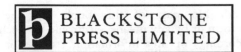
BLACKSTONE
PRESS LIMITED

This edition published in Great Britain 1998 by Blackstone Press Limited, Aldine Place, London W12 8AA. Telephone: 0181-740 2277

First edition, 1986
Second edition, 1989
Reprinted 1990
Third edition, 1991
Reprinted 1992
Fourth edition, 1993
Reprinted 1993, 1994, 1995
Fifth edition, 1996
Reprinted 1997
Sixth edition, 1998

ISBN: 1 85431 844 6

British Library Cataloguing in Publication Data
A CIP cataloguing record for this book is available from the British Library

Typeset by Style Photosetting Ltd, Mayfield, East Sussex
Printed by Ashford Colour Press, Gosport, Hampshire

Contents

Preface   ix
Abbreviations of titles of books   xi
Table of Cases   xiii
Table of Statutes   xlvii

1   PERSPECTIVES   1

1.1 Scope of tort   **1.2 Malice, intention and fault**   **1.3 Role of insurance**   **1.4 Objectives of tort**   1.4.1 Appeasement and justice   **1.4.2 Deterrence and efficiency**   1.4.3 Compensation and loss distribution   **1.5 Accident compensation**

2   NEGLIGENCE I: DUTY OF CARE   25

2.1 General principles   2.1.1 The neighbour principle   **2.1.2 Foreseeability and proximity**   2.1.3 Duty and the unforeseeable plaintiff   **2.1.4 Policy and the function of duty**   **2.2 Excluded interests and limited duties**   2.2.1 Omissions — 2.2.1.1 Undertaking — 2.2.1.2 Relationship between plaintiff and defendant — 2.2.1.3 Control over third parties — 2.2.1.4 Control of land or dangerous things   **2.2.2** Types of plaintiff   **2.2.3** Types of defendant — 2.2.3.1 Legal proceedings — 2.2.3.2 Exercise of statutory powers   **2.2.4** Types of loss — 2.2.4.1 Economic loss: statements — 2.2.4.2 Economic loss: acts — 2.2.4.3 Nervous shock — 2.2.4.4 Other types of loss

3   NEGLIGENCE II: BREACH OF DUTY   172

3.1 The reasonable man   3.1.1 The objective standard   **3.1.2 Unforeseeable harm**   **3.1.3** Foreseeable harm: risk — 3.1.3.1 Magnitude of the risk — 3.1.3.2 Defendant's purpose — 3.1.3.3 Practicability of precautions   **3.1.4 General practice**   **3.2 Special standards**   3.2.1 Professionals   **3.2.2 Sport**   **3.2.3 Children**   **3.2.4 Design**   **3.3 Proof of breach**   3.3.1 Burden of proof   **3.3.2** *Res ipsa loquitur* — 3.3.2.1 Application — 3.3.2.2 Effect

4 NEGLIGENCE III: CAUSATION AND REMOTENESS 201
OF DAMAGE

4.1 Factual causation **4.1.1** The 'but for' test **4.1.2** Proof of causation
4.1.3 Loss of a chance **4.2 Causation in law** **4.2.1** Successive sufficient
causes **4.2.2** Intervening acts — 4.2.2.1 By third parties — 4.2.2.2 By the
plaintiff **4.3 Remoteness of damage** **4.3.1** Foreseeability and directness
4.3.2 Manner of the occurrence **4.3.3** Type of harm **4.3.4** Extent of the
harm — 4.3.4.1 Eggshell skulls — 4.3.4.2 Plaintiff's impecuniosity **4.3.5**
Reflections on *The Wagon Mound* **4.3.6** Other torts

5 NEGLIGENCE IV: EMPLOYERS' LIABILITY   250

5.1 Common law duties **5.1.1** Competent staff **5.1.2** Safe place of work
5.1.3 Proper plant and equipment **5.1.4** Safe system of work **5.2**
Statutory duties **5.3 Defences** **5.3.1** *Volenti non fit injuria* **5.3.2**
Contributory negligence

6 NEGLIGENCE V: DANGEROUS PREMISES   264

6.1 Liability of occupiers to visitors **6.1.1** Occupiers **6.1.2 Visitors**
6.1.3 The common duty of care — 6.1.3.1 Children — 6.1.3.2 Skilled visitors
— 6.1.3.3 Independent contractors — 6.1.3.4 Warning **6.1.4** Acceptance
of risk **6.1.5** Exclusion of liability **6.1.6** Contributory negligence **6.2**
Liability of occupiers to other entrants **6.2.1** Persons other than visitors
6.2.2 Existence of the duty **6.2.3** Content of the duty **6.2.4** Warning
6.2.5 Acceptance of risk **6.2.6** Exclusion of liability **6.3 Liability of**
non-occupiers to entrants **6.3.1** Independent contractors **6.3.2** Landlords **6.3.3** Builders and architects

7 NUISANCE   298

7.1 Private nuisance **7.1.1** Definition and scope **7.1.2** Constituents of
liability — 7.1.2.1 Physical damage — 7.1.2.2 Interference with enjoyment of
land — 7.1.2.3 Interference with servitudes **7.1.3** Unreasonable user —
7.1.3.1 Locality — 7.1.3.2 Abnormal sensitivity — 7.1.3.3 Duration of the
interference — 7.1.3.4 Public benefit — 7.1.3.5 Malice — 7.1.3.6 Natural
condition of the land — 7.1.3.7 Negligence **7.1.4** Who can sue? **7.1.5**
Who is liable? — 7.1.5.1 Creator — 7.1.5.2 Occupier — 7.1.5.3 Landlord —
7.1.6 Defences — 7.1.6.1 Prescription — 7.1.6.2 Statutory authority —
7.1.6.3 Other defences — 7.1.6.4 Ineffective defences **7.1.7** Remedies —
7.1.7.1 Damages — 7.1.7.2 Injunction — 7.1.7.3 Abatement **7.1.8**
Standard of liability **7.2 Public nuisance** **7.2.1** Definition **7.2.2**
Distinguished from private nuisance **7.2.3** The public rights protected —
7.2.3.1 Public health — 7.2.3.2 Convenience: obstruction of the highway —
7.2.3.3 Safety: dangers to the highway **7.2.4** Particular damage **7.2.5**
Standard of liability

8 STRICT LIABILITY 348

8.1 *Rylands* v *Fletcher* **8.1.1 Dangerous things** **8.1.2** Accumulation **8.1.3** Escape **8.1.4** Non-natural use **8.1.5** Who can sue? **8.1.6** Type of damage **8.1.7** Defences — 8.1.7.1 Consent — 8.1.7.2 Plaintiff's default — 8.1.7.3 Act of God — 8.1.7.4 Act of stranger — 8.1.7.5 Statutory authority — 8.1.7.6 Necessity **8.1.8** Remoteness of damage **8.1.9** Future of strict liability for hazardous activities **8.2 Fire** **8.2.1** Liability at common law **8.2.2** Statute **8.3 Animals** **8.3.1** Liability at common law **8.3.2** Animals Act 1971 **8.3.3** Dangerous species **8.3.4** Non-dangerous species **8.3.5** Defences **8.3.6** Straying livestock **8.3.7** Injury to livestock by dogs **8.3.8** Straying on to the highway **8.3.9** Remoteness of damage **8.4 Vicarious liability** **8.4.1** Justification **8.4.2** Basis of liability **8.4.3** Who is a servant? — 8.4.3.1 Lending a servant — 8.4.3.2 Vehicle drivers **8.4.4** Course of employment — 8.4.4.1 Implied and ostensible authority — 8.4.4.2 Express prohibition — 8.4.4.3 Criminal acts **8.4.5** Master's indemnity **8.5 Liability for independent contractors** **8.5.1** Basic rule **8.5.2** Primary liability **8.5.3** Statutory duties **8.5.4** Common law duties — 8.5.4.1 Withdrawal of support — 8.5.4.2 Public nuisance — 8.5.4.3 Hazardous activities — 8.5.4.4 Private nuisance — 8.5.4.5 Master and servant — 8.5.4.6 Bailees — 8.5.4.7 Landlord? **8.5.5** Collateral negligence

9 BREACH OF STATUTORY DUTY 399

9.1 Is the breach actionable? **9.1.1** Statutory remedy **9.1.2** Common law remedy **9.1.3** Benefit of a class **9.1.4** Public rights and particular damage **9.1.5** Public utilities **9.2 Statutory negligence** **9.3 Ambit of the statute** **9.4 Causation** **9.5 Defences**

10 DEFECTIVE PRODUCTS 416

10.1 Common law **10.1.1** Manufacturers' duty **10.1.2** Extending the duty **10.1.3** Intermediate inspection **10.1.4** Causation and contributory negligence **10.1.5** Warning **10.1.6** Continuing duty **10.1.7** Proof **10.1.8** Type of loss **10.2 Statute** **10.2.1** Plaintiffs **10.2.2** Defendants **10.2.3** Products **10.2.4** Defects **10.2.5** Type of loss **10.2.6** Causation **10.2.7** Defences and limitation 10.2.7.1 Miscellaneous defences — 10.2.7.2 Development risks — 10.2.7.3 Limitation

11 TRESPASS TO LAND 442

11.1 Nature of the action **11.1.1** Intention **11.1.2** Damage **11.1.3** Trespass and nuisance **11.2 The interference** **11.2.1** Types of trespass **11.2.2** Airspace and subsoil **11.2.3** Highways **11.3 Justification** **11.3.1** Licence **11.3.2** Rights of entry **11.3.3** Trespass *ab initio* **11.4 Possession: who can sue?** **11.5 Remedies**

12   TRESPASS TO THE PERSON   453

12.1 Trespass and negligence   12.2 Assault and battery   12.3 Criminal injuries   12.4 False imprisonment   12.5 Defences   12.5.1 Consent **12.5.2** Lawful arrest   **12.5.3** Self-defence   **12.6 Malicious prosecution 12.6.1** Initiating proceedings   **12.6.2** Prosecution ended in the plaintiff's favour   **12.6.3** No reasonable and probable cause   **12.6.4** Malice   **12.6.5** Damage

13   DEFAMATION   485

13.1 The cause of action   13.1.1 What is defamatory?   **13.1.2** Reference to the plaintiff   **13.1.3** Publication   **13.1.4** Libel and slander   **13.2 Defences   13.2.1** Truth (or justification)   **13.2.2** Absolute privilege — 13.2.2.1** Parliamentary proceedings — **13.2.2.2** Judicial proceedings — **13.2.2.3** Official communications   **13.2.3** Qualified privilege — 13.2.3.1 Statements in pursuance of a duty — **13.2.3.2** Protection of an interest — **13.2.3.3** Privileged reports   **13.2.4** Fair comment — **13.2.4.1** Matters of public interest — **13.2.4.2** Comment and fact — **13.2.4.3** What is 'fair' comment?   **13.2.5** Malice

14   DEFENCES AND LIMITATION   522

14.1 *Volenti non fit injuria*   14.1.1 Voluntary   **14.1.2** Agreement **14.1.3** Knowledge   **14.1.4** Drunken drivers and sporting events   **14.2 Excluding liability   14.3 Illegality   14.4 Other defences   14.4.1** Mistake   **14.4.2** Inevitable accident   **14.4.3** Necessity   **14.5 Contributory negligence   14.5.1** Scope of the Law Reform (Contributory Negligence) Act 1945   **14.5.2** Causation   **14.5.3** Standard of care — 14.5.3.1 Children — 14.5.3.2 The infirm — 14.5.3.3 Workmen — 14.5.3.4 Emergency   **14.5.4** Apportionment   **14.6 Contribution between tortfeasors   14.7 Limitation   14.7.1** Personal injuries and death   **14.7.2** Latent damage   **14.7.3** Deliberate concealment   **14.7.4** Persons under a disability

15   REMEDIES AND DEATH   574

15.1 Damages   15.1.1 Types of damages — **15.1.1.1** Nominal and contemptuous — **15.1.1.2** General and special — **15.1.1.3** Aggravated and exemplary   **15.1.2** A single action and the lump sum   **15.1.3** Personal injuries — **15.1.3.1** Medical and other expenses — **15.1.3.2** Loss of earnings — **15.1.3.3** Pain and suffering — **15.1.3.4** Loss of faculty and amenity **15.1.4** Damage to property   **15.1.5** Economic loss from misstatements **15.1.6** Mitigation   **15.1.7** Interest on damages **15.2 Injunction   15.3 Death in relation to tort   15.3.1** Survival of actions   **15.3.2** Fatal accidents and loss of dependency — **15.3.2.1** The action — **15.3.2.2** Dependants — 15.3.2.3 Damages

Index   621

Preface

The appellate courts have, as usual, been kept busy over the last couple of years adding to the volume of case law in torts. Sometimes the effect is greater clarity, but on other occasions, unfortunately the result is more confusion. The House of Lords has effectively re-written the law of private nuisance in *Hunter* v *Canary Wharf Ltd* (1997) (having previously emasculated what was left of the rule in *Rylands* v *Fletcher* in *Cambridge Water* v *Eastern Counties Leather plc* (1994)). This has undoubtedly created greater conceptual clarity, but arguably at the cost of some entirely arbitrary consequences. Indeed, on one theory the law of nuisance no longer belongs in a book on Torts but in a textbook on Land Law, but it would be a pity to cede the subject to the property lawyers, and readers may be reassured to see that this book retains a chapter on Nuisance. In *Bolitho* v *City and Hackney Health Authority* (1997) the House of Lords has restated the basic propositions of the *Bolam* test for the purposes of professional liability, but with much clearer guidance on when the courts are entitled to discount expert evidence on the question of whether a professional person has acted negligently; and the very recent decision of the House of Lords in *Wells* v *Wells* (1998) is of enormous practical significance for the assessment of damages in personal injury actions. In this edition I have been able to include more detailed discussion of the House of Lords' decision in *Stovin* v *Wise* (1996), which only became available at the proof stage of the last edition.

The Court of Appeal has also been active with decisions on the liability of (*Capital and Counties plc* v *Hampshire County Council* (1997)) and liability to (*Frost* v *Chief Constable of South Yorkshire* (1997)) professional rescuers. *Frost*, in particular, raises far more questions than it even begins to answer about liability for negligently inflicted psychiatric damage, creating yet more anomalous rules in one of the most troubling areas of tort liability. We still await the ruling of the House of Lords in *Frost*, but, if history is anything to go by, it would be expecting far too much for their Lordships to put this area of negligence onto a rational basis. The government should act to implement the Law Commission's proposals with all speed. The Court of Appeal also appears to have extended the immunity from suit of advocates, probably unnecessarily, in *Kelley* v *Corston* (1997), and has taken somewhat divergent approaches to the defence of *ex turpi causa* in *Clunis* v *Camden and Islington Health Authority* (1998) and *Reeves* v *Commissioner of Police of the Metropolis* (1998). In the tort of defamation, the Court seems to be inching towards a general defence of privilege for comments made about public figures, which would bring English law more into line with the position in the United States and Commonwealth jurisdictions (see *Reynolds* v *Times Newspapers* (1998); though note that discussion of this case in chapter 13 is not based on the full report).

I am delighted to welcome my colleague, Alan Sprince, as Assistant Editor for this edition. I am sure that his contributions have improved the book at numerous points. As ever, thanks go to Blackstone for their amazing efficiency in turning manuscript into text, which makes it possible to keep the book right up-to-date, and accordingly the law is stated as at August 1998.

Michael Jones
Liverpool
September 1998

Abbreviations of titles of books

Atiyah	P. Cane, *Atiyah's Accidents, Compensation and the Law*, 5th ed., 1994.
Buckley	R.A. Buckley, *The Law of Nuisance*, 2nd ed., 1996.
Burrows	A.S. Burrows, *Remedies for Torts and Breach of Contract*, 2nd ed., 1994.
Charlesworth and Percy	R.A. Percy, *Charlesworth and Percy on Negligence*, 8th ed., 1990.
Clerk and Lindsell	M. Brazier (general editor), *Clerk and Lindsell on Torts*, 17th ed., 1995.
Dugdale and Stanton	A.M. Dugdale and K.M. Stanton, *Professional Negligence*, 2nd ed., 1989.
Faulks	Report of the Committee on Defamation, Cmnd 5909, 1975.
Fleming	J.G. Fleming, *The Law of Torts*, 8th ed., 1992.
Hepple and Matthews	B.A. Hepple and M.H. Matthews, *Tort: Cases and Materials*, 4th ed., 1991.
Jackson and Powell	R.M. Jackson and J.L. Powell, *Professional Negligence*, 4th ed., 1997
Pearson	Royal Commission on Civil Liability and Compensation for Personal Injury, Cmnd 7054, 1978.
Salmond and Heuston	R.F.V. Heuston and R.A. Buckley, *Salmond and Heuston on the Law of Torts*, 21st ed., 1996.

Stanton   K.M. Stanton, *Breach of Statutory Duty in Tort*,
                           1986.

Street   M. Brazier, *Street on Torts*, 9th ed., 1993.

Weir   Tony Weir, *A Casebook on Tort*, 8th ed., 1996.

Williams and Hepple   G. Williams and B.A. Hepple, *Foundations of the
                           Law of Tort*, 2nd ed., 1984.

Winfield and Jolowicz   W.V.H. Rogers, *Winfield and Jolowicz on Tort*, 14th
                           ed., 1994.

Table of Cases

A.C. Billings & Sons Ltd v Riden [1958] AC 240 — 290
AB Marintrans v Comet Shipping Co. Ltd [1985] 3 All ER 442 — 547
AB v South West Water Services Ltd [1993] 1 All ER 609 — 577, 579, 580
AB v Tameside & Glossop Health Authority [1997] 8 Med LR 91 — 164
Abbassy v Commissioner of Police of the Metropolis [1990] 1 All ER 193 — 479
Acton v Graham Pearce & Co. [1997] 3 All ER 909 — 63, 68
Adam v Ward [1917] AC 309 — 506
Adams v Southern Electricity Board, The Times, 21 October 1993 — 287
Adams v Ursell [1913] 1 Ch 269 — 332
Addis v Crocker [1961] 1 QB 11 — 505
Addis v Odhams Press Ltd [1958] 2 QB 275 — 516, 517
Admiralty Commissioners v SS Amerika [1917] AC 38 — 615
Admiralty Commissioners v SS Volute [1922] 1 AC 129 — 551
Adsett v West [1983] 2 All ER 985 — 597
Airedale NHS Trust v Bland [1993] 1 All ER 821, HL — 470, 471, 474
Akerhielm v De Mare [1959] AC 789 — 91
Al-Kandari v J.R. Brown & Co. [1988] 1 All ER 833, CA — 66, 122
Al Saudi Banque v Clark Pixley [1989] 3 All ER 361 — 107
Albert v Lavin [1982] AC 546; [1981] 1 All ER 628 — 477, 479, 481
Alcock v Chief Constable of the South Yorkshire Police [1991] 4 All ER 907 — 144, 145, 148, 149, 152, 155, 160, 165, 166
Alcock v Wraith, The Times, 23 December 1991 — 395
Alderson v Booth [1969] 2 QB 216 — 465
Alexander v North Eastern Railway Co. (1865) 6 B & S 340 — 501
Alexandrou v Oxford [1993] 4 All ER 328, CA — 69, 71
Allan v Liverpool Overseers (1874) LR 9 QB 180 — 449
Allan v New Mount Sinai Hospital (1980) 109 DLR (3d) 635 — 474
Allason v Campbell, The Times, 8 May 1996 — 485
Allason v Haines (1995) 145 NLJ 1576 — 504
Allen v Flood [1898] AC 1 — 26
Allen v Gulf Oil Refining Ltd [1981] AC 1001; [1979] 3 All ER 1008 — 326, 327, 328, 329, 335
Alliance and Leicester Building Society v Edgestop Ltd [1994] 2 All ER 38 — 545
Allied Finance & Investments Ltd v Haddow & Co. [1983] NZLR 22 — 102
Allied Maples Group Ltd v Simmons & Simmons [1995] 4 All ER 907 — 205, 217, 218, 221
Allin v City & Hackney Health Authority [1996] 7 Med LR 167 — 164
Allsop v Church of England Newspaper Ltd [1972] 2 QB 161 — 493
Alston v Marine & Trade Insurance Co. Ltd 1964 (4) SA 112 — 228

Amann v Damm (1860) 8 CB (NS) 597   510
American Cyanamid Co. v Ethicon Ltd [1975] AC 396   613
AMF International Ltd v Magnet Bowling Ltd [1968] 1 WLR 1028   273
Ancell v McDermott [1993] 4 All ER 355, CA   69
Anchor Brewhouse Developments Ltd v Berkley House
   (Docklands Developments) Ltd (1987) 38 BLR 82   444, 445, 449, 450
Anderson v Coutts (1894) 58 JP 369   268
Andrews v Hopkinson [1957] 1 QB 229   419, 423
Andrews v Schooling [1991] 3 All ER 723   296
Angus v Dalton (1881) 6 App Cas 740   322
Anns v Merton London Borough Council [1978] AC 728   28, 29, 32, 37, 45, 48, 49,
          52, 77, 78, 124, 128, 132, 133, 134, 136, 137, 140, 141, 144, 293, 296, 533, 568
Applegate v Moss [1971] 1 QB 406   572
Appleton v Garrett [1996] PIQR P1   476, 577
Archer v Brown [1984] 2 All ER 267   580
Arenson v Casson Beckman Rutley & Co. [1977] AC 405   63
Argentino, The (1889) 14 App Cas 519   227
Argy Trading Development Co. Ltd v Lapid Developments Ltd [1977] 3 All ER 785   101
Armagas Ltd v Mundogas SA [1985] 3 All ER 795; [1986] 2 All ER 385, HL   386, 390
Armstrong v Sheppard & Short Ltd [1959] 2 QB 384   447, 449, 612, 613
Arnold v Teno (1978) 83 DLR (3d) 609   54
Arora v Bradford City Metropolitan Council [1991] 3 All ER 545   580
Arpad, The [1934] P 189   224, 243
Arthur v Anker [1996] RTR 308, CA   526
Ashcroft v Mersey Regional Health Authority [1983] 2 All ER 245   185, 195, 199
Ashdown v Samuel Williams & Sons Ltd [1957] 1 QB 409   253, 275
Asher v Whitlock (1865) LR 1 QB 1   450
Ashton v Turner [1981] QB 137   59, 526, 528, 529, 536, 539, 541, 542
Aspro Travel Ltd v Owners Abroad Group plc [1995] 4 All ER 728, CA   490, 495, 502
Associated Newspapers Group plc v Insert Media Ltd [1988] 2 All ER 420   613
Associated Provincial Picture Houses Ltd v Wednesbury Corporation [1948] 1 KB 223   78
Aswan Engineering Establishment Co. v Lupdine Ltd [1987] 1 All ER 135
                                                            134, 420, 421, 429, 436
Athey v Leonati [1997] 1 WWR 97   212, 244
Atkinson v Newcastle Waterworks Co. (1877) 2 ExD 441   403, 410
Attia v British Gas [1987] 3 All ER 455   144, 151, 160
Attorney-General of St Christopher v Reynolds [1980] AC 637   578
Attorney-General's Reference (No. 6 of 1980) [1981] QB 715   470, 481
Attorney-General v Birmingham Corporation (1858) 4 K & J 528   334
Attorney-General v Brighton & Hove Co-operative Supply Association [1890] 1 Ch 276   342
Attorney-General v Cory Brothers & Co. Ltd [1921] 1 AC 521   358
Attorney-General v Gastonia Coaches Ltd [1977] RTR 219   342
Attorney-General v Keymer Brick & Tile Co. Ltd (1903) 67 JP 434   341
Attorney-General v PYA Quarries Ltd [1957] 2 QB 169   340
Attwood v Chapman [1914] 3 KB 275   505
Audsley v Leeds City Council, The Times, 2 June 1988   567
Austin v Dowling (1870) LR 5 CP 534   481
Awad v Pillai [1982] RTR 266   36

B (A minor) (Wardship: sterilisation) [1987] 2 All ER 206   472
B v Curry (1997) 146 DLR (4th) 72   390
B v Islington Health Authority [1992] 3 All ER 833, CA   58
Baddeley v Earl Granville (1887) 19 QBD 423   414
Baker v Bolton (1808) 1 Camp 493   615
Baker v James Bros & Sons Ltd [1921] 2 KB 674   261
Baker v Kaye [1997] IRLR 219   116, 117
Baker v Market Harborough Cooperative Society Ltd [1953] 1 WLR 1472   195

Baker v T. Clarke (Leeds) Ltd [1992] PIQR P262 257
Baker v T.E. Hopkins & Son Ltd [1959] 3 All ER 225; [1958] 3 All ER 147 60, 61, 525
Baker v Willoughby [1970] AC 467 208, 215, 224, 225, 226
Balfour v Barty-King [1957] 1 QB 496 364, 395
Ballard v North British Railway Co. 1923 SC (HL) 43 198
Ballina Shire Council v Ringland (1994) 33 NSWLR 680 488
Bamford v Turnley (1862) 3 B & S 66 308
Bank of Montreal v Dominion Gresham Guarantee & Casualty Co. [1930] AC 659 182
Bank of Nova Scotia v Hellenic Mutual War Risks Association (Bermuda) Ltd
 [1991] 3 All ER 1, HL; [1989] 3 All ER 628 5, 101
Bank voor Handel en Scheepvart NV v Slatford [1953] 1 QB 248 378
Banque Bruxelles Lambert SA v Eagle Star Insurance Co. Ltd [1995] 2 All ER 769 608
Barbara v Home Office (1984) 134 NLJ 888 576
Barclays Bank plc v Fairclough Building Ltd [1995] 1 All ER 289, CA;
 (1995) 76 BLR 1 6, 8, 547
Barclays Bank plc v Khaira [1992] 1 WLR 623 101
Barkway v South Wales Transport Co. Ltd [1950] 1 All ER 392 198
Barnes v Hampshire County Council [1969] 3 All ER 746 55, 193
Barnes v Lucille Ltd (1907) 96 LT 680 371
Barnes v Nayer, The Times, 19 December 1986 470, 535, 545
Barnes v Ward (1850) 9 CB 392 345
Barnett v Chelsea & Kensington Hospital Management Committee [1969] 1 QB 428 47, 203
Barnett v Cohen [1921] 2 KB 46 1 619
Barnett v H. and J. Packer & Co. Ltd [1940] 3 All ER 575 419
Barrett v Enfield London Borough Council [1997] 3 All ER 171 40, 84
Barrett v Lounova (1982) Ltd [1989] 1 All ER 351 292
Barrett v Ministry of Defence [1995] 3 All ER 87, CA 47, 54, 523, 528
Barrow v Bankside Members Agency Ltd [1996] 1 WLR 257 582
Barwick v English Joint Stock Bank (1867) LR 2 Ex 259 390
Basebé v Matthews (1867) LR 2 CP 684 483
Basildon District Council v J. E. Lesser (Properties) Ltd [1985] 1 All ER 20 547
Batty v Metropolitan Property Realisations Ltd [1978] QB 554 4, 128
Baxter v Woolcombers Ltd (1963) 107 SJ 553 553
Bayley v Manchester, Sheffield & Lincolnshire Railway Co. (1873) LR 8 CP 148 384
Bayoumi v Protim Services Ltd [1996] EGCS 187 296
Beach v Freeson [1972] 1 QB 14 510, 512
Beard v London General Omnibus Co. [1900] 2 QB 530 384, 385
Beasley v Buckinghamshire County Council [1997] PIQR P473 86
Beaumont v Humberts [1990] 49 EG 46 104, 105
Bechard v Haliburton (1991) 84 DLR (4th) 668 148, 149
Beckford v R [1987] 3 All ER 425 480, 481
Beecham v Hughes (1988) 52 DLR (4th) 625 BCCA 158
Behrens v Bertram Mills Circus Ltd [1957] 2 QB 1 367, 368
Bell-Booth Group Ltd v Attorney-General [1989] 3 NZLR 148 170, 500, 508
Bell v Peter Browne & Co. [1990] 3 All ER 124 560, 569
Ben Stansfield (Carlisle) Ltd v Carlisle City Council (1982) 265 EG 475 26
Benjamin v Storr (1874) LR 9 CP 400 345, 346
Bennett v Commissioner of Police of the Metropolis [1995] 1 WLR 488 468
Bennett v Tugwell [1971] 2 QB 267 526, 527
Benning v Wong (1968) 43 ALJR 467 362
Benson v Lee [1972] VR 879 149
Bentley v Bristol & Western Health Authority [1991] 2 Med LR 359 562
Bentley v Wright [1997] 2 VR 175 101
Berg Sons & Co. Ltd v Adams (1992) 8 PN 167 108
Bergin v David Wickes Television [1994] PIQR P167, 168 199
Berkoff v Burchill [1996] 4 All ER 1008 490
Bernstein v Skyviews & General Ltd [1978] QB 479 445

Berntt v Vancouver City [1997] 4 WWR 505   480
Berriello v Felixstowe Dock & Railway Co. [1989] 1 WLR 695   602
Berry v British Transport Commission [1962] 1 QB 306   484
Best v Wellcome Foundation Ltd [1994] 5 Med LR 81   208, 422, 426
Bhoomidas v Port of Singapore Authority [1978] 1 All ER 956   381
Bigsharles v Merkel [1973] 1 WWR 324   535
Birch v Mills [1995] 9 CL 354   367
Bird v Holbrook (1828) 4 Bing 628   288, 481
Bird v Jones (1845) 7 QB 742   465
Bird v King Line Ltd [1970] 2 Lloyd's Rep 349   272
Birkett v Hayes [1982] 2 All ER 710   612
Bishop v Arts & Letters Club of Toronto (1978) 83 DLR (3d) 107   244
Blackshaw v Lord [1983] 2 All ER 311   510, 514
Blake v Barnard (1840) 9 C & P 626   455
Bliss v Hall (1838) 4 Bing NC 183   332
Blue Circle Industries plc v Ministry of Defence [1998] 3 All ER 385, CA   363
Blyth v Birmingham Waterworks Co. (1856) 11 Exch 781   173
Blyth v Bloomsbury Area Health Authority (1987) 5 PN 167;
     [1993] 4 Med LR 151, CA   472
Boardman v Sanderson [1964] 1 WLR 1317   147
Bognor Regis Urban District Council v Campion [1972] 2 QB 169   488
Bolam v Friern Hospital Management Committee [1957] 2 All ER 118   183, 205, 473
Bolitho v City and Hackney Health Authority [1997] 4 All ER 771   185, 187, 205, 206, 220
Bolton v Stone [1951] AC 850, HL   33, 177, 178, 181, 269, 312, 345
Bond v Chief Constable of Kent [1983] 1 All ER 456   464
Bone v Seal [1975] 1 All ER 787   300, 333
Bonnard v Perryman [1891] 2 Ch 269   613
Bonnington Castings Ltd v Wardlaw [1956] AC 613   145, 209, 210, 212, 214, 414
Boothman v British Northrop Ltd (1972) 13 KIR 112   555
Boston v W.S. Bagshaw & Sons [1966] 2 All ER 906   514
Botterill v Whytehead (1879) 41 LT 588   510, 520
Bottomley v Bannister [1932] 1 KB 458   292
Bottomley v Brougham [1908] 1 KB 584   503
Bottomley v F.W. Woolworth & Co. Ltd (1932) 48 TLR 521   497
Bourhill v Young [1943] AC 92   25, 35, 59, 147, 149, 244
Bova v Spring [1994] 5 Med LR 120, 122   189
Bow Valley Huskey (Bermuda) Ltd v Saint John Shipbuilding Ltd
     (1997) 153 DLR (4th) 385   125, 126
Bowater v Rowley Regis Corporation [1944] KB 476   524
Bower v Peate (1876) 1 QBD 321   322, 394
Bowman v Harland and Wolff plc [1992] IRLR 349   213
Box v Jubb (1879) 4 ExD 76   359, 361
Boyd v Great Northern Railway Co. [1895] 2 IR 555   345
Boyle v Kodak Ltd [1969] 2 All ER 439   257, 262, 414, 415
Bradburn v Great Western Railway (1874) LR 10 Ex 1   601
Bradburn v Lindsay [1983] 2 All ER 408   317
Bradford Corporation v Pickles [1895] AC 587   313, 314
Bradford v Robinson Rentals Ltd [1967] 1 All ER 267   241
Bradley v Eagle Star Insurance Co. Ltd [1989] 2 WLR 568   13
Brady v Department of Environment for Northern Ireland [1990] 5 NIJB 9   282
Brandeis Goldschmidt & Co. Ltd v Western Transport Ltd [1981] QB 864   607
Brandon v Osborne, Garrett & Co. Ltd [1924] 1 KB 548   229
Bray v Palmer [1953] 1 WLR 1455   195
Brazier v Skipton Rock Co. Ltd [1962] 1 WLR 471   260
Brent Walker Group plc v Time Out Ltd [1991] 2 All ER 753   516
Brew Brothers Ltd v Snax (Ross) Ltd [1970] 1 QB 612   325
Brewer Bros v The Queen in right of Canada (1991) 80 DLR (4th) 321   52

Brice v Brown [1984] 1 All ER 997   149, 243
Bridlington Relay Ltd v Yorkshire Electricity Board [1965] 1 All ER 264   303
Bristol and West Building Society v Fancy and Jackson [1997] 4 All ER 582   548, 609
Bristol and West Building Society v Mothew [1996] 4 All ER 698   91, 109, 609
Bristow v Grout, The Times, 9 November 1987, CA   582
Britannia Building Society v Hallas (t/a Wilds and Griffiths) [1997] EGCS 117   548
British Celanese Ltd v A.H. Hunt (Capacitors) Ltd [1969] 1 WLR 959;
      [1969] 2 All ER 1252;   126, 311, 353, 357
British Columbia Electric Railway Co. Ltd v Loach [1916] 1 AC 719   545
British Railways Board v Herrington [1972] AC 877
                                 58, 267, 270, 278, 279, 282, 283, 288, 291, 315
British Road Services Ltd v A. V. Crutchley & Co. Ltd [1967] 1 WLR 835   396
British Road Services v Slater [1964] 1 WLR 498   324
British Telecommunications plc v James Thomson & Sons (Engineers) Ltd
      (1996) 82 BLR 1   5, 534
British Transport Commission v Gourley [1956] AC 185   592
Broadley v Guy Clapham & Co. [1994] 4 All ER 439   562
Broadway Approvals Ltd v Odhams Press Ltd [1965] 1 WLR 805   520
Broome v Cassell & Co. Ltd [1972] AC 1027   576, 578, 579, 581
Brown v Hawkes [1891] 2 QB 718   483, 484
Brown v National Coal Board [1962] AC 574   260, 412
Brown v Rolls-Royce Ltd [1960] 1 WLR 210   182
Browne v D.C. Thomson & Co. 1912 SC 359   495
Browne v Dawson (1840) 12 A & E 624   449
Browning v War Office [1963] 1 QB 750   602
Brunsden v Humphrey (1884) 14 QBD 141   582, 584
Brushett v Cowan (1990) 69 DLR (4th) 743   474
Bryan v Maloney (1995) 128 ALR 163   143
Bryanston Finance Ltd v De Vries [1975] QB 703   512
Bryce v Swan Hunter Group plc [1988] 1 All ER 659   214
Buchan v Ortho Pharmaceuticals (Canada) Ltd (1986) 25 DLR (4th) 658   423, 424, 425
Buck v English Electric Co. Ltd [1977] 1 WLR 806   562
Buckland v Guildford Gas Light & Coke Co. [1944] 1 KB 410   290, 291
Bull v Devon Area Health Authority (1989), [1993] 4 Med LR 117   392
Bulli Coal Mining Co. v Osborne [1899] AC 351   445
Bunker v Charles Brand & Sons Ltd [1969] 2 QB 480   265, 275
Burgess v Gray (1845) 1 CB 578   343
Burke v Tower Hamlets Health Authority, The Times, 10 August 1989   584
Burmah Oil Co. Ltd v Lord Advocate [1965] AC 75   544
Burnett v British Waterways Board [1973] 2 All ER 631   275, 276, 525
Burnett v George (1986), [1992] 1 FLR 525   458
Burnie Port Authority v General Jones Pty Ltd (1994) 120 ALR 42   352
Burns v Edman [1970] 2 QB 541   540
Burris v Azadani [1995] 4 All ER 802   343, 459, 613
Burton v Winters [1993] 1 WLR 1077   335, 336, 452
Business Computers International Ltd v Registrar of Companies [1987] 3 All ER 465   63
Butterfield v Forrester (1809) 11 East 60   544
Bux v Slough Metals Ltd [1974] 1 All ER 262   204, 260, 412
Byrne v Boadle (1863) 2 H & C 722   197
Byrne v Deane [1937] 1 KB 818   490, 496
Bywell Castle (1879) 4 PD 219   190, 555

C (adult: refusal of treatment), Re [1994] 1 WLR 290   470
C v S [1987] 1 All ER 1230   471
Calascione v Dixon (1993) 19 BMLR 97   145
Calgarth, The [1927] P 93   268
Calliope, The [1970] P 172   233, 556

Caltex Oil (Australia) Pty Ltd v Dredge Willemstad (1976) 136 CLR 529   125, 126
Calveley v Chief Constable of the Merseyside Police [1989] 1 All ER 1025, 1030   42, 69
Cambridge Water Co. v Eastern Counties Leather [1994] 2 WLR 53
        249, 300, 307, 321, 336, 337, 339, 350, 351, 352, 353, 354, 355, 357, 359, 361, 362
Caminer v Northern & London Investment Trust Ltd [1951] AC 99   345
Campbell v Spottiswoode (1863) 3 B & S 769   518
Campbelltown City Council v Mackay (1989) 15 NSWLR 501   158
Canadian National Railway Co. v Norsk Pacific Steamship Co. Ltd
    (1992) 91 DLR (4th) 289   125
Canadian Pacific Hotels Ltd v Bank of Montreal (1988) 40 DLR (4th) 432   5
Canadian Pacific Railway Co. v Lockhart [1942] AC 591   386
Candler v Crane Christmas & Co. [1951] 2 KB 164   106
Candlewood Navigation Corporation Ltd v Mitsui OSK Lines Ltd
    [1985] 2 All ER 935, PC   126, 130
Caparo Industries plc v Dickman [1990] 1 All ER 568
        30, 31, 32, 33, 34, 36, 89, 95, 97, 104, 108, 110, 115, 151, 222
Capital & Counties Bank Ltd v Henty & Son (1882) 7 App Cas 741   490
Capital and Counties plc v Hampshire County Council [1997] 2 All ER 865   40, 44, 48, 70
Capps v Miller [1989] 2 All ER 333   549, 555, 557
Carmarthenshire County Council v Lewis [1955] AC 549   54, 55, 193
Carpenters' Co. v British Mutual Banking Co. Ltd [1937] 3 All ER 811   182
Carr-Glynn v Frearsons [1997] 2 All ER 614   122
Carr v Mercantile Produce Co. Ltd [1949] 2 KB 601   553
Carroll v Fearon, The Times, 26 January 1998, CA   425
Carslogie Steamship Co. Ltd v Royal Norwegian Government
    [1952] AC 292   223, 224, 226
Carson v John Fairfax and Sons Ltd (1993) 67 ALJR 634   486
Cartledge v E. Jopling & Sons Ltd [1963] AC 758   561, 566
Cassidy v Daily Mirror Newspapers Ltd [1929] 2 KB 331   489, 492, 494
Cassidy v Ministry of Health [1951] 2 KB 343   195, 197, 378, 379, 380, 392
Castle v St Augustine's Links (1922) 38 TLR 615   312, 345
Castorina v Chief Constable of Surrey [1988] NLJ Law Rep 180   479
Caswell v Powell Duffryn Associated Collieries Ltd [1940] AC 152   414, 554
Cattle v Stockton Waterworks Co. (1875) LR 10 QB 453   125
Cavalier v Pope [1906] AC 428   291
Cavanagh v Ulster Weaving Co. Ltd [1960] AC 145   182
CBS Songs Ltd v Amstrad Consumer Electronics plc [1988] 2 All ER 484   29
Cekan v Haines (1990) 22 NSWLR 296   181
Central Trust Co. v Rafuse (1986) 31 DLR (4th) 481   4, 8
Century Insurance Co. Ltd v Northern Ireland Road Transport Board [1942] AC 509   384
Chadwick v British Railways Board [1967] 1 WLR 912   59, 147, 150, 153, 154
Chamberlain v Boyd (1883) 11 QBD 407   498
Chaplain of Gray's Inn Case (1400) YB 2 Hen 4   480
Chaplin v Hicks [1911] 2 KB 786   216, 219
Chaplin v Westminster Corporation [1901] 2 Ch 329   346
Chapman v Ellesmere [1932] 2 KB 431   510
Chappell v Cooper [1980] 2 All ER 463   565
Chaproniere v Mason (1905) 21 TLR 633   197
Charing Cross Electricity Supply Co. v Hydraulic Power Co. [1914] 3 KB 772, CA   357
Charleston v News Group Newspapers Ltd [1995] 2 All ER 313   491
Charlton v Forrest Printing Ink Co. Ltd [1980] IRLR 331   54
Chasemore v Richards (1859) 7 HL Cas 349   313
Chatterton v Gerson [1981] 1 All ER 257   204, 471, 475
Chatterton v Secretary of State for India [1895] 2 QB 189   506
Chaudhry v Prabhaker [1988] 3 All ER 718   98, 99
Chic Fashions (West Wales) Ltd v Jones [1968] 2 QB 299   448
China & South Sea Bank Ltd v Tan Soon Gin [1989] 3 All ER 839   170

Chipchase v British Titan Products Co. Ltd [1956] 1 QB 545 413
Christie v Davey [1893] 1 Ch 316 313
Christie v Leachinsky [1947] AC 573 479
Church of Jesus Christ of Latter Day Saints (Great Britain) v Yorkshire Fire
  and Civil Defence Authority [1997] 2 All ER 865 70
Church of Scientology of California v Johnson-Smith [1972] 1 QB 522 503
Cinnamond v British Airports Authority [1980] 2 All ER 368 448
City of Kamloops v Nielsen (1984) 10 DLR (4th) 641 52, 143
City of Richmond v Scantelbury [1991] 2 VR 38 316, 335
Claridge v Mackenzie (1842) 4 Man & G. 142 450
Clark v Chambers (1878) 3 QBD 327 343
Clark v MacLennan [1983] 1 All ER 416 199, 211
Clark v Molyneux (1877) 3 QBD 237 520
Clarke v Bruce Lance & Co. [1988] 1 All ER 364 102, 122
Clarke v Rotax Aircraft Equipment Ltd [1975] 1 WLR 1054 604
Clay v Crump & Sons Ltd [1964] 1 QB 533 118
Clayards v Dethick (1848) 12 QB 439 527
Clayton v Woodman & Sons (Builders) Ltd [1962] 2 QB 533 118
Clegg Parkinson & Co. v Earby Gas Co. [1896] 1 QB 592 410
Clegg v Dearden (1848) 12 QB 576 444
Clifford v Charles H. Challen & Son Ltd [1951] 1 KB 495 257
Clippens Oil Co. v Edinburgh & District Water Trustees [1907] AC 291 611
Close v Steel Co. of Wales Ltd [1962] AC 367 259, 260, 413
Clough v Bussan [1990] 1 All ER 431 69
Clunis v Camden & Islington Health Authority [1998] 3 All ER 180 84, 236, 539
Co-Operative Wholesale Society Ltd v British Railways Board, The Times,
  20 December 1995 335
Coad v Cornwall and Isles of Scilly Health Authority [1997] 1 WLR 189 562
Cockcroft v Smith (1705) 11 Mod 43 480
Cocks v Thanet District Council [1983] 2 AC 286 402
Cohen v Daily Telegraph Ltd [1968] 1 WLR 916 517
Cole v Turner (1704) 6 Mod 149 456
Coleridge v Miller Construction Ltd 1997 SLT 485 123
Colledge v Bass Mitchells & Butlers Ltd [1988] 1 All ER 536 603
Collier v Anglian Water Authority, The Times, 26 March 1983 266
Collins v Hertfordshire County Council [1947] KB 598 377
Collins v Renison (1754) 1 Say 138 452, 481
Collins v Wilcock [1984] 3 All ER 374 455, 456, 457, 456, 464
Coltman v Bibby Tankers Ltd [1988] AC 276 255
Colvilles Ltd v Devine [1969] 1 WLR 475 198
Commission of the European Communities v UK (C300/95)
  [1997] All ER (EC) (1) 481 440
Commissioners of Inland Revenue v Hoogstraten [1984] 3 All ER 25 63
Condon v Basi [1985] 2 All ER 453 191, 469, 529
Connolly v Camden & Islington Area Health Authority [1981] 3 All ER 250 597
Constantine v Imperial Hotels Ltd [1944] KB 693 575
Control Risks Ltd v New English Library Ltd [1989] 3 All ER 577 516
Conway v George Wimpey & Co. Ltd [1951] 2 KB 266 388, 443
Cook v Beal (1697) 1 Ld Raym 176 480
Cook v Cook (1986) 68 ALR 353 174, 189
Cook v Lewis [1952] 1 DLR 1 195, 207, 215
Cook v Square D Ltd [1992] ICR 262 254
Cookson v Harewood [1932] 2 KB 478n 500, 502
Cookson v Knowles [1979] AC 556 592, 593, 612
Cooper v Firth Brown Ltd [1963] 1 WLR 418 592
Coote v Stone [1971] 1 WLR 279 344
Cope v Sharpe [1912] 1 KB 496, 510 543

Corbett v Barking, Havering & Brentwood Health Authority [1991] 1 All ER 498
                                                              612, 618, 619
Corfield v D. S. Bosher & Co. [1992] 1 EGLR 163   216
Cork v Kirby MacLean Ltd [1952] 2 All ER 402   222
Cornish v Midland Bank plc [1985] 3 All ER 513   101
Corporacion Nacional del Cobre de Chile v Sogemin Metals Ltd [1997] 1 WLR 1396   545
Costello v City of Calgary (1997) 152 DLR (4th) 453   443
Cotic v Gray (1981) 124 DLR (3rd) 641   245
Cotton v Derbyshire Dales District Council, The Times, 20 June 1994   274
Couch v Steel (1854) 3 E & B 402   400
Coventry Building Society v William Martin and Partners [1997] 48 EG 159   548
Crawford v Board of Governors of Charing Cross Hospital, The Times,
    8 December 1953   188
Crocker v Sundance Northwest Resorts Ltd (1988) 51 DLR (4th) 321,
    Supreme Court of Canada   54
Croke v Wiseman [1981] 3 All ER 852   597
Cronin v Redbridge London Borough Council, The Times, 20 May 1987   604
Crook v Derbyshire Stone Ltd [1956] 1 WLR 432   384
Crossley v Rawlinson [1981] 3 All ER 674   33, 60, 240
Crown River Cruises Ltd v Kimbolton Fireworks Ltd [1996] 2 Lloyd's Rep 533   312, 352
Cumbernauld and Kilsyth District Council v Dollar Land (Cumbernauld) Ltd
    1993 SLT 1318   281
Cummings v Grainger [1977] 1 All ER 104   368, 370, 371, 372, 535
Cunningham v Harrison [1973] QB 942, 952   591
Cunningham v Reading Football Club Ltd [1992] PIQR P141   56, 269
Curran v Northern Ireland Co-ownership Housing Association Ltd
    [1987] 2 All ER 13   28, 53
Curtis Publishing v Butts (1967) 388 US 130   503
Curtis v Betts [1990] 1 All ER 769   368, 369, 370
Cutler v McPhail [1962] 2 QB 292   249, 512
Cutler v United Dairies (London) Ltd [1933] 2 KB 297   60, 235, 525
Cutler v Wandsworth Stadium Ltd [1949] AC 398   400, 402, 408

D & F Estates Ltd v Church Commissioners for England [1988] 2 All ER 992
                    128, 130, 132, 133, 136, 140, 141, 296, 392, 428, 568
D (A minor) (Wardship: sterilisation) [1976] 1 All ER 326   472
D. W. Moore & Co. Ltd v Ferrier [1988] 1 All ER 400   569
D'Amato v Badger (1996) 137 DLR (4th) 129 (SCC)   125
Daborn v Bath Tramways Motor Co. Ltd [1946] 2 All ER 333   179
Dakhyl v Labouchere [1908] 2 KB 325n   519
Dallison v Caffery [1965] 1 QB 348   479, 480, 483
Dalton v Angus (1881) 6 App Cas 740   394
Daly v General Steam Navigation Co. Ltd [1981] 1 WLR 120   591
Daly v Liverpool Corporation [1939] 2 All ER 142   553
Daniel v Ferguson [1891] 2 Ch 27   613
Daniels v Whetstone Entertainments Ltd [1962] 2 Lloyd's Rep 1   390
Daniels v White & Sons Ltd [1938] 4 All ER 258   426
Dann v Hamilton [1939] 1 KB 509   526, 528, 529
Darbishire v Warran [1963] 1 WLR 1067   607, 610, 611
Darley Main Colliery Co. v Mitchell (1886) 11 App Cas 127   583
Darling v Attorney-General [1950] 2 All ER 793   394
Davey v Harrow Corporation [1958] 1 QB 60   300, 316, 443
Davidson v Barclays Bank Ltd [1940] 1 All ER 316   507
Davidson v Chief Constable of the North Wales Police [1994] 2 All ER 597   465, 481, 482
Davie v New Merton Board Mills Ltd [1959] AC 604   13, 252, 254, 255, 396, 419
Davies v Bennison (1927) 22 Tas LR 52   445
Davies v Mann (1842) 10 M & W 546   544

Davies v Powell Duffryn Associated Collieries Ltd [1942] AC 601   617
Davies v Solomon (1871) LR 7 QB 112   498
Davies v Swan Motor Co. (Swansea) Ltd [1949] 2 KB 291   556
Davies v Taylor [1974] AC 207   219, 618
Davis v Barking, Havering and Brentwood Health Authority [1993] 4 Med LR 85   474
Davis v City and Hackney Health Authority [1991] 2 Med LR 366   562
Davis v Radcliffe [1990] 2 All ER 536   53, 83
Davison v Gent (1857) 1 H & N 744   451
Dawkins v Lord Paulet (1869) LR 5 QB 94   506
Dawkins v Lord Rokeby (1875) LR 8 QB 255   504
Dawson v Bingley Urban District Council [1911] 2 KB 149   403
De Buse v McCarthy [1942] 1 KB 156   508, 512
De Keyser's Royal Hotel Ltd v Spicer Bros Ltd (1914) 30 TLR 257   311
de la Giroday v Brough [1997] 6 WWR 585   217
De Meza and Stuart v Apple, Van Straten, Shena and Stone [1974] 1 Lloyd's Rep 508   547
Deane v Clayton (1817) 7 Taunt 489   288
Deane v Ealing London Borough Council [1993] ICR 329   580
Deerness v John Keeble & Son Ltd [1983] 2 Lloyd's Rep 260   565
Defreitas v O'Brian [1995] 6 Med LR 108   187
Delaney v T.P. Smith Ltd [1946] KB 393   449
Demarco v Ungaro (1979) 95 DLR (3d) 385   67
Denny v Supplies and Transport Co. Ltd [1950] 2 KB 374   421
Denton v United Counties Omnibus Co. Ltd, The Times, 6 May 1986   56
Department of the Environment v Thomas Bates & Son Ltd [1990] 2 All ER 943   134
Department of Transport v North West Water Authority [1983] 1 All ER 892   327
Derbyshire County Council v Times Newspapers Ltd [1993] 1 All ER 1011   487, 488, 500
Dering v Uris [1964] 2 QB 669   497
Derry v Handley (1867) 16 LT 263   496
Derry v Peek (1889) 14 App Cas 337   91, 92, 93
Deshane v Deere & Co. (1993) 106 DLR (4th) 385 (Ont CA)   424
Dews v National Coal Board [1987] 2 All ER 545   592
Deyong v Shenburn [1946] KB 227   170
Dickinson v Jones Alexander & Co. [1990] Fam Law 137   605
Dixon v King [1975] 2 NZLR 357   528
Dobbie v Medway Health Authority [1994] 4 All ER 450   562
Dobell v Stevens (1825) 3 B & C 623   90
Docker v Chief Constable of West Midlands Police, The Times, 29 April 1998   62
Dodd Properties (Kent) Ltd v Canterbury City Council [1980] 1 All ER 928
                                                                        247, 607, 608, 611
Dodds v Dodds [1978] QB 543   616
Dodwell v Burford (1670) 1 Mod 24   456
Doe d Bishop of Rochester v Bridges (1831) 1 B & Ad 847   401
Doe d Carter v Barnard (1849) 13 QB 945   450
Doe d Johnson v Baytup (1835) 3 A & E 188   450
Doe d Smith v Webber (1834) 1 A & E 119   450
Dollman v Hillman [1941] 1 All ER 355   344
Dolson v Hughes (1980) 107 DLR (3d) 343   534, 541
Dominion Mosaics & Tile Co. Ltd v Trafalgar Trucking Co. Ltd [1990] 2 All ER 246   608
Dominion Natural Gas Co. v Collins and Perkins [1909] AC 640   56
Donaghey v Boulton & Paul Ltd [1968] AC 1, 26   413
Donelan v Donelan and General Accident Fire and Life Insurance [1993] PIQR P205   528
Donelan v Donelan and General Accident Fire and Life Insurance   549
Donnelly v Jackman [1970] 1 WLR 562   457
Donnelly v Joyce [1974] QB 454   590, 591
Donoghue v Stevenson [1932] AC 562   26, 27, 29, 118, 128, 132, 133, 137, 139,
                                         142, 293, 295, 416, 417, 419, 425, 428, 430, 568
Donovan v Gwentoys Ltd [1990] 1 All ER 1018   564

Dooley v Cammell Laird & Co. Ltd [1951] 1 Lloyd's Rep 271   148, 153, 154, 163
Dorset Yacht Co. Ltd v Home Office [1969] 2 QB 412   37, 79
Doughty v Turner Manufacturing Co. Ltd [1964] 1 QB 518   240, 248
Downs v Chappell [1996] 3 All ER 344   90, 109, 558
Doyle v Olby (Ironmongers) Ltd [1969] 2 QB 158   249, 610
DPP v Hawkins [1988] 3 All ER 673   480
Drane v Evangelou [1978] 2 All ER 437   450, 581
Draper v Hodder [1972] 2 QB 556   242, 366
Dube (Litigation Guardian of) v Penlon Ltd (1994) 21 CCLT (2d) 268   158
Duchess of Argyll v Beuselinck [1972] 2 Lloyd's Rep 172   190
Duke of Brunswick v Harmer (1849) 14 QBD 185   496
Dulieu v White [1901] 2 KB 669   146, 153
Dunbar v A & B Painters Ltd [1986] 2 Lloyd's Rep 38   12
Duncan v British Coal Corp. [1997] 1 All ER 540   161, 163, 256
Dunlop Rubber Co. Ltd v Dunlop [1921] 1 AC 367   490
Dunlop v Commissioners of Customs and Excise, The Times,
   17 March 1998, CA   482
Dunne v North Western Gas Board [1964] 2 QB 806   327, 358
Dutton v Bognor Regis Urban District Council [1972] 1 QB 373   128, 142, 293, 567, 568
Dwyer v Rodrick, The Times, 12 November 1983   195
Dyer v Munday [1895] 1 QB 742   390
Dymond v Pearce [1972] 1 QB 496   343, 344, 347

E. Hulton & Co. v Jones [1910] AC 20   493, 494
Earl of Harrington v Derby Corporation [1905] 1 Ch 205   612
Easson v London & North Eastern Railway Co. [1944] KB 421   196
East Suffolk Rivers Catchment Board v Kent [1941] AC 74   48, 50, 76
E (a minor) v Dorset County Council [1995] 3 WLR 152   86
East Suffolk Rivers Catchment Board v Kent   48, 77
Eastern & South African Telegraph Co. Ltd v Cape Town Tramways Companies Ltd
   [1902] AC 381, PC   359
Eastwood v Holmes (1858) 1 F & F 347   495
Eaton v Haney Speedways Ltd (1963) 39 DLR (2d) 48   340
Eaves v Morris Motors Ltd [1961] 2 QB 385   259
Edgington v Fitzmaurice (1885) 29 ChD 459   90
Edgson v Vickers plc [1994] ICR 510   215
Edmondson v Birch [1907] 1 KB 371   512
Edward Wong Finance Co. Ltd v Johnson, Stokes and Master [1984] AC 296   186
Edwards v Bell (1824) 1 Bing 403   501
Edwards v Lee, Independent, 1 November 1991   114, 546
Edwards v National Coal Board [1949] 1 All ER 743   259
Edwards v Railway Executive [1952] AC 737   267
Egger v Viscount Chelmsford [1965] 1 QB 248   521
Eglantine Inn Ltd v Smith [1948] NI 29   495, 498
Electrical, Electronic, Telecommunication & Plumbing Union v Times Newspapers Ltd
   [1980] QB 585   488
Elguzouli-Daf v Commissioner of Police of the Metropolis [1995] 1 All ER 833
                                                                  18, 40, 41, 66, 70
Elias v Pasmore [1934] 2 KB 164   448
Elliott v London Borough of Islington [1991] 10 EG 145   334, 335
Ellis v Home Office [1953] 2 All ER 149   55
Ellis v Sheffield Gas Consumer's Co. (1853) 2 E & B 767   392
Ellison v Ministry of Defence (1997) 81 BLR 101   300, 306, 338, 351, 354
Emeh v Kensington & Chelsea & Westminster Area Health Authority
   [1984] 3 All ER 1044, CA   235
Empire Jamaica, The [1957] AC 386   207
Esanda Finance Corporation Ltd v Peat Marwick Hungerfords (1997) 142 ALR 750   106

Esso Petroleum Co. Ltd v Hall Russell & Co. Ltd [1989] 1 All ER 37   126, 380
Esso Petroleum Co. Ltd v Mardon [1976] QB 801   4, 99, 102
Esterhuizen v Allied Dunbar Assurance plc, The Times, 10 June 1998   121
Euro-Diam Ltd v Bathurst [1988] 2 All ER 23   534, 537
Evans v London Hospital Medical College [1981] 1 All ER 715   62, 482
Evans v Triplex Safety Glass Co. Ltd [1936] 1 All ER 283   421, 426
Everett v Ribbands [1952] 2 QB 198   483
Eyre v Measday [1986] 1 All ER 488   183

F. E. Callow (Engineers) Ltd v Johnson [1971] AC 335   259
F (in utero) [1988] 2 All ER 193   471
F v West Berkshire Health Authority [1989] 2 WLR 1025; [1989] 2 All ER 545
                                                           457, 472, 473, 475, 543
F v Wirral Metropolitan Borough Council [1991] 2 All ER 648, CA   170
Fardon v Harcourt-Rivington (1932) 146 LT 391   146
Farr v Butters Bros & Co. [1932] 2 KB 606   420, 421
Farrell v John Mowlem & Co. Ltd [1954] 1 Lloyd's Rep 437   343, 347
Farrell v Secretary of State for Defence [1980] 1 All ER 166   480, 541
Farrington v Leigh, The Times, 10 December 1987   495
Farrugia v Great Western Railway Co. [1947] 2 All ER 565   446
Fayed v Al-Tajir [1987] 2 All ER 396   506
Fenna v Clare & Co. [1895] 1 QB 199   345, 481
Ferguson v Dawson Partners (Contractors) Ltd [1976] 1 WLR 1213   377
Ferguson v Welsh [1987] 3 All ER 777   273
Fetter v Beale (1701) 1 Ld Raym 339   582
Filliter v Phippard (1847) 11 QB 347   365
Fineux v Hovenden (1598) Cro Eliz 664   342
Firman v Ellis [1978] QB 886   565, 566
First Interstate Bank of California v Cohen Arnold & Co., The Times,
    11 December 1995   220
Fitzgerald v Cooke Bourne (Farms) Ltd [1964] 1 QB 249   370
Fitzgerald v Cooke Bourne (Farms) Ltd   370
Fitzgerald v Ford [1996] PIQR Q72, CA   591, 605
Fitzgerald v Lane [1987] 2 All ER 455   213, 214, 556
Flower v Ebbw Vale Steel Iron & Coal Ltd [1934] 2 KB 132   263
Forrester v Tyrrell (1893) 9 TLR 257   498
Forsikringsaktieselskapet Vesta v Butcher [1986] 2 All ER 488   547
Forster v Oughtred & Co. [1982] 1 WLR 86   569, 571
Forward v Hendricks [1997] 2 All ER 397   565
Foster v Tyne & Wear County Council [1986] 1 All ER 567   603, 604
Foulkes v Chief Constable of Merseyside Police [1998] 3 All ER 705   478
Fowell v National Coal Board, The Times, 28 May 1986   564
Fowler v Lanning [1959] 1 QB 426   454, 542
Fowles v Bedfordshire County Council [1995] PIQR P380   194
Foxcroft v Lacey (1613) Hob 89   495
Francome v Mirror Group Newspapers Ltd [1984] 2 All ER 408   613
Franklin v British Railways Board [1993] IRLR 441, CA   602
Franklin v South Eastern Railway Co. (1858) 3 H & N 211   618
Fraser-Armstrong v Hadow, The Times, 21 February 1994, CA   520
Fraser v Evans [1969] 1 All ER 8   613
Freeman v Home Office [1983] 3 All ER 589; [1984] 1 All ER 1036, CA   469, 474
Fritz v Hobson (1880) 14 ChD 542   342
Froom v Butcher [1976] QB 286   549, 552, 557
Frost v Chief Constable of South Yorkshire [1997] 1 All ER 540   69, 149, 159, 160, 256
Fullam v Newcastle Chronicle & Journal Ltd [1977] 3 All ER 32   493
Furniss v Fitchett [1958] NZLR 396   164

G v Chief Superintendent of Police, Stroud (1986) 86 Cr App R 92   478
Gala v Preston (1991) 100 ALR 29   541
Galashiels Gas Co. Ltd v Millar [1949] AC 275   247
Galoo Ltd v Bright Grahame Murray [1995] 1 All ER 16   108
Gammell v Wilson [1982] AC 27   597, 615
Gardner v Grace (1858) 1 F & F 359   553
Gardner v Moore [1984] AC 548   12
Gartside v Sheffield, Young & Ellis [1983] NZLR 37   121
Gascoine v Ian Sheridan & Co. [1994] 5 Med LR 437, 444   185, 188
Gaskin v Balls (1879) 13 ChD 324   612
Gayler & Pope Ltd v Davies & Son Ltd [1924] 2 KB 75   373
Geddis v Proprietors of the Bann Reservoir (1878) 3 App Cas 430   74
Geier v Kujawa [1970] 1 Lloyd's Rep 364   277
General Cleaning Contractors Ltd v Christmas [1953] AC 180   182, 253, 254, 257, 263
General Engineering Services Ltd v Kingston and Saint Andrew Corp.
    [1988] 3 All ER 867   384
Gerald v Commissioner of Police of the Metropolis, The Times, 26 June 1998   577
Gibb v United Steel Companies Ltd [1957] 1 WLR 668   381
Gilbert v Stone (1647) Style 72   443
Giles v Walker (1890) 24 QBD 656   352
Gillespie Brothers & Co. Ltd v Roy Bowles Transport Ltd [1973] 1 QB 400   532
Gillick v West Norfolk & Wisbech Area Health Authority [1985] 3 All ER 402   468, 472
Gillingham Borough Council v Medway (Chatham) Dock Co. Ltd [1992] 3 WLR 449
                                                       310, 328, 329, 340
Ginty v Belmont Building Supplies Ltd [1959] 1 All ER 414   262, 414, 415, 551, 554
Glasgow Corporation v Muir [1943] AC 448   36, 173, 176, 179
Glasgow Corporation v Taylor [1922] 1 AC 44   178, 269
Glass v Cambridge Health Authority [1995] 6 Med LR 91   197
Glinski v McIver [1962] AC 726   483, 484
Gold v Haringey Health Authority [1987] 2 All ER 888   184, 472
Goldman v Hargrave [1967] 1 AC 645   56, 314, 315, 323, 339, 365
Goldsmith v Bhoyrul [1997] 4 All ER 268   489
Good-Wear Treaders Ltd v D & B Holdings Ltd (1979) 98 DLR (3d) 59   425
Goodwill v British Pregnancy Advisory Service [1996] 2 All ER 161   117
Gorris v Scott (1874) LR 9 Ex 125   207, 249, 413
Gough v Thorne [1966] 3 All ER 398   552
Gouriet v Union of Post Office Workers [1978] AC 435   410
Graham and Graham v ReChem International Ltd [1996] Env LR 158   300, 355
Graham v Dodds [1983] 2 All ER 953   618
Gran Gelato Ltd v Richcliff (Group) Ltd [1992] 2 WLR 867   102, 122, 546
Grand Restaurants of Canada Ltd v Toronto (1981) 123 DLR (3d) 349   546
Grant v Australian Knitting Mills Ltd [1936] AC 85   418, 420, 425, 426
Grappelli v Derek Block (Holdings) Ltd [1981] 2 All ER 272   493
Gravesham Borough Council v British Railways Board [1978] Ch 379   345
Gray v Jones (1939) 55 TLR 437   499
Greater Nottingham Co-operative Society Ltd v Cementation Piling
    and Foundations Ltd [1988] 2 All ER 971   5, 42, 100, 131, 533
Green v Building Scene Ltd [1994] PIQR P259   182
Green v Goddard (1702) 2 Salk 641   456
Greenhalgh v British Railways Board [1969] 2 QB 286   268, 280, 282
Greenock Corporation v Caledonian Railway Co. [1917] AC 556   359
Gregory v Kelly [1978] RTR 426   529, 549
Gregory v Piper (1829) 9 B & C 591   444
Griffin v Kingsmill [1998] PIQR P24   65, 68
Griffin v Mersey Regional Ambulance [1998] PIQR P34   179
Griffiths v Arch Engineering Co. Ltd [1968] 3 All ER 217   420
Griffiths v Commonwealth (1985) 72 FLR 260   225

Griffiths v Williams, The Times, 24 November 1995   605
Grimshaw v Ford Motor Co. (1981) 119 Cal App 3d 757   18
Groves v Lord Wimborne [1898] 2 QB 402   250, 400, 403, 404
Guay v Sun Publishing Co. [1953] 4 DLR 577   164
Gulf Oil (GB) Ltd v Page [1987] 3 All ER 14   613
Gunn v Wallsend Slipway & Engineering Co. Ltd, The Times, 23 January 1989   35
Guppys (Bridport) Ltd v Brookling (1983) 269 EG 846   404, 579

H. & N. Emanuel Ltd v Greater London Council [1971] 2 All ER 835   361, 364
H. West & Son Ltd v Shephard [1964] AC 326   604, 605, 606
H v Norfolk County Council [1997] 1 FLR 384   84
H v Secretary of State for the Home Department, The Times, 7 May 1992   468
Hale v Jennings Bros. [1938] 1 All ER 579   357
Haley v London Electricity Board [1965] AC 778   36, 178, 276, 553
Halford v Brookes [1992] PIQR P175   195
Hall v Brooklands Auto Racing Club [1933] 1 KB 205   529, 530
Hall v Hebert [1993] 4 WWR 113, 126   537, 538
Hallam-Eames v Merrett Syndicates Ltd [1996] 7 Med LR 122, CA   563, 570
Halsey v Esso Petroleum Co. Ltd [1961] 2 All ER 145   300, 310, 340, 341, 346, 357
Hall v Brooklands Auto Racing Club [1933] 1 KB 205   173
Hambrook v Stokes Bros [1925] 1 KB 141   147, 165
Hamlin v Edwin Evans (1996) 80 BLR 85   570
Hanson v Wearmouth Coal Co. Ltd [1939] 3 All ER 47   360
Hardy v Motor Insurers' Bureau [1964] 2 QB 745   12, 236
Harnett v Bond [1925] AC 669   466
Harper v Haden & Sons Ltd [1933] Ch 298   342
Harris v Birkenhead Corporation [1976] 1 All ER 341   266, 278, 283
Harris v Empress Motors Ltd [1983] 3 All ER 561   596, 597
Harris v Evans [1998] 3 All ER 522   40, 44, 83, 86
Harris v James (1876) 45 LJ QB 545   324
Harris v Wyre Forest District Council [1988] 1 All ER 691   112
Harris v Wyre Forest District Council   104, 112
Harrison v British Railways Board [1981] 3 All ER 679   61, 525
Harrison v Bush (1856) 5 E & B 344   512
Harrison v Duke of Rutland [1893] 1 QB 142   446
Harrison v Michelin Tyre Co. Ltd [1985] 1 All ER 919   253
Harrison v Southwark & Vauxhall Water Co. [1891] 2 Ch 409   311
Harrison v Vincent [1982] RTR 8   190
Harrold v Watney [1898] 2 QB 322   344
Hartley v Birmingham City District Council [1992] 2 All ER 213   566
Hartley v Mayoh & Co. [1954] 1 QB 383   413
Hartt v Newspaper Publishing plc, The Times, 9 November 1989   491
Harvey v R. G. O'Dell Ltd [1958] 2 QB 78   384
Haseldine v C.A. Daw & Son Ltd [1941] 2 KB 343   273, 418, 420, 423
Hasselblad (GB) Ltd v Orbinson [1985] 1 All ER 173   505
Hawkins v Clayton (1988) 78 ALR 69   121
Hay v Hughes [1975] 1 All ER 257   619
Hayden v Hayden [1992] 1 WLR 986   591
Haynes v Harwood [1935] 1 KB 146   57, 60, 229, 525
Hayward v Thompson [1982] QB 47   493
Headford v Bristol and District Health Authority [1995] 6 Med LR 1   573
Heap v Ind Coope & Allsopp Ltd [1940] 2 KB 476   325
Heasmans v Clarity Cleaning Co. Ltd [1987] IRLR 286   389
Heath v Keys (1984) 134 NLJ 888   450
Heath v Mayor of Brighton (1908) 98 LT 718   311
Hebditch v MacIlwaine [1894] 2 QB 54   496
Hebridean Coast, The [1961] AC 545   607

Hedley Byrne & Co. Ltd v Heller & Partners Ltd [1964] AC 465   6, 8, 9, 37, 85, 86,
      88, 89, 90, 92, 93, 94, 95, 96, 98, 99, 101, 103, 104, 105, 106, 110,
          112, 114, 115, 117, 121, 124, 125, 129, 130, 131, 140, 143, 572
Hegarty v E.E. Caledonia Ltd [1997] 2 Lloyd's Rep 259   154, 155, 163
Hegarty v Shine (1878) 14 Cox CC 145   475, 476
Hemmens v Wilson Browne [1994] 2 WLR 323   121
Hemmings v Stoke Poges Golf Club [1920] 1 KB 720   451
Hempler v Todd (1970) 14 DLR (3d) 637   55
Henderson v Henderson (1843) 3 Hare 100   5, 7, 9, 582
Henderson v Henry E. Jenkins & Sons [1970] AC 282   198, 199
Henderson v Merrett Syndicates Ltd [1994] 3 All ER 506
         5, 7, 89, 94, 95, 99, 101, 102, 110, 120, 124, 532, 571
Henderson v Temple Pier Co. Ltd [1998] 3 All ER 324   564
Henderson v The Wakefield Shirt Company Ltd [1997] PIQR P413   181, 252
Hepworth v Kerr [1995] 6 Med LR 139   242
Herald of Free Enterprise, The: Appeal by Captain Lewry, Re, Independent,
  18 December 1987   187
Hercules Managements Ltd v Ernst & Young (1997) 146 DLR (4th) 577   96
Herd v Weardale Steel, Coal & Coke Co. Ltd [1915] AC 67   466
Herniman v Smith [1938] AC 305   483
Heron II, The [1969] 1 AC 350   239
Herring v Boyle (1834) 1 Cr M & R 377   467
Herrington v British Railways Board [1971] 1 QB 107   285
Herschtal v Stewart & Arden Ltd [1940] 1 KB 155   418, 420
Hevican v Ruane [1991] 3 All ER 65   152, 157
Hewett v Alf Brown's Transport Ltd [1992] ICR 530   35, 244
Hey v Moorhouse (1839) 6 Bing NC 52   444
Hickman v Maisey [1900] 1 QB 752   446
Hicks v Chief Constable of South Yorkshire Police [1992] 2 All ER 65   615
Hicks v Faulkner (1878) 8 QBD 167   483
Hilder v Associated Portland Cement Manufacturers Ltd [1961] 1 WLR 1434   178
Hill v Baxter [1958] 1 QB 277   175
Hill v Chief Constable of South Yorkshire Police [1990] 1 All ER 1046   468
Hill v Chief Constable of West Yorkshire [1988] 2 All ER 238;
  [1987] 1 All ER 1173, CA;   18, 29, 34, 39, 42, 44, 53, 55, 69, 70, 83
Hill v Church of Scientology of Toronto (1995) 126 DLR (4th) 129   487
Hill v James Crowe (Cases) Ltd [1978] 1 All ER 812   426
Hill v Tupper (1863) 2 H & C 121   449
Hill v Van Erp (1997) 142 ALR 687   121
Hillen v ICI (Alkali) Ltd [1936] AC 65   444
Hills v Potter [1983] 3 All ER 716   204
Hilton v Thomas Burton (Rhodes) Ltd [1961] 1 WLR 705   384
Hindustan Steam Shipping Co. Ltd v Siemens Bros & Co. Ltd
  [1955] 1 Lloyd's Rep 167   194
Hinz v Berry [1970] 2 QB 40   604
Hoare & Co. v McAlpine [1923] 1 Ch 167   300
Hobbs (Farms) Ltd v Baxenden Chemical Co. Ltd [1992] 1 Lloyd's Rep 54
                  361, 365, 395, 425
Hodge & Sons v Anglo-American Oil Co. (1922) 12 Ll LR 183   416
Hodgson v Trapp [1988] 3 All ER 870   14, 587, 595, 597
Holden v Chief Constable of Lancashire [1986] 3 All ER 836   578
Holden v White [1982] QB 679; [1982] 2 All ER 328   268, 280, 281
Holgate v Lancashire Mental Hospitals Board [1937] 4 All ER 19   55
Holian v United Grain Growers Ltd (1980) 112 DLR (3d) 611   56
Hollebone v Midhurst & Fernhurst Builders Ltd [1968] 1 Lloyd's Rep 38   607
Holliday v National Telephone Co. [1899] 2 QB 392   394, 397
Holling v Yorkshire Traction Co. [1948] 2 All ER 662   344

Hollis v Dow Corning Corporation (1993) 103 DLR (4th) 520 (BCCA);
   (1995) 129 DLR (4th) 609, SCC   423, 424
Hollywood Silver Fox Farm Ltd v Emmett [1936] 2 KB 468   313
Holman Construction Ltd v Delta Timber Co. Ltd [1972] NZLR 1081   99
Holmes v Ashford [1950] 2 All ER 76   420, 422
Holmes v Bagge (1853) 1 E & B 782   481
Holmes v Mather (1875) LR 10 Ex 261   10, 454
Holmes v Wilson and others (1839) 10 A & E 503   444
Holt v Payne Skillington (a firm) (1995) 77 BLR 51   9
Holtham v Commissioner of Police of the Metropolis, The Times,
   28 November 1987, CA   612
Home Brewery plc v William Davis & Co. (Loughborough) Ltd [1987] 1 All ER 637   314
Home Office v Dorset Yacht Co. Ltd [1970] AC 1004   28, 33, 53, 55, 76, 231
Honeywill & Stein Ltd v Larkin Bros Ltd [1934] 1 KB 191   364, 395
Hooper v Rogers [1975] Ch 43   613
Hopkins v Mackenzie [1995] 6 Med LR 26   569
Hopper v Reeve (1817) 7 Taunt 698   456
Hopwood v Muirson [1945] KB 313   499
Horbury v Craig Hall & Rutley (1991) 7 PN 206   570
Hornal v Neuberger Products Ltd [1957] 1 QB 247   92, 195
Horrocks v Lowe [1975] AC 135   520
Horsley v MacLaren [1970] 1 Lloyd's Rep 257   48, 54, 61
Hosie v Arbroath Football Club Ltd 1978 SLT 122   56
Hoskin v Rogers, The Times, 25 January 1985   374
Hosking v De Havilland Aircraft Co. Ltd [1949] 1 All ER 540   393
Hotson v East Berkshire Area Health Authority [1987] 1 All ER 210
                  211, 215, 217, 220, 221, 222
Hough v London Express Newspaper Ltd [1940] 2 KB 507   489
Hourihane v Metropolitan Police Commissioner, The Independent,
   18 January 1995, CA   483
Housecroft v Burnett [1986] 1 All ER 332   589, 591, 605
Howard Marine & Dredging Co. Ltd v Ogden & Sons (Excavations) Ltd
   [1978] QB 574   92, 98, 99, 102
Howard v Furness Houlder Argentine Lines Ltd [1936] 2 All ER 781   419
Howard v Shirlstar Container Transport Ltd [1990] 3 All ER 366   537
Hubbard v Pitt [1976] QB 142   342, 446
Hucks v Cole (1968), [1993] 4 Med LR 393, 397   186, 187
Hudson v Ridge Manufacturing Co. Ltd [1957] 2 QB 348   55, 253, 375
Hughes v Lord Advocate [1963] AC 837   239, 240, 241, 244, 249, 413
Hughes v McKeown [1985] 3 All ER 284   604
Hughes v National Union of Mineworkers [1991] 4 All ER 278   69
Hunt v Severs [1994] 2 All ER 385   591, 592, 602
Hunt v Star Newspaper Co. Ltd [1908] 2 KB 309   519
Hunt v Wallis (1991), [1994] PIQR P128   371
Hunter v British Coal Corp. [1998] 2 All ER 97   154, 163
Hunter v Butler, The Times, 28 December 1995, CA   619
Hunter v Canary Wharf Ltd [1997] 2 All ER 426   299, 318, 330, 458, 459
Hunter v Chief Constable of West Midlands [1981] 3 All ER 727   67, 68
Huntingdon Life Sciences Ltd v Curtin, The Times, 11 December 1997   460
Hurditch v Sheffield Health Authority [1989] 2 All ER 869   585
Hurley v Dyke [1979] RTR 265   419, 423
Hurst v Picture Theatres Ltd [1915] 1 KB 1   446, 447
Hussain v Lancaster City Council, The Times, 27 May 1998   324
Hussain v New Taplow Paper Mills Ltd [1988] 1 All ER 541, HL   602, 603
Hussien v Chong Fook Kam [1970] AC 942   477, 479
Hutchinson v London & North Eastern Railway Co. [1942] 1 KB 481   17
Huth v Huth [1915] 3 KB 32   496

Huxford v Stoy Hayward (1989) 5 BCC 421   107
Hyde v Tameside Area Health Authority (1981) 2 PN 26   234
Hyett v Great Western Railway Co. [1948] 1 KB 345   61

Ilkiw v Samuels [1963] 1 WLR 991   385, 387
Imperial Chemical Industries Ltd v Shatwell [1965] AC 656   261, 262, 376, 414, 525, 528
Independent Broadcasting Authority v EMI Electronics Ltd (1980) 14 BLR 1   194
Innes v Wylie (1844) 1 Car & Kir 257   456
Interallianz Finanz AG v Independent Insurance Co. Ltd [1997] EGCS 91   548
Invercargill City Council v Hamlin [1996] 1 All ER 756   142
Inverugie Investments Ltd v Hackett [1995] 3 All ER 841   451
Investors in Industry Commercial Properties Ltd v South Bedfordshire District Council
    [1986] 1 All ER 787   132
Iqbal v London Transport Executive (1973) 16 KIR 329   386, 387
Iron Trade Mutual Insurance Co. Ltd v J. K. Buckenham Ltd [1990] 1 All ER 808
    8, 569, 571
Irving v Post Office [1987] IRLR 289   389
Island Records Ltd [1978] Ch 122   399, 401
Islander Trucking Ltd v Hogg Robinson & Gardner Mountain (Marine) Ltd
    [1990] 1 All ER 826   569
Issa v Hackney LBC [1997] 1 WLR 956, CA   402, 404
Iveagh v Martin [1961] 1 QB 232   446
Iveson v Moore (1699) 1 Ld Raym 486   342

J (A minor) (Wardship: medical treatment) [1990] 3 All ER 930   472
J. Nunes Diamonds Ltd v Dominion Electric Protection Co.
    (1972) 26 DLR (3d) 699   99
Jackson v Harrison (1978) 19 ALR 129   536, 541
Jacobs v London County Council [1950] AC 361   280, 281, 291
Jacobs v Morton (1994) 72 BLR 92   137, 295, 296, 429
Jaensch v Coffey (1984) 54 ALR 417   34, 149, 151, 152, 156, 158
James McNaughton Papers Group Ltd v Hicks Anderson & Co. [1991] 1 All ER 134
    30, 97, 107
James v Campbell (1832) 5 C & P 372   457
Jameson v CEGB [1997] 4 All ER 38   557
Jane Doe v Metropolitan Toronto (Municipality) Commissioners of Police
    (1990) 72 DLR (4th) 580   69
Janiak v Ippolito (1985) 16 DLR (4th) 1   611
Janvier v Sweeney [1919] 2 KB 316, CA   458, 459
Jarvis v T. Richards & Co. (1980) 124 SJ 793   247
Jaundrill v Gillett, The Times, 30 January 1996   368, 370, 372
Jayes v IMI (Kynoch) Ltd [1985] ICR 155   262, 421, 554
Jayne v National Coal Board [1963] 2 All ER 220   260
JEB Fasteners Ltd v Marks Bloom & Co. [1981] 3 All ER 289   104, 108, 204, 546
Jefford v Gee [1970] 2 QB 130   612
Jobling v Associated Dairies Ltd [1982] AC 794   225, 226
Joel v Morison (1834) 6 C & P 501   383
John Lewis & Co. Ltd v Tims [1952] AC 676   480
John Munroe (Acrylics) Ltd v London Fire and Civil Defence Authority,
    The Times, 22 May 1996   40, 70
John Summers & Sons Ltd v Frost [1955] AC 740   259, 260, 412
John Trenberth Ltd v National Westminster Bank Ltd (1979) 253 EG 151   448
John v Mirror Group Newspapers Ltd [1996] 2 All ER 35   486, 579, 606
Johnson v Bingley, The Times, 28 February 1995   183
Johnson v Tennant Bros Ltd (1954) unreported, CA   555
Johnstone v Bloomsbury Health Authority [1991] 2 All ER 293
    6, 252, 256, 261, 275, 278, 524, 526, 531

Jolley v Sutton London Borough Council [1998] 3 All ER 559   269, 271
Jolliffe v Willmett & Co. [1971] 1 All ER 478   576
Jones v Boyce (1816) 1 Stark 493   190, 555
Jones v Department of Employment [1988] 1 All ER 725   42
Jones v Festiniog Railway Co. (1868) LR 3 QB 733   361
Jones v Great Western Railway Co. (1930) 47 TLR 39   196
Jones v Liverpool Health Authority [1996] PIQR P251   564
Jones v Livox Quarries Ltd [1952] 2 QB 608   550, 551
Jones v Llanrwst Urban District Council [1911] 1 Ch 393   449
Jones v Manchester Corporation [1952] 2 QB 852   189, 190, 391, 392
Jones v Northampton Borough Council, The Times, 21 May 1990   59
Jones v Skelton [1963] 1 WLR 1362   490
Jones v Stroud District Council [1986] 1 WLR 1141   607
Jones v Tower Boot Co. Ltd [1997] 2 All ER 406, CA   383
Jones v Williams (1843) 11 M & W 176   335
Jones v Wright [1991] 3 All ER 88   25, 154, 156
Jordan House Ltd v Menow and Honsberger (1973) 38 DLR (3d) 105   54
Jordan v Norfolk County Council (1994) 93 LGR 50   450
Joyce v Sengupta [1993] 1 All ER 897, CA   485
Joyce v Wandsworth Health Authority [1996] PIQR P121;
    [1995] 6 Med LR 60, 64   185, 206
Junior Books Ltd v Veitchi Co. Ltd [1983] 1 AC 520   4, 124, 128, 129, 132, 140, 532, 567

K v JMP Co. Ltd [1976] QB 85   619
K v P (J, third party) [1993] 1 All ER 521   558
Kandalla v British European Airways Corporation [1981] QB 158   619
Kapfunde v Abbey National plc, The Times, 6 April 1998   116
Kars v Kars (1996) 141 ALR 37   592
Kay v Ayrshire and Arran Health Board [1987] 2 All ER 417   208
Kay v ITW Ltd [1968] 1 QB 140   384, 385
Kaye v Robertson [1991] FSR 62   459
Kelley v Corston [1997] 4 All ER 466   64
Kelly v Chief Constable of Hampshire, The Independent, 25 March 1993, CA   478
Kelly v Dawes, The Times 27 September 1990   587
Kelly v O'Malley (1889) 6 TLR 62   513
Kelsen v Imperial Tobacco Co. Ltd [1957] 2 QB 334   445, 612
Kemsley v Foot [1952] AC 345   517
Kennaway v Thompson [1981] QB 88   334, 335
Keppel Bus Co. Ltd v Sa'ad bin Ahmad [1974] 1 WLR 1082, PC   390
Kerby v Redbridge Health Authority [1994] PIQR Q1   604
Khan v Ahmed [1957] QB 149   513
Khorasandjian v Bush [1993] 3 WLR 476; [1993] 3 All ER 669
                                                    304, 317, 318, 343, 458, 459
Kiam v Neil, The Times, 14 December 1994, CA   486
Kimber v Press Association Ltd [1893] 1 QB 65   513
King v Liverpool City Council [1986] 1 WLR 890   45, 232, 323
King v Phillips [1953] 1 QB 429   33, 148
King v Smith [1995] ICR 339   258
Kingshott v Associated Kent Newspapers Ltd [1991] 2 All ER 99   513
Kingsway, The [1918] P 344   607
Kirby v Leather [1965] 2 QB 367   573
Kirkham v Chief Constable of the Greater Manchester Police[1990] 3 All ER 246, CA;
    [1989] 3 All ER 882   55, 234, 525, 534, 537
Kitchen v Royal Air Force Association [1958] 1 WLR 563   216, 217, 219, 220, 572
Kite, The [1933] P 154   195
Kite v Napp, The Times, 1 June 1982   370
Knapp v Railway Executive [1949] 2 All ER 508   413

Knight v Gibbs (1834) 1 A & E 43   512
Knight v Home Office [1990] 3 All ER 237   55, 181
Knightley v Johns [1982] 1 All ER 851   60, 68, 71, 229, 230, 231, 234
Knowles v Liverpool City Council [1993] 4 All ER 321   255
Knupffer v London Express Newspaper Ltd [1944] AC 116   495
Konskier v Goodman Ltd [1928] 1 KB 421   444
Kooragang Investments Pty Ltd v Richardson & Wrench Ltd [1981] 3 All ER 65   386
Kralj v McGrath [1986] 1 All ER 54   145, 576, 604
Kubach v Hollands [1937] 3 All ER 907   419, 421

L. Shaddock and Associates Pty Ltd v Parramatta City Council (1981) 36 ALR 385   101
La Banque Financière de la Cité SA v Westgate Insurance Co. Ltd
    [1988] 2 Lloyd's Rep 513   42, 100, 112
Lady Gwendolen, The [1964] P 294   176
Laferrière v Lawson (1991) 78 DLR (4th) 609   221
Lagan Navigation Co. v Lambeg Bleaching, Dyeing & Finishing Co. Ltd
    [1927] AC 226   335, 336
Lam v Brennan and Borough of Torbay [1997] PIQR P488, CA   83, 85
Lamb v Camden London Borough Council [1981] QB 625
                               15, 33, 37, 57, 202, 228, 231, 232, 239
Lambert v Lewis [1981] 1 All ER 1185   194, 417, 428, 547
Lambert v West Devon Borough Council (1997) 96 LGR 45   86
Lambton v Mellish [1894] 3 Ch 163   333
Lancashire County Council v Municipal Mutual Insurance Ltd [1996] 3 All ER 545   578
Landall v Dennis Faulkner & Alsop [1994] 5 Med LR 268   62
Lane v Dixon (1847) 3 CB 776   449
Langbrook Properties Ltd v Surrey County Council [1969] 3 All ER 1424   26, 170, 313
Lange v Australian Broadcasting Corporation (1997) 71 ALJR 818   503
Langley v Dray and M.T. Motor Policies at Lloyds [1997] PIQR P508   175
Langridge v Levy (1837) 2 M & W 519; (1838) 4 M & W 337   91
Lanphier v Phipos (1838) 8 C & P 475   183
Larner v British Steel plc [1993] 4 All ER 102   260
Latchford v Spedeworth International Ltd, The Times, 11 October 1983   527
Latham v R. Johnson & Nephew Ltd [1913] 1 KB 398   269, 270, 553
Latimer v AEC Ltd [1953] AC 643   180, 253, 260
Latter v Braddell (1881) 50 LJ QP 448   474
Laws v Florinplace Ltd [1981] 1 All ER 659   301, 310
Le Fanu v Malcolmson (1848) 1 HL Cas 637   495
Leach v British Oxygen Co. (1965) 109 SJ 157   255
Leadbitter v Hodge Finance Ltd [1982] 2 All ER 167   564
League Against Cruel Sports Ltd v Scott [1985] 2 All ER 489   366, 443
Leakey v National Trust for Places of Historic Interest or Natural Beauty
    [1980] QB 485   315, 317, 331
Lee Ting San v Chung Chi-Keung [1990] IRLR 236   378
Lee v Thompson (1989) 6 PN 91   569
Leeds Industrial Co-operative Society v Slack [1924] AC 851   613
Leeman v Montagu [1936] 2 All ER 1677   301, 366
Leeson v General Council of Medical Education (1889) 43 ChD 366   505
Leigh & Sillavan Ltd v Aliakmon Shipping Co. Ltd [1986] 2 All ER 145, HL;
    [1985] 2 All ER 44, CA   4, 15, 28, 43, 126, 127, 130, 428, 532, 533
Leigh v Gladstone (1909) 26 TLR 139   543
Lemon v Webb [1895] AC 1   335
Lemos v Kennedy Leigh Development Co. Ltd (1961) 105 SJ 178   613
Letang v Cooper [1965] 1 QB 232   443, 454, 542, 561
Letang v Ottawa Electric Railway Co. [1926] AC 725   527
Lewis v Chief Constable of Greater Manchester, The Independent, 23 October 1991   477
Lewis v Chief Constable of the South Wales Constabulary [1991] 1 All ER 206, CA   480

Lewis v Daily Telegraph Ltd [1964] AC 234   490, 492
Liddle v Yorkshire (North Riding) County Council [1934] 2 KB 101   446
Liesbosch Dredger v SS Edison [1933] AC 449   223, 246, 247, 606, 607
Lim Poh Choo v Camden & Islington Area Health Authority [1980] AC 174
                                                              584, 588, 589, 593, 606
Limbrick v French [1993] PIQR P121   549
Limpus v London General Omnibus Co. (1862) 1 H & C 526   386, 388
Linden Gardens Trust Ltd v Lenesta Sludge Disposals Ltd [1993] 3 All ER 417   127
Lindsay v Mid-Western Health Board [1993] 2 IR 147, 181   197
Lister v Romford Ice & Cold Storage Co. Ltd [1957] AC 555   13, 391, 559
Liverpool City Council v Irwin [1977] AC 239   292
Livingstone v Ministry of Defence [1984] NI 356, NICA   457
Livingstone v Rawyards Coal Co. (1880) 5 App Cas 25   574
Lloyd Cheynham & Co. Ltd v Littlejohn & Co. (1985) 2 PN 154   182
Lloyd v Grace, Smith & Co. [1912] AC 716   390
Lloyde v West Midlands Gas Board [1971] 1 WLR 749   196, 198, 199
Lloyds Bank Ltd v E.B. Savory & Co. [1933] AC 201   182, 186
Lloyds Bank plc v Rosset [1990] 1 All ER 1111, HL   320
Lochgelly Iron & Coal Co. Ltd v M'Mullan [1934] AC 1   25, 410
Lodge Holes Colliery Co. Ltd v Wednesbury Corporation [1908] AC 323   450
Logan v Uttlesford District Council (1984) 136 NLJ 541   559
London, Brighton & South Coast Railway Co. v Truman (1886) 11 App Cas 45   327
London Artists Ltd v Littler [1969] 2 QB 375   516
London Association for Protection of Trade v Greenlands Ltd [1916] 2 AC 15   509
London Corporation, The [1935] P 70   607
London County Council v Cattermoles (Garages) Ltd [1953] 1 WLR 997   386
London Graving Dock Co. Ltd v Horton [1951] AC 737   253
London Passenger Transport Board v Upson [1949] AC 155   173, 408, 412, 555
Londonwaste Ltd v Amec Civil Engineering Ltd (1997) 83 BLR 136   123
Long v Hepworth [1968] 1 WLR 1299   561
Longden v British Coal Corporation [1998] 1 All ER 289   602
Lonrho Ltd v Shell Petroleum Co. Ltd [1981] 2 All ER 456   401, 404, 407, 408, 409, 410
Loughans v Odhams Press Ltd [1963] CLY 2007   502
Love v Port of London [1959] 2 Lloyd's Rep 541   244
Loveday v Renton [1990] 1 Med LR 117   208, 422
Lowery v Walker [1911] AC 10   267
Lucas-Box v News Group Newspapers Ltd [1986] 1 All ER 177   502
Lucas v Mason (1875) LR 10 Ex 251   385
Luxmoore-May v Messenger May Baverstock [1990] 1 All ER 1067   184
Lynch v Ministry of Defence [1983] NI 216   470, 526, 542
Lynch v Nurdin (1841) 1 QB 29   552
Lyon v Daily Telegraph Ltd [1943] KB 746   519, 521
Lyon v Fishmongers Co. (1876) 1 App Cas 662   346
Lyons v Gulliver [1914] 1 Ch 631   342

M (a minor) v Newham London Borough Council [1994] 2 WLR 554   40, 62, 83, 117
M. Isaacs & Sons Ltd v Cook [1925] 2 KB 391   506
MacDonald v York County Hospital (1973) 41 DLR (3d) 321   221
Macintosh v Dun [1908] AC 390   509
Mains v Uniroyal Englebert Tyres Ltd, The Times, 29 September 1995,
    Court of Session   260
Malcolm v Broadhurst [1970] 3 All ER 508   245
Malec v J. C. Hutton Proprietary Ltd (1990) 169 CLR 638   221
Malette v Shulman (1990) 67 DLR (4th) 321   543
Mallett v McMonagle [1970] AC 166   217, 617
Mallory v Butler [1991] 2 All ER 889   584
Malone v Laskey [1907] 2 KB 141   317

Malyon v Plummer [1964] 1 QB 330   619
Manchester Corporation v Farnworth [1930] AC 171   326
Mann v Saulnier (1959) 19 DLR (2d) 130   443
Mansfield v Weetabix Ltd [1997] PIQR P526   175
Mapp v News Group Newspapers Ltd [1998] 2 WLR 260   491
Marc Rich & Co. v Bishop Rock Marine Co. Ltd [1995] 3 All ER 307   6, 34, 40, 41, 295
March v E. & M. H. Stramare Pty Ltd (1991) 99 ALR 423   233
Margereson v J. W. Roberts Ltd [1996] PIQR P358   36
Mariola Marine Corporation v Lloyd's Register of Shipping [1990] 1 Lloyd's Rep 547   106
Market Investigations Ltd v Minister of Social Security [1969] 2 QB 173   378
Marks v Chief Constable of Greater Manchester Police, The Times, 28 January 1992   576
Marlor v Ball (1900) 16 TLR 239   371
Marshall v Curry [1933] 3 DLR 260   474
Marshall v Osmond [1983] QB 1034   175, 536
Martin d Tregonwell v Strachan (1742) 5 D & E 107 n   450
Martin v Watson [1996] 1 AC 74   482
Martindale v Duncan [1973] 1 WLR 574' HL   247, 606
Mason v Levy Auto Parts of England Ltd [1967] 2 QB 530   354, 364, 365
Mason v Williams & Williams Ltd [1955] 1 WLR 549   426
Massey v Crown Life Insurance Co. [1978] 2 All ER 576   377
Masters v Brent London Borough Council [1978] QB 841   317
Matania v National Provincial Bank Ltd [1936] 2 All ER 633   300, 311, 322, 395
Mathew v Maughold Life Assurance Co. Ltd (1984) 1 PN 142   569
Matrix-Securities Ltd v Theodore Goddard (1997) 147 NLJ 1847   190
Matthews v Wicks, The Times, 25 May 1987   373
Mattocks v Mann [1993] RTR 13, CA   247, 607
Maynard v West Midlands Regional Health Authority [1984] 1 WLR 634;
     (1981), unreported   184, 185, 190, 200
MB (Medical Treatment), Re [1997] 2 FLR 426   471
McAuley v Bristol City Council [1992] 1 All ER 749, CA   292
McAuley v London Transport Executive [1957] 2 Lloyd's Rep 500, 505   611
McC v Mullan [1984] 3 All ER 908   61
McCafferty v Metropolitan Police District Receiver [1977] 1 WLR 1073   253, 562
McCain Foods Ltd v Grand Falls Industries Ltd (1991) 80 DLR (4th) 252   425
McCall v Abelesz [1976] QB 585   404, 408
McCamley v Cammell Laird Shipbuilders Ltd [1990] 1 All ER 854   591, 602
McCarey v Associated Newspapers Ltd [1964] 1 WLR 855   506
McCreesh v Courtaulds plc [1997] PIQR P421   414
McCullagh v Lane Fox and Partners Ltd [1996] 18 EG 104   106, 113, 532
McDermid v Nash Dredging and Reclamation Co. Ltd
     [1987] 2 All ER 878, HL   258, 393, 396
McEllistrum v Etches (1956) 6 DLR (2d) 1   192
McFarlane v E.E. Caledonia Ltd [1994] 2 All ER 1   153, 155, 163
McFarlane v Wilkinson [1997] 2 Lloyd's Rep 259, CA   64
McGeown v Northern Ireland Housing Executive [1994] 3 All ER 53   266, 268, 281, 282
McGhee v National Coal Board [1972] 3 All ER 1008   210, 211, 214, 221, 222
McHale v Watson (1966) 115 CLR 199   192
McKay v Essex Area Health Authority [1982] QB 1166   58, 170
McKew v Holland & Hannen & Cubitts (Scotland) Ltd
     [1969] 3 All ER 1621   33, 232, 233, 550
McKinnell v White 1971 SLT 61   553
McKinnon Industries Ltd v Walker [1951] 3 DLR 577   311
McLaren v Bradstreet (1969) 119 NLJ 484   245
McLaughlin v Pryor (1842) 4 Mac & G 48   392
McLeod v Commissioner of Police of the Metropolis [1994] 4 All ER 553   447
McLoughlin v O'Brian [1982] 2 All ER 298, HL; [1981] 1 All ER 809
                  33, 37, 38, 144, 148, 149, 151, 152, 156, 157, 166

McNamara v Duncan (1979) 26 ALR 584   469
McNerny v Lambeth London Borough Council (1988) 21 HLR 188, CA   291
McPhail v Persons Unknown [1973] Ch 447   449
McQuire v Western Morning News Co. Ltd [1903] 2 KB 100   518
McWilliams v Sir William Arrol & Co. Ltd [1962] 1 WLR 295   91, 204, 211, 217,
                                                                       218, 254, 414
Meade's Case (1823) 1 Lew CC 184   455
Meah v McCreamer (No. 2) [1986] 1 All ER 943   12, 236, 540, 590
Mediana, The [1900] AC 113   607
Meering v Grahame-White Aviation Co. Ltd (1920) 122 LT 44   467
Mehmet v Perry [1977] 2 All ER 529   619
Mercer v South Eastern & Chatham Railway Companies' Managing Committee
   [1922] 2 KB 549   47
Merivale v Carson (1887) 20 QBD 275   517
Merlin v British Nuclear Fuels plc [1990] 3 All ER 711   363
Merricks v Nott-Bower [1965] 1 QB 57   506
Mersey Docks & Harbour Board v Coggins & Griffith (Liverpool) Ltd [1947] AC 1 380, 381
Mersey Docks and Harbour Board v Procter [1923] AC 253   268
Messenger Newspapers Group Ltd v National Graphical Association [1984] IRLR 397
                                                                              576, 580
Metropolitan Asylum District v Hill (1881) 6 App Cas 193   327
Metropolitan Saloon Omnibus Co. v Hawkins (1859) 4 H & N 87   488
Middleton v Elliott Turbomachinery Ltd, Independent, 16 November 1990, CA   586
Midland Bank plc v Bardgrove Property Services Ltd (1992) 60 BLR 1, 20   614
Midland Bank Trust Co. Ltd v Hett Stubbs & Kemp [1979] Ch 384
                                                        4, 7, 95, 101, 120, 124, 560,
Midland Bank v Bardgrove Property Services [1992] 37 EG 126   305, 309, 335, 584
Midwood v Manchester Corporation [1905] 2 KB 597   339
Miles v Forest Rock Granite Co. (Leicestershire) Ltd (1918) 34 TLR 500, CA   353, 357
Miliangos v George Frank (Textiles) Ltd [1976] AC 443   608
Miller v Jackson [1977] QB 966   2, 178, 312, 332, 334
Mills v Silver [1991] 1 All ER 449   447
Mills v Winchester Diocesan Board of Finance [1989] 2 All ER 317   42
Minister of Health v Bellotti [1944] KB 298   446
Ministry of Defence v Ashman [1993] 2 EGLR 102   451
Ministry of Housing & Local Government v Sharp [1970] 2 QB 223   111, 118, 412
Minories Finance Ltd v Arthur Young (a firm) (Bank of England, third party)
   [1989] 2 All ER 105   39, 53
Mint v Good [1951] 1 KB 517   292, 325, 339, 344, 347
Minter v Priest [1930] AC 558   505
Mitchell v Liverpool Area Health Authority, The Times, 17 June 1985   603
Mobil Oil Hong Kong Ltd v Hong Kong United Dockyards Ltd [1991] 1 Lloyd's Rep 309 34
Moeliker v Reyrolle & Co. Ltd [1977] 1 All ER 9   603
Mogul Steamship Co. v McGregor, Gow & Co. [1892] AC 25   26
Molinari v Ministry of Defence [1994] PIQR Q33   585
Moloney v Lambeth London Borough Council (1966) 64 LGR 440   269
Mond v Hyde [1998] 3 All ER 833   62
Monk v Warbey [1935] 1 KB 75   383, 400, 405, 406, 407, 412
Monson v Tussauds Ltd [1894] 1 QB 671   492, 498
Montreal v Montreal Locomotive Works Ltd [1947] 1 DLR 161   378
Moore v DER Ltd [1971] 1 WLR 1476   606
Moore v R. Fox & Sons [1956] 1 QB 596, CA   198
More v Weaver [1928] 2 KB 520   505
Morgan Crucible Co. plc v Hill Samuel Bank Ltd [1991] 1 All ER 148   97, 108
Morgan v Lingen (1863) 8 LT (NS) 800   489
Morgan v Odhams Press Ltd [1971] 1 WLR 1239   489, 492, 493
Morgans v Launchbury [1973] AC 127   13, 316, 382

Morrell v Owen, The Times, 14 December 1993   178
Morris v Breaveglen Ltd [1993] PIQR P294, CA   258, 381
Morris v C. W. Martin & Sons Ltd [1966] 1 QB 716   389, 396
Morris v Ford Motor Co. Ltd [1973] QB 792   391
Morris v Murray [1990] 3 All ER 801   526, 527, 529
Morris v Redland Bricks Ltd [1970] AC 652   613
Morris v West Hartlepool Steam Navigation Co. Ltd [1956] AC 552   181
Morrison Steamship Co. Ltd. v Greystoke Castle [1947] AC 265   125
Morton v Wheeler (1956) unreported, CA   341
Morton v William Dixon Ltd 1909 SC 807   181
Motherwell v Motherwell (1976) DLR (3d) 62   318
Motorworks Ltd v Alwahbi [1977] RTR 276   606
Mount Albert BC v Johnson [1979] 2 NZLR 234   584
Mount Carmel Investments Ltd v Peter Thurlow Ltd [1988] 3 All ER 129   449, 451
Mount Isa Mines Ltd v Pusey (1970) 125 CLR 383   148, 164
Muirhead v Industrial Tank Specialities Ltd [1985] 3 All ER 705
                               33, 123, 130, 234, 241, 427, 532
Muirhead v Industrial Tank Specialities Ltd   428
Mulcahy v Ministry of Defence [1996] 2 All ER 758   170, 253
Mulholland v McRae [1961] NI 135   616
Mulholland v Mitchell [1971] AC 666   584
Mullard v Ben Line Steamers Ltd [1970] 1 WLR 1414   553
Mullin v Richards [1998] 1 All ER 920   192
Munro v Porthkerry Park Holiday Estates Ltd, The Times, 9 March 1984   54
Murdoch v Glacier Metal Co. Ltd, The Times, 21 January 1998   309, 310, 311
Murphy v Brentwood District Council [1990] 2 All ER 908   15, 32, 34, 49, 78, 123, 125,
   127, 128, 130, 134, 135, 136, 139, 140, 141, 144, 293, 294, 295, 428, 429, 568, 569, 572
Murphy v Culhane [1977] QB 94   286, 470, 534, 535, 536, 545
Murray v Harringay Arena Ltd [1951] 2 KB 529   530
Murray v McMurchy [1949] 2 DLR 442   473
Murray v Ministry of Defence [1988] 2 All ER 521   467, 477
Musgrove v Pandelis [1919] 2 KB 43   353, 365
Mutual Life & Citizens' Assurance Co. Ltd v Evatt [1971] AC 793   98, 102

Nader v Urban Transit Authority of New South Wales [1985] 2 NSWLR 501   245
Nahhas v Pier House (Cheyne Walk) Management Ltd (1984) 270 EG 328   389
Nance v British Columbia Electric Railway Co. Ltd [1951] AC 601   549
Nash v Calthorpe [1905] 2 Ch 237   90
Nash v Eli Lilly & Co. [1993] 1 WLR 782   562, 563, 564, 565
Nash v Sheen [1953] CLY 3726   456, 474
National Bank of Greece SA v Pinios Shipping Co. (No. 1) [1989] 1 All ER 213, 223, 232   5
National Coal Board v England [1954] AC 403   534
National Union of General and Municipal Workers v Gillian [1946] KB 81   488
Nelhams v Sandells Maintenance Ltd [1996] PIQR P52   258, 382
Nettleship v Weston [1971] 2 QB 691   173, 174, 188, 526, 528, 552
Neufeld v Landry (1975) 55 DLR (3d) 296   555
Newstead v London Express Newspaper Ltd [1940] 1 KB 377   493
New York Times, The v Sullivan (1964) 376 US 254   503
Newstead v London Express Newspaper Ltd   494
Newton v Edgerley [1959] 1 WLR 1031   55
Ng Chun Pui v Lee Chuen Tat [1988] RTR 298   175, 199
Nicholls v Ely Beet Sugar Factory [1936] Ch 343; [1931] 2 Ch 84   309, 449
Nicholls v F. Austin (Leyton) Ltd [1946] AC 493   259, 413
Nicholls v Rushton, The Times, 19 June 1992   145
Nichols v Marsland (1876) 2 ExD 1   359
Nicholson v Atlas Steel Foundry & Engineering Co. Ltd [1957] 1 All ER 776 209, 213
Nicholson v John Deere Ltd (1986) 34 DLR (4th) 542   424, 425

Nimmo v Alexander Cowan & Sons Ltd [1968] AC 107   260
Nitrigin Eireann Teoranta v Inco Alloys Ltd [1992] 1 All ER 854   131, 138, 568
Noble v Harrison [1926] 2 KB 332   324, 345
Nocton v Lord Ashburton [1914] AC 932   92
Nolan v Dental Manufacturing Co. Ltd [1958] 1 WLR 936   257
Nor-Video Services Ltd v Ontario Hydro (1978) 84 DLR (3d) 221, 231   303
Norris v W. Moss & Sons Ltd [1954] 1 WLR 346   551, 554
Northern Sandblasting Pty Ltd v Harris (1997) 71 ALJR 1428   291, 395, 396
Northwestern Utilities Ltd v London Guarantee & Accident Co. Ltd [1926] AC 108   360
Norwich & Peterborough Building Society v Steed [1991] 2 All ER 880   584
Norwich City Council v Harvey [1989] 1 All ER 1180   5, 131, 533
Nottingham Health Authority v Nottingham City Council [1988] 1 WLR 903   559
Nova Mink Ltd v Trans-Canada Airlines [1951] 2 DLR 241   36, 37
NWL Ltd v Woods [1979] 1 WLR 1294   613
Nykredit Mortgage Bank plc v Edward Erdman Group Ltd (No. 2)
    [1981] 1 All ER 305   569

O'Connell v Jackson [1972] 1 QB   549
O'Grady v Westminster Scaffolding Ltd [1962] 2 Lloyd's Rep 238   607
O'Reilly v National Rail & Tramway Appliances Ltd [1966] 1 All ER 499   253
O'Rourke v Camden LBC [1997] 3 WLR 86, HL   401, 402, 409
Ocean Estates Ltd v Pinder [1969] 2 AC 19   449
Oceangas (Gibraltar) Ltd v Port of London Authority, The Times, 24 May 1993   380
Ogston v Aberdeen District Tramways Co. [1897] AC 111   307
Ogwo v Taylor [1987] 2 WLR 988   149, 272
Oke v Weide Transport Ltd (1963) 41 DLR (2d) 53   48
Oliver v Ashman [1962] 2 QB 210   596
OLL Ltd v Secretary of State for Transport [1997] 3 All ER 897   73
Olotu v Secretary of State for the Home Department [1997] 1 All ER 385, CA   467
Olutu v Home Office [1997] 1 All ER 385   403
Oman v McIntyre 1962 SLT 168   245
Omega Trust Co. Ltd v Wright Son & Pepper [1997] 18 EG 120   113, 532
Ontario Hospital Services Commission v Borsoski (1974) 54 DLR (3d) 339   55
Orchard v South Eastern Electricity Board [1987] 1 All ER 95   66
Orme v Associated Newspapers Ltd, The Times, 4 February 1981   495
Ormiston v Great Western Railway Co. [1917] 1 KB 598   499
Ormrod v Crossville Motor Services Ltd [1953] 1 WLR 1120   382
Oropesa [1943] P 32   227, 229
Osborne v London & North Western Railway Co. (1888) 21 QBD 220   527
Osborne v Thomas Boulter & Son [1930] 2 KB 226   498, 512
Osman v Ferguson [1993] 4 All ER 344   69
Otto v Bolton & Norris [1936] 2 KB 46   292
Ould v Butler's Wharf Ltd [1953] 2 Lloyd's Rep 44   60
Overseas Tankship (UK) Ltd v Miller Steamship Co. Pty Ltd,
    The Wagon Mound (No. 2) [1967] 1 AC 617   180, 239
Overseas Tankship (UK) Ltd v Morts Dock & Engineering Co.,
    The Wagon Mound [1961] AC 388   237, 240
Owen v Martin [1992] PIQR Q151 1992   618
Owens v Brimmell [1977] QB 859   528, 549
Owens v Liverpool Corporation [1939] 1 KB 394   244
Oyston v Blaker [1996] 2 All ER 106   560

P. Perl (Exporters) Ltd v Camden London Borough Council
    [1984] QB 342   14, 45, 54, 57, 232
Pacific Associates Inc. v Baxter [1989] 2 All ER 159   5, 30, 42, 97, 100, 112, 113, 131
Padbury v Holliday & Greenwood Ltd (1912) 28 TLR 492   323, 397, 398
Page Motors Ltd v Epsom & Ewell Borough Council (1982) 80 LGR 337   323, 324

Page v Enfield and Haringey Area Health Authority, The Times, 7 November 1986 — 604
Page v Smith (No. 2) [1996] 3 All ER 272   145, 146, 148, 149, 153, 165, 213, 242, 243, 245
Palacath Ltd v Flanagan [1985] 2 All ER 161 — 63
Palmer v Durnford Ford [1992] 2 All ER 122 — 62
Palmer v Tees Health Authority, The Times, 1 June 1998 — 55
Pamplin v Express Newspapers Ltd (No.2) [1988] 1 All ER 282 — 575
Pannett v McGuinness & Co. Ltd [1972] 2 QB 599 — 284, 288
Pape v Cumbria County Council [1992] 3 All ER 211 — 257
Paris v Stepney Borough Council [1951] AC 367 — 179, 182, 252
Parker-Tweedale v Dunbar Bank plc (No. 1) [1990] 2 All ER 577 — 170
Parkes v Prescott (1869) LR 4 Ex 169 — 496
Parkins v Scott (1862) 1 H & C 153 — 489
Parkinson v Liverpool Corporation [1950] 1 All ER 367 — 175
Parkinson v Lyle Shipping Co. [1964] 2 Lloyd's Rep 79 — 255
Parry v Cleaver [1970] AC 1 — 601, 602
Parslow v Masters [1993] 6 WWR 273 (Sask QB) — 117
Pasley v Freeman (1789) 3 D & E 51 — 90
Pass of Ballater, The [1942] P 112 — 392, 393
Patel v Patel [1988] 2 FLR 179 — 343
Patel v W.H. Smith (Eziot) Ltd [1987] 2 All ER 569, CA — 450
Paterson Zochonis Ltd v Merfarken Packaging Ltd [1986] 3 All ER 522 — 38
Paton v British Pregnancy Advisory Service [1978] 2 All ER 987 — 471
Payne v Rogers (1794) 2 B1 R 350 — 325
Payton v Brooks [1974] RTR 169 — 607
Peabody Donation Fund v Sir Lindsay Parkinson & Co. Ltd [1984] 3 All ER 529
                                                    28, 39, 128, 132, 295
Pearson v Coleman Bros [1948] 2 KB 359 — 268
Peek v Gurney (1873) LR 6 HL 377 — 90
Pennington v Brinsop Hall Coal Co. (1877) 5 ChD 769 — 334
Penny v Northampton Borough Council (1974) 72 LGR 733 — 279
Percy v Hall [1996] 4 All ER 524, CA — 477
Performance Cars Ltd v Abraham [1962] 1 QB 33 — 223, 224, 226
Perrett v Collins, The Times, 23 June 1998, CA — 39, 53
Perry v Clissold [1906] AC 73 — 450
Perry v Kendricks Transport Ltd. [1956] 1 WLR 85, 92, CA   353, 357, 358, 360, 361
Perry v Sidney Phillips & Son [1982] 3 All ER 705 — 247, 607
Perry v Tendring District Council (1984) 2 PN 58 — 546, 567
Petch v Customs and Excise Commissioners [1993] ICR 789 — 179, 256
Peter Walker Ltd v Hodgson [1909] 2 KB 239 — 519
Peters v Prince of Wales Theatre (Birmingham) Ltd [1943] KB 73 — 358, 359
Pettersson v Royal Oak Hotel Ltd [1948] NZLR 136 — 390
Phelps v Hillingdon London Borough Council (1997) 96 LGR 1 — 86
Phelps v Kemsley (1942) 168 LT 18 — 507
Philco Radio & Television Corporation of Great Britain Ltd v J. Spurling Ltd
  [1949] 2 All ER 882 — 230
Philcox v Civil Aviation Authority, The Times, 8 June 1995 — 39, 53
Philips v William Whiteley [1938] 1 All ER 566 — 188
Phillips Products Ltd v Hyland [1987] 2 All ER 620 — 381, 531
Phillips v Britannia Hygienic Laundry Co. Ltd [1923] 2 KB 832   404, 408, 409, 413
Phipps v Brooks Dry Cleaning Service Ltd [1996] PIQR Q100 — 596
Phipps v Rochester Corporation [1955] 1 QB 450 — 270, 276, 287
Photo Production Ltd v Securicor Transport Ltd [1980] AC 827 — 15
Pickard v Smith (1861) 10 CB (NS) 470 — 394
Pickering v Liverpool Daily Post & Echo Newspapers plc [1991] 1 All ER 622, HL — 400
Pickering v Rudd (1815) 4 Camp 219 — 445
Pickett v British Rail Engineering Ltd [1980] AC 136 — 596, 615, 616
Pickford v Imperial Chemical Industries plc [1998] 3 All ER 462 — 208

Pigney v Pointer's Transport Services Ltd [1957] 1 WLR 1121   145, 234, 245, 616
Pike v Wallis, The Times, 6 November 1981   374
Pinn v Rew (1916) 32 TLR 451   392
Pirelli General Cable Works Ltd v Oscar Faber & Partners [1983] 2 AC 1
                                                          125, 140, 567, 568, 571, 572
Pitcher v Martin [1937] 3 All ER 918   367
Pittman Estate v Bain (1994) 112 DLR (4th) 257   56
Pitts v Hunt [1990] 3 All ER 344   529, 536, 538, 541, 542, 554
Plange v Chief Constable of South Humberside Police, The Times, 23 March 1992   479
Platform Home Loans Ltd v Oyston Shipways Ltd (1997) 14 PN 56, CA   548, 610
Poland v Parr & Sons [1927] 1 KB 236   385
Polemis and Furness, Withy & Co. Ltd, Re [1921] 3 KB 560
                                               237, 238, 241, 245, 246, 247, 248
Polly Peck (Holdings) plc v Trelford [1986] 2 All ER 84   501
Pontardawe Rural District Council v Moore-Gwyn [1929] 1 Ch 656   352
Porter v Barking & Dagenham London Borough Council, The Times, 9 April 1990   194
Poseidon Ltd v Adelaide Petroleum NL (1968) 68 ALJR 313   221
Possfund Custodian Trustee Ltd v Diamond [1996] 2 All ER 774   107
Pounder v London Underground Ltd [1995] PIQR P217   616
Powell v Fall (1880) 5 QBD 597   19, 306, 353, 365
Powell v Gelston [1916] 2 KB 615   495
Prebble v Television New Zealand [1994] 3 All ER 407   504
Price v Milawski (1977) 82 DLR (3d) 130   245
Prichard v Ministry of Defence, The Times, 27 January 1995   465
Pride of Derby & Derbyshire Angling Association Ltd v British Celanese Ltd
      [1952] 1 All ER 1326; [1953] Ch 149   332, 333, 334, 612
Priest v Manchester Corporation (1915) 84 LJ KB 1734   342
Priestley v Fowler (1837) 3 M & W 1   250
Pritchard v Cobden Ltd [1987] 1 All ER 300; [1987] 2 FLR 56   590
Progress & Properties Ltd v Craft (1976) 51 ALJR 184   536
Public Transport Corporation v Sartori [1997] 1 VR 168, Victoria CA   54, 253
Pullman v Walter Hill & Co. Ltd [1891] 1 QB 524   496
Punjab National Bank v de Boinville [1992] 1 WLR 1138   7, 32, 118
Purdew v Seress-Smith [1993] IRLR 77   505
Pursell v Horn (1838) 8 A & E 602   456
Pyrenees Shire Council v Day (1998) 151 ALR 147   52

Qualcast (Wolverhampton) Ltd v Haynes [1959] AC 743, HL   172, 257
Quartz Hill Consolidated Gold Mining Co. v Eyre (1883) 11 QBD 674   484
Queen in Right of Canada v Saskatchewan Wheat Pool (1983) 143 DLR (3d) 9   411
Queen v Cognos Inc. (1993) 99 DLR (4th) 626   99
Quinn v Burch Brothers (Builders) Ltd [1966] 2 QB 370   233, 547
Quinn v Leatham [1901] AC 495   249
Quintas v National Smelting Co. Ltd [1960] 1 All ER 104   556

R. A. Lister & Co. Ltd v E. G. Thomson (Shipping) Ltd (No.2) [1987] 3 All ER 1032   559
R (A minor) (Wardship: medical treatment) [1991] 4 All ER 177   472
R v Billinghurst [1978] Crim LR 553   469
R v Bournewood Community and Mental Health NHS Trust, ex parte L
      [1998] 3 All ER 289   465, 473, 543
R v Brown [1993] 2 All ER 75   469, 470
R v Caldwell [1982] AC 341   9
R v Carden (1879) 5 QBD 1   517
R v Clarence (1888) 22 QBD 23   475
R v Criminal Injuries Compensation Board, ex parte Warner [1986] 2 All ER 478   461
R v Daly [1974] 1 WLR 133   464
R v Duffy [1967] 1 QB 63   480

R v Flattery (1877) 2 QBD 410   475
R v Governor of Brockhill Prison, ex parte Evans (No. 2), The Times, 6 July 1998, CA   467
R v Howell [1981] 3 All ER 383   477
R v Ireland [1997] 3 WLR 534, HL   459
R v Johnson [1997] 1 WLR 367   340
R v Jones (1813) 3 Camp 230   342
R v Kneeshaw [1975] 1 QB 57   464
R v Lawrence [1982] AC 510   10
R v Linekar [1995] 3 All ER 69   475
R v Longton Gas Co. (1860) 2 E & E 651   342
R v Manchester City Magistrates' Court, ex parte Davies [1989] 1 All ER 90   61
R v Rahman [1985] Crim LR 596   468
R v Reid [1992] 1 WLR 793   10
R v Richardson, The Independent, 3 April 1998, CA   476
R v Russell (1805) 6 East 427   342
R v Secretary of State for the Home Department ex parte Fire Brigades Union
    [1995] 2 WLR 1   462, 463
R v Self [1992] 3 All ER 476   478
R v St George (1840) 9 C & P 483   455
R v Train (1862) 2 B & S 640   343
R v Vivian [1979] 1 All ER 48   464
R v Ward (1836) 4 A & E 384   343
R v Wilson [1955] 1 WLR 493   455
Racz v Home Office [1994] 2 WLR 23, HL   468, 578
Rae v Mars (UK) Ltd [1990] 3 EG 80   274
Rainham Chemical Works Ltd v Belvedere Fish Guano Co. Ltd [1921] 2 AC 465   354
Ramsden v Lee [1992] 2 All ER 204   566
Ramwade Ltd v Emson & Co. Ltd (1986) 2 PN 197, CA   247, 606
Rance v Mid-Downs Health Authority [1991] 1 All ER 801   538
Randall v Tarrant [1955] 1 WLR 255   446
Rantzen v Mirror Group Newspapers [1993] 4 All ER 975   486
Rapier v London Tramways Co. [1893] 2 Ch 588   317, 338
Ratcliffe v Plymouth & Torbay Health Authority [1998] PIQR P170   197
Ravenscroft v Rederiaktiebolaget Transatlantic [1991] 3 All ER 73   30, 152, 157, 158
Razzel v Snowball [1954] 1 WLR 1382   380
RCA Corporation v Pollard [1983] Ch 135   401, 408
Read v Coker (1853) 13 CB 850   455
Read v Croydon Corporation [1938] 4 All ER 631   403, 410, 411
Read v J. Lyons & Co. Ltd [1947] AC 156   177, 338, 352, 353, 354, 357, 358, 362
Ready Mixed Concrete (South East) Ltd v Minister of Pensions & National Insurance
    [1968] 2 QB 497   378, 379
Reay v British Nuclear Fuels plc [1994] 5 Med LR 1   208
Redland Bricks Ltd v Morris [1970] AC 652   333
Redpath v Belfast & Co. Down Railway [1947] NI 167   601
Reeves v Commissioner of Police of the Metropolis [1998] 2 All ER 381   55, 234, 525, 534
Reffell v Surrey County Council [1964] 1 All ER 743   402
Regan v Williamson [1976] 1 WLR 305   590, 619
Reid v Rush & Tompkins Group plc [1989] 3 All ER 228, CA   6, 7, 110, 170, 252
Resolute Maritime Inc. v Nippon Kaiji Kyokai [1983] 2 All ER 1   92
Revill v Newbery [1996] 1 All ER 291   265, 279, 286, 287, 535, 540, 541
Reynolds v Clarke (1725) 1 Str 634   453
Reynolds v Times Newspapers Ltd (1998) 148 NLJ 105   511
Rhodes v Canadian National Railway (1990) 75 DLR (4th) 248   158
Rialas v Mitchell, The Times, 17 July 1984   589
Richards v Cresswell, The Times, 24 April 1987   505
Richards v Naum [1967] 1 QB 620   506
Richardson v Pitt-Stanley [1995] ICR 303   12, 251, 405, 407, 408, 409

Richardson v West Lindsey District Council [1990] 1 All ER 296   132, 295
Riches v News Group Newspapers Ltd [1985] 2 All ER 845   580
Rickards v Lothian [1913] AC 263   353, 360
Ricketts v Thos. Tilling Ltd [1915] 1 KB 644   385
Rickless v United Artists Corporation [1987] 1 All ER 679   406, 408
Riddick v Thames Board Mills Ltd [1977] QB 881   489
Rigby v Chief Constable of Northamptonshire [1985] 2 All ER 985
                                            68, 71, 352, 353, 361, 543, 544
Rimmer v Liverpool City Council [1984] 1 All ER 930   291, 293, 294, 421
River Wear Commissioners v Adamson (1877) 2 App Cas 743   443
Riverstone Meat Co. Pty Ltd v Lancashire Shipping Co. Ltd [1961] AC 807   393
Rivtow Marine Ltd v Washington Iron Works (1973) 40 DLR (3d) 530   141, 143, 425
Roach v Yates [1938] 1 KB 256   590, 592
Roberge v Bolduc (1991) 78 DLR (4th) 666, SCC   186
Robert Addie & Sons (Collieries) Ltd v Dumbreck [1929] AC 358   267, 278
Roberts v Johnstone [1988] 3 WLR 1247   589
Roberts v Ramsbottom [1980] 1 All ER 7   175
Roberts v Roberts (1864) 5 B & S 384   498
Roberts v Rose (1865) LR 1 Ex 82   336
Robertson v Forth Road Bridge Joint Board [1995] IRLR 251   163
Robertson v Ridley [1989] 2 All ER 474   59
Robinson v Balmain Ferry Co. Ltd [1910] AC 295   466
Robinson v Kilvert (1889) 41 ChD 88   311
Robinson v Post Office [1974] 2 All ER 737   203, 228, 245
Robinson v Ward (1958) 108 LJ 491   499
Robson v Hallett [1967] 2 QB 939   446
Robson v Liverpool City Council [1993] PIQR Q78, CA   603
Roe v Minister of Health [1954] 2 QB 66   176, 195, 197, 436
Rogers v Night Riders [1983] RTR 324   395, 396
Rogers v Whitaker (1992) 109 ALR 625   472
Roles v Nathan [1963] 1 WLR 1117   269, 272, 274
Romney Marsh v Corporation of the Trinity House (1870) LR 5 Ex 204   544
Rondel v Worsley [1969] 1 AC 191   29, 63, 66, 68
Rookes v Barnard [1964] AC 1129   576, 578, 579, 581
Rose v Miles (1815) 4 M & S 101   342, 345
Rose v Plenty [1976] 1 WLR 141   387, 388
Ross v Associated Portland Cement Manufacturers Ltd [1964] 1 WLR 768   262, 415
Ross v Caunters [1980] Ch 297   3, 89, 118, 121, 124, 126, 569
Rost v Edwards [1990] 2 All ER 654   503
Rothwell v Raes (1988) 54 DLR (4th) 193; aff'd (1990) 76 DLR (4th) 280 (Ont CA)   422
Rouse v Squires [1973] QB 889   230
Rowe v Herman [1997] 1 WLR 1390, CA   394, 397
Rowling v Takaro Properties Ltd [1988] 1 All ER 163   29, 30, 40, 42, 78
Royal Aquarium & Summer & Winter Garden Society Ltd v Parkinson [1892] 1 QB 431   505
Royscot Trust Ltd v Rogerson [1991] 3 All ER 294   92
Rozario v The Post Office [1997] PIQR P15   257
Rushton v Turner Bros. Asbestos Co. Ltd [1960] 1 WLR 96   414, 554
Ryeford Homes Ltd v Sevenoaks District Council (1989) 46 BLR 34   83
Rylands v Fletcher (1866) LR 1 Ex 265; (1868) LR 3 HL 330
                 249, 264, 300, 316, 331, 339, 341, 349, 350, 355, 357, 358, 361, 366, 395, 543

S (adult: refusal of medical treatment), Re [1992] 4 All ER 671   470
S v Clement (1995) 122 DLR (4th) 449   55
S v Distillers Co. (Biochemicals) Ltd [1970] 1 WLR 114   603
S v London Borough of Newham, The Independent, 26 February 1998   508
Sadgrove v Hole [1901] 2 KB 1   496
Saif Ali v Sydney Mitchell & Co. [1980] AC 198   63, 66, 67, 68

Saif Ali v Sydney Mitchell & Co.   67
Saipem SpA and Conoco (UK) Ltd v Dredging VO2 BV and Geosite Surveys Ltd
    (The 'Volvox Hollandia') (No. 2) [1993] 2 Lloyd's Rep 315   533
Salmon v Seafarer Restaurants Ltd [1983] 3 All ER 729   272
Salsbury v Woodland [1970] 1 QB 324   394
Sampson v Hodson-Pressinger [1981] 3 All ER 710   324
Sanderson v National Coal Board [1961] 2 QB 244   260
Sarch v Blackburn (1830) 4 C & P 297   276
Saunders v Edwards [1987] 2 All ER 651   537, 539, 541, 612
Saunders v Leeds Western Health Authority (1984), [1993] 4 Med LR 355   197
Savill v Roberts (1698) 12 Mod 208   484
Sayers v Harlow Urban District Council [1958] 1 WLR 623   233, 547, 555
Scally v Southern Health and Social Services Board [1991] 4 All ER 563   7, 252
Schenck v Province of Ontario (1982) 131 DLR (3d) 310   306, 310
Schneider v Eisovitch [1960] 2 QB 430   147, 153
Schofield v Chief Constable of West Yorkshire, The Times, 15 May 1998, CA   163
Schweizer v Central Hospital (1975) 53 DLR (3d) 494   474
SCM (United Kingdom) Ltd v W.J. Whittall & Son Ltd [1971] 1 QB 337;
    [1970] 1 WLR 1017   123, 311
Scott v London & St Katherine Docks Co. (1865) 3 H & C 596   197
Scott v Shepherd (1773) 2 Bl R 892   229, 249, 453
Scruttons Ltd v Midland Silicones Ltd [1962] AC 446   532, 533
Seaman v Netherclift (1876) 2 CPD 53   505
Secretary of State for the Environment v Essex Goodman & Suggitt [1986] 2 All ER 69   569
Sedleigh-Denfield v O'Callaghan [1940] AC 880   300, 310, 316, 321, 323
Selfe v Ilford & District Hospital Management Committee (1970) 114 SJ 935   55
Selvanayagam v University of the West Indies [1983] 1 All ER 824   610
Shah v Standard Chartered Bank, The Times, 13 May 1998, CA   502
Shearman v Folland [1950] 2 KB 43   589
Sheldon v R.H.M. Outhwaite (Underwriting Agencies) Ltd [1995] 2 All ER 562   573
Shelfer v City of London Electric Lighting Co. [1895] 1 Ch 287   333, 334
Shelfer v City of London Electric Lighting Co   335
Shelley v Paddock [1980] QB 348   91
Shepherd v Post Office, The Times, 15 June 1995, CA   616
Sheppard v Glossop Corporation [1921] 3 KB 132   50, 75
Shiffman v Order of the Hospital of St John of Jerusalem [1936] 1 All ER 557   357
Shoreham Urban District Council v Dolphin Canadian Proteins Ltd (1972) 71 LGR 261   326
Sidaway v Bethlem Royal Hospital Governors [1985] 1 All ER 643;
    [1985] 1 All ER 1018   182, 184, 204, 472, 475
Silkin v Beaverbrook Newspapers Ltd [1958] 1 WLR 743   518
Sim v Stretch (1936) 52 TLR 669   489
Simaan General Contracting Co. v Pilkington Glass Ltd (No. 2) [1988] 1 All ER 791
                                                                            42, 131, 533
Simkiss v Rhondda Borough Council (1983) 81 LGR 460   271
Simmons v Mitchell (1880) 6 App Cas 156   499
Simms v Leigh Rugby Football Club Ltd [1969] 2 All ER 923   269, 274
Simpson & Co. v Thomson (1877) 3 App Cas 279   126
Simpson v Chief Constable of South Yorkshire Police, The Times, 7 March 1991   468
Simpson v Norwest Holst Southern Ltd [1980] 2 All ER 471   564
Simpson v Robinson (1848) 12 QB 511   520
Sims v Foster Wheeler Ltd [1966] 1 WLR 769   559
Singh v Gillard [1988] NLJ Law Rep 144   487
Sion v Hampstead Health Authority [1994] 5 Med LR 170   158
Sirros v Moore [1975] QB 118   61, 505
Six Carpenters' Case (1610) 8 Co Rep 146a   448
Skinner v London, Brighton & South Coast Railway Co. (1850) 5 Exch 787   197
Skinner v Secretary of State for Transport, The Times, 3 January 1995   18, 40, 44, 72

Slater v Clay Cross Co. Ltd [1956] 2 QB 264   523
Slim v Daily Telegraph Ltd [1968] 2 QB 157   487, 490, 516, 517
Slingsby v District Bank Ltd [1932] 1 KB 544   390
Slipper v British Broadcasting Corporation [1991] 1 All ER 165   496, 498
Smith New Court Securities Ltd v Scrimgeour Vickers (Asset Management) Ltd
    [1996] 4 All ER 769, HL   610
Smith v Ainger, The Times, 5 June 1990   368, 370
Smith v Austin Lifts Ltd [1959] 1 WLR 100   254, 527
Smith v Baker [1891] AC 325   254, 261
Smith v Bush [1989] 2 WLR 790   14, 30, 99, 104, 105, 110, 113, 121, 141, 142, 531, 546
Smith v Cammell Laird & Co. Ltd [1940] AC 242   393
Smith v Charles Baker & Sons [1891] AC 325   250, 523, 524, 526
Smith v Crossley Bros Ltd (1951) 95 SJ 655   253
Smith v Drumm [1996] EGCS 192   296
Smith v Giddy [1904] 2 KB 448   300, 336, 443
Smith v Jenkins (1970) 44 ALJR 78   536
Smith v Leech Brain & Co. Ltd [1962] 2 QB 405   243, 244, 246, 249
Smith v Linskill [1996] 2 All ER 353   67, 68
Smith v Littlewoods Organisation Ltd [1987] 1 All ER 710   45, 46, 54, 57, 232, 323
Smith v London & South Western Railway Co. (1870) LR 6 CP 14   243
Smith v Manchester Corporation (1974) 17 KIR 1   603
Smith v North Metropolitan Tramways Co. (1891) 55 JP 630   390
Smith v Prendergast, The Times, 18 October 1984   367
Smith v Scott [1973] Ch 314   323, 324
Smith v Stages [1989] 2 WLR 529   384
Smith v Stone (1647) Style 65   443
Smithwick v Hall & Upson Co. (1890) 59 Conn 261   550
Smoker v London Fire & Civil Defence Authority [1991] 2 All ER 449   601
Smoldon v Whitworth [1997] PIQR P133   54, 191, 529
Snell v Farrell (1990) 72 DLR (4th) 289   212
Sochaki v Sas [1947] 1 All ER 344   197, 365
Société Commerciale de Réassurance v ERAS (International) Ltd (Note)
    [1992] 2 All ER 82   571
Sole v W. J. Hallt Ltd [1973] QB 574   547
Solloway v Hampshire County Council (1981) 79 LGR 449   316, 339
Solomons v Gertzenstein Ltd [1954] 2 QB 243   408
Somasundaram v M. Julius Melchior & Co. [1989] 1 All ER 129   63, 68
Somerville v Hawkins (1851) 10 CB 583   511
South Australia Asset Management Corporation v York Montague Ltd
    [1996] 3 All ER 365   103, 548, 608, 610
South Hetton Coal Co. Ltd v North Eastern News Association Ltd [1894] 1 QB 133   488
Southern Portland Cement Ltd v Cooper [1974] AC 632   279, 287
Southern Water Authority v Carey [1985] 2 All ER 1077   533
Southport Corporation v Esso Petroleum Co. Ltd [1954] 2 QB 182;
    [1953] 3 WLR 773, QBD   321, 347, 444, 543
Southwark London Borough Council v Williams [1971] Ch 734   447, 543
Sparham-Souter v Town & Country Developments (Essex) Ltd [1976] QB 858   567
Sparrow v Fairey Aviation Co. Ltd [1964] AC 1019   259
Spartan Steel & Alloys Ltd v Martin & Co. (Contractors) Ltd [1973] 1 QB 27
                                                 37, 123, 124, 125, 126, 140, 141, 151, 427
Speed v Thomas Swift & Co. Ltd [1943] KB 557   255
Speidel v Plato Films Ltd [1961] AC 1090   501
Speight v Gosnay (1891) 60 LJ QB 231   498
Spencer-Ward v Humberts [1995] 06 EG 148, CA   570
Spicer v Smee [1946] 1 All ER 489   322, 365
Spillane v Wasserman (1992) 13 CCLT (2d) 267 (Ontario HC)   56
Spittle v Bunney [1988] 3 All ER 1031   619

Spring v Guardian Assurance plc [1994] 3 All ER 129, HL; 3 WLR 354
                                    40, 42, 95, 114, 116, 219, 500, 505, 508, 520
Square v Model Farm Dairies (Bournemouth) Ltd [1939] 2 KB 365   403
St Anne's Well Brewery Co. v Roberts (1929) 140 LT 1   323, 326
St George's Healthcare NHS Trust v S [1998] 3 All ER 673, CA   468, 471
St Helens Smelting Co. v Tipping (1865) 11 HL Cas 642   300, 305, 310, 312, 313, 338
Stafford v Conti Commodity Services Ltd [1981] 1 All ER 691   197
Stanley v Powell [1891] 1 QB 86   454
Stanley v Saddique [1991] 1 All ER 529   619
Stansbie v Troman [1948] 2 KB 48   54
Staples v West Dorset District Council (1995) 93 LGR 536   274
Stapley v Gypsum Mines Ltd [1953] AC 663   222, 262, 551, 554, 556
Staveley Iron & Chemical Co. Ltd v Jones [1956] AC 627   263, 376, 553, 554
Stennett v Hancock [1939] 2 All ER 578   393, 395, 419
Stephen v Riverside Health Authority [1990] 1 Med LR 261   563, 565
Stephens v Anglian Water Authority [1987] 3 All ER 379   170, 314
Stephens v Myers (1830) 4 C & P 349   455
Stephenson v Waite, Tileman Ltd [1973] 1 NZLR 152   248
Stern v Piper [1996] 3 All ER 385   502, 513
Stevenson Jordan & Harrison Ltd v Macdonald & Evans [1952] 1 TLR 101   378
Stevenson v Nationwide Building Society (1984) 272 EG 663   105
Stewart v Pettie [1994] 1 WWR 372   549
Stewart v West African Terminals Ltd [1964] 2 Lloyd's Rep 371   240
Stokes v Guest, Keen & Nettlefold (Bolts & Nuts) Ltd [1968] 1 WLR 1776 178, 182
Stone v Bolton [1950] 1 KB 201; [1949] 1 All ER 237   308, 312
Stone v Taffe [1974] 3 All ER 1016   268, 388
Storey v Ashton (1869) LR 4 QB 476   383
Stovin v Wise [1996] 3 All ER 801; [1994] 3 All ER 467   41, 49, 74, 80
Stovold v Barlows, The Times, 30 October 1995   219
Street v Mountford [1985] 2 All ER 289   449
Strover v Harrington [1988] 1 All ER 769   109, 546
Stuart v Bell [1891] 2 QB 341   508, 510
Stubbings v UK [1997] 1 FLR 105   561
Stubbings v Webb [1993] 1 All ER 322   561
Sturge v Hackett [1962] 1 WLR 1257   364
Sturges v Bridgman (1879) 11 ChD 852   310, 326, 332
Sullivan v South Glamorgan County Council (1985) 84 LGR 415   240
Summers v Salford Corporation [1943] AC 283   232
Sumner v William Henderson & Sons Ltd [1964] 1 QB 450   396
Sun Life Assurance Co. of Canada v W.H. Smith & Son Ltd (1934) 150 LT 211   497
Sunbolf v Alford (1838) 3 M & W 248   466
Sutcliffe v Pressdram Ltd [1990] 1 All ER 269   486, 576
Sutcliffe v Thackrah [1974] AC 727   63
Sutherland Shire Council v Heyman (1985) 60 ALR 1; (1985) 157 CLR 424
                                              32, 33, 49, 51, 77, 144
Sutherland v British Telecommunications plc, The Times, 30 January 1989   509
Swain v Natui Ram Puri [1996] PIQR P442   283
Swanson v The Queen in right of Canada (1991) 80 DLR (4th) 741   53, 78
Swindle v Harrison [1997] 4 All ER 705   610
Swinney v Chief Constable of Northumbria Police [1996] 3 All ER 449   70
Sylvester v Chapman Ltd (1935) 79 SJ 777   371
Szalatnay-Stacho v Fink [1946] 1 All ER 303   506

T (a minor) v Surrey County Council [1994] 4 All ER 577   85
T (Adult: refusal of medical treatment), Re [1992] 4 All ER 649   471, 475, 476
T v T [1988] 1 All ER 613   456, 473
Taff Vale Railway Co. v Jenkins [1913] AC 1   618

Tai Hing Cotton Mill Ltd v Liu Chong Hing Bank Ltd [1986] AC 80   4, 6, 7, 9, 99, 100
Tait v Pearson [1996] PIQR Q92   604
Talbot v Berkshire County Council [1994] QB 290   582
Targett v Torfaen Borough Council [1992] 3 All ER 27   139, 294, 421
Tarry v Ashton (1876) 1 QBD 314   344, 347, 394
Tate & Lyle Industries Ltd v Greater London Council [1983] 1 All ER 1159   130, 328, 346
Tate v Swan Hunter & Wigham Richardson Ltd [1958] 1 WLR 39   260
Taylor v Metropolitan Police Commissioner, The Times, 6 December 1989   463
Taylor v O'Connor [1971] AC 115   593
Taylor v Rover Co. Ltd [1966] 1 WLR 1491   420
Taylor v Somerset Health Authority [1993] 4 Med LR 34; [1993] PIQR P262   156
Taylorson v Shieldness Produce Ltd [1994] PIQR P329   158
Telnikoff v Matusevitch [1991] 4 All ER 817   517, 520, 521
Tempest v Snowden [1952] 1 KB 130   483
Tennant Radiant Heat Ltd v Warrington Development Corporation (1988) 11 EG 71   548
Tennent v Earl of Glasgow (1864) 2 M (HL) 22   359
Tesco Stores Ltd v Wards Construction (Investment) Ltd (1995) 76 BLR 94   49, 134, 295
Tetley v Chitty [1986] 1 All ER 663   324, 334
Thackwell v Barclays Bank plc [1986] 1 All ER 676   537, 539, 541
Thake v Maurice [1986] 1 All ER 497   7, 117, 183
Theaker v Richardson [1962] 1 WLR 151   496
Theophanous v Herald and Weekly Times Ltd (1994) 182 CLR 104   503
Thomas v Bath District Health Authority [1995] PIQR Q19, CA   611
Thomas v Bradbury Agnew & Co. Ltd [1906] 2 KB 627   519
Thomas v British Railways Board [1976] QB 912   282
Thomas v Lewis [1937] 1 All ER 137   359
Thomas v National Union of Mineworkers (South Wales Area) [1985] 2 All ER 1   342, 455
Thomas v Quartermaine (1887) 18 QBD 685   528
Thomas v Sorrell (1673) Vaugh 330   446, 447
Thomas v Wignall [1987] 1 All ER 1185   595
Thomas Witter Ltd v TBP Industries Ltd [1996] 2 All ER 573   91
Thompson-Schwab v Costaki [1956] 1 WLR 335; [1956] 1 All ER 652   301, 310
Thompson v Brown Construction (Ebbw Vale) Ltd [1981] 2 All ER 296   565, 566
Thompson v Commissioner of Police of the Metropolis [1997] 2 All ER 762   581
Thompson v Gibson (1841) 7 M & W 456   321
Thompson v London, Midland & Scottish Railway Co. [1930] 1 KB 41   277
Thompson v Park [1944] KB 408   446
Thompson v Smiths Shiprepairers (North Shields) Ltd [1984] 1 All ER 881   182, 213, 256
Thompson v T Lohan (Plant Hire) Ltd [1987] 2 All ER 631, CA   381
Thompson v Toorenburgh (1975) 50 DLR (3d) 717   234
Thomsen v Davison [1975] Qd R 93   117
Thorne v University of London [1966] 2 QB 237   170
Thornton v Kirklees Metropolitan Borough Council [1979] QB 626   402
Thorpe v Brumfitt (1873) LR 8 Ch App 650   332
Three Rivers District Council v Bank of England (No. 3) [1996] 3 All ER 558   468
Tims v John Lewis & Co. Ltd [1951] 2 KB 459   483
Tinsley v Milligan [1993] 3 All ER 65; [1992] Ch 310   536, 537, 538, 539
Titchener v British Railways Board [1983] 3 All ER 770   270, 289, 523, 526
Tito v Waddell (No. 2) [1977] 3 All ER 129   572
Todd v Hawkins (1837) 8 C & P 88   510
Tolley v J. S. Fry & Sons Ltd [1931] AC 333   492
Tolley v Morris [1979] 2 All ER 561   573
Tolstoy Miloslavsky v United Kingdom (1995) 20 EHRR 442   487
Tomlinson v Harrison (1972) 24 DLR (3d) 26   541
Toogood v Spyring (1834) 1 CrM & R 181   507, 512
Topp v London Country Bus (South West) Ltd [1993] 1 WLR 976   56
Toronto Power Co. v Paskwan [1915] AC 734   254

Toronto Railway Co. v King [1908] AC 260   555
Trecarrell, The [1973] 1 Lloyd's Rep 402   246, 248
Tredget v Bexley Health Authority [1994] 5 Med LR 178   159
Tremain v Pike [1969] 3 All ER 1303   240, 242, 248
Trevett v Lee [1955] 1 All ER 406   342, 343
Tri-Line Expressways v Ansari [1997] 5 WWR 342   126
Tsikata v Newspaper Publishing plc [1997] 1 All ER 655   510
Tuberville v Savage (1669) 1 Mod 3   455, 456
Turner v Ambler (1847) 10 QB 252   484
Turner v Metro- Goldwyn-Mayer Pictures Ltd [1950] 1 All ER 449   480, 512, 518
Tutin v Chipperfield Promotions Ltd (1980) 130 NLJ 807   367
Tutton v A.D. Walter Ltd [1986] QB 61   280
Twine v Bean's Express Ltd (1946) 62 TLR 458   386, 387, 388
Tysoe v Davies [1984] RTR 88   344

UBAF Ltd v European American Banking Corporation [1984] 2 All ER 226   569
Ultramares Corporation v Touche (1931) 174 NE 441, 444; 255 NY 170   87, 124
Urbanski v Patel (1978) 84 DLR (3d) 650   235
US v Carroll Towing Co. (1947) 159 F 2d 169   180
Uxbridge Permanent Benefit Building Society v Pickard [1939] 2 KB 248   390

Vacwell Engineering Co. Ltd v BDH Chemicals Ltd [1971] 1 QB 88   241, 243, 244, 418
Vail v MacDonald (1976) 66 DLR (3d) 530, 536 (Supreme Court of Canada)   221
Van Gervan v Fenton (1992) 109 ALR 283   591
Van Oppen v Clerk to the Bedford Charity Trustees [1989] 3 All ER 389   54, 170
Vancouver General Hospital v McDaniel (1934) 152 LT 56   392
Vasey v Surrey Free Inns [1996] PIQR P373   390
Veinot v Kerr-Addison Mines Ltd (1975) 51 DLR (3d) 533   286
Vernon v Bosley (No. 1) [1997] 1 All ER 577   145, 159, 213
Verrall v Great Yarmouth Borough Council [1981] QB 202   447
Videan v British Transport Commission [1963] 2 QB 650   60, 61
Vincent v Lake Erie Transportation Co. (1910) 109 Minn 456, 124 NW 221   544
Virgo Steamship Co. SA v Skaarup Shipping Corporation [1988] 1 Lloyd's Rep 352   428
Vizetelly v Mudie's Select Library Ltd [1900] 2 QB 170   497

W (A minor) (medical treatment) [1992] 4 All ER 627, CA   472
W.B. Anderson & Sons Ltd v Rhodes (Liverpool) Ltd [1967] 2 All ER 850   92
W v Essex County Council [1998] 3 All ER 111   84, 85
Wagner v International Railway Co. (1921) 133 NE 437; 232 NY 176   60, 235
Wagon Mound, The (No. 2) [1967] 1 AC 617   33, 178, 180, 239, 248, 336, 345, 347
Wagon Mound, The [1961] AC 388   238, 239, 241, 243, 245, 246, 247, 248, 249
Wain v F. Sherwood and Sons Transport Ltd, The Times, 16 July 1998   583
Waldick v Malcolm (1991) 83 DLR (4th) 114   275, 526
Walker v Northumberland County Council [1995] 1 All ER 737   179, 256
Walkley v Precision Forgings Ltd [1979] 1 WLR 606   565
Wallace v Newton [1982] 2 All ER 106   370
Walmsley v Humenick [1954] 2 DLR 232   193
Walpole v Partridge & Wilson [1994] 1 All ER 385   68
Walter v Selfe (1851) 4 De G & Sm 315   309
Walton v British Leyland UK Ltd (1978) unreported   425
Wandsworth Board of Works v United Telephone Co. (1884) 13 QBD 904   445
Waple v Surrey CC [1998] 1 All ER 624, CA   504
Ward v Cannock Chase District Council [1985] 3 All ER 537   232, 608
Ward v London County Council [1938] 2 All ER 341   179
Ward v Tesco Stores Ltd [1976] 1 WLR 810   198, 265
Ward v The Ritz Hotel (London) Ltd [1992] PIQR P315   182
Ward v Weeks (1830) 7 Bing 211   496, 498

Warder v Cooper [1970] Ch 495   404, 412
Ware v Garston Haulage Co. [1944] KB 30   343
Warner v Riddiford (1858) 4 CB NS 180   464
Warren v Henlys Ltd [1948] 2 All ER 935   390
Warren v Scruttons Ltd [1962] 1 Lloyd's Rep 497   245
Wason, ex parte (1869) LR 4 QB 573   503
Wason v Walter (1868) LR 4 QB 73   513
Wasson v Chief Constable of the Royal Ulster Constabulary [1987] 8 NIJB 34   455, 545
Waters v Metropolitan Police [1997] ICR 1073, CA   69
Watson v Buckley, Osborne Garrett & Co. Ltd [1940] 1 All ER 174   418, 419
Watt v Hertfordshire County Council [1954] 1 WLR 835   179, 180
Watt v Longsdon [1930] 1 KB 130   508, 512
Watters v Pacific Delivery Service Ltd (1963) 42 DLR (2d) 661, 669   482
Watts v Times Newspapers Ltd [1996] 1 All ER 152, CA   509
Waugh v James K. Allan Ltd [1964] 2 Lloyd's Rep 1   175
Webb v Times Publishing Co. Ltd [1960] 2 QB 535   513
Weir v Wyper 1992 SLT 579   541
Weld-Blundell v Stephens [1920] AC 956   55, 227, 228, 238
Weldon v Home Office [1991] 3 All ER 733, HL   467
Weller & Co. v Foot & Mouth Disease Research Institute [1966] 1 QB 569   125, 357
Wells v Cooper [1958] 2 QB 265   176
Wells v Wells [1998] 3 All ER 481   584, 593, 612
Welsh v Chief Constable of the Merseyside Police [1993] 1 All ER 692   66, 70
Welton v North Cornwall District Council [1997] 1 WLR 570, CA   85
Wenman v Ash (1853) 13 CB 836   495
Wennhak v Morgan (1888) 20 QBD 635   495
Wentworth v Wiltshire County Council [1993] 2 WLR 175   281, 346, 402
West Leigh Colliery Co. Ltd v Tunnicliffe & Hampson Ltd [1908] AC 27   584
Westlake v Bracknell District Council (1987) 282 EG 868   572
Westripp v Baldock [1938] 2 All ER 799   444
Westwood v Post Office [1974] AC 1; [1973] 1 QB 591   285, 288, 289, 555, 556
Whatley v Lancashire & Yorkshire Railway Co. (1884) 13 QBD 131   352
Whatman v Pearson (1868) LR 3 CP 422   383
Wheat v E. Lacon & Co. Ltd [1966] AC 552   265, 266, 291
Wheeler v Copas [1981] 3 All ER 405   265, 329
Wheeler v J.J. Saunders Ltd [1995] 2 All ER 697   329
Wheeler v New Merton Board Mills Ltd [1933] 2 KB 669   261
Wheeler v Somerfield [1966] 2 QB 94   492
White v Blackmore [1972] 2 QB 651   274, 275, 531
White v Glass, The Times, 18 February 1989, CA   565
White v J. & F. Stone (Lighting & Radio) Ltd [1939] 2 KB 827   496
White v Jameson (1874) LR 18 Eq 303   322
White v Jones [1995] 1 All ER 691   95, 110, 111, 119, 121
White v Metropolitan Police Commissioner, The Times, 24 April 1982   463
White v St Albans City & District Council, The Times, 12 March 1990   283
Whiteford v Hunter [1950] WN 553, HL   188
Whitehouse v Jordan [1981] 1 All ER 267   184, 188
Whitfield v North Durham Health Authority [1995] 6 Med LR 32   565
WHPT Housing Association Ltd v Secretary of State for Social Services [1981] ICR 737   378
Wickberg v Patterson [1997] 4 WWR 591   551
Wieland v Cyril Lord Carpets Ltd [1969] 3 All ER 1006   224, 233, 240
Wiffen v Bailey [1915] 1 KB 600   484
Wigg v British Railways Board (1986) 136 NLJ 446   147, 151, 153
Wilchick v Marks [1934] 2 KB 56   325, 326
Wilkes v Hungerford Market Co. (1835) 2 Bing NC 281   345
Wilkes v Wood (1763) Lofft 1   578
Wilkinson v Ancliff (BLT) Ltd [1986] 3 All ER 427   562, 563

Wilkinson v Downton [1897] 2 QB 57   319, 453, 457, 458, 459
Wilks v Cheltenham Home Guard Motor Cycle & Light Car Club [1971] 2 All ER 369   190
Williams v Birmingham Battery and Metal Co. [1899] 2 QB 338   261
Williams v Humphrey, The Times, 20 February 1975   193
Williams v Natural Life Health Foods Ltd [1998] 2 All ER 577   89, 110, 111
Williamson v John I. Thornycroft & Co. Ltd [1940] 2 KB 658   618
Willson v Ministry of Defence [1991] 1 All ER 638   585
Wilsher v Essex Area Health Authority [1986] 3 All ER 801, CA
                           175, 176, 181, 188, 190, 199, 211, 214, 392
Wilson v Pringle [1986] 2 All ER 440   454, 456, 457
Wilson v Tyneside Window Cleaning Co. [1958] 2 QB 110   254, 257
Wilsons & Clyde Coal Co. Ltd v English [1938] AC 57   252, 396
Wimpey Construction UK Ltd v Poole [1984] 2 Lloyd's Rep 499   190
Winnik v Dick 1984 SLT 185   529
Winnipeg Condominium Corporation No. 36 v Bird Construction Co. Ltd
    (1995) 121 DLR (4th) 193   143, 144
Winter Garden Theatre (London) Ltd v Millennium Productions Ltd [1948] AC 173 446, 447
Winter v Cardiff Rural District Council [1950] 1 All ER 819   252, 256
Winterbottom v Lord Derby (1867) LR 2 Ex 316   345
Winterbottom v Wright (1842) 10 M & W 109   27, 416
Wise v Kaye [1962] 1 QB 638   604, 605
Withers v Perry Chain Co. Ltd [1961] 1 WLR 1314   181, 252
Wood v Leadbitter (1845) 13 M & W 838   446, 447
Woodley v Metropolitan District Railway Co. (1877) 2 ExD 384   526
Woodrup v Nicol [1993] PIQR Q104, 114, CA   589
Woodward v Mayor of Hastings [1945] KB 174   273
Wooldridge v Sumner [1963] 2 QB 43   190, 191, 523, 526, 527, 529, 530
Woolfall v Knowsley Borough Council, The Times, 26 June 1992   345
Woolins v British Celanese Ltd (1966) 1 KIR 438   272
Workvale Ltd (No. 2), Re [1992] 2 All ER 627   565
Wright Estate v Davidson (1992) 88 DLR (4th) 698, BCCA   245
Wright v British Railways Board [1983] 2 AC 773   612
Wright v Dunlop Rubber Co. Ltd (1972) 13 KIR 255   425, 426
Wright v Lodge [1993] 4 All ER 299   231
Wringe v Cohen [1940] 1 KB 229   300, 325, 339, 344, 347
Wynbergen v Hoyts Corporation Pty Ltd (1997) 149 ALJR 25   555
Wyngrove v Scottish Omnibuses Ltd 1966 SC (HL) 47   194
Wynston v Macdonald (1979) 105 DLR (3d) 527   102

X (minors) v Bedfordshire County Council [1995] 3 WLR 152
               18, 40, 41, 44, 62, 74, 78, 84, 117, 399, 401, 402, 409

Yachuk v Oliver Blais Co. Ltd [1949] AC 386   553
Yianni v Edwin Evans & Sons [1982] QB 438; [1981] 3 All ER 592   105, 546
York, The [1929] P 178   607
Yorkshire Dale Steamship Co. Ltd v Minister of War Transport [1942] AC 691   223
Youell v Bland Welch & Co Ltd (No 2) [1990] 2 Lloyd's Rep 431   548
Young & Woods Ltd v West [1980] IRLR 201   377
Young v Charles Church (Southern) Ltd, The Times, 1 May 1997, CA   163
Young v Edward Box & Co. Ltd [1951] 1 TLR 789   388
Youssoupoff v Metro-Goldwyn-Mayer Pictures Ltd (1934) 50 TLR 581   489, 498
Yuen Kun-yeu v A-G of Hong Kong [1987] 2 All ER 705   29, 30, 40, 41, 52, 53, 83

Zelenko v Gimbel Bros (1935) 158 Misc 904, 287 NYS 134   47
Zuijs v Wirth Brothers Pty Ltd (1955) 93 CLR 561   377

Table of Statutes

Abortion Act 1967   170, 538
Access to Neighbouring Land Act 1992
   448
Administration of Justice Act 1982   24
   s.1(1)
      (a)   604, 617
      (b)   604
   s.3   617, 620
   s.4(2)   615
   s.5   589
Animals Act 1971   249, 359, 366, 367,
      368, 369, 370, 371, 372, 373, 374
   s.2   368, 371
   s.2(1)   367, 370, 374
   s.2(2)   368, 369, 370, 371, 373, 374
   s.2(2)(a)   368, 369
   s.2(2)(b)   368, 369, 370, 372
   s.2(2)(c)   371
   s.3   368, 373
   s.4   368, 372, 373
   s.4(2)   372
   s.5   368
   s.5(1)   371, 372, 373
   s.5(2)   371
   s.5(3)   371, 372
   s.5(3)(b)   371
   s.5(4)-(5)   373
   s.5(6)   372, 373
   s.6(2)   367
   s.6(2)(b)   367
   s.6(3)   368
   s.6(5)   371
   s.7   372
   s.8(1)-(2)   374
   s.9   373, 481
   s.9(3)-(4)   373
   s.10   371, 372, 373
   s.11   367, 370, 372
Animals (Scotland) Act 1987
   s.2(2)   371

Betting and Lotteries Act 1934   408
Broadcasting Act 1990
   s.166   498
   s.201   498
   Sch.20
      para.1   513
Building Act 1984
   s.38   296

Carriage by Air Act 1961   560
Carriage of Goods by Sea Act 1971   532
Carriage of Goods by Sea Act 1992   127
Chancery Amendment Act 1858   333
   s.2   614
Child Care Act 1980   409
Children Act 1989   409
Children and Young Persons Act 1933
   s.1(7)   468
Children and Young Persons Act 1969
   409
Civil Aviation Act 1982   445
   s.76   363
   s.76(1)-(2)   445
   s.76(3)   446
Civil Evidence Act 1968   502
   s.11   196
   s.13   502
Civil Liability (Contribution) Act 1978
      417, 420, 428, 437, 544, 557, 559
   s.1(1)-(5)   559
   s.2(1)-(3)   558
   s.3-s.4   558
   s.6(1)   558
   s.7(3)   559
Clean Air Act 1993   341
Companies Act 1985
   s.110   90
   s.651   13
Companies Act 1989
   s.141   13

Congenital Disabilities (Civil Liability) Act
    1976 58
  s.1(1) 58
  s.1(2) 58
  s.1(2)(a)-(b) 170
  s.1(3) 58
  s.1(4) 59, 528
  s.1(5) 182
  s.1(6)-(7) 59
  s.1A 58
  s.2 58, 59
Consumer Protection Act 1961 432
Consumer Protection Act 1987 417, 431,
    432, 433, 434, 437, 438, 439, 440, 441,
    560
  Part I 430, 432, 532
  Part II 432
  s.1(1) 430
  s.1(2) 432, 433, 434
  s.1(3) 433
  s.2 436
  s.2(1) 432
  s.2(2) 432, 438
  s.2(2)(b)-(c) 433
  s.2(3) 432, 433, 434, 438
  s.2(4) 434
  s.3(1) 434, 438
  s.3(2) 435, 437
  s.3(2)(c) 435, 436
  s.4 438
  s.4(1)(a)-(c) 438
  s.4(1)(d) 435, 438
  s.4(1)(e) 439, 440, 441
  s.4(1)(f) 433, 439
  s.4(2)(a) 438, 439
  s.4(2)(b) 438
  s.5(1) 436
  s.5(2) 134, 430, 434, 436
  s.5(3)-(4) 437
  s.6(3) 432
  s.6(4) 439
  s.7 438, 532
  s.11 426
  s.41 432
  s.45 433
  s.46 433
  s.46(3)-(4) 434
  s.50(7) 430
  Sch.1 441
Consumer Safety Act 1978 432
Control of Pollution Act 1974 341
  s.88 363
Courts and Legal Services Act 1990
  Part II 506
  s.8 486
  s.62 63
  s.69(2) 506

Courts and Legal Services Act 1990 –
    continued
  s.108 62
Criminal Injuries Compensation Act 1995
    460, 461, 462
  s.1(1) 462
Criminal Justice Act 1988 462
  s.107 464
  s.108 460
  s.109 460, 462
  s.110-s.117 460
  Sch.6 460
  Sch.7 460
Criminal Justice and Public Order Act 1994
  s.61 442
  s.68 442
  s.72-s.73 442
  s.76 442
Criminal Law Act 1967
  s.2 479
  s.3 542
  s.3(1) 480
Criminal Law Act 1977
  s.6 442, 452
  s.7-s.10 442

Damages Act 1996
  s.2 587
  s.3 586
  s.5 587
Dangerous Dogs Act 1991 371
Dangerous Wild Animals Act 1976 13, 368
Defamation Act 1952 510, 514
  s.2 499
  s.3 485
  s.4 9, 493, 494
  s.4(5) 494
  s.5 501, 560
  s.6 516
  s.9(1) 513
  s.10 512
  s.16 498
Defamation Act 1996 487, 495,
    497, 500
  s.1 497
  s.1(5) 498
  s.2 494, 499
  s.2(5) 495
  s.3 494, 499
  s.4 494, 499
  s.4(4) 494
  s.4(5) 495
  s.8-s.10 487
  s.12 502
  s.13 504
  s.13(1) 504
  s.13(4) 504

Defamation Act 1996 – *continued*
s.14   505, 506
s.15   513
s.15(2)-(4)   513
Sch.1   513
  para.14   510
  Part I   513
  Part II   514
Defective Premises Act 1972   142, 326
s.1   296, 297
s.3   293
s.4   264, 266, 280, 292, 317, 325, 344
s.4(1)   291, 292
s.4(2)   283, 292
s.4(4)-(6)   292
s.6(3)   292
Dramatic and Musical Performers'
  Protection Act 1958   409

Education Act 1944   402
Employers' Liability (Compulsory
  Insurance) Act 1969   12, 251, 255,
  405, 406, 407, 409
s.5   251, 405, 406, 407
Employers' Liability (Defective Equipment)
  Act 1969   396, 419
s.1(1)   255
Environmental Protection Act 1990   341

Factories Act 1961   258, 259, 406, 413
s.14   414
s.14(1)   259
s.28(1)   259
s.29(1)   259, 260
Factories Acts   553
Family Law Reforn Act 1969
s.8(1)   472
Fatal Accidents Act 1846   615
Fatal Accidents Act 1976   58, 168, 557,
  566, 574, 586, 590, 591, 596, 597, 600,
  614, 615, 616, 617, 620
s.1   616
s.1(1)   616
s.1A   144, 617
s.2   617
s.3(1)   617, 620
s.3(3)-(4)   618
s.4   592, 620
Finance Act 1995
s.142   587
Fire Prevention (Metropolis) Act 1774
  365
s.86   365
Fire Services Act 1947
s.30   71
Food and Drugs (Adulteration) Act 1928
  403

Food Safety Act 1990   86

Gas Act 1964
s.14   363
Guard Dogs Act 1975   371, 372, 399
Gulf Oil Refining Act 1965   327

Health and Safety at Work etc. Act 1974
  83, 258, 261
s.47(1)-(2)   258
s.71   296
Highways Act 1959
s.59   402
Highways Act 1980   49, 80
s.41   281, 346, 347, 402
s.56   402
s.58   281, 347, 402
s.58(2)   394
Highways (Miscellaneous Provisions) Act
  1961
s.1   280, 346, 402
Housing Act 1961
s.32   325
Housing Act 1985
  Part III   402
s.63(1)   402
Housing Act 1988
s.16   292
s.27-s.28   404
Housing (Homeless Persons) Act 1977
  402
Human Fertilisation and Embryology Act
  1990
s.44   58

Income and Corporation Taxes Act 1988
s.329A-s.329B   587
Industrial Injuries and Diseases (Old Cases)
  Act 1975   598
Inheritance (Provision for Family and
  Dependants) Act 1975
s.1   616

Justices of the Peace Act 1979
s.45   62

Land Compensation Act 1973   328
Landlord and Tenant Act 1985
s.8   292
s.11-s.12   292, 325
Latent Damage Act 1986   8, 142, 568, 570,
  571
s.1   570
s.2(1)   573
s.3   127, 572
s.3(1)   572, 573
s.3(3)   573
s.4(3)-(4)   572

Law Reform (Contributory Negligence) Act
   1945 278, 331, 545–9, 555, 556, 558
  s.1 554
  s.1(1) 439, 545, 555
  s.4 545
Law Reform (Miscellaneous Provisions) Act
   1934 566, 574, 614, 616, 620
  s.1(1) 614
  s.1(2)(a) 615
  s.1(2)(c) 615
  s.1(4) 614
Law Reform (Personal Injuries) Act 1948
  s.1 250
  s.2(1) 597, 603
  s.2(4) 589
Limitation Act 1980 13, 441, 559, 560,
   561, 616
  s.2 560, 561, 573
  s.4A 560
  s.5 573
  s.9 561
  s.10 559
  s.11 561, 564, 565, 571
  s.11(1) 561
  s.11(4) 560
  s.11(5) 566
  s.11(7) 566
  s.11A(3)-(4) 441
  s.12 564
  s.12(2) 566
  s.13(1) 566
  s.14 565, 570
  s.14(1) 441, 561, 562, 570
  s.14(1)(a)-(b) 562
  s.14(1A) 441
  s.14(2) 562
  s.14(3) 564
  s.14A 563, 570, 571, 572
  s.14A(1) 571
  s.14A(3)-(4) 570
  s.14A(5) 570, 573
  s.14A(6)-(10) 570
  s.14B 570, 571, 573
  s.15 449, 451
  s.28 561, 573
  s.28(1) 573
  s.28A 573
  s.32 573
  s.32(1) 572
  s.32(1)(b) 573
  s.32(2) 572
  s.32A 560
  s.33 441, 561, 562, 565, 566
  s.33(1) 564
  s.33(3) 564
  s.33(3)(e) 562
  s.33(4) 566

Limitation Act 1980 – *continued*
  s.38(2) 573
  s.38(3) 573
  s.38(3)(d) 573
Local Government Act 1974
  s.32 506
London Hackney Carriages Act 1843 380
Lord Cairns' Act *see* Chancery Amendment
  Act 1858
Lord Tenterden's Act *see* Statute of Frauds
  Amendment Act 1882

Maritime Conventions Act 1911
  s.1 544
Matrimonial Causes Act 1973 64, 65
Matrimonial Homes Act 1983 319, 320,
   321
Mental Health Act 1983 236, 465, 468,
   470, 471, 573
  s.117 84, 236, 237
Merchant Shipping (Oil Pollution) Act 1971
   363
Mines and Quarries Act 1954 258, 259
  s.48 260
  s.157 259
Misrepresentation Act 1967 92, 399
  s.2(1) 89, 92, 99, 546, 547
  s.3 531

National Health Service Act 1946
  s.3 380
National Health Service Act 1977
  s.3(1) 380
National Insurance (Industrial Injuries) Act
   1946 251
National Parks and Access to the
   Countryside Act 1949 268
  s.60 280, 447
Nuclear Installations Act 1965 363, 399

Occupiers' Liability Act 1957 167, 264,
   265, 266, 268, 275, 280, 281, 282, 285,
   288, 289, 290, 291, 299, 399
  s.1(1) 265, 279
  s.1(2) 265, 266
  s.1(3)(a) 265
  s.1(3)(b) 265, 280
  s.1(4) 268
  s.2(1) 265, 275, 526
  s.2(2) 268
  s.2(3) 269
  s.2(3)(a) 194, 269
  s.2(3)(b) 271
  s.2(4)(a) 274, 275, 288
  s.2(4)(b) 272
  s.2(5) 274, 275, 526
  s.2(6) 268

Occupiers' Liability Act 1957 – *continued*
  s.3(1) 277
  s.5(1) 267
Occupiers' Liability Act 1984 58, 167,
    264, 276, 279, 280, 282, 284, 285, 286,
    287, 288, 289, 290, 291, 295, 299, 372
  s.1 280, 286
  s.1(1) 279
  s.1(1)(a) 280
  s.1(2) 280
  s.1(2)(a) 280
  s.1(3) 282, 283, 284, 285
  s.1(3)(a) 282, 283, 284
  s.1(3)(b) 282, 283, 284, 285, 286
  s.1(3)(c) 282, 284, 286
  s.1(4) 284, 286, 288
  s.1(5)-(9) 288
  s.2 277
Occupiers' Liability (Northern Ireland) Act
    1957 281
Occupiers' Liability (Scotland) Act 1960
    284, 285
Offences against the Person Act 1861
  s.42-s.45 464
Offices, Shops and Railway Premises Act
    1963 258

Parliamentary Commissioner Act 1967
  s.10(5) 506
Parliamentary Papers Act 1840
  s.1 503
  s.3 503, 513, 520
Party Wall etc Act 1996 448
  s.8 448
Pilotage Act 1913
  s.15(1) 380
Pilotage Act 1987 380
Police Act 1964
  s.48 380
Police and Criminal Evidence Act 1984
    477, 479
  s.1-s.3 477
  s.16-s.18 447
  s.24 477
  s.24(1) 478
  s.24(2) 477, 478
  s.24(3)-(6) 478
  s.24(7) 479
  s.25 477
  s.25(1) 479
  s.25(3) 479
  s.26 477
  s.28 479
  s.28(5) 479
  s.32 477
  s.117 480
  s.245 478

Police and Criminal Evidence Act 1984 –
    continued
  Sch.2 477
Powers of Criminal Courts Act 1973
  s.35 3, 462, 464, 600
  s.35(1) 464
  s.35(3) 464
  s.35(3B) 464
  s.35(3D) 464
  s.36-s.38 3, 464
  s.43A 464
Prison Act 1952
  s.12 467
Property Misdescriptions Act 1991 114
Prosecution of Offences Act 1985 403
Protection from Eviction Act 1977
  s.1 404, 452
  s.3 404
Protection from Harassment Act 1997
    305, 343, 459, 460, 477, 561, 612
  s.1(1) 459, 460
  s.1(2) 459
  s.1(3) 460
  s.3(1) 459
  s.3(6) 460
  s.6 561
  s.7(2) 459
  s.74 459
Public Health Act 1875
  s.66 403
Public Health Act 1936 341, 402
  Part III 402
Public Health Act 1961 341
Public Order Act 1986 477
Public Passenger Vehicles Act 1981
  s.29 532

Railway Fires Act 1905 361
Railway Fires Act 1923 361
Rehabilitation of Offenders Act 1974 462
  s.8 500
Reservoirs Act 1975
  s.28 361
  Sch.2 361
Riding Establishment Act 1964 13
Riding Establishment Act 1970 13
Road Traffic Act 1930 407
  s.35 405
Road Traffic Act 1972
  s.148(3) 529
Road Traffic Act 1988 277
  s.14-s.15 552
  s.143-s.145 12, 532
  s.149 277, 529, 532, 542
  s.151 12
  s.151(4) 12, 542
  s.152 12

Road Traffic Act 1988 – *continued*
Safety of Sports Grounds Act 1975   399
Sale of Goods Act 1979
  s.12-s.13   3
  s.14   3, 130, 417
Sale and Supply of Goods Act 1994   417
Slander of Women Act 1891   499
Social Security Act 1989   597
Social Security Administration Act 1992
  251
  Part IV   597
Social Security Contributions and Benefits
  Act 1992   251
Social Security (Recovery of Benefits) Act
  1997   598, 599, 600
  s.6   599
  s.15   599
  Sch.1   600
  Sch.2   599
Solicitors' Act 1974
  s.37   13
Southern Rhodesia Act 1965   410
Statute of Frauds Amendment Act 1828
  92
  s.6   92
Supply of Goods and Services Act 1982
  s.4   417
  s.13   183
Supreme Court Act 1981
  s.32A   585
  s.35A   611
  s.50   333, 614
  s.51   63

Theatres Act 1968
  s.4   498
  s.7   498
Theft Act 1968   464
Third Parties (Rights Against Insurers) Act
  1930   13, 417
Town Police Clauses Act 1847   380
Trade Union and Labour Relations Act 1974
  s.2(1)   488
  s.2(1)(c)   488
Trade Union and Labour Relations
  (Consolidation) Act 1992
  s.10   488

Unfair Contract Terms Act 1977   112,
  113, 114, 121, 275, 277, 289, 290,
  531, 532
  s.1(1)(b)   289
  s.1(1)(c)   277, 289
  s.1(3)   112, 277
  s.1(3)(a)   531
  s.2   112, 381, 423, 531
  s.2(1)   59, 112, 261, 275, 277, 278, 526,
    531
  s.2(2)   14, 112, 277, 381, 526, 531
  s.2(3)   278, 526, 528, 531
  s.5   531
  s.6   417
  s.11   277
  s.11(3)   112, 531
  s.11(4)   113, 532
  s.13(1)   112, 531
  s.14   277

Vaccine Damage Payments Act 1979   24,
  349, 600

War Damage Act 1965   544
Water Act 1981
  s.6   363
Waterworks Clauses Act 1847   403
Wills Act 1837
  s.15   118
Workmen's Compensation Act 1897
  251

European legislation

Directive 85/374/EEC (Product
  Liability)   430, 433, 439, 440
  art.7(e)   440
Directive 89/391/EEC (Framework on
  Health and Safety)   259
European Convention on Human Rights
  561
  art.10   487, 511
Strasbourg Convention on Products Liability
  430

ONE

Perspectives

1.1 SCOPE OF TORT

The law of tort is primarily concerned with providing a remedy to persons who have been harmed by the conduct of others. In any society conflicts of interest are bound to lead to the infliction of losses, a process that, not surprisingly, tends to increase with the level of social interaction. The allocation, and in some instances the prevention, of these losses is the principal function of tort law. It can be misleading, however, to think of losses being 'allocated', because in real terms the damage that has been done will still constitute a net social or economic loss irrespective of the outcome of any litigation. If A negligently destroys B's car, A will be ordered to pay money compensation to B for the value of the vehicle, and B can then replace it with another. As between A and B the financial consequences of the loss have been 'allocated' to A, but there is still a net loss of social resources. The point is more obvious in the case of personal injuries. If A's negligence caused B to lose a leg, then no amount of compensation will 'restore' B's loss or 'allocate' it to A. Again, A can be required to meet the financial consequences of the injury, such as B's loss of earnings or medical expenses and even a sum in respect of pain and suffering and loss of amenity, but the real loss cannot be removed by the payment of money.

Tort may prevent losses in two ways. First, by the remedy of an injunction a person can be restrained from behaving in a manner which interferes with another's interests. This is a common feature of the tort of nuisance (chapter 7) and the economic torts. Secondly, the possibility of liability in tort may induce people to modify their behaviour so as to avoid damaging others. This is the concept of deterrence, which, as will be seen, is far from uncontroversial.

The payment of compensation by A to B does not in itself involve a social cost, although clearly it produces a private cost to A. It is what an economist would call a transfer payment. However, the process by which a decision is reached that A *should* pay, does consume resources in the form of the time and effort of lawyers, the courts, insurance companies, witnesses and the parties. Therefore, it is usually argued, there has to be some reason or justification for transferring the loss to A, rather than letting it lie where it falls, i.e., with B. It might be thought that if B has suffered harm and A caused it, this would be sufficient justification. There are two problems with this approach. First, identifying the cause of damage is not necessarily a simple exercise. If both A and B were engaged in activities which came into conflict (e.g., A was a motorist and B a pedestrian) then which activity 'caused' the damage? The tendency here is to look for the person who was 'at fault' in some way. Even where B is passive and A is 'active' it does not necessarily follow that A 'caused' the harm. For example, A builds a factory on a site located well beyond any residential area. Subsequently, B purchases adjoining land and builds a house. He then complains about the noise and fumes from A's factory. Who caused the damage? Is it the product of A's land use or B's, and should it make any difference which use was first in time? (See, e.g., *Miller* v *Jackson* [1977] QB 966, para. 7.1.3.4.)

The second problem is that A's activity may be regarded as socially or economically valuable, and B's damage an unfortunate but unavoidable consequence. A liability rule that required A to compensate B might deter or restrict A's activity to such an extent as to produce a net social loss. Strict rules on defamation, for example, will limit freedom of speech. So, just as rules of non-liability impose costs on the people who suffer damage, liability rules also involve costs by restricting freedom of action. The problem is to strike a balance between competing claims and values. It is not for every loss, then that the law will grant a remedy. Indeed, in a capitalist economy some harm, such as the losses attributable to trade competition, is regarded as desirable. There has to be some basis for deciding what types of loss are to be actionable and the circumstances in which someone who has caused such loss will be liable to pay compensation. This is the role of tort, which marks out the conditions of both liability and non-liability.

The interests which the law of tort will protect include physical harm, both to the person and to property, a person's reputation, or dignity, or liberty, or use and enjoyment of land, or even his financial interests. Whether a particular type of harm will entitle the victim to redress varies considerably with the manner in which it occurred. In broad terms there is a spectrum of conduct ranging from intentional through careless to accidental. The deliberate infliction of damage usually, but not always, entails liability. As a general rule intentional wrongs have no social utility and thus there is little to weigh in the balance against the plaintiff's claim to redress. At the other end of the scale, strict liability specifies compensation simply for the causation of damage. However, this is comparatively rare, and there is no coherent basis to explain when or why strict liability will be applied in the English law of tort (see chapter 8). The historical trend has been a gradual move away from strict to fault liability.

It is traditional in a tort textbook to offer a definition of tort which will distinguish it from other branches of the law such as contract, restitution and criminal law. The problem is that most definitions are either at too high a level of abstraction or are too cumbersome to be of any practical value. *Flemming,* p. 1, for example, suggests that 'In very general terms, a tort is an injury other than a breach of contract, which the law will redress with damages'. The author concedes that this is far from informative nor even strictly accurate. The distinctions can best be seen in the light of the different functions of these categories of law, although there can be considerable overlap. Thus the criminal law punishes the perpetrator and vindicates the public interest in the maintenance of law and order, whereas tort compensates the victim of a private wrong. Many criminal offences, however, are also torts; the effect of an award of damages may be to punish the defendant (and in the case of exemplary damages this is the purpose, para. 15.1.1.3); and the criminal courts can make limited compensation orders to the victims of crime (Powers of Criminal Courts Act 1973, ss. 35 to 38, para. 12.3). Restitution is not so much concerned with compensating the plaintiff's loss, as recovering the defendant's unjust gains. The boundaries of tort have often been fixed by its historical development. The equitable remedy for breach of trust, for example, was established by the courts of Chancery rather than the common law courts and the modern distinctions between breach of trust and tort probably have as much to do with this as any functional differences.

Perhaps the most difficult distinction to draw, and the one with most practical significance, is that between tort and contract. Broadly speaking contract deals with the enforcement of mutually binding promises, and so the obligations are created by the parties to the contract. In tort duties are fixed by the law rather than the parties. This is only partially true, because some tort duties depend upon the parties voluntarily 'entering into' a relationship (see, e.g., negligent statements, para. 2.2.4.1.3; employers' liability, chapter 5; and occupiers' liability, chapter 6). Some tort duties can be varied by the parties (see, e.g., paras 14.1 and 14.2), and certain contractual obligations are fixed by statute (e.g., Sale of Goods Act 1979, ss. 12 to 14). Perhaps the most helpful distinction is that between the aim of an award of damages in contract and tort. Tort protects the status quo, in that the plaintiff's position should not be worsened by the defendant's conduct. This is expressed in terms of the measure of damages, namely that the plaintiff should be restored to the position he would have been in had the tort not been committed. In contract the defendant is liable for not making the plaintiff's position better, for not fulfilling the plaintiff's expectation of benefit from the contract. This is only a broad generalisation because tort can be used to protect certain types of expectation of advantage (see *Ross* v *Caunters* [1980] Ch 297, para. 2.2.4.1.4). Indeed, a typical tort action in respect of personal injuries, which is usually regarded as a clear example of returning the plaintiff to the status quo ante, often contains a substantial element of expectation loss, in the form of 'loss' of future earnings. The plaintiff cannot have lost what he is not yet entitled to receive, but what has been harmed is his expectation that his capacity to earn will continue into the future. Similarly, in some circumstances contract provides a remedy where the plaintiff's position has been worsened, e.g., where a carrier has negligently damaged the plaintiff's goods in transit—the contract supplies the defendant's obligation to act, and the duty to act *carefully* can be categorised as contractual or tortious. (For a more sophisticated analysis of the distinction between 'status quo' and 'expectation' interests see Burrows (1983) 99 LQR 217–32. For an alternative classification see Stapleton (1997) 113 LQR 257, and for criticism of Stapleton's approach see Friedmann (1997) 113 LQR 424 and Smith (1997) 113 LQR 426.)

Until comparatively recently the trend has been for the differences between contract and tort to be minimised (see Holyoak (1983) 99 LQR 59 1). In *Junior Books Ltd* v *Veitchi Co. Ltd* [1983] 1 AC 520 (see para. 2.2.4.2.2), for example, Lord Roskill said (at p. 545) that:

> today the proper control lies not in asking whether the proper remedy should lie in contract . . . or tort, not in somewhat capricious judicial determination whether a particular case falls on one side of the line or the other . . . but in the first instance in establishing the relevant principles and then in deciding whether the particular case falls within or without those principles.

Nonetheless, there remain some important practical differences, such as different rules for the commencement of the limitation period, different measures of damages, possibly different tests for remoteness of damage, and quite distinct approaches to the question of purely financial losses. In the 1970s the courts decided that the existence of a contractual relationship did not preclude tortious duties arising between the parties, and the plaintiff could opt for the more advantageous action (*Esso Petroleum Co. Ltd* v *Mardon* [1976] QB 801; *Batty* v *Metropolitan Property Realisations Ltd* [1978] QB 554; *Midland Bank Trust Co. Ltd* v *Hett Stubbs & Kemp* [1979] Ch 384; see also *Central Trust Co.* v *Rafuse* (1986) 31 DLR (4th) 481, Supreme Court of Canada). This emphasised the considerable overlap between contract and tort. In the 1980s the courts were less sanguine about superimposing tortious obligations on contractual relationships (see, e.g., *Leigh & Sillavan Ltd* v *Aliakmon Shipping Co. Ltd* [1985] 2 All ER 44, CA; [1986] 2 All ER 145, HL; cf. Goff LJ in the Court of Appeal).

In *Tai Hing Cotton Mill Ltd* v *Liu Chong Hing Bank Ltd* [1986] AC 80 Lord Scarman, giving the opinion of the Privy Council, said (at p. 107):

> Their Lordships do not believe that there is anything to the advantage of the law's development in searching for a liability in tort where the parties are in a contractual relationship. This is particularly so in a commercial relationship. Though it is possible as a matter of legal semantics to conduct an analysis of the rights and duties inherent in some contractual relationships . . . either as a matter of contract law when the question will be what, if any, terms are to be implied or as a matter of tort law when the task will be to identify a duty arising from the proximity and character of the relationship between the parties, their lordships believe it to be correct in principle and necessary for the avoidance of confusion in the law to adhere

to the contractual analysis: on principle because it is a relationship in which the parties have, subject to a few exceptions, the right to determine their obligations to each other, and for the avoidance of confusion because different consequences do follow according to whether liability arises from contract or tort, e.g., in the limitation of action.

The courts have demonstrated an increasing reluctance to impose a duty in tort where this would be wider than the parties' contractual obligations, on the basis that the parties had the opportunity to define the extent of their liability in the contract and did just that by entering into the contract. They cannot then rely on the law of tort to provide greater protection than that for which, either expressly or impliedly, they have contracted (*National Bank of Greece SA* v *Pinios Shipping Co. (No. 1)* [1989] 1 All ER 213, 223, 232; *Bank of Nova Scotia* v *Hellenic Mutual War Risks Association (Bermuda) Ltd* [1989] 3 All ER 628 (reversed on other grounds [1991] 3 All ER 1, HL); *Greater Nottingham Co-operative Society Ltd* v *Cementation Piling and Foundations Ltd* [1988] 2 All ER 971, 984, 991; see also *Canadian Pacific Hotels Ltd* v *Bank of Montreal* (1988) 40 DLR (4th) 432 in which the Canadian Supreme Court rejected the existence of a duty of care in tort when the same duty had been denied or excluded by the court as an implied term of a particular class of contracts, though accepting that in other classes of contract there could be concurrent liability in tort). Similar reasoning has been employed to deny the existence of a duty of care in the tort of negligence between an employer and a subcontractor under a building contract (where there is normally no direct contractual relationship, i.e., no privity of contract). Thus, in *Pacific Associates Inc.* v *Baxter* [1989] 2 All ER 159, 170 Purchas LJ said that 'where the parties have come together against a contractual structure which provides for compensation in the event of a failure of one of the parties involved, the court will be slow to superimpose an added duty of care beyond that which was in the contemplation of the parties at the time that they came together'. This approach has been adopted by the Court of Appeal even in respect of physical damage to property by the negligence of a subcontractor, allowing the subcontractor to take the benefit of the terms of the main contract—putting the risk of fire on the plaintiff—to which the subcontractor was not a party (*Norwich City Council* v *Harvey* [1989] 1 All ER 1180; see also *British Telecommunications plc* v *James Thomson & Sons (Engineers) Ltd* (1996) 82 BLR 1; Convery 1997 SLT 113).

In *Henderson* v *Merrett Syndicates Ltd* [1994] 3 All ER 506 the House of Lords held that sub-agents acting on behalf of 'indirect' Lloyd's names owed a duty of care in negligence to the names, despite the fact that they were not in a contractual relationship with the names, in other words notwithstanding that the parties had chosen a particular structure of obligations in which the names had no direct relationship with the sub-agents (i.e., the names contracted with the agents who then contracted with the sub-agents). Lord Goff acknowledged that the 'contractual structure' argument still had force. The facts of *Henderson*, his Lordship thought, may be quite unusual. In many cases in which a contractual chain comparable to that on the facts of

Henderson is constructed 'it may well prove to be inconsistent with an assumption of responsibility which has the effect of, so to speak, short-circuiting the contractual structure so put in place by the parties' ([1994] 3 All ER 506, 534). In the case of an ordinary building contract the owner contracts with a main contractor who will then contract with subcontractors for the provision of materials or certain aspects of the work. If the subcontracted work or materials did not conform to the required standard, it would not ordinarily be open to the building owner to sue the subcontractor or supplier direct under *Hedley Byrne*. There is generally no assumption of responsibility by the subcontractor or supplier direct to the building owner, the parties having so structured their relationship that it is inconsistent with any such assumption of responsibility (though there may be an assumption of responsibility between parties who are in privity of contract under a building or repair contract: see *Barclays Bank plc* v *Fairclough Building Ltd* (1995) 76 BLR 1). Unfortunately, his Lordship did not explain why the ordinary building contract differs from the contractual structure established in *Henderson* nor offer any criteria by which to assess whether or not the contractual structure argument should apply in any given case. The distinction is not based on a difference between economic loss and physical damage, because in *Marc Rich & Co.* v *Bishop Rock Marine Co. Ltd* [1995] 3 All ER 307 the House of Lords concluded that a classification society does not owe a duty of care to the owner of the cargo on a vessel which has been negligently certified as seaworthy, when subsequently the vessel sinks, partly because if a duty of care was held to exist the cost of insuring against potential claims would ultimately be passed on to shipowners, thereby outflanking the contractual structure governing dealings between shipowners and cargo owners. It remains to be seen whether the courts will attempt to lay down guidelines for determining when the 'contractual structure' is to be enforced and when it can be ignored.

It is possible that many of these cases can be explained by the fact that they were concerned with commercial contracts in circumstances where in any event the availability of a tortious remedy was doubtful (see Holyoak (1990) 6 PN 113). Thus, where a plaintiff is seeking to *extend* the defendant's obligations beyond the express or implied terms of the contract and beyond the defendant's previously acknowledged duties in tort the court will be extremely cautious about finding an additional tortious duty (*Reid* v *Rush & Tompkins Group plc* [1989] 3 All ER 228, CA—no duty of care owed by employers to an employee posted overseas either to provide personal accident insurance or to advise the employee to obtain such insurance himself). On the other hand, as Stuart-Smith LJ commented in *Johnstone* v *Bloomsbury Health Authority* [1991] 2 All ER 293, 298, where there is no question of importing from the law of tort some hitherto unrecognised duty not provided for in the express contract terms or inconsistent with them the *Tai Hing* approach should be irrelevant. Thus, an employer's tortious duty to exercise reasonable care for the health and safety of his employee would not necessarily be overriden by an express contractual term to work a specific number of hours per week which was harmful to the employee's health. However,

Leggatt LJ took the view that since the scope of the relevant duties owed was delimited by the contract the plaintiff could not be in a better position by couching his claim in tort, and Browne-Wilkinson V-C said (at p. 304) that:

> In my judgment the approach adopted in the *Tai Hing* case shows that where there is a contractual relationship between the parties their respective rights and duties have to be analysed wholly in contractual terms and not as a mixture of duties in tort and contract. It necessarily follows that the scope of the duties owed by one party to the other will be defined by the terms of the contract between them.

Accordingly, if the contract were to impose an absolute obligation to work 88 hours per week on average this would preclude an argument that there was a breach of an implied duty of care for the employee's health. If this view of the relationship between employer and employee is correct, it would seem that the whole of the law of employers' liability should be a matter of contract not tort. It must be doubtful whether Lord Scarman's dictum in *Tai Hing*, which was made in the context of a banker-customer relationship where the bank was seeking to argue that the customer owed a duty of care to the bank to manage its account carefully, can support such a radical shift (see Weir [1991] CLJ 397, 399; Dolding and Fawlk (1992) 55 MLR 562, 565). Moreover, it is not clear how precisely contractual terms invalidate the operation of tortious duties between contracting parties (Holyoak (1990) 6 PN 113, 117), particularly duties imposed by law for the protection of the health and safety of employees. On the other hand, it is worth bearing in mind that in some circumstances a contractual analysis of the problem may be more advantageous to a plaintiff than attempting to frame the issue in terms of tort (see, e.g., *Scally* v *Southern Health and Social Services Board* [1991] 4 All ER 563 where the House of Lords was prepared to imply a term into a contract of employment requiring the employer to inform employees of the existence of a valuable contingent right under the contract which required action by the employees to obtain the benefit of the right. It is unlikely that this obligation could have been cast in terms of a duty of care in the tort of negligence, since it involved a claim for purely economic loss: see per Lord Bridge at p. 569 and *Reid* v *Rush & Tompkins Group plc*, above).

In *Henderson* v *Merrett Syndicates Ltd* [1994] 3 All ER 506 one of the central issues was whether a professional person could owe a *concurrent* duty in both contract and tort. The relationship between professional and client has long been considered to be the paradigm example of concurrent liability, the client being entitled to sue either in the tort of negligence or for breach of an implied contractual term that the professional would exercise reasonable care in performing the contract (*Midland Bank Trust Co. Ltd* v *Hett Stubbs & Kemp* [1979] Ch 384—solicitors; *Thake* v *Maurice* [1986] 1 All ER 497—doctors; *Punjab National Bank* v *de Boinville* [1992] 1 WLR 1138, 1152—insurance brokers). Lord Scarman's comments in *Tai Hing* had given rise to some doubts about this. In *Henderson* the House of Lords held that an assumption of responsibility by a person rendering professional or quasi-professional services coupled with reliance by the person for whom the services were rendered could give rise to a tortious duty of care under the principle of *Hedley Byrne & Co. Ltd* v *Heller Partners Ltd* [1964] AC 465, para. 2.2.4.1.3, irrespective of whether there was a contractual relationship between the parties. There was no reason to limit the tortious duty of care to cases where the relevant services were rendered gratuitously. Indeed, insisting on a contractual analysis to the exclusion of tort whenever the parties are in a contractual relationship would make it impossible to apply the provisions of the Latent Damage Act 1986 to contractual negligence, since it has been held that the legislation does not cover breach of contract (*Iron Trade Mutual Insurance Co. Ltd* v *J. K. Buckenham Ltd* [1990] 1 All ER 808; see para. 14.7.2), whereas a third party who was not in a contractual relationship with the defendant might be able to sue in tort and would be able to invoke the more favourable rules on limitation. A concurrent liability in tort would not be accepted if its effect would be to permit the plaintiff to circumvent or escape a contractual exclusion or limitation of liability for the act or omission that would otherwise constitute the tort, but, subject to this, a plaintiff who had concurrent remedies in contract and tort was entitled to choose the remedy which appeared to him to be the most advantageous in respect of any particular legal consequence, e.g., the limitation period is more favourable to plaintiffs in the tort of negligence than in contract (*Henderson* v *Merrett Syndicates Ltd* [1994] 3 All ER 506, 530 per Lord Goff, citing *Central Trust Co.* v *Rafuse* (1986) 31 DLR (4th) 481, 522 per Le Dain J, Supreme Court of Canada). Lord Goff commented (at pp. 532–3) that:

> The result may be untidy; but given that the tortious duty is imposed by the general law, and the contractual duty is attributable to the will of the parties, I do not find it objectionable that the claimant may be entitled to take advantage of the remedy which is most advantageous to him, subject only to ascertaining whether the tortious duty is so inconsistent with the applicable contract that, in accordance with ordinary principle, the parties must be taken to have agreed that the tortious remedy is to be limited or excluded.

In *Barclays Bank plc* v *Fairclough Building Ltd* (1995) 76 BLR 1 a sub-subcontractor (T) was held to have been negligent in the manner in which it performed the task of cleaning an asbestos roof causing extensive contamination of the surrounding area. The subcontractor (C) was liable in contract up the chain of contracts for the cost of dealing with the contamination, and T was held liable in contract in respect of this economic loss (i.e., C's liability under the contract). T argued that it also owed a concurrent duty of care in tort to C because T sought to claim that C had been contributorily negligent (thus reducing the damages payable by T to C) which it would be unable to do unless it could demonstrate that its own contractual breach of duty corresponded to a common law duty in tort (see para. 14.5.1). The Court of Appeal held that T did owe a concurrent duty of care in tort applying

Henderson, on the basis that a skilled contractor undertaking maintenance work to a building assumes a responsibility which invites reliance no less than a financial adviser does in undertaking his work. The finding of a concurrent duty would not expose T to the risk of an unrestricted number of claims or to claims greater in extent than those for which it was potentially liable in contract. It just so happened on the facts of this case that the finding of a concurrent duty worked in favour of T (the defendant in the third party proceedings brought by C. See further Whittaker (1997) 17 LS 169, discussing *Barclays Bank* v *Fairclough Building* and *Holt* v *Payne Skillington*, below).

In *Henderson* Lord Goff said that Lord Scarman's comments in *Tai Hing* were addressed to the question of whether a tortious duty of care could be established which was more extensive than that provided under the contract, as opposed to co-extensive. In *Holt* v *Payne Skillington (a firm)* (1995) 77 BLR 51, however, the Court of Appeal held that where a duty of care in tort arose between parties to a contract wider obligations *could* be imposed by the duty of care in tort than those arising under the contract. The duty in tort was imposed by the general law, whereas the contractual obligations resulted from the common intention of the parties (a point that had been made by Lord Goff in *Henderson*). There was no reason, said Hirst LJ, why a *Hedley Byrne* duty could not arise in a set of circumstances where the parties entered into a contractual relationship involving more limited obligations than those imposed by the duty in tort. The duties would be concurrent but not co-extensive. The difference in scope between the two would reflect the more limited factual basis which gave rise to the contract and the absence of any term in the contract which precluded or restricted the wider duty of care in tort.

1.2   MALICE, INTENTION AND FAULT

Malice can have two meanings in tort: (a) intentional wrongdoing, and (b) improper motive. When used in the first sense the word is superfluous. For example, in the tort of defamation it is said that the defamatory words must be 'maliciously' published, but this is regarded as mere verbiage. Even an 'innocent' publication will suffice (subject to the defence of the Defamation Act 1952, s. 4). The defendant's motive is usually irrelevant to his liability in tort. 'The law in general asks merely what the defendant has done, not why he did it' (*Salmond and Heuston*, p. 19). In some instances an improper motive may be a prerequisite to liability. The best example is an action for malicious prosecution (para. 12.6). It will also defeat a defence of qualified privilege in defamation (para. 13.2.5), and in some circumstances may be relevant to liability in nuisance (para. 7.1.3.5).

Intention refers to the defendant's knowledge that the consequences of his conduct are bound to occur, where the consequences are desired or, if not desired, are foreseen as a certain result. 'Recklessness' is usually categorised with intention, where it used to signify the defendant's advertence to a risk that the consequences will result from his act (although the House of Lords has said that recklessness can include some forms of inadvertence: *R* v

Caldwell [1982] AC 341; *R v Lawrence* [1982] AC 510; *R v Reid* [1992] 1 WLR 793). In tort the concept of intention has not created the problems that have bedevilled the criminal law. The much wider range of liability for careless conduct has, to a large extent, removed the need for fine distinctions. If a defendant is responsible when he ought to have foreseen that harm would result from his actions, it becomes irrelevant whether in fact he did foresee the possibility of harm, or even whether he desired it.

The term 'fault liability', though including intentional wrongs, usually refers to liability for careless conduct as opposed to strict liability or 'no-fault' compensation schemes. Liability in negligence shifts the focus of the courts' attention away from the nature of the plaintiff's interest that has been infringed, as in older actions such as trespass, to the nature of the defendant's conduct. In trespass the defendant was liable if by some positive act he directly interfered with an interest protected by the law. These were fairly well defined—the plaintiff's person, his liberty or his possession of land or goods. The defendant could escape liability if he could justify his conduct, for example, by showing that the plaintiff consented to the interference, or that he was maintaining law and order, or that it was a matter of urgent necessity. He could not justify the interference simply by proving that he acted reasonably in the circumstances, which is the measure of careful conduct. Historically, the action known as 'trespass on the case' or simply 'case', developed to fill gaps left by trespass, particularly as a remedy for damage which was a consequential rather than direct result of the defendant's act (see chapter 12). In the course of time case came to be associated with negligence, and when procedural changes allowed case to be used for direct damage the scene was set for the emergence of negligence as the dominant form of liability (Winfield and Goodhart (1933) 49 LQR 359; Prichard [1964] CLJ 234).

Once the emphasis had been transferred from the deed itself to the manner of its commission, it became almost self-evident that liability should be founded on 'faulty' behaviour rather than mere causation of damage. Whilst it is true that liability at common law was never absolute (see Winfield (1926) 42 LQR 37), the historical trend has been a movement away from forms of strict liability to fault (Winfield (1926) 42 LQR 184; Malone (1970) 31 La L Rev 1). Fault liability corresponded with the social and economic values of the 19th century. Economic liberalism and rugged individualism suggested that fault liability was a moral principle, and that it was unjust to hold a person responsible for causing harm that could not have been avoided by the exercise of reasonable care. Fault also had the convenient effect of transferring the risk of non-negligent injury from the person who created the risk to the victim. In *Holmes v Mather* (1875) LR 10 Ex 261, for example, Bramwell B commented (at p. 267) that people must put up with 'such mischief as reasonable care on the part of others cannot avoid', and that this was 'for the convenience of mankind in carrying on the affairs of life'. Of course, the 'affairs of life' that tended to cause most mischief were commercial organisations such as factories and railway companies, and so the move from strict to fault liability represented a considerable subsidy to industry (for analysis of this process in the USA see Horwitz, *The Transformation of American Law 1780–1860* (1977), ch. 3; Abel (1981) 8 Br J Law and Soc 199; cf. Schwartz (1981) 90 Yale LJ 1717; see also chapter 5 for other techniques of reducing employers' costs). As *Fleming* (6th ed.) put it (p. 300):

> 'No liability without fault' became the banner of an individualistic society set on commercial exploitation and valuing property rights more highly than legal protection against physical injury.

Today, despite the predominance of fault as the basis of compensation in tort, there are few who would attempt to defend it as a moral principle. The objective standard of care in negligence (para. 3.1.1) means that a person can be held responsible for failing to achieve a standard of conduct that he was physically incapable of reaching. The amount of compensation payable (the 'punishment' for the defendant's faulty behaviour) bears no relation either to the degree of fault or the defendant's means. But in any event it is rare for the person found to be at fault to be the one who pays compensation. Liability insurance has effectively undermined the whole moral basis of fault liability. The operation of the fault system produces arbitrary and inequitable differences of treatment between plaintiffs, and as between plaintiffs and defendants in general. Thus the wholly innocent plaintiff who cannot find someone to blame for his injury will get nothing from tort, whereas a plaintiff who was himself negligent will usually receive some compensation, reduced for his contributory negligence, if he can point to someone else who was also careless. The plaintiff may in fact have been injured by the negligence of another but be unable to prove it because of the difficulties of adjudication. Finally, and perhaps most fundamentally, the fairness or justice argument for fault liability is suspect. It is not obvious why plaintiffs, but not defendants, must bear the burden of non-negligently inflicted loss or injury. Society as a whole derives economic benefits from certain activities, such as high-speed transport and manufacturing, with which a substantial degree of risk is associated. Indeed, the risk is often such that harm to others is regarded as statistically inevitable. Each isolated event is treated as an 'accident', but for the purpose of tort these 'accidents' are divided into 'fault-caused' and 'pure' accidents. Thus, individuals who cannot prove fault bear a disproportionate burden of the inevitable risks created by socially desirable activities (for a detailed critique, see *Atiyah,* ch. 7).

1.3 ROLE OF INSURANCE

The role of insurance is crucial to the operation of the tort system. The courts regularly make awards of compensation running into tens or hundreds of thousands of pounds which would be beyond the capacity of individuals, and even many companies, to pay. Insurance spreads the risk of a particular type of loss among all the premium payers. There are two broad categories of insurance, first-party (or loss) insurance and third-party (or liability) insurance. First-party insurance protects the insured against damage to himself or his property irrespective of whether the loss is caused by the insured or someone else (although deliberate damage by the insured is generally excluded). Common examples are house contents and building insurance, fire insurance, and comprehensive motor vehicle insurance. This is a form of no-fault compensation, and is much more significant as a source of compensation for property damage than the tort system.

Third-party insurance protects the insured against his liability for causing damage to others, and takes effect through the mechanism of the tortfeasor's liability. This also protects the victim because it ensures that a judgment for damages against the insured will be satisfied. Thus liability insurance serves both to spread risks among potential defendants and meet the compensation objective of tort. Protection for victims is the rationale behind legislation making insurance against some forms of liability to third parties compulsory. This applies to personal injuries and property damage up to £250,000 caused by the use of a motor vehicle on a road (Road Traffic Act 1988, ss. 143 to 145) and the liability of employers for injury to their employees (Employers' Liability (Compulsory Insurance) Act 1969; see chapter 5; though cf. *Richardson* v *Pitt-Stanley* [1995] ICR 303, para. 9.1.2 which suggests that protecting employees is not the purpose of this legislation). Road traffic accident victims are treated particularly favourably because they are entitled to enforce a judgment insurer could refuse indemnity for breach of some material term of the contract (Road Traffic Act 1988, ss. 151 to 152, though note s. 151(4)). Moreover, where the driver of the vehicle was uninsured or the plaintiff was the victim of a 'hit-and-run' driver, the Motor Insurers' Bureau (MIB) will meet an unsatisfied judgment. The bureau was set up in an agreement between the motor vehicle insurers and the government, and is funded from motor insurance premiums (*see Atiyah*, pp. 212–16; Lewis (1985) 48 MLR 275, 279–81; and *Hepple and Matthews*, p. 898). It is a non-statutory scheme which, strictly speaking, is not enforceable by the accident victim, but the MIB do not rely on this point in practice. Formerly the scheme was limited to claims for personal injuries or death, but under a new agreement, applying to accidents occurring on or after 31 December 1988, the MIB will consider claims for property damage up to a maximum value of £250,000, excluding the first £175. Property damage claims will be met only in respect of uninsured, not untraced, drivers. The MIB will be responsible even where the driver used the vehicle with the deliberate intention of causing injury (*Hardy* v *MIB* [1964] 2 QB 745; *Gardner* v *Moore* [1984] AC 548), thus relieving taxpayers from compensating the victims of this particular type of violent crime under the Criminal Injuries Compensation Scheme (for another way of making motor insurance pay for crimes of violence, *see Meah* v *McCreamer* [1985] 1 All ER 367, para. 4.2.2.2).

There is no equivalent of the MIB for employers' liability insurance, nor do employees have any direct claim against the insurers should indemnity be revoked and the employers be unable to satisfy judgment. This creates a gap in the protection afforded to employees, which is inconsistent with the policy objective of requiring insurance (see the comments of Balcombe LJ in *Dunbar* v *A & B Painters Ltd* [1986] 2 Lloyd's Rep 38, 43–4). Employment and road accidents are the two most significant examples of compulsory liability insurance, but there are others, such as the Dangerous Wild Animals Act 1976 and the Riding Establishment Acts 1964 and 1970 (see also Solicitors Act 1974, s. 37, providing for compulsory professional indemnity insurance for solicitors).

The Third Parties (Rights against Insurers) Act 1930 provides further protection for the victims of tortfeasors who have insured against their liability (whether compulsory or not) where the tortfeasor has gone bankrupt or into liquidation. The Act transfers the tortfeasor's rights against the insurer under the contract of insurance to the third party to whom the tortfeasor was liable, thereby avoiding the general creditors taking a share of the compensation at the expense of the victim. However, the House of Lords has held that under a policy of insurance against liability to third parties the insured tortfeasor cannot sue for an indemnity from the insurer unless and until the existence and amount of his liability to the third party has been established by court action, arbitration or agreement. Thus, where an insured company has been wound up and dissolved before the existence and extent of its liability has been established, the third party cannot rely on the Act to sue the insurers direct (*Bradley* v *Eagle Star Insurance Co. Ltd* [1989] 2 WLR 568). In the absence of even a nominal defendant the plaintiff cannot assert that the 'true defendant' is the insurer. The Companies Act 1985, s. 651 allows a plaintiff to apply to the court to restore a company to the register of companies for the purpose of bringing an action against the company. This did not assist the plaintiff in *Bradley* because the application must be made within two years of the dissolution of the company. Section 651 was amended by the Companies Act 1989, s. 141, to allow a plaintiff claiming damages in respect of personal injuries or death to make an application at any time after the dissolution of the company. This change applies retrospectively for 20 years, i.e., it applies to companies dissolved from 1969, but not earlier. This procedure allows plaintiffs to rely on the Third Parties (Rights against Insurers) Act 1930, although a claim brought after many years could well be statute barred under the Limitation Act 1980 (see para. 14.7.1) and may face difficulties in proving a breach of duty by the defendants.

As a rule, first-party insurance is a cheaper way of spreading risks than liability insurance combined with tort. With first-party insurance the extent of the risk can be assessed more easily and accurately, whereas it can be very difficult if not impossible to assess the extent of potential liability to others. This can lead to either over- or under-insurance. Secondly, liability insurance requires the third party to establish the insured's liability, through the courts if necessary, and this can be a very expensive process. With loss insurance the insured simply has to prove the loss. Of course, the courts do not usually consider the problems that come before them in these terms. There are a number of judicial statements, of high authority, that in determining the respective rights of plaintiff and defendant the fact that one of them is insured should be disregarded (*Lister* v *Romford Ice & Cold Storage Co. Ltd* [1957] AC 555; *Davie* v *New Merton Board Mills Ltd* [1959] AC 604, 626–7; *Morgans* v *Launchbury* [1973] AC 127, 136–7). This express refusal to look at the insurance position suggests that an action in tort focuses exclusively on the equity between the parties—should this loss be *shifted* from plaintiff to defendant? The reality is that in the vast majority of cases the defendant will not bear the loss because it has already been distributed via his insurance premium. It has been estimated that 80% of the work of the Queen's Bench Division consists of personal injury actions, and of these over 90% are either road accidents or employers' liability cases, where insurance is compulsory (*Pearson*, vol. 2, para. 83; *Atiyah*, pp. 167–70). The courts are obviously aware of this, and in some instances this knowledge influences the shape of legal rules (for an analysis of the historical development of the symbiotic relationship between liability insurance and the duty of care in negligence, see Davies (1989) 9 Legal Stud 67). The best example is the very high objective standard of care required of motorists (see para. 3.1.1). There are signs that the courts' attitude to liability insurance is changing. In *Hodgson* v *Trapp* [1988] 3 All ER 870, 876, for example, Lord Bridge, in deciding that certain social security benefits should be deducted from damages for personal injuries, commented that the court should 'have regard to the realities' that such damages are met from the insurance premiums of motorists, employers, occupiers of property, professionals and others. More recently, in *Smith* v *Bush* [1989] 2 WLR 790, 810 Lord Griffiths said:

> There was once a time when it was considered improper even to mention the possible existence of insurance cover in a lawsuit. But those days are long past. Everyone knows that all prudent professional men carry insurance, and the availability and cost of insurance must be a relevant factor when considering which of two parties should be required to bear the risk of a loss.

This view, expressed in the context of whether a surveyor's exclusion of liability was reasonable under the Unfair Contract Terms Act 1977, s. 2(2), was quite explicitly based on principles of loss distribution.

In the case of tortious damage to property, the owner may have first-party insurance which would compensate him for the loss. Under the equitable doctrine of subrogation the insurer is then entitled to pursue any claim that the insured would have had against third parties in respect of the insured loss. This is done in the name of the insured. So not only are defendants in tort actions frequently nominal, the real defendant being an insurance company, but in some cases the plaintiff is also nominal, and the substance of the action is which of two insurance companies should bear the loss. There is little social or economic advantage in allowing the expensive panoply of the law to be used to transfer losses between insurance companies in this way, but the courts are usually stuck with the fiction that they are resolving a dispute between the nominal parties to the action. They do occasionally take some account of these issues where the circumstances are such that it is very likely that *the plaintiff* was insured or ought to have been insured against the loss particularly where the 'plaintiff' is arguing for an extension of liability (this was the underlying premise of *P. Perl (Exporters) Ltd* v *Camden London*

Borough Council [1984] QB 342 (para. 2.2.1); *Lamb* v *Camden London Borough Council* [1981] QB 625 (para. 4.2.2.1) per Lord Denning MR; *Leigh & Sillavan Ltd* v *Aliakmon Shipping Co. Ltd* [1986] 2 All ER 145; see also *Photo Production Ltd* v *Securicor Transport Ltd* [1980] AC 827, 851 per Lord Diplock, a case in contract; and *Murphy* v *Brentwood District Council* [1990] 2 All ER 908, 923 per Lord Keith).

Stapleton (1995) 58 MLR 820, in a cogent argument, points out that there is no broad formulation of where and why liability insurance or insurability should be a factor relevant to the imposition and shape of liability, which suggests that commentators deploy it selectively, and therefore unconvincingly. Similarly, arguments about who is the cheapest insurer make the assumption that tort is simply about the cheapest way to insure and distribute risks, and that tort entitlements are not about corrective justice (remedying 'wrongs') or deterrence of certain types of undesirable conduct. This is a controversial assumption, and suggests that although insurance is the context within which much of the tort system functions it is not a reliable guide to making decisions about where tort liability should lie (whether in favour of plaintiffs or defendants):

> Commentators and judges should think twice before making off-hand comments that insurance should be relevant to the scope of tort liability, that judges should take into account 'the realities of insurance' or that they should address the comparative insurability of parties. Such statements are dangerous. They are not only indeterminate criteria but can mislead us into suppressing any corrective justice or deterrence goals we may have for tort liability . . . (*ibid.*, p. 843).

1.4 OBJECTIVES OF TORT

Glanville Williams (1951) 4 CLP 137 identified four possible objectives of an action for damages in tort: appeasement, justice, deterrence and compensation. To these could be added loss distribution and economic efficiency. These aims can overlap, but may also conflict.

1.4.1 Appeasement and justice

Appeasement, i.e., buying off the victim's instinct for revenge, may be a feature of primitive law, but few informed commentators would give it much significance today. Any psychological benefits derived from a successful action would probably be more than offset by the worry and distress caused by the uncertainties of protracted litigation.

Justice has two aspects. First, retribution against a wrongdoer, and secondly compensation for the victim. The notion of retribution is not fashionable these days, even in the criminal law, but in any event tort is not well adapted to matching the penalty to the degree of wrongdoing so as to produce a level of retribution that could be described as 'just'. Once liability is established, retribution is subordinated to the compensatory function of an award of damages which is dictated by the measure of the plaintiff's loss, whether large or small. It is true that there is a penal element in the limited circumstances where exemplary damages may be awarded, but this is restricted in practice and is probably better justified by the aim of deterrence. The justice of providing compensation for a person who has sustained damage at the hands of a tortfeasor is ambiguous. Does justice require compensation because he has suffered a wrong or because he has suffered a loss? If justice specifies compensation for loss *per se,* rather than wrongful loss, the law of tort cannot satisfy this objective and an alternative compensation system would be required. A conception of justice which required compensation only for wrongful loss would have to provide a rational justification for distinguishing between claims to compensation for identical losses on the basis of the manner in which they were inflicted. For example, from a plaintiffs point of view is a broken leg caused by the defendant's negligence any different from a broken leg caused by accident? The wrongfulness or lawfulness of the defendant's conduct does not change the nature of the plaintiff's claim, in justice, to compensation, although it might change his claim that the defendant is the person who should pay compensation. But in the present tort system the tortfeasor himself rarely pays the damages. Liability insurance removes the connection between the wrongdoer and the plaintiff's compen-sation (para. 1.3). Thus the claim that tort satisfies the aim of justice is suspect, to say the least.

1.4.2 Deterrence and efficiency
In theory almost any liability rule should be capable of deterring the conduct that would lead to the imposition of liability. Certainly some torts do provide an effective deterrent. Defamation, for example, has a salutary effect on the world of publishing. Once again, it is in the realm of liability for negligence that the arguments about deterrence are most controversial, particularly the claim that by applying a standard of reasonable care negligence contributes to accident prevention. If, the argument runs, people are held liable in damages for failing to take reasonable care, they will have an incentive to act carefully and thereby avoid accidents. There are several flaws, however, in this proposition. First, the standard of care is objective. A person doing his 'incompetent best' to meet the standard will be liable although he is unable to adjust his behaviour to the required level. Secondly, a general exhortation to 'be careful' is not specific enough to give useful guidance as to how people should behave, and the courts must inevitably rule on whether the defendant has been sufficiently careful after the event (hence, there is some emphasis on usual or common practice). Thirdly, most cases of negligence consist of inadvertence to the dangerous consequences of the defendant's conduct. If in fact he does not foresee the danger, even though he ought reasonably to have foreseen it, he will hardly be inclined to take precautions against it. The point is easily illustrated by the negligent motorist. If the prospect of serious injury or death to himself does not encourage the motorist to drive carefully, how can the threat of an award of damages against him do so? It has been suggested that where the negligence consists of a fault in a system or method of working, where there is an opportunity to consider safety aspects in

advance, then the threat of liability will lead to greater precautions. One example of this is an employer's liability for breach of his personal (as opposed to vicarious) obligation with respect to employees' safety (see chapter 5; *Hutchinson* v *London & North Eastern Railway Co.* [1942] 1 KB 481 per Goddard LJ commenting (at p. 488) that the 'real incentive' for employers to comply with their statutory duties was the possibility of heavy damages claims rather than fines).

This argument, together with most of the theory of deterrence, is undermined by the widespread availability (and in road and employment accidents the compulsory requirement) of liability insurance. Since it is not the defendant who pays the damages the prospect of tort liability is unlikely to deter carelessness. It is true that insurance premiums can be varied to reflect the risk and that a bad claims record will lead to higher premiums, but the link between variable rates and accident prevention is tenuous in the extreme (see *Atiyah*, pp. 369–74). The best known example is the 'no-claims discount' for motor insurance, but the point made above in relation to inadvertent motorists and the payment of damages applies *a fortiori* to insurance premiums. It is even more difficult to produce accurate risk rating for employers' liability insurance, and any increase will generally be absorbed as part of the overheads of the business and passed on to customers or employees as higher prices or lower wages. Insurers could have a more direct role in accident prevention by inspecting premises or systems of work. In theory this should reduce insured losses but in practice there is little financial incentive for insurance companies to run such an expensive service (*Atiyah*, ibid.). As *Williams and Hepple* observe (p. 170), 'If insurance makes any contribution to deterrence, then, this is largely fortuitous'.

Where a finding of negligence could adversely affect the defendant's commercial or professional reputation then, possibly, potential liability in tort may have some deterrent effect. This is strongest, perhaps, in the case of professional liability, but again its value should not be over-emphasised. Inadvertence, the careless slip, is difficult to deter when by definition the defendant is unaware that he is making a mistake. To the extent that this type of error is the product of pressure of work reducing the time available to devote to each particular problem, a finding of negligence might provide an incentive to reduce workloads or employ more staff, thus improving the quality of service. Of course, this involves an economic judgment about the costs of improving the service compared with the costs of a claim for damages against the professional (see Veljanovski and Whelan (1983) 46 MLR 700 for discussion in the context of the legal profession). Where the damage is not the result of inadvertent carelessness, but of a conscious and deliberate exercise of professional judgment then, in theory, tort should deter the taking of an 'unreasonable risk'. This has led to claims, particularly by the medical profession, that the threat of liability induces 'defensive' practices, which are contrary to the interests of the client, by practitioners who wish to protect themselves from negligence actions. The difficulty with this argument is that the standard of care, i.e., the measure of what constitutes negligence, is in substance set by the profession itself, and a professional judgment will not be condemned as negligence unless there is *no* body of responsible professional opinion that would support the judgment, even though others within the profession would not have acted in that way (see para. 3.2.1). Thus, in principle, tort should not be capable of deterring practices that are accepted as proper within the profession concerned (see, e.g., Jones (1987) 3 PN 43, 45). There is some evidence that doctors practice 'defensive medicine' in this country, but there is no consensus about what this somewhat emotive concept entails (see Tribe and Korgaonkar (1991) 7 PN 2; Jones and Morris (1989) 5 J of the MDU 40; Summerton (1995) 310 BMJ 27). In recent years the courts have been increasingly willing to conclude that the imposition of a duty of care in negligence upon a body exercising a public function could lead to that function being performed in an 'unduly defensive frame of mind', to the detriment of the service in question (see, e.g., *X (minors)* v *Bedfordshire County Council* [1995] 3 WLR 152—child protection agencies; *Hill* v *Chief Constable of West Yorkshire* [1988] 2 All ER 238—police; *Skinner* v *Secretary of State for Transport, The Times*, 3 January 1995—coastguard; *Elguzouli-Daf* v *Commissioner of Police of the Metropolis* [1995] 1 All ER 833—Crown Prosecution Service; *Marc Rich & Co.* v *Bishop Rock Marine Co. Ltd* [1995] 3 All ER 307—ship classification society). This is essentially a judgment that imposing liability for negligence will tend to 'over deter' the defendants in question, though this is an intuitive judgment rather than one based on empirical evidence. Logically, the same argument would apply to any defendant who is held accountable in the tort of negligence, but no one suggests that imposing a duty of care on, say, motorists makes them drive *too* carefully.

The link between tort liability and damage to commercial reputation is even more difficult to establish. In a famous American case a motor vehicle manufacturer discovered a design defect in a car which rendered it susceptible to an explosion when struck from the rear. The company decided that it would be cheaper to pay damages to the victims than to redesign the vehicle, presumably taking the view that its commercial reputation would not be seriously affected by tort actions. The courts were outraged that the manufacturer had so cynically calculated the cost of human life (though the courts regularly have to calculate this cost when awarding damages in fatal accident cases, of course) and awarded exemplary damages (*Grimshaw* v *Ford Motor Co.* (1981) 119 Cal App 3d 757—$125 million punitive damages awarded by jury, reduced to $3.5 million on appeal). Arguably, it is the prospect of adverse publicity that acts as the greatest deterrent when companies consider their commercial reputation, and in many respects it is entirely coincidental whether this stems from a judgment to pay damages. The manufacturers of thalidomide, for example, never conceded liability for the damage caused by the drug and so were never adjudged to have been 'at fault', but eventually they came to a settlement with the victims, in the face of widespread public criticism of the company.

Economic efficiency as an objective of tort is a variant of deterrence. It has been argued, for example, that to the extent that an activity imposes costs on others for which it does not have to pay, the activity is being subsidised and its price does not reflect its true cost. This distorts the market mechanism, because the activity is underpriced, and this leads to inefficiency. The solution is to require activities to 'internalise' these external costs by imposing strict liability for the damage caused by the specific risks created by a particular activity. This increases the price, thereby reducing the level of the activity and hence the amount of damage associated with it. The object is not to eliminate all damage but to achieve an efficient amount, taking into account the costs of prevention. In other words, tort should aim to minimise the sum of accident costs and the costs of preventing accidents (Calabresi, *The Cost of Accidents* (1970); for discussion see *Atiyah,* pp. 374–94; see *Powell v Fall* (1880) 5 QBD 597, 601 per Bramwell B for an example of an argument favouring the 'internalisation' of costs). It is not necessarily a simple task to identify specific risks with particular activities, because risks are often the product of competing activities. For example, is the risk of a collision at a level crossing attributable to running trains or driving cars?

This theory is known as general deterrence because it seeks to influence behaviour through the pricing of activities, rather than deterring individuals from specific acts. Other theories rely on the deterrent effect of liability rules on individuals. For example, it has been suggested that the tort of negligence leads to efficient results because the standard of reasonable care encourages people to take only those precautions that are justified on the grounds of cost, whereas strict liability might lead people to devote more resources to damage prevention than is warranted by the risk (Posner, *The Economic Analysis of Law,* 3rd ed. (1986); for a general introduction see Burrows and Veljanovski, *The Economic Approach to Law* (1981), chs 1 and 5).

Ultimately, all economic theorising about tort rests on assumptions about the deterrent effect of liability rules, which have not been empirically tested. Even if the courts were inclined to look for 'efficient' solutions they can only achieve this through imposing liability on one of the parties, but it might be that a more efficient result could be achieved by requiring some third party to pay compensation for the loss. For example, administrative regulation combined with a no-fault compensation fund might be more cost-effective as a method of reducing the costs of accidents and the costs of prevention while still compensating losses. Perhaps the most fundamental point of departure between lawyers and economists relates to the justice or fairness of legal rules. The economist is not concerned with fairness as such, only efficiency. The legal system is seen, not as a system for compensating losses, but as an elaborate incentive scheme. The loss that a plaintiff has sustained is a 'sunk cost', and the resources consumed cannot be restored to the economy by an award of damages, which is merely a transfer payment. Thus the payment of compensation by the defendant is generally irrelevant to the economist, except in so far as it forms part of a liability rule that is intended to influence future behaviour. Lawyers, on the other hand, often argue for or against a particular rule by reference to its fairness. Moreover, economists usually disclaim any expertise in determining what the distribution of income and wealth *should* be, because the very definition of 'efficiency' is by reference to a *given* distribution of income and wealth. If the distribution changes, the requirements of efficiency will change. However, the allocation of legal rights, in the form of liability rules, forms part of that distribution (e.g., if A is liable for polluting B's stream, B has the 'right' to an unpolluted stream and is richer than he would be if A were not liable for the pollution). Thus economic efficiency, which by definition is a function of the distribution of 'wealth' (in this case 'legal rights'), cannot be used as a criterion for determining what the distribution of legal rights should be.

1.4.3 Compensation and loss distribution

Compensating the victim of a wrong is commonly regarded as the main objective of tort. The principle of full compensation, namely that the plaintiff is entitled to be compensated to the full extent of his loss irrespective of the degree of the defendant's culpability, emphasises this. Similarly, statutory provisions requiring compulsory liability insurance further the compensatory aim by ensuring that funds will be available to satisfy a judgment. Intuitively most people expect to be compensated for *wrongs* and see no objection in requiring the wrongdoer to pay. In tort, 'wrongdoing' is generally measured by the culpability of the defendant's behaviour, and not simply by its tendency to inflict damage on others. Thus to say that tort aims to compensate for losses pure and simple would be misleading, and to say that it *should* aim to compensate for such losses would be highly controversial. Tort can only operate in the two-dimensional world of loss shifting, where the deliberate fiction is maintained that either the individual plaintiff or the individual defendant must bear the loss, and some justification, fault, is required before it can be transferred to the defendant.

In the real world losses are not, on the whole, shifted, they are distributed or spread either through private insurance or the social security system. This tends to change the nature of the question from: Who was to blame? to: Who can most easily bear this cost? It is usually considered socially desirable that the 'accidental' victims of modern social conditions should not be left to bear the full brunt of their misfortune, and loss distribution is the principal mechanism by which this is achieved. It is difficult to regard loss distribution as an objective of tort in itself, although it is probably the best explanation for the principle of vicarious liability, whereby an employer is held responsible for the torts of employees committed in the course of employment (see para. 8.4.1). Compulsory liability insurance also contributes to loss spreading, though this is not its primary purpose. It is the combination of tort and liability insurance that distributes certain types of losses, those that are 'fault-caused'. But once the central issue changes from the behaviour of the parties to the way in which compensation is financed, and it is realised that it is the exception for defendants themselves to pay damages (an uninsured defendant is rarely worth suing) then distinguishing between plaintiffs on the basis of the defendants' culpability begins to look purely arbitrary. Add to this the fact that the tort system is extremely expensive to administer, and it is scarcely surprising to find tort under repeated attack, particularly as a method of compensating personal injuries, by reformers who would like to see a fairer, more rational and more efficient means of achieving the compensation aim.

1.5 ACCIDENT COMPENSATION

Accident compensation is a term applied to systems for compensating people who have suffered personal injury as a result of 'accident'. An 'accident' can refer to injury sustained through negligence (including the victim's negligence), 'pure' accident, where no one is at fault, and even intentionally inflicted harm. Congenital disability may be included within the definition of accident, but disease due to natural causes usually is not (for the problems of distinguishing between natural and 'man-made disease', and the consequences of the 'accident preference' when discussing personal injury compensation see Stapleton (1985) 5 OJLS 248, and more generally, Stapleton, *Disease and the Compensation Debate*, OUP, 1986). This is not a book about accident compensation (see generally, *Atiyah*) rather, it deals with liability in tort, which is concerned with a wider range of interests than personal injury. Conversely, tort plays only a subsidiary role in the provision of compensation for accident victims. Nonetheless, claims in respect of personal injury account for the vast majority of tort actions, and it is helpful to consider tort in the broader context of accident compensation.

The Pearson Commission estimated that each year some three million people suffer injuries which are sufficiently serious to lead to four or more days off work or to an equivalent degree of incapacity for those not in work, and about 21,000 die as a result of injury (*Pearson, vol.* 1, ch. 3). Of the three million injuries about a million occur at work or on the road. Approximately 1,700,000 receive some form of compensation for their injuries, of which about half of the total of £800 million a year (at 1977 prices) comes from social security. A quarter of the total comes from the tort system, with the remainder being provided by occupational sick pay and pensions, private insurance, criminal injuries compensation, and other miscellaneous sources including charities. About a quarter of a million tort claims in respect of personal injury are made each year, of which 85% to 90% are successful (a more recent estimate put this figure at 340,000 per year: *Civil Justice Review* Cm 394, 1988, para. 391). This amounts to about 6.5% of the total number of people suffering injury. Thus, 6.5% of accident victims receive 25% of the compensation paid for accidental injury. Even allowing for the fact that tort victims are more likely to suffer serious injury (41% of tort claims are for motor vehicle injuries and 47% for work injuries or illness) they are treated particularly generously in the compensation stakes. The principle of 'full' compensation in tort provides compensation for non-pecuniary losses such as pain and suffering and loss of amenity, in addition to pecuniary losses, generally medical and other expenses and loss of earnings. The social security system is restricted to meeting pecuniary losses, although the industrial injuries scheme does provide disablement benefit based on an objective assessment of the degree of disablement (*Atiyah*, pp. 284–90). In addition, social security, unlike tort, does not meet pecuniary losses in full because there are upper limits placed on benefits.

There have been many criticisms of tort as a method of accident compensation, based on its expense, delay, unpredictability and capricious distribution of compensation. The Pearson Commission found that the administrative costs of the tort system represented 85% of the sum paid to accident victims, whereas the costs of running the social security system came to 11% of the total paid out (for an explanation of why tort is so expensive see *Atiyah*, pp. 337–42). The *Civil Justice Review* Cm 394 estimated that legal costs alone amounted to up to 75% of the sums recovered in the High Court, and up to 175% of the sums recovered in the County Court (paras 427–32, though see para. 439(xii)). Tort is very slow in obtaining compensation. Delay is inherent in an adversarial system, and the more serious the case the greater is the delay (average time from accident to trial is over five years in the High Court and almost three years in the County Court: *Civil Justice Review* Cm 394, para. 42 1). The Pearson Commission found that this was the most important reason for dissatisfaction with the legal system. The outcome of legal proceedings can be unpredictable. Even an apparently straightforward case can run into problems of proof. This, combined with the risk that even a successful plaintiff may have to pay a substantial sum in costs if the award of damages at trial is less than a sum that may have been paid into court by the defendants' insurers, places plaintiffs in an unequal bargaining position. This puts pressure on them to settle claims for less than would be awarded if the case went to trial (see Phillips and Hawkins (1976) 39 MLR 497). Only 1% of claims reach the courts, though personal injury actions make up over 75% of cases set down for hearing in the Queen's Bench Division (*Pearson*, vol. 1, para. 79). This under-compensation tends to be greater in the more serious cases where the plaintiff has more at risk, whereas small claims tend to be over-compensated, because the administrative cost to insurance companies of processing them is disproportionately large compared to the sums involved and so they will make more generous offers to settle the claims quickly. The award of damages as a single lump sum also tends to contribute to under-compensation (though in some cases over-compensation) because awards are discounted to take account of future vicissitudes which might never materialise.

A review of the civil justice system by Lord Woolf has suggested radical reform of civil litigation procedure to speed up the process and reduce the costs (*Access to Justice*, 1996). This would involve a new 'fast track' procedure for personal injury cases up to £10,000, with tight procedural timescales and fixed costs. The fast track would apply to non-personal injury cases valued between £3,000 and £10,000, with the small claims jurisdiction of the court being extended to £3,000. Trials would have to take place after a maximum of 30 weeks, and last hours rather than days. There would be a new 'multi-track' procedure with judicial case management and timetables set by the court for cases worth more than £10,000 and complex cases below that figure, such as medical negligence. In order to attempt to prevent wealthy defendants or insurers grinding out the proceedings in the hope that the plaintiff will either abandon the claim or settle for a low sum, a new procedure would be introduced to give a plaintiff additional interest on damages if the plaintiff makes an offer of settlement which is not accepted by the defendant but the offer is equalled or exceeded at trial. This is the equivalent of the defendant's payment into court, which puts the plaintiff on risk as to costs after the payment in. In order to succeed in reducing delay and cost the new procedures will require a significant change in the attitudes of the legal profession to accommodate a more cooperative approach by the parties to resolving the dispute in issue, in contrast to the current adversarial system, and, perhaps more significantly, appropriate training and funding for a more interventionist judiciary. (For analysis of Lord Woolf's proposals for reducing the cost of litigation see Zuckerman (1996) 59 MLR 773; and, more generally, Zander (1998) 61 MLR 382). It is anticipated that some of the changes proposed in *Access to Justice* will be implemented in 1999.

It has already been pointed out that tort selects its beneficiaries in a particularly arbitrary manner, looking, in the first instance, not to the needs of the accident victim but the 'fault' of the defendant. But, due to the fact that in some circumstances social security benefits are not deducted in full from an award of damages and that collateral benefits such as occupational pensions and charitable payments are not deducted at all (see para. 15.1.3.2), some tort victims have their needs met twice over and are actually better off after the accident. Other accident victims may not receive any compensation at all from either the tort or social security system (e.g., non-earners who are injured at home).

Dissatisfaction with the inefficiences and inequities of tort has led to proposals for alternative methods of accident compensation. In New Zealand a comprehensive no-fault accident compensation scheme was introduced in 1972, and corresponding rights of action in tort were abolished. This replaces the victim's financial loss at 80% of his pre-accident earnings, subject to a maximum amount, and this is payable weekly. Until 1992 it was possible for a lump sum to be awarded for permanent loss or impairment of bodily function, though the sums were modest by comparison to tort awards for pain and suffering and loss of amenity (the maximum was NZ$27,000). This award was abolished in 1992 and replaced with an 'independence allowance' for persons with a permanent disability of 10% or more. The scheme is funded by a levy on vehicles for motor accidents, levies on employees and the self-employed for accidents to earners (at differential rates for different occupational risks), a levy on health care providers in respect of personal injury from medical error or medical mishap, and out of general taxation for other accidents. It is limited to personal injury by 'accident' (which includes occupational discase), but does not cover disease or the consequences of the ageing process. The distinction between accident and disease has caused some problems in practice, and is open to the objection that it is wrong in principle when the underlying rationale of a no-fault scheme is that attention should focus on the disability itself, not the *cause* of the disability (see Todd and Black (1993) 1 Tort L Rev 197; McLean [1985] JSWL 31; Stapleton (1985) 5 OJLS 248; *Atiyah*, p. 404; the pragmatic objection to extending compensation to sickness is the cost).

In England the Pearson Commission did not recommend a comprehensive no-fault scheme, although it did propose an extension of the existing industrial injuries scheme to road accident victims, to be financed by a tax on petrol. The tort action would remain, however, in effect allowing high earners to 'top up' the benefits received under the no-fault scheme. The abolition of tort in New Zealand and the upper earnings limit works to the disadvantage of high earners, but can be justified by the argument that the chance of 'full' compensation, or indeed of no compensation, under tort has been traded off against the certainty of some, albeit lower, compensation under the scheme. High earners are also in a position to protect their income through insurance. The Commission's proposal has been criticised for selecting another group of victims for preferential treatment to the exclusion of others with similar disabilities (see Atiyah, 'What Now?', in Allen, Bourn and Holyoak, *Accident Compensation after Pearson* (1979); for the Commission's justification of the road accident scheme see *Pearson, vol.* 1, para. 996). Of course, this argument applies to any scheme of compensation that differentiates between people with similar disabilities on the basis of the cause of the disability (such as the Criminal Injuries Compensation Scheme, see para. 12.3, the Vaccine Damage Payments Act 1979, or the industrial injuries scheme). A no-fault compensation system for road accident victims would no doubt produce some savings in administration costs, particularly if combined with the Commission's proposals for the assessment of tort damages to require full deduction of social security benefits and the abolition of damages for non-pecuniary loss suffered during the first three months after the injury (*Pearson*, vol. 1, paras 482 and 388). Most claims are small: 60% are for less than £500 and only 1% for more than £10,000, at 1977 prices. But the report fell short of the expectations of many reformers and has been roundly criticised (Atiyah, *supra*; Hasson (1979) 6 Br J Law and Soc 119; Fleming (1979) 42 MLR 251; Ogus, Corfield and Harris (1978) 7 ILJ 143; see also Harris et al., *Compensation and Support for Illness and Injury* (1984) ch. 12, for alternative proposals).

It is possible that some limited no-fault schemes to deal with particular categories of injured people could be adopted (see *Atiyah*, pp. 400–404). For example, the British Medical Association has called for a scheme for the victims of medical accidents (Jones (1987) 3 PN 83; Bolt (1989) 139 NLJ 109; BMA, *No Fault Compensation Working Party Report*, 1991; Royal College of Physicians, *Compensation for the Adverse Consequences of Medical Intervention*, 1990), and the government did consider the feasibility of a no-fault scheme for minor road accidents. Such schemes usually envisage that compensation through tort will continue to be available, but a fundamental objection that they usually fail to address is how preferential treatment for one particular group of accident victims could be justified, especially if it were to be publicly funded.

Most of the Pearson Commission's 188 recommendations are unlikely ever to be implemented, although a few minor changes to the assessment of damages were introduced by the Administration of justice Act 1982. With all its anomalies and inadequacies, it is likely that the law of tort will continue to have a role in accident compensation for the foreseeable future (see generally Fleming (1984) 58 ALJ 131).

TWO

Negligence I: duty of care

Negligence has at least three possible connotations for the lawyer. It may signify a state of mind, a person's inadvertence to the consequences of his conduct. It can be a standard or measure of behaviour, where a person has been careless in that he did not behave as a prudent man would have done, whether by inadvertence or otherwise. Lastly, it may refer to the tort of negligence whereby persons who by carelessness have caused damage to others may be held liable to pay compensation. The tort of negligence always requires some form of careless conduct which is usually, although not necessarily, the product of inadvertence. Not all careless conduct which causes damage, however, will give rise to an action. As a tort negligence consists of a legal duty to take care and breach of that duty by the defendant causing damage to the plaintiff (*Lochgelly Iron Co.* v *M'Mullan* [1934] AC 1, 25 per Lord Wright).

Duty determines whether the type of loss suffered by the plaintiff in the particular way in which it occurred can ever be actionable. Breach of duty is concerned with the standard of care that ought to have been adopted in the circumstances, and whether the defendant's conduct fell below that standard, i.e., whether he was careless (see chapter 3). The negligence must have caused the plaintiff's loss, but a defendant is not necessarily responsible for all the loss that he has 'caused'. Where the type of damage is different from that which could reasonably have been anticipated it may be regarded as too 'remote' a consequence of the defendant's negligence to be actionable (see chapter 4). Lastly, the loss must be calculated in financial terms, and this is called the measure of damages (chapter 15). The division of negligence into duty, breach and consequent damage is convenient for the purpose of exposition, but it can be confusing because the issues will often overlap. It is not uncommon to conceptualise negligence as the breach of an antecedent duty, but in practical terms the duty question always arises after the event. ('It is . . . a question of what the hypothetical reasonable man, viewing the position, I suppose *ex post facto*, would say it was proper to foresee': *Bourhill* v *Young* [1943] AC 92, 110 per Lord Wright; see also *Jones* v *Wright* [1991]

3 All ER 88, 113–14 per Stocker LJ.) In many respects it is more illuminating to consider the nature of the damage first. Damage is the gist of the action, and so without damage there is no tort. There can be no liability 'in the air'. Negligence does not impose a duty to act carefully, it is a duty not to inflict damage carelessly. A motorist, for example, may drive as carelessly as he pleases but will not be liable in tort unless he damages another, although there could be no dispute that motorists 'owe' a duty of care to other road users.

Other nominate torts such as trespass to the person or to land, nuisance, or defamation protect specific interests that may be infringed (e.g., bodily integrity, civil liberty, enjoyment of land, reputation). Negligence is not tied to the protection of any particular interest. It is not so much an act as a way of acting, and so cuts across other classifications. That is one reason why it has become such a predominant tort. As Lord Macmillan observed: 'The grounds of action may be as various and manifold as human errancy; and the conception of legal responsibility may develop in adaptation to altering social conditions and standards. The criterion of judgment must adjust and adapt itself to the changing circumstances of life. The categories of negligence are never closed' (*Donoghue* v *Stevenson* [1932] AC 562, 619). Yet there are many actions which a person is perfectly entitled to take for which there will be no liability in tort, even with the intention of causing harm to others (e.g., *Mogul Steamship Co.* v *McGregor, Gow & Co.* [1892] AC 25—trade competition) or even where actuated by malice (*Allen* v *Flood* [1898] AC 1). If there is no liability for intentionally causing a particular kind of damage then *a fortiori* there can be no liability for inflicting the same harm negligently (*Langbrook Properties Ltd* v *Surrey County Council* [1969] 3 All ER 1424, see para. 7.1.3.5; cf. the remarkable case of *Ben Stansfield (Carlisle) Ltd* v *Carlisle City Council* (1982) 265 EG 475 which is probably wrongly decided: Murdoch (1983) 99 LQR 178). Moreover, it does not follow that where there is liability for intentionally inflicted damage the same damage should be actionable when caused by negligence.

The duty of care defines the interests that are protected by the tort of negligence. It does not provide a justification or reason for imposing liability, but rather marks out the boundaries of what is or is not actionable. Justifications for setting the boundary at any particular point have to be sought elsewhere (see para. 2.1.4). The trend in recent years has been to reduce the number of situations in which the courts will say that no duty of care is owed. As a general rule, there is no question that a person owes a duty not to cause (or expressed another way, 'will be liable for causing') physical damage, either to people or property, by some positive action. The difficult areas relate primarily to non-physical harm, such as economic loss or psychiatric damage, and liability for omissions.

2.1 GENERAL PRINCIPLES

2.1.1 The neighbour principle

Before 1932 there was no generalised duty of care in negligence. The tort was applied to damage caused in very particular circumstances where the courts had decided that a duty should be owed, e.g., road accidents, bailments or chattels regarded as dangerous *per se*. In *Donoghue* v *Stevenson* [1932] AC 562 the House of Lords held (by a bare majority) that the manufacturer of ginger beer could be liable in negligence for injury to an ultimate consumer of the product as a result of its defective condition (allegedly the remains of a decomposed snail in the bottle, the consumption of which caused the plaintiff's illness, but see *Hepple and Matthews*, p. 50, n. 1). In other words the negligent manufacturer of a defective article could be liable in tort ('owes a duty of care') to someone other than the person with whom he was in a contractual relationship, who would usually be a wholesaler or retailer but probably not the user. *Donoghue* v *Stevenson* disposed of the 'privity of contract fallacy', usually attributed to *Winterbottom* v *Wright* (1842) 10 M & W 109, that where there was a contractual relationship between a manufacturer and another then there could be no liability in tort to a third party injured by the negligent performance of the contract, because the third party was seeking to take the benefit of a contract to which he was not privy. The fallacy lay in the fact that the third party's claim is in tort not contract, and there is no reason why a contractual relationship between A and B should preclude a tortious duty of care as to C's safety in carrying out the contract.

This is all very well, but it does not explain why *Donoghue* v *Stevenson* is regarded as such a landmark in the tort of negligence and not simply as establishing another particular situation (the manufacturer-consumer relationship) in which negligence would be actionable. In the course of his speech Lord Atkin attempted (at p. 580) to find a general principle which would encompass all the circumstances in which the courts had previously held that there could be liability for negligence:

> The rule that you are to love your neighbour becomes in law, you must not injure your neighbour; and the lawyer's question, Who is my neighbour? receives a restricted reply. You must take reasonable care to avoid acts or omissions which you can reasonably foresee would be likely to injure your neighbour. Who, then, in law is my neighbour? The answer seems to be—persons who are so closely and directly affected by my act that I ought reasonably to have them in contemplation as being so affected when I am directing my mind to the acts or omissions which are called in question.

The test, then, is reasonable foresight of harm to persons whom it is foreseeable are likely to be harmed by my carelessness. As a principle of liability this statement is too wide, because it is not true, even today, that in all circumstances the infliction of foreseeable damage is actionable in negligence. The whole point of the 'duty problem' is to determine when foreseeable damage is actionable. As Lord Macmillan expressed it (at p. 619):

> Where there is room for diversity of view, it is in determining what circumstances will establish such a relationship between the parties as to give rise, on the one side, to a duty to take care, and on the other side to a right to have care taken.

What Lord Atkin's 'neighbour principle' did, however, was to provide a
unifying thread for those situations in which liability for negligent conduct
was imposed, allowing lawyers to talk in terms of the *tort* of negligence. This
in turn made it easier to argue that there should be liability for negligently
inflicting damage in new situations, not covered by previous case law, *because*
the damage was foreseeable. By 1970 it was possible for Lord Reid to say that
Lord Atkin's dictum ought to apply unless there is some justification or valid
explanation for its exclusion (*Home Office* v *Dorset Yacht Co. Ltd* [1970] AC
1004, 1027), and in *Anns* v *Merton London Borough Council* [1978] AC 728
the House of Lords confirmed this. Lord Wilberforce said (at pp. 751–2)
that:

> in order to establish that a duty of care arises in a particular situation, it is
> not necessary to bring the facts of that situation within those of previous
> situations in which a duty of care has been held to exist. Rather the
> question has to be approached in two stages. First one has to ask whether,
> as between the alleged wrongdoer and the person who has suffered damage
> there is a sufficient relationship of proximity or neighbourhood such that,
> in the reasonable contemplation of the former, carelessness on his part may
> be likely to cause damage to the latter—in which case a prima facie duty
> of care arises. Secondly, if the first question is answered affirmatively, it is
> necessary to consider whether there are any considerations which ought to
> negative, or to reduce or limit the scope of the duty or the class of person
> to whom it is owed or the damages to which a breach of it may give rise.

This two-stage approach makes the problem appear much simpler than it is.
The first stage corresponds to Lord Atkin's neighbour principle, but the
second stage tends to obscure the fact that considerations of policy (which
seem to be raised only at that stage) are inherent in the neighbour principle
itself (see para. 2.1.4). In *Peabody Donation Fund* v *Sir Lindsay Parkinson &
Co. Ltd* [1984] 3 All ER 529 the House of Lords warned against the danger
of treating these statements as definitive. 'A relationship of proximity in Lord
Atkin's sense must exist before any duty of care can arise, but the scope of
the duty must depend on all the circumstances of the case', and 'in
determining whether or not a duty of care of particular scope was incumbent
on a defendant it is material to take into consideration whether it is just and
reasonable that it should be so' (per Lord Keith at p. 534).

These comments of Lord Keith marked the beginning of a remarkable
retreat from the implications of the Wilberforce test by appellate courts (see
Kidner (1987) 7 Legal Stud 319). In *Leigh & Sillavan Ltd* v *Aliakmon
Shipping Co. Ltd* [1986] 2 All ER 145, 153 Lord Brandon said that Lord
Wilberforce's words could not provide 'a universally applicable test of the
existence and scope of a duty of care in the law of negligence', and in *Curran*
v *Northern Ireland Co-ownership Housing Association Ltd* [1987] 2 All ER 13,
17 Lord Bridge described *Anns* as the 'high-water mark' of a trend elevating
Lord Atkin's neighbour principle 'into one of general application from which
a duty of care may always be derived unless there are clear countervailing

considerations to exclude it'. Then in *Yuen Kun-yeu* v *A-G of Hong Kong* [1987] 2 All ER 705 the Privy Council, in a judgment delivered by Lord Keith, said (at p. 710):

> Their Lordships venture to think that the two-stage test formulated by Lord Wilberforce for determining the existence of a duty of care in negligence has been elevated to a degree of importance greater than it merits, and greater perhaps than its author intended.

Thus, 'for the future it should be recognised that the two-stage test in *Anns* is not to be regarded as in all circumstances a suitable guide to the existence of a duty of care' (at p. 712). There were two possible interpretations of the Wilberforce test, said Lord Keith. On the first view, foreseeability of damage was in itself sufficient to create a relationship of 'proximity or neighbour-hood', subject only to such limitations on the existence of a duty of care as 'policy' might dictate. The second (and, in the opinion of the Privy Council, correct) view is that Lord Wilberforce intended the expression 'proximity or neighbourhood' to be a composite one importing the whole concept of necessary relationship between the plaintiff and defendant described by Lord Atkin in *Donoghue* v *Stevenson*.

The result would seem to be that factors which formerly might have been considered at the second stage of Lord Wilberforce's test, policy consider-ations which ought to 'negative, or to reduce or to limit the scope of the duty', should be taken into account at an earlier point when deciding whether a relationship of proximity between plaintiff and defendant exists. The second stage of the test will apply only rarely, 'in a limited category of cases where, notwithstanding that a case of negligence is made out on the proximity basis, public policy requires that there should be no liability' (*Yuen Kun-yeu* at p. 712; see, e.g., *Rondel* v *Worsley* [1969] 1 AC 191, para. 2.2.3.1—barristers' immunity; *Hill* v *Chief Constable of West Yorkshire* [1988] 2 All ER 238—police immunity).

This approach represents a shift of emphasis rather than a new substantive test for the existence of a duty of care. In *Rowling* v *Takaro Properties Ltd* [1988] 1 All ER 163, 172 Lord Keith (again) explained that the underlying rationale of *Peabody Donation Fund* and *Yuen Kun-yeu* was the fear that a too literal application of the Wilberforce test could produce a failure to have regard to, and to analyse and weigh, all the relevant considerations when deciding whether to impose a duty of care. Lord Templeman has put this point somewhat more colourfully, commenting that since *Anns* 'put the floodgates on the jar, a fashionable plaintiff alleges negligence. The pleading assumes that we are all neighbours now, Pharisees and Samaritans alike, that foreseeability is a reflection of hindsight and that for every mischance in an accident-prone world someone solvent must be liable in damages' (*CBS Songs Ltd* v *Amstrad Consumer Electronics plc* [1988] 2 All ER 484, 497). Rather than starting from a prima facie assumption that where a defendant's carelessness causes foreseeable damage a duty of care will exist, subject to policy considerations which may negative such a duty, the courts now determine the duty issue on a case by case basis, looking in particular at the nature of the relationship between the parties to determine whether it is sufficiently 'proximate'. That question, said Lord Keith, is 'of an intensely pragmatic character, well suited for gradual development but requiring most careful analysis' (*Rowling* v *Takaro Properties Ltd* at p. 172).

The formal requirements that it now appears must be satisfied before a duty of care is held to exist are:

(a)   foreseeability of the damage;
(b)   a sufficiently 'proximate' relationship between the parties; and
(c)   even where (a) and (b) are satisfied it must be 'just and reasonable' to impose such a duty (see *Caparo Industries plc* v *Dickman* [1990] 1 All ER 568, 573–4 per Lord Bridge; *Smith* v *Bush* [1989] 2 WLR 790, 816 per Lord Griffiths; *Pacific Associates Inc.* v *Baxter* [1989] 2 All ER 159, 189 per Russell LJ).

This formulation of the test for the existence of a duty of care is apt, once again, to make the problem seem simpler than it is, for at least two reasons. First, because there is an unavoidable interrelationship between the three limbs of the test. For example, the more foreseeable the harm, the more likely a court will be to hold that the relationship is 'proximate' (see *Caparo Industries plc* v *Dickman* [1989] 1 All ER 798, 803 per Bingham LJ), and, arguably, the more likely a court will be to hold that it is just and reasonable to impose a duty. Similarly, notwithstanding Lord Keith's comment in *Yuen Kun-yeu* that policy would only rarely need to be invoked to deny a duty of care, it would seem that some courts are treating the 'just and reasonable' requirement as equivalent to Lord Wilberforce's 'policy' stage (see *Caparo Industries plc* v *Dickman* [1989] 1 All ER 798, 803; *Pacific Associates Inc.* v *Baxter* [1989] 2 All ER 159, 170), and, moreover, some of the factors taken into account in determining what is just and reasonable may be equally relevant to the proximity of the relationship between the parties, and vice versa (see, e.g., the comments of Neill LJ in *James McNaughton Papers Group Ltd* v *Hicks Anderson & Co.* [1991] 1 All ER 134, 142: 'fairness' is 'elusive and may indeed be no more than one of the criteria by which proximity is to be judged'; and Ward J in *Ravenscroft* v *Rederiaktiebolaget Transatlantic* [1991] 3 All ER 73, 84–5: 'Proximity requires such a relation between the parties as renders it fair, just and reasonable that liability be imposed . . . the policy factors should now be considered as part and parcel of the relationship of proximity'). In other words, the three limbs of the test are not watertight compartments, but flexible components of Lord Atkin's neighbour principle, any one of which may be invoked to deny the existence of a duty of care (see *Pacific Associates Inc.* v *Baxter* [1989] 2 All ER 159, 180 per Purchas LJ). This point was specifically recognised by Lord Oliver in *Caparo Industries plc* v *Dickman* [1990] 1 All ER 568, 585:

Indeed, it is difficult to resist a conclusion that what have been treated as three separate requirements are, at least in most cases, in fact merely facets of the same thing, for in some cases the degree of forseeability is such that it is from that alone that the requisite proximity can be deduced, whilst in others the absence of that essential relationship can most rationally be attributed simply to the court's view that it would not be fair and reasonable to hold the defendant responsible. 'Proximity' is, no doubt, a convenient expression so long as it is realised that it is no more than a label which embraces not a definable concept but merely a description of circumstances from which, pragmatically, the courts conclude that a duty of care exists.

Secondly, for all the courts' efforts to elucidate and refine the neighbour principle, it remains a *general* and quite *indeterminate* principle. What is 'just and reasonable', for example, is no more determinate than policy consider-ations which 'ought to negative, or reduce or limit the scope of the duty' (the second stage of Lord Wilberforce's test). This problem has also been acknowledged by the House of Lords in *Caparo Industries plc v Dickman* [1990] 1 All ER 568, 574 where Lord Bridge observed that the concepts of proximity and fairness are not susceptible of any such precise definition as would be necessary to give them utility as practical tests, but amount in effect to little more than convenient labels to attach to specific situations which the law recognises pragmatically as giving rise to a duty of care. Lord Roskill commented (at pp. 581–2) that:

> . . . it has now to be accepted that there is no simple formula or touchstone to which recourse can be had in order to provide in every case a ready answer to the questions whether, given certain facts, the law will or will not impose liability for negligence or, in cases where such liability can be shown to exist, determine the extent of that liability. Phrases such as 'foreseeabil-ity', 'proximity', 'neighbourhood', 'just and reasonable', 'fairness', 'volun-tary acceptance of risk' or 'voluntary assumption of responsibility' will be found used from time to time in the different cases. But . . . such phrases are not precise definitions. At best they are but labels or phrases descriptive of the very different factual situations which can exist in particular cases and which must be carefully examined in each case before it can be pragmatically determined whether a duty of care exists and, if so, what is the scope and extent of that duty.

Here is explicit recognition that the language that the courts adopt when considering the duty of care does not provide any meaningful criteria with which to determine the existence of a duty of care. The new orthodoxy is that there is simply no general principle which can be applied to an infinite variety of circumstances to decide this question (*Caparo Industries plc v Dickman* at pp. 585–6 per Lord Oliver), and any attempt to find one is doomed to failure. The flesh can be put on the bones of the duty of care only by looking to the cases to see how 'general principles' have been applied in specific fact-situations. The 'Wilberforce test' is no longer valid, and the future develop-ment of the tort of negligence will take place according to a more traditional categorisation of distinct and recognisable situations as guides to the existence, scope and limits of various discrete duties of care (ibid. at p. 574 per Lord Bridge, citing Brennan J in *Sutherland Shire Council v Heyman* (1985) 60 ALR 1, 43–4). This is a process of incremental development by analogy with established categories, rather than by a sweeping extension of a prima facie duty of care restrained only by vague 'considerations which ought to negative, or to reduce or limit the scope of the duty' (*Murphy v Brentwood District Council* [1990] 2 All ER 908, 915 per Lord Keith, also citing Brennan J in *Sutherland Shire Council v Heyman*). In *Caparo Industries plc v Dickman* Lord Roskill commented (at p. 582) that a return to the traditional categorisation of cases was infinitely preferable to recourse to 'wide generalisations which leave their practical application matters of difficulty and uncertainty'. It is not clear from the decisions of the House of Lords in *Caparo* and *Murphy* whether the return to 'traditional categories' is intended to replace, or merely supplement, the tripartite test for the duty of care developed in the 1980s. The concepts of 'proximity' or what is 'just and reasonable' or 'fair' are just as empty of content and beg as many questions as Lord Wilberforce's wide generalisations, and thus are open to many of the objections directed at the *Anns* two-stage test. It is doubtful whether the practical application of the duty of care is any easier or more certain now that future extensions of liability can occur only on an *ad hoc*, incremental basis.

Developments in the 1960s and 1970s undoubtedly had the effect of expanding the tort of negligence into areas of loss that were traditionally regarded as either a ground of immunity or subject only to a limited duty (see in particular paras 2.2.4.1.3, 2.2.4.2 and 2.2.4.3). The 1980s witnessed a reaction to that process, particularly in the realm of claims for pure economic loss, in which the 'language' of duty of care changed. In the long run the change of terminology is probably less significant than the shift in judicial attitudes that the new orthodoxy reflects. The courts are now more cautious, even conservative, in their approach to the duty of care (although this will not necessarily prevent an incremental extension of the categories in which a duty of care may be held to exist, in an appropriate case: see, e.g., *Punjab National Bank v de Boinville* [1992] 1 WLR 1138).

2.1.2 Foreseeability and proximity

The concept of foreseeability, i.e., what a hypothetical 'reasonable man' would have foreseen in the circumstances, is ubiquitous in the tort of negligence. It is the foundation of the neighbour principle, but it is also used as a test of breach of duty and remoteness of damage. The fact that particular consequences were 'unforeseeable' may lead to the conclusion that the defendant's behaviour was not careless, and, even where negligence is patent, damage of an unforeseeable kind will be regarded as 'too remote' and therefore not actionable. This is partly related to the notion of fault liability. It can hardly be said that someone is blameworthy if harm to others could not reasonably have been anticipated. (The other strand to fault liability is whether the conduct was 'reasonable' in the face of *foreseeable* damage.)

It is important to realise, however, that foreseeability is a very flexible concept. One man's reasonable foresight is another man's flight of fancy, and so the bounds of what is foreseeable can be stretched or narrowed as the case may be. The likelihood that a particular event may occur in a given set of circumstances may range from almost certainty to virtual impossibility, and deciding whether it was 'foreseeable' involves a choice. There is 'no fixed point at which the law requires people to take account of a possibility' (*Atiyah* p. 35, see generally pp. 34–7). It is not a totally unprincipled choice since the degree of foreseeability required may be varied with the kind and extent of the damage, and the nature of the relationship between the parties. But the language of the courts is indeterminate. The loss must be 'reasonably' foreseeable, which may mean that it must be foreseeable as a 'possibility', or 'probable', or 'more probable than not', or 'likely', or 'very likely' (for examples of the use of language in this way see *Bolton* v *Stone* [1951] AC 850; *The Wagon Mound (No. 2)* [1967] 1 AC 617, 641–2; *Lamb* v *Camden London Borough Council* [1981] QB 625). This scope for ambiguity allows the concept of foreseeability to be used as a control mechanism to admit or deny recovery in certain types of case. This becomes most apparent when the courts feel constrained, either by authority or reasons of policy, to deny liability and do so by relying on an absence of reasonable foreseeability which attributes to the reasonable man 'an abnormal degree of myopia' (see the comments of Stephenson LJ in *McLoughlin* v *O'Brian* [1981] 1 All ER 809, 819, CA; *King* v *Phillips* [1953] 1 QB 429 (see para. 2.2.4.4); *Crossley* v *Rawlinson* [1981] 3 All ER 674; (1982) 45 MLR 342). But as Lord Reid observed in *McKew* v *Holland & Hannen & Cubitts (Scotland) Ltd* [1969] 3 All ER 1621, 1623:

> It only leads to trouble if one tries to graft on to the concept of foreseeability some rule of law to the effect that a wrongdoer is not bound to foresee something which in fact he could readily foresee as quite likely to happen.

The modern tendency is for the courts to be more explicit about resorting to policy arguments (para. 2.1.4), but it is as well to be aware of the possibility of concealing choices in the language of foreseeability.

'Proximity' is usually used as shorthand for Lord Atkin's neighbour principle. This refers to legal not physical proximity. Physical proximity may be relevant in deciding whether the parties should be treated as 'neighbours' in law (see, e.g., *Home Office* v *Dorset Yacht Co. Ltd* [1970] AC 1004; *McLoughlin* v *O'Brian* [1982] 2 All ER 298, HL), but it is not an essential requirement. The manufacturer is probably many miles from the consumer but there is a relationship of proximity if the product causes injury. In *Muirhead* v *Industrial Tank Specialities Ltd* [1985] 3 All ER 705 Goff LJ said that proximity is used as a convenient label to describe a relationship between the parties by virtue of which the defendant can reasonably foresee that his act or omission is liable to cause damage to the plaintiff of the relevant type. 'In this context, the word "relationship" refers to no more than the relative situations of the parties, as a consequence of which such foreseeability of damage may exist' (at p. 714; but cf. the analysis of Deane J *in Sutherland Shire Council* v *Heyman* (1985) 60 ALR 1, 54–6). In *Caparo Industries plc* v

Dickman [1990] 1 All ER 568, 599 Lord Oliver commented that proximity 'is an expression used not necessarily as indicating literally "closeness" in a physical or metaphorical sense but merely . . . a convenient label to describe circumstances from which the law will attribute a duty of care' (see also per Lord Jauncey at p. 602). His Lordship has also said that proximity is an expression which 'persistently defies definition' (*Murphy* v *Brentwood District Council* [1990] 2 All ER 908, 935), although this is perhaps not surprising as it is regarded as merely a 'label' which applies to describe the parties' relationship whenever the court concludes that a duty of care exists, since the duty of care also defies definition. The circularity of this reasoning is quite apparent. As Martin (1991) 7 PN 37, 38 comments: 'There is a duty of care where there is proximity, and proximity means that the facts give rise to a duty of care'. The ingredients necessary to establish a sufficiently proximate relationship vary with the circumstances of the case (see *Hill* v *Chief Constable of West Yorkshire* [1988] 2 All ER 238, 241; *Caparo Industries plc* v *Dickman* [1989] 1 All ER 798, 803). Thus, although it is often said that foreseeability is not in itself a sufficient criterion, where the defendant causes physical harm to the plaintiff or his property foreseeability of the harm will normally be sufficient to establish a duty of care. As Lord Oliver commented in *Murphy* v *Brentwood District Council* [1990] 2 All ER 908, 934: 'In the straightforward case of the direct infliction of physical injury by the act of the plaintiff [sic, query "defendant"] there is, indeed, no need to look beyond the foreseeability by the defendant of the result in order to establish that he is in a "proximate" relationship with the plaintiff'; and in *Mobil Oil Hong Kong Ltd* v *Hong Kong United Dockyards Ltd* [1991] 1 Lloyd's Rep 309, 328–9, Lord Brandon observed that: 'In most claims in respect of physical damage to property the question of the existence of a duty of care does not give rise to any problem, because it is self-evident that such a duty exists and the contrary view is unarguable', giving the example of physical damage to property arising out of driving a motor vehicle on a road (see also *Caparo Industries plc* v *Dickman* [1990] 1 All ER 568, 587–8 on negligent statements giving rise to direct physical injury: 'In such cases it is not easy to divorce foreseeability *simpliciter* and the proximity which flows from the virtual inevitability of damage if the advice is followed'; see also *Jaensch* v *Coffey* (1984) 54 ALR 417, 442 per Deane J, High Court of Australia). On the other hand, the foreseeability of physical damage is not invariably sufficient to establish a duty of care. In *Marc Rich & Co.* v *Bishop Rock Marine Co. Ltd* [1995] 3 All ER 307 the House of Lords held that a classification society did not owe a duty of care to the owner of the cargo on a vessel that had been negligently certified as seaworthy when the vessel subsequently sank. Their Lordships considered that all three elements of the tripartite test, foreseeability, proximity and questions of justice and reasonableness were relevant 'whatever the nature of the harm sustained by the plaintiff' (p. 326), although it was accepted that these issues overlap and are 'facets of the same thing'. Although the defendants did not *directly* cause the physical damage, the facts effectively involved a negligent statement ('this vessel is seaworthy') causing physical damage, and it is not obvious that a person who negligently labels a noxious substance as 'safe' should be in any different position from the person who negligently manufactured and put into circulation a noxious substance, when the consequences of the negligence may be identical (see Tan Keng Feng (1996) 112 LQR 209). Where the defendant's negligence consists of failing to prevent a third party from inflicting physical harm on the plaintiff (i.e., it involves an omission), foreseeability of the damage is never sufficient in itself to establish a duty of care; and *a fortiori* where the plaintiff is claiming in respect of pure economic loss which requires a very close relationship of 'proximity' in addition to it being 'just and reasonable' to impose a duty of care.

Sometimes the word 'proximate' is used, not to describe the relationship between the parties, but the connection between the defendant's negligence and the plaintiff's damage. Here it is being used as a test of causation to determine which of a number of causes is to be treated as the cause in law of the damage.

2.1.3   Duty and the unforeseeable plaintiff

The word 'duty' is used in at least three different senses. First, 'duty of care' may signify the recognition of liability for careless conduct in the abstract—is this type of harm occurring in this kind of situation ever actionable? Where the courts deny liability by holding that there is no duty of care even though the neighbour principle appears to be satisfied they are setting the limits of actionability in negligence as a matter of policy. Foreseeability may be necessary, but it is not a sufficient criterion of liability. The remaining paragraphs of this chapter are concerned with the duty of care in this sense.

Secondly, even where it is accepted that a particular type of loss is capable of giving rise to liability in negligence, the court may conclude that the defendant did not owe a duty of care to the particular plaintiff, if the plaintiff was unforeseeable. The plaintiff cannot rely on a duty that the defendant may have owed to others. In *Bourhill* v *Young* [1943] AC 92 the defendant motor-cyclist was killed in a crash caused by his own negligence. The plaintiff heard the crash but did not see it, and subsequently saw the scene of the accident after the defendant's body had been removed. The House of Lords held that the defendant was not liable for the nervous shock that the plaintiff suffered because he did not owe the plaintiff a duty of care. Although it was foreseeable that negligent driving might endanger other road users, the particular injury to the plaintiff was not foreseeable. It would have been different if she had been struck by a piece of debris from the crash. In *Hewett* v *Alf Brown's Transport Ltd* [1992] ICR 530 an employee's wife suffered from lead poisoning through contact with her husband's working clothes which were contaminated with lead oxide. The Court of Appeal held that the employers did not owe a duty of care to the plaintiff in respect of lead poisoning, because the exposure of her husband to the lead oxide had been 'insignificant', and the plaintiff's condition was a consequence of her special susceptibility to the effects of lead in her blood (see also *Gunn* v *Wallsend Slipway & Engineering Co. Ltd, The Times,* 23 January 1989, where it was held that employers owed no duty of care to an employee's wife who contracted mesothelioma as a result of inhaling asbestos dust from the employee's working clothes, because at the time such a risk was unforeseeable; cf. *Margereson v J. W. Roberts Ltd* [1996] PIQR P358, where the Court of Appeal held that the danger associated with inhaling large quantities of asbestos dust was foreseeable to the owner of an asbestos factory in 1933, and that accordingly the defendants owed a duty of care to children who played in the dust of a factory loading bay; for comment see Steele and Wikeley (1997) 60 MLR 265). The same principle applies to damage to property. In *Nova Mink Ltd v Trans-Canada Airlines* [1951] 2 DLR 241 it was held that the operator of an aircraft did not owe a duty of care to the owner of a mink ranch in respect of injury to the mink caused by the noise of the aircraft. It was not that there could never be such a duty, but that on the particular facts the defendants had no reason to anticipate that there was any need to keep a greater distance than would be necessary for an ordinary farm.

This second usage of 'duty of care' has sometimes been called the duty 'in fact' to distinguish it from the first sense of a 'notional duty', which deals with general actionability rather than specific fact-situations. This is merely an instance of moving from the general to the particular, and illustrates the point that negligence in the abstract is not sufficient to ground liability—the defendant's conduct must be negligent with respect to the plaintiff, which it cannot be if the particular plaintiff or damage is unforeseeable: 'It is not a duty to take care in the abstract but a duty to avoid causing to the particular plaintiff damage of the particular kind which he has in fact sustained' (per Lord Oliver in *Caparo Industries plc v Dickman* [1990] 1 All ER 568, 599). (Note that it is not necessary to foresee the specific plaintiff if he belongs to a class of individuals who were foreseeably likely to be harmed in the same way as the plaintiff, see *Haley v London Electricity Board* [1965] AC 778 (see para. 3.1.3.1.1); *Awad v Pillai* [1982] RTR 266, the true owner of a motor vehicle damaged by the defendant is the person foreseeably affected by his negligence even though the defendant believed the car belonged to someone else.)

The third sense in which the word duty is sometimes used is in the context of breach of duty. Where the question is whether the precautions against a particular risk taken by the defendant fall below the standard that a reasonable man would have undertaken, the court may ask: was the defendant under a duty to take further precautions? Here 'duty' is superfluous, it merely signifies the obligation to be careful by adopting the standard of care of a reasonable man (see, e.g., *Glasgow Corporation v Muir* [1943] AC 448, 458 per Lord Macmillan, 'There was no duty incumbent on her to take precautions against the occurrence of such an event', i.e., she was not careless in the circumstances—for criticism of the use of the word 'duty' in this way see Howarth [1991] CLJ 58, 72).

2.1.4 Policy and the function of duty

It has been said that the concept of duty of care adds nothing to the tort of negligence. In some circumstances a person is held liable for the negligent infliction of damage, and in other circumstances he is not. In the first set of circumstances it is said that a person owes a duty of care, and in the second set that there is no duty. Thus to say that a duty of care exists is to state as a conclusion that (not as a reason why) this damage ought to be actionable. It is circular to argue that there is no liability because there is no duty.

> When . . . a court holds that the defendant was under a duty of care, the court is stating as a conclusion of law what is really a conclusion of policy as to responsibility for conduct involving unreasonable risk. It is saying that such circumstances presented such an appreciable risk of harm to others as to entitle them to protection against unreasonable conduct by the actor. (*Nova Mink Ltd* v *Trans-Canada Airlines* [1951] 2 DLR 241, 255 per MacDonald J.)

This view has been increasingly accepted by the courts in this country. In *Hedley Byrne & Co. Ltd* v *Heller & Partners Ltd* [1964] AC 465 Lord Pearce observed (at p. 536) that: 'How wide the sphere of the duty of care in negligence is to be laid depends ultimately on the courts' assessment of the demands of society for protection from the carelessness of others'. Lord Denning in particular has been forthright in his criticism of the language of duty, causation and remoteness in negligence, taking the view (in *Dorset Yacht Co. Ltd* v *Home Office* [1969] 2 QB 412, 426) that it is all:

> at bottom a matter of public policy which we, as judges, must resolve. This talk of 'duty' or 'no duty' is simply a way of limiting the range of liability for negligence.

This statement was approved by Lord Diplock [1970] AC 1004, 1058, who added (at p. 1059) a 'choice is exercised by making a policy decision whether or not a duty of care ought to exist' (see also *Spartan Steel & Alloys Ltd* v *Martin & Co. (Contractors) Ltd* [1973] 1 QB 27, 37; *Lamb* v *Camden London Borough Council* [1981] QB 625, 634).

The policy element was explicitly recognised by Lord Wilberforce's two-stage test in *Anns* v *Merton London Borough Council* [1978] AC 728 (see para. 2.1.1) but it should be noted that policy considerations are not confined to the second part of the test. They are inherent in the neighbour principle itself. First, at the more general level, imposing liability only for 'faulty' conduct rather than on the basis simply that the defendant caused the harm involves a policy judgment that fault liability better reflects or serves certain social or economic values (see para. 1.4). Secondly, the decision as to what circumstances will give rise to 'a sufficient relationship of proximity or neighbourhood' allows scope for concealed policy choices. In *McLoughlin* v *O'Brian* [1982] 2 All ER 298 Lord Wilberforce observed (at p. 303) that 'Foreseeability . . . is a formula adopted by English law, not merely for defining, but also for limiting the persons to whom duty may be owed, and the consequences for which an actor may be held responsible'. Foreseeability of *physical* damage to others may be sufficient even as between strangers, but in the case of financial loss the courts will look at the nature of the relationship between the parties *before* the damage occurred (see para. 2.2.4.1.3). In the latter case foreseeability of the damage will not of itself be enough to create a relationship of 'proximity'.

In *McLoughlin* v *O'Brian,* at pp. 310–11, Lord Scarman commented that although policy considerations have to be weighed, the objective of the judges is the formulation of principle. ('Principle' can broadly be described as applying the formal logic of legal rules, whereas 'policy' allows pragmatic considerations to limit this verbal logic, e.g., by denying liability even though damage was reasonably foreseeable and so apparently within the formulation of the rule.) 'And, if principle inexorably requires a decision which entails a degree of policy risk, the court's function is to adjudicate according to principle, leaving policy curtailment to the judgment of Parliament.' His Lordship added that:

> the policy issue where to draw the line is not justiciable. The problem [of liability for 'nervous shock'] is one of social, economic, and financial policy. The considerations relevant to a decision are not such as to be capable of being handled within the limits of the forensic process.

If this statement purports to describe the way in which the courts operate it is patently incorrect. Indeed, in the same case Lord Edmund-Davies observed that the proposition that 'the policy issue is not justiciable' was 'as novel as it is startling'. It is true that the courts are not particularly well equipped to assess all the ramifications of a policy decision (see *Paterson Zochonis Ltd* v *Merfarken Packaging Ltd* [1986] 3 All ER 522, 540 per Robert Goff LJ) but Parliament will not necessarily provide any (let alone a speedy) solution to problems created by an unrestrained application of 'principle'. Moreover policy and principle are not mutually exclusive. The indeterminacy of such concepts as 'foreseeability', 'proximity', and the requirements of what is 'just and reasonable', allows considerable scope for policy manipulation within the confines of legal rules. It is better to recognise this, even at the cost of exposing the judiciary to 'political' criticism, than to pretend that the logical structure of the tort of negligence somehow demands a particular result.

The function of the duty of care, then, is to define the limits of liability for negligence, a role which is shared by the concept of remoteness of damage. It is a duty not to cause *actionable* damage by carelessness, and what is actionable is sometimes determined by 'duty' and sometimes by 'remoteness'. The nature of the exercise is the same in each case, and as long as this is kept in mind there is no harm in retaining the language of duty. Duty determines whether a generalised type of loss is ever actionable, whereas remoteness determines whether a particular loss, which is generally actionable, has occurred in such an unusual manner that it should not be actionable.

It must be remembered, however, that decisions about the existence of a duty of care in a new fact-situation are not unfettered or unprincipled. They are taken against the background of the existing law bearing in mind the practical implications. It is not sufficient for the courts to invoke the magic incantation 'policy' in order to deny liability, any more than the word 'proximity' will provide an easy test for duty of care. The policy of the law must be founded upon underlying justifications that will stand up to careful scrutiny. Thus arguments that an extension of liability for negligence would lead to a flood of litigation or to fraudulent claims were once granted greater credence than they are today. But other arguments, such as the possible commercial or financial consequences, the prospect of indeterminate liability, the possibility of risk-spreading (e.g., through insurance; see Davies (1989) 9 Legal Stud 67 for an attempt to establish a conceptual link between liability insurance and the duty of care) and potential conflicts with rights in property or other social or moral values, are given due consideration (for an earlier discussion see Symmons (1971) 34 MLR 394, 528; Buckley, *The Modern Law of Negligence*, 2nd ed., 1993, pp. 17–26).

In recent years the courts have identified a wide range of factors that may be relevant to the denial of a duty of care, though it is not always clear whether these factors render the relationship insufficiently proximate or whether they fall under the just and reasonable limb. The result, in practice, is the same. For example, a duty of care may not exist where:

(a) The plaintiff is the author of his own misfortune (*Peabody Donation Fund* v *Sir Lindsay Parkinson & Co. Ltd* [1984] 3 All ER 529; *Minories Finance Ltd* v *Arthur Young (a firm) (Bank of England, third party)* [1989] 2 All ER 105). Thus, in *Philcox* v *Civil Aviation Authority, The Times*, 8 June 1995 the Court of Appeal held that the Civil Aviation Authority did not owe a duty of care to the owner of an aircraft to ensure that he maintained his aircraft properly. The CAA's supervisory role over the safety of aircraft was for the protection of the public from the owner's failures and the duty, if any, was owed to the public. It was the owner's task to maintain his aircraft properly, and the CAA's supervisory function was not intended to protect an owner against his own failures. Clearly, it is possible for a plaintiff who has been careless to be held contributorily negligent, with an appropriate reduction in the damages awarded (para. 14.5), but denying the existence of a duty of care prevents the claim from ever getting that far. This factor tends to be raised in situations where the claim is against a 'secondary' defendant having a regulatory role, where the allegation is that the defendant should have prevented someone else (the 'primary' defendant) from inflicting damage upon the plaintiff (see para. 2.2.1.1). If under the regulatory framework the plaintiff is also in breach of an obligation to comply with certain requirements it is not a convincing plea that the defendant should compensate the plaintiff for failing to make *the plaintiff* observe the regulations (cf. the situation where the action is brought by a passenger who is not the owner of the aircraft: *Perrett* v *Collins, The Times*, 23 June 1998, where the Court of Appeal held that an inspector and a regulatory body which had negligently issued a certificate of airworthiness for a light aircraft could owe a duty of care to a passenger injured when the aircraft crashed).

(b) A duty of care would lead to unduly defensive practices by defendants seeking to avoid claims for negligence with detrimental effects on their performance of some public duty (*Hill* v *Chief Constable of West Yorkshire*

[1988] 2 All ER 238; *Rowling* v *Takaro Properties Ltd* [1988] 1 All ER 163, 173; *Yuen Kun-yeu* v *A-G of Hong Kong* [1987] 2 All ER 705, 715–16). Although initially invoked almost in passing, the courts now appear to rely on the notion of defendants performing their functions in an 'unduly defensive frame of mind' almost routinely to deny the existence of a duty of care in the context of claims against public bodies, on the basis that this would be to the detriment of the service in question (see, e.g., *X (minors)* v *Bedfordshire County Council* [1995] 3 WLR 152—child protection agencies; *Skinner* v *Secretary of State for Transport, The Times,* 3 January 1995—coastguard; *Elguzouli-Daf* v *Commissioner of Police of the Metropolis* [1995] 1 All ER 833—Crown Prosecution Service; *Marc Rich & Co.* v *Bishop Rock Marine Co. Ltd* [1995] 3 All ER 307—ship classification society; *Harris* v *Evans* [1998] 3 All ER 522—Health and Safety Executive). This argument is difficult to assess, or perhaps to give much credibility to, given that it usually consists of little more than mere assertion. It suggests that imposing a duty of care will lead to over-deterrence, damaging the service, rather than contributing to an improvement in standards of conduct. Why should the courts consider that imposing a duty of care is damaging to standards of behaviour in some cases but makes a positive contribution to the adoption of appropriate standards in others (see, e.g., the comments of Lord Woolf in *Spring* v *Guardian Assurance plc* [1994] 3 WLR 354, 395 in the context of imposing liability for negligent employment references)? Given that negligence requires people to exercise only *reasonable* care it is not clear why requiring defendants to meet this standard would be detrimental. The 'state of mind' with which any person undertakes a task is irrelevant if objectively he conforms to standards of reasonable care. For example, it matters not whether a motorist observes the speed limit because he believes it right and proper to do so, or because he is worried that he will be caught if he exceeds it. Moreover, as Sir Thomas Bingham MR pointed out in his dissenting judgment in *M (a minor)* v *Newham London Borough Council* [1994] 2 WLR 554, 571, it is a fallacy to suggest, as a general proposition, that the imposition of a duty of care makes no contribution to the maintenance of high standards, and some judges clearly do not attach much weight to this particular factor (see *Barrett* v *Enfield London Borough Council* [1997] 3 All ER 171, 181 per Evans LJ; *Capital and Counties plc* v *Hampshire County Council* [1997] 2 All ER 865, 890–91, CA). It is possible that concerns about 'defensive practice' are linked to the courts' perception that such defendants are 'peripheral parties' who could be exposed to a liability wholly out of proportion to their degree of responsibility for the loss (see Stapleton (1995) 111 LQR 301, 314; *John Munroe (Acrylics) Ltd* v *London Fire and Civil Defence Authority, The Times,* 22 May 1996, per Rougier J), although this is more explicitly acknowledged by the next factor.

(c)   Awards of damages against a public authority exercising a public function would have an impact upon the resources available to the authority to perform its duties, both in terms of the damages and costs, and in terms of the resources required to investigate and defend spurious claims. Thus, in *X (minors)* v *Bedfordshire County Council* [1995] 3 WLR 152, the House of

Lords held that a social services authority and those engaged in child protection (including social workers and doctors) did not owe a duty of care in negligence to children who were the subject of their intervention in respect of the manner in which they conducted the investigation or made a decision to remove a child into care, because the impact of litigation would be detrimental to the proper functioning of the child protection agencies and might impede their statutory function in that they would have even fewer funds for child protection activities than is currently the case (see also *Elguzouli-Daf* v *Commissioner of Police of the Metropolis* [1995] 1 All ER 833 on the impact of potential liability of the Crown Prosecution Service). In *Stovin* v *Wise* [1996] 3 All ER 801, 832, Lord Hoffmann commented:

> In my view the creation of a duty of care upon a highway authority, even on the grounds of irrationality in failing to exercise a power, would inevitably expose the authority's budgetary decisions to judicial inquiry. This would distort the priorities of local authorities, which would be bound to try to play safe by increasing their spending on road improvements rather than risk enormous liabilities for personal injury accidents. They will spend less on education or social services. I think that it is important, before extending the duty of care owed by public authorities, to consider the cost to the community of the defensive measures which they are likely to take in order to avoid liability.

(d) A duty of care would cut across a complex statutory framework established by Parliament for regulating particular circumstances, such as the protection of children at risk (*X (minors)* v *Bedfordshire County Council* [1995] 3 WLR 152) or the regulation of financial markets (*Yuen Kun-yeu* v *A-G of Hong Kong* [1987] 2 All ER 705). Indeed, in *X (minors)* v *Bedfordshire County Council* Lord Browne-Wilkinson (at pp. 184–5) went so far as to suggest that regulatory agencies charged with the task of protecting society from the wrongdoings of others should not normally be held liable in negligence. A similar type of concern was expressed by the majority of their Lordships in *Marc Rich & Co.* v *Bishop Rock Marine Co. Ltd* [1995] 3 All ER 307 where the House of Lords concluded that a classification society does not owe a duty of care to the owner of the cargo on a vessel which has been negligently certified as seaworthy, when subsequently the vessel sinks. Classification societies were independent non-profit making entities, operating for the sole purpose of promoting the collective welfare, namely the safety of ships and lives at sea. If a duty of care was held to exist the cost of insuring against potential claims would ultimately be passed on to shipowners, thereby cutting across the contractual structure governing dealings between shipowners and cargo owners, which was based on the system of double or overlapping insurance of cargo and the limitation of shipowners' liability to cargo owners under the Hague Rules, the Hague Visby Rules and tonnage limitation provisions. Lord Steyn said that if a duty of care were to be recognised it would enable cargo owners, or their insurers, to disturb the balance created by the Hague Rules and the Hague Visby Rules by enabling them to recover in tort against a peripheral party to the prejudice of the protection of shipowners under the existing system. This would have a substantial impact on international trade (see, however, the strong dissenting judgment of Lord Lloyd; and for comment see Cane [1995] LMCLQ 433).

(e)   There is an alternative remedy available to an aggrieved plaintiff, such as a statutory right of appeal from the decision of a government officer or department (*Jones* v *Department of Employment* [1988] 1 All ER 725; *Mills* v *Winchester Diocesan Board of Finance* [1989] 2 All ER 317), or judicial review (*Rowling* v *Takaro Properties Ltd* at p. 172), or another source of compensation, such as the Criminal Injuries Compensation Scheme (*Hill* v *Chief Constable of West Yorkshire* [1987] 1 All ER 1173, CA) or another cause of action, such as a claim for breach of contract, even where the action would be against a different defendant (*La Banque Financière de la Cité SA* v *Westgate Insurance Co. Ltd* [1988] 2 Lloyd's Rep 513, 563; *Simaan General Contracting Co.* v *Pilkington Glass Ltd (No. 2)* [1988] 1 All ER 791, 804–6). On the other hand, the courts must be sensitive to the realities of the alternative remedy which in practice may fall short of the advantages provided by the tort of negligence (Stapleton (1995) 111 LQR 301, 320).

(f)   Where a duty of care would tend to undermine the requirements of other causes of action, particularly in the case of complex commercial contracts where the parties have had the opportunity to negotiate a detailed structure of contractual obligations (*Greater Nottingham Co-operative Society Ltd* v *Cementation Piling and Foundations Ltd* [1988] 2 All ER 971; *Pacific Associates Inc.* v *Baxter* [1989] 2 All ER 159; see also *Calveley* v *Chief Constable of the Merseyside Police* [1989] 1 All ER 1025, 1030 per Lord Bridge—'Where no action for malicious prosecution would lie, it would be strange indeed if an acquitted defendant could recover damages for negligent investigation' of the alleged criminal offence). In *Spring* v *Guardian Assurance plc* [1994] 3 WLR 354 the Court of Appeal had held that an employer does not owe a duty of care in respect of an employment reference to the employee, because otherwise 'the defence of qualified privilege in an action for defamation where a reference was given, or the necessity for the plaintiff to prove malice in an action for malicious falsehood, would be bypassed' (for criticism of this reasoning see Weir [1993] CLJ 376). The House of Lords reversed this decision, however, on the basis that the employer who gives such a reference voluntarily undertakes responsibility for the reference being given with reasonable care, and there was no reason why the possibility that on the same facts the plaintiff would not succeed in an action for defamation or malicious falsehood should mean that no duty of care was owed. Lord Woolf commented (at p. 395) that the result of the requirement to prove malice was that an action for defamation provided a wholly inadequate remedy for an employee who suffered damage as a result of a negligent reference.

In certain areas the policy issues at stake may be manifold: some pointing to, and others against, the imposition of liability (see, e.g., Symmons (1987) 50 MLR 269 discussing actions for 'wrongful birth'). This does not necessarily mean that the courts have a free hand in setting the limits of actionability. As

Oliver LJ commented in *Leigh & Sillavan Ltd* v *Aliakmon Shipping Co. Ltd* [1985] 2 All ER 44, 57:

> But policy is not arbitrary and I do not read Lord Wilberforce's formulation as absolving the court, at any rate at any level below the House of Lords, from inquiring into the basis in logic or in precedent for the adoption of a particular policy . . .

Nor, it might be added, should the House of Lords be absolved from this aspect of the judicial function. Moreover, the substitution of the requirements of what is 'just and reasonable' for 'policy' does not alter the nature of the exercise. In reality, changes in the ambit of actionability through the duty of care, whether as an expansion or contraction of liability, reflect the fact that, over time, judicial perceptions about the strengths of the respective policy arguments favouring liability or non-liability may change, in response to social and economic developments. (For discussion of how judicial views have altered, reflecting shifts in social ideologies and moral and economic values since the nineteenth century, see Hepple [1997] CLP 69, who argues that the conceptual framework of the tort of negligence, particularly the notion of 'duty of care', seeks to draw artificial lines between law and policy which produces both formal and functional incoherence.)

2.2 EXCLUDED INTERESTS AND LIMITED DUTIES

There has been a dramatic reduction over the past 25 years or so in the fact-situations in which the courts are likely to conclude that there was no duty of care. Sometimes old immunities have been brought within the mainstream of negligence liability, and in other cases more restricted forms of duty have been developed. The main problem areas will be considered in the remainder of this chapter, but it should be remembered that it is always open to the courts to make further inroads into the limits of non-actionability. Conversely, new fact-situations may arise where, for policy reasons, it is held that no duty of care should exist.

There are four broad categories corresponding to the nature of the defendant's conduct (act or omission), the type of plaintiff, type of defendant and the type of damage sustained. Some fact-situations can cut across two or more of these categories.

2.2.1 Omissions

The law has always drawn a disctinction between the infliction of harm through some positive action and merely allowing harm to occur by failing to prevent it. This is the distinction between misfeasance and nonfeasance, but it is not always easy to make. In many cases an omission may simply be part and parcel of a course of conduct that constitutes a negligent way of acting. The motorist who fails to stop at red traffic lights has 'omitted' to brake, but this is not regarded as an omission, merely the negligent performance of the activity of driving. Negligent acts can always be described in terms of a failure to take the appropriate precautions, but this is not what is meant by an omission in this context. An omission is characterised by passive inaction, and the general rule is that there is no liability for nonfeasance. In other words there is no general obligation to take positive steps to confer a benefit on others, by preventing harm befalling them. The conferment of benefits, it is said, lies in the realm of contract whereas tortious obligations are limited to not worsening someone's position. The usual example is that there is no obligation to rescue someone in danger, even if rescue would involve little or no effort (e.g., shouting a warning to a blind man) and no danger to the rescuer.

The reasons for this are partly historical, partly practical. The early common law was hard put to deal with the intentional infliction of harm, and sins of omission are popularly regarded as less culpable than sins of commission. This is probably related to notions of causation—failing to prevent harm is not in the same category as causing harm through positive actions. How can it be said that a totally passive defendant has 'caused' anything to happen at all? Two other arguments are invoked in support of the rule. First, how is the defendant to be identified? Generally a person who causes damage through his negligent behaviour identifies himself as the potential defendant. If, like the priest and the Levite, 10 or 20 members of the public pass by the injured man without rendering assistance, which of them is responsible? Why pick on one rather than the other 19? Secondly, it is argued that the imposition of liability for omissions would create burdensome duties of affirmative action which interfere with individual liberty. Negligence does not normally compel specific actions, rather, it requires one who chooses to act to do so carefully. What if a rescue would involve expending time and money or even incurring a risk to one's personal safety? How nicely is a defendant to be allowed to calculate the risk to himself before he can refuse to act? (see Logie [1989] CLJ 115, 116–20). The rule applies, however, even when the burden is minimal and there is no risk to the defendant, as where a passer-by can decline to assist a child who is drowning in a foot of water without incurring tortious liability. More recently, in the case of public services exercising a 'rescue' function, it has been said that imposing a duty of care would tend to lead to the services being carried out in a 'defensive' frame of mind and that imposing liability would lead to a drain on resources to the detriment of the service itself and contrary to the public interest (see, e.g., *Hill* v *Chief Constable of West Yorkshire* [1988] 2 All ER 238—the police; *X (minors)* v *Bedfordshire County Council* [1995] 3 WLR 152—child protection agencies; *Harris* v *Evans* [1998] 3 All ER 522—Health and Safety Executive; *Skinner* v *Secretary of State for Transport, The Times*, 3 January 1996—the coastguard; cf. *Capital and Counties plc* v *Hampshire County Council* [1997] 2 All ER 865, 890–91).

The mere-omissions rule has been criticised, particularly in the context of non-rescue (*Atiyah*, pp. 63–7; Linden (1971) 34 MLR 241; Weinrib (1980) 90 Yale LJ 247; see also Logie, op. cit., who distinguishes between failure to warn and failure to rescue), but it also has its supporters. Smith and Burns (1983) 46 MLR 147, for example, argue that Lord Atkin's neighbour principle has, in many instances, been misapplied by the courts in order to provide a duty to act to prevent harm instead of the usual (doctrinally correct) duty to be careful when acting (see also Bowman and Bailey [1984] PL 277). Stapleton (1995) 111 LQR 301 suggests that the omissions rule is understandable in the context of judicial attempts to contain an expanding tort of negligence by denying liability where the defendant is not causally important but is a 'peripheral party'. The courts generally avoid imposing duties of affirmative action on peripheral parties because such duties dilute any moral and economic deterrent signals of tort liability in general. In recent years there have been increasing numbers of claims made against peripheral parties, as plaintiffs seek 'deep pocket' defendants, arguing that the defendants were in a position to control or modify the conduct of the principal culprit who has inflicted damage on the plaintiff (the classic example of this is *Anns* v *Merton London Borough Council* [1978] AC 728 where the plaintiffs were suing the local authority in respect of negligently supervising the activities of a builder who constructed a building with defective foundations). As Stapleton points out, this problem is compounded where the defendant is a public authority, because imposing liability could give rise to a disproportionate liability (since the principle of joint and several liability holds the defendant who is only partially to blame responsible for the whole loss *vis-à-vis* the plaintiff) with a corresponding distorting effect upon the finances of public authorities.

It is clear that foreseeability of damage cannot *per se* provide the necessary obligation to act, as the decision of the Court of Appeal in *P. Perl (Exporters) Ltd* v *Camden London Borough Council* [1984] QB 342 illustrates. Thieves entered the plaintiff's premises by knocking a hole through the wall of an adjoining flat, which belonged to the defendants. It was accepted that the defendants had been careless in failing to secure the flat from entry by vagrants, and there had been complaints about the lack of security from other occupants of the block of flats. The defendants were not liable for the theft. Oliver LJ objected that the 'foreseeability of damage to property is, by itself, being treated as the foundation of the duty'. The decision was clearly influenced by the policy consideration that redress for this type of loss is better left to first-party insurance rather than imposing a wide-ranging obligation on property owners to protect neighbours from the depredations of burglars (see Jones (1984) 47 MLR 223). But more fundamentally the claim was in respect of a pure omission, the defendants' 'failure to impede' entry to their own premises (see also *King* v *Liverpool City Council* [1986] 1 WLR 890 where the Court of Appeal said that the fact that it was impossible to take effective steps against the activities of vandals 'should operate to restrict the ambit of the duty to take any positive steps to secure the property'; see Joslin (1986) 136 NLJ 543).

In *Smith* v *Littlewoods Organisation Ltd* [1987] 1 All ER 710 the defendants purchased a cinema intending to demolish it and build a supermarket. The property remained empty and unattended for over a month, during which time vandals obtained entry and on two occasions there were attempts to start fires. Neither the police nor the defendants were informed about this. Finally, a fire was deliberately started in the cinema by vandals and the fire spread and caused serious damage to the plaintiff's adjacent property. The House of Lords was unanimous that the plaintiff's action must fail, but for apparently different reasons. Only Lord Goff dealt with the case in terms of a pure omission—the defendants' failure to prevent a third party from causing damage to the plaintiff by deliberate wrongdoing. 'In such a case, it is not possible to invoke a general duty of care; for it is well recognised that there is no *general* duty of care to prevent third parties from causing such damage' (at pp. 728–9). This is so even if there is a high degree of foreseeability that the damage may occur—the problem in this type of case could not be solved 'simply through the mechanism of foreseeability. When a duty *is* cast on a person to take precautions against the wrongdoing of third parties, the ordinary standard of foreseeability applies; and so the possibility of such wrongdoing does not have to be very great before liability is imposed' (at p. 735). There are some 'special circumstances' in which a defendant may be held responsible for deliberate wrongdoing by another (see especially at pp. 730–1), but the degree of foreseeability of damage, however great, is not *in itself* sufficient to create an affirmative duty to act. One example of such a special circumstance is where the defendant carelessly creates a source of danger and it is reasonably foreseeable that a third party may interfere with it and spark off the danger causing damage to the plaintiff. Another example is where an occupier of property knows or ought to know that a third party (or even an act of nature) has created a risk on his land, and the occupier fails to take reasonable steps to avert the danger. But neither circumstance applied to the facts of *Smith* v *Littlewoods Organisation Ltd* because, since the defendants were unaware of the entry by the vandals, the risk could not be said to be foreseeable.

Lord Brandon, Lord Griffiths and Lord Mackay appear to have expressed the defendants' duty in more positive terms. Lord Griffiths, for example, said (at p. 713): 'The duty of care owed by Littlewoods was to take reasonable care that the condition of the premises they occupied was not a source of danger to neighbouring property'. But because there was nothing inherently dangerous stored in the premises and they did not know of the activities of the vandals there was no foreseeable danger. 'People do not mount 24-hour guards on empty properties and the law would impose an intolerable burden if it required them to do so save in the most exceptional circumstances' (per Lord Griffiths at p. 714). This more positive formulation of a general duty of care has led one commentator to suggest that this case may have produced an unnoticed revolution, which ultimately might lead to the abolition of the distinction between acts and omissions (Markesinis (1989) 105 LQR 104). This seems unlikely, however, at least in the short term. It is possible, of course, that the exceptions to the mere-omissions rule may be extended to the point at which the 'rule' is honoured more in the breach than the observance. On the other hand, the majority of their Lordships in *Smith* v *Littlewoods Organisation Ltd* may simply have taken as the starting point for their analysis the exception which applies to the occupation of land. There is a general positive duty which arises from the occupation and control of land, but whether that general duty gives rise to a specific duty to the plaintiff depends upon the facts of each case: how was the damage caused, how foreseeable was it, could the defendant have reasonably prevented it? Lord Goff, however, analysed the problem at a higher level of generality, starting from the mere-omissions rule and then considering the exceptions to the rule and their application to the facts. In practice there is very little, if any, difference between these approaches, though, with great respect, Lord Goff's speech provides the clearest exposition of the issues (see, however, the comment of Howarth (1994) 14 LS 88).

It is not true, then, to say that there can never be liability for a pure omission, because in some circumstances the courts have established duties of affirmative action. These may arise where:

(a)   there is an undertaking by the defendant;
(b)   there is a special relationship between plaintiff and defendant;
(c)   the defendant has control over a third party who causes damage to the plaintiff; or
(d)   the defendant has control over land or something likely to be dangerous if interfered with.

2.2.1.1 Undertaking A person who undertakes to perform a task, even gratuitously, assumes a duty to act carefully in carrying it out. So a hospital casualty department can be responsible for making an incorrect diagnosis and sending a patient away without treatment (*Barnett* v *Chelsea & Kensington Hospital Management Committee* [1969] 1 QB 428, see para. 4.1.1). In *Barrett* v *Ministry of Defence* [1995] 3 All ER 87, a naval airman became so intoxicated, having consumed a large amount of cheap alcohol provided at one of the defendants' naval bases, that he fell into a coma and subsequently choked to death on his own vomit. The Court of Appeal held that the defendants did not owe a duty of care to the deceased to prevent him from consuming an excessive volume of alcohol, because he assumed responsibility for his own actions in consuming alcoholic drink and it was not just or reasonable to dilute self-responsibility by blaming one adult for another's lack of self-control. Nonetheless, the defendants were liable in respect of the death because once the deceased had collapsed and was incapable of looking after himself the defendants had assumed responsibility for his care but had not called a doctor, and the supervision of the deceased had been inadequate by the defendants' own standards. Damages were reduced by two thirds for the deceased's contributory negligence.

If the defendant's conduct in commencing a rescue, deters or prevents others (or even the plaintiff) from effecting a rescue, the defendant will be liable if he does not complete the task (*Zelenko* v *Gimbel Bros* (1935) 158 Misc 904, 287 NYS 134). This is founded upon 'detrimental reliance', i.e., reliance to his detriment by the plaintiff on the defendant properly carrying out the duty he has undertaken. In *Mercer* v *South Eastern & Chatham Railway Companies' Managing Committee* [1922] 2 KB 549 the defendants' practice of keeping a wicket-gate locked when a train was passing induced members of the public to believe that it was safe to cross the line when the gate was unlocked. The defendants were liable for leaving the gate unlocked although under no obligation to keep it locked. These cases are probably more correctly classified as instances of misfeasance. Where the defendant was active in creating a hazardous situation, even without negligence, the court may treat this as a sufficient ground for requiring him to take some steps to remove the danger (see, e.g., *Oke v Weide Transport Ltd* (1963) 41 DLR (2d) 53).

It is more problematic where the plaintiff's position has not been altered by the defendant's conduct. If, for example, he commences the rescue but then abandons the attempt, is the defendant liable, even though he would not be liable had he done nothing and his actions have not changed the plaintiff's circumstances? In *Horsley v MacLaren* [1970] 1 Lloyd's Rep 257, the Ontario Court of Appeal held that a person who embarks on a rescue is not liable unless his intervention, or the discontinuance of his efforts, leaves the rescuee in a worse condition than when he commenced (see also Restatement, Second, Torts, ss. 323 and 324). In the Supreme Court of Canada this point was left open, but it is consistent with the traditional interpretation of the decision of the House of Lords in *East Suffolk Rivers Catchment Board v Kent* [1941] AC 74 that a public body that acts in the exercise of a statutory power is not liable unless it increases the damage that would have been sustained had it chosen to do nothing. This was based on the argument that, since there was no duty to act (i.e., exercise the power) and there was no liability for failing to act (i.e., for omissions), there should be no liability for acting negligently unless this increased the harm. Thus, it is arguable (though admittedly the argument is not particularly attractive) that a doctor who comes across a man who is bleeding to death, who could easily prevent this but is careless in his attempts, is not liable in negligence for the man's death, unless his intervention prevented other, more effective, aid reaching the deceased ('If he volunteers his assistance, his only duty as a matter of law is not to make the victim's condition worse': *Capital and Counties plc* v *Hampshire County Council* [1997] 2 All ER 865, 883, CA). In these circumstances there is no practical difference between the negligent doctor and a doctor who simply ignores the deceased and passes by, and imposing liability on the former but not the latter could be seen as deterring medical intervention. For this reason some North American jurisdictions have enacted 'Good Samaritan' legislation, which generally provides for immunity where emergency medical treatment is given where facilities are inadequate, unless there is 'gross negligence', though this does not normally apply to treatment in hospital.

East Suffolk Rivers Catchment Board v Kent must now be read in the light of *Anns v Merton London Borough Council* [1978] AC 728 (see para. 2.2.3.2) in which it was held that a public body could be liable for an omission to exercise a statutory power where this was both *ultra vires* the statute and negligent with respect to the plaintiff. This can be taken as an exception to the mere-omissions rule, particularly as on the facts of *Anns v Merton London Borough Council* the defendants were liable for failing to confer a benefit, i.e., they failed to prevent the damage caused by the negligent construction of property by a builder (see Bowman and Bailey [1984] PL 277). Whether this is treated as *sui generis* or as a case of undertaking and reliance (though it is difficult to see in what sense it can be said that a purchaser 'relied' on the local authority to inspect building foundations, any more than he 'relied' on the builder or the architect not to act negligently), it seems clear that the affirmative duty is delineated by the statutory context and would not apply to private individuals. *Anns* has now been overruled by the House of Lords in *Murphy* v *Brentwood District Council* [1990] 2 All ER 908, para. 2.2.4.2, to the extent that it held that local authorities owed a duty of care to a building owner to avoid damage to the building which creates a present or imminent danger to the health and safety of occupants, arising out of the authorities' powers to require compliance with building regulations. The damage was held to be pure economic loss and therefore irrecoverable. Their Lordships specifically left open the question of whether the local authority would owe a duty of care in respect of physical damage, either to persons or property other than the building, caused by a latent defect in the building (see *Tesco Stores Ltd* v *Wards Construction (Investment) Ltd* (1995) 76 BLR 94, para. 6.3.3). On this basis, it is possible that the approach adopted in *Anns* is still relevant to this issue.

In *Sutherland Shire Council* v *Heyman* (1985) 60 ALR 1, on essentially similar facts to *Anns,* the High Court of Australia held that a local authority did not owe a duty of care in respect of an allegedly negligent inspection or failure to inspect a defectively constructed building. Deane J commented (at p. 58) that 'the distinction between a failure to act and positive action remains a fundamental one. The common law imposes no prima facie general duty to rescue, safeguard or warn another from or of reasonably foreseeable loss or injury or to take reasonable care to ensure that another does not sustain such loss or injury'. Cases in which such a duty will be imposed are 'exceptional'. Apart from cases involving an assumption of an obligation (undertaking) and special relationships, 'they are largely confined to cases involving reliance by one party upon care being taken by the other in the discharge or performance of statutory powers, duties or functions, or of powers, duties or functions arising from or involved in the holding of an office or the possession or occupation of property' (ibid. at p. 59).

In *Stovin* v *Wise* [1994] 3 All ER 467, a bank on land adjacent to the highway obstructed visibility and created a danger to the highway. The highway authority decided to take action to remove the bank, under powers conferred by the Highways Act 1980, but some 11 months later no further action had been taken. The Court of Appeal held that the authority owed a duty of care in negligence to the plaintiff who was injured in an accident caused partly by the limited visibility. Since the authority had become aware of the danger, which it alone had the physical and financial resources to eliminate, and had decided to seek the cooperation of the adjacent land-owner, it owed a duty of care to road users to press forward with its proposal with reasonable expedition. The authority argued that although it had a statutory power to act, that did not create a common law duty to act, because the common law does not impose liability for a failure to act even if damage is readily foreseeable. This was not a danger that the authority had itself created, and its activities could not give rise to liability unless the activities created additional danger which caused the injury, relying on *Sheppard* v *Glossop Corporation* [1921] 3 KB 132 and *East Suffolk Rivers Catchment Board* v *Kent* [1941] AC 74. The Court of Appeal considered that it was not true that the highway authority had simply failed to act: it had decided positively to proceed by seeking the agreement of the adjacent landowner, and its failure to pursue that course was not an omission on which it could rely to escape liability (per Kennedy LJ at p. 480). Roch LJ considered that the highway authority's position was analogous to that of an occupier of premises in relation to visitors, because it was the only person who could deal with a danger of physical damage to users of the highway due to the construction and layout of the highway. On appeal ([1996] 3 All ER 801) the House of Lords reversed this decision, by a bare majority, concluding that no duty of care was owed, on the basis that there was no public law duty to do the work and the alleged negligence consisted of a pure omission. Lord Hoffmann said that there were sound reasons why omissions require different treatment from positive conduct. It was one thing for the law to say that a person who undertakes some activity should take reasonable care not to cause damage to others. It was another thing for the law to require that a person who is doing nothing in particular shall take steps to prevent another from suffering harm from the acts of third parties (like Mrs Wise) or natural causes. The problem of how a defendant is to be identified in the case of a mere omission (or as Lord Hoffmann expressed it, the 'why pick on me?' argument) did not apply to a highway authority. The authority alone had the financial and physical resources, as well as the legal powers, to eliminate the hazard. But that in itself was not sufficient to create a common law duty of care. Nor was the existence of the authority's statutory powers to deal with the danger sufficient to create the 'proximity' between the parties which would not otherwise have existed. There were many instances, said Lord Hoffmann (at p. 827), where even statutory *duties* have been held not to give rise to common law rights of action:

> In terms of public finance, this is a perfectly reasonable attitude. It is one thing to provide a service at the public expense. It is another to require the public to pay compensation when a failure to provide the service has resulted in loss. Apart from cases of reliance . . . the same loss would have been suffered if the service had not been provided in the first place. To require payment of compensation increases the burden on public funds. Before imposing such an additional burden, the courts should be satisfied that this is what Parliament intended.

If, continued his Lordship, legislation which creates a statutory duty does not create a statutory liability to pay compensation, the same policy should ordinarily exclude the existence of a common law duty of care. The difficulty with this approach is that legislation very rarely creates a statutory compensation scheme for breach of its provisions, and moreover, if a particular statute did provide for compensation the likelihood is that the court would conclude that it was unnecessary to add a further common law remedy, which is close to saying that there should never be a common law duty of care. His Lordship did not take such an extreme view. There could be a duty to act if the defendant has undertaken to do something or has induced a person to rely upon his doing something. In the context of public authorities, a good example of this was where a lighthouse authority has created an expectation in mariners that the light from a lighthouse will warn them of danger. The authority would owe a duty of care requiring it not to extinguish the light without giving reasonable notice. This was based on representation and reliance, and did not depend upon the public nature of the authority's powers. There was a broader sense, however, in which the public may 'rely' on public authorities' decisions, namely general dependence on an authority's performance of its function with reasonable care, without the need for contributing conduct by the defendant or action to his detriment by the plaintiff (citing *Sutherland Shire Council* v *Heyman* (1985) 157 CLR 424, 464, where Mason J gave the examples of air traffic control, safety inspection of aircraft, and a fire authority fighting a fire). This was the concept of 'general reliance', which had little in common with the ordinary doctrine of reliance. Under this theory, the plaintiff does not need to have relied upon the expectation that a statutory power would be used, or even have known that it existed. It appeared to refer to general expectations in the community, which the individual plaintiff may or may not have shared (per Lord Hoffmann at p. 829). But on the facts of *Stovin* v *Wise* there was no question of reliance on the highway authority having improved the junction. Everyone could see that it was still the same. The plaintiff was not arbitrarily denied a benefit which was routinely provided to others (which was central to the notion of general reliance); he was treated in exactly the same way as any other road user. The foundation of the doctrine of general reliance was absent because it was not a case of provision of a uniform identifiable benefit or service. Lord Hoffmann commented (at p. 833) that: 'Drivers of vehicles must take the highway network as they find it. Everyone knows that there are hazardous bends, intersections and junctions. It is primarily the duty of drivers of vehicles to take due care. And if . . . they do not, there is compulsory insurance to provide compensation to the victims. There is no reason of policy or justice which requires the highway authority to be an additional defendant.' With respect, this last point proves too much. The fact that hazards are known does not preclude an action against the highway authority if by some act of misfeasance the authority has created or increased the hazard; nor, indeed, should it. A highway authority should be no more immune from the consequences of creating a hazard in the highway than a private citizen. And, moreover, the question of 'compensating' insurance companies from public funds (since the effect of holding the authority liable would have been to reduce the liability of the defendant's insurers to compensate the plaintiff) would not be a factor in the courts' determination of a duty of care. Ultimately the majority view in *Stovin* v *Wise* rested on the basis that there was no *public law* duty on the highway authority to remove the danger; but even if there had been such a duty there were no grounds for imposing a common law liability for nonfeasance. (See also the discussion of *Stovin* v *Wise* in the context of the exercise of statutory powers, at para. 2.2.3.2. Note also the dissenting speech of Lord Nicholls, taking the view that public authorities could be liable in negligence for an omission to exercise a statutory power, even where there has not been a specific assumption of responsibility or undertaking to the plaintiff, though in his Lordship's view there were no fixed categories of case. The greater the discretion involved, the less readily would a common law duty be superimposed, and *vice versa*. See further the majority decision of High Court of Australia in *Pyrenees Shire Council* v *Day* (1998) 151 ALR 147, holding a local authority liable for a fire, having failed to follow up a written warning to the occupier of premises that a chimney was dangerous and that the fireplace should not be used unless it was repaired.)

Actions by members of the public against allegedly negligent statutory regulatory agencies will tend to fall into the category of omissions (see McLean (1988) 8 OJLS 442). The agency may have failed adequately to supervise a third party, be it a builder or financial organisation, with resulting loss to the plaintiff. In some cases the statutory framework has been used by the court to justify the imposition of an affirmative, common law duty of care (as in *Anns,* a decision followed by a majority of the Supreme Court of Canada in *City of Kamloops* v *Nielsen* (1984) 10 DLR (4th) 641), but in others it has been said that since the statute has pointedly failed to confer a remedy in damages on the plaintiff the court should not superimpose a common law duty. For example, in *Yuen Kun-yeu* v *A-G of Hong Kong* [1987] 2 All ER 705 the plaintiffs deposited substantial sums of money with a registered deposit-taking company which subsequently went into liquidation. The Commissioner of Deposit-taking Companies regulated deposit-taking businesses in Hong Kong and had wide discretionary powers to refuse to register or revoke the registration of a company considered to be unfit to take deposits. The plaintiffs alleged that the company had been run fraudulently and speculatively. They sued the commissioner alleging that he either knew or ought to have known how the company was being run, and that he either should never have registered the company or should have revoked the registration before they deposited their money. The Privy Council held that the commissioner owed no duty of care to the plaintiffs. Amongst a number of reasons given for denying the existence of a duty, their Lordships said that they were unable to discern any legislative intention that the commissioner should owe any statutory duty to potential investors, and it 'would be strange that a common law duty of care should be superimposed on such a statutory framework' (at p. 713; cf. *Brewer Bros* v *The Queen in right of Canada* (1991) 80 DLR (4th) 321 where the relevant statutory provisions were found to have expressly provided for the protection of a defined group against economic loss). There was, moreover, no voluntary assumption of responsibility by the commissioner to the plaintiffs. He had a duty to supervise deposit-taking companies in the general public interest, but no special responsibility towards individual members of the public. Nor could the plaintiffs' reliance on the fact of registration as a guarantee of the soundness of a particular company establish a special relationship which would give rise to a duty of care. Such reliance was neither reasonable nor justifiable (see also *Davis* v *Radcliffe* [1990] 2 All ER 536; *Minories Finance Ltd* v *Arthur Young (a firm) (Bank of England, third party)* [1989] 2 All ER 105).

The commissioner's position in *Yuen Kun-yeu* was analogous to that of the police in *Hill* v *Chief Constable of West Yorkshire* [1988] 2 All ER 238. The mother of a victim of a notorious serial murderer sued the police, alleging that by their negligence they failed to apprehend the murderer before he killed her daughter. The House of Lords held that the police owed no duty of care to individual members of the public who may suffer injury as a result of the failure to identify and apprehend unknown criminals (see Bailey (1987) 50 MLR 956 commenting on the decision of the Court of Appeal). This was based partly on public policy, that the threat of litigation might have an adverse impact on the conduct of criminal investigations, and partly on the fact that the murderer was never in police custody and so never under their control. If he had been in custody and had escaped through the police's negligence they might have owed a duty in respect of damage caused during the course of the escape, but not for his subsequent criminal career (applying *Home Office* v *Dorset Yacht Co. Ltd* [1970] AC 1004, para. 2.2.3.2). In *Yuen Kun-yeu* the fact that the commissioner did not have any power to control the day-to-day management of any registered company was a significant factor in denying the existence of a duty of care (see also *Curran* v *Northern Ireland Co-ownership Housing Association Ltd* [1987] 2 All ER 13, 19 and *Davis* v *Radcliffe* [1990] 2 All ER 536, 541 on the absence of control over the third party).

Where a regulatory agency has been established with the specific objective of protecting the public from dangerous practices then, arguably, it should be easier to find a duty of care owed to individual members of the public injured or killed by the agency's negligent failure to regulate. For example, in *Swanson* v *The Queen in right of Canada* (1991) 80 DLR (4th) 741, Transport Canada had the responsibility for regulating the safety of commercial airlines, with extensive powers to enforce compliance with safety standards up to and including suspension of an airline's operating licence. A small commercial airline operated with safety irregularities. Following complaints, Transport Canada made inspections, and reports listed serious deficiencies. They issued warnings to the airline but did not take further action. In an action brought by family members of two passengers killed in a subsequent plane crash the Federal Court of Appeal held Transport Canada liable for negligently allowing the airline to continue its unsafe practices (cf. *Philcox* v *Civil Aviation Authority, The Times*, 8 June 1995 where the Court of Appeal held that the Civil Aviation Authority did not owe a duty of care to the owner of an aircraft that crashed because it was the owner's responsibility to maintain the aircraft, and the CAA's supervisory role was for the protection of the public against an owner's failures. Where, however, the claim is by a passenger injured in a crash a regulatory agency can owe a duty of care in respect of a negligently issued certificate of airworthiness—*Perrett* v *Collins, The Times*, 23 June 1998, CA).

2.2.1.2 Relationship between plaintiff and defendant There are a number of relationships that give rise to an affirmative duty to prevent harm. These include employer and employee (*Public Transport Corporation* v *Sartori* [1997] 1 VR 168, Victoria CA; *Charlton* v *Forrest Printing Ink Co. Ltd* [1980] IRLR 331—duty to take precautions against attacks on employees), parent and child (*Carmarthenshire County Council* v *Lewis* [1955] AC 549; even ice-cream vendor and child: *Arnold* v *Teno* (1978) 83 DLR (3d) 609; though the duty does not extend to protecting the child's economic interests: *Van Oppen* v *Clerk to the Bedford Charity Trustees* [1989] 3 All ER 389), captain (or carrier) and passenger (*Horsley* v *MacLaren* [1971] 2 Lloyd's Rep 410; Maritime Conventions Act 1911, s. 6), referee and player in a colts rugby match (*Smoldon* v *Whitworth* [1997] PIQR P133), hotelier and patron (*Jordan House Ltd* v *Menow and Honsberger* (1973) 38 DLR (3d) 105; *Munro* v *Porthkerry Park Holiday Estates Ltd*, *The Times*, 9 March 1984—duty to prevent harm to the plaintiff resulting from excessive consumption of alcohol where the defendant knew that the customer was so intoxicated as to be incapable of taking care of himself), the organiser of a dangerous competition and a visibly drunken participant (*Crocker* v *Sundance Northwest Resorts Ltd* (1988) 51 DLR (4th) 321, Supreme Court of Canada) and occupier and visitor (chapter 6). In *Barrett* v *Ministry of Defence* [1995] 3 All ER 87, 95 the Court of Appeal said that the characteristic which distinguishes the relationships of employer/employee, schoolmaster/pupil or occupier/visitor was reliance, expressed or implied in the relationship, which the party to whom the duty of care is owed is entitled to place on the other party to make provision for his safety. That did not mean that a responsible adult was entitled to blame another adult for his own lack of self-control in drinking an excessive amount of alcohol, even where the defendant provided that alcohol. *Jordan House Ltd* v *Menow* and *Crocker* v *Sundance Northwest Resorts Ltd* were different, said the Court, because there were factors additional to the mere provision of alcohol by the defendant in those cases (the occupier/visitor relationship in *Jordan* and the fact that the defendant took the positive step of providing the plaintiff with the equipment to take part in a dangerous race knowing that he was intoxicated in *Crocker*).

In *Stansbie* v *Troman* [1948] 2 KB 48, a decorator was left alone in a house by the householder's wife. He was asked to lock the door if he left the premises but he failed to do so, and a thief entered and stole some jewellery. The decorator was held liable for the loss. The case has been interpreted as depending on an implied term of the contract to decorate the house that the defendant would exercise reasonable care in respect of the contents (*P. Perl (Exporters) Ltd* v *Camden London Borough Council* [1984] QB 342, 357 and 359 per Oliver and Goff LJJ). More recently, however, it has been suggested that there might be liability in such a case where there was no contractual relationship between plaintiff and defendant, where, for example, the person left alone in the house had entered as a licensee of the occupier, or where property belonging to a guest had been stolen and the guest sued the decorator (*Smith* v *Littlewoods Organisation Ltd* [1987] 1 All ER 710, 730, 724 per Lord Goff and Lord Mackay respectively). In such a case the duty of care would seem more firmly to be based on an undertaking, whether express or implied, to secure the plaintiff's property.

The relationship between plaintiff and defendant may be such that the defendant has a duty to exercise reasonable care to prevent the plaintiff from harming himself. This is certainly true of the parent/child relationship (*Barnes v Hampshire County Council* [1969] 3 All ER 746). The police and prison authorities also owe a duty of care to a person in their custody who is a known suicide risk, to take precautions against a suicide attempt, though this may be based on an assumption of responsibility by the defendant rather than relationship (*Kirkham v Chief Constable of the Greater Manchester Police* [1990] 3 All ER 246; *Reeves v Commissioner of Police of the Metropolis* [1998] 2 All ER 381; *Knight v Home Office* [1990] 3 All ER 237). Medical staff will owe a similar duty to a patient who is a known suicide risk (*Selfe v Ilford & District Hospital Management Committee* (1970) 114 SJ 935; see Jones (1990) 6 PN 107). Such an action might be defeated by a defence of *volenti non fit injuria* or *ex turpi causa*, but this may depend on the state of the suicide's mind at the time (see paras 14.1.1 and 14.3).

2.2.1.3 Control over third parties As a general rule 'even though A is in fault, he is not responsible for injury to C which B, a stranger to him, deliberately chooses to do' (*Weld-Blundell v Stephens* [1920] AC 956, 986 per Lord Sumner). In some circumstances, however, A is in such a relationship with B as to have a duty to control B's conduct in order to prevent harm to C. These include employer and employee (*Hudson v Ridge Manufacturing Co. Ltd* [1957] 2 QB 348), parent and child (*Newton v Edgerley* [1959] 1 WLR 1031; *Carmarthenshire County Council v Lewis* [1955] AC 549), gaoler and prisoner (*Home Office v Dorset Yacht Co. Ltd* [1970] AC 1004; *Ellis v Home Office* [1953] 2 All ER 149; *S v Clement* (1995) 122 DLR (4th) 449—attack by an escaped prisoner; cf. *Hill v Chief Constable of West Yorkshire* [1988] 2 All ER 238, para. 2.2.1.1), mental hospital and patient (*Holgate v Lancashire Mental Hospitals Board* [1937] 4 All ER 19; see de Haan (1986) 2 PN 86; cf. *Palmer v Tees Health Authority, The Times*, 1 June 1998 — no duty of care owed by defendant health authority to the mother of a young child abducted and killed by a mental patient in respect of alleged negligent failure to diagnose that the patient constituted a serious risk to children) and even car owner and an incompetent or drunken driver (*Ontario Hospital Services Commission v Borsoski* (1974) 54 DLR (3d) 339; *Hempler v Todd* (1970) 14 DLR (3d) 637; *P. Perl (Exporters) Ltd v Camden London Borough Council* [1984] QB 342, 359, per Robert Goff LJ; see Horder (1988) 51 MLR 735).

It is not so much the *control* over the third party that gives rise to the obligation to act (although in the case of prisoners and detained mental patients the fact of control is clearly important), but knowledge that the third party is, in the particular circumstances, a potential danger to others and in a relationship with the third party that enables and thereby requires the defendant to take reasonable steps to avoid the foreseeable damage. The defendant has the power to avoid the damage and in this sense can exercise 'control' over the third party. For example, a doctor does not exercise control over the behaviour of a patient but in some situations injury to others is plainly foreseeable and the doctor/patient relationship gives rise to an obligation to take reasonable precautions to avoid it. Those precautions may be as simple as giving a warning to the patient to avoid certain activities, for example if the patient's medical condition (such as epilepsy) or the side-effects of a drug that has been prescribed render certain conduct (such as driving a motor vehicle) hazardous. If the doctor fails to do so and as a result the patient causes an accident injuring others the doctor would be responsible, both to the patient and the third parties. In *Spillane* v *Wasserman* (1992) 13 CCLT (2d) 267 (Ontario HC) the defendant W suffered an epileptic seizure whilst driving a heavy goods vehicle, passed through a red light, and killed a cyclist. W had a long history of epileptic seizures and should not have been driving at the time of the accident. He frequently neglected to take the medication prescribed for his condition and misrepresented his medical condition when renewing his driver's licence. Two doctors had been involved in treating W's epilepsy for years, but had failed to identify W's lax attitude to taking the medication, had not warned W not to drive commercial vehicles, nor not to drive at all except in specified circumstances, and had not reported W's condition to vehicle registration authorities. The doctors were held liable in negligence to the deceased's estate, being found 40% responsible, with W being 60% responsible (see also *Pittman Estate* v *Bain* (1994) 112 DLR (4th) 257 where a general practitioner was held liable for failing to inform his patient that there was a high risk that the patient was HIV positive, as a result of which the patient's spouse also contracted HIV).

2.2.1.4 Control of land or dangerous things An occupier's control of land may give rise to an affirmative duty in relation to the behaviour of visitors (*Hosie* v *Arbroath Football Club Ltd* 1978 SLT 122; *Cunningham* v *Reading Football Club Ltd* [1992] PIQR P141—defendants liable for injuries inflicted by football hooligans who broke pieces of concrete off the structure of the premises for use as missiles) or even acts of nature (*Goldman* v *Hargrave* [1967] 1 AC 645, see para. 7.1.3.6). Where the defendant has control over some object which is likely to be particularly dangerous if interfered with by a third party he may be under a duty to prevent such an interference (*Dominion Natural Gas Co.* v *Collins and Perkins* [1909] AC 640, 646). This has been applied to the theft of a poisonous chemical by young children (*Holian* v *United Grain Growers Ltd* (1980) 112 DLR (3d) 611). On the other hand, the Court of Appeal has held that where a bus company leaves a bus unattended with the key in the ignition it is not liable for the damage caused by a third party who steals the vehicle and drives it dangerously (*Topp* v *London Country Bus (South West) Ltd* [1993] 1 WLR 976; *Denton* v *United Counties Omnibus Co. Ltd, The Times,* 6 May 1986). This was a different case, said Dillon LJ, from the example given by Goff LJ in *P. Perl (Exporters) Ltd* v *Camden London Borough Council* [1984] QB 342, 359 of the defendant who presents the wrongdoer with the means to commit the wrong in circumstances where it is obvious or very likely that he will do so, for example by handing over a car to be driven by a person who is drunk, or plainly incompetent, who then runs over the plaintiff (for criticism see Fleming (1994) 110 LQR 187; and generally Howarth (1994) 14 LS 88).

In this context the word 'control' is used in the broad sense of control over the circumstances which lead to the damage, rather than control over the third party. In *Smith* v *Littlewoods Organisation Ltd* [1987] 1 All ER 710, 730 Lord Goff expressed this as a general principle. Liability would arise 'where the defendant negligently causes or permits to be created a source of danger, and it is reasonably foreseeable that third parties may interfere with it and, sparking off the danger, thereby cause damage to persons in the position of the plaintiff'. His Lordship gave the example of *Haynes* v *Harwood* [1935] 1 KB 146 in which a horse-drawn van was left unattended in a crowded street and the horses bolted when a boy threw a stone at them. The defendant was in 'control' in so far as he had created a foreseeable danger, which could have been sparked off by an innocent event. It was irrelevant that it was deliberate misconduct that did so. Lord Goff gave a further, hypothetical example (at p. 731) of a defendant who stores a large quantity of fireworks in an unlocked garden shed. If mischievous, trespassing boys entered the shed, set off the fireworks and started a fire that spread to adjacent property, the defendant might well be liable because interference by mischievous children was the very thing which he ought to have guarded against. Lord Goff's general principle, or some modified version of it, may explain the potential liability of a car owner who gives the keys to a drunken driver (para. 2.2.1.3) or the barman who continues to serve alcohol to a visibly intoxicated customer until he is incapable of taking care for his own safety (para. 2.2.1.2).

Sometimes the problems that arise in relation to affirmative duties are discussed in terms of intervening acts or remoteness of damage (see para. 4.2.2.1). It is simpler, however, to deal with the actions of third parties as a 'duty question'. In *P. Perl (Exporters) Ltd* v *Camden London Borough Council* [1984] QB 342, Oliver LJ observed (at p. 353) that 'if there be a duty to take reasonable care to prevent damage being caused by a third party then I find it difficult to see how damage caused by the third party consequent upon the failure to take such care can be too remote a consequence of the breach of duty' (see also *Haynes* v *Harwood* [1935] 1 KB 146, 156, para. 2.2.2). Lord Goff has made the same point in relation to causation: 'Of course, if a duty of care is imposed to guard against deliberate wrongdoing by others, it can hardly be said that the harmful effects of such wrongdoing are not caused by such breach of duty. We are therefore thrown back to the duty of care' (*Smith* v *Littlewoods Organisation Ltd* [1987] 1 All ER 710, 730). It follows that where there is no such duty the defendant is not responsible, and it is otiose to consider whether the intervention was *novus actus* or too remote (cf. Oliver LJ in *Lamb* v *Camden London Borough Council* [1981] QB 625, see para. 4.2.2.1).

2.2.2 Types of plaintiff

There are now few circumstances in which plaintiffs as a class are granted no, or limited, redress. At common law the dependants of a deceased person had no claim in respect of the death, but this problem was dealt with long ago by the Fatal Accidents Acts (para. 15.3.2). Trespassers were not looked upon favourably, but they are now owed a common law duty to be treated with common humanity (*British Railways Board* v *Herrington* [1972] AC 877, see para. 6.2, put into statutory form for the occupiers of premises by the Occupiers' Liability Act 1984). It is an open question whether this is any different from a duty to take reasonable care, although *British Railways Board* v *Herrington* adopted a subjective rather than objective standard of care. The common law duty probably does not apply to trespassers' property, and the statutory duty certainly does not.

For many years it was undecided in this country whether at common law a duty of care was owed to an unborn child in respect of injuries inflicted whilst *en ventre sa mère*, although the point had been conceded in a number of cases. It has now been held that such a duty does exist at common law (*B* v *Islington Health Authority* [1992] 3 All ER 833, CA; Whitfield (1993) 1 Med L Rev 28 discusses some of the implications of this decision), although this can apply only to births before 22 July 1976 when the Congenital Disabilities (Civil Liability) Act 1976 came into force. The Act, which replaces the common law for births after its commencement, grants a right of action to a child who is born alive and disabled in respect of the disability, if it is caused by an occurrence which affected either parent's ability to have a normal, healthy child, or affected the mother during pregnancy or the mother or child during labour, causing disabilities which would not otherwise have been present (s. 1(2)). A defendant is liable to the child if he is or would have been (if sued in time or if actionable injury had been sustained) liable in tort to the parent (s. 1(3)). The Act also covers negligence in the course of the selection or handling of an embryo or gametes for the purpose of assisted conception during treatment for infertility (s. 1A, added by the Human Fertilisation and Embryology Act 1990, s. 44). The child's mother is not liable under the Act, except where the injury is attributable to her negligent driving of a motor vehicle (ss. 1(1) and 2; the mother will normally be insured against this liability). The Act applies only to children born alive, with disabilities that would not otherwise have been present (see Murphy (1994) 10 PN 94 who argues that there is a distinction between being injured or damaged and suffering a 'disability'). This excludes claims by children with non-tortious disabilities that they should have been given an opportunity to be aborted (usually called a 'wrongful life' action, see para. 2.2.4.5). This view is supported by comments of the Court of Appeal in *McKay* v *Essex Area Health Authority* [1982] QB 1166, though it has been argued that this interpretation of the Act is incorrect (Fortin [1987] JSWL 306, 312).

The child's action is unusual, in that it is derived from the defendant's tortious duty to the parents, except that it is not necessary to show that the parent suffered any actionable injury, provided that the defendant would have been liable to the parent if he or she had suffered injury. This avoids any argument that a child damaged by a drug taken by its mother during pregnancy cannot sue the manufacturer because the mother did not suffer any harm. The derivative nature of the duty is emphasised by the defences available. The child is bound by a contractual exclusion or limitation clause that would have applied to the parent's action (s. 1(6); but this will be of very limited application in view of the Unfair Contract Terms Act 1977, s. 2(1), see para. 14.2). Damages can be reduced to take account of the parent's share of the responsibility for the child being born disabled (s. 1(7)), except where the damage is caused by the mother in the course of driving a motor vehicle (s. 2). Finally, where the disability is the result of a preconception occurrence affecting the parents' ability to have a normal healthy child, the defendant is not responsible to the child if either or both of the parents knew of the risk of disability, except that if the child's father is the defendant and he knew of the risk but the mother did not he will be answerable to the child (s. 1(4)). This seems to make the parents' knowledge defeat the child's claim even where objectively it would be reasonable for them to attempt to have a normal, healthy child (e.g., if the defendant's negligence has created a one-in-ten chance of them producing a disabled child). The Act raises a number of problems (see Pace (1977) 40 MLR 141; *Hepple and Matthews*, pp. 144–5), but in practice one of the most difficult to overcome is establishing causation (*Pearson*, vol. 1, para. 1452 and annexes 12 and 13; only a 'minute proportion' of those born with congenital defects establish causation and prove negligence; the Commission recommended a disability allowance for all severely handicapped children: *Pearson*, vol. 1, ch. 27).

Certain other types of claim may be excluded or restricted. In *Ashton* v *Turner* [1981] QB 137, Ewbank J said that in some circumstances a participant in a crime may not be owed a duty of care by a fellow participant in the same crime. This is related to the illegality of the plaintiff's conduct, but it is submitted that this issue is probably better left to the defence of *ex turpi causa*, rather than being dealt with as a 'duty' problem, in order to achieve some consistency between negligence and other torts where the duty concept could not be employed in this way (see para. 14.3). In the absence of express provision in the club rules, a member of an unincorporated members' club cannot sue the club in respect of personal injuries resulting from the defective condition of the club premises (*Robertson* v *Ridley* [1989] 2 All ER 474; cf. *Jones* v *Northampton Borough Council, The Times,* 21 May 1990, CA—a club member who undertakes a task on behalf of other club members, and acquires actual knowledge of circumstances which create a risk of injury to members, has a duty to inform them of that risk). This anomalous immunity derives from the law of unincorporated associations by which the club has no separate legal identity from that of its members (for comment see Capper (1993) 44 NILQ 388).

The final category of plaintiff meriting some consideration is the rescuer. Although the law does not oblige a person to undertake a rescue, as a general rule the courts will be favourably disposed to someone who does attempt a rescue and is injured in the process (e.g., in the context of nervous shock compare the position of the rescuer—*Chadwick* v *British Railways Board* [1967] 1 WLR 912—with that of the inquisitive bystander—*Bourhill* v *Young* [1943] AC 92—see para. 2.2.4.3 and generally Linden (1971) 34 MLR 241). This was not always the case. The concepts of *novus actus interveniens* and *volenti non fit injuria* (paras 4.2.2 and 14.1) have been used to deny the claims of rescuers who come to the aid of a person imperilled by the defendant's negligence. This approach was rejected, however, by the Court of Appeal in *Haynes* v *Harwood* [1935] 1 KB 146 and *Baker* v *T.E. Hopkins & Son Ltd* [1959] 3 All ER 225.

In *Haynes* v *Harwood* the defendants left a horse-drawn van unattended in a busy street and the horses bolted when a boy threw a stone at them. A policeman was injured in bringing the horses to a halt, thereby averting a serious danger to pedestrians. The defendants were liable. Neither the act of the boy nor that of the plaintiff constituted *novus actus* because they were foreseeable as the 'very kind of thing . . . likely to happen' as a result of the defendants' negligence. In *Baker* v *T.E. Hopkins & Son Ltd* a doctor was killed by carbon monoxide fumes having gone down a well to rescue two of the defendants' employees who had also been overcome by fumes. In response to an argument that the plaintiff's action could not have been foreseen and constituted *novus actus*, Morris LJ said: 'Those who put men in peril can hardly be heard to say that they never thought that rescue might be attempted or be heard to say that the rescue attempt was not caused by the creation of the peril'. Moreover, it was ungracious even to suggest that in these circumstances the rescuer was a 'volunteer'. Willmer LJ cited the celebrated dictum of Cardozo J in *Wagner* v *International Railway Co.* (1921) 133 NE 437 (232 NY 176, 180):

> Danger invites rescue. The cry of distress is the summons to relief. The law does not ignore these reactions of the mind in tracing conduct to its consequences. It recognises them as normal. It places their effects within the range of the natural and probable. The wrong that imperils life is a wrong to the imperilled victim; it is a wrong also to his rescuer.

Provided the rescuer did not act with a wanton disregard for his own safety the defendant will be responsible. The defendant could plead contributory negligence, but he would have to prove that the rescuer's conduct was so foolhardy as to amount to a wholly unreasonable disregard for his own safety and 'the court should not be astute to accept criticism of the rescuer's conduct from the wrongdoer who created the danger' (per Willmer LJ).

Foreseeability of the particular emergency that arose is unnecessary, provided some emergency is foreseeable (*Videan* v *British Transport Commission* [1963] 2 QB 650, 669) or, alternatively, provided the emergency is of the same 'kind or class' as those that might have been anticipated (*Knightley* v *Johns* [1982] 1 All ER 851, 860; cf. *Crossley* v *Rawlinson* [1981] 3 All ER 674, see para. 4.3.2). Nor is it necessary for the victim to be in actual danger provided that the rescuer's perception of danger was reasonable in the circumstances (*Ould* v *Butler's Wharf Ltd* [1953] 2 Lloyd's Rep 44). Otherwise, if the victim was beyond help (e.g., if he was dead) the defendant would not owe a duty to the 'rescuer'. But if the danger has passed, the rescuer's intervention may be unreasonable (see, e.g., *Cutler* v *United Dairies (London) Ltd* [1933] 2 KB 297).

The duty owed to a rescuer is an independent duty, it is not derived from the duty owed by the defendant to the victim. The significance of this is that a defendant may be liable to a rescuer even though he is not liable to the victim, e.g., because liability to the victim has been effectively excluded or because he owed no duty to the victim (*Videan* v *British Transport Commission* [1963] 2 QB 650—victim a trespasser and (at that time) not owed a duty; rescuer still entitled to succeed). A further consequence of the non-derivative nature of the duty is that if someone negligently imperils himself, in circumstances where it is foreseeable that there may be an attempt to rescue him he will be liable for the rescuer's injuries, even though no one owes a duty to preserve his own safety (*Baker* v *T.E. Hopkins & Son Ltd* [1958] 3 All ER 147, 153 per Barry J; applied in *Harrison* v *British Railways Board* [1981] 3 All ER 679 where the rescuer was held 20% contributorily negligent). In *Horsley* v *MacLaren* [1971] 2 Lloyd's Rep 410 the Supreme Court of Canada considered the liability of a first rescuer, R1, to a second rescuer, R2. Delivering the majority opinion, Ritchie J said that in order for R2 to succeed, R1's negligence must have been such that the rescuee was placed 'in an apparent position of increased danger subsequent to and distinct from the danger to which he had been initially exposed by his accidental fall'. This requirement of a 'new situation of peril' is questionable. It may be appropriate to R1's liability to the rescuee (based on the mere-omissions rule, para. 2.2.1), but it should be irrelevant to his liability to R2, because the duty owed to R2 is not derived from the duty R1 owes to the rescuee and, with respect to R2, a negligent rescue attempt is not an omission. The duty owed to a rescuer is based on the tendency of the defendant's negligence to induce the rescue attempt, not on its tendency to imperil the rescuee (per Laskin J, dissenting—in most cases these aspects converge). Thus the 'increased danger' requirement, it is submitted, should be unnecessary.

The duty of care also extends to the rescuers of property, although a rescuer would have to be more circumspect about the risks that he could legitimately accept without being regarded as wanton or foolhardy, and hence *volens* or contributorily negligent (*Hyett* v *Great Western Railway Co.* [1948] 1 KB 345).

2.2.3 Types of defendant

The policy considerations that have underlain the courts' attitudes to certain types of plaintiff are clear enough. Rescuers benefit from a general social approval, whereas the treatment of criminals and to a lesser extent trespassers reflects public condemnation. The policy factors limiting actions against certain defendants are of a different nature. They are generally based on the notion that a duty of care would conflict with some more important duty, or would allow private individuals to challenge the decisions of public officials which have been properly taken within the limits of a discretion conferred by Parliament.

2.2.3.1 Legal proceedings Judges have immunity from an action in negligence, and this extends to a judge of an inferior court provided there is an honest belief that he was acting within his jurisdiction (*Sirros* v *Moore* [1975] QB 118; but see *McC* v *Mullan* [1984] 3 All ER 908 and *R* v

Manchester City Magistrates' Court, ex parte Davies [1989] 1 All ER 90 on the
liability of magistrates acting in excess of jurisdiction). In an action against a
magistrate for acting outside his jurisdiction the plaintiff must prove that the
defendant acted in bad faith (Justices of the Peace Act 1979, s. 45, as
substituted by the Courts and Legal Services Act 1990, s. 108. See generally
on judicial immunity Olowofoyeku (1990) 10 LS 271). Similarly, witnesses
in legal proceedings have immunity, not only in respect of evidence given in
court but also in respect of the collection and analysis of material relevant to
the proceedings (*Evans* v *London Hospital Medical College* [1981] 1 All ER
715; Hervey (1985) 1 PN 102; *Mond* v *Hyde* [1998] 3 All ER 833—official
receiver in bankruptcy proceedings). This extends to conduct which can fairly
be said to be part of the investigatory and preparatory process of investigating
a crime or possible crime with a view to the possible prosecution in respect
of the matter being investigated (*Docker* v *Chief Constable of West Midlands
Police, The Times*, 29 April 1998). This immunity is based on public policy so
that witnesses may give their evidence fearlessly, and to avoid a multiplicity
of actions in which the truth of their evidence would be tried over again.
Since the immunity is conferred to prevent a witness from being inhibited
from giving truthful and fair evidence in court, in the case of an expert witness
the immunity only extends to what can fairly be said to be preliminary to
giving evidence in court. Thus, the production of a report for the purpose of
disclosure to the other side will be immune, but work done for the principal
purpose of advising the client, for example, as to the merits of the claim, will
not (*Palmer* v *Durnford Ford* [1992] 2 All ER 122, 127). In *Landall* v *Dennis
Faulkner & Alsop* [1994] 5 Med LR 268 it was held that reports provided by
a medical expert on the plaintiff's medical condition for the purpose of a
claim being brought by the plaintiff against a third party were covered by the
immunity. The plaintiff's argument that the reports had a dual purpose, in
that they also constituted medical advice as to the future treatment of his
condition, was rejected. In *M (a minor)* v *Newham London Borough Council*
[1994] 2 WLR 554 a child and her mother brought an action for negligence
against a psychiatrist and social worker in respect of the manner in which they
conducted an interview with the child for the purpose of identifying whether,
and if so by whom, the child had been sexually abused. The psychiatrist and
social worker were negligent in ascertaining the identity of the abuser, with
the result that the child was needlessly removed from her mother's home for
a lengthy period, and it was alleged that this had caused psychiatric harm.
The defendants claimed that they were protected by witness immunity
because at the time of the interview the psychiatrist would have appreciated
that there might very well be court proceedings in which she would be a
witness. Although this argument was rejected in the Court of Appeal, on the
apparently reasonable ground that witness immunity does not apply to those
who have never become involved in the administration of justice, the House
of Lords concluded that witness immunity should apply to the psychiatrist
(*sub. nom. X (minors)* v *Bedfordshire County Council* [1995] 3 WLR 152, 188).
The policy considerations which applied to witnesses in criminal proceedings
were equally applicable to a local authority's investigation, in the performance

of a public duty, of whether or not there was evidence on which to bring proceedings for the protection of children from child abuse. The psychiatrist knew that if abuse was discovered her findings would be the evidence on which proceedings by the local authority would be based. The investigations had an immediate link with possible proceedings in pursuance of a statutory duty, and therefore could not be the subject of a subsequent action in negligence.

A litigant does not owe a duty of care to another litigant regarding the manner in which the litigation is conducted, because the safeguards against impropriety in the conduct of litigation are to be found in the rules and procedures of the court rather than the law of tort (*Business Computers International Ltd* v *Registrar of Companies* [1987] 3 All ER 465). The judicial immunity extends to those exercising a quasi-judicial function such as an arbitrator where a decision is made on the basis of the evidence and submissions of the parties, rather than a direct investigation of the facts (*Sutcliffe* v *Thackrah* [1974] AC 727; see Olowofoyeku (1990) 6 PN 2). This does not apply where there is no defined dispute between the parties. So there is no immunity for an accountant appointed to value a company (*Arenson* v *Casson Beckman Rutley & Co.* [1977] AC 405), an architect who issues certificates of 'work properly executed' under a building contract (*Sutcliffe* v *Thackrah*), a surveyor appointed to determine the rent under a rent review clause of a lease (*Palacath Ltd* v *Flanagan* [1985] 2 All ER 161), or a sequestrator appointed as an officer of the court under a writ of sequestration (*Commissioners of Inland Revenue* v *Hoogstraten* [1984] 3 All ER 25).

Advocates, whether barristers or solicitors, do not owe a duty of care to their client in respect of the manner in which a case is conducted in court (*Rondel* v *Worsley* [1969] 1 AC 191). (Note, however, that the court has the power to order a legal representative to pay 'wasted costs', which includes costs incurred as a result of incompetence: Supreme Court Act 1981, s. 51.) This immunity was extended in *Saif Ali* v *Sydney Mitchell & Co.* [1980] AC 198 to pre-trial work which is so intimately connected with the conduct of the case in court that it can fairly be said to be a preliminary decision affecting the way that the action is to be conducted at the hearing. However, the scope of this immunity is unclear. Advising who was to be a party to the proceedings and settling pleadings in accordance with the advice was held to be outside the immunity. Advice as to a plea in a criminal case is within the immunity, although the Court of Appeal has said that this applies only to barristers, not to solicitors, a ruling that must raise a serious question mark about the purpose of the immunity (*Somasundaram* v *M. Julius Melchior & Co.* [1989] 1 All ER 129; Evans (1989) 5 PN 48). However, the Courts and Legal Services Act 1990, s. 62 now provides that any advocate who lawfully provides legal services in relation to any proceedings shall have the same immunity from liability for negligence as a barrister.

The precise scope of the advocate's immunity remains uncertain. It does not apply to a solicitor who is not acting as an advocate in the case; *a fortiori* where the solicitor fails to act on counsel's advice or has failed to bring relevant matters to the attention of counsel (*Acton* v *Graham Pearce & Co.* [1997] 3 All ER 909). On the other hand, it does apply to the failure by counsel to include in pleadings a cause of action which has a 'nuisance value' (and hence a chance of producing an offer of settlement) but which has no reasonable prospects of success at trial (*McFarlane* v *Wilkinson* [1997] 2 Lloyd's Rep 259, CA, though it is not clear why this should be a matter of *immunity* rather than a question of breach of duty). In *Kelley* v *Corston* [1997] 4 All ER 466, the defendant barrister advised the plaintiff to compromise a claim for ancillary relief in divorce proceedings. At a hearing in court the following day, a consent order was made under the provisions of the Matrimonial Causes Act 1973. The plaintiff subsequently sued the barrister on the basis that the advice to settle had been given negligently. The Court of Appeal held that the plaintiff's claim fell within the advocate's immunity, but there were different views as to the basis of this immunity. Judge LJ took the view that the settlement of litigation is not normally within the principles on which the immunity is based. There were no public policy considerations which justified a blanket immunity from suit for negligent advice to a client which results in a settlement of his claim, whether the advice was given by counsel or a solicitor (whether advocate or not) and whether the settlement was reached before the hearing or at the door of the court. This proposition was subject to two exceptions:

(a)   where there is a settlement after the hearing has begun, in the sense that the judge has begun to consider the plaintiff's claim, because at that stage any settlement is intimately connected with the conduct of the case in the presence of the judge; and

(b)   settlements which are subject to or required the approval of the court. This included settlements of ancillary proceedings under the Matrimonial Causes Act 1973 and also the settlement of a claim by a person under a disability.

This was because 'such settlements involve the direct participation of the judge who is invited to indicate his approval, and who is not bound to give it.' If litigation on such matters were permitted, the defendant advocate would seek to call the judge to demonstrate that the settlement was reasonable, and it was contrary to public policy that judges should be required to explain their decisions in this manner. His Lordship made it clear that this exception did not include settlements which do not *require* the approval of the court but which are settled and followed by an order made by consent, because in these circumstances the judge does not participate by approving the settlement. Judge LJ did not accept that settlements at the door of the court should have 'blanket immunity' because the immunity should be drawn as narrowly as was consistent with the underlying policy which justified its existence:

Whatever the basis for the immunity of the advocate and whatever its ambit, the starting point remains that the immunity constitutes an exception to the fundamental principle that those who have suffered loss and damage as a result of the negligence of their professional advisers should normally be entitled to their remedy. Therefore the immunity should be confined as closely as possible to those circumstances where notwithstanding the possible merit of an individual claim the public interest requires that immunity should be recognised. (at p. 475)

Pill LJ was unable to accept that an immunity which would not otherwise exist was created by judicial intervention by way of approval of the settlement in this case (i.e., the immunity did not depend on the form of the settlement in a particular case). But his Lordship held that the scope of the advocate's immunity did extend to a settlement at the door of the court when the trial on the merits was about to begin. The conduct at the door of the court was intimately connected with the conduct of the cause in court. It would be difficult to see how advice as to plea in a criminal case (as in *Somasundaram*), which could be based on a misunderstanding of the law or the evidence, was covered by the immunity but advice at the door of the court as to whether to settle a civil case was not. Butler-Sloss LJ expressly agreed with Pill LJ that 'door of the court' settlements fall within the immunity, if it could be said that the settlement was closely connected with the litigation which was about to start, because it was important to have a clear rule about whether the advocate was or was not covered by immunity from suit at the door of the court. It should not depend upon the impact of the judge on proceedings by way of approving the settlement, since that was too uncertain. This might create some 'illogicality in protecting the advocate in giving his advice on the day of the hearing and not protecting him in giving the same advice in chambers or the office on the day before' (at p. 496), but that was the price of certainty in applying the rule. The difficulty with Butler-Sloss LJ's judgment is that she also appeared to accept Judge LJ's approach, stating that the judge was right to have dismissed the appeal from the district judge and to hold that the plaintiff's case disclosed no reasonable cause of action, on the grounds which she had set out, namely that consent orders in ancillary relief proceedings under the Matrimonial Causes Act 1973 are so intimately connected with the conduct of the cause in court that they fall within the test approved in *Saif Ali* v *Sidney Mitchell & Co.* (see pp. 493–4). Similarly, the special categories of civil cases where the approval of the court was required for a settlement were indistinguishable from consent orders in ancillary relief applications.

The potential problem that *Kelley* v *Corston* has created—leaving aside the 'illogicality' of distinguishing between settlement at the door of the court and settlement in chambers or the office on the day before—is that in cases where approval of the court is a requirement for a settlement, it would appear that the immunity should apply to the advice to settle irrespective of how close to the door of the court the parties are. Since any settlement of a claim involving a minor (or indeed any other person under a disability) requires the approval of the court, the danger would be that such plaintiffs would be unable to claim against their advocate for negligent advice to settle an action on unfavourable terms. This point arose almost immediately in *Griffin* v *Kingsmill* [1998] PIQR P24, where the plaintiff, who was a minor, settled a claim for personal injuries on the defendants' advice. The settlement was approved by the court under the normal procedure for minors. The plaintiff subsequently alleged that the claim was worth much more than the sum that she was advised to settle for, and sued the defendants in negligence. The defendants argued that, in the light of *Kelley* v *Corston*, the claim was caught by the advocate's immunity. Timothy Walker J considered *Kelley* v *Corston* and concluded that the *ratio* of the case was to be found in the judgments of Pill and Butler-Sloss LJJ, that an advocate was immune in respect of 'door of the court' settlements, and that the views expressed as to the immunity resting on the nature of the court's order were *obiter*. The advice in *Griffin* v *Kingsmill* had been prepared four months before the hearing at which the settlement was approved. Timothy Walker J held that to apply *Kelley* v *Corston* would involve an extension of the Court of Appeal's reasoning, since it would mean that no matter how remote in time and space the advice to settle is from the courthouse door and the eventual court order, the advice to settle would be immune just because of the court order. As his Lordship commented: 'I am far from satisfied that such a result could have been intended.' It would also mean that the advice would be immune depending on the age of the client—advice to a client under 18 which was approved before the age of majority would effectively always be immune. Accordingly, the immunity did not apply to the facts of *Griffin* v *Kingsmill*.

Barristers do not owe a duty to an opposing litigant in civil litigation (*Orchard* v *South Eastern Electricity Board* [1987] 1 All ER 95, 99), though solicitors have been held to owe such a duty on very unusual facts which did not fall within either *Rondel* v *Worsley* or *Saif Ali* (see *Al-Kandari* v *J.R. Brown & Co.* [1988] 1 All ER 833, CA, in which there was an express undertaking of responsibility by the solicitors). In *Welsh* v *Chief Constable of the Merseyside Police* [1993] 1 All ER 692 the plaintiff was arrested and held in custody for failing to answer to his bail in the magistrates' court, despite the fact that the offences for which he was bailed had previously been dealt with in the Crown Court. This was due to an administrative mix-up, the magistrates not having been informed about the outcome of the Crown Court proceedings. Tudor Evans J held that, although the Crown Prosecution Service (CPS) was immune from any action based on the failure of its advocate at the magistrates' hearing to inform the bench that the plaintiff's offences had been dealt with, the immunity did not extend to a failure by the CPS to carry out its general administrative responsibility as prosecutor to keep a court informed as to the state of an adjourned criminal case, nor where a prosecutor had in practice assumed such a responsibility. In *Elguzouli-Daf* v *Commissioner of Police of the Metropolis* [1995] 1 All ER 833 the Court of Appeal accepted that *Welsh* had been correctly decided, but it was limited to its special facts where the CPS, by its conduct, had voluntarily assumed responsibility to the plaintiff. As a general rule the CPS did not owe a duty of care to private individuals aggrieved by careless decisions by CPS lawyers. Although there may be an element of injustice to deny a remedy when an individual was deprived of his liberty by carelessness of the CPS, there were countervailing policy considerations which militated against imposing a duty of care, including a risk of prosecutors taking a defensive approach to their duties and having to spend valuable time and resources preventing or dealing with negligence claims, which would divert CPS lawyers from their central function of prosecuting offenders.

Several grounds for the immunity of advocates have been advanced (for criticism of these justifications see Veljanovski and Whelan (1983) 46 MLR 700, 711–18). Perhaps the most convincing is that a duty of care to the client might conflict with an advocate's duty to the court and to the administration of justice. Other arguments, such as the fact that barristers cannot choose their clients, or that the prospect of liability would lead to prolixity in the conduct of trials, or having to retry the action, seem weak by comparison. The prospect of having to retry actions arises in other contexts. In Ontario, for example, it has been held that it was contrary to the public interest to confer immunity 'exclusively on lawyers engaged in court work, an immunity possessed by no other professional person' (*Demarco* v *Ungaro* (1979) 95 DLR (3d) 385). Miller (1981) 97 LQR 127, 138 observes that the public perception may be that 'the immunity is an anachronism maintained by lawyers for lawyers' (see generally, *Dugdale and Stanton*, ch. 10).

In *Saif Ali* v *Sydney Mitchell & Co.* Lord Diplock suggested that if a court of coordinate jurisdiction had to decide whether another court had reached an incorrect decision this would bring the administration of justice into disrepute. This could be seen as a justification for the advocate's immunity, but it is probably more accurate to treat it as a separate ground of immunity based on public policy. In *Hunter* v *Chief Constable of West Midlands* [1981] 3 All ER 727, 733 Lord Diplock described as an abuse of process the initiation of proceedings for the purpose of mounting a collateral attack on a final decision against the intending plaintiff, which has been made by another court of competent jurisdiction in previous proceedings, in which the intend-ing plaintiff had a full opportunity of contesting the decision. Despite featuring in Lord Diplock's formulation of the rule, the intending plaintiff's 'purpose' in bringing the proceedings is not crucial. Thus, it is irrelevant that his only purpose is to recover damages for professional negligence and not to attack the validity of the earlier decision (*Walpole* v *Partridge & Wilson* [1994] 1 All ER 385, 396). The existence of an ulterior purpose provides a strong additional ground for holding the proceedings to be an abuse of process, but an ulterior motive is not a necessary element for the claim to be struck out as an abuse. The rule rests on public policy, the basis of which is:

(a) the affront to any coherent system of justice which would necessarily arise if there subsisted two final but inconsistent decisions of courts of competent jurisdiction;

(b) the virtual impossibility of fairly retrying at a later date the issue before the court on the earlier occasion; and

(c) the importance of finality in litigation (per Sir Thomas Bingham MR in *Smith* v *Linskill* [1996] 2 All ER 353).

The undesirable effects of re-litigating actions are not mitigated by the plaintiff's motive being to recover damages rather than to establish that the earlier decision was wrong (ibid.). The Court of Appeal has held that even where a barrister would not be immune from suit under *Saif Ali*, nonetheless 'where there has in fact been a decision on the merits by a court of competent jurisdiction public policy requires that the decision should not be impugned either directly or indirectly' (*Somasundaram* v *M. Julius Melchior & Co.* [1989] 1 All ER 129, 133). This, in effect, extends the immunity under *Rondel* v *Worsley* and *Saif Ali* because even where the claim did not fall within that immunity (where it was not 'intimately connected with the conduct of the cause in court') there would be no liability if there had been a decision on the merits and an action in negligence would represent a direct or indirect challenge to that decision. (Where the decision was in the plaintiff's favour an action in negligence would not constitute a challenge to the decision: *Acton* v *Graham Pearce & Co.* [1997] 3 All ER 909, where the plaintiff had been convicted of a criminal offence, the conviction had been overturned on appeal and the plaintiff then sued his solicitors for negligence in handling the trial.) Thus the disappointed client's right to sue might depend upon whether there had been a decision on the merits or whether the case had been lost on a technical procedural point, such as expiry of the limitation period or dismissal for want of prosecution. The rule in *Hunter* is not absolute. There are exceptions where:

(a)   there is fresh evidence which was not available or could not reasonably have been obtained at the first trial which 'entirely changes the aspect of the case';

(b)   in a civil case, where a party has not had an opportunity to resist a hostile claim, for example where judgment was entered against him because of a procedural default (*Smith* v *Linskill* [1996] 2 All ER 353 per Sir Thomas Bingham MR, i.e., it was not a decision on the merits; the approval by the court of a settlement on behalf of a person under a disability is not a decision on the merits: *Griffin* v *Kingsmill* [1998] PIQR P24, P31); and

(c)   where the solicitors acting for the plaintiff in the earlier proceedings failed, in breach of duty, to advance an appeal on a point of law which would have caused the decision against the plaintiff to be set aside (*Walpole* v *Partridge & Wilson* [1994] 1 All ER 385).

An immunity which is analogous to that of the advocate applies to the police in the course of investigating crime. If during the course of their operations the police negligently cause direct harm to another they will be liable for that damage (*Rigby* v *Chief Constable of Northamptonshire* [1985] 2 All ER 985—negligent use of CS gas cannister; *Knightley* v *Johns* [1982] 1 All ER 851—traffic accident). But the police do not owe a duty to road users to protect them from, or to warn them against, hazards created by others on the road, because, in the absence of a special relationship, it was exceptional to impose a duty to control a third party's actions to prevent harm to a stranger; such a duty would impose potentially unlimited liability; and it would hamper the performance of ordinary police duties by diverting police resources to the defence of the many civil actions that would ensue (*Ancell* v *McDermott* [1993] 4 All ER 355, CA; *Clough* v *Bussan* [1990] 1 All ER 431—no duty owed to motorists simply because the police were unaware that traffic lights at a junction were malfunctioning). Nor is there any duty of care owed to individual members of the public in respect of the conduct of an investigation if the police fail to identify and apprehend a criminal, who in the meantime causes damage to a member of the public (*Hill* v *Chief Constable of West Yorkshire* [1988] 2 All ER 238, para. 2.2.1.1; *Alexandrou* v *Oxford* [1993] 4 All ER 328, CA—no duty owed to the owners of premises with a burglar alarm system connected to a police station to protect the owner from theft; cf. *Jane Doe* v *Metropolitan Toronto (Municipality) Commissioners of Police* (1990) 72 DLR (4th) 580—plaintiff attacked by serial rapist alleged that the police were negligent in failing to give any warning of the risk, and had, in effect, used her as 'bait' in an attempt to catch the rapist; held that in these circumstances the police could owe a duty of care). In *Osman* v *Ferguson* [1993] 4 All ER 344 the Court of Appeal held that the immunity applied even in the case of a known and identified individual who had been conducting a campaign of harassment against the plaintiff, ultimately with fatal consequences. On the facts, the Court was prepared to accept that there was a sufficient relationship of proximity between the plaintiff's family and the investigating officer (cf. *Hill* v *Chief Constable of West Yorkshire*), but the public policy immunity applied even if there was sufficient proximity, and was not limited merely to conduct in the investigation of crime but extended to conduct relating to the prevention of crime (see further Dugdale (1993) 9 PN 85; Tregilgas-Davey (1993) 56 MLR 732; Steele and Cowan [1994] PL 4). Similarly, the police do not owe a duty of care to a suspect as to the manner in which a criminal investigation is conducted, and *a fortiori* when the investigation is in relation to a disciplinary offence by a fellow police officer (*Calveley* v *Chief Constable of the Merseyside Police* [1989] 1 All ER 1025, HL; *Waters* v *Metropolitan Police* [1997] ICR 1073, CA). Where a police officer is injured in the course of policing a serious incident of public disorder, senior police officers charged with the task of deploying a force of officers to control the disorder do not owe a duty of care to the injured officer (*Hughes* v *National Union of Mineworkers* [1991] 4 All ER 278). The fear of such a claim would be likely to affect the decisions taken and prejudice the very task that the decisions were intended to advance, and accordingly public policy required that senior police officers should not generally be liable to subordinates who may be injured by rioters for on the spot operational decisions taken in the course of attempts to control serious public disorder (ibid. at p. 288. But cf. the decision of the Court of Appeal in *Frost* v *Chief Constable of South Yorkshire* [1997] 1 All ER 540, para. 2.2.4.3, where police officers on duty at the Hillsborough disaster succeeded in actions in respect of psychiatric damage from witnessing the events which were caused by the negligence of fellow officers in making operational decisions about crowd control. Note also that in *Osman* v *Ferguson* the Court of Appeal refused to draw any distinction between policy decisions and operational decisions in respect of the applicability of the public policy immunity).

The immunity of the police is not total. In *Swinney* v *Chief Constable of Northumbria Police* [1996] 3 All ER 449 the Court of Appeal held that the immunity could be displaced by other considerations of public policy for the protection of the public. The first plaintiff supplied confidential information to the police relating to a serious crime, and the police were aware of the violent character of the person(s) named in that information. The information was left in a police vehicle and stolen when the vehicle was broken into. It came into the hands of the alleged person(s) and as a result the plaintiffs were threatened with violence and arson, and suffered psychiatric injury. It was at least arguable, said Hirst LJ, that a special relationship existed between the plaintiff and the police which rendered the plaintiff distinguishable from the general public as being particularly at risk (thus distinguishing *Hill* v *Chief Constable of West Yorkshire* [1988] 2 All ER 238) such that the police could owe a duty in respect of negligently failing to keep secure the confidential information supplied to them. Moreover, the Court did not accept that the police had a 'blanket immunity' in these circumstances. There were countervailing considerations of public policy, such as the need to encourage informants to come forward without an undue fear of the risk that their identities will subsequently become known to the suspect or his associates. It was also arguable that on the pleaded facts the police had voluntarily assumed a responsibility to the plaintiff to maintain confidentiality (an exception to the immunity of the Crown Prosecution Service acknowledged in *Elguzouli-Daf* v *Commissioner of Police of the Metropolis* [1995] 1 All ER 833 and applied in *Welsh* v *Chief Constable of the Merseyside Police* [1993] 1 All ER 692).

The public policy immunity of the police has been applied to other emergency services, including the fire service and the coastguard, though the Court of Appeal has doubted whether policy should confer immunity on the fire brigade. In *Capital and Counties plc* v *Hampshire County Council*; *John Munroe (Acrylics) Ltd* v *London Fire and Civil Defence Authority*; *Church of Jesus Christ of Latter Day Saints (Great Britain)* v *Yorkshire Fire and Civil Defence Authority* [1997] 2 All ER 865, three consolidated appeals were heard in respect of claims against the fire brigade for negligence in carrying out their fire-fighting functions. In the *Capital Counties* case, a fire officer at the scene of a fire had ordered that a sprinkler system in a burning building be turned off, with the result that the fire spread and caused more extensive damage. In *John Munroe (Acrylics) Ltd*, the fire brigade turned up in response to a call for assistance and then left the scene believing that the fire was out, but they had not checked the premises thoroughly and burning embers re-ignited causing further damage. In *Church of Jesus Christ of Latter Day Saints*, the alleged negligence consisted of failing to take reasonable steps to ensure that an adequate supply of water was available at the scene of the fire. The Court of Appeal held that, except in a case where the fire service negligently increase the damage or cause additional damage, there is no proximity of relationship between the fire brigade and a building owner in respect of negligence in the tackling of a fire. The fire brigade are not under a common law duty to answer a call for help, and are not under a duty to take care to do so: 'if therefore they fail to turn up or fail to turn up in time because they have carelessly misunderstood the message, got lost on the way or run into a tree, they are not liable' (at p. 878, applying *Alexandrou* v *Oxford* [1993] 4 All ER 328). Nor were the fire brigade under a duty of care once they arrived at the scene and started to fight the fire. There was no assumption of responsibility to a particular owner, and 'general reliance' by the owner on the fire service could not create a duty of care. The fire brigade's duty was owed to the public at large to prevent the spread of fire, and this could involve a conflict between the interests of various owners of premises. The statutory authority conferred on the senior fire officer present to take charge and control of fire-fighting operations, by s. 30 of the Fire Services Act 1947, did not involve the fire officer in undertaking a voluntary assumption of responsibility to the owner of the premises on fire, whether or not the owner in fact relies upon the fire brigade. Again, this was for the benefit of the public generally. Accordingly there was no duty of care owed in either the *John Munroe (Acrylics)* or the *Church of Jesus Christ of Latter Day Saints* cases. In the *Capital Counties* case, however, the defendants had negligently increased the risk of damage by turning off the sprinkler system. This created a fresh danger, albeit of the same kind or nature, for which the fire service could owe a duty of care, just as the police can owe a duty of care in respect of the positive, direct infliction of damage in the course of their operations (see *Rigby* v *Chief Constable of Northamptonshire* [1985] 2 All ER 985; *Knightley* v *Johns* [1982] 1 All ER 851). This, essentially, is an application of the mere omissions rule. In the absence of some special relationship or undertaking, a rescuer is not liable for failing to effect a rescue, or for carrying out a rescue negligently, unless the negligence causes additional damage over and above that which would have been caused in the absence of the rescue attempt.

On the question of a public policy immunity for the fire brigade, the Court of Appeal accepted counsel for the plaintiffs' submission that the courts should not grant immunity simply because the judge may have a 'visceral dislike' for allowing possibly worthless claims to be made against public authorities whose activities involve the laudable operation of rescuing people or property in conditions of great danger. Any immunity 'must be based on principle'. In the *John Munroe (Acrylics)* case the trial judge, Rougier J, had identified several considerations of policy that militated against a duty of care, including:

(a) no additional standard of care would be achieved;
(b) a common law duty could lead to 'defensive firefighting';
(c) the efficiency of emergency services should not be tested in private litigation;
(d) a fire brigade acted in the collective welfare; and
(e) the floodgates would open to numerous claims which ultimately would have to be paid for by the general public (reported at *The Times*, 22 May 1996).

Similarly, in *Church of Jesus Christ of Latter Day Saints* the trial judge had also relied on policy factors to exclude a duty of care (reported at *The Times*,

9 May 1996). Such a duty might impede the statutory duties of the fire service, impose a burden detrimental to the service, and prove a distraction from their proper task of fighting fires. It would create the possibility of massive financial claims which would be an unreasonable burden on the taxpayer. It was for the individual to insure his property against fire; it was not for the community to do this for him. The Court of Appeal considered these policy grounds for granting immunity and the criticisms made by counsel for the plaintiffs (see [1997] 2 All ER 865, 890–91), concluding that there was no basis for excluding the duty of care simply on the ground of policy:

> In our judgment there is considerable force in the criticisms made. If we had found a sufficient relationship of proximity in the [*John Munroe (Acrylics)* and *Church of Jesus Christ of Latter Day Saints*] cases, we do not think that we would have found the arguments for excluding a duty of care on the grounds that it would not be just fair and reasonable convincing. The analogy with the police exercising their functions of investigating and suppressing crime is not close. The floodgates argument is not persuasive; nor is that based on insurance. Many of the other arguments are equally applicable to other public services for example the National Health Service.

Of course, many of the arguments that are deployed in the context of claims to 'policy immunity' are difficult to test empirically (even if the court had the luxury of being able to do this, which it does not). The arguments about defensive firefighting, distracting fire officers from their task, or that there would be no improved standard of care are, at best, equivocal, since it is equally possible to argue that tort does have an important deterrent effect and can lead to higher standards (arguments that are occasionally deployed when courts do impose a duty of care). The floodgates argument is again empirically unproven, and in any event consists of the assertion that there are too many plaintiffs who are the victims of a legal wrong to confer a remedy, an argument that does lie well in the mouth of a negligent defendant. The point that large financial claims would be an unreasonable burden on the taxpayer is, as counsel for the plaintiffs observed, ultimately an argument for the immunity from suit of government departments and all public authorities. Lastly, the argument about insurance tends to prove too much, since on this basis it would be possible to argue that the courts should never permit recovery for property damage, because 'the plaintiff could have insured'. It also tends to ignore the reality that in some areas insurance against property damage may be unobtainable, and in the case of personal injuries is much less common (see also Stapleton (1995) 58 MLR 820, commenting that statements about the significance of insurance are 'dangerous').

The coastguard have also been said to have immunity from suit for negligence. In *Skinner* v *Secretary of State for Transport, The Times*, 3 January 1995, it was held that the coastguard did not owe a duty of care to a mariner when exercising their ordinary functions of watching and listening and their rescue coordination activities, even in an emergency. The court distinguished cases of pure omission from positive acts which create a dangerous situation.

The public policy concerns raised in *Hill* v *Chief Constable of West Yorkshire* applied with even greater force to the coastguard. The effects of possible legal action would not lead to more caution but would lead to defensiveness, and the resources taken up in dealing with claims would be detrimental to the coastguard service, contrary to the public interest. It is not clear whether, in the light of the Court of Appeal's decision in *Capital and Counties plc*, the policy arguments for immunity would no longer be considered to have force in the case of the coastguard, though it is apparent that the coastguard will not normally owe a duty of care. In *OLL Ltd* v *Secretary of State for Transport* [1997] 3 All ER 897, May J applied the Court of Appeal's analysis in *Capital and Counties plc* to the coastguard, without any need to resort to a public policy immunity. There was no obvious distinction, said his Lordship, between the fire brigade responding to a fire where lives are at risk and the coastguard responding to an emergency at sea: 'On this basis, the coastguard would be under no enforceable private law duty to respond to an emergency call, nor, if they do respond, would they be liable if their response was negligent, unless their negligence amounted to a positive act which directly caused greater injury than would have occurred if they had not intervened at all' (at p. 905). The plaintiff alleged that there had been negligent coordination of a rescue attempt by the coastguard, in that they had diverted the plaintiff's manager from a rescue attempt, misdirected the lifeboat and a Royal Navy helicopter, and had failed to mobilise a second helicopter. It was argued that the coastguard had positively made things worse by removing the potential for other services to make an earlier rescue; and that once they intervened they assumed responsibility for coordinating the search and rescue operation. The intervention crossed the line from an omission to a positive act. This argument was rejected. Misdirections given by the coastguard to other rescue services were not to be equated with the fire officer turning off the sprinkler system in *Capital and Counties*. The effect of *Capital and Counties* was that no duty of care would arise if the coastguard were to misdirect their own staff or equipment. If the coastguard were potentially liable for misdirections given to others the result would be artificial: 'If there were two helicopters, one belonging to the coastguard and the other to the Royal Navy, it would be nonsensical if the coastguard were liable for misdirections given to one but not the other.' Misdirecting other rescuers did not, of itself, inflict direct physical injury, any more so than misdirecting the coastguard's own services (at p. 908). With respect, the argument about the 'direct' infliction of physical harm, while being a good illustration of the potential circumstances in which a rescuer can be held liable for negligence, is rather too narrow. The usual proposition applied to cases of rescue, under the mere omissions rule, is that the rescuer will not be liable if he has not worsened the victim's position. Where there is only one potential rescuer, incompetence cannot worsen the victim's position unless it prevents the victim from effecting his own rescue (there is an analogy here with the turning off of the sprinklers in the plaintiff's building in *Capital and Counties*), or it involves the positive infliction of additional damage (e.g., negligently dropping the plaintiff from a stretcher while carrying him to an ambulance). Where, however, there is more than one potential rescuer, negligence by one rescuer may worsen the plaintiff's position by preventing the other(s) from undertaking the rescue. Thus, if rescuer A has been correctly informed and is acting on the assumption that the victim is at position X, but rescuer B then negligently informs A that the victim is at position Y, diverting A from the rescue, as a result of which the victim suffers additional harm beyond that which would have occurred by the time A would have reached point X, B has negligently worsened the victim's position, i.e. by a positive intervention he has increased the risk of damage to the victim (as in *Capital and Counties*). The damage has not been 'directly' inflicted by B, since it is the result of A being delayed in effecting the rescue, but, nonetheless, it would seem that B should be held to owe a duty of care in these circumstances. The result in *OLL Ltd* v *Secretary of State for Transport* might be consistent with this principle where, notwithstanding that there were a number of services involved in the rescue, the coastguard were solely responsible for coordinating the rescue activity. In such circumstances, negligent coordination would be no different from negligent non-rescue, because the plaintiff's position has not been worsened, and in the absence of a duty to rescue there can be no liability for a negligent rescue attempt. May J rejected the plaintiff's argument that there was a 'general expectation' that the coastguard would act, and act carefully, giving rise to a duty to act (the plaintiff was relying on the example given by Lord Hoffmann in *Stovin* v *Wise* [1996] 3 All ER 801, 828, of a lighthouse authority which creates in mariners an expectation that its light will warn them of danger). There was a difference, said his Lordship, between a 'particular duty derived from a specific expectation publicly induced and relied on that a lighthouse authority will not withdraw an existing light without giving due notice' and 'a general duty on the coastguard to conduct any search and rescue operation they may undertake without negligence' (at p. 907).

2.2.3.2 Exercise of statutory powers Breach of a statutory duty may give rise to a separate action in tort (chapter 9) and, generally speaking, where a statute has authorised the defendant's activity, negligence will defeat a defence of statutory authorisation (*Geddis* v *Proprietors of the Bann Reservoir* (1878) 3 App Cas 430, 455; see para. 7.1.6.2). Where a public authority acts in the exercise of a statutory power (which authorises but does not compel particular actions) negligence may, but will not necessarily, be held to be actionable. The 'mere' careless exercise of a statutory power does not, in itself, establish a claim for damages. The plaintiff either has to demonstrate that the statute gives rise to an action for breach of statutory duty or must show that the circumstances are such as to raise a duty of care at common law (*X (minors)* v *Bedfordshire County Council* [1995] 3 WLR 152, 169 per Lord Browne-Wilkinson). One of the central problems, as perceived by the courts, has been how to avoid the prospect of an action for damages undermining the statutory discretion that Parliament has conferred on the authority. This has taken the courts into an analysis of public law principles, although this is not the only issue that arises out of the exercise of statutory powers, and there can be many factors to weigh in deciding whether a body exercising a public law function should be held accountable in damages for negligence.

Public bodies are often granted discretionary powers which confer a certain degree of freedom in the development of suitable policies for the implementation of that body's statutory functions. For example, an authority charged with the duty to provide street lighting for a particular district may not have the resources to maintain lights on all streets during all the hours of darkness. It will have to make a 'policy' decision as to how the resources at its command are to be employed: should all streets be lit for the same length of time; should the main streets be lit during all the hours of darkness and others not at all; or some fully and others partially? (See *Sheppard* v *Glossop Corporation* [1921] 3 KB 132.) Whatever decision is reached, the courts would refuse to allow an objector to challenge the decision on administrative (or 'public') law grounds provided the discretion had been properly exercised. Even if the court's assessment as to the correct policy differed from that of the authority the court would not substitute its own view because that would subvert the intention of Parliament which granted the discretion to the authority. A challenge would be permitted only where the decision was *ultra vires* the statute, applying the principles of administrative law (e.g., the authority had acted in bad faith, or had considered irrelevant matters, or failed to consider relevant matters or the decision was one which no reasonable authority could have reached).

It will be seen, however, that in determining what constitutes careless conduct for the purpose of the tort of negligence the courts will assess the magnitude of a particular risk against the burden of taking precautions against that risk (para. 3.1.3). This exercise is similar in nature to that undertaken by a public authority charged with the task of balancing the demand for public services such as street lighting, against the requirements of thrift and efficiency. An allegation that the authority were negligent in failing to light a particular area because they failed to take reasonable precautions against a foreseeable risk (i.e., injury to persons who might fall in the dark) claims, in effect, that the authority's decision of policy was wrong. How, then, can a private law action in negligence be accommodated to the principles of public law?

A second problem that has featured in claims against public authorities in respect of the alleged negligent exercise, or failure to exercise, a statutory power is the 'mere omissions' rule. A private individual is not normally liable in negligence for a mere omission in the absence of some special feature, such as a particular relationship with the plaintiff or an undertaking of responsibility (see paras 2.2.1 to 2.2.1.4). The powers conferred on public authorities, often in a regulatory capacity, may permit the authority to intervene to prevent harm to others. If there has been negligence in performing the regulatory function with the result that someone suffers damage that could have been prevented, the tendency will be for that person to seek redress against the public authority (often because the principal culprit whom the authority has failed to prevent causing the harm is not worth suing, and a public authority is perceived to have 'deep pockets', or at least to be solvent and capable of satisfying a judgment). A claim in negligence is, of course, a claim in private law, but it is relatively rare for private individuals to be placed in the position of being charged with responsibility for preventing harm to a plaintiff, in the absence of a contract between the parties. The public authority's position derives from the statutory context which gave it the powers, and sometimes the duty, to intervene to protect the plaintiff. If the statute did not explicitly create a private law remedy for aggrieved individuals, the plaintiff will be seeking to argue that the statutory context has, somehow, created a *private law* duty (a duty of care in negligence) to intervene to protect the plaintiff from harm in circumstances where a comparable duty would not be imposed upon a private individual. In other words, the plaintiff is seeking to convert a *public law* responsibility (which may be expressed in terms of a duty, i.e. a mandatory obligation to act, or a power, i.e. a discretion to act) into a common law duty of care in private law.

One response has been to say that there should be no liability for the negligent exercise of a statutory power (as opposed to a statutory duty) unless the negligence increased the damage beyond that which would have occurred if the power had not been exercised. Since there could be no liability for failing to exercise the power (a 'mere omission'), there should be no liability unless a negligent exercise of the power worsened the plaintiff's position (*East Suffolk Rivers Catchment Board* v *Kent* [1941] AC 74—defendants' incompetence in effecting repairs to sea defences resulted in plaintiff's land being flooded for 178 days instead of 14 days; defendants were not liable because they had not 'caused' the flooding and the damage would still have been sustained had they done nothing).

This approach will work only where the substance of the plaintiff's complaint is that the authority, although empowered to do so, failed to confer some benefit on him. It may be, however, that the exercise of a power does inflict damage that would not otherwise have been incurred. In *Home Office* v *Dorset Yacht Co. Ltd* [1970] AC 1004, due to negligent supervision some Borstal trainees escaped and in the process damaged the plaintiffs' yacht. The preliminary point of law raised by these assumed facts was whether the Borstal officers owed any duty of care to the plaintiffs. The relationship between the officers and the trainees was sufficient to create a duty of affirmative action, so this was not a case of a pure omission. The House of Lords held that there could be a duty of care, but this would depend on the precise circumstances (for comment see *Weir,* p. 96). There was no general duty to keep Borstal boys in detention, because the prison authorities had a statutory discretion as to the regime that would be adopted. The authorities had to reach a balance between the need to protect the public and the public interest in promoting the rehabilitation of offenders, which might involve a more relaxed scheme of supervision to allow the boys to develop a sense of responsibility. It was not the function of the court, said Lord Diplock, to substitute its own view of the appropriate means for that of the department by granting a private law remedy to a citizen adversely affected by the way in which the discretion had been exercised. It was a condition precedent to liability that the defendant's conduct was *ultra vires* on public law principles.

This was amplified by the subsequent decision of the House of Lords in *Anns* v *Merton London Borough Council* [1978] AC 728. Under the Public Health Act 1936 the defendant authority had power to make by-laws to regulate the construction of buildings in its area, together with powers (but no duty) of inspection to require compliance. The plaintiffs alleged that the authority had been negligent in the inspection of, or had negligently failed to inspect, the foundations of a block of flats, which, being inadequately constructed by the builder, had caused structural damage to the building. It was held that depending on the facts there could be liability in this situation. It was not sufficient, said Lord Wilberforce (at p. 755), to say (as in *East Suffolk Rivers Catchment Board* v *Kent*) that the defendants were under no duty to inspect:

> They are under a duty to give proper consideration to the question whether they should inspect or not. Their immunity from attack, in the event of failure to inspect, in other words, though great is not absolute. And because it is not absolute, the necessary premise for the proposition 'if no duty to inspect, then no duty to take care in inspection' vanishes.

(Note that the 'duty to give proper consideration' is a *public law* duty derived from the statutory context and any 'attack' would be on administrative law grounds. It is not obvious why this should supply the necessary affirmative duty at *common law* to impose liability for omitting to act; see *Sutherland Shire Council* v *Heyman* (1985) 60 ALR 1, 31 per Mason J.)

If a decision not to inspect was *ultra vires* the court would not be placed in the position of having to 'second-guess' the authority's decision on a matter of policy if it allowed an action for negligence. Moreover, there was a distinction between policy decisions in which an authority exercised its statutory discretion, and the practical execution of those policy decisions, described by Lord Wilberforce as the 'operational area'. Although only a distinction of degree, because many operational powers or duties would have in them an element of discretion, nonetheless 'the more "operational" a power or duty may be, the easier it is to superimpose on it a common law duty of care' (p. 754). (For criticism of this distinction see Bailey and Bowman [1986] CLJ 430, who convincingly argue that the ordinary principles applicable to breach of duty would have been sufficient to cope with this problem.) Thus, if the defendants did inspect the foundations but were careless in doing so, this would be negligence at the operational level and there was no reason to distinguish between statutory duties and statutory powers when the power was actually exercised. If the defendants had omitted to inspect at all, liability would depend on the *reason* for the omission. If it was the result of a policy decision, e.g., to inspect only certain types of new building because of a lack of resources, there would be no liability if this was a valid exercise of the authority's discretion, i.e., the decision was *intra vires*. In order to maintain an action in negligence the decision would have to be challenged on public law grounds, and the plaintiff would have to show that it was both *ultra vires* and negligent, i.e., that it created an unreasonable risk of harm to the plaintiff. On the other hand, if the failure to inspect was due to a careless oversight this would be negligence at the operational level which was no different from a careless inspection. At the operational level negligence itself would render the act or omission *ultra vires*, because negligence in the implementation of a policy will normally consist of inadvertent carelessness, where there is no question of a conscious balancing of the available resources against foreseeable risks, and so no prospect of undermining the statutory discretion. Parliament cannot be taken to have authorised inadvertent negligence because this serves no useful purpose (see the statutory authorisation defence, para. 7.1.6.2). *Anns* has been overruled in *Murphy* v *Brentwood District Council* [1990] 2 All ER 908, para. 2.2.4.2.2, on the basis that the loss suffered by the plaintiff was purely economic. There was no discussion of the policy/operational distinction in *Murphy*, and it would seem that this has been unaffected by the overruling of *Anns* (*Hepple & Matthews*, p. 105; *X (minors)* v *Bedfordshire County Council* [1995] 3 WLR 152, 170). Another way of looking at this problem is to say that a government is entitled to govern free of the constraints of the law of tort, but that when it is merely supplying services to the public it should be subject to the ordinary principles of negligence (*Swanson* v *The Queen in right of Canada* (1991) 80 DLR (4th) 741, 749–50, where it was held that airline inspectors, who did not make policy, but rather implemented it, although they had some discretion and exercised judgment in their work, were engaged in operational not policy matters since they were not involved in any decisions which had to weigh 'social, political or economic factors').

Although the approach in *Anns* to distinguish between policy and operational decisions has not been expressly overruled, the courts have subsequently retreated from this type of analysis. In *Rowling* v *Takaro Properties Ltd* [1988] 1 All ER 163, 172 Lord Keith said that the distinction between policy and operational decisions 'does not provide a touchstone of liability, but rather is expressive of the need to exclude altogether those cases in which the decision under attack is of such a kind that a question whether it has been made negligently is unsuitable for judicial resolution, of which notable examples are discretionary decisions on the allocation of scarce resources or the distribution of risks'. Thus, classification of the relevant decision as a policy or planning decision may exclude liability 'but a conclusion that it does not fall within that category does not . . . mean that a duty of care will necessarily exist'. On this view, the fact that the public authority's conduct involved a 'policy' aspect represents a preliminary filter to deny a duty of care. But even if this hurdle is overcome the duty must be established on the usual basis of foreseeability of damage, proximity of relationship and the requirements of what is just and reasonable. In *X (minors)* v *Bedfordshire County Council* [1995] 3 WLR 152, 170–71, Lord Browne-Wilkinson said that it was neither helpful nor necessary to introduce public law concepts as to the validity of a decision into the question of liability at common law for negligence, because in public law a decision can be *ultra vires* for reasons other than *Wednesbury* unreasonableness (*Associated Provincial Picture Houses Ltd* v *Wednesbury Corporation* [1948] 1 KB 223) which have no relevance to the question of negligence. In seeking to establish that a local authority is liable at common law for negligence in the exercise of a discretion conferred by statute, the first requirement was to show that the decision was outside the ambit of the discretion altogether: if it was not, a local authority could not itself be in breach of any duty of care owed the plaintiff:

> In deciding whether or not this requirement is satisfied, the court has to assess the relevant factors taken into account by the authority in exercising the discretion. Since what are under consideration are discretionary powers conferred on public bodies for public purposes the relevant factors will often include policy matters, for example social policy, the allocation of finite financial resources between the different calls made upon them or (as in *Dorset Yacht*) the balance between pursuing desirable social aims as against the risk to the public inherent in so doing. It is established that the courts cannot enter upon the assessment of such 'policy' matters. The difficulty is to identify in any particular case whether or not the decision in question is a 'policy' decision.

The effect, said his Lordship, was that nothing which the authority does within the ambit of the discretion can be actionable at common law. If the decision complained of falls outside the statutory discretion, it can (but not necessarily will) give rise to common law liability. If the factors relevant to the exercise of the discretion include matters of policy the court cannot adjudicate on such policy matters and therefore cannot reach the conclusion that the decision was outside the ambit of the statutory discretion. 'Therefore a common law duty of care in relation to the taking of decisions involving policy matters cannot exist' (p. 173). This leaves open the question of precisely what the terms 'policy' and 'discretion' mean, since it is apparent that they do not simply correspond with situations where someone has to make a judgment. His Lordship added that if the plaintiff's complaint alleges carelessness not in the taking of a discretionary decision to do some act, but in the practical manner in which that act has to be performed (e.g. the running of a school) the question whether or not there is a common law duty of care falls to be decided by applying the usual principles, i.e., those laid down in *Caparo Industries plc* v *Dickman* [1990] 1 All ER 568. But as Cane (1996) 112 LQR 13, 16 points out, those who run the day-to-day activities of schools are confronted with a multitude of choices about how to do it, and thus Lord Browne-Wilkinson cannot have meant that the implementation of policy decisions may not require the person carrying them out to make choices between alternative courses of action. Clearly, those choices involve an exercise of 'discretion' of some kind. Thus, without some clarification of the precise sense in which his Lordship was using the word 'discretion', the statement that 'nothing which the authority does within the ambit of the discretion can be actionable at common law' is either unhelpful or positively misleading (see further, Wright (1998) 18 OJLS 1, discussing *X (Minors)* v *Bedfordshire CC* in the context of the European Convention on Human Rights).

In *Stovin* v *Wise* [1996] 3 All ER 801, the House of Lords held, by a bare majority, that a highway authority was not liable in negligence for failing to remove a hazard to the highway under statutory powers conferred by the Highways Act 1980, on the basis that the authority owed no private law duty of care to road users to exercise its powers to confer a benefit (see also the discussion of this case at para. 2.2.1.1; for comment see Hopkins [1996] CLJ 425, Harris (1997) 113 LQR 398, Convery (1997) 60 MLR 559, Mullender (1997) 5 Tort L Rev 180). This was the position even though the authority was aware of the danger and had decided that it would be appropriate to remove the hazard, but had carelessly delayed implementing the decision:

> If the public authority was under no duty to act, either by virtue of its statutory powers or on any other basis, it cannot be liable because it has acted but negligently failed to confer a benefit on the plaintiff or to protect him from loss. The position is of course different if the negligent action of the public authority has left the plaintiff in a worse position than he would have been in if the authority had not acted at all. (per Lord Hoffmann at p. 824)

The plaintiff's claim sought to create liability for a 'mere omission' on the ground that the existence of the statutory powers created a 'proximity' between the parties which in the absence of the statute would not have existed. Lord Hoffmann observed that until *Anns*, there was no authority for treating a statutory power as giving rise to a common law duty of care; and though *Anns* was overruled by *Murphy*, that case left open the question of whether the council might have a duty of care in respect of physical injury. However, Lord Wilberforce's point in *Anns* that the authority had a public law duty to 'give proper consideration to the question whether they should inspect or not' could not in itself give rise to a common law duty of care. Lord Hoffmann considered that the distinction between policy and operations was an inadequate tool with which to discover whether it was appropriate to impose a duty of care or not (at p. 826, citing *Rowling* v *Takaro Properties Ltd*), for two reasons. First, the distinction was often elusive. But even where the distinction was clear-cut, and it could be argued that it would be irrational (in the sense of public law irrational) for the public authority not to exercise its power, it did not follow that the law should superimpose a common law duty of care. There were many instances where statutory *duties*, let alone powers, have been held not to give rise to common law rights of action. The fact that Parliament had conferred a discretion (a power) should be taken as some indication that the policy of the legislation conferring the power was not to create a right to compensation. The need to have regard to the policy of the statute meant that exceptions to this would be rare. Thus, in his Lordship's view (at p. 828) the minimum preconditions for basing a duty of care upon the existence of a statutory power, if it could be done at all, were:

> first, that it would in the circumstances have been irrational not to have exercised the power, so that there was in effect a public law duty to act,

and secondly, that there are exceptional grounds for holding that the policy of the statute requires compensation to be paid to persons who suffer loss because the power was not exercised.

On the facts, there was no basis for saying that there were exceptional grounds for imposing a duty of care. Even if it could be said that the authority's conduct was irrational in public law (the hazard could have been removed at relatively low cost), a duty of care would distort the budgetary priorities of local authorities in that they would probably act defensively by allocating resources to road improvements rather than, say, to education or social services. As his Lordship commented when discussing the possible liability of a fire brigade for negligence in responding to a fire, in circumstances where the likelihood is that the owner of premises has insurance against the risk of fire, 'the only reason would be to provide a general deterrent against inefficiency. But there must be better ways of doing this than by compensating insurance companies out of public funds' (at pp. 829–30, since the insurance company would be subrogated to the rights of the property owner).

In a dissenting speech Lord Nicholls (with whom Lord Slynn agreed) said that the highway authority was not a mere bystander, because it had a statutory power to remove the danger. Where action would call for the expenditure of resources, the court could have regard to the financial resources of the defendant: 'The law must recognise the need to protect the public exchequer as well as private interests' (at p. 810). But, said his Lordship, Parliament confers powers on public authorities for a purpose; an authority is entrusted and charged with responsibilities, for the public good. The powers are intended to be exercised in a suitable case, and thus compelling a public authority to act does not represent an intrusion into private affairs in the same way as when a private individual is compelled to act. A common law obligation on the facts of *Stovin* v *Wise* would march hand in hand with the authority's public law obligations. The authority had already decided to act, and the matter was overlooked. Given the decision to act, the only proper course open to the council was to proceed to implement the decision. The council failed to fulfil its public law obligations just as much as if it were in breach of a statutory duty. Hence a concurrent common law duty would not impose on the authority any greater obligation to act than the obligation already imposed by its public law duties. The common law duty would impose not a duty to act differently, but a liability to pay damages if the council failed to act as it should have done. Breach of its public law duties was not sufficient to justify the imposition of a duty of care. There must be some special circumstance, beyond the mere existence of the statutory power, rendering it fair and reasonable for the authority to be under a concurrent common law duty. What would constitute a special circumstance defied definition or exhaustive categorisation. The factors included: the subject matter of the statute; the intended purpose of the statutory duty or power; whether a common law duty might inhibit the proper and expeditious discharge of the statutory functions; the nature of the loss; the ability of the plaintiff to protect himself; the adequacy of public law remedies; and the presence or absence of a particular reason why the plaintiff was relying on or dependent on the authority. Where the authority could reasonably foresee that the plaintiff would reasonably rely on the authority acting in a particular way, the authority can be taken to have assumed responsibility to act in that way: 'Reliance may be actual, in the case of a particular plaintiff, or more general, in the sense that persons in the position of the plaintiff may be expected to act in reliance on the authority exercising its powers' (at p. 813). Reliance would not always be a sufficient basis for a duty of care, nor would it always be a necessary ingredient:

> Proximity cannot be confined by fixed restraints applicable in all cases. Some statutory powers, of their nature, are less susceptible to a concurrent common law duty than others. More is needed by way of special circumstance. This does not mean that powers are capable of being assigned to fixed categories. There are no hard and fast boundary lines here. The approach, rather, is that as the part played by broad discretionary considerations in the exercise of the power grows, the less readily will a common law duty be superimposed, and *vice versa*. At the discretionary edge of the spectrum will be powers whose nature and purpose make it difficult to envisage any likely circumstances where a common law duty, sounding in damages, could be superimposed. A local authority's powers to decide what schools there should be, and where, and of what type, may be a example of this. At the other edge of the spectrum will be powers where comparatively little extra may be needed to found a common law duty owed to a particular person or class of persons. A power to remove dangers from public places must be near this edge of the spectrum. A power to control air safety may be another example, as in *Swanson* v *The Queen in right of Canada* (1991) 80 DLR (4th) 741. (ibid. at pp. 813–14)

This approach, which is inherently more flexible and expansive in terms of potential liability than that of the majority, is open to the objection that it is so vague as to provide little in the way of guidance to potential litigants as to their rights and responsibilities. It would represent an open invitation to plaintiffs (or indeed, defendants' insurers seeking to shift part of their liability to a public authority in third party proceedings, as occurred in *Stovin* v *Wise*) to bring private law actions against public authorities. On the other hand, while recognising the genuine concern that the courts have repeatedly expressed in recent years for protecting the finances of public authorities from the effects of litigation, the majority view tends to assume that there will usually be another remedy available to a plaintiff, in the form of either first party insurance or another potential defendant, which will not necessarily be the case (see per Lord Nicholls at p. 816) . The alternative, a willingness to leave the loss to 'lie where it falls', is also occasionally evident, and though this may be conceptually satisfactory in the case of a 'mere omission' (why should the public purse bear the loss?) there are circumstances where the distinction between acts and omissions can be extremely artificial. As Lord Nicholls commented in *Stovin* v *Wise* (at p. 815):

A highway authority is liable in damages for failing to take reasonable care to keep the highway safe [in relation to non-repair of the highway]. But no sound distinction can be drawn between dangers on the highway itself, where the authority has a statutory duty to act, and other dangers, where there is a statutory power but no statutory duty. The distinction would not correspond to the realities of road safety. On the council's argument a highway authority would be liable if it carelessly failed to remove a dead tree fallen into the road, but not liable if it carelessly failed to act after learning of a diseased overhanging tree liable to fall at any moment. Such a legalistic distinction does not commend itself. It would be at variance with ordinary persons' expectations and perceptions.

Moreover, there are circumstances where by any measure the negligence of a public authority has inflicted damage on a plaintiff that would not have occurred in the absence of the statutory power, where the desire to protect public finances has been a significant factor in denying the existence of a duty of care (as in *M (a minor)* v *Newham London Borough Council*, which was heard in the House of Lords together with a *X (minors)* v *Bedfordshire County Council*, in which a child was negligently removed into local authority care).

Of course, many public bodies perform functions which have no counterpart in private law and there may well be good policy reasons, apart from the mere omissions rule, for excluding a duty of care (see, e.g., *Hill* v *Chief Constable of West Yorkshire* [1988] 2 All ER 238; *Yuen Kun-yeu* v *A-G of Hong Kong* [1987] 2 All ER 705). A regulatory agency, for example, will often have to make decisions in which competing considerations have to be carefully weighed and balanced in the public interest, and this 'militates strongly against the imposition of a duty of care . . . on such an agency in favour of any particular section of the public' (*Davis* v *Radcliffe* [1990] 2 All ER 536, 541, PC). Thus, the power to grant or refuse planning permission under the Town and Country Planning Act 1971, s. 29, does not give rise to a common law duty of care because it is inevitable in granting planning permission that some members of the public might be adversely affected, whereas a planning authority has to consider a range of other factors in reaching its decision in the public interest (*Lam* v *Brennan and Borough of Torbay* [1997] PIQR P488, CA; *Ryeford Homes Ltd* v *Sevenoaks District Council* (1989) 46 BLR 34). Similarly, in *Harris* v *Evans* [1998] 3 All ER 522, the Court of Appeal held that an inspector of the Health and Safety Executive did not owe a duty of care to the owner of a business when making recommendations as to whether a particular activity should be authorised under the Health and Safety at Work etc. Act 1974. The statute was concerned with public safety, and it was implicit in the statutory regime that enforcement decisions could have adverse economic consequences for a business enterprise. The legislation provided a suitable appeals mechanism, and moreover, the imposition a duty of care would probably have a detrimental effect on the system created in the interests of public safety by producing an unduly cautious and defensive approach by inspectors to the use of their enforcement powers under the Act.

A common law duty of care cannot be superimposed on a statutory duty if the observance of the common law duty of care would be inconsistent with,

or have a tendency to discourage, the due performance by the public
authority of its statutory duties (*X (minors)* v *Bedfordshire County Council*
[1995] 3 WLR 152, 173; *Clunis* v *Camden and Islington Health Authority*
[1998] 3 All ER 180—statutory context of s. 117 of the Mental Health Act
1983 providing for after-care for mental patients on discharge from hospital
held to be inconsistent with a duty of care to the patient where there is a
negligent failure to provide after-care). The decision in *X (minors)* v *Bedfordshire*, that no duty of care was owed by a social services authority in relation
to decisions whether to take children into local authority care under its
statutory powers to protect children at risk of abuse or neglect, has been
applied to claims by a foster child that an authority was negligent in the way
it made and supervised foster placements (*Barrett* v *Enfield London Borough
Council* [1997] 3 All ER 171, where the allegation was that the plaintiff had
suffered emotional and psychiatric damage as result of inadequate and
inappropriate care; *H* v *Norfolk County Council* [1997] 1 FLR 384, where the
allegation was that the child was sexually abused by one of the foster parents),
and to a claim by foster parents that the local authority placed a 15-year-old
boy, who was a known sexual abuser, with a family without informing the
parents of his full history, with the result that the family's children were
sexually abused (*W* v *Essex County Council* [1998] 3 All ER 111). In *H* v
Norfolk County Council, the policy factors were similar, though not quite
identical, to those applied in *X (minors)* v *Bedfordshire*; whereas in *Barrett* v
Enfield London Borough Council, the Court of Appeal held that the local
authority was *in loco parentis* and it was contrary to the public interest to
impose a duty of care in respect of decisions about the upbringing of a child,
which often required a difficult and delicate balancing of conflicting interests.
Lord Woolf MR said that 'parents are daily making decisions with regard to
their children's future and it seems to me that it would be wholly inappropriate that those decisions, even if they could be shown to be wrong should be
ones which give rise to a liability for damages'. This was not a 'blanket
immunity', but an immunity in relation to the making of those decisions as
to the future of a child which are normally made by a parent:

> Social workers and other members of staff could, however, be negligent in
> an operational manner. They could, for example, be careless in looking after
> property belonging to the child or in reporting what they had observed for
> the purposes of an inter-disciplinary assessment of what action should be
> taken in relation to the child. They could also be negligent in failing to carry
> out instructions properly. If in implementing their decisions or the decisions
> of the authority, a social worker was careless, I accept there *would* be a case
> for the defendant being vicariously liable if the necessary causation of injury
> or other damage could be established. (at p. 179, original emphasis).

(Note, however, the comment of Stuart-Smith LJ in *W* v *Essex County Council*
[1998] 3 All ER 111, 125, that Lord Woolf's statement was 'clearly obiter',
and apparently contrary to the decision in *X* v *Bedfordshire* that the distinction
between policy and operational decisions is not the touchstone of liability.)

On the other hand, in *W v Essex County Council* [1998] 3 All ER 111, a majority of the Court of Appeal held that the claims for negligence by the children abused by the 15-year-old foster child, should not be struck out as disclosing no reasonable cause of action because the authority was not exercising any statutory function in respect of these children. It was not just and reasonable to impose a duty of care to *the parents*, having regard to the fact that:

(a)   a common law duty of care would cut across the statutory arrangements for the fostering of children in care;

(b)   the local authority's task in dealing with such children is 'extraordinarily difficult and delicate';

(c)   local authorities might adopt a more defensive approach to their duties;

(d)   the relationship between parents and social workers was frequently one of conflict;

(e)   the children had an alternative remedy, i.e. to claim compensation under the Criminal Injuries Compensation Scheme (all factors which had influenced the House of Lords in *X* v *Bedfordshire*).

But in relation to the children's actions, the Court placed emphasis on the fact that the parents had relied on oral assurances from the local authority that a suspected or known sexual abuser would not be placed with them, and in answer to a specific question about the boy were told, wrongly, that he was not known or suspected of being a sexual abuser. It was held that the local authority assumed a responsibility for the accuracy of the statements that it gave about the boy placed with the family. The question of 'whether it would be just and reasonable to superimpose a duty of care should not be decided as if the misleading assurances had not been given when they had' (per Judge LJ at p. 138; query, however, why this consideration was relevant to the children's claims, but not the parents?).

The argument that the defendants have assumed a responsibility to the plaintiff, upon which the plaintiff relies, thereby giving rise to a duty of care under *Hedley Byrne & Co. Ltd* v *Heller & Partners Ltd* [1964] AC 465 (see para. 2.2.4.1.3), has been applied in a number of cases involving public authorities. It will usually involve some positive action by the authority, taking its conduct outside the normal statutory context. There must be something more than simply the performance of the statutory function (*Lam v Brennan and Borough of Torbay* [1997] PIQR P488, P504, CA). So, for example, where a local authority actively advised a parent that there was no reason why a child should not be placed with a particular child-minder, the authority was held liable for negligent misstatement when the child suffered injury in the child-minder's care (*T (a minor) v Surrey County Council* [1994] 4 All ER 577). Similarly, in *Welton* v *North Cornwall District Council* [1997] 1 WLR 570, CA, the local authority was held liable under the principle of *Hedley Byrne* where an environmental health officer negligently required the owner of food premises to undertake unnecessary works to secure compliance with the Food Safety Act 1990, causing the owner to incur substantial unnecessary expenditure. By purporting to impose detailed requirements, enforced by threat of closure and close supervision, the officer had assumed a responsibility to exercise reasonable care in the statements made to the plaintiffs as to the necessary works for compliance with the legislation. The fact that the relationship between the parties arose out of the exercise of statutory functions by the defendant was no reason for immunity in a case which would otherwise fall within common law principles for the existence of a duty of care (though see the comments of Sir Richard Scott V-C on this case in *Harris* v *Evans* [1998] 3 All ER 522, 538). Again, although as a general proposition there is no duty of care owed in respect of decisions made about planning permission, it is possible for a local authority planning officer to act in a manner which constitutes an assumption of responsibility to the plaintiff, upon which the plaintiff relies, thereby giving rise to a duty under *Hedley Byrne* (*Lambert* v *West Devon Borough Council* (1997) 96 LGR 45).

It is also arguable that where a public authority takes on the role of providing a quasi-professional service, which corresponds to a service that might well be provided by the private sector, the authority can be liable for negligence in the provision of that service. In *E (a minor)* v *Dorset County Council* [1995] 3 WLR 152, 195, the House of Lords held that a local authority could be both directly liable in negligence and vicariously liable for the negligence of an educational psychologist in assessing a child's special educational needs. The direct duty of care arose because the authority held itself out as offering a specialist service (psychological advice) to the public: 'By opening its doors to others to take advantage of the service offered, it comes under a duty of care to those using the service to exercise care in its conduct. The position is directly analogous with a hospital conducted, formerly by a local authority now by a health authority, in exercise of statutory powers.' The educational psychologist owed a duty of care because there was no potential conflict of duty between the professional's duties to the plaintiff and his duty to the education authority. Nor was there any obvious conflict, said Lord Browne-Wilkinson, between the professional being under a duty of care to the plaintiff and the discharge by the authority of its statutory duties (see also *Phelps* v *Hillingdon London Borough Council* (1997) 96 LGR 1—local authority vicariously liable for negligence of an educational psychologist in failing to diagnose dyslexia as a result of which the plaintiff's education was seriously prejudiced). Similarly, in *Beasley* v *Buckinghamshire County Council* [1997] PIQR P473, it was held that a local authority can owe a duty of care to a foster parent in respect of its negligence in failing to provide advice and training to the foster parent in dealing with a severely disabled and heavy child, in particular lifting the child, and in failing to provide suitable equipment. The injury to the plaintiff's back occurred in circumstances which were not far removed from claims by nurses in respect of back injuries sustained when lifting patients, which were commonplace in the NHS, which itself is engaged in discharging statutory duties and powers. This was a quasi employer/employee relationship, and there was nothing in the legislation which was inconsistent with such a duty of care. It was not a case of having to balance delicate considerations of policy or discretion.

Thus, where the claim arises in the context of statutory duties and/or powers it will be easier to argue that a duty of care should exist if the circumstances correspond to a situation in which a private law duty of care already exists. In this situation, the statute merely provides the background context (or the authority for the public body to be engaged in this type of activity at all) for the common law action. An 'assumption of responsibility' by the public authority (or someone for whom the authority is vicariously liable) to the plaintiff may also constitute an exceptional ground for imposing a duty of care in respect of the exercise of statutory powers, even where the authority's conduct does not correspond to circumstances where there would be an existing common law duty of care. Beyond this, it is very difficult to predict which statutory powers are likely to be the subject of a parallel common law duty of care, except to suggest that such a duty will probably be rare. It is a precondition of liability that the authority's conduct is irrational, on public law grounds, and, in the light of the majority decision in *Stovin* v *Wise*, it would appear that there can never be liability in respect of conduct characterised as a 'pure omission'. Lastly, it should be noted that even if a duty of care is held to exist, the statutory context will place limits on the nature of the duty of care and the persons to whom it is owed. In *Anns* v *Merton London Borough Council*, for example, Lord Wilberforce expressed the duty narrowly, in terms of securing that the builder does not cover foundations which do not comply with the by-laws; and in *Home Office* v *Dorset Yacht Co. Ltd*, the duty was owed only to persons in the vicinity whose property was foreseeably likely to be stolen or damaged in the course of the immediate escape.

2.2.4 Types of loss

It is impossible to give a complete catalogue of all the types of loss that may be held not to be actionable or subject to a restricted duty, because new forms of harm can arise at any time. Some miscellaneous examples are provided in para. 2.2.4.4, but historically the two principal types of damage that the courts have been particularly wary of admitting are 'pure' economic loss and 'nervous shock'. Claims in respect of economic loss have been the most prominent in taxing the ingenuity of both judiciary and academics alike.

The courts have long accepted that financial loss consequent upon physical damage either to the person or to property is recoverable. The injured plaintiff can claim his loss of earnings during the period of his incapacity. The owner of a damaged chattel can claim for the loss of profits that the chattel would have earned during the time when it is being repaired. The problems arise with pure economic loss, i.e., financial loss unconnected with physical damage to the plaintiff's person or property. (Note that there may be physical damage to someone else's property which causes purely economic loss to the plaintiff, e.g., by making the plaintiff's contract with that person more onerous or less profitable.) The difficulty has been how to frame a liability rule that will avoid burdening the defendant with 'liability in an indeterminate amount for an indeterminate time to an indeterminate class' (*Ultramares Corporation* v *Touche* (1931) 174 NE 441, 444; 255 NY 170, 179 per Cardozo

CJ). If the defendant negligently interrupts a power supply or gives negligent investment advice, the potential loss may be enormous, not simply for a single plaintiff but in terms of the number of plaintiffs. Reluctance to impose such crushing liability is not based merely on concern for the welfare of defendants. The courts have been traditionally wary of actions which might lead to a flood of claims inundating them with work (the 'floodgates' argument). From a practical point of view there is little or no advantage to plaintiffs in having a right of action where judgment is likely to remain unsatisfied because the sheer volume of claims has forced the defendant into bankruptcy or liquidation. Insurance against such widespread liability may be prohibitively expensive or even impossible to obtain. Moreover, in many instances the plaintiff may be in a better position to spread the risk. A business for which a continuous supply of power is important can insure against the risk of interruption, and pass on the cost in the price of its products, and first-party insurance is likely to be cheaper because the insured can more accurately assess the extent of the risk to his business.

A liability rule based on reasonable foreseeability of financial loss is too wide. Some mechanism was required to limit potential claims, both in terms of the range of plaintiffs and the circumstances in which liability might be imposed. In *Hedley Byrne & Co. Ltd* v *Heller & Partners Ltd* [1964] AC 465 the House of Lords adopted the concept of 'reasonable reliance' by the plaintiff on the defendant's skill and judgment as the basis of tortious liability for negligent statements (though more recently this has been restated on the basis of an assumption of responsibility by the defendant). This was the first occasion on which the House of Lords sought to establish a general principle of liability for economic loss in negligence, though apparently limited to statements. Attempts to identify a wider principle applicable to both negligent statements and negligent conduct have generally fallen on stony ground, however, and the courts have now largely abandoned the search for general principles and retreated to what may be considered, perhaps, to be the less ambitious task of specifying discrete categories of liability or non-liability. It is possible to identify four broad categories of cases where the plaintiff may sustain economic loss:

(1) economic loss as a result of the plaintiff relying on the accuracy of a statement made by the defendant;

(2) loss to the plaintiff caused by a third party relying on the accuracy of a statement made by the defendant;

(3) loss to the plaintiff as a result of physical damage to a third party's property caused by the defendant; and

(4) loss as a result of the plaintiff acquiring a defective item of property, so that he has to expend money in repairing the property or replacing it.

In categories 1 and 2 economic loss may be recoverable in some circumstances, whereas in categories 3 and 4 the loss will be irrecoverable (leaving aside the possibility of occasional anomalous exceptions). It can be seen that the distinction between categories 1 and 2, on the one hand, and categories 3 and

4, on the other, is a distinction between negligent words and negligent deeds. The distinction is undoubtedly arbitrary, and in some cases, particularly those involving the liability of professional persons, may be extremely difficult to draw. For example, where an auditor is careless in carrying out an audit of a company's accounts, is this a negligent statement (contained in the misleading audit report) or negligent conduct in performing the audit carelessly (see *Caparo Industries plc* v *Dickman* [1990] 1 All ER 568, para. 2.2.4.1.3)? If a solicitor is negligent in preparing a will is this a negligent act, or might it be a negligent statement if the will simply reflects the testator's wishes following negligent advice by the solicitor (see *Ross* v *Caunters* [1980] Ch 297, para. 2.2.4.1.4, where the facts were slightly different)? If, on the other hand, liability for pure economic loss under *Hedley Byrne* is based upon a principle of voluntary assumption of responsibility by the defendant in circumstances where the defendant can foresee that negligence on his part will cause economic loss to the plaintiff (see *Henderson* v *Merrett Syndicates Ltd* [1994] 3 All ER 506, below, para. 2.2.4.1.3) this could explain the liability in negligence of professionals for economic loss to both clients and third parties irrespective of the classification of the nature of the conduct as statement or act (see the comment of Lord Steyn in *Williams* v *Natural Life Health Foods Ltd* [1998] 2 All ER 577, 581 that *Henderson* had extended *Hedley Byrne* to cases of economic loss caused by the negligent performance of services), though it is not necessarily obvious why this should be limited to those acting in a professional or quasi-professional capacity.

Allowing or disallowing the recovery of pure economic loss on the basis of how the loss was caused (negligent statement or negligent act), though clearly arbitrary, might be justifiable if it reflected some underlying policy that the law was attempting to uphold or develop. The problem is that there does not appear to be any policy rationale in the distinction. As Stapleton (1991) 107 LQR 249 points out in her penetrating analysis, the organisation of cases into discrete 'pockets' of liability 'fails to generate a wider and consistent treatment of cases which are alike on policy grounds to the case in question. This would be odd but workable if the chosen groupings of cases could be kept separate; but this is impossible' (at p. 295). The result is 'confusion, complexity and high levels of litigation'. Nonetheless, given that the distinction between statements and acts is essentially the basis on which the courts currently deal with the subject, this structure will be followed here. Categories 1 and 2 are dealt with in paras 2.2.4.1.3 and 2.2.4.1.4 respectively, and categories 3 and 4 are considered in paras 2.2.4.2.1 and 2.2.4.2.2 respectively.

2.2.4.1 Economic loss: statements There are three possible causes of action in respect of financial loss caused by reliance on statements made by the defendant: (a) the intentional tort of deceit; (b) the Misrepresentation Act 1967, s. 2(1), where the plaintiff has entered a contract following a misrepresentation; and (c) the tort of negligence. Damage to the plaintiff's reputation is the subject of an action in defamation (chapter 13). Strictly speaking, deceit, which is an intentional tort, does not belong in a chapter on

negligence, but it provides a helpful basis for understanding the development
of liability for negligent statements. In practical terms the action in deceit has
been largely superseded by *Hedley Byrne & Co. Ltd* v *Heller & Partners Ltd*
[1964] AC 465.

2.2.4.1.1 Deceit Liability for fraudulent statements predates liability for
negligent statements by almost two centuries (*Pasley* v *Freeman* (1789) 3 D
& E 51). The requirements of an action for deceit are that the defendant
knowingly or recklessly made a false representation to the plaintiff intending
him to act on the representation, and that the plaintiff did act on it to his
detriment. The representation may be oral, in writing or by conduct, but as
a general rule mere silence does not constitute a representation. In some
instances, however, there may be a duty to speak (see, e.g., Companies Act
1985, s. 110), and in other cases the withholding of some information can
render what is represented false (*Peek* v *Gurney* (1873) LR 6 HL 377, 392).
Similarly, a defendant may be under an obligation to correct a representation
which, although true or believed to be true when it was made, he has
subsequently discovered to be false (*Salmond and Heuston*, p. 370; *Winfield
and Jolowicz*, p. 284).

The representation may be as to matters of fact, of law or of opinion, where
this includes an implied representation as to the facts on which the opinion
is based. A promise which the defendant has no intention of fulfilling is
sufficient, because 'the state of a man's mind is as much a fact as the state of
his digestion' (*Edgington* v *Fitzmaurice* (1885) 29 ChD 459, 483 per Bowen
LJ). An unfulfilled promise, which was a true representation of the defendant's intention when it was made, is not actionable in deceit. The plaintiff's
remedy, if any, lies in contract. Nor does the failure to inform the plaintiff of
the defendant's change of intention as to fulfilling the promise constitute
deceit, otherwise many breaches of contract would be fraudulent.

The defendant must have intended the plaintiff, or a class of persons to
which the plaintiff belongs, to act on the representation. He is not liable to
someone outside the intended class who acts on it (*Peek* v *Gurney*). If the
defendant intended the plaintiff to rely on the misrepresentation it is no
defence that the plaintiff acted foolishly or carelessly in doing so, or could
easily have checked the true position (*Dobell* v *Stevens* (1825) 3 B & C 623).
In *Downs* v *Chappell* [1996] 3 All ER 344, 351, Hobhouse LJ said that,
strictly, the word 'reliance' is not the correct criterion. The question should
be 'Was the plaintiff "induced" to act to his detriment?', though the terms
have similar meaning. If the plaintiff was induced to act to his detriment it is
sufficient if the representation substantially contributed to his actions. It need
not be the sole cause of his loss (*Nash* v *Calthorpe* [1905] 2 Ch 237; *Edgington*
v *Fitzmaurice*). Moreover, in *Downs* v *Chappell* the Court of Appeal held that
once it is proved that the plaintiff was in fact induced to act to his detriment
by a material misrepresentation, the question of what the plaintiff would have
done but for the representation becomes irrelevant: 'The judge was wrong to
ask how [the plaintiffs] would have acted if they had been told the truth. They
were never told the truth. They were told lies in order to induce them to enter

into the contract. The lies were material and successful' (at p. 351). This appears to run counter to the normal rules on causation in tort, where, if the plaintiff would in any event have acted in the same way and suffered the same damage even if the wrong had not been committed, the action will fail on causation on the basis that the wrong did cause the plaintiff's loss (see, e.g., *McWilliams* v *Sir William Arrol & Co. Ltd* [1962] 1 WLR 295, para. 4.1.1). Although there may be an element of policy in the approach adopted in *Downs* v *Chappell* in the context of an action for deceit (where, of course the defendant, by definition, has been fraudulent and therefore it may be thought appropriate to refuse to permit him to argue too assiduously about what might have happened in different, hypothetical circumstances), the same 'test' of causation was applied in that case to the second defendants who were guilty only of negligence. Nonetheless, in *Bristol and West Building Society* v *Mothew* [1996] 4 All ER 698, 705–6 the Court of Appeal confirmed that *Downs* v *Chappell* applies to actions in negligence (see para. 2.2.4.1.3 (f) *Causation*). There is no requirement that the defendant intended to cause damage to the plaintiff, although damage as a consequence of reliance on the representation must be proved. This is usually financial loss but can include personal injuries or property damage (*Langridge* v *Levy* (1837) 2 M & W 519; (1838) 4 M & W 337—exploding gun; *Shelley* v *Paddock* [1980] QB 348—mental distress).

The most significant restriction on the tort of deceit is that the plaintiff must prove fraud, i.e., that the defendant made the representation knowing that it was false, or recklessly, not caring whether it was true or false. In *Derry* v *Peek* (1889) 14 App Cas 337 the House of Lords held that dishonesty, in the sense that the defendant had no genuine belief in the truth of the representation, was essential to an action in deceit. A statement which is made not caring whether it be true or false is made without any real belief in its truth, and this is different from a statement honestly believed to be true which, through lack of care, is false (per Lord Herschell). It is not sufficient to show that there were no reasonable grounds for the defendant's belief in its truth. This can be *evidence* from which fraud *may* be inferred, but it is not conclusive. Therefore, although recklessness as to the truth of the representation may suffice, it must be such as to lead to the conclusion that the defendant was *dishonest* (*Thomas Witter Ltd* v *TBP Industries Ltd* [1996] 2 All ER 573, 587). Where a statement is ambiguous the plaintiff must establish that the defendant intended it to be understood in a sense which is untrue, or deliberately used the ambiguity to deceive. The plaintiff's interpretation, even if more obvious or reasonable, is irrelevant if the defendant did not intend the statement to be interpreted in that way, and honestly believed that his own interpretation was true (*Akerhielm* v *De Mare* [1959] AC 789, 805). Again, if the defendant's interpretation bears little or no relation to the meaning that a reasonable man would put upon the words, this *may* be evidence that he did not honestly hold that belief (for discussion of the mental element in deceit, see Hoyano (1996) 75 Can Bar Rev 474).

Although the standard of proof is the usual civil standard of the balance of probabilities, an allegation of fraud requires a 'higher degree of probability'

(*Hornal* v *Neuberger Products Ltd* [1957] 1 QB 247, 258). This makes an action in deceit extremely difficult to establish, and for most practical purposes the tort has been rendered superfluous by the development of an action for negligent misrepresentation (note, however, that deceit is theoretically of wider application because fraud removes any problem about what constitutes a 'special relationship' under *Hedley Byrne & Co. Ltd* v *Heller & Partners Ltd* [1964] AC 465). The point is typified by the Statute of Frauds Amendment Act 1828 (Lord Tenterden's Act), s. 6, which provides a defence to an action in deceit for misrepresentations as to the credit of third persons which are not made in writing. The Act does not apply to negligent statements giving rise to liability under *Hedley Byrne & Co. Ltd* v *Heller & Partners Ltd* (*W.B. Anderson & Sons Ltd* v *Rhodes (Liverpool) Ltd* [1967] 2 All ER 850), and this provides an unusual example of liability in negligence for conduct that would not be actionable if intentional.

2.2.4.1.2 Misrepresentation Act 1967 Section 2(1) of the Misrepresentation Act 1967 provides that where a person has entered into a contract after a misrepresentation has been made to him by another party to the contract, and has suffered loss as a result, if the person making the misrepresentation would be liable to damages had the misrepresentation been made fraudulently, that person shall be so liable notwithstanding that the misrepresentation was not made fraudulently, unless he proves that he had reasonable grounds to believe and did believe up to the time the contract was made that the facts represented were true. This extends the tort of deceit, creating in effect a statutory tort. Provided the other elements of deceit are present the plaintiff will succeed without proving fraud. The plaintiff is in a better position under the Act than in a common law action for negligent misstatement because there is no question whether a duty of care exists, and the defendant bears the burden of proof, which is a heavy one (*Howard Marine & Dredging Co. Ltd* v *Ogden & Sons (Excavations) Ltd* [1978] QB 574. Damages under the Act are measured under tortious rather than contractual principles, but the measure is that for the tort of deceit rather than negligence, and so includes unforeseeable losses: *Royscot Trust Ltd* v *Rogerson* [1991] 3 All ER 294; Hooley (1991) 107 LQR 547). The Act does not apply, however, where the plaintiff did not enter a contract or the representation was made by a person who was not a party (including an agent: *Resolute Maritime Inc.* v *Nippon Kaiji Kyokai* [1983] 2 All ER 1—the principal who is a party to the contract will be responsible for the agent's misrepresentation if the agent acted within his actual or ostensible authority). In this situation the plaintiff must resort to the common law.

2.2.4.1.3 Negligent statements relied upon by the plaintiff *Derry* v *Peek* (1889) 14 App Cas 337 established that dishonesty is an essential requirement for the tort of deceit, but in subsequent cases it was interpreted as holding that there could never be liability at common law, in the absence of a contract, for a careless yet honest statement leading to economic loss (unless there was a fiduciary relationship between the parties (*Nocton* v *Lord Ashburton* [1914] AC 932), where the remedy is, strictly speaking, equitable): In *Hedley Byrne*

& Co. Ltd v *Heller & Partners Ltd* [1964] AC 465 the House of Lords concluded that *Derry* v *Peek* had decided no such thing. Heller & Partners Ltd were bankers to Easipower Ltd, which was a client of the plaintiffs, who were advertising agents. Through their own bank the plaintiffs made an enquiry to the defendants as to the financial standing of Easipower, mentioning an advertising contract for £100,000. The reply was headed 'Confidential. For your private use and without responsibility on the part of the bank or its officials'. The letter said that Easipower was a 'respectably constituted company, considered good for its ordinary business engagements. Your figures are larger than we are accustomed to see'. Relying on this the plaintiffs incurred expenditure on behalf of Easipower and lost £17,000 when the company went into liquidation. The plaintiffs alleged that the reference had been made carelessly and that the defendants owed them a duty to take reasonable care in giving this information. The House of Lords agreed that in the appropriate circumstances there could be such a duty. The defendants were not liable on the facts, however, because the disclaimer of responsibility made it unreasonable for the plaintiffs to place reliance on the statement.

When will such a duty of care arise? The House referred to 'special relationships', which Lord Reid described (at p. 486) as:

> all those relationships where it is plain that the party seeking information or advice was trusting the other to exercise such a degree of care as the circumstances required, where it was reasonable for him to do that, and where the other gave the information or advice when he knew or ought to have known that the inquirer was relying on him.

Lord Morris of Borth-y-Gest said (at p. 503) that where a person:

> is so placed that others could reasonably rely upon his judgment or his skill or upon his ability to make careful inquiry, [and] a person takes it upon himself to give information or advice to, or allows his information or advice to be passed on to, another person who, as he knows or should know, will place reliance upon it, then a duty of care will arise.

Lord Devlin considered such relationships to be 'equivalent to contract', i.e., where there is an assumption of responsibility in circumstances in which, but for the absence of consideration, there would be a contract.

It is not sufficient to invoke the term 'special relationship' in dealing with liability for negligent statements, any more than the word 'proximity' provides a simple solution to general liability in negligence. The crucial question is what constitutes a special relationship? Following *Hedley Byrne & Co. Ltd* v *Heller & Partners Ltd* it appeared that there were three requirements:

(a)   the plaintiff relied on the defendant's skill and judgment or his ability to make careful enquiry;
(b)   the defendant knew, or ought reasonably to have known, that the plaintiff was relying on him; and

(c) it was reasonable in the circumstances for the plaintiff to rely on the defendant.

Arguably, the first two requirements could be treated as elements of the third, which can be summed up in the phrase 'reasonable reliance'.

For many years the notion of reasonable reliance has been understood to be the underlying principle of *Hedley Byrne*, and much of the case law is concerned with identifying the circumstances in which it was reasonable for the plaintiff to place such reliance on the defendant. More recent pronouncements of the House of Lords have tended to emphasise another aspect of *Hedley Byrne*, however, namely the voluntary assumption of responsibility by the defendant. In *Henderson* v *Merrett Syndicates Ltd* [1994] 3 All ER 506 the House of Lords held that an assumption of responsibility by a person rendering professional or quasi-professional services coupled with reliance by the person for whom the services were rendered could give rise to a tortious duty of care irrespective of whether there was a contractual relationship between the parties. Accordingly, subagents acting on behalf of 'indirect' Lloyd's 'names' owed a duty of care in negligence to the 'names' because they had assumed such a responsibility, despite the fact that they were not in a contractual relationship with the names, in other words notwithstanding that the parties had chosen a particular structure of obligations through their contractual relationships. Lord Goff said that the *Hedley Byrne* principle rests upon a relationship between the parties, which may be general or specific to the particular transaction, and which may or may not be contractual in nature. It depended upon one party having assumed or undertaken a responsibility towards the other. In *Hedley Byrne* Lord Morris had spoken of that party being possessed of special skill which he undertakes to apply for the assistance of another who relies on such skill. This concept of special skill must be understood broadly enough to include special knowledge, and the *Hedley Byrne* principle of liability extended beyond the provision of information and advice to include the performance of other services (per Lord Goff at p. 520). The question of whether in any particular case responsibility should be held to have been assumed by the defendant to the plaintiff is to be measured by an objective test. It is not a question of what the defendant subjectively believes he has undertaken. The concept, said Lord Goff (at p. 521), provides its own explanation for why in such cases there is no problem with pure economic loss:

for if a person assumes responsibility to another in respect of certain services, there is no reason why he should not be liable in damages for that other in respect of economic loss which flows from the negligent performance of those services.

It followed that, once a case was identified as falling within the *Hedley Byrne* principle, there was no need to embark upon any further inquiry as to whether it was 'fair, just and reasonable' to impose liability for economic loss. The concept could also explain why a professional person could be liable in respect of negligent omissions as much as negligent acts of commission. Similar views as to the basis of liability have been expressed by Lord Browne-Wilkinson and Lord Goff in *White* v *Jones* [1995] 1 All ER 691 and by Lord Goff again in *Spring* v *Guardian Assurance plc* [1994] 3 WLR 354.

This approach has some advantages in that it seeks to provide a more general principle of liability which can explain the recovery of pure economic loss in the context of both negligent statements and professional liability (which may encompass both statements and negligent acts). Actions nominally based on *Hedley Byrne* have long been extended to include what are essentially negligent acts or omissions in the case of claims for professional negligence, even though *Hedley Byrne* was thought of in terms of liability for statements (see, e.g., *Midland Bank Trust Co. Ltd* v *Hett Stubbs & Kemp* [1979] Ch 384—solicitors liable in tort for failing to register an option to purchase land as a C(iv) land charge). However, the concept of voluntary undertaking of responsibility is not without its difficulties (see the discussion below at (g) *Voluntary undertaking*), and the tone of their Lordships' speeches in *Henderson* v *Merrett Syndicates Ltd, Spring* v *Guardian Assurance plc* and *White* v *Jones* (in all of which the plaintiffs' action succeeded) appears to be at odds with the more restrictive approach adopted only four years earlier in *Caparo Industries plc* v *Dickman* [1990] 1 All ER 568. This may reflect a subtle swing in the pendulum that tends to move back and forth between pro-plaintiff and pro-defendant attitudes over time, but it could also represent part of a continuing process of seeking, in the *ad hoc*, case by case method of the common law, to establish workable principles which both explain and justify the sometimes intuitive judgments that have to be made about the boundaries of liability (for discussion of the proposition that liability under *Hedley Byrne* should be based in fiduciary obligations rather than the tort of negligence see McBride and Hughes (1995) 15 LS 376).

In *Caparo Industries plc* v *Dickman* [1990] 1 All ER 568 the House of Lords had restated the duty of care which may arise under *Hedley Byrne & Co. Ltd* v *Heller & Partners Ltd* in more limited terms. The plaintiffs owned shares in a public company whose accounts were audited by the defendants. The plaintiffs made a successful takeover bid for the company, and subsequently brought an action against the auditors alleging that the accounts were inaccurate and misleading so that the company was overvalued, that they had purchased shares in the company in reliance on the accuracy of the accounts, and had suffered a substantial loss as a result. In the Court of Appeal, a majority held that there was no sufficiently proximate relationship between an auditor and a potential investor such as to give rise to a duty of care, but that there was such a relationship between an auditor and existing shareholders, so that an individual shareholder who suffered loss by acting in reliance on the audited accounts, whether by selling or retaining his shares or by purchasing more shares, could maintain an action in negligence against the auditors. The House of Lords reversed this decision, holding that there was no duty of care owed either to the public at large who might rely on the accounts in deciding whether to purchase shares or to existing shareholders. The auditor's statutory duty to prepare accounts was owed to the body of shareholders as a whole for the purpose of enabling shareholders as a body to exercise informed control of the company. It was not to enable individual shareholders to buy shares with a view to profit (see also the decision of the Supreme Court of Canada in *Hercules Managements Ltd* v *Ernst & Young* (1997) 146 DLR (4th) 577 adopting a similar rationale for denying the existence of a duty of care, though employing the two-stage test for duty of care established in *Anns* v *Merton London Borough Council*, above, para. 2.1.1).

Lord Bridge considered (at p. 576) that the duty of care would arise if the defendant knew that his statement would be communicated to the plaintiff, either as an individual or as a member of an identifiable class, specifically in connection with a particular transaction or transactions of a particular kind, and that the plaintiff would be very likely to rely on it for the purpose of deciding whether or not to enter into the transaction. The emphasis here is on the defendant's knowledge of a specific transaction for which the plaintiff would be very likely to rely on the defendant's statement or advice. Mere knowledge (foreseeability) that the information could be relied on by a plaintiff in connection with any one of a number of possible transactions was not sufficient to establish a duty of care. Thus, the fact that it is highly probable that a company is vulnerable to a takeover bid was irrelevant, since that went merely to foreseeability which is not sufficient to create the requisite relationship of proximity between plaintiff and defendant (see also per Lord Oliver at p. 598, and Lord Jauncey at p. 608). Lord Oliver expressed (at p. 589) the duty in the following terms:

> What can be deduced from the *Hedley Byrne* case, therefore, is that the necessary relationship between the maker of a statement or giver of advice (the adviser) and the recipient who acts in reliance on it (the advisee) may typically be held to exist where (1) the advice is required for a purpose, whether particularly specified or generally described, which is made known, either actually or inferentially, to the adviser at the time when the advice is given, (2) the adviser knows, either actually or inferentially, that his advice will be communicated to the advisee, either specifically or as a member of an ascertainable class, in order that it should be used by the advisee for that purpose, (3) it is known, either actually or inferentially, that the advice so communicated is likely to be acted on by the advisee for that purpose without independent inquiry and (4) it is so acted on by the advisee to his detriment. That is not, of course, to suggest that these conditions are either conclusive or exclusive, but merely that the actual decision in the case does not warrant any broader propositions.

Although it is possible to state, in the abstract, a test for the existence of a duty of care in cases of negligent statements the courts are now wary of attempting to identify a single touchstone which can apply in all cases. Lord Oliver commented (at p. 587) that even within the limited category of negligent statement cases:

. . . circumstances may differ infinitely and, in a swiftly developing field of law, there can be no necessary assumption that those features which have served in one case to create the relationship between the plaintiff and the defendant on which liability depends will necessarily be determinative of liability in the different circumstances of another case.

This may look like a counsel of despair at ever achieving consistency, but the reality is that there are various criteria which can be adapted to the particular circumstances of each case (*Pacific Associates Inc. v Baxter* [1989] 2 All ER 159, 169 per Purchas LJ). In *James McNaughton Papers Group Ltd v Hicks Anderson & Co.* [1991] 1 All ER 134, 144–5, Neill LJ identified a number of headings which may be relevant to the existence of a duty of care following *Caparo Industries plc v Dickman,* though his Lordship accepted that there could be considerable overlap amongst these headings:

(a)   *The purpose for which the statement was made*—was it made for the specific purpose of being communicated to the advisee or was it made for a different purpose and for the benefit of someone else? (This was the crucial point in *Caparo Industries plc v Dickman.* The statement by the auditors had not been given for the purpose for which the plaintiff had relied on it: see *Morgan Crucible Co. plc v Hill Samuel Bank Ltd* [1991] 1 All ER 148, 158 per Slade LJ.)

(b)   *The purpose for which the statement was communicated*—the court must consider the purpose and circumstances surrounding the communication: was it for information only? Was it for the purpose of action and if so by whom? Who requested the communication?

(c)   *The relationship between the adviser, the advisee and any third party*—did the advisee look to the third party and through him to the adviser for advice or guidance, or was the advisee wholly independent and in a position to make any necessary judgments himself?

(d)   *The size of any class to which the advisee belongs*—where there is a single advisee or he is a member of a small class, it may be easier to infer a duty of care than where he is a member of a large class, particularly where the statement was initially made for someone outside the class.

(e)   *The state of knowledge of the adviser*—the adviser's knowledge of the purpose for which the statement was made and his knowledge of the purpose for which it was communicated to the advisee may be one of the most important factors. Knowledge includes actual knowledge, and the knowledge that would be attributed to a reasonable person in the adviser's circumstances. The duty is limited to transactions or types of transactions of which the adviser had knowledge, where the adviser knew or ought to have known that the advisee would rely on the statement in connection with that transaction. It is also relevant whether the adviser knew that the advisee would rely on the statement without obtaining independent advice.

(f)   *Reliance by the advisee*—did the advisee in fact rely on the statement? To what extent was he entitled to rely on it to take the action that he did take? Should he have used his own judgment or obtained independent advice?

These headings provide a helpful basis for analysis, but they do not necessarily correspond with or specify all the factors that the courts have previously had to address in determining whether a duty of care under *Hedley Byrne & Co. Ltd* v *Heller & Partners Ltd* should be held to exist. What, for example, is the effect of advice tendered outside a business or professional context? What is the position where there is a contractual relationship? Can silence constitute a representation? What constitutes reasonable reliance by the plaintiff? Does the duty depend upon a voluntary assumption of responsibility by the defendant? What is the effect of a disclaimer? In considering these factors it should be borne in mind that there may often be an interrelationship between them, particularly with concepts such as voluntary undertaking, reliance and disclaimer.

(a)   *Social occasions*   It would not be reasonable to rely on opinions expressed on social or informal occasions, nor even in a professional or business context unless it was clear that the plaintiff was seeking considered advice (*Mutual Life & Citizens' Assurance Co. Ltd* v *Evatt* [1971] AC 793, 812 per Lords Morris of Borth-y-Gest and Reid, dissenting). So an impromptu opinion given offhand or 'off the cuff' over the telephone does not create a duty (*Howard Marine & Dredging Co. Ltd* v *Ogden & Sons (Excavations) Ltd* [1978] QB 574, 591 per Lord Denning MR). But where the plaintiff enquires about a specific fact which he has no direct means of checking, this may indicate the 'gravity of the enquiry or the importance and influence attached to the answer' (ibid. p. 600 per Shaw LJ). In *Chaudhry* v *Prabhaker* [1988] 3 All ER 718 the plaintiff, who knew nothing about cars, asked a friend who had some knowledge of cars, though not a mechanic, to find a suitable second-hand car for her to buy. She said that it should not have been involved in an accident. The defendant found a car which he recommended highly. The plaintiff purchased it but subsequently it was discovered that the car had been involved in a serious accident, had been poorly repaired, and was unroadworthy. The Court of Appeal held the defendant liable. Stocker LJ said (at p. 723) that 'in the absence of other factors giving rise to such a duty, the giving of advice sought in the context of family, domestic or social relationships will not in itself give rise to any duty in respect of such advice'. Counsel for the defendant had conceded that the defendant owed a duty to the plaintiff to take such care as he would have done if he had been looking for a car for himself. May LJ doubted whether this concession was rightly made and was worried that the existence of a duty of care in such circumstances 'will make social regulations and responsibilities between friends unnecessarily hazardous'. Stocker and Stuart-Smith LJJ, however, would have held that a duty existed even without the concession. The relationship of principal and agent between plaintiff and defendant, even though gratuitous, was 'powerful evidence that the occasion is not a purely social one, but . . . is in a business connection' (per Stuart-Smith LJ at p. 722). The standard of care would be the same as that required of an unpaid agent, namely such care as it is reasonable to expect in the light of his actual skills and experience, and, if he has represented his skill and experience to be greater than it is, it may be reasonable to expect him to demonstrate the standard that he claims to possess.

(b) *Contract* The relationship that is nearest to being 'equivalent to contract' is a contractual relationship, for as Lord Devlin observed in *Hedley Byrne & Co. Ltd* v *Heller & Partners Ltd,* payment for information or advice is very good evidence that it is being relied on. Accordingly, the duty has been held to apply to pre-contract negotiations (*Esso Petroleum Co. Ltd* v *Mardon* [1976] QB 801; *Howard Marine & Dredging Co. Ltd* v *Ogden & Sons (Excavations) Ltd*; *Queen* v *Cognos Inc.* (1993) 99 DLR (4th) 626, Supreme Court of Canada—representation made to a prospective employee at a job interview; cf. *Holman Construction Ltd* v *Delta Timber Co. Ltd* [1972] NZLR 1081 where the plaintiff relied on a mistaken offer by the defendant which was withdrawn before it was accepted, and the defendant was not liable). Where the parties have entered into a contract the Misrepresentation Act 1967, s. 2(1), now provides a better remedy for a pre-contract misrepresentation. Once the parties have entered into a contractual relationship then it seems likely that their obligations will be defined by reference to the terms of the contract, whether express or implied, rather than any additional tortious duty (see especially *Tai Hing Cotton Mill Ltd* v *Liu Chong Hing Bank Ltd* [1986] AC 80, 107 cited at para. 1.1; see also *J. Nunes Diamonds Ltd* v *Dominion Electric Protection Co.* (1972) 26 DLR (3d) 699, Supreme Court of Canada—defendants not liable for negligently stating that the alarm previously hired to the plaintiff was burglar-proof, because a tort claim would have effectively changed the contract from a hiring contract to an insurance contract). This does not mean, however, that there cannot be concurrent liability in tort, merely that in normal circumstances the defendant's liability will not be more extensive in tort than under the contract, though the 'incidental' consequences may be different, e.g., as to the limitation period (*Henderson* v *Merrett Syndicates Ltd* [1994] 3 All ER 506).

It is not entirely clear how the term 'equivalent to contract' should be interpreted, since there are many relationships where, with the addition of consideration, there would be a contract. So in *Chaudhry* v *Prabhaker* [1988] 3 All ER 718 Stuart-Smith LJ was able to characterise the relationship between two friends as equivalent to contract, 'save only for the absence of consideration'. In other situations there may well be consideration but no privity of contract, and it is arguable, in some types of case at least, that where the consideration paid to the defendant has come from the plaintiff, but indirectly, the relationship is equivalent to contract. In *Smith* v *Bush* [1989] 2 WLR 790 the plaintiff sued a firm of surveyors in respect of a negligent house valuation report. The report had been prepared on the instructions of a building society which granted a mortgage to the plaintiff, secured on the house, to enable the plaintiff to purchase the house. The plaintiff purchased the property in reliance on the valuation, having paid a fee to the building society in relation to the report. The House of Lords held that the defendants owed a duty of care to the plaintiff, as well as the building society, under the principle of *Hedley Byrne*. Lord Templeman described the relationship between the purchaser and valuer as akin to contract: 'The valuer knows that the consideration which he receives derives from the purchaser and is passed on by the mortgagee, and the valuer also knows that the valuation will determine whether or not the purchaser buys the house' (at p. 798; see also per Lord Griffiths at p. 811).

The contractual 'setting' can be used in a different fashion to deny the existence of a duty of care, especially in the case of complex commercial transactions where there will often be a detailed written contract. In *Pacific Associates Inc.* v *Baxter* [1989] 2 All ER 159 the plaintiffs were contractors engaged in dredging and reclamation work for the ruler of Dubai (the employer). The work was supervised by a consultant engineer retained by the employer. There was no contractual relationship between the plaintiffs and the engineer, and, moreover, the contract between the plaintiffs and the employer contained a clause disclaiming responsibility on the part of the engineer in respect of obligations under the contract. The plaintiffs sued the engineer claiming that inaccurate geological information supplied at the tender stage had resulted in the work being more difficult than expected and that consequently the tender price had been too low. The contract also provided for additional payments to be made to the plaintiffs if they encountered unforeseen hard material in the course of dredging. Repeated claims for such payments were rejected by the engineer on the basis that hard material should have been foreseen from the information provided. The plaintiffs claimed that the engineer had been negligent or in breach of a duty to act fairly and impartially in administering the contract.

The Court of Appeal held that the engineer did not owe a duty of care to the contractors. Purchas LJ said (at p. 170) that 'where the parties have come together against a contractual structure which provides for compensation in the event of a failure of one of the parties involved, the court will be slow to superimpose an added duty of care beyond that which was in the contemplation of the parties at the time that they came together' (for a similar approach in relation to negligent acts see *Greater Nottingham Co-operative Society Ltd* v *Cementation Piling and Foundations Ltd* [1988] 2 All ER 971, para. 2.2.4.2). The contractors had a remedy in respect of the hard material claims because they could have referred them to arbitration under the contract with the employer. The employer might then have had a contractual claim against the engineer if he had been at fault in rejecting the claims. Purchas LJ considered this to be a policy argument for denying a duty of care—it was not 'just and reasonable' to grant the contractors rights in tort in excess of the rights that they were content to acquire against the employer under the contract. But this 'contractual structure' argument was also employed to find that the contractors had not relied on the engineer, and that the engineer had not assumed any responsibility to the contractors, particularly in view of the disclaimer (per Purchas LJ at p. 179; and Ralph Gibson LJ at p. 187).

(c) *Silence* In *Tai Hing Cotton Mill Ltd* v *Liu Chong Hing Bank Ltd* [1986] AC 80, 110 Lord Scarman said that mere silence or inaction could not amount to a misrepresentation unless there was a duty to disclose or act. The difficulty is to determine when there will be such a duty. In *La Banque Financière de la Cité SA* v *Westgate Insurance Co. Ltd* [1988] 2 Lloyd's Rep

513, 559 the Court of Appeal accepted that a mere failure to speak could give rise to liability under *Hedley Byrne* provided there has been a voluntary assumption of responsibility by the defendant and reliance by the plaintiff on that assumption. Such a voluntary assumption would be much more difficult to infer in a case of mere silence than a case of misrepresentation. The distinction between acts and omissions remained fundamental, and in some cases an obligation to speak would undermine a basic principle of contract law that there is no obligation to speak in the context of negotiations for an ordinary commercial contract. Accordingly, insurers did not have any obligation to inform the plaintiff banks of the fraudulent conduct of an insurance broker which was likely to cause substantial loss to the banks. This decision was affirmed by the House of Lords on the basis that the broker was the plaintiffs' agent, the silence did not amount to an assertion that the agent was trustworthy, and the plaintiffs did not rely on the defendants (see [1990] 2 All ER 947, 954–5). The action also failed on causation. See also *Bank of Nova Scotia* v *Hellenic Mutual War Risks Association (Bermuda) Ltd* [1989] 3 All ER 628, CA (reversed on different grounds [1991] 3 All ER 1, HL); for criticism see Trindade (1989) 105 LQR 191). Similarly, in *Argy Trading Development Co. Ltd* v *Lapid Developments Ltd* [1977] 3 All ER 785 a landlord was held not liable to the tenant for failing to advise that insurance cover on the premises had lapsed. In *Bentley* v *Wright* [1997] 2 VR 175, the Victoria Court of Appeal held that a farmer who looked after, but did not own, an ostrich did not owe a duty of care to prospective purchasers of the bird to volunteer the information that the bird had not laid an egg for 12 months. Although she did have a duty to exercise reasonable care in answering the plaintiffs' specific questions, she had not 'set herself up as an information centre' and had not voluntarily assumed a responsibility to the plaintiffs. Moreover, since the owner of the bird would not have been liable in tort for a *mere* omission to volunteer information about when the bird had last laid (*'caveat emptor'*), there was no reason why the farmer should be in a different position.

On the other hand, in *Cornish* v *Midland Bank plc* [1985] 3 All ER 513, 523 it was said that mere silence may not be consistent with the duty owed by a bank to its customer in some circumstances, although this view was criticised in *Barclays Bank plc* v *Khaira* [1992] 1 WLR 623, 637 where it was said that, in the normal course of events, a bank has no duty to proffer explanations or to advise a person who is about to sign a security to take independent advice. In *Midland Bank Trust Co. Ltd* v *Hett Stubbs & Kemp* [1979] Ch 384 Oliver J suggested that liability under *Hedley Byrne* could arise from misfeasance or nonfeasance in the context of a professional relationship between solicitor and client, a view approved by the House of Lords in *Henderson* v *Merrett Syndicates Ltd* [1994] 3 All ER 506, on the basis that a defendant who voluntarily assumes a responsibility to the plaintiff can be liable for a pure omission. Perhaps the clearest example of liability for mere silence arose in *L. Shaddock and Associates Pty Ltd* v *Parramatta City Council* (1981) 36 ALR 385 in which the defendant council were under a statutory duty to provide information in response to enquiries from prospective purchasers of land. The duty did not apply to information concerning road widening plans, but in practice this information was given if plans existed. The High Court of Australia held the council liable for negligently failing to refer to such plans in reply to a specific request from the plaintiffs' solicitor. In the circumstances, the omission amounted to a representation that there were no road widening proposals affecting the plaintiffs' land.

(d)   *Advice*   In *Mutual Life & Citizens' Assurance Co. Ltd* v *Evatt* [1971] AC 793 a majority of the Privy Council held that the duty applied only to defendants who were in the business of giving advice or information or who claimed that they had the requisite expertise. It was assumed that the imposition of the duty would unfairly require others to achieve the same standard of competence as those in the business of giving advice. A duty to be reasonably careful, however, is not a duty to meet a professional standard of competence. Lords Reid and Morris of Borth-y-Gest dissented, objecting that passages from their own speeches in *Hedley Byrne* were being misconstrued by the majority. In their Lordships' opinion the duty could arise when an enquirer consulted a businessman in the course of his business and made it plain that he was seeking considered advice and intended to act on that advice. If the businessman chooses to give advice without any warning or qualification he would be under a duty to take such care as is reasonable in the circumstances. The minority view has been followed by the Court of Appeal (*Esso Petroleum Co. Ltd* v *Mardon; Howard Marine & Dredging Co. Ltd* v *Ogden & Sons (Excavations) Ltd*). In *Esso Petroleum Co. Ltd* v *Mardon*, although the defendants were not in the business of giving advice, it was significant that they were experienced and had special knowledge and skill in estimating the petrol throughput at a filling station, whereas the plaintiff did not. On the other hand, where both parties have similar skill and experience and are negotiating at arms' length it would usually be unreasonable for one to rely on the other's representations without verification (*Wynston* v *Macdonald* (1979) 105 DLR (3d) 527; cf. *Allied Finance & Investments Ltd* v *Haddow & Co.* [1983] NZLR 22; Todd (1985) 1 PN 2; see also *Clarke* v *Bruce Lance & Co.* [1988] 1 All ER 364, 370, on the position of a solicitor giving advice where there is a conflict of interest between his client and the plaintiff; *Gran Gelato Ltd* v *Richcliff (Group) Ltd* [1992] 2 WLR 867—solicitor acting for a vendor on the sale of property does not owe a duty of care to the purchaser in relation to replies given to 'enquiries before contract', though the vendor will be liable for a negligent misrepresentation to the buyer by his solicitor, who acts as the vendor's agent; for criticism of this decision see Cane (1992) 109 LQR 539).

It has been clear for many years that *Hedley Byrne* applies not only to the giving of *advice* but also to the provision of *information* in circumstances where the plaintiff enquires about a specific fact which he has no direct means of checking (as in *Howard Marine & Dredging Co. Ltd* v *Ogden & Sons (Excavations) Ltd* [1978] QB 574, 600). In *Henderson* v *Merrett Syndicates Ltd* [1994] 3 All ER 506, 520 Lord Goff said that the concept of special skill which a defendant undertakes to apply for the assistance of another who relies on such skill must be understood broadly enough to include special knowledge. On the other hand, although most judicial statements about the distinction between the giving of advice and the provision of information address the inclusive nature of the duty of care (i.e., merely giving information can fall within the *Hedley Byrne* duty) the distinction between advice and information may be important in terms of defining the *scope* of the defendant's duty. A duty to exercise reasonable care in giving advice will normally cover a broader range of matters than a duty to be careful in providing information. The difference in scope of the duty can have significant consequences in terms of assessing the loss for which the defendant is held responsible. In *South Australia Asset Management Corporation* v *York Montague Ltd* [1996] 3 All ER 365 the House of Lords held that a valuer engaged to provide a valuation of property was providing information upon which a lender could base a decision, taking into account a number of other matters, as to whether to advance a loan secured on the property to a borrower. The valuer was not advising the lender whether to advance the loan. Their Lordships distinguished between *providing information* for the purpose of enabling someone else to decide upon a course of action and a duty to *advise* someone as to what course of action he should take. In the case of advice the adviser must take reasonable care to consider all the potential consequences of that course of conduct, and if he is negligent he will be responsible for all the foreseeable loss which is a consequence of that course of action, but if the duty is only to supply information he must take reasonable care to see that the information is correct, and if he is negligent he will be responsible for the foreseeable consequences of the information being wrong. Thus, in assessing the lender's loss when the borrower defaulted on the loan repayments and the value of the property turned out to be insufficient to cover the outstanding loan, the court should take into account only the difference between the negligent valuation and the correct property valuation at the time of the valuation, and not the fall in market value of the property in the interim even if, had the borrower known the true value of the property, he would never have advanced the loan. A defendant is not responsible for all the consequences of the events that result from his conduct, but only for those consequences that fall within the scope of his duty of care. Losses due to falls in the market value of the property were unforeseeable consequences of the defendant's negligence in providing the valuation, outside the scope of the duty, and therefore were not caused by the defendant's negligence. If the defendant had been engaged to give advice about whether to enter the transaction a wider range of potential risks, including the risk of falls in market value, would have been considered to be foreseeable. (On the distinction between an 'informer' and an 'adviser' see Dugdale (1996) 12 PN 71, 75; and generally on *South Australia Asset Management*, Stapleton (1997) 113 LQR 1.)

(e) *Reliance* The concept of 'reasonable reliance' gives the courts a control mechanism with which to place limits on the range of liability for negligent statements (see further Barker (1993) 109 LQR 461, 475). There are two points to bear in mind about reliance. First, the defendant must have knowledge that the plaintiff will rely on the information or advice, and secondly, the plaintiff's reliance must be reasonable in the circumstances. In *Caparo Industries plc v Dickman* [1990] 1 All ER 568 Lord Bridge stressed that the adviser must have knowledge that his statement or advice would be communicated to the plaintiff, either as an individual or as a member of an identifiable class, in connection with a particular transaction, and that the plaintiff would be very likely to rely on it. This appears to require actual knowledge on the part of the defendant. Lord Oliver was prepared to admit actual or *inferential* knowledge of: the purpose of the advice; that it would be communicated to the advisee; and that the advice was likely to be acted on by the advisee for that purpose without independent enquiry (at p. 589). Mere foreseeability that the plaintiff might rely on the advice was insufficient. In *JEB Fasteners Ltd v Marks Bloom & Co.* [1981] 3 All ER 289 Woolf J had held that auditors who prepared a company's accounts, knowing that the company was in difficulty and needed finance, ought to have foreseen that a takeover was a possible source of finance and that someone contemplating a takeover might rely on the accuracy of the accounts. Accordingly, the auditors owed a duty of care to that person in preparing the accounts. In *Caparo Industries plc v Dickman* this decision was said to be wrong to the extent that it was based on foreseeability alone, although it was possible that on the facts of the case the necessary proximity to found a duty of care could be derived from the actual knowledge on the part of the auditors of the specific purpose for which the plaintiffs intended to use the accounts (per Lord Bridge at p. 579 and Lord Oliver at p. 597).

A requirement for *actual* knowledge that the advice would be communicated to the plaintiff and was likely to be relied upon would probably be unworkable. It would restrict liability under *Hedley Byrne & Co. Ltd v Heller & Partners Ltd* to an extremely narrow field of cases, it would put a premium on ignorance on the part of advisers, and it would be out of line with most other areas of the tort of negligence where the question of what the defendant ought reasonably to have done or known is as relevant to his liability as what he in fact did or knew. It is reasonably clear from Lord Oliver's speech that his reference to inferential knowledge included the knowledge that the defendant 'ought' to have or is 'presumed' to have (see at pp. 590 and 592), and none of the other speeches are inconsistent with this. This was certainly the view of Staughton LJ in *Beaumont v Humberts* [1990] 49 EG 46, 48 where he said that: 'The question . . . is whether such knowledge [i.e., that the plaintiff was likely to rely on a valuation] can be inferred from other evidence or (which is in practice much the same thing) whether he ought to have known'. But the question of what an adviser ought to have known is almost inevitably bound up with the question of what he could reasonably have foreseen, so that 'inferential knowledge' that the plaintiff would rely on the advice may simply be a version of foreseeability (see Mullis and Oliphant (1991) 7 PN 22, 25). In *Harris v Wyre Forest District Council* (which was heard by the House of Lords at the same time as, and is reported with, *Smith v Bush* [1989] 2 WLR 790), a house purchaser brought an action against the local authority in respect of a negligent survey of the house conducted by an in-house surveyor of the defendants. The survey report was never communicated to the purchaser, who simply inferred from the advance by the defendants of a mortgage on the property that the valuation was favourable. The imputation to the surveyor of 'knowledge' that the plaintiff would rely on the valuation report must depend on the foreseeability of reliance in such circumstances. Moreover, in *Caparo Industries plc* v *Dickman* Lord Oliver commented (at pp. 589–90) that the decision in *Smith* v *Bush* demonstrated that the absence of a positive intention that the advice shall be acted on by someone other than the immediate recipient, or even an expressed intention that it should not be acted on by anyone else, cannot prevail against actual or presumed knowledge that it is in fact likely to be relied on in a particular transaction without independent verification. The defendant's 'presumed knowlege' must be derived from the likelihood, or foreseeability, that the plaintiff would rely on the advice notwithstanding the defendant's intention that he should not do so.

In *Smith* v *Bush* [1989] 2 WLR 790 it was crucial to the finding that the surveyor owed a duty of care to the purchaser that the purchaser relied, to the surveyor's knowledge, on the valuation report in deciding to purchase the property, and that such reliance was reasonable. Lord Griffiths stressed (at p. 816) that 'in cases where the advice has not been given for the specific purpose of the recipient acting upon it, it should only be in cases where the adviser knows that there is a high degree of probability that some other identifiable person will act upon the advice that a duty of care should be imposed'. Evidence given in the earlier case of *Yianni* v *Edwin Evans & Sons* [1981] 3 All ER 592 indicated that less than 15% of house purchasers have an independent survey. Thus, the vast majority of house purchasers do rely on building society valuation reports, assuming that if the building society is willing to rely on the surveyor's valuation there is no reason why they should not do so also. In both cases this was an important factor in categorising the plaintiff's reliance as reasonable. Other points included the fact that the plaintiff paid the surveyor's fee, albeit indirectly; a second, independent survey would simply duplicate the work involved; and this would inhibit house purchase by increasing the cost and causing delay (see Kaye (1989) 52 MLR 841; Allen (1989) 105 LQR 511; James (1989) 5 PN 73). On the other hand, it may not be reasonable for all purchasers to rely on a mortgagee's valuer. With different types of property, such as industrial property, large blocks of flats or very expensive houses, 'it may well be that the general expectation of the behaviour of the purchaser is quite different. With large sums of money at stake prudence would seem to demand that the purchaser obtain his own structural survey . . .' (per Lord Griffiths at p. 811; see also *Stevenson* v *Nationwide Building Society* (1984) 272 EG 663 where the plaintiff was an estate agent; query how expensive is a 'very expensive house'? See *Beaumont* v *Humberts* [1990] 49 EG 46 where the property was neither at the lower end of the housing market nor in the 'very expensive' category). It is not entirely clear whether Lord Griffiths was indicating that in these circumstances the purchaser's reliance would be unreasonable, or alternatively that it would render a disclaimer of liability by the surveyor reasonable, though in the context of liability under *Hedley Byrne* this may be a very fine distinction (see (h) *Disclaimers,* below). In *McCullagh* v *Lane Fox and Partners Ltd* [1996] 18 EG 104, for example, the Court of Appeal held that a disclaimer in an estate agent's sale particulars made it unreasonable for a prospective purchaser to rely on the accuracy of statements made in the particulars, since a reasonable person would understand that because of the disclaimer there was no assumption of responsibility by the estate agent. Indeed, two members of the Court (Sir Christopher Slade and Nourse LJ) would have concluded that no duty of care arose in respect of an oral statement, which was also contained in the particulars of sale, even in the absence of a disclaimer, because the estate agent did not know at the time, either actually or inferentially, that it was likely that the purchaser would rely on the representation without further independent inquiry.

It is unlikely that it would be reasonable for a purchaser of property to rely on a survey conducted before the specific transaction in question was contemplated, even if the seller has commissioned the survey himself with a sale in mind. In *Mariola Marine Corporation* v *Lloyd's Register of Shipping* [1990] 1 Lloyd's Rep 547 it was held that a survey of a vessel conducted by Lloyd's for classification purposes was not carried out for the benefit of a specific individual purchaser who subsequently came on the scene. The plaintiffs were not intended to act on the result of the survey, 'they were merely one of an indeterminate class of persons who might do so' (per Phillips J at p. 561).

It is clearly unreasonable for members of the public to rely on a company's accounts when purchasing shares, otherwise liability would be indeterminate. In *Candler* v *Crane Christmas & Co.* [1951] 2 KB 164, 181 Denning LJ, in a dissenting judgment which was subsequently approved by the House of Lords in both *Hedley Byrne & Co. Ltd* v *Heller & Partners Ltd* and *Caparo Industries plc* v *Dickman,* said that an auditor's duty does not extend to 'strangers of whom they have heard nothing and to whom their employer without their knowledge may choose to show their accounts'. It is clear from *Caparo Industries plc* v *Dickman* [1990] 1 All ER 568, however, that the auditor's duty is much narrower than this. A duty does not arise simply from the fact that the company is vulnerable to a takeover at the time the auditor is preparing his report. This may increase the foreseeability of a third party relying on the accounts, but foreseeability alone cannot be a sufficient criterion for liability (see *Esanda Finance Corporation Ltd* v *Peat Marwick Hungerfords* (1997) 142 ALR 750 where the High Court of Australia applied *Caparo*). Lord Oliver commented (at p. 593) that:

> To apply as a test of liability only the foreseeability of possible damage without some further control would be to create a liability wholly indefinite in area, duration and amount and would open up a limitless vista of uninsurable risk for the professional man.

All of their Lordships considered that the purpose of the statutory audit of a public company's accounts was the crucial issue. This purpose was said to be to protect the company itself from the consequences of undetected errors and to provide shareholders as a body with reliable information to enable them to scrutinise the conduct of the company's affairs, not to assist those who might be minded to profit from dealings in the company's shares, whether existing shareholders or not (for criticism of the view that Parliament could not have intended the statutory audit to benefit investors see Mullis and Oliphant (1991) 7 PN 22, 26; Fleming (1990) 106 LQR 349, 351). Defining the 'purpose' of the report narrowly made it simple to conclude that there was no duty of care, since it makes reliance by the plaintiff for another purpose unreasonable. The same technique was applied in *Al-Nakib Investments (Jersey) Ltd* v *Longcroft* [1990] 3 All ER 321 where it was held that a prospectus which invites shareholders in a company to subscribe for additional shares in the company by way of a rights issue is issued for that specific purpose, and no other. Thus, if a shareholder buys additional shares in the stock market in reliance on statements made in the prospectus he is not owed a duty of care (cf. *Possfund Custodian Trustee Ltd* v *Diamond* [1996] 2 All ER 774). Similarly, the auditors of a company owe no duty of care to a bank which lends money to the company, regardless of whether the bank is an existing creditor or a potential one, since the auditors do not make their report to the creditors or to any other person with the intention or knowledge that the report will be communicated to the creditors (*Al Saudi Banque* v *Clark Pixley* [1989] 3 All ER 361. To avoid this problem banks now commonly make it a condition of a loan that the auditor of the borrower state in writing that the audited accounts can be relied on for this purpose: see Martin (1991) 7 PN 37, 38). This is also the position where accountants are retained by the creditor to advise on the financial position of a company. The accountants do not owe a duty of care to the directors of the company or guarantors of the company's debts (*Huxford* v *Stoy Hayward* (1989) 5 BCC 421).

In *James McNaughton Papers Group Ltd* v *Hicks Anderson & Co.* [1991] 1 All ER 134 the Court of Appeal applied *Caparo Industries plc* v *Dickman* in another case involving a successful but financially unprofitable takeover bid. The defendants were accountants to a company (MK) which was the subject of an agreed takeover by the plaintiffs. MK asked the defendants to prepare draft accounts for use in the negotiations, and the accounts were shown to the plaintiffs. At a meeting between the negotiating parties a representative of the defendants stated in response to a question by the plaintiffs that MK was breaking even or doing marginally worse. After the takeover the plaintiffs discovered discrepancies in the accounts and sued the accountants. It was held that the defendants owed no duty of care to the plaintiffs because the accounts were produced for MK not the plaintiffs; they were merely draft accounts and it could not be reasonably foreseen that the plaintiffs would regard them as final accounts; the defendants did not take part in the negotiations; and the plaintiffs were aware that MK was in a poor financial condition and could be expected to consult their own accountants. The statement made by the defendants' representative was a very general answer and did not affect the specific figures in the accounts, and it was not reasonable to rely on that statement without further enquiry or advice. Neill LJ commented (at p. 145) that:

In business transactions conducted at arms' length it may sometimes be difficult for an advisee to prove that he was entitled to act on a statement without taking any independent advice or to prove that the adviser knew, actually or inferentially, that he would act without taking such advice.

There is clearly a distinction to be drawn here between a corporate 'predator', seeking to make a profit in a high-risk entrepreneurial venture, who discovers that the deal is not as lucrative as was anticipated and then seeks to take the benefit of professional services without having paid for them by suing the auditors in tort, and the purchaser of a house who relies on a valuation conducted by the mortgagee's surveyor, having paid a fee to the mortgagee to cover the cost of the survey report. The former is in a much better position to protect his own financial interests than the latter. This is a policy judgment, of course, but it can be translated into legal form simply by asking whether it was reasonable for the plaintiff to rely on the defendant's valuation without taking independent advice (for discussion of further policy issues surrounding the liability of auditors: see Mullis and Oliphant (1991) 7 PN 22, 26; Percival (1991) 54 MLR 739; Gwilliam (1992) 8 PN 147; Dugdale (1992) 8 PN 160 discussing *Berg Sons & Co. Ltd* v *Adams* (1992) 8 PN 167).

Caparo Industries plc v *Dickman* was distinguished, however, in *Morgan Crucible Co. plc* v *Hill Samuel Bank Ltd* [1991] 1 All ER 148 in which the Court of Appeal held on a preliminary point of law that it was at least arguable that where, during the course of a contested takeover bid, the directors and financial advisers of the target company make express representations after an identified bidder has emerged, intending that the bidder would rely on those representations, they owe a duty of care not to be negligent in making representations which might mislead the bidder. The distinction between this case and *Caparo Industries plc* v *Dickman* was that the representations were made after, not before, the bidder had emerged, and the representations were made in the knowledge and *with the intention* that they should be relied on by the bidder in deciding whether or not to make an increased bid (see also *Galoo Ltd* v *Bright Grahame Murray* [1995] 1 All ER 16; for criticism of the view that a plaintiff should be unable to rely on expert advice in connection with a transaction entered into before the advice was given see Stapelton (1991) 107 LQR 249, 280–1).

(f)   *Causation*   The fact that the plaintiff placed reliance on the defendant's statement does not, in itself, prove that the defendant's negligence caused the damage. The defendants in *JEB Fasteners Ltd* v *Marks Bloom & Co.* [1983] 1 All ER 583 were held not liable because although the plaintiffs had 'relied' on the accounts this was not the *cause* of the loss, because they would have taken over the company even if they had known the true financial position. The plaintiff's reliance will constitute a cause of his loss 'as long as a misrepresentation plays a real and substantial part, though not by itself a decisive part, in inducing the plaintiff to act' (per Stephenson LJ at p. 589). (Query whether a plaintiff who has acted carelessly and therefore would normally be regarded as contributorily negligent can still be treated as placing *reasonable* reliance on the defendant's statement: see para. 14.5.1. See also

Strover v *Harrington* [1988] 1 All ER 769, 780–1, where it was held that
carelessness by the plaintiff will defeat a claim on the basis that the defendant's misrepresentation did not *cause the* loss.)

In *Downs* v *Chappell* [1996] 3 All ER 344, the Court of Appeal held that
in relation to an action for deceit, once it is proved that the plaintiff was in
fact induced by a material misrepresentation to act to his detriment, the
question of what the plaintiff would have done but for the representation was
irrelevant. The trial judge had been wrong to ask, hypothetically, what the
plaintiffs would have done if they had been told the truth. Although this
would seem to run contrary to the normal principles applicable to causation
(see para. 4.1.1), it could be justified on the basis that a defendant in an
action for deceit has acted fraudulently, and since he intended to persuade
the plaintiff to act in a particular manner he should not be permitted to argue
that the plaintiff would have so acted in any event. The difficulty is that the
same view on causation was taken in relation to the second defendants in
Downs v *Chappell*, a firm of accountants, who were held liable in negligence.
Once it was proved that the plaintiffs had acted in reliance on inaccurate
information provided by the defendants causation was established, and the
question of whether the plaintiffs would have gone ahead with the purchase
of a business if the correct figures had been supplied was irrelevant. The
decision of the Court of Appeal in *JEB Fasteners Ltd* v *Marks Bloom & Co.*,
though cited, was not referred to in the judgments. In *Bristol and West
Building Society* v *Mothew* [1996] 4 All ER 698, 705–6, the Court of Appeal
considered itself bound by the decision in *Downs* v *Chappell* and accepted
that, in an action for negligent misrepresentation, where the plaintiff proves
that he relied on the defendant's incorrect advice or information, i.e. that he
would not have acted as he did if he had not been given that advice or
information, it is not necessary for him to go on to prove that he would not
have acted as he did if he had been given proper advice or the correct
information. *JEB Fasteners Ltd* was not cited or referred to in the judgments
in *Mothew*. Millett LJ distinguished between the situation where the defendant has negligently given incorrect advice or incorrect information, where the
'but for' test of causation appears not to apply, and the case where the
plaintiff's claim is based on a failure to give appropriate advice or information.
In the latter situation the plaintiff must show what advice or information
ought to have been given and prove (on a balance of probabilities) that if the
missing advice or information had been given he would not have entered into
the relevant transaction or would not have done so on disadvantageous terms.
This difference in approach appears to rest on a distinction between
omissions and acts. If there is a complete failure to provide advice or
information, in breach of duty, the plaintiff must prove what he would have
done in the hypothetical situation of the advice or information having been
given in order to establish a causal link between the negligence and the
damage. If advice or information was provided, but it was incorrect, the
plaintiff need only prove that he relied on it in fact, not that he would have
acted differently had the advice or information been correct. The difficulty
with this is that the general proposition when considering causation in tort,

and particularly in negligence, is that if the defendant's breach of duty would have made no difference to the outcome (i.e., the damage would have occurred in any event) the breach is not treated as the cause of the loss. It is not clear why this basic principle should be any different in cases of negligent misrepresentation, nor what advantage is brought by an excess of subtlety in classifying different types of negligence (acts and omissions) for the purpose of causation.

(g)   *Voluntary undertaking*   In *Hedley Byrne & Co. Ltd* v *Heller & Partners Ltd* Lord Reid said that a reasonable man who knew that his skill and judgment were being relied on had three options. He could keep silent; he could reply without accepting responsibility for the accuracy of the answer; or he could answer without qualification. If he adopted the last course he must 'be held to have accepted some responsibility for his answer being given carefully'. Lord Devlin suggested that this responsibility was something voluntarily undertaken, not imposed by law. The concept of a 'voluntary assumption of responsibility' is ambiguous, however, and can give rise to confusion (for detailed analysis see *Barker* (1993) 109 LQR 461; and Whittaker (1997) 17 LS 169). It does not mean that the defendant is free to choose whether to accept legal responsibility for his statements, except in so far as he is free to and does in fact disclaim liability. It means that if he behaves in a certain manner he will be subject to a duty of care. Ralph Gibson LJ has said that the concept 'as used in *Hedley Byrne* seems to me to refer to an act [sic] by a defendant whereby he voluntarily does something, which affects the plaintiff, and it is such an act that a reasonable man would recognise that in the circumstances he is required to perform it with due care' (*Reid* v *Rush & Tomkins Group plc* [1989] 3 All ER 228, 241). Used in this way it scarcely distinguishes the *Hedley Byrne* defendant from the negligent motorist. Indeed, in *Smith* v *Bush* [1989] 2 WLR 790 Lord Griffiths suggested that 'voluntary assumption of responsibility' is not a helpful or realistic test for liability. It 'can only have any real meaning if it is understood as referring to the circumstances in which the law will *deem* the maker of the statement to have assumed responsibility to the person who acts upon the advice' (at p. 813, emphasis added). Similarly, in *Caparo Industries plc* v *Dickman* [1990] 1 All ER 568, 589, Lord Oliver said that the phrase 'means no more than that the act of the defendant in making the statement or tendering the advice was voluntary and that the law attributes to it an assumption of responsibility if the statement or advice is inaccurate and is acted on. It tells us nothing about the circumstances from which such attribution arises' (see also per Lord Roskill at p. 582).

In *Henderson* v *Merrett Syndicates Ltd* [1994] 3 All ER 506 and *White* v *Jones* [1995] 1 All ER 691 both Lord Goff and Lord Browne-Wilkinson said that the criticism of the concept of a voluntary assumption of responsibility in *Smith* v *Bush* and *Caparo* was misplaced (see also Lord Steyn in *Williams* v *Natural Life Health Foods Ltd* [1998] 2 All ER 577, 581 — 'the general criticism is overstated'). Lord Browne-Wilkinson suggested that the criticism had proceeded on the basis that 'assumption of responsibility' refers to the defendant having assumed legal responsibility rather than responsibility for the task, but the assumption of responsibility referred to is the defendant's assumption of responsibility for the task, not the assumption of legal liability. Even in cases of *ad hoc* relationships, it is the undertaking to answer the question posed which creates the relationship. If the responsibility for the task is assumed by the defendant he thereby creates a special relationship between himself and the plaintiff in relation to which the law (not the defendant) attaches a duty to carry out carefully the task so assumed (*White* v *Jones* [1995] 1 All ER 691, 715–16). With respect, this appears to be a matter of semantics. If it is a question of the law attaching legal responsibility to the defendant's conduct it is difficult to see what the concept of assumption of responsibility adds to the notion that the courts simply decide when and in what circumstances a duty of care will be owed. This is simply a restatement of the proposition that if the defendant chooses to act, and does so negligently, the law deems him to be liable, just as when someone chooses to drive a motor car and does so carelessly the law holds him liable for the resulting damage. As Stanton (1995) 3 Tort L Rev 85, 87 comments:

> Once it is accepted that the duty is imposed by law on the basis of the circumstances, there seem to be compelling reasons for not reviving the fiction of assumption of responsibility with its implication that we are dealing with a voluntary form of tort liability.

The value of Lord Goff's analysis of *Hedley Byrne* in terms of voluntary assumption of responsibility lies, it is submitted, in its attempt to state a general principle which applies to negligently caused economic loss, since *Hedley Byrne* assumptions of responsibility can apply to negligent acts as well as negligent words and in circumstances where the plaintiff does not rely on defendant (as, e.g., in *White* v *Jones*, see para. 2.2.4.1.4). Thus, in *Williams* v *Natural Life Health Foods Ltd* [1998] 2 All ER 577, 581 Lord Steyn said that 'The extended *Hedley Byrne* principle [established in *Henderson*] is the rationalisation or technique adopted by English law to provide a remedy for the recovery of damages in respect of economic loss caused by the negligent performance of services'.

If the duty of care is imposed by law it is irrelevant that the defendant was under a statutory obligation to speak and could not realistically be said to be acting voluntarily (*Ministry of Housing & Local Government* v *Sharp* [1970] 2 QB 223, 268). Similarly, the fact that the defendant was under a contractual obligation to make the statement to someone else does not mean that he has not 'voluntarily' assumed responsibility to the plaintiff. In *Smith* v *Bush,* for example, the surveyor was under a contractual obligation to supply a valuation report to the building society. The voluntary element of his conduct was the decision to enter that contract: 'the valuer assumes responsibility to both mortgagee and purchaser by agreeing to carry out a valuation for mortgage purposes knowing that the valuation fee has been paid by the purchaser and knowing that the valuation will probably be relied upon by the purchaser in order to decide whether or not to enter into a contract to purchase' (per Lord Templeman at p. 799).

Where, however, the plaintiff claims that the defendant's silence constituted a misrepresentation it will be much more difficult to infer that there has been a voluntary assumption of responsibility (*La Banque Financière de la Cité SA* v *Westgate Insurance Co. Ltd* [1988] 2 Lloyd's Rep 513, 559). In this context the court will look for some 'conduct by the party signifying that he assumes responsibility for taking due care', although the Court of Appeal was prepared to accept that in some, if rare, cases, having regard to special circumstances and the relationship between the parties, a defendant should be treated in law (even though not in fact) as having assumed a responsibility to the plaintiff which is capable of giving rise to a claim for damages for pure economic loss (ibid. at p. 561; see also *Pacific Associates Inc.* v *Baxter* [1989] 2 All ER 159 185c per Ralph Gibson LJ).

(h)   *Disclaimers*   Since in many instances potential defendants are unable simply to remain silent, e.g., because they are under a statutory or contractual obligation to make the statement to someone else, the ability to disclaim responsibility is particularly important. Here, the Unfair Contract Terms Act 1977 has had a significant impact. Section 2(2) subjects contract terms and general notices purporting to exclude or restrict liability for negligence to a 'reasonableness' test (at least, in relation to 'business liability': s. 1(3); liability for death or personal injuries cannot be excluded at all: s. 2(1)). It was arguable that s. 2(2) did not apply to a *Hedley Byrne* type disclaimer because the disclaimer does not seek to exclude an accrued *liability,* rather it prevents the duty of care from arising by making the plaintiff's reliance unreasonable. There is thus no 'liability' upon which s. 2(2) can 'bite'. This argument was accepted by the Court of Appeal in *Harris* v *Wyre Forest District Council* [1988] 1 All ER 691, but the decision was reversed by the House of Lords ([1989] 2 WLR 790). Lord Templeman pointed out that this interpretation would not give effect to the manifest intention of the Act but would emasculate it. By s. 11(3), when considering whether it is fair and reasonable to allow reliance on an exclusionary notice the court must take account of 'all the circumstances obtaining when the liability arose or (but for the notice) would have arisen' and s. 13(1) extends s. 2 to the exclusion of liability 'by reference to terms and notices which exclude or restrict the relevant obligation or duty'. Both these provisions, said Lord Templeman, support the view that the Act subjects all exclusion notices which at common law would provide a defence to an action for negligence to a requirement of reasonableness (for an earlier discussion of the arguments see Stanton (1985) 1 PN 132).

Their Lordships went on to hold in both *Harris* v *Wyre Forest District Council* and *Smith* v *Bush* (in which the appeals were heard together) that it was not fair and reasonable to allow a surveyor to rely on a general exclusion of liability to a house purchaser in respect of a negligent mortgage valuation (see per Lord Templeman at pp. 801–6, per Lord Griffiths at pp. 809–11; see further para. 14.2, and Harwood (1987) 50 MLR 588). Moreover, it was irrelevant whether the valuation was undertaken by an independent surveyor instructed by the mortgagee or by an 'in-house' surveyor employed by the mortgagee. It does not follow, of course, that it would always be unreasonable for a professional person to seek to exclude or limit liability, particularly if the damages would be very large and it was impossible to obtain adequate insurance cover (per Lord Griffiths at p. 810; Gwilliam (1988) 4 PN 8; see also Unfair Contract Terms Act 1977, s. 11(4)). But in an ordinary contract for the supply of professional services it would be extremely difficult to justify an exclusion of liability for negligence, and where the plaintiff has paid for the service, albeit indirectly, as in *Smith* v *Bush*, this may be a good reason for saying both that his reliance was reasonable and that an exclusion of liability was unreasonable. In *Omega Trust Co. Ltd* v *Wright Son & Pepper* [1997] 18 EG 120, the Court of Appeal accepted that it was reasonable for valuers to rely on a clause in a valuation report stating that it was for the private and confidential use of their client and should not be relied upon by third parties for any use whatsoever without the express written authority of the valuers. The defendants' client, Omega, had, unknown to the defendants, passed the report to the second plaintiffs who had advanced a loan to a third party against the security of property valued in the defendants' report. The plaintiffs suffered loss when the third party defaulted on the loan, and the property, which had been negligently overvalued, was insufficient to cover the debt. The Court of Appeal accepted that if the disclaimer was valid it would effectively negative any duty of care that might arise under *Hedley Byrne*, and therefore the question turned upon whether it satisfied the requirements of reasonableness under the Unfair Contract Terms Act. The crucial distinction between this case and *Smith* v *Bush* was that it was a commercial setting rather than a domestic householder purchasing his home: 'in a transaction involving a lot of money in a commercial context, both parties are well able to look after themselves, and it is not necessary to have any statutory protection for them' (per Henry LJ at p. 122). The parties were of equal bargaining power and it would have been easy for the second plaintiffs to obtain their own independent advice or ask the defendants if they could rely on their valuation. The defendants were entitled to know who their clients were and to whom their duty was owed (see also *Pacific Associates Inc.* v *Baxter* [1989] 2 All ER 159 (above, (b) *Contract*) where in a complex commercial contract the 'contractual structure', including a disclaimer, was held to negative both reliance and assumption of responsibility; the contract predated the Unfair Contract Terms Act, but the tenor of the judgments suggests that the same conclusion would be reached after the Act).

In *McCullagh* v *Lane Fox and Partners Ltd* [1996] 18 EG 104 the Court of Appeal held that it was not unfair or unreasonable to allow an estate agent to rely on a standard disclaimer contained in particulars of sale to the effect that 'none of the statements contained in these particulars as to this property are to be relied on as statements or representations of fact'. The plaintiff had relied on a statement as to the overall area of the site in deciding to purchase the property. Hobhouse LJ pointed out that the transaction involved a sophisticated member of the public (the purchase price had been £875,000) who had had ample opportunity to regulate his conduct having regard to the disclaimer and who would have been assumed by all concerned to have had the benefit of legal advice before exchanging contracts. Moreover, the use of disclaimers to insulate estate agents and their principals from responsibility for representations was commonplace and the normal basis on which house sales were carried out. In these circumstances it would not be unfair to allow the defendants to rely on the disclaimer, and this was the position even in respect of an oral statement made by the agent which repeated a statement made in the written particulars. The situation might be different, said his Lordship, if the representation had been about something not, or not expected to be, included in the particulars. The purchase in *McCullagh* pre-dated the coming into force of the Property Misdescriptions Act 1991, which makes it a criminal offence to give false or misleading statements about the measurements of a property. Although the Act does not create any civil liability, it is arguable that it would be unreasonable (under the Unfair Contract Terms Act 1977) to exclude liability in civil law for conduct which is a breach of the criminal law (see Hartshorne [1997] Conv 229, 235).

Similarly, where a plaintiff relies on gratuitous advice from a defendant who has no direct commercial interest in the relevant transaction it will probably be easier to conclude that the defendant should be permitted to invoke a disclaimer. As Weir [1963] CLJ 216, 218 wryly observed in commenting on *Hedley Byrne & Co. Ltd* v *Heller & Partners Ltd* the plaintiffs' claim to redress was not indisputably high:

> They made bad business deals, having taken only a free opinion before hazarding their wealth in the hope of profit, no part of which, had it eventuated, would they have transferred to the honest person whom they now seek to saddle with their loss.

In such cases, notwithstanding the effect of the Unfair Contract Terms Act 1977, it is difficult to see how the reasonableness of a disclaimer can be divorced from consideration of the reasonableness of the plaintiff's reliance, in circumstances where he has been effectively informed that he should not rely on the defendant's statement.

2.2.4.1.4 Negligent statements relied upon by a third party   In some circumstances a negligent statement made by A to B and acted upon by B causes financial loss to C. The classic example is a reference given by A to B about C, normally for employment purposes. An employer who gives a negligent reference about an employee to a prospective employer would clearly owe a *Hedley Byrne* duty, subject to any disclaimers, to the prospective employer (see, e.g., *Edwards* v *Lee, Independent*, 1 November 1991). May the employer, A, also owe a duty of care to the employee, C, if as a result of the negligent reference the prospective employer, B, refused to employ C? In *Spring* v *Guardian Assurance plc* [1994] 3 WLR 354 the Court of Appeal had held that as a matter of policy an employer does not owe a duty of care in respect of an employment reference to the employee, because otherwise it would undermine the defence of qualified privilege in an action for defamation (which would normally apply in the context of a reference). The defence of qualified privilege can be defeated by proof of the defendant's malice, but allowing a cause of action in negligence would mean that the plaintiff would only have to prove carelessness on the part of the defendant. The House of Lords reversed this decision, however, with the majority of their Lordships applying the tripartite test of *Caparo Industries plc v Dickman* [1990] 1 All ER 568 for the duty of care. Foreseeability of the damage, and proximity of the relationship were easily satisfied in the context of the employment relationship. The real issue was whether it was just and reasonable to impose a duty of care given the possible overlap with the rules in the tort of defamation. In concluding that it was just and reasonable to impose a duty of care Lord Woolf said that an action for defamation provided a wholly inadequate remedy for an employee who sustained loss as a result of a negligently inaccurate reference, because it placed a wholly disproportionate burden on the employee to prove malice, which is extremely difficult to establish. Both Lord Woolf and Lord Slynn considered that it would be unacceptable that the recipient of a reference might be able to sue if he relied on the statement (applying *Hedley Byrne*) but that the employee who was refused employment because the recipient relied on a reference given negligently should have no remedy unless he could prove malice. Their Lordships emphasised that the decision was founded in the employment context, and that there might be a difference between this situation and the giving of a reference about someone known socially, though the duty was not limited to references about persons who were, strictly speaking, 'employees'. It could also apply to someone employed under a contract for services and to ex-employees. Their Lordships emphasised the fact that the provision of references for employees is a feature of the modern employment market and that both employees and employers benefit from this (employers indirectly, by being able to rely on references provided by other employers). The overlap with defamation was apparent rather than real, since the two torts do not cover the same ground. The tort of negligence requires foreseeability of damage, proximity of relationship, proof of actual damage and proof of carelessness by the defendant. Defamation required none of these. They were separate torts, with separate requirements and separate defences. There was no reason why a plaintiff's claim for economic loss flowing from a negligent employment reference should be barred, simply because if he were suing in respect of the damage to his reputation he would have to prove malice on an occasion of qualified privilege. (Of course, there could be no action in negligence if the contents of the reference were true, presumably on the basis that the plaintiff would be unable to establish carelessness by the defendant. Truth is a defence to a defamation action, but the burden of proving the truth of a defamatory imputation is the defendant's). Lord Goff, while agreeing in the result, held that liability could be derived from *Hedley Byrne & Co. Ltd v Heller & Partners Ltd* [1964] AC 465, which rested on a wide principle of an assumption or undertaking of responsibility by the defendant towards the plaintiff, coupled with reliance by the plaintiff on the exercise by the defendant of reasonable care and skill. *Hedley Byrne* itself was concerned with the provision of information and advice but, said his Lordship, it was clear that the principle was not limited in this way and extended to the performance of other services, as for example the professional services rendered by a solicitor to his client. 'Special skill' was to be understood in a broad sense, at least broad enough to include 'special knowledge' which an employer would have when writing a reference. An employer who gave a reference voluntarily undertook responsibility for the reference being given with reasonable care. (For comment on *Spring* see Allen (1995) 58 MLR 553 and Stanton (1995) 3 Tort L Rev 85.)

The reasoning in *Spring* could also be applied in the context of a doctor who carries out a pre-employment medical assessment on behalf of a company. Such an assessment is carried out at the request of the company, and the doctor clearly owes a duty of care (probably concurrently with a duty in contract) to the company in respect of the advice provided. If the examination or report is negligent, as a result of which the doctor advises the company that the prospective employee is unsuitable for the job, the prospective employee may suffer economic loss as a result of failing to obtain the employment. In *Baker* v *Kaye* [1997] IRLR 219, it was held that in such circumstances a doctor could owe a duty of care to the prospective employee (although, on the facts, there had been no breach of duty). Although *Spring* is analogous, in the sense that it involved a duty of care where the plaintiff had not acted to his detriment in reliance on the defendant's advice (his 'reliance' was entirely passive), the judge, Mr Robert Owen QC, did not regard it as determinative because the duty of care in *Spring* had its foundation in the former contractual relationship of employer and employee between the plaintiff and the defendant. There was no comparable contractual relationship between the plaintiff and the defendant doctor in *Baker* v *Kaye*. Nonetheless, the duty of care applied because the loss was clearly foreseeable, there was sufficient proximity between the parties (the plaintiff provided detailed medical information to the defendant, who regarded himself as under a duty of confidentiality and under a duty to advise the plaintiff to seek further medical advice if his assessment revealed a medical condition which required treatment), and it was just and reasonable to impose the duty because there was no conflict between such a duty and the duty that the defendant owed to the company. Indeed, the duty owed to the plaintiff could be couched in virtually identical terms to the duty the defendant owed to the company. On the other hand, in *Kapfunde* v *Abbey National plc*, *The Times*, 6 April 1998, the plaintiff applied for a job and filled in a medical questionnaire, which was considered by a doctor who took the view that the plaintiff would have a higher than average level of absence from work. The plaintiff was not offered the job. The Court of Appeal held that there was no proximity of relationship between the doctor and the plaintiff because the doctor had never seen the plaintiff, the loss was purely economic, and the prospective employer did not owe a duty to exercise reasonable care in selecting employees. Clearly, there is a distinction between *Kapfunde* and *Baker* v *Kaye*, in that the plaintiff was not physically examined. Nonetheless, the Court of Appeal expressed a firm view that *Baker* v *Kaye* was wrongly decided on the question of the duty of care (in the light of comments made in *X* v *Bedfordshire County Council*, below).

In *Baker* v *Kaye* the judge suggested that the assumption of responsibility by the doctor for advising the plaintiff to seek further medical advice if he discovered anything requiring further medical treatment 'could of itself be said to imply a duty to take reasonable care in carrying out the assessment'. This observation is not entirely unproblematic. In *M (a minor)* v *Newham London Borough Council* [1994] 2 WLR 554, a majority of the Court of Appeal suggested that where a medical examination is conducted for the purpose of a life insurance proposal, with the doctor advising the proposed insurers, the doctor would owe no duty to the individual in the advice he gave to the insurers, even though for the purpose of confidentiality he might treat the individual as a patient. On appeal to the House of Lords (sub. nom. *X (minors)* v *Bedfordshire County Council* [1995] 3 WLR 152, 186) Lord Browne-Wilkinson agreed that a doctor instructed by an insurance company to examine an applicant for life insurance does not, simply by examining the applicant, come under any general duty of care to the applicant. He was under a duty not to damage the applicant in the course of the examination, but beyond this his duties were owed to the insurance company, not to the applicant. Notwithstanding these *obiter* comments, it is arguable that if the doctor discovers something seriously wrong with the individual then he should come under a duty at least to alert the individual to the problem (see, e.g., *Thomsen* v *Davison* [1975] Qd R 93; *Parslow* v *Masters* [1993] 6 WWR 273 (Sask QB)) bearing in mind that this would involve physical harm rather than economic loss, though in the light of the Court of Appeal's views in *Kapfunde*, above, the argument may not be well received.

Goodwill v *British Pregnancy Advisory Service* [1996] 2 All ER 161 was a case where the plaintiff, who was not the doctor's patient, relied upon advice by the doctor to the patient and suffered economic loss. Clearly, a situation which involves reliance by C on advice given by A to B is closer to a traditional *Hedley Byrne* analysis than *Spring*. The patient, M, had undergone a vasectomy arranged by the defendants in 1984. Three months later, in 1985, M was advised by the defendants that the operation had been successful and that he did not need to use contraception in the future. In 1988 the plaintiff began a sexual relationship with M and he told her that he had been sterilised. As a result they did not use any form of contraception (although the plaintiff did also seek advice from her own doctor). In 1989 the plaintiff became pregnant and subsequently gave birth. She claimed damages from the defendants for the economic loss resulting from the cost of bringing up the child and loss of earnings. The Court of Appeal held that there was no duty of care owed to the plaintiff because the defendants could not have known that their advice to M would be communicated to the plaintiff and acted on by her as a warranty of M's sterility without independent inquiry. They could know nothing about the likely conduct of M's future sexual partners, and had not voluntarily assumed any responsibility to the plaintiff. It would have been different if the plaintiff had been M's current sexual partner at the time of the advice, and that advice had been given directly to both of them (per Peter Gibson LJ at p. 168; see *Thake* v *Maurice* [1986] 1 All ER 497).

The concept of voluntary assumption of responsibility, which is now treated as the broad principle underpinning *Hedley Byrne*, has also been used to explain the liability of a solicitor to a beneficiary under a will who has lost a legacy due to the solicitor's negligence in carrying out the testator's instructions. The issue was first addressed in *Ross v Caunters* [1980] Ch 297 where Megarry V-C held that solicitors who had failed to warn a testator not to allow the spouse of a beneficiary to witness a will drawn up by the solicitors were liable in negligence to the named beneficiary who lost her bequest as a result of the effects of the Wills Act 1837, s. 15. Clearly, the plaintiff beneficiary had not 'relied' on the solicitors at all. If anyone had relied on the solicitors it was the testator who was in a contractual relationship with them, and it could be argued that the plaintiff, by suing in tort, was in effect seeking to obtain the benefit of a contract to which she was not a party, thereby undermining the doctrine of privity of contract. For Megarry V-C the significance of *Hedley Byrne* did not lie in establishing liability for negligent words. The courts had already reached that position where a careless statement had caused physical damage (see *Clayton* v *Woodman & Sons (Builders) Ltd* [1962] 2 QB 533; *Clay* v *Crump & Sons Ltd* [1964] 1 QB 533). Rather, *Hedley Byrne* opened up the possibility of claims in negligence for purely financial loss in circumstances where the conceptual tools were available to place a limit on the extent of liability, and thus the absence of reliance by the plaintiff was not determinative. His Lordship considered that the solicitors' duty of care could be based on *Donoghue* v *Stevenson* [1932] AC 562. Four points were important. First, the close degree of proximity between the parties—as a named beneficiary the plaintiff was easily foresee-able as likely to be affected by the defendants' negligence. Secondly, this was not accidental, it was the product of the duty owed by the defendants to the testator. Thirdly, there was no prospect of unlimited liability—it was to a specific individual for a specific sum. Lastly, all the parties were 'on the same side' so there was no conflict of interest between the defendants' duty to the testator and a duty to the plaintiff.

The Vice-Chancellor relied on the earlier decision of the Court of Appeal in *Ministry of Housing & Local Government* v *Sharp* [1970] 2 QB 223, which was another three-party situation, in which the defendant negligently issued a local land charges search, omitting a land charge in favour of the plaintiffs. The prospective purchaser bought the land in reliance on the search and thereby took the land free of the charge. The clerk who had issued the search was held liable for the plaintiffs' financial loss. Similarly, in *Punjab National Bank* v *de Boinville* [1992] 1 WLR 1138 the Court of Appeal held that an insurance broker owed a duty of care to the specific person whom he knew was to become an assignee of the policy, at all events if that person actively participated in giving instructions for the insurance to the broker's knowl-edge. Staughton LJ commented that there was a greater degree of proximity between the broker and the assignee than that which existed between the solicitor and the beneficiary under the will in *Ross v Caunters*, since the beneficiary may have known nothing of the will or the solicitor and would not have derived any benefit from it if it had later been revoked.

The trend of decisions in the late 1980s and early 1990s on liability for pure economic loss consequent upon negligent acts (para. 2.2.4.2.2) appeared to have gone some way to undermining the authority of *Ross* v *Caunters*, so that it was possible to question whether *Ross* v *Caunters* was still good law. The issue was finally addressed by the House of Lords in *White* v *Jones* [1995] 1 All ER 691 where the defendant solicitors had negligently delayed drawing up an amended will in accordance with a client's instructions to do so, and the client died not having amended the earlier will, with the result that the two plaintiffs were deprived of gifts of £9,000 each. By a bare majority it was held that the solicitors did owe a duty of care to the disappointed 'beneficiaries', principally because it was considered unjust that the solicitors would otherwise escape any responsibility for the consequences of their negligence because the deceased testator and his estate had suffered no loss and therefore would have no claim in contract (other than for nominal damages). The approach adopted in *Ross* v *Caunters* to the conceptual basis for the imposition of a duty of care was rejected, however, their Lordships preferring to rest liability upon the broader principle of an assumption of responsibility derived from *Hedley Byrne* (for comment see: Weir (1995) 111 LQR 357; Haydon [1995] CLJ 239; Hedley [1995] 1 Web JCLI; Brady (1995) 46 NILQ 434; Collins (1995) 11 PN 97; Dwyer (1996) 4 Tort L Rev 77; Murphy [1996] CLJ 45).

Lord Goff pointed out some of the conceptual difficulties in recognising a duty of care owed by the solicitors to the intended beneficiaries:

(1)   A solicitor will owe a duty to his client, and when performing his duty to the client he will generally owe no duty of care to third parties.

(2)   The plaintiffs were effectively seeking damages for the solicitor's breach of contract with the testator, and their claim was in respect of pure economic loss which is not generally recoverable (except under the principle of *Hedley Byrne*). This is particularly so where the plaintiff is claiming a loss of 'expectation' which is the preserve of the law of contract. The plaintiffs had not lost something that they once had, such as money which had been badly invested. They had been deprived of an expected benefit, which is a form of damage that traditionally has not been the subject of an action in tort. The plaintiffs' failed bequest would pass to the residuary beneficiaries under the previous will, and so the effect of an award of damages against the solicitors would be to produce a windfall increase in the testator's estate.

(3)   There would be no sensible boundaries to the cases in which such a form loss would be recoverable. The duty of care would apply to an irrevocable *inter vivos* transaction in which the solicitor's client intended to benefit the third party, and would have to be extended beyond specific named beneficiaries to indeterminate classes of persons who might have been affected.

(4)   On the particular facts of *White* v *Jones* (though arguably not *Ross* v *Caunters*) there was no act of the defendant solicitors which could be characterised as being negligent. It was the omission to do anything to amend the will before the testator died that produced the loss, but as a general rule there is no liability in tort for a pure omission unless the defendant is under some pre-existing duty.

The countervailing reasons which supported imposing liability were:

(1)   If such a duty was not recognised the only persons who had a valid claim (the testator and the estate) have suffered no loss, and the only person who had suffered a loss (the disappointed beneficiary) has no claim. The testator, through the estate, has a claim for breach of contract but is entitled only to nominal damages since there is no financial loss to the estate—it is simply not distributed in accordance with the testator's intentions. This point had influenced Megarry V-C in *Ross* v *Caunters*, who had described the result as 'striking'. As Lord Goff commented (at p. 702), if the solicitor owes no duty to the intended beneficiaries, there is a lacuna in the law which needs to be filled. This was a point which his Lordship regarded as being of 'cardinal importance' (as it had been for Sir Donald Nicholls V-C in the Court of Appeal when he stated that in these circumstances a 'coherent system of law demands there should be an effective remedy against the solicitor', at [1993] 3 All ER 481, 489).

(2)   The importance of legacies in a society which recognises the right of citizens to leave their assets to whom they please indicated that it would be unjust to deny a remedy. The evidence of similar claims notified to the Solicitors' Indemnity Fund was that the value of such claims was of a comparatively modest size, suggesting that mistakes of this nature most affected people of modest means where a testator instructed a small firm of solicitors.

(3)   The solicitors' profession could not complain if such a liability were to be imposed on their members. If a solicitor has been negligent in such a way which defeats his client's testamentary intentions he must regard himself as lucky if the effect of the law is that he is not liable to pay damages in the ordinary way. It involved no injustice to the solicitor to impose liability, even if the damages did not go the estate but to the disappointed beneficiary. This view was reinforced by the professional role of solicitors in society, since in practice the public relies on solicitors to prepare effective wills.

In these circumstances, said Lord Goff, there was a strong impulse to achieve practical justice by creating an effective remedy for the solicitor's breach of professional duty to his client (echoing the remarks of Sir Donald Nicholls V-C in the Court of Appeal). Thus, to fill the gap, the law should extend to the intended beneficiary a remedy under the *Hedley Byrne* principle by holding that the assumption of responsibility by the solicitor towards his client should be held in law to extend to the intended beneficiary who, as a result of the solicitor's negligence, was reasonably foreseeably deprived of the intended legacy in circumstances where neither the testator nor his estate would have a remedy against the solicitor (at p. 710). Since *Hedley Byrne* liability is founded upon an assumption of responsibility the solicitor may be liable for negligent omissions as well as negligent acts (per Lord Goff, citing *Midland Bank Trust Co. Ltd* v *Hett Stubbs & Kemp* [1979] Ch 384, 416 and *Henderson* v *Merrett Syndicates Ltd* [1994] 3 All ER 506, 521) and, moreover, damages for loss of expectation were not excluded in cases of negligence arising under *Hedley Byrne*. This was a matter of practical justice, rather than legal doctrine, because refusing to admit the beneficiaries' claim would mean that there was no sanction in respect of the solicitors' breach of professional duty. (Though note that this duty is not limited to actions against solicitors but can also apply to lay will-writers: *Esterhuizen* v *Allied Dunbar Assurance plc, The Times*, 10 June 1998. The defendants were offering a similar service to that of solicitors and should not be judged by a lesser standard than applied to solicitors.) This appears to have been the primary factor influencing the majority opinions in *White* v *Jones*. Moreover, it is clear that the 'voluntary assumption of responsibility' that the defendant undertakes is *deemed* to have occurred by law, irrespective of the defendant's intentions in the matter. This is simply another way of saying that if in these circumstances the defendant is negligent in performing his task he will owe a duty of care to someone who suffers loss as a result. On this basis it is difficult conceptually to distinguish between the negligent solicitor and the negligent motorist (except that the solicitor may in some circumstances be liable for not acting at all, whereas the motorist cannot be liable in respect of his driving if he does not get into the car).

The result in *White* v *Jones* is generally supported by Commonwealth authority. *Ross* v *Caunters* has been followed by the New Zealand Court of Appeal (*Gartside* v *Sheffield, Young & Ellis* [1983] NZLR 37), and in *Hill* v *Van Erp* (1997) 142 ALR 687 the High Court of Australia held a negligent solicitor liable on virtually identical facts to those of *Ross* v *Caunters*, although there was some reluctance to base the decision upon a 'voluntary assumption of responsibility' as espoused by the majority in *White* v *Jones* (see also *Hawkins* v *Clayton* (1988) 78 ALR 69 where the High Court of Australia, by a bare majority, held that solicitors who had drafted and retained custody of a will were liable in tort for the loss occasioned by a substantial delay in notifying the executor of the will of the testatrix's death).

There are limits to the solicitor's duty of care to third parties. The solicitor's assumption of responsibility is subject to any term of the contract between the solicitor and the testator which might exclude or restrict the solicitor's liability to the testator under *Hedley Byrne* (though Lord Goff accepted that such a term is most unlikely to arise in practice. It would also be subject to the Unfair Contract Terms Act 1977, see *Smith* v *Bush* [1989] 2 WLR 790, above, para. 2.2.4.1.3 (h)). Lord Goff also said that the duty will not arise in cases where the defect in the will comes to light before the death of the testator, and the testator either leaves the will as it is or otherwise continues to exclude the previously intended beneficiary from the relevant benefit. This was effectively the position in *Hemmens* v *Wilson Browne* [1994] 2 WLR 323, though in a case involving an *inter vivos* gift. It was accepted that a solicitor could owe a duty of care to a third party in respect of an irrevocable *inter vivos* transaction in which the solicitor's client intended to benefit the third party (e.g., an irrevocable deed of settlement conferring benefits on X instead of, as intended, Y), but there was no duty of care owed to a third party where, the solicitor having negligently drafted a document so as to confer no enforceable rights on the third party, it remained within the power of the client/settlor to remedy the situation and the only reason he did not do so was that he had changed his mind about conferring the benefit. It was not just and reasonable to impose liability on the solicitor in these circumstances, bearing in mind the client's ability, but unwillingness, to rectify the situation, and the fact that it was not a case where there would be no remedy against the negligent solicitor, since the client had an adequate remedy for breach of contract.

In *Clarke* v *Bruce Lance & Co.* [1988] 1 All ER 364 the plaintiff was a beneficiary under a will drawn up by the defendant solicitors by which he was to receive an interest in a service station owned by the testator. The testator subsequently granted an option to a third party to purchase the service station at a fixed price on his death, and the defendants had drawn up that option. On the testator's death the service station was worth substantially more than the fixed price. The plaintiff contended that the defendants owed both the testator and himself a duty to advise the testator that the fixed price option was an uncommercial transaction, and that it would adversely affect his interest under the will. The Court of Appeal held that there was no such duty for four reasons. First, the relationship between the plaintiff and the defendants was not sufficiently close. The testator was free to deal with the property during his lifetime in any way he wished, and the defendants' duty was to carry out his instructions. They could not be expected to contemplate the plaintiff as a person likely to be affected by their negligence. Second, the transaction (the grant of the option) on which the defendants advised the testator was not intended to benefit the plaintiff. There was a conflict of interest between the testator and the plaintiff in this respect (cf. *Al-Kandari* v *J.R. Brown & Co.* [1988] 1 All ER 833 where despite a potential conflict of interest between solicitors and an opposing litigant there was a very clear assumption of responsibility). Third, if a duty were owed it would have been owed to an indeterminate class of all potential donees or beneficiaries, not just the plaintiff, opening up the prospect of indeterminate liability. Finally, it was not a case where there was no other effective remedy, since the testator during his life, and his personal representatives after his death, would have a cause of action if the solicitors were negligent (see further Goddard (1988) 4 PN 129; see also *Gran Gelato Ltd* v *Richcliff (Group) Ltd* [1992] 2 WLR 867—solicitor acting for a vendor of property owes no duty of care to the purchaser in respect of statements about the property). This last point was central to the decision in *Carr-Glynn* v *Frearsons* [1997] 2 All ER 614, where it was held that if a solicitor's negligence in advising a testator about a will caused loss to the estate there would be no duty of care owed to an intended beneficiary whose gift under the will failed as a result. The plaintiff was left a share in a property under the testatrix's will, but there was some doubt as to whether the testatrix held her share as a joint tenant or a tenant in common. The defendants advised the testatrix that the gift would be ineffective unless she severed the joint tenancy, but this was not followed up, and on her death the property, which was held on a joint tenancy, passed to the other joint tenant by survivorship. Lloyd J held that the estate had suffered a loss in not being enhanced by the testatrix's share of the property and therefore no duty of care was owed by the solicitor to the intended beneficiary because it was unacceptable that the solicitor should be exposed to two separate claims for the identical loss.

2.2.4.2 Economic loss: acts Until the 1970s the rules on liability for economic loss as a result of negligent acts were simple to state: there was generally no liability in respect of 'pure' economic loss. Economic loss consequent upon physical damage to the plaintiff's property has always been actionable (*SCM (United Kingdom) Ltd* v *W.J. Whittall & Sons Ltd* [1971] 1 QB 337). The distinction between pure economic loss and economic loss consequent upon physical damage is illustrated by *Spartan Steel & Alloys Ltd* v *Martin & Co. (Contractors) Ltd* [1973] 1 QB 27 where the defendants negligently damaged an electricity cable, cutting off the power supply to the plaintiffs' premises. In order to avoid damage to their electric furnace the plaintiffs had to remove a 'melt' from it, and this caused physical damage to the melt itself and a loss of profit on that melt. The power cut also prevented four other melts being processed. By a majority, the Court of Appeal held that the plaintiffs could recover for the damaged melt and the loss of profit on that melt, but not for the loss of profit on the other four melts that would have been processed but for the power cut (see also *Muirhead* v *Industrial Tank Specialities Ltd* [1985] 3 All ER 705 for another application of this rule). This is undoubtedly a pragmatic and somewhat arbitrary result (see the comments of Lord Oliver on this case in *Murphy* v *Brentwood District Council* [1990] 2 All ER 908, 934). Lord Denning MR considered it justified on the grounds of policy. It was better that the risk of this sort of economic loss be borne by the whole community, usually in comparatively small amounts, than that the defendants should shoulder a disproportionate burden. Moreover, 'if claims for economic loss were permitted for this particular hazard, there would be no end of claims'. Edmund Davies LJ, dissenting, considered that the whole loss of profit was an equally foreseeable and equally direct consequence of the defendants' negligence. The fact that part of the loss of profit resulted from physical damage was 'purely fortuitous' and, in his Lordship's view, had nothing to do with legal principle. (See further *London-waste Ltd* v *Amec Civil Engineering Ltd* (1997) 83 BLR 136, where the plaintiffs' incinerator suffered physical damage as a result of the defendants severing electricity cables, but they were not entitled to recover loss of income from the sale of electricity because this was a consequence of the severed cables not the physical damage to their equipment. See also the Scottish case of *Coleridge* v *Miller Construction Ltd* 1997 SLT 485, where it was held that the pursuers could not recover for physical damage to glass produced at their factory following a negligent interruption of the electricity supply, because there was no plea that the defenders were aware of the nature of the pursuers' business as glass manufacturers or that it required a constant supply of electricity; and moreover the distinction between physical and purely economic loss was artificial, so that a duty of care could be denied in respect of the *physical* damage for the policy reasons identified by Lord Denning in *Spartan Steel* in relation to economic loss (consumers needing a continuous supply of electricity could install a standby system or insure against the risk). But query whether this approach would apply in English law.)

These comments of Lord Denning MR and Edmund Davies LJ reflect a persistent tension in cases of economic loss between reaching what are regarded as sensible results while reconciling that with a logically coherent structure of negligence theory. The simple, if arbitrary, test of *Spartan Steel & Alloys Ltd* v *Martin & Co. (Contractors) Ltd* was undermined by a number of trends in the 1970s and early 1980s. The distinction between statements and acts, never clear-cut at the best of times, was virtually extinguished by such cases as *Midland Bank Trust Co. Ltd* v *Hett Stubbs & Kemp* [1979] Ch 384 and *Ross* v *Caunters* [1980] Ch 297 (see para. 2.2.4.1.4; Craig (1976) 92 LQR 213). These cases concerned professional liability (the liability of solicitors) where it can be very difficult to decide whether the negligent conduct consists of an act or a statement (which may in any event be based on earlier acts, e.g., an audit report, which can be characterised as a statement, must be based on the prior act of carrying out the audit). In *Henderson* v *Merrett Syndicates Ltd* [1994] 3 All ER 506 the House of Lords took the view that the underlying principle of liability under *Hedley Byrne & Co. Ltd* v *Heller & Partners Ltd* [1964] AC 465 was a voluntary assumption of responsibility by the defendant for the affairs of another, and this could explain why a professional person may be held liable in tort for pure economic loss to both his client or a third party. If liability in respect of negligent acts could arise for professionals, why not in other cases where the conceptual tools for avoiding the prospect of indeterminate liability could be fashioned? A further innovation was the imposition of liability in respect of defectively constructed buildings, which blurred the boundary between damage to property and economic loss. Such claims represented a form of product liability in which the damage was not inflicted by the product on other property or people, but was sustained by the product itself, because the action was in respect of repairing the defect in the building. This was justified on the basis that the defects constituted a danger to health or safety and the repairs were intended to remove that danger, but this explanation ignored the fact that a product ceases to be dangerous if it is not used, whereas the plaintiffs were seeking the cost of putting the product into a safe, usable condition.

These developments, combined with Lord Wilberforce's attempt to state a single unifying test for the existence of a duty of care in negligence in *Anns* v *Merton London Borough Council* [1978] AC 728 (see para. 2.1.1), seemed to suggest that it was only a matter of time before the courts established a workable principle of liability that would allow for recovery of pure economic loss without the prospect of 'liability in an indeterminate amount for an indeterminate time to an indeterminate class' (*Ultramares Corporation* v *Touche* (1931) 174 NE 441, 444 per Cardozo CJ). Indeed, the decision of the House of Lords in *Junior Books Ltd* v *Veitchi Co. Ltd* [1983] 1 AC 520 represented an attempt to identify such a test. The recent trend in the appellate courts of this country, however, has been to abandon the search for an all-embracing principle as the foundation of the tort of negligence, and to retreat into a more pragmatic approach in which discrete categories of negligence are considered separately. This pragmatism has produced a return to what, in effect, was the previous state of the law, namely that, apart from cases which can be brought under the umbrella of *Hedley Byrne & Co. Ltd* v *Heller & Partners Ltd*, which includes cases of professional liability, or cases that can be confined to the category of an anomalous exception to the rule (which was how the House of Lords dealt with the case of *Morrison Steamship Co. Ltd.* v *Greystoke Castle* [1947] AC 265 in *Murphy* v *Brentwood District Council* [1990] 2 All ER 908; see particularly per Lord Keith at p. 920, and cf. Lord Oliver at p. 934), there is no liability in respect of pure economic loss caused by a negligent act.

If professional liability is explained as a species of liability under *Hedley Byrne & Co. Ltd* v *Heller & Partners Ltd* (see, e.g., the explanation of *Pirelli General Cable Works Ltd* v *Oscar Faber & Partners* [1983] 2 AC 1 by Lord Keith in *Murphy* v *Brentwood District Council* at p. 919), there are two broad categories of case in which the plaintiff sustains economic loss as a result of a negligent act, namely: (a) as a consequence of physical damage to a third party's property; and (b) as a consequence of acquiring a defective item of property. Adopting these categories for the purpose of exposition does not mean that, combined with the negligent statement category, they represent a coherent or rational approach to the problem of economic loss in the tort of negligence. Indeed, they probably do more to confuse and obstruct a sensible examination of the policy issues (see Stapleton (1991) 107 LQR 249).

2.2.4.2.1   Economic loss suffered by the plaintiff as a consequence of physical damage to a third party's property   There are at least three different ways (or subcategories) in which the plaintiff may suffer economic loss as a result of damage to someone else's property. First, the damage may interrupt the plaintiff's ability to carry on his business, as in *Spartan Steel & Alloys Ltd* v *Martin & Co. (Contractors) Ltd* [1973] 1 QB 27 (above) where the defendant's negligence cut off the power supply to the plaintiffs' premises, or *Weller & Co.* v *Foot & Mouth Disease Research Institute* [1966] 1 QB 569 where the plaintiffs were unable to continue their business of livestock auctioneers because of an outbreak of foot and mouth disease in the area (see also *Cattle* v *Stockton Waterworks Co.* (1875) LR 10 QB 453). The courts in this country have consistently refused to allow recovery for economic loss in these circumstances (cf. *Caltex Oil (Australia) Pty Ltd* v *Dredge Willemstad* (1976) 136 CLR 529, High Court of Australia; *Canadian National Railway Co.* v *Norsk Pacific Steamship Co. Ltd* (1992) 91 DLR (4th) 289 where, by a majority, the Supreme Court of Canada allowed the plaintiff railway company to recover its economic loss in re-routing its trains while a bridge damaged by the defendants was repaired, the bridge being owned by a third party; for comment see Markesinis (1993) 109 LQR 5; McInnes [1993] CLJ 13; Rafferty (1993) 9 PN 87; and cf. *D'Amato* v *Badger* (1996) 137 DLR (4th) 129 (SCC), discussed by Rafferty (1997) 13 PN 42. See further *Bow Valley Huskey (Bermuda) Ltd* v *Saint John Shipbuilding Ltd* (1997) 153 DLR (4th) 385, where the Supreme Court of Canada took a rather more restrictive view of when claims for 'contractual relational economic loss' should be permitted, than in its earlier decision in *Norsk Pacific*, though the position in Canada is still more generous to plaintiffs than in England; for comment, see Duncan Wallace (1998) 114 LQR 370). On the other hand, where the plaintiff can frame his claim in another cause of action, such as nuisance, the position may be different (see, e.g., *British Celanese Ltd* v *A.H. Hunt (Capacitors) Ltd* [1969] 2 All ER 1252).

Secondly, the plaintiff may have a contractual right to use the property for the purposes of his business, but no proprietary interest in it. Damage to the property may put him to the expense of repairing it (depending on the terms of the contract with the third party) and will interfere with his ability to use the property for profitable purposes. In *Candlewood Navigation Corporation Ltd* v *Mitsui OSK Lines Ltd* [1985] 2 All ER 935 the Privy Council upheld a long line of authority that a time charterer of a vessel, with no proprietary interest in the ship, cannot sue for loss of profits during the period when it is being repaired following a collision caused by the defendant's negligence. Their Lordships rejected as unworkable a test for limiting the range of liability for economic loss based on foreseeability of loss to the plaintiff as a particular individual rather than as a member of an unascertained class (cf. *Ross* v *Caunters* [1980] Ch 297, para. 2.2.4.1.4; the test is derived from the judgments of Gibbs and Mason JJ in *Caltex Oil (Australia) Pty Ltd* v *Dredge Willemstad* (1976) 136 CLR 529; see Cane (1977) 93 LQR 333; Thomson (1977) 40 MLR 714; *Leigh & Sillavan Ltd* v *Aliakmon Shipping Co. Ltd* [1985] 2 All ER 44, 75 per Robert Goff LJ). The result is that the owner or charterer by demise of a vessel can recover for such losses, based on *Spartan Steel & Alloys Ltd* v *Martin & Co. (Contractors) Ltd* [1973] 1 QB 27, but a time charterer, who has no proprietary interest in the vessel, cannot (for comment see Jones (1986) 102 LQR 13; and cf. the simpler, possibly simplistic, approach to this issue taken by the British Columbia Court of Appeal, on analogous facts, in *Tri-Line Expressways* v *Ansari* [1997] 5 WWR 342; though see *Bow Valley Huskey (Bermuda) Ltd* v *Saint John Shipbuilding Ltd* (1997) 153 DLR (4th) 385, where the Supreme Court of Canada, without referring to *Candlewood Navigation*, took essentially the same approach as the Privy Council on very similar facts).

Thirdly, the plaintiff may suffer loss as a result of damage to property belonging to a third party where the plaintiff is 'at risk' as to the loss at the time of the damage under a contract with the third party. A typical example of this situation is a contract of insurance. The insurer has no direct right of action against the negligent tortfeasor when he suffers loss by indemnifying the insured for damage to the property covered by the insurance contract, although he is entitled to exercise rights of subrogation under the contract and sue the tortfeasor in the name of the insured (*Simpson & Co.* v *Thomson* (1877) 3 App Cas 279). This principle is not limited to insurance contracts, but will apply to any liability to pay another person for physical damage to his property (see *Esso Petroleum Co. Ltd* v *Hall Russell & Co. Ltd* [1989] 1 All ER 37). It is irrelevant that the plaintiff may have become the owner of the property after it was damaged. In *Leigh & Sillavan Ltd* v *Aliakmon Shipping*

Co. Ltd [1986] 2 All ER 145 the House of Lords affirmed the rule that a plaintiff who was not the owner of property at the time when it was damaged, but subsequently became the owner, could not recover the financial loss attributable to the fact that the property was at his risk when the damage occurred. This was so, even though there was no prospect of indeterminate liability since on the facts of the case there could only be one plaintiff claiming for the cost of the physical damage, and the owner of the goods had no action against the defendants because he had suffered no loss. There were good policy grounds for reaching this conclusion, namely that liability in tort would have disturbed a long-established allocation of commercial risk in circumstances where certainty in the law is particularly important, i.e., carriage of goods by sea.

The rule that a person who is not the owner of property when it is damaged cannot sue in respect of the damage applies generally to all forms of property. This is now subject to the Latent Damage Act 1986, s. 3, which creates a new cause of action for a purchaser of property from the date he acquired his interest in it, provided that the damage was not discoverable by the owner (see para. 14.7.2). This provision was intended to deal with the possibility that purchasers of defective buildings which were the subject of latent damage at the time of purchase would have no cause of action. Its significance in that field is substantially reduced by the decision in *Murphy* v *Brentwood District Council* [1990] 2 All ER 908, but it is not entirely redundant, and it is possible that the facts of *Leigh & Sillavan Ltd* v *Aliakmon Shipping Co. Ltd* might fall within the terms of s. 3 (see Griew (1986) 136 NLJ 1201; Stapleton (1988) 104 LQR 213, 237–8; however, the problem that arose on the particular facts of *The Aliakmon* would not now occur, following the passing of the Carriage of Goods by Sea Act 1992). Another possible solution to this problem is that the purchaser may be able to take an assignment from the vendor of the vendor's rights against third parties in respect of damage to the property, although this is not without its difficulties (see Wallace (1993) 109 LQR 82; *Linden Gardens Trust Ltd* v *Lenesta Sludge Disposals Ltd* [1993] 3 All ER 417; Wallace (1994) 110 LQR 42).

2.2.4.2.2 Economic loss suffered by the plaintiff as a consequence of acquiring a defective item of property In this category the plaintiff owns the property, but it is discovered after he has acquired it that the property has a defect and the plaintiff has to expend money in repairing or replacing it. The defect may be one of quality or it may render the property potentially dangerous, creating a risk of personal injury or damage to other property. It is this category of cases which has produced the most marked shifts of judicial attitudes in relation to claims for economic loss, first in favour of allowing plaintiffs to recover for such losses where the property consisted of a dangerously defective building, then allowing plaintiffs to succeed for the loss where the defect could not be categorised as dangerous, and finally returning to a more orthodox approach in *Murphy* v *Brentwood District Council* [1990] 2 All ER 908, where the House of Lords held that the damage in both cases was purely economic and therefore irrecoverable. In order fully to understand the views expressed by their Lordships in *Murphy*, however, it is necessary to consider the earlier case law, which concentrated largely on claims in respect of defective buildings.

In *Dutton* v *Bognor Regis Urban District Council* [1972] 1 QB 373 the Court of Appeal held that a local authority was liable to a building owner in respect of negligent inspection of inadequate foundations constructed by a builder, in the course of exercising its statutory powers to require compliance with building regulations. The defective foundations resulted in damage to the building itself. On similar, though assumed, facts the House of Lords in *Anns* v *Merton London Borough Council* [1978] AC 728 approved the decision in *Dutton*, holding that a local authority could owe a duty of care to the building owner in so far as the defect or damage constituted a present or imminent danger to the health or safety of the occupants of the building. One of the novel features of both *Dutton* and *Anns* was the nature of the damage. The plaintiffs were complaining, not that they had suffered personal injury nor that the defective dwelling had damaged some other property, but that a defect in the house had damaged the house itself. This was the equivalent of Mrs Donoghue discovering the snail in the ginger beer before drinking it, and then suing Stevenson in tort for the cost of replacing the bottle, in effect succeeding in tort for a defect which, having been discovered, was dangerous neither to herself nor her property. In *Dutton*, however, Lord Denning MR had characterised the plaintiff's loss as physical damage to the house, and in *Anns* Lord Wilberforce said that if classification was required the relevant damage was material physical damage, and the plaintiff could recover the cost of restoring the dwelling to a condition in which it was no longer a danger to the health or safety of the occupants.

On the face of it, the notion of endangering health or safety seems to bring *Anns* within the principle of *Donoghue* v *Stevenson* [1932] AC 562. One interpretation of the loss treats it as a mitigation of the potential physical damage to persons or property that might occur if the premises were left in a dangerous condition. This is 'preventive damage', i.e., the 'expenditure necessary to avert injury to safety or health' (*Peabody Donation Fund* v *Sir Lindsay Parkinson & Co. Ltd* [1984] 3 All ER 529, 535 per Lord Keith). It was arguable, however, that the 'health and safety of the occupants' test constituted a form of economic loss, since it could apply even where there had, as yet, been no physical damage, e.g., where a dangerous defect was discovered before it had caused any physical damage to the building (see Wallace (1978) 94 LQR 60, 66). This became apparent in *Batty* v *Metropolitan Property Realisations Ltd* [1978] QB 554 in which a house was built on land that was liable to landslips. The house was undamaged, though part of the garden had slipped away and the house was likely to suffer the same fate within a few years. The builders were held liable partly on the basis of the (incidental) damage to the garden and partly on the basis of the present or imminent danger to occupants test. The case clearly involved a form of economic loss (see Wallace (1978) 94 LQR 331; *D & F Estates Ltd* v *Church Commissioners for England* [1988] 2 All ER 992, 1013; *Murphy* v *Brentwood District Council* [1990] 2 All ER 908, 918).

In *Junior Books Ltd* v *Veitchi Co. Ltd* [1983] 1 AC 520 the House of Lords went one step further than *Anns*. The defendants were specialists in laying floors. They were the nominated subcontractors under a building contract concluded between the plaintiffs and the main building contractors. The plaintiffs alleged that the defendants had negligently laid a factory floor which, as a result, was defective and they claimed the cost of replacing the floor plus consequential financial loss. There was no allegation that the floor was *dangerously* defective, or that it posed any threat whether imminent or otherwise to the safety of users of the building. This was a defect in *quality*, equivalent to Mrs Donoghue complaining that Stevenson's ginger beer was flat and seeking to sue the manufacturer in tort for the cost of replacing it. The usual remedy for the plaintiffs in this situation would have been to sue the main contractors under the building contract (or in Mrs Donoghue's case to sue the retailer under the contract of sale if she had purchased the ginger beer), who would then seek an indemnity under the subcontract from the defendants. Where, however, the contractual 'chain' is broken for some reason, the plaintiff cannot sue the subcontractors in contract because of the doctrine of privity. The majority of the House of Lords treated the case as a claim in respect of pure economic loss, and on a preliminary point of law held that the defendants did owe a duty of care. The proximity of the relationship between the plaintiffs and the defendants was extremely close: 'almost as close a commercial relationship . . . as it is possible to envisage short of privity of contract' (per Lord Roskill). The defendants were specialists, and as nominated subcontractors they must have known that the plaintiffs would rely on their skill and experience. Moreover, there was no question of indeterminate liability because the plaintiffs were plainly foreseeable as an identified individual likely to be affected by the defendants' negligence.

Junior Books Ltd v *Veitchi Co. Ltd* represented an attempt to establish a general duty of care in respect of pure economic loss resulting from a negligent act, based on the closeness of the relationship between the parties and reliance by the plaintiffs on the defendants' skill and experience. The difficulties that the case created, however, were immediately apparent (see Palmer and Murdoch (1983) 46 MLR 213; Holyoak (1983) 99 LQR 591). Would the manufacturer of chattels now be liable in tort to the ultimate consumer for non-dangerous defects of quality? The decision, said Lord Brandon, dissenting, would impose a non-contractual warranty that goods were as 'well designed and as fit for their contemplated purpose as the exercise of reasonable care could make them'. By what standard of quality would such a duty be measured? A duty not to produce a dangerous product sets a standard which is comparatively simple to determine, but a duty not to produce goods with defects in quality sets a standard which can only be judged by reference to the contract itself, and in a chain of contracts from manufacturer, through distributor and retailer to purchaser, which contract would be relevant? (See, however, Cane (1989) 52 MLR 200, 209–10.) Could a defendant sued in tort rely on an exclusion clause in the contract when sued by a person who was not a party, and therefore traditionally not bound by its terms? Lord Roskill tentatively suggested that, by analogy with the disclaimer in *Hedley Byrne & Co. Ltd* v *Heller & Partners Ltd* [1964] AC 465, the plaintiff would be bound by a suitably drafted exclusion clause,

although this was subsequently doubted by the House of Lords (*Leigh &
Sillavan Ltd* v *Aliakmon Shipping Co. Ltd* [1986] 2 All ER 145, 155; see
further para. 14.2).

The use of the concept of reliance in *Junior Books Ltd* v *Veitchi Co.
Ltd* as a control mechanism for avoiding liability was also suspect. Their Lordships
distinguished the facts of that case from the everyday transaction of purchasing chattels 'when it is obvious that in truth the real reliance was upon the
immediate vendor and not upon the manufacturer' (per Lord Roskill at p.
547). It is far from obvious, however, that consumers place real reliance on
the retailer when, in modern marketing conditions, manufacturers go to great
lengths to promote the quality, reliability and performance of their products,
and in reality reliance on the retailer is often merely a fiction to preserve the
consumers' remedies under the Sale of Goods Act 1979, s. 14 (Palmer and
Murdoch (1983) 46 MLR 213, 217). Reliance was being used in *Junior Books
Ltd* v *Veitchi Co. Ltd* in a different sense from that in *Hedley Byrne & Co. Ltd*
v *Heller & Partners Ltd*. The plaintiffs did not change their position as a result
of anything that the defendants said or did. They relied on the defendants'
skill and experience in just the same way that a client or a patient relies on
the skill of a solicitor or doctor. Used in this way reliance is deprived of much
of its meaning—it simply connotes the reasonable expectation that others will
act with reasonable care, just as road users 'rely' on motorists to drive
carefully (see *Muirhead* v *Industrial Tank Specialities Ltd* [1985] 3 All ER 705,
714–16; Cane (1989) 52 MLR 200, 201–3, 213).

The courts began to retreat from the implications of *Junior Books Ltd* v
Veitchi Co. Ltd almost immediately. In *Tate & Lyle Industries Ltd* v *Greater
London Council* [1983] 1 All ER 1159, 1165 the House of Lords characterised
it, somewhat remarkably, as a case of physical damage. It has repeatedly been
described as limited to its own facts (*Candlewood Navigation Corporation Ltd*
v *Mitsui OSK Lines Ltd* [1985] 2 All ER 935, PC; *Muirhead* v *Industrial Tank
Specialities Ltd* [1985] 3 All ER 705, 715, CA; *Leigh & Sillavan Ltd* v
Aliakmon Shipping Co. Ltd [1986] 2 All ER 145, HL). In *D & F Estates Ltd*
v *Church Commissioners for England* [1988] 2 All ER 992, 1003, 1013 the
House of Lords said that *Junior Books Ltd* v *Veitchi Co. Ltd* was so far
dependent on the 'unique' relationship between the plaintiff and the defendant that it cannot be regarded as laying down any general principle in the law
of tort (though it is unclear how the relationship between a building owner
and a nominated subcontractor under a building contract can be considered
to be 'unique'). The case appears now to have been 'reclassified' by the
House of Lords as a species of liability for negligent statements under *Hedley
Byrne & Co. Ltd* v *Heller & Partners Ltd* [1964] AC 465 (see *D & F Estates
Ltd* v *Church Commissioners for England* [1988] 2 All ER 992, 1013 per Lord
Oliver; *Murphy* v *Brentwood District Council* [1990] 2 All ER 908, 919 per
Lord Keith; cf. Lord Bridge at p. 930), though as Wallace (1991) 107 LQR
228, 242 comments this explanation is 'singularly inappropriate' to the great
majority of ordinary nominated subcontract relationships.

Junior Books Ltd v *Veitchi Co. Ltd* has been distinguished by the Court of
Appeal on a number of occasions. In *Muirhead* v *Industrial Tank Specialities*

Ltd [1985] 3 All ER 705 a manufacturer of electric pumps that were not suitable for use with the United Kingdom voltage was held not liable to the ultimate purchaser for pure economic loss. There was a chain of supply involving at least four intermediary companies, and it could not be said that the plaintiff relied on the manufacturer simply because the suitability of the voltage was of fundamental importance. In *Simaan General Contracting Co.* v *Pilkington Glass Ltd (No. 2)* [1988] 1 All ER 791 it was held that the manufacturers of glass panels were not liable to a main contractor for economic loss caused by the building owner rejecting the panels as defective and withholding payment under the main contract. There was no contractual relationship between the plaintiffs and the defendants, and it was not just and reasonable, said the Court of Appeal, to impose a duty of care in tort which would be inconsistent with the contractual structure under which the panels were supplied. The chain of contractual relationships was deliberately arranged without any direct relationship between the plaintiffs and defendants, and a duty in tort which might be unaffected by the contractual terms would make a 'mockery of contractual negotiation'. Then, in *Greater Nottingham Co-operative Society* v *Cementation Piling & Foundations Ltd* [1988] 2 All ER 971 a building owner sued a subcontractor in respect of the negligent operation of piling equipment which resulted in delay in completing the work and a need for a revised piling scheme. The plaintiffs had entered into a collateral contract with the subcontractor, which required the defendants to exercise reasonable care in designing the piling works and the selection of materials, but was silent on the manner in which the works were to be performed. Even though the relationship between the parties could be said to have been closer than that in *Junior Books Ltd* v *Veitchi Co. Ltd,* because there was a direct contractual link, the Court of Appeal held that there was no duty of care with respect to the economic loss. The parties had had an opportunity to define their legal relationship through the contract, but this was 'significantly silent' about liability for the manner in which the work was executed. Thus, the contractual structure was inconsistent with a duty of care in tort (see further *Pacific Associates Inc.* v *Baxter* [1989] 2 All ER 159; *Norwich City Council* v *Harvey* [1989] 1 All ER 1180, para. 14.2). It is perhaps surprising, in view of subsequent developments in the law, that *Junior Books* has not been overruled by the House of Lords. In practice, however, it is difficult to envisage circumstances in which the decision might be followed, even if it is treated as a form of *Hedley Byrne* liability, particularly since the 'contractual structure' approach has effectively outflanked the case. If the facts of *Junior Books Ltd* v *Veitchi Co. Ltd* were to recur, 'unique' as they are, the court could simply conclude that the parties had had an opportunity to structure their legal relationship through contract, and since they had deliberately chosen not to enter into a direct contractual relationship the law of tort should not be used to add to their respective rights and responsibilities. In *Nitrigin Eireann Teoranta* v *Inco Alloys Ltd* [1992] 1 All ER 854, 861 May J said that it would be 'intellectually dishonest' to attempt to distinguish *Junior Books,* but he simply declined to apply it on the basis that it was unique, and depended upon the *Hedley Byrne* doctrine of reliance, which was not relevant to the facts of *Nitrigin.*

The seeds of *Junior Books Ltd* v *Veitchi Co. Ltd,* it will be recalled, were sown in *Anns* v *Merton London Borough Council* [1978] AC 728 which was concerned with the liability of a local authority for failing to ensure compliance with building regulations in the course of the construction of a building. The effects of *Anns* on the liability of local authorities were gradually restricted as it was made clear that the duty did not apply to property developers (*Peabody Donation Fund* v *Sir Lindsay Parkinson & Co. Ltd* [1984] 3 All ER 529) or non-resident owners, even where there was a present or imminent danger to the health and safety of users of the building (*Investors in Industry Commercial Properties Ltd* v *South Bedfordshire District Council* [1986] 1 All ER 787, 805–6). Nor did the duty apply to the original building owner who, *ex hypothesi,* was himself in breach of the building regulations, even if he relied on independent expert advice and assistance in constructing the building (*Peabody Donation Fund* v *Sir Lindsay Parkinson & Co. Ltd*; *Richardson* v *West Lindsey District Council* [1990] 1 All ER 296). The courts continued, however, to sidestep the question of the nature of the damage suffered by the plaintiff in such actions. Finally, in *D & F Estates Ltd* v *Church Commissioners for England* [1988] 2 All ER 992 the House of Lords began to address the issue in an action against a builder. The defendant builders employed a subcontractor to carry out plastering work in a block of flats. The plaintiffs were lessees and occupiers of one of the flats. Fifteen years after construction they found that the plaster in their flat was loose and sued the builder for the cost of the remedial work. The House of Lords held that this was pure economic loss which was not recoverable in tort. Lord Bridge drew a distinction between a product which causes personal injury or damage to property other than itself, for which liability in tort would follow from *Donoghue* v *Stevenson* [1932] AC 562, and a product which is dangerously defective where the defect is discovered before any such damage is caused. In the latter case there was:

> no longer any room for the application of the *Donoghue* v *Stevenson* principle. The chattel is now defective in quality, but is no longer dangerous. It may be valueless or it may be capable of economic repair. In either case the economic loss is recoverable in contract by a buyer or hirer of the chattel entitled to the benefit of a relevant warranty of quality, but is not recoverable in tort by a remote buyer or hirer of the chattel (at p. 1006).

The same principle applied to a permanent structure which was dangerously defective: 'If the defect is discovered before any damage is done, the loss sustained by the owner of the structure, who has to repair or demolish it to avoid a potential source of danger to third parties, would seem to be purely economic' (ibid.). This appeared to rule out the possibility of 'preventive damage' and so raised serious doubts about *Anns* v *Merton London Borough Council,* in which, it will be recalled, a duty was said to arise when there was a 'present or imminent' danger to health or safety, a test which clearly includes preventive damage. It also left open the question whether physical damage could include damage to the product or building itself. Lord Bridge 'explained' *Anns* by distinguishing between simple and complex structures. It was arguable, he said ([1988] 2 All ER at pp. 1006–7), that:

> in the case of complex structures, and indeed possibly in the case of complex chattels, one element of the structure should be regarded . . . as distinct from another element, so that damage to one part of the structure caused by a hidden defect in another part may qualify to be treated as damage to other property.

It might then be possible to treat cracking walls caused by defective foundations as damage to 'other property' and therefore within the ordinary principles of *Donoghue* v *Stevenson*.

Lord Oliver said that in the case of defective chattels there could be no non-contractual warranty of fitness attached to the goods for the benefit of first or subsequent owners. Thus, the owner of a motor car could not sue the manufacturer of a dangerously defective tyre in tort if the defect was discovered before it burst, or if it burst without causing any damage other than to itself. Under *Anns* v *Merton London Borough Council* such a warranty seemed to apply to the construction of a building, however, and this was explicable only on the basis of Lord Bridge's complex structure hypothesis, treating the constituent parts as distinct items of property. But this reinterpretation of *Anns* did not bring it entirely within the orthodoxy of *Donoghue* v *Stevenson*, because the cause of action accrued when the building becomes a 'present or imminent danger', which does not necessarily depend on damage to the building itself, but rather the perception of potential but avoidable damage to the occupants in the future. This, said Lord Oliver, was either pure economic loss or a new species of the tort of negligence in which actual damage was no longer the gist of the action but was replaced by the perception of the risk of damage (see further Stapleton (1988) 104 LQR 213, 221). *Anns* might be explicable, said his Lordship, if it was understood in terms of an action arising from breach of statutory duty (though this was not the basis on which the House of Lords decided the case), but where there was no question of breach of statutory duty (as on the facts of *D & F Estates Ltd* v *Church Commissioners for England*) a builder should be liable for negligence only where 'actual damage' to person or property resulted from his carelessness in the course of construction. It was anomalous that this could include damage to the defective structure itself, but not in the case of a defective chattel, but this could be accounted for by Lord Bridge's complex structure theory (cf. Lord Bridge who would possibly have included chattels). Damage to the defective part of the structure itself would not be actionable except where it caused damage to a separate part of the structure, when the award of damages could include the cost of repairing the defective part so far as that was necessary to remedy the damage caused to other parts. Thus, 'to remedy cracking in walls and ceilings caused by defective foundations necessarily involves repairing or replacing the foundations themselves' (per Lord Oliver at p. 1012—but query whether this was *necessarily* the case).

The decision in *D & F Estates Ltd* v *Church Commissioners for England* added to the confusion in an already complex area of law (see Wallace (1989)

105 LQR 46; Cane (1989) 52 MLR 200; Ross (1989) 5 PN 11). It was clearly in conflict with *Anns* and it was difficult to reconcile the two decisions in readily comprehensible terms. Moreover, there were inconsistencies between the speeches of Lords Bridge and Oliver, though the other judges agreed with both. The complex structure theory was likely to lead to much litigation, as plaintiffs would inevitably seek to argue that the defect in the building had caused damage to a distinct part of the structure. The Court of Appeal had already had some difficulty distinguishing a plastic pail from its contents in *Aswan Engineering Establishment Co.* v *Lupdine Ltd* [1987] 1 All ER 135, 152, where Lloyd LJ considered that a car could constitute 'other property' if damaged by a defective tyre, as would a bottle of wine if damaged by a defective cork (cf. the Consumer Protection Act 1987, s. 5(2), para. 10.2.5).

In *Murphy* v *Brentwood District Council* [1990] 2 All ER 908 the House of Lords took *D & F Estates Ltd* v *Church Commissioners for England* to its logical conclusion and overruled *Anns*, in so far as it held that local authorities were under a duty of care in tort to avoid damage to property which causes a present or imminent danger to the health and safety of owners or occupiers, arising out of the authorities' function of supervising compliance with building regulations. The plaintiff purchased a newly constructed house in 1970. The plans and calculations for the foundations had been submitted to the local authority for building regulation approval prior to construction, and the council referred the plans and calculations to a firm of consulting engineers for checking, and on their recommendation approved the design under the building regulations. In 1981 the plaintiff discovered that the foundations were defective, and in 1986 sold the house for £35,000 less than its market value had it been in sound condition. He sued the local authority alleging that it was liable in respect of the consulting engineers' negligence in recommending approval of the plans, and claiming that he and his family had been subjected to an imminent risk to their health and safety because gas and soil pipes had broken as a result of differential settlement of the house, and there was a risk of further breaks. A specially constituted House of Lords, consisting of the Lord Chancellor and six Lords of Appeal in Ordinary, held that the local authority were not liable because the cost of remedying a dangerous defect in a building which had become apparent before the defect caused physical injury was economic loss not physical damage, consisting of the expenditure necessary to remedy the structural defect to avert the danger or of abandoning the building as unfit for habitation. (The question of the local authority's liability for personal injuries or damage to property other than the building itself caused by a latent defect was expressly left open by their Lordships: see *Tesco Stores Ltd* v *Wards Construction (Investment) Ltd* (1995) 76 BLR 94, para. 6.3.3.) A dangerous defect, once it was no longer latent, constituted merely a defect in quality, and to allow recovery in tort for a defect in quality would introduce a non-contractual warranty of quality attached to buildings or chattels. This decision was immediately applied by the House of Lords in *Department of the Environment* v *Thomas Bates & Son Ltd* [1990] 2 All ER 943 where a building in which low-strength concrete had been used was found to be incapable of supporting its design load, although it was not dangerous with its existing load. The plaintiffs were not entitled to recover from the builders the cost of remedial work to strengthen the building to enable it to support its design load, because this was economic loss incurred in rectifying a defect in quality.

In *Murphy* v *Brentwood District Council* Lord Bridge repeated his observations in *D & F Estates Ltd* v *Church Commissioners for England* that a manufacturer's liability in respect of products which are merely defective in quality arises only in contract. There is no liability in tort to persons who suffer economic loss because of the defect. The position is the same with a dangerous defect in a chattel which is discovered before it causes any personal injury or damage to property. Once the danger is known, the chattel cannot be safely used unless the defect is repaired, and the defect becomes merely a defect in quality. His Lordship commented ([1990] 2 All ER 908 at p. 927) that:

> If I buy a second-hand car and find it to be faulty, it can make no difference to the manufacturer's liability in tort whether the fault is in the brakes or in the engine, i.e. whether the car will not stop or will not start. In either case the car is useless until repaired. The manufacturer is no more liable in tort for the cost of the repairs in the one case than in the other.

In other words, in these circumstances it is irrelevant whether the defect renders the car dangerously defective or simply defective for its purpose of going from A to B. The same principles applied to buildings. If a dangerous defect becomes apparent before any injury or damage has been caused (the 'present or imminent danger' test) the loss sustained by the building owner is purely economic. Lord Oliver pointed out (at p. 935) that once a dangerous defect ceases to be latent the plaintiff's expenditure in repairing the defect:

> is not expenditure incurred in minimising the damage or in preventing the injury from occurring. The injury will not now ever occur unless the plaintiff causes it to do so by courting a danger of which he is aware and his expenditure is incurred not in preventing an otherwise inevitable injury but in order to enable him to continue to use the property or the chattel.

Lord Keith said that it was difficult to draw a distinction in principle between an article which was useless or valueless and one which suffered from a defect which would render it dangerous in use but which is discovered by the purchaser in time to avert any possibility of injury. 'The purchaser may incur expense in putting right the defect, or, more probably, discard the article. In either case the loss is purely economic' (at p. 918).

It should be noted that the word 'economic' is being used in a particular sense here. A plaintiff whose motor car is damaged by the negligent driving of the defendant will either incur expense in putting right the damage or discard the vehicle, i.e., write it off as uneconomic to repair. This is a paradigm example of *physical damage* to property. It is not called 'economic loss' simply because it costs money to put it right or replace it. The point of *Murphy* is that the 'damage' (discovery of the defect which renders the product useless) has occurred to the product itself, and whether it is a defect which simply makes the product fail to perform as intended (a defect of 'quality'), or whether it is a defect which makes it potentially dangerous to persons or other property (a dangerous defect), or whether it is a defect which causes physical damage to the product itself, either by a gradual deterioration or a catastrophic failure (which could be either a defect of quality or a dangerous defect), it is still categorised as 'economic loss'.

Lord Bridge was prepared to make an exception to the general proposition that there was no duty with respect to dangerous defects which are no longer latent:

> The only qualification I would make to this is that, if a building stands so close to the boundary of the building owner's land that after discovery of the dangerous defect it remains a potential source of injury to persons or property on neighbouring land or on the highway, the building owner ought, in principle, to be entitled to recover in tort from the negligent builder the cost of obviating the danger, whether by repair or demolition, so far as that cost is necessarily incurred in order to protect himself from potential liability to third parties (at p. 926).

Why distinguish a potential liability to adjoining occupiers or users of the highway from the potential liability that an owner of the building might incur to, say, visitors to the building if he continued to use it in its defective condition? Lord Bridge offered no explanation for this, but it can possibly be traced to the fact that the owner can avoid liability to visitors simply by not using the building for its purpose, but he cannot avoid liability to third parties on adjoining land or the highway by not using the building, which will continue to present a danger. In this sense a building is not like a chattel, because it cannot be 'taken out of circulation' quite so easily. Nonetheless, the distinction drawn by Lord Bridge is an extremely fine one, and Lord Oliver was not entirely convinced by it (ibid. at p. 936; see also Sir Robin Cooke (1991) 107 LQR 46, 51–2).

The 'complex structure' theory that Lord Bridge had advanced in *D & F Estates Ltd* v *Church Commissioners for England* as a possible explanation of *Anns* v *Merton London Borough Council* was rejected in *Murphy* v *Brentwood District Council* as artificial. As Lord Bridge himself observed:

> The reality is that the structural elements in any building form a single indivisible unit of which the different parts are essentially interdependent. To the extent that there is any defect in one part of the structure it must to a greater or lesser degree necessarily affect all other parts of the structure. Therefore any defect in the structure is a defect in the quality of the whole (at p. 928; see also per Lord Keith at p. 922 and Lord Jauncey at p. 942).

Thus, damage to a building caused by defective foundations cannot be treated as damage to 'other property' so as to bring it within the orthodoxy of *Donoghue* v *Stevenson*. Lord Bridge distinguished, however, between an integral part of the structure which does not perform its proper function of sustaining the other parts and a distinct item incorporated in the structure which positively malfunctions so as to inflict positive damage on the structure:

> Thus, if a defective central heating boiler explodes and damages a house or a defective electrical installation malfunctions and sets the house on fire, I see no reason to doubt that the owner of the house, if he can prove that the damage was due to the negligence of the boiler manufacturer in the one case or the electrical contractor in the other, can recover damages in tort on *Donoghue* v *Stevenson* principles (at p. 928).

This has nothing to do with a theory about complex structures. The manufacturer of the boiler and the electrical contractor would have been liable for negligently damaging the building even before *Anns*. Lord Jauncey, however, considered the complex structure theory might apply:

> where one integral component of the structure was built by a separate contractor and where a defect in such a component had caused damage to other parts of the structure, e.g., a steel frame erected by a specialist contractor which failed to give adequate support to floors or walls (at p. 942; see, however, the comments of Sir Robin Cooke (1991) 107 LQR 46, 51 and Wallace (1991) 107 LQR 228, 237 on this point).

His Lordship agreed that defects in ancillary equipment such as central heating boilers or electrical installations would be subject to liability under *Donoghue* v *Stevenson* if the defects caused damage to other parts of the building.

The distinction between an integral part of the structure and a distinct item incorporated into the structure, although necessary for the theory of negligence applied in *Murphy,* may not be so easy to draw in practice. If the crucial distinction is between structural and ancillary elements of a building there could be many features of a building which, though essential for its use, are not part of the structure in terms of its overall stability or safety. Moreover, on Lord Jauncey's interpretation the important distinction is not between 'structure' and 'ancillary equipment', but whether different contractors erected the particular 'component' that has failed and the part of the structure that has suffered damage. This could be a matter of pure chance. In *Jacobs* v *Morton* (1994) 72 BLR 92 the plaintiffs' predecessor in title retained the defendants, who were consulting civil and structural engineers, to advise them about remedial work for cracking in their property due to ground movement. The defendants approved the design for the construction of a piled raft foundation and supervised the work which was completed before the plaintiffs acquired the property. After they acquired the property further cracking occurred, caused by heave and the failure of the remedial works to allow sufficiently for this. The only solution was to demolish and rebuild the property. Mr Recorder Jackson QC held that the damage suffered by the plaintiffs constituted damage to property, not economic loss, because it fell within the complex structure exception. Whether any particular case fell within the complex structure exception was a matter of fact and degree taking into account: (1) whether the defective item was constructed by someone other than the main contractor responsible for the construction of the building as a whole; (2) whether the defective item retained its separate identity; (3) whether the defective item had positively inflicted damage on the building (e.g., faulty electrical wiring causing a fire) as opposed to simply failing to perform its function, thus permitting damage to occur; (4) whether the defective item was constructed at a different time from the rest of the building. On this basis the new raft foundation was a distinct item of property which had caused positive damage, and therefore the complex structure exception applied. The judge accepted that the complex structure theory was a limited exception, which should not be allowed to outflank the general principle.

These are not the only difficulties of interpretation that confront the courts when applying *Murphy*. In *Nitrigin Eireann Teoranta* v *Inco Alloys Ltd* [1992] 1 All ER 854 May J drew a distinction between the plaintiffs' knowledge of a defect and the physical damage caused by the defect. The plaintiffs discovered cracking in steel tubing supplied by the defendants and incorporated into a primary reformer in the plaintiffs' chemical plant, but they were unable to discover the cause of the cracking despite reasonable investigation. The cracks were repaired, but subsequently the tubing cracked again, causing an explosion and damaging the plant around the tubing. May J held that the original cracks constituted damage to the property supplied by the defendants and therefore did not give rise to a cause of action since it was economic loss, but that the physical damage to the surrounding plant (which it was accepted was 'other property') was actionable in negligence. Since the plaintiffs were unable to discover the cause of the original cracking they did not have knowledge of the defect which caused the physical damage, and therefore they were not caught by *Murphy*. His Lordship added that even if the plaintiffs had been negligent in failing to discover the cause of the original cracking, the plaintiffs would still have a cause of action in respect of the physical damage to 'other property', subject to a defence of contributory negligence. This statement is, perhaps, surprising given the views clearly expressed in *Murphy* that once a dangerous defect has been discovered it becomes merely a defect in quality which is not actionable in negligence. It is not immediately apparent why a negligent plaintiff, who should have but carelessly failed to discover the dangerous defect, should be in a 'better position' than the diligent plaintiff who did discover the defect and repaired it before it caused any physical damage to other property. The explanation for this difference would appear to be that the careless plaintiff is not entitled to claim for the cost of repairing the defect (i.e., the economic loss), in just the same way that the careful plaintiff is not entitled to claim, but the careless plaintiff's claim is for the *physical damage* caused to other property by the dangerous defect before the defect was in fact discovered, not the cost of repairing the defect. That physical damage is attributable to the original negligence of the defendant (in creating the dangerous defect) and the subsequent negligence of the plaintiff (in failing to discover the defect), but that is not necessarily a good reason to attribute the whole loss to the plaintiff by denying the claim.

This point is even more apparent in a case such as *Targett* v *Torfaen Borough Council* [1992] 3 All ER 27, para. 6.3.3, where the plaintiff knew of the dangerously defective condition of the property throughout, but nonetheless was held entitled to recover for personal injuries when he fell down a flight of steps that had no handrail and was unlit. *Murphy,* said the Court of Appeal, held that there could be no action to recover the cost of making good a defective product which had not yet caused any physical harm, but did not preclude a cause of action for physical damage caused by the defect, even where the plaintiff was aware of the danger. Although *Donoghue* v *Stevenson* depended upon the defective condition of the ginger beer remaining latent, it was not always the case that a reasonable opportunity for inspection of the defective product would exculpate the negligent defendant, where for example the plaintiff was not free to remove or avoid the danger and it was not unreasonable to run the risk.

Murphy v *Brentwood District Council* has not had a good academic or, indeed, judicial press (see Sir Robin Cooke (1991) 107 LQR 46; Stapleton (1991) 107 LQR 249; Wallace (1991) 107 LQR 228; Howarth [1991] CLJ 58; O'Dair (1991) 54 MLR 561; Fleming (1990) 106 LQR 525; Giles and Szyszczak (1991) 11 LS 85; Brown (1990) 6 PN 150; Olowofoyeku (1990) 6 PN 158; cf. Weir [1991] CLJ 24). There is a variety of reasons for this but they can, perhaps, be grouped into three broad bands. First, the general approach to the question of pure economic loss that the decision represents; secondly, the attitude adopted to the specific question of compensation for defective premises; and finally, dissatisfaction with the reasoning process employed by their Lordships to dismiss or even ignore some of the policy issues involved. In *Murphy* Lord Oliver commented (at p. 934) that:

The infliction of physical injury to the person or property of another universally requires to be justified. The causing of economic loss does not. If it is to be categorised as wrongful it is necessary to find some factor beyond the mere occurrence of the loss and the fact that its occurrence could be foreseen. Thus the categorisation of damage as economic serves at least the useful purpose of indicating that something more is required . . .

It is not true, of course, even in cases of physical injury, that the mere occurrence of the damage and the fact that it could be foreseen is sufficient to establish a duty of care, let alone liability (which requires duty, breach of duty and damage which is not too remote). Moreover, it is the assumptions which underlie the first two sentences which require analysis. *Why* do the courts consider that the careless infliction of economic loss does not necessarily require justification? In other words, what are the policy factors at stake? The commonest reason given for excluding such claims from the ambit of a duty of care is the possibility of indeterminate liability. This may justify adopting a clear 'bright-line' rule of no recovery (Stapleton (1991) 107 LQR 249, 256), a rule which creates a degree of certainty in the law even if its application may seem arbitrary. *Spartan Steel & Alloys Ltd v Martin & Co. (Contractors) Ltd* [1973] 1 QB 27 is an example of just such a bright-line rule. The question then arises why claims for economic loss should be precluded when there is no prospect of indeterminate liability, as in a case such as *Murphy v Brentwood District Council?* It cannot simply be a matter of seeking to avoid indeterminate liability.

There has been a marked shift of judicial attitudes, in recent years, to the boundary between contract and tort, with a clear attempt to reassert the primacy of contractual principles in relation to economic loss. Thus, the more orthodox doctrinal approach to the distinction between the role of contract and tort adopted in *Murphy v Brentwood District Council* and *D & F Estates Ltd v Church Commissioners for England* asserts that to allow recovery in tort for a defect in quality would be to introduce a transmissible non-contractual warranty of quality attached to buildings, *and this is impermissible.* Why, it might be asked? Because such a warranty belongs in the realm of the law of contract not tort. But this is mere assertion which does not in itself provide a justification. As Sir Robin Cooke (1991) 107 LQR 46 comments, the common law has in the past been capable of adaptation to the current social needs, without necessarily being ossified into a rigid distinction between contract and tort. It is not that this distinction is unimportant, rather that the doctrinal argument misses the underlying policy issues (see generally Stapleton (1991) 107 LQR 249 on the strategies available). The 'more difficult to explain' tort cases have been recategorised as versions of *Hedley Byrne* (see, e.g., the explanation of *Junior Books Ltd v Veitchi Co. Ltd* and *Pirelli General Cable Works Ltd v Oscar Faber & Partners* [1983] 2 AC 1 given by Lord Keith in *Murphy v Brentwood District Council* [1990] 2 All ER 908, 919) or as anomalous exceptions to the general rule of non-liability (For an alternative analysis of *Junior Books* in a Scottish context see Thomson (1994) 110 LQR 361.) The effect has been to restore the importance of the distinction between negligent statements and negligent conduct in the tort of negligence. However, the logic of this distinction is, in itself, elusive and the underlying policy is obscure (Cane (1989) 52 MLR 200, 213–14). This is most apparent in areas where the distinction breaks down, as with professional liability. The courts apparently have little appreciation of the anomalies that the law now creates by distinguishing between negligent statements and negligent acts (see Stapleton (1991) 107 LQR 249, 277–83).

The overruling of *Anns v Merton London Borough Council* leaves many home-owners without any redress for serious defects in their properties caused by negligence. A rather basic question which the House of Lords chose not to ask in *Murphy* was *should* home-owners be protected from damage to their homes as a result of negligent design or construction by a builder or approval by a local authority? The answer to this question does not necessarily have to depend upon precisely how the loss is characterised. As Sir Robin Cooke (1991) 107 LQR 46, 50 put it: 'Is there much profit in arguing about whether this should be classified as physical damage or purely economic loss?' The underlying issue is a question of social policy. *Anns* patently reflected a policy of consumer protection, particularly given the restrictions subsequently applied to it. In a 'property-owning democracy' the importance attached by the average individual to home ownership suggests that it is a social value to which the courts should give some protection, at least from the consequences of *negligent* conduct, when the individual is not in a position to protect himself against latent defects (Hayes (1992) 12 OJLS 112). First-party buildings insurance may not cover subsidence due to inadequately constructed foundations (see Dugdale (1991) 7 PN 91; and O'Dair (1991) 54 MLR 561, 564), and having a survey conducted at the time of purchase will rarely reveal latent defects. On the other hand, despite judicial concern about the financial impact of liability under *Anns* on impoverished local authorities, in practice the effect on their insurance premiums appears to have been minimal (see Howarth [1991] CLJ 58, 66, n. 33; Olowofoyeku (1990) 6 PN 158, 164). Paradoxically, the courts have accepted that the same economic interests of a home-owner may be worthy of protection if the negligence takes a different form (as in *Smith* v *Bush* [1989] 2 WLR 790, para. 2.2.4.1.3. For an attempt to explain the difference between *Smith* v *Bush* and *Murphy* see Stapleton (1995) 111 LQR 301, 335–7).

Why, it may be asked, should local authorities underwrite negligent builders? Perhaps because they are in a position to check on the work *before it is covered up,* and it is well-known that in the construction industry there are economic pressures to cut corners in the knowledge that defects will probably not come to light immediately (see O'Dair (1991) 54 MLR 561; Wallace (1991) 107 LQR 228). *Murphy* v *Brentwood District Council* (and *D & F Estates Ltd* v *Church Commissioners for England*) ignores or discounts the value of deterrence, particularly in denying recovery for 'preventive damage' where the defect creates a danger of personal injury, and so 'downplays the paramount goal of accident prevention by not encouraging investment for safety before an accident has actually happened' (Fleming (1990) 106 LQR 525, 527; see also Stapleton (1988) 104 LQR 213, 221–4; Cane (1989) 52 MLR 200, 207; see further the dissenting judgment of Laskin J in *Rivtow Marine Ltd* v *Washington Iron Works* (1973) 40 DLR (3d) 530, relied upon by Lord Wilberforce in *Anns,* though described as 'wholly unconvincing' by Lord Bridge in *Murphy*).

If the court had been willing to address such policy issues the 'technical' legal problems could, no doubt, have been resolved. There was no prospect of indeterminate liability under *Anns,* a factor which is significant in denying liability in a case like *Spartan Steel & Alloys Ltd* v *Martin & Co. (Contractors) Ltd* [1973] 1 QB 27. The loss was limited to the damage to the building and it was recoverable only by the owner of the property. Nor did it necessarily follow that chattels would have to be treated in the same way as buildings. Real property and personal property may have different rules applied to them. A consumer may well be able to discard a defective chattel, but in the real world he is probably not in a position to discard his house. 'An owner of an unsafe house, a ship or an aircraft cannot be expected to cease to use them or throw them away like a useless refrigerator or a ginger beer bottle. . .' (Wallace (1991) 107 LQR 228, 235; see also O'Dair (1991) 54 MLR 561, 563). If he cannot afford to repair it, he must continue to live in it exposed to the risk of injury. The point here is that the court had a choice. It was not simply that having identified the 'correct' doctrinal analysis it followed inexorably that the plaintiff must be denied a remedy.

It has been argued that some of the incidental reasons given by their Lordships in *Murphy* did not adequately support the decision to overrule *Anns* (see, e.g., O'Dair (1991) 54 MLR 561; and more generally Markesinis and Deakin (1992) 55 MLR 619). Thus, an assertion that *Anns* constituted an instance of 'judicial legislation' (per Lord Keith at p. 923) simply begs the question of when it is permissible for the courts to intervene to create a new remedy. The same criticism could be directed at *Donoghue* v *Stevenson* which extended the tort of negligence to the manufacturer of a defective chattel. Similarly, the suggestion that consumer protection should be left to Parliament (per Lord Jauncey at p. 943) raises the question: Why? Does this mean that a manufacturer's responsibility for the safety of his products should have been left to Parliament? How can *Smith* v *Bush* [1989] 2 WLR 790, which is patently a 'consumer protection' decision, be explained if this is Parliament's responsibility? Lord Mackay took the view that in the light of the Defective Premises Act 1972 an extension of liability beyond the limits of that legislation was 'not a proper exercise of judicial power' (see also per Lord Bridge at p. 930, Lord Oliver at p. 938 and Lord Jauncey at p. 943). There was no attempt to assess whether the Defective Premises Act 1972 confers adequate protection on 'consumers' (see para. 6.3.3). It is arguable that the Act has only limited application because it imposes a strict obligation in respect of defects in the construction, conversion or enlargement of a dwelling. It says nothing about restricting liability for negligent construction. Moreover, it is possible to discern a Parliamentary policy in favour of the form of liability established by *Dutton* v *Bognor Regis Urban District Council* [1972] 1 QB 373 and *Anns* in the Latent Damage Act 1986, which was enacted specifically to deal with problems of limitation and accrual of actions to subsequent purchasers in such actions. *Murphy* renders this legislation virtually redundant in the context of defective buildings (see para. 14.7.2).

The response of other common law jurisdictions to the question of liability for defective buildings demonstrates that *Murphy* is not necessarily the last word on the subject. Indeed, a series of decisions in the highest courts of Australia, Canada and New Zealand have left English law looking distinctly out of line. In *Invercargill City Council* v *Hamlin* [1996] 1 All ER 756 the plaintiffs sued the local authority in respect of the negligence of a building inspector in approving inadequate foundations, because the original builder had gone out of business. The New Zealand Court of Appeal held the local authority liable in negligence taking the view that *Murphy* did not represent the law in New Zealand on the basis that different circumstances applied in that jurisdiction, because house purchasers relied on the proper exercise of building control supervision by local authorities and the employment of independent surveyors was almost unheard of ([1994] 3 NZLR 513). The Privy Council dismissed the local authority's appeal, holding that local conditions in New Zealand were such that the Court of Appeal was entitled to develop common law principles in a manner that was appropriate. The perception in New Zealand was that community standards and expectations demanded the imposition of a duty of care on the local authority and builders alike to ensure compliance with local building regulations. There was a line of authority based on the linked concepts of control by the local authority of building works through enforcement of by-laws and reliance on that control by purchasers. The Privy Council endorsed that approach taken by the New Zealand courts notwithstanding *Murphy* (see Wallace (1995) 111 LQR 285, commenting on the Court of Appeal decision; and Wallace (1996) 112 LQR 369, for comment on the Privy Council's decision, pointing out, at p. 374, that the 'reliance' drawn upon is a perceived or notional general reliance, rather than a form of *Hedley Byrne* reliance; Martin (1997) 60 MLR 94; James (1996) 12 PN 94). In *Winnipeg Condominium Corporation No. 36* v *Bird Construction Co. Ltd* (1995) 121 DLR (4th) 193 the Supreme Court of Canada held that a builder was liable in respect of defective cladding, parts of which had fallen into the street below, on the basis that there was a real and substantial danger to the occupants of the building. The subsequent owner was entitled to the cost of putting the building back into a non-dangerous condition (the Supreme Court had already followed *Anns* in respect of the local authority's liability in *City of Kamloops* v *Nielsen* (1984) 10 DLR (4th) 641). La Forest J said that persons who participate in the construction of a large and permanent structure which has the capacity to cause serious damage to other persons or property should be held to a reasonable standard of care. The duty in *Bird* does not extend to 'safe but shoddy' work but is limited to dangerous defects, applying Laskin J's dissenting judgment in *Rivtow Marine* (a judgment that had been influential in *Anns*). Thus, it must be foreseeable that the defect would pose a substantial danger to the health and safety of the occupants, but once this state arises the owner can recover for preventive damage: 'Where negligence is established and such defects manifest themselves before any damage to persons or property occurs, they should, in my view, be liable for the reasonable cost of repairing the defects and putting the building back into a non-dangerous state', (per La Forest J at p. 216). As Professor Fleming has observed the English courts' refusal to permit recovery for preventive damage gives plaintiffs no incentives to mitigate potential losses (Fleming (1995) 111 LQR 362, 363. For trenchant criticism of *Bird* see Palmer (1995) 3 Tort L Rev 240; cf. Hoyano (1995) 58 MLR 886, 892 commenting that the Supreme Court was 'entirely justified in concluding that the superior knowledge and expertise of builders dictate that they are in the best position to ensure the reasonable safety of buildings, such that imposition of tort liability will provide an important incentive for care in the construction industry').

In *Bryan* v *Maloney* (1995) 128 ALR 163 the High Court of Australia has gone one step further and held that a builder of a house owes a duty of care in tort to subsequent purchasers with respect even to non-dangerous defects in the construction of the property. It was foreseeable to the builder that negligent construction of a house with inadequate foundations was likely to cause foreseeable economic loss to the owner when the inadequacies in the foundations became apparent, measured by the diminution in value of the property. The only connection between the builder and the subsequent owner was likely to be the house itself, but it was a substantial link. The house is a permanent structure and probably the most significant investment that most people make during their lifetime. The causal proximity between the loss and the builder's negligence was unextinguished by either the lapse of time or change of ownership. The existence of a contract did not prevent a duty of care in tort arising in the performance of the contract. The decision was expressly limited to dwelling-houses, and the court was careful to state that the result should not apply to chattels (for comment see Clifford and Sharp (1995) 3 Tort L Rev 173; Miller [1995] LMCLQ 326; Wallace (1995) 3 Tort L Rev 231; Fleming (1995) 111 LQR 362; Martin (1996) 59 MLR 116). Interestingly, Brennan J dissented, although his Honour would have been willing to adopt the approach of the Supreme Court of Canada in *Bird*, imposing a duty of care in respect of dangerous defects. It was Brennan J's judgment in *Sutherland Shire Council* v *Heyman* (1985) 60 ALR 1 that provided much of the intellectual impetus to the House of Lords' decision to overrule *Anns* in *Murphy*. (See Stychin (1996) 16 LS 387 for an argument that the Commonwealth case law should be used to persuade English courts to fill the 'gap' created by *Murphy*, to permit recovery for dangerous defects.)

2.2.4.3 Nervous shock It is now well established that a tortfeasor who has negligently killed or injured A, or put A in peril of injury or death, may be liable to B for a psychiatric illness resulting from the perception of the events (for a detailed analysis see generally Mullany and Handford, *Tort Liability for Psychiatric Damage*, 1993; and Napier and Wheat, *Recovering Damages for Psychiatric Injury*, 1995). The term 'nervous shock' is used by lawyers to signify a medically recognised psychiatric illness or disorder arising in these circumstances, although the phrase has been described as a 'misleading and inaccurate expression' (*Attia* v *British Gas* [1987] 3 All ER 455, 462 per Bingham LJ; *Alcock* v *Chief Constable of the South Yorkshire Police* [1991] 4 All ER 907, 912, 922). 'Psychiatric damage' encompasses 'all relevant forms of mental illness, neurosis and personality change' (ibid.). This is distinguished from emotional distress or grief which normal individuals may suffer when someone else is injured or killed, though the distinction may sometimes be difficult to draw (see Trindade [1986] CLJ 476). There can be no claim for emotional distress, anguish or grief unless this leads to a positive psychiatric illness, such as an anxiety neurosis or reactive depression, or physical illness, such as a heart attack (*McLoughlin* v *O'Brian* [1982] 2 All ER 298, 311, per Lord Bridge; *Alcock* v *Chief Constable of the South Yorkshire Police* [1991] 4 All ER 907, 925 per Lord Oliver. There is a statutory exception to this rule in the form of damages for bereavement under the Fatal Accidents Act 1976, s. 1A; see para. 15.3.2.3). Thus, a plaintiff involved in a road traffic accident who has sustained no physical injury, but suffered a nervous reaction falling short of an identifiable psychological illness cannot recover damages for 'shock and shaking up' (*Nicholls* v *Rushton, The Times,* 19 June 1992). Normal human emotions, together with their normal physical consequences, do not constitute either psychiatric illness or physical injury (*Reilly* v *Merseyside Regional Health Authority* [1995] 6 Med LR 246). On the other hand, where the plaintiff has suffered mental illness which has been contributed to partly by the defendant's negligence (the plaintiff witnessing the death of a loved one caused by the defendant's negligence) and partly by pathological grief attributable to the death itself the plaintiff is entitled to damages for the mental illness, with no discount for the consequences of the grief and the consequences of bereavement, even though the mental illness was partly caused by the grief (*Vernon* v *Bosley (No. 1)* [1997] 1 All ER 577, CA, applying *Bonnington Castings Ltd* v *Wardlaw* [1956] AC 613, see para. 4.1.2; cf. *Calascione* v *Dixon* (1993) 19 BMLR 97, where the Court of Appeal did distinguish between post-traumatic stress disorder, which was held to be compensatable, being attributable to the events the plaintiff had witnessed, and a pathological grief disorder which could not be causally linked to the immediate aftermath of the accident).

Emotional distress or anguish are compensatable where the plaintiff has sustained *physical injuries,* and will be dealt with through the award of non-pecuniary damages for pain and suffering. If the plaintiff's mental distress or grief exacerbates other physical injuries which the plaintiff sustained in the same incident, preventing the plaintiff from making a recovery as quickly as would otherwise have occurred, this can be reflected in the award of damages for pain and suffering in respect of the physical injuries (*Kralj* v *McGrath* [1986] 1 All ER 54, 62). Moreover, where the plaintiff has sustained physical injury and suffers psychiatric damage as a consequence there is no question of whether a duty of care in respect of the psychiatric damage is owed. It is then regarded as a matter of causation and remoteness, and even where the plaintiff commits suicide as a result of depression brought on by physical injury the death may be actionable as caused by the initial injury (*Pigney* v *Pointer's Transport Services Ltd* [1957] 1 WLR 1121, para. 4.2.2.2).

It is now clear that the plaintiff does not even have to suffer physical injury, provided physical injury was foreseeable, in order to recover for psychiatric illness. In *Page* v *Smith* [1995] 2 All ER 736 the House of Lords, by a majority, held that in the case of a 'primary victim' (i.e., where the plaintiff was involved either mediately or immediately as a participant in the events: see Lord Oliver's classification in *Alcock* v *Chief Constable of South Yorkshire* [1991] 4 All ER 907, discussed below) if personal injury of some kind to the plaintiff was foreseeable the defendant was liable for psychiatric injury sustained as a result of the defendant's negligence, irrespective of whether psychiatric injury was foreseeable. The plaintiff was involved in a road traffic accident of moderate severity but was physically unhurt in the collision. The accident resulted in a recrudescence of myalgic encephalomyelitis (ME) from which he had suffered for about 20 years but which was then in remission. The defendant admitted that he had been negligent but argued that the psychiatric injury (the ME) was unforeseeable and therefore irrecoverable as a head of damage. Their Lordships disagreed. In the case of 'primary victims' of an accident the test was whether the defendant could reasonably foresee that his conduct would expose the plaintiff to the risk of personal injury, whether physical or psychiatric. If the answer was yes, it was irrelevant that physical injury did not occur or that the psychiatric injury was unforeseeable because the plaintiff had an 'eggshell personality'. The defendant had to take his victim as he found him (see para. 4.3.4.1). This treats psychiatric injury as damage of the same type or kind as physical injury. Lord Lloyd commented (at p. 759) that:

> In an age when medical knowledge is expanding fast, and psychiatric knowledge with it, it would not be sensible to commit the law to a distinction between physical and psychiatric injury, which may already seem somewhat artificial, and may soon be altogether outmoded. Nothing will be gained by treating them as different 'kinds' of personal injury, so as to require the application of a different test (see also the comments of Lord Browne-Wilkinson at p. 754).

Lord Ackner while agreeing with the majority opinion of Lord Lloyd on this point, considered (at p. 742) that psychiatric injury *was* foreseeable as a real risk on the facts, applying the principle that the risk could not be said to be so far-fetched or fantastic as to be a 'mere possibility which would never occur to the mind of a reasonable man' (per Lord Dunedin in *Fardon* v *Harcourt-Rivington* (1932) 146 LT 391, 392). The effect of the decision in *Page* v *Smith* is that the distinction between 'primary victims' and 'secondary victims' (where the plaintiff sustains psychiatric illness as a result of witnessing events in which another person is placed at risk of injury by the defendant's negligence) is absolutely crucial in determining the requirements of a duty of care for psychiatric harm. Secondary victims face considerable hurdles in establishing such a duty that primary victims simply do not have to leap. Whether this is a sensible basis upon which to determine who ought to be compensated for sustaining psychiatric harm as a consequence of the defendant's negligence is another matter (for discussion of *Page* v *Smith* see Sprince (1995) 11 PN 124; Trindade (1996) 112 LQR 22; Handford (1996) 4 Tort L Rev 5; Hopkins [1995] CLJ 491).

Historically, the courts have been extremely cautious about admitting claims for psychiatric harm which was not the result of physical injury to the plaintiff. This was partly due to judicial scepticism about the authenticity of psychiatric harm, based to some extent upon doubts about the validity of psychiatry as a medical discipline. The initial fear of a flood of fraudulent claims was gradually replaced with the fear of a multiplicity of genuine claims if the neighbour principle was applied in an unqualified manner to this type of harm. This is reflected in the case law. The first response was to deny any action for psychiatric harm which was not the product of some form of physical impact with the plaintiff. Then in *Dulieu* v *White* [1901] 2 KB 669 the plaintiff succeeded for harm sustained as a result of being put in fear for her own safety by the defendant's negligence. In *Hambrook* v *Stokes Bros* [1925] 1 KB 141 a mother suffered psychiatric injury when she saw a runaway lorry going down a hill and round a bend, where she had just left her three children who were walking to school. She did not see a collision but feared that the lorry may have injured her children, and was subsequently told that there had been an accident with one of the children involved fitting the description of her daughter. A majority of the Court of Appeal held that the defendant driver was liable for the injury if it was induced by what the mother had seen with her own eyes rather than what she had been told. It would be absurd, it was said, not to compensate a mother who suffered psychiatric harm as a result of fearing for her children's safety, when on similar facts another mother could succeed if, not thinking about her children, she was frightened only for her own safety.

Once having admitted the possibility of claims for psychiatric harm by such 'ricochet victims' the courts faced the problem of determining how wide the scope of liability should be drawn. Scepticism about the nature of psychiatric damage and concerns about a possible flood of claims led to more or less strict limits as to who could recover and in what circumstances. Several limiting factors emerged:

(a) The psychiatric injury must have been the product of what the plaintiff perceived with his or her own unaided senses. There would be no action in respect of harm sustained as a result of what the plaintiff was told by others (*Hambrook* v *Stokes Bros* [1925] 1 KB 141; cf. *Schneider* v *Eisovitch* [1960] 2 QB 430—plaintiff injured and knocked unconscious in a road traffic accident in which her husband was killed; she was subsequently informed about the death of her husband, and was held entitled to 'add' her claim for psychiatric damage to the undoubted claim that she had for her own physical injuries). The effect was to limit claims to plaintiffs who were in fairly close physical proximity to the accident, although it was not essential that they had seen the accident itself. In *Boardman* v *Sanderson* [1964] 1 WLR 1317 the plaintiff heard the accident and came upon the scene immediately afterwards; and in *Chadwick* v *British Railways Board* [1967] 1 WLR 912 the plaintiff witnessed the aftermath of a major train crash while assisting in the rescue of the victims.

(b) The nature of the relationship between the accident victim and the person who suffered the psychiatric injury was important. A parent or spouse of the accident victim would more readily be accepted as a person likely to be affected, and accordingly within the range of a duty of care owed by the defendant. On the other hand, a bystander who was a total stranger to the accident victim was likely to be treated as an unforeseeable plaintiff (*Bourhill* v *Young* [1943] AC 92). This was not an invariable rule. In *Chadwick* v *British Railways Board* [1967] 1 WLR 912 the plaintiff was not related to the victims of the train disaster that he witnessed. The fact that he was assisting the victims at the scene and therefore could be regarded as a 'rescuer' undoubtedly influenced the Court of Appeal's decision to accept his claim for psychiatric injury. This is also the explanation of *Wigg* v *British Railways*

Board (1986) 136 NLJ 446 in which a train driver suffered psychiatric injury on seeing the body of a passenger killed by the defendants' negligence. The plaintiff searched the track, found the victim (whom he mistakenly believed was still alive) and attempted to comfort him until medical assistance arrived. More problematic was the case of *Dooley* v *Cammell Laird & Co. Ltd* [1951] 1 Lloyd's Rep 271 in which the cable of a crane snapped and the load being carried fell to the ground. The plaintiff was the crane operator who, seeing the load fall, thought that his fellow employees below would be injured (although no injuries were in fact caused) and suffered psychiatric injury as a consequence. Donovan J held the defendants liable even though there could not be said to be a close emotional tie between the primary 'victims' (the fellow employees) and the plaintiff (see also *Mount Isa Mines Ltd* v *Pusey* (1970) 125 CLR 383, HC of Australia, where the plaintiff suffered psychiatric damage having witnessed serious injuries to a fellow employee, although he also rendered assistance by carrying the injured worker to an ambulance and so might be said to fall within the 'rescuer principle'; *Bechard* v *Haliburton* (1991) 84 DLR (4th) 668 Ontario CA where, following a motor accident in which a motor-cyclist was injured and thrown into the middle of the road, the plaintiff attempted unsuccessfully to warn the defendant to stop his vehicle by screaming and waving her arms, and then saw the defendant's car strike and kill the motor-cyclist; the plaintiff was held to be acting as a 'rescuer' and therefore the defendant was liable for her psychiatric injury).

(c)   In *King* v *Phillips* [1953] 1 QB 429, 441 Denning LJ said that the test of liability for shock is foreseeability of injury by shock, thus separating psychiatric damage from other forms of personal injury as a type of damage. It was apparent, however, that 'foreseeability' was being given a restricted meaning in order to limit the potential number of claimants, first by excluding those who did not witness the event, and thus were not in close physical proximity to the accident, and secondly by (normally) excluding bystanders not related in some way to the accident victim. Moreover, the courts' assessment of what could be regarded as foreseeable tended to be based on a particularly myopic 'reasonable man'. In *King* v *Phillips* itself it was held that a negligent taxi driver who reversed over a child's tricycle would not have been able to foresee the reaction of a mother who witnessed the event from a distance of 70 yards, again suggesting a stringent requirement for *physical* proximity (for criticism see Goodhart (1953) 69 LQR 347. The result on the facts of *King* v *Phillips* would be different today: *McLoughlin* v *O'Brian* [1982] 2 All ER 298, 316; *Alcock* v *Chief Constable of the South Yorkshire Police* [1991] 4 All ER 907, 926). In *Page* v *Smith* [1995] 2 All ER 736, 764 Lord Lloyd said that Denning LJ's dictum in *King* v *Phillips* was wrong in two respects—it was both too wide and too narrow. It is too wide where the plaintiff is a 'secondary victim' because foreseeability of injury by shock is not the sole test. The test was also too narrow where the plaintiff is a 'primary victim', because if the plaintiff was within the range of foreseeable physical injury the defendant must take his victim as he found him.

(d)   When applying the test of foreseeability of injury by shock it has to be demonstrated that the plaintiff is a person of reasonable fortitude and is not unduly susceptible to some form of psychiatric reaction (*Bourhill* v *Young* [1943] AC 92, 110; *McLoughlin* v *O'Brian* [1982] 2 All ER 298, 309), although this rule does not apply where the plaintiff falls into the category of a 'primary victim' since the defendant must take his victim as he finds him (*Page* v *Smith* [1995] 2 All ER 736, 760). This excludes persons who are abnormally sensitive to psychiatric injury. If, however, a person of ordinary fortitude would have sustained psychiatric injury in the circumstances, the particularly sensitive plaintiff can also recover (*Jaensch* v *Coffey* (1984) 54 ALR 417). Moreover, the particularly sensitive plaintiff whose claim succeeds in these circumstances is entitled to damages for the full extent of his injuries, even if they are exacerbated by a predisposition to a psychiatric reaction and thus are more severe than an ordinary individual would have experienced (*Brice* v *Brown* [1984] 1 All ER 997; *Benson* v *Lee* [1972] VR 879; *Bechard* v *Haliburton* (1991) 84 DLR (4th) 668). At one time the position of 'professional rescuers', such as police officers, fire officers or medical staff, was thought to be more problematic. It was arguable that, since it is part of their job to attend scenes involving death and serious injury to others, they should be expected to be rather more 'thick-skinned' than ordinary members of the public when confronted with gruesome sights. Possibly, they could be regarded as having accepted the risk of witnessing such events (para. 14.1). On the other hand, in *Ogwo* v *Taylor* [1987] 2 WLR 988, para. 6.1.3.2, which was not a psychiatric damage case, the House of Lords held that an occupier of premises owes the same duty of care to a fireman fighting a fire at his premises as is owed to any other visitor, although he could reasonably expect a fireman to exercise the ordinary skills of his profession. There was no 'fireman's rule' in English law requiring firemen to accept the ordinary risks incidental to fighting a fire, having claims only in respect of unusual or extraordinary risks. In *Frost* v *Chief Constable of South Yorkshire* [1997] 1 All ER 540, the trial judge held that police officers could not recover for psychiatric damage attributable to witnessing distressing events because they were hardened to events which would cause an ordinary person distress. The Court of Appeal allowed the plaintiffs' appeal, however. Rose LJ cited *Ogwo* v *Taylor* and commented (at p. 550) that: 'if firemen should not be at any disadvantage in relation to compensation for injury . . . there is to my mind no reason why policemen should be at a disadvantage.' Moreover, since rescuers are categorised as 'primary victims' (see the discussion of *Alcock* v *Chief Constable of South Yorkshire*, below) the rule that the plaintiff must be of reasonable fortitude will not apply, at least where the rescuer is exposed to a foreseeable risk of physical injury (applying *Page* v *Smith*). *Frost* now indicates that where there is no risk of *physical* injury to the rescuer, the professional rescuer is in the same position as the volunteer, at least with regard to requirement for 'reasonable fortitude'.

The purpose of these restrictions was to narrow the potential number of claimants. They have been considered by the House of Lords on two further occasions in *McLoughlin* v *O'Brian* [1982] 2 All ER 298 and *Alcock* v *Chief Constable of the South Yorkshire Police* [1991] 4 All ER 907. In *McLoughlin* v

O'Brian the plaintiff's husband and her three children were involved in a road accident caused by the defendant's negligence. One child was killed and her husband and other two children were badly injured. The plaintiff was informed about the accident two hours after the event, and she was taken to the hospital where she was told about the death of her child and saw the injuries to her family in extremely distressing circumstances, before they had been attended to by the medical staff. At first instance it was held that the plaintiff's psychiatric illness was not reasonably foreseeable. The Court of Appeal decided that the shock was foreseeable, but as a matter of policy the defendant did not owe a duty of care to someone who was not at or near the scene of the accident. The House of Lords was unanimous in holding that the plaintiff's claim for psychiatric harm should succeed, but there was a difference of opinion as to the appropriate test of liability.

The central problem was the fact that the plaintiff had not been at the scene of the accident. All members of the appellate tribunals agreed that the illness was readily foreseeable, but the question was whether as a matter of policy there should be some other limit on the duty of care. Lord Wilberforce, with whom Lord Edmund-Davies agreed, adopted an 'aftermath test'. Foreseeability of psychiatric harm was not sufficient. There had to be some additional limits based on:

(a)   The class of persons who could sue—the closer the emotional tie the greater the claim for consideration.

(b)   Physical proximity to the accident, which must be close both in time and space, although this could extend to persons who did not witness the accident but came upon the 'aftermath' of events. By analogy with the 'rescue cases' persons who would normally come to the scene, such as a parent or spouse, would be within the scope of the duty.

(c)   The means by which the psychiatric harm was caused—it must come through the plaintiff's own sight or hearing of the event or its immediate aftermath; communication by a third party would not be sufficient.

Lord Bridge, with whom Lord Scarman agreed, preferred a test based upon foreseeability alone, 'untrammelled by spatial, physical or temporal limits' (per Lord Scarman). The drawing of a line by reference to the criteria suggested by Lord Wilberforce would impose a largely arbitrary limit of liability. The factors identified in the 'aftermath test' would have a bearing on the *degree* to which psychiatric damage was foreseeable, but they would not necessarily preclude a claim. So a bystander of normal fortitude would not normally be foreseeably affected, but if the events were particularly horrific then a spectator might be foreseeably affected (e.g., an uninjured passenger on the train in *Chadwick* v *British Railways Board*). Lord Bridge could see no logic in denying an action to a mother who read a newspaper report of a fire at a hotel where her children were staying, and who subsequently learned of their deaths, simply because 'an important link in the chain of causation of her psychiatric illness was supplied by her imagination of the agonies of mind and body in which her family died, rather than direct perception of the event' (at p. 320). Indeed, this may be a more likely cause of psychiatric damage than witnessing the events (Teff (1983) 99 LQR 100, 107).

It was not clear whether Lord Russell was in favour of a test based on foreseeability of injury by psychiatric damage *simpliciter,* or whether liability should be restricted by arbitrary factors such as the physical circumstances of the manner in which it occurred. Policy considerations were 'rooted in a fear of floodgates opening', an argument with which his Lordship was not impressed.

Following *McLoughlin* v *O'Brian* it was at least arguable that liability for psychiatric harm had been brought within the mainstream of the neighbour principle, depending upon foreseeability of psychiatric harm alone. For example, in *Wigg* v *British Railways Board* (1986) 136 NLJ 446 Tucker J said that the plaintiff could be described as a 'rescuer', but that this was unnecessary since the psychiatric illness was reasonably foreseeable, and that was the 'fundamental question in each case'. In *Jaensch* v *Coffey* (1984) 54 ALR 417 the High Court of Australia, on very similar facts to *McLoughlin* v *O'Brian,* held that reasonable foreseeability of some recognisable psychiatric illness induced by shock was sufficient. Brennan J commented that the cases reflected a growing contemporary acceptance of the foreseeability of shock-induced psychiatric illness (although it has been suggested that here foreseeability still had a 'coded meaning': see Kidner (1987) 7 LS 319, 325).

In *Attia* v *British Gas* [1987] 3 All ER 455 the plaintiff sustained psychiatric illness as a result of witnessing a fire which caused extensive damage to her home, although there were no personal injuries to anyone else and the plaintiff had not been at risk of physical injury to herself. On a preliminary point of law, the Court of Appeal held that the illness could not be regarded as unforeseeable *as a matter of law;* rather it was a question of fact on the medical evidence to be given at trial whether the psychiatric damage was reasonably foreseeable. Since the defendants undoubtedly owed the plaintiff a duty of care not to inflict physical damage to her house, the question of liability for psychiatric injury was a matter of remoteness of damage rather than duty of care. With respect, the existence of a duty of care with regard to one type of damage says nothing about a duty of care in relation to a different type of damage. In *Caparo Industries plc* v *Dickman* [1990] 1 All ER 568, 599 Lord Oliver observed that 'the duty of care is inseparable from the damage which the plaintiff claims to have suffered from its breach. It is not a duty to take care in the abstract but a duty to avoid causing to the particular plaintiff damage of the *particular kind* which he has in fact sustained' (emphasis added; see also per Lord Bridge at p. 581). So, for example, a duty in respect of 'pure economic loss' cannot be inferred from the fact that a duty was owed not to cause physical harm (see *Spartan Steel & Alloys Ltd* v *Martin & Co.* [1973] 1 QB 27, para. 2.2.4.2). Psychiatric harm has always been treated as a distinct type of damage, distinct even from other forms of personal injury. The effect of 'piggy-backing' the duty as in *Attia* is to make it much easier to overcome the threshold of foreseeability.

If witnessing damage to property could give rise to an action for psychiatric injury, it was difficult to see what policy grounds could possibly justify denying liability where a plaintiff sustained foreseeable psychiatric injury as a result of being told about the death or injury of a loved one, even if the plaintiff did not witness Lord Wilberforce's 'aftermath'. Why, for example, should a mother who is informed of the death of her husband and children but who does not witness the 'aftermath' of the events fail in a claim for psychiatric harm? (see, e.g., *Jaensch* v *Coffey* (1984) 54 ALR 417, 463; Trindade [1986] CLJ 476, 484–5). Given that, from a medical viewpoint, the crucial determinant of whether a plaintiff is likely to suffer psychiatric harm is almost invariably the nature of his or her relationship with the accident victim (see Teff (1983) 99 LQR 100), foreseeability *simpliciter* should be easily satisfied in such a case. The logic of the foreseeability test was applied in *Hevican* v *Ruane* [1991] 3 All ER 65, where Mantell J held that a plaintiff who had identified his son's body at the mortuary was entitled to succeed for psychological trauma following the death, although he was not present at the scene of the accident or the aftermath. The trauma was foreseeable as a likely consequence of the defendant's negligence, and this was sufficient. This was taken a stage further in *Ravenscroft* v *Rederiaktiebolaget Transatlantic* [1991] 3 All ER 73 where a mother who had been called to the hospital, and on arrival was informed by her husband that her son was dead, was held entitled to succeed for a reactive depression, not having even seen her son's body.

In *Alcock* v *Chief Constable of the South Yorkshire Police* [1991] 4 All ER 907 the central issue was the status of the decision in *McLoughlin* v *O'Brian*: did it establish a test of liability based on foreseeability of psychiatric harm alone, or were there additional policy factors that had to be taken into account in determining the ambit of liability? Actions for psychiatric damage were brought against the police arising out of the Hillsborough stadium disaster in April 1989, where 95 people were killed and over 400 injured by crushing when too many people were allowed to crowd into a confined area of the football stadium. The events were shown in a live television broadcast, and some scenes were repeated in news broadcasts. The actions were brought by 16 people, some of whom were at the stadium but not in the area where the disaster occurred, and some of whom identified bodies at the mortuary. All the plaintiffs were relatives, or in one case a fiancée, of people who were in the disaster area, but none of them were either a spouse or parent of the victims. The police admitted liability for negligence in respect of those who were killed and injured in the disaster, but denied that they owed a duty of care to the plaintiffs. On the assumption that the plaintiffs had suffered psychiatric illness, the question of whether the plaintiffs were owed a duty of care was tried as a preliminary issue. The plaintiffs argued that reasonable foreseeability of the risk of injury to them, in the form of psychiatric illness, was all that was required. The House of Lords, applying Lord Wilberforce's 'aftermath test', dismissed the plaintiffs' actions. Psychiatric harm arising from the apprehension of physical injury or the risk of physical injury to another person was actionable only if the plaintiff satisfied *both* the test of reasonable foreseeability that he would be affected by psychiatric illness, because of his close relationship of love and affection with the accident victim, *and* the test of proximity of relationship to the tortfeasor in terms of a physical and temporal connection between the plaintiff and the event.

Lord Oliver said that 'nervous shock' cases could be divided broadly into two categories: (a) cases in which the injured plaintiff was involved, either mediately or immediately, as a participant ('primary victims'); and (b) those in which the plaintiff was simply a passive and unwilling witness of injury caused to others ('secondary victims'). Cases falling into the first category included: *Dulieu* v *White & Sons* where the plaintiff was put in fear for her own safety; *Schneider* v *Eisovitch,* where the plaintiff was told that her husband had been killed, but she herself was directly involved as a victim suffering physical injuries in the accident in which her husband was killed; and the 'so-called "rescue cases"' such as *Chadwick* v *British Railways Board.* These were all cases where the plaintiff was, to a greater or lesser degree, personally involved in the incident out of which the claim arose, either through the direct threat of bodily injury to the plaintiff or by coming to the aid of others injured or threatened. Lord Oliver placed into the same category cases such as *Dooley* v *Cammell Laird & Co. Ltd* [1951] 1 Lloyd's Rep 271 and *Wigg* v *British Railways Board* (1986) 136 NLJ 446 on the basis that the negligent act of the defendant had put the plaintiff in the position of being, or thinking that he was about to be or had been, the involuntary cause of another's death or injury, and the illness stemmed from the shock to the plaintiff of the consciousness of this supposed fact. Here, the fact that the defendant's negligent conduct had foreseeably put the plaintiff in the position of being an unwilling participant in the event was sufficient to establish a proximate relationship between them. The principal question then was simply whether injury of that type to that plaintiff was reasonably foreseeable.

Now, following *Page* v *Smith* [1995] 2 All ER 736, the *type* of damage that has to be reasonably foreseeable where the plaintiff falls within this category as a 'primary victim' has been broadened. If the plaintiff was in the area of physical danger such that physical injury to the plaintiff was foreseeable it is irrelevant that psychiatric harm may not have been foreseeable (though defining the 'area of physical danger' may raise nice questions of fact: see *McFarlane* v *E.E. Caledonia Ltd* [1994] 2 All ER 1). The defendant must take the plaintiff as he finds him with respect to his 'eggshell personality'. This would cover cases such as *Schneider* v *Eisovitch* and, probably, *Dulieu* v *White* (although in *McFarlane* v *E.E. Caledonia Ltd* [1994] 2 All ER 1, 10 the Court of Appeal considered that *Dulieu* fell into a category of 'primary victims' where the plaintiff was not actually in danger, but because of the sudden and unexpected nature of the event, in the agony of the moment, he reasonably thinks that he is). Clearly, in many instances if physical injury was foreseeable then so also will psychiatric harm be foreseeable. However, the practical effect of *Page* v *Smith* will not be limited to those rare cases where the plaintiff's psychiatric damage was unforeseeable in circumstances where physical injury, though foreseeable, has not occurred. It removes from debate all those cases where there was doubt about the foreseeability of the psychiatric damage. Provided that some physical injury to the plaintiff was foreseeable, damages for the psychiatric harm will be recoverable. This simple, indeed some would argue simplistic, analysis will deal with most cases falling within Lord Oliver's category of 'primary victim', but not all. In some of the rescue cases it may be stretching the imagination to suggest that the 'rescuer' was in danger of foreseeable physical harm. This is probably true of *Chadwick* v *British Railways Board*. Similarly, in cases where the plaintiff's categorisation as a primary victim depends upon having been an involuntary participant in the events, as in *Dooley* v *Cammell Laird & Co. Ltd* where the plaintiff was clearly not in physical danger himself, there may well be no foreseeable physical injury to the plaintiff. In these circumstances the plaintiff will have to prove that the psychiatric harm was itself foreseeable.

In *Hunter* v *British Coal Corp.* [1998] 2 All ER 97, Brooke LJ identified three categories of 'primary victim':

(a)   those who are caused to fear physical injury to themselves;
(b)   those who come to the rescue of the injured; and
(c)   those who believe that they are about to be, or have been, the involuntary cause of another's death or injury.

The Court of Appeal held that a plaintiff who was not himself at risk of physical injury, and was not a rescuer, could not be categorised as a 'primary victim' simply because he considered himself responsible, incorrectly, for the death of a workmate. The plaintiff was 30 metres from a water hydrant when it exploded. He ran from the immediate vicinity to find a stop valve to turn the water off. He only discovered that his workmate had been killed 15 minutes later when informed by another worker. This did not fall into the third category of 'primary victim' because the plaintiff's psychiatric illness was an abnormal reaction to the news of his colleague's death, triggered off by his own irrational feeling of responsibility. His belief that he was responsible for the death had to be a reasonable belief. Similarly, in both *McFarlane* v *E.E. Caledonia Ltd* [1994] 2 All ER 1 and *Hegarty* v *E.E. Caledonia Ltd* [1997] 2 Lloyd's Rep 259, the plaintiffs genuinely believed that they were in danger of physical injury to themselves (indeed, they believed that they were going to die) but the Court of Appeal held that, on the particular facts, their belief was irrational. Brooke LJ said that: 'The law does not, however, accommodate people who are not directly threatened but who genuinely and irrationally believe they are, because their dilemma is not reasonably foreseeable' (*Hegarty* v *E.E. Caledonia Ltd*, at p. 271).

In *Alcock* Lord Oliver took the view that cases involving 'primary victims' were relatively straightforward. His second category of cases, where the psychiatric injury was attributable simply to witnessing the misfortune of another person in an event by which the plaintiff was not personally threatened or in which he was not directly involved as an actor, required a more complex analysis, however. Their Lordships in *Alcock* identified four essential elements in claims by 'secondary victims':

(a)   *The nature of the relationship between the plaintiff and the primary victim*   In the Court of Appeal it had been held that the class of persons who could sue was restricted to spouses and persons in a parent/child relationship to the accident victim (*sub. nom. Jones* v *Wright* [1991] 3 All ER 88). More remote relationships (such as brother/sister, uncle-aunt/nephew-niece, grand-children/grandparents, and fiancés) were excluded on the basis that such relations would possess the customary fortitude and phlegm. In the House of Lords it was held that the class of persons to whom a duty could be owed was not limited by reference to a particular relationship, such as husband and wife or parent and child, but it must be within the defendant's contemplation as foreseeable. The crucial factor was the existence of a relationship between the accident victim and the plaintiff which involved close ties of love and affection. There was a rebuttable presumption that such ties would be present between spouses and in the parent/child relationship, though they could be present in other family relationships or those of close friendship, and may be stronger in the case of engaged couples than in that of persons who have been married to each other for many years (per Lord Keith at p. 914). The closeness of the tie would have to be proved by a plaintiff. This is unfortunate. The spectacle of a detailed enquiry into the emotional ties of love and affection between relatives is unedifying, and, moreover, unnecessary given that the plaintiff has to prove that he has suffered a genuine psychiatric illness in very specific and restrictive circumstances.

Psychiatric injury to a bystander unconnected with the accident victim would not ordinarily be reasonably foreseeable, but Lords Keith, Ackner and Oliver contemplated the possibility that a bystander who suffered psychiatric harm after witnessing a particularly horrific catastrophe close to him might be entitled to claim damages from the person whose negligence caused the catastrophe, if a reasonably strong-nerved person would have been so affected. Lord Ackner (with whom Lord Oliver agreed) gave the example of a petrol tanker careering out of control into a school in session and bursting into flames, as one where a potential claim by a passer-by, so shocked at the scene as to suffer psychiatric illness, could not be ruled out. It is not clear, however, how a bystander could be regarded as being foreseeably affected in these hypothetical circumstances when their Lordships concluded that *relatives* of the victims who were present in the stadium were not within the reasonable contemplation of the defendant in *Alcock* as they watched the catastrophic events at Hillsborough unfold (Nasir (1992) 55 MLR 705, 710). This point is further emphasised by the decision of the Court of Appeal in *McFarlane* v *E.E. Caledonia Ltd* [1994] 2 All ER 1, where it was held that no duty was owed to a person of ordinary fortitude who witnessed at close range the 'horrific catastrophe' of the *Piper Alpha* oil rig disaster in which 164 men died. In any event the plaintiff was not in fact a person of ordinary fortitude, although the same result was reached in *Hegarty* v *E.E. Caledonia Ltd* [1997] 2 Lloyd's Rep 259, where the plaintiff, who was on the same support vessel as Mr McFarlane and witnessed similar events, was found to be a person of ordinary fortitude. Both plaintiffs were 'mere bystanders' on a vessel which, though close to being in danger, was never actually in danger. This tends to suggest that a 'mere bystander' outside the area of danger could never recover, despite the dicta in *Alcock* (for comment on *McFarlane* see Tan Keng Feng (1995) 111 LQR 48; Oughton and Lowry (1995) 46 NILQ 18). Of course, if they had been in the actual area of danger such that physical injury was foreseeable they would have been entitled to claim for unforeseeable psychiatric harm, applying *Page* v *Smith* [1995] 2 All ER 736.

(b)   *The proximity of the plaintiff to the accident or its immediate aftermath*   This was the second element of Lord Wilberforce's test in *McLoughlin* v *O'Brian*, requiring proximity of the plaintiff to the accident to be close, in both time and space. In *McLoughlin* the requirement that the plaintiff be at the scene of the accident was extended to the 'immediate aftermath', which was held to include seeing the victims at the hospital two hours later, before they had been properly attended to by medical staff. In *Jaensch* v *Coffey* (1984) 54 ALR 417, 462–3 Deane J said that the 'aftermath' extended to the hospital to which the injured person was taken, and persisted for so long as he remained in the state produced by the accident up to and including immediate post-accident treatment. In *Alcock* their Lordships refused to extend the meaning of 'immediate aftermath' to include the identification of a victim's body at a mortuary some eight or nine hours after death. This failed the test on the ground that even if the identification could be described as part of the 'aftermath', it could not be described as part of the 'immediate aftermath' (per Lord Ackner at p. 921). *McLoughlin* was a case 'upon the margin' of what was acceptable as the aftermath. But as Teff (1992) 12 OJLS 440, 446 comments: 'Invidious distinctions are inevitable when the "immediate aftermath" is treated in isolation, as a crude notion of temporal proximity'.

Lord Jauncey said that to attempt a comprehensive definition of the 'immediate aftermath' would be a fruitless exercise. His Lordship emphasised that in *McLoughlin* v *O'Brian* the victims were waiting to be attended to, and were in very much the same condition as they would have been had the plaintiff found them at the scene of the accident, a point that had been stressed by the Court of Appeal in distinguishing Mrs McLoughlin's visit to the hospital from the visits to the mortuary. The scene at the hospital was 'part of the catastrophe itself for none of the victims had been cleaned up or attended to' (*Jones* v *Wright* [1991] 3 All ER 88, 97, 123 per Parker and Nolan LJJ, respectively). Moreover, the visits to the mortuary were not made for the purpose of rescuing or giving comfort to the victim but purely for the purpose of identification (see also *Taylor* v *Somerset Health Authority* [1993] 4 Med LR 34; [1993] PIQR P262 where the plaintiff was informed by medical staff at a hospital that her husband was dead, and shortly afterwards she identified his body in the mortuary. Auld J held that the plaintiff did not witness the 'immediate aftermath' of the events; the purpose of the visit to the mortuary was to confirm the information that her husband was dead, and settle her disbelief; accordingly the defendants were not liable for her psychiatric illness, applying *Alcock*). The emphasis on the fact that in *McLoughlin* the victims had not been cleaned up or attended to by medical staff when the plaintiff saw them makes too much hang on an entirely arbitrary circumstance. Should liability for psychiatric harm depend upon a race between the plaintiff and the ambulance? (see the comment of Brennan J in *Jaensch* v *Coffey* (1984) 54 ALR 417, 439).

(c)   *The means by which the plaintiff perceived the events or received the information*   Their Lordships in *Alcock* confirmed that a plaintiff must either see or hear the event or its immediate aftermath. Psychiatric damage induced by communication of events by a third party was outside the ambit of liability. In *McLoughlin* v *O'Brian* Lord Wilberforce had contemplated the possibility that watching a live television broadcast might satisfy the requirements of proximity, without expressing any concluded view. In *Alcock* it was held that since the scenes broadcast on television did not depict the suffering of recognisable individuals, this being excluded by the broadcasting code of ethics (a fact known to the defendant), the viewing of these scenes could not be equated with the plaintiff being within sight or hearing of the event or its immediate aftermath. Although the television pictures certainly gave rise to feelings of the deepest anxiety and distress, it was equivalent to being told about the events by a third party, and therefore it was excluded from the ambit of compensation.

In the Court of Appeal ([1991] 3 All ER 88, 122) Nolan LJ did not exclude the possibility, in principle, of a duty of care extending to the viewers of a television programme:

> If a publicity seeking organisation made arrangements for a party of children to go up in a balloon, and for the event to be televised so that their parents could watch, it would be hard to deny that the organisers were under a duty to avoid mental injury to the parents as well as physical injury to the children, and that there would be a breach of that duty if through some careless act or omission the balloon crashed.

Both Lord Ackner and Lord Oliver agreed that simultaneous broadcasts of a disaster could not always be ruled out as providing the equivalent of the actual sight or hearing of the event or its immediate aftermath. The circumstances outlined by Nolan LJ was one example: 'Many other such situations could be imagined where the impact of the simultaneous television pictures would be as great, if not greater, than the actual sight of the accident' (per Lord Ackner at p. 921). It is not entirely clear, however, why the impact of viewing the events at Hillsborough should have been thought to be less significant. Their Lordships did not identify the factors that were thought to be relevant to the severity of the 'impact'.

The correctness of the decisions in both *Hevican* v *Ruane* [1991] 3 All ER 65 and *Ravenscroft* v *Rederiaktiebolaget Transatlantic* [1991] 3 All ER 73 was doubted in *Alcock*, 'since in both of these cases the effective cause of the psychiatric illness would appear to have been the fact of a son's death and the news of it' (per Lord Keith at p. 915; see also per Lords Ackner and Oliver at pp. 917 and 932 respectively). *Ravenscroft* was subsequently reversed on appeal, on the ground that the plaintiff's illness had not come about through sight or hearing of the relevant event or its immediate aftermath, applying *Alcock* (see [1992] 2 All ER 470n; Steele (1993) 56 MLR 244).

(d) *The manner in which the psychiatric illness was caused* The term 'nervous shock' itself tends to suggest that the plaintiff's psychiatric illness must be caused by a single event, which in colloquial terms can be regarded as 'shocking', notwithstanding that medical understanding of the mechanisms by which psychiatric injury may occur does not correspond with this approach. In *Alcock*, Lord Keith said that the scenes witnessed on television could not reasonably be regarded as giving rise to shock, in the sense of a sudden assault on the nervous system. Lord Ackner agreed (at p. 917) that:

> Even though the risk of psychiatric illness is reasonably foreseeable, the law gives no damages if the psychiatric injury was not induced by shock. Psychiatric illnesses caused in other ways, such as from the experience of having to cope with the deprivation consequent upon the death of a loved one, attracts no damages. Brennan J in *Jaensch's* case (1984) 54 ALR 417 at 429 gave as examples: the spouse who has been worn down by caring for a tortiously injured husband or wife and who suffers psychiatric illness as a result, but who, nevertheless, goes without compensation; a parent made distraught by the wayward conduct of a brain-damaged child and who suffers psychiatric illness as a result also has no claim against the tortfeasor liable to the child.

'Shock' meant the sudden appreciation by sight or sound of a horrifying event, which violently agitates the mind. It did not include psychiatric illness caused by the accumulation over a period of time of more gradual assaults on the nervous system (at p. 918; see also *Rhodes* v *Canadian National Railway* (1990) 75 DLR (4th) 248, 298; *Dube (Litigation Guardian of)* v *Penlon Ltd* (1994) 21 CCLT (2d) 268; *Campbelltown City Council* v *Mackay* (1989) 15 NSWLR 501, 503; cf. *Beecham* v *Hughes* (1988) 52 DLR (4th) 625 BCCA). This requirement seems to be based on an 'outmoded scientific view' about the causal mechanism for suffering psychiatric harm (*Campbelltown City Council* v *Mackay* (1989) 15 NSWLR 501, 503 per Kirby P) and, given that the legal expression 'nervous shock' has been described as inaccurate and misleading, it is undoubtedly artificial to re-introduce the notion of 'shock' as an element in the chain of causation (*Ravenscroft* v *Rederiaktiebolaget Transatlantic* [1991] 3 All ER 73, 77–8 per Ward J).

The requirement of a specific 'shocking' event results in the drawing of fine distinctions which are simply not defensible. In *Sion* v *Hampstead Health Authority* [1994] 5 Med LR 170 the plaintiff was unable to recover for psychiatric illness allegedly caused by sitting at his 23-year-old son's hospital bedside for 14 days, as his son gradually deteriorated and eventually died. There was no 'sudden appreciation by sight or sound of a horrifying event, which violently agitates the mind'. There was a process, said the Court of Appeal, which continued for some time, from first arrival in the hospital to the appreciation, after the inquest, that there may have been medical negligence. The son's death, when it occurred, was not surprising but expected (see also *Taylorson* v *Shieldness Produce Ltd* [1994] PIQR P329, where the parents of a 14-year-old boy who had been crushed under a vehicle went to the hospital where he was being treated and stayed with him in hospital for two days, until he died. The Court of Appeal held that the events were not sufficiently immediate: the parents' psychiatric illnesses grew out of a whole sequence of events extending over an appreciable period of time, not 'one shocking event', and accordingly there could be no liability). On the other hand, in *Tredget* v *Bexley Health Authority* [1994] 5 Med LR 178 the parents of a child born with serious injuries as a result of medical negligence, from which it died two days later, were held entitled to recover in respect of their psychiatric illness. The defendants disputed that the parents' psychiatric illness was the result of 'shock', as opposed to stress, strain, grief or sorrow from either a gradual or a retrospective realisation of events. The judge concluded that it was unrealistic to isolate the delivery as an event from the other sequence of happenings. Although lasting for over 48 hours from the onset of labour to the death, 'this effectively was one event'. The birth, with its 'chaos' or 'pandemonium', the sense that something was wrong, and the arrival of the child in a distressed condition requiring immediate resuscitation, was frightening and horrifying for the parents. The parents were also participants in the events rather than passive witnesses. These fine distinctions between the precise circumstances of particular plaintiffs are impossible to justify on principle, and reflect a continuing concern to place arbitrary limits, for policy reasons, on the scope of recovery for psychiatric harm (see Teff (1996) 4 Tort L Rev 44 for cogent criticism of the 'sudden shock' requirement).

It is clear that the law on liability for negligently inflicted psychiatric harm is dictated largely by policy factors which have little or no basis in logic or, indeed, medical understanding of the causes of psychiatric harm (see Teff (1992) 12 OJLS 440, 442 who points out that generally speaking it is the closeness of the *actual* bond between plaintiff and primary victim which is the key indicator of whether psychiatric illness will ensue. Focusing on precisely how the shock is experienced is 'artificial'). Lord Oliver commented that he could not 'regard the present state of the law as either entirely satisfactory or as logically defensible'. But it is not obvious what policy factors motivate the judgments. Is it fear of fraudulent claims or fear of a flood of genuine claims (see Davie (1992) 43 NILQ 237, 261; Hedley [1992] CLJ 16, 19; see, however, *Frost* v *Chief Constable of South Yorkshire* [1997] 1 All ER 540, 565, per Henry LJ dismissing the risk of fraudulent claims as no greater than that from cases involving back injuries 'where there is often a wide gap between observable symptoms and complaints')? Is it that the courts do not trust the medical profession to make the correct diagnosis or that they refuse to acknowledge the growing understanding of the causes of traumatic psychiatric harm, being imprisoned by intuitive, but mistaken, thinking about causal mechanisms (Teff (1992) 32 Med Sci & Law 250; on post-traumatic stress disorder see Weller (1993) 143 NLJ 878; O'Brien [1994] JPIL 257; Turnbull [1997] JPIL 234; and the Court of Appeal's discussion of the condition in *Vernon* v *Bosley (No. 1)* [1997] 1 All ER 577; Law Commission, *Liability for Psychiatric Illness*, Law Com. No. 249, 1998, paras 3.4–3.14)? For 'secondary victims' *Alcock* enshrines a restrictive test of liability, requiring positive psychiatric harm which is caused by witnessing in person a sudden, horrific event, with the plaintiff present at the scene or immediate aftermath, and having a close emotional tie with the primary victim. But policy does not *dictate* that a plaintiff's entitlement to compensation should hang on fine distinctions about how soon he managed to arrive at the aftermath, how precisely he learned of the events, how horrific the catastrophe was, or whether the psychiatric illness was the product of an immediate emotional response or a gradual realisation of the nature of the event or its consequences. Nor can it be acceptable that plaintiffs with genuine psychiatric illness should be denied compensation, for example, because they did not see the 'immediate' aftermath of traumatic events, but that others might be compensated for witnessing the destruction of their property (distressing though that may be). *Attia* v *British Gas* [1987] 3 All ER 455 was cited in argument in the House of Lords but their Lordships did not refer to it in their speeches. Lord Oliver doubted (at p. 932; see also Lord Ackner at pp. 917–18) whether a claim would be entertained as a matter of law in a case where the accident victim was the negligent defendant himself and the psychiatric harm to the plaintiff arose from witnessing the victim's self-inflicted injury. If so, said his Lordship, 'the limitation must be based upon policy rather than logic'. One wonders what policy could dictate such an illogical result, which would be even more anomalous where the accident victim's injuries were partially contributed to by the negligence of another defendant, who would, presumably, be liable for the plaintiff's psychiatric harm.

These objections might be overcome if *Alcock* had succeeded in fixing a 'bright-line' rule, which increased certainty in the law. Unfortunately, it does not even achieve this, leaving considerable scope for drawing fine distinctions about the meaning of the 'aftermath', the closeness of the emotional tie between plaintiff and accident victim, how suddenly the emotional reaction occurred or how horrific the events were. Even the distinction between primary and secondary victims can be difficult to draw in practice. When, precisely, is a person acting as a 'rescuer'? Following the decision in *Alcock* a number a claims brought by police officers who were actually on the terraces at Hillsborough dealing with the dead and injured were settled with the payment of compensation (see *The Times*, 4 February 1995 and *The Independent*, 4 June 1996). It is assumed, though not known, that these claims were settled on the basis that officers who entered the enclosed pens or rendered assistance at the pens' fence were rescuers. In *Frost* v *Chief Constable of South Yorkshire* [1997] 1 All ER 540, claims were brought by police officers who were engaged in activity further away from the pens, and, in one case, by an officer who was in the hospital mortuary. By a majority the Court of Appeal held that all the plaintiffs (apart from the officer at the hospital) were entitled to succeed, some on the basis of being a rescuer and some, who were not categorised as rescuers, by virtue of 'being directly involved, in the course of their employment, in the consequences flowing from their employer's negligence' (per Rose LJ at p. 549; for discussion of this case see Mullany and Handford (1997) 113 LQR 410; Teff (1997) 5 Tort L Rev 184; Hilson (1998) 6 Tort L Rev 37; Dunford and Pickford (1997) 48 NILQ 364; Hedley [1997] CLJ 254). This raises two important issues: first, how one should categorise

a 'rescuer'; and, secondly, in what circumstances an employee will be
regarded as falling within the phrase 'being directly involved . . . in the
consequences flowing from their employer's negligence.'

Dealing with the question of who qualifies as a rescuer, Rose LJ said (at
p. 550) that this was a question of fact to be decided in the light of all the
circumstances of the case:

> Among the factors to be considered, although none is in itself decisive, are
> the following: the character and extent of the initial incident caused by the
> tortfeasor; whether that incident has finished or is continuing; whether
> there is any danger, continuing or otherwise, to the victim or to the
> plaintiff; the character of the plaintiff's conduct, in itself and in relation to
> the victim; and how proximate, in time and place, the plaintiff's conduct is
> to the incident.

Henry LJ, agreeing, said that public policy favoured a wide rather than a
narrow definition to ensure that those brave and unselfish enough to go to
the help of their fellow men would be properly compensated if they suffered
damage as a result (at pp. 567–8). Given this approach, it is perhaps a little
surprising that the Court did not consider that the plaintiff in *Duncan* v *British
Coal Corp.* [1997] 1 All ER 540, which was a conjoined appeal with *Frost*,
qualified as a rescuer. The plaintiff was 275 metres away when one of his men
was crushed to death. He was contacted by telephone and arrived at the scene
within four minutes. There was no sign of any injury or blood. The deceased
had no pulse and made no noise. The plaintiff had been trained in first aid
and gave mouth to mouth resuscitation for about two hours. The Court of
Appeal held that the plaintiff was not a rescuer, and had not observed
horrifying circumstances. He was proximate in time to the trapping of the
deceased, but he was not geographically proximate when the incident occurred. When he arrived at the scene there was no danger to him or to the
deceased. The first aid that he administered was 'plainly within the normal
scope of his employment and was not attended by any unusually distressing
features.' (at p. 554). Accordingly, he was 'outside the area of risk of physical
or psychiatric injury when the deceased was injured and he was not exposed
to any unnecessary risk of injury when he attended the scene'. In *Frost* the
officer at the hospital mortuary was not a rescuer. She had labelled two or
three bodies for identification and dealt with relatives of the dead. Officers in
the temporary mortuary at the ground were not regarded as rescuers either,
nor was an officer who assisted at the far end of the ground away from the
pens where the crushing took place, though he had carried three bodies to
the temporary mortuary. They were not rescuers because they were 'not
sufficiently closely involved in the crushing incident or its immediate aftermath'. On the other hand, an officer who approached to within 20 yards of
the pens' fencing and tried resuscitate two victims on the pitch who were
already dead was considered to be a rescuer. The only clear difference
between this plaintiff and the plaintiff in *Duncan* was the extent of the
incident (the numbers of victims) and the gruesome nature of the sights that

confronted the police officer. It is arguable that the 'degree of horror' is an issue that should go to the foreseeability of the psychiatric damage rather than the categorisation of the plaintiff as a rescuer.

The second issue raised by *Frost* is the ruling that an employee may be entitled to claim for psychiatric damage against a negligent employer if the employee has been directly involved, in the course of his employment, in the consequences flowing from the employer's negligence. The police officers who did not succeed on the basis of being rescuers were entitled to claim on this ground, with the exception of the officer at the hospital mortuary: 'She was not at the ground when the negligent loss of control occurred and she was not therefore within the category of those officers to whom, being within the area of risk when the incident occurred, a duty of care was owed by virtue of the master and servant relationship' (per Rose LJ at p. 551). The phrase 'being within the area of risk when the incident occurred' is ambiguous. None of the officers who recovered in *Frost* was within the area of risk of suffering physical injury, since, if they had been, they would have recovered on the basis of *Page* v *Smith*, because if physical injury had been foreseeable it would be irrelevant that psychiatric injury might not be foreseeable. Thus the 'area of risk', if not concerned with physical risk, must mean risk of psychiatric harm. What, it might be asked, is the *area* of risk of psychiatric harm in circumstances where there is no risk of physical harm to the plaintiff? Presumably it is that area where the sight of gruesome events or circumstances gives rise to a risk of developing psychiatric illness as a consequence of what has been witnessed. But this area is, as a question of fact, not limited to what was seen at the ground. In other words, if a plaintiff of reasonable fortitude could reasonably foreseeably suffer psychiatric illness as a consequence of what was witnessed and done in a hospital mortuary, that plaintiff was, at least as a question of fact, within the 'area of risk' of developing psychiatric illness. Thus, the 'area of risk' of developing psychiatric illness must be a legal concept. Unfortunately, the Court of Appeal gave very little indication as to the content of this concept. Rose LJ commented that the officer at the hospital was doing 'no more than could properly be asked of any police officer in the ordinary carrying out of her duties following a serious incident', but, with respect, this is not to the point. Precisely the same point could be used against the other police officers whom Rose LJ considered should recover. Indeed, the argument is not far removed from the 'fireman's rule', to the effect that professional rescuers should be rather more robust in dealing with emergencies than volunteers, since that is what they are paid to do, which Rose LJ had already rejected as inapplicable. Henry LJ said that he regarded the police officers at the ground as participants in the events, and therefore 'primary victims', because they were on duty under their service contracts, 'at the ground close to the centre of the horror, dealing with the dead and the injured and the fans, whether distressed or abusive. They had no choice but to be there and be involved' (at p. 560). This emphasis on the police officers' lack of choice, deriving from the employment relationship, is somewhat puzzling. It would seem almost to amount to a reversal of the 'fireman's rule', so that a plaintiff would be in a *better* position by virtue of having no choice as to whether he acts as a rescuer because he is a 'professional rescuer' (i.e. he has a contract of employment under which his employers could require him to attend the scene). Their Lordships denied, however, that the different outcomes in *Alcock* and *Frost* represented the courts treating police officers more favourably than the relatives at the Hilisborough disaster. It also proves too much, since presumably the officer at the hospital mortuary also had no choice about the scenes that she witnessed, and moreover Henry LJ said (at p. 565) that: 'I do not imagine that police officers in the calm of the control room, watching TV monitors, would recover.' They too would have had no choice. His Lordship also commented (at p. 567) that: 'My emphasis has been on the police officers as direct victims because of the employer/employee relationship. While that duty of care to them is a factor in a case such as this where their employer was negligent, I would expect a duty to be owed to them by any defendant who caused such a disaster as this.' If a defendant was not in an employer/employee relationship with the plaintiffs in *Frost*, and the plaintiffs did not qualify as 'primary victims' under Lord Oliver's classification (fear of physical injury to themselves; rescuer; or a reasonable belief that they have been the involuntary cause of injury to another), Henry LJ's suggestion comes very close to holding the defendants liable for foreseeable psychiatric injury to a person who has witnessed gruesome events, without the requirement for a close tie of love and affection for the victims.

It is clear that the employer/employee relationship is not *per se* sufficient to take employees outside the category of 'mere bystanders' who must be assumed to possess sufficient fortitude to enable them to endure witnessing accidents to their fellow workers (see, e.g., *McFarlane* v *E.E. Caledonia Ltd* [1994] 2 All ER 1; *Hegarty* v *E.E. Caledonia Ltd* [1997] 2 Lloyd's Rep 259; *Hunter* v *British Coal Corp.* [1998] 2 All ER 97; *Duncan* v *British Coal Corp.* [1997] 1 All ER 540; *Robertson* v *Forth Road Bridge Joint Board* [1995] IRLR 251). But employees may fall into the category of 'primary victim' in a number of ways:

(a)   they may have been exposed to the risk of physical injury in the same incident in which a fellow worker is injured or killed (*Young* v *Charles Church (Southern) Ltd, The Times*, 1 May 1997, CA — plaintiff was working alongside a man who was electrocuted and killed; *Schofield* v *Chief Constable of West Yorkshire, The Times*, 15 May 1998, CA—plaintiff, a police officer, exposed to the risk of physical injury when a fellow police officer negligently discharged a gun);

(b)   they may qualify as a rescuer (*Frost*), but not simply by being present at the scene, particularly if they are off duty (*McFarlane* v *E.E. Caledonia Ltd*), nor even necessarily by attending the scene and rendering first aid (*Duncan* v *British Coal Corp.*);

(c)   they may be involved as a participant in the events as an involuntary cause of the injury to the fellow employee (as in *Dooley* v *Cammell Laird & Co. Ltd* [1951] 1 Lloyd's Rep 271), but not where the plaintiff's belief that he is responsible for the injury or death is unreasonable (*Hunter* v *British Coal Corp*);

(d)   they may qualify as 'being directly involved, in the course of their employment, in the consequences flowing from their employer's negligence' (*Frost*; see also *Schofield* v *Chief Constable of West Yorkshire*, where it was held that the plaintiff police officer was 'directly involved' as a participant in the incident).

It is apparent that the scope for litigation by plaintiffs seeking to qualify as 'primary victims' has multiplied in the few years since the House of Lords' decision in *Alcock*.

A further issue that was not directly touched upon in *Alcock* is the position where a plaintiff is negligently given distressing news and sustains psychiatric damage as a result. This was probably not considered relevant given that, for 'secondary victims' at least, it was clear that merely being informed of events could not give rise to liability—the plaintiff must perceive the accident with his own unaided senses. But it is at least arguable that in some cases the plaintiff will be a 'primary victim' of a negligent statement, where in theory the test is simply foreseeability of psychiatric damage. In *Guay* v *Sun Publishing Co.* [1953] 4 DLR 577 the Supreme Court of Canada held that a newspaper that negligently published a false report of the deaths of the plaintiff's family was not liable for the plaintiff's resulting psychiatric illness. Moreover, it has also been said that, where the information is true, there is no duty to break bad news gently, even if it is foreseeable that the person will be shocked by it (*Mount Isa Mines Ltd* v *Pusey* (1970) 125 CLR 383, 407, High Court of Australia; cf. *Furniss* v *Fitchett* [1958] NZLR 396—doctor held to owe a duty of care to prevent true information about a patient being disclosed to his patient where this resulted in foreseeable psychiatric harm to the patient). These propositions may now be challenged. In *AB* v *Tameside & Glossop Health Authority* [1997] 8 Med LR 91 the defendants conceded that they owed a duty of care to break distressing, though truthful, news to patients in a manner which reduced the risk of patients developing psychiatric illness in response to the news, though the defendants were held not to have been negligent in choosing to inform patients that there was a small risk that they might have contracted HIV from a doctor by letter rather than face-to-face. It may be questioned whether the defendants' concession in this case was appropriate (see Dziobon and Tettenborn (1997) 13 PN 70; cf. Mullany (1998) 114 LQR 380). In *Allin* v *City & Hackney Health Authority* [1996] 7 Med LR 167, as a result of the defendants' negligence, the distressing information was *inaccurate* and the plaintiff claimed to have suffered psychiatric harm from this distressing 'news', subsequently corrected, although the incorrect information was imparted in a sensitive and appropriate manner (i.e., if it had been correct—the plaintiff had undergone a very difficult labour and was told that her baby was dead when in fact it was not dead). Again, counsel for the defendants conceded the existence of a duty of care, but in this case the defendants were held liable on the facts. The basis of this concession of a duty of care is not clear (see Jones (1997) 13 PN 111), but if it is correct the somewhat odd consequence would be that a plaintiff who is correctly informed about the death of a loved one killed by the defendant's negligence has no claim against the person who killed that loved one for the psychiatric damage which results (applying *Alcock*), whereas a person who is incorrectly, and negligently, informed that a loved one has died may have a claim for psychiatric harm against the careless informant, even though no one has died and there was no negligence in respect of the loved one. On the other hand, Mullany (1998) 114 LQR 380, 385 comments that: 'It is unquestionably right for the common law to insist that those who communicate objectively distressing (indeed, potentially life-shattering) news take all reasonable precautions to ensure that such news is accurate.'

A more fundamental problem, perhaps, than the fact that the scope for ever more litigation seems to grow with each new decision is that the distinction between primary victims and secondary victims is deeply flawed. In so far as the courts persist in applying different rules to the recovery of compensation for negligence depending upon whether the plaintiff suffers physical injury or psychiatric injury they appear to support a proposition that physical injury is somehow superior to or morally more worthy of compensation than psychiatric illness. If one accepts that psychiatric illness is just as substantial and disabling as physical injury and is just as much a subject for compensation under the tort system then the distinction between those suffering physical injury and those who suffer psychiatric illness should be irrelevant. A mother who suffers psychiatric illness on witnessing the death of her child is as much a victim of the defendant's negligence as the child. The *causal mechanism* by which the mother sustains the damage is different, involving as it does the impact of witnessing the event on the working of the mother's mind rather than, say, the impact of metal on flesh and bone in a road traffic accident. To treat the causal mechanism as a reason for describing one victim as 'secondary' is merely to conclude that it is somehow 'less deserving'. Secondly, the distinction drawn by Lord Oliver in *Alcock* between 'primary' and 'secondary' victims is also false. It is a means of categorising plaintiffs in order to explain the present legal structure, but it is not a *justification* for the present legal structure. The view expressed in *Hambrook* v *Stokes Bros* that it would be wrong not to compensate the mother solicitous for her children's safety (the 'secondary' victim) when another mother could succeed in a claim if she feared only for her own safety (the 'primary' victim) is, it is submitted, correct and reflects sentiments that are probably widely held in the community. Following *Page* v *Smith* in the case of a 'primary' victim psychiatric damage need not even be foreseeable provided physical injury to the plaintiff is foreseeable, and the distinction between the 'selfish mother' and the mother solicitous for her children's welfare appears even more untenable. The 'selfish mother' will recover almost automatically, whereas the 'solicitous mother' will have to jump all the hurdles of proximity in time and space, the suddenness of the event, the aftermath, the closeness of the tie of love and affection, etc. It is absurd that this artificial legal categorisation, a product of the history of the law's development, should produce discrete tests for recovery of damages. A 'primary' victim, whether it be a person who fears for his own safety, a rescuer, or an involuntary participant in the event, has suffered psychiatric illness *as a consequence of what (s)he has witnessed/*

experienced, just as the relatives in *Alcock* suffered psychiatric illness as a result of what they had witnessed/experienced. They may not have observed the events at close quarters, but nonetheless the *mechanism* by which the psychiatric illness was caused is essentially the same in the case of both 'primary' and 'secondary' victims. The categorisation merely states a conclusion rather than a basis for the distinction (see Jones [1995] 4 Web JCLI where this argument is developed in more detail; for an extended discussion of why recovery for negligently inflicted psychiatric harm should be put on a more rational basis, see Teff [1998] CLJ 91; and for discussion of the relationship between medical and legal understanding of psychiatric damage and its implications for the law, see Sprince (1998) 18 LS 59).

The one policy ground that appears most strongly to underpin the present arbitrary rules is the fear that the number of claims for genuine psychiatric illness, as opposed to grief or distress, will far outstrip the ability of defendants, through their insurance arrangements, to meet the costs, i.e., the floodgates argument. Unfortunately, there is no empirical evidence about the likely cost of applying the ordinary principles of liability in negligence to psychiatric injury. No one knows whether the cost would be crippling or readily absorbed through the insurance mechanism.

The criticisms of the present state of the law might be addressed if legislative reform introduced greater certainty into the categories of plaintiff and the circumstances in which they might claim for psychiatric harm. Both Lord Scarman in *McLoughlin* v *O'Brian* and Lord Oliver in *Alcock* favoured a legislative response similar to that of New South Wales which provides a statutory cause of action for psychiatric harm for parents or spouses of the accident victim (whether or not they witnessed the events), or other family members who were within sight or hearing of the victim (see *Hepple and Matthews*, p. 131). The Law Commission has also recommended legislative reform in this area (see *Liability for Psychiatric Illness*, Law Com No. 249, 1998). The Commission took the view that the problematic area of recovery for psychiatric illness concerned Lord Oliver's 'secondary victims', and that the problem lies with the 'duty of care' rather than with any other aspect of such claims, such as breach of duty or remoteness of damage. In order to deal with some of these issues the Commission has recommended a novel solution of creating a statutory 'duty of care' superimposed upon the existing elements of the tort of negligence. Where statutory duties create private rights of action for compensation the statute will normally be the exclusive measure of the ambit of the tort (see chapter 9). The Commission's proposals would graft a new statutory *duty of care* onto the tort of negligence, leaving the common law to supply the remaining features such as the necessary requirements for breach of that duty, remoteness of damage, and any defences. Under the proposed statutory duty of care, a plaintiff who suffered a reasonably foreseeable psychiatric illness as a result of the death, injury or imperilment of a person with whom he had a close tie of love and affection, would be entitled to recover damages from the negligent defendant regardless of the plaintiff's closeness in time and space to the accident or its aftermath or the means by which the plaintiff learned of it. Thus, it would no longer be a requirement that the plaintiff be close to the accident in time and space and directly perceive the event. It would still be necessary for the plaintiff to prove that the psychiatric illness was reasonably foreseeable, but this would not change the rule in *Page* v *Smith* that reasonable foreseeability of psychiatric illness is not required where physical injury was reasonably foreseeable. The requirement that the plaintiff be a person of 'reasonable fortitude' might continue to be used, but merely as an aspect of the assessment whether the psychiatric illness was reasonably foreseeable, as in cases of physical injury.

The Commission recommends that the requirement that the plaintiff have a close tie of love and affection with the immediate victim should be retained. There would be a fixed list of relationships covered by the statutory duty of care, creating an irrebuttable presumption that there was a close tie of love and affection. The list would include: spouse; parent; child (including sons and daughters over 18); brother or sister (but not step-brother or step-sister); and cohabitant (i.e., a person who although not married to the immediate victim, had lived with him or her as man and wife, or 'if of the same gender, in the equivalent relationship', for a period of at least two years). It would be open to a plaintiff outside this list (such as a grandparent or brother-in-law) to prove that a close tie of love and affection did in fact exist between himself and the immediate victim. The proposed statutory duty would not apply if the court was satisfied that its imposition would not be just and reasonable, either because of any factor by virtue of which the defendant owed no duty of care to the *immediate victim*, or because the immediate victim voluntarily accepted the risk that the defendant's act or omission might cause his death, injury or imperilment. Nor would the duty be imposed where *the plaintiff* voluntarily accepted the risk, excluded the duty, or was engaged in conduct that was illegal or contrary to public policy (the *ex turpi causa* defence, see para. 14.3). It is also recommended that the statutory duty of care should not apply where a statutory provision regulates the defendant's duty to the plaintiff in place of the common law rules of the tort of negligence (e.g., Occupiers' Liability Acts 1957 and 1984, where the assumption is that the Acts would cover psychiatric illness, see Law Com Report No. 249, para. 6.48).

The Law Commission considered the position where the psychiatric illness is caused by the death, injury or imperilment of the defendant himself (a point that was raised in *Alcock* by Lord Oliver), and recommended that it should not be an absolute bar to recovery, but that the courts should have scope to decide not to impose a duty of care where satisfied that its imposition would not be just and reasonable because the defendant chose to cause his own death, injury or imperilment. This would be dealt with by the creation of a new, distinct, statutory duty of care.

Under these proposals, where there was no overlap with the proposed statutory duty of care the common law duty of care in relation to psychiatric illness would continue to exist, but the statutory duty of care would replace the common law duty of care to the extent that it would overlap with it. There was no need for legislation, said the Commission, in relation to recovery by rescuers, involuntary participants, employees, bystanders, for stress at work, for psychiatric illness suffered as a result of damage or danger to property, or for psychiatric illness suffered as a result of the negligent communication of distressing news. These areas would continue to be governed by the common law and the proposed legislation should not be construed as impeding judicial development of the common law duty of care. The one recommendation that would cover all types of plaintiff was that the proposed legislation should remove the requirement that psychiatric illness be induced by 'shock'. This would apply to cases governed by the new statutory duty of care and those continuing to be covered by the common law duty of care (i.e., the 'shock' requirement would be removed for both 'primary' and 'secondary' victims). Although the Commission did not recommend formally removing the distinction between 'primary' and 'secondary' victims, it did suggest that the courts should abandon attaching practical significance to the distinction.

If the Law Commission's recommendations are enacted they will remove some of the worst anomalies that currently bedevil the law on recovery for negligently inflicted psychiatric damage. For example, most of the relatives in *Alcock* would probably succeed under the proposed statutory duty of care, as would the plaintiff in *Sion* v *Hampstead Health Authority*, assuming of course that they could prove the causal link between the defendant's negligence and their illness.

2.2.4.3.1 Summary The limiting factors for liability in respect of 'nervous shock' can be summarised as follows:

(a) The plaintiff must suffer a recognised psychiatric illness. With the exception of damages for bereavement awarded under the Fatal Accidents Act 1976, grief, distress or anxiety are not actionable unless they accompany other injuries.

(b) If the plaintiff is a 'primary victim' and the circumstances are such that physical injury to the plaintiff was foreseeable, the plaintiff can succeed for unforeseeable psychiatric harm, even if physical injury did not occur. If physical injury was unforeseeable (which could be the case for some 'primary victims', and by definition will always be the case with 'secondary victims') the psychiatric harm must be a foreseeable result of the defendant's negligence. A 'primary victim' is someone who:

(i)   was exposed to reasonably foreseeable physical injury; or
(ii)   was caused to fear physical injury to himself; or
(iii) was a rescuer; or
(iv)   reasonably believed he was the involuntary cause of death or injury to another; or
(v)   was directly involved, in the course of his employment, in the consequences flowing from his employer's negligence.

(c) With 'secondary victims' (but not 'primary victims' where physical damage is foreseeable) the plaintiff must be an individual of 'reasonable fortitude' or 'customary phlegm'. If the injury is attributable to the plaintiff's peculiar susceptibility to psychiatric damage it is unforeseeable. On the other hand, if a person of reasonable fortitude would have suffered psychiatric illness the plaintiff is not excluded from recovery simply because he was particularly susceptible, and he can recover to the full extent of the harm even if this is exacerbated by a predisposition to psychiatric injury.

(d) The psychiatric illness must have been caused by a sudden assault upon the psyche (a 'shocking' event). Illness attributable to a gradual accumulation of events, such as looking after a seriously injured spouse, is not actionable even though it may be clearly foreseeable. The shocking event may be fear of imminent injury or death to the plaintiff or to others, but it is not necessary for actual physical harm to occur provided that the plaintiff's apprehension was reasonable in the circumstances.

(e) The relationship between the plaintiff and the accident victim:

(i) this must normally be a close tie of love and affection; the relationship between spouses or parent and child will suffice, and there is a rebuttable presumption that such a relationship gives rise to a close tie of love and affection; other relationships require specific proof of the closeness of the emotional tie;

(ii) a bystander will not normally be within the range of foreseeable injury by shock, but may possibly be so if the events witnessed are particularly catastrophic or horrific;

(iii) where the plaintiff has become a 'participant' in the events, either as a rescuer or as an unwilling 'instrument' of the injuries to the accident victim, a close relationship between the plaintiff and the accident victim is not necessary.

(f) Proximity in time and space: the plaintiff must witness the event causing injury to the accident victim or its immediate aftermath. The 'aftermath' includes seeing the victims two hours after the initial accident (provided they have not been attended to by medical staff?), but not identifying the victims at a mortuary or in a hospital.

(g) The plaintiff must perceive the events with his or her own unaided senses, either sight or hearing. Being told about the events after they have occurred is not sufficient (unless the plaintiff was also involved in the events as a 'primary victim'). Perception of events from live television or radio broadcasts will not normally be sufficient, though it may be in exceptional circumstances.

(h) Possibly, where the plaintiff suffers psychiatric illness in consequence of witnessing damage to his or her property, the plaintiff can be regarded as being involved in the events as a 'primary victim' suffering physical damage (albeit property damage), with the result that liability for the psychiatric harm depends upon foreseeability of psychiatric harm, as a matter of remoteness of damage.

(i) Possibly, a plaintiff can recover for psychiatric damage caused as a result of being given accurate but distressing news in a negligent manner, or for negligently being given inaccurate, distressing news.

2.2.4.4   Other types of loss   There are a number of miscellaneous types of loss that the courts have held not to be actionable in negligence, but it is not possible to give more than a few examples. There is no duty of care in respect of trade competition, or in relation to the abstraction of percolating water by the defendant from his own land (*Langbrook Properties Ltd* v *Surrey County Council* [1969] 3 All ER 1424; *Stephens* v *Anglian Water Authority* [1987] 3 All ER 379, para. 7.1.3.5). A university does not owe a duty to its students with respect to the conduct of examinations (*Thorne* v *University of London* [1966] 2 QB 237), nor an employer to his employees in relation to theft of their property (*Deyong* v *Shenburn* [1946] KB 227). A school is under no duty to insure pupils against accidental (i.e., non-negligent) injury or to advise parents to purchase such insurance (*Van Oppen* v *Clerk to the Bedford Charity Trustees* [1989] 3 All ER 389). Similarly, an employer owes no duty to an employee posted overseas to provide personal accident insurance against special risks arising from the overseas posting or to advise the employee to obtain such cover (*Reid* v *Rush & Tomkins Group plc* [1989] 3 All ER 228; see Todd (1989) 5 PN 89). A mortgagee does not owe a duty of care in the tort of negligence when exercising a power of sale under the mortgage to either a surety or a beneficiary under a trust of the mortgaged property (*China & South Sea Bank Ltd* v *Tan Soon Gin* [1989] 3 All ER 839; *Parker-Tweedale* v *Dunbar Bank plc (No. 1)* [1990] 2 All ER 577). There is no duty to take reasonable care to avoid injuring the plaintiff's reputation by the publication of true statements (*Bell-Booth Group Ltd* v *Attorney-General* [1989] 3 NZLR 148, New Zealand CA), and there is no right of action in tort, whether in negligence or for breach of statutory duty, for interference with parental rights (*F* v *Wirral Metropolitan Borough Council* [1991] 2 All ER 648, CA). A serviceman owes no duty of care to fellow servicemen in battle conditions since it is not fair, just or reasonable to impose a duty of care on a soldier in respect of his conduct towards a fellow soldier when engaging the enemy during hostilities (*Mulcahy* v *Ministry of Defence* [1996] 2 All ER 758, where the plaintiff was a member of a howitzer gun team actively engaging the enemy during the Gulf War when he was injured). The position might be different if the injury was not incurred during 'battle conditions'.

In *McKay* v *Essex Area Health Authority* [1982] QB 1166 tests conducted on a pregnant woman failed to disclose that she had contracted German measles and her child was born severely disabled. The Court of Appeal held that a doctor did not owe a duty of care to the child to advise the mother to undergo an abortion. The child's action claimed a right to be aborted, and this was contrary to public policy. These 'wrongful life' claims are now barred by the Congenital Disabilities (Civil Liability) Act 1976, s. 1(2)(b) for births after the commencement of the Act (but cf. Fortin [1987] JSWL 306, 312; and note that s. 1(2)(a) of the Act does allow recovery for preconception negligence, which appears to recognise a legal interest in not being conceived: Pace (1977) 40 MLR 141, 153). Somewhat paradoxically, a doctor does owe a duty of care to the mother in these circumstances to advise her of her right to an abortion under the Abortion Act 1967. Thus, claims for 'wrongful birth' on behalf of the parents may provide some redress for families in this situation (see Robertson (1982) 45 MLR 697; Slade (1982) 132 NLJ 874; and more generally Symmons (1987) 50 MLR 269; Grainger (1994) 2 Tort L Rev 164).

THREE

Negligence II: breach of duty

This chapter is concerned with whether the defendant's conduct can be characterised as careless. When jury trials were common in civil litigation this was a matter for the jury to decide, and so it was regarded as a question of fact. However, an assertion that the defendant was negligent is a two-stage process. First, it involves an assessment by the court of how, in the circumstances, the defendant *ought* to have behaved—what standard of care should he have exercised? This is a question of law requiring a value judgment, which today is made by the judge. The courts approach this question by relying on the standards of a hypothetical 'reasonable man', but it should not be thought that he is anything other than a mythical figure which at times obscures the policy element of a judicial decision (for criticism see *Atiyah*, pp. 28–31, 152–5). The whole concept of 'reasonableness' is consciously indeterminate to allow for flexibility in its application. What is reasonable conduct must always depend upon *all the circumstances of the case,* and so it is a mistake to rely on previous cases as precedents for what constitutes negligence (*Qualcast (Wolverhampton) Ltd v Haynes* [1959] AC 743, HL).

Secondly, there must be a decision about whether on the facts the defendant's conduct fell below the appropriate standard. Generally it is for the plaintiff to prove this, on the balance of probabilities, but in some cases the plaintiff may have little or no knowledge of how the damage occurred. In this event he may be able to rely on the principle of *res ipsa loquitur* which requires the defendant to furnish a reasonable explanation of the events.

Breach of duty is commonly the most important aspect of the tort of negligence in practical terms, since in the vast majority of cases the existence of a duty of care or questions about causation or remoteness of damage are not in issue. 'Common sense' will often provide a useful indication of whether the defendant was in breach of duty, but this should be informed by the general principles that have been developed by the courts.

3.1 THE REASONABLE MAN

'Negligence is the omission to do something which a reasonable man, guided upon those considerations which ordinarily regulate the conduct of human affairs, would do, or doing something which a prudent and reasonable man would not do' (*Blyth* v *Birmingham Waterworks Co.* (1856) 11 Exch 781, 784, per Alderson B). The reasonable man, being an abstraction, may be imbued with qualities that can rarely be consistently maintained in the real world. He is 'free both from over-apprehension and from over-confidence' (*Glasgow Corporation* v *Muir* [1943] AC 448, 457); he anticipates the negligence of others where experience suggests that it is common (*London Passenger Transport Board* v *Upson* [1949] AC 155, 173); he remains cool, calm and collected despite a sudden emergency (*Charlesworth and Percy*, para. 3–51, n. 69). He is, protested Sir Alan Herbert, devoid 'of any human weakness, with not one single saving vice, *sans* prejudice, procrastination, ill-nature, avarice and absence of mind, as careful for his own safety as he is for that of others, this excellent but odious character stands like a monument in our courts of justice, vainly appealing to his fellow citizens to order their lives after his own example' (*Uncommon Law*, p. 4).

This tongue-in-cheek description rather overstates the case, and there are many judicial pronouncements to the effect that the reasonable man is not a paragon or a clairvoyant. He is the ordinary man, the average man, or the man on the Clapham omnibus (*Hall* v *Brooklands Auto Racing Club* [1933] 1 KB 205, 217). None of these expressions indicates anything about the standard of care that the court will require in any particular situation. Indeed, in practice, 'reasonable care' can be manipulated to produce standards which range from very low to almost strict liability. It must be remembered that the correct test is always 'reasonable care in all the circumstances', not 'average care'. The fact that most people behave in a certain way may be good evidence that that conduct is reasonable, but this is not necessarily the case. Although the courts give considerable weight to the common practices of mankind, the average standard of care can constitute negligence in some circumstances (see para. 3.1.4 and cf. para. 3.2.1).

3.1.1 The objective standard

The standard of care expected of the reasonable man is objective. It does not take account of the particular idiosyncrasies or weaknesses of the defendant (*Glasgow Corporation* v *Muir* [1943] AC 448, 457 per Lord Macmillan but, his Lordship added, there is a subjective element in that it is left to the individual judge to decide what is reasonable or what could have been foreseen. 'What to one judge may seem far-fetched may seem to another both natural and probable.') The point is well illustrated by *Nettleship* v *Weston* [1971] 2 QB 691 where the defendant was a learner-driver who crashed into a lamp-post, injuring the front-seat passenger. The defendant was convicted of driving without due care and attention, but at first instance the plaintiff's claim was dismissed because the defendant had been doing her best to control the car. The Court of Appeal held that the standard of care required of a learner-driver is the same as that required of any other driver, namely that of a reasonably competent and experienced driver. (His 'incompetent best is not good enough'.) The defendant's driving had fallen below this standard and it was irrelevant that this was because of her inexperience. A variable standard for different levels of experience, or competence, or temperament would create much uncertainty and, indeed, unfairness for plaintiffs, and result in the court having the impossible task of specifying a subjective level of competence for each defendant. It is irrelevant, said Megaw LJ, that this attributes liability to someone who is not morally blameworthy because tortious liability has in many cases ceased to be based on moral blameworthiness. Of course, driving a motor vehicle is an activity for which liability insurance is compulsory and so the additional risk that a learner-driver creates for other road users by venturing on to the road will be spread via the insurance company. If this is thought to be unfair to insurers, remember that they accept the risk on the basis that a much higher premium is charged to inexperienced drivers.

Salmon LJ dissented in *Nettleship* v *Weston* on the question of the standard of care that a passenger is normally entitled to expect from a learner-driver (although he agreed with the result on the particular facts of the case). This was on the basis that the duty of care springs from the relationship between the parties, and in the case of an inexperienced learner-driver the passenger/ instructor knows that the driver does not possess the skill and competence of an experienced driver. Thus, the learner-driver should not be liable for an accident which results from 'some mistake which any prudent beginner doing his best can be expected to make'. This approach was adopted by the High Court of Australia in *Cook* v *Cook* (1986) 68 ALR 353 where the driver, to the knowledge of the passenger, was both unlicensed to drive and inexperienced. It was held that, while the personal skill or characteristics of the individual driver are not directly relevant to the standard of care, special and exceptional facts may so transform the relationship between driver and passenger that it would be unreal to treat it as the ordinary relationship of driver and passenger, and unreasonable to measure the standard of skill and care by reference to the skill and care of an experienced and competent driver (for criticism see Todd (1989) 105 LQR 24). Such special relationships would be rare, but an example would be that between a professional driving instructor and a pupil having his first driving lesson. On this view the standard of care is still objective, but it is adjusted to take account of the relationship between the plaintiff and defendant. The mere fact that the passenger knew that the driver had some physical disability, was below average expertise or was commonly careless, would not in itself be sufficient to create a special relationship—that would be a departure from the objective standard by taking account of the characteristics of the particular driver. *A fortiori* the relationship between an inexperienced driver and other road users or pedestrians could never be such a special relationship and the defendant must then reach the standard of the reasonably competent and experienced driver. Moreover, even applying the reduced standard of care the defendant will be liable if the accident was the result of carelessness over and above what could be attributed merely to inexperience. *Cook* v *Cook* illustrates an alternative approach to the problem of inexperienced defendants. It does not represent the law in England, although there have been attempts to modify the standard of care applicable to inexperienced doctors (*Wilsher* v *Essex Area Health Authority* [1986] 3 All ER 801, CA).

The objective standard also applies to a driver who becomes physically incapable of controlling the vehicle carefully because of an impairment of consciousness, e.g., as a result of a stroke. In *Roberts* v *Ramsbottom* [1980] 1 All ER 7, Neill J held that this would be the position even if the driver was unaware of his condition, except where he was in a state of automatism or had completely lost consciousness so that he could not be said to have any control of the vehicle. In *Mansfield* v *Weetabix Ltd* [1997] PIQR P526, however, the Court of Appeal held that a driver who becomes unable to control a vehicle will not be liable for damage caused by his loss of control if he is unaware of the disabling condition from which he is suffering, whether the disabling event is sudden or gradual. On this point, said the Court, *Roberts* v *Ramsbottom* had been wrongly decided, though the decision in that case could be supported on the alternative ground that the defendant continued to drive when he was unfit to do so, and when he should have been aware of his unfitness. Leggatt LJ commented that to apply an objective standard in a way which did not take account of the defendant's condition in *Mansfield* (of which he was unaware) would be to impose strict liability. Aldous LJ said of the defendant: 'He did not know and could not reasonably have known of his infirmity which was the cause of the accident. Therefore he was not at fault.' Of course, if the defendant knew that he was susceptible to such attacks he will be liable for harm resulting from a loss of control (*Hill* v *Baxter* [1958] 1 QB 277); and similarly if he ought to have known that he was subject to a condition rendering him unfit to drive (*Waugh* v *James K. Allan Ltd* [1964] 2 Lloyd's Rep 1).

Since what is reasonable varies with the circumstances, the fact that a police driver was in pursuit of a stolen car may indicate that the level of care that he could reasonably be expected to demonstrate for the safety of the occupants of that car would not be as great as in ordinary traffic (*Marshall* v *Osmond* [1983] QB 1034). Though query what standard would be applied if a bystander were injured by a police officer pursuing an offender (cf. the policy objectives of *Nettleship* v *Weston*). An offender who is being pursued by the police owes a duty of care to the police officers giving chase and can be liable for injury to an officer if he acts carelessly or recklessly, even in the absence of a direct collision between the defendant and the plaintiff (*Langley* v *Dray and M.T. Motor Policies at Lloyds* [1997] PIQR P508—where the plaintiff's car, in pursuit of the defendant, skidded on black ice and collided with a lamp post).

The objective standard will take account of the particular situation as it presented itself to the defendant as part and parcel of 'all the circumstances of the case'. So a defendant faced with an emergency or a dilemma, having to act on the spur of the moment, will not be judged too critically simply because with hindsight a different course of action might have avoided the harm (*Parkinson* v *Liverpool Corporation* [1950] 1 All ER 367; *Ng Chun Pui* v *Lee Chuen Tat* [1988] RTR 298, 302). The same principle applies to an action for professional negligence (*Wilsher* v *Essex Area Health Authority* [1986] 3 All ER 801, 812) and to contributory negligence (see para. 14.5.3.4).

Where a person undertakes a task which requires a particular skill he will be judged by the standards of a person who is reasonably competent in the exercise of that skill (para. 3.2.1). So a householder who decides to carry out work on his property that involves carpentry skills must achieve the standards of a reasonably competent carpenter. He cannot claim that he did the job to the best of his ability if he did not reach this level of competence (*Wells* v *Cooper* [1958] 2 QB 265—but this is not, apparently, the same standard as a professional carpenter working for reward; see also *The Lady Gwendolen* [1964] P 294—brewers who engage in shipping must behave as reasonably competent shipowners). If it were otherwise the protection from injury afforded to visitors would vary with the skills of the householder. The mere fact that the defendant did not employ someone with appropriate skill to carry out the work will not necessarily constitute negligence, unless the work requires very specialised skills and there would be a serious danger if the work was not properly executed. Similarly, an inexperienced doctor must achieve the standard of a reasonably competent doctor filling the post which he occupies. This standard is tailored to the task that the doctor undertakes, not his individual level of experience (*Wilsher* v *Essex Area Health Authority* [1986] 3 All ER 801, see para. 3.2.1).

3.1.2 Unforeseeable harm
If a particular danger could not reasonably have been anticipated, the defendant has not acted negligently, because a reasonable man would not take any precautions against unforeseeable consequences. This is measured by reference to knowledge at the time of the event. In *Roe* v *Minister of Health* [1954] 2 QB 66, during the course of an operation, the plaintiff was paralysed by anaesthetic which had become contaminated by disinfectant. The anaesthetic had been kept in glass ampoules which were stored in the disinfectant, and became contaminated by seepage through invisible cracks in the glass. At the time of the accident in 1947 this risk was not known. The Court of Appeal held that the hospital authorities were not liable because the danger was not reasonably foreseeable. The court 'must not look at the 1947 accident with 1954 spectacles' (per Denning LJ), but it would have been negligence to adopt the same practice in 1954. (See also *Glasgow Corporation* v *Muir* [1943] AC 448, in which the defendants were not liable for a spillage of scalding water because there was no reason to anticipate the accident and therefore no precautions were reasonably necessary.) It is not necessary, however, that the particular damage that occurred be foreseeable if damage of the same type was foreseeable and, similarly, it is not necessary that the precise manner in which the accident happened was foreseeable if it was of a type which was foreseeable in a general way (see paras 4.3.2 and 4.3.3).

3.1.3 Foreseeable harm: risk
A defendant is not negligent if the damage was not a foreseeable consequence of his conduct. It does *not* follow, however, that a defendant is negligent if

the damage was foreseeable. In *Bolton* v *Stone* [1951] AC 850, Lord Oaksey commented (at p. 863) that a reasonable man can:

> foresee the possibility of many risks, but life would be almost impossible if he were to attempt to take precautions against every risk which he can foresee. He takes precautions against risks which are reasonably likely to happen.

So it may be reasonable not to take any precautions against some foreseeable risks. But even where some precautions are required the standard of care that can reasonably be expected will vary according to the magnitude of the risk, the purpose of the defendant's activity and the practicability or cost of the precautions.

Here the courts are engaged in a balancing exercise to determine whether the risk of harm to others which the defendant's conduct created was justified. Most activities entail some degree of risk, but that is not a reason *per se to* condemn them as negligent. The concept of safety, for example, is relative. It 'would be perverse to insist on 'absolute' safety if the cost in resources of achieving it would be astronomic. Levels of safety are traded off against other valued uses for those resources. This is also true of non-physical losses. A professional person, such as a lawyer or accountant, must exercise reasonable, not absolute, care in performing his work because to demand more would be too costly in social resources (i.e., time and effort) to justify the additional benefits.

3.1.3.1 Magnitude of the risk 'The law in all cases exacts a degree of care commensurate with the risk created' (*Read* v *J. Lyons & Co. Ltd* [1947] AC 156, 173 per Lord Macmillan). The greater the risk of harm the more precautions must be taken. The magnitude of the risk is the product of two factors: (a) the likelihood of the risk materialising and (b) the potential severity of the damage if it should occur.

3.1.3.1.1 Likelihood of the harm In *Bolton* v *Stone* [1951] AC 850 the plaintiff was struck by a cricket ball driven from the defendants' cricket ground on to a quiet road. It was rare for balls to be hit out of the ground. It had happened perhaps six times in 30 years. The risk of such an accident was foreseeable but the chance that it would actually occur was very small. The House of Lords held that the defendants were not liable because in the circumstances it was reasonable to ignore such a small risk. Lord Reid said that reasonable men take into account the degree of risk and do not act on a bare possibility as they would if the risk were more substantial. 'In the crowded conditions of modern life even the most careful person cannot avoid creating some risks and accepting others. What a man must not do . . . is to create a risk which is substantial' (p. 867). Lord Radcliffe commented that a reasonable man, taking account of the chances against an accident happening, would have done what the defendants did, in other words he would have done nothing. He would not have increased the height of the fences around the ground and he would not have abandoned the use of the ground for cricket. His Lordship added that he could see nothing unfair in requiring the defendants to compensate the plaintiff, but 'the law of negligence is concerned less with what is fair than with what is culpable'.

This case should be contrasted with *Miller* v *Jackson* [1977] QB 966 where cricket balls were hit out of the defendants' ground eight or nine times a season, damaging the plaintiffs' property on a number of occasions. A high fence did not prevent this because the pitch was too close. By a majority the Court of Appeal held that the risk of harm was so great that the defendants were negligent 'on each occasion when a ball comes over the fence and causes damage'. (Note that the court did not say that it was negligent to carry on playing cricket at all on this ground, which was the logical conclusion, because it wanted to allow cricket to continue being played. But if it is reasonable to play cricket at all it can hardly be unreasonable conduct for a batsman to attempt to hit the ball for six, which is one of the objects of the game. Compare *Hilder* v *Associated Portland Cement Manufacturers Ltd* [1961] 1 WLR 1434 where a motor-cyclist was killed when a football was kicked on to the road. The occupiers of the adjoining piece of land were liable in negligence for allowing children to play football on the land.)

Bolton v *Stone* is not authority for the view that it is always reasonable to ignore a small risk. The risk must still be measured against the defendant's purpose and the practicability of precautions (see *The Wagon Mound (No. 2)* [1967] 1 AC 617 discussed in para. 3.1.3.3).

If the defendant had knowledge of some fact which makes harm to the plaintiff more likely than would otherwise be the case, then as a reasonable man he must take account of that. A greater than average knowledge of the risks will entail more than the average or standard precautions (*Stokes* v *Guest, Keen & Nettlefold (Bolts & Nuts) Ltd* [1968] 1 WLR 1776, 1783 per Swanwick J). In *Haley* v *London Electricity Board* [1965] AC 778 the plaintiff, who was blind, fell into a hole in the pavement that had been dug by the defendants. The precautions taken to warn the public of the danger were adequate for sighted persons but not for the blind. The defendants were held liable. It was common knowledge that blind people walk alone on city pavements and there was no difficulty in providing adequate warning. It could not be said that the risk of causing them injury was so small as to be ignored. Lord Reid approved a dictum of Lord Sumner in *Glasgow Corporation* v *Taylor* [1922] 1 AC 44, 67 that 'a measure of care appropriate to the inability or disability of those who are immature or feeble in mind or body is due from others, who know of or ought to aniticipate the presence of such persons within the scope and hazard of their own operations' (see also para. 3.2.3). Thus, the organisers and coaches of a disabled persons' sports event have an obligation to exercise greater care in the implementation of safety measures than would be required where the participants were able bodied (*Morrell* v *Owen, The Times*, 14 December 1993), and where an employer can reasonably foresee that a particular employee might suffer a nervous breakdown because of the stress and pressures of his workload the employer has an obligation to take reasonable steps to avoid causing psychiatric damage to that employee (*Walker* v *Northumberland County Council* [1995] 1 All ER 737) but not where psychiatric damage to the particular employee was not foreseeable (*Petch* v *Customs and Excise Commissioners* [1993] ICR 789).

3.1.3.1.2 Severity of the damage The more serious the potential consequences, the greater the precautions that should be taken. 'Those who engage in operations inherently dangerous must take precautions which are not required of persons engaged in the ordinary routine of daily life' (*Glasgow Corporation* v *Muir* [1943] AC 448, 456 per Lord Macmillan). In *Paris* v *Stepney Borough Council* [1951] AC 367 the defendants knew that the plaintiff employee was blind in one eye. In the course of the plaintiff's work a chip of metal entered his good eye rendering him totally blind. He alleged that the defendants were negligent in failing to provide goggles, although it was not usual to do so for that type of work. In the House of Lords the defendants were held liable. The duty of an employer was owed to each particular employee and in determining the requisite degree of care an employer must have regard to the gravity of the consequences of the potential injury to each employee. An injury to the plaintiff's good eye was a much more serious consequence than a similar injury to a fully sighted man, and a reasonable man would take account of the risk of greater injury as well as the greater risk of injury (per Lord Simonds).

3.1.3.2 Defendant's purpose The social utility of the defendant's activity may justify taking greater risks than would otherwise be the case. So, in *Daborn* v *Bath Tramways Motor Co. Ltd* [1946] 2 All ER 333, it was held that it was not negligent to use a left-hand-drive vehicle as an ambulance in wartime when there was a shortage of vehicles for the task, even though it was difficult to give hand signals and this had caused an accident. Asquith LJ said that in assessing what is reasonable care the risk must be balanced against the consequences of not assuming the risk. 'The purpose to be served, if sufficiently important, justifies the assumption of abnormal risk', and so the need for ambulances justified the risks involved in using the vehicle. Similarly, in *Watt* v *Hertfordshire County Council* [1954] 1 WLR 835, the plaintiff was a fireman called out to an emergency where a woman was trapped under a lorry. A vehicle designed to carry a heavy lifting jack was not available so the jack was taken on an ordinary lorry with three firemen steadying it. The jack slipped, injuring the plaintiff. His employers were not liable. The risk had to be balanced against the end to be achieved and the saving of life or limb justifies taking considerable risk. Denning LJ added that if the accident had occurred in a commercial enterprise without any emergency the plaintiff would have succeeded, but 'the commercial end to make profit is very different from the human end to save life or limb'. This does not mean that the purpose of saving life or limb justifies taking any risk. There is little point racing to save one person if in the process others are killed and injured. Thus it can be negligence for the driver of a fire engine to ignore a red traffic-light (*Ward* v *London County Council* [1938] 2 All ER 341; *Griffin* v *Mersey Regional Ambulance* [1998] PIQR P34, where the plaintiff motorist crossing a junction

on a green light collided with an ambulance crossing against a red light, but
was held 60% contributorily negligent).

Where, on the other hand, the defendant's activity has no social utility or,
indeed, is unlawful then he will have to exercise a very high degree of care to
justify even a small risk of harm to others (see *The Wagon Mound (No. 2)*
[1967] 1 AC 617 discussed in para. 3.1.3.3).

3.1.3.3 Practicability of precautions
Some risks are unavoidable.
Others can be eliminated or reduced only at great expense. The question that
arises is at what point the cost of precautions would justify a reasonable man
in not taking them. In *Latimer* v *AEC Ltd* [1953] AC 643 the defendants'
factory was flooded after a heavy rainfall, and water became mixed with oil
leaving the floor very slippery when the flooding subsided. Sawdust was
spread over the surface but there was not enough to cover the entire area. A
workman slipped on the uncovered part and was injured. The trial judge held
the defendants liable for failing to close down that part of the factory. The
House of Lords agreed that this might be necessary if the risk to employees
was sufficiently grave, but that had not been the position in this case. The
test was, remedial steps not being possible, would a reasonably prudent
employer have closed down the factory rather than allow his employees to run
the risks involved in continuing work? It may be asked, however, at what
point would a reasonable employer choose to lose profit instead of subjecting
employees to additional risk? Here, the comment of Denning LJ in *Watt* v
Hertfordshire County Council [1954] 1 WLR 835 (see para. 3.1.3.2) that
commercial profit is in a different category from life or limb is very apposite.

Nonetheless, reasonableness remains a matter of achieving a balance, and
the practical problem is to determine what weight will be given to the
respective factors in achieving that balance. If a large reduction of risk could
be obtained by a small expenditure, the defendant has acted unreasonably if
he does not take the precautions. If great expense would only produce a very
small reduction in risk it will be reasonable to do nothing (cf. the approach
of the American judge Learned Hand in *US* v *Carroll Towing Co.* (1947) 159
F 2d 169, 173: 'if the probability be called P; the injury, L; and the burden,
B; liability depends upon whether B is less than L multiplied by P: i.e.
whether B < PL'). It is a question of degree. But even where the risk is very
small it would be careless to ignore it if it could be avoided at virtually no
cost.

In *Overseas Tankship (UK) Ltd* v *Miller Steamship Co. Pty Ltd, The Wagon
Mound (No. 2)* [1967] 1 AC 617 a large quantity of bunkering oil was spilled
in Sydney harbour as a result of the carelessness of the defendants' engineer.
With a high flash-point the oil was very difficult to ignite in the open, but it
did catch fire causing extensive damage (probably as a consequence of hot
metal falling to the water from welding operations carried out on a wharf).
The Privy Council concluded that a reasonable engineer would have foreseen
the possibility of the oil catching fire but the likelihood of it doing so was
extremely small. It did not follow, however, that, no matter what the
circumstances, it is justifiable to neglect a small risk. 'A reasonable man

would only neglect such a risk if he had some valid reason for doing so, e.g., that it would involve considerable expense to eliminate the risk. He would weigh the risk against the difficulty of eliminating it' (p. 642). It would have been simple to stop the discharge of oil—it was a matter of closing a valve. A reasonable man would not ignore even a small risk 'if action to eliminate it presented no difficulty, involved no disadvantage and required no expense'. Moreover, the defendants' activity, unlike the playing of cricket (*Bolton* v *Stone* [1951] AC 850, see para. 3.1.3.1), was unlawful and involved considerable financial loss to the defendants. There was no question of balancing the advantages and disadvantages. All the indications pointed the same way.

When precautions are not practicable then the risks of continuing the activity have to be weighed against the disadvantages of stopping the activity altogether. Where it was not possible to give an employee who was susceptible to dermatitis work which did not involve a risk of contracting this disease it was held that the employers were not liable (*Withers* v *Perry Chain Co. Ltd* [1961] 1 WLR 1314). There were no further precautions that the employers could have taken short of dismissing the plaintiff, and there was no obligation to do this in order to avoid an action in negligence. If an employee developed work-related symptoms, a reasonable employer would reconsider whether the equipment provided or the particular system of work created any particular risk to the employee. But if there were no reasonable changes that could be made, the employer does not have to offer a wholly different job to the employee (*Henderson* v *Wakefield Shirt Co. Ltd* [1997] PIQR P413).

As a general rule a defendant's lack of resources will not justify a failure to take the precautions demanded by the exercise of reasonable care. Impecuniosity is not a defence. It may be relevant, however, where the plaintiff seeks to hold a public authority liable in negligence for failing to provide an adequate service. In *Knight* v *Home Office* [1990] 3 All ER 237 it was held that prison authorities were not negligent in failing to provide the same level of staffing for prisoners suffering from psychiatric illness that would be found in a psychiatric hospital outside prison (see further Fleming (1992) 108 LQR 9, commenting on the Australian case of *Cekan* v *Haines* (1990) 22 NSWLR 296). The lack of resources to provide a better staff/patient ratio, however, would not necessarily be a complete defence. Pill J commented that if it had been claimed that there was no funds to provide any medical facilities for prisoners there would be a breach of the duty of care, just as lack of funds would not excuse a public body which operated its vehicles on public roads without any system of maintenance, if an accident occurred due to lack of maintenance (see also the comments of Browne-Wilkinson V-C in *Wilsher* v *Essex Area Health Authority* [1986] 3 All ER 801, 833–4).

3.1.4 General practice
Where the defendant has acted in accordance with the common or general practice of others in a similar situation this will be strong evidence that he has not been negligent (*Morton* v *William Dixon Ltd* 1909 SC 807, 809; *Morris* v *West Hartlepool Steam Navigation Co. Ltd* [1956] AC 552, 579). It is not, however, conclusive. The court may find that a common practice is itself

negligent (see, e.g., *Lloyds Bank Ltd* v *E.B. Savory & Co.* [1933] AC 201; *Cavanagh* v *Ulster Weaving Co. Ltd* [1960] AC 145). There may be many reasons (e.g., convenience, habit, cost) for following a common practice, which have nothing to do with the exercise of reasonable care for the safety of others; but as Lord Tomlin observed: 'Neglect of duty does not cease by repetition to be neglect of duty' (*Bank of Montreal* v *Dominion Gresham Guarantee & Casualty Co.* [1930] AC 659, 666; *Carpenters' Co.* v *British Mutual Banking Co. Ltd* [1937] 3 All ER 811, 820 per Slesser LJ). There is also an obligation to keep up to date and to change practices in the light of new knowledge (*Stokes* v *Guest, Keen & Nettlefold (Bolts & Nuts) Ltd* [1968] 1 WLR 1776, 1783). On the other hand, although the defendant must keep reasonably abreast of developing knowledge and not be slow to apply it (per Swanwick J, ibid.), where the omission involves an absence of initiative in seeking out knowledge of facts which are not in themselves obvious 'the court must be slow to blame him for not ploughing a lone furrow' (*Thompson* v *Smiths Shiprepairers (North Shields) Ltd* [1984] 1 All ER 881, 894 per Mustill J). It is comparatively rare for the courts to condemn a commonly accepted practice as negligent. Only where the risk was obvious, such that it would be folly to disregard it, will the practice to held negligent (see *Paris* v *Stepney Borough Council* [1951] AC 367, 382; *General Cleaning Contractors Ltd* v *Christmas* [1953] AC 180, 193; *Sidaway* v *Bethlem Royal Hospital Governors* [1985] 1 All ER 643, 663; see further Holyoak (1990) 10 LS 201, and para. 3.2.1).

Conversely, the fact that the defendant has departed from common practice is not necessarily negligence either. It may be prima facie *evidence* of negligence, but it is not conclusive (*Brown* v *Rolls-Royce Ltd* [1960] 1 WLR 210; see also Congenital Disabilities (Civil Liability) Act 1976, s. 1(5)). There may well be more than one approved practice and it is not negligent to follow one rather than another (see para. 3.2.1). Codes of practice issued by professional bodies may constitute significant evidence of what constitutes reasonable care. In *Lloyd Cheynham & Co. Ltd* v *Littlejohn & Co.* (1985) 2 PN 154 Woolf J said of accounting and audit standards that:

> While they are not conclusive, so that a departure from their terms necessarily involves a breach of a duty of care, and they are not rigid . . . rules, they are very strong evidence as to what is the proper standard which should be adopted and unless there is some justification, a departure from this will be regarded as constituting a breach of duty.

In *Ward* v *The Ritz Hotel (London) Ltd* [1992] PIQR P315 the Court of Appeal held that a failure to comply with the British Standards Institution's recommendation as to the height of a balustrade on a balcony was strong evidence of negligence. But, again, such standards are not necessarily determinative. Thus, in *Green* v *Building Scene Ltd* [1994] PIQR P259 the Court of Appeal held that although a failure to comply with Building Regulations or the British Standards Institution's recommendations about the safety of a staircase was evidence which the court should take into account, because it represented current professional opinion as to what was desirable to avoid accidents, it was not conclusive. There was a difference between laying down standards and defining what is reasonably safe in all the circumstances of the case. Similarly, in *Johnson* v *Bingley, The Times*, 28 February 1995, it was held that breach of the *Guide to Professional Conduct of Solicitors* published by the Law Society was not *per se* proof of negligence. The *Guide* was proper and accepted practice for solicitors, but negligence was a legal concept, and neither the Law Society nor any other body could, by issuing rules or codes of conduct, alter the law.

3.2 SPECIAL STANDARDS

3.2.1 Professionals

A person who professes a special skill is not judged by the standard of the man on the Clapham omnibus, but by the standards of his peers. He does not undertake to use the highest possible degree of skill, 'he undertakes to bring a fair, reasonable and competent degree of skill' (*Lanphier* v *Phipos* (1838) 8 C & P 475 per Tindal CJ). A professional person is not an insurer. The lawyer does not guarantee to win the case. The doctor does not guarantee a cure. It is theoretically possible for a professional to give a contractual warranty that he will achieve a particular result, but, in the case of a doctor at least, the court will be slow to infer such a warranty in the absence of an express term because medicine is an inexact science and it is unlikely that a responsible doctor would intend to give such a warranty (*Eyre* v *Measday* [1986] 1 All ER 488; *Thake* v *Maurice* [1986] 1 All ER 497). In the absence of an express term, a term will be implied into a contract for the supply of a service that the service will be performed with reasonable care and skill (Supply of Goods and Services Act 1982, s. 13). The standard of care required to satisfy this obligation is the same as in the tort of negligence.

The classic statement of the test of negligence in a situation which involves the use of some special skill or competence is the direction to the jury of McNair J in *Bolam* v *Friern Hospital Management Committee* [1957] 2 All ER 118, 121:

> The test is the standard of the ordinary skilled man exercising and professing to have that special skill. A man need not possess the highest expert skill at the risk of being found negligent . . . it is sufficient if he exercises the ordinary skill of an ordinary competent man exercising that particular art.

His Lordship agreed that (in the context of the medical profession) negligence 'means failure to act in accordance with the standards of *reasonably competent* medical men at the time' (emphasis added) provided that it is remembered that there may be one or more perfectly proper standards. Then, referring to professional practice McNair said (at p. 122) that:

> A doctor is not guilty of negligence if he has acted in accordance with a practice accepted as proper by a responsible body of medical men skilled

in that particular art . . . Putting it the other way round, a doctor is not negligent, if he is acting in accordance with such a practice, merely because there is a body of opinion that takes a contrary view.

This test, which has come to be known as the '*Bolam* test', has been approved by the House of Lords on at least three occasions in respect of actions for medical negligence (*Whitehouse* v *Jordan* [1981] 1 All ER 267—treatment; *Maynard* v *West Midlands Regional Health Authority* [1984] 1 WLR 634—diagnosis; *Sidaway* v *Bethlem Royal Hospital Governors* [1985] 1 All ER 643—disclosure of information about risks of proposed procedures by doctors to patients). The test is not limited to doctors, however, but is of general application to any profession or calling which requires special skill, knowledge or experience (*Gold* v *Haringey Health Authority* [1987] 2 All ER 888, 894, CA; *Luxmoore-May* v *Messenger May Baverstock* [1990] 1 All ER 1067, provincial auctioneer engaged in the valuation of a painting. In the case of property valuers there has been a tendency to use a 'margin of error' or 'bracket' as an indication of negligence or reasonable care. This involves judging the outcome rather than the reasonableness of the method employed. For criticism of this see Crosby, Lavers and Murdoch [1998] 14 EG 125).

Despite the authority with which the *Bolam* test has been imbued it contains an inherent ambiguity. It could mean that negligence is a departure from the practices which *in fact* are commonly adopted by the profession (the standards of the 'ordinary skilled man'). Alternatively negligence may be a departure from standards that *ought* to be adopted by the profession, whether or not they are in fact practised (the standards of the 'reasonably competent' man). This distinction was identified at the time of *Bolam* (see Montrose (1958) 21 MLR 259—'is negligence an ethical or a sociological concept?') and can be seen in some cases, although it is often overlooked or conflated (see *Jackson and Powell* para. 1.95). The question is most likely to arise in the context of the second limb of the *Bolam* test: does compliance with a common practice of the profession absolve the defendant from a finding of negligence or may the court condemn a common professional practice as unreasonable and therefore negligent? Lord Scarman, for example, has suggested that a practitioner whose actions have received the seal of approval of distinguished professional opinion, 'truthfully expressed, honestly held' is not negligent (*Maynard* v *West Midlands Regional Health Authority* [1984] 1 WLR 634, 639G; see also the same judge in *Sidaway* v *Bethlem Royal Hospital Governors* [1985] 1 All ER 643, 649e, commenting that the *Bolam* test 'leaves the determination of a legal duty to the judgment of doctors'). Nonetheless, it is submitted that the second alternative is the correct approach. A professional person must conform to the standards of a reasonably competent individual exercising and professing to have that professional skill (*Jackson and Powell* para. 1.96; *Dugdale and Stanton* para. 15.22). What is reasonable is ultimately a question of law to be determined by the court, but not surprisingly the courts place heavy reliance on expert evidence which is usually crucial to the outcome of an action (Codified professional standards may also be significant evidence of what constitutes reasonable care; see Gwilliam (1986) 2 PN 175.)

Once a body of professional opinion supporting the defendant's conduct is characterised as a 'responsible' body of opinion the court will not choose between conflicting views (see, e.g., *Ashcroft* v *Mersey Regional Health Authority* [1983] 2 All ER 245; *Maynard* v *West Midlands Regional Health Authority*). But before any question of complying with accepted practice can arise the court must be satisfied on the evidence that there is a responsible body of professional opinion which supports the practice. It is always open to the court to reject expert evidence applying ordinary principles of credibility. Moreover, the fact that a number of expert witnesses give evidence to the same effect does not automatically constitute an established alternative 'school of thought' if the reasons given to substantiate the views expressed do not stand up to sensible analysis (*Gascoine* v *Ian Sheridan & Co.* [1994] 5 Med LR 437, 444 per Mitchell J; *Joyce* v *Wandsworth Health Authority* [1995] 6 Med LR 60, 64 per Overend J, approved by the Court of Appeal at [1996] PIQR P121, 140).

This issue was at the heart of the plaintiff's appeal in *Bolitho* v *City and Hackney Health Authority* [1997] 4 All ER 771. A two-year-old boy suffered brain damage as a result of cardiac arrest caused by an obstruction of the bronchial air passages. The plaintiff was in hospital at the time for the treatment of croup. The defendants admitted that there had been negligence, in that a doctor who had been summoned for assistance on more than one occasion had failed to attend. It was also common ground that had the plaintiff been seen by a doctor and intubated, clearing the obstruction, the brain damage could have been avoided. There were two schools of thought, however, as to whether in the circumstances it was appropriate to intubate. The doctor who failed to attend said that had she attended the plaintiff she would not have intubated, and therefore the cardiac arrest and subsequent brain damage would have occurred in any event. There was evidence from one expert for the defendants, which the trial judge and the Court of Appeal chose to characterise as a responsible body of professional opinion, that he would not have intubated in the circumstances, although five medical experts for the plaintiff said that the child should have been intubated, and it was agreed that this was the only course of action that would have prevented the damage in this case. In the House of Lords the plaintiff submitted that the judge had been wrong in law to treat the *Bolam* test as requiring him to accept the views of one truthful body of expert professional advice, even though he was unpersuaded of its logical force, and that ultimately it was for the court, not for medical opinion, to decide what was the standard of care required of a professional in the circumstances of each particular case. Lord Browne-Wilkinson agreed that the court was not bound to conclude that a doctor can escape liability for negligent treatment or diagnosis just because he leads evidence from a number of medical experts who are genuinely of the opinion that the defendant's treatment or diagnosis accorded with sound medical practice. The court had to be satisfied that the opinion had a logical basis, which would involve the weighing of risks against benefits, in order to reach a defensible conclusion:

. . . in cases of diagnosis and treatment there are cases where, despite a body of professional opinion sanctioning the defendant's conduct, the defendant can properly be held liable for negligence (I am not here considering questions of disclosure of risk). In my judgment that is because, in some cases, it cannot be demonstrated to the judge's satisfaction that the body of opinion relied upon is reasonable or responsible. In the vast majority of cases the fact that distinguished experts in the field are of a particular opinion will demonstrate the reasonableness of that opinion. In particular, where there are questions of assessment of the relative risks and benefits of adopting a particular medical practice, a reasonable view necessarily presupposes that the relative risks and benefits have been weighed by the experts in forming their opinions. But if, in a rare case, it can be demonstrated that the professional opinion is not capable of withstanding logical analysis, the judge is entitled to hold that the body of opinion is not reasonable or responsible. (at p. 779)

However, it would very seldom be right, said his Lordship, for a judge to reach the conclusion that views genuinely held by a competent medical expert were unreasonable. It would be wrong to allow the assessment of medical risks and benefits, which was a matter of clinical judgment, to deteriorate into seeking to persuade the judge to prefer one of two views both of which are capable of being logically supported: 'It is only where a judge can be satisfied that the body of expert opinion cannot be logically supported at all that such opinion will not provide the bench mark by reference to which the defendant's conduct falls to be assessed.'

Nonetheless, *Bolitho* affirms the view that ultimately it is for the court to decide what is 'responsible' opinion, even where none of the expert evidence is critical of the defendant's conduct (*Sidaway* v *Bethlem Royal Hospital Governors* [1985] 1 All ER 643, 663 per Lord Bridge). In *Hucks* v *Cole* (1968), [1993] 4 Med LR 393, 397 Sachs LJ said that:

When the evidence shows that a lacuna in professional practice exists by which risks of grave danger are knowingly taken, then, however small the risks, the courts must anxiously examine that lacuna—particularly if the risks can be easily and inexpensively avoided. If the court finds, on an analysis of the reasons given for not taking those precautions that, in the light of current professional knowledge, there is no proper basis for the lacuna, and that it is definitely not reasonable that those risks should have been taken, its function is to state that fact and where necessary to state that it constitutes negligence. In such a case the practice will no doubt thereafter be altered to the benefit of patients.

Accordingly, although likely to be rare, the courts will sometimes condemn a common professional practice as negligent (see, e.g., *Lloyds Bank Ltd* v *E. B. Savory & Co.* [1933] AC 201; *Roberge* v *Bolduc* (1991) 78 DLR (4th) 666, SCC). In *Edward Wong Finance Co. Ltd* v *Johnson, Stokes and Master* [1984] AC 296 the Privy Council held that a solicitor who had followed a standard

Hong Kong conveyancing practice was negligent, and in *Re The Herald of Free Enterprise: Appeal by Captain Lewry, Independent,* 18 December 1987, the Divisional Court held the general practice of ships' masters commanding roll-on roll-off ferries to set sail without checking that the bow doors of the ferry were closed was not evidence of the required standard of care, but rather of a general and culpable complacency in respect of elementary safety precautions.

On the other hand, the number of cases in which it can be said that the court has declared a professional practice to be negligent is comparatively small, and there is a suggestion that the judges tend to be particularly deferential to the views medical experts in medical negligence cases in comparison to the approach adopted in other jurisdictions (see, e.g., Giesen (1993) 1 Med Law Int 3, 5, and the comments of Lord Denning MR in *Hucks* v *Cole* (1968), [1993] 4 Med LR 393, 396: 'A doctor is not to be held negligent simply because something goes wrong . . . He is not liable for mischance, or misadventure. Nor is he liable for an error of judgment . . . He is only liable if he falls below the standard of a reasonably competent practitioner in his field—so much so that his conduct may fairly be held to be—I will not say deserving of censure, but, at any rate, inexcusable'). This approach may change. The effect of the decision of the House of Lords in *Bolitho* v *City and Hackney Health Authority* [1997] 4 All ER 771 is that expert opinion about the defendant's conduct (whether favourable or unfavourable) should be measured against the general principles applied to the question of breach of duty. Lord Browne-Wilkinson commented (at p. 778) that:

> the court has to be satisfied that the exponents of the body of opinion relied upon can demonstrate that such opinion has a logical basis. In particular in cases involving, as they so often do, the weighing of risks against benefits, the judge before accepting a body of opinion as being responsible, reasonable or respectable, will need to be satisfied that, in forming their views, the experts have directed their minds to the question of comparative risks and benefits and have reached a defensible conclusion on the matter.

Thus, medical experts will have to be able to demonstrate that they have undertaken a form of risk–benefit analysis of the particular medical practice in question, and that their opinion stands up to logical analysis.

The question of how many experts constitutes a body of opinion that can be characterised as a 'responsible body of professional opinion' was raised in *Defreitas* v *O'Brian* [1995] 6 Med LR 108. The Court of Appeal rejected the plaintiff's argument that the defendant could not simply rely on a small number of experts in the field as supporting a particular practice. The test of whether there was a 'responsible body' of opinion could not be measured in purely quantitative terms. On the facts, a body of 11 doctors who specialised in spinal surgery, out of a total of well over 1,000 orthopaedic and neuro-surgeons in the country, could represent a responsible body of opinion. This could make it reasonable for a specialist in spinal surgery to undertake intricate exploratory surgery, on the basis that this conformed to a practice accepted as proper by a responsible body of surgeons in the sub-specialty, in circumstances where other surgeons engaged in a more generalised practice might consider the procedure to be too risky.

Professional practice may change over time so that what was once accepted as the correct procedure is no longer considered to be respectable or responsible. A professional person cannot 'obstinately and pig-headedly carry on with some old technique if it has been proved to be contrary to what is really substantially the whole of informed [professional] opinion' (Bolam, p. 122). This imposes an obligation to keep up to date in the exercise of a particular skill. But a professional does not have to read every article appearing in the professional literature nor must he adopt every suggested new technique. It will only be negligence not to adopt it when it is a proved and accepted practice of the profession (Crawford v Board of Governors of Charing Cross Hospital, The Times, 8 December 1953, CA—doctor not liable for failing to adjust his practice following an article published in the Lancet six months previously). In Gascoine v Ian Sheridan & Co. [1994] 5 Med LR 437, 447 Mitchell J said that a 'shop floor gynaecologist' had a responsibility to keep himself generally informed about mainstream changes in diagnosis, treatment and practice through the mainstream literature, such as the leading textbooks and the Journal of Obstetrics and Gynaecology, but it was unreasonable to expect him to acquaint himself with the content of the more obscure journals. On the same basis, it is not negligent to use the methods and equipment normally employed in this country, even if the harm could have been avoided by using equipment commonly available in another country although rare here (Whiteford v Hunter [1950] WN 553, HL).

At one time it was believed that a 'mere error of professional judgment' would not amount to negligence. This, however, is not correct. 'To say that a surgeon committed an error of clinical judgment is wholly ambiguous, for while some such errors may be completely consistent with the due exercise of professional skill, other acts or omissions in the course of exercising 'clinical judgment' may be so glaringly below proper standards as to make a finding of negligence inevitable' (Whitehouse v Jordan [1981] 1 All ER 267, 276 per Lord Edmund-Davies).

Where a person holds himself out as having a specialist skill he will be judged by the objective standards of a reasonably competent man exercising that skill, even though he does not in fact possess the requisite skill (though care must be taken in determining just what the defendant has held himself out as capable of performing, see, e.g., Philips v William Whiteley [1938] 1 All ER 566—a jeweller must exercise the degree of care appropriate to a jeweller, not a surgeon, when piercing ears). Therefore, as with learner-drivers (Nettleship v Weston [1971] 2 QB 691, see para. 3.1.1), the inexperienced professional is negligent if he does not achieve the standards of a reasonably competent and experienced man. In Wilsher v Essex Area Health Authority [1986] 3 All ER 801 a premature baby in a special care baby unit received excess oxygen due to an error in monitoring its oxygen supply. A junior and inexperienced doctor inserted a catheter into a vein rather than an artery and then asked a senior registrar to check its position. The registrar failed to spot the error. The baby was subsequently discovered to be blind, possibly as a result of the excess oxygen (the decision of the Court of Appeal was reversed on the causation issue: [1988] 1 All ER 871, see para. 4.1.2). On the question of the standard of care applicable to the junior doctor, Browne-Wilkinson V-C, in his dissenting judgment, commented (at p. 833) that 'so long as the English law rests liability on personal fault, a doctor who has properly accepted a post in a hospital in order to gain necessary experience should only be held liable for acts or omissions which a careful doctor with his qualifications and experience would not have done or omitted'. This subjective standard would mean that the standard of care that a patient could legitimately expect would depend upon the experience of the particular doctor who treated him. (Note that this is not the equivalent of the special relationship which the High Court of Australia considered justified a subjective test in *Cook* v *Cook* (1986) 68 ALR 353, see para. 3.1.1.)

The majority in the Court of Appeal (Mustill and Glidewell LJJ) adhered to the objective standard. Mustill LJ said (at p. 813) that 'this notion of a duty tailored to the actor, rather than to the act which he elects to perform, has no place in the law of tort'. However, his Lordship, having said that the degree of skill should be appropriate to the task undertaken, added that the standard of care should be related, not to the individual, but to the post which he occupies, though differentiating 'post' from 'rank' or 'status'. Thus, 'the standard is not just that of the averagely competent and well-informed junior houseman (or whatever the position of the doctor) but of such a person who fills a post in a unit offering a highly specialised service. But, even so, it must be recognised that different posts make different demands.' This statement is puzzling since, having rejected a subjective test, Mustill LJ seems to reintroduce variable standards of care by reference to the 'posts' occupied by different doctors. Glidewell LJ applied the *Bolam* test without any gloss, commenting (at p. 831) that 'the law requires the trainee or learner to be judged by the same standard as his more experienced colleagues. If it did not, inexperience would frequently be urged as a defence to an action for professional negligence.' With respect, it is submitted that this is the correct (and long-established) approach (see, e.g., *Jones* v *Manchester Corporation* [1952] 2 QB 852; *Bova* v *Spring* [1994] 5 Med LR 120, 122—minimum standard of care expected of a trainee general practitioner no lower than that expected of an experienced one). A single standard of care for patients can only be achieved by relating the reasonableness of the defendant's conduct to the task that is undertaken, and what is objectively reasonable does not change with the experience of the defendant. As a matter of practice and common sense the inexperienced doctor, or lawyer, or accountant, will normally undertake less complex tasks than his experienced colleagues, but if he does perform tasks beyond the level of his competence the 'fault' lies not so much in not having the skills, which by definition he does not possess, but in undertaking the task at all. Moreover, in any event, an inexperienced professional will often satisfy the standard of care by seeking the assistance of his superiors to check his work, even though he may himself have made a mistake. It was on this basis that the junior doctor was found not to have been negligent in *Wilsher*, although the registrar was liable. (Note that an employer may be directly liable in negligence for permitting an inexperienced employee to undertake tasks which he is not competent to perform without proper supervision: *Jones* v *Manchester Corporation*; *Wilsher* v *Essex Area Health Authority* [1986] 3 All ER 801, 833.)

A question to which no clear answer has yet emerged is whether a defendant who is particularly experienced or eminent who practises in a highly specialised field within his profession must exercise greater care than the ordinarily competent man. In *Maynard* v *West Midlands Regional Health Authority* [1984] 1 WLR 634 Lord Scarman said that 'a doctor who professes to exercise a special skill must exercise the ordinary skill of his speciality' (see also *Duchess of Argyll* v *Beuselinck* [1972] 2 Lloyd's Rep 172, 183 per Megarry J in relation to a specialist solicitor, though the action was in contract; cf. *Wimpey Construction UK Ltd* v *Poole* [1984] 2 Lloyd's Rep 499, 506 where Webster J applied the *Bolam* test 'without qualification' for the experienced specialist; see, however, *Matrix-Securities Ltd* v *Theodore Goddard* (1997) 147 NLJ 1847—a lawyer advising in tax matters must exercise the standard of care appropriate to that sector of the profession specialising in tax matters). This variable standard may be more appropriate to professions that have a number of specialised subdisciplines such as medicine or engineering (cf. *Dugdale and Stanton,* para. 15.20, who treat the issue as a question of fact, and *Jackson and Powell,* paras 1.98 and 1.99, who express the standard of care by reference to 'reasonably competent members of the profession, who have the same rank and profess the same specialisation (if any) as the defendant').

3.2.2 Sport
In *Wooldridge* v *Sumner* [1963] 2 QB 43 the plaintiff was a photographer at a horse show who was knocked down when a horse that was being ridden in a competition got out of control. The Court of Appeal held that a spectator at a game or competition takes the risk of any damage caused by the act of a participant in the course of and for the purposes of the game, unless the participant's conduct shows a reckless disregard of the spectator's safety. This appears to set a lower standard than 'reasonable care in all the circumstances', and for this reason the case has been criticised (Goodhart (1962) 78 LQR 490), and was followed with some diffidence in *Wilks* v *Cheltenham Home Guard Motor Cycle & Light Car Club* [1971] 2 All ER 369. However, in *Harrison* v *Vincent* [1982] RTR 8 the Court of Appeal extended the 'reckless disregard of safety' test from spectators to fellow competitors in the sport, at least where the injury was caused 'in the flurry and excitement of the sport'. The negligence in that case consisted of a failure to maintain a motor-cycle combination, but this occurred 'in the relative calm of the workshop' and so the ordinary standard of reasonable care applied.

The analogy here is with a person who, confronted with an emergency or dilemma, has to decide on a course of action. If he takes a reasonable decision he is not negligent although with hindsight his choice turns out to be wrong (*The Bywell Castle* (1879) 4 PD 219; *Jones* v *Boyce* (1816) 1 Stark 493, see para. 14.5.3). In *Wooldridge* v *Sumner* itself, Diplock LJ pointed out that where decisions have to be made on the spur of the moment, as many decisions in the course of a game or competition are, then this is one of the circumstances that will be taken into account in determining whether the conduct was reasonable. It is unclear, then, why a standard based on recklessness was adopted. The concept of reasonable care *in all the circumstances* is flexible enough to allow for conduct which occurs in the heat of the moment when competitors are concentrating their efforts on the game. It may be that the difficulty stems from the interpretation to be put upon the word 'reckless'. Is it confined to conscious appreciation of the risk of harm (which would entail a difference in kind from the reasonable-man test) or does it extend to serious inadvertent negligence? It has been argued that, on the basis of Lord Diplock's own subsequent statements, 'recklessness' can include some inadvertent conduct, and that in *Wooldridge* v *Sumner* the use of the word 'was merely an emphatic expression of the fact that all circumstances must be taken into account in assessing negligence and that players under competitive stress would not be held to answer by standards applicable in normal conditions' (Hudson (1982) 98 LQR 545, 548).

This suggestion receives some support from the decision of the Court of Appeal in *Condon* v *Basi* [1985] 2 All ER 453 which applied the ordinary standard of reasonable care to participants in an amateur football match. The *Wooldridge* v *Sumner* test was not referred to, but it is possible to reconcile the two cases if it is accepted that 'recklessness' is not used in any technical sense, but merely describes the fact that the flexibility of the standard of reasonable care 'demands less for its fulfilment at sporting events than in other circumstances of everyday life' (Hudson (1986) 102 LQR 11, 13; note also the comment of Sir John Donaldson MR in *Condon* v *Basi* at p. 454 that there would be 'a higher degree of care required of a player in a First Division football match than of a player in a local league football match'; cf. the discussion of professional liability in para. 3.2.1).

In *Smoldon* v *Whitworth* [1997] PIQR P133 it was held that a referee of a colts rugby match owed a duty of care to a player injured due to a collapsed scrum. It was well known that collapsing scrums carried a high risk of injury to players. The referee had failed to take a tight grip on the manner in which the players were scrummaging, and in circumstances where there was a known risk of serious injury, which administrators, referees, coaches and players had in general taken steps to avoid, there was no objection to the law of tort seeking also to protect players from unnecessary and potentially highly dangerous aspects of the game of rugby by imposing a duty of care in negligence. Both the trial judge and the Court of Appeal emphasised that this ruling related to colts, not senior, rugby, as it was played under the rules in 1991–92. The judge had adopted the test applied by Sir John Donaldson MR in *Condon* v *Basi* that the standard of care was that degree of care that was reasonable in the circumstances. The Court of Appeal held that this was the right test:

> The level of care required is that which is appropriate in all the circumstances, and the circumstances are of crucial importance. Full account

must be taken of the factual context in which a referee exercises his functions, and he could not be properly held liable for errors of judgment, oversights or lapses of which any referee might be guilty in the context of a fast-moving and vigorous contest. The threshold of liability is a high one. It will not easily be crossed.

There is in our judgment no inconsistency between this conclusion and that reached by the Court of Appeal in *Wooldridge* v *Sumner* and *Wilks* v *Cheltenham Cycle Club*. In these cases it was recognised that a sporting competitor, properly intent on winning the contest, was (and was entitled to be) all but oblivious of spectators. It therefore followed that he would have to be shown to have very blatantly disregarded the safety of spectators before he could be held to have failed to exercise such care as was reasonable in all the circumstances. The position of a referee *vis-à-vis* the players is not the same as that of a participant in a contest *vis-à-vis* a spectator. One of his responsibilities is to safeguard the safety of the players. So although the legal duty is the same in the two cases, the practical content of the duty differs according to the quite different circumstances. (at p. P139)

If it is accepted that a referee can potentially owe a duty of care to the participants in the sport that is being refereed, then the standard of care will, presumably, be that of a reasonably competent referee in the circumstances. Nonetheless, in practice referees may face some difficult judgments about when precisely to intervene. For example, could a boxer who suffers injury at the hands of his opponent claim that the referee should have stopped the bout sooner than he did? Could a footballer who sustains injury in a dangerous tackle sue the referee on the basis that the player who made the tackle had been playing dangerously throughout the match and should have been warned or even sent off prior to the tackle in which the injury was sustained?

3.2.3 Children

There are few cases in this country in which a child features as a defendant. It may be that children are not often worth suing, but infancy is not as such a defence (*Gorely* v *Codd* [1967] 1 WLR 19, 16-year-old negligent in using an air rifle). The standard of care applied when assessing *contributory negligence* by children is such care as can reasonably be expected of an ordinary child of the same age as the plaintiff (see para. 14.5.3). In *McHale* v *Watson* (1966) 115 CLR 199, the High Court of Australia held that this was the appropriate standard to apply to a child defendant. The standard is adjusted only for the child's age, but is otherwise objective. It is no answer 'to say that the harm he caused was due to his being abnormally slow-witted, quick-tempered, absent-minded or inexperienced' (per Kitto J). Owen J stated that conduct should be assessed by reference to a reasonable child 'of the same age, intelligence and experience'. Adjusting the standard for the child's intelligence and experience would seem to be a more subjective test, and this approach is applied in Canada (*McEllistrum* v *Etches* (1956) 6 DLR (2d) 1). In *Mullin* v *Richards* [1998] 1 All ER 920, the Court of Appeal adopted the view taken in *McHale* v *Watson*. Two 15-year-old schoolgirls were playing at fencing with plastic rulers when one of the rulers broke and a piece of plastic entered the plaintiff's eye. The trial judge considered that they were equally to blame and held the defendant liable, with 50% contributory negligence by the plaintiff. The Court of Appeal held that given the history of events at the school (such games were common, were not prohibited, and had not caused any injuries in the past) the risk of injury was not reasonably foreseeable by a 15-year-old schoolgirl (though it might conceivably be foreseeable as a remote risk) and accordingly there was no negligence. Hutchison LJ said (at p. 924):

> The question for the judge is not whether the actions of the defendant were such as an ordinarily prudent and reasonable adult in the defendant's situation would have realised gave rise to a risk of injury, it is whether an ordinarily prudent and reasonable 15-year-old schoolgirl in the defendant's situation would have realised as much.

His Lordship referred to the judgments of Kitto and Owen JJ in *McHale* v *Watson*, and, while querying the use of the word 'intelligence' by Owen J, concluded that they were essentially making the same point that allowance has to be made for the age of the child. Butler-Sloss LJ cited a passage from the judgment of Kitto J:

> in the absence of any relevant statutory provision, children, like everyone else, must accept as they go about in society the risks from which ordinary care on the part of others will not suffice to save them. One such risk is that boys of twelve may behave as boys of twelve . . .

adding that 'girls of 15 playing together may play as somewhat irresponsible girls of 15'.

Of course, some risks may be obvious, even to children, and in some cases an older child may appear to be judged by the standards of an adult (*Williams* v *Humphrey, The Times*, 20 February 1975—15-year-old pushed the plaintiff into a swimming-pool), but this will simply be on the basis that the risk was reasonably foreseeable both to adults *and* children of the defendant's age. On the other hand, very young children may be incapable of negligence, being unable to foresee the harm (*Walmsley* v *Humenick* [1954] 2 DLR 232—five-year-old playing with bow and arrow not liable), but there is no fixed age.

A parent is generally not liable for the torts of his children, but he may be liable for his own negligence in failing to supervise the child whereby the child causes injury to a third party or himself (*Barnes* v *Hampshire County Council* [1969] 3 All ER 746; *Carmarthenshire County Council* v *Lewis* [1955] AC 549). Persons who have control over children, such as an education authority, are in the same position. It is usually said that the standard required is that of a 'reasonably prudent parent', but this is no different from the ordinary standard of reasonable care in the circumstances. It merely emphasises the fact that parents are aware that children tend to get into mischief and do not exercise the same degree of responsibility for safety as adults. This is simply one of the circumstances that has to be taken into account when a parent, or indeed any other potential defendant, is considering what precautions are appropriate when dealing with the actions of children (see, e.g., Occupiers' Liability Act 1957, s. 2(3)(a), para. 6.1.3.1). A reasonably prudent parent has to strike a balance which does not stifle the initiative and independence of teenagers by an excess of caution (*Porter* v *Barking & Dagenham London Borough Council, The Times*, 9 April 1990, allowing two 14-year-old boys to practise putting the shot unsupervised not negligent; cf. *Fowles* v *Bedfordshire County Council* [1995] PIQR P380—local authority negligent in permitting young persons at a youth centre to engage in gymnastics without supervision or a proper system of instruction).

3.2.4 Design

Traditionally the courts have been more reluctant to make findings of negligence in respect of the design of a product or structure, than in relation to its manufacture or operation. There is no rule of law to this effect, but in practice it is simply more difficult to establish negligence where a product is functioning as it was intended. Design problems are frequently related to cost and there will often be an element of policy for the designer in choosing a level of safety for which consumers are prepared to pay. For example, the financial consequences of a finding that a particular motor vehicle has an unsafe design could be very serious (see, e.g., *Wyngrove* v *Scottish Omnibuses Ltd* 1966 SC (HL) 47). In effect, purchasers of the vehicle will be required to pay more for a safety feature that, if given the choice, they may have preferred not to have. This is in the nature of a legislative act, particularly if the vehicle conforms to safety standards laid down by Parliament, which the courts are not necessarily in the best position to undertake. It may be that the courts do not wish to become involved in this type of exercise, for reasons which are essentially similar to their approach to the liability of public authorities (see para. 2.2.3.2; *Atiyah*, pp. 42–5).

This is not to suggest that there can never be liability for negligent design (see, e.g., *Hindustan Steam Shipping Co. Ltd* v *Siemens Bros & Co. Ltd* [1955] 1 Lloyd's Rep 167; *Lambert* v *Lewis* [1981] 1 All ER 1185). Indeed, this is a not uncommon complaint against architects (*Jackson and Powell*, para 2.106), and where the design is novel or experimental, amounting to a 'venture into the unknown', a high degree of care may be required to meet the standard of reasonableness. This involves an obligation to identify the problems and, think things through' (*Independent Broadcasting Authority* v *EMI Electronics Ltd* (1980) 14 BLR 1).

3.3 PROOF OF BREACH

3.3.1 Burden of proof

The burden of proof, on the balance of probabilities, that the defendant has been careless rests with the plaintiff. As a general rule it is not for the defendant to show that he was not negligent. So where there are two equally possible explanations for an accident, one of which indicates that the accident occurred without negligence by the defendant, the plaintiff's action will fail (*The Kite* [1933] P 154; *Ashcroft* v *Mersey Regional Health Authority* [1983] 2 All ER 245). In *Cook* v *Lewis* [1952] 1 DLR 1 two people on a hunting trip discharged their guns simultaneously and the plaintiff was hit by one of them, but he was unable to prove which one. The Supreme Court of Canada held that in circumstances where two defendants have acted negligently and this has prevented the plaintiff from proving whose negligence caused the damage then the burden of proof is reversed and it is for the defendants to establish that they did not cause the damage. If neither could do so then both would be liable. This could be hard on an entirely innocent defendant, and it is not clear whether the rule would apply in this country (cf. *Baker* v *Market Harborough Cooperative Society Ltd* [1953] 1 WLR 1472, 1475 per Somervell LJ suggesting that it would not, and *Roe* v *Minister of Health* [1954] 2 QB 66, 82 per Denning LJ implying that it would and citing *Baker* v *Market Harborough Cooperative Society Ltd* in support). It may be that the rule would be confined to joint tortfeasors involving some element of concerted action (*Salmond and Heuston,* p. 242; see para. 14.6). In any event where a defendant is vicariously liable for the negligence of all the potential defendants the plaintiff does not have to establish which defendant caused the harm (*Cassidy* v *Ministry of Health* [1951] 2 KB 343).

If the evidence indicates that the damage was caused by the negligence of two persons but there is nothing to show which of them was more at fault the inference should be that they are equally to blame (*Baker* v *Market Harborough Cooperative Society Ltd*). Where the accident was due entirely to the fault of one or the other, but not both, but the judge cannot decide which, then again the court may infer that both are equally to blame (*Bray* v *Palmer* [1953] 1 WLR 1455). This is a rule of practical convenience rather than strict logic.

The civil burden of proof—'on the balance of probabilities'—tends to hide the fact that the cogency of the evidence required to satisfy this test can vary with the issues at stake (see, e.g., Pattenden (1988) 7 CJQ 220). It is more difficult, for example, to establish fraudulent than negligent behaviour (*Hornal* v *Neuberger Products Ltd* [1957] 1 QB 247), and an allegation of murder made in civil proceedings requires the criminal standard of proof (*Halford* v *Brookes* [1992] PIQR P175). Similarly, professional negligence may be more difficult to prove. In *Dwyer* v *Rodrick, The Times,* 12 November 1983, May LJ commented:

> Professional men . . . are entitled to no special preference before the law, to no rule requiring a highier standard of proof on the balance of probabilities than any other. But it is to shut one's eyes to the obvious if one denies that the burden of achieving something more than that mere balance of probabilities is greater when one is investigating the complicated and sophisticated actions of a qualified and experienced lawyer, doctor, accountant, builder or motor engineer than when one is enquiring into the momentary inattention of the driver of a motor car in a simple running-down action.

In some circumstances the burden of proof may be reversed. By the Civil Evidence Act 1968, s. 11, proof that a person has been convicted of an offence shall be taken as proof that he committed the offence unless the contrary is proved. Provided the conviction is relevant to the facts in issue this means that a defendant will have to disprove negligence. This can be an important advantage for the plaintiff, particularly in road traffic accident cases where negligence is more likely to lead to a prosecution for driving without due care and attention (see also para. 3.3.2.2 on the effect of establishing *res ipsa loquitur*).

The plaintiff does not necessarily have to provide direct evidence of negligence by the defendant. He may rely upon any legitimate inferences that can be drawn from the proved facts, and in the absence of evidence to the contrary the inference may be that the defendant was negligent. An inference is a deduction from the evidence which, if it is a reasonable deduction, may have the validity of legal proof, as opposed to conjecture which, even though plausible, has no value, since it amounts to a mere guess (*Jones* v *Great Western Railway Co.* (1930) 47 TLR 39, 45 per Lord Macmillan).

3.3.2 Res ipsa loquitur

Sometimes an accident may occur in circumstances in which accidents do not normally happen unless there has been negligence by someone. Where the plaintiff has no or insufficient knowledge about how the accident occurred it would be unfair to require him to prove negligence, particularly if the defendant does know what happened and could choose not to give any evidence. Thus the fact of the accident itself may give rise to an inference of negligence by the defendant which, in the absence of evidence in rebuttal, would be sufficient to impose liability. This is referred to by the Latin maxim *res ipsa loquitur* ('the thing speaks for itself'), although there is no magic in the phrase—it is simply a submission that the facts establish a prima facie case of negligence against the defendant (*Roe* v *Minister of Health* [1954] 2 QB 66, 87–8 per Morris LJ). There are two questions to be determined: (a) when does the maxim apply? and (b) what is its effect?

3.3.2.1 Application

3.3.2.1.1 Control The defendant or someone for whom he is responsible must have been in control of the thing that caused the damage. The *res* must speak of negligence *by the defendant*, which it will not do if the circumstances were under the control of others as well as the defendant. The test is whether outside interference was likely. If it is improbable that some unauthorised person could have interfered with the thing that caused the damage, the defendant has sufficient control (*Lloyde* v *West Midlands Gas Board* [1971] 1 WLR 749). In *Easson* v *London & North Eastern Railway Co.* [1944] KB 421 a boy fell through a door in a train during the journey. It was 'impossible to say that the doors of an express corridor train travelling from Edinburgh to London are continuously under the sole control of the railway company' (per Goddard LJ at p. 424). Passengers could have interfered with the door, and so *res ipsa loquitur* did not apply.

Where the events were under the control of two independent persons, but the plaintiff cannot say which, it may be that he can call on each of them for an explanation (*Roe* v *Minister of Health* [1954] 2 QB 66, 82 per Denning LJ; cf. *Salmond and Heuston*, p. 244).

3.3.2.1.2 Accident must be such as would not normally happen without carelessness In *Scott* v *London & St Katherine Docks Co.* (1865) 3 H & C 596 several bags of sugar fell from a hoist on to the plaintiff. Erle CJ said (at p. 601) that:

> where the thing is shown to be under the management of the defendant or his servants, and the accident is such as in the ordinary course of things does not happen if those who have the management use proper care, it affords reasonable evidence, in the absence of explanation by the defendants, that the accident arose from want of care.

Common experience indicates that barrels of flour do not fall from warehouse windows into the street in the absence of negligence (*Byrne* v *Boadle* (1863) 2 H & C 722), that stones are not usually found in buns (*Chaproniere* v *Mason* (1905) 21 TLR 633) and that trains do not usually collide (*Skinner* v *London, Brighton & South Coast Railway Co.* (1850) 5 Exch 787). For further examples *see Charlesworth and Percy*, paras 5–108 to 5–116. On the other hand, losses on the commodity market are not *per se* evidence of negligence by brokers (*Stafford* v *Conti Commodity Services Ltd* [1981] 1 All ER 691) nor is a spark from a domestic fire (*Sochaki* v *Sas* [1947] 1 All ER 344).

Res ipsa loquitur can apply to events which are outside the common experience of mankind, such as medical negligence. A patient who goes into hospital to be cured of two stiff fingers and comes out with four stiff fingers is entitled to put the hospital to an explanation of how that could have happened without negligence (*Cassidy* v *Ministry of Health* [1951] 2 KB 343, 365 per Denning LJ), and a failure to return a patient to consciousness from a normal general anaesthetic in the course of a routine medical procedure calls for an explanation from the defendants (*Lindsay* v *Mid-Western Health Board* [1993] 2 IR 147, 181 per O'Flaherty J, Supreme Court of Ireland; *Saunders* v *Leeds Western Health Authority* (1984), [1993] 4 Med LR 355). In *Glass* v *Cambridge Health Authority* [1995] 6 Med LR 91 *res ipsa loquitur* was held to apply where the heart of a healthy man went into cardiac arrest while under general anaesthesia, though the defendants' explanation of events showed that they had not been negligent. It will be rare for *res ipsa loquitur* to apply in a case of medical negligence, except in very simple situations, because in practice the parties will have obtained relevant evidence, e.g. from the medical records, and have expert medical opinion available. In these circumstances the question is what weight should be given to the evidence and whether an inference of negligence is appropriate (see the Court of Appeal's discussion in *Ratcliffe* v *Plymouth & Torbay Health Authority* [1998] PIQR P170).

3.3.2.1.3 Cause must be unknown When all the facts as to the cause of the accident are known the maxim does not apply. The question then is whether on the facts negligence by the defendant is to be inferred (*Barkway* v *South Wales Transport Co. Ltd* [1950] 1 All ER 392).

3.3.2.2 Effect There are two views as to the effect of the plaintiff establishing *res ipsa loquitur*. The first is that it raises a prima facie inference of negligence which requires the defendant to provide a reasonable explanation of how the accident could have occurred without negligence on his part. If he does this then the inference is rebutted and the plaintiff is back to the original position of having to prove the defendant's negligence (*Ballard* v *North British Railway Co.* 1923 SC (HL) 43, 54). The reality, of course, is that the plaintiff will be unable to do so because he would not have relied on *res ipsa loquitur* if he had positive evidence of the defendant's carelessness. This was the position adopted by the House of Lords in *Colvilles Ltd* v *Devine* [1969] 1 WLR 475, 479 where it was said that the defendants had to show that the accident was just as consistent with their having exercised due diligence as with negligence. There was no suggestion that the defendants' explanation had to be more likely than the inference of negligence raised by the maxim. Thus if the probabilities are equally balanced the plaintiff, having the burden of proving negligence, would lose (see also per Megaw LJ in *Lloyde* v *West Midlands Gas Board* [1971] 1 WLR 749, 755—'it is no more than an exotic, although convenient, phrase to describe what is in essence no more than a common-sense approach . . . to the assessment of the effect of evidence'; and *Ward* v *Tesco Stores Ltd* [1976] 1 WLR 810, 816).

The second view is that the maxim reverses the burden of proof requiring the defendant to show that the damage was not caused by his failure to take reasonable care. On this approach, where the probabilities are equal the defendant would lose. In *Henderson* v *Henry E. Jenkins & Sons* [1970] AC 282 the hydraulic brakes on a lorry failed when it was travelling downhill and there was an accident in which the plaintiff's husband was killed. The brake failure was caused by corrosion of the brake pipe at a point that was hidden from ordinary visual inspection. The vehicle had been regularly maintained, and neither the manufacturers nor the Ministry of Transport recommended removing the pipe for inspection. The defendants argued that this was a latent defect which could not have been discovered by the exercise of reasonable care. By a bare majority the House of Lords held the defendants liable, because they had given no evidence about the history of the vehicle. If, for example, it had been used to carry corrosive chemicals, reasonable precautions would have included removing the pipe for inspection. On the evidence it was impossible to say whether the defendants had been negligent or not, and therefore the decision to impose liability must have been on the basis that they had failed to establish that they had exercised reasonable care. Indeed, Lord Reid and Lord Donovan said that the burden of proof lay with the defendants (see also *Moore* v *R. Fox & Sons* [1956] 1 QB 596, CA). Moreover, it has been argued that despite statements to the contrary in *Colvilles Ltd* v *Devine* the effect of the *decision* in that case was to reverse the burden of proof (see Atiyah, (1972) 35 MLR 337, 342–4). Similarly in *Ward* v *Tesco Stores Ltd* [1976] 1 WLR 810 the defendants were held liable when the plaintiff slipped on some yoghurt that had been spilled on the floor of a supermarket. There was no evidence as to how long the yoghurt had been there. The only evidence was that the plaintiff had slipped, and as Ormrod LJ (dissenting) observed, that could have happened no matter what degree of care had been taken.

In *Ng Chun Pui* v *Lee Chuen Tat* [1988] RTR 298, however, the Privy Council has stated quite explicitly that the burden of proof does not shift to the defendant, but rests throughout the case on the plaintiff. The 'so-called doctrine of *res ipsa loquitur* . . . is no more than the use of a Latin maxim to describe the state of the evidence from which it is proper to draw an inference of negligence' (at p. 300). In an appropriate case the plaintiff can establish a prima facie inference of negligence from the mere fact of the accident. The 'burden' on the defendant is to adduce evidence that is capable of rebutting the prima facie case, just as he would have to do in the face of positive evidence from the plaintiff raising an inference of negligence. The duty of the court is to examine all the evidence and decide whether on the proved facts and legitimate inferences negligence has been established (ibid. at p. 301, approving Megaw LJ in *Lloyde* v *West Midlands Gas Board*). In *Bergin* v *David Wickes Television* [1994] PIQR P167, 168 Steyn LJ observed that *res ipsa loquitur* 'is in truth not a doctrine, nor a principle, nor a rule. It is simply a convenient label for a group of situations in which an unexplained accident is, as a matter of common sense, the basis for an inference of negligence'. But, just as the plaintiff is not entitled to rely on conjecture or speculation to establish his case on the balance of probabilities, so the defendant cannot resort to this when he is called upon for an explanation of events. Where an inference of negligence does arise from the circumstances of the accident, a general denial by way of defence will not be sufficient to rebut the inference of negligence.

If *res ipsa loquitur* did reverse the burden of proof the strange consequence would be that a plaintiff who relied on the maxim to raise a prima facie case would be in a better position than a plaintiff who established a prima facie case in some other way, e.g., by adducing affirmative evidence of negligence. It may be that the differences between the two views of the effect of *res ipsa loquitur* are exaggerated. After all, it is a fine line between the probabilities being equally balanced and tipping the scale one way or the other. The issue will turn upon the cogency that the court attributes to particular pieces of evidence and this is necessarily a subjective judgment which it is virtually impossible to quantify (as the speeches in *Henderson* v *Henry E. Jenkins & Sons* demonstrate). However, in cases of professional negligence, where as a matter of law the court is precluded from choosing between responsible bodies of professional opinion as to the correct professional practice, the location of the burden of proof will, in effect, decide the case (cf. *Clark* v *MacLennan* [1983] 1 All ER 416 and *Ashcroft* v *Mersey Regional Health Authority* [1983] 2 All ER 245, though note that the reasoning in *Clark* v *MacLennan*, in which the judge reversed the burden of proof, but not the decision itself that the defendants were liable, has been strongly criticised in *Wilsher* v *Essex Area Health Authority* [1986] 3 All ER 801, 814 per Mustill

LJ). It remains, nonetheless, for the court to decide whether a particular view constitutes a 'responsible' body of professional opinion, and this must depend on the cogency of the evidence which may be influenced, for example, by the unimpressive demeanour of a witness or the defective logic of an argument advanced by one or more experts (*Maynard* v *West Midlands Regional Health Authority* (1981), unreported, CA, per Sir Stanley Rees).

FOUR

Negligence III: causation and remoteness of damage

Causation and remoteness of damage are of general relevance in the law of tort. Even in torts which are actionable *per se* the plaintiff must prove that the tort caused the loss of which he complains if he wants to obtain substantial, rather than nominal, damages. In practice most of the problems that have arisen on this subject have involved the tort of negligence, and many of the cases demonstrate a persistent tension between notions of fault liability and the objective of compensating the plaintiff.

Causation is concerned with the physical connection between the defendant's negligence and the plaintiffs damage. No matter how gross the defendant's negligence he will not be liable if, as a question of fact, his conduct was not a cause of the damage. The 'but for' test serves to exclude from consideration factors which have made no difference to the final outcome of events. This is normally a comparatively simple exercise (para. 4.1). Problems occur where the conduct satisfies the 'but for' test, yet is merely one of a number of events that could rightly be regarded as causing the harm. There are two broad categories of circumstances. First, where each event is a sufficient cause of the damage and the question is which event is to be treated as the effective cause—the cause 'in law' (para. 4.2.1). Secondly, where the defendant's conduct sets off a sequence of events that ultimately results in harm to the plaintiff. Here the issue is whether the subsequent events should be regarded as severing the causal link—the 'chain of causation'—between the conduct and the damage (para. 4.2.2). Again it is a question of deciding whether the conduct was the cause 'in law' of the harm.

It is important to appreciate from the outset that in neither of these situations is the problem a pure question of fact. Clearly the facts must have a bearing on the decision, but in the final analysis the court has to make a choice as to which events are to be regarded as having sufficient causative potency. This is not a scientific inquiry but a process of attributing responsibility, and this involves value judgments and policy decisions (see *Atiyah*, pp. 101–6). The point becomes more obvious with remoteness of damage. Even when it is patent that the defendant's negligence 'caused' the harm, it may be said that the damage was too 'remote' if it is not of the same type as would normally be anticipated in similar circumstances, or if it occurred in an unusual way. There has to be some limit, it is said, and therefore it would be wrong to hold a person liable for all the consequences of his negligence however bizarre or freakish they might be.

Strictly speaking, causation in law and remoteness of damage are separate issues, but in practice they tend to merge. This is partly due to the rather casual use of the word 'remoteness', which is often employed to describe a causation problem, rather than being confined to setting the limits of actionability for damage admittedly caused by the defendant's carelessness. Where there has been an intervening event, for example, the damage may be designated as 'too remote' a consequence of the negligence. This is simply a way of saying that the defendant's conduct was not the cause in law of the damage. The word 'remoteness' is being used here in a non-technical sense to mean far removed in causative effect from the original wrong (see further para. 4.2.2).

'Remoteness' has at least three other meanings. First, to place limits on a defendant's liability for damage that he admittedly caused, but which is unusual either in the manner of its occurrence or its type. 'Remoteness' is used in this sense in paragraph 4.3. Secondly, it is sometimes used to indicate the non-actionability of a particular type of damage. Pure financial loss, for example, may be described as too remote. When used in this way it is performing precisely the same function as the notional duty of care, i.e., excluding certain types of negligently inflicted loss from the ambit of actionability (see para. 2.1.4). Thirdly, remoteness has sometimes been used where harm to a particular plaintiff is unforeseeable. Here the word performs the same function as duty 'in fact' (see para. 2.1.3). The courts are not necessarily explicit about the meaning that is attributed to the term 'remoteness', although it is generally not very difficult to spot from the context, provided the reader is aware of the possible interpretations.

Given the variety of conceptual tools available for regulating liability, it is hardly surprising that the law sometimes becomes confused. 'The truth', said Lord Denning MR, 'is that all these three—duty, remoteness and causation—are all devices by which the courts limit the range of liability for negligence or nuisance' (*Lamb* v *Camden London Borough Council* [1981] QB 625, 636). Lines have to be drawn somewhere:

> Sometimes it is done by limiting the range of the persons to whom duty is owed. Sometimes it is done by saying that there is a break in the chain of causation. At other times it is done by saying that the consequence is too remote to be a head of damage. All these devices are useful in their way. But ultimately it is a question of policy for the judges to decide.

Indeed, ultimately it is, and it is not difficult to discern the policy choices that have been made in many of the cases that follow in this chapter. But that does not absolve the courts from making decisions that can be justified, wherever possible, by a coherent structure of principle. It will be seen, however, that policy and principle do not always correspond, and this, compounded by a confused and confusing use of language, has made causation and remoteness of damage one of the most difficult areas in the law of tort.

4.1 FACTUAL CAUSATION

The first question to be determined is whether the defendant's conduct was in any way causally relevant to the plaintiff's loss. This is essentially an explanatory inquiry—how in fact did the damage occur? The result of this inquiry may, but will not necessarily, indicate where *responsibility* for causing the damage should be attributed. Lawyers take a very pragmatic approach even to this comparatively simple exercise, which is shaped by the ultimate objective of allocating responsibility. Take a common example of a pedestrian run down by a negligent motorist. To a scientist the pedestrian's presence at that time and place was a 'cause' of the accident. It was a necessary condition for the occurrence of the event. To an economist also the pedestrian's presence is significant. Injury to pedestrians is not 'caused' by the activity of driving motor vehicles but by the conflict between the uses which motorists and pedestrians wish to make of the highway. It is not simply a matter of drivers imposing costs on pedestrians, because from the drivers' point of view pedestrians impose costs on drivers by requiring them to drive more carefully (for the same point in the context of private nuisance see para. 7.1.2. 1). For the lawyer the mere presence of the pedestrian is causally neutral. It may have been a *sine qua non* of the accident but it is causally irrelevant to the allocation of responsibility for the accident. If, however, the pedestrian had carelessly stepped into the road without warning, the lawyer would regard his presence at that point in time and space as an important element in the events leading to the accident. Thus, in the law of tort, causes assume significance to the extent that they assist the court in deciding how to attribute responsibility for the plaintiff's damage (cf. *Weir,* p. 254: 'How can you solve a problem of causation by asking: "Whose fault was it?"?'). The first step is to eliminate irrelevant causes, and this is the purpose of the 'but for' test.

4.1.1 The 'but for' test
If harm to the plaintiff would not have occurred 'but for' the defendant's negligence then that negligence is a cause of the harm. It is not necessarily *the* cause because there may well be other events which are causally relevant. Putting this another way, if the loss would have been incurred in any event, the defendant's conduct is not a cause. In *Barnett* v *Chelsea & Kensington Hospital Management Committee* [1969] 1 QB 428 a doctor in a casualty department sent a patient away without treatment, telling him to see his own doctor. The patient died from arsenic poisoning. It was held that the doctor's conduct was negligent, but the expert evidence indicated that the patient was beyond help and would have died in any event. Therefore the doctor's negligence did not cause the death. Similarly, in *Robinson* v *Post Office* [1974]

2 All ER 737 a doctor's omission to test for an allergic reaction to an anti-tetanus vaccination was not causally related to the patient's subsequent reaction, because the test would not have revealed the allergy in time.

It is easier to say what would have happened in the absence of negligence by the defendant where events depend on physical reactions which are amenable to objective scientific proof. Where speculation as to what might have occurred turns on how a person would have behaved, conclusions may be more difficult to draw, but they are not impossible. In *McWilliams* v *Sir William Arrol & Co. Ltd* [1962] 1 WLR 295 a steel erector who was not wearing a safety belt fell to his death. His employers were in breach of a statutory duty to supply safety belts, but the House of Lords held that they were not liable because it was probable that the deceased would not have worn the belt if it had been available. The deceased had rarely, if ever, used a safety belt in the past and so it was a natural inference that he would not have worn a belt on this occasion. Lord Reid commented that it would not be right to draw such an inference too readily because people do sometimes change their minds unexpectedly, but the evidence in this case was 'overwhelming' (for criticism see *Atiyah*, p. 98; and cf. *Bux* v *Slough Metals Ltd* [1974] 1 All ER 262—employers liable for failing to instruct and supervise plaintiff in use of safety equipment).

This type of causation problem also arises in cases where a patient alleges that his doctor has been negligent in failing to disclose information about the risks of a proposed medical procedure. Even if the plaintiff overcomes the problems of establishing negligence (see *Sidaway* v *Bethlem Royal Hospital Governors* [1985] 1 All ER 643; Clements (1985) 1 PN 136), he still has to prove that had the information been disclosed he would have declined the treatment, thereby avoiding the risk. (It has been said that this does not apply to an action in trespass to the person where medical treatment has been given without the patient's consent: *Chatterton* v *Gerson* [1981] 1 All ER 257, 265 per Bristow J; Robertson (1981) 97 LQR 102, 107. But this is questionable. Causation of the damage is relevant to all torts, including torts actionable *per se* if the plaintiff wants more than nominal damages.) In practice this is difficult to prove because the courts are wary of a disappointed patient forming judgments about what he would have done with the benefit of hindsight (*Chatterton* v *Gerson* [1981] 1 All ER 257, 267; *Hills* v *Potter* [1983] 3 All ER 716; cf. *Sidaway* v *Bethlem Royal Hospital Governors* where at trial Skinner J concluded that the plaintiff would have declined treatment if the risks had been disclosed; for further discussion of this issue in the context of medical treatment see Jones (1994) 10 PN 24). Similarly, in the case of negligent statements the plaintiff must establish not only that he placed reasonable reliance on the defendant's advice but also that the reliance, not some other consideration, caused him to act to his detriment (*JEB Fasteners Ltd* v *Marks Bloom & Co.* [1983] 1 All ER 583).

This issue is not limited to circumstances where the question is what the plaintiff would have done, but for the breach of duty. A question may arise as to what the *defendant* would have done in hypothetical circumstances, which have not arisen because of the defendant's own negligence. The courts' approach to causation is the same in this situation: the plaintiff must still prove that but for the negligence the damage would not have occurred (although the Court of Appeal has recently suggested that where the loss turns upon what a *third party* would have done in hypothetical circumstances the correct approach is to assess the value of the chance of benefit or avoiding a detriment that the plaintiff has lost: *Allied Maples Group Ltd* v *Simmons & Simmons* [1995] 4 All ER 907; see para. 4.1.3). In *Bolitho* v *City and Hackney Health Authority* [1997] 4 All ER 771 a two-year-old boy, who was in hospital, suffered brain damage as a result of cardiac arrest caused by an obstruction of the bronchial air passages. The defendants admitted negligence because a doctor had not attended to the plaintiff in response to calls for assistance. The damage could have been avoided if the plaintiff had been seen by a doctor and 'intubated', clearing the obstruction. The doctor who failed to respond said that had she attended she would not have intubated, and therefore the cardiac arrest and subsequent brain damage would have occurred in any event. There was evidence that a responsible body of professional opinion would have supported a decision not to intubate, although five medical experts for the plaintiff said that he should have been intubated, and it was agreed that this was the only course of action that would have prevented the damage. By a majority, the Court of Appeal held that the action failed on the ground of causation. In a case of breach of duty by omission it was necessary to decide what would have happened had the defendant's duty been discharged. Whether the doctor's omission to attend caused the plaintiff's damage depended upon what she would have done had she turned up. The plaintiff had to prove that the doctor would probably have intubated, or that if, as she claimed, she would not have intubated that this omission would have been itself negligent in that it was contrary to accepted medical practice. Simon Brown LJ expressed a strong dissenting judgment, however, arguing that in determining matters of causation the question that should be asked is what probably would have happened, not whether a responsible body of professional opinion agrees with what the defendant says she would have done. On appeal to the House of Lords it was urged on behalf of the plaintiff that the *Bolam* test (see *Bolam* v *Friern Hospital Management Committee* [1957] 2 All ER 118, para. 3.2.1), which is used as a measure of whether a professional person is in breach of duty, had no relevance in determining questions of causation. Lord Browne-Wilkinson agreed, that as a general proposition that was correct. In all cases the primary question is one of fact: did the wrongful act cause the injury? But in cases where the breach of duty consists of an omission to do an act which ought to have been done (such as the failure of a doctor to attend the patient) the factual enquiry is necessarily hypothetical. The question is 'What would have happened if an event, which by definition did not occur, had occurred?'. The first question is: 'What would have happened?'—either the doctor would have intubated, had she attended, or she would not. The *Bolam* test was not, and could not, be relevant to that question. The defendant doctor said that she would not have intubated, and therefore the plaintiff would in any event have sustained the brain damage. But she could not escape liability by proving that she would have failed to act as any reasonably competent doctor would have acted in the circumstances: 'A defendant cannot escape liability by saying that the damage would have occurred in any event because he would have committed some other breach of duty thereafter.' ([1997] 4 All ER 771, 776–7).

Lord Browne-Wilkinson adopted the reasoning of Hobhouse LJ in *Joyce* v *Wandsworth Health Authority* [1996] PIQR P121 in explaining the majority decision of the Court of Appeal in *Bolitho*. In *Joyce* the plaintiff underwent an operative procedure which resulted in a partially occluded artery, leading three months later to an upper brain stem infarction causing almost total paralysis. Although the procedure was not necessarily negligent the Court of Appeal considered that the immediate follow-up care that the plaintiff had received was negligent, in that he was discharged from hospital without proper instructions and advice. It was accepted that the only thing that could have prevented the damage was if within the first 48 hours the plaintiff had been seen by a vascular surgeon and the surgeon had decided to operate to deal with the occlusion. The Court of Appeal held that to succeed on causation the plaintiff had to prove either that had the vascular surgeon at the hospital been summoned he would in fact have re-operated, or that it would have been negligent for him not to do so. Hobhouse LJ said that where the negligence consisted of an act which is alleged to have had physical consequences, the question to be asked is straightforward even though its answer may not be: was the act a cause of the injury? Where the negligence consists of an omission, or an act which does not in itself have physical consequences, identifying the correct question is less easy. These cases could be further subdivided into (a) cases where the question is: what steps would have been taken if proper care had been taken? and (b) cases where the question is: what would have been the outcome of any further steps that ought to have been taken? In *Joyce* the facts fell into the first of these categories, (a), which was the same type of question that *Bolitho* raised. Hobhouse LJ summarised the position (at p. 152) in the following terms:

> Thus a plaintiff can discharge the burden of proof on causation by satisfying the court *either* that the relevant person would in fact have taken the requisite action (although she would not have been at fault if she had not) *or* that the proper discharge of the relevant person's duty towards the plaintiff required that she take that action. The former alternative calls for no explanation since it is simply the factual proof of the causative effect of the original fault. The latter is slightly more sophisticated: it involves the factual situation that the original fault did not itself cause the injury but that this was because there would have been some further fault on the part of the defendants; the plaintiff proves his case by proving that his injuries would have been avoided if proper care had continued to be taken . . . Properly viewed, therefore, this rule is favourable to a plaintiff because it gives him two routes by which he may prove his case—either proof that the exercise of proper care would have necessitated the relevant result, or proof that if proper care had been exercised it would in fact have led to the relevant result. (original emphasis)

In *Bolitho* Lord Browne-Wilkinson, having cited Hobhouse LJ, concluded that there were two questions for the judge to decide on causation: (1) what would the doctor have done, or authorised to be done, if she had attended the plaintiff? and (2) if she would not have intubated, would that have been negligent? The *Bolam* test had no relevance to the first question but was central to the second. Another way of putting this is to say that causation is about *what in fact happened*, which in turn depends upon the hypothetical question of what would have happened had there been no negligence ('but for' the negligence would the damage have occurred?). In *Bolitho* the plaintiff was claiming that had the doctor not been negligent and attended he would not have suffered brain damage, because the doctor would have intervened to prevent it. The doctor denied that she would have intervened, so that the damage would have occurred in any event (no 'but for' causation). The plaintiff alleged that a hypothetical failure to intervene would itself have been negligent, and a defendant cannot avoid a finding of causation by arguing that, in the hypothetical situation being considered, she would have acted negligently. The defendant then replies that a failure to intervene would not have been negligent because it was supported by a responsible body of professional opinion. Thus, in these circumstances the causation issue *appears* to turn on a question of negligence and the *Bolam* test. In reality *Bolitho* is about whether the failure to intubate, for whatever reason (non-attendance or conscious professional judgment), was negligent. The defendant's evidence that she would not have intubated simply moved the focus of the argument about negligence, i.e. breach of duty, from the non-attendance to the non-intubation.

The 'but for' test operates as a preliminary filter to exclude events which did not affect the outcome. It cannot, however, resolve all the problems of factual causation. In the case of two simultaneous wrongs to the plaintiff, each of which would have been sufficient to cause the damage, the test produces the ludicrous conclusion that neither wrong caused the harm (see Strachan (1970) 33 MLR 386, 391; consider also the facts of *Cook* v *Lewis* [1952] 1 DLR 1, para. 3.3.1). The only sensible answer here is that both caused the harm.

Another approach to factual causation is to ask whether the damage was within the risk envisaged by the defendant's fault. This can be illustrated by the case of *Gorris* v *Scott* (1874) LR 9 Ex 125 which was an action for breach of statutory duty. The defendant was in breach of a statutory obligation to keep animals being imported by ship in pens. The purpose of the legislation was to protect against the animals developing and spreading contagious disease. The plaintiffs sheep were washed overboard because of the absence of pens, but this was not actionable because the loss was 'altogether different' from the purpose of the legislation. This case was not argued on the basis of causation but it can be supported on this ground. Although the loss would not have occurred but for the breach of duty it was not caused by the breach, which envisaged an entirely different risk. Similarly in *The Empire Jamaica* [1957] AC 386 the defendant's fault consisted of failing to obtain a certificate of exemption for a ship's mate. This was not relevant because in fact the mate was fully competent and an exemption would have been granted if it had been applied for. Therefore the defendant's fault was not a cause of the collision which occurred while the mate was in charge of the ship. This can be treated as an application of the 'but for' test, but equally the risk envisaged by the legislation was that ships might be under the control of incompetent persons, and this was not the cause of the particular collision.

Take another example. A decayed tree falls on to a police car which is in pursuit of a burglar. Is the burglar responsible? True the police car would not have been at that point in time and space but for the chase, but that damage is not within the risk created by the burglar (*Fleming*, p. 195). Similarly, where the defendant's tort results in the plaintiff having to change his job, the tort is not *per se* a 'cause' of subsequent damage sustained by the plaintiff in the course of his new employment (see *Baker* v *Willoughby* [1970] AC 467, para. 4.2.1). Here factual causation shades into causation in law, where it is more obvious that the courts are making a selection from two or more possible causes.

4.1.2 Proof of causation

It is for the plaintiff to prove, on the balance of probabilities, that the defendant's breach of duty caused the damage. So where there are conflicting explanations for the plaintiff's condition, neither of which is wholly satisfactory, the defendant does not have to prove that his explanation is the correct one, though failure to prove it may be a factor in deciding whether the plaintiff's explanation of the cause should be accepted (*Pickford* v *Imperial Chemical Industries plc* [1998] 3 All ER 462, HL). In some instances the precise cause of the damage may be unknown, and even where it is possible in principle to establish a link between the type of harm suffered by the plaintiff and a specific hazard it may be very difficult to show that the individual plaintiff's condition was caused by exposure to that hazard rather than some other factor for which the defendant was not responsible. An obvious example is the problem of proving that an individual contracted cancer as a result of exposure to radiation, rather than other causes, although it is well known that radiation can cause cancer (see Brahams (1988) 138 NLJ 570). For example, in *Reay* v *British Nuclear Fuels plc* [1994] 5 Med LR 1 the plaintiffs failed to prove, on the balance of probabilities, that paternal *pre-conception* irradiation of the gonads produced mutation of spermatagonia causing a predisposition to cancer in children. In practice these problems are most acute in cases of man-made, usually industrial, disease (see Stapleton, *Disease and the Compensation Debate*, 1986, OUP, chapter 3), and some types of medical negligence claims (see, e.g., *Kay* v *Ayrshire and Arran Health Board* [1987] 2 All ER 417—plaintiff failed to prove that an overdose of penicillin could cause deafness; *Loveday* v *Renton* [1990] 1 Med LR 117—plaintiff failed to show, on a balance of probabilities, that pertussis vaccine could cause brain damage in young children, although it was 'possible' that it did; cf. *Best* v *Wellcome Foundation Ltd* [1994] 5 Med LR 81, para. 10.1.4, however, where the Supreme Court of Ireland drew an inference that the administration of pertussis vaccine caused the plaintiff's brain damage from the fact that there was a close temporal connection between the child's first convulsion and the injection of the vaccine, when the vaccine was proved to be from a defective batch). The Pearson Commission, for example, reported that the 'Medical Research Council said that while future research was likely to establish more causal relationships it would also reveal increasingly complex interactions which would heighten the problems of proving causation in the individual case' (*Pearson, vol.* 1, para. 1364; see also para. 1449: 'As the boundary of knowledge increases, so does the area of uncertainty'). Faced with this kind of factual uncertainty the plaintiff may have an impossible burden of proving causation on the balance of probabilities.

In *Bonnington Castings Ltd* v *Wardlaw* [1956] AC 613 the House of Lords held that the plaintiff does not have to establish that the defendant's breach of duty was the main cause of the damage provided that it materially contributed to the damage. The plaintiff contracted pneumoconiosis from inhaling air which contained silica dust at his workplace. The main source of the dust was from pneumatic hammers for which the employers were not in breach of duty (the 'innocent dust'). Some of the dust (the 'guilty dust') came from swing grinders for which they were responsible by failing to maintain the dust-extraction equipment. There was no evidence as to the proportions of innocent dust and guilty dust inhaled by the plaintiff. Indeed, such evidence as there was indicated that much the greater proportion came from the innocent source. On the evidence the plaintiff could not prove 'but for' causation, in the sense that it was more probable than not that had the dust-extraction equipment worked efficiently he would not have contracted the disease. Nonetheless, the House of Lords drew an inference of fact that the guilty dust was a contributory cause, holding the employers liable for the full extent of the loss. The plaintiff did not have to prove that the guilty dust was the sole or even the most substantial cause if he could show, on a balance of probabilities (the burden of proof remaining with the plaintiff), that the guilty dust had materially contributed to the disease. Anything which did not fall within the principle *de minimis non curat lex* would constitute a material contribution. Subsequently, in *Nicholson* v *Atlas Steel Foundry & Engineering Co. Ltd* [1957] 1 All ER 776, on virtually identical facts, the House of Lords held the defendants liable for an employee's pneumoconiosis, even though, in the words of Viscount Simonds, it was 'impossible even approximately to quantify' the respective contributions of guilty and innocent dust.

These cases are significant in easing the plaintiff's burden of proof for two reasons. First, they represent a departure from 'but for' causation—the plaintiff does not have to prove that he would not have suffered the 'damage' (i.e. the injury or illness) but for the breach of duty. What has to be proved is redefined as 'material contribution' to the injury or illness. But, notwithstanding that the courts redefined the 'damage' to which the plaintiff must establish a causal link in more limited terms than the outcome (injury or illness), the plaintiff still recovers *damages* for the whole loss, i.e., the outcome, having proved causation in respect of a part only of that loss (see Stapleton (1988) 104 LQR 389, 404–5). Second, the courts were willing to draw an *inference* of fact that there had been a material contribution when it was in reality impossible to say whether there had been any such contribution, or even to make a statistical guess.

McGhee v *National Coal Board* [1972] 3 All ER 1008 appeared to take *Bonnington Castings* one step further. The plaintiff, who worked at the defendants' brick kilns, contracted dermatitis as a result of exposure to brick dust. The employers were not at fault for the exposure during working hours, but they were in breach of duty by failing to provide adequate washing facilities. This increased the period of time during which the plaintiff was exposed to contact with the brick dust while he bicycled home. It was agreed that the brick dust had caused the dermatitis, but the current state of medical knowledge could not say whether it was probable that the plaintiff would not have contracted the disease if he had been able to take a shower after work (i.e., he could not establish 'but for' causation in respect of the 'guilty' exposure). At best it could be said that the failure to provide washing facilities materially increased the risk of the plaintiff contracting dermatitis. The House of Lords held the defendants liable on the basis that it was sufficient for a plaintiff to show that the defendants' breach of duty made the risk of injury more probable even though it was uncertain whether it was the actual cause.

A majority of their Lordships treated a 'material increase in the risk' as equivalent to a 'material contribution to the damage'. Lord Simon of Glaisdale, for example, said that 'a failure to take steps which would bring about a material reduction of the risk involves, in this type of case, a substantial contribution to the injury' (at p. 1014; see also per Lords Reid and Salmon at pp. 1011, 1017). Lord Wilberforce explicitly recognised that this process involves overcoming an 'evidential gap' by drawing an inference of fact which, strictly speaking, the evidence does not support (as was done in *Bonnington Castings*), and, moreover that this 'fictional' inference is drawn for policy reasons. Why, his Lordship asked (at p. 1012), should a man who is able to show that his employer should have taken certain precautions, because without them there is a risk or an added risk of injury or disease, and who in fact sustains exactly that injury or disease, have to assume the burden of proving more? In many cases it is impossible to prove causation because medical opinion cannot segregate the causes of an illness between compound causes.

> And if one asks which of the parties, the workman or the employers, should suffer from this inherent evidential difficulty, the answer as a matter of policy or justice should be that it is the creator of the risk who, *ex hypothesi*, must be taken to have foreseen the possibility of damage, who should bear its consequences.

The potential in this line of reasoning for reversing the burden of proof of causation was enormous—the plaintiff does not have to show that the defendant's breach of duty caused his injury, merely that it increased the risk of injury (see Weinrib (1975) 38 MLR 518). Indeed, Lord Wilberforce seemed to suggest that the burden of disproving causation would shift to the defendant in such cases. The decision has not had as significant an impact, however, as might have been expected. This may be due in part to the fact that, if applied literally, it could lead to results that look distinctly odd. Say, for example, there has been a leak of a carcinogenic chemical from a factory and the expert evidence is that statistically there will be a 20% increase in the number of people who develop cancer in that locality over the next five years. The factory has 'caused' the disease in one of every six people who contract cancer, but it is extremely unlikely that any one individual could prove that his illness was caused by the leak. Clearly the factory's carelessness has materially increased the risk but if the burden of proof is reversed it would be very difficult for the factory to disprove, except by pointing to the balance of probabilities, that a particular plaintiff's illness was not caused by the leak. The balance of probabilities, however, would disprove each individual's case in turn (see, e.g., the comments of Croom-Johnson LJ in *Hotson* v *East Berkshire Area Health Authority* [1987] 1 All ER 210, 223 on the use of statistical evidence; Hill (1991) 54 MLR 511; but cf. Stapleton (1988) 104 LQR 389, at 399 n. 23). The overall result would seem to be that either the factory is not liable for the additional cancers that it has caused or it is liable for all the cancers in the locality. This example illustrates the intractability of certain types of causation problem, and highlights the conflict between *McGhee* and the 'but for' test. (Did the failure to supply safety belts increase the risk of an accident in *McWilliams* v *Sir William Arrol & Co. Ltd* [1962] 1 WLR 295, para. 4.1.1?)

In *Clark* v *MacLennan* [1983] 1 All ER 416, a case of medical negligence, the principle of *McGhee* was extended to proof of breach of duty. Pain J held that where there is a general practice to take a particular precaution against a specific, known risk but the defendant fails to take that precaution, and the very damage against which it is designed to be a protection occurs, then the burden of proof lies with the defendant to show both that he was not in breach of duty and that the breach did not cause the damage. This approach to the question of proving negligence, as opposed to causation, was criticised by Mustill LJ in *Wilsher* v *Essex Area Health Authority* [1986] 3 All ER 801, 814, although his Lordship accepted that in some instances breach and causation are so closely linked that in practice it may be difficult to maintain a different rule for proof of breach of duty when the *McGhee* rule is applicable to proof of causation.

In *Wilsher* itself the question was whether *McGhee* could be applied to a case where there were up to five discrete causes of the plaintiff's injury, any one of which might have caused the damage. The plaintiff was a premature baby who, through the defendants' negligence, received an excessive concentration of oxygen. It is known that excessive oxygen can damage the retina of a premature baby leading to a condition called retrolental fibroplasia (RLF) which results in blindness. The plaintiff contracted RLF. However, RLF can occur in premature babies who have not been given additional oxygen and there is evidence of some correlation between RLF and several other conditions from which premature babies can suffer, all of which afflicted the plaintiff. As Mustill LJ put it (at p. 828): 'What the defendants did was not to enhance the risk that the known factors would lead to injury, but to add to the list of factors which might do so.' The majority of the Court of Appeal held that *McGhee* could apply in these circumstances, although recognising that this represented an extension of the principle (see per Mustill LJ at pp. 828–9, per Glidewell LJ at p. 832). Browne-Wilkinson V-C, dissenting, took the view that the position was 'wholly different' from that in *McGhee:* 'A failure to take preventive measures against one out of five possible causes is no evidence as to which of those five caused the injury' (at p. 835).

The House of Lords reversed the decision of the Court of Appeal on the causation issue, approving the judgment of the Vice-Chancellor ([1988] 1 All ER 871). It was held that *McGhee* did not establish any new principle of law and did not have the effect of reversing the burden of proof. The burden of proof remained with the plaintiff throughout, and he must establish that the breach of duty was at least a material contributory cause of the harm (applying *Bonnington Castings* v *Wardlaw*). What the House of Lords did in *McGhee,* said Lord Bridge, was to adopt a robust and pragmatic approach to the undisputed primary facts of the case and draw a legitimate, common-sense inference of fact that the additional period of exposure to brick dust had probably materially contributed to the plaintiff's dermatitis (at pp. 880, 881–2). (See also *Snell* v *Farrell* (1990) 72 DLR (4th) 289 where the Supreme Court of Canada adopted the same approach to *McGhee* while pointing out that the court was entitled to draw an inference even where there was no firm expert evidence supporting the plaintiff's theory of causation, since experts normally determine causation in terms of scientific certainties, whereas the courts deal with the matter on the balance of probabilities. See further *Athey* v *Leonati* [1997] 1 WWR 97, where the Supreme Court of Canada held that the defendants' negligence, which the trial judge had concluded was no more than a 25% contributory factor to the plaintiff's injury, constituted a material contribution to the damage and held the defendants liable for the full loss.)

This interpretation of *McGhee,* however, does not address the substantive legal issue raised by these cases, which is how the plaintiff can succeed in recovering his whole loss from the defendant while establishing causation in respect of an indeterminate part only of that loss (Stapleton (1988) 104 LQR 389, 404). *Wilsher* also leaves unanswered the very real practical problem of how these cases should be applied. *McGhee,* it seems, is still good law, subject to the formal requirement that the burden of proof remains with the plaintiff. But it must still be open to argue that proof of a material increase in the risk of harm due to the defendant's negligence is sufficient proof of a material contribution to the damage, at least when the court can be persuaded to take a robust and pragmatic approach to the drawing of inferences of fact. Although in theory a material contribution to the damage is one step beyond a material increase of risk in a chain of logical reasoning about causation, in practice, where the evidence is so uncertain, it is simply unreal to attempt to draw a sensible distinction between them (see per Lord Salmon in *McGhee* at pp. 1017, and 1018f). Indeed, bearing in mind the paucity of the evidence on which the House of Lords held that a material contribution to the damage had been proved in *Bonnington Castings,* it might seem to be a matter of semantics whether the test should be material contribution to the damage or material increase of the risk. Certainly, the correlation between these concepts, which was made explicit in *McGhee*, had been anticipated in *Nicholson v Atlas Steel Foundry & Engineering Co. Ltd* [1957] 1 All ER 776 by Viscount Simonds and Lord Cohen (at pp. 781 and 782 respectively).

This still leaves two obvious questions: (a) What constitutes a 'material contribution' to the damage? and (b) When is it legitimate to draw *admittedly fictional* inferences about causation when confronted by factual uncertainty? (Note that the inference is no less fictional simply for being described as 'common sense' or 'pragmatic'.) If the court is prepared to draw such an inference the burden of proof is *irrelevant*, because the defendant, faced with the same factual uncertainty as the plaintiff, is unable to adduce evidence which would rebut the inference. There is, so far, simply no answer to the first question, which in many respects seems to be bound up with the answer to the second.

In what circumstances, then, will *Bonnington Castings* and/or *McGhee* be applied? (see Boon (1988) 51 MLR 508, 513–16). First, and most obviously, there must be uncertainty about the causal connection between the defendant's negligence and the plaintiff's damage. Where the extent of the defendant's contribution is known the defendant is liable to that extent and no more (*Thompson v Smiths Shiprepairers (North Shields) Ltd* [1984] 1 All ER 881—plaintiff suffered progressive hearing impairment due to industrial noise. Defendants liable only for that part of the deafness occurring after the exposure to noise became a breach of duty; *Bowman v Harland and Wolff plc* [1992] IRLR 349, 359). Second, in *Fitzgerald v Lane* [1987] 2 All ER 455 the Court of Appeal held that *McGhee* was not limited to factual uncertainties due to gaps in medical knowledge about the cause of injuries or diseases, but could apply to other types of factual uncertainty. This proposition seems still to be correct after *Wilsher*. Third, *Bonnington Castings* can apply to psychiatric injuries. In *Page v Smith (No. 2)* [1996] 3 All ER 272 the plaintiff developed a recrudescence of chronic fatigue syndrome (also known as myalgic encephalomyelitis) following a road traffic accident of 'moderate severity' in which he suffered no physical injuries. The Court of Appeal accepted that on the evidence there were other possible causes which had contributed to an exacerbation of the plaintiff's symptoms, but nonetheless considered that the trial judge was entitled to conclude that the accident had materially contributed to the plaintiff's symptoms, converting his illness from a mild and sporadic state to one of chronic intensity and permanence. This was the position notwithstanding that the plaintiff's nervous reaction to the accident was 'not necessarily proportional to the trauma' (see also *Vernon v Bosley (No. 1)* [1997] 1 All ER 577 applying *Bonnington Castings* to psychiatric damage). Fourth, there would appear to be a distinction of some kind between cumulative causes and discrete causes. In *Bonnington Castings* the guilty dust and the innocent dust were concurrent and (it was presumed) cumulative causes. In *McGhee* the innocent and guilty periods of exposure to brick dust were consecutive. They might both have contributed to the cause of the disease (cumulative effect) or, one or other may have been the sole (discrete) cause, although in *Wilsher* Lord Bridge seems to have presumed that the inference drawn in *McGhee* was that they contributed cumulatively to the dermatitis (see [1988] 1 All ER 871, 880). In *Wilsher* there were five possible discrete causes, and the House of Lords regarded this as an important distinction from *McGhee*. Yet it may be pure chance whether a defendant's negligence enhances an existing risk or adds a new risk factor, even if it is possible to distinguish between such risks. In some cases, for example, it may simply be unknown whether an illness is the result of a cumulative effect or of a single event the risk of which has been enhanced by the defendant (see *Bryce v Swan Hunter Group plc* [1988] 1 All ER 659, 665—mesothelioma caused by exposure to asbestos dust). In the face of such uncertainty it would seem strange to attach much significance to the distinction between cumulative and discrete causes (see Stapleton (1988) 104 LQR 389, 402 and 406 n. 40), although it may be conceded that in practice, if not in logic, it may be easier to infer that 'there must have been some contribution' in cases of cumulative causes. Possibly the *number* of risk factors involved will be regarded as important, although again, this would appear to be an arbitrary basis for drawing distinctions. In *Fitzgerald v Lane* the Court of Appeal applied *McGhee* to a case involving *three* discrete possible causes of injury, namely three distinct impacts in a road traffic accident involving a pedestrian and two vehicles. It is unclear to what extent this decision is affected by the House of Lords' ruling in *Wilsher* (*see Dugdale and Stanton,* para. 18.14).

Another possibility is that *McGhee* will apply where the specific risk which has materialised (for which there would have to be some prima facie evidence) has been enhanced by the defendant's breach of duty, but not where the negligence enhanced a general risk to the plaintiff (though query whether this is simply a more conceptualised version of the distinction between cumulative and discrete causes). This requires a narrow interpretation of the 'risk'. So, for example, in *Wilsher* the risk created by the defendants was 'RLF caused *by excess oxygen*', not simply an enhancement of an existing risk of RLF from other causes. Until it can be shown that the RLF was caused by excess oxygen the injury cannot be said to fall squarely within the risk created by the defendants (per Browne-Wilkinson V-C [1986] 3 All ER 801, 835). Thus '*McGhee* saves the court from the impossibility of separating the 'guilty' and 'innocent' components of a single risk, not from the impossibility of determining the causal impact of distinct risks, even if these risks may have the same consequences on maturity' (Boon (1988) 51 MLR 508, 513). This approach is unconvincing for the same reason that the distinction between cumulative and discrete causes remains unconvincing, particularly when it is recalled that *Bonnington Castings* represents a patent departure from orthodox 'but for' causation. Why, it might be asked, should the courts want to make such fine distinctions when dealing with different types of factual uncertainty, given that *McGhee*, *Wilsher* in the Court of Appeal, and *Fitzgerald v Lane* are quite explicitly based upon policy considerations of fairness to plaintiffs faced with otherwise insuperable problems of proof? *Fleming,* p. 175, for example, comments that: 'Whatever the technical allocation and standard of proof, in practice causal uncertainty is apt to be resolved by the strong sympathetic bias for the victim of a proven wrongdoer' (see also Nourse LJ in *Fitzgerald v Lane*

[1987] 2 All ER 455, 464: 'A benevolent principle smiles on these factual uncertainties and melts them all away'). Lord Bridge, on the other hand, considered that the forensic process would be rendered ,still more unpredictable and hazardous by distorting the law to accommodate the exigencies of what may seem hard cases' (*Wilsher* [1988] 1 All ER 871, 883). Despite Lord Bridge's caution it is clear that the demands of justice or simple fairness to plaintiffs may persuade the court to adopt a sympathetic approach. In *Edgson v Vickers plc* [1994] ICR 510 there were two defendants, both of whom were in breach of duty with respect to precautions that should have been taken to reduce the deceased's exposure to asbestos dust. It was held that *Bonnington Castings* could be applied to draw an inference of causation (on the basis that the tortious act(s) made a material contribution to the plaintiff's damage) where there is more than one defendant. Jeffrey Burke QC, sitting as a deputy High Court judge, commented (at p. 525) that:

> The difficulties faced by a plaintiff if he has to prove which of different consecutive or concurrent exposures to danger caused his injuries as a matter of probability are not reduced by the presence in his case of more than one defendant; if the principle did not apply in such a case, there would be a clear risk that a plaintiff might fail to establish causation against any of the parties against whom he had brought his claim—in other words that he might fall between two or several stools.

This echoes the concern of the House of Lords in *Baker* v *Willoughby* [1970] AC 467, para. 4.2.1, that a plaintiff should not, in effect, fall between two tortfeasors, receiving less in damages than would have been the case had the two torts not been separated in time. (See also *Cook* v *Lewis* [1952] 1 DLR 1, para. 3.3.1 where the plaintiff was negligently shot by one of two defendants who discharged their guns at the same time, but the plaintiff could not prove which defendant shot him. The Supreme Court of Canada reversed the burden of proof, requiring the defendants to prove which of them did not shoot the plaintiff. This was clearly a policy decision to prevent the plaintiff falling between two tortfeasors on the question of causation.) (See Price (1989) 38 ICLQ 735 and Stauch (1997) 17 OJLS 205 for further discussion of these issues and cases involving 'loss of a chance', considered in para. 4.1.3.)

4.1.3 Loss of a chance
An alternative, and arguably better, approach to problems of factual uncertainty would be to deal with them in terms of the measure of damages by reference to the chance of loss, rather than liability on an all or nothing basis. In *Hotson* v *East Berkshire Area Health Authority* [1987] 1 All ER 210, CA the plaintiff suffered an accidental injury to his hip in a fall which created a 75% risk that he would develop a permanent disability. Due to negligent medical diagnosis the hip was not treated for five days, and the delay made the disability inevitable. The plaintiff contended that the doctor's negligence had deprived him of a 25% chance of making a good recovery, whereas the

defendant argued that the plaintiff had failed to prove, on the balance of probabilities, that the negligence caused the disability. The trial judge held that where a 'substantial chance' of a better medical result had been lost it was not necessary to prove that the adverse medical result was directly attributable to the breach of duty because the issue was the proper quantum of damage rather than causation. The plaintiff could prove causation of the lost chance and accordingly he was entitled to damages on the basis of 25% of the value of the claim for the full disability. This approach was upheld by the Court of Appeal, where Sir John Donaldson MR characterised the plaintiff's claim as the loss of the *benefit* of timely treatment (rather than the *chance* of successful treatment), commenting that: 'As a matter of common sense, it is unjust that there should be no liability for failure to treat a patient, simply because the chances of a successful cure by that treatment were less than 50%' (at pp. 215–16; see also per Dillon LJ at p. 219).

The House of Lords, however, reversed the Court of Appeal decision on the basis that the judge's finding that there was a high probability, put at 75%, that even with correct diagnosis and treatment the plaintiff's disability would have occurred, amounted to a finding of fact that the accidental injury was the sole cause of the disability ([1987] 2 All ER 909). In other words this was not a 'lost chance' case, it was an all or nothing case—either the fall or the misdiagnosis caused the disability, and on the balance of probabilities (75/25) it was the fall. The valuation of a 'lost chance' would only arise once 'causation' had been established. But as Stapleton (1988) 104 LQR 389, 393 points out, this decision failed to address the essence of the plaintiff's argument, which was whether a claim formulated as a loss of a chance was acceptable. If the nature of the damage could be redefined as the loss of a *chance* of a successful outcome, rather than the outcome itself (the disability), then on a traditional causation test the defendants' negligence clearly did cause the damage (i.e., the lost chance). Logically, the question of whether the negligence caused the damage is an issue that can only be dealt with *after* the nature of the damage has been defined (cf. Price (1989) 38 ICLQ 735, 748 who argues, that redefining the injury 'is merely to indulge in semantic juggling'; Hill (1991) 54 MLR 511).

The question of whether it would ever be possible to claim for loss of a chance in tort was specifically left open by their Lordships. It is long established that a lost chance may be actionable in contract (*Chaplin* v *Hicks* [1911] 2 KB 786). Where, for example, through a solicitor's negligence a client has lost the opportunity to bring proceedings (e.g., because the limitation period has been allowed to expire), the client in an action against the solicitor does not have to prove that he would have won the other case, merely that he has lost 'some right of value, some chose in action of reality and substance' (*Kitchen* v *Royal Air Force Association* [1958] 1 WLR 563). Damages are then discounted to reflect his chances of success in the original action. This applies notwithstanding that the plaintiff's chance of success in the original action is put at less than 50% (see, e.g., *Corfield* v *D. S. Bosher & Co.* [1992] 1 EGLR 163, where damages were awarded on the basis that the plaintiff had a one third chance of success). It scarcely seems arguable that the basis of a distinction between *Kitchen* and *Hotson* is that one was a claim in contract and the other in tort, when the duties in each instance are the same (i.e., a duty to exercise reasonable skill and care, see para. 3.2.1). It would lead to the untenable result that, in identical circumstances, a patient who had received treatment privately might have a claim but a patient who received treatment under the national health service would not (see [1987] 1 All ER 210, 216 and 222 per Sir John Donaldson MR and Croom-Johnson LJ respectively; though see *de la Giroday* v *Brough* [1997] 6 WWR 585, where the British Columbia Court of Appeal accepted that the loss of a chance approach was not available in tort but could apply to breach of a contractual obligation to exercise reasonable care and skill).

In the House of Lords the analogy of *Kitchen* was dismissed as irrelevant, though it is not entirely clear why it was irrelevant, particularly as their Lordships did not give any reasons. The trial judge, for example, was unable to see any sensible distinction between the solicitor/client relationship and the doctor/ patient relationship in these circumstances ([1985] 1 All ER 167, 176). One possible explanation is that *Hotson* was concerned with uncertainty as to past facts whereas *Kitchen* concerned uncertainty about hypothetical facts (*Dugdale and Stanton*, paras 18.05–18.06). Uncertainty about the past is decided on the balance of probabilities. Anything that is more probable than not is treated as certainty (*Mallett* v *McMonagle* [1970] AC 166, 176 per Lord Diplock, cited by Lord Ackner in *Hotson* [1987] 2 All ER 909, 921). On the other hand, where 'the uncertainty is as to the facts that would have occurred had there been no negligence, i.e., hypothetical facts, English Law has been prepared to regard the plaintiff's loss as that of the chance of a favourable outcome' (*Dugdale and Stanton*, para. 18.06). With great respect, this distinction does not seem so clear-cut, because in each case the issue can be reformulated as uncertainty about either 'hypothetical facts' or 'past facts'. In *Hotson*, for example, the uncertainty was as to what *would* have happened in the absence of negligence ('hypothetical fact'), i.e., whether the plaintiff would have fallen into the category of the 25% of patients in his circumstances who would have benefited from prompt treatment. Conversely, in *Kitchen*, the uncertainty was as to a past fact, i.e., did the solicitor's negligence cause the plaintiffs loss of the action? That question can only be answered by answering another, hypothetical, question about what would have happened in the absence of negligence. But this is true of any causal inquiry which employs the 'but for' test. For example, in *McWilliams* v *Sir William Arrol & Co. Ltd* [1962] 1 WLR 295, para. 4.1.1, the answer to the question 'Did the failure to supply safety belts cause the workman's death?' (apparently uncertainty as to a past fact) depended on the answer to the further, and clearly hypothetical, question 'Would he have worn a safety belt if supplied?' It seems doubtful, then, that the distinction between past and hypothetical facts can explain the different approaches in *Hotson* and *Kitchen*.

An alternative categorisation was suggested by the Court of Appeal in *Allied Maples Group Ltd* v *Simmons & Simmons* [1995] 4 All ER 907. The plaintiffs sought to acquire particular businesses and commercial properties of a rival company, G. Four of the properties could not be conveyed directly to the plaintiffs because there were covenants against alienation or planning consents which were personal to K, a subsidiary of G, in which the properties were vested. The defendant solicitors advised that the plaintiffs should acquire all the shares in K and then hive off the unwanted properties and liabilities to another company, retaining the four properties they wanted. After completion of the sale it became apparent that K had liabilities for which the plaintiffs were responsible. The plaintiffs were unable to reclaim this liability from G under the terms of the sale. The trial judge held that the defendants had been negligent in failing to warn the plaintiffs about a potentially open-ended liability and that if they had known of this risk the plaintiffs would have taken steps to obtain a warranty from G or protect themselves in some other way. The judge also concluded that, on the balance of probability, if asked G would have given some form of warranty or protection from the liability, and that if K's properties had not been included in the sale the whole deal would not have proceeded. Stuart-Smith LJ said (at pp. 914–16) that the classification of the causation issue into all or nothing on the balance of probabilities or the quantification of the loss of a chance depends upon whether the negligence consists in some positive act or misfeasance, or an omission or nonfeasance:

(1)   In the case of a positive act of misfeasance the question of causation is one of historical fact, which once established on the balance of probability is taken as true. The plaintiff recovers damages in full. Quantifying the plaintiff's loss, however, may depend upon uncertain future events, such as the degree to which the plaintiff's medical condition will deteriorate or improve, whether he would have continued to earn at the same rate etc. These issues are dealt with on the basis of an assessment of the risk often expressed in percentage terms, that the event will or will not occur.

(2)   Where the defendant's negligence consists of an omission, e.g., to provide proper equipment, or to give proper instructions or advice, causation depends, not upon a question of historical fact, but on the answer to the hypothetical question: what would the plaintiff have done if the equipment had been provided or the instruction or advice given? This will be a matter of inference to be determined from all the circumstances. The plaintiff's own evidence that he would have acted to obtain the benefit or avoid the risk, while important, may not be believed by the judge, especially if there is compelling evidence that he would not (as, e.g., in *McWilliams v Sir William Arrol & Co. Ltd* [1962] 1 WLR 295, para. 4.1.1). Although the question is a hypothetical one, the plaintiff must prove on the balance of probability that he would have taken action to obtain the benefit or avoid the risk, and as with positive acts of misfeasance, if he does establish that, there is no discount of the damages because the balance is only just tipped in his favour.

(3)   Where, as in *Allied Maples* itself, *the plaintiff's loss depends on the hypothetical action of an independent third party*, either in addition to action by the plaintiff or independently of it, the plaintiff does not have to prove on the balance of probability that the third party *would* have acted so as to confer the benefit or avoid the risk to the plaintiff. The plaintiff succeeds if he shows that

he had a substantial chance, as opposed to a speculative one, that he would have been successful in negotiating total or partial protection, the evaluation of the substantial chance being a question of quantification of damages. There was 'no difference in principle between the chance of gaining a benefit and the chance of avoiding a liability'. Nor does it depend upon the plaintiff proving that the chance of success was over 50%. Provided the chance is substantial it may be less than 50%.

Stuart-Smith LJ cited both *Chaplin* v *Hicks* and *Kitchen* v *Royal Air Force Association*, and therefore it might be thought that *Allied Maples* adds nothing to the debate about whether loss of a chance can be pursued in tort. But his Lordship also relied upon a dictum of Lord Lowry in *Spring* v *Guardian Assurance plc* [1994] 3 WLR 354, 377 a case involving a negligent employment reference about a former employee:

> Once the duty of care is held to exist and the defendants' negligence is proved, the plaintiff only has to show that by reason of that negligence he has lost a reasonable chance of employment (which would have to be evaluated) and has thereby sustained loss . . . He does not have to prove that, but for the negligent reference, [the third party] *would* have employed him. (original emphasis)

Spring v *Guardian Assurance plc* is undoubtedly a tort case, as is the decision of the House of Lords in *Davies* v *Taylor* [1974] AC 207, also relied upon by Stuart-Smith and Hobhouse LJJ. The plaintiff claimed for loss of financial dependency under the Fatal Accidents Act following the death of her husband. Five days before his death she had left the marital home, and the question was whether there was any prospect of a reconciliation between the plaintiff and her deceased husband. This obviously depended not only on the conduct of the plaintiff, but also on that of the deceased husband. Lord Reid said at p. 213:

> But here we are not and could not be seeking a decision either that the wife would or that she would not have returned to her husband. You can prove that a past event happened, but you cannot prove that a future event will happen and I do not think that the law is so foolish as to suppose that you can. All that you can do is to evaluate the chance. Sometimes it is virtually 100 per cent, sometimes virtually nil. But often it is somewhere in between. And if it is somewhere in between I do not see much difference between a probability of 51 per cent and a probability of 49 per cent . . .

In two subsequent cases the Court of Appeal has followed the approach adopted n *Allied Maples*. In *Stovold* v *Barlows*, *The Times*, 30 October 1995, the sale of the plaintiff's property fell through because of the negligence of his solicitors. The trial judge had assessed damages on the basis that if the plaintiff succeeded in demonstrating on the balance of probabilities that but for the negligence the sale would have proceeded he was entitled to the difference between what the prospective purchaser would have paid and what he eventually received for the property when it was sold later. The Court of Appeal held that this was the wrong approach to causation, where the loss depended upon the action of an independent third party in circumstances which *ex hypothesi* did not arise. The proper approach was to evaluate the loss of the plaintiff's chance that but for the defendant's negligence the sale would have gone ahead, applying *Allied Maples*. If the plaintiff proved that he had lost a real or substantial chance as opposed to a speculative one the evaluation of that chance was part of the assessment of the quantum of damage. In *First Interstate Bank of California* v *Cohen Arnold & Co., The Times*, 11 December 1995, the plaintiffs had lent money to X, a client of the defendants, who were accountants. The defendants negligently told the plaintiffs that X was much wealthier than in fact he was. As a consequence of this misrepresentation the plaintiffs delayed calling in the loan. During the period of the delay the value of the property upon which the loan was secured fell and was therefore insufficient to cover the plaintiffs' loss when X defaulted on the loan. The trial judge assessed damages on the basis of the difference in value between the actual sale price and what the property would have fetched if there had not been a delay in putting it on the market. The Court of Appeal held that the judge should have proceeded on the basis of the chance of selling at the full price before the delay, which was estimated at two to one (i.e, a two-thirds chance). Although *Stovold* v *Barlows* involved a claim against solicitors and is therefore analogous to *Kitchen, First Interstate Bank of California* was undoubtedly a claim based in the tort of negligent misrepresentation.

The effect of the Court of Appeal's approach is that where causation depends upon what the plaintiff himself would have done in a 'past' hypothetical situation the plaintiff has to establish this on the balance of probabilities (e.g., *McWilliams* v *Arrol*). This is also the position where the question turns upon what the defendant would have done in a 'past' hypothetical situation (as in *Bolitho* v *City and Hackney Health Authority* [1997] 4 All ER 771, para. 4.1.1). But where it depends upon the independent act of a third party the plaintiff need only establish that there was a chance. This could mean that in some cases causation depends upon *both* proof of what the plaintiff or defendant would have done in a hypothetical situation (on the balance of probabilities) and what an independent third party would have done (was there a substantial chance?). Although these distinctions 'fit the facts' of *Hotson* and *Kitchen* and therefore in one sense 'explain' them, unfortunately, there is little in the cases to indicate *why* the approach should differ depending upon whose hypothetical conduct has to be taken into account. (For an interesting attempt to explain the distinction between lost chance cases and balance of probabilities cases see Reece (1996) 59 MLR 188, who argues that lost chances are 'quasi-deterministic' whereas 'but for' causation applies to 'quasi-indeterministic' cases. *Allied Maples* was 'quasi-indeterministic' and therefore correctly dealt with in terms of lost chances, but on Reece's analysis Stuart-Smith LJ was incorrect to treat the cases involving assessment of the hypothetical conduct of the plaintiff, or defendant, as cases to be dealt with on the balance of probabilities, because they involve human conduct in a hypothetical chain of events and the result at the end of the chain is inherently unpredictable. This makes them 'quasi-indeterministic', and therefore to be treated as lost chance cases. Whether, ultimately, this view proves useful may depend upon how readily the distinction between 'quasi-indeterministic' and 'quasi-deterministic' events can be drawn or indeed whether the distinction is accepted as being relevant. The fact that the outcome of a chain of events cannot be predicted with certainty does not necessarily mean that the courts, taking the common law's traditional pragmatic and 'common sense' attitude to such matters, should treat it as being for practical purposes unpredictable. See further Stauch (1997) 17 OJLS 205, 217–24)

In Canada the Supreme Court has rejected the loss of a chance approach (*Laferrière* v *Lawson* (1991) 78 DLR (4th) 609), and where causation turns upon the acts of a third party the courts still deal with it on a balance of probabilities (see, e.g., *MacDonald* v *York County Hospital* (1973) 41 DLR (3d) 321; affd *sub. nom. Vail* v *MacDonald* (1976) 66 DLR (3d) 530, 536 (Supreme Court of Canada) where the negligence of nurses in failing to notify a doctor (who was also a defendant) about the plaintiff's symptoms of circulatory impairment was held not to be a contributory cause of the patient's injury because the doctor gave evidence that even if he had been informed he would not have taken any action at that time). In Australia, however, the High Court has held that the ordinary standard of proof, on the balance of probabilities, applied to the proof of historical facts, whereas for the proof of past hypothetical situations and future possibilities the court should assess the degree of probability that an event would have occurred or might occur and adjust the award of damages to reflect the degree of probability (*Malec* v *J. C. Hutton Proprietary Ltd* (1990) 169 CLR 638; see also *Poseidon Ltd* v *Adelaide Petroleum NL* (1968) 68 ALJR 313, on which see Lunney (1995) 15 LS 1).

In this country there remains uncertainty about the circumstances in which a lost chance claim may be accepted (*Allied Maples* notwithstanding) and the conceptual basis for the distinction between cases where proof on the balance of probabilities is essential and those where a lost chance is a valid head of claim. There is also a number of related questions that the lost chance approach raises:

(a) What is the relationship between *McGhee* v *National Coal Board* [1972] 3 All ER 1008, para. 4.1.2, and lost chance claims—would *McGhee* apply where it was impossible to determine the extent of the increased risk, but the lost chance approach when the risk was quantifiable (with the result that the less that was known about the risk the greater the potential award of damages, which would not be discounted)?

(b) Is *McGhee* really a lost chance case? (See per Lord Mackay in *Hotson* [1987] 2 All ER 909 at p. 916e; Price (1989) 38 ICLQ 735, the differences are not differences of substance 'only of terminology'.)

(c) Is *Hotson* really a case of a 'material contribution to the damage', treating the disability as having two causes, the fall and the negligent delay in treatment? (See per Lord Bridge at p. 913—the case was not argued on this basis.)

(d) If lost chance claims were accepted, would all cases be dealt with in this way, so that defendants could argue that damages should be discounted to the extent that the plaintiff has failed to prove causation with 100% certainty? (Answer, no: see per Lords Bridge and Ackner at pp. 914 and 922 respectively; but see Stapleton (1988) 104 LQR 389, 396 who comments that this question misreads the 'lost chance' argument. The loss is payable in full, not discounted. It is simply a different *type* of loss, which coincidentally may be calculated approximately by a discount of the damages that would be awarded if the 'damage' were formulated as the outcome.)

(e)   Would plaintiffs be able to bring speculative claims for lost chances, even where the outcome has not materialised?

One consequence of *Hotson* is that a patient whose chances of a successful outcome to his treatment were less than 50% will not have an action against the doctor no matter how negligent the doctor. In the Court of Appeal Sir John Donaldson MR commented that, as a matter of common sense, this was unjust. Moreover, it leads to what is, in effect, an unenforceable duty (to exercise reasonable care), a factor which had influenced both Lord Simon and Lord Salmon to impose liability in *McGhee*. As Bingham LJ has observed, in the very different context of whether a statutory auditor of a public company should owe a duty of care to shareholders: 'It is just and in principle desirable that those who fail to perform their professional duties in accordance with professional standards should compensate those foreseeably injured by their failure' (*Caparo Industries plc* v *Dickman* [1989] 1 All ER 798, 809–10).

4.2   CAUSATION IN LAW

'Two causes may both be necessary preconditions of a particular result—damage to X—yet the one may, if the facts justify that conclusion, be treated as the real, substantial, direct or effective cause, and the other dismissed as at best *a causa sine qua non* and ignored for the purposes of legal liability' (*Stapley* v *Gypsum Mines Ltd* [1953] AC 663, 687 per Lord Asquith of Bishopstone; see also per Lord Reid at p. 681, para. 14.5.2). Having eliminated irrelevant factual 'causes' by the 'but for' test the court is still faced with the task of selecting which of two or more factual causes are to be regarded as the cause in law of the plaintiffs damage, i.e., *the* cause for the purpose of attributing legal responsibility. It is not necessary for the court to alight upon a single event as the sole legal cause—the whole concept of apportionment in contributory negligence proceeds on a contrary assumption (para. 14.5.4). There is a tendency, however, for the courts to look for a single cause, at least where the plaintiff has not been at fault and this can be something of a fiction.

'Common sense' is often said to be the starting point in this selection process (see, e.g., *Cork* v *Kirby MacLean Ltd* [1952] 2 All ER 402, 407;

Yorkshire Dale Steamship Co. Ltd v *Minister of War Transport* [1942] AC 691, 706 per Lord Wright) but common sense is not necessarily a matter of arbitrary assertions. There may be underlying principles that would support, at least in part, the causal notions of the ordinary man (Hart and Honoré, *Causation in the Law*, 2nd ed., ch. 2). As *Salmond and Heuston*, p. 509, points out, however, these principles:

> cannot provide conclusive answers to the complex causal questions which the courts are sometimes obliged to answer, but serve rather as an organising framework within which a choice may be made according to whatever considerations of policy the law may consider to be relevant.

For the ordinary man the language of causation is the language of metaphor. Has the 'chain of causation' been broken? Is the damage 'too remote'? Was the tort a 'proximate' or 'direct' or 'substantial' or 'effective' cause, the *causa causans* not merely a *causa sine qua non?* The law reports are replete with such terms, but they should not disguise the fact that ultimately the court must make a choice, which may be influenced either by common usages of speech or by considerations of policy (see *Atiyah*, pp. 101–6). This is inevitably a pragmatic exercise. As Lord Wright observed in *Liesbosch Dredger* v *SS Edison* [1933] AC 449, 460: 'In the varied web of affairs, the law must abstract some consequences as relevant, not perhaps on grounds of pure logic but simply for practical reasons'.

4.2.1 Successive sufficient causes

Where two independent events, each of which would be sufficient to cause the harm, occur simultaneously the practical solution is to say that both caused the harm (see para. 4.1.1). Where the two events are separated in time it might be thought that the simple answer would be that the first event should be treated as the cause. Certainly this is so where it is the tort that comes second. In *Performance Cars Ltd* v *Abraham* [1962] 1 QB 33 the defendant collided with the plaintiffs' Rolls-Royce and the damage would have necessitated a respray of part of the vehicle. However, the car had previously been damaged in the same position in an earlier accident and would have needed a respray to repair that damage. The defendant was not liable for the cost of the respray because, having damaged an already damaged car, his negligence was not the cause of the loss.

Even when the tort occurs first a subsequent event may supervene, removing the causative potency of the original wrong. In *Carslogie Steamship Co. Ltd* v *Royal Norwegian Government* [1952] AC 292 the plaintiffs' ship was damaged in a collison caused by the defendants' negligence. Temporary repairs rendered the ship seaworthy, and it was sent to the United States for permanent repairs. On the voyage the ship suffered further damage due to heavy weather. The collision damage and the heavy-weather damage were repaired together, taking 51 days. The collision damage alone would have taken 10 days. The House of Lords held that the plaintiffs could not claim for the loss of use of the vessel for the 10 days attributable to the collision damage because the ship was in any event out of use at that time for the heavy-weather damage repairs. This is a very literal application of the 'but for' test since, clearly, it was logically possible to attribute 10 of the 51 days to *two* causes, the collision and the heavy weather. Thus even the 'but for' test may conceal policy decisions. (Note that 'but for' the tort the ship would not have made that voyage and so would not have sustained heavy-weather damage. However, the tort was merely part of the history of events that placed the ship in that place at that time, and this in itself is not a 'cause' of harm that arises from some independent mechanism. Compare the situation in which collision damage renders the ship more susceptible to storm damage, if a storm should occur. See *Wieland* v *Cyril Lord Carpets Ltd* [1969] 3 All ER 1006, para. 4.2.2.2.)

In *Carslogie Steamship Co. Ltd* v *Royal Norwegian Government* the whole loss was attributed to the subsequent innocent cause. Where the second event is also a tort this is not possible because of the principle that a tortfeasor ,takes his victim as he finds him'. The negligent motorist who runs down a shabby-looking millionaire must compensate him for the full extent of his loss of earnings (*The Arpad* [1934] P 189, 202 per Scrutton LJ). Conversely, if the victim was a tramp with no earnings this is the tortfeasor's good fortune. If the plaintiff or his property is already damaged in some way the defendant is responsible only for the additional damage that he has caused (*Performance Cars Ltd* v *Abraham*). This stems from the basic rule that the object of an award of damages in tort is to restore the plaintiff to the position he would have been in if he had not sustained the tort. The effect of these principles where there are two successive torts is demonstrated by *Baker* v *Willoughby* [1970] AC 467. The plaintiff's left leg was injured in a road accident caused by the defendant's negligence. This affected his mobility and reduced his earning capacity. Subsequently the plaintiff was shot in the same leg during the course of an armed robbery at his place of work, and the leg had to be amputated. The defendant argued that the amputation submerged or obliterated the original injury so that he should only have to compensate for the loss up to the date of the robbery. Thereafter the loss of mobility and earning capacity was the result of the shooting. The House of Lords held that the defendant remained responsible for the initial disability after the amputation.

If the robbers had been sued they would have been liable only for the *additional* loss that they had inflicted, not the whole disability. The defendant's argument would have left the plaintiff undercompensated because he would not have been compensated at all for the original injury after the robbery occurred (see per Lord Pearson at p. 495). It was clearly wrong that the plaintiff should fall between two tortfeasors in this way, receiving less in damages than he would have received had there been no interval between the two torts. Lord Reid said that the defendant's argument was based on an incorrect view of what is the subject of compensation. A man is not compensated for the physical injury. He is compensated for the loss which he suffers as a result of that injury. His loss is not in having a stiff leg, it is in his inability to enjoy those amenities of life that depend on freedom of movement and his inability to earn as much as he could have earned. The second injury did not reduce these losses, so why should it be regarded as having obliterated them? Lord Pearson added that the plaintiff should not have less damages through being made worse off.

It is not difficult to conceive of an event as having two concurrent causes. This happens whenever a court decides that a plaintiff was contributorily negligent. Mr Baker's total disability was caused in part by the defendant and in part by the thieves. It is possible to argue, however, that for the period after the shooting the *initial* part of the disability was caused by both the defendant and the robbers. If the shooting had not happened that disability would obviously have been attributable to the road accident. If the road accident had not occurred it would have been attributed to the shooting. As in the case of two simultaneous causes the 'but for' test produces the absurd result that neither is the cause (see para. 4.1.1). The pragmatic solution would suggest that both torts are causes and that the loss could be apportioned between the tortfeasors. The time interval between the torts should not necessarily preclude that conclusion (cf. *Griffiths* v *Commonwealth* (1985) 72 FLR 260, 273 applying the preferred solution of the Court of Appeal in *Baker* v *Willoughby* that the second tortfeasor is liable for the whole loss, having caused the plaintiff to 'lose' his right of action against the original wrongdoer; and for comment on *Griffiths* see Hudson (1987) 38 NILQ 190–3).

In *Jobling* v *Associated Dairies Ltd* [1982] AC 794 the facts were similar to *Baker* v *Willoughby*, except that the second event was non-tortious. In 1973 the plaintiff sustained a back injury as a result of his employers' negligence which reduced his earning capacity by 50%. In 1976 he was found to be suffering from a disease, unconnected with the accident, which prevented him from working at all. The House of Lords held that the defendants were liable only for the reduced earning capacity between 1973 and 1976, when the supervening disease terminated their responsibility. This result was justified, not on the basis of causation but on what might be termed the 'vicissitudes argument'. When assessing damages for future loss of earnings the award is 'discounted' for the possibility that other contingencies might, in any event, have reduced the plaintiff's earning capacity or working life. A subsequent illness is one of these 'vicissitudes of life', and, applying the principle that the court will not speculate about future events when the facts are known, the illness must be taken into account.

Their Lordships in *Jobling* were critical of *Baker* v *Willoughby*, but much of the criticism was unjustified. It was suggested, for example, that if the plaintiff had received an award from the Criminal Injuries Compensation Board in respect of the shooting he would have been over-compensated (per Lords Wilberforce and Edmund-Davies). But since the Board assesses an award on a similar basis to a court it would have taken account of the plaintiff's existing disability, so there would have been no double compensation. Lord Wilberforce observed that the interaction of damages awards and the social security system meant that there was no means of knowing whether the plaintiff in *Jobling* would be over-compensated if he were awarded damages for the period after 1976 or under-compensated if left to his benefit. This is true of many other personal injury actions; it is not the basis of a distinction between

Jobling v *Associated Dairies Ltd* and *Baker* v *Willoughby*. It would seem that *Baker* v *Willoughby* will apply where the supervening event is a tort, but that *Jobling* v *Associated Dairies Ltd* will apply where it is non-tortious. There is no logical or rational justification for this distinction, however, as Lord Wilberforce explicitly recognised. (Lord Keith of Kinkel suggested that a supervening tort might not be regarded as one of the ordinary vicissitudes of life, and so not be taken into account. This rationalisation is a clear example of *post hoc ergo propter hoc* reasoning. Note that where there is dispute about whether the second event is tortious, the court will be faced with the problem of deciding whether *Baker* v *Willoughby* or *Jobling* v *Associated Dairies Ltd* applies.)

Jobling v *Associated Dairies Ltd* is a policy decision based on the idea that compensation for the period after the supervening illness would 'put the plaintiff in a better position than he would be in if he had never suffered the tortious injury' (per Lord Bridge of Harwich). This is only notionally true in the sense that anyone who has suffered a tortious injury is in a 'better position', in terms of getting compensation, than someone who has suffered the same injury in a non-tortious manner. The reality is that *Jobling* v *Associated Dairies Ltd* creates the possibility of under-compensation, by the plaintiff 'falling between', not two tortfeasors as in *Baker* v *Willoughby,* but tort and non-tortious compensation (see Hervey (1981) 97 LQR 210, 211–12); and it allows a defendant to escape responsibility for damage that, on causation arguments, he has wrongfully inflicted, as a result of the plaintiff becoming worse off in real terms. Moreover it achieves this by appealing to 'justice', vicissitudes and practicalities, while ignoring the fact that risk-spreading, in the form of insurance against an employer's liability to his employees, has been compulsory since 1972.

The net result of these cases seems to be that where there are two successive sufficient causes of damage, one of which is tortious and the other non-tortious, responsibility in law will be attributed to the innocent, non-tortious cause and the defendant will not be liable *no matter in what order they occur* (*Carslogie Steamship Co. Ltd* v *Royal Norwegian Government*; *Jobling* v *Associated Dairies Ltd* — tort first in time; *Performance Cars Ltd* v *Abraham* — tort second in time, in fact the first event in this case was tortious, but the result could not possibly have been different if it had been non-tortious). Where consecutive sufficient causes are both tortious, responsibility will be attributed to the first in time (*Baker* v *Willoughby* — first tortfeasor liable; *Performance Cars Ltd* v *Abraham* — second tortfeasor not liable).

4.2.2 Intervening acts
Sometimes the defendant's negligence forms part of a sequence of events leading to harm to the plaintiff. Where the act of another person, without which the damage would not have occurred, intervenes between the defendant's negligence and the damage, the court has to decide whether the defendant remains responsible or whether the act constitutes a *novus actus interveniens,* i.e., whether it can be regarded as breaking the causal connection between the negligence and the damage. Was there 'such a direct relationship between the act of negligence and the injury that the one can be treated as

flowing directly from the other' (*The Oropesa* [1943] P 32, 36 per Lord Wright)? Again, metaphor and 'common sense' are invoked. Did the intervening event 'isolate', or 'insulate' or 'eclipse' the defendant's fault so that it was merely the occasion of the harm rather than the cause of it? Was the act of some third party 'no mere conduit pipe through which consequences flow from [defendant to plaintiff], no mere part of a transmission gear set in motion by [the defendant]'? (*Weld-Blundell* v *Stephens* [1920] AC 956, 986 per Lord Sumner). Lord Wright has said (*The Oropesa* at p. 39):

> To break the chain of causation it must be shown that there is something which I will call ultroneous, something unwarrantable, a new cause which disturbs the sequence of events, something which can be described as either unreasonable or extraneous or extrinsic.

The very proliferation of expressions suggests that there is no simple test, and though common sense may point the way, the language of causation tends to obscure the evaluative nature of the decisions that the courts must inevitably make. It is 'in reality only a screen behind which judges have all too often in the past retreated to avoid the irksome task of articulating their real motivation' (*Fleming*, p. 217). It is not surprising, then, to find some confusion in the principles applied to determine whether an intervention constituted a *novus actus*. There are two broad approaches, causation and fault (cf. apportionment in contributory negligence, para. 14.5.4). The causation test asks whether the act was 'reasonable' in the circumstances. Was it part of 'the ordinary course of things' which flowed from the wrongful act (*The Argentino* (1889) 14 App Cas 519, 523)? This has to be measured against the nature of the risk created by the defendant. 'Reasonable' in this context tends to relate to the *voluntariness* of the act, not whether it was careless. The more voluntary the act the less reasonable it is, and the more potent is its causative effect. Even deliberate actions may be 'Involuntary' in this sense, e.g., where a person is 'forced' to make some response in a situation brought about by the defendant's negligence (see, e.g., *The Oropesa*, para. 4.2.2.1). Careless behaviour will generally be less potent causally than a voluntary act, even if the act can be called 'reasonable' (*Weir*, p. 245). The fault approach turns on the foreseeability of the intervention. If reasonableness were the sole test then a deliberate (i.e., voluntary) or reckless act, and *a fortiori* criminal conduct, would always amount to a *novus actus*. But this is not necessarily so. However, foreseeability is not an entirely satisfactory test either, because there are many forms of intentional conduct that are eminently foreseeable for the consequences of which the courts would hesitate long and hard before imposing responsibility on another. Here the issue resolves itself into a problem of 'duty'. Was the defendant under a duty to prevent the very intervention that occurred (see para. 2.2.1.4)? Each of these methods involves a choice, a process that requires the court to make an assessment of the relative effect of the defendant's conduct and the intervening act. In both cases this means assessing the comparative blameworthiness of the parties (again, cf. contributory negligence).

The two approaches can overlap. Clearly if the intervention was both reasonable and foreseeable the defendant will be liable, and if it was both unreasonable and unforeseeable it will constitute a *novus actus interveniens*. A third possibility is that the intervention was reasonable but unforeseeable. It could be argued that reasonable conduct is never unforeseeable, but more realistically it may not have been possible to anticipate the consequences of otherwise reasonable actions. For example, a particular reaction to certain forms of reasonable medical treatment may not have been specifically foreseeable (see, e.g., *Alston* v *Marine & Trade Insurance Co. Ltd* 1964 (4) SA 112—cheese eaten by plaintiff reacted with a drug he was taking and caused a stroke; defendants who caused initial injury necessitating treatment not liable for stroke; cf. *Robinson* v *Post Office* [1974] 2 All ER 737). It is submitted that in this situation the defendant *should* be liable on the basis that (a) the intervention was reasonable, arising in the ordinary course of events, and so did not break the chain of causation, or (b) the unforeseeable consequences of a foreseeable and reasonable intervention are within the risk created by the defendant's negligence, or (c) some complication from medical treatment is foreseeable and it is not necessary to foresee the precise manner of its occurrence. Each of these formulae takes a very different approach to foreseeability. The first treats it as irrelevant, the second considers it relevant to the occurrence of the intervening act but not its consequences (on this argument reasonable conduct might always be foreseeable), and the third takes a broad view of what has to be foreseen. Whichever justification is adopted the conclusion that the defendant should be liable involves a value judgment.

The fourth possible combination of the causation and culpability approaches is that the intervening act was foreseeable but unreasonable. It is at this point that the confusion created by two different tests becomes most intense. In some cases foreseeable intervening acts which are unreasonable or negligent are regarded as breaking the chain of causation, whereas in other cases even criminal acts may not absolve the defendant. This can only be understood by reference to the nature of the defendant's duty. The general rule is that a person is not liable for harm caused by the deliberate actions of another (*Weld-Blundell* v *Stephens* [1920] AC 956, 986 per Lord Sumner). A special relationship between the defendant and the plaintiff, or the defendant and the third party may create a duty to prevent harm to the plaintiff. This, however, is the exception (see para. 2.2.1) . The classification of intervening acts ranges from the involuntary (and therefore 'reasonable'), through carelessness (which may or may not be 'reasonable' depending on the circumstances), to the deliberate, in the sense that the act has not been forced upon the actor by the defendant's negligence. There is no liability for deliberate intervention unless the defendant was under a duty to prevent that very occurrence. The courts find themselves in considerable difficulty when they try to deal with this type of problem solely as a matter of foreseeability or remoteness of damage, rather than causation and duty, because they have to resort to increasingly subtle distinctions between degrees of foreseeability in order to reach a sensible result (see *Lamb* v *Camden London Borough Council* [1981] QB 625, para. 4.2.2.1).

Remoteness of damage is frequently confused with causation in law, particularly when there is an intervening act. There are three possible explanations for this. First, the word 'remote' in its colloquial sense of 'far removed' is often used in the context of causation in order to *justify* a decision that the defendant's negligence should not be treated as the 'cause in law' of the damage (see, e.g., *Knightley* v *Johns* [1982] 1 All ER 851, 866). Secondly, before 1961 the test of remoteness of damage was 'directness' of consequence which is a test based on causation (see para. 4.3.1). In the older cases causation in law and remoteness of damage were simply different aspects of the same problem. Finally, foreseeability, which is sometimes used as a test for causation, is now also the test of remoteness of damage. Confusion is hardly surprising when the same yardstick is used, and the concepts of remoteness of damage and causation in law perform essentially similar functions, namely to place what are considered to be fair or just limits on liability for wrongful conduct. Whilst appreciating the similarities, it nonetheless seems sensible to maintain a distinction between cases of multiple cause, where the question is which cause is to be treated as having legal significance, and cases where on any view the defendant's negligence was *the* cause of the harm, but it is thought to be unfair to hold him responsible because it occurred in some unusual or bizarre fashion.

These comments should be kept in mind when considering the cases discussed in the next two paragraphs. The division into intervening acts by third parties and by the plaintiff is largely a matter of convenience, since the principles of law applied to these situations are essentially the same. Where it is the plaintiff whose act has intervened the position is slightly complicated by the possibility of using other conceptual tools, such as contributory negligence, *volenti non fit injuria* and mitigation of damage, instead of causation.

4.2.2.1 By third parties Faced with an emergency or dilemma created by the defendant's wrong a reasonable response by a third party will not constitute *novus actus,* even though with hindsight an alternative action might have been preferable (cf. contributory negligence, para. 14.5.3.4). This applies not only to involuntary or instinctive reactions in the alarm of the moment (*Scott* v *Shepherd* (1773) 2 Bl R 892; *Brandon* v *Osborne, Garrett & Co. Ltd* [1924] 1 KB 548) but also where there is an opportunity for a more considered decision. In *The Oropesa* [1943] P 32 there was a collision between two ships due to the negligent navigation of the *Oropesa.* The other ship was badly damaged and the captain set out in a lifeboat to consult the captain of the *Oropesa* about saving the ship. The lifeboat capsized in heavy seas and some of the crew were drowned. It was held that in the circumstances the captain's decision was reasonable and did not break the chain of causation. Those in charge of the *Oropesa* were liable for the deaths. Similarly, where the intervention is by a person who is not fully responsible for his actions, such as a young child, it will not absolve the defendant. In *Haynes* v *Harwood* [1935] 1 KB 146 the defendant left a horse-drawn van unattended in a busy street. A mischievous boy threw a stone at the horses and they bolted. The plaintiff was injured in attempting to bring them to a halt, and the defendant was held liable. Greer LJ said that the maxim *novus actus interveniens* is no defence if the intervention 'is the very kind of thing which is likely to happen if the want of care which is alleged takes place'. This shifts the analysis from the reasonableness of the act to its foreseeability. No doubt such conduct by an adult might be *less* foreseeable, but it is hardly unforeseeable. However, it would certainly be more unreasonable where the actor is fully responsible for his actions.

Philco Radio & Television Corporation of Great Britain Ltd v *J. Spurling Ltd* [1949] 2 All ER 882 provides an unusual example of deliberate and wrongful conduct by an adult being held *not* to constitute *novus actus* even though it was unforeseeable. The defendants negligently delivered some cases of highly flammable scrap film to the wrong address. One of the plaintiffs' employees touched the film with a lighted cigarette, probably (according to the trial judge) intending to make a 'small and innocuous bonfire'. There was an explosion and fire which caused serious damage to the plaintiffs' premises. The Court of Appeal held the defendants liable. The evidence as to the employee's intentions was obscure and Jenkins and Singleton LJJ might have allowed the appeal if the defendants had established that the employee intended to cause the fire. (Jenkins LJ said: 'There is really no evidence except her observation: "What a lovely bonfire that would make!"' *No* evidence?) Tucker LJ said that even if the act was deliberate there was no evidence that the employee knew the nature of the scrap and the consequences of setting light to it, so there was no 'conscious act of volition'. The act could hardly be said to have been foreseeable but it was not so unreasonable as to obliterate the risk created by the defendants' original negligence (*Clerk and Lindsell*, para. 2–29).

Negligent intervening acts may or may not break the chain of causation. No categorical answer can be given. In *Knightley* v *Johns* [1982] 1 All ER 851 the Court of Appeal said (at p. 865) that the question to be asked is whether the whole sequence of events is a natural and probable consequence of the defendant's negligence and whether it was reasonably foreseeable, not foreseeable as a mere possibility. In answering this question it was 'helpful but not decisive' to consider which events were deliberate choices to do positive acts and which were mere omissions, which acts and omissions were innocent mistakes or miscalculations and which were negligent. 'Negligent conduct is more likely to break the chain of causation than conduct which is not; positive acts will more easily constitute new causes than inaction.' The defendant, who had negligently caused a traffic accident at the exit of a tunnel, was held not liable for a subsequent accident when a police officer, who had forgotten to close the tunnel, ordered a policeman to ride his motor cycle the wrong way down the tunnel in order to close the entrance (cf. *Rouse* v *Squires* [1973] QB 889 where a driver negligently caused a motorway accident and later another negligent driver collided with the stationary vehicles—the first driver was held 25% responsible for the additional harm inflicted in the second crash). In this type of case the courts seek refuge in 'common sense rather than logic on the facts and circumstances of each case' (per Stephenson LJ in *Knightley* v *Johns*). Where the intervening conduct can be characterised as reckless, as opposed to merely negligent, it is far more likely to be treated as a *novus actus interveniens* (*Wright* v *Lodge* [1993] 4 All ER 299; Jones (1994) 2 Tort L Rev 133—reckless lorry driver collided with the stationary car of a negligent motorist in fog, careered onto the opposite carriageway of a dual carriageway and collided with several vehicles. Negligent motorist not liable for the subsequent collisions which would not have occurred if the lorry driver had been merely driving negligently).

The foreseeability of an intervening act may be a useful guide to assessing comparative blameworthiness, but it cannot be decisive. This becomes most apparent when the intervention is a criminal act. In *Home Office* v *Dorset Yacht Co. Ltd* [1970] AC 1004, Lord Reid said (at p. 1030) that:

> Where human action forms one of the links between the original wrong-doing of the defendant and the loss suffered by the plaintiff, that action must at least have been something very likely to happen if it is not to be regarded *as novus actus interveniens*.

This caused some perplexity in *Lamb* v *Camden London Borough Council* [1981] QB 625. The defendants negligently damaged a water main which led to serious subsidence of the plaintiff's house, causing the tenant to move out. Subsequently, squatters moved in and caused considerable damage to the property. The defendants admitted liability for the subsidence but denied responsibility for the criminal damage inflicted by the squatters. The arbitrator had found that squatting was a reasonably foreseeable risk but it was not likely.

The Court of Appeal concluded that the defendants were not liable for the squatters' damage. Oliver LJ said that Lord Reid may have 'understated the *degree* of likelihood required before the law can or should attribute the free act of a responsible third person to the tortfeasor'. In some (unspecified) circumstances the court would 'require a degree of likelihood amounting almost to inevitability'. Watkins LJ, adopting a 'robust and sensible approach', had an 'instinctive feeling that the squatters' damage is too remote'. Lord Denning MR rejected Lord Reid's test as leading to too wide a range of liability (as had Watkins LJ) and held that as a matter of policy the plaintiffs action should fail because it was her responsibility, not the council's, to keep squatters out of her own property. The very diversity of these judgments is instructive because it suggests that there is something awry with the court's analysis. The case was argued on the basis of remoteness of damage where, as will be seen, the test is reasonable foreseeability of the harm. Foreseeability cannot resolve this problem, however, without resorting to fictional degrees of foresight which are chosen to 'fit' the result that the court considers appropriate (Oliver LJ) or judicial 'instinct' (Watkins LJ) which is probably the same thing. *Lamb* is a problem in causation and duty. The council did not inflict criminal damage on the plaintiffs property, the squatters did. The council's negligence created the opportunity for the squatters' damage but it did not *cause* it, unless it could be said that they were under a *duty* of care to prevent the squatters' behaviour. If there is such a duty then the defendant cannot complain that the intervention is a *novus actus*. The third party's act is the occasion of the defendant's breach of duty, not a separate cause. Such duties arise only in special circumstances which were not present in *Lamb* (see para. 2.2.1). To the extent that the existence of a duty of care is ultimately a matter of policy, Lord Denning's view was probably the most appropriate, but his judgment did not adopt this analysis, and vague appeals to 'policy' are arguably as indeterminate as judicial instinct (Jones (1981) 78 LS Gaz 1292; cf. *P. Perl (Exporters) Ltd* v *Camden London Borough Council* [1984] QB 342, para. 2.2.1, where on very similar facts the case was analysed in terms of duty not remoteness, although Oliver LJ commented that these were 'simply two facets of the same problem'; see further, Jones (1984) 47 MLR 223; *King* v *Liverpool City Council* [1986] 1 WLR 890; *Smith* v *Littlewoods Organisation Ltd* [1987] 1 All ER 710, para. 2.2.1; for some of the problems created by treating duty and remoteness as merely interchangeable mechanisms for dealing with the same problem see Kidner (1989) 9 Legal Stud 1).

In *Ward* v *Cannock Chase District Council* [1985] 3 All ER 537 the defendants were held liable for damage to the plaintiffs property by vandals and thieves. The council had allowed adjoining property to fall into disrepair, and it collapsed, damaging the plaintiff's premises which had to be vacated. The council accepted responsibility but negligently failed to carry out repairs promptly. This made it 'virtually certain' that the property would be vandalised in that particular locality. Applying both reasonable foreseeability and 'common sense', Scott J distinguished *Lamb* v *Camden London Borough Council*, because the likelihood of the intervention was much greater and that likelihood was related not only to the original negligence but to the council's continuing failure to repair the initial damage (but does this deal with Lord Denning's observation in *Lamb*—whose responsibility was it to keep vandals out?).

4.2.2.2 By the plaintiff When it is the plaintiff whose act intervenes the same principles apply, although the emphasis seems to be on whether he acted reasonably rather than whether his conduct was foreseeable. It will not be *a novus actus* 'even though the accident and damage would not have happened but for some action of the plaintiff, so long as his action was in the ordinary course of things and, at least generally speaking, was not blameworthy' (*Summers* v *Salford Corporation* [1943] AC 283, 296 per Lord Wright). In *McKew* v *Holland & Hannen & Cubitts (Scotland) Ltd* [1969] 3 All ER 1621 the defendants negligently injured the plaintiff's leg, which as a result was liable to give way without warning. Without asking for assistance he attempted to descend a steep flight of stairs without a handrail and he fell suffering further serious injuries. The House of Lords held that the defendants were not liable for this additional injury because the plaintiff's conduct was unreasonable and constituted a *novus actus*. It was not a question of what was foreseeable, because it was not at all unlikely or unforeseeable that in these circumstances someone might take just such an unreasonable risk (per Lord Reid). But it did not follow that a defendant was liable for every foreseeable consequence.

McKew v *Holland & Hannen & Cubitts (Scotland) Ltd* can be contrasted with *Wieland* v *Cyril Lord Carpets Ltd* [1969] 3 All ER 1006 where the plaintiff had to wear a surgical collar as a result of the initial injury. This restricted the movement of her head which reduced her ability to use her bifocal glasses. Eveleigh J held the defendants liable for further injuries sustained in a fall down some steps on the basis that it was foreseeable that one injury may affect a person's ability to cope with the vicissitudes of life and thereby be a cause of another injury. It would seem that the distinction between these two cases is that in *Wieland* v *Cyril Lord Carpets Ltd* the plaintiff did not act unreasonably in attempting to descend the steps.

It is clear that in *McKew* v *Holland & Hannen & Cubitts (Scotland) Ltd* Lord Reid used the word 'unreasonable'to describe a distinction between careless and careful conduct, not voluntary and involuntary conduct. The usual technique for dealing with negligent plaintiffs is the defence of contributory negligence, which allows responsibility to be apportioned (note that other conceptual devices include *volenti non fit injuria,* para. 14. 1, and failure to mitigate the damage, para. 15.1.6). Why, it might be asked, was contributory negligence not employed in *McKew* (Millner (1971) 22 NILQ 168, 176–9, but note that Millner regards *novus actus* as a form of remoteness of damage governed by foreseeability)? Negligence by an intervening third party will not necessarily break the chain of causation, and in *Sayers* v *Harlow Urban District Council* [1958] 1 WLR 623 the plaintiff's negligence did not constitute *novus actus.* She had become trapped in a public lavatory by a faulty door lock. After calling for assistance without response she decided to climb out, but fell when she placed her weight on a toilet-roll holder which gave way. On any interpretation it was reasonable to attempt the escape but she was careless in the manner of performing the attempt, for which she was held contributorily negligent. It is difficult to see a tenable distinction between *Sayers* and *McKew.* (See also *The Calliope* [1970] P 172 discussed by Millner (1971) 22 NILQ 168, 178–9; cf. *Quinn* v *Burch Brothers (Builders) Ltd* [1966] 2 QB 370 where the Court of Appeal held that an unreasonable risk taken by the plaintiff, although foreseeable, broke the chain of causation. The claim was contractual, however, and contributory negligence would not have applied, see para. 14.5.1.)

As with intervention by a third party, once the court has determined that the defendant was in breach of a duty to exercise reasonable care for the plaintiffs safety, the plaintiff's negligent conduct should not lead to a finding of *novus actus* but should be dealt with as a question of contributory negligence. In *March* v *E. & M. H. Stramare Pty Ltd* (1991) 99 ALR 423 the defendant parked a truck across the centre line of a six lane street, partially blocking the offside lane in each direction. The plaintiff motorist, who was intoxicated at the time, was injured when he collided with the stationary truck. The Supreme Court of South Australia held that the defendant's negligence did not cause the injuries, the negligence of the plaintiff being the 'real cause'. The High Court of Australia allowed the plaintiff's appeal on the basis that the defendant owed a duty of care to all road users, 'including the inattentive and those whose faculties were impaired by alcohol'. The plaintiff's negligence did not take him outside the class of persons to whom the defendant owed a duty of care—on the contrary, the plaintiff's 'intoxication and associated carelessness took him within the class of inattentive drivers to whom the truck represented the greatest hazard' (per Deane J at p. 434). Once it is accepted that the defendant owed a duty of care to take reasonable precautions against negligent conduct by others, he cannot assert that the circumstances which give rise to a breach of that duty constitute a *novus actus interveniens*. The plaintiff was held contributorily negligent to the extent of 70%.

A dictum in *Muirhead* v *Industrial Tank Specialities Ltd* [1985] 3 All ER 705, 718–19 suggests that where the plaintiffs negligence consists of a failure to prevent damage caused by the defendant's wrong it will not constitute a *novus actus*. (cf. the distinction drawn between omissions and acts in *Knightley* v *Johns* [1982] 1 All ER 851, para. 4.2.2.1). This approach was taken in *Thompson* v *Toorenburgh* (1975) 50 DLR (3d) 717 where it was said that the failure to provide an *actus interveniens* which would have saved an accident victim's life was not the same as committing an *actus interveniens* that caused her death. The defendant who caused the accident was liable for the death.

'Reasonableness' is also used to indicate an element of involuntary conduct, as well as carelessness, when the plaintiff's act intervenes. In *Pigney* v *Pointer's Transport Services Ltd* [1957] 1 WLR 1121 the plaintiff's husband sustained a head injury which produced a depressive mental illness leading to his suicide. The defendants were held liable for his death because the act was not sufficiently unreasonable to constitute *novus actus*. By most objective criteria suicide is usually an unreasonable act. Indeed, at the time it was a crime. But the accident had affected the deceased's capacity for rational judgment and so removed the necessary voluntary element of a *novus actus*. Similarly, in *Kirkham* v *Chief Constable of the Greater Manchester Police* [1989] 3 All ER 882 (affirmed [1990] 3 All ER 246, CA) Tudor Evans J rejected the defendant's argument that the deceased's own deliberate and conscious act of suicide broke the chain of causation, on the basis that the suicide was the very thing that the police were under a duty to take precautions against. Although the deceased's act was deliberate, his 'mental balance' was affected at the time. By way of contrast, in *Hyde* v *Tameside Area Health Authority* (1981) 2 PN 26 Lord Denning MR commented that as a matter of policy the courts should discourage actions in respect of suicides and attempted suicides, a view clearly influenced by his Lordship's opinion that 'medical malpractice cases should not get out of hand' in this country. However, O'Connor LJ said that suicide or attempted suicide would not necessarily break the chain of causation; and in *Kirkham* v *Chief Constable of the Greater Manchester Police* [1990] 3 All ER 246, 250 Lloyd LJ doubted Lord Denning's comments in *Hyde* v *Tameside Area Health Authority*. This issue has recently been considered again by the Court of Appeal in *Reeves* v *Commissioner of Police of the Metropolis* [1998] 2 All ER 381, where a prisoner in police custody committed suicide. By a majority it was held that a *novus actus interveniens* must be an event of such impact that it obliterates the defendant's wrongdoing. The suicide was not an *intervening* cause, or was not a *new* act, said

Buxton LJ (at p. 389) because foresight of its possible occurrence was the most important part of the reason for placing the defendants under their duty of care to the deceased in the first place. Lord Bingham CJ commented (at p. 403) that:

> Since an act of self-destruction by the deceased was the very risk against which the defendant was bound in law to take reasonable precautions, I cannot see how that act can be regarded as a *novus actus*. So to hold would be to deprive the duty of meaningful content. This was, after all, the very thing against which the defendant was duty-bound to take precautions. It can make no difference that the deceased was mentally 'normal' (assuming he was), since it is not suggested that the defendant's duty was owed only to the abnormal.

Morritt LJ, in a dissenting judgment, accepted that if the deceased was not of sound mind the defendants would be liable, but took a different view in the case of a sane prisoner (at p. 398):

> But where the prisoner is wholly of sound mind I find it hard to see how there is any material increase in the risk in any causative sense. It is true that the failure to take reasonable care provides the opportunity for the suicide but the occurrence of that event depends wholly on the will and intention of the prisoner. In my view the voluntary, deliberate and in-formed act of a plaintiff (or one whom the plaintiff represents) intended to exploit the situation created by the defendant albeit in breach of duty precludes a causative link between the breach of duty and the consequences of the plaintiff's action. If the law is otherwise then those who fail to take reasonable care will become insurers for the deliberate actions of those to whom they owe their duty of care. In my view this would extend the law of negligence far beyond its proper scope.

A plaintiff injured in a rescue attempt is not *novus actus interveniens* (unless the emergency has passed: *Cutler* v *United Dairies (London) Ltd* [1933] 2 KB 297). 'The risk of rescue, if only it be not wanton, is born of the occasion. The emergency begets the man.' (*Wagner* v *International Railway Co.* (1921) 133 NE 437, 437; 232 NY 176, 180) This can be justified either on the basis that rescue is foreseeable or it is a reasonable intervention. A rescue will not necessarily be undertaken on the spur of the moment, but conscious deliberation will neither break the chain of causation nor render the rescuer *volenti*, even where injury is inevitable. In *Urbanski* v *Patel* (1978) 84 DLR (3d) 650 a doctor negligently removed a patient's only kidney, believing it to be an ovarian cyst. He was liable to the patient's father who donated one of his own kidneys to save her life.

The refusal of a plaintiff who is pregnant, following a negligently performed sterilisation operation, to undergo an abortion is not unreasonable and so does not constitute a *novus actus interveniens* (*Emeh* v *Kensington & Chelsea & Westminster Area Health Authority* [1984] 3 All ER 1044, CA). Arguably, a woman's refusal to undergo an abortion should never be considered unreasonable.

In *Meah* v *McCreamer* [1985] 1 All ER 367 the plaintiff suffered brain damage in an accident caused by the defendant's negligence. This produced a personality change which led the plaintiff to commit a series of violent sexual attacks for which he was convicted and sentenced to life imprisonment. He was awarded damages to compensate him for being imprisoned. This remarkable result was reached solely on the basis of principles for the assessment of damages. *Novus actus* was not even argued, although it is difficult to conceive of more unreasonable behaviour. Nor is it easy to justify on the ground that his conduct was an involuntary reaction produced by his injury, because that ought to have undermined the *mens rea* necessary for his conviction (see Banakas [1985] CLJ 195). Subsequently, two of Meah's victims sued him and were awarded damages for their injuries. He then sought to recover these sums from the defendant. The same judge, Woolf J, held that this loss was too remote (*Meah* v *McCreamer (No. 2)* [1986] 1 All ER 943). This is, frankly, illogical. If the plaintiff's own criminal actions did not break the chain of causation between the defendant's negligence and his imprisonment, how can those same actions break the link between the negligence and the compensation payable to the victims of the very crimes for which the plaintiff was imprisoned? Both in terms of causation and foreseeability the losses are of the same calibre. The distinction upon which Woolf J relied was that damages for the imprisonment were in respect of the plaintiff's *direct* financial loss, whereas the claim for the damages paid to the victims was an indirect loss. It is not apparent, however, why the consequences of criminal proceedings should be regarded as any more direct than the consequences of civil proceedings arising from the same acts.

Woolf J considered that policy also supported this conclusion. It was contrary to public policy that the plaintiff should be compensated for the consequences of his own crime in the second action, but this did not apply to the first action, partly because that award provided a fund which enabled the victims to recover the damages to which they were entitled. His Lordship did not explain quite why motor insurers should be compensating the victims of violent crime in this way (Banakas [1985] CLJ 195, 198; but see *Hardy* v *Motor Insurers' Bureau* [1964] 2 QB 745 in which a vehicle was used as an instrument of violence). *Meah* v *McCreamer* is a clear example of 'policy', however well-intentioned, making a nonsense of legal principle.

It may be that *Meah* v *McCreamer* would not now be followed in the light of the decision of the Court of Appeal in *Clunis* v *Camden & Islington Health Authority* [1998] 3 All ER 180. The plaintiff was a man with a history of mental disorder and seriously violent behaviour. He had been detained under the Mental Health Act 1983, and following his discharge from hospital the defendants came under a duty, by virtue of s. 117 of that Act, to provide after-care services, but he did not receive any after-care. Three months after his discharge from hospital the plaintiff killed a stranger in a sudden and completely unprovoked attack. He was charged with murder, but a plea of manslaughter on the ground of diminished responsibility was accepted by the prosecution and he was ordered to be detained in a special hospital. Clunis brought an action against the defendants alleging that they were in breach of a common law duty of care to treat him with reasonable professional care and skill. He claimed that if he had received an appropriate assessment he would not have gone on to commit the crime because he would either have consented to become a voluntary patient or would have been detained under the Act. As a result he would now be detained for much longer than he would otherwise have been. The Court of Appeal struck out the claim as disclosing no reasonable cause of action, on the grounds that: (1) the action was based the plaintiff's own illegal act, and therefore the maxim *ex turpi causa non oritur actio* applied (see para. 14.3); and (2) the statutory obligation to provide after-care created by s. 117 of the Mental Health Act 1983 did not give rise to a duty of care at common law. The fact that the plaintiff was found guilty of manslaughter is most obviously relevant to the defence of *ex turpi causa*, but it appears also to have influenced the Court's view of the duty of care: 'Nor do we think that it would be fair or reasonable to hold the defendant responsible for the consequences of the plaintiff's criminal act' (at p. 192). Although it was accepted that the plaintiff's mental responsibility was substantially impaired, nonetheless a plea of diminished responsibility did not remove liability for his criminal act. He had to be taken to have known what he was doing and that it was wrong: 'public policy would preclude the court from entertaining the plaintiff's claim unless it could be said that he did not know the nature and quality of his act or that what he was doing was wrong' (at p. 188). In passing, the Court commented that *Meah* v *McCreamer* could no longer be regarded as authoritative on this issue.

4.3 REMOTENESS OF DAMAGE

In order that the defendant may be held in breach of duty it must have been reasonably foreseeable that his conduct might cause harm to someone. What is the position where objectively the defendant has acted carelessly, but the resulting damage is more extensive, or of a different type, or occurred in a different manner from that which would normally be expected from such conduct? In a system of fault liability, holding a person liable for the unpredictable or freakish consequences of his negligence may seem unfair because of a sense of disproportion between the fault and the harm. To drop a plank into a ship's hold is careless. It could be expected to cause a dent in the ship, or impact damage to any cargo or people in the hold. But should the defendant be responsible for an explosion by a spark igniting petrol vapour and the consequent destruction of the ship (as in *Re Polemis and Furness, Withy & Co. Ltd* [1921] 3 KB 560)? To spill oil in a harbour is careless, even criminal. It may foul the wharfs and require expensive cleaning operations. But if it is extremely difficult to set alight on open water should the defendant be responsible for the destruction of a wharf by fire? (Not so in *Overseas Tankship (UK) Ltd* v *Morts Dock & Engineering Co., The Wagon Mound* [1961] AC 388.)

There are two broad approaches to this problem. The first states that a defendant is liable for all the direct consequences of his negligence, no matter how unusual or unexpected. This is essentially a test based on causation. Some independent intervening cause, either voluntary conduct or coincidence (Hart and Honoré, *Causation in the Law,* 2nd ed., p. 164) would render the damage indirect. The second holds that a person is only responsible for consequences that could reasonably have been anticipated. Although in theory it is now accepted that foreseeability is the correct test, in reality decisions as to exactly how foreseeable the consequences must be, in combination with the principle that a tortfeasor must 'take his victim as he finds him', mean that the limits of actionability set by remoteness of damage lie somewhere between these two approaches.

4.3.1 Foreseeability and directness
The directness of consequence test is usually attributed to the decision of the Court of Appeal in *Re Polemis and Furness, Withy & Co. Ltd* [1921] 3 KB 560. Bankes LJ said that given the damage was a direct result of the negligence 'the anticipations of the person whose negligent act has produced the damage appear to me to be irrelevant'. Similarly, Scrutton LJ observed that 'once the act is negligent, the fact that its exact operation was not foreseen is immaterial'. On this view foreseeability 'goes to culpability, not to compensation' (*Weld-Blundell* v *Stephens* [1920] AC 956, 984 per Lord Sumner).

In *The Wagon Mound* [1961] AC 388 the Privy Council described this proposition as fundamentally false. The trial judge had found that it was not reasonably foreseeable that bunkering oil with such a high flash-point would catch fire when spread on water. Indeed, the plaintiffs' works manager had made enquiries and then allowed welding to continue on the wharf. Viscount Simonds said (at p. 425) that although an action for negligence can be analysed in terms of duty, breach of duty and consequent damage, there can be no liability until the damage has been done.

> It is not the act but the consequences on which tortious liability is founded. just as . . . there is no such thing as negligence in the air, so there is no such thing as liability in the air. . . . [T]he only liability that is in question is the liability for damage by fire. It is vain to isolate the liability from its context and to say that [the defendant] is or is not liable, and then to ask for what damage he is liable. For his liability is in respect of that damage and no other. If, as admittedly it is, [the defendant's] liability (culpability) depends on the reasonable foreseeability of the consequent damage, how is that to be determined except by the foreseeability of the damage which in fact happened—the damage in suit? And, if that damage is unforeseeable so as to displace liability at large, how can the liability be restored so as to make compensation payable?

Reasonable foreseeability, said his Lordship, corresponds with the common conscience of mankind whereas the direct consequence test 'leads to nowhere but the never-ending and insoluble problems of causation' (but see *Weir,* p. 231, question 5). Despite being only a persuasive authority (as a decision of the Privy Council) the strong disapproval of *Re Polemis in The Wagon Mound* has led subsequent courts to adopt foreseeability as the test of remoteness of damage in negligence. The same test was extended to nuisance in *Overseas Tankship (UK) Ltd v Miller Steamship Co. Pty Ltd, The Wagon Mound (No. 2)* [1967] 1 AC 617 in which the owners of two ships damaged in the same fire that damaged the wharf sued the owners of *The Wagon Mound*. The plaintiffs in this case were successful on the basis that damage by fire was foreseeable, albeit only as a remote risk, notwithstanding the fact that the Privy Council had concluded in *The Wagon Mound* that the fire was unforeseeable (for an explanation of how this remarkable conclusion was reached see Dias [1967] CLJ 62, and especially pp. 66–76). For the purpose of remoteness, once it is established that the damage sustained by the plaintiff was foreseeable, the *likelihood* that it would have occurred is irrelevant. In *The Heron II* [1969] 1 AC 350, 422, for example, Lord Upjohn said that 'the tortfeasor is liable for any damage which he can reasonably foresee may happen as a result of the breach however unlikely it may be, unless it can be brushed aside as far-fetched' (cf. the *degrees* of foreseeability to which Oliver LJ was forced to resort in *Lamb v Camden London Borough Council* [1981] QB 625 (para. 4.2.2.1) by trying to deal with intervening criminal acts as a problem in 'remoteness'). The likelihood of the occurrence or degree of foreseeability relates to the determination of whether the defendant acted carelessly in the face of the risk (*Clerk and Lindsell,* para. 7–188); which is why *The Wagon Mound (No. 2)* looks like a case on breach of duty, see para. 3.1.3.3). The somewhat surprising consequence of this is that *The Wagon Mound (No. 2)* has gone some way to restoring causation as the test of remoteness, because many things which could be regarded as unlikely are foreseeable and yet are not necessarily 'far-fetched' (on 'variable degrees' of foresight applied to the duty of care and remoteness of damage see Kidner (1989) 9 LS 1).

It is hardly sufficient, therefore, to say that the test of remoteness of damage is foreseeability because the crucial question is, what is it, precisely, that has to be foreseen? Foreseeability gives the court scope to manipulate the outcome of a particular case by defining what has to be foreseen either broadly or narrowly. The narrower the range of events or damage that must be anticipated the more difficult it is for the plaintiff to overcome the remoteness hurdle. After *The Wagon Mound* the courts quickly came to the conclusion that, provided the type or kind of harm sustained by the plaintiff could have been foreseen, it did not matter that its extent or the precise manner of its occurrence could not have been foreseen. Moreover the case did not abolish the 'eggshell-skull' (or 'thin-skull') rule, and this has the practical effect of putting a wide interpretation on the *type* of damage that must be foreseen.

4.3.2 Manner of the occurrence
The fact that damage occurred in an unforeseeable way does not necessarily mean that it was not foreseeable. In *Hughes v Lord Advocate* [1963] AC 837 employees of the Post Office negligently left a manhole open in the street.

This was covered by a canvas tent and surrounded by paraffin warning lamps. Out of curiosity, two young boys entered the tent, taking one of the lamps with them. The lamp was knocked into the hole and there was a violent explosion in which one of the boys suffered severe burns. The evidence indicated that an explosion was unforeseeable in the circumstances, although burns from a conflagration could have been anticipated. The House of Lords held the defendants liable. Lord Guest said that it was not necessary that the precise details leading up to the accident should have been reasonably foreseeable, 'it is sufficient if the accident which occurred is of a type which should have been foreseeable by a reasonably careful person'. The accident was simply a variant of the foreseeable' (per Lord Pearce) and, having been caused by a known source of danger, it was no defence that it was caused in a way which was unforeseeable (per Lord Reid).

Thus the precise concatenation of events need not be anticipated if the harm is within the general range of what is reasonably foreseeable (*Stewart* v *West African Terminals Ltd* [1964] 2 Lloyd's Rep 371, 375; see also *Sullivan* v *South Glamorgan County Council* (1985) 84 LGR 415). Similarly, in *Wieland* v *Cyril Lord Carpets Ltd* [1969] 3 All ER 1006, 1009 (see para. 4.2.2.2), where a disability caused by the defendant's negligence led to a further injury, Eveleigh J said that *Overseas Tankship (UK) Ltd* v *Morts Dock & Engineering Co., The Wagon Mound* [1961] AC 388 did not require foreseeability of the manner in which the original injury caused harm to the plaintiff. 'Indeed, the precise mechanics of the way in which the negligent act results in the original injury do not have to be foreseen.'

Two cases appear to run contrary to this line of reasoning. In *Doughty* v *Turner Manufacturing Co. Ltd* [1964] 1 QB 518 an asbestos cover was knocked into a bath of molten liquid. Shortly after, due to a chemical reaction which was unforeseeable at the time, there was an eruption of the molten liquid that burned the plaintiff who was standing nearby. The Court of Appeal, distinguishing *Hughes* v *Lord Advocate*, held that burning by an unforeseeable chemical eruption was not a variant of burning by splashing, which was within the foreseeable risk created by knocking the cover into the liquid. With great respect, it is difficult to see the distinction between these cases. They clearly illustrate that the framing of the question will determine the answer to a remoteness question. In *Doughty* v *Turner Manufacturing Co. Ltd*, the question answered in the negative was: was burning *by eruption* foreseeable? In *Hughes* v *Lord Advocate* the question was expressed differently: was burning foreseeable? If the House of Lords had asked: was burning *by explosion* foreseeable? the result in *Hughes* v *Lord Advocate* would have been different. (See also *Tremain* v *Pike* [1969] 3 All ER 1303 (para. 4.3.3) for another example of how narrowing the scope of the question produces the result that harm was unforeseeable. Note that the result in *Doughty* v *Turner Manufacturing Co. Ltd* might be justified on other grounds, e.g., that, on the facts, burning by splashing was unforeseeable and so there was no negligence (*Clerk and Lindsell*, para. 7–190)).

The second case is *Crossley* v *Rawlinson* [1981] 3 All ER 674 in which the plaintiff, whilst running towards a burning vehicle with a fire extinguisher, tripped in a concealed hole and was injured. It was held that because the plaintiff had not reached the scene of the danger the injury was unforeseeable and therefore too remote. Rescuers are usually accorded more sympathetic treatment than this by the courts. The distinction between rescuers at the scene of the danger and those attempting to get to the scene is arbitrary and inconsistent with *Hughes* v *Lord Advocate* since the injury is within the risk created by the defendant's negligence (see further, Jones (1982) 45 MLR 342; para. 2.2.2).

4.3.3 Type of harm

The damage will be too remote if it is not of the same type or kind as the harm that could have been foreseen. The difficulty is to know how to categorise the 'type' of damage that must be foreseeable, and this is at the centre of most of the problems concerning remoteness. It is possible to take a broad view of the classification of harm, dividing it into personal injury, property damage and financial loss. So far as property damage is concerned *The Wagon Mound* [1961] AC 388 indicates that there is a distinction between damage by impact and damage by fire (because of the disapproval of *Re Polemis and Furness, Withy & Co. Ltd* [1921] 3 KB 560), and damage by fouling and damage by fire. Beyond that it gives no guidance about how to categorise harm. *Hughes* v *Lord Advocate* [1963] AC 837 (see para. 4.3.2) makes it clear that burning by explosion is the same type of harm as burning by conflagration, and this would presumably be equally applicable to property damage. In *Vacwell Engineering Co. Ltd* v *BDH Chemicals Ltd* [1971] 1 QB 88, Rees J said (at p. 100; emphasis is added):

It would also be foreseeable that *some* damage to property would or might result. In my judgment the explosion and the *type* of damage being foreseeable, it matters not in the law that the magnitude of the former and the extent of the latter were not.

This suggests a wide classification of 'damage to property', at least where the manner of the occurrence is foreseeable (see also *Muirhead* v *Industrial Tank Specialities Ltd* [1985] 3 All ER 705, 718).

In the context of personal injuries it would have been theoretically open to the courts to adopt a very wide categorisation and state that if personal injury was foreseeable it is irrelevant that the precise injury was unforeseeable. This has not been done, but in practice the eggshell-skull rule (para. 4.3.4.1) produces a very similar result. Under that rule if injury of a foreseeable type occurs and this leads to injury of a different, unforeseeable type the defendant is responsible. He is not liable, however, if there is no injury of a foreseeable type, so it remains important to know how the 'type of harm' will be categorised. Again, the decision as to whether harm is foreseeable depends upon how the court chooses to frame the question. Two cases will illustrate the point.

In *Bradford* v *Robinson Rentals Ltd* [1967] 1 All ER 267 the plaintiff suffered frostbite when he was sent on a journey by his employers in a vehicle without a heater, at a time of very severe winter weather. Rees J held that frostbite was damage of the same kind as that which was a foreseeable consequence of exposure to extreme cold. In *Tremain* v *Pike* [1969] 3 All ER 1303, on the other hand, a farm employee contracted a rare disease transmitted by contact with rats' urine. Payne J said that although injury by rat bites or from contaminated food was foreseeable, this particular disease was unforeseeable, and by implication harm of a different type. If the question had been: Was illness from some rat-transmitted disease foreseeable? the answer would surely have been yes. Rats are associated with disease but few people could specify which diseases are foreseeable. *Tremain* v *Pike* requires too precise a degree of foresight and is probably wrong on this point (Dias [1970] CLJ 28). By contrast, in *Draper* v *Hodder* [1972] 2 QB 556 Edmund Davies LJ said (at p. 573) that 'the proper test in negligence is not whether the particular type of physical harm actually suffered ought reasonably to have been anticipated, but whether broadly speaking it was within the range of likely consequence'. Thus, in *Hepworth* v *Kerr* [1995] 6 Med LR 139, 170–1 McKinnon J held that a spinal stroke was within the range of foreseeable consequences from an experimental anaesthetic technique, when the known complications from this procedure included cerebral (though not spinal) stroke. The technique created a foreseeable risk of damage, and the injury that occurred was but 'a variant of the foreseeable', applying *Hughes* v *Lord Advocate* [1963] AC 837.

It was formerly the view that there was a difference in kind between physical injury and psychiatric injury, but in *Page* v *Smith* [1995] 2 All ER 736 the House of Lords held that if physical injury to the plaintiff was foreseeable the defendant was liable for any psychiatric damage which the plaintiff sustained as a result of the defendant's negligence, even though physical injury did not in the event occur and the psychiatric damage was itself unforeseeable. Lord Lloyd said (at p. 761) that there was no justification for regarding physical and psychiatric injury as different 'kinds' of injury: 'Once it is established that the defendant is under a duty of care to avoid causing personal injury to the plaintiff it matters not whether the injury in fact sustained is physical, psychiatric or both'. *Page* v *Smith* was a case where the plaintiff was a 'primary victim', i.e., was involved as a participant in the accident caused by the defendant's negligence. In cases of 'secondary victims' the plaintiff suffers psychiatric injury as a result of witnessing an event in circumstances where, by definition, physical injury to the plaintiff was unforeseeable (see para. 2.2.4.3). In these circumstances, psychiatric injury must be foreseeable in order to establish a duty of care, but provided the duty has been established (whether to a 'primary victim' or a 'secondary victim') it is irrelevant that the illness takes a rare form or is of unusual severity (per Lord Lloyd at p. 768). Any recognised psychiatric illness will be sufficient, and the defendant need not foresee the particular illness developed by the plaintiff.

One possible implication of *Page* v *Smith*, though not discussed in the House of Lords, is that the courts will now increasingly approach the determination of the type of damage with a very broad brush, possibly going so far as to treat all forms of personal injury as foreseeable as a result of the occurrence of any foreseeable form of personal injury. If there is to be no distinction between *physical* injury and *psychiatric* injury, there is little obvious justification for distinguishing between different types of physical injury, at least in the case of personal injuries. It might be said that, strictly speaking, *Page* v *Smith* was a case concerning the existence of a duty of care, rather than remoteness of damage, and that it should be confined to the duty question. But this would be to take too rigid an approach to the categories of duty and remoteness, and to ignore the frequent references in the majority speeches to notions that are normally to be found when dealing with questions of remoteness of damage (such as 'the defendant must take his victim as he finds him'; see paras 4.3.4 and 4.3.4.1).

4.3.4 Extent of the harm

If the type of harm and the manner of its occurrence were foreseeable it is irrelevant that the physical extent of the damage was unforeseeable. That rule was not changed by *The Wagon Mound* [1961] AC 388 (*Smith* v *Leech Brain & Co. Ltd* [1962] 2 QB 405, 414 per Lord Parker CJ). So in *Hughes* v *Lord Advocate* [1963] AC 837, Lord Reid said (at p. 845):

> No doubt it was not to be expected that the injuries would be as serious as those which the appellant in fact sustained. But a defender is liable, although the damage may be a good deal greater in extent than was foreseeable. He can only escape liability if the damage can be regarded as differing in kind from what was foreseeable.

This applies as much to psychiatric injury as it does to other types of personal injury, and irrespective of any predisposition on the plaintiffs part which, unknown to the defendant, increases the likelihood of more extensive harm (*Page* v *Smith* [1995] 2 All ER 736; *Brice* v *Brown* [1984] 1 All ER 997).

The same principle applies to property damage. In *Vacwell Engineering Co. Ltd* v *BDH Chemicals Ltd* [1971] 1 QB 88 it was known that a chemical distributed by the defendants reacted with water to produce toxic vapour. Some of the chemical came into contact with water and the reaction led to an explosion of unforeseeable violence causing extensive damage. Rees J held that it was irrelevant that the magnitude of the explosion and resulting damage was unforeseeable (see the quotation in para. 4.3.3).

Liability for the unforeseeable *physical* extent of otherwise foreseeable harm should be distinguished from the *measure* of damages, in financial terms, required to compensate the plaintiff's loss. If the defendant injures someone with a large income, or damages a very valuable piece of property, he cannot object that the monetary cost of compensation is greater than if he had injured someone on a low income or if the property was a piece of junk (*Smith* v *London & South Western Railway Co.* (1870) LR 6 CP 14, 22–3; *The Arpad* [1934] P 189, 202). This is responsibility, not for unexpected consequences, but for the unexpectable cost of expected consequences (*Fleming*, p. 206). This principle is sometimes expressed in the maxim, 'The tortfeasor must take his victim as he finds him'. Although usually invoked on the plaintiffs behalf the principle can also work to the defendant's advantage in some cases.

4.3.4.1   Eggshell skulls   The same maxim is also used to describe the notion that where the plaintiff is suffering from a latent physical or psychological predisposition to a particular injury or illness which the harm inflicted by the defendant triggers off, the defendant is responsible for the additional, unforeseeable damage that his negligence has produced. This is commonly called the 'thin-skull' or the 'eggshell-skull' rule. The rule can apply to almost any type of weakness or predisposition, such as a fragile skull (*Owens* v *Liverpool Corporation* [1939] 1 KB 394, 401), a weak heart (*Love* v *Port of London* [1959] 2 Lloyd's Rep 541), a weak back (*Athey* v *Leonati* [1997] 1 WWR 97, 110) or haemophilia (*Bishop* v *Arts & Letters Club of Toronto* (1978) 83 DLR (3d) 107), provided *some* harm was foreseeable to establish breach of duty (see *Bourhill* v *Young* [1943] AC 92, 109; *Hewett* v *Alf Brown's Transport Ltd* [1992] ICR 530, where the plaintiff's special susceptibility to lead poisoning resulted in a finding that her injury was unforseeable and accordingly the defendants did not owe a duty of care).

The eggshell-skull rule overlaps, but is not coextensive, with the general principle that the extent of the harm need not be foreseeable. Where the plaintiffs predisposition simply exacerbates the otherwise foreseeable type of harm, then it is little more than the mechanism by which that principle comes into effect. And clearly, the general principle can apply in the absence of any predisposition in the plaintiff (*Vacwell Engineering Co. Ltd* v *BDH Chemicals Ltd* [1971] 1 QB 88; *Hughes* v *Lord Advocate* [1963] AC 837). The eggshell-skull rule arguably goes beyond this, however, by allowing recovery for harm of a different type from that which is foreseeable.

In *Smith* v *Leech Brain & Co. Ltd* [1962] 2 QB 405 the plaintiff's husband was burned on the lip by a piece of molten metal. The burn was treated and healed, but due to a premalignant condition the burn promoted a cancerous growth which ultimately led to his death. Lord Parker CJ held the defendants liable for the death.

> The test is not whether these [defendants] could reasonably have foreseen that a burn would cause cancer and that [Mr Smith] would die. The question is whether these [defendants] could reasonably foresee the type of injury he suffered, namely, the burn. What, in the particular case, is the amount of damage which he suffers as a result of that burn, depends upon the characteristics and constitution of the victim.

Lord Parker classified the type of injury as 'the burn'. The 'type' of injury that caused the death, admittedly triggered off by the burn, was cancer. If ever there was a case in which the unforeseeable harm which caused the loss was different in kind from the harm that was foreseeable this is it. Only if the harm had been categorised as 'personal injury' could the loss be regarded as merely greater in extent than the foreseeable damage (although Lord Parker's reference to 'the amount of damage' suggests that he was seeking to treat cancer and death as simply more extensive harm of the same type as a burn).

Whatever the theoretical reconciliation of *The Wagon Mound* [1961] AC 388 and the eggshell-skull rule, subsequent cases have confirmed Lord Parker's view that the rule survived the sinking of *Re Polemis and Furness, Withy & Co. Ltd* [1921] 3 KB 560 (see, e.g., *Oman v McIntyre* 1962 SLT 168; *Warren v Scruttons Ltd* [1962] 1 Lloyd's Rep 497). In *Robinson v Post Office* [1974] 2 All ER 737 the plaintiff was injured as a result of the defendant's negligence. When he sought medical treatment he suffered a serious allergic reaction to an anti-tetanus injection given to him by a doctor. The Court of Appeal held the defendants liable for this injury, stating that a person who could reasonably foresee that the victim of his negligence may require medical treatment is liable for the consequences of the treatment 'although he could not reasonably foresee those consequences or that they could be serious'. (Negligent treatment will usually constitute *novus actus interveniens*, but see *Price v Milawski* (1977) 82 DLR (3d) 130 where a negligent doctor was held liable for the subsequent negligence of another doctor—on the particular facts it was a possibility that a reasonable doctor would not have brushed aside as far-fetched.) No question here of the *type* of consequence being foreseeable, provided the need for treatment is foreseeable. The rule has even been applied to an 'eggshell personality' (*Page v Smith* [1995] 2 All ER 736; *Malcolm v Broadhurst* [1970] 3 All ER 508 where the injury merely aggravated a pre-existing nervous condition). This approach will also explain a case such as *Pigney v Pointer's Transport Services Ltd* [1957] 1 WLR 1121 in which the defendants were held liable for the suicide of the plaintiff's husband during a depressive mental illness induced by a severe head injury, for which the defendants were responsible. Williams (1961) 77 LQR 179, 196 observed that: 'Either the victim's suicide was a normal reaction to his injuries, or it was abnormal. If it was normal, it should be taken as reasonably foreseeable; if it was abnormal, it comes within the thin-skull rule as applied to [psychological] states'. This view was applied by the Ontario Court of Appeal in *Cotic v Gray* (1981) 124 DLR (3rd) 641 where, on similar facts to *Pigney*, it was held that either suicide was generally within the realm of foreseeable consequences following personal injury, or the suicide fell within the thin-skull rule which was an exception to the requirement of foreseeability, but it was unnecessary to decide which test applied (cf. *Wright Estate v Davidson* (1992) 88 DLR (4th) 698, BCCA—deceased's suicide amounting to a *novus actus interveniens* where there was no evidence of disabling mental illness). The thin-skull rule does not extend, however, to the plaintiff's family (*McLaren v Bradstreet* (1969) 119 NLJ 484—plaintiffs could not recover for 'family hysteria' resulting from mother's neurotic reaction to minor injuries to her children caused by defendant's negligence; cf. *Nader v Urban Transit Authority of New South Wales* [1985] 2 NSWLR 501, noted by Hudson (1987) 38 NILQ 190, 193–8).

It must be conceded that the eggshell-skull rule contains a strong element of policy, particularly in the case of personal injuries. Although the premise usually remains inarticulate, the courts are not unaware that in most personal injury actions that come before them the defendant (commonly a driver or employer) is in the best position to distribute the loss via compulsory insurance. Moreover, 'human bodies are too fragile and life too precarious to permit a defendant nicely to calculate how much injury he might inflict' (*Fleming*, p. 206). What, then, of damage to property? Does the thin-skull rule apply? It probably does (*Salmond and Heuston*, p. 520), at least where the damage is of the same type as the foreseeable harm, but is unforeseeable in its extent. It would be difficult to apply *Smith* v *Leech Brain & Co. Ltd* to property damage, in so far as that case allowed recovery for damage of an unforeseeable type, without undermining *The Wagon Mound* completely. If a ship with a hold full of petrol vapour could be regarded as property having a predisposition to explode if it sustained an impact, and impact damage was a foreseeable consequence of the defendant's negligence, *Smith* v *Leech Brain & Co. Ltd* would resurrect *Re Polemis and Furness, Withy & Co. Ltd.* Consider, for example, the facts of *The Trecarrell* [1973] 1 Lloyd's Rep 402 where a contractor's employee dropped a drum of highly inflammable vinyl lacquer on to an electricity cable. The cable was cut and sparks from the resulting short-circuit ignited the lacquer which escaped from the broken drum. The fire spread to other drums of lacquer which burst and added fuel to the fire. This caused extensive damage to a ship under repair and the quay where the drum was dropped. The contractor was held liable on the basis that dropping the drum created a foreseeable fire hazard, and the type of damage being foreseeable it was irrelevant that the particular source of ignition, the damaged cable, was unforeseeable.

It is worth bearing in mind that the thin-skull rule, as with all rules which function as guides to causation (such as the 'but for' test or the 'material contribution to the damage' test), is concerned with the extent of the *damage* for which the defendant is liable. In other words, it goes to liability. When it comes to the assessment of *damages* as compensation for the damage caused by the defendant, an existing predisposition of the plaintiff to a particular injury may result in a reduction, or 'discount', of the damages awarded if there is evidence to show that the plaintiff would probably have developed the condition in any event. For example, if the plaintiff has constitutional, degenerative changes in his spine and suffers injury to his back as a result of the defendant's negligence, he is entitled to an assessment of damages for the injury to his back even if a normal back would not have suffered, or not have suffered such extensive, injury; but the damages will be reduced to reflect the chances (which may be less than 50%) that he would have developed disabling symptoms from the constitutional causes in any event.

4.3.4.2 Plaintiff's impecuniosity

In *Liesbosch Dredger* v *SS Edison* [1933] AC 449 the plaintiffs' dredger was sunk due to the defendants' fault. The plaintiffs could not afford to purchase a new vessel and so hired a substitute at an exorbitant rate, and this made the performance of their contractual obligations much more expensive. The House of Lords held that they were not entitled to claim this additional expense because it was not an immediate physical consequence of the negligence, but was the result of their own want of means which was an 'extraneous matter'. The defendant did not have to take the plaintiff as he found him with respect to his impecuniosity.

It is not easy to reconcile this with either the thin-skull rule or the rule that the plaintiff must be compensated for the loss of his personal earning capacity, whatever its level. Nor does it sit well with the plaintiff's obligation to mitigate his loss (where the plaintiff's impecuniosity can be taken into account: *Dodd Properties (Kent) Ltd* v *Canterbury City Council* [1980] 1 All ER 928, 935, 941) because in *The Liesbosch* the plaintiffs would have been under an obligation to mitigate by obtaining a replacement vessel. They could not have done nothing and charged the defendants for the loss of profits on the work they would have carried out but for the sinking. It may be that *The Liesbosch* can be justified on the basis that for pure financial loss, only the foreseeable extent of the damage is recoverable (but see *Ramwade Ltd* v *Emson & Co. Ltd* (1986) 2 PN 197, CA, where foreseeable financial loss was held irrecoverable, applying *The Liesbosch;* for criticism see Jones (1987) 3 PN 76, and more generally *Burrows* pp. 87–92).

The case has been distinguished (see *Martindale* v *Duncan* [1973] 1 WLR 574) and does not apply where a decision not to effect early repairs to property, because it would lead to 'financial stringency', is based on 'commercial prudence' rather than lack of resources (*Dodd Properties (Kent) Ltd* v *Canterbury City Council*; see also *Perry* v *Sidney Phillips & Son* [1982] 3 All ER 705), nor where the impecuniosity is caused by the defendant's tort (*Jarvis* v *T. Richards & Co.* (1980) 124 SJ 793; see generally, Davies [1982] JBL 21). In *Mattocks* v *Mann* [1993] RTR 13 Beldam LJ said that the law of damages had not stood still since 1933 and the authority of *The Liesbosch* was consistently being attenuated in more recent decisions. Accordingly, the plaintiff was entitled to recover the cost of hiring a replacement vehicle during a period of delay caused by insurers failing to pay the repair costs of her own vehicle, notwithstanding her own inability to pay the repair costs. It would clearly be contemplated that with substantial repair costs the parties would look to insurers to meet that cost, and the plaintiff's impecuniosity could not be regarded as the sole cause of her having to incur additional hire charges.

4.3.5 Reflections on *The Wagon Mound*
Re Polemis and Furness, Withy & Co. Ltd [1921] 3 KB 560 had been subjected to much criticism, both judicial and academic. In *The Wagon Mound* [1961] AC 388, Viscount Simonds (at p. 422) was scathing. It did:

> not seem consonant with current ideas of justice or morality that for an act of negligence, however slight or venial, which results in some trivial foreseeable damage the actor should be liable for all the consequences however unforeseeable and however grave, so long as they can be said to be 'direct'.

This was 'neither logical nor just'. There is nothing inherently illogical, however, about combining a liability rule based on foreseeability with a remoteness rule based on causation (nor, indeed, combining a liability rule based on causation—strict liability—with a remoteness rule based on fore-seeability, see, e.g., *Galashiels Gas Co. Ltd* v *Millar* [1949] AC 275; Dias

[19671 CLJ 62, 68). As for the justice of the matter, it should be remembered that the extent of *foreseeable* damage rarely corresponds with the degree of a defendant's fault, and the measure of damages, even for damage of the same physical extent, will vary from case to case. Thus foreseeability too can lead to dire consequences from a venial act of negligence. Moreover, fairness for defendants may overlook the question of what is fair for plaintiffs. If a choice has to be made as to where the loss should lie, then as between an innocent plaintiff and a defendant who *ex hypothesi* is guilty of wrongful conduct it is not obviously unfair to make the defendant responsible. This is particularly so where the defendant is better placed to distribute the loss through liability insurance (though see Stapleton (1995) 58 MLR 820 for criticism of this type of argument). Where hard choices have to be made the criterion of fairness merely begs the question to whom the court should be fair.

Viscount Simonds also considered that foreseeability would be simpler to apply than the 'never-ending and insoluble problems of causation'. Unfortunately, experience has proved him wrong. *The Wagon Mound (No. 2)* [1967] 1 AC 617 illustrates how unpredictable and convoluted foreseeability can be. *The Wagon Mound* [1961] AC 388 effectively increased the uncertainties of litigation because the categorisation of the type of harm that must be foreseen has become more indeterminate (e.g., *Tremain* v *Pike* [1969] 3 All ER 1303 (para. 4.3.3); *Doughty* v *Turner Manufacturing Co. Ltd* [1964] 1 QB 518 (para. 4.3.2)).

Much of the criticism of *Polemis* was misdirected (see Davies (1982) 45 MLR 534). This may have been partially due to misunderstanding about what the case actually decided. It has been argued, for example, that the decision is open to two possible interpretations. The first, 'wide' principle, is that the defendant is liable for all the damage directly resulting from his careless behaviour, even to an unforeseeable plaintiff. The second, 'narrow' principle, is that as long as the plaintiff was in foreseeable danger, the defendant is liable to him to the full extent of the damage that directly results, though neither the manner of its incidence nor its extent were foreseeable. The first, erroneous interpretation has been the source of all the difficulty, whereas the second, correct, interpretation fits the facts of the case and is consistent with the case law (Dias [1962] CLJ 151). This second formulation is virtually identical to the test that has been developed since *The Wagon Mound*. If the damage was of a foreseeable type or kind (and remember that foreseeability as a 'possibility' will suffice) it is irrelevant that the extent or the precise manner of the occurrence were unforeseeable. The thin-skull rule looks even more like *Polemis*. Once it is established that the initial injury was of a foreseeable type the defendant is responsible for the ultimate consequences, even of a different type, simply on the basis of causation, i.e., provided there is a causal link between the two (see the comment of Richmond J in *Stephenson* v *Waite, Tileman Ltd* [1973] 1 NZLR 152, 168). For the purpose of remoteness, then, foreseeability is given a very wide interpretation, and is not tempered by the policy elements that encumber the reasonableness of foresight when considering breach of duty.

What, then, is the difference between *Re Polemis* and *The Wagon Mound*? The answer seems to be, very little (see, e.g., *The Trecarrell* [1973] 1 Lloyd's

Rep 402, para. 4.3.4.1). Indeed, having castigated *Polemis* as unfair and unjust, no longer 'good law', Viscount Simonds observed that it was 'not probable that many cases will for that reason have a different result'. Only at the extreme margin, where the accident is truly bizarre, should *The Wagon Mound* produce a difference. The only 'clear' point to emerge from the case is that damage by fire is somehow different in kind from damage by impact or fouling. But even this conclusion depends upon the level of abstraction at which the courts *choose* to define the harm that must be foreseen. It may be wondered whether, if the case had involved personal injuries, the Privy Council would have been so sanguine. A person is killed in a motor accident. Is the damage 'death' or 'death by impact'? The vehicle had burst into flames: 'death by impact' or 'death by fire'? Both are probably foreseeable and so in a motor accident the classification would be immaterial. But say, for example, that due to negligence a sealed crate falls from a warehouse window into the street. It is about to land on a passing pedestrian when, unforeseeably, it explodes killing him. Is 'death by explosion' damage of a different kind from 'death by crushing', and more importantly *should* it make any difference to the defendant's responsibilities?

The nature of this example indicates that remoteness deals with the problems that arise at the very edge of human experience. Nonetheless the solutions proffered by the courts are symptomatic of underlying values. *The Wagon Mound* represents the apotheosis of fault liability, but the subsequent retrenchment in cases such as *Hughes* v *Lord Advocate* [1963] AC 837 and *Smith* v *Leech Brain & Co. Ltd* [1962] 2 QB 405 suggests that the courts are conscious that there are other, and perhaps more worthy, principles at stake. In the final analysis the limits of actionability are as much a policy choice as the initial decision to impose liability through a duty of care.

4.3.6 Other torts

In the case of intentional torts the test of remoteness is causation because an intention to injure the plaintiff 'disposes of any question of remoteness' (*Quinn* v *Leatham* [1901] AC 495, 537 per Lord Lindley; *Doyle* v *Olby (Ironmongers) Ltd* [1969] 2 QB 158). This is so even where the damage is caused by the intervention of a third party, if the defendant intended that the intervention would occur (see *Cutler* v *McPhail* [1962] 2 QB 292), or even where he was negligent as to the occurrence of the intervention (*Scott* v *Shepherd* (1773) 2 Bl R 892). Similarly, torts of strict liability, such as liability under the Animals Act 1971, are not governed by foreseeability (para. 8.3.9), although in *Cambridge Water Co.* v *Eastern Counties Leather* [1994] 2 WLR 53 the House of Lords held that the test of remoteness for actions under the rule in *Rylands* v *Fletcher*, as in the tort of nuisance, does rest on foreseeability (see para. 8.1.8).

Problems of remoteness seldom arise in actions for breach of statutory duty because the nature of the action limits claims to damage which is of a kind that the statute was intended to prevent, by plaintiffs within the class that the statute was intended to protect (*Gorris* v *Scott* (1874) LR 9 Ex 125). This will effectively exclude unforeseeable harm.

FIVE

Negligence IV: employers' liability

This chapter deals with the liability of an employer to his employees in respect of work injuries. Employers will be vicariously liable for torts committed by employees in the course of employment, and this applies both to claims by third parties and by fellow employees. At one time the doctrine of 'common employment' precluded a worker's action against his employer for harm inflicted by fellow employees. This doctrine, which can be traced back to *Priestley* v *Fowler* (1837) 3 M & W 1, was based on a judicial fiction that an employee impliedly agreed to accept the risks incidental to his employment, including the risk of negligence by other employees. The underlying assumption was that compensation for the victims of the vast numbers of industrial accidents would place a heavy financial burden on employers, putting a brake on economic growth.

The 'unholy trinity' of common employment, *volenti non fit injuria* and contributory negligence prevented virtually any action by employees, but the harshness of this rule was gradually circumvented. The concept of an employer's personal, non-delegable duty for the safety of his workers was developed specially to avoid the common employment defence. Similarly, it was held that the defence did not apply to an action for breach of statutory duty (*Groves* v *Lord Wimborne* [1898] 2 QB 402), and in *Smith* v *Charles Baker & Sons* [1891] AC 325 the House of Lords pulled the teeth of the *volenti* defence as applied to employees, by insisting on truly free consent to run the risk. Common employment was finally abolished by the Law Reform (Personal Injuries) Act 1948, s. 1, but it has left its mark on the shape of employers' liability. This now takes one of three forms: (a) vicarious liability for the negligence of fellow employees (para. 8.4); (b) primary liability for breach of a personal, non-delegable duty (para. 5.1; see para. 8.5.2 for the nature of non-delegable duties); (c) liability for breach of statutory duty (para. 5.2). *Atiyah*, p. 188, points out that the distinction between an employer's vicarious and primary liability corresponds in general terms to that between misfeasance and nonfeasance. A more helpful distinction is probably that between casual acts of negligence for which vicarious liability is appropriate, and some failure in the managerial system to provide for employees' safety. This will often be the result of an omission for which it is difficult to attribute responsibility to a specific employee. For most practical purposes, the abolition of common employment has removed the need to differentiate between an employer's vicarious and primary liability, but it can still be important for two reasons. First, if a fellow employee's tort is committed outside the course of employment the employer is not vicariously liable, but this does not prevent a breach of an employer's primary duty to provide competent staff (para. 5.1.1). Secondly, an employer is not vicariously liable for the torts of an independent contractor, but he will be responsible where the contractor's negligence produces a breach of the employer's primary duty (see, e.g., para. 5.1.3).

In addition to any claim in tort an injured worker will usually be entitled to compensation in the form of social security benefits from the industrial injuries scheme (*Atiyah,* pp. 279–96). Some form of no-fault compensation for work accidents has been available since the Workmen's Compensation Act 1897. That scheme was incorporated into the range of benefits available under the welfare state (National Insurance (Industrial Injuries) Act 1946, and now the Social Security Contributions and Benefits Act 1992 and the Social Security Administration Act 1992), but there remains what is known as 'the industrial preference' whereby those injured at work receive more generous benefits than others with similar injuries (for criticism see Lewis (1980) 43 MLR 514; *Atiyah,* pp. 297–8). With the abolition of industrial injury benefit the preference has been reduced, but it remains for the long-term industrially disabled. Despite the fact that only some 12.5% of those injured at work receive any compensation through the tort system, the Pearson Commission recommended that the common law action should be retained (*Pearson,* vol. 1, para. 913). The result is that, because of the way in which the tort actions have been developed, particularly the action for breach of statutory duty and the less stringent application of contributory negligence (para. 5.3.2), people injured at work are much more likely to receive compensation, and in more generous terms, than others who suffer identical injuries outside the context of work (except for the victims of road accidents: *Atiyah,* p. 84). Far from being a burden to economic development, industrial injuries are now regarded as simply another cost of production, a view that is reflected in the fact that insurance against liability for personal injury to employees is compulsory (Employers' Liability (Compulsory Insurance) Act 1969). A failure to insure is a criminal offence under s. 5 of the Act, although in *Richardson* v *Pitt-Stanley* [1995] ICR 303 the Court of Appeal held that the directors and secretary of a company employer which subsequently went into liquidation were not liable in tort for breach of statutory duty where an employee was unable to recover an award of damages against the company because of the defendants' failure to comply with the terms of the 1969 Act. This ruling runs contrary to the policy of the Act, which is to protect the financial position of injured employees bringing actions against their employers (see further para. 9.1.2).

5.1 COMMON LAW DUTIES

The employer's duty to his employees is personal and non-delegable. He can delegate the performance of the duty to others, whether employees or independent contractors, but not responsibility for its negligent performance (see para. 8.5.4.5). This is the case even though by legislation the employer is required to delegate the task to a suitably qualified person and is not permitted to interfere (*Wilsons & Clyde Coal Co. Ltd v English* [1938] AC 57). It is not, however, a duty of strict liability (except in so far as the employer may be liable for the acts of others without being personally at fault). It will be fulfilled by the exercise of reasonable care for his employees' safety. The standard of care required has been described as 'high' (*Winter v Cardiff Rural District Council* [1950] 1 All ER 819, 822 per Lord Porter), but this means no more than that the precautions required vary with the circumstances, and the dangers involved in a work situation may require considerable care (*Davie v New Merton Board Mills Ltd* [19591 AC 604, 620 per Viscount Simonds: 'the subject-matter may be such that the taking of reasonable care may fall little short of absolute obligation'). Essentially, the courts apply those factors which are considered relevant to breach of duty (see paras 3.1.3 and 3.1.4) within the specific context of the employment relationship. So, for example, the duty is owed to the individual employee and must take account of his circumstances (*Paris v Stepney Borough Council* [1951] AC 367 (see para. 3.1.3.1.2)) but reasonableness allows for the practicability of precautions and for the principle that it is not the duty of the employer to go so far as to offer a wholly different job or to dismiss so as to avoid a claim in negligence (*Withers v Perry Chain Co. Ltd* [1961] 1 WLR 1314; *Henderson v The Wakefield Shirt Company Ltd* [1997] PIQR P413 (see para. 3.1.3.3)). Requiring an employee to work such long hours that his health is reasonably foreseeably affected by stress and sleep deprivation may constitute a breach of the employer's duty (*Johnstone v Bloomsbury Health Authority* [1991] 2 All ER 293; see further para. 5.1.4), although the implied contractual duty to take reasonable care for the health and safety of an employee is subject to any express terms in the contract of employment imposing a duty on the employee to work certain specified hours (ibid., per Leggatt LJ and Browne-Wilkinson V-C; but query this latter point).

The employer's duty is commonly dealt with under four headings, the provision of: (a) competent staff; (b) a safe place of work; (c) proper plant and equipment; and (d) a safe system of work. These are simply aspects of the broader duty to see that reasonable care for the safety of employees is taken. The duty applies only to employees' physical and mental safety. In the absence of an express or implied term in the contract of employment the employer has no duty to protect the employee from economic loss, for example, by providing an employee posted overseas with personal accident insurance or advising the employee to obtain such insurance (*Reid v Rush & Tompkins Group plc* [1989] 3 All ER 228 CA; cf. *Scally v Southern Health and Social Services Board* [1991] 4 All ER 563 where the House of Lords was prepared to imply a term into a contract of employment requiring an employer to take reasonable steps to bring the existence of a contingent right to the notice of an employee, even though the effect of this was to sustain a claim for purely economic loss).

Other policy considerations linked to the question of the existence of a duty of care may also arise in the context of employers' liability. For example, in *Mulcahy* v *Ministry of Defence* [1996] 2 All ER 758 the Court of Appeal held that as a matter of policy, despite the proximity of the relationship and the forseeability of damage, a soldier does not owe a duty of care to a fellow soldier when engaging the enemy in armed hostilities, i.e., where an injury was sustained in battle conditions. Accordingly, the employer could not be vicariously liable for the negligence of one soldier to another. The same policy considerations also precluded any direct liability on the part of the employer to the injured soldier for failure to maintain a safe system of work.

5.1.1 Competent staff

The employer has an obligation to select competent fellow employees, and a correlative duty to give them proper instruction in the use of equipment (*General Cleaning Contractors Ltd* v *Christmas* [1953] AC 180). This is a continuing duty which might require the dismissal of incompetent employees. This particular head is of less significance since the abolition of common employment, because the employer will normally be vicariously liable for the incompetent's negligence. It could be important where the fellow employee's conduct does not fall within the course of employment. In *Hudson* v *Ridge Manufacturing Co. Ltd* [1957] 2 QB 348 the plaintiff was injured by an employee with a reputation for persistently engaging in practical jokes. Possibly this deliberate conduct was not within the course of employment (cf. *Harrison* v *Michelin Tyre Co. Ltd* [1985] 1 All ER 919) but the employers were held liable for not taking any steps to curb his proclivities. On the other hand, an isolated incident of horseplay would not be sufficient (*Smith* v *Crossley Bros Ltd* (1951) 95 SJ 655) and the employer would not be liable unless the act could be regarded as within the course of employment.

5.1.2 Safe place of work

An employer must take such steps as are reasonable to see that the premises are safe (*Latimer* v *AEC Ltd* [1953] AC 643 (see para. 3.1.3.3)), and this duty may also apply to the means of access (*Ashdown* v *Samuel Williams & Sons Ltd* [1957] 1 QB 409, 430 CA). It is not necessarily discharged by giving a warning of the danger (*London Graving Dock Co. Ltd* v *Horton* [1951] AC 737, 746), nor is it any answer that the plaintiff was experienced and familiar with the danger, and had made no complaints about the safety of the premises (*McCafferty* v *Metropolitan Police District Receiver* [1977] 1 WLR 1073). In the case of a temporary danger the reasonableness of the employer's conduct will depend on both the degree of risk and the employer's knowledge of the risk (*O'Reilly* v *National Rail & Tramway Appliances Ltd* [1966] 1 All ER 499—unexploded shell of which employer had no knowledge, held not liable; see also *Latimer* v *AEC Ltd*). The duty can also extend to taking reasonable steps to secure the premises from intruders, to protect employees from physical attack (*Public Transport Corporation* v *Sartori* [1997] 1 VR 168).

The employer is also under a duty with respect to the premises of a third party even though he has no control over the premises, but the steps required to discharge the duty will vary with the circumstances (*Wilson* v *Tyneside Window Cleaning Co.* [1958] 2 QB 110, 124 per Parker LJ). In some cases a warning to his workers about the danger may be sufficient, whereas in others it may not be reasonable to allow them to work on the premises until the occupier has made them safe (*Smith* v *Austin Lifts Ltd* [1959] 1 WLR 100, 117). Alternatively, in occupations where the same type of danger is often encountered the employer may have to devise a safe system of work for dealing with it and instruct the employees in the use of that system (*General Cleaning Contractors Ltd* v *Christmas* [1953] AC 180; cf. *Wilson* v *Tyneside Window Cleaning*). The circumstances that have to be taken into account include the place where the work is to be done, the nature of the building (if any) on the site concerned, the experience of the employee, the nature of the work he is required to carry out, the degree of control that the employer can reasonably exercise in the circumstances, and the employer's own knowledge of the defective state of the premises (*Cook* v *Square D Ltd* [1992] ICR 262, 268). Thus, where an employee was sent to Saudi Arabia on a two-month contract and the employer was satisfied that the site occupiers and the general contractors were both reliable companies and aware of their responsibility for the safety of workers on the site, the employer could not be expected to be held responsible for daily events on the site; though if a number of employees were going to work on a foreign site or one or two employees were going to work there for a considerable period of time, it may be that the employer would be required to inspect the site and satisfy himself that the occupiers were conscious of their safety obligations (ibid. p. 271).

5.1.3 Proper plant and equipment

An employer has a 'duty of taking reasonable care to provide proper appliances, and to maintain them in a proper condition' (*Smith* v *Baker* [1891] AC 325, 362 per Lord Herschell). So if necessary equipment is unavailable and this leads to an accident he will be liable, although he is not necessarily bound to adopt the latest improvements and equipment (*Toronto Power Co.* v *Paskwan* [1915] AC 734, 738). This duty is subject to arguments about causation, so that if the employee would not have used the safety equipment if it had been supplied the employer's breach of duty is not the cause of the injury (*McWilliams* v *Sir William Arrol & Co. Ltd* [1962] 1 WLR 295 (see para. 4.1.1), but cf. the duty to provide a safe system of work (para. 5.1.4), which may require the employer to instruct employees on safety procedures and supervise their implementation). The duty applies to the provision of safety appliances, and to maintaining equipment in a proper state of repair. This is not an absolute obligation, however, and so the employer is not liable for a latent defect that could not have been detected on a reasonable inspection (*Toronto Power Co.* v *Paskwan*).

In *Davie* v *New Merton Board Mills Ltd* [1959] AC 604 the plaintiff was injured when a fragment of metal broke off a drift on being struck by a hammer and entered his eye. The manufacturer had been negligent, but the plaintiffs employers had purchased the tool from a reputable supplier and the defect was not discoverable by reasonable inspection. The House of Lords held that the employers were not liable for the manufacturer's negligence. The point at issue was not whether the employers were liable for a latent defect, but the nature and extent of the employers' non-delegable duty, and the effect of the decision is that the manufacturer of tools cannot be regarded as a person for whose acts an employer is responsible. Viscount Simonds asked 'by what use or misuse of language can the manufacturer be said to be a person to whom the employer delegated a duty which it was for him to perform?' The decision was reversed by the Employers' Liability (Defective Equipment) Act 1969, s. 1(1), which makes an employer liable if an employee suffers personal injury in the course of his employment in consequence of a defect in equipment provided by the employer, and the defect is attributable wholly or partly to the fault of a third party, whether identifiable or not. The word 'equipment' has been given a broad interpretation in order to give effect to the purpose of the Act, which is to protect an employee from 'falling between two stools' where the employer has exercised reasonable care by relying upon a reliable supplier but the employee has manifestly been exposed to a dangerous chattel. Thus, it includes a defective merchant ship (*Coltman* v *Bibby Tankers Ltd* [1988] AC 276) and has been extended to defective material, such as a flagstone, with which the employee was working (*Knowles* v *Liverpool City Council* [1993] 4 All ER 321). Indeed it applies to any article of whatever kind provided by the employer for the purposes of the business (ibid. at p. 326). This is not an absolute duty, because the employee must establish fault on the part of someone, but it alleviates the employee's problem of identifying and suing the manufacturer. The employer would be entitled to an indemnity from the person at fault (but see Lang (1984) 47 MLR 48 who argues that employers are rarely found liable under the Act due to the problems of proving third-party fault and causation). *Davie* v *New Merton Board Mills Ltd* cannot be taken to suggest that the employer's general duty with respect to plant and equipment may be delegated. So if he employs an independent contractor to maintain and repair equipment he will be responsible for the contractor's negligence.

An employer will not be liable if a worker fails to make proper use of the equipment supplied (*Parkinson* v *Lyle Shipping Co.* [1964] 2 Lloyd's Rep 79), nor where the employee acted foolishly in choosing the wrong tool for the job (*Leach* v *British Oxygen Co.* (1965) 109 SJ 157), assuming that, where necessary, the employee has been given adequate instruction in the use of the equipment.

5.1.4   Safe system of work
It is a question of fact whether a particular operation requires a system of work in the interests of safety, or whether it can reasonably be left to the employee charged with the task. It is usually applied to work of a regular type where the proper exercise of managerial control would specify the method of working, give instruction on safety and encourage the use of safety devices (*see Speed* v *Thomas Swift & Co. Ltd* [1943] KB 557, 563). The duty can

apply to an isolated task, however, where it is complicated or highly dangerous or prolonged or involves a number of men performing different functions (*Winter* v *Cardiff Rural District Council* [1950] 1 All ER 819, 823).

Although normally thought of in terms of physical safety, it is clear that the obligation to provide a safe system of work also extends to an employee's mental health. In *Petch* v *Customs and Excise Commissioners* [1993] ICR 789 the defendants conceded, and the Court of Appeal accepted, that employers owe a duty to take reasonable care not to damage an employee's mental health by adopting a system of work which is such that the stress created by the workload of the job gives rise to a real risk of foreseeable mental breakdown. On the facts, however, the plaintiff's action failed because his breakdown was held to be unforeseeable. In *Walker* v *Northumberland County Council* [1995] 1 All ER 737 the plaintiff's action in respect of a second nervous breakdown attributable to the stress of work was successful because he had suffered an earlier breakdown. Following that breakdown the second breakdown was more readily foreseeable when the employers did not respond to his requests for assistance to reduce the burden of his work as a social work manager. This fact makes the outcome in *Walker* unusual because in many cases of this nature the employer will simply be unaware of the particular circumstances which give rise to a risk of psychiatric injury to the particular employee, given that many 'white collar' managerial jobs are stressful or 'pressured', and it may be argued that, unknown to the employer, the plaintiff was unduly susceptible to the risk of psychiatric illness. There is also scope for arguing that the employee has voluntarily accepted the risk (cf. *Johnstone* v *Bloomsbury Health Authority* [1991] 2 All ER 293). Moreover, proving causation will also be problematic for many employees, because they would have to demonstrate that their psychiatric illness was attributable to stress at work rather than the many other stressful factors of ordinary life that can contribute to mental breakdown. (For analysis of the subtleties of bringing claims based upon 'occupational stress' see Sprince (1995) 17 Liverpool Law Rev 189; Dolding and Mullender (1996) 59 MLR 296.) In *Frost* v *Chief Constable of South Yorkshire* [1997] 1 All ER 540 the Court of Appeal held that an employee may be entitled to claim for psychiatric damage against a negligent employer if the employee had been directly involved, in the course of his employment, in the consequences flowing from the employer's negligence. The plaintiffs were police officers on duty at the Hillsborough stadium disaster in 1989 and suffered psychiatric damage as a result of what they had witnessed. Not all were categorised as 'rescuers' but those at the ground succeeded in their claims on the basis of their 'direct involvement', a phrase which remains to be clarified (cf. *Duncan* v *British Coal Corp.* [1997] 1 All ER 540, and see the discussion at para. 2.2.4.3).

Where an employer has followed a general practice of a particular trade or industry the plaintiff will have some difficulty in establishing that the practice was negligent (see para. 3.1.4). In *Thompson* v *Smiths Shiprepairers (North Shields) Ltd* [1984] 1 All ER 881 it was said that the test was what would have been done by a reasonable and prudent employer who was properly but not extraordinarily solicitous for his workers' safety, in the light of what he knew or ought to have known at the time. The employer was not liable having adopted a recognised practice which had been followed throughout the industry as a whole for a substantial period, when, at that time, the consequences of a particular type of risk were regarded as an inescapable feature of the industry.

On the other hand, the House of Lords has said that where a practice of ignoring an obvious danger has grown up it is not reasonable to expect an individual workman to devise precautions. Where the problem varies from job to job it is reasonable to leave a great deal to the man in charge, but where the danger is constantly found it calls for a system to meet it (*General Cleaning Contractors Ltd* v *Christmas* [1953] AC 180). The employer must consider the situation, devise a suitable system and instruct his employees how best to avoid the dangers. He must allow for the fact that employees may be inadvertent or become heedless of the risks, particularly where they are encountered on a regular basis. This will involve taking reasonable steps, not only to instruct employees on safety procedures, but also to ensure that the procedures are followed (*Clifford* v *Charles H. Challen & Son Ltd* [1951] 1 KB 495). This may require strict orders as to the use of safety equipment and reasonable supervision to ensure the orders are obeyed (*Nolan* v *Dental Manufacturing Co. Ltd* [1958] 1 WLR 936, 941–2; *Pape* v *Cumbria County Council* [1992] 3 All ER 211—employers liable for plaintiff's dermatitis caused by contact with cleaning products, notwithstanding the provision of protective gloves, on the basis of a failure to warn cleaning staff of the danger of sustained exposure of the skin to the chemicals and a failure to instruct staff to wear protective gloves at all times; cf. *Qualcast (Wolverhampton) Ltd* v *Haynes* [1959] AC 743 where the employer provided protective boots against the obvious danger of splashes of molten metal, but did not urge employees to wear them; the plaintiff wore his own boots and so the employer was not liable). In some cases a warning of the danger to a skilled employee will be sufficient to discharge the employer's duty, and in others it may be reasonable to expect experienced workers to guard against obvious dangers (*Wilson* v *Tyneside Window Cleaning Co.* [1958] 2 QB 110; *Baker* v *T. Clarke (Leeds) Ltd* [1992] PIQR P262, 267—not necessary 'for an employer to tell a skilled and experienced man at regular intervals things of which he is well aware unless there is reason to believe that that man is failing to adopt the proper precautions or, through familiarity, becoming contemptuous of them', per Stuart-Smith LJ. To similar effect, see *Rozario* v *The Post Office* [1997] PIQR P15, in which the Court of Appeal held that the employers were not in breach of a duty to supervise and instruct the plaintiff who had injured his back lifting a box. Though he had not long returned to such work after a period on lighter duties following an earlier accident, the lifting in question was a simple task which the plaintiff had previously done for many years and so it was not necessary for there to be repeated instruction or regular supervision to prevent him falling into bad habits). Conversely, the more remote the danger the greater the need to instruct the employee or remind him of the application of statutory regulations (*Boyle* v *Kodak Ltd* [1969] 2 All ER 439, 447–8). In some circumstances the risk may be so great that the

employer has a duty to issue an absolute prohibition against using a dangerous method of working (*King* v *Smith* [1995] ICR 339—window cleaner
standing on the exterior sill of a second-floor window, with no means of
attaching a safety harness).

There are two aspects to the provision of a safe system of work: (a) the
devising of a system; and (b) its operation. Even if the system itself is safe a
negligent failure to operate the system, whether by another employee or an
independent contractor, will render the employer liable (*McDermid* v *Nash
Dredging and Reclamation Co. Ltd* [1987] 2 All ER 878, HL). An employer
who sends his employee to work on a site under the direction and control of
another 'employer' remains liable to his employee if the system of work is
unsafe, particularly where in the past the employer has allowed the employee
to operate plant or equipment without proper instruction and the injury was
caused by the lack of instruction when the employee was using the second
employer's plant (*Morris* v *Breaveglen Ltd* [1993] PIQR P294). Where the
second 'employer' has also been negligent then that 'employer' is liable to the
employee and there may be an apportionment of the loss between the two
defendants under the Civil Liability (Contribution) Act 1978 (*Nelhams* v
Sandells Maintenance Ltd [1996] PIQR P52). In an appropriate case this may
amount to a full indemnity of the employer by the second 'employer'.

5.2 STATUTORY DUTIES

Breach of statutory duty is an entirely separate tort from an action in
negligence (see generally, chapter 9), but it is particularly important in the
realm of employers' liability. Indeed, industrial safety legislation, which is
penal in nature, is the one area where the courts have consistently allowed
such common law actions (Williams (1960) 23 MLR 233). Initially it was a
means of avoiding the defence of common employment, but today it is used
to impose stricter standards of care than in negligence. It is impossible in this
book to give detailed consideration to the huge volume of legislation on the
subject (see Munkman, *Employers' Liability at Common Law*, 11th ed., 1990),
but it is important to be aware of the possibility of this action, which can be
more useful to an injured employee than a claim in negligence. Indeed, it has
been argued that the present uncertainties in the common law, particularly in
relation to those who seek compensation for negligently inflicted psychiatric
damage, may result in an increasing reliance on a system of civil actionability
for breach of statutory duties (Barratt (1998) 27 ILJ 59).

It is intended that regulations made under the Health and Safety at Work
etc. Act 1974 will gradually replace the variety of statutes which now govern
specific types of premises, such as the Factories Act 1961, the Mines and
Quarries Act 1954 and the Offices, Shops and Railway Premises Act 1963.
The 1974 Act imposes a number of very general duties in relation to safety
at work, breach of which does not give rise to a civil action (s. 47(1)). Breach
of the regulations that the Secretary of State is empowered to make under the
1974 Act to replace the existing legislation would be actionable before the
civil courts, except where the regulations provide otherwise (s. 47(2)). The

process of introducing the regulations was initiallly very slow, though the pace has quickened with regulations having been introduced to comply with EC health and safety directives (most particularly the EC Framework Directive on Health and Safety—Council Directive 89/391), including the Management of Health and Safety at Work Regulations 1992, the Health and Safety (Display Screen Equipment) Regulations 1992, the Noise at Work Regulations 1989, the Control of Substances Hazardous to Health Regulations 1994, and the Workplace (Health, Safety and Welfare) Regulations 1992. Until further regulations are implemented, the earlier legislation, with its uncertainty as to (or even express denial of) the availability of a civil action remains relevant.

The two earlier statutes most commonly relied upon are the Factories Act 1961 and the Mines and Quarries Act 1954. The degree of protection conferred by an action for breach of statutory duty varies considerably with the wording of the particular provision and perhaps more importantly with the interpretation of the courts (accurately described by *Hepple and Matthews*, p. 561, as 'complex, capricious and vague'). Section 14(1) of the Factories Act 1961 will illustrate the point. This provides that every dangerous part of any machinery must be securely fenced. It has been held that this obligation is absolute, in the sense that it is not a defence to show that it was impracticable to fence, even though fencing would make the machine unusable (*John Summers & Sons Ltd* v *Frost* [1955] AC 740). On the other hand, the section does not apply to materials in the machine (*Eaves* v *Morris Motors Ltd* [1961] 2 QB 385), to tools which come into contact with the machine, as opposed to the worker's clothes (*Sparrow* v *Fairey Aviation Co. Ltd* [1964] AC 1019) nor to bits flying out of the machine (*Close* v *Steel Co. of Wales Ltd* [1962] AC 367—part of the machine; *Nicholls* v *F. Austin (Leyton) Ltd* [1946] AC 493—material on which the machine was working: 'The fence is intended to keep the worker out, not to keep the machine or its product in', per Lord Simonds at p. 505). Even the courts have recognised that these distinctions are arbitrary and illogical (see *F. E. Callow (Engineers) Ltd* v *Johnson* [1971] AC 335, 343).

Some duties are qualified by the phrase 'so far as is reasonably practicable' (see, e.g., Factories Act 1961, s. 28(1)—duty to keep floors, passages and stairs free from obstruction or slippery substances; s. 29(1)—safe means of access). The assessment of what is reasonably practicable must involve a calculation similar to that in deciding what constitutes 'reasonable care' (see para. 3.1.3), although it is possibly a stricter standard than negligence. In *Edwards* v *National Coal Board* [1949] 1 All ER 743, Asquith LJ said (at p. 747) that where there is a gross disproportion between the risk and the measures necessary for avoiding the risk, the risk being 'insignificant' in relation to the cost, then the measures are not reasonably practicable. Other provisions require an employer to do what is 'practicable' to achieve a particular result. For example, the Mines and Quarries Act 1954, s. 157, provides a defence to all the duties laid down in that Act if it was impracticable to avoid or prevent the contravention. This is probably a stricter standard than 'reasonably practicable', but in both cases the test is vague (for interpretations of 'practicable' and 'reasonably practicable' see *Jayne* v *National Coal Board* [1963] 2 All ER 220; *Sanderson* v *National Coal Board* [1961] 2 QB 244). The onus of proving that it was impracticable or not reasonably practicable to comply with the statutory requirement is the defendant's (*Nimmo* v *Alexander Cowan & Sons Ltd* [1968] AC 107). This in itself gives the employee an advantage over a claim based on negligence.

In addition to specific qualifications of the statutory duties, other terms are used which allow scope for interpretation along the lines of fault liability. A machine is 'dangerous' only if it is foreseeably likely to injure someone, taking account of carelessness by the worker (*Close* v *Steel Co. of Wales Ltd* [1962] AC 367; *John Summers & Sons Ltd* v *Frost* [1955] AC 740), though in *Larner* v *British Steel plc* [1993] 4 All ER 102 the Court of Appeal held that in determining whether a place of work had been kept 'safe' for any person working there under the Factories Act 1961, s. 29(1), it would be wrong to import a test of 'reasonable foreseeability' of danger. The obligation imposed by the section was strict, with no reference to foreseeability, reasonable or otherwise, and such a requirement would have the effect of limiting successful claims for breach of statutory duty to circumstances where the worker would also succeed in a parallel claim for negligence, reducing the utility of the section. It is for the defendant specifically to plead and prove that it was not reasonably practicable to keep the premises safe, and because this involves weighing the degree and extent of risk on the one hand against the time, trouble and expense of avoiding it on the other, foreseeability will come into the equation at this point since it is impossible to assess the degree of risk without considering foreseeability (see *Mains* v *Uniroyal Englebert Tyres Ltd, The Times*, 29 September 1995, Court of Session). A duty to take such steps as may be necessary for keeping the road or working place secure, under the Mines and Quarries Act 1954, s. 48, is not an absolute duty but a duty to exercise care in the light of the knowledge at the time (*Brown* v *National Coal Board* [1962] AC 574; cf. the interpretation of s. 108(1) in *Brazier* v *Skipton Rock Co. Ltd* [1962] 1 WLR 471). In *Latimer* v *AEC Ltd* [1953] AC 643 the question of whether a floor was maintained in an 'efficient state' was treated as a matter of degree depending on the foreseeability of injury. Thus apparently strict provisions can be interpreted so as to produce forms of 'statutory negligence'.

It will be clear, even from this brief discussion, that there is little consistency in the standards applied to breaches of industrial safety legislation. Williams (1960) 23 MLR 233 commented (at p. 243) that the language used in legislation seems to be largely haphazard, yet it is upon the accident of language that the issue is made to turn. Moreover, unless the facts of the case fall within the precise statutory wording the plaintiff will be unable to maintain an action for breach of statutory duty (see, e.g., *Tate* v *Swan Hunter & Wigham Richardson Ltd* [1958] 1 WLR 39), even though the facts may be analogous and objectively might warrant such protection. The plaintiff would then have to rely on an action in negligence. (The fact that a claim for breach of statutory duty has failed does not prevent a successful claim in negligence, see *Bux* v *Slough Metals Ltd* [1974] 1 All ER 262.) This inconsistency, it might be said, is the product of adapting legislation with one purpose (the promotion of industrial safety through penal sanctions) to an entirely different purpose, namely providing compensation for injured workers. However, this process has been in progress for over 90 years now, and the courts have shown little interest in establishing a uniform approach to the problem. The apparent satisfaction of the Pearson Commission with the present basis of liability is hardly reassuring (*Pearson*, vol. 1, paras 914–17). It remains to be seen whether, in the long run, the regulations issued under the Health and Safety at Work etc. Act 1974 will lead to more rational results.

5.3 DEFENCES

At one time the defences of common employment, *volenti non fit injuria* and contributory negligence combined to prevent virtually any claim against employers for work injuries. Common employment has been abolished and *volenti* now has only limited application to employees. Contributory negligence is no longer a complete defence (para. 14.5), and moreover is applied more favourably for employees than for other plaintiffs (para. 14.5.3.3).

5.3.1 *Volenti non fit injuria*
The doctrine of voluntary assumption of risk held that a worker who knew of the risks involved in the job, yet continued in his employment, had 'assumed' the risk himself, thereby absolving the employer from any responsibility. In *Smith* v *Baker* [1891] AC 325 the House of Lords finally recognised that this was a fiction, because economic realities compel most people to accept the risks of their employment, removing the essential voluntary element. Subsequent cases stressed the obvious point that an employee's knowledge of the existence of a danger does not in itself amount to consent to run the risk (see, e.g., *Baker* v *James Bros & Sons Ltd* [1921] 2 KB 674; *Williams* v *Birmingham Battery and Metal Co.* [1899] 2 QB 338). It is also arguable that an express term in the contract of employment which has the effect in substance, whatever language may be used, of raising a plea of voluntary assumption of risk by the employee may be subject to s. 2(1) of the Unfair Contract Terms Act 1977, which prevents the exclusion or restriction of liability for death or personal injury resulting from negligence (*Johnstone* v *Bloomsbury Health Authority* [1991] 2 All ER 293; see para. 14.2). Since *Smith* v *Baker, volenti* has been of little significance in employers' liability actions, although it is still possible to invoke the defence on appropriate facts ('if there was a genuine full agreement, free from any kind of pressure, to assume the risk of loss' *Imperial Chemical Industries Ltd* v *Shatwell* [1965] AC 656, 687 per Lord Pearce; see generally para. 14.1). This does not mean that employers must remove all risks. Many jobs are inherently dangerous and the employer will have done enough, at least for the purposes of negligence, if he acts reasonably to minimise the risks.

As a matter of public policy *volenti* is not a defence to an action for breach of statutory duty brought by a worker against his employer (*Wheeler* v *New Merton Board Mills Ltd* [1933] 2 KB 669; *Imperial Chemical Industries Ltd* v

Shatwell; but note the possibility of a finding of 100% 'contributory negligence', which in effect undermines this policy, see *Jayes* v *IMI (Kynoch) Ltd* [1985] ICR 155 (para. 14.5.3.3)). A limited exception was admitted in *Imperial Chemical Industries Ltd* v *Shatwell* where two shot-firers of equal rank collaborated in a method of work which they both knew to be dangerous and contrary to statutory regulations. They were both injured, and one of the men sued the employers on the basis of their vicarious liability for the conduct of the other shot-firer. The House of Lords considered that it would be unfair not to allow the employers to rely on *volenti.* Lord Pearce said that the defence should be available where the employer was not himself in breach of statutory duty and was not vicariously in breach of statutory duty through the fault of an employee whose commands the plaintiff was bound to obey, and where the plaintiff assented to and took part in the breaking of the statutory duty.

This is closely analogous to the position where it is the plaintiff's own wrongful act which puts the employer in breach of statutory duty. In *Ginty* v *Belmont Building Supplies Ltd* [1959] 1 All ER 414 the plaintiff's failure to use crawling boards while working on an unsafe roof constituted a breach of statutory regulations by both the plaintiff and his employer. The only wrongful act was the plaintiff's, the employer being vicariously responsible. Pearson J, holding the employer not liable, said that it would be absurd if a workman who deliberately disobeyed his employer's orders and thereby put the employer in breach of a regulation, could claim damages for injury, caused to him solely by his own wrongdoing. 'To say "You are liable to me for my own wrongdoing" is neither good morals nor good law' (*Boyle* v *Kodak Ltd* [1969] 2 All ER 439, 446 per Lord Diplock). This defence will apply only where the plaintiff is the *sole* author of his own misfortune. The employer will be liable if he was himself at fault (e.g., in failing to explain the regulations or warn about dangers: *Boyle* v *Kodak Ltd)* or if he is vicariously responsible for the conduct of another employee (*Ross* v *Associated Portland Cement Manufacturers Ltd* [1964] 1 WLR 768, 777—employer failed to give proper instructions). The plaintiff's conduct will then be treated as contributory negligence. The difference between *Ginty* v *Belmont Building Supplies Ltd* and *Imperial Chemical Industries Ltd* v *Shatwell* is that in the latter case the court could not say that the injury was caused *solely* by the plaintiff's conduct, and therefore *volenti* was invoked in order to prevent the concept of vicarious liability producing the result that was avoided in *Ginty* v *Belmont Building Supplies Ltd* by causation arguments (cf. the similar case of *Stapley* v *Gypsum Mines Ltd* [1953] AC 663 (para. 14.5.2) where a joint decision by two employees to continue working, having failed to remove a known danger, was dealt with on the basis of contributory negligence).

5.3.2 Contributory negligence
Contributory negligence is a defence both to an action in negligence and breach of statutory duty (see para. 14.5.3.3; Fagelson (1979) 42 MLR 646). In general, however, the carelessness of employees as plaintiffs is treated more leniently than the negligence of employers, even where liability rests upon the

vicarious responsibility of the employer for the negligence of another employee (ibid.). 'It is not for every risky thing which a workman in a factory may do in his familiarity with the machinery that a plaintiff ought to be held guilty of contributory negligence' (*Flower* v *Ebbw Vale Steel Iron & Coal Ltd* [1934] 2 KB 132, 140, per Lawrence J, approved by Lord Wright [1936] AC 206, 214). The House of Lords has viewed with equanimity the possibility that precisely the same conduct by an employee might lead to a different conclusion on negligence, depending upon whether the employee is suing as a plaintiff or whether a third party (possibly another employee) is suing the employer as vicariously liable for the employee's conduct (*Staveley Iron & Chemical Co.* v *Jones* [1956] AC 627, 642, 648). Indeed, an allegation of contributory negligence may point to a breach of the employer's personal duty to take reasonable precautions to protect employees from their own carelessness or inadvertence (*General Cleaning Contractors Ltd* v *Christmas* [1953] AC 180). Nonetheless, in practice, contributory negligence is often successfully invoked as a defence.

SIX

Negligence V: dangerous premises

Liability for dangerous premises is not a separate tort, but a compound of liability in negligence, nuisance, the rule in *Rylands* v *Fletcher* and breach of statutory duty. This reflects the historical development of the law of tort, and the fact that property rights were regarded as significant in determining the obligations that an owner or occupier ought to owe to others. The basic question to ask in order to determine the cause of action is: where did the damage occur? If it occurred on the premises the common law action was a form of negligence. If the damage occurred off the premises (although arising from some event on the premises) the action will usually be in nuisance or *Rylands* v *Fletcher*. This chapter deals with liability for damage which occurs on the premises. Liability to third parties is commonly called 'occupiers' liability' and it is usually, though not exclusively, concerned with personal injuries. Occupiers' liability is further divided into liability to lawful visitors, which is governed by the Occupiers' Liability Act 1957 (para. 6.1), and liability to persons other than visitors under the Occupiers' Liability Act 1984 (para. 6.2). Although this legislation imposes statutory duties on the occupiers of premises with respect to the safety of entrants, the standard of care required is very similar to the common law of negligence. Indeed, the Occupiers' Liability Acts could be regarded as simply 'applied negligence'. The liability of non-occupiers for dangers they have created on the premises is largely a matter of common law negligence, although the Defective Premises Act 1972, s. 4, creates special rules for landlords (para. 6.3). Liability in tort to the owners of buildings in respect of defective construction is a recent innovation concerned with damage to property or economic loss, and has been discussed above (para. 2.2.4.3).

It will be seen that in many of the cases the defendant is held responsible for failing to act. The reason is that the occupier is in control of the premises and the fact of control imposes a duty to take positive steps to keep the premises in good repair. This provides an exception to the 'mere omission' rule in negligence.

6.1 LIABILITY OF OCCUPIERS TO VISITORS

At common law the duty owed by an occupier to an entrant varied according
to which of four categories the entrant came within. These were (a) entry
pursuant to a contract; (b) an invitee, who had some common interest with
the occupier; (c) a licensee, who had the occupier's express or implied
permission to enter but no common interest; and (d) a trespasser, who had no
permission. The level of precautions expected of an occupier for an entrant's
safety ranged from very high in the case of entry under a contract to very low
in the case of a trespasser. The Occupiers' Liability Act 1957 (OLA 1957)
abolished the distinction between invitees and licensees, and provided, in
effect, that there would be only two categories: (a) lawful visitors, and (b), by
implication, persons who were not lawful visitors, mostly trespassers.

An occupier owes a single 'common duty of care' to all his visitors (OLA
1957, s. 2(1)). In spite of the wording of s. 1(1) that the duty relates to the
risk arising from 'any danger due to the state of the premises or to things done
or omitted to be done on them', it is generally accepted that the duty applies
only to dangers arising from the condition of the land itself, and not activities
carried out on the land. The careless driving of a motor vehicle or the careless
discharge of a gun on private land, for example, would be the subject of a
common law action (see *Revill* v *Newbery* [1996] 1 All ER 291, 298). In
practice the differences between an action in negligence and an action under
the Act are minimal and in some instances plaintiffs have succeeded in
ordinary negligence where the Act might have seemed more appropriate (e.g.,
Ward v *Tesco Stores Ltd* [1976] 1 WLR 810).

The common duty of care applies to property damage, including damage
to the property of persons who are not themselves visitors (s. 1(3)(b)). If, for
example, the plaintiff's car had been loaned to a friend when it was damaged
due to the defective condition of the defendant's premises, the plaintiff would
have an action. This would include consequential financial loss applying the
ordinary rules of remoteness of damage.

Section 1(3)(a) defines 'premises' to include any fixed or movable structure, including any vessel, vehicle or aircraft. This has been held to include
both mundane and esoteric objects (e.g., *Wheeler* v *Copas* [1981] 3 All ER
405—a ladder; *Bunker* v *Charles Brand & Sons Ltd* [1969] 2 QB 480—a
tunnel-cutting machine).

6.1.1 Occupiers
The Occupiers' Liability Act 1957 does not define an 'occupier' but provides
that the rules of the common law shall apply (s. 1(2)). The test is occupational control over the premises, i.e., 'control associated with and arising from
presence in and use of or activity in the premises' (*Wheat* v *E. Lacon & Co.
Ltd* [1966] AC 552, 589 per Lord Pearson). Control does not have to be
complete or exclusive, for as Lord Denning has said, 'wherever a person has
a sufficient degree of control over premises that he ought to realise that any
failure on his part to use care may result in injury to a person lawfully coming
there, then he is an "occupier"'. . . . (ibid. at p. 578).

An owner who has let premises to a tenant and parted with possession will not usually be an occupier (although he may have some responsibility as a landlord by virtue of the Defective Premises Act 1972, s. 4; see para. 6.3.2). The grant of a licence to occupy, however, will not divest the owner of control. In *Wheat* v *E. Lacon & Co. Ltd* the defendants owned a public house which was run by a manager. They granted him a licence to use the first floor as his private accommodation, retaining the right to repair. A paying guest of the manager fell down some unlit stairs in the private area of the premises and was killed. The House of Lords held that the defendants had sufficient control over the private accommodation to be occupiers along with the manager. There is no difficulty in having more than one occupier at one and the same time, each of whom owes a duty to visitors. Dual occupation can arise for different purposes. In *Collier* v *Anglian Water Authority, The Times,* 26 March 1983, the plaintiff was injured on a seaside promenade which was in disrepair. The promenade formed part of the sea defences for which the water authority was responsible, although the local authority owned the land and looked after the promenade by sweeping it and removing rubbish. The Court of Appeal concluded that the water authority was an occupier because they asserted control over the condition of the structure and its state of repair, and even though this was for the purpose of maintaining the sea defences they knew that the safety of the public, who were allowed access to the promenade by the local authority, depended upon its control of the state of repair. If, on the other hand, the plaintiff had been injured by a piece of broken glass the local authority would have been responsible because that was a matter under its control.

An absentee owner may be in occupation through his servants (this is the only way that a company can occupy premises), and in some instances physical occupation itself will be unnecessary. In *Harris* v *Birkenhead Corporation* [1976] 1 All ER 341 the local authority made a compulsory purchase order and served notices of entry on the tenant and owner of a house. Subsequently the tenant left the house which remained unoccupied. The Court of Appeal rejected the local authority's argument that it was not an occupier because there had been no actual or symbolic taking of possession. The authority became an occupier when the tenant vacated the premises, because the house was uninhabited and the tenant had left as a result of the authority's lawful assertion of an immediate right to enter and control the property.

6.1.2 Visitors
Visitors are those persons who at common law would be treated as invitees or licensees (OLA 1957, s. 1(2)). This removes for practical purposes the distinction between invitees and licensees, though some commentators have argued that the relevance of the distinction might have been preserved as a result of the speech of Lord Browne-Wilkinson in *McGeown* v *Northern Ireland Housing Executive* [1994] 3 All ER 53, such that it might provide the basis for a user of a public right of way to claim a cause of action under the 1957 Act (Murphy [1997] Conv 362; for full discussion and counter-arguments see

para. 6.2.1). This remote possibility aside, the conventional approach now is simply to distinguish visitors from 'non-visitors'. Where a person enters pursuant to a contract a term will be implied into the contract that the visitor is owed the common duty of care (s. 5(1)). If the contract provides for greater protection the visitor is entitled to that under the contract. Where the occupier has given an express invitation or permission there is no difficulty in classifying the entrant as a visitor. Problems can arise when the occupier has not granted express permission to enter, because it may be possible to find an implied permission. A person entering for the purpose of communicating with the occupier, for example, will be taken to have an implied permission to do so. The occupier can revoke the permission, but the entrant has a reasonable time in which to depart, after which he will become a trespasser.

It is essentially a question of fact whether the occupier's conduct can be interpreted as the grant of an implied licence. Mere knowledge of entry is not consent, but in some cases the courts have been prepared to 'stretch' the facts to find an implied licence. In *Lowery* v *Walker* [1911] AC 10 members of the public had used a short cut across the defendant's field for many years. He had attempted to prevent this but did not take any legal proceedings. The plaintiff was savaged by a horse and the House of Lords held that he was an implied licensee. The mere tolerance of repeated entry may be so pronounced as to lead to the conclusion that it was tantamount to permission. In *Robert Addie & Sons (Collieries) Ltd* v *Dumbreck* [1929] AC 358, 372, Lord Dunedin suggested that if an occupier put up a notice stating 'No trespassers' but took no further steps when people regularly entered his land, it would be possible to find an implied licence.

This approach has been criticised, however, by the House of Lords in *Edwards* v *Railway Executive* [1952] AC 737 where Lord Goddard observed (at p. 746) that 'repeated trespass of itself confers no licence'. How can it be said, his Lordship added, that an occupier has licensed that which he cannot prevent? It is true that, as many commentators have suggested, the courts have strained to find an implied licence on dubious facts, particularly with child plaintiffs, in order to avoid the harshness of the rules that applied to trespassers. Now that trespassers have a greater degree of protection the temptation to employ this particular 'legal fiction' will have been reduced (see *British Railways Board* v *Herrington* [1972] AC 877, 933). Nonetheless, it is significant that in *Edwards* v *Railway Executive* the defendants had taken steps to deter entry by repairing the fence. It must surely be incumbent upon an occupier faced with repeated entry to take reasonable steps to indicate that he does not condone the trespass, and though he does not have to turn his premises into a fortress, if he does nothing at all he may be taken to have impliedly permitted the entry.

Children do not form a special category of entrant and the fact that some dangerous object on the premises constituted an 'allurement' to children will not necessarily convert a child trespasser into an implied licensee. The concept of allurement was simply an aspect of the implied-licence 'legal fiction' to avoid the rules applicable to trespassers. The notion of an object which is both a concealed danger and attractive to children is still important, however, when considering both the precautions that an occupier ought reasonably to take for the safety of a child visitor, and the foreseeability of the presence of a child trespasser.

The occupier may set limits on the visitor's permission as to the time, place or purpose of the visit. The common duty of care is specifically restricted to 'the purposes for which [the visitor] is invited or permitted by the occupier to be there' (s. 2(2)). If the visitor abuses his permission he will become a trespasser. In *The Calgarth* [1927] P 93 Scrutton LJ said (at p. 110) that 'when you invite a person into your house to use the stairs, you do not invite him to slide down the bannisters'. So a visitor may become a trespasser by entering a part of the premises that he has been warned not to enter (*Anderson* v *Coutts* (1894) 58 JP 369) even though he may have strayed there accidentally (*Mersey Docks and Harbour Board* v *Procter* [1923] AC 253) or by staying after the time specified for his departure (*Stone* v *Taffe* [1974] 3 All ER 1016). The occupier must give a clear indication that the visit is subject to some limitation as to time or place (see, e.g., *Pearson* v *Coleman Bros* [1948] 2 KB 359, 375–6).

Section 2(6) provides that persons who enter premises for any purpose in the exercise of a right conferred by law are to be treated as visitors for that purpose, whether the occupier has in fact given permission or not. This will include a fireman attending a fire, a policeman executing a warrant, and many other officers of public agencies exercising statutory rights of entry. It also includes members of the public using public premises such as public parks and libraries. This section does not extend, however, to persons lawfully exercising a public right of way (*Greenhalgh* v *British Railways Board* [1969] 2 QB 286; *McGeown* v *Northern Ireland Housing Executive* [1994] 3 All ER 53; cf. Murphy [1997] Conv 362, who argues that the protection of the 1957 Act might be available to such persons, if they are invitees; see also para. 6.2.1 for full discussion of the generally limited causes of action available to users of unadopted public rights of way) nor a private right of way (*Holden* v *White* [1982] 2 All ER 328). Additionally, a person who enters premises in the exercise of rights conferred by an access agreement or order under the National Parks and Access to the Countryside Act 1949 is not a visitor (OLA 1957, s. 1(4)).

In summary, the categories of entrant who do *not* qualify as a visitor under the OLA 1957 are: (a) trespassers, (b) persons entering under an access agreement or order, (c) persons using a private right of way, and (d) persons using a public right of way. The first three categories are governed by the OLA 1984; the fourth remains the subject of the common law (see para. 6.2.1).

6.1.3 The common duty of care
The common duty of care is a duty to take such care as in all the circumstances of the case is reasonable to see that the visitor will be reasonably safe in using the premises for the purposes for which he is invited or permitted by the occupier to be there (OLA 1957, s. 2(2)). The standard of care expected of an occupier is the same as that in an ordinary action in

negligence and the same factors that were considered in chapter 3 will be relevant here (para. 3.1.3). For example, the occupier does not have to guard against improbable, even if foreseeable, events (*Simms* v *Leigh Rugby Football Club Ltd* [1969] 2 All ER 923; cf. *Bolton* v *Stone* [1951] AC 850, para. 3.1.3.1.1). In an appropriate case an occupier may be liable for injuries to visitors caused deliberately by other visitors to the premises where the conduct was foreseeable as a likely consequence of the occupier's breach of duty (*Cunningham* v *Reading Football Club Ltd* [1992] PIQR P141—defendants liable for injuries sustained by police officers caused by football hooligans hurling pieces of concrete which had been broken off the premises by hand or foot). Similarly, the same principles of remoteness of damage apply to an action under the Act as apply to a common law action for negligence (*Jolley* v *Sutton London Borough Council* [1998] 3 All ER 559). It is not the premises but the *visitor* who must be made reasonably safe, and the precautions required to fulfil this duty will vary with the particular visitor (*Roles* v *Nathan* [1963] 1 WLR 1117). This, indeed, is implicit in OLA 1957, s. 2(3), which provides that one of the relevant circumstances is the degree of care which would ordinarily be looked for in such visitors. Two categories are singled out by the Act, children (para. 6.1.3.1) and skilled visitors (para. 6.1.3.2). The Act also provides some guidance on the circumstances in which an occupier will be liable for the negligence of an independent contractor (para. 6.1.3.3) and the effect of a warning given to the visitor (para. 6.1.3.4).

6.1.3.1 Children An occupier must be prepared for children to be less careful than adults (OLA 1957, s. 2(3)(a); see Kidner (1988) 39 NILQ 150). An object which poses no threat to an adult may be dangerous to a child as, for example, in *Moloney* v *Lambeth London Borough Council* (1966) 64 LGR 440 where a boy aged four fell through a gap in the railings protecting a stairwell. An adult could not have fallen through the gap. The occupier was held liable. Dangers which might be obvious to an adult and so easily avoided, can present serious risks to children who may simply be unable to appreciate the nature or extent of the danger. An occupier must also take account of the fact that children are naturally curious and inquisitive, and may be attracted to objects or situations which are outside the limits of the permission granted by the occupier. There is a duty not to lead children into temptation (*Latham* v *R. Johnson & Nephew Ltd* [1913] 1 KB 398, 415). A good example is *Glasgow Corporation* v *Taylor* [1922] 1 AC 44 in which a boy aged seven died after eating poisonous berries picked from a shrub in a botanical garden. The defendants knew the berries were poisonous but did not fence off the shrub or give any warning. It was held that the attractive-looking berries constituted an 'allurement' to children for which the defendants were liable. Technically, the child was a trespasser in that he had no permission to pick berries from the shrubs in the garden, but where the object is an allurement this is no answer. The fact that it was a temptation to children is the very reason that the occupier should have taken adequate precautions. It is the basis of the occupier's breach of the common duty of care.

It is sometimes said that where there is no allurement there is no liability. This is not strictly correct, since a child could be injured by an object that would have been regarded as equally dangerous to an adult. The concept of allurement is relevant only where the occupier would not have been liable to an adult, and even then it should not be treated as an easy solution to the question of the occupier's liability to children. To say that an occupier is liable for an allurement is simply another way of saying that he has failed to take reasonable precautions for the safety of child visitors, bearing in mind the particular circumstance that children were likely to be tempted by an object which is both 'fascinating and fatal'. An object which could not possibly constitute a 'trap' (in the sense not only of physically concealed danger but also 'unappreciated' danger), such as a heap of stones (*Latham* v *R. Johnson & Nephew Ltd*), will not amount to an allurement. But, again, this is just another way of saying that in the circumstances the precautions taken by the occupier were reasonable and he is not in breach of duty. In the past the allurement cases served a useful purpose as a variant of the implied-licence device, which was employed to circumvent the harsh rule that trespassers could not sue for negligence. Now that the law applying to trespassers has been changed, the characterisation of a dangerous object as an allurement is simply part of the overall calculation of whether the occupier has fulfilled the common duty of care.

Older children tend to be treated in the same way as adults (see, e.g., *Titchener* v *British Railways Board* [1983] 3 All ER 770—15-year-old girl). Very young children (i.e., 'children of tender years' who have not reached the age of reason or understanding: *Phipps* v *Rochester Corporation* [1955] 1 QB 450, 458) present a problem, however, because even the most innocuous objects can be a potential danger to them. There is a genuine conflict here between the prospect of leaving very young children without any remedy for their injuries and requiring occupiers to maintain their property to the standards of a nursery. One solution to this problem, adopted in *Latham* v *R. Johnson & Nephew Ltd* is to make the child's licence to enter conditional on being accompanied by a person capable of looking after him and avoiding obvious dangers. The difficulty is to know in what circumstances this condition should apply. Perhaps more significantly, an unaccompanied child would automatically become a trespasser, and (prior to *British Railways Board* v *Herrington* [1972] AC 877) would have had no action even if injured by a danger for which an older child or adult would have recovered.

In *Phipps* v *Rochester Corporation* [1955] 1 QB 450, Devlin J took a different approach, looking not at the nature of the licence but at the content of the occupier's duty. The defendants were developing a housing estate and had dug a trench two and a half feet wide and eight feet deep. The plaintiff aged five and his sister aged seven crossed the land in order to pick berries. The plaintiff fell into the trench and broke his leg. The trench was not an allurement or a concealed danger, but Devlin J accepted that so far as the plaintiff was concerned the danger was 'concealed from his understanding'. His Lordship stated that an occupier who tacitly permits the public to use his land must assume that the public may include little children, but he is also entitled, when considering what precautions he ought reasonably to take for their safety, to take into account the habits of prudent parents who will not normally allow their little children to go out unaccompanied. This places the primary responsibility for the safety of young children upon parents, but it is a more flexible approach than the conditional licence because the occupier may have to take into account the social habits of the neighbourhood (it was not as if the site 'were the only green place in the centre of a city'), and there may well be places, such as public parks or recognised playing grounds, where prudent parents might reasonably allow their children to go unaccompanied.

This reasoning was applied by the Court of Appeal in *Simkiss v Rhondda Borough Council* (1983) 81 LGR 460 in which a girl aged seven was injured while trying to slide down a steep bluff on a blanket. There was no concealed danger so the defendants were not under a duty to fence the area—otherwise they would be under a duty to fence every climbable tree in the area in case a child fell from one. The defendants were entitled to assume that prudent parents would warn children not to play where it was dangerous. The plaintiff's father had stated in evidence, however, that he did not consider the bluff to be dangerous. The court concluded on that basis that the defendants had no reason to believe that the bluff was dangerous because an occupier should not be required to achieve a higher standard of care than a reasonably prudent parent. In this situation the parent of a young child is faced with a dilemma. If he says that he considered the defendant's premises to be dangerous, he will be asked why he let the child go there unaccompanied. If he says he thought the place was safe then, in the absence of a hidden trap, the occupier will probably have complied with the standard of a reasonably prudent parent.

Even where there is a clearly foreseeable risk of injury to children the occupier will not be liable if the plaintiff's injury occurred in an unforeseeable manner, applying the normal principles of remoteness of damage (see para. 4.3.2). In *Jolley v Sutton London Borough Council* [1998] 3 All ER 559 a rotten boat had been abandoned on the defendants' land, to their knowledge, for at least two years. The boat was attractive for children to play on and in a dangerous condition, creating a foreseeable risk of injury. The plaintiff, a 14-year-old boy, and a friend decided to repair the boat, and jacked it up with a car jack. The boat fell on the plaintiff while he was working underneath it. The Court of Appeal held that, even allowing for the unpredictability of children's behaviour at play, it was not foreseeable that an accident would occur in this manner as a result of two boys deciding to work under a propped-up boat. The damage was too remote because it occurred in an unforeseeable manner.

6.1.3.2 Skilled visitors An occupier is entitled to expect that a person in the exercise of his calling will appreciate and guard against any special risk ordinarily incidental to it so far as the occupier allows him to do so (OLA 1957, s. 2(3)(b)). Just as children can be expected to be less able than the average adult to look after themselves, the skilled visitor should be better able to take care for his own safety, but only with respect to the risks associated with his specialism. In *Roles* v *Nathan* [1963] 1 WLR 1117 two chimney-sweeps died from carbon monoxide poisoning while cleaning the flue of a boiler. They had been warned not to continue working while the boiler was alight. The Court of Appeal held that the occupier was not liable (a) because the sweeps had been warned, and (b) because it is reasonable to expect a specialist to appreciate and guard against the dangers arising from the very defect that he has been called in to deal with. If, on the other hand, the stairs leading to the cellar had given way the occupier would have been responsible because that is not a special risk incidental to the trade of chimney-sweep.

The risks incidental to a Post Office engineer's job include live wiring, but not defective roofing, which is a risk incidental to the premises, even though the job may involve climbing on roofs sometimes (*Woolins* v *British Celanese Ltd* (1966) 1 KIR 438; see also *Bird* v *King Line Ltd* [1970] 2 Lloyd's Rep 349—risks incidental to working on a ship do not include falling over refuse carelessly left on deck, *aliter* if the plaintiff had tripped on a cable or rope).

The fact that the visitor is skilled is not sufficient *per se* to absolve the occupier from responsibility. In *Salmon* v *Seafarer Restaurants Ltd* [1983] 3 All ER 729 the defendants argued that an occupier's duty to a fireman attending a fire at his premises was limited to protecting him from special or exceptional risks over and above the ordinary risks incidental to fighting fires. Woolf J rejected this contention. The occupier owed the same duty as he did to any other visitor, but, in determining whether there was any breach of that duty, a fireman could be expected to exercise the ordinary skills of a fireman. If he did so, but nonetheless suffered injury as a foreseeable consequence of the negligence, the occupier will be liable. This approach has been expressly approved by the House of Lords in *Ogwo* v *Taylor* [1987] 2 WLR 988. There is no distinction between injuries caused by ordinary and exceptional risks if they are attributable to the defendant's negligence, but if the fireman took a foolhardy and unnecessary risk in fighting the fire this might break the chain of causation.

6.1.3.3 Independent contractors The general rule in tort is that a person is not responsible for the negligence of his independent contractor (see para. 8.5.1). The faulty execution of any work of construction, repair or maintenance by an independent contractor employed by the occupier will not put the occupier in breach of the common duty of care provided that (a) it was reasonable to entrust the work to an independent contractor, (b) the occupier had taken reasonable care to see that the contractor was competent, and (c) the occupier had taken reasonable care to check that the work was properly done (OLA 1957, s. 2(4)(b)).

(a) Was it reasonable to entrust the work to a contractor? This will depend upon the circumstances of the occupier (e.g., was he an ordinary householder or a large public authority?) and the nature of the work to be done. The more technical the work the more reasonable it will be, and in some circumstances where the occupier has no technical skill and cannot rely on his own judgment he would be negligent *not* to obtain and follow good technical advice (*Haseldine* v *C.A. Daw & Son Ltd* [1941] 2 KB 343, 356 per Scott LJ—occupier not liable for negligence of contractor in maintaining a lift in a block of flats). In *Woodward* v *Mayor of Hastings* [1945] KB 174 a child at a school slipped on a step which had been negligently left in an icy condition by a cleaner. The defendants were responsible since there was no technical knowledge required for the cleaning of a step.

(b)   Was the contractor competent to carry out the work? The ability of the average householder to check the competence of tradesmen is obviously limited. The more extensive or technical the work the more reasonable it will be to expect some inquiry, perhaps of trade associations, to be made. So a local authority undertaking demolition work should use reputable and careful contractors, and should not 'countenance the unsafe working methods of cowboy operators' (*Ferguson* v *Welsh* [1987] 3 All ER 777, 784).

(c)   Did the occupier check that the work was properly carried out? Again, the more technical the task the less reasonable it would be to expect an occupier to supervise the contractor. In some circumstances the occupier may have to delegate supervision to a properly qualified professional person, such as an architect, in order to avoid a finding of negligence (*AMF International Ltd* v *Magnet Bowling Ltd* [1968] 1 WLR 1028, 1044). In that case AMF were to instal bowling equipment in a bowling centre being built by the defendants' contractors. After the contractors had said that the installation could begin, heavy rain flooded the partially constructed building and damaged the plaintiffs equipment. The defendants were held liable because they had not taken any steps to check on the contractors' work before allowing AMF to enter the premises. The contractors were also liable under the Act as they had a sufficient degree of control over the premises to be an occupier.

In *Ferguson* v *Welsh* the plaintiff was an employee of a demolition contractor. He suffered serious injury as a result of the contractor's unsafe system of work, and sued the local authority as occupiers of the premises. In the House of Lords, Lord Keith said that it would not ordinarily be reasonable to expect an occupier, having engaged a contractor whom he has reasonable grounds for regarding as competent, to supervise the contractor's activities in order to ensure that he was discharging his duties to his employees to observe a safe system of work. In special circumstances, however, where the occupier knows or has reason to suspect that the contractor is using an unsafe system, it might be reasonable for the occupier to take steps to see that the system was made safe. It is debatable whether in this situation the defendant's liability would arise from his capacity as an occupier or whether he would be, for some other reason, a joint-tortfeasor (per Lords Oliver and Goff). In any event it is arguable that an ordinary householder would not be liable merely because he knew or had reason to suspect that a contractor, such as an electrician, was using a system of work that was unsafe for his employees (per Lord Goff).

6.1.3.4 Warning   An occupier may discharge his duty to a visitor by giving a warning of the danger, but the warning is not to be treated without more as absolving the occupier from liability unless in all the circumstances it was enough to enable the visitor to be reasonably safe (OLA 1957, s. 2(4)(a)). The mere fact that a warning was given will not necessarily suffice. In *Roles* v *Nathan* [1963] 1 WLR 1117 Lord Denning MR gave (at p. 1124) an example of a warning that the only means of access to premises over a rotten footbridge was dangerous. This would not enable the visitor to be reasonably safe, because he has no option but to use the bridge for access and egress. But if there were two footbridges, and a warning at the dangerous bridge advising the visitor to use the other, safe bridge, this would be sufficient to enable the visitor to be reasonably safe. Similarly, where the nature of the risk is not obvious a warning notice stating simply 'Danger' would probably not be enough. The warning should give some indication of the nature and location of the danger in order to enable the visitor to avoid it.

In some instances even a specific warning about an exceptional danger may not be sufficient to discharge the occupier's duty, and he may have to set a physical barrier to protect a visitor from an immediate danger such as a deep pit at the entrance of a dark shed with no artificial lighting (*Rae* v *Mars (UK) Ltd* [1990] 3 EG 80, 84). On the other hand, there is no obligation to warn of an obvious danger which is known to the visitor and he is free to take appropriate precautions for his own safety (*Staples* v *West Dorset District Council* (1995) 93 LGR 536—plaintiff slipped on a sea wall covered in algae and visibly slippery; *Cotton* v *Derbyshire Dales District Council, The Times*, 20 June 1994—no duty to warn an adult that it is dangerous to go near the edge of an obvious cliff). Moreover, the fact that the defendant has erected a warning notice after the accident to the plaintiff is not an indication that the omission to warn the plaintiff was negligent (*Staples* v *West Dorset District Council*).

At this stage it is worth bearing in mind the distinction between different types of 'warning notice'. A sign which states 'Danger—steps slippery when wet' seeks not to avoid the occupier's responsibility for visitors' safety, but to fulfil it by giving a warning to enable them to negotiate the danger safely. A notice which states 'Persons enter at their own risk' does not attempt to discharge the occupier's duty, but to raise the defence of *volenti nonfit injuria*. If the notice states 'All liability for any accident howsoever caused is hereby excluded', this is an attempt to exclude a liability which must already have accrued by virtue of the occupier's breach of duty. Although, if effective, each of these notices could produce the same result, in that the occupier will not be held liable, the effect in law of each of these devices (and the circumstances in which they are likely to succeed) is conceptually distinct (see *White* v *Blackmore* [1972] 2 QB 651, para. 6.1.5).

6.1.4 Acceptance of risk
An occupier does not have any obligation to a visitor in respect of risks willingly accepted as his by the visitor (OLA 1957, s. 2(5)). This is a specific application of the general defence of *volenti non fit injuria* (para. 14.1). In *Simms* v *Leigh Rugby Football Club Ltd* [1969] 2 All ER 923, for example, it was held that the plaintiff, a professional rugby player, had accepted the risk of playing on a rugby ground that complied with the by-laws of the Rugby

League. In *Bunker* v *Charles Brand & Sons Ltd* [1969] 2 QB 480, O'Connor J stated that s. 2(5) had to be read in conjunction with s. 2(4)(a) (para. 6.1.3.4), so that knowledge of the danger is not sufficient to establish *volenti* unless it was enough to enable the visitor to be reasonably safe. This probably does no more than restate the common law rule that knowledge does not of itself amount to consent. The plaintiffs knowledge must cover the specific risk that causes the injury; so knowledge that jalopy car racing is dangerous does not mean that the plaintiff has accepted the risk of negligence in the setting out of safety arrangements (*White* v *Blackmore* [1972] 2 QB 651). Indeed, it is arguable that mere knowledge, even of a specific risk, is never sufficient *per se* to establish *volenti*, on the basis that in addition to knowledge of the risk the defence requires a willingness on the part of the plaintiff to accept the legal risk; i.e., to waive the legal rights that would otherwise arise from the damage caused by the defendant's unreasonable conduct (*Waldick* v *Malcolm* (1991) 83 DLR (4th) 114, 126–9, Supreme Court of Canada; see further paras 14.1.2, 14.1.3). Where the plaintiff has no real choice about entering premises he cannot be taken to have accepted the risk (*Burnett* v *British Waterways Board* [1973] 2 All ER 631 where the compulsion derived from the plaintiff's employment, not the occupier). Moreover, it is possible that an express notice stating that the visitor enters at his own risk will be caught by the Unfair Contract Terms Act 1977, s. 2(1) (*Johnstone* v *Bloomsbury Health Authority* [1991] 2 All ER 293, 301; see para. 6.1.5).

6.1.5 Exclusion of liability

The Occupiers' Liability Act 1957 provides that an occupier owes the common duty of care to his visitors 'except in so far as he is free to and does extend, restrict, modify or exclude his duty to any visitor or visitors by agreement or otherwise' (s. 2(1)). The ability of business occupiers to exclude liability has been severely restricted by the Unfair Contract Terms Act 1977, but the private occupier still has some freedom to do so. Liability can be excluded 'by agreement or otherwise' and in *Ashdown* v *Samuel Williams & Sons Ltd* [1957] 1 QB 409 the Court of Appeal sanctioned the use of a notice. The plaintiff, who was on the defendants' land as a licensee, was injured by the negligent shunting of railway trucks. Notices had been posted on the land excluding the defendants' liability for negligence. The court held that the plaintiff had entered the land subject to the conditions set out in the notice, i.e., she was a conditional licensee. The defendants had taken reasonable steps to bring to the plaintiff's attention the conditions which they attached to their permission, and therefore they were not liable. Since an occupier could exclude a licensee altogether by refusing permission to enter, there was nothing wrong with allowing entry subject to conditions stipulated by the occupier. If the entrant did not like the terms, he could choose either to stay out or to enter as a trespasser.

Although the logic of this argument can be criticised (see Gower (1956) 19 MLR 536) the decision is still good law. In *White* v *Blackmore* [1972] 2 QB 651 the plaintiff's husband was killed at a jalopy race when a car became entangled in the safety ropes, with the result that stakes holding the ropes were pulled up, and he was catapulted about 20 feet through the air. A notice at the entrance to the course and at other points about the field specified that the organisers were to be absolved from all liabilities arising out of accidents causing damage or personal injury howsoever caused. A majority of the Court of Appeal concluded that this was an effective defence. The deceased had entered the premises subject to the conditions of the notice.

There are, however, certain limits on the freedom of a private occupier to exclude the common duty of care:

(a)   Since the ability of the occupier to exclude liability appears to rest on his right to prohibit entry there should be no right to exclude liability to persons who enter in the exercise of rights conferred by law, because the occupier has no right to prevent their entry (P.M. North, *Occupiers' Liability* pp. 130–1; para. 6.1.2).

(b)   Where the plaintiff has no real choice about whether to enter the premises on the terms of an exclusionary notice there can be no implied agreement that he will be bound by its terms (*Burnett* v *British Waterways Board* [1973] 2 All ER 631—employee on a barge entering the defendants' dock had no choice).

(c)   There is an argument that the duty owed to trespassers, now contained in the OLA 1984, is a minimum standard of duty which as a matter of public policy should be unexcludable (see para. 6.2.6). If this is correct it must also apply to lawful visitors, even where the common duty of care has been excluded, because it would be very strange if trespassers were to be in a better position in this respect than visitors.

(d)   Although the effectiveness of the defence does not depend upon actual notice of the condition by the plaintiff, because the occupier will have done enough if he takes reasonable steps to bring the condition to the visitor's attention, it is difficult to see how an exclusionary notice can operate against children who may not be able to read, let alone comprehend the notice. (This is true also of warning notices and notices raising *volenti*.) If constructive notice of an exclusion of liability were always effective, the visitor who has no choice but to enter would be caught by the condition. It seems reasonable then to look for some element of agreement in the application of the defence. An adult fixed with constructive notice has at least had an opportunity to consider the effect of the term excluding liability before entering the premises. A child may have had no opportunity to do so. If this argument is correct, then, unless *Phipps* v *Rochester Corporation* [1955] 1 QB 450 (para. 6.1.3.1), were to be extended to older children for this very purpose, the exclusion of liability may well be ineffective against many children. A similar argument might apply if the plaintiff were illiterate. This may seem harsh on the occupier who has done all he can to bring the notice to public attention, but what if there were evidence that more people suffer from illiteracy in this country than blindness? A reasonable man takes account of the fact that a cross-section of the public will include some who are blind (*Haley* v *London Electricity Board* [1965] AC 778, para. 3.1.3.1.1). Would it not also be reasonable to take account of the illiterate? (See *Sarch* v *Blackburn* (1830) 4

C & P 297; *Geier* v *Kujawa* [1970] 1 Lloyd's Rep 364—German girl who spoke little English did not consent to an exempting notice in a motor vehicle; see now Road Traffic Act 1988, s. 149. Cf. the position in contract: *Thompson* v *London, Midland & Scottish Railway Co.* [1930] 1 KB 41.)

(e) OLA 1957, s. 3(1), provides that where an occupier is bound by a contract to permit third parties, who are strangers to the contract, to enter or use the premises, the duty of care owed to the third parties as visitors cannot be restricted or excluded by that contract. If the contract specifies a higher standard than the common duty of care the third parties are entitled to the benefit of the additional protection, unless the contract specifically excludes this. There is some doubt whether the occupier can exclude his duty to the third parties by other means, such as a notice, but the better view is that he cannot because this would undermine the purpose of s. 3(1) (although the original aim of the section was to avoid the possibility that a visitor could find the occupier's duty to him excluded by a contract term of which he had no knowledge, and he would have at least constructive knowledge of a notice).

The clearest restriction on the occupier's freedom to limit or exclude liability is the Unfair Contract Terms Act 1977 (UCTA 1977), but the Act applies only to 'business liability' (UCTA 1977, s. 1(3)). This includes liability for breach of duty arising from the occupation of premises used for business purposes of the occupier (the purpose of the visitor is generally irrelevant). The problem is to know what constitutes a business purpose. It includes a profession and the activities of a government department or local or public authority (UCTA 1977, s. 14). It does *not* include the granting of access for recreational or educational purposes unless granting such access falls within the business purposes of the occupier (UCTA 1977, s. 1(3) as amended by OLA 1984, s. 2). This provision applies only to loss or damage caused by the dangerous state of the premises, not to activities carried out on the land in a negligent manner; nor does it apply where the occupier's business is recreational or educational. There is no other guidance in the Act as to the meaning of 'business purpose' and it is a matter of some considerable doubt (see Mesher [1979] Conv 58–60). Would the activities of a charitable organisation, for example, be covered by the Act? It is unclear whether partial use of premises for business purposes would result in the application of UCTA 1977 to the premises in all their uses, but a strict reading of s. 1(3) would appear to produce this conclusion.

Where UCTA 1977 applies the occupier cannot by reference to any contract term or to a notice given to persons generally or to particular persons exclude or restrict his liability for death or personal injury resulting from negligence (UCTA 1977, s. 2(1)). In the case of other loss or damage, liability for negligence cannot be excluded or restricted except in so far as the term or notice satisfies the requirement of reasonableness (UCTA 1977, s. 2(2)). (For the 'reasonableness' test see s. 11, and para. 14.2.) Negligence includes breach of the common duty of care (UCTA 1977, s. 1(1)(c)), but not, it should be noted, the statutory duty created by the OLA 1984 (see para. 6.2.6). A person's agreement to or awareness of an exclusionary term or notice is not of itself to be taken as indicating his voluntary acceptance of any risk (UCTA 1977, s. 2(3)). This prevents the business occupier from relying on an invalid exclusion clause to raise the *volenti* defence, although, in any event, it may now be arguable that a notice purporting to raise *volenti* is subject to s. 2(1) of UCTA 1977 (see *Johnstone* v *Bloomsbury Health Authority* [1991] 2 All ER 293, 301).

6.1.6 Contributory negligence
The Law Reform (Contributory Negligence) Act 1945 applies to an action for breach of the common duty of care, and damages will be apportioned, if the visitor has been careless for his own safety, in the same manner as in an ordinary negligence action (see para. 14.5).

6.2 LIABILITY OF OCCUPIERS TO OTHER ENTRANTS

At one time the common law took a very Draconian view of the degree of protection an occupier could be expected to offer persons he had not invited or permitted on to his land. The occupier owed no duty to trespassers other than to refrain from inflicting damage intentionally or recklessly on a trespasser known to be present on the land (*Robert Addie & Sons (Collieries) Ltd* v *Dumbreck* [1929] AC 358). This was a harsh rule and led to the invention of several techniques for avoiding its effect, e.g., the distinction between occupancy duties, and 'activity' duties to which ordinary negligence applied; the rule that independent contractors were liable in negligence to persons injured on another's land; the concept of 'allurements' to children; the facility with which some licences were implied.

In *British Railways Board* v *Herrington* [1972] AC 877 the House of Lords changed the law and established what came to be known as the duty of 'common humanity' owed by occupiers to trespassers. A six-year-old boy was badly burned by an electrified rail while trespassing on the defendants' land. He had obtained access through a gap in a fence created by members of the public who used a short cut across the railway line. The defendants knew that in the past children had been seen on the line, but they had no system for checking the fence. The defendants were held liable, but their Lordships refused to impose a duty of care in negligence on occupiers because it was thought that this would infringe the rights of property owners. A trespasser forces himself into a relationship of proximity with the occupier and therefore must accept a lower standard of precautions against injury than a visitor. An occupier did owe a duty, however, to act humanely. This duty would be owed when a reasonable man knowing the physical facts which the occupier actually knew would appreciate that a trespasser's presence at the point and time of danger was so likely that in all the circumstances it would be inhumane not to give an effective warning of the danger. This is a combination of an objective and subjective test, since it is measured by the conduct of a 'reasonable man', but only with reference to the knowledge of the particular occupier. The knowledge that a hypothetical reasonable occupier ought to have acquired was irrelevant (but see *Harris* v *Birkenhead Corporation* [1976] 1 All ER 341, para. 6.2.2).

A similar test applied to the occupier's knowledge of the existence of danger, i.e., actual knowledge of the physical facts which a reasonable man would appreciate involved danger of serious injury to the trespasser. There was no obligation, then, for an occupier to inspect his premises either for the presence, or likely presence, of trespassers or for circumstances that might be dangerous to trespassers. Whether, on the known facts, a reasonable man would have considered it inhumane not to offer some protection is an objective judgment, which depends upon the potential gravity of the injury and the likelihood of its occurrence (factors which are normally used to decide whether a person is in *breach* of a *duty of care* in negligence, see para. 3.1.3).

The content of the occupier's duty, i.e., the level of precautions expected of him, also contained subjective considerations. The occupier's duty varied according to his knowledge, ability and resources because trespassers force a 'neighbour' relationship on him. Thus a trespasser could expect an impoverished occupier to take fewer precautions than a wealthy one. Where the occupier created the danger, however, as opposed to allowing his premises to fall into disrepair, the standard of care was objective and his personal resources were irrelevant (*Southern Portland Cement Ltd* v *Cooper* [1974] AC 632, 644). There has been no reported decision in this country in which an occupier's lack of resources has been treated as a basis for absolving him from liability, although the cost and practicability of taking precautions, measured on an objective basis, can be significant, just as it is relevant to the question of breach of duty in negligence (*Penny* v *Northampton Borough Council* (1974) 72 LGR 733).

Following a Law Commission Report (Law Com. No. 75, Cmnd 6428, 1976) *British Railways Board* v *Herrington* has been replaced by the Occupiers' Liability Act 1984, but the similarities between the new statutory duty and the common law far outweigh the differences. For this reason *Herrington* and the cases that followed it are still useful as illustrations of how the Act may be applied, but it must be remembered that they are *only* illustrative and it is the statutory duty that governs accidents which occurred on or after 13 May 1984.

The Occupiers' Liability Act 1984 determines (a) whether an occupier of premises owes any duty to persons other than his visitors in respect of any risk of their suffering injury on the premises by reason of any danger due to the state of the premises or to things done or omitted to be done on them, and (b) if so, what that duty is (s. 1(1)). This wording is similar to that of the OLA 1957, s. 1(1), the effect of which is that an act or omission not in itself affecting the safety of the premises falls outside the scope of the Act. If, for example, while shooting rabbits an occupier injured a trespasser, liability would turn upon the common law not the Act, although the fact that the plaintiff was a trespasser would be relevant to the foreseeability of the injury. In *Revill* v *Newbery* [1996] 1 All ER 291, 298 in which the defendant negligently shot a burglar, Neill LJ said that although the issue should be dealt with under the common law, the defendant's status as occupier of the premises being irrelevant, nonetheless the scope of the duty owed at common

law to an intruder who comes onto premises in the middle of the night should
be determined as if one were considering a breach of duty under OLA 1984,
s. 1. 'Premises' are defined in OLA 1984 in the same terms as under OLA
1957 (OLA 1984, s. 1(2) and (9); see para. 6.1), as is an 'occupier' (OLA
1984, s. 1(2)(a); para 6.1.1). There is no liability under OLA 1984 for loss
of or damage to property (s. 1(8); cf. OLA 1957, s. 1(3)(b); but see the
strange case of *Tutton* v *A.D. Walter Ltd* [1986] QB 61—landowner liable in
negligence at common law for damage to 'trespassing' bees caused by crop
insecticide; see Spencer [1986] CLJ 15).

6.2.1   Persons other than visitors

An occupier may owe a duty under OLA 1984 to 'persons other than his
visitors' (s. 1(1)(a)), hereafter 'non-visitors'). This category of entrants
includes (a) trespassers, (b) persons who enter land in the exercise of rights
conferred by an access agreement or order under the National Parks and
Access to the Countryside Act 1949, s. 60, and (c) persons lawfully exercising
a private right of way.

In *Holden* v *White* [1982] QB 679 the Court of Appeal decided that persons
using a private right of way were not the visitors of the occupier of the servient
land under the OLA 1957. This meant that a milkman who was injured by a
defective manhole cover could not sue the owner of the land over which the
right of way passed. The defendant had conceded that she was the occupier
of the defective cover, but the court doubted whether this concession was
correct. The Law Commission clearly intended that persons using a private
right of way should be within the new statutory duty, but if the owner of the
servient land is not an occupier the Act cannot apply, and at common law
there would probably be no liability for nonfeasance such as a mere omission
to repair (*Greenhalgh* v *British Railways Board* [1969] 2 QB 286). This raises
the possibility of an injured person being left with no one to sue (unless the
owner of the dominant tenement had sufficient control to qualify as an
occupier). This would be particularly anomalous since, in some circumstances, the user of a private right of way may have the benefit of the common
duty of care under OLA 1957. Where a landlord retains control of the means
of access to premises or of the common parts he will be treated as an occupier
owing the common duty of care to the tenants, their families and their visitors
(*Jacobs* v *London County Council* [1950] AC 361). Additionally, the landlord
qua landlord may owe a duty of care to persons exercising a right of way by
virtue of the Defective Premises Act 1972, s. 4 (para. 6.3.2).

Another anomaly was specifically retained by OLA 1984. In *Greenhalgh* v
British Railways Board [1969] 2 QB 286 it was held that persons using a *public*
right of way were not visitors under OLA 1957. Section 1(7) of OLA 1984
states that this Act also does not apply to persons using the highway. The
effect of this is that the occupier's liability is governed by the common law,
which provides that he will be liable for negligent misfeasance but not for
nonfeasance. A mere failure to repair a public way will not incur liability. In
practice this rule applies only to public rights of way maintainable at private
expense because the Highways (Miscellaneous Provisions) Act 1961, s. 1 (see

now Highways Act 1980, ss. 41 and 58), changed the position of highway authorities, imposing liability for both negligent misfeasance and non-feasance, though the Act grants an action only in respect of personal injuries or physical damage to property, not for pure economic loss (*Wentworth* v *Wiltshire County Council* [1993] 2 WLR 175). The Law Commission considered that the potential burden of repair that would be imposed upon the owners of servient land would be excessive if the law were changed. This point was emphasised by the House of Lords in *McGeown* v *Northern Ireland Housing Executive* [1994] 3 All ER 53. The plaintiff broke her leg when she tripped in a hole in a footpath over open land forming part of a housing estate. At some unspecified point in time the public had acquired a right of way over the path, but it had not been adopted by the highway authority. Lord Keith appears to have accepted that if the path had not become the subject of a public right of way the defendants would have owed the plaintiff the common duty of care under the Occupiers Liability (Northern Ireland) Act 1957 (which is in the same terms as the OLA 1957), and would have been liable accordingly (at p. 60, although if the path was a *private* right of way then, presumably, *Holden* v *White* [1982] 2 All ER 328 would have applied). It was held that the common law rule that a person exercising a public right of way is neither the licensee nor the invitee of the occupier of the soil over which the right of way runs was still good law, and that there was no liability for mere nonfeasance. Lord Keith commented (at p. 59) that: 'Rights of way pass over many different types of terrain, and it would place an impossible burden upon landowners if they not only had to submit to the passage over them of anyone who might choose to exercise them but also were under a duty to maintain them in a safe condition'. Moreover, once the public right of way was established, any licence that the defendant might have been held to have granted to the plaintiff to use the path before it became subject to the right of way is merged in the public right of way and thereby extinguished. Once the public right of way is established there is no question of permission being granted by the owner of the soil to those who choose to use it. In the absence of any requirement for permission from the occupier the entrant is not a licensee or visitor. Lord Browne-Wilkinson was uncomfortable with the conclusion that a duty of care which had formerly existed on the facts of *McGeown* (because the defendants had laid out the paths as a means of access to the houses on the estate occupied by its tenants: see *Jacobs* v *London County Council* [1950] AC 361) could be extinguished by the acts of third parties, i.e., members of the public using the path otherwise than to gain access to the houses, thereby, over a period of time, creating a public right of way. This could lead to the undesirable extinction of duties of care which public policy would indicate should be held to exist. His Lordship gave the example of a public right of way through the middle of an artificial structure which was in part a shopping centre (as in *Cumbernauld and Kilsyth District Council* v *Dollar Land (Cumbernauld) Ltd* 1993 SLT 1318). It would be unfortunate if the owner of a shopping centre could, by either expressly dedicating the land as a public highway or submitting to long public user, free himself from liability to users whose presence he had invited and encouraged:

'Who, other than the occupier, is to maintain these artificial structures and protect from injury those encouraged to use them by the occupier for the occupier's own business reasons?' (pp. 63–64). His Lordship considered that the existence of a public right of way was not incompatible with the owner of the soil owing a duty of care to an invitee, as opposed to a licensee, the invitation giving rise to the duty (a view supported by Murphy [1997] Conv 362). On the other hand, restoring the sometimes fine distinction between invitees and licensees would run counter to the policy of the OLA 1957, and, moreover, the other members of the House of Lords did not appear to share Lord Browne-Wilkinson's concerns (for a detailed discussion of the interaction between property rules and liability rules in this context see Barker and Parry (1995) 15 LS 335).

The effect of both *Greenhalgh* v *British Railways Board* and *McGeown* is that there is a significant lacuna in the protection of personal safety accorded to members of the public that is difficult to justify even under a system of fault liability. Not only do the users of a public right of way have no action in respect of defects in the state of repair (due to nonfeasance, as opposed to misfeasance) of the land over which the right of way runs, but the creation of a public right of way also extinguishes any existing, more onerous, duty of the occupier. Their Lordships did not refer in *McGeown* to the decision of the Court of Appeal in *Thomas* v *British Railways Board* [1976] QB 912 which, on one interpretation had undermined the effect of *Greenhalgh* v *British Railways Board*. A public footpath ran across a railway line. The plaintiff, a two-year-old child who had wandered through a broken stile, was hit by a train. It was held that in operating a railway the defendants owed a duty to take reasonable care to reduce or avert danger to those who may reasonably be expected to be on the line, 'whether they be trespassers, visitors, or persons exercising their right to use a public highway' (per Scarman LJ at p. 927). The Court was clearly influenced by *British Railways Board* v *Herrington*, and on principle it would be strange if an occupier were liable only for misfeasance to a person lawfully exercising a public right of way, whereas he could be liable for both acts and omissions if that person abused the right of way and became a trespasser. In *Brady* v *Department of Environment for Northern Ireland* [1990] 5 NIJB 9, however, it was considered that *Greenhalgh* had been unaffected by the decision in *Thomas*, which was concerned with misfeasance in the operation of the railway (a negligent activity carried out on the land) as opposed to nonfeasance in the defendants' capacity as an occupier of land (for criticism of the decision in *Brady* see McMillen (1991) 42 NILQ 138; for argument that 'public bodies' ought to be liable at common law for nonfeasance in respect of unadopted public rights of way over their land, see Murphy [1997] Conv 362).

6.2.2 Existence of the duty

The Occupiers' Liability Act 1984 adopts a separate test for the existence of the duty owed to a non-visitor and the content of the duty, if it is found to exist. Section 1(3) stipulates that the occupier owes the statutory duty if:

(a)   he is aware of the danger or has reasonable grounds to believe that it exists;

(b)   he knows or has reasonable grounds to believe that the [non-visitor] is in the vicinity of the danger concerned or that he may come into the vicinity of the danger (in either case, whether the [non-visitor] has lawful authority for being in that vicinity or not); and

(c)   the risk is one against which, in all the circumstances of the case, he may reasonably be expected to offer the [non-visitor] some protection.

Paragraph (c) corresponds substantially with the test proposed by the Law Commission and is clearly objective. Paragraphs (a) and (b) appear to create a subjective test. The phrase 'he knows or has reasonable grounds to believe' would apply to the situation where the occupier knows or is aware of the primary facts but fails to draw the reasonable inference that the premises are dangerous or that the non-visitor's presence is likely, or where he *deliberately* shuts his eyes to such facts. The basis for such an understanding of the phrase can be partially traced back to *Harris* v *Birkenhead Corporation* [1976] 1 All ER 341, 352 where Lawton LJ construed the requirement of actual knowledge under *British Railways Board* v *Herrington* [1972] AC 877 to include cases where the occupier ignores the obvious or fails to draw reasonable inferences from known facts. In turn, Lawton LJ's judgment in that case has subsequently been reconsidered in the specific context of s. 1(3)(b) of the 1984 Act (the defendants having conceded awareness of danger for the purpose of s. 1(3)(a)) by the Court of Appeal in *Swain* v *Natui Ram Puri* [1996] PIQR P442. It is now clear that ignorance of the obvious in the context of that section carries a highly restricted meaning, and one which does not allow for a simple objective determination of what the occupier ought to know. In *Swain*, the Court of Appeal confirmed that the section required actual knowledge of the actual risk or of the primary facts from which an inference could be drawn, and that such knowledge did include 'shut-eye' knowledge but not constructive knowledge, the distinction being that, in the former situation, the occupier deliberately shuts his eyes to the relevant facts whereas, in the latter, he negligently does so. It is difficult, however, to see how (a) and (b) could apply to the occupier who is unaware of the primary facts in circumstances where the reasonable occupier would have been so aware (cf. Defective Premises Act 1972, s. 4(2): 'if the landlord knows . . . or if he ought in all the circumstances to have known'). Both the Law Commission and the Lord Chancellor intended the test to be objective (see Jones (1984) 47 MLR 713, 718), but it has been open to the courts to interpret s. 1(3) as a subjective test, in virtually identical terms to that laid down in *British Railways Board* v *Herrington*. As such, the occupier is under no obligation to inspect his premises either for the presence of trespassers or the existence of dangers, and to this extent the knowledge that the hypothetical reasonable occupier would have acquired will be irrelevant.

In *White* v *St Albans City & District Council, The Times,* 12 March 1990, the Court of Appeal held that the fact that an occupier has taken precautions to stop people getting onto land where there was a danger does not necessarily mean that he had reason to believe that someone was likely to come into the vicinity of the danger for the purposes of s. 1(3)(b). The question had to be determined by looking at the actual state of affairs on the ground when the injury occurred. Where the accident occurred on private land surrounded by a fence the court was justified in holding that the occupier had no reason to believe that the plaintiff would come into the vicinity of the danger. On the other hand, this conclusion might not be appropriate if the fence was in disrepair and there was evidence that people used the land as a short cut.

Whether the risk is one against which the occupier may reasonably be expected to offer some protection will depend upon factors which are more usually taken into account when assessing the standard of care, e.g., the nature and extent of the risk, practicability of precautions and, possibly, the type of entrant. If s. 1(3) is satisfied the court will then consider the content of the occupier's duty.

6.2.3 Content of the duty

By OLA 1984, s. 1(4), the duty is to take such care as is reasonable in all the circumstances of the case to see that the non-visitor does not suffer injury on the premises by reason of the danger concerned. This is an objective negligence standard which does not depend upon the skill or resources of the particular occupier. It had been doubted whether there was any real difference between the concept of common humanity and a duty to take reasonable care (see the judgment of Lord Denning MR in *Pannett* v *McGuinness & Co. Ltd* [1972] 2 QB 599; Law Com. No. 75, para. 11). Now it is clear that, at least so far as the content of the duty is concerned, they are the same. What constitutes reasonable care will vary considerably with the circumstances including the nature and character of the entry, the age of the entrant, the nature of the premises, the extent of the risk and the cost of precautions. There is an inevitable overlap here between the considerations relevant to the existence of the duty in s. 1(3) and those relevant to breach of the duty under s. 1(4). An alternative approach would have been to specify that an occupier will automatically owe a duty to all non-visitors, or even all entrants, and vary the content of the duty according to the nature of the entry. Under the Occupiers' Liability (Scotland) Act 1960 Scottish occupiers owe the same duty of care to all entrants, visitors and non-visitors alike. There is no evidence that unmeritorious plaintiffs have succeeded in actions in Scotland, because the negligence standard of *reasonable* care in *all the circumstances* of the case is flexible enough to take account of different types of entry.

It may be that, in theory, the difference between the Scottish legislation and the OLA 1984 is one of form rather than substance. This is the case where the test for the existence of the duty employs criteria that would in any event be taken into account when assessing whether there had been a breach of duty. If, for example, an occupier owed the common duty of care to all entrants it is inconceivable that he could be in *breach* of this duty if the circumstances were such that he could not reasonably have known of either the danger (s. 1(3)(a)) or the presence of the plaintiff (s. 1(3)(b)), or if it was unreasonable to expect him to take precautions against the risk (s. 1(3)(c)).

In terms of liability the result should be the same. Employing a separate test for the existence of the duty simply shifts the process of assessment of some of the factors that go to liability to a different theoretical level. Why have such a test? The answer to this question probably has more to do with the symbolic function of law than its substance. The layman appears to have great difficulty in appreciating that the imposition on occupiers of a single duty of care as a matter of *law* does not mean that the standard of care will be the same in every case as a matter of *fact*. Section 1(3) demonstrates to the world that there is a difference between the duties owed to trespassers and lawful visitors.

It is important to note, however, that in practice there could be different results on the same facts under the Scottish Act and the OLA 1984, for two reasons. First, the measure of the occupier's knowledge in OLA 1984, s. 1(3), probably contains a subjective element, unlike the Scottish legislation or OLA 1957. Secondly, the existence of two separate Occupiers' Liability Acts could produce unfortunate consequences in terms of the foreseeability of the presence of trespassers.

This latter point can be illustrated by *Westwood* v *Post Office* [1973] 1 QB 591 (reversed on other grounds [1974] AC 1) where an employee who was technically a trespasser failed in an action in circumstances in which a lawful visitor would have succeeded. It is very difficult to justify this result on principle (except where the occupier does not allow visitors access to the area where the accident occurred). Two common reasons given for placing trespassers in a different category from visitors are, first, that they are unforeseeable, and secondly that liability would impose an unduly heavy repairing obligation on the occupier. Where a trespasser is injured in circumstances that would render the occupier liable to a visitor, how can it be said that the trespasser's presence is unforeseeable? Usually, if it is foreseeable that some individual will suffer injury in consequence of a specific danger, the plaintiff's injury will be foreseeable. The defendant does not have to be able to foresee precisely who he is or what he is doing. 'The fact that [the occupier] does not foresee their status or the class to which they belong should be no more relevant, in my view, than that he does not foresee the colour of their hair' (*Herrington* v *British Railways Board* [1971] 1 QB 107, 121 per Salmon LJ). The occupier's burden of precautions can hardly have been increased either, if he ought reasonably to have taken similar precautions to protect his visitors. The fact that the plaintiff was a trespasser is, from the defendant's point of view, purely fortuitous. If there is a reason for treating the two categories of entrant differently it must be in order to penalise the trespasser's 'wrongdoing'. That may be very well in the case of the burglar, but it is not so obviously just in the case of the accidentally, or even intentionally, errant adult. The existence of two distinct statutory duties owed to visitors and non-visitors respectively will provide some justification for the approach adopted in *Westwood* v *Post Office*. Under OLA 1984 the foresight required is foresight of the presence of the non-visitor (s. 1(3)(b)). The fact that a visitor's presence was foreseeable will presumably be irrelevant to the question of whether a trespasser's presence was foreseeable, so that *Westwood* v *Post Office* would probably be decided in the same way under the Act.

Of the factors that the courts will take into account in deciding whether the occupier has exercised reasonable care one of the most important, at least in the case of trespassers, tends to be the age of the entrant. There is no reported case in this country where an adult trespasser has succeeded under *British Railways Board* v *Herrington* [1972] AC 877, although an adult has succeeded in Canada (see *Veinot* v *Kerr-Addison Mines Ltd* (1975) 51 DLR (3d) 533). There is no reason in theory, however, why an adult trespasser should not succeed, nor is there any reason to think that the OLA 1984 has changed the common law position in this respect. If the adult trespasser was a burglar or thief the court might be inclined to take the view that it would be unreasonable to expect an occupier to take any precautions for his safety, and it is arguable that the plaintiff could be met by the defence of *ex turpi causa non oritur actio* (*Murphy* v *Culhane* [1977] QB 94, 98; para. 14.3). In *Revill* v *Newbery* [1996] 1 All ER 291, however, the Court of Appeal held that a burglar was entitled to bring a claim in the tort of negligence when he was shot by the occupier. The defendant was sleeping in a brick shed on his allotment in order to protect his property from burglars. When he was awoken in the night by the sound of the plaintiff trying to break into the shed he fired a shotgun through a small hole in the door without being able to see whether he was likely to hit anyone. The plaintiff brought an action for the injuries caused to his arms and chest by the blast, both under the OLA 1984 and at common law for negligence. The claim under the Act was rejected on the basis that the legislation imposed a duty upon the occupier as occupier. It is concerned with the safety of the premises and with dangers due to things done or omitted to be done on the premises, not with activities such as shooting a gun. Accordingly, the defendant's status as an occupier was irrelevant. Nonetheless, in considering the defendant's liability at common law the Court held that the issue should be determined on the same lines as if one was considering a breach of duty under s. 1 of the Act. Having said that, Neill LJ then proceeded to address only the question posed by s. 1(3)(b), namely: did the defendant know or have reasonable grounds to believe that the plaintiff was in the vicinity of the danger or that he might come within the vicinity of the danger, the danger being the gun which was about to be discharged? The Court did not ask whether the risk was one against which, in all the circumstances, the defendant might reasonably be expected to offer the trespasser some protection (s. 1(3)(c)), nor whether under s. 1(4) there was a breach of the duty to take such care as was reasonable in all the circumstances to see that the trespasser did not suffer injury on the premises by reason of the danger concerned, i.e., the gun. The implication of the finding that the defendant was liable, however, must be that there was a breach of such a duty (or its common law equivalent). The Court was clearly concerned that the fact that the plaintiff was a burglar should not mean that he effectively became an outlaw, beyond the protection of the civil law. This underlies the Court's rejection of the defence of *ex turpi causa non oritur actio* on the facts (see para. 14.3). A similar effect would have been produced if the Court had taken a blanket view that it was not reasonable to offer burglars some protection against being shot by householders. There are some who might take the view that this is entirely reasonable, as evidenced by the fact that the defendant was prosecuted and acquitted by a jury on a charge of wounding, and the fact that there was subsequently a public collection for the defendant which paid the damages awarded in favour of the plaintiff. The Court did acknowledge the plaintiff's responsibility for his own injuries by reducing the damages by two thirds for his contributory negligence. *Revill* v *Newbery* should not be taken as authority for the proposition that burglars, nor indeed even innocent adult trespassers, will always be owed a duty with respect to their safety. There is a world of difference between taking a gun and firing it in the vicinity of a trespasser, even without an intention to harm the trespasser, and simply omitting to repair the premises or give an adequate warning of danger. If the plaintiff in *Revill* v *Newbery* had fallen through a defective floorboard in the shed and broken his leg it is unlikely that the Court would have taken such a strong line against the defendant. It was the perception that the defendant's reaction was out of proportion to the circumstances that influenced the Court's judgment.

In the case of an 'innocent' adult trespasser, the plaintiff may be found to have assumed the risk of injury (para. 6.2.5), whereas young children may simply not appreciate the danger even when warned (*Pannett* v *McGuinness & Co. Ltd* [1972] 2 QB 599—child aged five did not appreciate the danger from fires burning on a demolition site). As with lawful visitors, the precautions that would protect an adult will not necessarily be effective to protect a child, and the presence of an allurement will greatly increase the risk that children will be attracted to a danger and injured by it, which in turn will increase the level of precautions that an occupier ought reasonably to undertake (*Southern Portland Cement Ltd* v *Cooper* [1974] AC 632). This principle will also apply to older children. In *Adams* v *Southern Electricity Board, The Times*, 21 October 1993, the plaintiff, who was almost 15 years old was electrocuted climbing a pole-mounted, high voltage electrical installation. The plaintiff knew that climbing up the pole was dangerous. Despite the fact that he was old enough to be responsible for his actions and that climbing onto an electrical transformer had been an act of 'crass stupidity' the Court of Appeal held the defendants liable because an anti-climbing device, required by statutory regulations to deter children from climbing, was defective. If properly maintained the device would have been effective to prevent the plaintiff from climbing the pole and accordingly the defendants were in breach of their common law duty to exercise reasonable care for the plaintiff's safety (the accident occurred before the OLA 1984 came into force). Damages were reduced by two thirds for the plaintiff's contributory negligence.

One matter which appears to have evaded the attention of the courts is the possibility that unaccompanied young children are more likely to succeed in an action if they are classified as trespassers than if they are lawful visitors. The courts have not expressly applied the reasoning of Devlin J in *Phipps* v *Rochester Corporation* [1955] 1 QB 450 (para. 6.1.3.1) to trespassing children. (Master Herrington, it will be recalled, was aged six at the time of his accident. Where were his parents?) There is no obvious reason, however, why an occupier should not be entitled to take into account the habits of prudent parents, when considering what precautions he ought reasonably to take for the protection of young children under OLA 1984. Otherwise, his obligations under this Act would be greater than under OLA 1957.

The other factors that will be considered when applying OLA 1984, s. 1(4), include (a) the gravity and likelihood of the probable injury—the greater the risk the greater the precautions that must be taken; (b) the nature of the premises—an electrified railway line or a demolition site is in a different category from a private house; and (c) the foreseeability of the entrant—the more likely the presence of non-visitors the more precautions are required (*Pannett* v *McGuinness & Co. Ltd* [1972] 2 QB 599, 607 per Lord Denning MR applying the common law duty of humanity).

6.2.4 Warning

In an 'appropriate case' the occupier may discharge his duty by taking reasonable steps to give a warning of the danger concerned, or to discourage persons from incurring the risk (OLA 1984, s. 1(5)). Warning notices will often be inadequate for children, either because the child cannot read or because he is incapable of appreciating the danger. In that event the occupier may have to take additional steps to 'discourage persons from incurring the risk', such as erecting an obstacle, particularly if the danger is an allurement (*British Railways Board* v *Herrington* [1972] AC 877, 940 per Lord Diplock). In the case of devices designed to keep trespassers out, the common law distinguished between deterrence, which was permissible (*Deane* v *Clayton* (1817) 7 Taunt 489), and concealed retributive dangers, which were not (*Bird* v *Holbrook* (1828) 4 Bing 628). That distinction will still be valid under OLA 1984.

Warning notices have been more successful with adults, and it would seem that almost any notice will suffice. In *Westwood* v *Post Office* [1973] 1 QB 591 Lawton LJ considered (at p. 601) that a notice fixed to a lift motor room door stating 'Only the authorised attendant is permitted to enter' would be understood by an intelligent person to mean keep out because of some danger. It could be argued, however, that this type of notice merely informs unauthorised persons that they enter as trespassers. There might be many reasons for posting such a notice which have nothing to do with a concern for safety. Even if the word 'Danger' is added, the reasonable inference is that the hazard consists of the machinery of the lift motor, not that entrants were likely to be fatally precipitated through a defective trapdoor in the floor. A reasonable warning ought to be sufficient to enable a non-visitor to appreciate and avoid the danger, and it should not be open to an occupier to argue that the non-visitor could have avoided the danger merely by obeying an instruction to keep out (cf. OLA 1957, s. 2(4)(a), para. 6.1.3.4).

6.2.5 Acceptance of risk

The defence of *volenti non fit injuria* is preserved by OLA 1984, s. 1(6). As a general rule the defendant must establish not only that the plaintiff consented to the risk but also that he agreed that if he was injured the loss should be his not the defendant's. In addition, the plaintiff should appreciate both the nature and extent of the risk, not simply the fact that there is some risk (see para. 14.1.3). In cases involving trespassers, however, the courts have adopted an objective rather than subjective test of agreement, so that it is possible to argue that knowledge of a risk plus entry on to the land renders a trespasser *volenti* (*Westwood* v *Post Office* [1973] 1 QB 591, 605; *Titchener* v *British Railways Board* [1983] 3 All ER 770; for criticism see Jaffey [1985] CLJ 87, 91). It would be more difficult to argue that knowledge plus entry constitutes *volenti* in the case of lawful non-visitors. Under OLA 1957 knowledge of a danger is insufficient to establish consent unless it is enough to enable the visitor to be reasonably safe (para. 6.1.4). It would be odd if this principle did not also apply to OLA 1984, because otherwise the concept of assumption of risk would vary with the category of entrant.

6.2.6 Exclusion of liability
The Occupiers' Liability Act 1984 makes no reference to the question of whether an occupier can exclude or restrict his potential liability under the Act. This is in marked contrast to OLA 1957 which specifically reserves an occupier common law right to 'restrict, modify or exclude' his duty to visitors. Although there was some doubt about whether the Unfair Contract Terms Act 1977 applied to the duty of common humanity it is clear that it cannot apply to the statutory duty created by OLA 1984, because UCTA 1977, s. 1(1)(b) and (c) refers only to common law duties to take reasonable care and the statutory common duty of care under OLA 1957. Whether any occupier can exclude the new duty, therefore, is open to debate.

The omission of any reference to the occupier's right to exclude liability (contrary to the recommendation of the Law Commission, Law Com. No. 75 paras 73–4) suggests that this cannot be a defence under the Act. This view is supported by the contrast with OLA 1957, and the possibility that at common law the occupier could not exclude the duty owed to a trespasser. The technical device by which the courts have permitted the exclusion of liability to visitors, the conditional licence, cannot be applied to a trespasser because there is no licence to which conditions can be attached. Moreover, it has been argued that since the duty owed to trespassers is the very minimum imposed by the law, as a matter of public policy the occupier should not be permitted to exclude that obligation (Mesher [1979] Conv 58, 63–4). This point has not been tested in the courts. There is some force in the argument that occupiers should not be allowed to act less than humanely, even to a 'wrongdoer', but whether this has the same appeal now that the duty is expressed in terms of reasonable care remains to be seen.

On the other hand, if the duty were held to be unexcludable this would have implications for the extent to which a non-business occupier could exclude the common duty of care, since Parliament surely cannot have intended that visitors should be in a worse position than non-visitors in this respect. Bearing in mind the similarities in the standard of care owed to visitors and non-visitors, this would effectively undermine the non-business occupier's right to exclude the duty owed to visitors. This might indicate that the new duty *is* excludable, because it could be argued that Parliament cannot have intended to remove by stealth rights that have been expressly preserved by OLA 1957 and impliedly preserved 20 years later by UCTA 1977.

If this is correct the courts will have to develop some basis for assessing when an exclusion of liability will be valid. Reasonable steps to bring a notice to the attention of the non-visitor would probably be sufficient. There may be some limit upon the type of conduct for which liability could be excluded. It would be strange if an occupier could exclude the statutory duty and thereby avoid all liability, even for reckless acts or omissions. The argument that there is a minimum standard which as a matter of public policy should be unexcludable would carry greater weight here. Additionally, if it is correct that an occupier's power to exclude liability rests upon a right to prohibit entry (para. 6.1.5), liability to lawful non-visitors could not be excluded. The occupier has no right to prevent the entry of a person exercising a public right of access or a person lawfully exercising a private right of way. Thus, even if the duty owed to non-visitors can be excluded it would probably be effective only against trespassers for careless, as opposed to reckless, conduct. (It is debatable whether an occupier would be under a residuary common law obligation to act with humanity towards trespassers. See Buckley [1984] Conv 413, 422).

6.3 LIABILITY OF NON-OCCUPIERS TO ENTRANTS

6.3.1 Independent contractors

An independent contractor may have sufficient control over the premises to qualify as an occupier for the purposes of the Occupiers' Liability Acts 1957 and 1984 (paras 6.1.1, 6.1.3.3). Where the contractor is not an occupier his liability turns on the common law of negligence. The plaintiff's status as a visitor or non-visitor *vis-à-vis* the occupier is irrelevant. In *A.C. Billings & Sons Ltd* v *Riden* [1958] AC 240 the House of Lords held that contractors did not owe the same duty as an occupier to a licensee. A contractor owed a duty to take reasonable care to avoid harm to persons he could reasonably expect to be affected by his work. Now that occupiers owe the same common duty of care to all visitors the practical significance of this case is small, given that the standard of care in negligence and under OLA 1957 is virtually identical.

A similar approach is taken in the case of non-visitors. In *Buckland* v *Guildford Gas Light & Coke Co.* [1944] 1 KB 410 the defendant contractors ran an electricity cable through the foliage of a tree on a farmer's land. The plaintiff was electrocuted when she climbed the tree and came into contact with the cable. The defendants were held liable because, even if the plaintiff was a trespasser on the farmer's land, they should have foreseen the possibility that someone might climb the tree and they had not taken reasonable care to protect her from the cable. Of course, the fact that the plaintiff is a trespasser may affect the foreseeability of his presence at the site of danger, applying the ordinary principles of negligence.

Some doubt was cast upon the status of *Buckland* v *Guildford Gas Light &
Coke Co.* in *British Railways Board* v *Herrington* [1972] AC 877, 914, 929 (per
Lords Wilberforce and Pearson; cf. Lord Diplock at p. 943), where it was
suggested that the distinction between occupiers and non-occupiers in this
respect was unjustified. The OLA 1984 does not apply to non-occupiers,
however, and it might be thought a somewhat retrograde step if *British
Railways Board* v *Herrington* were to be applied to independent contractors,
thereby lowering the standard of care that they would owe to entrants.

6.3.2 Landlords

A landlord who grants a licence to occupy premises may retain sufficient
control to constitute himself an occupier for the purpose of the Occupiers'
Liability Acts 1957 and 1984 (*Wheat* v *E. Lacon & Co. Ltd* [1966] AC 552;
para. 6.1.1) but a landlord who lets premises on a tenancy will not be treated
as an occupier, except where he has retained control of the common parts of
a building in multiple occupation (*Jacobs* v *London County Council* [1950] AC
361).

At one time a landlord could not be liable in tort to an entrant in respect
of dangers that he had created before the letting. That immunity has now
been removed (see para. 6.3.3) but any liability arises from his capacity as the
creator of the danger, not from his status as a landlord. A 'bare landlord', i.e.,
a lessor who did not create the dangerous defect, does not owe a duty in
respect of the state of the premises at the time of the letting (*Cavalier* v *Pope*
[1906] AC 428; *Rimmer* v *Liverpool City Council* [1984] 1 All ER 930,
938–40; *McNerny* v *Lambeth London Borough Council* (1988) 21 HLR 188,
CA). The mere omission to put premises into a safe condition prior to the
letting will not render a landlord responsible in tort at common law
(cf. *Northern Sandblasting Pty Ltd* v *Harris* (1997) 71 ALJR 1428, in which
the High Court of Australia, by a 4:3 majority, held a landlord liable when
the tenant's child electrocuted herself due to a combination of defective earth
wiring that pre-dated the tenancy and shoddy kitchen wiring work by an
electrical contractor hired by the landlord that post-dated it. Two of the
majority judges, Brennan CJ and Gaudron J, held the landlord liable in
negligence for letting out the premises in a reasonably discoverable unsafe
state of repair. The other two majority judges, Toohey and McHugh JJ, held
the landlord personally liable for the electrical contractor's negligence after
letting, on which see para. 8.5.2. For comment on *Northern Sandblasting*, see
Feng (1998) 114 LQR 193.)

A landlord can be liable for both acts and omissions where they constitute
a failure to carry out his obligation to the tenant to maintain and repair the
premises. By s. 4(1) of the Defective Premises Act 1972, where the landlord
has an obligation to the tenant under the tenancy for the maintenance or
repair of premises, the landlord owes to all persons who might reasonably be
expected to be affected by defects in the state of the premises a duty to take
such care as is reasonable in all the circumstances to see that they are
reasonably safe (see Spencer [1975] CLJ 48, 71–8). The duty, which covers
both personal injury and damage to property, is owed if the landlord knows

or if he ought in all the circumstances to have known of the defect (Defective
Premises Act 1972, s. 4(2)). A landlord who has a power to enter and repair
is treated as if he were under an obligation to repair for the purposes of the
section, except that he will not owe a duty to the tenant in respect of the
tenant's breach of a repairing covenant (Defective Premises Act 1972,
s. 4(4)). This is an important extension of the landlord's potential liability
because there are many tenancies where the lessor is not under an obligation
to repair but reserves a power to enter and repair, either expressly or by
implication (e.g., in *Mint* v *Good* [1951] 1 KB 517 the Court of Appeal held
that a power to carry out structural repairs would be implied at common law
into a weekly tenancy of a dwelling; see now Landlord and Tenant Act 1985,
s. 11; and *Barrett* v *Lounova (1982) Ltd* [1989] 1 All ER 351—landlord's
obligation to repair outside of premises can be implied into a tenancy where
it is necessary to give business efficacy to the agreement; *McAuley* v *Bristol
City Council* [1992] 1 All ER 749, CA—in order to give business efficacy to
a weekly tenancy agreement a term may be implied into the agreement that
the landlord has the right to carry out repairs to remedy any defects in the
premises, including defects in the garden, which might expose the tenants or
visitors to the risk of injury, and the tenant could be required to grant the
landlord access for this purpose. This implied right to repair carries with it,
by virtue of s. 4(4), the duty imposed by s. 4(1)). The landlord's obligation
to repair may be express or implied and includes obligations imposed by
statute (Defective Premises Act 1972, s. 4(5)). The most important statutory
obligation is to be found in the Landlord and Tenant Act 1985, ss. 11 and
12 (as amended by the Housing Act 1988, s. 16), which require the lessor of
a dwelling-house for a term of less than seven years to keep in repair the
structure and exterior of the premises, together with the installations for the
supply of water, gas and electricity and for sanitation, space heating or water
heating. This obligation cannot be excluded except by application to the
county court (see also Landlord and Tenant Act 1985, s. 8—covenant that
dwelling let at a very low rent is fit for human habitation; and *Liverpool City
Council* v *Irwin* [1977] AC 239).

The duty created by s. 4 of the Defective Premises Act 1972 is a statutory
form of negligence which is quite extensive in its application. It cannot be
excluded or restricted by any term of an agreement (s. 6(3)), and it applies
to occupational licences granted by contract or by statute, as well as tenancies
(s. 4(6)). The duty is owed to all persons who might reasonably be expected
to be affected by defects in the premises. This must include not only entrants
(visitors and non-visitors alike, including the tenant) but also persons using
the highway and on adjoining land. Thus the duty overlaps with occupiers'
liability, public nuisance and private nuisance.

6.3.3 Builders and architects
At common law a builder who did not own the premises was liable in
negligence for injury caused by his defective work. Where the builder owned
the premises, however, but had sold or let them he was not liable in tort for
dangers he had created (*Bottomley* v *Bannister* [1932] 1 KB 458; *Otto* v *Bolton*

& *Norris* [1936] 2 KB 46). This rule was probably based on the privity of contract fallacy that a vendor or lessor's obligations sounded in contract, with which a duty in tort could not coexist. Section 3 of the Defective Premises Act 1972 removed this anomaly, providing that any duty of care arising from construction, repair, maintenance, demolition or any other work on or in relation to premises shall not be abated by the subsequent disposal of the premises. Coincidentally, at the same time the common law position was changed and a builder/vendor was said to owe a duty of care in negligence by the Court of Appeal in *Dutton* v *Bognor Regis Urban District Council* [1972] 1 QB 373, a decision approved by the House of Lords in *Anns* v *Merton London Borough Council* [1978] AC 728. In *Rimmer* v *Liverpool City Council* [1984] 1 All ER 930 the plaintiff was the tenant of a council flat which had been designed and built by the council. He tripped and put his hand through a thin, breakable glass panel which was found to be dangerous to occupants of the flat. The Court of Appeal held that a designer or builder of premises owes a duty of care to all persons who might reasonably be expected to be affected by the design or construction of the premises. This was a duty to take reasonable care to see that such persons would not suffer injury as a result of faults in the design or construction of the premises. The defendants owed this duty in their capacity as designers and builders of the flat. The only significance of their status as landlords was that it did *not* confer any immunity to the plaintiff's action.

Both *Dutton* v *Bognor Regis Urban District Council* and *Anns* v *Merton London Borough Council* have been overruled by the House of Lords in *Murphy* v *Brentwood District Council* [1990] 2 All ER 908 insofar as those cases held that a local authority could be liable in negligence for damage to the building itself which produces a present or imminent danger to the health or safety of the occupants as a result of failing to ensure that a builder complied with building regulations (see para. 2.2.4.2.2). Their lordships in *Murphy* v *Brentwood District Council* had no doubt, however, that a builder could be liable in negligence under the ordinary principles of *Donoghue* v *Stevenson* [1932] AC 562. Lord Keith commented ([1990] 2 All ER 908 at p. 917) that:

> In the case of a building, it is right to accept that a careless builder is liable, on the principle of *Donoghue* v *Stevenson*, where a latent defect results in physical injury to anyone, whether owner, occupier, visitor or passer-by, or to the property of any such person.

The important point here is that the defect must normally be latent, as was the case in *Donoghue* v *Stevenson*, and the damage must be personal injury or damage to property other than the building itself (damage to the building itself is regarded as economic loss which is not recoverable: see para. 2.2.4.2.2). Once the occupier is aware of the extent of the defect, he is in the position of a person who is injured through consuming or using a product which he knows to be defective, who has no remedy against the manufacturer (*Murphy* v *Brentwood District Council* [1990] 2 All ER 908, 917; see paras 10.1.3 and 10.1.4). If he continues to use a building which he knows to be dangerous with the result that visitors to the premises are injured, he will be liable in his capacity as occupier, but logically the builder would not be responsible. In *Targett* v *Torfaen Borough Council* [1992] 3 All ER 27, however, the Court of Appeal distinguished *Murphy* on the ground that *Murphy* was concerned with a claim to recover the cost of making good a defective product which had not yet caused any physical injury to persons or damage to other property. In *Targett* the plaintiff was the tenant of a council house designed and built by the defendants. He sustained personal injuries when he fell down a flight of exterior steps which had no handrail and were unlit. The Court of Appeal upheld the trial judge's finding that the defendants were liable for the injury attributable to the defective steps, subject to a finding of 25% contributory negligence, applying *Rimmer* v *Liverpool City Council*. *Rimmer*, which had not been cited in *Murphy*, had not been impliedly overruled. Moreover, it was not invariably true to say that once the plaintiff becomes aware of a potential danger there could be no liability under *Donoghue* v *Stevenson*. In *Rimmer* the plaintiff knew that the glass panel was dangerously thin before the accident; indeed, he had complained about the danger to the landlord. Nonetheless, it was held that an opportunity for inspection of a dangerous defect would not exonerate the defendant unless the plaintiff was free to remove or avoid the danger in the sense that it was reasonable to expect him to do so, and unreasonable for him to run the risk of being injured by the danger. Similarly, in *Targett* it was not considered reasonable to expect the plaintiff to remove or avoid the danger (e.g. by leaving the house or providing a handrail or fixed lighting himself), nor was it unreasonable for him to run the risk of being injured by the danger. Sir Donald Nicholls V-C commented (at p. 37) that:

> . . . knowledge of the existence of a danger does not always enable a person to avoid that danger. In simple cases it does. In other cases, especially where buildings are concerned, it would be absolutely unrealistic to suggest that a person can always take steps to avoid a danger once he knows of its existence, and that if he does not do so he is the author of his own misfortune. Here, as elsewhere, the law seeks to be realistic.

The combined effect of *Murphy* and *Targett* would seem to be that a builder is not liable in negligence for the cost of removing a patently dangerous defect, but he will be liable for personal injuries or damage to other property caused by that defect if it is unreasonable to have expected the occupier to remove the danger and not unreasonable for the plaintiff (whether the occupier himself or a visitor) to run the risk of injury by the danger.

In *Murphy* v *Brentwood District Council* counsel for the local authority conceded that where a local authority approved defective plans or inspected defective foundations but negligently failed to discover the defect, its potential liability in tort would be coextensive with that of the builder, so that if a plaintiff sustained personal injury or damage to property (other than the defective building itself) the authority could be liable for that damage if it was caused by a latent defect attributable to a failure to secure compliance with the building regulations. This point was specifically reserved by their Lordships, however, for future consideration. The question arose for consideration in *Tesco Stores Ltd* v *Wards Construction (Investment) Ltd* (1995) 76 BLR 94 in which there was a fire at a new shopping centre. The plaintiffs alleged that the speed of the spread of the fire was caused by defects in the design and construction of the development. Proceedings were issued against, *inter alia*, the local authority, alleging that the local authority was in breach of a duty owed to the plaintiffs in respect of its approval of design drawings and inspection of the construction to ensure that proper fire prevention precautions were taken and that the building regulations were complied with. In the High Court it was held that the local authority did not owe a duty of care with respect to damage to property. The building regulations were concerned with protecting the health, safety and welfare of persons, not the protection of property or chattels, and therefore the local authority owed no common law duty of care to avoid causing loss of or damage to property of the owners or occupiers. Moreover, even if the purpose of the building regulations was to avoid damage to property it was not fair, just or reasonable to impose a duty of care on the local authority (applying *Marc Rich & Co.* v *Bishop Rock Marine Co. Ltd* [1995] 3 All ER 307). The courts do not normally distinguish between personal injuries and physical damage to property—if physical damage is foreseeable it usually matters not that the damage was to property rather than persons (though the OLA 1984 provides a statutory precedent for distinguishing injury to persons and injury to property). As counsel for the plaintiffs pointed out, on this approach the defendants' liability will depend upon the quite unpredictable consequences of a fire. But the judge, Mr Recorder Mauleverer QC, was persuaded that the local authority's common law duty of care, if any, arose in the context of the statutory framework, i.e., the building regulations, and was limited by the purpose of the regulations. The question of whether the local authority owed a duty with respect to personal injuries or death was left open. Even if a duty in respect of physical damage to property owed by the local authority is subsequently held to exist (e.g., by Court of Appeal) it is possible that it would not be owed to an owner-occupier who was himself in breach of the building regulations, since a local authority can reasonably expect an owner who is embarking on a building project to obtain independent advice and assistance to enable him to comply with the building regulations and to carry out the job properly, and it is not reasonable to expect the local authority to assume this role (*Peabody Donation Fund* v *Sir Lindsay Parkinson & Co. Ltd* [1984] 3 All ER 529; *Richardson* v *West Lindsey District Council* [1990] 1 All ER 296).

A plaintiff wishing to claim in respect of damage to the building itself may have three options. First, where the damage to the building is caused by the negligence of a subcontractor in installing some feature of the building which is not integral to its structure, such as defective wiring or a defective boiler, the owner may succeed under the ordinary principles of *Donoghue* v *Stevenson* provided the building can be characterised as 'other property', i.e., distinct from the defective item (*Murphy* v *Brentwood District Council* [1990] 2 All ER 908, 922, 928, 942; see para. 2.2.4.2.2). Thus, in *Jacobs* v *Morton* (1994) 72

BLR 92 the plaintiffs were successful in bringing a piled raft foundation within the 'complex structure' exception. The foundation had been constructed to remedy defects in the original foundations, but was itself defective, causing further damage to the property which was characterised as (recoverable) physical damage rather than (irrecoverable) economic loss. Secondly, the builder may be subject to an action for breach of statutory duty. The Building Act 1984, s. 38, provides that breach of a duty imposed by the building regulations shall be actionable as a breach of statutory duty (re-enacting the Health and Safety at Work etc. Act 1974, s. 71), but the section has not yet been brought into force. In *Anns* Lord Wilberforce suggested that in these circumstances there might be an action at common law for breach of statutory duty, but this was always a matter of some uncertainty, and the dictum may not have survived the overruling of *Anns* (see the comments of Lord Oliver in *D & F Estates Ltd* v *Church Commissioners for England* [1988] 2 All ER 992; Wallace (1989) 105 LQR 46, 72–74; *Dugdale and Stanton*, para. 11.11; Stanton (1986) 2 PN 13).

Finally, the builder may be liable under s. 1 of the Defective Premises Act 1972 which provides that a person taking on work for or in connection with the provision of a dwelling owes a duty to see that the work is done in a workmanlike or professional manner, and with proper materials, so that as regards that work the dwelling will be fit for habitation when completed (see *Smith* v *Drumm* [1996] EGCS 192—converted flat without gas or electricity was not 'fit for habitation'). The duty applies to the construction, conversion or enlargement of a dwelling (not industrial or other premises), and is owed by any person taking on the work, for example, the builder, architect, engineer, surveyor (though possibly not a local authority surveyor) and subcontractors. It applies as much to a failure to carry out necessary remedial work as to the carrying out of the work badly (*Andrews* v *Schooling* [1991] 3 All ER 723), although it has been held that the duty does not apply to rectification of an existing dwelling, as opposed to the creation of a new dwelling (*Jacobs* v *Morton* (1994) 72 BLR 92, 105). The duty is owed to the person who orders the work and every person who subsequently acquires an interest in the dwelling. As for causation, the Court of Appeal in *Bayoumi* v *Protim Services Ltd* [1996] EGCS 187 confirmed that the correct test is whether the defendant's breach of the section is a significant cause of or factor in the dwelling's unfitness. It need not be the sole cause. In the same case, the Court of Appeal also confirmed the proper measure of damages under the Act as all losses naturally consequent upon the breach, not merely the cost of repair or the diminution in value. The obligations imposed by the section are stricter than in negligence, essentially extending the implied warranties in a contract to build a house to subsequent purchasers. This clearly applies to defects in quality. There are two significant drawbacks, however, to this statutory obligation. First, it does not apply to a dwelling covered by an approved scheme which confers a remedy on the owner. For many years the National House Building Council insurance scheme, which applies to the majority of new dwellings, was an approved scheme, with the result that s. 1 was largely confined to conversions and extensions. It may be, however, that the NHBC scheme is no longer approved for this purpose (see Wallace (1991) 107 LQR 228, 243). Secondly, the limitation period is six years from the time when the building was complete. In negligence the period runs from the date of the damage, which may be long after the building was completed, and may be extended where the damage was latent (see generally Spencer [1974] CLJ 307, who points out in an addendum [1975] CLJ 48 that if the action for breach of statutory duty in respect of breach of the building regulations were to be brought into effect, s. 1 would be largely redundant).

SEVEN
Nuisance

Nuisances are divided into private nuisance and public nuisance. Although they share the same name, and sometimes the same facts can produce liability in both private and public nuisance, the two actions are conceptually distinct. Private nuisance regulates unreasonable interference with an occupier's use or enjoyment of his rights over his land. The law seeks to draw a balance between the legitimate but conflicting interests of landowners—the right of an occupier to use his land as he chooses and the right of his neighbour not to have his use of land interfered with. The litigants are usually 'neighbours' in the popular sense of the word. Public nuisance is a crime which protects certain public rights, principally the right to an unobstructed and safe use of the highway. It becomes actionable in tort only if the plaintiff suffers 'particular damage' over and above the damage suffered by the public generally (see Spencer [1989] CLJ 55 arguing that public nuisance should be abolished).

'Reasonableness' is a term that crops up frequently in relation to both private and public nuisance, but the word is not necessarily used in the same sense as it is used in the tort of negligence. In private nuisance, for example, the issue is not whether the defendant's conduct has fallen below the standard of the reasonable man, but whether the interference with the plaintiff's use or enjoyment of his rights over his land is unreasonable bearing in mind the nature of the defendant's activity. This can be translated into the question: was the defendant's *use* of land reasonable? The focus shifts from the quality of the defendant's act, in negligence (was it careless?), to the nature of the plaintiff's damage and the reasonableness of the defendant's *activity*, in nuisance (although the distinction between activities and acts may be difficult to draw at times). Carelessness may be relevant to the reasonableness of the defendant's activity, but not necessarily so. An activity which is carried on with all reasonable precautions to prevent harm to others may nonetheless interfere unreasonably with the plaintiff's rights. This is also true of public nuisance where an unreasonable user of the highway can constitute a

nuisance even where there is no foreseeable risk of harm to others (para. 7.2.5). The 'balancing exercise' which takes place in the tort of negligence (see particularly chapter 3) takes a different form in nuisance. In negligence the court will look at the defendant's behaviour and measure it against his duty, whereas in nuisance the court will look at the damage and measure it against the plaintiff's right. Another way of putting this is to say that liability in negligence is conduct-based whereas liability in nuisance (particularly for amenity nuisance such as noise or smell) is fairness-based (see Cane (1982) 2 OJLS 30; para. 7.1.8). (For an interesting account of how the nature of the balancing exercise altered in response to the industrial revolution see McLaren (1983) 3 OJLS 155.)

It is important to note that this conduct/fairness dichotomy has emerged as a means of distinguishing negligence and nuisance *within* the framework of the law of obligations. In the light of the House of Lords' landmark decision in *Hunter* v *Canary Wharf Ltd* [1997] 2 All ER 426 (to deny actions in private nuisance to spouses and children of tenants who complained of dust and poor television reception caused by the erection of a large building nearby), it is now legitimate to question whether private nuisance, at least, better occupies a place *outside* that framework altogether, and whether, as Cane has speculated, it might be 'more properly viewed as an adjunct to the law of property . . .?' ((1997) 113 LQR 515; for other comment on *Hunter* in the House of Lords, see Hedley [1997] 3 Web JCLI; Oliphant (1998) 6 Tort L Rev 21; O'Sullivan [1997] CLJ 483; see paras 7.1.1 and 7.1.4). This would in turn carry more than mere classifactory signifance. In reiterating the principle that private nuisance was fundamentally 'a tort against land' (per Lord Hoffmann, at p. 458) and, as a consequence, insisting that a plaintiff must both possess a recognisable proprietary interest in the land affected and establish damage with a similarly proprietary quality (the latter pronouncements probably being *obiter*—para. 7.1.1), their Lordships in *Hunter* have probably put the brakes on a period in which the tort had expanded into the wider personal protection of the plaintiff.

As with liability under the Occupiers' Liability Acts 1957 and 1984, the question to ask in order to determine the cause of action is: where did the damage occur? If it occurred on the defendant's premises then one of the Occupiers' Liability Acts will be appropriate (chapter 6). If it occurred on the highway the action will be in public nuisance, provided the damage is attributable to circumstances that historically have been characterised as public nuisances (para. 7.2.3). If the damage occurs on the plaintiff's premises the action is private nuisance. (For the distinction between *private* nuisance and trespass to land see para. 11.1.3.) The tort of negligence cuts across all these classifications and can overlap with nuisance. Traditionally, the nature of the relationship between negligence and nuisance has been one of the most difficult questions in the law of tort (paras 7.1.8 and 7.2.5). *Hunter*, however, may have gone some way to 'unblurring the boundaries of nuisance' (Oliphant, op. cit.), particularly where negligence is concerned. In reasserting the rule that private nuisance plaintiffs must establish a qualifying proprietary interest in the land affected, and linking that *ratio* to strong *obiter* pronouncements as to the corresponding need for qualifying damage to a proprietary interest, *Hunter* seems to have effected a stricter demarcation between the torts than before, the necessary corollary of its limitations being that negligence, and not private nuisance, is the proper place for most personal injury actions (see paras 7.1.1 and 7.1.4). Nuisance can overlap with liability under the rule in *Rylands* v *Fletcher* (this is well-illustrated by *Halsey* v *Esso Petroleum Co. Ltd* [1961] 2 All ER 145, para. 7.2.3.1, *Ellison* v *Ministry of Defence* (1997) 81 BLR 101, paras 7.1.2.1, 8.1.2 and 8.1.4, and *Graham and Graham* v *ReChem International Ltd* [1996] Env LR 158, para. 8.1.4). Indeed, in *Cambridge Water Co.* v *Eastern Counties Leather plc* [1994] 2 WLR 53 the House of Lords considered that the rule in *Rylands* v *Fletcher* was merely a species of liability in nuisance, extended to cases of isolated escape.

7.1 PRIVATE NUISANCE

7.1.1 Definition and scope

A judicially approved definition of private nuisance is 'an unlawful interference with a person's use or enjoyment of land, or some right over, or in connection with it' (*Winfield and Jolowicz,* p. 404). The word 'unlawful' is crucial to this definition because it indicates that not all interferences with another's enjoyment of land will be actionable. It is applied in an *ex post facto* manner, however, since the interference normally derives its unlawful nature from the fact that it is held to be a nuisance. Most of the activities that give rise to claims in nuisance are, in themselves, perfectly lawful. It is only when the activity interferes with another's enjoyment of land to such a degree as to be an unreasonable interference that it will be regarded as a nuisance, and thereby 'unlawful'.

In *Sedleigh-Denfield* v *O'Callaghan* [1940] AC 880 Lord Wright commented (at p. 903) that: 'The forms which nuisance may take are protean. Certain classifications are possible, but many reported cases are no more than illustrations of particular matters of fact which have been held to be nuisances'. Examples of the types of interference that have been held to amount to a nuisance include:

(a)   Encroachment on the plaintiff's land, e.g., by tree branches or roots (*Smith* v *Giddy* [1904] 2 KB 448; *Davey* v *Harrow Corporation* [1958] 1 QB 60).

(b)   Physical damage to the plaintiff's land or property on it, e.g., by flooding (*Sedleigh-Denfield* v *O'Callaghan* [1940] AC 880), vibration (*Hoare & Co.* v *McAlpine* [1923] 1 Ch 167), collapse of neighbouring buildings (*Wringe* v *Cohen* [1940] 1 KB 229), or noxious fumes which damage vegetation (*St Helens Smelting Co.* v *Tipping* (1865) 11 HL Cas 642).

(c)   Interference with an easement, such as obstructing a private right of way.

(d)   Interference with the plaintiff's comfort or convenience, e.g., through smells (*Bone* v *Seal* [1975] 1 All ER 787), dust (*Matania* v *National Provincial Bank Ltd* [1936] 2 All ER 633), vibration, noise (*Halsey* v *Esso Petroleum Co.*

Ltd [1961] 2 All ER 145; *Leeman* v *Montagu* [1936] 2 All ER 1677), using premises as a brothel (*Thompson-Schwab* v *Costaki* [1956] 1 WLR 335) or a sex shop (*Laws* v *Florinplace Ltd* [1981] 1 All ER 659).

The House of Lords in *Hunter* v *Canary Wharf* may have placed some limits on this relatively unstructured approach to private nuisance, by attempting to shape the tort according to more formal demarcations, particularly as to *who* can claim (where their Lordships' pronouncements are part of the *ratio* of the case—para. 7.1.4) and, of equal importance, as to precisely *what* such plaintiffs can sue for (where their pronouncements may be treated as *obiter*). In that latter regard, the somewhat ominous starting point (for plaintiffs) is Lord Hoffmann's remark in *Hunter* that, in cases of nuisances such as those in (d) above, that are 'productive of sensible discomfort', the private nuisance action does 'not constitute a separate tort of causing discomfort to *people*, but [it is] merely part of the single tort of causing injury to *land*' (p. 452, emphasis added). This is, in part, a reference to the distinction (para. 7.1.2) between nuisances that cause material injury to the property (para. 7.1.2.1) (such as those in (b) above, e.g. flooding) and those (as in (d) above, e.g. smells) that affect its enjoyment (often termed 'sensible', 'intangible' or 'amenity' damage; para. 7.1.2.2). This is a distinction conventionally drawn so as to except the former class of nuisances from the 'locality test' (para. 7.1.2.1), and it is apparent that Lord Hoffmann in *Hunter* was keen to curb the potential for that division to be developed more generally into one between *property* and *personal* damage. His general caution that nuisance is fundamentally a tort against land may, however, be of greater significance than the fact that it afforded him the opportunity to assert that 'sensible' damage is actionable because it is actually a species of property damage. Indeed, employing this particular line of reasoning in *Hunter* in the specific context of actionable damage may prove to be as significant a restraint on the role of the private nuisance action as their Lordships' corresponding decision in that case to deny private nuisance actions to those without a legally recognisable interest in the land affected (para. 7.1.4). This is to recognise that Lord Hoffmann's pronouncement also encompasses a wider concern, voiced some time earlier by Professor Newark, that nuisance might have had a tendency to expand beyond its intended boundaries, in particular by a failure by courts to appreciate that private nuisance was fundamentally 'a tort to land' which should not be available as a remedy for personal injury ((1949) 65 LQR 480; cited, in the context of *Hunter*, by Oliphant (1998) 6 Tort L Rev 21; for criticism of Newark see para. 7.2.5). In *Hunter*, there is express approval of Newark's assertions, which Lord Goff suggested ought to be 'nailed to the doors of the law courts and defended against all comers' (p. 435). The effect of their Lordships' adoption of this rationale in the context of actionable damage would be that, for the purposes of identifying that damage, the court's initial and axiomatic focus ought to be on the land itself, rather than on the land owner, Lord Hoffmann expressly rejecting the notion that 'the plaintiff's interest in the land becomes no more than a qualifying condition or a springboard which entitles him to sue for injury to himself' (p. 451). In short, on this reasoning, in private nuisance the land owner claims, in effect, on behalf of his land rather than his person, *whichever* side of the material damage/amenity divide his case happens to fall on. As such, he must be able to identify a means by which the land has been affected, whether by way of a diminution in its capital value or *its* amenity (as opposed simply to that of its occupier).

Such principles and distinctions are relatively easy to state, but they barely stand up to scrutiny and would prove difficult to apply (for extensive criticism and comment see Cane (1997) 113 LQR 515; Hedley [1997] 3 Web JCLI; Oliphant (1998) 6 Tort L Rev 21; O'Sullivan [1997] CLJ 483). What is clear is that they are essentially exclusionary in nature and would demand much of would-be private nuisance plaintiffs in all but the most clear-cut of material property interference cases (such as flooding). They may even be employed to exclude personal injury and damage to the landowner's personal property from the ambit of private nuisance altogether. In such cases, the inevitable arguments would be that such damage would not affect the capital value of the land and that the undoubted 'inconvenience' is only as a result of the plaintiff's coincidental presence on the land rather than being the product of some harm to the land's utility, which would, presumably (but somewhat curiously), be actionable whether the plaintiff is present or not. Indeed, Lord Lloyd and Lord Hoffmann stated unequivocally in *Hunter* that an action could not lie in private nuisance for personal injury, though the other judges did not go that far (Lord Cooke pointedly remarking that it would be anomalous for personal injuries to be recoverable in public but not private nuisance—p. 463). In *Hunter*, the express retention within the ambit of the private nuisance action of the 'productive of sensible discomfort' cases is, by contrast, on the basis that their inconvenience damages the *property*'s utility in that 'persons upon it are *liable to* suffer inconvenience, annoyance or illness' (p. 452, per Lord Hoffmann, emphasis added).

Diminution in the value of the land and damage to its utility may thus provide the theoretical basis for identifying and quantifying allowable damage in private nuisance, but their potential, post-*Hunter*, to exclude most personal injury (and personal property damage) cases and to include those involving 'sensible' damage seems to rest on an unrealistic and unduly harsh distinction between person and property, or, more precisely, the no less strained distinction between the *property*'s provision of enjoyment and a *person*'s enjoyment while on the property. It takes little to expose the fictions upon which these distinctions are based. For instance, it is unlikely that a landowner would appreciate that bad smells actually harm his land first and him second, and that other injuries to his person or personal property might not. Lord Hoffmann's attempts (p. 451) to explain away what he admits to be a fiction that the land might, in the former situation, suffer 'sensible' injury, by the assertion that 'its utility has been diminished by the existence of the nuisance', may be designed to preserve the necessary proprietary basis for such claims, but it succeeds more as an acknowledgement that the only realistic basis for them is their essentially personal impact. Diminution in value as a basis for quantification may assist in determining initial actionability in amenity cases and non-actionability in other personal harm situations, but this does not make the distinction which this quantification is meant to support any more real. Moreover, Lord Hoffmann's assertion (p. 451) that he would quantify damage in the case of a transitory amenity nuisance by reference to the diminution in value during the period for which the nuisance persists, even though the property's value recovers and is thus ultimately unaffected, serves only to compound the artificiality.

The fragility of such distinctions is what makes their Lordships' pronouncements on qualifying damage in *Hunter* both confusing and potentially vulnerable. Quite simply, by asserting that amenity claims are still actionable in private nuisance *only because* they have the *necessary* proprietary quality, their Lordships in *Hunter* cannot have it both ways should such claims' real foundation be found to lie elsewhere. In that event, either the strictness of the proprietary criterion is unnecessary (as well as unrealistic) in such cases, which would re-introduce into the ambit of the private nuisance action the other personal claims that their Lordships in *Hunter* were keen to exclude, or it is necessary and they are excluded too. Equally, it should be recognised that the neatness that might be achieved by consigning the excluded personal injury and personal property cases to other torts, such as negligence, might, for the plaintiff, be at the expense of his chances of establishing liability, negligence, for instance, requiring only reasonable care whereas nuisance rests on the more plaintiff-friendly concept of reasonable user.

It may be that some of the potential harshness of the *Hunter* pronouncements on damage might be mitigated if they came to be regarded as *obiter*, the case neither involving personal injury nor conventional sensible damage, but rather a claim for interference with television reception. Their Lordships' decision and reasoning on the question of whether such damage could be the subject of a claim in private nuisance, however, is largely consistent with their overall assessment of the modern law of private nuisance as being concerned with interference with the enjoyment of property and not person, thus making it naturally antipathetic to claims for damage that lack adequate property characteristics. In *Hunter*, the House of Lords held unanimously that an action did not lie in private nuisance for interference with television reception which had been caused by the erection of a large building. Though it is apparent that the decision does not rule out the possibility that a future television reception case might qualify as a private nuisance action, the circumstances in which it might do so seem extremely limited, with their Lordships' conclusions and reasoning on the point by no means universal. Lord Goff (at p. 431), for instance, expressly refused to adopt the dictum of Buckley J in *Bridlington Relay Ltd* v *Yorkshire Electricity Board* [1965] 1 All ER 264 to the effect that television viewing was purely recreational, and preferred to recognise that nowadays 'television transcends the function of mere entertainment' and that interference with it has been held capable of protection through nuisance in some circumstances in Canada (*Nor-Video Services Ltd* v *Ontario Hydro* (1978) 84 DLR (3d) 221, 231). From the rest of his speech, however, and that of Lord Lloyd, it seems that such concessions might, at best, serve only to allow the potential for a television interference claim where, as in *Bridlington* itself (electrical interference with television reception caused by the activities of the defendant electricity board), the television interference is caused other than by the simple presence of a building (where, according to their Lordships, the building owner's freedom to build on his land would prevail). Lord Hoffmann (p. 453) expressly left the *Bridlington* point open, but, together with Lord Hope, was more categorical as to the unavailability of a private nuisance action in the case of a claim for television interference caused by the simple presence of a neighbouring building. Unlike Lord Goff and Lord Lloyd, Lord Hoffmann (p. 454) and Lord Hope (p. 470) did not see such a case as involving an exercise of balancing competing property rights, but rather as one in which the right to claim in nuisance could never arise. They reasoned that, because a right to unaffected television reception could not be acquired by long usage (prescription), it was not invested with the necessary proprietary quality for an interference with it to be actionable in private nuisance. Lord Cooke's suggested exceptions to *Hunter's* presumption of non-actionability in building-induced television interference cases (malice and breach of planning law) seem more broadly based than the activity-dependent approach favoured by Lord Goff and Lord Hoffmann. It may prove unwise, however, for distressed television viewers in future cases to rely too heavily on Lord Cooke's speech, given that its underlying reasoning on the damage issue differs fundamentally from that of the other judges in the case. For, as Cane (op. cit.) has observed, where the majority all took a decidedly 'property-based' view of nuisance (an 'interference with rights in land'—Cane, op. cit.) and decided (to various degrees of exclusion) that, as a general rule, television interference claims would not be actionable *ab initio* for want of the necessary proprietary characteristics, Lord Cooke started from the proposition that private nuisance remains traditionally 'obligation-based' (an obligation 'not to cause injury to others in their use and enjoyment of land'—Cane, op. cit.) such that interference by a building with television reception would potentially be actionable as a private nuisance, though most cases (save where malice or breach of planning law could be identified) would fall at the 'reasonable user' hurdle.

The extent to which Lord Cooke's approach is out of line with that of the other judges in *Hunter* on the property-based reasoning that may serve to exclude most personal injury and damage to personal property cases from the ambit of private nuisance, becomes even clearer when seen in the context of the *locus standi* question also considered in the case (para. 7.1.4). On this, the majority maintained their strict property-based approach to the tort—the harm is, first and foremost, to the land. For them, the necessary corollary of this was that only those with a recognisable interest in the land thus affected could claim in private nuisance. Lord Cooke dissented, his obligation-based approach (the gist of which being that harm is occasioned primarily to the land user) not demanding such a limitation. It was, notably though, the majority's findings on *locus standi* that were employed in *Hunter* to overrule the Court of Appeal's earlier decision in *Khorasandjian* v *Bush* [1993] 3 All ER 669 to allow a plaintiff an action in private nuisance even though she did not have a proprietary interest. Moreover, even if she had had such an

interest, a decision to have then granted her a cause of action in private
nuisance would have been extremely vulnerable. This is because the plaintiff
in that case claimed in relation to harassment from persistent telephone calls.
Such a claim would not sit well with the majority's general approach in
Hunter to private nuisance, and their pronouncements on damage in particular. As such, post-*Hunter*, it would probably be held to lack the necessary
proprietary quality and even to exemplify the excess that Lord Hoffmann
sought to curb with his reference to the property-based heritage of *both* sides
of the material damage/amenity damage divide and his caution that private
nuisance should not be developed as a means of protecting essentially
personal interests, which he considered are better dealt with elsewhere (e.g.,
the Protection from Harassment Act 1997—see paras 7.1.4 and 12.2). By
contrast, Lord Cooke's express willingness to allow such a claim to be
mounted in private nuisance, as a breach of an obligation not to injure a land
user, may illustrate his liberal approach to the tort's capacity to develop in
parallel with other causes of action (p. 459), but it is undoubtedly out of line
with the concern for stricter demarcations preferred by the majority.

7.1.2   Constituents of liability

Damage to the plaintiff's use or enjoyment of his rights over his land is the
gist of an action in private nuisance. Accordingly, there is no cause of action
in respect of a present risk of potential future damage (see, e.g., *Midland Bank
v Bardgrove Property Services* [1992] 37 EG 126). It is often said that the law
of nuisance is concerned with achieving a balance between the competing
claims of neighbours to use their property as they see fit, and that an occupier
is entitled to reasonable comfort in his use of land but no more. However, a
distinction is drawn between different forms of damage when assessing what
that balance should be. This is the distinction referred to above (para. 7.1.1)
between physical damage to property such as pollution damage to crops or
structural damage by vibration, on the one hand, and personal discomfort
attributable to offensive smells or excessive noise (intangible or amenity
damage), on the other.

7.1.2.1   Physical damage

In *St Helens Smelting Co. v Tipping* (1865) 11
HL Cas 642 the plaintiff's estate was located in a manufacturing area. Fumes
from a copper smelting works damaged the trees on the estate. In the House
of Lords, Lord Westbury differentiated between physical damage and intangible damage. One should not expect to breathe the clean air of the Lake
District in an industrial town such as St Helens, and so in the case of amenity
damage the degree of the interference has to be measured against the
surrounding circumstances, particularly the nature of the locality. Where the
nuisance causes physical damage to property, however, the nature of the
locality is irrelevant. An occupier is entitled to expect protection from
physical damage no matter where he lives. This suggests that almost any
amount of physical damage would suffice for liability in nuisance, subject to
the *de minimis* principle. The balancing exercise which is undertaken for the
purpose of determining whether the defendant's user of land was reasonable

simply does not take place where the damage is physical. An alternative interpretation is that the existence of physical damage normally tips the balance irretrievably in the plaintiff's favour (see Ogus and Richardson [1977] CLJ 284, 297). Neither proposition, of course, amounts to an assertion that the defendant's use of land in such cases can never be reasonable, but, realistically, robbed of the opportunities afforded by the locality test and the balancing exercise (wholly or partially), such a possibility is remote at best (for a rare instance where reasonable use appeared to be found in such a case see *Ellison* v *Ministry of Defence* (1997) 81 BLR 101 below and paras 8.1.2 and 8.1.4). Moreover, there are, anyway, exceptions where elements of the balancing exercise traditionally employed only (or mainly) in cases of intangible damage are also relevant in cases of material physical damage. For instance, the abnormal sensitivity of the plaintiff's property to physical damage will be taken into account, and in cases where liability depends upon the proof of negligence the balancing involved in setting the standard of reasonable care will be relevant (see paras 7.1.3.2, 7.1.3.6 and 7.1.3.7).

One possible justification for this approach is to say that the damage to the plaintiff's property was part of the cost of producing copper. If the plaintiff had to bear that cost then copper would be over-produced, because its price would not reflect its true social cost. The solution is to make the defendant 'internalise' this external cost by requiring him to compensate the plaintiff. This sort of reasoning can be traced back to the 19th century (see *Powell* v *Fall* (1880) 5 QBD 597, 601 per Bramwell B), but the Canadian case of *Schenck* v *Province of Ontario* (1982) 131 DLR (3d) 310 provides a modern example. The plaintiff complained that his fruit orchards had been partially destroyed by the application of salt to an adjacent highway during the winter months. From the point of view of the highway authority the use of salt in the interests of public safety on the highway was perfectly reasonable. The damage was simply an unfortunate incident of life in a modern society, the defendants argued. The High Court of Ontario held that this type of interference with the plaintiff's proprietary rights was not comparable to the ordinary interferences associated with highways, such as noise, dust or exhaust fumes. The damage to the orchards was in reality a cost of highway maintenance, and the burden imposed on fruit farmers by the public (via the highway authority) for their own benefit should be borne by the public generally, not by fruit farmers.

The problem with this reasoning is that it oversimplifies the question of causation. The damage to the orchards was not solely the product of the defendants' land use, but was the result of the conflict between the competing uses as an orchard and a highway. If the plaintiff happened to use his property for another purpose which would have been unaffected by salt (industrial use, for example), there would have been no damage and therefore no external cost attributable to the use of salt. So it would be equally true to say that fruit farmers impose the cost of maintaining their particular use of land (i.e., as an orchard) on the public, in the form of either compensation to farmers or more road accidents if the use of salt is stopped. The point becomes more obvious when it is combined with the rule that the fact that the plaintiff 'came to the nuisance' is no defence (para. 7.1.6.4.1). If the plaintiff had changed his land use from industrial to agricultural the 'cost of highway maintenance' attributable to salt would only then have become apparent. Who 'caused' the damage in these circumstances? Yet the plaintiff would still succeed in private nuisance (for an example of salt damage creating liability in public nuisance see *Ogston* v *Aberdeen District Tramways Co.* [1897] AC 111).

The distinction drawn between physical damage and personal discomfort, and the general refusal to engage in a balancing exercise in the case of physical harm, can be criticised (Ogus and Richardson [1977] CLJ 284, 299; *Buckley*, pp. 8–9; if an intangible nuisance reduces the value of the premises without physically damaging the building, is this damage to property or personal inconvenience?) but it has been reaffirmed on many occasions by the courts. If justification is required it can be found in the view that it sets a minimum standard for the protection of proprietary rights which is comparatively certain in its application. This is not the case where liability turns upon questions of degree. On the other hand, it has been argued that physical harm should fall under the remit of the tort of negligence, leaving private nuisance to deal with non-physical interference with an occupier's enjoyment of land (Gearty [1989] CLJ 214). This would undoubtedly make private nuisance a logically 'neater' tort, at the possible expense of reducing protection for occupiers who would then have to prove negligence in all, rather than, as at present, some cases of physical damage.

Even if a distinction between physical and amenity damage does operate so as to allow a balancing exercise and the locality test in the latter case only, *Ellison* v *Ministry of Defence* (1997) 81 BLR 101 (see also paras 8.1.2 and 8.1.4) indicates that it is unsafe to assume that use of land that causes physical damage cannot be found to be reasonable. *Ellison* concerned claims in nuisance and under the rule in *Rylands* v *Fletcher* for flooding to the plaintiffs' land caused by the defendants' construction of bulk fuel installations on their land (an airfield). The plaintiffs lost, for two main reasons. First, because the damage was not foreseeable (which, therefore, under *Cambridge Water Co.* v *Eastern Counties Leather plc* [1994] 2 WLR 53, put paid to the claims in nuisance and under *Rylands* v *Fletcher*; see paras 7.1.5.1, 7.1.8 and 8.1) and, secondly, because the flooding was by water (rainwater) which had accumulated naturally (and not, as required under *Rylands* v *Fletcher*, artificially) on the defendants' land. The court also considered, *obiter*, that the defendants' construction work did not amount to a non-natural user of the land for the purposes of liability under *Rylands* v *Fletcher*, in that there was nothing extraordinary about it to make it anything other than a necessary adjunct to its ordinary use as an airfield. Interestingly, while in no way formally disregarding the general proposition that an activity which causes foreseeable physical damage to another's land should be difficult to justify as a 'reasonable use' for the purposes of private nuisance, the court nonetheless considered that, in the context of the parallel nuisance action, the defendants' construction works did amount to a 'reasonable use' of the land. This was, again, said to be because they were a necessary part of the use of the land as an airfield, which, itself, was not challenged as an unreasonable use. Though the nuisance action had already, strictly, been disposed of by the court's other findings on foreseeability, the court's willingness to countenance a finding of reasonable use in such circumstances is still remarkable, not the least for the way in which the supporting rationale appeared to equate, on the particular facts at least, reasonable use in nuisance with natural user under *Rylands* v *Fletcher*. This would be an interesting, but surely unintended, consequence of the House of Lords' assertion in *Cambridge Water* that *Rylands* v *Fletcher* liability was merely a species of liability in nuisance. There may be many instances where a defendant's physically damaging activity might be part of the ordinary functioning of their property. Moreover, it seems equally absurd to suggest that an activity that was not a natural and ordinary use of land (such as the industrial chemical process described by Lord Goff in *Cambridge Water*) would thereby become an unreasonable user, for this would be to declare unreasonable many modern industrial processes that planning and other regulatory authorities must presumably have considered reasonable (see Layard (1997) 113 LQR 254, commenting on *Graham and Graham* v *ReChem* [1996] Env LR 158, para. 8.1.4). As such, it is submitted that the dictum in *Ellison* as to reasonable use is either wrong, *obiter* or relevant only in the context of a case (like *Ellison*) where nuisance and *Rylands* v *Fletcher* liability overlap.

7.1.2.2 Interference with enjoyment of land   Where the plaintiff complains of an interference with his comfort or convenience in his use of land (intangible damage) then liability in nuisance is almost entirely a matter of degree. It is here that the question of the reasonableness of the defendant's user, and the balancing of conflicting interests becomes most prominent. 'The convenience of such a rule may be indicated by calling it a rule of give and take, live and let live' (*Bamford* v *Turnley* (1862) 3 B & S 66, 84 per Bramwell B). It is also appropriate to note Lord Hoffmann's caution in *Hunter* v *Canary Wharf Ltd* that the inconvenience in issue in such cases ought properly to be regarded as inconvenience to the land first and the landowner second (para. 7.1.1). Most of the activities which discomfort or inconvenience an occupier in this way are in themselves perfectly lawful and only become actionable when they are carried on in such a way as to exceed reasonable limits. What those limits are in any particular case cannot be determined in advance. The comment of Pollock CB in *Bamford* v *Turnley* at p. 79 is not untypical: 'The question . . . entirely depends on the surrounding circumstances—the place where, the time when, the alleged nuisance, what, the mode of committing it, how, and the duration of it, whether temporary or permanent, occasional or continual' (see also *Stone* v *Bolton* [1949] 1 All ER 237, 238–9). Personal discomfort is not measured by the standards of the plaintiff, but must be substantial by reference to the standards of any ordinary person who might occupy the plaintiff's property. It must be 'an inconvenience materially interfering with the ordinary comfort physically of human existence, not merely according to elegant or dainty modes and habits of living, but according to plain and sober and simple notions among the

English people' (*Walter* v *Selfe* (1851) 4 De G & Sm 315, 322 per Knight Bruce V-C). This proposition is subject to the 'locality principle', however, for plain and sober and simple notions of what is acceptable vary from area to area (see para. 7.1.3.1).

An example of the operation of that principle and the subtlety of the balancing exercise inherent in determining actionability in nuisance in a case of alleged intangible damage is *Murdoch* v *Glacier Metal Co. Ltd, The Times,* 21 January 1998. In that case, the Court of Appeal held that night-time factory noise did not, on the facts, constitute an actionable nuisance to a family living close by, notwithstanding the fact that the noise was of a droning nature from which there was no escape, and that it was at a level greater than that which the World Health Organisation had indicated could affect the restorative value of sleep. The Court of Appeal were keen to confirm generally that it was still possible, in the particular circumstances of any case, for there to be counterbalancing factors that would result in even substantial and measurable intangible damage not qualifying as actionable damage in nuisance. As such, they stated that, though sleep was a matter of importance, there was no proposition of law that there was an automatic common law nuisance if sleep was disturbed. They held that the overall circumstances, including the proximity of the plaintiff's property to a busy by-pass and the paucity of complaints from others living nearby, were, in fact, capable of negativing even a strong suggestion that the noise was an actionable nuisance.

7.1.2.3 Interference with servitudes Private nuisance provides a remedy for interferences with servitudes, i.e., easements, profits à prendre and natural rights (see Megarry and Wade, *The Law of Real Property,* 5th ed., p. 834). Examples of these property rights are private rights of way, rights of support of land and buildings, and riparian (water) rights (but not the 'right' to uninterrupted television reception: *Hunter* v *Canary Wharf Ltd*—see para. 7.1.1). If the interference is substantial it is treated on the same basis as physical damage to property. There is no balancing exercise, since the purpose of the action is to protect the proprietary right, and liability is strict. Some instances of this type of nuisance (and nuisance by encroachment) are actionable *per se* (*Nicholls* v *Ely Beet Sugar Factory Ltd* [1936] Ch 343). This is contrary to the general rule in nuisance that liability requires proof of actual damage, but in this situation there is a close analogy with trespass to land, where the plaintiff may simply be vindicating the existence of his proprietary rights (see *Buckley,* p. 123). In the case of interference with a neighbour's right to the support of his land, physical damage to the land is a necessary ingredient of the cause of action; an established potential risk of future physical damage is not sufficient (*Midland Bank* v *Bardgrove Property Services* [1992] 37 EG 126).

7.1.3 Unreasonable user
It is worth emphasising again that in determining whether the defendant's user of land was reasonable the question is *not*: did the defendant act reasonably? There are many instances where, viewed objectively, the defendant

acted in a reasonable manner but was nonetheless liable in nuisance (e.g., *Schenck* v *Province of Ontario,* para. 7.1.2.1). Reasonableness is the test for striking the balance between conflicting interests. It is not to be equated with an absence of negligence. This does not mean that negligence is never relevant—in some types of nuisance it is essential to the defendant's liability—but, as a general rule, it is only one of the circumstances that are taken into account. This is particularly so where the action is in respect of amenity damage which the plaintiff is trying to halt by injunction. The reasonableness of the defendant's user is treated as a question of fact. The following factors give some indication of how the courts will approach this question.

7.1.3.1 Locality In the case of intangible damage the nature of the locality will be taken into account (see, for example, the way in which the proximity of the plaintiff's property to a busy by-pass was one of the factors employed by the Court of Appeal in *Murdoch* v *Glacier Metal Co. Ltd, The Times,* 21 January 1998, to deny liability in nuisance; see para. 7.1.2.2). A person living in an industrial area cannot expect the same level of comfort in terms of the purity of the atmosphere or noise levels as someone living in a secluded residential area. As Thesiger LJ expressed it in *Sturges* v *Bridgman* (1879) 11 ChD 852, 865 'what would be a nuisance in Belgrave Square would not necessarily be so in Bermondsey'. This does not mean that a person living in a manufacturing area can never succeed in an action for amenity damage. He will do so if the interference substantially exceeds the prevailing standards of the neighbourhood (see, e.g., *Halsey* v *Esso Petroleum Co. Ltd* [1961] 2 All ER 145), though the prevailing standards of the locality may change, for example, if the planning authority grants planning permission for commercial or industrial use (see *Gillingham Borough Council* v *Medway (Chatham) Dock Co. Ltd* [1992] 3 WLR 449). 'Trifling inconveniences' are disregarded but the locality sets the measure of what is regarded as trifling and what is substantial. The principle does not apply to physical damage to property, of course, applying *St Helens Smelting Co.* v *Tipping,* para. 7.1.2.1.

In *Laws* v *Florinplace Ltd* [1981] 1 All ER 659 the plaintiffs obtained an interim injunction against the opening of a 'sex centre and cinema club' in an area described as 'a residential enclave, albeit in a commercially developed area'. Vinelott J observed that nuisance is not confined to cases where there is some physical emanation of a damaging kind from the defendant's premises, but extends to cases where the defendant's use is an affront to the reasonable susceptibilities of ordinary men and women. Such an affront, carried on in a way that makes its nature apparent to neighbours and visitors constitutes an interference with the reasonable domestic enjoyment of property (see also *Thompson-Schwab* v *Costaki* [1956] 1 All ER 652—interim injunction granted restraining the use of premises in a 'good-class residential street' for the purpose of prostitution). The appropriate test is 'what is reasonable according to the ordinary usages of mankind living in society, or more correctly, in a particular *society*' (*Sedleigh-Denfield* v *O'Callaghan* [1940] AC 880, 903 per Lord Wright).

7.1.3.2 Abnormal sensitivity If either the plaintiff or his property is abnormally sensitive he cannot complain about interferences that would not have troubled an individual of ordinary susceptibilities. In *Robinson v Kilvert* (1889) 41 ChD 88, for example, heat from the defendant's manufacturing process raised the temperature of the plaintiff's premises situated above the defendant's premises. This damaged some paper stored on the plaintiffs premises which was sensitive to heat, but it would not have damaged ordinary paper. The Court of Appeal held that the defendant was not liable, because the plaintiff was carrying on an exceptionally delicate trade and the defendant's activity was perfectly lawful. This principle also applies to intangible damage, such as noise (*Heath v Mayor of Brighton* (1908) 98 LT 718).

On the other hand, if the defendant's activity would have interfered with an ordinary use of land in any event, he will be liable, notwithstanding the delicate nature of the plaintiff's operations. Thus, if fumes from the defendant's premises would have damaged flowers of ordinary sensitivity the defendant will also be responsible for damage to delicate plants, such as orchids (*McKinnon Industries Ltd v Walker* [1951] 3 DLR 577).

7.1.3.3 Duration of the interference The duration of the alleged nuisance will be taken into account. If it is of a temporary nature this might indicate that the injury is trivial and therefore part of the price of social existence. The execution of building work may cause a considerable temporary annoyance to neighbours but provided the work is carried out in a reasonable manner, i.e., with reasonable care, it will not generally be held to be a nuisance (*Harrison v Southwark & Vauxhall Water Co.* [1891] 2 Ch 409, 13–14 per Vaughan Williams J). It does not follow, however, that no temporary interference will be actionable. If the interference is sufficiently substantial it can amount to a nuisance (see *Matania v National Provincial Bank Ltd* [1936] 2 All ER 633—liability for dust and noise caused by building work). Thus, the temporary nature of the alleged nuisance must be measured against the gravity of the interference. For example, a temporary nuisance carried on at night, thereby interrupting the plaintiff's sleep, will normally be unreasonable (*De Keyser's Royal Hotel Ltd v Spicer Bros Ltd* (1914) 30 TLR 257—injunction granted restraining pile-driving at night; cf. *Murdoch v Glacier Metal Co. Ltd, The Times*, 21 January 1998, para. 7.1.2.1).

The existence of a nuisance is usually associated with a continuing 'state of affairs' rather than a single act of the defendant. What is the position where there is an isolated event, such as a single escape of something which damages the plaintiff's property? In *British Celanese Ltd v A.H. Hunt (Capacitors) Ltd* [1969] 2 All ER 1252 the defendants stored strips of metal foil used for making electrical components on their premises. Some of these strips were blown on to an electricity substation by the wind, causing a power failure. Lawton J held that an isolated happening by itself can create an actionable nuisance, and there is no rule that a plaintiff cannot sue for the first escape. In *SCM (United Kingdom) Ltd v W.J. Whittall & Son Ltd* [1970] 1 WLR 1017 Thesiger J made it clear (at p. 1031) that although a single escape may constitute a nuisance, the nuisance must arise from the condition of the defendant's land or from activities carried out on the land, i.e., it must be attributable to a 'state of affairs'. A single negligent act, damaging an electric cable for instance, would not be a nuisance.

This explains how an action in nuisance can be brought in respect of cricket balls or golf balls struck on to neighbouring land or the highway (see *Stone* v *Bolton* [1950] 1 KB 201, 213, CA; *Miller* v *Jackson* [1977] QB 966; *Castle* v *St Augustine's Links* (1922) 38 TLR 615). The basis of the claim is not the specific act of hitting a ball on to adjoining land, but the activity of organising a game which creates a danger. The frequency with which balls are struck beyond the defendants' land will indicate just how dangerous the activity is, and therefore whether the 'state of affairs' constitutes a nuisance (cf. *Miller* v *Jackson*—cricket balls struck on to the plaintiff's property eight or nine times a season—and *Bolton* v *Stone* [1951] AC 850, HL—cricket balls struck out of the ground perhaps six times in 30 years). In *Crown River Cruises Ltd* v *Kimbolton Fireworks Ltd* [1996] 2 Lloyd's Rep 533 it was held that a firework display constituted a nuisance in circumstances where it was inevitable that for 15 or 20 minutes debris of a flammable nature would fall upon nearby property, thereby damaging the property in the ensuing fire.

7.1.3.4 Public benefit It is no defence that the defendant's activity, which would otherwise constitute a nuisance, is justified by the public benefit derived from that activity. Public benefit is relevant, however, in a limited sense as one of the circumstances to be considered in determining whether the defendant's user is reasonable. In *St Helens Smelting Co.* v *Tipping* (1865) 11 HL Cas 642 (see para. 7.1.2.1) Lord Westbury said (at p. 650):

> If a man lives in a town, it is necessary that he should subject himself to the consequences of those operations of trade which may be carried on in his immediate locality, which are actually necessary for trade and commerce and also for the enjoyment of property, and for the benefit of the inhabitants of the town and of the public at large.

Although this could be regarded as part and parcel of the locality principle, it is clear that the utility of the defendant's activity is a factor, albeit a small factor, that is weighed in the balancing process (cf. malicious acts, para. 7.1.3.5).

It is in this light, perhaps, that Lord Denning's judgment in *Miller* v *Jackson* [1977] QB 966 should be approached. The Master of the Rolls held that the defendants' user of their cricket ground was reasonable because cricket had been played there for over 70 years to the great benefit of the community as a whole and, prior to the construction of houses adjoining the ground, to the injury of no one. In balancing the conflicting interests of neighbours, the need to protect the environment by preserving playing fields in the face of increasing development should take priority. On this point, however, this was a dissenting judgment, but the decision of the majority of the Court of Appeal that the defendants were liable in nuisance should not be taken as indicating that public benefit is never relevant to the liability issue. Rather it affirms the traditional view that where the interference is *substantial* (the plaintiffs were subject to the real risk of damage to property and personal injury by cricket balls which fell 'like thunderbolts from the heavens' per Cumming-Bruce LJ) public benefit will not excuse the nuisance. It may be relevant, however, to the question of whether an injunction should be granted (see para. 7.1.7.2).

7.1.3.5 Malice Where the defendant's conduct is motivated by malice this may convert acts which would not otherwise amount to a nuisance into an actionable nuisance. In *Christie* v *Davey* [1893] 1 Ch 316 the defendant was annoyed by music lessons given by his neighbour, the plaintiff. In retaliation he banged on the party-wall, beat trays and shouted. North J granted an injunction against the defendant indicating that he would have taken a different view of the case if the defendant's acts had been 'innocent'.

The facts of *Christie* v *Davey* were such that even in the absence of malice the defendant's behaviour would have amounted to a nuisance, because it was carried on both day and night. In *Hollywood Silver Fox Farm Ltd* v *Emmett* [1936] 2 KB 468, however, the circumstances were different. The plaintiffs bred silver foxes, which during the breeding season are very nervous creatures, likely to devour their young if disturbed. The defendant fired a gun on his own land as near as possible to the breeding pens with the malicious intention of causing damage. Macnaghten J held the defendant liable. This decision might be criticised because it runs contrary to the principle that the plaintiff's abnormal sensitivity should not create a liability for damage that would not have been suffered had the plaintiff's use of land been a normal use. The defendant's motive should not change a lawful act into an unlawful act. The difficulty with this argument is that no one has a *right* to make noise. It is a privilege based on mutual forbearance, and this is related to the social utility of the activity generating the noise (see the dictum of Lord Westbury in *St Helens Smelting Co.* v *Tipping* (1865) 11 HL Cas 642 quoted in para. 7.1.3.4). Malicious acts have no social utility, and therefore in balancing the competing interests of landowners a lesser degree of interference than would otherwise be required will suffice. Malice tips the balance towards finding the defendant's user unreasonable. If the plaintiff's use had been 'ordinary' then, no doubt, the defendant would have chosen other means of expressing his spite.

These cases can be contrasted with *Bradford Corporation* v *Pickles* [1895] AC 587 where the House of Lords held that the defendant had acted lawfully when he deliberately interfered with percolating water on his own land in order to reduce the supply of water to the plaintiffs' land. His intention was to persuade the plaintiffs to purchase his land at a price that was acceptable to himself. The plaintiffs had no right to an uninterrupted supply of water and thus the defendant had not interfered with a legally recognised interest of the plaintiffs (the position is different where the water flows in defined channels: *Chasemore* v *Richards* (1859) 7 HL Cas 349). A bad motive could not in itself create a cause of action (but it may be questioned whether the motive was malicious, *see Buckley*, p. 16). In *Langbrook Properties Ltd* v *Surrey County Council* [1969] 3 All ER 1424 the defendants abstracted percolating water from their own land by pumping, with a consequential abstraction of water from the plaintiffs' land. This caused buildings on the land to settle. The plaintiffs' claim in both nuisance and negligence failed. Plowman J, applying *Bradford Corporation* v *Pickles*, commented (at p. 1440) that 'since it is not actionable to cause damage by the abstraction of underground water, even where this is done maliciously, it would seem illogical that it should be actionable if it were done carelessly. Where there is no duty not to injure for the sake of inflicting injury, there cannot, in my judgment, be a duty to take care not to inflict the same injury.' The Court of Appeal reached the same conclusion on virtually identical facts in *Stephens* v *Anglian Water Authority* [1987] 3 All ER 379 (an action framed solely in negligence). The Court rejected an argument that there was a difference between being prevented from abstracting percolating water for one's own use (which is what happened to the plaintiffs in *Bradford Corporation* v *Pickles*) and physical damage to one's property, as 'a distinction without any essential difference'. This view is clearly open to question (see Fleming (1988) 104 LQR 183; *Weir*, p. 445), and it is arguable that proprietary rights should no longer confer absolute immunity in the face of careless conduct which causes foreseeable physical harm to one's neighbours. This is certainly the position in relation to nuisances which arise from natural causes, where the action is a form of negligence (para. 7.1.3.6).

Although an occupier may have the right to abstract percolating water regardless of the consequences to his neighbours, he does not have the right to require his neighbours to receive the water. A lower occupier may put up a barrier or pen the water back even if this causes damage to the higher occupier (*Home Brewery plc* v *William Davis & Co. (Loughborough) Ltd* [1987] 1 All ER 637). This right to reject percolating water, however, is not absolute. If a barrier was erected maliciously and not for the purpose of reasonable use of the land, this may amount to a nuisance (ibid. at p. 646). Negligence may render the use unreasonable, although the mere fact that damage was reasonably foreseeable is not sufficient if the use was otherwise reasonable. Building a housing estate, for example, is reasonable even if it is a commercial enterprise with a view to profit. But there is a difference between preventing water draining naturally from the plaintiff's land to the defendant's, and forcing water from the defendant's land on to the plaintiff's. In the latter instance the defendant will be liable either for nuisance by encroachment or for trespass to land (ibid. at p. 648).

7.1.3.6 Natural condition of the land The general rule of the common law was that an occupier was not under any duty to abate a nuisance that arose on his land from natural causes, although he did have to permit his neighbour reasonable access for the purpose of abating the nuisance. This was changed by the Privy Council in *Goldman* v *Hargrave* [1967] 1 AC 645. A tree on an occupier's land in Australia was struck by lightning and began to burn. The occupier had it cut down but did not extinguish the fire. Subsequently the wind increased and the fire spread to the plaintiff's premises. The occupier was held liable for failing to take adequate precautions to extinguish the fire in the face of a foreseeable risk. The positive nature of this duty is apparent from Lord Wilberforce's statement (at p. 661) that: 'The basis of the occupier's liability lies not in the use of his land; in the absence of "adoption" there is no such use; but in the neglect of action in the face of something which may damage his neighbour'. This is a form of liability in negligence. Indeed, Lord Wilberforce considered the classification of the action as nuisance or negligence to be irrelevant—liability rested on negligence and nothing else. The existence of the duty is based upon the occupier's knowledge of the hazard, ability to foresee the consequences of not checking or removing it, and the ability to abate it.

In *Leakey v National Trust for Places of Historic Interest or Natural Beauty* [1980] QB 485 the Court of Appeal applied *Goldman v Hargrave* to a case where natural erosion of a steep, natural hill caused landslips of soil and rock which threatened the safety of buildings at the foot of the hill. 'If', exclaimed Megaw LJ, 'as a result of the working of the forces of nature there is poised above my land, or above my house, a boulder or a rotten tree, which is liable to fall at any moment of the day or night, perhaps destroying my house, and perhaps killing or injuring me or members of my family, am I without remedy? . . . Must I, in such a case, if my protests to my neighbour go unheeded, sit and wait and hope that the worst will not befall?' Their Lordships answered this question in the negative. An occupier was under a duty to do that which is reasonable in all the circumstances to prevent or minimise a known risk of damage to his neighbour or his neighbour's property. Although agreeing 'with diffident reluctance' in this conclusion, Shaw LJ pointed out that the justice of imposing liability for naturally occurring dangers was by no means obvious, when the occupier's only connection with the danger was that he owned the land on which by chance it originated. The question is not, as Megaw LJ implied, whether the unfortunate adjoining occupier must wait for the worst, but rather who should meet the cost of averting the danger. The National Trust had been willing to permit the plaintiffs to enter on to the land to abate the nuisance, but the plaintiffs wanted the National Trust to bear the cost (for two different justifications for the imposition of liability, see Smith and Burns (1983) 46 MLR 147, 158, and *Atiyah*, p. 70).

Some account is taken of these considerations in terms of the standard of care imposed. It is not an objective duty to take such precautions as a reasonable occupier would have done, but a duty to take such care as is reasonable taking into account the circumstances of the particular occupier (not the average occupier), including the expenditure required and the means of the occupier (cf. *British Railways Board v Herrington* [1972] AC 877, para. 6.2). Less will be expected of the infirm than the able-bodied. An impoverished occupier upon whose land a hazard arises may have satisfied his duty by notifying his more substantial neighbour and requesting additional resources to deal with the danger (*Goldman v Hargrave* [1967] 1 AC 645, 663). But as Megaw LJ emphasised in *Leakey v National Trust etc.* this subjective assessment of what is reasonable can only be made on a broad basis. Detailed inquiry into the state of the bank balances of the respective parties would be inappropriate. The subjective duty is clearly intended to ameliorate the full impact of a potentially harsh rule, but as a principle of law it is extremely suspect. It makes the existence of liability turn upon the relative wealth of the parties to the action. Whatever the merits of the result in terms of the redistribution of wealth, it is startling as a principle of civil liability. The courts have rarely been willing to contemplate the notion that a defendant's capacity to pay is at all relevant to his liability (a point reflected in the judicial attitude to insurance: see *Morgans* v *Launchbury* [1973] AC 127, para. 8.4.3.2).

Several questions about the nature of this new duty remain to be answered. Does it apply to all naturally occurring nuisances? Would it apply, for example, to cases of amenity damage as well as physical damage? Would the locality principle apply, even in cases of physical damage, where, for example, the nuisance is the product of natural forces which are characteristic of the particular environment in which the plaintiff has chosen to live? (see *Buckley*, p. 44, who argues that the locality principle should apply. On the question of the plaintiff's consent see para. 7.1.6.3.) Does the duty in negligence apply to nuisance by the encroachment of tree roots or branches, which had previously been regarded as a duty of strict liability? (see *Davey* v *Harrow Corporation* [1958] 1 QB 60.) In *Leakey* v *National Trust etc.* Megaw LJ approved *Davey* v *Harrow Corporation* subject to the proviso that, where a nuisance is not brought about by human agency, the duty does not arise unless and until the defendant has or ought to have had knowledge of the existence of the defect. The Court of Appeal has approved this dictum (*Solloway* v *Hampshire County Council* (1981) 79 LGR 449), so that knowledge that the encroachment constitutes a foreseeable risk is a prerequisite to liability, though constructive knowledge will suffice (ibid; *City of Richmond* v *Scantelbury* [1991] 2 VR 38). In *Solloway* Dunn LJ commented that this approach is consistent with *Sedleigh-Denfield* v *O'Callaghan* [1940] AC 880, para. 7.1.5.2.4, and 'confines strict liability for nuisance to cases where there has been some non-natural user of the land as stated in *Rylands* v *Fletcher* (1868) LR 3 HL 330'. Accordingly, in considering whether there has been a breach of duty, the extent of the risk and its foreseeable consequences must be balanced against the practicable measures required to minimise the damage and its consequences (per Dunn LJ at p. 457). What is not clear from these cases, however, is whether the subjective standard of care, measured by reference to the particular occupier, will apply to this type of encroachment. If not, on what basis will the courts distinguish different types of naturally occurring nuisance?

The concept of 'natural use of land' is more familiar in the context of the rule in *Rylands* v *Fletcher* (para. 8.1) where some 'non-natural use' is one of the elements of liability. But liability for a naturally occurring nuisance does not depend upon any 'user' as such by the occupier. Mere continuance of the nuisance will suffice. The reasonableness of the occupier's 'user' is not measured by balancing competing activities, unless the occupation of land is treated as an 'activity' *per se*. Rather, it is measured against a positive obligation to act, created by the tort of negligence and founded upon the occupation and control of land (see Gearty [1989] CJL 214, 240–1, arguing that negligence is the appropriate action, not nuisance). In *Leakey* v *National Trust etc.* Shaw LJ commented that the 'development of "the good neighbour" concept has . . . blurred the definition of rights and liabilities between persons who stand in such a relationship as may involve them in reciprocal rights and liabilities'. His Lordship's point is well-illustrated by *Bradburn* v *Lindsay* [1983] 2 All ER 408 in which, relying on *Leakey* v *National Trust etc.*, it was held that the owner of a semidetached house owed a duty of reasonable care in respect of the state of repair and support for a party-wall. Just as the tort of negligence is capable of outflanking the law of contract, *Bradburn* v *Lindsay* demonstrates that it is capable of making inroads into the law of property (see Jackson [1984] Conv 54).

7.1.3.7 Negligence The fact that an occupier has acted with all reasonable care does not necessarily indicate that his use of land was reasonable. If the interference with the plaintiff's use or enjoyment of his rights over his land is such as to constitute a nuisance in spite of the defendant's exercise of reasonable care, then the user is unreasonable (*Rapier* v *London Tramways Co.* [1893] 2 Ch 588, 590). On the other hand, where the defendant has been negligent this may be evidence of unreasonable user, since it will not usually be reasonable to expect adjoining owners to put up with interferences that could be avoided by the exercise of reasonable care. Finally, in some forms of nuisance, negligence is an essential requirement of liability (see para. 7.1.8).

7.1.4 Who can sue?
If private nuisance protects interests in land, then it would seem to follow that only those with an interest in the land affected can maintain an action (see generally Kodilinye (1989) 9 LS 284). This has been confirmed as a strict rule in *Hunter* v *Canary Wharf Ltd* (para. 7.1.1), in which the House of Lords denied actions in nuisance on this basis to the spouses and children of tenants of property affected by dust and interference with television reception. In the case of continuing nuisance, such as encroachment by tree roots, a plaintiff with such an interest can sue for damage inflicted prior to the acquisition of his interest, even if he knew about the damage at the time of acquisition (*Masters* v *Brent London Borough Council* [1978] QB 841).

The rule that a person who does not have a proprietary or possessory interest in the land cannot sue can be traced back to *Malone* v *Laskey* [1907] 2 KB 141, in which it was held that members of the occupier's family did not have *locus standi* for that reason (note that they might have an action in negligence or under the Defective Premises Act 1972, s. 4 (paras 6.3.2 and 7.1.5.3.3)). However, there were competing lines of authority on the issue (see Bridgman and Jones (1994) 14 LS 180, 186–9), and in *Khorasandjian* v *Bush* [1993] 3 WLR 476 a majority of the Court of Appeal had held that a plaintiff who had no proprietary interest in the property (she was a teenager residing with her parents) was entitled to a *quia timet* injunction to restrain a private nuisance in the form of harassment by persistent unwanted telephone calls (adopting the approach of the Appellate Division of the Alberta Supreme Court in *Motherwell* v *Motherwell* (1976) DLR (3d) 62). Dillon LJ commented that it would be 'ridiculous' if in the present age the law is that the making of deliberately harassing and pestering telephone calls to a person is only actionable in the civil courts if the recipient of the calls happens to have the freehold or a leasehold proprietary interest in the premises in which he or she has received the calls: 'The court has at times to reconsider earlier decisions in the light of changed social conditions' (cf. the dissenting judgment of Peter Gibson J: 'Given that the purpose of an action in nuisance is to protect the right to use and enjoyment of land . . . it seems to me to be wrong in principle if a mere licensee or someone without such right could sue in private nuisance'). The approach of the majority in *Khorasandjian* v *Bush* was then adopted by the Court of Appeal in *Hunter* v *Canary Wharf Ltd* [1996] 1 All ER 482 (for comment on *Hunter* in the Court of Appeal, see O'Sullivan [1996] CLJ 184; English (1996) 59 MLR 726; Ghandhi [1997] Conv 145). Pill LJ said (at p. 498) that 'a substantial link between the person enjoying the use and the land on which he or she is enjoying it is essential but . . . occupation of property, as a home, does confer upon the occupant a capacity to sue in private nuisance'. Given the trend of the law to grant additional protection to occupiers, and the inconsistencies between members of a family which insisting on a proprietary or possessory interest created, the Court of Appeal considered that it was no longer tenable to require a plaintiff to demonstrate a proprietary or possessory interest in the land to sue in nuisance. As such, they held that occupation of property *as a home* should provide a sufficient link with the property to enable the plaintiff to sue.

When *Hunter* came before the House of Lords ([1997] 2 All ER 426), however, only Lord Cooke (who dissented on the point) was willing to embrace such laudable sentiments and to countenance a private nuisance action for one without a recognisable proprietary interest. The majority (Lords Hoffmann, Lloyd, Goff and Hope) were less convinced and, in a barely disguised attempt to return the tort to its property-based roots, reasserted the rule in *Malone* v *Laskey* and, with it, overruled *Khorasandjian* v *Bush*. They held that, doctrinally, it was proper that a plaintiff should establish a right to the land affected in order to sue in private nuisance. In turn, such a right could either be *proprietary* (a legal title or a beneficial/ equitable interest) or *possessory*.

It would be a mistake to read the House of Lords' reference to 'possessory' as in any way analogous to the Court of Appeal's ostensibly similar notion of residential occupation. Far from it. In the House of Lords, it is clear that the majority's conception of a 'possessory' basis for establishing standing in nuisance is intended largely to reflect (rather than in any meaningful way to add to) the governing 'proprietary' criterion. Lord Hoffmann for instance, explains its inclusion simply on the basis that '. . . so far as land is concerned there is in England no law of ownership, but only a law of possession' (at p. 449, citing *Cheshire and Burn's Modern Law of Real Property*, 15th ed., 1994), and he expressly limits its application in the nuisance context to those with the '*right* to *exclusive* possession' (at p. 447, emphasis added). In turn, their Lordships considered that such a right would be established in the case of a freeholder, a reversioner (insofar as his reversionary interest was affected), a tenant in possession, a licensee with exclusive possession, and even a person who was in exclusive possession of the land but who was unable to prove title to it as against a third party. The right to exclusive possession would not, however, be established in the case of mere licensees or other occupiers, who (like the plaintiffs in *Hunter* itself—spouses and children of tenants) might occupy but without a sufficient possessory right to do so. Similarly, though perhaps even more pedantically, their Lordships considered that a non-owning spouse's right, following marital breakdown, to be awarded exclusive possession under the Matrimonial Homes Act 1983 did not amount to a qualifying right to exclusive possession for the purposes of *locus standi* in private nuisance until it was formally granted by the court (Lord Hoffmann, at p. 453).

The House of Lords majority in *Hunter* also drew upon several other seemingly more practical grounds in order to bolster the doctrinal neatness of their confirmation that *locus standi* in a tort against land necessitated an interest in the land affected (Cane (1997) 113 LQR 515). Lord Goff (at p. 439), for instance, was concerned that extending the right to sue to 'anybody who lived in the relevant property as a home' might put practical obstacles in the way of 'sensible' agreements that the creator of the nuisance might otherwise reach with would-be injunction-seeking plaintiffs, by making it difficult for him to be sure that all necessary consents had been sought and obtained. To similar, but more general, effect, Lord Hope warned as to the 'chilling effect' that multiple plaintiff actions might have on builders of large residential buildings. Significantly and, it is suggested, ultimately most controversially, Lord Goff (at p. 438) and Lord Hoffmann (at p. 453) were also satisfied that would-be plaintiffs denied standing in private nuisance on proprietary grounds would not be left without an action elsewhere. They suggested that they could, for example, proceed in negligence or, in the *Khorasandjian* v *Bush* context, under the Protection from Harassment Act 1997 (para. 12.2) or, perhaps, even under the rule in *Wilkinson* v *Downton* [1897] 2 QB 57 (para. 12.2), which, being a species of deliberate harm, Lord Hoffmann (at p. 452) saw no reason to restrict by rules in negligence that required plaintiffs to suffer a recognisable psychiatric illness.

The most fundamental conceptual objections to the *Hunter* ruling on *locus standi* are simply that it unnecessarily stultifies the law of private nuisance and reduces the scope of meaningful protection available to plaintiffs. Such fears, of course, were articulated by the Court of Appeal in *Hunter* and were clearly instrumental in their having come to a contrary view on the law. They also resonate throughout Lord Cooke's dissenting speech in the House of Lords, central to which are his assertions that it is because nuisance remains fundamentally 'obligation-based' (Cane (1997) 113 LQR 515, 517; see para. 7.1.1) that it does not have to deny relief to those in 'substantial occupation' only and that, as a result, it can adapt to do justice to relevant contemporary concerns. His Lordship thought it incongruous for such plaintiffs to be excluded from the ambit of private nuisance when they were at the same time afforded sufficient status to qualify for protection under international human rights treaties and certain key domestic legislation ('. . . current statutes give effect to current perception', at p. 458). Concerns for maintaining the capacity of private nuisance to evolve in the face of society's changing priorities presumably also underlie his remark, in the context of '. . . the lineaments of the law of nuisance', that '. . . public consciousness of the need to protect the environment [is] among the factors falling to be taken into account in evolving the law' (at p. 456). On similar grounds, the theoretical availability of other causes of action to the sort of people now denied a parallel claim in nuisance might do little practical justice to any notion that society today might generally be more inclined to recognise and protect them. The negligence action, for example, could prove, at best, more difficult to establish (given the defendant-friendly governing criterion of 'reasonable care', as opposed to nuisance's 'reasonable user') and, at worst, even incapable of providing redress (in that many amenity damage cases would require damages for loss of enjoyment, which Lord Hoffmann conceded would not be recoverable in negligence—p. 452).

The practical anomalies and difficulties with the potential strictness of the *Hunter* rule seem no less remarkable. For instance, in what sort of circumstances will a spouse (whether married or 'common law') be able to assert a relevant 'proprietary' interest? If a spouse holds a legal title, the difficulty does not arise, but what of the 'non-owning' spouse (i.e., the not uncommon situation in which the legal title is held in the other spouse's sole name)? There, it might be largely correct for Lord Hoffmann in *Hunter* to state that 'the answer . . . lies in the law of property, not the law of tort', but surely something of an exaggeration, at the very least, for him to assert (at p. 453) that '[t]he courts today will readily assume that a wife has acquired a beneficial interest in the matrimonial home'. This may sound reassuring for non-owning spouses, for whom the court's consequent presumption of such a beneficial (equitable) interest would then provide the proprietary right to sue in nuisance. As a conclusion, however, on the state of the law upon which such a presumption would have to rest, it would be barely recognisable to property law students grappling with the intricacies of modern trust law decisions that tend to require non-owning spouses to jump through hoops in order to persuade a court to grant them a beneficial interest (see *Lloyds Bank plc* v *Rosset* [1990] 1 All ER 1111, HL). Though divorce legislation typically enables courts to carve up a property's beneficial ownership on the more pragmatic lines that Lord Hoffmann suggests, this would not help in the case of an unmarried couple. Moreover, his reference to 'the law of property, not the law of tort' suggests that it is unlikely that he had this in mind in the context of the married would-be nuisance plaintiff, or that, even if he did, he would really require him/her to institute divorce proceedings first (though his assertions on the contingent-only basis of the non-owning spouse's right to exclusive possession under the Matrimonial Homes Act 1983 do make such a conclusion difficult to resist). Indeed, Lord Cooke's assessment (at p. 458) that '[a]s between spouses and *de facto* partners the question whether contributions in money or services give a proprietary equitable interest in a matrimonial home is a notoriously difficult one today, wrestled with throughout the common law world' seems an altogether more appropriate and realistic assessment of the non-owning spouse's uncertain path to the establishment of a beneficial interest in this context. If so, then, coupled with their Lordships' largely negative pronouncements on the Matrimonial Homes Act 1983, this results in the curious possibility that he/she may well have less chance of establishing *locus standi* in private nuisance than a person in exclusive possession who is unable to prove title, an anomaly neatly summed up in O'Sullivan's comment that 'it may prove difficult to swallow a rule that excludes spouses but includes squatters' ([1997] CLJ 483, 485).

7.1.5 Who is liable?
There are three potential defendants in a private nuisance action, the person who created the nuisance, the occupier of the land from which it emanates and the occupier's landlord. These categories are not mutually exclusive. The occupier can be jointly and severally liable with the creator, and will almost always be liable in the circumstances in which a landlord will be responsible.

7.1.5.1 Creator The person who creates a nuisance by some positive act (not merely allowing the nuisance to arise, e.g., letting premises fall into disrepair) is liable, and remains so even though he is not in occupation of the land from which it emanates and even though he has no power to abate it (*Thompson* v *Gibson* (1841) 7 M & W 456). This statement of the traditional view that the creator of the nuisance is strictly liable, even when he is not in a position to remedy the situation, must now be read in the light of the decision of the House of Lords in *Cambridge Water Co.* v *Eastern Counties Leather plc* [1994] 2 WLR 52. Chemicals escaped from the defendants' premises into the aquifer beneath, and over a considerable period of time percolated to the plaintiffs' borehole, contaminating the drinking water. At the time of the escape into the ground the escape was unforeseeable, but when the source of the pollution was identified the circumstances were clearly known. No further escapes of the chemical into the aquifer were occurring at that stage, though chemical from the accumulated pool in the aquifer was continuing to percolate to the plaintiffs' property. The House of Lords held that the defendants were not liable for the continuing pollution once it became foreseeable to them. When they created the conditions which led to the pollution the defendants could not have foreseen damage of that type, and the chemical had subsequently become irretrievably lost below ground. In those circumstances the defendants should not be under any greater liability than for negligence (see Lord Goff at p. 81; see however the comment of Wilkinson (1994) 57 MLR 799, 807–8 on this point). It is not necessary for the creator to have any interest in the land from which the nuisance emanates, nor need it arise on private land (*Southport Corporation* v *Esso Petroleum Co. Ltd* [1953] 3 WLR 773, QBD; cf. *Sedleigh-Denfield* v *O'Callaghan* [1940] AC 880, 896–7 per Lord Atkin).

7.1.5.2 Occupier The occupier of the land from which the nuisance emanates will be the usual defendant in private nuisance. The occupier will be liable not only for his own acts or omissions but also, in appropriate circumstances, the acts or omissions of others. He is responsible for (a) persons under his control; (b) independent contractors where the duty is 'non-delegable'; (c) predecessors in title; (d) trespassers; and (e) acts of nature. In cases (c), (d) and (e) the occupier will only be liable if he either adopts the nuisance or continues it. An occupier 'adopts' a nuisance if he makes use of it, and 'continues' a nuisance if he knows or ought reasonably to have known (i.e., was negligent in not knowing) of its existence, and fails to take reasonable steps to abate it (*Sedleigh-Denfield* v *O'Callaghan* [1940] AC 880, 897).

7.1.5.2.1 Persons under his control An occupier is liable for the acts of his servants, applying the principles of vicarious liability (para. 8.4). He is also responsible for the acts of lawful visitors because he can exercise control by preventing their entry, but knowledge or means of knowledge of the nuisance is probably required (*Winfield and Jolowicz*, p. 423). Authorising a licensee's activity, which creates a nuisance, will suffice (*White* v *Jameson* (1874) LR 18 Eq 303).

7.1.5.2.2 Independent contractors The general rule in tort is that an employer is not liable for the acts of an independent contractor. There is an exception where the employer's duty is 'non-delegable', i.e., the employer can delegate the performance of the task but not the responsibility for its performance (see para. 8.5.2). Where the nuisance is an inevitable, or even a reasonably foreseeable (*Clerk and Lindsell*, para. 18–47), consequence of the work that is undertaken the occupier cannot avoid liability by employing a contractor to do the work. In *Matania* v *National Provincial Bank Ltd* [1936] 2 All ER 633 the dust and noise from building operations caused a nuisance. The evidence was that the noise and dust were an inevitable consequence of the work. The Court of Appeal held the defendants liable. Slesser LJ said (at p. 646) that 'if the act done is one which in its very nature involves a special danger of nuisance being complained of, then . . . the employer of the contractor will be responsible if there is a failure to take the necessary precautions that the nuisance shall not arise'. The duty to maintain support for the adjoining land is also non-delegable (*Bower* v *Peate* (1876) 1 QBD 321; but there. is no liability for a contractor's negligence where the work, if properly carried out, involves no risk to the neighbour's premises: *Angus* v *Dalton* (1881) 6 App Cas 740, 831). *Spicer* v *Smee* [1946] 1 All ER 489 is sometimes cited as authority for the proposition that an occupier will be generally liable in nuisance for the acts of his independent contractor (*Winfield and Jolowicz*, p. 422, *Buckley*, p. 97). Although a dictum in the case supports this view (at p. 495 per Atkinson J), the facts do not, since the decision concerned liability for the escape of fire, which itself gives rise to a non-delegable duty (para. 8.5.4.3). Thus, the proposition is too widely expressed, at least for private nuisance (*Clerk and Lindsell*, para. 18–47).

Even when an occupier is responsible for a nuisance created by an independent contractor, he will not be liable for negligence which is not related to the dangerous element of the work that the contractor is employed to perform (i.e., collateral negligence: *Padbury* v *Holliday & Greenwood Ltd* (1912) 28 TLR 492; para. 8.5.5).

7.1.5.2.3 Predecessors in title Where the nuisance existed before the occupier acquired his interest in the land he will be liable if he knows or ought reasonably to have known of its existence, on the basis that he has continued the nuisance. But where he has not been negligent in failing to discover the nuisance he will not be liable (*St Anne's Well Brewery Co* v *Roberts* (1929) 140 LT 1). Arguably, the same standard of care should apply as for naturally occurring nuisances (*Winfield and Jolowicz*, p. 426).

7.1.5.2.4 Trespassers An occupier is not liable for a nuisance created by a trespasser on his land, unless he either adopts or continues the nuisance. In *Sedleigh-Denfield* v *O'Callaghan* [1940] AC 880 the defendant owned an open ditch that ran alongside the plaintiff's land. Without the defendant's permission (and therefore as trespassers) the local authority laid a drainage pipe in the ditch. There was no grid at the mouth of the pipe to stop it getting blocked. After a rainstorm the pipe became blocked with debris and the plaintiff's land was flooded as a result. The House of Lords held the defendant liable because he was aware of its presence and ought to have appreciated the risk of flooding. The defendant had also made use of the drain for his own purposes, since it drained water from his own land. He had both continued the nuisance and adopted it (for criticism of the label 'nuisance' in this situation see Gearty [1989] CLJ 214, 235–7).

The occupier is not an insurer and thus there must be some degree of personal responsibility (per Lord Atkin). Passive continuance of the nuisance will suffice for this purpose, but knowledge of the existence of the nuisance is not enough. The occupier must have failed 'to take any reasonable means to bring it to an end, though with ample time to do so' (per Viscount Maugham). The duty exists only to the extent that the occupier can reasonably abate the nuisance. If there are no effective steps that he could have taken to avoid the harm he will not be liable (see *King* v *Liverpool City Council* [1986] 1 WLR 890; and *Smith* v *Littlewoods Organisation Ltd* [1987] 1 All ER 710, para. 2.2.1, a case argued solely in negligence). An obvious question that arises here is whether reasonableness is to be measured objectively, or whether, as with naturally occurring nuisances, the particular occupier's abilities and resources will be taken into account. There is no logical justification for distinguishing between the two situations, since the rationale for the subjective approach is the fact that the occupier has 'had this hazard thrust upon him through no seeking or fault of his own' (*Goldman* v *Hargrave* [1967] 1 AC 645, 663). The decision of the Court of Appeal in *Page Motors Ltd* v *Epsom & Ewell Borough Council* (1982) 80 LGR 337 now supports the view that a subjective test is to be applied to an occupier's responsibility for the acts of third parties over whom he has no control. In that case a local authority was held liable for failing to take steps to halt the activities of gypsies camped on their land, which interfered with the plaintiff's business (cf. *Smith* v *Scott* [1973] Ch 314, para. 7.1.5.3.1).

7.1.5.2.5 Acts of nature The occupier's liability for naturally occurring nuisances has been discussed in para. 7.1.3.6.

Where the nuisance is latent then, clearly, there will be no liability (*Noble v Harrison* [1926] 2 KB 332—latent defect in tree branch), and even where the defect is patent and there to be seen, the defendant is not liable unless he knew or ought reasonably to have known of the danger (*British Road Services v Slater* [1964] 1 WLR 498).

7.1.5.3 Landlord The general rule is that a landlord who has parted with possession and control of the demised premises is not liable for nuisances arising on them. There are three situations, however, in which a landlord will be liable in nuisance: (a) where he authorised the nuisance; (b) where the nuisance existed prior to the letting; and (c) where the landlord has an obligation to repair or has reserved the right to enter and repair.

7.1.5.3.1 Landlord authorised the nuisance Where the nuisance is the result of the tenant's use of the premises in a normal and usual manner for the purposes for which they were let, the landlord will be taken to have authorised the nuisance. The landlord is responsible under the general principle that a person who authorises another to commit a tort is liable as a principal. In *Harris v James* (1876) 45 LJ QB 545, for example, the landlord was liable for a nuisance caused by his tenant's working of a quarry in the normal fashion. The test is whether the nuisance was an ordinary (or natural) and necessary consequence of the purpose for which the premises were let (*Tetley v Chitty* [1986] 1 All ER 663, 671). An assignee of the reversion who knows of the existence of the nuisance at the time of acquisition will be in the same position as the original landlord (*Sampson v Hodson-Pressinger* [1981] 3 All ER 710—tiled terrace of a flat used in a normal way caused nuisance by noise to tenant of the flat below).

Where the landlord takes a covenant from the tenant not to cause a nuisance, and the nuisance is not an inevitable consequence of the letting, the landlord will not be liable. In *Smith v Scott* [1973] Ch 314, a local authority let a house to a 'problem family', who by their behaviour caused a nuisance to the plaintiffs, who in the end had to move out of their own house. Although the local authority knew about their tenants' behaviour they were not liable because a covenant in the lease prohibited the tenants from creating a nuisance, and the nuisance was not a consequence of the purpose of the letting but of the persons to whom the premises were let (for criticism see Merritt [1973] JPL 154; *Weir*, p. 444; cf. *Page Motors Ltd v Epsom & Ewell Borough Council* (1982) 80 LGR 337, para. 7.1.5.2.4, though note that *Smith v Scott* was applied by the Court of Appeal in *Hussain v Lancaster City Council*, *The Times*, 27 May 1998)).

7.1.5.3.2 Nuisance existed before the letting Where the nuisance existed at the date of the letting the landlord will be liable if he knew or ought reasonably to have known about it. Even if the tenant has covenanted to repair, the landlord remains responsible because the landlord cannot 'shuffle off' his liability to a third party by signing a contract which, as between landlord and tenant, puts the burden of remedying the defect on the tenant (*Brew Brothers Ltd* v *Snax (Ross) Ltd* [1970] 1 QB 612, 638–9 per Sachs LJ).

7.1.5.3.3 Obligation to repair or reservation of right to enter If the nuisance arises after the commencement of the tenancy the landlord's liability will depend upon the degree of control that he exercises over the state of repair of the premises. An express covenant to repair by the landlord clearly gives sufficient control (*Payne* v *Rogers* (1794) 2 Bl R 350). In the case of a dwelling-house let for a term of less than seven years there is implied an unexcludable covenant that the landlord will keep in repair the structure and exterior of the dwelling-house (including drains, gutters and external pipes) and certain installations for the supply of water, gas, electricity, sanitation and for space or water heating (Landlord and Tenant Act 1985, ss. 11 and 12). The landlord will be liable for disrepair whether he knew or ought to have known of the defect or not, unless it was due to the act of a trespasser or a latent defect, in which event he is liable if he continues the nuisance (*Wringe* v *Cohen* [1940] 1 KB 229).

Where the landlord reserves a right to enter and repair this will also be sufficient, even though he has no obligation to repair (*Wilchick* v *Marks* [1934] 2 KB 56), and even though he was unaware of the disrepair (*Heap* v *Ind Coope & Allsopp Ltd* [1940] 2 KB 476, 484, i.e., applying the rule in *Wringe* v *Cohen*). In *Mint* v *Good* [1951] 1 KB 517, where a wall collapsed on to a highway, the landlord did not reserve a right to enter and repair but the Court of Appeal held that in a weekly tenancy a term to this effect would be implied, at least with respect to defects in the structure. Denning LJ observed that the occupying tenant of a small dwelling-house does not in practice do the structural repairs, but the owner does. 'This practical responsibility means that he has *de facto* control of the structure for the purpose of repairs and is therefore answerable in law for its condition.' This common law implied right (which is, in effect, an implied obligation) is of less significance since the enactment of the Housing Act 1961, s. 32 (now Landlord and Tenant Act 1985, s. 11).

In addition to his common law liability in nuisance, where a landlord has an obligation or a power to maintain or repair premises he owes a duty of reasonable care to all persons who might reasonably be expected to be affected by defects in the state of the premises (Defective Premises Act 1972, s. 4, para. 6.3.2). This duty will be owed to adjoining owners and persons on the premises themselves. The duty is owed in addition to the landlord's common law duties, although in practice this will only be significant to a potential plaintiff in circumstances where liability in nuisance could be regarded as stricter than in negligence. Section 4 of the Defective Premises Act 1972 is more extensive than liability in private nuisance in that the duty is owed to any person foreseeably affected, and is not limited to persons with an interest in land (see para. 7.1.4).

Where the tenant has covenanted to repair and there is no express or implied power to enter and repair the landlord will not be liable, either in nuisance or under the Defective Premises Act 1972. In all the situations in which the landlord is liable, the tenant in occupation will also be liable for the nuisance, as an occupier. This is so, even where it is the landlord who has covenanted to repair (*Wilchick* v *Marks* [1934] 2 KB 56, 68; *St Anne's Well Brewery Co.* v *Roberts* (1929) 140 LT 1, 8). Thus, the obligations in the lease may regulate liability between landlord and tenant but cannot alter their respective liabilities to third parties, unless the landlord has no control over the state of repair.

7.1.6 Defences

7.1.6.1 Prescription The continuation of a private nuisance for 20 years will, in theory, entitle the defendant to claim a prescriptive right to commit the nuisance, but in practice this plea has rarely succeeded (*Buckley*, p. 99). In order to acquire such an easement the defendant must establish that the interference amounted to an actionable nuisance throughout the 20-year period. It is not sufficient that he has carried on the activity for 20 years. In *Sturges* v *Bridgman* (1879) 11 ChD 852 the noise and vibration from the defendant's business as a confectioner, which had been carried on for more than 20 years, did not constitute a nuisance until the plaintiff built a consulting room in his garden for use in his medical practice. Time ran from that date and therefore the defendant failed to establish the defence (for discussion of this case, see Ogus and Richardson [1977] CLJ 284, 301–3). In addition, the nuisance must have been exercised as of right, i.e., neither forcibly, secretly nor with permission, for the 20-year period.

A defendant must not abuse his prescriptive right and therefore must carry on his activity in a way that causes the least practicable nuisance applying reasonable contemporary standards, not the standards that existed at an earlier period (*Shoreham Urban District Council* v *Dolphin Canadian Proteins Ltd* (1972) 71 LGR 261, 267).

7.1.6.2 Statutory authority If a statute authorises the defendant's activity the defendant will not be liable for interferences that are an inevitable result of the activity. It is for the defendant to prove that the interference was inevitable and the test is whether it could have been avoided by the exercise of reasonable care, i.e., without negligence (*Manchester Corporation* v *Farnworth* [1930] AC 171). In this context the word 'negligence' is used in a special sense of requiring the defendant, as a condition of obtaining immunity, 'to carry out the work and conduct the operation with all reasonable regard and care for the interests of other persons' (*Allen* v *Gulf Oil Refining Ltd* [1981] AC 1001, 1011 per Lord Wilberforce). In *Allen* v *Gulf Oil Refining Ltd* Lord Edmund-Davies suggested that in determining what was unavoidable no regard should be paid to the expense that would be involved. This is a strange proposition since most nuisances could probably be avoided if money were no object. The better view, it is submitted, is that the cost of avoiding the nuisance is a relevant factor in determining whether it is 'inevitable' (*Manchester Corporation* v *Farnworth* [1930] AC 171, 183 per

Lord Dunedin). Whether a nuisance is avoidable may turn on the degree of discretion given by the statute, e.g., as to the location of the activity. If there is a wide discretion the defendant will be liable if he could have located his undertaking elsewhere without causing a nuisance to neighbours (*Metropolitan Asylum District* v *Hill* (1881) 6 App Cas 193—smallpox hospital; cf. *London, Brighton & South Coast Railway Co.* v *Truman* (1886) 11 App Cas 45—location of cattle yards limited by requirement of proximity to railway station).

The authority must be either expressly stated or be necessarily implied from the legislation. This will depend upon the interpretation of the particular statute in question. A recent example of an implied authority is provided by *Allen* v *Gulf Oil Refining Ltd* [1981] AC 1001 in which the plaintiffs alleged that the noise, smell and vibrations from an oil refinery caused a nuisance. The Gulf Oil Refining Act 1965 authorised the defendants to purchase land compulsorily for the construction of the refinery and defined all the ancillary works such as jetties and railways, but it did not specifically authorise the refinery itself. Relying on the rule that a private Act of Parliament should be construed strictly *contra proferentum* the Court of Appeal held that the statute did not authorise the construction or use of the refinery. By a majority, the House of Lords reversed this decision, holding that the construction and operation of the refinery must have been impliedly authorised. Lord Diplock commented that 'Parliament can hardly be supposed to have intended the refinery to be nothing more than a visual adornment to the landscape in an area of natural beauty'. The plaintiffs' action would still succeed if they could establish that a nuisance had been committed and the defendants failed to establish that the interference could not be avoided by the exercise of reasonable care. But in assessing the level of interference that would be regarded as reasonable, the prevailing standards of the locality would be that of a neighbourhood in which an oil refinery was situated. In other words, the interference must be *both* in excess of what would be reasonable for a locality with a refinery and avoidable (although admittedly, in most instances these issues will tend to coincide).

Some statutes contain a specific proviso that the statutory undertakers are to be liable for nuisance. The effect of this depends on whether the undertakers operate under a statutory duty or a power. Where there is a mandatory obligation (e.g., to maintain a supply of water, electricity or gas) there can be no liability for anything expressly required by the statute or reasonably incidental to it, if it is done without negligence, even if there is a proviso imposing liability for nuisance. Where there is a power but no nuisance clause the position is the same. But where there is a power *with* a nuisance clause the undertakers are liable for nuisance even if they are not negligent (*Dunne* v *North Western Gas Board* [1964] 2 QB 806; see the summary of Webster J in *Department of Transport* v *North West Water Authority* [1983] 1 All ER 892, 895 approved by the House of Lords [1983] 3 All ER 273, 275–6).

Statutory authorisation is a complete defence. In *Allen* v *Gulf Oil Refining Ltd* [1979] 3 All ER 1008 Lord Denning MR suggested (at p. 1016) that, even where the defence applies, the plaintiff should be entitled to damages to compensate for his loss, but not an injunction, because private rights might then be used to prevent publicly authorised activities:

> Just as in principle property should not be taken compulsorily except on proper compensation being paid for it, so also in principle property should not be damaged compulsorily except on proper compensation being made for the damage done. No matter whether the undertakers use due diligence or not, they ought not to be allowed, for their own profit, to damage innocent people or property without paying compensation.

The House of Lords rejected this approach, restating the traditional view which can be traced back to decisions in the 19th century that were particularly favourable to railway companies (Davies (1974) 90 LQR 361, 362–5). The reason for this is that a successful action in nuisance will normally lead to an injunction almost 'as of right'. The courts are extremely reluctant to award damages in lieu of an injunction, taking the view that it would amount to a compulsory purchase by the defendant of the plaintiff's rights (see para. 7.1.7.2). Paradoxically, then, in order to prevent the exercise of private rights bringing a halt to authorised works, statutory authorisation is treated as a complete defence, leaving the plaintiff without any remedy, even by way of damages. If the plaintiff in *Allen* v *Gulf Oil Refining Ltd* had been affected by public works she would probably have had a claim for compensation under the Land Compensation Act 1973. It seems odd that she should have no claim where the defendants are a private organisation seeking to make a profit.

Even where the defence of statutory authorisation fails because the defendant has been negligent, it will still be relevant to the *measure* of damages. In *Tate & Lyle Industries Ltd* v *Greater London Council* [1983] 1 All ER 1159 the defendants were negligent in the design and construction of a ferry terminal which caused an obstruction in the River Thames. The plaintiffs were awarded only 75% of their loss because a proper design would inevitably have caused 25% of the obstruction that actually occurred.

Most changes to the use of land require planning permission from the local planning authority which acts under delegated powers granted by Parliament. The planning authority is charged with the task of balancing the interests of the community against those of individuals, and of holding the scales between individuals in weighing up requests to change the use of land. Can it be said that the grant of planning permission has authorised the new use, thereby precluding an action in nuisance? In *Gillingham Borough Council* v *Medway (Chatham) Dock Co. Ltd* [1992] 3 WLR 449 Buckley J held that planning permission is not a licence to commit a nuisance and a planning authority has no jurisdiction to authorise a nuisance. On the other hand, through its development plans and decisions a planning authority can alter the character of a neighbourhood, and thus where the planning authority had granted the defendants planning permission for the use of a naval dockyard as a commercial port this had changed the character of the neighbourhood such that the inevitable disturbance to the residents from the noise and vibration of heavy goods vehicles travelling to and from the port was not actionable (although it would have amounted to a nuisance prior to the grant of planning permission). In assessing the nature of the locality the court would look to the situation *after* the grant of permission, just as in *Allen* v *Gulf Oil Refining Ltd* the House of Lords considered that in assessing the level of interference that would be regarded as reasonable, the prevailing standards of the locality would be that of a neighbourhood with an oil refinery. Interference which was not the inevitable result of the planning permission, i.e., which could have been avoided with reasonable care, would not be taken into account as part of the nature of the locality.

In *Wheeler* v *J.J. Saunders Ltd* [1995] 2 All ER 697 the defendants obtained planning permission to build two pig housing units on their land, close to the plaintiff's property. This was not a new use but a more intensive use of the land. The smell from the pigs created what was undoubtedly a nuisance to the plaintiffs and the question was whether the grant of the planning permission effectively authorised the defendants' activity. The Court of Appeal re-affirmed the traditional view that a grant of planning permission cannot *per se* authorise a nuisance, apparently accepting Buckley J's approach to the possible effect of a planning permission on the nature of the locality. On the facts, however, the permission to intensify a particular use, namely increasing the number of pigs that could be kept on the land, on a comparatively small scale, did not in itself change the character of the locality. It was not a strategic planning decision affected by considerations of public interest. Staughton LJ left open the possibility that some planning permissions may authorise some nuisances, but his Lordship did not specify the circumstances in which this might occur. Peter Gibson LJ said that *Gillingham Borough Council* v *Medway (Chatham) Dock Co. Ltd*, if rightly decided, had called into question the previous assumption that private rights to claim in nuisance were unaffected by the permissive grant of planning permission, at least in cases where there was a major development altering the character of the neighbourhood with wide consequential effects such as required a balancing of competing public and private interests before permission was granted. In such a case the argument that the public interest should prevail was persuasive and it would be inappropriate to grant an injunction (though it should not necessarily preclude the award of damages in lieu of an injunction). But the principle applied in the *Gillingham* case did not apply to every planning decision: 'The court should be slow to acquiésce in the extinction of private rights without compensation as a result of administrative decisions which cannot be appealed and are difficult to challenge' (at p. 711). (A person who unsuccessfully objects to the grant of a planning permission, such as the plaintiff in *Wheeler* v *Saunders*, has no right of appeal and would have to bring a challenge to the decision by way of judicial review.) The planning decisions taken in *Wheeler* did not involve considerations of community or public interest, said his Lordship, but merely whether the private interests of the applicants for planning permission should prevail over the private interests of the plaintiff objectors. Sir John May took the view that a planning permission could not even authorise an inevitable nuisance. If the planning authority were, with notice, to grant a permission the inevitable consequence of which would be the creation of a nuisance, then it was arguable, said his Lordship, that the grant would be subject to judicial review on the ground of irrationality. The approach of Peter Gibson LJ was approved by the Court of Appeal in *Hunter* v *Canary Wharf Ltd* [1996] 1 All ER 482 where the plaintiffs were complaining that the erection of a tall building had interfered with their reception of television signals. The building had been erected under a planning permission granted pursuant to a 'fast track' procedure for obtaining planning permission laid down in statutory regulations creating the London Docklands Development Corporation for the purpose of regenerating the London docklands area. However, the Court could find no necessary implication that Parliament had authorised a particular structure to enjoy immunity from an action in nuisance. The permission did not authorise the nuisance, although if the erection of the building had changed the character of the locality that could be taken into account in assessing whether the interference with television signals constituted a nuisance at all. (The Court of Appeal's decision in *Hunter* was reversed by the House of Lords [1997] 2 All ER 426 (see paras 7.1.1 and 7.1.4), on the grounds that the plaintiffs did not have *locus standi* and that, in the circumstances of their case, interference with television reception by the presence of a nearby building was not capable of constituting an action in private nuisance. Note, though, Lord Cooke's assertion (at p. 465) that such an interference might be actionable where the building had been erected in *breach* of planning law.)

The effect of these cases is not entirely satisfactory. They create uncertainty in that some planning permissions will have the effect of changing the nature of the locality and some will not, but the parties to a potential action are not in a position to identify which planning consents will have this effect. The type and scale of the change will be relevant to assessing this, as will the extent to which the decision involves weighing the public interest, as opposed to weighing competing private interests. But beyond that it is difficult to say how the courts will react to the planning authority's decision. If the character of the neighbourhood has not changed, the planning permission can have no effect on a plaintiff's right of action in nuisance. By looking at the locality in the light of the new permitted use, however, it is arguable that the effect of a planning permission almost becomes determinative. As Tromans [1995] CLJ 494 comments, 'the argument tries to pull itself up by its own bootstraps: if a major industrial facility is built in a previously residential area and is held to change the character of the neighbourhood in the process, the facility would, by its very presence, be providing itself with a defence against nuisance. The character of the locality must surely be judged as it was before the alleged nuisance began'. The consequence will tend to be that, in those cases where the planning permission is taken into account, the practical effect will not in reality be very different from a statutory authority (see Steele and Jewell (1993) 56 MLR 568, 571). Of course, the theoretical difference between statutory authority and grants of planning permission lies in the assumption that Parliament is sovereign and can abolish or restrict the civil rights of individuals, whereas a planning authority, although acting under powers delegated to it by Parliament, is an administrative body making administrative decisions which must be taken within the framework of existing legal rights. There is now a danger that private rights could effectively be removed by administrative fiat. Finally, it is worth noting that, where it applies, the grant of planning permission is clearly a more restricted defence than statutory authorisation, relying simply on the change in the nature of the locality. Since the locality principle applies only to intangible damage, the grant of planning permission should be irrelevant where the plaintiff is complaining of physical damage to his property, though the defence of statutory authority may apply to physical damage if it is an inevitable result of the authorised activity.

7.1.6.3 Other defences There are a number of other defences which, on appropriate facts, might be pleaded. The Law Reform (Contributory Negligence) Act 1945 applies to nuisance (para. 14.5). Consent, in the form of a specific agreement to accept the interference, will be a defence. *Volenti non fit injuria* could apply to public nuisance, but it is more difficult to see how it could be relevant to private nuisance, particularly as the plea that the plaintiff has 'come to the nuisance' is not a defence (para. 7.1.6.4.1). In *Leakey* v *National Trust etc.* [1980] QB 485, para. 7.1.3.6, Megaw LJ considered that it was a pleadable defence that the plaintiffs, knowing of the danger to their property, by word or deed, had shown their willingness to accept that danger. This dictum must be understood in the light of the scope of the duty that was applied in that case. It will be recalled that, where the defendant's resources are modest, he may fulfil his duty with respect to naturally occurring nuisances by drawing the attention of his more substantial neighbour to the existence of the danger and inviting the neighbour to provide the resources to deal with it. If the neighbour refused, that could be taken to indicate his acceptance of the risk, although the defence would be somewhat redundant since the defendant would in any event have discharged his obligation. Another possibility is that, if the plaintiff has made use of the nuisance, he will be deemed to have accepted the risk, by analogy with the 'common benefit' defence to liability under *Rylands* v *Fletcher* (para. 8.1.7.1).

Act of God or act of a third party may provide a defence, subject to possible liability for negligence in adopting or continuing the nuisance. Where the liability depends on proof of negligence, inevitable accident will be a defence but this amounts to little more than a plea that the defendant was not negligent. Ignorance of the nuisance is not, strictly speaking, a defence to an accrued liability but part of the question whether the defendant should be liable in the first place, e.g., for a latent defect (cf. *Clerk and Lindsell,* para. 18–59).

7.1.6.4 Ineffective defences It is something of a paradox to speak of 'defences' that are ineffective. Rather they are pleas that in the past have been raised by defendants, but which the courts have refused to accept as valid.

7.1.6.4.1 Coming to the nuisance It is not a defence to say that the defendant had carried on his activity before the plaintiff arrived and that the plaintiff therefore knew of and consented to the nuisance by choosing to move into the area. This is the effect of *Sturges* v *Bridgman* (1879) 11 ChD 852 in which the plaintiff doctor obtained an injunction against a confectioner who had carried on business for many years before the plaintiff built his consulting room which was the subject of the interference. The justification for the rule is that it would be unreasonable to expect someone not to purchase land because a neighbour was abusing his rights (*Bliss* v *Hall* (1838) 4 Bing NC 183). Alternatively, it is not for one landowner unilaterally to determine the uses to which neighbouring land can be put simply because he was the first to commence his particular use (*Buckley,* p. 117). The rule can work harshly, however, and has been the subject of criticism. In *Miller* v *Jackson* [1977] QB 966 a cricket ground had been in use for over 70 years before some houses were built in an adjoining field. Lord Denning MR (dissenting on this point) considered that the fact that the plaintiffs had chosen to purchase a house knowing that there was a risk that cricket balls would be hit on to the property was a good reason for holding that the defendants were not liable in nuisance. Geoffrey Lane LJ would have agreed with the Master of the Rolls, but for the authority of *Sturges* v *Bridgman* ('It may be that this rule works injustice'). Cumming-Bruce LJ agreed with Geoffrey Lane LJ that the defendants were liable, but then agreed with Lord Denning that an injunction should not be granted, partly on the ground that the plaintiffs had come to the nuisance. Thus the effectiveness of the rule in *Sturges* v *Bridgman* was considerably undermined by the refusal of injunctive relief (for criticism see Buckley (1978) 41 MLR 334).

It should be noted that the locality rule does, to some extent, ameliorate the absence of a defence of 'coming to the nuisance'. Someone who built residential property in an industrial area would not necessarily be able to put a stop to the industrial activities, since he would be expected to accept such intangible interferences with his enjoyment of property as were reasonable for that particular locality.

7.1.6.4.2 Public benefit The fact that the defendant's activity is useful to the public in general is no defence to an otherwise unreasonable interference (*Adams* v *Ursell* [1913] 1 Ch 269—injunction granted against fish and chip shop situated in a residential part of a street). It will be considered, however, in deciding whether the defendant's user is reasonable, and may be relevant to the question of whether an injunction should be granted.

7.1.6.4.3 Contribution of others It is not a defence that the nuisance is the result of the separate actions of several people, even though the actions of each of them would not, taken individually, amount to a nuisance (*Thorpe* v *Brumfitt* (1873) LR 8 Ch App 650). This is probably the case even where the act of one of them is sufficient to constitute a nuisance (*Pride of Derby & Derbyshire Angling Association Ltd* v *British Celanese Ltd* [1952] 1 All ER 1326, 1333). The rule is subject to the locality principle (para. 7.1.3.1) and the requirement that each of the contributors should have some awareness of what the others are doing (*Lambton* v *Mellish* [1894] 3 Ch 163, 166).

7.1.7 Remedies

There are three possible remedies available to the victim of a nuisance: damages, injunction and a form of self-help known as abatement.

7.1.7.1 Damages An award of damages in the case of physical damage to property or to the person will be calculated on the same basis as awards in other torts (see chapter 15). With nuisances that cause personal discomfort and inconvenience, such as noise or smell, it will be more difficult to apply general principles. In *Bone* v *Seal* [1975] 1 All ER 787 the Court of Appeal suggested that damages awarded for loss of amenity in personal injury cases might provide an analogy, so that interference by a noxious smell could be compared with a loss of sense of smell caused by an accident (an award of £6,000 for smell emanating from a pig farm over 12 years was reduced to £1,000). Lord Hoffmann, however, in *Hunter* v *Canary Wharf Ltd* [1997] 2 All ER 426, 451 (paras 7.1.1 and 7.1.4) has expressly disapproved of the *Bone* v *Seal* approach to quantification of damages in private nuisance amenity cases. In line with the majority's approach in *Hunter*, that private nuisance is essentially a 'tort against land' and not 'against the person', Lord Hoffmann asserted that it was, therefore, inappropriate to measure damages by reference to personal injury. Instead, he considered that damages in such a case should be fixed by reference to the diminution in capital value of the property as a result of the amenity damage. He acknowledged that '[t]o some extent this involves placing a value on intangibles', but was reassured that 'estate agents do this all the time'. He reinforced his faith in this basis of quantification by asserting that it could even be employed in a case of a transitory nuisance, where the capital value of the property would probably recover, to allow for compensation for the diminution in the amenity value of the property during the period for which the nuisance persisted.

Damages for past losses can be combined with a claim for an injunction, and if an injunction is refused damages can be awarded for future loss (as in *Miller* v *Jackson* [1977] QB 966).

7.1.7.2 Injunction Although, being an equitable remedy, the award of an injunction is discretionary, in practice where the nuisance is continuing the plaintiff is entitled to an injunction almost as a matter of course (*Redland Bricks Ltd* v *Morris* [1970] AC 652, 664; *Pride of Derby & Derbyshire Angling Association Ltd* v *British Celanese Ltd* [1953] Ch 149, 181). Since Lord Cairns's Act of 1858 the court has had the power to award damages in lieu of an injunction (Chancery Amendment Act 1858; see now Supreme Court Act 1981, s. 50). This power has been severely restricted, however, by adherence to the principles laid down by A.L. Smith LJ in *Shelfer* v *City of London Electric Lighting Co.* [1895] 1 Ch 287, 322 to determine when damages should be substituted. This would be:

(1)   If the injury to the plaintiff's legal rights is small,

(2)   And is one which is capable of being estimated in money,

(3)   And is one which can be adequately compensated by a small money payment,

(4)   And the case is one in which it would be oppressive to the defendant to grant an injunction.

At times, the courts have treated this statutory discretion as virtually coextensive with the general equitable discretion (a recent example is *Kennaway* v *Thompson* [1981] QB 88). But where the case does not satisfy the conditions set out in *Shelfer* v *City of London Electric Lighting Co.* it does not necessarily follow that the plaintiff is automatically entitled to an injunction (see *Buckley*, p. 149). Other, more general equitable principles might justify the refusal of this discretionary remedy.

Traditionally, where the plaintiff has established a substantial interference the courts have been extremely reluctant to permit extrinsic considerations, such as the effect of an injunction on the defendant or the public, to influence the relief granted. This stems from respect for private property rights and an intuitive objection to what is regarded as compulsory purchase of the plaintiff's rights if he is left to his remedy in damages. Claims that an injunction would cause an immensely disproportionate loss to the defendant, or would result in heavy job losses from the closure of a factory, or even that the city of Birmingham would be turned into a vast cesspit have all fallen on deaf ears (*Pride of Derby & Derbyshire Angling Association Ltd* v *British Celanese Ltd* [1953] Ch 149; *Pennington* v *Brinsop Hall Coal Co.* (1877) 5 ChD 769; *Attorney-General* v *Birmingham Corporation* (1858) 4 K & J 528). As a general rule an injunction will be refused only where the interference with plaintiff's right is trifling or slight. For example, in *Elliott* v *London Borough of Islington* [1991] 10 EG 145 the Court of Appeal held that interference with the plaintiff's garden wall by tree roots was not a small or relatively minor matter justifying the substitution of damages for an injunction. Lord Donaldson MR said (at p. 146) that though compulsory purchase under statute was well known and subject to specific protections for the individual, it was 'not for the courts to add to that burden on the citizen a system whereby . . . they will grant, for a fee payable to the plaintiff, a compulsory lease of land to accommodate the roots of this tree in addition to putting up with the nuisance which it creates'.

In *Miller* v *Jackson* [1977] QB 966, para. 7.1.3.4, a majority of the Court of Appeal (Lord Denning MR and Cumming-Bruce LJ) refused an injunction on the ground that the public interest in preserving playing fields for recreation in the face of increasing development outweighed the plaintiffs' private interest in not having their house and garden peppered with cricket balls. Cumming-Bruce LJ also considered that the fact that the plaintiffs had 'come to the nuisance' was a factor to be weighed when considering the equities between the parties (see also *Tetley* v *Chitty* [1986] 1 All ER 663, 675). Whether this heralds a more flexible approach is an open question, for in the later case of *Kennaway* v *Thompson* [1981] QB 88 a differently constituted Court of Appeal criticised *Miller* v *Jackson*, and in granting the plaintiff an injunction against the noise created by power-boat racing, restated the principles of *Shelfer* v *City of London Electric Lighting Co.* In *Elliott* v *London Borough of Islington* [1991] 10 EG 145, 149 Lord Donaldson MR commented that 'it is not generally appropriate that specific private rights should be denied in order to give rise to indefinite advantages to the general public. Were it otherwise, the court would . . . be legislating to deprive people of their rights'.

It is certainly arguable that the courts ought to be more flexible in their choice of remedies, taking account of wider social and economic considerations (see Ogus and Richardson [1977] CLJ 284, 305–14 and Tromans [1982] CLJ 87), though in some circumstances the court may be willing to consider granting an injunction, *quia timet*, where it would not be possible to award damages because the cause of action does not arise until damage occurs despite the fact that there is a present risk of damage occurring in the future (*Midland Bank* v *Bardgrove Property Services* [1992] 37 EG 126). In certain instances the law of remedies has had an adverse effect on the substantive law: 'If the only way in which a court can avoid imposing an injunction is by denying liability altogether, then plaintiffs run the risk of being left with no remedy at all' (Tromans, op. cit., p. 105; consider *Allen* v *Gulf Oil Refining Ltd* [1981] AC 1001, para. 7.1.6.2). On the other hand, the severity of an injunction can be mitigated by suspending its operation to give the defendant time to comply or by the terms of the order limiting its application in certain ways (see, e.g., *Kennaway* v *Thompson*). Moreover, it may be that there are certain values which are not reducible to a monetary compensation and yet are worthy of the courts' protection even in the face of substantial economic costs.

7.1.7.3 Abatement

Abatement, i.e., removal of the nuisance by the victim, is not encouraged by the law. Normally, notice must be given to the wrongdoer before exercising the right of abatement unless (a) it is an emergency, or (b) the nuisance can be removed without entering the wrongdoer's land, or (c) the person who created the nuisance still occupies the premises (*Jones* v *Williams* (1843) 11 M & W 176; *Lemon* v *Webb* [1895] AC 1; *Lagan Navigation Co.* v *Lambeg Bleaching, Dyeing & Finishing Co. Ltd* [1927] AC 226). Abatement is appropriate only in clear and simple cases of nuisance, such as an overhanging branch or an encroaching root, which would not justify the expense of legal proceedings, and urgent cases which require an immediate remedy (*Burton* v *Winters* [1993] 1 WLR 1077, 1081 CA). A person who abates a nuisance forgoes his right of action in respect of the nuisance (ibid. at p. 1080), although he may be entitled to damages for the harm suffered before the abatement (*City of Richmond* v *Scantelbury* [1991] 2 VR 38; *Clerk and Lindsell*, para. 24–29) and for the cost incurred in carrying out the abatement provided the expenditure was justifiably and reasonably incurred to remove a potential source of danger to the plaintiff's property or persons on the property (*Co-Operative Wholesale Society Ltd* v *British Railways Board, The Times*, 20 December 1995; for comment see

Murdoch [1996] 36 EG 142). Yet there is a right to abate even in the absence of a right of action, e.g., where a tree spreads over a boundary but has caused no damage (*Smith* v *Giddy* [1904] 2 KB 448). If a plaintiff brings an action seeking an injunction to remove the nuisance but an injunction has been refused by the court, the plaintiff cannot then resort to abatement, since the court has determined the issue and the justification for the remedy of self-redress has gone (*Burton* v *Winters* [1993] 1 WLR 1077, 1082). In exercising the right unnecessary damage must not be caused, except that where the alternative method of abatement would damage an innocent person the interference must be with the property of the wrongdoer (*Lagan Navigation Co.* v *Lambeg Bleaching, Dyeing & Finishing Co. Ltd* [1927] AC 226, 246; *Roberts* v *Rose* (1865) LR 1 Ex 82, 89).

7.1.8 Standard of liability
The relationship between the torts of private nuisance and negligence is problematic. In some cases negligence is regarded as an essential requirement for liability, and in others it is treated as irrelevant. Judicial pronouncements support both fault-based and strict liability, and there is little to be gained from listing authorities on each side of the divide. Some of the confusion is attributable to a statement made by Lord Reid in *The Wagon Mound (No. 2)* [1967] 1 AC 617, 639: 'It is quite true that negligence is not an essential element in nuisance. Nuisance is a term used to cover a wide variety of tortious acts or omissions and in many negligence in the narrow sense is not essential.' However, 'although negligence may not be necessary, fault of some kind is almost always necessary and fault generally involves foreseeability'.

Lord Reid's distinction between 'negligence in the narrow sense' and 'fault of some kind' appears to differentiate between the tort of negligence involving duty of care, breach of duty and consequent damage, and the degree of personal responsibility required for liability in nuisance. This could mean simply that the torts of nuisance and negligence are not coextensive (an interpretation that seems more compelling in the light of the House of Lords' decision and pronouncements in *Hunter* v *Canary Wharf Ltd* [1997] 2 All ER 426; see paras 7.1.1 and 7.1.4), although that observation might have been more carefully expressed. An alternative view is that the statement is dealing with remoteness of damage and seeks to draw a distinction between the degree of foreseeability required in negligence and nuisance (Dias [1967] CLJ 62), a view apparently endorsed by Lord Goff in *Cambridge Water Co.* v *Eastern Counties Leather plc* [1994] 2 WLR 53, 76. The case was primarily concerned with remoteness of damage in nuisance, and is authority for the proposition that the test is reasonable foreseeability of damage, as in negligence. Lord Reid's statement, however, is directed at the standard of liability in nuisance. Counsel had argued that foreseeability should not be employed as a test of remoteness in all cases of nuisance, because it was not an element of liability in all cases of nuisance. In seeking to refute this contention Lord Reid agreed that 'negligence in the narrow sense' was not essential, but some kind of 'fault' is, and fault 'generally involves foreseeability'.

The question that remains, however, is what is encompassed by the word 'fault', and is it any stricter than the standard that would be applied to a claim in negligence? It has already been emphasised that unreasonable user of land is not synonymous with a failure to exercise reasonable care (paras 7.1.3 and 7.1.3.7), so the fact that the defendant has taken all reasonable precautions will not necessarily excuse him. The usual explanation for this is that the factors that are taken into account when assessing whether the user of land was reasonable relate primarily to intangible nuisances such as noise or smell, where the defendant's conduct is probably quite deliberate, but he has miscalculated the degree of interference that he may legitimately inflict upon his neighbours. The principal remedy sought by the plaintiff will be an injunction, so the defendant will know about the interference at the latest when proceedings are issued. At this stage there can be no question of the defendant being unable to foresee the consequences of his activity, and the issue before the court will be whether the interference is sufficiently substantial to constitute a nuisance warranting an injunction. Thus, statements in injunction cases to the effect that liability in nuisance is strict can be discounted (*Winfield and Jolowicz,* p. 414; *Buckley,* p. 20; Law Com. No. 32, p. 25), and cases involving claims for damages are more relevant when looking to the standard of liability.

In *Cambridge Water Co.* v *Eastern Counties Leather plc* [1994] 2 WLR 53, 75 Lord Goff acknowledged that it was axiomatic that there is a distinction between injunction cases and cases claiming damages for past harm, and that conclusions about the standard of liability should not be drawn from injunction cases. An injunction is significant only in terms of the defendant's knowledge, however, which relates to the foreseeability of the consequences of his activity. 'Strict liability' is sometimes equated with liability in the absence of knowledge or foresight of the harm by the defendant, but a defendant who has taken reasonable precautions to avoid foreseeable harm, who nonetheless is held liable, is clearly subject to a stricter duty than in negligence. Despite the fact that in *Cambridge Water* the House of Lords held that foreseeability of the type of damage is a prerequisite of liability in damages for nuisance, nonetheless Lord Goff agreed (at p. 75) that in the case of a nuisance created by someone for whose actions the defendant was responsible:

> . . . the fact that the defendant has taken all reasonable care will not of itself exonerate him from liability, the relevant control mechanism being found within the principle of reasonable user.

The principle of reasonable user—the principle of give and take as between neighbouring occupiers of land—functions as a control mechanism for tempering the strictness of liability in nuisance, said his Lordship, because if the user is reasonable the defendant will not be liable but if the user is not reasonable he will be liable, even though he may have exercised reasonable care to avoid the interference. On the whole, however, the balancing exercise which the principle of reasonable user implies only takes place in the context of amenity damage, as opposed to physical damage. Whereas the reasonableness of an interference by, say, noise or smell is inevitably a matter of degree, the courts have generally taken the view that if the defendant's use of land is causing physical damage to his neighbour the user cannot be reasonable (cf. *Ellison* v *Ministry of Defence* (1997) 81 BLR 101; see para. 7.1.2.1).

Another possible explanation for judicial statements to the effect that reasonable care is not a defence to a proved nuisance (e.g., *Rapier* v *London Tramways Co.* [1893] 2 Ch 588, 599; *Read* v *J. Lyons & Co. Ltd* [1947] AC 156, 183) is that liability for intangible nuisance is strict, whereas liability for physical damage depends on proof of negligence (Cane (1982) 2 OJLS 30, 55–9). Most injunction cases are cases of amenity nuisance, hence the apparent connection between injunctions and strict liability. The justification for these different standards lies in competing conceptions of justice, one fairness-based the other conduct-based. The conduct-based conception puts the emphasis on the causation of damage, and the 'prime modern embodiment' of this conception is the tort of negligence. Because of the dominance of negligence within the conduct-based theory, liability for physical damage depends on proof of negligence. Justice as fairness involves the reciprocal sharing of benefits and burdens among the members of a society. Cane states (at pp. 56–7) that:

> The conception of justice underlying amenity nuisance is fairness-based. The test of reasonableness in this form of nuisance is concerned with fair accommodation of competing land use claims. . . .
>
> [I]t is no defence that one could not foresee the excessive level of interference because the gist of the action is not conduct-based. For the same reason, it is no defence to say that one took all reasonable care to reduce the level of interference to a minimum.

This is an elegant theory, but it appears to rest upon a somewhat hazy distinction between physical damage caused by *acts* (where the conception of justice is conduct-based, hence fault liability) and amenity damage caused by *activities* (where the conception is fairness-based, hence strict liability). 'The focus of the amenity-nuisance action is damage caused by activities rather than acts' (ibid.). What conception of justice, it might be asked, underlies an action for physical damage caused by an activity? It can hardly be suggested that activities do not cause physical damage (*St Helens Smelting Co.* v *Tipping* (1865) 11 HL Cas 642 provides a classic example). If the act/activity distinction is the basis for different standards of liability then in some forms of nuisance where physical damage occurs, liability must be stricter than in others. If this is not the appropriate distinction then the theory becomes little more than an assertion that where physical damage has occurred the courts tend to look for fault. This is a proposition with which no one would disagree, but it is not particularly helpful in elucidating the circumstances in which liability will be imposed notwithstanding the defendant's exercise of reasonable care.

There is no general rule as to the standard of liability applicable in all cases of nuisance. Different circumstances give rise to different standards. Where the nuisance is attributable to an act of nature or the act of a third party for whom the defendant is not responsible, liability turns on negligence, the standard of care being subjective (*Goldman* v *Hargrave* [1967] 1 AC 645). Where the defendant has created the nuisance there are several possibilities. First, the nuisance may be obvious, in which case there is no difficulty over the foreseeability of harm to the plaintiff. The defendant has simply miscalculated the degree of interference he can lawfully inflict. It is no defence that he took reasonable care to avoid the nuisance. Secondly, where the nuisance is not obvious but develops as a result of the defendant's otherwise lawful activity going awry, the defendant will be liable if he was negligent in that he ought to have foreseen the likelihood of the mishap and the damage. It makes no difference whether the action is called nuisance or negligence, and the exercise of reasonable care will avoid liability. The rule in *Wringe* v *Cohen* [1940] 1 KB 229 (para. 7.2.3.3.2) is usually regarded as an anomalous exception to this principle, in that an occupier of defective premises adjoining the highway can be liable whether he knew of the defect or not. Liability, however, is based on the failure to repair, and it is difficult to see how it can be argued that damage attributable to the occupier's neglect of his repairing obligations was unforeseeable. As Denning LJ observed in *Mint* v *Good* [1951] 1 KB 517 when structures fall into dangerous disrepair 'there must be some fault on the part of someone or other'. Finally, in some situations, where the defendant's activity is particularly hazardous, nuisance may overlap with the rule in *Rylands* v *Fletcher* (see, e.g., *Midwood* v *Manchester Corporation* [1905] 2 KB 597; *Solloway* v *Hampshire County Council* (1981) 79 LGR 449, 453). Liability is then strict in that the exercise of reasonable care is not a defence, although the damage must be of a type that was reasonably foreseeable (*Cambridge Water Co.* v *Eastern Counties Leather plc* [1994] 2 WLR 53). It has been observed (Smithers and Seal [1998] 02 EG 115) that nuisance in this context can become a form of environmental liability and that, given increasing environmental awareness, it may prove more difficult generally for defendants to contend that such damage was not foreseeable. Even if this is so, what it gives may, in the nuisance action, have effectively been taken away by the House of Lords' confirmation in *Hunter* v *Canary Wharf Ltd* [1997] 2 All ER 426 (see paras 7.1.1 and 7.1.4) that an action can be maintained in private nuisance only if a plaintiff can establish a recognisable proprietary or possessory interest in the land affected.

7.2 PUBLIC NUISANCE

7.2.1 Definition

Public nuisance has been defined as 'an act not warranted by law or an omission to discharge a legal duty, which act or omission obstructs or causes damage or inconvenience to the public in the exercise of rights common to all Her Majesty's subjects' (Stephen, *Digest of the Criminal Law*, 1883). This definition suggests that public nuisance is concerned with the infringement of 'public rights', but it does not indicate which public rights, nor the type of conduct that will constitute a public nuisance (see generally, Spencer [1989] CLJ 55). More recently, Romer LJ defined a public nuisance as an act or omission 'which materially affects the reasonable comfort and convenience of life of a class of Her Majesty's subjects' (*Attorney-General* v *PYA Quarries Ltd* [1957] 2 QB 169, 184), but this does not take the matter much further. The courts tend to approach the question of the existence of a nuisance, whether public or private, as a question of fact. This is partly because it is difficult to embrace all the different fact-situations regarded as nuisances within a useful definition, and partly because the courts are reluctant to place conceptual limits on the discretion that a reasonableness test permits. Thus the defendant's conduct or activity can be measured against the degree of interference with public rights. It is not essential that the defendant's conduct be an independently unlawful act since public nuisance is 'primarily concerned with the effect of the act complained of as opposed to its inherent lawfulness or unlawfulness' (*Gillingham Borough Council* v *Medway (Chatham) Dock Co. Ltd* [1992] 3 WLR 449, 458 per Buckley J). For example, excessive noise and vibration from heavy goods vehicles passing along the highway could amount to a public nuisance notwithstanding that the use of the highway for passage and repassage is itself lawful.

Whether a sufficient number of people have been affected by the nuisance to constitute a 'class' of Her Majesty's subjects is also a question of fact, but it is not necessary that all members of the class have been affected; it will be sufficient if a representative cross-section of the class have been inconvenienced (*Attorney-General* v *PYA Quarries Ltd*; in *Attorney-General of British Columbia, ex rel. Eaton* v *Haney Speedways Ltd* (1963) 39 DLR (2d) 48 the members of seven neighbouring families amounted to a class of the public). In *R* v *Johnson* [1997] 1 WLR 367 the Court of Appeal held that hundreds of obscene telephone calls to at least 13 women over a period of five years constituted a public nuisance.

7.2.2 Distinguished from private nuisance

Although the same conduct can amount to both a private and public nuisance (see, e.g., *Halsey* v *Esso Petroleum Co. Ltd* [1961] 2 All ER 145) the two actions rest upon conceptually different foundations. The tort of private nuisance protects a person's enjoyment of land, but public nuisance is not necessarily connected with an interference with the use of land, and therefore the plaintiff need not have an interest in land to be entitled to sue in public nuisance. Public nuisance is primarily a crime, for which the remedy is a prosecution or a relator action by the Attorney-General on behalf of the public. A plaintiff must suffer 'particular damage' over and above the damage sustained by the public generally before he can maintain an action in tort for public nuisance. Such 'particular damage' often takes the form of personal injury or damage to personal property, the right to claim for which in private nuisance has been cast into doubt by the House of Lords in *Hunter* v *Canary Wharf Ltd* [1997] 2 All ER 426 (see para. 7.1.1). 'Particular damage' is not a requirement in private nuisance. Finally, the defence of prescription does not apply to public nuisance because no one can acquire the right to commit a crime.

7.2.3 The public rights protected

Historically the crime of public nuisance covered four broad categories: public decency, public health, public convenience and public safety. Crimes such as keeping a disorderly house, displaying one's naked body to a crowd or exposing a corpse in a public place are now regulated by statute and were never significant in the realm of tort. Public health is also largely the subject of legislative regulation. Public convenience and public safety are essentially concerned with nuisance to the highway.

7.2.3.1 Public health The tort of public nuisance plays only a residual role in the control of pollution, which is now the subject of extensive statutory control. (The principal statutes are the Public Health Acts 1936 and 1961, the Control of Pollution Act 1974, the Environmental Protection Act 1990 and the Clean Air Act 1993. For an account of the emergence of legislation to protect health in the 19th century see Brenner (1974) 3 J Legal Stud 403, 424–32). It is not necessary to prove damage to health from noxious emissions in order to establish a nuisance. It will be sufficient to show that there has been 'a material interference with the comfort and convenience of life' (*Attorney-General* v *Keymer Brick & Tile Co. Ltd* (1903) 67 JP 434, 435 per Joyce J; but the plaintiff must establish that he has suffered 'particular damage', see para. 7.2.4).

A modern example is provided by the judgment of Veale J in *Halsey* v *Esso Petroleum Co. Ltd* [1961] 2 All ER 145 which illustrates the relationship between both public and private nuisance and an action under *Rylands* v *Fletcher*. The plaintiff complained about the operation of the defendants' oil depot. Acid smuts had damaged clothing hung out to dry in his garden and the paintwork of the plaintiff's car parked in the highway. There was a nauseating smell, and noise, from both the boilers in the depot and oil tankers arriving and departing during the night, interfered with the plaintiff's sleep. Veale J held the defendants liable in *public* nuisance for the damage to the car and the noise created by the tankers on the night shift (unreasonable use of the highway). The defendants were liable in *private* nuisance for the damage to the clothing, the noxious smell and the noise emanating from the depot itself, and under *Rylands* v *Fletcher* for the escape of the acid smuts in relation to *both* the car and the clothing. (Note that, following *Hunter* v *Canary Wharf Ltd*—para. 7.1.1—the damage to clothing might be deemed inherently personal, rather than proprietary, damage and so not actionable in private nuisance. Note also that, though the noise and smells would remain allowable as actionable amenity damage, the loss would be quantified by reference to the diminution in value of the *land*, rather than the personal discomfort of the land user—para. 7.1.7.1.)

7.2.3.2 Convenience: obstruction of the highway Nuisance to the highway takes two forms: (a) obstructions other than obstructions which are also dangerous, and (b) acts alleged to be a public nuisance because they produce a risk of physical harm (*Morton* v *Wheeler* (1956) unreported, CA per Denning LJ). An obstruction may be both inconvenient and dangerous and its categorisation often depends upon the pure chance of whether an accident has occurred. Thus a gully in a street may be dangerous (*Priest* v *Manchester Corporation* (1915) 84 LJ KB 1734) while a ditch may be a simple obstruction (*Fineux* v *Hovenden* (1598) Cro Eliz 664). This rather obvious distinction would not be of any particular significance were it not for the fact that the basis of liability for the same nuisance differs according to the nature of the damage sustained by the plaintiff. Where the nuisance has caused an obstruction and the plaintiff has suffered economic loss as a result, liability turns upon proof of particular damage over and above that suffered by the public at large (para. 7.2.4). Where the plaintiff has suffered personal injury or damage to property there can be no dispute that this constitutes particular damage (*Trevett* v *Lee* [1955] 1 All ER 406, 409) but the courts will generally look for negligence or some 'fault' on the part of the defendant (see para. 7.2.5).

Obstruction of the highway, or the failure to repair it where such a duty exists, have been criminal offences since the 11th century. Examples include the deliberate obstruction of the highway with rocks and rubble (*Iveson* v *Moore* (1699) 1 Ld Raym 486), obstructing a public navigable river with a barge (*Rose* v *Miles* (1815) 4 M & S 101) and digging ditches in the highway without authority for the purpose of laying pipes (*R* v *Longton Gas Co.* (1860) 2 E & E 651). Convenience is, by definition, concerned with relative ease of passage and the question of whether a nuisance exists must be a matter of degree. This is particularly so where the obstruction is of a temporary nature. The issue is whether the defendant's user of the highway was reasonable (*Fritz v Hobson* (1880) 14 ChD 542, 552 per Fry J).

In *R* v *Russell* (1805) 6 East 427 the defendant was prosecuted for leaving wagons standing in the street for several hours at a time for the purposes of loading and unloading. This was held to be a nuisance because he was seeking to conduct his business in the street, the primary object of which is the free passage of the public (for a modern example see *Attorney-General* v *Gastonia Coaches Ltd* [1977] RTR 219). Even where the defendant's use is essential for the purpose of carrying on his business it will not necessarily be a reasonable user of the highway (*Attorney-General* v *Brighton & Hove Co-operative Supply Association* [1890] 1 Ch 276, 285; *R* v *Jones* (1813) 3 Camp 230). On the other hand, where the obstruction is reasonable in both its extent and duration it will not amount to a nuisance (*Harper* v *Haden & Sons Ltd* [1933] Ch 298—temporary scaffolding and hoarding on the highway which obstructed access to the plaintiff's premises held not to be a nuisance). The same principle of reasonable user applies to obstruction by gathering a crowd together, and it is no defence that the defendant did not intend the crowd to gather if that was the probable consequence of his actions, even by something lawfully done on his premises (*Lyons* v *Gulliver* [1914] 1 Ch 631—a theatre queue obstructing access to the plaintiff's premises). Peaceful picketing of the plaintiff's premises by way of protesting against his business practices may, in some circumstances, constitute a nuisance (*Hubbard* v *Pitt* [1976] QB 142 and 171; in the context of a trade dispute see the case of *Thomas* v *National Union of Mineworkers (South Wales Area)* [1985] 2 All ER

1 in which Scott J, unable to find facts supporting an action in nuisance, 'invented' a new 'tort' of unreasonable harassment. Subsequently the Court of Appeal stated, albeit in the setting of domestic rather than industrial strife, that there is no tort of harassment in English law: *Patel* v *Patel* [1988] 2 FLR 179; but in *Khorasandjian* v *Bush* [1993] 3 WLR 476 a majority of the Court of Appeal considered that this proposition was too wide, holding that a defendant could be liable in private nuisance for harassment by persistent unwanted telephone calls; and in *Burris* v *Azadani* [1995] 4 All ER 802 the Court of Appeal took the view that the court in *Patel* v *Patel* had not intended to lay down a general principle. Sir Thomas Bingham MR appeared to accept that harassment was capable of being treated as an independent tort, listing it along with a number of recognised torts as providing the basis for an injunction. *Khorasandjian* v *Bush* has now been overruled by the House of Lords in *Hunter* v *Canary Wharf Ltd* [1997] 2 All ER 426, on the basis that the plaintiff had insufficient standing to sue in private nuisance, but not before its common law recognition of a tort of harassment had effectively been codified by the Protection from Harassment Act 1997, which provides for both a tort and crime of harassment; see para. 12.2).

It is no defence that the public benefit derived from the defendant's activity exceeds the inconvenience which the nuisance creates (*R* v *Train* (1862) 2 B & S 640; *R* v *Ward* (1836) 4 A & E 384, 404). Nonetheless, the benefit to the public may be taken into account when the court considers whether in all the circumstances of the case the defendant's user of the highway was reasonable. If the inconvenience was trifling the court would be unlikely to find that a nuisance existed. Where the inconvenience was great the defendant would have difficulty in demonstrating that the benefit from his activity was sufficient to make the user reasonable.

7.2.3.3 Safety: dangers to the highway Dangers to the highway can be divided into two categories: (a) dangers on the highway itself, and (b) dangers arising from premises adjoining the highway.

7.2.3.3.1 Dangers on the highway Almost any obstruction can create a source of danger, such as a heap of rubble (*Burgess* v *Gray* (1845) 1 CB 578) or an unlit spiked barrier (*Clark* v *Chambers* (1878) 3 QBD 327). The principle of reasonable user applies to obstructions which lead to physical damage. In *Trevett* v *Lee* [1955] 1 All ER 406, for example, the plaintiff was injured when she tripped over a hosepipe which had been laid across a country lane during daylight. The Court of Appeal held that this was not an unreasonable user and did not amount to a public nuisance (cf. *Farrell* v *John Mowlem & Co. Ltd* [1954] 1 Lloyd's Rep 437—plaintiff tripped over a rubber pipeline laid on the pavement; defendant liable). An unlit vehicle parked so as to obstruct the highway at night may constitute a public nuisance (*Ware* v *Garston Haulage Co.* [1944] KB 30). If the vehicle is left in a position which makes it a foreseeable source of danger to other road users there would be liability in negligence in any event. But in *Dymond* v *Pearce* [1972] 1 QB 496 it was said that a vehicle parked so as to constitute an obstruction can be a nuisance even though it does not create a foreseeable risk. The defendant parked a lorry overnight on a dual carriageway under a street light with its lights on. The Court of Appeal found that this was an unreasonable user because it had been done solely for the defendant's convenience. It might have been different if the vehicle had broken down (cf. *Coote* v *Stone* [1971] 1 WLR 279). The plaintiff in *Dymond* v *Pearce* was a pillion passenger on a motor cycle that collided with the stationary lorry, but he did not succeed in his action because although the lorry was a nuisance it was not the *cause* of the accident. Responsibility lay with the motor cyclist who had not been watching where he was going. As Sachs LJ observed, it would be rare to find that something which was not a foreseeable cause of an accident would in law be regarded as the actual cause of the accident (i.e., in the absence of negligence by the defendant).

The danger to the highway need not take the form of an obstruction. In *Dollman* v *Hillman* [1941] 1 All ER 355 a piece of fat from a butcher's shop upon which the plaintiff slipped was held to be a nuisance, and clouds of smoke which obscure the vision of drivers may constitute a nuisance (*Holling* v *Yorkshire Traction Co.* [1948] 2 All ER 662; *Tysoe* v *Davies* [1984] RTR 88).

7.2.3.3.2 Dangers arising from premises adjoining the highway An occupier whose premises adjoin the highway is responsible for the state of repair of the premises, because the public should not be prejudiced by the occupier's neglect of his property (*Tarry* v *Ashton* (1876) 1 QBD 314, 320 per Quain J). A lamp projecting over the highway which fell on a passer-by was a nuisance (*Tarry* v *Ashton*), and a rotten fence close to a highway is an 'obvious nuisance' (*Harrold* v *Watney* [1898] 2 QB 322; see also *Mint* v *Good* [1951] 1 KB 517—wall adjoining footpath collapsed on to plaintiff).

In *Wringe* v *Cohen* [1940] 1 KB 229 the Court of Appeal stated a general rule that where premises on a highway become dangerous from want of repair, the person under a duty to repair is liable for damage caused by their collapse whether he knew or ought to have known of the danger or not. (The rules that apply to a landlord's liability in private nuisance, including the duty created by the Defective Premises Act 1972, s. 4, also apply in public nuisance. See para. 7.1.5.3.3.) Where, however, the nuisance is created by a trespasser or by a secret and unobservable operation of nature (a latent defect), the occupier or owner will not be liable unless he knew or ought to have known of the danger, i.e., unless he negligently permitted the nuisance to continue. The rule in *Wringe* v *Cohen,* as it has come to be known, has been criticised both for setting a stricter standard of liability than the previous case law justified, and for undermining that standard through the exceptions of latent defect and act of a trespasser. There is some force in this latter point since it is unlikely that an occupier will be unaware of the existence of a danger, where it is not attributable to a latent defect or the act of a trespasser, unless he was negligent. In *Mint* v *Good* [1951] 1 KB 517 Denning LJ stated that the occupier is liable when structures fall into dangerous disrepair 'because there must be some fault on the part of someone or other for that to happen; and he is responsible for it to persons using the highway, even though he was not actually at fault himself'. Where a tree, as opposed to an artificial projection, overhangs the highway it will be easier to infer that the fall was caused by a latent defect (*Noble* v *Harrison* [1926] 2 KB 332; *Caminer* v *Northern & London Investment Trust Ltd* [1951] AC 99).

Danger to the highway may arise not only from the defective state of repair of premises but also from the nature of the premises. Thus, a low wall mounted with spikes (*Fenna* v *Clare & Co.* [1895] 1 QB 199) or an unfenced excavated area adjacent to the highway (*Barnes* v *Ward* (1850) 9 CB 392) are nuisances, even though the danger consists of an accidental deviation from the road. In *Castle* v *St Augustine's Links* (1922) 38 TLR 615 the defendants were held liable in nuisance when a golf ball was struck through the windscreen of a motor car. The evidence indicated that golf balls had been repeatedly sliced on to the highway and this was a substantial interference with the public's use of the highway (cf. *Bolton* v *Stone* [1951] AC 850).

It is no defence to claim that the dangerous state of affairs came about as a result of industrial action. In *Woolfall* v *Knowsley Borough Council, The Times,* 26 June 1992 the plaintiff, who was standing on the highway, was injured by a fragment from an aerosol can which exploded on a burning rubbish tip on land adjoining the highway. The rubbish had not been cleared from the tip because the local authority had not wanted to aggravate an industrial dispute with its employees. Nonetheless, the Court of Appeal held that the local authority remained under a duty to protect the public who might be endangered from activities on the land.

7.2.4 Particular damage

The requirement that the plaintiff suffer particular damage over and above the injury suffered by the public at large goes back to the origins of public nuisance as a tort (*Anon.* (1535) YB 27 Hen 8, Mich pl 10; Newark (1949) 65 LQR 480). The infringement of public rights could lead to extensive damage and numerous claims, which it might be unreasonable to expect the defendant to meet. Particular damage operates as a control device which both crystallises tortious liability and at the same time limits its extent to the damage suffered by the plaintiff. The damage must be both direct and substantial (*Benjamin* v *Storr* (1874) LR 9 CP 400, although it is not clear precisely what the word 'direct' means in this context: *The Wagon Mound (No. 2)* [1967] 1 AC 617, 636).

Personal inconvenience caused by delay will not be sufficient (*Winterbottom* v *Lord Derby* (1867) LR 2 Ex 316; but cf. *Boyd* v *Great Northern Railway Co.* [1895] 2 IR 555—doctor delayed for 20 minutes at a level crossing succeeded on the basis that his time was 'of substantial value'). The fact that the plaintiff's business is more expensive to run can amount to particular damage (*Gravesham Borough Council* v *British Railways Board* [1978] Ch 379, 398). In *Rose* v *Miles* (1815) 4 M & S 101, for example, the plaintiff's barges were obstructed and he had to unload the cargo and transport it by land at additional cost. This expense constituted particular damage. Loss of custom attributable to members of the public being obstructed in obtaining access to the plaintiff's shop may be particular damage (*Wilkes* v *Hungerford Market Co.* (1835) 2 Bing NC 281; there are two divergent lines of authority on this point: *Clerk and Lindsell,* para. 18–97, n. 28; see also *Salmond and Heuston,*

p. 88). In *Benjamin* v *Storr* (1874) LR 9 CP 400 the defendant was liable for parking wagons outside the plaintiff's coffee shop which interfered with the light and air to the premises and obstructed access. Here, particular damage shades into interference with an occupier's private rights, such as the private right of access to the highway which is distinct from the occupier's right to use the highway as a member of the public (*Lyon* v *Fishmongers Co.* (1876) 1 App Cas 662; *Chaplin* v *Westminster Corporation* [1901] 2 Ch 329). In *Tate & Lyle Industries Ltd* v *Greater London Council* [1983] 1 All ER 1159 the House of Lords failed to draw any clear distinction between public rights and private rights, and held the defendants liable in public nuisance for obstructing access to the plaintiffs' property, although there had been no interference with private proprietary rights. (For comment see Samuel (1983) 99 LQR 529; Jones (1983) 34 NILQ 341; and generally on particular damage Kodilinye (1986) 6 LS 182.) (Note that the statutory right of action against a highway authority in respect of non-repair of the highway created by the Highways (Miscellaneous Provisions) Act 1961, s. 1 [now the Highways Act 1980, s. 41] is limited to claims in respect of personal injury or physical damage to property attributable to the fact that the highway was 'dangerous to traffic'. Claims for pure economic loss are not actionable: *Wentworth* v *Wiltshire County Council* [1993] 2 WLR 175.)

Where the plaintiff's loss is not purely financial but takes the form of physical damage to property or personal injury, there can be no dispute that he has suffered particular damage. In a case such as *Halsey* v *Esso Petroleum Co. Ltd* [1961] 2 All ER 145 (see para. 7.2.3.1) the court will tend to look at the reasonableness of the defendant's behaviour, in a manner analogous to private nuisance. Where personal injury has been occasioned, however, the court will generally require some element of fault, but it is not clear whether the standard of liability is the same as in the tort of negligence.

7.2.5 Standard of liability

As with private nuisance, the question of the standard of liability in public nuisance is confused. Newark (1949) 65 LQR 480 argued that much of this confusion was attributable to changes that occurred after 1840, when nuisance concepts were grafted on to actions which had previously been dealt with in negligence. Unfortunately, the cases he cites do not support this theory, which is inherently implausible since it runs contrary to the historical trend, which was to move away from stricter forms of liability to fault liability (see Winfield (1926) 42 LQR 184). More likely is that the courts began to import the requirement of fault into actions in public nuisance, particularly in cases of danger to the highway where the analogy with ordinary 'running-down' actions was too obvious to be overlooked. There developed what Winfield called a 'hybrid action of nuisance and negligence. Sometimes it looks as if negligence were the substance of the action, and nuisance were an untechnical term; sometimes the exact reverse would be the truth' (ibid. p. 197; see also Winfield (1931) 4 CLJ 189, 197–201). The result is that it is possible to point to one line of cases favouring strict liability and to another line of cases favouring fault liability (*Buckley*, pp. 68–70).

In *Farrell* v *John Mowlem & Co. Ltd* [1954] 1 Lloyd's Rep 437 Devlin J said (at p. 440) that 'any person who actually creates a nuisance is liable for it and for the consequences which flow from it, whether he is negligent or not'. This statement was approved by the Privy Council in *The Wagon Mound (No. 2)* [1967] 1 AC 617, 638, although it will be recalled (see para. 7.1.8) that Lord Reid qualified this with the observation that 'although negligence may not be necessary, fault of some kind is almost always necessary and fault generally involves foreseeability'. It is not clear in what sense Lord Reid was using the words 'fault' and 'negligence', but if he intended a substantive distinction between the terms, it must be possible for a defendant to have acted as a reasonable man would have done and yet still be 'at fault' for the purpose of liability in public nuisance. In *Dymond* v *Pearce* [1972] 1 QB 496 (see para. 7.2.3.3.1) Sachs LJ stated that although it would be rare to find that an obstruction of the highway which did not create a foreseeable risk of injury (for which the defendant could not be liable in negligence) was the *actual* cause of an accident, nonetheless, if there had been a supervening event, such as fog or failure of the lighting, a defendant could be liable even though he was not negligent. This was because the risk of injury should be borne by the person who created the nuisance rather than a person who was using the highway in a proper manner. Stephenson LJ agreed that there may still be rare cases when a plaintiff could succeed in public nuisance when an action in negligence would fail.

In the context of defective premises the rule in *Wringe* v *Cohen* appears to set an intermediate standard of liability, somewhere between negligence and strict liability, at least for man-made structures (*Winfield and Jolowicz*, p. 439). The comment of Denning LJ in *Mint* v *Good* [1951] 1 KB 517 (see para. 7.2.3.3.2) that when premises fall into dangerous disrepair there must have been 'some fault on the part of someone or other' is hardly conclusive, however, since it raises the same problem about the distinction between 'fault' and 'negligence' as Lord Reid's statement. (In *The Wagon Mound (No. 2)* the Privy Council expressly excluded *Wringe* v *Cohen* from their deliberations. For criticism of *Wringe* v *Cohen* see *Buckley*, pp. 68–9). If nothing else, *Wringe* v *Cohen* shifts the burden of proof from the plaintiff to the defendant, since it is the occupier who must establish that the nuisance was caused by a trespasser or a secret unobservable process of nature. This is consistent with dicta from both Sachs LJ in *Dymond* v *Pearce* [1972] 1 QB 496, 502 and Denning LJ in *Southport Corporation* v *Esso Petroleum Co. Ltd* [1954] 2 QB 182, 197 that proof of a prima facie nuisance lays the onus on the defendant to establish some justification or excuse. (Similarly the statutory duty to maintain and repair the highway placed on highway authorities by the Highways Act 1980, s. 41, is subject to a specific defence that all reasonable care was taken, reversing the normal burden of proof: see s. 58.)

Whatever the merits of the arguments about the standard of liability there is one long-established distinction between public nuisance and negligence. The duty in public nuisance, at least in respect of dangers to the highway, is 'non-delegable' in nature and so, unlike the ordinary rule in negligence, the occupier is responsible for the actions of an independent contractor (*Tarry* v *Ashton* (1876) 1 QBD 314, see para. 8.5.4.2).

EIGHT

Strict liability

Strict liability is a general term used to describe forms of liability that do not depend upon proof of fault. Where a defendant is held responsible for unforeseeable harm or where he is liable despite having taken all reasonable care to avoid foreseeable harm then liability can be said to be strict. The distinction between fault and strict liability is not rigid. Strict duties may range from almost absolute liability, allowing virtually no defence, to duties which amount to little more than a high standard of care in negligence. Indeed, the objective standard of care in negligence divorces 'fault liability' from the notion of moral blameworthiness (for discussion of the moral basis of strict liability and its relationship to fault liability see Honoré (1988) 104 LQR 530). Yet, on the whole, the courts do not favour strict liability. The language of 'fault' creates an almost instinctive judicial antipathy to holding a person responsible for causing harm that could not reasonably have been avoided.

There is no obvious unity of purpose in the areas of social conduct that are subjected to stricter duties. If there is a discernible theme it is that people who engage in particularly hazardous activities should bear the burden of the greater risk of damage, or the risk of greater damage, that their activities generate. Strict liability focuses on the nature of the defendant's activity rather than, as in negligence, the way in which it is carried on, but it should not be assumed that strict liability is synonymous with 'liability without fault'. An activity which creates an unusual or exceptional risk may be justified by its social utility, and therefore may be reasonable on a negligence theory, but the defendant has imposed this risk on others for his own purpose and so his conduct is not necessarily blameless. This idea of the allocation of the burden of the risk to the person who created it is sometimes used as a justification for strict liability. But this usually rests on certain unstated assumptions about causation. For example, if a housing estate is built alongside an existing munitions factory, who created the risk of damage to the houses from an explosion? Moreover, negligence is also concerned with risk allocation. The 'risk' of suffering a non-negligent injury is the victim's, whereas the risk of causing harm by carelessness is the actor's. Thus analysis in terms of risk allocation does not explain why particular kinds of risk are dealt with on the basis of fault, whereas others merit strict liability. Appeals to the notion of extra-hazardous activities appear somewhat specious when it is recalled that in practical terms driving a motor vehicle is one of the most risky activities that the vast majority of the population ever undertakes, and yet it is the paradigm of a negligence action (consider Spencer [1983] CLJ 65).

A more plausible explanation of strict liability is that it operates as a loss distribution mechanism. Accidental damage arising from the materialisation of a risk inherent in a particular activity is paid for by the person or enterprise carrying on the activity. That person is in the best position to spread the loss via insurance and higher prices for the products that the activity creates, and so the true social cost of those products is borne by the consumers in small amounts. Vicarious liability (para. 8.4) is a good example of this process. However, fault liability can be regarded as a loss distribution mechanism too, at least in conjunction with insurance against liability. The only difference between strict and fault liability in this respect is the question of *which* losses are distributed—under fault liability non-negligent damage lies where it falls, whereas under strict liability accidental harm is distributed.

The language of loss distribution and risk allocation does not provide a solution to the problem of how losses are to be distributed (see *Atiyah*, pp. 354–8), but more particularly it does not explain the rather haphazard incidence of strict liability in the law of tort. The rule in *Rylands* v *Fletcher* (para. 8.1), the common law's response to hazardous activities which cause an escape of something dangerous, is now so hedged with exceptions and limitations as to be almost a species of fault. Vicarious liability, the liability of employers for the torts of their employees acting in the course of employment, is strict from the defendant's point of view—the employer is responsible in the absence of any fault on his part. But the plaintiff still has to prove that the employee committed a tort, which will almost certainly require proof of fault. This is also true of liability for independent contractors (para. 8.5). Liability for animals (para. 8.3), particularly those belonging to a dangerous species, is truly strict.

The Pearson Commission recommended the introduction of strict liability for death or personal injuries arising in a number of circumstances. These were: railway transportation; volunteers for medical research; vaccine damage (see the Vaccine Damage Payments Act 1979, which was intended to be an interim measure; Dworkin [1978–9] JSWL 330); exceptional risks (see para. 8.1.9); and defective products. With the exception of defective products (see chapter 10) none of these recommendations have been implemented.

Strict liability can arise in the form of an action for breach of statutory duty (see chapter 9), but the strictness of the obligation tends to vary with the statute in question and the interpretation that the courts put on its provisions. Some legislation explictly imposes strict liability in tort (see, e.g., para. 8.1.9). It will also be recalled that liability in nuisance may in some circumstances be stricter than in negligence (paras 7.1.8, 7.2.5).

8.1   *RYLANDS* v *FLETCHER*

In *Rylands* v *Fletcher* (1866) LR 1 Ex 265; (1868) LR 3 HL 330 the
defendants were mill owners who employed independent contractors to build
a reservoir. Beneath the site there were some disused mine shafts leading to
old coal workings which, unknown to the defendants, were connected to the
plaintiff's mine. Due to the contractors' negligence in failing to block the
shafts the plaintiff's mine was flooded when the reservoir was filled. The
defendants were not themselves negligent but the House of Lords held them
liable.

In the Exchequer Chamber Blackburn J said:

> We think that the true rule of law is, that the person who for his own
> purposes brings on his lands and collects and keeps there anything likely to
> do mischief if it escapes, must keep it in at his peril, and, if he does not do
> so, is prima facie answerable for all the damage which is the natural
> consequence of its escape.

This statement has come to be known as the rule in *Rylands* v *Fletcher*. The
House of Lords approved Blackburn J's judgment, but Lord Cairns added
that the defendant's use of land was 'non-natural'. In subsequent cases the
requirement of non-natural use was established as part of the rule. This
limited the scope for development of this form of strict liability, because
Blackburn J had referred to a person bringing on to his property something
'which was not naturally there'. This is clearly a wider test than non-natural
use, in that something may be brought on to land to be used in a natural or
ordinary manner even though it was 'not naturally there'.

There has been much academic ink spilt on the question of the origin of
the rule. Certainly Blackburn J did not regard it as a new principle, but
probably considered it to be an example of liability in nuisance. This was also
the view of the House of Lords in *Cambridge Water Co.* v *Eastern Counties
Leather plc* [1994] 2 WLR 53. The defendants used a solvent in degreasing
pelts at their tannery, which was located 1.3 miles from the plaintiffs'
borehole from which water was extracted for domestic use. Sometimes the
solvent was spilled onto the concrete floor of the defendants' premises.
Unknown to the defendants the solvent seeped into the ground below the
tannery and was then conveyed in percolating water to the borehole, contaminating the water. The Court of Appeal held the defendants liable in nuisance
on the basis that liability was strict where the nuisance consisted of an
interference with a natural right incidental to the plaintiffs' ownership of the
land (i.e., the right to extract percolating water). The House of Lords held
that it was an essential element in an action to recover damages in the tort of
nuisance and under the rule in *Rylands* v *Fletcher* that harm of the relevant
type was foreseeable by the defendant. Lord Goff, with whom their Lordships
agreed, said that the general tenor of Blackburn J's judgment was that
knowledge, or at least foreseeability of the risk, is a prerequisite of the
recovery of damages under the rule, although the rule is one of strict liability

in the sense that the defendant may be held liable notwithstanding that he has exercised all due care to prevent the escape from occurring (p. 77). The historical connection with the law of nuisance also pointed to the same conclusion. Since contamination of the plaintiffs' water supply was not foreseeable at the time of the spillages the defendants were not liable. The link between *Rylands* v *Fletcher* and nuisance was expressly endorsed by Lord Goff, who commented (at p. 80) that:

> It would moreover lead to a more coherent body of common law principles if the rule were to be regarded essentially as an extension of the law of nuisance to cases of isolated escapes from land, even though the rule as established is not limited to escapes which are in fact isolated.

As Wilkinson (1994) 57 MLR 799 observes, there is a difference between the statement: (1) that a defendant is liable for only that damage caused by the escape which a reasonable bystander would have foreseen, since on this test the escape itself must be foreseeable; and (2) that a defendant is liable for foreseeable damage, but in determining what is foreseeable the escape is to be assumed (whether or not foreseeable). In these circumstances the defendant is liable for the damage caused by the escape that a reasonable bystander, on being informed of the escape, would have anticipated. Foreseeability of the escape is irrelevant. *Cambridge Water* endorses (1), because Lord Goff specifies that the seepage of the chemical was unforeseeable (i.e., the escape), and in *Ellison* v *Ministry of Defence* (1997) 81 BLR 101 (see paras 7.1.2.1, 8.1.2 and 8.1.4) the trial judge stated (at p. 124), albeit *obiter*, that the defendants were 'not in any way at fault for failing to foresee the risk of what in fact happened or that damage would result'. Wilkinson argues that (2) is the correct test implicit in Blackburn J's judgment, because '. . . once we acknowledge the foreseeability of the escape (as opposed to the foreseeability of the damage alone), it is difficult to argue that the keeper of a dangerous thing can realistically be said to do so "at his peril"' (ibid. at p. 805). Professor Fleming (1995) 3 Tort L Rev 56, 58, n. 10 points out that the House of Lords did not advert to the fact that *Rylands* v *Fletcher* itself would have been decided *against* the plaintiff if the damage had to be foreseeable, since neither the defendant nor his contractor had any reason to suspect that the water in the reservoir would leak into the plaintiff's mines through underground passages. Moreover, the decision to impose strict liability was not accidental, it was a deliberate response to the menace of high risk enterprises of the industrial age, and particularly a response to the fact that there had been a number of calamitous burstings of reservoirs constructed for industrial purposes in the mid-19th century. It was a deliberate decision to impose strict liability for extra-hazardous activities, which if it were not for their social usefulness would probably have been condemned as negligent (ibid. pp. 60–1).

Shortly after the ruling of the House of Lords in *Cambridge Water* the High Court of Australia effectively abolished the rule in *Rylands* v *Fletcher* in Australia by declaring that it should be seen as having been absorbed by the general principles of the tort of negligence (*Burnie Port Authority* v *General Jones Pty Ltd* (1994) 120 ALR 42; Heuston and Buckley (1994) 110 LQR 506). Thus a person who took advantage of his control of premises to introduce a dangerous substance, to carry on a dangerous activity, or to allow someone else to do one of these things, would owe a duty of care to avoid a reasonably foreseeable risk of damage to another. Although at times the restrictions and limitations placed upon the rule in *Rylands* v *Fletcher* by the English courts have had the effect of making it look little more than a variant of negligence, *Cambridge Water* makes it clear that provided the damage was foreseeable the exercise of reasonable care by the defendant is irrelevant.

8.1.1 Dangerous things
The rule applies to 'anything likely to do mischief if it escapes'. Conventionally, this has meant not that the thing has to be likely to escape, but that it has to be likely to cause damage if it should escape. In some cases this has been interpreted to mean that the thing must be 'dangerous', but it is not easy to distinguish between dangerous and non-dangerous things because many things which are ordinarily safe are potentially dangerous if they escape. The rule has been applied to water, fire, gas, electricity, chemicals, explosions, fumes, flag-poles, fairground roundabouts, and even gypsies. In *Read* v *J. Lyons & Co. Ltd* [1947] AC 156 Lord Porter said (at p. 176) that it is a question of fact in each case. It may, however, no longer be necessary for the courts to spend any time resolving it. Since *Cambridge Water* states that the relevant damage must be foreseeable, there is no need to retain the concept of 'dangerous things' because this must be subsumed within the notion of whether the damage was foreseeable.

8.1.2 Accumulation
Rylands v *Fletcher* applies to things which the defendant deliberately accumulates ('brings on his lands and collects and keeps there'). It does not apply to things naturally on the land or natural accumulations. For example, there will be no liability under the rule for self-sown weeds which blow from the defendant's to the plaintiff's land (*Giles* v *Walker* (1890) 24 QBD 656), for rocks which fall from a natural outcrop as a result of weathering (*Pontardawe Rural District Council* v *Moore-Gwyn* [1929] 1 Ch 656) or for flooding by rainwater (*Ellison* v *Ministry of Defence* (1997) 81 BLR 101, see paras 7.1.2.1, 8.1.4). There may be liability in nuisance or negligence in these circumstances, but this will not constitute strict liability (see para. 7.1.3.6). If, however, an occupier deliberately causes something which was naturally on his land to escape he will be responsible under the rule (*Whatley* v *Lancashire & Yorkshire Railway Co.* (1884) 13 QBD 131), although it has been doubted whether *Rylands* v *Fletcher*, as opposed to trespass to land, applies to an intentional or voluntary release of a dangerous thing (*Rigby* v *Chief Constable of Northamptonshire* [1985] 2 All ER 985, 996). On the other hand, in *Crown River Cruises Ltd* v *Kimbolton Fireworks Ltd* [1996] 2 Lloyd's Rep 533, 547, Potter J said that there was no good reason for limiting the liability to an accidental escape as opposed to an intentional release, at least where the release was not

deliberately aimed in the direction of the plaintiff or with the intention of impinging upon his property.

8.1.3 Escape

There must be an 'escape', which means 'escape from a place where the defendant has occupation or control over land to a place which is outside his occupation or control' (*Read* v *J. Lyons & Co. Ltd* [1947] AC 156, 168 per Viscount Simon). In that case the plaintiff was a munitions inspector who was injured by an explosion at the defendants' factory. The House of Lords held that *Rylands* v *Fletcher* did not apply because there had been no escape from the defendants' premises, and in the absence of any allegation of negligence the plaintiff's action failed.

The thing that escapes and causes damage need not be the 'dangerous thing' that has been brought on to the land, provided the escape occurs during the course of a non-natural user. In *Miles* v *Forest Rock Granite Co. (Leicestershire) Ltd* (1918) 34 TLR 500 the plaintiff was injured by rocks thrown on to the highway as a result of blasting explosives on the defendants' land. The rock had not been accumulated (though the explosives had) yet the defendants were liable.

It is not necessary for the defendant to have a proprietary interest in the land from which the dangerous thing escapes. It is sufficient if he is in control of the dangerous thing. An escape from the highway, for example, will suffice (*Powell* v *Fall* (1880) 5 QBD 597; *Rigby* v *Chief Constable of Northamptonshire* [1985] 2 All ER 985, 996).

8.1.4 Non-natural use

The courts have interpreted natural use to mean something which is ordinary and usual, even though it may be artificial (Newark (1961) 24 MLR 557, 558). Non-natural use is equated with 'extraordinary use'. In *Rickards* v *Lothian* [1913] AC 263, 280, Lord Moulton said that it 'must be some special use bringing with it increased danger to others and must not merely be the ordinary use of the land or such a use as is proper for the general benefit of the community', but in *Cambridge Water Co.* v *Eastern Counties Leather plc* [1994] 2 WLR 53 Lord Goff commented that the term 'ordinary use of land' lacks precision, although his Lordship did not consider it necessary to attempt a definition of natural use. It has been treated as a flexible concept, taking into account the degree of risk created by the defendant's use and the prevailing standards of the time. In *Musgrove* v *Pandelis* [1919] 2 KB 43, for example, it was held that keeping a car in a garage with a full tank of petrol was a non-natural use. This would not be applied today (cf. *Perry* v *Kendricks Transport Ltd* [1956] 1 WLR 85, para. 8.1.7.4). In *British Celanese Ltd* v *A. H. Hunt (Capacitors) Ltd* [1969] 1 WLR 959 strips of metal foil used for making electrical components were blown on to an electricity substation and caused a power failure. Lawton J held that in 1964 this was a natural use of land because there were no special risks incidental to the storage of foil or the manufacture of electrical components and this use was beneficial to the community. This flexibility in its application has led to the suggestion that non-natural user is analogous to the concept of unreasonable risk in negligence, the courts balancing the magnitude of the risk against the social utility of the defendant's activity (Williams [1973] CLJ 310). A clear example of this approach is the case of *Mason* v *Levy Auto Parts of England Ltd* [1967] 2 QB 530 where the defendants stored large quantities of combustible material on their premises. MacKenna J held that the use was non-natural because of the quantity of material, the way in which it was stored and the character of the neighbourhood. His Lordship added that 'it may be that these considerations would also justify a finding of negligence'.

The benefit to the community from the manufacture of munitions in wartime clearly influenced some members of the House of Lords in *Read* v *J. Lyons & Co. Ltd* in suggesting that the use might be natural (although the point was not expressly decided; cf. *Rainham Chemical Works Ltd* v *Belvedere Fish Guano Co. Ltd* [1921] 2 AC 465 where the House of Lords held that such use was non-natural). The use of land for military-related purposes can, of course, also be natural in peacetime. In *Ellison* v *Ministry of Defence* (1997) 81 BLR 101 (see paras 7.1.2.1, 8.1 and 8.1.2), the trial judge dismissed the plaintiff's claims in nuisance and under the rule in *Rylands* v *Fletcher* for flooding caused by the defendant's construction of bulk fuel installations on their land (the Greenham Common airfield). Though the *Rylands* v *Fletcher* claim was dismissed because the water which caused the flood was rainwater which had accumulated naturally on the airfield and not water artificially kept there (para. 8.1.2), the trial judge stated (p. 119), *obiter*, that he would also have rejected the plaintiff's claim on the basis that the construction works were an ordinary use of the land and not a non-natural use. He was satisfied that the construction works were a necessary part of the use of the land as an airfield, which, itself, he considered not to be a non-natural use in turn, largely because of its benefit to the community in the wider sense of 'the national community as a whole'. (Moreover, he could find no evidence that the construction of the bulk fuel installations had materially increased the risk of danger so as to be treated as a severable non-natural use.) Benefit to the community is not a literal test, however, for any useful activity could be regarded as natural on that basis no matter how great the risks it created. No one would dispute the value to the community of public utilities supplying electricity, gas or water, but *Rylands* v *Fletcher* has nonetheless been applied to each of these uses. In *Cambridge Water* the trial judge had considered that the creation of employment in the locality was a benefit to the community which justified a finding of natural use. Lord Goff was unable to accept this. The storage of chemicals in substantial quantities, said his Lordship, and their use in the manner employed at the defendants' premises could not fall within the exception:

> The mere fact that the use is common in the tanning industry cannot . . . be enough to bring the use within the exception, nor the fact that Sawston contains a small industrial community which is worthy of encouragement or support . . . [T]he storage of substantial quantities of chemicals on industrial premises should be regarded as an almost classic case of non-

natural use; and I find it very difficult to think that it should be thought objectionable to impose strict lability for damage caused in the event of their escape. ([1994] 2 WLR 53, 83.)

Lord Goff expressed the hope that, since foreseeability was now to form part of the test for *Rylands* v *Fletcher*, the courts would feel less pressure to extend the concept of non-natural use to circumstances such as those in *Cambridge Water*, and that in due course it might become easier to control this exception and ensure that it has a more recognisable basis of principle. On the other hand, his Lordship drew an analogy between non-natural use of land in *Rylands* v *Fletcher* and the concept of unreasonable user in the tort of nuisance, suggesting that they had a similarity of function as a 'control' mechanism (though cf. Cross (1995) 111 LQR 445, 448). It is probably but a short step from this observation on the general function of the two concepts to a determination that, in *application*, there need be no difference between them. Indeed, in *Ellison* v *Ministry of Defence*, the trial judge seemed to find such a conclusion irresistible, for he employed exactly the same reasoning in order to find that the defendant's construction of bulk fuel installations on their airfield was both a natural use and a reasonable user for the purposes of *Rylands* v *Fletcher* and nuisance respectively (see para. 7.1.2.1). Similarly, though this time in the plaintiffs' favour, in *Graham and Graham* v *ReChem International Ltd* [1996] Env LR 158, Forbes J was content to use a non-natural use rationale to support an unreasonable user finding. He accepted that the defendant's user (the incineration of chemical waste) was unreasonable for the purposes of the plaintiffs' nuisance action expressly on the basis that such a use was not 'necessary for the common and ordinary use and occupation of the land *and was thus* an activity which [did not come] within the principle of "give and take as between neighbouring occupiers of land"' (emphasis added). It should be noted, though, that, in *Ellison*, the finding in relation to *Rylands* v *Fletcher* was expressly *obiter* and the observation in relation to nuisance probably so, and that in *Graham*, Forbes J went on to find against the plaintiffs on causation. The current lack of unequivocal authority for treating Lord Goff's observation as the green light for conflating the non-natural use and unreasonable user tests might prove a welcome opportunity to reconsider whether this would in fact be such a worthwhile development. Conceptually, it would undoubtedly amount to something of a change of approach, but, post-*Cambridge Water*, probably one that would not be too difficult to justify. Conventionally, the relative applicability of a balancing exercise akin to that inherent in the breach of duty equation in negligence has been the main means of distinguishing between the non-natural use and unreasonable user concepts.

'Reasonable user' in nuisance involves the court engaging in a balancing exercise as between the nature and extent of the interference with the plaintiff's use of his land against the use being made by the defendant. Although strictly speaking the exercise of reasonable care is not a defence, the balancing exercise does resemble in some respects the process by which the courts determine questions of negligence. It is true that in negligence the greater the risk then the greater the precautions that a defendant must undertake in order to avoid liability, and it may be that for very hazardous conduct the standard of care is so high that the duty will almost be treated as strict. By contrast, it has not been easy to equate non-natural use with negligence in this way. This is because the significance of strict liability has conventionally been that a defendant will be held responsible for damage caused by activities that create abnormal or extraordinary risks, irrespective of the care with which they are carried on and any balancing exercise inherent to it. This has essentially resulted from a policy decision that certain activities create such risks for others that the defendant ought to act as an insurer against any damage that occurs. The fact, however, that, post-*Cambridge Water*, foreseeability now clearly forms part of the rule in *Rylands* v *Fletcher* makes any basis of distinction that rests on a negligence/fault characteristic less compelling. This has, in turn, reduced significantly the conceptual distance between the non-natural use and unreasonable user tests, thereby theoretically paving the way for further development and alignment. Practically, though, a wholesale denial of any distinctiveness between the two tests would bring wider and more difficult considerations sharply, and perhaps uncomfortably, into focus (see Layard (1997) 113 LQR 254). For instance, in such an environment, Lord Goff's assertion that an industrial chemical process would be the paradigm non-natural use would make it difficult to resist concluding that most modern chemical processes are also unreasonable uses for the purposes of a nuisance action. That might obviously seem an attractive proposition for an environmentalist plaintiff (at least one who has the requisite proprietary standing to mount an action—para. 7.1.4). Ultimately, though, it might do more to reveal the extent to which planning laws and other forms of environmental regulation distort the neatness of a common law picture that has to pretend that the appropriate allocation of risk between the parties themselves (currently through the partial application of the fault principle) is the only relevant determination to be made. Thus, a defendant would argue that it would be incongruous for the court to be able to use the non-natural use methodology as a simple means of declaring unreasonable industrial chemical processes that society, through the granting of planning permissions and pollution permits, must presumably have determined to be necessary and, indeed, reasonable (see para. 7.1.2.1). Plaintiffs too could complain that, from their perspective, it would be equally incongruous if any benefits that they had been handed by a fusion of the non-natural use and unreasonable user tests were then taken away by the operation of a foreseeability requirement. Such a schizophrenic approach to protecting plaintiffs in industrial pollution cases would actually show up the limitations of those tests, both individually and when fused, and would contrast markedly with society's general approach to environmental regulation as incorporating a far more broadly based, community-centred 'cost–benefit' analysis. The parties' and society's dilemmas are neatly summarised by Layard (op. cit.) as encapsulating two choices: 'We can either face up to our polluting ways squarely and take responsibility for their effects, perhaps instituting legislative reform. Or we can continue to shy away from the reality of our daily societal choices, apparently protecting plaintiffs by identifying hazardous activities as unreasonable, but then raising the question of reasonable foresight.'

8.1.5 Who can sue?

There has been some doubt about whether a plaintiff must have an interest in land affected by the escape in order to maintain an action under *Rylands* v *Fletcher*. Dicta of some members of the House of Lords in *Read* v *J. Lyons & Co. Ltd* [1947] AC 156, 173, 186 suggest that the plaintiff must be an occupier, and in *Weller & Co.* v *Foot & Mouth Disease Research Institute* [1966] 1 QB 569, Widgery J held that the plaintiffs could not succeed under *Rylands* v *Fletcher* because they did not have an interest in land affected by the escape. Yet there have been many cases in which dicta to the contrary have been expressed (*Miles* v *Forest Rock Granite Co. (Leicestershire) Ltd* (1918) 34 TLR 500, CA; *Shiffman* v *Order of the Hospital of St John of Jerusalem* [1936] 1 All ER 557; *Perry* v *Kendricks Transport Ltd.* [1956] 1 WLR 85, 92, CA; *British Celanese Ltd* v *A.H. Hunt (Capacitors) Ltd* [1969] 1 WLR 959, 964) and some decisions where non-occupiers have succeeded under the rule (*Halsey* v *Esso Petroleum Co. Ltd* [1961] 2 All ER 145—in respect of damage to a car parked on the highway; *Charing Cross Electricity Supply Co.* v *Hydraulic Power Co.* [1914] 3 KB 772, CA—licensee).

The doubt over a qualifying proprietary interest arises from the absence of a definitive ruling on the specific point. It is therefore theoretically possible to argue that the rule in *Rylands* v *Fletcher* was conceived as a separate species of strict liability for harm caused by the escape of dangerous things, under which there would be no need to insist that the plaintiff must be an occupier. It is suggested, though, that the more likely finding in such a case would be that such an interest *is* required. This would be the natural consequence of the modern tendency to equate the rule with liability in nuisance (*Cambridge Water Co.* v *Eastern Counties Leather plc* [1994] 2 WLR 53), in which it has been accepted that a plaintiff must have an interest in land (see para. 7.1.4).

8.1.6 Type of damage

In *Read* v *J. Lyons & Co. Ltd* [1947] AC 156 doubts were raised about whether the rule in *Rylands* v *Fletcher* could be used for a claim for personal injuries, particularly by Lord Macmillan who considered that negligence was an essential requirement for such damage. It has been said that until this case there had never been any doubt that personal injuries were recoverable (*Clerk and Lindsell*, para. 19–15; *Charlesworth and Percy*, para. 12–31). Indeed, in *Hale* v *Jennings Bros.* [1938] 1 All ER 579, the tenant of a fairground stall succeeded for injuries caused by the escape of a 'chair-o-plane' from a roundabout. The issue was not finally decided in *Read* v *J. Lyons & Co. Ltd,* but it is likely that the House of Lords' pronouncements in *Hunter* v *Canary Wharf Ltd* [1997] 2 All ER 426, that have cast doubt on the recoverability of damages for personal injuries in a nuisance action, may, in turn, have provided contemporary support for the doubts expressed in *Read* v *Lyons* in the *Rylands* v *Fletcher* context (cf. Lord Cooke in *Hunter*, who saw no reason why personal injuries could not be actionable in nuisance, though he dissented on the primary finding in the case that nuisance was essentially a tort against land and that, therefore, a proprietary interest in the land affected was necessary for *locus standi*). If this is so, then it would obviously also put paid to personal injury claims under *Rylands* v *Fletcher* by non-occupiers, whose claims may not be actionable in any event if, as is likely, a proprietary interest is required (see para. 8.1.5). Indeed, many of the cases which have dealt with the question of whether the plaintiff must be an occupier involved claims for personal injuries. In *Perry* v *Kendricks Transport Ltd* [1956] 1 WLR 85, in which a 10-year-old boy was injured when the petrol tank of a disused bus exploded, Parker LJ (at p. 92) did not think that it was open to the Court of Appeal 'to hold that the rule applies only to damage to adjoining land or to a proprietary interest in land and not to personal injury'. This was in spite of the dicta in *Read* v *J. Lyons & Co. Ltd.* A similar view was expressed by the Court of Appeal in *Dunne* v *North Western Gas Board* [1964] 2 QB 806, 838 although the question was specifically left open. It is doubtful whether, in the light of *Hunter's* findings on *locus standi* and actionable damage in nuisance (paras 7.1.1 and 7.1.4) and *Cambridge Water's* concern for equating *Rylands* v *Fletcher* with nuisance, modern courts would be able to take the same line in contemporary versions of *Perry* or *Dunne*.

An exclusion of personal injury claims would initially seem a retrograde step. If the rule in *Rylands* v *Fletcher* were to be considered a practicable mechanism for the imposition of strict liability on extra-hazardous activities, then the exclusion of personal injuries from its ambit would have the unjustifiable effect of giving greater protection to property damage than to people. However, it is clear that *Rylands* v *Fletcher* has not in fact developed into a general principle of liability for 'ultrahazardous activities', as occurred in the United States (see Restatement, Torts, § 519). It might be argued, also, that to remove personal injuries from within the ambit of *Rylands* v *Fletcher* would hardly be the source of great hardship given its rather limited range of application. Moreover, there can be few cases where an action in *Rylands* v *Fletcher* would succeed where an action in negligence would fail.

8.1.7 Defences
There are a number of defences some of which were recognised by Blackburn J, and others which were developed later.

8.1.7.1 Consent There will be no liability where the plaintiff has consented to the accumulation, unless the defendant has been negligent in causing the escape (*Attorney-General* v *Cory Brothers & Co. Ltd* [1921] 1 AC 521). Consent may be implied. In *Peters* v *Prince of Wales Theatre (Birmingham) Ltd* [1943] KB 73, for example, it was held that the plaintiff consented on entering into occupation of property where the dangerous thing (a fire sprinkler system) had been installed. Where the accumulation is established for the common benefit of plaintiff and defendant, consent will generally be implied. This usually applies to multiple occupants of a building in respect of common utilities such as water, gas and electricity. The mutual benefit is taken to be evidence of consent, but it is not essential as *Peters* v *Prince of Wales Theatre (Birmingham) Ltd* demonstrates. Provided the plaintiff knows of the dangerous thing he 'takes the premises as they are, and, accordingly, consents to the presence there of the installed water system with all its advantages and disadvantages' ([1943] KB 73, 79 per Goddard LJ; many of the cases that discuss the defence of consent could have been dealt with on the basis that the defendant's use of the premises was a natural use).

Consent will not be implied simply because a person occupies property which is situated close to a known source of danger, such as a chemical plant or a quarry, unless, perhaps, the relationship of landlord and tenant exists between plaintiff and defendant (see *Thomas* v *Lewis* [1937] 1 All ER 137).

8.1.7.2 Plaintiff's default The defendant will not be liable where the damage is caused by the plaintiff's act or default. If the plaintiff is partially responsible the Law Reform (Contributory Negligence) Act 1945 will apply. Where the damage is attributable to the extra sensitivity of the plaintiff's property then, as in nuisance, there is no liability (*Eastern & South African Telegraph Co. Ltd* v *Cape Town Tramways Companies Ltd* [1902] AC 381, PC—defendants' use of electricity interfered with telegraph messages, plaintiffs' action failed). This can be treated as the plaintiffs' default, or alternatively it could be argued that the 'thing' was not dangerous because it was not 'likely to do mischief' if it escaped.

8.1.7.3 Act of God Act of God is a defence of very limited application. It refers to events caused by the forces of nature 'which no human foresight can provide against, and of which human prudence is not bound to recognise the possibility' (*Tennent* v *Earl of Glasgow* (1864) 2 M (HL) 22, 26 per Lord Westbury). Whether any particular natural phenomenon falls into this category will be treated as a question of fact, but it must have been impossible for human foresight to provide against. It is not sufficient to demonstrate that the occurrence could not reasonably have been foreseen (*Greenock Corporation* v *Caledonian Railway Co.* [1917] AC 556 in which on very similar facts the House of Lords criticised *Nichols* v *Marsland* (1876) 2 ExD 1 where the defence had been allowed when an extraordinarily heavy rainfall caused artificial lakes to break their banks).

It can be argued that natural occurrences are just the sort of events that ought to be within the scope of the risk created by the accumulation of dangerous things (Goodhart (1951) 4 CLP 177; cf. the position under the Animals Act 1971 where the defences are not available, para. 8.3.5). But since the damage must be reasonably foreseeable (*Cambridge Water Co.* v *Eastern Counties Leather plc* [1994] 2 WLR 53) this argument is effectively lost, and the Act of God defence will be subsumed within the requirement of foreseeability.

8.1.7.4 Act of stranger The unforeseeable act of a stranger over whom the defendant has no control is a defence. For example, in *Box* v *Jubb* (1879) 4 ExD 76 the defendant was not liable for the overflow of a reservoir caused by the owner of another reservoir emptying it into a stream that fed the defendant's reservoir. In *Rickards* v *Lothian* [1913] AC 263 someone deliberately blocked a basin in the defendant's premises and turned the taps on, flooding the plaintiff's premises below. The defendant was not responsible.

It has been said that the act of the third party must be intentional or deliberate, and there are a number of judicial statements to this effect (see *Clerk and Lindsell*, para. 19–23). The logic of this requirement is obscure. Would the defendant in *Rickards* v *Lothian* have been any more responsible if the flooding had been caused by a third party negligently leaving the taps running? It may be that the distinction rests upon the question of the *defendant's* negligence. The defendant will be liable if the stranger's act was foreseeable and the defendant failed to take precautions against it (*Northwestern Utilities Ltd* v *London Guarantee & Accident Co. Ltd* [1926] AC 108, where the defendants were liable for a gas explosion having failed to check whether any damage had been done to their gas main in the course of construction of a sewer by third parties). Negligence by third parties is more commonplace than malicious conduct, and therefore more foreseeable by the defendant. It is therefore more likely that the defence will not succeed where the third party's conduct is negligent rather than deliberate, but this is not a reason for making an intentional act an essential requirement (cf. causation, where deliberate conduct is more likely than negligence to constitute *novus actus interveniens*, para. 4.2.2.1). If it is argued that negligence by others is within the risk created by the defendant, then why are deliberate acts not within the risk? If non-culpability is the basis of the defence it is illogical to justify an arbitrary distinction on the basis of the concept of risk (In *Perry* v *Kendricks Transport Ltd* [1956] 1 WLR 85, 90 Jenkins LJ did not limit the defence to deliberate acts, but cf. Singleton LJ at p. 87.)

As Jenkins LJ observed in *Perry* v *Kendricks Transport Ltd* [1956] 1 WLR 85, 90, where liability depends on the defendant's failure to prevent the foreseeable act of a stranger a claim framed under *Rylands* v *Fletcher* merges into an action in negligence. The burden of proof, however, lies with the defendant who must show not only that the escape was caused by the act of an independent third party, but also that he was not negligent in failing to prevent the interference (*Hanson* v *Wearmouth Coal Co. Ltd* [1939] 3 All ER 47, 53 per Goddard LJ; *Northwestern Utilities Ltd* v *London Guarantee & Accident Co. Ltd* [1926] AC 108, 120; *Charlesworth and Percy*, para. 12–55; cf. *Clerk and Lindsell*, para. 19–24). In *Perry* v *Kendricks Transport Ltd* the plaintiff was injured by an explosion that occurred when two young boys, who were trespassing on the defendants' land, dropped a lighted match into the petrol tank of a disused bus. The Court of Appeal held that the defendants were not liable because they had no control over the trespassers and had not been negligent. Parker LJ said that once the defendant proves that the escape was caused by a stranger the burden of proving negligence rests with the plaintiff. It is submitted that this approach is inconsistent because it is clearly possible to exercise some 'control' over the conduct of others by the steps that are taken to prevent interference with the dangerous thing. If the defendant does not show that he has taken reasonable steps to prevent the foreseeable acts of third parties it can hardly be said that he has established that the escape was due to the conduct of others beyond his control. The burden of proof should be the defendant's. (Note, though, that nowadays the plaintiff in *Perry* may be denied an action under the rule in *Rylands* v *Fletcher* if, as is likely, a proprietary interest is necessary for a cause of action, and/or if personal injury is not actionable—see paras 8.1.5 and 8.1.6.)

Who is classified as a stranger? The test is whether the person was outside the defendant's control. Trespassers and persons who perform acts on land other than the defendant's (as in *Box* v *Jubb, supra*) will generally be regarded as strangers. Servants acting in the course of employment and independent contractors will not (*Hobbs (Farms) Ltd* v *Baxenden Chemical Co. Ltd* [1992] 1 Lloyd's Rep 54, 69). Members of the defendant's family and licensees are more difficult to classify, but applying *Perry* v *Kendricks Transport Ltd* the question appears to depend upon whether he had a sufficient degree of control to have prevented the act (see further *H. & N. Emanuel Ltd* v *Greater London Council* [1971] 2 All ER 835, para. 8.2.1).

The effect of this defence is to reduce the defendant's duty to 'one which, apart from the burden of proof, resembles a duty of care in negligence' (*Clerk and Lindsell,* para. 19–25). This, combined with the escape requirement, has rendered the rule virtually redundant in practical terms (*Pearson,* vol. 1, para. 1636).

8.1.7.5 Statutory authority Statutory authorisation is a defence to a claim under *Rylands* v *Fletcher* for the same reasons as apply in the case of nuisance. The same principles of law apply (see para. 7.1.6.2). The Reservoirs Act 1975, s. 28 and sch. 2, specifically provides that the defence shall not apply to reservoirs constructed after 1930, and in relation to the escape of fire the Railway Fires Acts 1905 and 1923 provide that statutory authority is not a defence where sparks from a railway engine cause damage by fire to crops or agricultural land up to the value of £3,000. Liability would be based on *Rylands* v *Fletcher* (*Jones* v *Festiniog Railway Co.* (1868) LR 3 QB 733). Beyond the £3,000 limit a plaintiff would have to prove negligence to defeat the defence of statutory authority.

8.1.7.6 Necessity Necessity can be a defence in the case of a deliberate release of a dangerous thing, assuming that *Rylands* v *Fletcher* would apply to an intentional escape (*Rigby* v *Chief Constable of Northamptonshire* [1985] 2 All ER 985, 996; see para. 14.4.3). It may be that the appropriate action in respect of a deliberate release is trespass to land. In any event, necessity will not apply to an involuntary escape (ibid.).

8.1.8 Remoteness of damage
Blackburn J said that a defendant is prima facie liable for all the damage which is the natural consequence of the escape. In *Cambridge Water Co.* v *Eastern Counties Leather plc* [1994] 2 WLR 53 the House of Lords held that the test of remoteness under *Rylands* v *Fletcher* is reasonable foreseeability of the damage. Whether in practice a test based on foreseeable consequences

will lead to different results from one based on natural consequences is another matter. The chances are that it will not.

8.1.9 Future of strict liability for hazardous activities

Liability under the rule in *Rylands* v *Fletcher* approximates to a form of liability in negligence despite the fact that the exercise of reasonable care is not necessarily a defence. The range of defences available, particularly act of a stranger and statutory authority, explicitly transform the action into an inquiry about the defendant's culpability. In addition the necessity for an escape can produce arbitrary results. The limitations of the rule as a mechanism for compensating accident victims have become more apparent with the growing criticism of the fault principle. In *Benning* v *Wong* (1968) 43 ALJR 467 Windeyer J said that to regard strict liability as unjust is to mistake both present social values and past history. When insurance is commonplace it can hardly be unjust to make people who carry on hazardous activities liable for the damage they cause. In *Cambridge Water Co.* v *Eastern Counties Leather plc* [1994] 2 WLR 53, 79 Lord Goff commented that it could be argued that the rule in *Rylands* v *Fletcher* should be treated as a developing principle of strict liability from which could be derived a general rule of strict liability for damage caused by ultra-hazardous operations which expose others to extraordinary risk. This would lead to the practical result that the cost of damage resulting from such operations would have to be absorbed as part of the overheads of the relevant business rather than be borne (where there is no negligence) by the injured person or his insurers, or even by the community at large. His Lordship considered that there were serious obstacles to the development of *Rylands* v *Fletcher* in this way, e.g., *Read* v *Lyons* limits it to escapes, whereas such a principle should be of general application. The Law Commission had also expressed misgivings about the adoption of a test for the application of strict liability involving a general concept of especially dangerous or ultra-hazardous activity (*Civil Liability for Dangerous Things and Activities*, Law Com. No. 32, 1970). It was more appropriate, said Lord Goff, for strict liability in respect of high risk operations to be imposed by Parliament. Legislation would enable the activities to be identified, could lay down precise criteria for establishing the incidence and scope of liability, and those concerned would know where they stood.

The ability to cover a risk by insurance was a factor considered by the Pearson Commission in recommending a statutory scheme of strict liability for personal injuries resulting from exceptional risks (*Pearson*, vol. 1, ch. 31, para. 1641). Under this scheme strict liability would be imposed on the controllers of things or operations in two categories: (a) those which by their unusually hazardous nature require close, careful and skilled supervision, e.g., explosives and flammable gases or liquids; and (b) those which, although normally safe, are likely to cause serious and extensive casualties if they do go wrong, e.g., large public bridges, dams, major stores and stadia, and other similar buildings. The scheme would operate by means of a parent statute with statutory instruments applying the general provisions of the statute to particular dangerous things and activities set out in a list. The recommendation to include a particular thing or activity on a list would be made by an advisory committee which could assess a variety of factors such as accident statistics, economic considerations and insurance. This would be much more flexible than judicial determination of what constitutes a non-natural use. In addition, there would be a power to require compulsory insurance to cover the specified risks.

Contributory negligence and voluntary assumption of risk would be general defences but statutory authority and act of a third party (whether negligent, malicious or criminal) would not. The fact that the plaintiff was a trespasser would not be a general defence but could be introduced as a defence to a specific type of exceptional risk when making the statutory instrument (cf. Animals Act 1971, s. 5(3), para. 8.3.5).

Such a scheme would create more certainty for both plaintiffs and defendants, but it is open to the objection that political and economic pressures from groups who might be subject to strict liability could lead to the exclusion of certain exceptional risks on grounds which have little if anything to do with the level of risk they generate. Plaintiffs would then be left to the common law for redress, presumably relying on *Rylands* v *Fletcher* since the Commission stopped short of recommending its abolition. In any event *Rylands* v *Fletcher* would be available for damage to property. The Pearson Commission's recommendation has not been implemented.

It should be noted that there are already a number of statutes which impose civil liability of varying degrees of strictness for certain hazards. Among the most prominent of these are: Nuclear Installations Act 1965 (on which see *Merlin* v *British Nuclear Fuels plc* [1990] 3 All ER 711—liability under the Act limited to personal injury and physical damage to property; the presence of ionising radiation in a house creating an increased risk of injury to the health of occupants in the future, and reducing the value of the house not actionable; cf. *Blue Circle Industries plc* v *Ministry of Defence* [1998] 3 All ER 385, CA—contamination of land by radioactive material constitutes physical damage to land, even though the consequence was economic in that the property was worth less and expenditure was incurred in removing the contaminated top soil); Merchant Shipping (Oil Pollution) Act 1971; Control of Pollution Act 1974, s. 88—poisonous waste; Gas Act 1964, s. 14—underground gas storage; Water Act 1981, s. 6—escape from water mains; Civil Aviation Act 1982, s. 76—things falling from aircraft (see para. 11.2.2). Detailed consideration of this legislation is beyond the scope of this book (see *Clerk and Lindsell*, ch. 19).

8.2 FIRE

8.2.1 Liability at common law
The early common law remedy for damage caused by fire was a form of trespass on the case for negligently allowing one's fire to escape. The word 'negligently' was not used in its modern sense and there is some doubt as to whether liability was strict or fault-based (cf. *Winfield and Jolowicz*, p. 463 with *Clerk and Lindsell*, para. 19–44 and *Charlesworth and Percy*, paras 12–105

to 12–109). Many of the judicial comments to the effect that a man must keep his fire 'at his peril' have been made in the context of actions which are analogous to the rule in *Rylands* v *Fletcher*, although liability for fire predates *Rylands* v *Fletcher*. Thus, there must be an escape; liability is based on the occupation and control of land and so an occupier is liable for the acts of others who are under his control; and act of a stranger or an unforeseeable Act of God are defences.

The modern tendency, then, has been to assimilate the common law liability for fire with the rule in *Rylands* v *Fletcher*. Yet it is not, as such, the escape of a 'dangerous thing' brought on to the land that causes the damage, but the spread of the fire. In *Mason* v *Levy Auto Parts of England Ltd* [1967] 2 QB 530, 542 MacKenna J held that a defendant would be liable if (a) he brought on to his land things likely to catch fire, and kept them there in such conditions that, if they did ignite, the fire would be likely to spread to the plaintiff's land, (b) he did so in the course of some non-natural use, and (c) the thing ignited and the fire spread. This was a more reasonable test to apply, 'since to make the likelihood of damage if the thing escapes a criterion of liability, when the thing has not in fact escaped but has caught fire, would not be very sensible'. This approach introduces a strong element of fault into the question of liability, since it is unlikely that something 'likely to catch fire' where 'the fire would be likely to spread' would be regarded as an unforeseeable cause of harm. If the concept of non-natural use is then equated with the reasonableness of the precautions taken by the defendant, there would be little to choose between an action under *Rylands* v *Fletcher* and negligence (see para. 8.1.4, and the judgment of Lord Denning MR in *H. & N. Emanuel Ltd* v *Greater London Council* [1971] 2 All ER 835, 838 'the occupier is not liable for the escape of fire which is not due to the negligence of anyone').

One significant difference between the two actions is that under *Rylands* v *Fletcher* liability for fire is founded upon the occupation and control of land (*Sturge* v *Hackett* [1962] 1 WLR 1257). The occupier is liable for the acts of persons under his control, which includes servants acting in the course of employment, visitors and independent contractors. 'Control' is used in a broad sense here. In *Balfour* v *Barty-King* [1957] 1 QB 496, para. 8.5.4.3, Lord Goddard CJ said that the defendants had 'control over the contractor in that they chose him, they invited him to their premises to work, and he could have been ordered to leave at any moment'. There is no liability, however, for the acts of a 'stranger', who is anyone who, in lighting a fire or in allowing it to escape, acts contrary to anything which the occupier could anticipate that he would do. 'Even if it is a man whom you have allowed or invited into your house, nevertheless, if his conduct in lighting a fire is so alien to your invitation that he should *qua* the fire be regarded as a trespasser, he is a "stranger"' (*H. & N. Emanuel Ltd* v *Greater London Council* [1971] 2 All ER 835, 839 per Lord Denning MR; see the comments of *Weir*, p. 480).

Where a person undertakes an operation which involves the risk of fire this will be regarded as a hazardous activity, imposing a non-delegable duty to see that care is taken to keep the fire safe (see para. 8.5.4.3; *Honeywill & Stein Ltd* v *Larkin Bros Ltd* [1934] 1 KB 191). This is not an absolute duty, in that it will be satisfied if there is no negligence. Its significance lies in the fact that a person will be liable for the negligence of his independent contractor, or indeed anyone who is not a stranger, in circumstances where *Rylands* v *Fletcher* would not apply (e.g., because there has been no escape).

Liability for damage by fire can also be based on the ordinary tort of negligence, and private nuisance (where again the obligation may be non-delegable, see *Spicer* v *Smee* [1946] 1 All ER 489). Moreover, where the fire arises from natural causes or the act of a stranger an occupier will be liable if he negligently fails to abate the danger (*Goldman* v *Hargrave* [1967] 1 AC 645, para. 7.1.3.6; possibly the occupier will have done enough if he calls the fire brigade).

8.2.2 Statute
The Fires Prevention (Metropolis) Act 1774, s. 86, which is of general application, provides that 'no action, suit or process whatever shall be had, maintained or prosecuted against any person in whose house, chamber, stable, barn or other building, or on whose estate any fire shall . . . accidentally begin'. The Act modified the common law, not by creating a cause of action but by granting immunity from liability for accidental fires (on the assumption, presumably, that liability at common law was not fault-based). In *Filliter* v *Phippard* (1847) 11 QB 347, however, it was held that 'accidentally begin' meant by mere chance or where the cause was unknown. It did not apply to fires started negligently (see *Hobbs (Farms) Ltd* v *Baxenden Chemical Co. Ltd* [1992] 1 Lloyd's Rep 54, 69), nor to fires started intention-ally which spread accidentally (cf. *Salmond and Heuston,* p. 321, but *per contra Clerk and Lindsell* para. 19–46; *Charlesworth and Percy* para. 12–111). Nor does it apply where the fire starts accidentally but is spread through negli-gence. In *Musgrove* v *Pandellis* [1919] 2 KB 43 a fire started in the carburettor of a car parked in a garage. If the defendant's servant had turned off the petrol tap the fire would have soon burned itself out, but he negligently omitted to do this and the fire spread to the plaintiff's premises. The Court of Appeal held that the word 'fire' in s. 86 referred to the fire which caused the damage, which was the fire spread by the servant's negligence, not the original fire in the carburettor. Thus the fire did not 'accidentally begin'.

On this approach it would be possible to argue that a fire started intentionally which spread accidentally was protected by the Act, since the fire which caused the damage began 'accidentally' (see *Sochaki* v *Sas* [1947] 1 All ER 344—no liability in the absence of negligence for fire caused by a spark from a domestic fire grate; see *Hepple and Matthews* p. 670, n. 1). The Act does not apply where liability is based on the rule in *Rylands* v *Fletcher* (*Musgrove* v *Pandelis*) nor where the fire starts from the highway (*Powell* v *Fall* (1880) 5 QBD 597).

The net result seems to be that the 1774 Act did little more than remove any doubts about the possibility of absolute liability at common law for purely accidental fires, possibly by reversing the burden of proving negligence, which now rests with the plaintiff (*Mason* v *Levy Auto Parts of England Ltd* [1967] 2 QB 530 at p. 539; see para. 8.2.1). The modern position is that there is no liability in the absence of negligence, unless the rule in *Rylands* v *Fletcher* applies, although even this action comes very close to fault liability. The strictness of the duty relates to the liability of an occupier or a person undertaking an operation involving the risk of fire for the negligence of others, particularly independent contractors. In practice the vast majority of fire losses are compensated through first-party insurance. Civil actions are likely to arise only where the plaintiff was underinsured or the insurance company decides to exercise its right of subrogation under the policy (see in general Ogus [1969] CLJ 104).

8.3 ANIMALS

The Pearson Commission found that there were approximately 50,000 injuries a year caused by animals, and a small number of deaths. Most injuries involve dogs or horses. Animals have always been put into a special category for the purpose of civil liability, for, unlike other chattels which may be the instrument in the commission of a tort, animals have a 'will' of their own. At common law this special category was known as a *scienter* action which was based on the keeper's knowledge of the animal's dangerous propensities. The keeper was strictly liable for damage caused by the animal if either (a) it belonged to a dangerous species, or (b) it did not belong to a dangerous species but the keeper knew that the individual animal was dangerous. The Animals Act 1971 abolished the *scienter* action and replaced it with a statutory code of strict liability.

Although an action under the Animals Act 1971 is the most obvious remedy for damage caused by animals, if for some reason the Act does not apply there may nonetheless be liability under the general principles of some other nominate tort.

8.3.1 Liability at common law
A person can commit many torts through the agency of an animal. For example, setting a dog on to someone may constitute assault and battery, a parrot may be taught to say something defamatory, dogs may trespass on another's land (*League Against Cruel Sports Ltd* v *Scott* [1985] 2 All ER 489), an escape by tigers may fall within the rule in *Rylands* v *Fletcher,* the smell of pigs or the crowing of cockerels may constitute a nuisance (*Leeman* v *Montagu* [1936] 2 All ER 1677), and the failure to control an animal may give rise to liability in negligence where there was a foreseeable risk of harm occurring.

An action in negligence can be particularly important in the case of animals belonging to a 'non-dangerous' species, where strict liability under the Animals Act 1971 depends upon *knowledge* by the keeper of some characteristic of the particular animal which is not normally found in that species. If the harm was foreseeable but the result of a normal characteristic of the species there is no liability under the Act. The keeper may be liable in negligence, however, as in *Draper* v *Hodder* [1972] 2 QB 556 where a pack of terriers attacked a child. The evidence indicated that terriers can be dangerous when roaming free in a pack, and the defendant was held liable for failing to take reasonable precuations against a foreseeable risk. In *Smith* v *Prender-gast, The Times,* 18 October 1984, CA, the owner of a scrapyard was held responsible for an attack by a stray Alsatian dog which had taken up residence in his yard three weeks earlier. The dog had not done anything in that time to indicate it might bite. The scrapyard owner was held to have been negligent in failing to supervise and control the dog for a reasonable period in order to observe whether it was docile (see also *Pitcher* v *Martin* [1937] 3 All ER 918—owner liable in nuisance and negligence when dog escaped from his control and tripped plaintiff in the course of chasing a cat; *Birch* v *Mills* [1995] 9 CL 354—defendant liable for an attack by a herd of cows upon the plaintiff while walking dogs on leads down a public road. If it was foreseeable that the cows would attack a dog it was foreseeable that a person attached to the dog was likely to get hurt).

8.3.2   Animals Act 1971
General liability in tort is concurrent with liability under the Animals Act 1971. The Act preserved the basic distinction of the *scienter* action between animals belonging to dangerous and non-dangerous species.

8.3.3   Dangerous species
Section 2(1) of the Animals Act 1971 provides that where any damage is caused by an animal which belongs to a dangerous species, any person who is a keeper of the animal is liable for the damage except as provided by the Act.

A dangerous species is a species (a) which is not commonly domesticated in the British Isles, and (b) whose fully grown animals normally have such characteristics that they are likely, unless restrained, to cause severe damage or that any damage they may cause is likely to be severe (s. 6(2); 'species' includes subspecies and variety: s. 11). There are a number of points to note about this definition. First, whether a species is dangerous is a question of law not fact. This was the position under the *scienter* action and there is no reason to think that the Act has changed this (*Behrens* v *Bertram Mills Circus Ltd* [1957] 2 QB 1, 15). This means that it is a matter for the judge, and expert evidence will not be decisive. The keeper's ignorance that the animal belongs to a dangerous species is irrelevant. Secondly, a species may be regarded as dangerous if it is not commonly domesticated in this country, even though it is domesticated abroad, e.g., camels (*Tutin* v *Chipperfield Promotions Ltd* (1980) 130 NLJ 807). Thirdly, s. 6(2)(b) is expressed in the alternative. A species may be dangerous even if such animals are not *likely* to cause severe damage provided that if damage is caused it is likely to be severe. For example, an elephant may not be likely to cause damage, but if it does the damage will probably be serious. Fourthly, if the animal belongs to a dangerous species it is irrelevant that the particular animal is tame.

This last point illustrates how strict liability under s. 2(1) is. It does not matter that the damage is not the result of the particular characteristic which renders the species as a whole dangerous. The section refers simply to 'any damage'. Thus, if a lion escaped from a zoo and in the course of its escape tripped someone up in the street quite accidentally, the keeper would be liable for the resulting injuries (*Behrens* v *Bertram Mills Circus Ltd* [1957] 2 QB 1, 18). Liability is strict, it is not absolute since the Act allows certain defences.

For the purpose of ss. 2 to 5 of the 1971 Act a 'keeper' is someone who (a) owns the animal, or (b) has it in his possession, or (c) is the head of a household of which a member under the age of 16 owns the animal or has it in his possession (s. 6(3)). Thus there can be more than one keeper of an animal at a time. Where an animal has ceased to be in the ownership or possession of a person, any person who immediately before that time was a keeper remains responsible as a keeper until another person becomes a keeper.

The Dangerous Wild Animals Act 1976 requires a keeper of a dangerous wild animal to be licensed by the local authority and to take out insurance against liability to third parties.

8.3.4 Non-dangerous species
Section 2(2) of the Animals Act 1971 provides that where damage is caused by an animal which does not belong to a dangerous species, a keeper of the animal is liable for the damage, except as provided by the Act, if:

(a) the damage is of a kind which the animal, unless restrained, was likely to cause or which, if caused by the animal, was likely to be severe; and

(b) the likelihood of the damage or of its being severe was due to characteristics of the animal which are not normally found in animals of the same species or are not normally so found except at particular times or in particular circumstances; and

(c) those characteristics were known to that keeper or were at any time known to a person who at that time had charge of the animal as that keeper's servant or, where that keeper is the head of a household, were known to another keeper of the animal who is a member of that household and under the age of 16.

This subsection has given rise to some difficulties of interpretation. The correct approach is to consider each part of the subsection separately and in turn (*Curtis* v *Betts* [1990] 1 All ER 769). Under s. 2(2)(a) it is not a requirement that the damage that the animal was likely to cause or, if caused, was likely to be severe, be the result of the abnormal characteristic specified in s. 2(2)(b) (cf. *Jaundrill* v *Gillett*, *The Times*, 30 January 1996, where the Court of Appeal held that there has to be a causal link between the animal's characteristic under s. 2 and the damage). The question is whether the damage is of a kind which the particular animal in question, unless restrained, was likely to cause, or which, if caused by that animal, was likely to be severe. Thus, where the animal is a dog of the bull mastiff breed or the Alsatian breed, if it did bite anyone the damage was likely to be severe and s. 2(2)(a) is satisfied (*Curtis* v *Betts* [1990] 1 All ER 769, 772; *Cummings* v *Grainger* [1977] 1 All ER 104, 108). In *Smith* v *Ainger*, *The Times*, 5 June 1990, the

Court of Appeal held that the words 'was likely' in s. 2(2)(a) should be given a wide meaning. They did not mean 'more probable than not' but could include an event that was 'such as might well happen' or 'where there is a material risk that it will happen'. The plaintiff was knocked over and broke his leg when the defendant's dog attacked the plaintiff's dog. The Court characterised the kind of damage as 'personal injury to a human being caused by the direct application of force'. Where the personal injury was the result of an attack by a dog it was unrealistic to distinguish between a bite and the consequences of a buffet. The defendant's dog had a history of attacking other dogs, and therefore it could be said that it was likely to attack another dog; if it did so there was a material risk that the owner of the other dog would intervene and would be bitten or buffeted as a result, and accordingly the plaintiff's injury did constitute damage of a kind which, unless restrained, the dog was likely to cause.

Greater problems have arisen over s. 2(2)(b). Arguably, the provision requires that the damage be caused by a characteristic of the particular animal which is not normally found in the same species, with the words 'or are not normally so found except at particular times or in particular circumstances' intended to preclude an argument by a defendant that it is normal for a particular species, say, to bite because at certain times (e.g., when the female has young to protect) it is common or normal behaviour. However, the words 'except at particular times or in particular circumstances' have been interpreted as a distinct 'abnormal' characteristic for the purpose of s. 2(2), even though, say, protecting its young is an otherwise perfectly normal characteristic of the species. In *Cummings* v *Grainger* [1977] 1 All ER 104 the defendant allowed an untrained Alsatian dog to roam free in his scrapyard at night as a guard dog. The dog savaged the plaintiff when she entered the yard at night with her boyfriend who worked there. The Court of Appeal held that the dog satisfied the requirements of s. 2(2)(b). Alsatians were not normally vicious except in the 'particular circumstances' of being used as a guard dog. It follows, then, that characteristics which are normally found in animals of the same species but only at 'particular times or in particular circumstances' will be regarded as abnormal characteristics. This view is confirmed by the approach of the Court of Appeal in *Curtis* v *Betts* [1990] 1 All ER 769. Stuart-Smith LJ said that s. 2(2)(b) has two alternative limbs, dealing with what may be called permanent characteristics and temporary characteristics. Dogs, for example, are not normally fierce or prone to attack humans; a particular dog which had a propensity to attack humans at all times and in all places would fall within the first limb, whereas an animal that was only aggressive in particular circumstances, for example, when guarding its territory or when guarding young, falls within the second limb.

A further problem with s. 2(2)(b) concerns the words '*the likelihood of* the damage *or of its being severe*'. The italicised words appear to suggest an element of foreseeability of the damage. Without the italicised words it would be clear that the subsection is concerned with causation, the Act requiring that the particular damage sustained by the plaintiff be caused by the animal's abnormal characteristic, and in *Curtis* v *Betts*, Stuart-Smith and Nourse LJJ held that this is how the subsection should be read, i.e., as if it said: 'the damage was due to characteristics of the animal which . . .' Thus, the effect of s. 2(2) is that in the case of an animal of a non-dangerous species the plaintiff must establish that the damage was caused by an abnormal characteristic of the animal, of which the keeper had actual or imputed knowledge. 'Damage' does not mean 'any damage' but damage due to the abnormal characteristic, and so there will be no liability for a dog that is known to be vicious which accidentally trips a pedestrian (cf. s. 2(1), para. 8.3.3) unless the accident occurs in the course of exhibiting its vicious tendency, as in *Smith* v *Ainger, The Times,* 5 June 1990.

Characteristics which have been held to be abnormal under s. 2(2)(b) include: a tendency of a dog to be vicious when defending what it regards as its own territory (*Cummings* v *Grainger,* Alsatian used as a guard dog; *Curtis* v *Betts,* a bull mastiff being loaded into the back of a Land Rover); a propensity of a dog to attack other dogs (*Smith* v *Ainger*), or to attack people carrying bags (*Kite* v *Napp, The Times,* 1 June 1982); and a horse with unpredictable behaviour (*Wallace* v *Newton* [1982] 2 All ER 106), although in *Jaundrill* v *Gillett, The Times,* 30 January 1996, Russell LJ had reservations about whether a horse which had a tendency to panic and gallop aimlessly when on a highway in the dark was displaying a characteristic under s. 2(2)(b). Before the Act the Court of Appeal had held that there must be a vicious or mischievous propensity on the part of the animal to attack people or other animals. Thus there was no liability for injury caused by a 'playful' filly which was merely engaging in its natural propensities (*Fitzgerald* v *Cooke Bourne (Farms) Ltd* [1964] 1 QB 249). In *Wallace* v *Newton* [1982] 2 All ER 106, however, Park J held that the words 'characteristics of the animal which are not normally found in animals of the same species' in s. 2(2)(b) do not mean that the animal must have a vicious propensity to attack people. It was sufficient if the damage was caused by a characteristic unusual in the species. The plaintiff succeeded for injuries sustained when a horse suddenly became violent and uncontrollable on being loaded into a trailer. The horse was known to be unreliable and unpredictable, which were characteristics not normally found in horses.

Although a vicious propensity to attack is not essential under the Act, it is not obvious that *Fitzgerald* v *Cooke Bourne (Farms) Ltd* would be decided differently today because it could be argued that playfulness is a normal characteristic of fillies (*Winfield and Jolowicz,* p. 478; cf. *Charlesworth and Percy,* para. 13–16). On the other hand, relying on the second limb of s. 2(2)(b), it could be argued that playfulness is not a normal characteristic of a horse except at a particular time, i.e, when it is young, and on this approach *Fitzgerald* v *Cooke Bourne (Farms) Ltd* would probably be decided differently under the Act.

Section 2(2)(b) requires a comparison to be made between the characteristics of the particular animal and those of animals of the same species, which includes subspecies and variety (s. 11). This is a biological concept, and so it would be wrong to treat 'guard dog' as a variety or subspecies (*Cummings* v *Grainger* [1977] 1 All ER 104, 110), but the term does apply to an identifiable breed of dog such as Alsatian or Border collie (*Hunt* v *Wallis* (1991), [1994] PIQR P128). Thus, the comparison that has to be made is with other dogs of the same breed and not with other dogs generally. On this basis it might be possible for a keeper to avoid liability for damage inflicted by a bad-tempered dog if dogs of that particular breed are normally bad-tempered.

The 'knowledge' that is required under s. 2(2)(c) is the keeper's actual knowledge or the knowledge of others that is imputed to him by the subsection. It will not be sufficient if a servant who does not have charge of the animal knows about its abnormal characteristics, nor where a minor under 16 who is not a keeper acquires knowledge, unless in fact that knowledge is passed to the keeper. It is not necessary to establish that the animal has caused similar damage in the past if it has shown a propensity to cause such harm and the keeper knows of its propensity (*Barnes* v *Lucille Ltd* (1907) 96 LT 680). Otherwise there could be no liability for a dog known to be vicious until after it had managed to savage someone. If the keeper did not have actual or imputed knowledge of the animal's characteristics, but ought reasonably to have known, there can be no liability under s. 2(2). The plaintiff would have to rely on an action in negligence.

Where all the requirements of s. 2(2) are satisfied, liability is strict. It is not necessary that the animal should have escaped from the keeper's control.

8.3.5 Defences

There are a number of defences to liability under s. 2 of the Animals Act 1971. A person is not liable for damage which is due 'wholly to the fault of the person suffering it' (s. 5(1); e.g., stroking a zebra: *Marlor* v *Ball* (1900) 16 TLR 239; entering a leopard's pen to remove a lighted cigarette: *Sylvester* v *Chapman Ltd* (1935) 79 SJ 777), and damages will be apportioned where the plaintiff has been guilty of contributory negligence (s. 10). Voluntary assumption of the risk is a defence (s. 5(2)), except that a person is not to be treated as accepting a risk voluntarily where he is employed by a keeper and incurs a risk incidental to his employment (s. 6(5)).

Where the plaintiff was trespassing on the premises the keeper is not liable if either (a) the animal was not kept there for the protection of persons or property, or (b) keeping it there for that purpose was not unreasonable (s. 5(3)). In *Cummings* v *Grainger* [1977] 1 All ER 104, para. 8.3.4, the trial judge held that it was unreasonable to keep a guard dog to protect a load of 'old broken-down scrap motor cars'. The Court of Appeal took a different view, finding that it was the only reasonable way of protecting the place. 'True, it was a fierce dog' said Lord Denning MR, 'But why not? A gentle dog would be no good'. The Guard Dogs Act 1975 now makes it a criminal offence to allow a guard dog to roam freely on premises unless it is under the control of a handler (see also Dangerous Dogs Act 1991). This does not create any civil liability, but in *Cummings* v *Grainger* it was suggested that breach of the Act might make it unreasonable to allow a guard dog loose and so deprive a keeper of the defence under s. 5(3)(b) of the Animals Act 1971 (see also the Animals (Scotland) Act 1987, s. 2(2), which makes compliance with the Guard Dogs Act 1975 a requirement of the defence to civil liability). It would not defeat a *volenti* defence, however, and in *Cummings* v *Grainger* it was held that the plaintiff had voluntarily accepted the risk of injury when she entered the premises knowing that the animal was there and having seen a notice stating 'Beware of the dog'. Where a defence under s. 5(3) succeeds a trespasser will have to rely on the Occupiers' Liability Act 1984, but it will be recalled that *volenti* is a defence under that Act also, and an appropriate warning will discharge the occupier's duty (paras 6.2.5 and 6.2.4).

Act of God and act of a third party are not defences to any of the liabilities created by the Animals Act 1971. Such an event is within the risk that a keeper must accept as a consequence of keeping the animal. In *Jaundrill* v *Gillett, The Times*, 30 January 1996, however, the keeper of horses which had been maliciously released onto a road in the dark was held not to be liable when they panicked and galloped into an oncoming car driven by the plaintiff. The Court of Appeal concluded that the real cause of the accident was the release of the animals onto the road, and that therefore it was the presence of the horses on the highway that was the cause of the damage, not any particular abnormal characteristic of the animals under s. 2(2)(b). Clearly this approach can only apply to animals belonging to a non-dangerous species where the plaintiff has to prove that the animal was known to have abnormal characteristics.

8.3.6 Straying livestock
The Animals Act 1971 abolished the ancient action of cattle-trespass which was quite distinct from the *scienter* action. Section 4 substituted a modern form of strict liability, providing that where livestock belonging to any person strays on to land in the ownership or occupation of another and (a) damage is done by the livestock to the land or to any property on it which is in the ownership or possession of the other person; or (b) any expenses are reasonably incurred by that other person in keeping the livestock while it cannot be restored to the person to whom it belongs or while it is detained in pursuance of s. 7, or in ascertaining to whom it belongs, the person to whom the livestock belongs is liable for the damage or expenses, except as otherwise provided by the Act.

This section protects a person who owns or occupies land from damage to his property by straying livestock or for the expenses of detaining the livestock. It does not apply to personal injuries. Livestock 'belongs' to the person in whose possession it is, not an owner out of possession (s. 4(2)). 'Livestock' means cattle, horses, asses, mules, hinnies, sheep, pigs, goats, poultry, and deer not in the wild state (s. 11). There is no liability under the section for straying dogs or cats, though if repeated this may constitute nuisance. Section 7 gives an occupier onto whose land livestock has strayed a power to detain and sell the livestock in order to recoup the cost of damage done to his property, but the power is subject to very detailed restrictions.

It is a defence to liability under s. 4 that the damage was due wholly to the fault of the plaintiff (s. 5(1); contributory negligence also applies: s. 10), but by virtue of s. 5(6) damage shall not be treated as due to the fault of the person suffering it by reason only that he could have prevented it by fencing.

However, there is no liability under s. 4 where it is proved that the straying of the livestock on to the land would not have occurred but for a breach by any other person, being a person having an interest in the land, of a duty to fence (s. 5(6)). The effect of this is that there is no general duty to fence to keep livestock out, but where such a duty does exist (e.g., arising from contract, custom, easement or statute) then if any person with an interest in the land (not necessarily the plaintiff) is in breach of the fencing obligation the defendant is not liable for the straying livestock (unless, of course, it is the defendant who was in breach of the duty to fence). It is not necessary that the duty was owed to the defendant, he can still rely on its breach as a defence (*Clerk and Lindsell*, para. 20–13).

It is also a defence to an action under s. 4 that the livestock strayed from a highway and the livestock was lawfully present on the highway (s. 5(5)). Lawful use of the highway is for passage and repassage. So the defence does not apply where the livestock have previously strayed onto the highway and are left to wander at will (*Matthews* v *Wicks, The Times,* 25 May 1987). A person who takes animals on the highway owes a duty of care to prevent them straying from the highway, and therefore will be liable for negligence (*Gayler & Pope Ltd* v *Davies & Son Ltd* [1924] 2 KB 75).

8.3.7   Injury to livestock by dogs

Section 3 of the Animals Act 1971 provides that where a dog causes harm by killing or injuring livestock, any person who is a keeper of the dog is liable for the damage, except as otherwise provided by the Act. This imposes strict liability and it is not necessary to show that the damage was the result of an abnormal characteristic or that the keeper had knowledge of the dog's propensity to attack livestock (cf. s. 2(2)). Thus livestock are given greater protection than people. It is a defence to liability under s. 3 that the livestock was killed or injured on land on to which it had strayed and the dog belonged to the occupier or its presence there was authorised by the occupier (s. 5(4)). That the damage was due wholly to the fault of the plaintiff and contributory negligence are also defences (ss. 5(1) and 10).

Section 9 is related to s. 3, in that it gives a defence to an action for killing or injuring a dog if it is proved that the defendant 'acted for the protection of livestock', and the livestock or the land on which it was situated belongs to the defendant or to any person under whose express or implied authority he is acting. The defendant must notify the police within 48 hours of the incident. The defence will not apply if the circumstances are such that the keeper of the dog would not have been liable for the dog killing or injuring the livestock by virtue of s. 5(4).

A person will only be regarded as acting for the protection of livestock if: (a) the dog is worrying or is about to worry the livestock and there are no other reasonable means of ending or preventing the worrying; or (b) the dog has been worrying livestock, has not left the vicinity and is not under the control of any person and there are no practicable means of ascertaining to whom it belongs (s. 9(3)). A reasonable belief that the conditions of s. 9(3) were satisfied will be sufficient for the purpose of the defence (s. 9(4)).

8.3.8 Straying on to the highway

At common law the occupier of land adjoining a highway had no duty in tort to prevent tame domestic animals from straying on to the highway. This immunity was abolished by s. 8(1) of the Animals Act 1971 so that liability is now determined by applying the ordinary rules of negligence (an interpretation confirmed by *Pike* v *Wallis, The Times,* 6 November 1981). The duty of care may, in effect, impose a duty to see that land is adequately fenced, but the fence need only be reasonably stock-proof and a landowner will not be liable unless he ought reasonably to have been aware that the fence was inadequate (*Hoskin* v *Rogers, The Times,* 25 January 1985). Liability is not limited to livestock straying on to the highway but applies to any animal, and 'damage' includes personal injuries.

By s. 8(2) where damage is caused by animals straying from unfenced land to a highway a person who placed them on the land will not be regarded as having committed a breach of the duty to take care by reason only of placing them there if (a) the land is common land, or is land situated in an area where fencing is not customary, or is a town or village green; and (b) he had a right to place the animals on that land. Of course, the duty to take care is a duty only to take *reasonable* care in all the *circumstances* and in many instances (e.g., open moorland) it would not be reasonable to expect the highway to be fenced.

8.3.9 Remoteness of damage

There are no specific provisions in the Animals Act 1971 dealing with the question of remoteness of damage. At common law a keeper was liable for all the damage caused by a dangerous animal and s. 2(1) preserves this position, stating simply that the keeper is liable for 'any damage'. The test would appear to be causation, not foreseeability. Although it is not impossible to apply foreseeability as a test of remoteness in torts of strict liability there is no good reason why words should be read into the statute to produce this result. Provided there is a causal connection the test of remoteness is directness (*Charlesworth and Percy,* para. 13–34). With animals belonging to a non-dangerous species liability will be limited to damage attributable to characteristics not usually found in the same species which were known to the keeper. But any damage caused by such known characteristics is within s. 2(2). It does not matter that the precise damage suffered by the plaintiff was unforeseeable.

8.4 VICARIOUS LIABILITY

An employer is responsible for damage caused by the torts of his employees acting in the course of employment. This is known as 'vicarious liability'. It is a form of strict liability because it arises from the employer-employee (or master-servant) relationship, without reference to any fault of the employer. Liability is imposed on A, not for a breach of duty owed by A to P, but for B's breach of a duty owed by B to P. There are some situations in which B's act causes a breach of A's duty to P. This is a primary not vicarious liability.

One example of this primary liability is the common law duty owed by an employer to an employee to provide competent fellow workers (para. 5.1.1). The act of an incompetent employee may put an employer in breach of this primary duty, even though the employer is not vicariously liable because the act was not within the course of employment (*Hudson* v *Ridge Manufacturing Co. Ltd* [1957] 2 QB 348—employer liable for failing to take reasonable steps to curb an employee's persistent practical joking). Another example is provided by those situations in which an employer is held liable for the acts of an independent contractor. It is said that where the law imposes such a 'non-delegable' duty, a person may delegate the performance of the duty but not responsibility for the manner in which it is performed (see para. 8.5.2). Where the contractor is negligent it is the employer's primary duty that is broken.

Vicarious liability and breach of an employer's primary duty may both arise on the same facts (e.g., where an employee is negligent in the performance of a non-delegable duty imposed on the employer), but they are conceptually quite distinct. Although the term 'vicarious' suggests a type of substituted liability in which the employer takes the place of the employee, in all cases of vicarious liability the employer is liable in addition to the employee, who remains legally responsible for his tort. From the plaintiff's point of view, however, the employer is much the more attractive defendant since he is more likely to have the resources (or to have insured against the risk) to meet an award of damages.

8.4.1 Justification
Several reasons have been advanced as a justification for the imposition of vicarious liability. First the master has 'the deepest pocket'. This emphasises the compensation function of the law of tort. The wealth of a defendant (or its assumed wealth in the case of public authorities), or the fact that he has access to resources via insurance, has in some cases had an unconscious influence on the development of legal principles. It has never been explicitly accepted by the courts, however, as a reason for imposing liability, in spite of the fact that without the insurance industry the present tort system could not operate.

Secondly, vicarious liability encourages accident prevention by giving an employer a financial interest in encouraging his employees to take care for the safety of others. This argument depends upon the validity of the more general claim that tort liability contributes to accident prevention.

A third reason is that since an employer makes a profit from the activities of his employees he should also bear any losses that those activities cause. This is an argument based on fairness, but it is closely linked to a fourth and more convincing justification, namely that vicarious liability functions as a loss distribution mechanism. The torts of employees committed in the course of employment can be regarded as part of the cost of producing the goods or services supplied by the employer. The employer is in the best position to insure against those costs, and the cost of insurance will be reflected in higher prices. The people who make use of the employer's goods or services, i.e., customers, will pay for the risks created by the enterprise rather than the innocent victims who would usually find that an action against the employee alone is worthless. This is also more efficient in economic terms, since by treating the 'external' risks created by an enterprise as a cost of production the price of the product reflects its true social cost.

It is possible that none of these reasons fully justifies vicarious liability, but as Lord Pearce said in *Imperial Chemical Industries Ltd* v *Shatwell* [1965] AC 656, 686 the doctrine is based on 'social convenience and rough justice'.

8.4.2 Basis of liability
At one time there was some confusion over the basis of an employer's vicarious liability. Originally the master was liable because he had commanded the servant to perform the act in question, either expressly or later impliedly. This is a primary liability, which can still arise today on appropriate facts, based upon the master's direct participation in the commission of a tort. By the middle of the 19th century it was accepted that vicarious liability derived from the master-servant relationship and did not depend on the master's own wrongdoing. There have been, nonetheless, some judicial pronouncements suggesting that a master can be vicariously liable irrespective of any breach of duty by the servant—the servant's act leads to a breach of the master's duty. Such an approach blurs the distinction between primary duties and vicarious liability. It is true that where the employer is under a non-delegable duty the act of an employee may produce a breach of the employer's duty, but this has nothing to do with the relationship of employer and employee. The employer would be equally responsible if the act had been performed by an independent contractor or even gratuitously by a friend. The range of non-delegable duties, though not fixed, is limited, and certainly does not cover all acts of an employee in the course of employment.

The House of Lords has expressly rejected the notion that vicarious liability depends on breach of an employer's personal duty (*Staveley Iron & Chemical Co. Ltd* v *Jones* [1956] AC 627; *Imperial Chemical Industries Ltd* v *Shatwell* [1965] AC 656). It is founded on the breach of the employee's duty and the employment relationship. Thus if the employee has not committed a tort the employer cannot be vicariously liable. Defences that would have been available to the employee can be relied upon by the employer.

The essential requirements of vicarious liability are: (a) a tort, (b) committed by an employee, (c) who was acting in the course of his employment.

8.4.3 Who is a servant?
A person who is paid to do something may be either an employee or an independent contractor. (The words 'employee' and 'servant' are used synonymously. 'Master' connotes the employment relationship, but 'employer' can have a wider meaning because the word is used in connection with liability for independent contractors.) It is easy to illustrate the distinction but it is more difficult to define it. A chauffeur is an employee but a taxi driver is not employed by his passengers. It would be strange if passengers were responsible for the negligent driving of a taxi driver, but an employer is

responsible for the negligence of his chauffeur. A servant, it is said, is employed under a contract of service whereas an independent contractor is employed under a contract for services. This merely reformulates the problem, however, since the difficulty then is to distinguish between contracts of service and contracts for services.

No single test is used. There are a number of possible approaches which include: (a) the intention of the parties, (b) the degree of control; (c) integration within the business; and (d) the allocation of financial risk.

(a) *Intention of the parties.* Whether the parties intended to create a master-servant relationship is obviously a relevant factor, but even an express intention is not necessarily conclusive. In *Ferguson v Dawson Partners (Contractors) Ltd* [1976] 1 WLR 1213 a building worker who at the time of hiring was expressed to be a 'labour only subcontractor' was held to be an employee because in all other respects he was treated as an employee. The statement had been made for tax and national insurance purposes (see also *Young & Woods Ltd v West* [1980] IRLR 201, worker engaged on a self-employed basis for tax purposes held to be an employee—the 'label' put on the relationship by the parties was a factor to be considered by the court, but it was not decisive; cf. *Massey v Crown Life Insurance Co.* [1978] 2 All ER 576, where there was a detailed written contract and the parties' intention prevailed). On the other hand, *Ferguson v Dawson Partners (Contractors) Ltd* should not be applied too literally. An occupier who hires a gardener, for example, to look after his garden on one day a week would not necessarily become his employer, even if the occupier supplied the tools, directed the work and paid an hourly rate, for as Lawton LJ has said 'I can see no reason why in law a man cannot sell his labour without becoming another man's servant even though he is willing to accept control as to how, when and where he will work' (*Ferguson v Dawson Partners (Contractors) Ltd* at p. 1226, dissenting).

(b) *Degree of control.* The traditional test of the employment relationship is the ability of the employer to control the work. A master can 'not only order or require what is to be done, but how it shall be done' (*Collins v Hertfordshire County Council* [1947] KB 598, 615 per Hilbery J). The other side of the coin is that a 'servant is an agent who works under the supervision and direction of his employer; an independent contractor is one who is his own master' (*Salmond and Heuston*, p. 435). Control can only be one factor. It is not the determining factor because in modern economic conditions employers often do not have the technical expertise to supervise and control the manner in which skilled employees carry out their work (see Kahn-Freund (1951) 14 MLR 504). The airline cannot tell its pilot how to fly the plane. The hospital cannot tell the surgeon how to conduct an operation. Inability to control precisely how the work is carried out does not necessarily mean that there is no employment relationship. Skilled workers can still be employees. Possibly the test should refer to control of the incidental features of the employment, the 'when and where', not how, the work is performed (Atiyah, *Vicarious Liability*, p. 47). In *Zuijs v Wirth Brothers Pty Ltd* (1955) 93 CLR 561 Dixon CJ said (at p. 571): 'little room for direction or command in detail may exist.

But that is not the point. What matters is lawful authority to command so far as there is scope for it.'

(c)   *Integration within the business.* In *Stevenson Jordan & Harrison Ltd* v *Macdonald & Evans* [1952] 1 TLR 101 Denning LJ said (at p. 111) that:

> One feature which seems to run through the instances is that, under a contract of service, a man is employed as part of the business, and his work is done as an integral part of the business; whereas, under a contract for services, his work, although done for the business, is not integrated into it but is only accessory to it.

A test based on this approach would appear to be: was the man employed as part of the business? ('It depends on whether the person is part and parcel of the organisation', per Denning LJ in *Bank voor Handel en Scheepvart NV* v *Slatford* [1953] 1 QB 248, 290. See also *Cassidy* v *Ministry of Health* [1951] 2 KB 343.) The difficulty with this is that, although it might be more realistic than a test based on control, it may be objected that it is too indeterminate to apply with confidence (for criticism see the *Ready Mixed Concrete* case below, [1968] 2 QB 497, 524 per MacKenna J: 'This raises more questions than I know how to answer.') Moreover, this approach may be misleading in the case of casual workers and those working for two or more employers concurrently who, not being on the permanent staff, may not be considered to be 'part and parcel of the organisation' but nonetheless may be held to be employees (*Lee Ting San* v *Chung Chi-Keung* [1990] IRLR 236, 240, PC).

(d)   *Allocation of financial risk.* In *Montreal* v *Montreal Locomotive Works Ltd* [1947] 1 DLR 161 Lord Wright suggested (at p. 169) a complex test involving (i) control; (ii) ownership of the tools; (iii) chance of profit; (iv) risk of loss. This corresponds more with economic reality, and indeed, common sense. As a general rule employees work for a wage which is calculated by reference to the time worked (piece work and bonuses are admittedly exceptions). They do not participate in the profits of the business or run the risk of losses. (On the other hand, independent contractors may work at an hourly rate, see *WHPT Housing Association Ltd* v *Secretary of State for Social Services* [1981] ICR 737, although the remuneration will probably be called a fee or charge rather than a wage, and some employees do enjoy the benefit of profit-sharing schemes). In *Market Investigations Ltd* v *Minister of Social Security* [1969] 2 QB 173, 184 Cooke J said that the fundamental test was: 'Is the person who has engaged himself to perform these services performing them as a person in business on his own account?' If the answer is yes, it is a contract for services; if no, it is a contract of service. There is no exhaustive list of considerations relevant to determining this question, and no strict rules about the relative weight the various considerations should carry in a particular case. Cooke J identified Lord Wright's four factors, adding: (v) whether the person hires his own helpers; and (vi) what degree of responsibility for investment and management he has. In *Lee Ting San* v *Chung Chi-Keung* [1990] IRLR 236, 238 the Privy Council expressly approved Cooke J's approach.

These factors were considered to be significant in *Ready Mixed Concrete (South East) Ltd* v *Minister of Pensions & National Insurance* [1968] 2 QB 497. The company organised a scheme for the delivery of concrete through 'owner-drivers' who were paid a fixed mileage rate. The contract required the driver to buy his vehicle on hire-purchase from an associated finance company; the vehicles had to be painted in the company's colours; the 'owner-driver' could not alter, charge or sell the vehicle without the company's permission and the company had an option to purchase the vehicle; it could not be used for private purposes or for any other haulage business; and the 'owner-driver' had to comply with the rules and regulations of the company and 'carry out all reasonable orders . . . as if he were an employee of the company'. MacKenna J said that there were three conditions for the existence of a contract of service: (i) the servant agrees that in consideration of a wage or other remuneration he will provide his own work and skill in the performance of some services for his master; (ii) he agrees, expressly or impliedly, that in the performance of that service he will be subject to the other's control in a sufficient degree to make that other master; (iii) the other provisions of the contract are consistent with its being a contract of service. In spite of the very extensive control that the contract gave the company over their 'owner-drivers' MacKenna J concluded that the obligations were more consistent with a contract of carriage than of service. In particular, the 'owner-driver' had to make the vehicle (with a replacement driver if necessary) available throughout the contract period, at his own expense, and, the ownership of the assets (the vehicle), the chance of profit and the risk of loss were the driver's. These factors were inconsistent with a master-servant relationship. His Lordship added: 'A man does not cease to run a business on his own account because he agrees to run it efficiently or to accept another's superintendence'.

The classification of an individual as an employee or an independent contractor is of crucial significance since it will determine whether an employer is vicariously liable for his acts or only responsible for acts that fall within a non-delegable duty. There is no clear-cut test for this distinction, and in borderline cases the answer can only be found by weighing a number of conflicting features. The problem with many of the criteria is that they either assume what they seek to prove or simply beg the question. How much control is sufficient? Which provisions are inconsistent with a contract of service? It may be that Somervell LJ was not far short of the mark when he suggested that a contract of service should be given 'the meaning which an ordinary person would give to the words' (*Cassidy* v *Ministry of Health* [1951] 2 KB 343, 353). It has been argued that the classification of a worker as an employee or an independent contractor should depend upon the context in which the decision has to be taken, so that workers may be employees for the purposes of the law of vicarious liability and independent contractors for tax or social security purposes (McKendrick (1990) 53 MLR 770; Kidner (1995) 15 LS 47). This might help to avoid the undermining of the policy objectives of vicarious liability, such as loss distribution, by the growth of an 'atypical' workforce consisting of the self-employed, part-time workers, casual workers, homeworkers and people on government training schemes.

Special rules apply to at least four categories of employment. First, hospital authorities are vicariously liable for all full-time staff (*Cassidy* v *Ministry of Health*) but probably not for visiting consultants (cf. *Street*, p. 447). But under the National Health Service a hospital authority is under a duty to provide medical services to the patient, and it has been held that this is a primary duty which is not discharged by delegating its performance to a competent independent contractor, such as a consultant (*Razzel* v *Snowball* [1954] 1 WLR 1382; National Health Service Act 1946, s. 3; see now National Health Service Act 1977, s. 3(1)). In practice, under a scheme known as 'NHS indemnity' health authorities and NHS trusts will normally accept vicarious responsibility for the negligence of a consultant doing NHS work. Secondly, before 1964 a police officer did not have a 'master' as such. The Police Act 1964, s. 48, provides that the chief officer of police for any police area is vicariously liable for torts committed by constables under his direction and control in the performance or purported performance of their functions (see Williams (1989) 139 NLJ 1664). Damages are paid out of the police fund, not by the chief constable personally. Thirdly, the owners of hackney carriages (but not private hire taxis) are vicariously liable for the torts of the driver committed in the 'course of employment', even though the relationship of master and servant does not exist (London Hackney Carriages Act 1843, in London, and Town Police Clauses Act 1847, outside London; the usual relationship is bailor and bailee, the driver paying the owner for the use of the cab). Finally, the general employer of a qualified licensed ship's pilot will normally not be vicariously liable to the owner of a ship damaged by negligence while under his pilotage (*Esso Petroleum Co. Ltd* v *Hall Russell & Co. Ltd* [1989] 1 All ER 37). This is because a pilot is an independent professional man who navigates the ship as a principal and not as an employee of his general employer, and the Pilotage Act 1913, s. 15(1) makes him the employee of the shipowner for all purposes connected with navigation. The same conclusion has been reached in relation to the duty imposed on a harbour authority by the Pilotage Act 1987. The duty is to provide a properly authorised pilot and the authority is not vicariously liable for his negligence (*Oceangas (Gibraltar) Ltd* v *Port of London Authority, The Times*, 24 May 1993).

8.4.3.1 Lending a servant Where an employer lends an employee to another employer on a temporary basis, which employer will be vicariously liable for the torts of the employee? This is treated as a question of fact, but as a general rule it will be difficult for the first employer to shift responsibility to the temporary 'employer'. The leading case is *Mersey Docks & Harbour Board* v *Coggins & Griffith (Liverpool) Ltd* [1947] AC 1 in which a crane together with a driver were hired out to a firm of stevedores. The driver was negligent in operating the crane and injured a third party. The contract between the Board and the stevedores provided that the driver was to be the servant of the stevedores, but the Board continued to pay his wages and had the power to dismiss him. The stevedores had immediate control over what the driver should do (e.g., load this cargo on to that ship), but no power over how the crane should be operated to achieve this. The House of Lords held that the driver remained the servant of the Board. The burden of proof rests upon the general or permanent employer to shift the prima facie responsibility to the hirer. 'This burden is a heavy one and can only be discharged in quite exceptional circumstances' (per Viscount Simon at p. 10).

Several factors have to be considered. 'Who is paymaster, who can dismiss, how long the alternative service lasts, what machinery is employed, have all to be kept in mind' (per Lord Porter at p. 17). The most important question, however, is 'who is entitled to give the orders as to how the work should be done'. It is not enough that the task to be performed is under the control of the temporary 'employer', he must also control the method of performing it. There will be a distinction between cases where sophisticated equipment and a skilled operator are lent and cases where labour only, especially unskilled labour, is lent. Where machinery is lent the operator remains responsible to the general employer for its safe keeping and it would be extremely difficult to infer that the hirer could control how the machine should be operated. This is less difficult to establish where labour only is hired out 'but the task in either case is likely to be formidable' (*Bhoomidas* v *Port of Singapore Authority* [1978] 1 All ER 956, 960, PC, where it was held that in the case of stevedoring services it had to be shown that the entire and absolute control of the employee had been transferred; for a rare example of a transfer upheld by the court see *Gibb* v *United Steel Companies Ltd* [1957] 1 WLR 668).

If the hirer were to give a specific order he would be responsible for harm resulting from negligent execution of the order, but he would be liable as a principal, not vicariously. The general employer would not be liable.

An express term in the contract of hire that the workman is to be the servant of the hirer, as in *Mersey Docks & Harbour Board* v *Coggins & Griffith (Liverpool) Ltd* itself, is clearly not conclusive as against a third party, but it may regulate the respective liabilities between the employers. Indeed, this is a common term in standard-form contracts for the hire of plant and machinery, together with an indemnity clause requiring the hirer to indemnify the general employer against all liabilities arising out of the use of the vehicle during the hire period. Moreover, a clause 'transferring' a servant, or even an indemnity clause, should not, logically, be treated as an exclusion clause and thus should not be caught by s. 2 of the Unfair Contract Terms Act 1977, at least as between the parties to the hire contract (*Thompson* v *T Lohan (Plant Hire) Ltd* [1987] 2 All ER 631, CA; cf. the earlier Court of Appeal decision in *Phillips Products Ltd* v *Hyland* [1987] 2 All ER 620 which treated an identical 'transfer' clause as an unreasonable exclusion of liability by virtue of s. 2(2) of UCTA 1977: see Morris (1987) 16 ILJ 264).

The test adopted in *Mersey Docks & Harbour Board* v *Coggins & Griffith (Liverpool) Ltd* applies where the court has to decide whether a temporary or the general employer is vicariously liable to a third party for damage caused by the employee. But if it is the employee himself who is injured, as a consequence of an unsafe system of work, the general employer remains liable as his employer because he is under a personal, non-delegable duty with respect to the safety of his employees (*Morris* v *Breaveglen Ltd* [1993] PIQR

P294, CA; see para. 8.5.4.5). This does not preclude an action by the employee against the temporary employer if there has been negligence by that employer (*Nelhams* v *Sandells Maintenance Ltd* [1996] PIQR P52).

8.4.3.2 Vehicle drivers The principles of vicarious liability have been extended beyond the master-servant relationship, to the situation in which A loans a chattel to B and B through negligent use of the chattel injures C. If A has an 'interest' in the use which is being made of the chattel he will be liable for B's negligence. The cases in which this rule has applied have almost all involved the loan of a motor vehicle. In *Ormrod* v *Crossville Motor Services Ltd* [1953] 1 WLR 1120 the owner of a car, A, asked B to drive it to Monte Carlo, where A would join him for a holiday. Shortly after setting off B was involved in an accident and A was held liable for B's negligence. A had an interest in getting the car to Monte Carlo for the holiday. Denning LJ said that the owner is 'liable if the driver is his agent, that is to say if the driver is, with the owner's consent, driving the car on the owner's business or for the owner's purposes'.

In *Morgans* v *Launchbury* [1973] AC 127 a husband often used his wife's car to go to work and to visit public houses. The husband had promised that if he was unfit through drink to drive he would get a friend to drive him home, which he did. The friend was not sober either and there was a serious accident. The issue before the court was whether the wife was vicariously liable for the negligent driving of the friend, although she did not know that he would drive the car on that occasion and to her he was merely an acquaintance. The House of Lords held that she was not. A mere permission to drive a motor vehicle without an interest in the purpose of the journey does not make an owner vicariously liable. The natural concern that a wife would have in the safe return of both her husband and the car were not sufficient to make either the husband or the friend her agent. Lord Wilberforce stated that 'in order to fix vicarious liability on the owner of a car in such a case as the present, it must be shown that the driver was using it for the owner's own purposes, under delegation of a task or duty'.

In the Court of Appeal, Lord Denning MR had said that the wife was liable, essentially because she was insured and had put the vehicle on the road where it was capable of doing damage. The notion of the driver's 'agency', as Lord Wilberforce agreed in the House, was merely a concept, the meaning and purpose of which is to say 'is vicariously liable', and . . . either expression reflects a value judgment—'*respondeat superior* is the law saying that the owner ought to pay' ([1973] AC 127, 135). But the House was unwilling to look beyond the immediate parties to the insurance position in order to develop a new principle of liability. The policy implications were so far-reaching that any change should be left to Parliament.

Morgans v *Launchbury* was a case where the plaintiff was attempting to reach the funds of an insurance policy via the person who held the policy, irrespective of fault. If the driver was covered by a policy of insurance there would usually be no need for such an action. Where the owner of a vehicle allows a person who is uninsured to use the vehicle, the owner will be liable for breach of statutory duty if the negligent driver cannot satisfy an award of damages to the victim (*Monk* v *Warbey* [1935] 1 KB 75, para. 9.1.2), and where the driver is uninsured or untraceable the Motor Insurers' Bureau may meet an unsatisfied judgment in respect of personal injuries (see *Weir*, pp. 325–6, for discussion of the relationship between insurance and civil and criminal liability; see also *Hepple and Matthews*, p. 825, question 7, and p. 891, nn. 2–7).

8.4.4 Course of employment

The tort must be committed in the course of the servant's employment. There is no single test, however, for deciding which acts fall within a servant's employment and which fall outside it. The courts approach the problem as a question of fact, and this means that the cases can only provide examples of conduct which falls on each side of the divide. Some of the cases are, frankly, irreconcilable. One test which has received judicial approval is that an act is within the course of employment if it is 'either (1) a wrongful act authorised by the master, or (2) a wrongful and unauthorised mode of doing some act authorised by the master' (*Salmond and Heuston*, p. 443). It should be noted that under the second limb of this test it is the act to which authorisation relates, not the tort, because if the master authorised the tort he would be jointly liable as a principal, which is the position under the first limb. It is the second limb which is difficult to apply because there is an unstated tension between unauthorised and improper modes of performing an authorised act and the question of whether the 'act' was authorised. In other words, it is the decision about which acts are authorised that is crucial, but in some cases it is the improper manner of their performance which leads to the decision that they were unauthorised. (For the growing disparity between the common law and statutory/employment protection approaches to this issue, see *Jones* v *Tower Boot Co. Ltd* [1997] 2 All ER 406, CA; for comment see Buckley (1997) 26 ILJ 158; Middlemiss and Mays 1997 SLT 95.)

In practice different results can be achieved depending on how widely the court is prepared to define the scope of the servant's employment. For example, in *Whatman* v *Pearson* (1868) LR 3 CP 422 an employee was not allowed to go home for dinner or leave his horse and cart unattended. He went home for dinner, making a deviation in his route of about a quarter of a mile. The unattended horse bolted and damaged the plaintiffs property. It was held that the scope of the employee's authority was to look after the horse and cart, and the employee was therefore still within the course of his employment. In *Storey* v *Ashton* (1869) LR 4 QB 476 a driver was instructed to deliver some wine and on the return journey after business hours, he was persuaded to set off in a different direction from the defendant's premises. The plaintiff was injured by the servant's negligent driving, but it was held that the driver was not acting in the course of his employment. It was an entirely new and independent journey which had nothing to do with his employment. This approach corresponds with a famous dictum of Parke B in *Joel* v *Morison* (1834) 6 C & P 501, 503 that the servant must be engaged on his master's business, not 'on a frolic of his own'. Again, this does not provide a satisfactory test, but rather represents a conclusion of fact in any particular case that the employee was acting outside the course of his employment. An unusually clear example of an employee's frolic occurred in *General Engineering Services Ltd* v *Kingston and Saint Andrew Corp.* [1988] 3 All ER 867 in which a fire engine took some 17 minutes to make a journey which would normally take $3\frac{1}{2}$ minutes, with the result that the plaintiffs' premises were completely destroyed by fire. The delay was due to the firemen, in furtherance of an industrial dispute, operating a 'go slow' policy (quite literally). The Privy Council had no hesitation in holding that this was not simply an unauthorised mode of performing an authorised act, i.e., driving to the scene as expeditiously as possible. It was not a mode of performing the act at all.

Meal breaks seem to produce particular problems. In *Crook* v *Derbyshire Stone Ltd* [1956] 1 WLR 432 it was held that a lorry driver, who was allowed to stop for his meals, ceased to be acting in the course of his employment from the moment he left the vehicle until he resumed the journey. Yet in *Harvey* v *R. G. O'Dell Ltd* [1958] 2 QB 78 a five-mile journey for the purpose of getting a meal was impliedly authorised and therefore within the course of employment (cf. *Hilton* v *Thomas Burton (Rhodes) Ltd* [1961] 1 WLR 705 where a similar journey for tea, but after the lunch break, was held not to be in the course of employment). An employee travelling on the highway will be acting in the course of employment if at the material time he is 'going about his employer's business'. There is a distinction between the duty to turn up for work and the concept of being 'on duty' while travelling to it (*Smith* v *Stages* [1989] 2 WLR 529, 551). So an employee travelling from his home to his regular place of work is not on duty, but if he is obliged by his contract of employment to use the employer's transport he will normally be regarded as acting in the course of employment. On the other hand an employee travelling *in the employer's time* from his home to a workplace other than his regular workplace, to the scene of an emergency, or between workplaces, or in the course of a peripatetic occupation will be acting in the course of employment (ibid. per Lord Lowry).

One question which it may be useful to ask is: what was the servant employed to do? In *Century Insurance Co. Ltd* v *Northern Ireland Road Transport Board* [1942] AC 509 the driver of a petrol lorry was transferring petrol from the lorry to a tank at a garage, and, having lit a cigarette, negligently threw the match to the floor. This caused an explosion and fire. The defendants were held responsible for the driver's negligence. The single negligent act could not be isolated from the circumstances in which it occurred. The driver was employed to deliver petrol and that was precisely what he was doing, albeit in a negligent fashion (see also *Bayley* v *Manchester, Sheffield & Lincolnshire Railway Co.* (1873) LR 8 CP 148—railway company liable for porter who mistakenly placed a passenger on a train to the wrong destination, having physically dragged the passenger from the correct train). Two cases that can be contrasted are *Beard* v *London General Omnibus Co.* [1900] 2 QB 530 and *Kay* v *ITW Ltd* [1968] 1 QB 140. In *Beard* v *London General Omnibus Co.* a bus conductor, in the driver's absence, decided to turn the bus around for its return journey. The employers were not vicariously liable for his negligence. It was not an improper manner of performing the duties of a conductor because conductors were not employed to drive buses. In *Kay* v *ITW Ltd* a storeman whose job involved driving a fork-lift truck and small vans moved a five-ton lorry that was in his way. There was no emergency and the storeman made no attempt to find the driver of the lorry. The Court of Appeal held that this act was within the course of the storeman's employment, because he was attempting to remove an obstruction in order to carry on with his work.

In *Ilkiw* v *Samuels* [1963] 1 WLR 991 a lorry driver allowed a third party to move the lorry a short distance without checking on his competence. The third party negligently injured the plaintiff who sued the lorry driver's employers. The employers were vicariously liable for the lorry driver's negligence in permitting the third party to drive. This was an improper manner of performing his duties because the lorry driver was employed not only to drive the vehicle but to be in charge of it (see *Ricketts* v *Thos. Tilling Ltd* [1915] 1 KB 644—bus conductor turned the bus around at the end of its journey and negligently killed a pedestrian; employers liable, not for the conductor's negligence, but for the driver's negligence in allowing the conductor to drive; cf. *Beard* v *London General Omnibus Co.*).

8.4.4.1 Implied and ostensible authority   Asking what an employee was employed to do will not necessarily produce a conclusive answer. In some instances an employee may perform an act which is different in kind from the class of acts which he is generally employed to do, but nonetheless he may still be acting within the course of employment. In *Poland* v *Parr & Sons* [1927] 1 KB 236, for example, an off-duty employee saw some boys apparently stealing from one of his employer's wagons. He struck one of the boys who fell and was run over. The employer was held liable on the basis that in an emergency a servant has implied authority to act for the protection of his master's property.

The language of implied authority is not particularly helpful because in many respects it is simply a restatement of the question whether the employee was acting in the course of his employment. In *Lucas* v *Mason* (1875) LR 10 Ex 251 Pollock B observed (at p. 253) that 'in most cases where a duty is to be performed or an act done by a servant, some discretion must be vested in him to whom the doing of it is committed, and, where this is so, the master cannot enjoy the benefit of his servant's acts which involve this discretion without being responsible for their result'. The granting of a discretion to employees necessarily requires some degree of express or implied authority as to the exercise of the discretion, and the question then becomes whether the employee was acting within the limits of the discretion, i.e., within the scope of his employment. If he was then he had implied authority, or, conversely, if he had implied authority he was acting in the course of employment. Again the issue is reduced to a question of fact and degree.

Where an employee has no actual authority, either express or implied, to perform the act in question he may still have apparent or ostensible authority. This arises where an employee is held out by the employer as having authority to act on his behalf, and a third party is misled and suffers damage in reliance on the employee's apparent authority. The employer is then estopped from denying that the employee did have authority. The important point here is that the representation as to the employee's authority must come from the employer, not the employee, since an employee cannot cloak himself with greater authority than he actually has (see, e.g., *Kooragang Investments Pty Ltd v Richardson & Wrench Ltd* [1981] 3 All ER 65; and especially *Armagas Ltd v Mundogas SA* [1985] 3 All ER 795; [1986] 2 All ER 385, HL, where the question of ostensible authority is dealt with in some detail).

8.4.4.2   Express prohibition   An act may be within the course of employment even though it has been expressly forbidden by the employer. At first sight this may seem strange, but if an express prohibition were always effective it would be easy for employers to avoid vicarious liability. A transport company, for example, could specify that drivers must not drive negligently. A prohibition will be effective only if it limits the scope of the servant's employment. It will not be effective where it merely circumscribes the method of performance of the employee's duties.

It will be a question of fact whether a particular prohibition has limited what the servant was employed to do or merely the mode in which he was to carry out his job. A number of examples will illustrate the point. In *Canadian Pacific Railway Co.* v *Lockhart* [1942] AC 591 an employee who was generally authorised to drive vehicles was forbidden to drive unless adequately insured. The employers were liable for damage caused when he drove an uninsured vehicle. In *Limpus* v *London General Omnibus Co.* (1862) 1 H & C 526 a bus driver was instructed not to race with or obstruct the buses of rival companies. He disobeyed this instruction, causing a collision. The employers were held liable since this was simply an improper method of performing his duties. Similarly, in *London County Council* v *Cattermoles (Garages) Ltd* [1953] 1 WLR 997 an employee was prohibited from driving vehicles but his duties involved moving them around the premises by hand. His negligence in driving a vehicle was held to be within the course of employment. It was a mode, although an unauthorised one, of doing his job (cf. *Iqbal* v *London Transport Executive* (1973) 16 KIR 329—prohibition against a bus conductor driving buses effective because driving is not a method of performing the duties of a conductor).

The courts have experienced some difficulty with cases in which drivers have given unauthorised lifts to passengers. Is the employer liable to the passenger for injuries caused by the driver's negligence? In *Twine* v *Bean's Express Ltd* (1946) 62 TLR 458 the employer was not liable to a hitch-hiker who had been given a lift contrary to express instructions. The Court of Appeal's reasoning, namely that the hitch-hiker was a trespasser *vis-à-vis* the employer and therefore was owed no duty of care, could not be supported today. Not only are trespassers owed a duty to be treated with common humanity (para. 6.2, and in the context of driving a motor vehicle it is difficult to see how this could be anything less than a duty to exercise reasonable care), but the existence of a duty owed to the plaintiff *by the employer* is irrelevant to the employer's vicarious liability. It is a breach of the *employee's* duty in the course of his employment that is significant. The prohibition on giving lifts is important only to the extent that it limits the scope of the driver's employment. The decision in *Twine* v *Bean's Express Ltd* can be justified only on the basis that the giving of a lift constituted 'an act of a class which [the driver] was not employed to perform at all' (per Lord Greene MR). But this conclusion depends upon how widely the court is prepared to construe the scope of employment.

This is demonstrated by the later decision of the Court of Appeal in *Rose* v *Plenty* [1976] 1 WLR 141. A milkman employed a boy aged 13 years to assist him on his milk round, contrary to the employers' express instruction not to allow children to assist or to allow passengers on the milk float. The boy was riding on the float when he was injured by the milkman's negligent driving. By a majority, the employers were held vicariously liable. Lord Denning MR said that:

> In considering whether a prohibited act was within the course of the employment, it depends very much on the purpose for which it is done. If it is done for his employers' business, it is usually done in the course of his employment, even though it is a prohibited act. . . . But if it is done for some purpose other than his masters' business, as, for instance, giving a lift to a hitch-hiker, such an act, if prohibited, may not be within the course of his employment.

This suggests that where a prohibited act is performed 'for the employer's business' it will be within the course of employment. This is an extremely wide test which would effectively permit employees to perform the duties of other employees and yet still be acting within the course of employment (reversing *Iqbal* v *London Transport Executive*, for example). It also begs the rather important question of what acts are done *for* the employer's business. The milkman's act was arguably done for his own convenience and benefit, not his employers'.

Taking a more traditional approach Scarman LJ concluded that enlisting the assistance of the plaintiff constituted a mode, albeit a prohibited mode, of doing the job with which the milkman was entrusted, namely to drive the float, deliver milk, collect empties and obtain payment. His Lordship observed that:

> if one confines one's analysis of the facts to the incident of injury to the plaintiff, then no doubt one would say that carrying the [plaintiff] on the float—giving him a lift—was not in the course of the servant's employment. But . . . the proper approach to the nature of the servant's employment is a broad one.

(Scarman LJ was applying a dictum of Diplock LJ in *Ilkiw* v *Samuels* [1963] 1 WLR 991, 1004: 'the matter must be looked at broadly, not dissecting the servant's task into its component activities'.) Even on this view the question remains as to what is the distinction between *Twine* v *Bean's Express Ltd* and *Rose* v *Plenty*. On a broad test the driver in *Twine* v *Bean's Express Ltd* was still doing what he was employed to do, i.e., drive his van (see the dissenting judgment of Lawton LJ in *Rose* v *Plenty* at p. 146). The only distinction that Scarman LJ could point to was that in *Twine* v *Bean's Express Ltd* (and the very similar case of *Conway* v *George Wimpey & Co. Ltd* [1951] 2 KB 266) 'the person lifted was not in any way engaged, in the course of the lift or indeed otherwise, in doing the master's business or in assisting the servant to do the master's business'. This brings Scarman LJ very close to the position adopted by Lord Denning MR. Such a test makes it virtually impossible to state in advance whether a prohibition is effective in limiting the scope of employment because each case would depend on the employee's purpose in disobeying his instructions. If a hitch-hiker assisted a driver by navigating, for example, a prohibition against giving lifts would be ineffective, limiting only the manner in which the driver was to perform his duties, but if the hitch-hiker did nothing, the instruction would be treated as limiting the scope of the driver's employment. This involves a patent fiction in the use of language, which can only be justified, if at all, by Scarman LJ's comment that it is 'important to realise that the principle of vicarious liability is one of public policy'.

A driver who is acting outside the course of employment in giving an unauthorised lift may nonetheless be acting within the course of employment in relation to third parties. Where a pedestrian is negligently run over, his action against the driver's employers would not be affected by the fact that at the time of the accident an unauthorised passenger was in the vehicle. Moreover, even where a prohibition is effective in removing actual authority an employee, such as a foreman, may have ostensible authority to consent to the giving of lifts, in which case the employers will be liable to a passenger for the driver's negligence (*Young* v *Edward Box & Co. Ltd* [1951] 1 TLR 789).

What is the effect if the plaintiff knows about the prohibition? In theory the plaintiff's knowledge should be irrelevant. Where the employer's instruction effectively limits the scope of employment the employer is not liable, whether the plaintiff was aware of it or not. If the prohibition merely limits the manner of carrying out the employee's duties it is difficult to see how the plaintiff's knowledge can take the servant's act outside the course of employment. In *Limpus* v *London General Omnibus Co.*, for example, the defendants would not have avoided liability by simply informing the rival bus companies about its instructions to drivers. In *Stone* v *Taffe* [1974] 3 All ER 1016, however, Stephenson LJ said (at p. 1022) that a plaintiff would not succeed where he knew (or it was likely that he knew) of the prohibition and had an opportunity to avoid the danger of injury from the prohibited act before he exposed himself to the danger. This is the language of the defence *volenti non fit injuria* (para. 14.1) and has little if anything to do with the course of employment.

8.4.4.3 Criminal acts It might have been thought that where the servant's wrongdoing involves the commission of a criminal offence the master could not be vicariously liable. This is not so, however, where the offence can be regarded as a manner of performing the servant's duties. Where an employee has been entrusted with the property of a third party by his employer and the employee steals the property, this is a mode, albeit a dishonest mode, of performing his duty to look after the property. In *Morris* v *C. W. Martin & Sons Ltd* [1966] 1 QB 716 the plaintiff's fur coat was sent to a firm of cleaners and it was stolen by the employee whose job it was to clean the coat. The Court of Appeal held the cleaners liable for the theft. The decision is complicated by the fact that the court placed considerable emphasis on the cleaners' non-delegable duty as bailees for reward (see para. 8.5.4.6). Indeed, the judgments tend to conflate the question of vicarious and primary liability. In either case an employer would only be liable for theft by an employee to whom the goods had been entrusted, not where the employment merely provided the opportunity for the theft. This can be explained on the basis that an employee who has not been entrusted with the property is either (a) not acting within the course of employment for the purpose of vicarious liability, or (b) is not a person to whom the employer's primary duty as a bailee for reward has been delegated. If, however, the bailment had been gratuitous (where the duty is not non-delegable) Lord Denning MR would not have held the employers liable, even though the employee to whom the property was entrusted would equally have been acting 'in the course of employment' in stealing it. Diplock LJ 'expressed no view' on the position of gratuitous bailees, but based his decision 'on the ground that the fur was stolen by the very servant whom the defendants as *bailees for reward* had employed to take care of it and clean it' (at p. 737, emphasis added; see also Salmon LJ at p. 740). This stress upon the defendants' position as bailees for reward is misplaced because under vicarious liability the nature of the *employer's* duty should be irrelevant. Vicarious liability rests on a breach of the *servant's* duty acting in the course of his employment (para. 8.4.2).

The better view, it is submitted, is that an employer will be vicariously liable for theft committed by an employee acting in the course of his employment, i.e., where the employee has been entrusted with the property for safe keeping or in order to carry out work on it. The character of the master's duty is irrelevant for this purpose (*Clerk and Lindsell*, para. 5–37; *Winfield and Jolowicz*, p. 608; *Charlesworth and Percy*, para. 2–278). Where an employee who has not been entrusted with the property uses the opportunity of his employment to steal the property the employer is not *vicariously* liable. In *Heasmans* v *Clarity Cleaning Co. Ltd* [1987] IRLR 286, for example, the Court of Appeal held that the employers of a cleaner who made an unauthorised use of the plaintiffs' telephone were not vicariously liable. It could not properly be regarded as cleaning the telephone in an unauthorised manner, it was an entirely separate act (see also *Irving* v *Post Office* [1987] IRLR 289—defendants not liable for employee's wilful misconduct in writing malicious, racist remarks on letters addressed to plaintiff). An employer may be liable, however, where an employee uses the opportunity created by his employment if (a) the theft puts him in breach of a primary duty to see that care is taken (e.g., in the case of a bailee for reward, where the employer or a person to whom he had delegated the care of the property was negligent in looking after it—the fact that the thief was a servant would be irrelevant here); or (b) the employer was negligent in the selection of the employee. In *Nahhas*

v *Pier House (Cheyne Walk) Management Ltd* (1984) 270 EG 328, for
example, a porter used keys entrusted to him by a tenant to gain entry to her
flat and steal her jewellery. The porter's employers were held liable both for
negligently employing a 'professional thief' in that position, and for breach of
a primary duty to protect the plaintiff's flat, the performance of which it had
delegated to the thief. This primary duty existed even though the employers
were not bailees of the stolen property. (References in the report to 'vicarious'
liability are, strictly speaking, inaccurate. The employers were liable for
breach of their own duty.)

An employer may also be vicariously liable for the fraud of his servant
(*Barwick* v *English Joint Stock Bank* (1867) LR 2 Ex 259). It was once thought
that liability depended upon some benefit accruing to the master from the
servant's wrong, but in *Lloyd* v *Grace, Smith & Co.* [1912] AC 716 the House
of Lords held that an employer may be liable even though the employee
intended only to benefit himself. A solicitors' clerk fraudulently induced a
client to transfer a mortgage into his name and stole the mortgage money.
The solicitors were liable because they had held the clerk out as having
authority to perform this type of transaction, and therefore he had ostensible
authority. It is irrelevant that the plaintiff was not in a contractual relationship
with the defendants or that the fraud involved forgery (*Uxbridge Permanent
Benefit Building Society* v *Pickard* [1939] 2 KB 248). But if the servant had
neither actual nor ostensible authority to perform acts of the type which
caused the loss, the master will not be liable (*Slingsby* v *District Bank Ltd*
[1932] 1 KB 544). Remember, also, that a servant's representations as to his
authority cannot constitute ostensible authority, where the transaction is not
of a type that would usually be performed by a servant in that position (see
Armagas Ltd v *Mundagas SA* [1985] 3 All ER 795; [1986] 2 All ER 385). The
representation as to the servant's authority must come from the master.

Where the servant's crime is an assault, the courts are reluctant to impose
vicarious liability even though the offence arises out of the employment. In
Keppel Bus Co. Ltd v *Sa'ad bin Ahmad* [1974] 1 WLR 1082, PC, a passenger
who objected to a bus conductor's insulting language was assaulted by the
conductor. The employers were not liable (cf. *Smith* v *North Metropolitan
Tramways Co.* (1891) 55 JP 630 where a conductor pushed a passenger off a
tram—employers liable; and *B* v *Curry* (1997) 146 DLR (4th) 72, in which
a non-profit foundation was held vicariously liable for acts of sexual abuse
committed by one of its employees on one of the boys resident in a children's
home that it ran). Where the assault furthers the employer's interests this will
usually be treated as within the course of employment (*Dyer* v *Munday* [1895]
1 QB 742), but not where it was an act of spite or personal vengeance (*Warren*
v *Henlys Ltd* [1948] 2 All ER 935; *Daniels* v *Whetstone Entertainments Ltd*
[1962] 2 Lloyd's Rep 1). If, however, the employee was in charge of
premises, such as a public bar, with responsibility for maintaining order the
employer may be liable even though the act was motivated primarily by spite
or malice (see Atiyah, *Vicarious Liability*, pp. 276–8; *Pettersson* v *Royal Oak
Hotel Ltd* [1948] NZLR 136). On this view *Keppel Bus Co. Ltd* v *Sa'ad bin
Ahmad* is probably wrongly decided. In *Vasey* v *Surrey Free Inns* [1996] PIQR

P373 the plaintiff was attacked by two doormen and a manager employed by the defendant after he had kicked a door, breaking the glass. The Court of Appeal held the defendants vicariously liable because the attack was a reaction to the damage to the door for the protection of the employer's property and was not a private quarrel unrelated to the employees' duties. Although it was an unlawful and unauthorised manner of carrying out their duty generally to preserve the integrity of the club, the employees were not on a frolic of their own. (See generally, Rose (1977) 40 MLR 420.)

8.4.5 Master's indemnity

There is an implied term in an employee's contract of employment that the employee will exercise reasonable care when performing his duties. Where an employee's negligence leads to the employer's vicarious liability then at common law the employer is entitled to be indemnified for the loss attributable to the employee's breach of contract. In *Lister* v *Romford Ice & Cold Storage Co. Ltd* [1957] AC 555 an employee negligently injured his father, who was also employed by the same company. The employers' insurers met the father's claim against the company for the negligence of the son, and then sued the son in the company's name, exercising their right of subrogation under the contract of insurance. By a majority the House of Lords held that the son was liable to indemnify the employers, and hence the insurers.

This case led to some concern at the prospect of insurers enforcing employers' rights against employees with detrimental consequences for industrial relations. Employers' liability insurers subsequently entered into a 'gentlemen's agreement' not to pursue such claims unless there was evidence of collusion or wilful misconduct (see Gardiner (1959) 22 MLR 552; *Hepple and Matthews*, p. 881).

In any event the principle of *Lister* v *Romford Ice & Cold Storage Co. Ltd* does not apply where the employer himself, either personally or through another employee, has been at fault (*Jones* v *Manchester Corporation* [1952] 2 QB 852). The employer would then be limited to claiming contribution under the Civil Liability (Contribution) Act 1978 (see para. 14.6). In *Morris* v *Ford Motor Co. Ltd* [1973] QB 792 a firm of cleaners were contractually bound to indemnify Ford in respect of the negligence of a Ford employee who injured one of the cleaners' employees. The cleaners (who clearly were not bound by the insurers' 'gentlemen's agreement') claimed to be subrogated to Ford's right of indemnity against the negligent employee. By a majority the Court of Appeal held that in an industrial setting it was unacceptable and unrealistic to allow subrogation, particularly as the cleaners had been advised to insure against their potential liability under the indemnity clause. The decision is difficult to reconcile with *Lister*, but represents a pragmatic approach to the financial background of industrial injury litigation.

8.5 LIABILITY FOR INDEPENDENT CONTRACTORS

8.5.1 Basic rule

The basic rule is that an employer is not liable for the torts of his independent contractors, but there are a number of exceptions to this general rule. None of these exceptions, however, are forms of vicarious liability, for in all of them it is the breach of a duty owed to the plaintiff *by the employer* that gives rise to liability. At this point it is important to distinguish between cases in which the employer has been personally at fault, and cases where he has not been at fault, but by the contractor's act a primary duty owed by the employer to the plaintiff has been broken. Where the employer is at fault liability cannot be said to be strict. If, for example, the contractor has been employed to do something unlawful, such as digging up the street without statutory authority the employer will be liable for damage resulting from the contractor's negligence (*Ellis* v *Sheffield Gas Consumer's Co.* (1853) 2 E & B 767—contractors failed to reinstate street properly). The employer is taken to have authorised or ratified the tort. Similarly, the employer is liable on the basis of his personal fault if he has himself been negligent in selecting an incompetent contractor, or in employing an inadequate number of men for the job, or has interfered with the manner in which the work was performed in such a way that damage is caused (*Pinn* v *Rew* (1916) 32 TLR 451; *McLaughlin* v *Pryor* (1842) 4 Mac & G 48). If the employer discovers that the contractor's work is being done in a defective and foreseeably dangerous way, he may be liable if he condones the contractor's negligence (*D & F Estates Ltd* v *Church Commissioners for England* [1988] 2 All ER 992, 1008). This is another instance of personal fault by the employer. Similarly, a hospital authority may be directly liable in negligence for some failure in the organisation of its services to patients, such as an inadequate system, for preventing cross-infection (*Vancouver General Hospital* v *McDaniel* (1934) 152 LT 56, 57) an unreliable system for summoning expert assistance in an emergency (*Bull* v *Devon Area Health Authority* (1989), [1993] 4 Med LR 117), or by employing inexperienced staff without proper supervision (*Jones* v *Manchester Corporation* [1952] 2 QB 852; *Wilsher* v *Essex Area Health Authority* [1986] 3 All ER 801, 833).

Where an employer has not been personally at fault but nonetheless is held responsible for the negligence of an independent contractor, liability is strict in the sense that the employer is liable for damage which he could not have avoided by taking reasonable precautions.

8.5.2 Primary liability
In *Cassidy* v *Ministry of Health* [1951] 2 KB 343 Denning LJ said (at p. 363) that:

> where a person is himself under a duty to use care, he cannot get rid of his responsibility by delegating the performance of it to someone else, no matter whether the delegation be to a servant under a contract of service or to an independent contractor under a contract for services.

This tends to blur the distinction between employees and independent contractors, but his Lordship was probably referring to those situations in which the courts impose a 'duty to provide that care is taken' (*The Pass of Ballater* [1942] P 112, 117 per Langton J), as opposed to a duty to take reasonable care. A duty to see that care is taken is usually referred to as a 'non-delegable' duty, because responsibility for its performance cannot be delegated to another, although the actual performance may be delegated. If care is not taken by the contractor, the employer's duty is broken (see Williams [1956] CLJ 180 who is critical of the language of non-delegable duties, regarding it as a 'logical fraud'). This simply means that the employer is liable for non-performance of the duty, and it is no defence to show that he delegated its performance to a person, whether his employee or not, whom he reasonably believed to be competent to perform it (*McDermid* v *Nash Dredging and Reclamation Co. Ltd* [1987] 2 All ER 878, 887 per Lord Brandon).

Where the duty is merely to take reasonable care the duty will generally be fulfilled by employing an apparently competent contractor to carry out the work. For example, the duty to take reasonable care for the safety of road users requires that a motor vehicle be in a roadworthy condition. That obligation is satisfied by employing a competent contractor to repair or maintain the vehicle, and the owner is not liable if as a result of the contractor's negligence the vehicle is dangerous and causes an accident (*Stennett* v *Hancock* [1939] 2 All ER 578).

The circumstances in which a non-delegable duty will be imposed are relatively fixed. Such duties arise under statute and at common law, but there is no guiding principle by which to determine precisely how and when they arise (see in particular McKendrick (1990) 53 MLR 770; 772–80; see also Jolowicz (1957) 9 Stan L Rev 690). What they have in common is that, in such situations, a prudent employer will appreciate the need to supervise the independent contractor's work, literally to ensure that reasonable care is taken (though, as Feng (1998) 114 LQR 193, 195 observes, in some situations the non-delegable duty relates to an obligation that is, itself, strict—such as that in relation to hazardous activities, para. 8.5.4.3—where the non-delegable duty might be better described as a 'duty to assume the inherent risk of injurious consequences'). The employer is liable in addition to the contractor and would normally be entitled to an indemnity, so the practical effect of imposing liability on the employer is to make him a 'guarantor' of the contractor's solvency.

8.5.3 Statutory duties

Where a statute imposes an 'absolute' duty on an employer, reponsibility for its performance cannot be delegated to a contractor (*Smith* v *Cammell Laird & Co. Ltd* [1940] AC 242; *The Pass of Ballater* [1942] P 112). The question of whether the duty is absolute for this purpose depends upon the construction of the particular statute, but it can include both strict duties (such as duties imposed by the Factories Act 1961: *Hosking* v *De Havilland Aircraft Co. Ltd* [1949] 1 All ER 540) and duties to take care. For example, in *Riverstone Meat Co. Pty Ltd* v *Lancashire Shipping Co. Ltd* [1961] AC 807 it was held that a statutory duty to use 'due diligence' to render a vessel seaworthy was not fulfilled by employing a competent contractor to repair the ship and having the work inspected by a Lloyd's surveyor.

In some instances the duty to take reasonable care in the exercise of a statutory power may be non-delegable, so that the employer is liable for the contractor's negligence in performing acts under the power (*Darling* v *Attorney-General* [1950] 2 All ER 793).

8.5.4   Common law duties

8.5.4.1   Withdrawal of support   The obligation to provide support for adjoining land is non-delegable. Where, in the course of carrying out work on the defendant's land, contractors removed support for neighbouring land the defendant was held liable (*Bower* v *Peate* (1876) 1 QBD 321). But the occupier is not liable for the contractors' negligence where, if properly conducted, the work 'can occasion no risk to his neighbour's house which he is under obligation to support' (*Dalton* v *Angus* (1881) 6 App Cas 740, 831 per Lord Watson).

8.5.4.2   Public nuisance   A person who carries out work on or adjoining the highway which involves danger to the public is responsible for the default of his contractor. In *Tarry* v *Ashton* (1876) 1 QBD 314, for example, a contractor was employed to repair a lamp which overhung the highway. The occupier was liable to a passer-by who was injured when the lamp fell, because he had failed in his duty to make the lamp reasonably safe. Employing a contractor could not shift the burden of responsibility (cf. *Rowe* v *Herman* [1997] 1 WLR 1390, CA—employers not responsible for highway danger caused by collateral negligence of independent contractor working on their land; see para. 8.5.5). Similarly, in *Holliday* v *National Telephone Co.* [1899] 2 QB 392 a telephone company which was laying wires in the highway was held responsible for a contractor who negligently dipped a blowlamp into a pot of molten solder, causing an explosion that injured the plaintiff (see also Highways Act 1980, s. 58(2), which provides that in an action against a highway authority for non-repair of the highway it is no defence that a contractor carried out maintenance unless the authority gave the contractor proper instructions and he carried them out).

This principle is not limited to highways, but has been extended to the creation of dangers in any place where the public may lawfully pass, such as a railway station platform (*Pickard* v *Smith* (1861) 10 CB (NS) 470). It does not apply, however, to work carried out *near* the highway. In *Salsbury* v *Woodland* [1970] 1 QB 324 an occupier employed a contractor to fell a tree which was 28 feet from the highway. The contractor was negligent and the tree struck some telephone wires which fell across the highway, causing an accident. The Court of Appeal held that the occupier was not liable because the work was not carried out on the highway and was not an inherently hazardous operation (see para. 8.5.4.3).

The ordinary use of the highway for passage and repassage is not subject to a non-delegable duty. Thus where an accident is caused by an unroadworthy vehicle the owner is not liable if the defect is attributable to the negligence of an apparently competent contractor employed to maintain it

(*Stennett* v *Hancock* [1939] 2 All ER 578). However, a person may by his conduct undertake a primary non-delegable duty in respect of a defective vehicle. In *Rogers* v *Night Riders* [1983] RTR 324 the defendants were a minicab hire firm, but all their drivers were independent contractors with responsibility for their own vehicles. The defendants were, in effect, little more than a booking agency. The plaintiff was injured when, riding as a passenger in a cab, the door flew open. The Court of Appeal held that the defendants had undertaken to provide a vehicle and driver to transport the plaintiff, and could foresee that she might be injured if the vehicle was defective. Therefore the defendants owed a non-delegable duty to ensure that the vehicle was properly maintained. The decision is based on a form of estoppel, created by the firm holding itself out to the general public as a car-hire firm. If the plaintiff had known the true nature of the firm's business the position would have been different (per Dunn LJ).

8.5.4.3 Hazardous activities The duty under *Rylands* v *Fletcher* is non-delegable, as is liability for the escape of fire (*Balfour* v *Barty-King* [1957] 1 QB 496—contractor attempting to thaw frozen water pipes with blowlamp negligently set fire to defendant's loft; defendant liable for spread of fire to plaintiff's property; *Hobbs (Farms) Ltd* v *Baxenden Chemical Co. Ltd* [1992] 1 Lloyd's Rep 54, 69). There is also a category of 'extra-hazardous operations' for which there will be liability for the acts of an independent contractor, because the operations are 'inherently dangerous' (*Honeywill & Stein Ltd* v *Larkin Bros Ltd* [1934] 1 KB 191, 200 per Slesser LJ). The difficulty is to know which acts 'in their very nature, involve . . . special danger to others' (ibid. at p. 197), but this, as with the categorisation of 'dangerous things' under *Rylands* v *Fletcher*, seems to be an open question for the court. In *Alcock* v *Wraith, The Times*, 23 December 1991 the Court of Appeal said that it was not possible to provide a list of activities which would be regarded as 'extra-hazardous', but the activity had to involve some special risk of damage or it had to be work which from its very nature was likely to cause damage. The defendant, the occupier of a terraced house, was held liable for the negligence of an independent contractor employed to re-roof his house which resulted in damage to an adjoining property through penetration of damp. The case was analogous to claims in respect of damage to party walls for which a defendant could be liable for the acts of an independent contractor, the basis for which was that the work involved a risk of damage to the adjoining property. In *Northern Sandblasting Pty Ltd* v *Harris* (1997) 71 ALJR 1428, the majority of the High Court of Australia found that the supply of electricity to domestic premises was not, on the facts, an extra-hazardous activity attracting this strictest form of primary liability for the acts of independent contractors (though the defendant was held liable on other grounds—see paras 6.3.2 and 8.5.4.7).

8.5.4.4 Private nuisance In *Matania* v *National Provincial Bank Ltd* [1936] 2 All ER 633 the defendants were held responsible for a nuisance by dust and noise caused by an independent contractor who was employed to carry out structural alterations to the defendants' premises. This was because the work in its very nature involved a special danger of creating a nuisance. This can probably be regarded as a specific instance of the principle applicable to hazardous activities (see para. 8.5.4.3), because there is no general rule that an occupier is liable in private nuisance for the acts of his independent contractor (see para. 7.1.5.2.2).

8.5.4.5 Master and servant An employer's common law duty in respect of the safety of his employees is non-delegable (*Wilsons & Clyde Coal Co. Ltd v English* [1938] AC 57, para. 5.1; see Williams [1956] CLJ 180, 1901). Some doubt was cast upon this proposition, however, by the later case of *Davie v New Merton Board Mills Ltd* [1959] AC 604 in which the House of Lords held that an employer was not liable for the negligence of the manufacturer of a defective tool which injured an employee. But it can hardly be said that an employer who purchases equipment has 'employed' the manufacturer or the vendor to fulfil a personal duty for the safety of his employees. The effect of the decision in *Davie v New Merton Board Mills Ltd* was reversed by the Employers' Liability (Defective Equipment) Act 1969, and it is generally accepted that an employer's common law duty with respect to the safety of employees is non-delegable, at least where it is a question of defective work rather than defective equipment (*Charlesworth and Percy*, para. 10–04; *Clerk and Lindsell*, para. 5–60; para. 5.1.3; and see *Sumner v William Henderson & Sons Ltd* [1964] 1 QB 450). Certainly that aspect of an employer's duty to his employees that requires the provision of a safe system of work (see para. 5.1.4) is non-delegable (*McDermid v Nash Dredging and Reclamation Co. Ltd* [1987] 2 All ER 878, HL, where Lord Hailsham regarded the contrary proposition 'unarguable'). Since the duty to provide a safe system of work is merely part of the employer's broader duty to his employees it would be illogical, if not perverse, to say that other elements of that broader duty are not non-delegable. It is possible that *McDermid v Nash Dredging and Reclamation Co. Ltd* extends the scope of an employer's non-delegable duty to his employees to the operation, as distinct from merely the provision, of a safe system of work, which would in effect be equivalent to establishing vicarious liability for the negligence of an independent contractor (McKendrick (1990) 53 MLR 770, 773).

8.5.4.6 Bailees The duty of a bailee for reward is non-delegable, unless the contract of bailment provides otherwise (*Morris v C. W. Martin & Sons Ltd* [1966] 1 QB 716, 725, para. 8.4.4.3). Thus, a warehouseman will be liable for the negligence of an independent contractor employed to protect the bailed goods (*British Road Services Ltd v A. V. Crutchley & Co. Ltd* [1967] 1 WLR 835). Liability is probably based on the defendant undertaking to see that care is taken rather than any notion of increased danger or risk (cf. *Rogers v Night Riders*, para. 8.5.4.2).

8.5.4.7 Landlord? In *Northern Sandblasting Pty Ltd v Harris* (1997) 71 ALJR 1428 (see Feng (1998) 114 LQR 193), the High Court of Australia may have opened the door for the development of a more broadly based common law notion of non-delegable liability for the default of independent contractors. By a 4:3 majority the court held a landlord liable when the tenant's child electrocuted herself due to a combination of defective wiring that pre-dated the tenancy and an independent contractor's shoddy wiring work that post-dated it. Two of the majority held the landlord liable in negligence, for letting out the premises in a reasonably discoverable unsafe state (para. 6.3.2). Significantly, perhaps, the other two majority judges (Toohey and McHugh JJ) based liability on the landlord's default *after* the letting, holding the landlord personally liable for the independent contractor's negligence expressly on the basis of a breach of a non-delegable duty to ensure that reasonable care was taken by them. The court had been satisfied that the landlord was not in breach of its (delegable) duty to take reasonable care in that it had appointed a qualified and licensed electrical contractor. Toohey and McHugh JJ, however, considered that, on the facts, the landlord had a non-delegable duty to go further and to ensure that the independent contractor performed the work with reasonable care. In turn, they held that this duty had arisen as a result of the defendant's control of the premises (by virtue of its status as landlord) and the vulnerability of the plaintiff and her implicit reliance on the landlord to protect her. Toohey and McHugh JJ were satisfied that the landlord/tenant situation before them was sufficiently analogous to the master/servant scenario in which a non-delegable liability for the default of an independent contractor has traditionally been recognised (para. 8.5.4.5). It is true that it is not difficult to recognise there an equivalent control/vulnerable reliance rationale, at least implicitly. It will be interesting, though, to see whether English courts would be willing to use such broad principles to cut across what has hitherto been a somewhat *ad hoc* species of liability, and develop common law non-delegable duties accordingly.

8.5.5 Collateral negligence
Even where an employer owes a non-delegable duty he is not liable for the collateral or casual negligence of an independent contractor. This is negligence which is not committed in performance of the very work that has been delegated to the contractor. In *Rowe* v *Herman* [1997] 1 WLR 1390, an independent contractor employed for contract work on private land had created an obstruction on the public highway by laying metal plates across it. The contractor had done this in order to protect the paving stones on the highway. The Court of Appeal found that the laying of the metal plates was not a necessary part of the contract work and so the employer was not responsible for the injuries caused to the plaintiff when he tripped over them. In practice it can be very difficult to distinguish between acts which are collateral and acts which constitute a manner of performing the delegated task. In *Padbury* v *Holliday & Greenwood Ltd* (1912) 28 TLR 492 a subcontractor's employee, in the course of installing a window, placed a tool on a window sill. The wind blew the window and the tool fell on to the plaintiff below. This was held to be collateral negligence. In *Holliday* v *National Telephone Co.* [1899] 2 QB 392 the contractor's employee negligently dipped a blowlamp into molten solder causing an explosion. The Court of

Appeal held that this was negligence in carrying out the act which he was employed to perform.

The simplest way to make the distinction is to ask whether the negligence was related to the dangerous element of the work, i.e., that aspect of the work which renders the employer's duty non-delegable. In *Padbury* v *Holliday & Greenwood Ltd* Fletcher Moulton LJ said that in order for the employer to be liable the task must be 'work the nature of which, and not merely the performance of which, cast on the superior employer the duty of taking precautions'. Thus where the negligence is incidental to the performance of the work and does not arise from the nature of the work itself, the employer will not be responsible. This constitutes a significant difference between liability for the acts of independent contractors and vicarious liability for the acts of employees, since casual negligence incidental to an employee's performance of his job is probably the most common event giving rise to vicarious liability.

NINE
Breach of statutory duty

A person who has suffered damage as a result of the breach of a statutory duty *may* have an action in tort, classified by Lord Browne-Wilkinson in *X (minors)* v *Bedfordshire County Council* [1995] 3 WLR 152 as an 'action for breach of statutory duty *simpliciter*'. In English law this is a specific common law action which is distinct from the tort of negligence (see para. 9.2), even where the negligence action is based on a common law duty of care arising either from the imposition of a statutory duty or from the performance of it (see para. 2.2.3.2). The careless performance of a statutory duty does not in itself give rise to any cause of action in the absence of either a 'right of action for breach of statutory duty *simpliciter*' or a common law duty of care in negligence (*X (minors)* v *Bedfordshire County Council* [1995] 3 WLR 152, 167). On the other hand, an 'action for breach of statutory duty *simpliciter*' does not depend upon proof of negligence by the defendant. Some statutes, such as the Occupiers' Liability Act 1957, are intended to clarify and amend existing common law duties. Others, such as the Misrepresentation Act 1967 or the Nuclear Installations Act 1965, expressly create new statutory torts. Yet others, like the Guard Dogs Act 1975 or the Safety of Sports Grounds Act 1975, expressly exclude a civil action for breach of their terms. In the vast majority of legislation, however, there is no express provision to indicate whether contravention will be actionable or not. Where the statute is silent the courts purport to 'discover' the intention of Parliament, but the truth is that, Parliament having pointedly omitted to express an intention, the construction of the statute, aided by certain 'presumptions', amounts to little more than judicial legislation. This in itself would not necessarily be a major ground of criticism, if it were possible to discern any coherent guiding principles employed by the courts to determine this question. However, there are so many conflicting 'presumptions' and contradictory statements as to the value of particular presumptions, that it is virtually impossible to predict how the courts will respond to a particular statute. 'You might as well toss a coin to decide it', said Lord Denning MR in *Ex parte Island Records Ltd* [1978] Ch

122, 135. 'In effect the judge can do what he likes, and then select one of the conflicting principles stated by his predecessors in order to justify his decision' (Williams (1960) 23 MLR 233, 246). These 'principles' are considered in para. 9.1.

One particular area, industrial safety legislation, tends to dominate the action for breach of statutory duty. Indeed, Williams, op. cit., commented that when it concerns industrial welfare, penal legislation results in absolute liability in tort, and in all other cases it is ignored. This statement was an admitted oversimplification, both as to the type of legislation which is treated as actionable and the standard of liability, but even today it is not an unreasonable working hypothesis with which to commence a study of this tort (though see *Stanton,* chapter 4). The standard of liability varies considerably with the wording of the statute, ranging from liability in negligence to strict liability (para. 9.2). As with other torts, the plaintiff must prove that the breach of statutory duty caused his loss, which he will fail to do if the damage would have occurred in any event (para. 9.4). In addition, it must be shown that the damage was of the type that the legislation was intended to prevent, and that the plaintiff belonged to the category of persons that the statute was intended to protect. It is not sufficient simply that the loss would not have occurred if the defendant had complied with terms of the statute (para. 9.3). This rule performs a function similar to that of remoteness of damage in the tort of negligence. The damage must also be of a type which the courts have accepted to be compensatable, namely personal injuries, damage to property or economic loss. Thus, the unauthorised publication of information in breach of the Mental Health Tribunal Rules 1983 about proceedings on a patient's application for discharge to a mental health tribunal, though adverse to the patient's interests, does not give the patient an action for breach of statutory duty because the loss or injury is not of a kind for which the law awards damages (*Pickering* v *Liverpool Daily Post & Echo Newspapers plc* [1991] 1 All ER 622, HL).

9.1   IS THE BREACH ACTIONABLE?

At one time the courts adopted a liberal approach to the imposition of civil liability for breach of a statutory duty (*Couch* v *Steel* (1854) 3 E & B 402, 415). This has been superseded by what may be termed the 'construction approach'. The leading authority is *Cutler* v *Wandsworth Stadium Ltd* [1949] AC 398, 407 where Lord Simonds said that 'the only rule which in all circumstances is valid is that the answer must depend on a consideration of the whole Act and the circumstances, including the pre-existing law, in which it was enacted'. The search for a fictional Parliamentary intention is confused by contradictory initial presumptions (see *Stanton,* chapter 3). In *Groves* v *Lord Wimborne* [1898] 2 QB 402, 407, A.L. Smith LJ said that proof that there has been a breach of the defendant's statutory duty, and that the plaintiff had been thereby injured would prima facie establish the plaintiff's cause of action (see also *Monk* v *Warbey* [1935] 1 KB 75, 81 per Greer LJ, but he later appeared to approve an opposite rule: Williams, op. cit., p. 244).

However, in *Lonrho Ltd* v *Shell Petroleum Co. Ltd* [1981] 2 All ER 456 the House of Lords approved the general rule laid down by Lord Tenterden CJ in *Doe d Bishop of Rochester* v *Bridges* (1831) 1 B & Ad 847, 859 that 'where an Act creates an obligation, and enforces the performance in a specified manner . . . that performance cannot be enforced in any other manner'. Lord Diplock recognised two exceptions to this general rule. First, where the obligation or prohibition was imposed for the benefit or protection of a particular class of individuals, and secondly, where the statute creates a public right and an individual member of the public suffers 'particular damage'. The House rejected a wider rule suggested by a majority of the Court of Appeal in *Ex parte Island Records Ltd* [1978] Ch 122 that interference with a private right as a result of a criminal act would justify a civil action. That case was an action for an injunction whereas *Lonrho Ltd* v *Shell Petroleum Co. Ltd* was a claim for damages, but in *RCA Corporation* v *Pollard* [1983] Ch 135 the Court of Appeal confirmed that the wide statement of principle in *Ex parte Island Records* was no longer correct.

The initial presumption, then, appears to be that if the Act provides for a penalty this is the only remedy (para. 9.1.1). This would tend to exclude many statutes which are criminal in nature and provide for some type of penalty, even if only a small fine. In some cases the availability of another common law remedy is regarded as significant (para. 9.1.2). Lord Diplock's two exceptions are considered in paras 9.1.3 and 9.1.4. Lastly, although not stated formally as a principle, the fact that the defendant is a public utility which might be subject to extensive liability is sometimes considered to be relevant (para. 9.1.5). The problem with all of these presumptions is that they are so vague and easily displaced that it is virtually impossible to detect a unifying theme or principle. On the whole, if the statute prescribes a safety standard which more or less corresponds to a common law duty it will be easier to infer an action, although there are exceptions both ways. But where a statute imposes general administrative functions on public bodies and involves the exercise of broad administrative discretion following subjective judgments, the courts are unlikely to find that Parliament intended to create a private law right of action for breach of the statutory duty (*X (minors)* v *Bedfordshire County Council* [1995] 3 WLR 152, 166; *O'Rourke* v *Camden LBC* [1997] 3 WLR 86, HL). The Law Commission recommended that an interpretation Act should create a statutory presumption in favour of legislation being actionable, unless civil liability was specifically excluded (Law Com. No. 21, 1969). Even if implemented, this would only apply to legislation enacted after the passing of the interpretation Act, which would still leave the courts hunting for a non-existent Parliamentary intention among the vast amount of previous legislation. But, as Williams, op. cit., p. 256 comments, why should the draftsman say what he does *not* intend the measure to do?

9.1.1 Statutory remedy
Where a statute imposes a duty but does not provide a remedy for its breach, or some other means of enforcement, the assumption is that there will be a

right of action for a breach of the duty (*Cutler* v *Wandsworth Stadium Ltd*
[1949] AC 398, 407 per Lord Simonds). Conversely, where the statute does
provide an adequate remedy there is a presumption against conferring a
common law action for breach of statutory duty (*Wentworth* v *Wiltshire County
Council* [1993] 2 WLR 175—no action against a highway authority in respect
of purely economic loss resulting from non-repair of a highway under the
Highways (Miscellaneous Provisions) Act 1961, s. 1, since the Highways Act
1959, s. 59 provided a procedure for enforcing the highway authority's
obligation to keep the highway in repair (see now Highway Act 1980, ss. 41,
56, 58); *Issa* v *Hackney LBC* [1997] 1 WLR 956, CA—no action against local
authority in respect of breach of Pt III of the Public Health Act 1936, since
that Act was a self-contained code dealing with the abatement of statutory
nuisances and it provided for a specified means of enforcement). Statutes
which provide no enforcement machinery at all are rare, and it has been
argued by Buckley (1984) 100 LQR 204, 217–20 that, far from justifying a
civil action, this type of legislation should not give rise to any liability because
it will usually consist of administrative instructions to public bodies which
have to exercise a wide discretion. Buckley's argument was in the context of
a criticism of *Thornton* v *Kirklees Metropolitan Borough Council* [1979] QB 626
in which the court awarded damages for breach of a local authority's
obligations under the Housing (Homeless Persons) Act 1977 which provided
no special remedy. The House of Lords in *O'Rourke* v *Camden LBC* [1997]
3 WLR 86 has since overruled *Thornton* v *Kirklees* and, with it, lent
considerable support to Buckley's argument. In *O'Rourke*, the House held
that a housing authority's duty to provide temporary accommodation under
s. 63(1) of the Housing Act 1985, although framed in objective terms, did
not confer any additional private law right to sue for damages. Their
Lordships also acknowledged that such a challenge to the exercise of
administrative discretion is likely to run into problems similar to those raised
by an action in negligence in respect of the exercise of statutory powers (see
para. 2.2.3.2). In doing so, their Lordships applied the earlier decision in
Cocks v *Thanet District Council* [1983] 2 AC 286, to the effect that challenges
to administrative decisions made by public authorities must be made by an
application for judicial review, under RSC Ord. 53, not an action for breach
of statutory duty. In *O'Rourke*, the House held that Pt III of the Housing Act
1985, as part of a scheme of social welfare providing housing assistance to
individuals for the benefit of society in general, which required in its
implementation an element of subjective judgment on the part of the housing
authority indicative of a public law function, had been intended by Parliament to be enforceable solely by way of judicial review. The broader the
discretion the less willing the court will be to permit a private law action (*X
(minors)* v *Bedfordshire County Council* [1995] 3 WLR 152).

The position is complicated by uncertainty as to what constitutes a
'remedy' for this purpose. In *Reffell* v *Surrey County Council* [1964] 1 All ER
743, for example, Veale J held that a student at one of the defendant
authority's schools, who was cut by a thin pane of glass, could maintain an
action for breach of the Education Act 1944. Referring to the 'strong

presumption' that an action would lie 'where the statute provides no penalty for the breach', Veale J said that this applied to the case because the remedy under the Act was an application for mandamus. The question was whether the special remedy provided by the statute was adequate for the protection of the person injured (cf. *Olutu* v *Home Office* [1997] 1 All ER 385, in which the Court of Appeal considered that the statutory right to apply for release on bail or *habeas corpus* and mandamus justified their denying a private law action for damages to a plaintiff who had been remanded in custody for an excessive period in breach of the Prosecution of Offences Act 1985 and the custody regulations made under it). There is a distinction, however, between providing no remedy and providing an inadequate remedy, although whether it justifies a different approach to statutory interpretation is perhaps debatable. Nonetheless, in *Atkinson* v *Newcastle Waterworks Co.* (1877) 2 ExD 441 the Court of Appeal held that a penalty of £10 under the Waterworks Clauses Act 1847 was the only sanction against a waterworks company that had failed to maintain sufficient pressure, with the result that the plaintiff's premises were burnt down because there was no water to extinguish the fire (see further para. 9.1.5). *Atkinson* v *Newcastle Waterworks Co.* was distinguished in *Dawson* v *Bingley Urban District Council* [1911] 2 KB 149 partly on the basis that the Public Health Act 1875, s. 66, which required local authorities to mark the position of fire-plugs for the purpose of fighting fires, contained no remedy for breach. The defendants were held liable for the additional damage to the plaintiff's premises caused by delay in locating the fire-plug. *Atkinson* v *Newcastle Waterworks Co.* was also distinguished in *Read* v *Croydon Corporation* [1938] 4 All ER 631 where Stable J held that breach of a different section of the Waterworks Clauses Act 1847 requiring the supply of pure and wholesome water was actionable despite provision for a penalty. The action was confined to ratepayers, however, although the defendants were also liable in negligence to non-ratepayers. In *Atkinson* v *Newcastle Waterworks Co.* the statutory duty to maintain water pressure was 'for the benefit of the community', whereas the supply of wholesome domestic water affected each householder individually (per Stable J at p. 653; cf. *Square* v *Model Farm Dairies (Bournemouth) Ltd* [1939] 2 KB 365—no action for supplying contaminated milk contrary to the Food and Drugs (Adulteration) Act 1928 because it was a penal statute).

The classic authority on the question of the adequacy of the statutory remedy is *Groves* v *Lord Wimborne* [1898] 2 QB 402 where an employee succeeded in an action against his employer for breach of statutory duty to fence dangerous parts of machinery. The legislation provided for a fine for breach of up to £100, all or part of which could be applied for the benefit of the injured person, but this was at the discretion of the Secretary of State. The fact that the employee might not receive any benefit, that the fine was a criminal sanction which should be assessed by reference to the nature of the offence rather than the severity of the injury, and the £100 limit, all pointed to the interpretation that Parliament had not intended to take away the common law remedy that the Factories Acts had prima facie conferred on injured workmen.

It would be unwise to treat *Groves* v *Lord Wimborne* as of general application in the 'interpretation' of legislation with an inadequate statutory remedy. In *Lonrho Ltd* v *Shell Petroleum Co. Ltd* [1981] 2 All ER 456, Lord Diplock regarded it as falling within the first exception to the general rule that if the legislation enforces performance in a specified manner then it cannot be enforced in another manner. The exception applies where the duty was imposed for the benefit of a particular class of individuals, in this case employees. Moreover, whatever the merits of the distinction the courts do interpret industrial safety legislation more favourably to the plaintiff than other legislation, even where the latter could aid public safety (cf. *Phillips* v *Britannia Hygienic Laundry Co. Ltd* [1923] 2 KB 832, para. 9.1.2).

9.1.2 Common law remedy

It has been said that the court should not admit an action for breach of statutory duty where the plaintiff's existing common law remedies would be sufficient redress. Thus, in *Phillips* v *Britannia Hygienic Laundry Co. Ltd* [1923] 2 KB 832 the Court of Appeal decided that breach of the construction and use regulations which govern the condition of motor cars on the highway did not give rise to a civil action. In support of this conclusion Atkin LJ observed that 'the obligations of those who bring vehicles upon highways have been already well provided for and regulated by the common law' (see also per Bankes LJ at p. 839). Similarly in *McCall* v *Abelesz* [1976] QB 585 the Court of Appeal held that there was no civil action for breach of what is now the Protection from Eviction Act 1977, s. 1, which creates a criminal offence of unlawful harassment of a residential occupier. The tenant could have sued the landlord for breach of the covenant for quiet enjoyment contained in the lease. However, some people who qualify as residential occupiers might not have this option, e.g., where the lease has been lawfully terminated by notice. It is possible that unlawful harassment would constitute private nuisance which would provide an alternative remedy (*Guppys (Bridport) Ltd* v *Brookling* (1983) 269 EG 846, 942), but this would depend upon the plaintiff having a sufficient interest in the premises to maintain the action (see para. 7.1.4). In *Warder* v *Cooper* [1970] Ch 495 it was held that breach of what is now s. 3 of the same Act, which prohibits the eviction of former tenants without a court order, was actionable in tort. It is difficult to see what other remedy would have been available to a person evicted in breach of s. 3 (see now Housing Act 1988, ss. 27 and 28 which create a statutory tort in respect of unlawful eviction, but not harassment short of eviction, in addition to existing common law remedies).

The availability of an alternative common law remedy has never been a decisive consideration. The existence of an action in negligence for breach of an employer's non-delegable duty (para. 5.1) did not preclude the employee's action for breach of statutory duty established by *Groves* v *Lord Wimborne* [1898] 2 QB 402. Conversely, the absence of a common law remedy has not necessarily persuaded the courts to allow an action for breach of a statute (Williams (1960) 23 MLR 233, 246; *Issa* v *Hackney LBC* [1997] 1 WLR 956, CA; cf. Barrett (1998) 27 ILJ 59, who argues that there may yet be a renaissance of civil actionability for breach of statutory duty for plaintiffs denied a common law remedy in actions for negligently inflicted psychiatric damage: see para. 5.2).

Another approach to existing remedies is to say that an action for breach of the statute should be allowed where it would supplement the common law rule, but not if it would undermine the common law (*Winfield and Jalowicz*, p. 197). In *Monk* v *Warbey* [1935] 1 KB 75 the defendant allowed an uninsured driver to drive his car contrary to the Road Traffic Act 1930, s. 35. The driver negligently injured the plaintiff, but the plaintiff's judgment against the driver remained unsatisfied. The defendant vehicle owner was held liable to compensate the plaintiff, even though his breach of statutory duty did not cause the plaintiff's injury, it merely prevented him from recovering damages from the driver. *Weir*, p. 207, comments that the decision fits well into the policy of the law that victims of negligence on the road should not only be entitled to compensation but should actually receive it (the case is now of little practical importance in view of the Motor Insurers' Bureau, see para. 1.3, although the MIB is entitled to recover sums paid out from the uninsured driver/owner: see the MIB Agreement, *Hepple and Matthews*, p. 899). On the other hand, an action for breach of statutory duty in *Phillips* v *Britannia Hygienic Laundry Co. Ltd* [1923] 2 KB 832 might have introduced a somewhat haphazard element of strict liability into road traffic accident cases, whereas the common law almost invariably requires negligence (per Atkin LJ; see also *Coote* v *Stone* [1971] 1 WLR 297; and cf. *London Passenger Transport Board* v *Upson* [1949] AC 155). But as Williams observed, there is no obvious reason why these regulations should be interpreted differently from the safety provisions in factory legislation (op. cit., p. 247).

The logic of *Monk* v *Warbey* [1935] 1 KB 75 was not followed in *Richardson* v *Pitt-Stanley* [1995] ICR 303. A failure by an employer to insure against liability for personal injury to employees is a criminal offence under s. 5 of the Employers' Liability (Compulsory Insurance) Act 1969. The plaintiff was unable to recover an award of damages against his former employer, a limited company which had gone into liquidation, because the company, in breach of the 1969 Act, had not taken out insurance against its liability to employees. The plaintiff brought an action for breach of statutory duty against the directors and secretary of the company, on the basis that it was their failure to comply with the terms of the Act which led to him being unable to recover damages for his personal injuries. On the face of it, this situation is directly analogous to that of *Monk* v *Warbey*. The clear and obvious purpose of the Employers' Liability (Compulsory Insurance) Act 1969 is to ensure that employees who suffer personal injuries as a result of negligence or breach of duty for which the employer is responsible in law are able to recover compensation from the employer or the employer's insurance company. Breach of the Act constitutes a criminal offence but this in itself does not help the injured employee. An action in tort for breach of statutory duty against those responsible for the fact that there is no insurance cover clearly supplements both the underlying policy of the Act and the common law rule which provides that the injured employee is entitled to compensation. But, by a majority (Russell and Stuart-Smith LJJ), the Court of Appeal held that the statute did not create any civil liability in addition to its criminal sanctions. This decision illustrates the sometimes tortuous process by which the courts seek the 'intention of Parliament'. A number of factors were taken as indicating that there should be no civil action for breach of statutory duty:

(1)   There was nothing in the Act which indicated that the employer company would be in breach of a civil obligation for failing to insure and therefore it would be strange if the directors and other officers of the company could be civilly liable for breach of the same provision. In his dissenting judgment, Sir John Megaw could see no objection to imposing civil liability for breach of s. 5 of the 1969 Act on the employer, though his Lordship recognised that in practice there would be no advantage to the plaintiff in doing so, since, almost by definition, in the circumstances when the plaintiff needs to resort to this particular breach of duty the employer will be insolvent.

(2)   The claim was for economic loss, namely the inability to recover damages against the employer in liquidation: 'The court will more readily construe a statutory provision so as to provide a civil cause of action where the provision relates to the safety and health of a class of persons rather than where they have merely suffered economic loss' (per Stuart-Smith LJ at p. 312). On the other hand, there is little or no point construing legislation (such as the Factories Act 1961) to provide a civil cause of action if the practical reality is that the plaintiff is denied a remedy in damages because the courts are not prepared to construe parallel legislation which is specifically designed to ensure that the plaintiff can recover damages against a solvent party as also conferring a civil cause of action. Moreover, the fact that the loss is economic is not necessarily a reason for denying the plaintiff a remedy (see, e.g., *Monk* v *Warbey* [1935] 1 KB 75; *Rickless* v *United Artists Corporation* [1987] 1 All ER 679).

(3)   The severity of the criminal sanction (a fine of up to £1,000 per day) was taken as being an indication against imposing civil liability, though arguably this merely indicates the importance which Parliament attaches to the object to be achieved and the seriousness with which it views breach of the statute, factors which are equally if not more indicative of a policy in favour of imposing civil liability (see O'Sullivan [1995] CLJ 241, 243).

(4)   The 1969 Act was not exclusively for the protection of employees but also for the protection of employers, particularly the small employer who might be bankrupted by a claim unless insured against it. The implication of this view is that it was the intention of Parliament to protect employers from the financial consequences (i.e, economic loss) of their own foolishness in failing to insure against their liability to employees, and moreover this Parliamentary benevolence to employers was to be enforced by a penalty of up to £1,000 per day for its breach, which, incidentally, might also bankrupt the small employer. The Court did not explain why Parliament should want to protect employers in this fashion, whilst

simultaneously declining to protect employees from economic loss by impliedly refusing to confer upon employees the benefit of a common law action for breach of statutory duty. Sir John Megaw, in his dissenting judgment, considered that the facts fell within Lord Diplock's first exception in *Lonrho Ltd* v *Shell Petroleum Co. Ltd* [1981] 2 All ER 456, namely that the obligation was imposed for the protection of a particular class of individuals, but this was not employers:

> The obligation to insure against bodily injury or disease sustained by employees was imposed by Parliament for one purpose, and one purpose only. The purpose was to give protection to a particular class of individuals, the employees, to eliminate, or, at least reduce, the risk to an injured employee of finding that he was deprived of his lawful compensation because of the financial position of the employer. (at p. 315.)

(5) The analogy of *Monk* v *Warbey* was distinguished on the grounds that: (a) the owner of a motor vehicle, unlike an employer, has no direct liability to the injured party in a road traffic accident caused by the negligence of the driver to whom the vehicle has been lent; (b) the wording of the two statutes was different, in that the Road Traffic Act rendered the conduct 'unlawful' and then attached criminal sanctions to that unlawful conduct, whereas the Employers' Liability (Compulsory Insurance) Act 1969 did not make the failure to insure 'unlawful' but 'merely' classified it as a criminal offence; (c) the Road Traffic Act deals only with the owner of the vehicle whereas the 1969 Act imposed criminal liability on the employer and any director or officer of the employer company who has consented to, connived or facilitated the company's omission to insure; and (d) the owner of a motor vehicle who permits another person to drive his vehicle puts into the hands of that person a potentially lethal object, which if not driven with proper care, may cause injury to members of the public on the road, but there is nothing similar in the action or inaction of a director who commits an offence under s. 5 of the 1969 Act. The relevance of these distinctions is something of a mystery. As Sir John Megaw commented of (b), 'Why should such subtle wording be used [by Parliament] to indicate that the breach of duty which it contemplates is not actionable when that intention can be expressed in clear and concise words?', and with regard to (d) it is not clear why the fact that a vehicle is potentially lethal can have any relevance to the owner's liability in respect of his failure to insure: in *Monk* v *Warbey* the defendant was held liable in respect of his failure to see that the vehicle was not used without appropriate insurance thereby preventing the plaintiff from recovering damages from the careless driver, not because he carelessly permitted an incompetent driver to use the car thereby causing personal injuries.

The poverty of the reasoning on display in *Richardson* v *Pitt-Stanley* is a sad indictment of the fiction that the courts are attempting to divine the Parliamentary intention, and though Parliament can be criticised for failing

to make its intention clear (whether for or against civil liability), it can hardly
have anticipated so many spurious reasons being advanced to achieve so
unjust a result. For as O'Sullivan [1995] CLJ 241, 243 comments if
Parliament leaves the issue of civil liability silent, ultimately the courts must
confront a policy decision, which in this case was:

> Who should bear the risk that a company, which has carried on business
> in breach of safety regulations (so that an employee is disabled) and
> without compulsory insurance, goes bust unable to meet the employee's
> damages? Should it be the culpable controllers of that company, skulking
> behind the corporate veil, or the injured employee? English law saddles the
> employee . . .

In making that policy decision (which in *Richardson* v *Pitt-Stanley* was
transparent on the face of the statute) the courts should not hide behind the
fiction that they are simply reflecting the will of Parliament.

9.1.3 Benefit of a class

Where the statute was passed for the benefit of an ascertainable class of
individuals the presumption is that an action will lie (*Solomons* v *Gertzenstein
Ltd* [1954] 2 QB 243, 261, 265). This has been criticised by Atkin LJ on the
basis that it 'would be strange if a less important duty which is owed to a
section of the public may be enforced by an action, while a more important
duty which is owed to the public at large cannot be so enforced' (*Phillips* v
Britannia Hygienic Laundry Co. Ltd [1923] 2 KB 832, 841; see also Buckley
(1984) 100 LQR 204, 21 1). Nevertheless, it was accepted as a specific
exception by Lord Diplock in *Lonrho Ltd* v *Shell Petroleum Co. Ltd* [1981] 2
All ER 456 (see para. 9.1). The problem is to know what constitutes an
'ascertainable class' and when the legislation was passed for the benefit of
such a group rather than the public at large.

Employees suing for breach of industrial safety legislation constitute such
a class as do visitors to premises which in breach of fire regulations do not
have an adequate fire escape (*Solomons* v *Gertzenstein Ltd*). The public using
the highway is not a class, 'it is the public itself and not a class of the public'
(per Bankes LJ in *Phillips* v *Britannia Hygienic Laundry Co. Ltd*), but
pedestrians using a pedestrian crossing apparently do constitute a class
(*London Passenger Transport Board* v *Upson* [1949] AC 155—civil action for
breach of Pedestrian Crossing Places (Traffic) Regulations, SR & O 1941/
397). In *Cutler* v *Wandsworth Stadium Ltd* [1949] AC 398 the Betting and
Lotteries Act 1934 required the occupiers of dog tracks to admit bookmakers
to the track. The plaintiff bookmaker was refused admission. The House of
Lords held that the Act was intended for the benefit of the public who visited
the track, not the bookmakers. (Cf. *McCall* v *Abelesz* [1976] QB 585 (para.
9.1.2)—for whose benefit was the offence of unlawful harassment of a
residential occupier created? See also *RCA Corporation* v *Pollard* [1983] Ch
135 and *Rickless* v *United Artists Corporation* [1987] 1 All ER 679—only
performers, not record companies, can sue for unauthorised recordings of live

performances contrary to the Dramatic and Musical Performers' Protection Act 1958.)

On the whole this presumption is not particularly helpful, since it can be invoked or excluded by an expedient choice of language when the court determines what constitutes a class of the public. (See, e.g., the Court of Appeal's approach in *Richardson* v *Pitt-Stanley* [1995] ICR 303 to the determination of the class protected by the Employers' Liability (Compulsory Insurance) Act 1969, discussed at para. 9.1.2.) Moreover, the fact that a statute was unquestionably passed for the protection of a specific class of individuals is not conclusive. In *X (minors)* v *Bedfordshire County Council* [1995] 3 WLR 152 the House of Lords held that a social services authority was not liable for breach of statutory duty in respect of the manner in which it conducted an investigation or made a decision whether or not to remove a child into care under the child protection legislation (the Children and Young Persons Act 1969, the Child Care Act 1980, and the Children Act 1989). This was despite the fact that the legislation was for the protection of a limited class, namely children at risk, and that until 1991 the legislation contained only limited machinery for enforcing those statutory duties. The legislation established an administrative system designed to promote the social welfare of the community, and involved difficult decisions about how to strike a balance between protecting children from immediate feared harm and disrupting the relationship between the child and its parents. Decisions would often have to be taken on the basis of inadequate and disputed facts. In such a context it required exceptionally clear statutory language to show a Parliamentary intention that social services authorities should be liable in damages if on subsequent investigation it was shown that they had reached an erroneous conclusion and therefore failed to discharge their statutory duties (per Lord Browne-Wilkinson at pp. 180–1). All the statutory provisions were dependent upon the subjective judgment of the local authority. Accordingly, it was not possible to treat such duties as being more than public law duties (see also *O'Rourke* v *Camden LBC* [1997] 3 WLR 86, para. 9.1.1).

9.1.4 Public rights and particular damage

Lord Diplock's second exception to the general rule in *Lonrho Ltd* v *Shell Petroleum Co. Ltd* [1981] 2 All ER 456 was where the statute creates a public right and an individual member of the public suffers 'particular damage'. The analogy here is with public rights existing at common law, breach of which will constitute a public nuisance (para. 7.2.3), and the particular damage that will make a public nuisance actionable in tort (para. 7.2.4). Lord Diplock described a public right as 'a right to be enjoyed by all those of Her Majesty's subjects who wish to avail themselves of it', but this is so indeterminate as to leave the question almost entirely open. For example, if the Construction and Use Regulations could be categorised as promoting a public 'right' to safety on the roads, would a breach which caused damage to the plaintiff be actionable under this heading thereby reversing the effect of *Phillips* v *Britannia Hygienic Laundry Co. Ltd* [1923] 2 KB 832? A mere prohibition on members of the public generally from doing what it would otherwise be lawful for them to do is not enough to create a public right. So in *Lonrho Ltd v Shell Petroleum Co. Ltd* itself, breach of sanctions orders made under the Southern Rhodesia Act 1965, which prohibited the supply of oil to Southern Rhodesia, did not give the plaintiffs a civil action, because the sanctions orders were instruments of State policy in external affairs. This distinction between statutes creating public rights (which are actionable on proof of particular damage) and 'mere prohibitions' on the public from doing what would otherwise be lawful (which are not) is somewhat opaque. Why does not any legislation creating a criminal offence create 'public rights', which would be enforceable by an individual if the Attorney-General should refuse to act? (See *Gouriet v Union of Post Office Workers* [1978] AC 435.) Lord Diplock's distinction simply asserts that some criminal legislation will be actionable on proof of particular damage, and some will not, but it is unclear what principle justifies the difference or even how the two categories are to be identified.

9.1.5 Public utilities
There is no specific presumption that applies to public utilities, but it is clear that the courts are reluctant to infer a civil action where it could lead to extensive liability (see *Clegg Parkinson & Co. v Earby Gas Co.* [1896] 1 QB 592, 594). In *Atkinson v Newcastle Waterworks Co.* (1877) 2 ExD 441 (see para. 9.1.1) the Court of Appeal considered it 'somewhat startling' that a company supplying water should be subject to individual actions by any householder because they had failed to maintain the water pressure. That would make them 'practically insurers, so far as water can produce safety from damage by fire'. It will be recalled that the statutory penalty of £10 was held to be the appropriate remedy, not a civil action. The reason for this, however, lay not in the esoteric process of statutory interpretation, but the court's concern to avoid an unduly heavy burden of liability. Householders would normally be insured against fire damage, but would rarely be insured against personal injuries, such as contracting typhoid, which might explain the different conclusion reached in *Read v Croydon Corporation* [1938] 4 All ER 631 (see para. 9.1.1) as to whether an action would lie for breach of the same Act.

9.2 STATUTORY NEGLIGENCE

In *Lochgelly Iron & Coal Co. Ltd v M'Mullan* [1934] AC 1 the House of Lords came close to equating an action for breach of statutory duty with an action in negligence. 'All that is necessary to show', said Lord Atkin (at p. 9), 'is a duty to take care to avoid injuring; and if the particular care to be taken is prescribed by statute, and the duty to the injured person to take the care is likewise imposed by statute, and the breach is proved, all the essentials of negligence are present'. Negligence did not depend on the court agreeing with the legislature that the precaution ought to have been taken, because the 'very object of the legislation is to put that particular precaution beyond controversy'. This is similar to the approach adopted in some American jurisdictions that breach of a statutory duty constitutes negligence *per se*. This is a rule that is used to determine which statutes will be actionable, since it is said to apply only to legislation which is designed to prevent a particular mischief in respect of which the defendant is already under a duty at common law (Williams (1960) 23 MLR 233, 252). Failure to meet the prescribed statutory standard is then treated as unreasonable conduct amounting to negligence, because a reasonable man would not ignore precautions required by statute, and the defendant cannot claim that the harm was unforeseeable because the legislature has already anticipated it. The statutory standard 'crystallises' the question of what constitutes carelessness. Where legislation does not deal with circumstances in which there is an existing common law duty, then, unless expressly stated, breach of the statute would not give rise to an action, because damages may greatly exceed the penalty considered appropriate by the legislature.

The advantage of the negligence *per se* rule, it is said, is that it avoids the search for a fictional parliamentary intention. But in reality it creates a presumptive parliamentary intent that when a statute fits the rule (i.e., covers the same ground as an existing common law rule) breach will give rise to civil liability. An alternative version of 'statutory negligence' is that breach of the statute is not conclusive as to liability, but provides prima facie evidence of negligence. On this version it is open to the defendant to argue that in spite of his contravention of the statute, nonetheless he acted reasonably in the circumstances and therefore should not be liable in negligence. This approach was adopted by the Supreme Court of Canada in *The Queen in Right of Canada* v *Saskatchewan Wheat Pool* (1983) 143 DLR (3d) 9, 23 principally, it seems, in order to avoid the imposition of strict liability (although 'absolute liability' in the case of industrial legislation was regarded as an exception). For all that the doctrine is called statutory 'negligence', it is clear that some statutory provisions will not be satisfied by the exercise of reasonable care. 'But there seems little in the way of defensible policy', said Dickson J, 'for holding a defendant who breached a statutory duty unwittingly to be negligent and obligated to pay even though not at fault. . . . Minimum fault may subject the defendant to heavy liability. Inconsequential violations should not subject the violator to any civil liability at all but should be left to the criminal courts for enforcement of a fine.'

There are two points of interest here. First, the notion of what constitutes 'fault'. A duty may be strict, in the sense that proof that the defendant exercised reasonable care to comply will not be a defence. But where a statute sets out in detail what the defendant must do it is difficult to argue that he is not in some way *culpable* for failing to comply. The more general the duty the more likely it is that the court will infer that the exercise of reasonable care will be sufficient to satisfy the provision (see Buckley (1984) 100 LQR 204, 223–4 discussing *Read* v *Croydon Corporation* [1938] 4 All ER 631). Conversely, industrial safety legislation, which is often regarded as imposing strict liability, is usually both detailed and specific as to what an employer must do. (See also *Fleming*, p. 128, who argues that this is a relevant factor in deciding whether the statute should be actionable. Where the statute prescribes specific safety standards, as opposed to general exhortations, it would be easier to infer an action.) Secondly, a blanket objection to strict liability seems misplaced, at least without some consideration of the respective policy objectives of fault and strict liability (see Matthews (1984) 4 OJLS 429, 431). On both versions of the statutory negligence doctrine the relevance of a statutory duty is confined to circumstances in which there is an existing common law duty of care. But as Matthews, op. cit., p. 432, points out, since the existence of a duty of care depends on a policy decision by the courts, there is no good reason why the policy objectives of a legislative provision should not be taken into account in deciding whether a breach should be actionable (see also Buckley, op. cit., pp. 208–9 for criticism of this aspect of statutory negligence).

The doctrine of statutory negligence has not taken root in English law (despite the pleas of Glanville Williams (1960) 23 MLR 233). There are 'fundamental differences' between breach of statutory duty and negligence.

> The statutory right has its origin in the statute, but the particular remedy of an action for damages is given by the common law in order to make effective, for the benefit of the injured plaintiff, his right to the performance by the defendant of the defendant's statutory duty. . . . It is not a claim in negligence in the strict or ordinary sense. (*London Passenger Transport Board* v *Upson* [1949] AC 155, 168 per Lord Wright.)

Thus, breach of statutory duty has not been limited to circumstances in which a common law duty of care already existed (*Monk* v *Warbey* [1935] 1 KB 75, para. 9.1.2; *Warder* v *Cooper* [1970] Ch 495, para. 9.1.2; *Ministry of Housing & Local Government* v *Sharp* [1970] 2 QB 223). The two actions may overlap, but failure by the plaintiff to establish breach of a relevant statute does not necessarily prevent a successful claim in negligence (*Bux* v *Slough Metals Ltd* [1974] 1 All ER 262). Indeed, statutory duties may be instrumental in suggesting to the courts what additional precautions a reasonable man would take. So if regulations require an employer to supply goggles to his workmen, reasonable care may require him to encourage their use (*Bux* v *Slough Metals Ltd*). Often the statutory obligation will extend beyond the requirements of reasonable care, and in many cases there would be little advantage to the plaintiff if it did not.

The standard of liability varies, not surprisingly, with the wording of the particular statutory provision in question. It ranges from standards that can truly be described as strict, where the defendant will be responsible irrespective of the efforts he made to avoid the occurrence (see, e.g., *John Summers & Sons Ltd* v *Frost* [1955] AC 740 where precautions would have rendered a machine unusable, defendant nonetheless liable), to duties requiring the exercise of reasonable care (see *Stanton*, chapter 5). Even where the wording appears to be strict, some element of fault may be imported into the courts' interpretation (see, e.g., *Brown* v *National Coal Board* [1962] AC 574—duty to take such steps as may be necessary for keeping the road secure, satisfied by obtaining relevant information and acting with due care and skill; see further para. 5.2). On the whole, strict duties are confined to industrial safety legislation, and even then there are no coherent principles underlying the distribution of strict liability and fault (Williams, op. cit., pp. 233–43; *Atiyah*, pp. 81–84, who points out that 'the strictness is of a fairly mild nature'). Moreover, the existence of an element of strict liability for industrial accidents may have influenced the courts in denying actions for breach of statutory duty in other areas (as in *Phillips* v *Britannia Hygienic Laundry Co. Ltd* [1923] 2 KB 832, para. 9.1.2; Williams, op. cit., p. 248). The 'construction of the statute' approach to determining whether breach of a particular piece of legislation is actionable, combined with the random distribution of strict duties, marks the action for breach of statutory duty as a prime example of the *ad hoc* nature of common law liability.

9.3 AMBIT OF THE STATUTE

It may seem obvious, but even when in theory breach of the statute is actionable, the circumstances in which the plaintiff sustains harm must fall within the terms of the defendant's statutory duty. Thus the Factories Act 1961 applies to factories and not, for example, to offices, shops or mines which are governed by different legislation. A duty that applies to platforms more than six feet and six inches from the ground does not apply to a platform that is only six feet from the ground (*Chipchase* v *British Titan Products Co. Ltd* [1956] 1 QB 545). Similarly, the plaintiff must fall within the class of persons that the statute is meant to protect. So regulations for the protection of persons employed in specific trades will not protect a visitor to the premises (*Hartley* v *Mayoh & Co.* [1954] 1 QB 383—fireman; *Knapp* v *Railway Executive* [1949] 2 All ER 508—duty to keep level crossing gates in the proper position to protect the public using the road, not the train driver).

In addition, the damage suffered by the plaintiff must be of the kind that the statute was intended to prevent. In *Gorris* v *Scott* (1874) LR 9 Ex 125 the plaintiff's sheep were washed overboard from the defendant's ship because there were no pens on the ship. The defendant was in breach of a statutory duty to keep animals being imported by ship in pens, but the object of the legislation was to prevent the animals developing and spreading contagious disease. It was held that the breach was not actionable because the statutory purpose had 'no relation whatever to the danger of loss by the perils of the sea'. Thus, even though but for the breach of duty the plaintiff would not have sustained the loss, the damage must fall within the ambit of the statute (see also *Close* v *Steel Co. of Wales Ltd* [1962] AC 367 and *Nicholls* v *F. Austin (Leyton) Ltd* [1946] AC 493, para. 5.2—fence on a dangerous machine intended to keep worker out not to keep the machine in). The rule in *Gorris* v *Scott* is analogous to that of remoteness of damage in negligence, which stipulates that the damage must be of the *type* which was reasonably foreseeable (para. 4.3.3). Provided the damage is of the type that the statute was meant to prevent, it is irrelevant that the precise manner in which it occurred was not envisaged (*Donaghey* v *Boulton & Paul Ltd* [1968] AC 1, 26; and see *Hughes* v *Lord Advocate* [1963] AC 837, para. 4.3.2). It is difficult to reconcile this statement, however, with the fine distinctions drawn in cases where the injury is the result of a failure to fence dangerous machinery as required by the Factories Act 1961, s. 14 (see para. 5.2).

9.4 CAUSATION

As in an action for negligence, the plaintiff must establish that the defendant's breach of statutory duty caused the damage (see *McWilliams* v *Sir William Arrol & Co. Ltd* [1962] 1 WLR 295, para. 4.1.1). The breach need not be the sole cause provided that it materially contributed to the damage (*Bonnington Castings Ltd* v *Wardlaw* [1956] AC 613, para. 4.1.2). Where it is the plaintiff's own wrongful act which puts the defendant in breach of statutory duty, the defendant will not be liable, provided the plaintiff is the sole cause of his own loss (*Ginty* v *Belmont Building Supplies Ltd* [1959] 1 All ER 414 and *Boyle* v *Kodak Ltd* [1969] 2 All ER 439, see para. 5.3.1, applied in *McCreesh* v *Courtaulds plc* [1997] PIQR P421).

9.5 DEFENCES

Volenti non fit injuria is not a defence to an action for breach of statutory duty brought by an employee against his employer, subject to the limited exception admitted in *Imperial Chemical Industries Ltd* v *Shatwell* [1965] AC 656 (see para. 5.3.1). There is some disagreement as to whether *volenti* will apply in other cases of breach of statutory duty (*Winfield and Jolowicz*, p. 203—yes; *Salmond and Heuston*, p. 255—no). It has been said that any agreement to contract out of a statutory duty is void (*Baddeley* v *Earl Granville* (1887) 19 QBD 423, 426 per Wills J), and so it could be argued that where the *volenti* defence rests upon agreement between the parties it should not apply. However, in some cases *volenti* has been held to apply where the plaintiff, knowing of the defendant's breach of duty, has nonetheless proceeded to encounter the risk (see para. 14.1.2). Even if this form of *volenti* was held inapplicable to an action for breach of statutory duty, the plaintiff might have some difficulty in establishing that the breach *caused* his loss, in circumstances where he would normally be regarded as having assumed the risk (e.g., where he engages in a deliberate act of folly: *Rushton* v *Turner Bros. Asbestos Co. Ltd* [1960] 1 WLR 96).

Contributory negligence is a defence, but special considerations operate in the case of an action by an employee against his employers (*Caswell* v *Powell Duffryn Associated Collieries Ltd* [1940] AC 152, 166; see paras 5.3.2 and 14.5.3.3).

As a general rule a person subject to a statutory duty cannot delegate responsibility for its performance to someone else. At one time it was accepted that delegation could be a defence where the performance of the duty had been delegated to the plaintiff, but this view is no longer correct. 'The important and fundamental question . . . is not whether there was a delegation, but simply the usual question: whose fault was it?' (*Ginty* v *Belmont Building Supplies Ltd* [1959] 1 All ER 414, 423–4 per Pearson J; but 'fault' is not necessarily equivalent to 'blameworthiness', it is a question of causation: *Ross* v *Associated Portland Cement Manufacturers Ltd* [1964] 1 WLR 768, 777). So where a statute imposes the same duty on both plaintiff and defendant, and it is the plaintiff's act that puts the defendant in breach, the defendant is not liable on the basis that he did not cause the loss (*Ginty* v *Belmont Building Supplies Ltd; Boyle* v *Kodak Ltd* [1969] 2 All ER 439; see para. 5.3.1).

TEN
Defective products

Liability for damage caused by defective products is an amalgam of liability in contract, the tort of negligence and, more recently, statutory provisions. In the nineteenth century contract tended to predominate in judicial patterns of thought. This produced what came to be known as the 'privity of contract fallacy', whereby it was said that a person injured by a dangerous chattel could not sue a negligent manufacturer in tort because he was seeking to take the benefit of a contract to which he was not a party (see *Winterbottom* v *Wright* (1842) 10 M & W 109). The remedy, if any, lay in contract not tort. Exceptionally, an action for negligence could be maintained if the chattel fell into a limited category of 'dangerous chattels' or if the defect was known to the supplier and he failed to warn of the danger. But the classification of chattels dangerous *per se* was arbitrary and illogical. In *Hodge & Sons* v *Anglo-American Oil Co.* (1922) 12 Ll LR 183, 187 Scrutton LJ said that he could 'not understand the difference between a thing dangerous in itself, as poison, and a thing not dangerous as a class, but by negligent construction dangerous as a particular thing. The latter, if anything, seems the more dangerous of the two; it is a wolf in sheep's clothing instead of an obvious wolf.'

Donoghue v *Stevenson* [1932] AC 562 removed the privity of contract fallacy by demonstrating that the tortious duty of care in negligence was independent of a contractual relationship; so the fact that A had produced a dangerously defective product and sold it to B should not prevent an injured third party, C, from suing A in tort. *Donoghue* v *Stevenson* provided the foundations for a general duty of care in negligence (see para. 2.1.1), but it was also the basis for the development of a more specific duty in relation to defective products. The nature of this specific common law duty is considered in the first part of this chapter (para. 10.1).

Donoghue v *Stevenson* established that there could be liability in negligence for defective products, but, in spite of some cases which suggested that in certain circumstances a high standard of care would be required, liability remained fault-based. The English courts did not follow the American example where strict liability in tort was established (see Restatement, *Torts*

(2d), s. 402A). In the 1970s a number of law reform bodies recommended that strict liability for defective products should be introduced, and now, following an EC initiative, the United Kingdom has a form of strict liability under the Consumer Protection Act 1987 (para. 10.2). In practice, however, this liability is not particularly 'strict'.

10.1 COMMON LAW

Where a contractual remedy is available it will often be more advantageous to the plaintiff than a claim in tort. A purchaser of goods will have the benefit of implied terms as to the quality and fitness for purpose of the goods (Sale of Goods Act 1979, s. 14; Supply of Goods and Services Act 1982, s. 4 as amended by the Sale and Supply of Goods Act 1994), which in the case of 'consumer' transactions cannot be excluded (Unfair Contract Terms Act 1977, s. 6). Liability is strict, in the sense that it does not have to be shown that the defect was the vendor's fault. Moreover, the contractual action is available for products which are defective in quality, though not dangerous, if the defect is such as to constitute a breach of warranty. This distinction between qualitative (i.e., non-dangerous) and dangerous defects is said to be one of the touchstones of the distinction between liability in contract and in tort, although in recent years the dividing line has become somewhat blurred.

A retailer sued in contract by the purchaser of defective goods will normally have a contractual claim for indemnity against his own vendor (wholesaler or distributor), and so on, up the contractual chain to the manufacturer who produced the defective goods (subject to any valid exemption clauses). In this way, in theory at least, liability will rest with the person responsible for the defect. In practice this contractual chain may break down if, for example, one link is missing, having gone into liquidation, or is simply untraceable through lack of records (as occurred in *Lambert* v *Lewis* [1981] 1 All ER 1185). The doctrine of privity of contract then prevents any further claims along the contractual chain (but see the Civil Liability (Contribution) Act 1978, para. 14.6, which may apply in this situation). From the plaintiff purchaser's point of view this will be irrelevant, unless of course it is the retailer who is no longer available to be sued, in which case the purchaser's contractual claim will be useless (subject to the Third Parties (Rights against Insurers) Act 1930, which is of only limited application, see para. 1.3). This will leave the purchaser in the same position as all other plaintiffs injured by a defective product, having to rely on an action in tort for negligence, or under the Consumer Protection Act 1987. Privity denied any claim in contract to members of the purchaser's family, donees or bystanders, and it is these categories of plaintiff who benefited from the consequences of *Donoghue* v *Stevenson*. Further discussion of contractual remedies is beyond the scope of this book, and it is the tort of negligence that will now be considered.

10.1.1 Manufacturers' duty
In *Donoghue* v *Stevenson* [1932] AC 562 the plaintiff drank a bottle of ginger beer, manufactured by the defendant, which had been purchased for her by

a friend. She alleged that the bottle contained the remnants of a decomposed snail and that she became ill as a consequence. The bottle was opaque and the snail could not be seen until most of the ginger beer had been consumed. The plaintiff could not sue the retailer, with whom she had no contract, and so sued the manufacturer, alleging negligence. The House of Lords held that on these allegations there could be a cause of action; the manufacturers owed a duty of care to the ultimate consumer.

In the course of his speech Lord Atkin (at p. 599) expressed the duty in these terms:

A manufacturer of products which he sells in such a form as to show that he intends them to reach the ultimate consumer in the form in which they left him, with no reasonable possibility of intermediate examination, and with the knowledge that the absence of reasonable care in the preparation or putting up of the products will result in injury to the consumer's life or property, owes a duty to the consumer to take that reasonable care.

Lord Thankerton said that the defendant brought himself into a direct relationship with the consumer by placing his ginger beer upon the market in a form which precluded interference with or examination of the product by any intermediate handler, with the result that the consumer was entitled to rely on the exercise of reasonable care by the manufacturer to secure that the product should not be harmful. Lord Macmillan put the duty in terms of the manufacturer of articles of food and drink intended for consumption by members of the public: 'He owes them a duty not to convert by his own carelessness an article which he issues to them as wholesome and innocent into an article which is dangerous to life and health.'

This duty with respect to dangerous products was clearly of much wider application than the previous category of things dangerous *per se*. Lord Macmillan suggested that it was inaccurate to regard 'dangerous things' as an exception to the principle that no one but a party to a contract can sue on that contract. Rather it was a special instance of negligence where the law extracts a degree of diligence so stringent as to amount practically to a guarantee of safety.

10.1.2 Extending the duty
The manufacturer's duty has been given a broad interpretation. 'Products' are not limited to food and drink, but include almost any item capable of causing damage, such as underpants (*Grant* v *Australian Knitting Mills Ltd* [1936] AC 85), motor cars (*Herschtal* v *Stewart & Arden Ltd* [1940] 1 KB 155), hair dye (*Watson* v *Buckley, Osborne Garrett & Co. Ltd* [1940] 1 All ER 174), lifts (*Haseldine* v *C. A. Daw & Son Ltd* [1941] 2 KB 343), and chemicals (*Vacwell Engineering Co. Ltd* v *BDH Chemicals Ltd* [1971] 1 QB 88). Similarly, 'ultimate consumer' seems to mean anyone foreseeably harmed by the defective product. This will include the user of the product, such as a donee, a member of the purchaser's family, or an employee of the purchaser

(*Davie* v *New Merton Board Mills Ltd* [1959] AC 604; see also Employers' Liability (Defective Equipment) Act 1969, para. 5.1.3); someone who handles the product, such as a storeman or a shopkeeper (*Barnett* v *H. and J. Packer & Co. Ltd* [1940] 3 All ER 575); and a bystander (*Stennett* v *Hancock* [1939] 2 All ER 578—pedestrian injured by part of a wheel flying off a passing lorry).

The range of potential defendants has also been extended to include not only manufacturers, but also repairers (*Stennett* v *Hancock; Haseldine* v *C.A. Daw & Son Ltd*) and assemblers (*Howard* v *Furness Houlder Argentine Lines Ltd* [1936] 2 All ER 781). A supplier of goods, such as a retailer or wholesaler, may be liable if the circumstances are such that he ought reasonably to have inspected the goods or tested them. For example, in *Andrews* v *Hopkinson* [1957] 1 QB 229 the defendant was a second-hand car dealer who sold an 18-year-old car to the plaintiff. The steering was defective and this caused an accident. The defendant was held liable because the defective steering could easily have been discovered by a competent mechanic, and, given the danger involved in allowing a car with a defective steering mechanism to be used on the road it was reasonable to expect the defendant to check it, or at least warn the plaintiff that it had not been checked (cf. *Hurley* v *Dyke* [1979] RTR 265, para. 10.1.5). Similarly, distributors who obtain goods from suppliers of doubtful reputation ought to test them (*Watson* v *Buckley, Osborne Garrett & Co.*), and *a fortiori* when the manufacturers' instructions suggest that the product should be tested (*Kubach* v *Hollands* [1937] 3 All ER 907). It is arguable that the same principles should apply in cases of gratuitous supply, though the precautions required to satisfy the standard of reasonable care may be quite low in the case of, say, a gift between friends. In any event, it should be remembered that the duty does not arise in all cases of supply, only where the circumstances indicate that an inspection or test is reasonably required. Clearly, if the dangerous defect was in fact known to the supplier he ought, at least, to give a warning to the recipient.

10.1.3 Intermediate inspection

Lord Atkins statement of the manufacturer's duty in *Donoghue* v *Stevenson* [1932] AC 562 applies to products which are intended to 'reach the ultimate consumer in the form in which they left him, with no reasonable possibility of intermediate examination'. The article there was a sealed, opaque bottle of ginger beer, but it was soon established that the goods need not reach the ultimate consumer in a sealed package for the duty to apply. In *Grant* v *Australian Knitting Mills Ltd* [1936] AC 85 the plaintiff contracted dermatitis due to excess sulphite present in a pair of underpants. He had not washed the underpants before wearing them. Lord Wright, delivering the judgment of the Privy Council, said that the essential factor was that the consumer must use the article exactly as it left the maker, in all material features, and use it as it was intended to be used. The fact that it was not in a sealed package was irrelevant if it reached the consumer subject to the same defect as it had when it left the manufacturer. It was not contemplated that the underpants should be washed before they were worn, so the presence of the chemicals was just as much a latent defect as were the remains of the snail in an opaque bottle.

The mere opportunity for inspection of the product after it has left the hands of the manufacturer will not exculpate the defendant (*Herschtal* v *Stewart & Arden Ltd* [1940] 1 KB 155; *Griffiths* v *Arch Engineering Co. Ltd* [1968] 3 All ER 217). Lord Atkins term 'reasonable possibility' of intermediate inspection has been interpreted to mean 'reasonable probability' of intermediate inspection (*Haseldine* v *C.A. Daw & Son Ltd* [1941] 2 KB 343, 376). So the manufacturer is liable if he has no reason to contemplate that an intermediate examination will occur, whether by a third party or the consumer. But if he has given a warning, for example, to test a product before use, this may be sufficient to discharge his duty. In *Holmes* v *Ashford* [1950] 2 All ER 76 the manufacturers of a hair dye were held not liable when a hairdresser disregarded an instruction to test the product before using it on a customer, and in *Kubach* v *Hollands* [1937] 3 All ER 907 the manufacturer of a chemical was held not liable to a schoolgirl injured in an explosion, having warned the retailer to examine and test the chemical before use. The retailer did not test the chemical or warn the teacher who purchased it that it should be tested. In both of these cases the warning did not reach the ultimate consumer but there was nonetheless a reasonable contemplation of intermediate examination. In *Aswan Engineering Establishment Co.* v *Lupdine Ltd* [1987] 1 All ER 135, 153–4, Lloyd LJ said that there is no independent requirement for the plaintiff to show that there was 'no reasonable possibility of intermediate examination'. Rather, this is merely a factor, usually an important factor, which the court must consider when determining whether the damage was reasonably foreseeable.

10.1.4 Causation and contributory negligence
The question of intermediate examination is closely related to the concepts of causation and contributory negligence. It has been held that there is no liability if the plaintiff knew of the danger and ignored it (*Farr* v *Butters Bros & Co.* [1932] 2 KB 606), nor if a third party knew of the danger, and, being under a duty to remove the product from circulation, failed to do so (*Taylor* v *Rover Co. Ltd* [1966] 1 WLR 1491). These cases can be explained in terms of causation rather than intermediate examination. The defendant's negligence was not the cause of the damage because the intervening conduct of the plaintiff or the third party broke the chain of causation (see *Grant* v *Australian Knitting Mills Ltd* [1936] AC 85, 105).

However, there is some force in the argument that a defendant who has created a dangerous situation should not be excused merely because someone else, whether an intermediary or the plaintiff, has failed to remove the danger. If both have been at fault then both should be held responsible. In the case of a negligent failure to inspect or test the product by an intermediary this could be achieved by apportioning liability between the manufacturer and the intermediary under the Civil Liability (Contribution) Act 1978 (para. 14.6), though an explicit and reasonable instruction by a manufacturer that an intermediary should inspect the product will usually discharge the manufacturer's duty of care (as in *Holmes* v *Ashford* [1950] 2 All ER 76 and *Kubach* v *Hollands* [1937] 3 All ER 907). If it is the plaintiff who has failed to use a reasonable opportunity to examine the goods, then it is a case of contributory negligence, for which damages can be apportioned (para. 14.5). In some instances the plaintiff's negligence may be such that he is considered 100% responsible, in which case the conclusion is that the defendant's breach of duty did not cause the damage (see, e.g., *Jayes* v *IMI (Kynoch) Ltd* [1985] ICR 155, para. 14.5.3.3). This might now be the explanation for cases such as *Farr* v *Butters Bros & Co.* where the plaintiff knew of the danger but disregarded it. However, knowledge of the danger will be irrelevant if there were no practical steps that the plaintiff could take to avoid it (see *Denny* v *Supplies and Transport Co. Ltd* [1950] 2 KB 374). In *Rimmer* v *Liverpool City Council* [1984] 1 All ER 930, 938 the Court of Appeal said that an opportunity for inspection by the plaintiff will not exonerate the defendant unless the plaintiff 'was free to remove or avoid the danger in the sense that it was reasonable to expect him to do so, and unreasonable for him to run the risk of being injured by the danger'. In that case it was held that it was not reasonable for the tenant of a council flat, designed and built by the defendants, to have removed a dangerous glass panel and he was not free to avoid the danger by leaving the flat. The defendants were held liable despite the plaintiff's knowledge of the danger (indeed, he had complained to the defendants about the danger). Similarly, in *Targett* v *Torfaen Borough Council* [1992] 3 All ER 27 the defendants were held responsible for injuries sustained by a tenant of a council house built by them when he fell down an external flight of steps which had no handrail and was unlit. Sir Donald Nicholls V-C said (at p. 37) that 'knowledge of the existence of a danger does not always enable a person to avoid the danger. In simple cases it does. In other cases, especially where buildings are concerned, it would be absurdly unrealistic to suggest that a person can always take steps to avoid a danger once he knows of its existence, and that if he does not do so he is the author of his own misfortune'.

If the consumer misuses the product in an unforeseeable fashion the defendant will not be liable. This is not because of contributory negligence or causation, but because the manufacturer is responsible only for dangers arising from a product's contemplated use. If misused, the product cannot be said to be 'defective', so there is no breach of duty (see *Aswan Engineering Establishment Co.* v *Lupdine Ltd* [1987] 1 All ER 135, 154 where Lloyd LJ gave the example of a car tyre fitted to a bus).

Apart from the question of intermediate examination, the plaintiff still has to prove that the defective product caused the injury of which he complains, applying the usual principles of causation (see para. 4.1.2). This will tend to be more difficult with certain types of product, such as defective drugs (see Newdick (1985) 101 LQR 405, 420), and certain types of harm, such as disease (Stapleton (1985) 5 OJLS 248, 250), but the issue may also be relevant in other instances. In *Evans* v *Triplex Safety Glass Co. Ltd* [1936] 1 All ER 283, for example, the plaintiffs sued the manufacturers of a car windscreen which disintegrated during a journey, injuring the occupants. The defendants were held not liable because the seller had had an opportunity of intermediate examination (the accident occurred about a year after the purchase), and there were a number of causes other than a defect in manufacture which could have caused the disintegration (such as the process of fitting the windscreen into the car). The plaintiffs simply failed to prove, on a balance of probabilities, that a defect in the windscreen had caused the injuries.

There may be difficulty in isolating drug-induced harm from the background incidence of such injuries. Merely proving an increased risk of injury does not in itself establish causation. The question is whether one can infer a causal link, taking a 'common sense' approach to attributing cause. In both *Loveday* v *Renton* [1990] 1 Med LR 117 and *Rothwell* v *Raes* (1988) 54 DLR (4th) 193; aff'd (1990) 76 DLR (4th) 280 (Ont CA) the plaintiffs were unable to prove, on the balance of probabilities, that pertussis vaccine can cause brain damage in children, although it was possible that there was a causal link. In *Best* v *Wellcome Foundation Ltd* [1994] 5 Med LR 81, however, the Supreme Court of Ireland was prepared to draw an inference that if there was a temporal connection between the child's first convulsion and the administration of the pertussis vaccine manufactured by the defendants then causation of the plaintiff's brain damage was established. The only alternative explanation offered for the plaintiff's condition was that he had suffered from 'infantile spasms, cause unknown', which, as O'Flaherty J pointed out, was a description rather than a diagnosis of the plaintiff's condition. The difference between this case, on the one hand, and *Loveday* v *Renton* and *Rothwell* v *Raes* on the other, would appear to be that in *Best* the defendants had been found negligent in distributing a *faulty* batch of the vaccine (which the defendants knew to have a particularly high potency and toxicity), i.e., a defect in manufacture, whereas in *Loveday* and *Rothwell* the plaintiffs were alleging that it was negligent to distribute a *normal* batch of the vaccine because it could foreseeably cause brain damage, i.e., a defect in design. While, logically, there should be no difference in the courts' approach to factual causation according to the nature of the defendant's breach of duty (the question is simply: did the negligence cause this plaintiff's damage?), in practice it may be easier to persuade the court to draw an inference that there must have been a causal link, at least in cases of drug injuries, where there is a defect in manufacture.

10.1.5 Warning

Warnings by the defendant are sometimes treated as part and parcel of the question of intermediate examination (as, e.g., in *Holmes* v *Ashford* [1950] 2 All ER 76, para. 10.1.3), but this will not necessarily be the case. For example, a warning as to the correct wiring contained in the instructions for use of an electrical appliance is not giving the consumer an opportunity to 'examine' the appliance for a defect. The appliance is not 'defective'; rather it must be used (wired) in a particular way.

An omission to provide proper instructions for use may be negligent, but conversely an adequate 'warning' may discharge the manufacturer's duty of care. Similarly, a warning that in its existing condition a product is unsafe may be sufficient to discharge the duty. In *Haseldine* v *C.A. Daw & Son Ltd* [1941] 2 KB 343, 380, Goddard LJ gave the following example: 'Suppose a lift repairer told the owner that a part was worn out, so that, while he could patch it up, he could not leave it in a safe condition. If he were told to do the best he could, and an accident then happened, I cannot conceive that the repairer would be held liable. He has fulfilled his duty by warning the employer, and, if the latter, in spite of that, chooses to allow the lift to be used, the liability rests on him.' It is not necessary that a warning be addressed directly to the consumer where a product is intended to be used under the supervision of an expert. A warning given to the expert will normally suffice to discharge the manufacturer's duty, as, for example, a warning of potentially harmful side-effects associated with a drug available only on prescription addressed to a doctor (*Buchan* v *Ortho Pharmaceuticals (Canada) Ltd* (1986) 25 DLR (4th) 658, 669, Ontario CA; an exception may apply to some prescription drugs, such as oral contraceptives, where the manufacturer may be under a duty to warn the ultimate consumer as well as the doctor: ibid., at pp. 668–9; for criticism of the 'learned intermediary' rule see Ferguson (1992) 12 OJLS 59). Of course, giving a warning to a 'learned intermediary' will discharge the manufacturer's duty only if the warning is adequate, and in some cases, particularly those involving medical products which are designed for ingestion or implantation in the consumer's body, this may be the case only when the intermediary's knowledge approximates that of the manufacturer (*Hollis* v *Dow Corning Corp.* (1995) 129 DLR (4th) 609, SCC).

In *Hurley* v *Dyke* [1979] RTR 265 the House of Lords apparently accepted that a defendant who sold a second-hand car knowing that it was potentially dangerous without further examination, was not liable to a third party injured in a subsequent accident because the car had been sold at auction subject to the caveat that it was sold 'as seen and with all its faults'. This warning, it was suggested, might even have been sufficient to fulfil the defendant's duty if he had known of a specific defect but had failed to advise the purchaser of the specific danger (but query this, and cf. *Andrews* v *Hopkinson* [1957] 1 QB 229, para. 10.1.2; consider whether such a warning constitutes a discharge of the defendant's duty or an attempt to exclude liability for negligence which would be subject to the Unfair Contract Terms Act 1977, s. 2; see para. 14.2, and in the context of occupiers' liability, paras 6.1.3.4, 6.1.5). A warning must be adequate, which means that it should be communicated clearly and understandably to inform the user of the nature and extent of the danger, it should be in terms commensurate with the gravity of the hazard, and it should not be negated or neutralised by collateral efforts on the part of the manufacturer, for example, promotional literature advertising the product as 'completely safe' (*Buchan* v *Ortho Pharmaceuticals (Canada) Ltd* (1986) 25 DLR (4th) 658, 667).

The same legal principles apply whatever the product in question, though drug injuries create their own special problems, because all drugs have some inherent risk. They are designed to interfere with the body's chemistry, and some patients may have idiosyncratic reactions. Many drugs cannot be made completely safe for their intended or ordinary use even when they are properly manufactured and are not impure, but nonetheless the marketing of such drugs may be justified by their utility for the majority of patients (*Buchan v Ortho Pharmaceutical (Canada) Ltd* (1986) 25 DLR (4th) 658, 668). In *Buchan* the defendants were held to have been negligent for failing to give adequate warning of the side-effects of an oral contraceptive drug, partly because the defendants' associated companies in other countries had given a much more comprehensive warning. Moreover, where there have been developments in the state of the manufacturer's knowledge there will be an obligation to keep the medical community (or consumers) advised of those developments. Thus, in *Hollis* v *Dow Corning Corporation* (1993) 103 DLR (4th) 520 (BCCA); aff'd (1995) 129 DLR (4th) 609 (SCC), the manufac-turers of breast implants became aware of the fact that an implant could rupture for a variety of reasons, including normal use, and that the life expectancy of implants was unpredictable, before the plaintiff received her implant in October 1983, but did not update their warning to surgeons until 1985. The statistical risk of rupture was less than 0.1%, though the conse-quences for the patient were serious. The manufacturers were held liable for failing to pass on this new information to doctors. It was not an obligation to issue a new warning each time a rupture occurred, but it was not expecting too much to require the manufacturers to issue updated information to the medical community on a yearly basis, or sooner if the circumstances war-ranted it. In the British Columbia Court of Appeal Prowse JA commented (at p. 544): 'A manufacturer should not be too coy about revealing the risks associated with its product and then expect to avoid liability by placing the full burden of those risks on either the medical community or the patient'. The Supreme Court of Canada agreed that the duty placed on the manufac-turers is a high one in this context. La Forest J said (at p. 623) that:

> To allow manufacturers to claim the benefit of the [learned intermediary] rule where they have not fully warned the physician would undermine the policy rationale for the duty to warn, which is to ensure that the consumer is fully informed of all risks. Since the manufacturer is in the best position to know the risks attendant upon the use of its product and is also in the best position to ensure that the product is safe for normal use, the primary duty to give a clear, complete, and current warning must fall on its shoulders.

(For comment on *Hollis* see Black and Klimchuck (1996) 75 Can Bar Rev 355.)

There is no duty to warn of an obvious danger which is known to the ultimate consumer (*Deshane* v *Deere & Co.* (1993) 106 DLR (4th) 385 (Ont CA)), although where a method exists of manufacturing the same product without risk of harm then no amount of or degree of specificity of warning will exonerate the manufacturer of an inherently dangerous article (*Nicholson* v *John Deere Ltd* (1986) 34 DLR (4th) 542, 549). If a seller knows that a purchaser will probably disregard a warning and misuse the product (such as using an inappropriate tyre on a heavy lorry) the warning will not defeat a claim by an injured third party against the seller (*Good-Wear Treaders Ltd* v *D & B Holdings Ltd* (1979) 98 DLR (3d) 59).

10.1.6 Continuing duty

Negligence depends upon foreseeability of injury. If at the time that a product was put on the market a *design* defect was unknown, the manufacturer was not negligent. If a danger becomes apparent (or ought to have been discovered) it will be negligent to continue to produce the same unmodified product, or at least to do so without attaching a warning (*Wright* v *Dunlop Rubber Co. Ltd* (1972) 13 KIR 255, 272). What is the position in relation to products already in circulation when the defect is discovered—does the manufacturer have a continuing duty in respect of products now known to be defective? The answer seems to be 'Yes'. The manufacturer must take reasonable steps either to warn users of the danger or recall the defective products (*Walton* v *British Leyland UK Ltd* (1978) unreported, cited in Miller, *Product Liability and Safety Encyclopaedia*, Div. III, para. 43.1; *Rivtow Marine Ltd* v *Washington Iron Works* (1973) 40 DLR (3d) 530; *Buchan* v *Ortho Pharmaceuticals (Canada) Ltd* (1986) 25 DLR (4th) 658, 678; *Hobbs (Farms) Ltd* v *Baxenden Chemical Co. Ltd* [1992] 1 Lloyd's Rep 54, 65: '. . . a manufacturer's duty of care does not end when the goods are sold. A manufacturer who realises that omitting to warn past customers about something which might result in injury to them must take reasonable steps to attempt to warn them, however lacking in negligence he may have been at the time the goods were sold'). This requires manufacturers to keep abreast of scientific developments concerning the safety of their products and to have an effective system for recalling unsafe products. Negligence in implementing the recall procedure may be actionable (see e.g. *Nicholson* v *John Deere Ltd* (1986) 34 DLR (4th) 542; *McCain Foods Ltd* v *Grand Falls Industries Ltd* (1991) 80 DLR (4th) 252). Moreover, where a product has not been recalled and there is strong evidence to suggest that problems in the manufacture of the product have been concealed to avoid the commercial repercussions that a recall will entail, the court will more readily infer that a defect in the product was due to negligence in the manufacturing process (*Carroll* v *Fearon, The Times*, 26 January 1998, CA).

10.1.7 Proof

The burden of proving negligence rests with the plaintiff. In *Donoghue* v *Stevenson* [1932] AC 562 Lord Macmillan said that there was no presumption of negligence nor any justification for applying the maxim *res ipsa loquitur* in such a case. But where a defect has arisen in the course of construction it will be virtually impossible for a plaintiff to show by affirmative evidence what went wrong. In *Grant* v *Australian Knitting Mills Ltd* [1936] AC 85 this difficulty was recognised. Lord Wright said (at p. 101):

[The manufacturing] process was intended to be foolproof. If excess sulphites were left in the garment, that could only be because someone was at fault. The appellant is not required to lay his finger on the exact person in all the chain who was responsible or to specify what he did wrong. Negligence is found as a matter of inference from the existence of the defects taken in connection with all the known circumstances.

The effect of this is that in cases of defective construction the plaintiff will normally establish negligence by proving the existence of the defect, and that this was probably not the result of events that occurred after the product left the manufacturer's possession (*Mason* v *Williams & Williams Ltd* [1955] 1 WLR 549). In *Carroll* v *Fearon*, *The Times*, 26 January 1998, the Court of Appeal commented that: '. . . once it was established that the tyre disintegrated because of an identified fault in the course of its manufacture the judge had to decide whether this fault was the result of negligence at Dunlop's factory. He did not have to identify any individual or group of employees or the acts or omissions which resulted in [the defect]. If the manufacturing process had worked as intended this defect should not have been present.' The possibility of intermediate deterioration or tampering with the product will be taken into account in terms of the degree of likelihood that the defect was present when it left the manufacturer (see, e.g., *Evans* v *Triplex Safety Glass Co. Ltd* [1936] 1 All ER 283, para. 10.1.4). It is irrelevant whether the inference of negligence is called *res ipsa loquitur* or not, because in some instances it amounts in practice to a form of strict liability. This is particularly true of products which formerly would have fallen into the category of chattels dangerous *per se*. The greater the danger, the greater the precautions that will be required to discharge a duty of care (see para. 3.1.3.1; *Wright* v *Dunlop Rubber Co. Ltd* (1972) 13 KIR 255, 273–4). The defendant may rebut the inference by proving how the defect occurred and showing that this was not due to lack of care on his part, but this may be difficult. Ironically, the stronger the evidence that his manufacturing system was 'foolproof', the stronger is the inference that the defect arose as a result of carelessness by one of his employees (the 'human factor'), for whose negligence he will be held vicariously liable (*Grant* v *Australian Knitting Mills Ltd*; *Hill* v *James Crowe (Cases) Ltd* [1978] 1 All ER 812, 816, criticising *Daniels* v *White & Sons Ltd* [1938] 4 All ER 258 where carbolic acid used in washing bottles contaminated lemonade, and the defendants were held not liable on proving the effectiveness of the system. *Daniels* is probably wrongly decided.).

The plaintiff will have greater difficulty in proving negligence where the product is defective in design rather than construction. It is easier to demonstrate that a product was defective if it does not meet the manufacturer's own standards because something has gone wrong during construction or production (e.g., where a manufacturer releases a faulty batch of vaccine which has excessively high potency and toxicity: *Best* v *Wellcome Foundation Ltd* [1994] 5 Med LR 81). Where, however, a product performs as it was designed and intended there is no obvious standard against which to compare it (unless specifically governed by statute, see, e.g., Consumer Protection Act 1987, s. 11). The design may have been the result of a conscious compromise between cost and safety, taking into account consumer preferences (e.g., are all cars which are not fitted with anti-lock brakes negligent in design because they are less safe than they could be?). So, although design defects can be negligent, the courts are more reluctant to hold defendants liable in such cases (see further para. 3.2.4; Newdick (1987) 103 LQR 288, 300–4).

It should also be remembered that the standard required to discharge the duty of care is reasonable care in all the circumstances. If a particular risk was unforeseeable it is not possible to take reasonable precautions against it, by, for example, amending the design. This is especially true of certain types of product such as drugs, where, despite extensive premarketing research, it may not be possible to predict all the potential reactions that might occur in a large population. Apart from the problem of proving causation, this will make it difficult to prove that the manufacturer was negligent, because at the time when the product was marketed the risk was unknown. On the other hand, if the risk was known it may be regarded as an unavoidable 'side-effect' which was 'acceptable' because of the otherwise beneficial effects of the drug, either for the plaintiff or other users. 'Side-effects' are part of the cost-benefit analysis undertaken when considering whether a drug has a safe design. There is no reported case in this country in which a court has had to make a finding of liability against a drug manufacturer. Claims have been made in respect of, *inter alia*, Thalidomide, Opren, Debendox, Myodil, pertussis vaccine, neomycin, and benzodiazepine, but the actions have, to date, either settled or failed for want of proof of causation. (For discussion of some of the difficulties faced by plaintiffs suing in respect of drug injuries 30 years after the thalidomide disaster see Ferguson [1992] JR 226; Newdick (1985) 101 LQR 405; and on the thalidomide tragedy itself see Teff and Munro, *Thalidomide: The Legal Aftermath*, 1976.)

10.1.8 Type of loss
Liability for defective products applies to personal injuries and physical damage to property other than the product itself, including economic loss consequential to the physical damage, applying the usual principles of the tort of negligence (*Spartan Steel & Alloys Ltd* v *Martin & Co. (Contractors) Ltd* [1973] 1 QB 27, see para. 2.2.4.2). Pure economic loss is not recoverable. In *Muirhead* v *Industrial Tank Specialities Ltd* [1985] 3 All ER 705 a manufacturer supplied pumps for pumping seawater through the plaintiff's lobster storage tanks. The pumps were the wrong voltage for the United Kingdom electricity supply, and they cut out, causing the lobsters to die. In a claim against the manufacturer the plaintiff recovered the value of the lobsters (physical damage) and the loss of profit on those lobsters. A claim for the cost of the pumps and the loss of profits on the operation as a whole failed on the basis that this was pure economic loss.

The rule against recovery of pure economic loss stems from the general antipathy to the recovery of economic loss in negligence, but it is not always clear what forms of loss will be categorised as purely economic. For example, economic loss suffered by a distributor in a chain of supply which consists of a liability to pay damages to the ultimate consumer for physical injuries, or to indemnify a distributor lower in the chain for his liability to the ultimate consumer for physical injuries, may be recoverable from the manufacturer under the principle of *Donoghue* v *Stevenson* (*Lambert* v *Lewis* [1981] 1 All ER 1185, 1192; *Virgo Steamship Co. SA* v *Skaarup Shipping Corporation* [1988] 1 Lloyd's Rep 352; cf. *Leigh & Sillavan Ltd* v *Aliakmon Shipping Co. Ltd* [1985] 2 All ER 44, 63, CA; note that a claim for contribution from the manufacturer under the Civil Liability (Contribution) Act 1978, para. 14.6, may avoid the potential difficulties of the distributor suing the manufacturer in tort). This is a limited exception to the rule against recovery of pure economic loss.

The general rule, however, is that pure economic loss is not recoverable in tort. The House of Lords has now made it clear in *D & F Estates Ltd* v *Church Commissioners for England* [1988] 2 All ER 992 and *Murphy* v *Brentwood District Council* [1990] 2 All ER 908 that both damage to the product itself caused by a defect in the product and 'preventive damage', i.e., the cost of avoiding threatened physical damage to other property or persons once a dangerous defect becomes apparent (either by repairing the product or taking it out of circulation), is to be regarded as pure economic loss and therefore irrecoverable (see para. 2.2.4.2.2). The important point about liability under *Donoghue* v *Stevenson* [1932] AC 562 is that the plaintiff sustains physical damage as a result of using a product with a latent, and dangerous, defect. Once the danger is known, the product cannot safely be used unless the defect is repaired, and the cost of repair is treated as merely a defect in quality. In *Murphy* v *Brentwood District Council* Lord Bridge commented (at p. 927) that if a car was found to be faulty it made no difference to a car manufacturer's liability in tort whether the fault was in the brakes or in the engine, i.e., whether the car will not stop or will not start. In either case the car was useless until repaired, and the manufacturer was no more liable in tort for the cost of repair in the one case than in the other. Their Lordships were anxious to avoid imposing a non-contractual warranty of qualify attached to products or buildings for the benefit of first or subsequent owners. The remedy for such defects lay in contract. Accordingly, a plaintiff cannot succeed in negligence for the cost of repairing the product, or the difference in value between the product in its defective state and its proper condition, or any loss of profits caused by the fact that it is not up to specification or functions inadequately (*Muirhead* v *Industrial Tank Specialities Ltd*).

In *D & F Estates Ltd* v *Church Commissioners for England* Lord Bridge had suggested that an exception might apply in the case of a 'complex structure', where a defect in one constituent part of a building, and possibly a chattel, could be treated as distinct from the damage caused to another constituent part of the structure. On this basis the damaged part could be regarded as 'other property' so that the builder or manufacturer would be liable for the damage as if the defective part were a separate product, applying *Donoghue* v *Stevenson*. This 'complex structure' theory was rejected in *Murphy* v *Brentwood District Council* [1990] 2 All ER 908 as artificial. Lord Bridge himself stated that the structural elements of a building form a single indivisible unit of which the different parts are essentially interdependent, and to the extent that there is a defect in one part of the structure it necessarily affects all other parts of the structure. Thus, any defect in the structure is a defect in the quality of the whole, and so damage to a building caused by defective foundations could not be treated as damage to 'other property'.

Lord Bridge distinguished, however, between a defect in an integral part of the structure and a distinct item incorporated into the structure which malfunctions, inflicting positive damage on the structure. A defective central heating boiler or a defective electrical installation which malfunctioned and damaged a building could fall within the principle of liability under *Donoghue* v *Stevenson,* if the damage was due to the negligence of the boiler manufacturer or the electrical contractor (at p. 928; see also per Lord Keith at p. 922 and Lord Jauncey at p. 942 on this particular example). Lord Jauncey was prepared to apply the complex structure theory to the structure itself 'where one integral component of the structure was built by a separate contractor and where a defect in such a component had caused damage to other parts of the structure, e.g., a steel frame erected by a specialist contractor which failed to give adequate support to floors or walls' (at p. 942). The effect of this, however, would be that a plaintiff's entitlement to compensation for damage to the structure caused by a defect in the structure itself would depend on whether the building or product was constructed by a single main contractor or whether more than one contractor had been employed (see Sir Robin Cooke (1991) 107 LQR 46, 51; Wallace (1991) 107 LQR 228, 237). This would clearly be completely arbitrary, and for this reason it is unlikely that Lord Jauncey's dictum would be applied, particularly given the approach of their Lordships to the whole question of economic loss in *Murphy* v *Brentwood District Council.* On the other hand, in *Jacobs* v *Morton* (1994) 72 BLR 92 the plaintiffs successfully argued that a raft foundation constructed for the purpose of remedying defects in the foundations of the plaintiffs' property, but which was itself defective, fell within the complex structure exception, the raft foundation having caused further damage to the property.

It remains open to plaintiffs, in an appropriate case, to argue that a defective product has caused physical damage to 'other property', bringing it within *Donoghue* v *Stevenson* principles. *Aswan Engineering Establishment Co.* v *Lupdine Ltd* [1987] 1 All ER 135 demonstrates that even in apparently simple instances it may be difficult to identify just what is 'the product' and what is 'other property'. The plaintiffs purchased a quantity of waterproofing compound from the first defendants for shipment to Kuwait. The compound was contained in heavy duty plastic pails manufactured and supplied by the second defendants. In Kuwait the pails were stacked five or six high and left on the quayside in the sun. The pails collapsed in the intense heat with the loss of the consignment of waterproofing compound. The plaintiffs' claim against the second defendants was that the pails were defective and caused damage to the contents which constituted 'other property'. Lloyd LJ (with whom Fox LJ agreed) assumed, without deciding the issue, that this was the correct approach, but held that the action failed because the damage was not reasonably foreseeable (at pp. 152–4). The purchaser of a defective car tyre which burst, said his Lordship, can sue the manufacturer of the tyre for damage to the car as well as personal injury. 'But what if the tyre was part of the original equipment? Presumably the car is *other* property of the plaintiff, even though the tyre was a component part of the car, and property in the tyre and property in the car passed simultaneously. Another example . . . would be if I buy a bottle of wine and find that the wine is undrinkable owing to a defect in the cork. Is the wine other property, so as to enable me to bring an action against the manufacturer of the cork in tort?' (at p. 152h, emphasis in original). Lloyd LJ's 'provisional view' was that in each of these examples there is damage to other property (cf. Consumer Protection Act 1987 s. 5(2), para. 10.2.5). This suggests that even 'simple' products may be divisible into component parts for the purpose of identifying 'other property'. Nicholls LJ agreed that the plastic pails and their contents were separate items of property, but questioned whether the failure of a container (whether a carrier bag, a plastic bag or an iron bucket) which leads to the loss of the contents should give rise to an action against the manufacturer of the container under *Donoghue* v *Stevenson*.

10.2 STATUTE

Although in some cases the liability of manufacturers under *Donoghue* v *Stevenson* [1932] AC 562 amounts, in effect, to a form of strict liability, the action for negligence remains essentially fault-based and subject to all the vagaries associated with such actions. Some plaintiffs simply fall through the compensation net due to an inability to prove negligence, particularly if the risk of injury was unforeseeable. Iatrogenic and teratogenic drug injuries are often in this category, and it was one of the most prominent and poignant examples of drug injuries, the thalidomide tragedy, which prompted calls for reform. Both the Law Commission and the Pearson Commission recommended the introduction of strict liability for defective products (Law Com. No. 82, Cmnd 6831, 1977; *Pearson* vol. 1, ch. 22).

The stimulus for reform finally came from Europe rather than domestic law reform bodies. The Strasbourg Convention on Products Liability in regard to Personal Injury and Death 1977, and two draft EEC Directives, led finally to the European Community Directive on Liability for Defective Products 1985 (85/374/EEC) which required member States to implement its terms within three years. This was done by Part I of the Consumer Protection Act 1987 which came into force on 1 March 1988 and applies to damage caused by products which were put into circulation by the producer after that date (SI 1987/1680; Consumer Protection Act 1987, s. 50(7)). Section 1(1) states that Part I of the Act 'shall have effect for the purpose of making such provision as is necessary in order to comply with the product liability Directive and shall be construed accordingly'. This is potentially important because there are some significant differences between the wording of the Directive and the wording of the Act (especially in relation to the development risks defence, see para. 10.2.7.2). It is arguable that, in the light of s. 1(1), where there is a conflict between the Act and the Directive then the Directive should prevail.

A number of justifications for strict liability have been advanced. The manufacturer, it is said, both benefits from the sale of his products and creates the risk of injury, and so he should bear the losses when the risk materialises. The cost of these losses, usually in the form of insurance premiums, is then reflected in the price of the product and paid for by all consumers rather than the unfortunate few who suffer injury. Thus, costs are internalised and this leads to greater economic efficiency, through the price mechanism and deterrence of 'unsafe' products. This 'thesis' involves elements of enterprise liability, loss distribution, economic efficiency, deterrence and 'fairness' (see further paras 1.4, 8.4.1). But each of these notions is question-begging, since they say little about the type of risk (whether arising through fault or no-fault) that should be distributed or deterred or to whom one is seeking to be 'fair'. Strict liability in tort, it is argued, simply extends to non-purchasers the benefit already available to purchasers of defective products of the strict warranties conferred by a contractual remedy. Thus, it removes an anomalous distinction between the rights of purchasers and non-purchasers who suffer some form of injury. The additional cost to manufacturers would not be great because they already have to insure against strict contractual liabilities and negligence claims by non-purchasers, and product liability claims represent only 1% of all tort claims for personal injuries (*Pearson*, vol. 1, para. 1201). But, at a policy level, it is legitimate to ask why this particular group of accident victims should have the advantage (if it is an advantage) of strict liability when others must prove fault. Enterprise liability, loss distribution, economic efficiency and deterrence might equally justify strict liability for injuries to employees, for example. However, the product liability regime which has been adopted is scarcely open to this line of criticism. Rather, the question is whether it differs in any significant respect from the action in negligence which, presumably, it was intended to be an improvement upon. The answer, apart from the reversal of the burden of proof in one area, seems to be 'No' (see the searching analysis of Stapleton (1986) 6 OJLS 392; Newdick (1987) 103 LQR 288; Newdick [1988] CLJ 455).

The very concept of a product which is 'defective' involves resorting to much the same approach as when deciding whether there has been negligence, particularly where it is alleged that a product is defective in design (Clark (1985) 48 MLR 325; Stapleton, op. cit.). This is even more obvious with the development risks defence, which effectively excludes liability for unforeseeable design defects (para. 10.2.7.2). Given that liability in negligence for most construction defects comes close to strict liability (i.e., negligence is inferred from the defect itself, see para. 10.1.7) it would seem that the Consumer Protection Act has not produced a marked change. Indeed, it is doubtful whether the victims of thalidomide, who provoked the initial cry for reform, would be in any better position under the Act than in the tort of negligence.

The Act has not replaced the common law, it is an additional remedy. It is important to remember that if for any reason the Act does not apply (e.g., if the plaintiff is injured by unprocessed agricultural produce, or commercial property has been damaged, or the special limitation periods under the Act have expired) a claim for negligence may still be available.

Part II of the Consumer Protection Act 1987 lays down general requirements for the safety of certain consumer goods and gives the Secretary of State power to make specific safety regulations. Breach of these regulations is a criminal offence, and by s. 41 any individual injured by an infringement of safety regulations (but not the general safety requirement) can bring an action for breach of statutory duty. Part II replaces earlier legislation containing similar provisions (Consumer Safety Act 1978, which itself replaced the Consumer Protection Act 1961). This right of action appears not to have been widely used.

The details of liability under Part I of the Consumer Protection Act 1987 are considered in the following paragraphs of this chapter. Section numbers refer to this Act, unless specified.

10.2.1 Plaintiffs

Section 2(1) provides that 'where any damage is caused wholly or partly by a defect in a product, every person to whom subsection 2 below applies shall be liable for the damage'. This section confers a right of action on *any* person who suffers damage as a result of a defective product (and this includes ante-natal injuries: s. 6(3)). There is no need to establish that the plaintiff was foreseeable as likely to be affected by the defect, nor that the defendant was negligent. Proof that the product was 'defective' and that the defect caused the damage puts the onus on the defendant to establish one of the specific defences. How strict the liability under this section will be depends on the meaning of 'defective' (para. 10.2.4) and the extent to which the defences, particularly the 'development risks' defence (para. 10.2.7.2) allow notions of fault liability to excuse the defendant.

10.2.2 Defendants

Liability is imposed on:

(a)   the producer of the product;
(b)   anyone who holds himself out as the producer;
(c)   an importer; and
(d)   in certain circumstances, the supplier (s. 2(2) and (3)).

'Producer' means the manufacturer of the product, or the person who won or abstracted a substance which has not been manufactured (e.g., coal), or a processor where the 'essential characteristics' of a product are attributable to an industrial or other process (e.g., fish fingers) (s. 1(2)). 'Producer' includes the manufacturer of a component part (by virtue of the definition of 'product' in s. 1(2)). The component manufacturer will be liable *together with* the manufacturer of the finished product if the damage caused by the finished product is attributable to a defect in the component. Conversely, it would appear that the component manufacturer is not liable for damage caused by the finished product if the component was not defective. This is certainly the position where the defect in the finished product was wholly attributable to the design of that product, because s. 4(1)(f) provides a specific defence for the component manufacturer. The Act does not deal with the position of the component manufacturer where the defect in the finished product is a construction defect or the result of a defective component supplied by another manufacturer, but under the Directive a person is liable only for products which he has supplied, and the component manufacturer does not supply the finished product.

A person holds himself out as the producer of the product 'by putting his name on the product or using a trade mark or other distinguishing mark in relation to the product' (s. 2(2)(b); the 'own-brander'). Whereas a retail supplier will not normally be liable (see below), retailers who adopt the practice of putting their own brand name on goods produced by others will be liable for defects in those goods. This is now a common practice with large retail chain stores in the United Kingdom.

The importer of a product is liable if he imported it from a place outside the EEC into a member State in the course of any business of his, to supply it to another (s. 2(2)(c)). But an importer from another member State into the United Kingdom is not liable. So the importer of a defective car from Japan is liable for damage caused by the defect, but not the importer of a car from France. If the Japanese car had first been imported to France and then imported to England, the French importer would be liable, but not the English importer.

The supplier of goods, whether a retailer or intermediate distributor, is not normally liable under the Act. A supplier will be liable, however, if he fails, within a reasonable period of receiving a request from the person who suffered the damage, either to identify the producer, 'own-brander', or importer, or the person who supplied the product to him (s. 2(3); on the meaning of 'supply' see s. 46). The supplier is not liable under s. 2(3) merely because he cannot identify who provided the component parts or raw materials in a finished product supplied to him (s. 1(3)), rather it is the producer or supplier of the finished product that he must identify. The victim's request must be made within a reasonable period after the damage occurred, when it was not reasonably practical for the victim to identify them. This section is intended to give plaintiffs an identifiable defendant and puts the onus on suppliers to keep accurate records of their own sources of supply. If the supplier complies with the request he is not liable under the Act, even if the victim cannot pursue a remedy against the identified defendants, e.g., because they are in liquidation. The liability of suppliers in negligence is potentially wider than under the Act (see para. 10. 1.2).

10.2.3 Products
'Product' means any 'goods or electricity' and includes a product which is comprised in another product whether as a component part or raw material (s. 1(2)). 'Goods' includes substances, growing crops and things comprised in land by virtue of being attached to it, and any ship, aircraft or vehicle (s. 45). It is not clear whether human blood or organs will be treated

as 'products', though *Pearson*, vol. 1, para. 1276 recommended that they should.

Agricultural produce and game are excluded unless they have undergone an industrial process (s. 2(4)). Agricultural produce is defined as produce of the soil, of stock-farming or of fisheries (s. 1(2)), but there is no definition of an 'industrial process'. Whilst canning vegetables and making fishcakes may be regarded as industrial processes there are many 'processes' that may not be treated as 'industrial'. For example, is spraying crops with pesticides an industrial process? Or salting meat as a preservative? Or adding hormones to cattle-feed? An additional complication is that the processor is only liable as a producer if the 'essential characteristics' of the product are attributable to an industrial or other process (s. 1(2)). What, it might be asked, is the essential characteristic of tinned carrots? Is it that they are tinned or that they are carrots? This 'essential characteristic' requirement does not apply to other potential defendants in respect of processed food, the 'own-brander', the importer or the supplier. Nor is it necessary that the defect in the produce is the result of the industrial process. So food that is contaminated prior to processing can give rise to liability under the Act, once processed, whereas the same contaminated food sold to consumers unprocessed is not within the Act.

The definition of goods is wide enough to include buildings, but buildings are specifically excluded except in so far as a supply of goods involves incorporating the goods into a building or structure (s. 46(3)). A supply which involves the creation or disposal of an interest in land is excluded (s. 46(4)). The effect of this seems to be that a builder/vendor cannot be liable under the Act at all, because there is no relevant supply (s. 46(4)). A builder who is not a vendor cannot be liable for faulty construction or design under the Act. A producer of goods which are incorporated into a building or structure (such as bricks, concrete, door frames, girders, etc.) can be liable if the goods are defective and cause damage, and the builder may then be potentially liable as a supplier, i.e., if he fails to identify the producer, etc., or his supplier (under s. 2(3)). Damage, however, does not include damage to the building itself (s. 5(2), see para. 10.2.5).

10.2.4 Defects
Liability under the Act is 'strict', not absolute. The plaintiff does not succeed simply by showing that the product caused damage; he must prove that the damage was caused by a defect in the product. By s. 3(1) a product has a defect 'if the safety of the product is not such as persons generally are entitled to expect'. Safety includes safety with respect to component parts, and with respect to property damage as well as personal injury. The crucial question then is: what are persons generally entitled to expect by way of safety? The answer, almost inevitably, must be: it all depends on the circumstances of the case. They are entitled to expect that food and drink will not be contaminated with decomposed snails or acid, that clothes and hair dye will not contain skin irritants, that motor cars will not have defective steering, that dangerous chemicals will be adequately labelled, and so on. But are they entitled to

expect that no drugs will have any adverse side-effects, that all motor cars will be as safe as modern technology can make them, that circular saws will never accidentally saw a finger off? If this looks familiar from the tort of negligence it is because safety, like risk, is a relative concept. It is always a question of degree, in which levels of safety are traded off against both cost and the usefulness of the product, although this is more likely to be an intuitive judgment than a strict cost-benefit analysis (see Clark (1985) 48 MLR 325; Stoppa (1992) 12 LS 210, 225: 'the consumer expectations test . . . does not provide the interpreter with an objective standard against which the safety of a product can be assessed').

The similarity to negligence is even more apparent in s. 3(2), which provides that in determining what persons generally are entitled to expect all the circumstances shall be taken into account, including:

(a)   the manner in which, and purposes for which, the product has been marketed, its get-up, the use of any mark in relation to the product and any instructions for, or warnings with respect to, doing or refraining from doing anything with or in relation to the product;

(b)   what might reasonably be expected to be done with or in relation to the product; and

(c)   the time when the product was supplied by its producer to another, and nothing in this section shall require a defect to be inferred from the fact alone that the safety of a product which is supplied after that time is greater than the safety of the product in question.

All of these factors can arise in one form or another in a negligence action. A warning, for example, may render a product, otherwise 'defective', safe. But it does not make sense to speak of warnings against dangers which were unknown or unforeseeable by the producer, and once the question of foreseeability arises the concept of reasonable care is reintroduced (Clark (1987) 50 MLR 614, 617). Another problem will be the extent to which warnings or instructions addressed to intermediaries which do not reach the ultimate consumer will render the product safe (cf. negligence, paras 10.1.3, 10.1.4). Misuse of the product by the consumer will be taken into account. If the product is used in a way which could not 'reasonably be expected' then, as with negligence, it cannot be considered defective. Presumably, foreseeable misuse will make the product defective (negligence again), subject to a possible defence of contributory negligence.

The time at which the product was supplied (s. 3(2)(c)) involves two elements. First, the product may have deteriorated since it left the producer's hands, as a result of the passage of time (as with some foodstuffs), or repeated use (wear and tear), or misuse or mishandling (e.g., faulty repair). A product which has deteriorated in this way is not necessarily defective, though it is not necessarily safe either. It will depend upon the nature of the product, how much time has elapsed, how much use it has had, and so on (see also the defence in s. 4(1)(d), para. 10.2.7.1). Second, the fact that products supplied subsequently are safer, does not in itself mean that the product was defective.

So the fact that all new cars are now supplied with rear seat belts does not mean that all cars previously supplied without rear seat belts are defective (but see the analysis of Stapleton (1986) 6 OJLS 392, 410–11). In negligence, of course, carelessness is measured by reference to the knowledge and standards applicable at the time of the accident, ignoring subsequent improvements (*Roe* v *Minister of Health* [1954] 2 QB 66, para. 3.1.2; but the duty does at least extend beyond the date of putting the product into circulation: see para. 10.1.6). Section 3(2)(c) goes to the question of proof rather than creating a rule of law, otherwise all unforeseeable defects would be excluded from the ambit of the Act (as in negligence). Presumably, the facts of *Roe* are just the type of case which ought to be covered by strict liability, since persons generally are entitled to expect that anaesthetics will not be contaminated with paralysing agents (but see the development risks defence, para. 10.2.7.2).

The Act does not mention the cost of the product as a factor in determining defectiveness. Where the defect is a construction defect or a failure to warn or provide adequate instructions for use then cost is probably irrelevant. But it may well be a significant feature where it is claimed that the product is defective in design (see Stapleton (1986) 6 OJLS 392, 404; Newdick (1987) 103 LQR 288, 300–4).

Once it is established that the product was defective liability is strict, in the sense that it is not a defence for the producer to show that he exercised reasonable care. But many of the factors taken into account in deciding whether a manufacturer has discharged a duty of care in negligence are incorporated into the decision-making process about defectiveness under the Act. This, combined with the development risks defence, raises the question whether 'strict liability' amounts to little more than window dressing (Stapleton, op. cit. p. 422; Stoppa (1992) 12 LS 210, 226: 'an empty shell, a definition devoid of any objective signification, a semantic veneer concealing the interpreter's own conceptions').

10.2.5 Type of loss
The Act is designed to protect consumer expectations in the safety of products, and therefore there is no liability in respect of pure economic loss, damage to commercial property or damage to the product itself, even if the product is potentially dangerous. For the purpose of liability under s. 2, damage means 'death or personal injury or any loss of or damage to any property (including land)' (s. 5(1)). Loss of, or damage to, the product itself is specifically excluded, as is loss of, or damage to, a product caused by a defective component product which had been supplied with the product (s. 5(2)). Thus, if a tyre supplied with a new car is defective and causes an accident the tyre manufacturer is not liable for the damage to the car under the Act (cf. the position in negligence: *Aswan Engineering Establishment Co.* v *Lupdine Ltd* [1987] 1 All ER 135, 152, para. 10.1.8). The tyre manufacturer would be liable in respect of the occupants' personal injuries and the damage to other vehicles involved in the accident. If the tyre had been fitted as a replacement after the car was first supplied he would also be liable for the

damage to the car itself, since the car has not been supplied with the tyre 'comprised in it', and is therefore a distinct item of property.

By s. 5(3) property damage claims are limited to property which is:

(a) ordinarily intended for private use, occupation and consumption; and
(b) intended by the person suffering the loss or damage mainly for his own private use, occupation or consumption.

The object of s. 5(3) is to exclude property used for business purposes, although there is scope for disagreement about what forms of property are ordinarily intended for private use, and whether the property in question was intended 'mainly' for a person's own private use. The business user may, of course, sue in negligence.

Actions in respect of property damage (but not personal injury) below £275 are excluded, with a view to cutting down on trivial claims (s. 5(4)). There is no upper limit on liability, although the Directive would have permitted a limit on a producer's total liability for death or personal Injury caused by identical products with the same defect.

Although pure economic loss is clearly not recoverable, the Act makes no reference to economic loss consequential upon physical damage or personal injury. Presumably such loss is recoverable applying the ordinary principles for the assessment of damages in tort (cf. Buckley, *The Modern Law of Negligence*, 2nd ed., 1993, p. 357).

10.2.6 Causation
The plaintiff has the burden of proving that the product was defective and that the damage was caused 'wholly or partly' by the defect (s. 2(1)). The difficulty of proving factual causation will, in some instances, be just as great as in the tort of negligence (e.g., in the case of defective drugs, see para. 10.1.4).

The Act makes it clear that the producer remains liable where the damage is caused partly by the defect and partly by some other event. The other event may be entirely innocent or it may be the 'faulty' conduct of a third party, for example, the failure of a third party to examine or test the product or heed warnings in the manufacturer's instructions for use. It will be recalled that so far as the tort of negligence is concerned the failure to take advantage of a reasonable opportunity for intermediate inspection may be treated as breaking the chain of causation (see paras 10.1.3, 10.1.4). It is arguable that this will no longer be the position under the Act, because the damage is 'partly' caused by the defective product and 'partly' by the failure of the intermediate examination (*Street*, pp. 310–11). The manufacturer and the third party will be jointly and severally liable, and their respective responsibilities can be apportioned under the Civil Liability (Contribution) Act 1978. On the other hand, it is possible that where the manufacturer has good grounds for contemplating that an intermediate inspection will occur or that an intermediary will follow instructions then the product will not be categorised as *defective*. Section 3(2) provides that instructions, warnings, and 'what might reasonably be expected to be done with or in relation to the product' can be taken into account in determining what is defective. Thus, the consequences in law of intermediate examination may simply have been shifted from the causation stage of the inquiry to the earlier point of deciding whether the product was unsafe in all the circumstances. If the product is categorised as defective, then the omission of an intermediate examination will not defeat the action on grounds of causation.

Logically, the same approach should apply to 'faulty' conduct by the plaintiff. If he misuses the product in an unforeseeable fashion or disregards a warning the conclusion may simply be that the product was not defective. If it is found to be defective, the plaintiff's conduct should be treated as contributory negligence. The only circumstance in which the plaintiff's conduct can justifiably be regarded as the *sole* cause of his loss when the product is defective is where his misuse of the item is unrelated to the nature of the defect. If, for example, an electric fire has faulty wiring which may cause an electric shock it is clearly defective within s. 3(1), but if the consumer sustains injury when, standing on the fire to change a light bulb, it collapses under his weight, then the defect did not cause the damage.

10.2.7 Defences and limitation
Once the plaintiff proves that the product was defective and caused the damage the onus shifts to the defendant to establish one of the specific defences provided in s. 4. The Act also creates special rules for limitation periods.

One possible defence is expressly prohibited. By s. 7 liability cannot be 'limited or excluded by any contract term, by any notice or by any other provision'.

10.2.7.1 Miscellaneous defences It is a defence for the defendant to show that:

(a)   The defect was attributable to compliance with any statutory requirement or EEC obligation (s. 4(1)(a)).

(b)   He never supplied the product to another (s. 4(1)(b)), e.g., if it was stolen from him.

(c)   The only supply by him was otherwise than in the course of a business, and that if he is a producer, 'own-brander' or importer (under s. 2(2)) this is by virtue only of things done by him otherwise than with a view to profit (s. 4(1)(c)).

(d)   The defect did not exist in the product when he supplied it to another (s. 4(1)(d) and s. 4(2)(a)). If the defendant is a supplier, as opposed to a producer, an 'own-brander' or an importer (see s. 2(3)), it is a defence to show that the defect did not exist, not when *he* supplied it, but when it was last supplied by the producer, 'own-brander' or importer (s. 4(2)(b)).

(e)   A component manufacturer is not liable for a defect in the finished product which was wholly attributable to the design of the finished product (e.g., where the component product is normally safe in its contemplated use but is misused in the design of the finished product, for example, fitting car tyres to heavy lorries); nor where the defect is due to compliance by the component manufacturer with instructions given by the manufacturer of the finished product (s. 4(1)(f)).

(f) Contributory negligence is a partial defence (s. 6(4)). Equally, misuse of the product by the plaintiff may be relevant to the question of whether the product was defective at all, or whether an otherwise defective product caused the plaintiff's damage (see paras 10.2.4, 10.2.6). Conceptually these are distinct issues—*if* the product was defective, and *if* it was a cause, even a partial cause, of the damage the defendant is liable, and the plaintiff's fault is relevant only to apportionment of the damages. In practice, it may be difficult to separate these questions. In theory problems could arise as to the basis of apportionment of damages since the plaintiff is at fault and the defendant in breach of a strict duty which may not involve any negligence on his part. In such circumstances what is the 'claimant's share in the responsibility for the damage'? (Law Reform (Contributory Negligence) Act 1945 s. 1(1), see para. 14.5.4). This is not likely to be a major obstacle, however, because the courts have considerable experience of apportionment in other areas where the defendant may have been in breach of a strict duty (e.g., employers' liability).

10.2.7.2 Development risks Under s. 4(1)(e) it is a defence to prove that:

the state of scientific and technical knowledge at the relevant time was not such that a producer of products of the same description as the product in question might be expected to have discovered the defect if it had existed in his products while they were under his control.

The 'relevant time' is the time when the defendant supplied the product to another (s. 4(2)(a)), in effect, when it was put into circulation.

This so-called 'development risks defence' was one of the most controversial aspects of both the EEC Directive and the Consumer Protection Act 1987. Its effect is to excuse a defendant who can show that the defect was unknown and unforeseeable when he put the product into circulation, the justification being that if defendants were held responsible for unknown and unknowable risks this might deter the development of new products which might be beneficial to the public at large. The objection to the defence is that it represents a policy of allowing individual consumers to bear these development risks should they materialise, when the possibility of loss spreading through insurance and the price mechanism was readily available. It amounts to a retreat into negligence theory at precisely the point that strict liability is most useful (though see Stapleton (1986) 6 OJLS 392, 408–13 arguing that even without a development risks defence the same considerations have to be taken into account in a scheme which bases liability on *defectiveness*). Moreover, it is not a defence to the strictness of the contractual remedy, should it be a purchaser who happens to suffer injury.

Both the Law Commission and the Pearson Commission recommended that this defence should not be available. *Pearson*, vol. 1, para. 1259 commented that it would 'leave a gap in the compensation cover, through which, for example, the victims of another thalidomide disaster might easily slip' (see also Ferguson [1992] JR 226, 229). Indeed, the pharmaceutical industry will probably be one of the principal beneficiaries of this defence. It is arguable that if the absence of the defence would have 'deterred' producers then it would have resulted in more careful and thorough research and development programmes for new products, with stringent testing and monitoring, rather than manufacturers merely having to achieve a 'reasonable' standard which may be simply a matter of what is the common practice within the particular industry. The wording of the defence invites comparison with the 'scientific and technical knowledge' of a hypothetical producer of 'products of the same description as the product in question'. This is a subjective test of knowledge, by reference to the knowledge of the industry concerned, not general scientific and technical knowledge. The Act seemed to differ from the Directive on this point. Article 7(e) of the Directive permits the defence where 'the state of scientific and technical knowledge at the time when he put the product into circulation was not such as to enable the existence of the defect to be discovered'. This version of the defence appears to be narrower than s. 4(1)(e) of the Act: 'It is clearly easier for the producer to prove that no producer of similar products could have discovered the defect, than to prove that no one, considering the state of scientific and technical knowledge, could have discovered the defect' (Crossick (1988) 138 NLJ 223; cf. Newdick [1988] CLJ 455, 459–60 who argues that the Directive is ambiguous and that s. 4(1)(e) is the correct interpretation of the ambiguity). This discrepancy was referred to the European Commission on the basis that the Act did not fully implement the Directive, and the Commission took the issue to the European Court of Justice. The Court concluded, however, that there was no conflict between Article 7(e) and s. 4(1)(e). The UK courts would be able to achieve the purpose of Article 7(e) in interpreting s. 4(1)(e) (*Commission of the European Communities* v *UK* (C300/95) [1997] All ER (EC) (1) 481; for discussion of this case and its implications for the development risks defence see Hodges (1998) 61 MLR 560 and Mildred and Howells (1998) 61 MLR 570).

As it stands s. 4(1)(e) effectively excuses the defendant when he has not been negligent in failing to discover the defect, and amounts to little more than a reversal of the burden of proving negligence (Newdick op. cit. at pp. 460, 475—indeed, in certain respects the standard required may be lower than in negligence: ibid. p. 457 n. 11).

The major problem in applying s. 4(1)(e) is the interpretation of the words scientific and technical knowledge'. At what point does information become 'knowledge'? When it is accepted as scientific fact? When it is published in a scientific journal as a hypothesis? When a researcher in a laboratory considers it to be a remote possibility? How discoverable must the defect be? With the expenditure of moderate or reasonable or extensive resources? If the defect could have been discovered from existing information but the appropriate intellectual 'connections' have not been made by researchers, is this 'knowledge' from which the defect might be expected to have been discovered (cf. where the primary information has not been discovered)? In *Commission of the European Communities* v *UK* (C300/95) (above), the European Court of

Justice indicated that for the defence to be overcome the relevant knowledge must have been accessible at the time when the product was put into circulation. Of course, this leaves open the question of precisely how accessible the knowledge must be, but the possibility that this will be interpreted to mean 'reasonably accessible' to a hypothetical 'reasonable producer' cannot be discounted. This would be a negligence standard. A further question that arises on the interpretation of s. 4(1)(e) is whether the defence applies to manufacturing defects. On the face of it the defence is concerned with the producer's knowledge of the possibility that the defect might exist and excuses him from liability if he could not have known about the risk. Thus, it appears to be concerned with design defects rather than construction defects. However, it is arguable that the defence might also apply to construction defects which it is known can occur but the state of *technical* knowledge is such that it is impossible to devise a quality control system that will detect all defective items in the production line (see Newdick, op. cit. pp. 469–73). Although this argument runs contrary to the whole principle of strict liability for defective products, and so may not be accepted (ibid.), the different treatment given to construction defects and design defects is itself illogical and arbitrary (Stapleton, op. cit.). It is the development risks defence itself which undermines strict liability, and the result is that the Consumer Protection Act constitutes little more than a statutory version of negligence, with a reversed burden of proof.

10.2.7.3 Limitation   Special rules in respect of limitation periods apply to claims brought under the Act (sch. 1, amending the Limitation Act 1980; see generally para. 14.7). The plaintiff has three years within which to bring an action running from either the date on which the action accrued (i.e., when the damage occurred) or, if later, the date of his 'knowledge' (Limitation Act 1980, s. 11A(4)). His knowledge is defined in similar terms to that for an ordinary personal injuries claim, to include the fact that the damage was significant, the fact that it was caused by the defect, and the identity of the defendant (Limitation Act 1980, s. 14(1A); cf. s. 14(1), para. 14.7.1). The plaintiff's ignorance that as a matter of law the product was defective is irrelevant and does not prevent time running.

These rules apply both to personal injuries and property damage claims brought under the Consumer Protection Act 1987. In the case of personal injuries, however, the court has a discretion to override the three-year limit and allow the action to proceed (under the Limitation Act 1980, s. 33, see para. 14.7.1). But these limitation periods are subject to an overall longstop which expires 10 years after the product was put into circulation by the defendant (producer, 'own-brander' or importer) (Limitation Act 1980, s. 11A(3)). The longstop is an absolute bar, even in cases where there has been deliberate concealment or the plaintiff was under a disability (paras 14.7.3, 14.7.4), and the court has no discretion to override this limit in personal injuries cases. A plaintiff caught by the longstop (a situation which is more likely to arise with certain types of drug injury than with other products) will have to sue in negligence in order to invoke the court's discretion.

ELEVEN

Trespass to land

Trespass to land consists of an unauthorised interference with a person's possession of land. It is one of the oldest actions known to the common law, and in its origins was both a civil and criminal remedy for unwarranted intrusions. Trespass to land is no longer a crime at common law, although there are certain statutory offences (see in particular, the Criminal Justice and Public Order Act 1994, ss. 61, 68, 76 and the Criminal Law Act 1977, ss. 6–10, as amended by the 1994 Act ss. 72 and 73). The emphasis is on a direct invasion of the plaintiff's possession (as opposed to consequential injury), a point which is illustrated by the distinction between trespass and nuisance (para. 11.1.3). Once the invasion is proved it is for the defendant to justify his actions, which he will normally be unable to do simply by showing that he acted reasonably or with due care. Nor does the plaintiff have to prove that he has been damaged—the interference with his right is injury enough to establish liability. These features of the action enable its use for three distinct purposes: as a remedy for damage actually inflicted on the land, as a means of settling title to land and, to a lesser extent, as protection against abuse of the powers of officialdom.

11.1 NATURE OF THE ACTION

11.1.1 Intention
Trespass to land is regarded as an intentional tort, but somewhat paradoxically, perhaps, it can be committed innocently. This is because the intention refers to the voluntariness of the defendant's act in entering the plaintiff's land, not his intention to trespass. Thus, deliberate entry on to the land is sufficient, and it is irrelevant that the defendant did not know that he was entering the plaintiff's land, or believed the entry was authorised, or even honestly and reasonably believed that the land was his (*Conway* v *George Wimpey & Co. Ltd* [1951] 2 KB 266, 273; *Costello* v *City of Calgary* (1997) 152 DLR (4th) 453). An involuntary intrusion is not intentional and

therefore not actionable, e.g., where the defendant was pushed on to the land by someone else (*Smith* v *Stone* (1647) Style 65; but someone who enters under duress acts voluntarily for this purpose: *Gilbert* v *Stone* (1647) Style 72). However, it would seem that where the trespass is by staghounds in the course of hunting deer, it must be shown that the master of hounds either intended that the hounds should enter or negligently failed to exercise proper control over them (*League against Cruel Sports Ltd* v *Scott* [1985] 2 All ER 489, in which Park J rejected the plaintiffs' argument that the only question was whether the entry was voluntary or involuntary). In the case of unintentional entry there are two possibilities. Where it is the result of an accident on an adjoining highway the plaintiff must prove negligence (*River Wear Commissioners* v *Adamson* (1877) 2 App Cas 743, 767). In other cases inevitable accident is probably a defence. This would put the burden of disproving negligence on the defendant (para. 14.4.2), but it is arguable that by analogy with trespass to the person the plaintiff must now prove negligence (*Fleming*, p. 41; *Winfield and Jolowicz*, p. 384; this assumes that it is still possible to bring trespass for negligent conduct following *Letang* v *Cooper* [1965] 1 QB 232, see para. 12.1).

11.1.2 Damage
Trespass to land is actionable *per se*, i.e., without proof of damage, and so it is no defence to plead that the trespass was trivial (though an unmeritorious plaintiff might be penalised in costs). The reason for this lies in the historical origins of the action as a means of maintaining the peace and settling boundary disputes (which today are more easily resolved by an action for a declaration). If the plaintiff wants to recover more than nominal damages he must prove his loss in the usual way, but this can include a sum which represents the amount that the plaintiff might reasonably have charged the defendant for a licence to commit the trespass.

11.1.3 Trespass and nuisance
The actions in trespass and nuisance have similarities in that they both protect the use and enjoyment of land. They differ in that nuisance normally requires proof of damage to be actionable, and deals with consequential harm, whereas in trespass the interference with the plaintiff's land must be a direct result of the defendant's act. Again, these distinctions stem from the historical development of the actions from the writs of trespass and case (see *Salmond and Heuston*, pp. 4–7). Thus, it is trespass to throw stones on to another's land, but nuisance to allow a fence or a wall to become dilapidated so that it collapses on to his land (*Mann* v *Saulnier* (1959) 19 DLR (2d) 130, 132). It is trespass to plant a tree in his land, but only nuisance if a tree spreads over the boundary (*Smith* v *Giddy* [1904] 2 KB 448—branches; *Davey* v *Harrow Corporation* [1958] 1 QB 60—roots). It is not always a simple matter, however, to draw the distinction between direct and consequential harm. There was a marked judicial difference of opinion, for example, as to whether discharging oil in navigable waters which is subsequently carried to the shore by the elements constitutes trespass (in *Southport Corporation* v *Esso*

Petroleum Co. Ltd [1954] 2 QB 182, 195, 204; and [1956] AC 218, at 242, 244).

Trespass does not depend upon a balancing of the parties' rights, as occurs in nuisance (see para. 7.1.2.2). So the fact that the trespass is trifling and causes no harm to the plaintiff is irrelevant to the defendant's liability (unlike nuisance), and, moreover, the plaintiff will normally be entitled to an injunction to restrain a continuing trivial trespass, even if the consequences for the defendant are very serious (*Anchor Brewhouse Developments Ltd* v *Berkley House (Docklands Developments) Ltd* (1987) 38 BLR 82, though see the comments of Scott J at p. 104 lamenting this latter point).

11.2 THE INTERFERENCE

11.2.1 Types of trespass
The most usual type of trespass is entry by the defendant on to the plaintiff's land, but it can take other forms such as placing objects on the land, or even placing objects in contact with the property (*Gregory* v *Piper* (1829) 9 B & C 591—rubbish placed against a wall; *Westripp* v *Baldock* [1938] 2 All ER 799—ladder against a wall). A person who was lawfully on the land, because he had permission to be there or was exercising a right of entry, will become a trespasser if he abuses the permission or right by acting outside the purpose for which it was granted, or if he remains on the land after it has expired (*Hillen* v *ICI (Alkali) Ltd* [1936] AC 65; see also para. 6.1.2). On the other hand, a person who is lawfully in possession of the land does not become a trespasser on the termination of his interest, because trespass is a wrong to possession, e.g., a lessee holding over on the termination of his lease (*Hey* v *Moorhouse* (1839) 6 Bing NC 52; see para. 11.4).

A continuing trespass gives rise to a new cause of action from day to day as long as it lasts. In *Holmes* v *Wilson and others* (1839) 10 A & E 503, for example, the defendants built buttresses supporting a road on the plaintiff's land. The defendants paid damages for the trespass, but were held liable again in a further action for failing to remove the buttresses. The same rule applies where the entry was initially lawful, but has ceased to be so, e.g., on the termination of a licence. It is a continuing trespass to fail to remove the object once permission has ceased (*Konskier* v *Goodman Ltd* [1928] 1 KB 421). Continuing trespass applies only to the failure to remove things (or people if the defendant remains in person) wrongfully left on the land. It does not extend to failing to restore the land to its original condition. So where the trespass has caused damage to the land, it does not 'continue' simply because the damage has not been repaired, and the plaintiff can bring only one action (*Clegg* v *Dearden* (1848) 12 QB 576).

11.2.2 Airspace and subsoil
Rights in possession can extend both below the surface of the land and to the airspace above it. Entry below the surface at any depth constitutes trespass (*Bulli Coal Mining Co.* v *Osborne* [1899] AC 351—coal mining). Possession

of the surface and the subsoil may be separated, e.g., by the grant of mining rights. In this situation trespass to the subsoil will be actionable at the suit of the person in possession of the subsoil, not the person in possession of the surface, and vice versa. Breach of the horizontal boundary will also constitute trespass.

An invasion of the airspace above land may be a trespass, but this is limited to the height at which the intrusion would interfere with the full use of the land. In *Kelsen* v *Imperial Tobacco Co. Ltd* [1957] 2 QB 334 the defendants were required by mandatory injunction to remove an advertising sign which projected only eight inches over the plaintiff's property. An unauthorised telephone wire above the plaintiff's land is a trespass (*Wandsworth Board of Works* v *United Telephone Co.* (1884) 13 QBD 904), as is a crane that swings over the land (*Anchor Brewhouse Developments Ltd* v *Berkley House (Docklands Developments) Ltd* (1987) 38 BLR 82). Firing a bullet across the land should on principle constitute trespass even if not dangerous (*Davies* v *Bennison* (1927) 22 Tas LR 52—defendant shot plaintiff's cat on a shed roof, liable in trespass to land; cf. *Pickering* v *Rudd* (1815) 4 Camp 219—shot striking the property a trespass, but a shot passing over the land not actionable unless a nuisance). Overhanging eaves will be a trespass, but overhanging tree branches are treated as a nuisance which requires proof of damage to be actionable (though the branches can be cut in the exercise of the occupier's right of abatement, para. 7.1.7.3).

The owner's rights in the airspace above land are restricted, however, to 'such height as is necessary for the ordinary use and enjoyment of his land and the structures on it', and so it is not a trespass to fly an aircraft at a reasonable height which does not interfere with any use to which the land might be put (*Bernstein* v *Skyviews & General Ltd* [1978] QB 479, 488—'many hundreds of feet'; but a *structure* which is attached to an owner's adjoining land and which overhangs his neighbour's land is trespass, even if the interference is at such a height that it would not normally affect the neighbour's use of land: see *Anchor Brewhouse Developments Ltd* at pp. 94–5). Repeated overflying that was noisy, or polluted the atmosphere, or amounted to 'the harassment of constant surveillance' might constitute an actionable nuisance. The Civil Aviation Act 1982, s. 76(1), provides that no action shall lie in respect of trespass or nuisance by reason only of the flight of aircraft over any property at a height which is reasonable, having regard to wind, weather and all the circumstances of the case. This applies to any civil flight, and is not restricted to passage and repassage by analogy with the use of highways (*Bernstein* v *Skyviews & General Ltd*). The Act confers a statutory right of action in respect of physical damage caused by aircraft. Section 76(2) imposes strict liability, providing that where material loss or damage is caused to any person or property on land or water by, or by a person in, or an article, animal or person falling from, an aircraft while in flight, taking off or landing, damages in respect of the loss or damage shall be recoverable without proof of negligence or intention or other cause of action, as if the loss or damage had been caused by the wilful act, neglect or default of the owner of the aircraft. This section does not apply where the loss or damage was caused or contributed to by the negligence of the person who sustained it, and by s. 76(3) the owner is entitled to an indemnity from another person who is legally liable for the loss, e.g., if it was caused by someone else's negligence.

11.2.3 Highways
Lawful use of the highway is limited to the right of passage and repassage, and reasonably incidental purposes such as loading and unloading a vehicle or parking it for a temporary period (*Iveagh* v *Martin* [1961] 1 QB 232, 273; *Randall* v *Tarrant* [1955] 1 WLR 255). In addition to possible liability in public nuisance (see paras 7.2.3.2 and 7.2.3.3), a person who uses the highway for another purpose is a trespasser against the person in possession of the subsoil (*Harrison* v *Duke of Rutland* [1893] 1 QB 142—interfering with adjoining occupier's shooting rights; *Hickman* v *Maisey* [1900] 1 QB 752—racing tout watching the performance of racehorses in training; *Hubbard* v *Pitt* [1976] QB 142—picketing; cf. *Liddle* v *Yorkshire (North Riding) County Council* [1934] 2 KB 101, 127—stopping to sketch possibly not a trespass). Other users of the highway must exercise reasonable care for a person's safety, even though he may be trespassing on the highway (*Farrugia* v *Great Western Railway Co.* [1947] 2 All ER 565).

11.3 JUSTIFICATION

Trespass consists of an unjustified entry on to land in the possession of another, so there can be no trespass where the entry was authorised. Justification can be either a permission granted by the plaintiff, or a right of entry conferred by law or by the plaintiff or his predecessor in title.

11.3.1 Licence
A licence is a permission which renders lawful that which would otherwise have been unlawful, but without passing any interest in land (*Thomas* v *Sorrell* (1673) Vaugh 330, 351). A person who enters land under a licence, whether express or implied, is not a trespasser. If he exceeds his licence, or remains on the land after it has expired or been effectively revoked, he becomes a trespasser (*Wood* v *Leadbitter* (1845) 13 M & W 838), but he is allowed a reasonable time in which to leave and remove his goods (*Robson* v *Hallett* [1967] 2 QB 939; *Minister of Health* v *Bellotti* [1944] KB 298).

A gratuitous licence is revocable at any time on giving notice. It is unclear to what extent a contractual licence may be revoked. It has been held that a contractual licence may be revoked even though the licensor would be liable in an action for breach of contract (*Wood* v *Leadbitter*; *Thompson* v *Park* [1944] KB 408). However, where the licensee would be granted an equitable remedy to prevent revocation in breach of contract by the licensor, the licence will be regarded as irrevocable (*Hurst* v *Picture Theatres Ltd* [1915] 1 KB 1; *Winter Garden Theatre (London) Ltd* v *Millennium Productions Ltd* [1948] AC 173). This is essentially a matter of construing the contract to see whether the licensor has expressly or impliedly promised not to revoke the licence.

Generally speaking, where the licence is for a limited period and a specific purpose, such as watching a sporting event or a theatre performance, it will be irrevocable until the purpose is complete, provided the licensee acts in accordance with the terms by behaving properly. The significance of this is that a licensor who forcibly ejects the licensee cannot claim that he is using reasonable force to remove a trespasser, and so the licensee will be able to maintain an action for substantial damages in tort for assault and battery, rather than being left to an action for breach of contract where damages would probably be nominal, e.g., the price of the entrance ticket (see *Hurst* v *Picture Theatres Ltd*; *Wood* v *Leadbitter* can no longer be regarded as correct on this point: *Winter Garden Theatre (London) Ltd* v *Millennium Productions Ltd*; on *Hurst* v *Picture Theatres Ltd*, see *Weir*, p. 377). It has even been held that in 'a proper case' specific performance of a contractual licence may be ordered where the licence has been 'revoked' before the licensee entered the land (*Verrall* v *Great Yarmouth Borough Council* [1981] QB 202). But it should not be thought that a contractual licence given in general terms can never be terminated (*Winter Garden Theatre (London) Ltd* v *Millennium Productions Ltd* [1948] AC 173, 194).

A licence coupled with an interest, i.e., a grant of property, whether realty or chattels, is irrevocable (*Thomas* v *Sorrell* (1674) Vaugh 330, 351; see Megarry and Wade, *The Law of Real Property*, 5th ed, p. 800). Even a gratuitous licence is irrevocable once it has been executed in that the licensee cannot be compelled to undo what he has already lawfully done (*Armstrong* v *Sheppard & Short Ltd* [1959] 2 QB 384). Once the licence has been properly revoked the licensor can sue for any continuing trespass (as opposed to the continuing effect on the land of an act lawfully done prior to revocation: ibid.)

11.3.2 Rights of entry

Entry may be justified in the exercise of an easement, such as a private right of way, granted by the plaintiff or his predecessor in title, or a public right of way. (On the acquisition of private rights of way by prescription see *Mills* v *Silver* [1991] 1 All ER 449.) Rights of access may be conferred both by the common law (e.g., under customary rights or the right to abate a nuisance) and by statute. In addition to the powers of the police to enter and search premises (Police and Criminal Evidence Act 1984, ss. 16–18), numerous public officials have statutory powers of entry (see e.g., *Clerk and Lindsell*, para. 16–135). The police have a common law power to enter private premises without a warrant to prevent a breach of the peace occurring there, provided that they have a genuine belief that there was a real and imminent risk of a breach of the peace occurring (*McLeod* v *Commissioner of Police of the Metropolis* [1994] 4 All ER 553. For criticism see Feldman (1995) 111 LQR 562). Entry pursuant to an access agreement or order under the National Parks and Access to the Countryside Act 1949, s. 60, is not a trespass.

Necessity is a defence to trespass to land (para. 14.4.3), but homelessness does not constitute necessity (*Southwark London Borough Council* v *Williams* [1971] Ch 734). At common law an adjoining occupier had no right of access to neighbouring land for the purpose of repairing his own premises, even if the building became dangerous (*John Trenberth Ltd* v *National Westminster Bank Ltd* (1979) 253 EG 151). The Access to Neighbouring Land Act 1992 allows an occupier to make an application to the court for an access order enabling the occupier to enter adjoining or adjacent land to carry out works that are reasonably necessary for the preservation of the whole or any part of his land, provided that they cannot be carried out, or would be substantially more difficult to carry out, without entry. The court will not make such an order where the adjoining occupier would suffer interference with or disturbance of his use or enjoyment of his land, or would suffer hardship, to such a degree by reason of the entry that it would be unreasonable to make the order. The court may require an applicant for an access order to pay compensation for any loss or damage or any substantial loss of privacy or other substantial inconvenience; may require insurance against specified risks; and, except in the case of works to residential land, may require payment to the adjoining occupier by way of consideration for the privilege of entry. Similarly, the Party Wall etc. Act 1996, s. 8 confers a right of entry for the purpose of executing work under the Act.

11.3.3 Trespass *ab initio*

Where a person exceeds the permission that he has been given or abuses a right of entry (e.g., as with trespass to the highway), he becomes a trespasser from that point. However, there is a special rule that applies where the defendant entered by authority of the law (as opposed to the plaintiff's authority). If he abuses his authority he becomes a trespasser *ab initio* and he is treated as a trespasser from the time he entered, no matter how innocent his conduct up to the time of the abuse (*The Six Carpenters' Case* (1610) 8 Co Rep 146a). The rule applies only to a positive wrongful act and not mere nonfeasance. In *Elias* v *Pasmore* [1934] 2 KB 164 police entered the plaintiff's premises and seized documents, some lawfully and others unlawfully. It was held that the doctrine of trespass *ab initio* applied only to the documents unlawfully seized, and since they had a valid reason for entry in connection with the documents lawfully seized they were not liable as trespassers *ab initio* for the damage inflicted in entering the premises.

The doctrine has been criticised (by Lord Denning MR in *Chic Fashions (West Wales) Ltd* v *Jones* [1968] 2 QB 299), but subsequently applied by the same judge to mini-cab drivers unlawfully touting for business (*Cinnamond* v *British Airports Authority* [1980] 2 All ER 368). It is meant to provide some protection for the individual against abuses of authority by public officials, and, as *Winfield and Jolowicz*, p. 394, comments, it would seem to be unduly optimistic to suppose that the doctrine has outlived its usefulness.

11.4 POSSESSION: WHO CAN SUE?

Trespass to land is a wrong to possession not ownership, and so only the person in exclusive possession may sue. Possession connotes occupation or physical control of the land. Mere use without possession is not sufficient, nor is ownership without possession. Thus a landlord cannot sue for trespass while the lease subsists (unless there is damage to his reversionary interest: *Jones* v *Llanrwst Urban District Council* [1911] 1 Ch 393), and a lodger does not have exclusive possession of his rooms (*Allan* v *Liverpool Overseers* (1874) LR 9 QB 180, 191; nor does a licensee: *Hill* v *Tupper* (1863) 2 H & C 121) whereas a tenant or subtenant does (*Street* v *Mountford* [1985] 2 All ER 289; *Lane* v *Dixon* (1847) 3 CB 776). Where the true owner sues a wrongdoer alleged to be in possession, the slightest act by the owner or his predecessors in title indicating an intention to take possession is sufficient to enable the owner to maintain trespass (*Ocean Estates Ltd* v *Pinder* [1969] 2 AC 19). However, the mere sending and receipt of a letter demanding the delivery up of possession does not mean that the recipient of the letter ceases to be in possession and the sender acquires possession. Thus such a letter does not prevent a trespasser in actual possession from acquiring title by adverse possession under the Limitation Act 1980, s. 15 (*Mount Carmel Investments Ltd* v *Peter Thurlow Ltd* [1988] 3 All ER 129). But a trespasser who evicts the person in possession does not obtain possession as against the evicted person seeking repossession unless the latter acquiesces by delaying steps to remove the intruder (*Browne* v *Dawson* (1840) 12 A & E 624; *McPhail* v *Persons Unknown* [1973] Ch 447).

A person in *de facto* possession can maintain an action in trespass against anyone who does not have an immediate right to recover possession. Thus possession without title or with a defective title is sufficient against third parties. The defendant sued in trespass cannot plead someone else's better title to possession, unless he acted on his authority (*Nicholls* v *Ely Beet Sugar Factory* [1931] 2 Ch 84). This is usually expressed by saying that *jus tertii*, the right of another person, is no defence. It does not apply, of course, against the person entitled to immediate possession (*Delaney* v *T.P. Smith Ltd* [1946] KB 393). This protection of possession, even wrongful possession such as may be acquired by a trespasser, is founded upon the need to avoid breaches of the peace.

Where the true owner is out of possession, either because he has been dispossessed or he failed to take up possession, then in theory he cannot sue in trespass (but note *Ocean Estates Ltd* v *Pinder, supra*). However, once the person with the immediate right to possession enters the land thereby acquiring possession, he is deemed by a legal fiction known as trespass by relation, to have been in possession since his right to enter accrued. This allows him to sue for trespasses committed while he was out of possession.

11.5 REMEDIES

The plaintiff in an action for trespass to land may seek damages or an injunction or both. Where the trespass is trivial, damages may be nominal and an injunction may be refused (*Armstrong* v *Sheppard & Short Ltd* [1959] 2 QB 384). But even if there is no physical harm or interference with the plaintiffs plans as to the use of his property it is arguable that he suffers harm by being deprived of the opportunity to bargain with the defendant for the grant of a licence to commit the trespass (*Anchor Brewhouse Developments Ltd* v *Berkley*

House (Docklands Developments) Ltd (1987) 38 BLR 82, 102). This argument
is somewhat self-referential since it depends upon the courts' willingness to
find that even minor trespasses warrant absolute protection, and thereby they
may acquire a commercial value. It follows that where the trespass consists
of some use of the land without causing any damage, the damages will be
measured by the value of the defendant's use, e.g., the letting value of the
land. Where the trespass has caused physical damage, damages are measured
by the diminution in value of the land, not the cost of restoration (*Lodge Holes
Colliery Co. Ltd* v *Wednesbury Corporation* [1908] AC 323, 326; cf. *Heath* v
Keys (1984) 134 NLJ 888, see para. 15.1.4). A tenant unlawfully evicted by
his landlord may be entitled to exemplary damages (see *Drane* v *Evangelou*
[1978] 2 All ER 437, and para. 15.1.1.3).

A plaintiff is prima facie entitled to an injunction to restrain a continuing
trespass, unless there are exceptional circumstances. This principle applies
equally to an interlocutory injunction (*Patel* v *W.H. Smith (Eziot) Ltd* [1987]
2 All ER 569, CA). The fact that the trespass caused no harm, did not
interfere with the plaintiff's ordinary use of his property, or that the plaintiff
did not intervene to prevent the defendant erecting the structure of which he
now complains, are not exceptional circumstances (*Anchor Brewhouse Developments Ltd*). Where the plaintiff is granted a mandatory injunction requiring the defendant to restore the land to its previous condition the cost of the
works may be taken into account because the remedy must be reasonably
proportionate to the wrong suffered by the plaintiff (*Jordan* v *Norfolk County
Council* (1994) 93 LGR 50).

A person who has been dispossessed may bring an action for the recovery
of land, formerly known as ejectment. The plaintiff must establish a right to
immediate possession, but to do this he must recover by the strength of his
own title and not by the weakness of the defendant's (*Martin* d *Tregonwell* v
Strachan (1742) 5 D & E 107 n). However, proof of the plaintiff's prior
possession is treated as prima facie evidence of the plaintiff's better title, and
the presumption is not rebutted by showing that the plaintiff did not derive
possession from someone who did have title (*Doe* d *Smith* v *Webber* (1834) 1
A & E 119; *Asher* v *Whitlock* (1865) LR 1 QB 1; in other words, mere later
possession by the defendant does not defeat the plaintiff's claim). It is a
matter of some controversy whether *jus tertii* is a defence to this action. Does
the defendant succeed by showing that the right to possession is vested in a
third party? Or is it sufficient for the plaintiff to establish a relatively better
title than the defendant? The balance of opinion takes the view that *jus tertii*
is a defence (relying on *Doe* d *Carter* v *Barnard* (1849) 13 QB 945; criticised
in *Asher* v *Whitlock* (1865) LR 1 QB 1, 6 and *Perry* v *Clissold* [1906] AC 73,
79; see *Fleming*, p. 49; *Winfield and Jolowicz*, p. 397; cf. *Clerk and Lindsell*,
para. 17–70). In any event, there is an exception where the defendant
acquired possession through the plaintiff, or from a person through whom the
plaintiff claims, because the defendant is then estopped from relying on a
defect in the plaintiff's title (*Doe* d *Johnson* v *Baytup* (1835) 3 A & E 188),
though he can show that the title has since expired or been parted with
(*Claridge* v *Mackenzie* (1842) 4 Man & G. 142). A possible second exception

is that *jus tertii* cannot be relied on by a defendant who is a trespasser as against the plaintiff (*Fleming*, p. 49; *Salmond and Heuston*, p. 48, relying on *Davison* v *Gent* (1857) 1 H & N 744, though *Salmond and Heuston* relates this to the presumption that prior possession raises only prima facie evidence; cf. *Winfield and Jolowicz*, p. 398). There is a summary procedure available for the eviction of persons in unlawful occupation of premises ('squatters': RSC, Ord. 113) but not against tenants holding over on the termination of the lease.

An action for mesne profits, unlike ejectment, allows the plaintiff to claim damages for his loss during the period that he has been dispossessed. This is compensation for the value of the use and occupation of the land plus any damage to the land itself. Mesne profits are usually awarded against a tenant who stays on the land at the end of the lease, and the assessment of damages is based on a 'reasonable rent' for the use of the property. In *Inverugie Investments Ltd* v *Hackett* [1995] 3 All ER 841 the Privy Council held that even where the plaintiff has not suffered any *actual* loss by being deprived of the use of his property, he is still entitled to recover in damages a 'reasonable rent' for the wrongful use of the property. Similarly, the defendant may not have derived any *actual* benefit, but is still obliged to pay a reasonable rent. As Lord Lloyd explained (at p. 846): 'If a man hires a concrete mixer, he must pay the daily hire, even though he may not in the event have been able to use the mixer because of rain. So also must a trespasser who takes the mixer without the owner's consent. He must pay the going rate, even though in the event he has derived no benefit from the use of the mixer'. The same principle, said his Lordship, applies to residential property. This approach appears to depart from the traditional compensatory basis for awarding damages in tort, since the assessment is not based on what the plaintiff has actually lost as a result of the tort (though Lord Lloyd side-stepped this point by suggesting that it all depends upon how widely one defines the plaintiff's 'loss'. See Mitchell [1995] LMCLQ 343; and see further Cooke (1994) 110 LQR 420, commenting on the decision of the Court of Appeal in *Ministry of Defence* v *Ashman* [1993] 2 EGLR 102). Mesne profits is a type of action in trespass, and so if it is brought separately the plaintiff must first enter the land, and then by trespass by relation (para. 11.4) he is deemed to have been in possession and entitled to claim for the period of his dispossession. He is not required to enter if his title has expired, or the claim for mesne profits is joined with an action for the recovery of land (RSC, Ord. 15, r. 1). However, once the true owner's title to land is extinguished by 12 years' adverse possession under the Limitation Act 1980, s. 15, he cannot claim mesne profits in respect of the period during which the adverse possession was being established. The claim for mesne profits is also extinguished (*Mount Carmel Investments Ltd* v *Peter Thurlow Ltd* [1988] 3 All ER 129).

Finally, a person who has been wrongfully dispossessed may undertake a form of self-help known as re-entry. It would appear that for the purpose of the civil law he is entitled to use reasonable force to effect the eviction (*Hemmings* v *Stoke Poges Golf Club* [1920] 1 KB 720), but it must be emphasised that forcible entry is likely to constitute a criminal offence

(Criminal Law Act 1977, s. 6; see also Protection from Eviction Act 1977, s. 1; Ashworth [1978–79] JSWL 76). A person in possession is entitled to use reasonable force to expel a trespasser provided he has first asked him to leave (*Collins* v *Renison* (1754) 1 Say 138). In the case of trespass by encroachment the plaintiff may be entitled to exercise a form of self-redress by abatement. This is analogous to the right to abate a nuisance (see para. 7.1.7.3) and is justified only in clear and simple cases which would not justify the expense of legal proceedings or in an emergency (*Burton* v *Winters* [1993] 1 WLR 1077). The remedy is not appropriate where the damage that would be inflicted on the defendant is out of all proportion to the damage suffered by the plaintiff as a result of the trespass, nor where the plaintiff has already applied for and been refused a mandatory injunction (ibid.).

TWELVE

Trespass to the person

The action for trespass to the person is descended from the ancient writ of trespass, which was available for unlawful interference with the person, with goods or with the possession of land. The two most distinctive features of the writ of trespass were that an interference was actionable *per se,* i.e., without proof of damage, and that it had to be a direct result of the defendant's act. Indirect or consequential harm was the subject of an action in 'trespass on the case', later referred to as an action on the case, or simply 'case'. The traditional example of the distinction between direct and indirect harm is that of a man who throws a log on to the highway. If the log strikes someone the injury is direct and trespass would lie, but if it simply obstructs the highway and someone trips over it, the injury is indirect and the plaintiff would have to sue in case, and prove damage (*Reynolds* v *Clarke* (1725) 1 Str 634, 636). Although the distinction is clear enough in this example, it was not always so easy to draw (see, e.g., *Scott* v *Shepherd* (1773) 2 Bl R 892—lighted squib thrown by D finally exploding in front of P, having been thrown on by X and Y, who acted instinctively for their own preservation or the preservation of their goods; D liable in trespass).

While the medieval lawyer tended to classify torts by reference to causation, the modern approach is to emphasise the nature of the defendant's act: was it careless? This categorisation cuts across the direct/indirect division, and though it is reasonably accurate to suggest that there is a generalised principle of liability for careless conduct (in the tort of negligence) there is no general principle of liability known as intentionally inflicting harm. Thus, although trespass is frequently referred to as a tort of intention, there is still a tendency to insist on directness (but see *Wilkinson* v *Downton* [1897] 2 QB 57, para. 12.2).

There are three forms of trespass to the person: assault, battery and false imprisonment. In many cases the defendant's conduct will also constitute a criminal offence, and in practice a non-tortious remedy is often of much greater value to the victim (see para. 12.3). Lastly, it should be noted that the tort of malicious prosecution (para. 12.6) does not, strictly speaking, belong in a chapter on trespass to the person. It derives from the action on the case and proof of damage is essential, but it performs a similar function to false imprisonment and the two actions are often combined.

12.1   TRESPASS AND NEGLIGENCE

The standard of liability in trespass (i.e., whether there could be liability in the absence of negligence) is a matter of some historical dispute. There was no question, however, that trespass could be committed carelessly as well as intentionally. By the end of the 19th century the defence of inevitable accident (para. 14.4.2) was interpreted to mean that if the defendant could show that he had not been negligent the plaintiff would fail (*Stanley* v *Powell* [1891] 1 QB 86). This effectively meant that the difference between trespass and negligence was the burden of proof. But there was an exception to this with accidents on the highway, where the plaintiff could sue either in negligence or trespass, but if he chose trespass he had the burden of proving negligence (*Holmes* v *Mather* (1875) LR 10 Ex 261—with highway accidents an inquiry into the *cause* of the accident tended to resolve itself into the question of which party was at fault, and the burden of proving that the defendant caused the harm was always the plaintiff's).

This was the position until *Fowler* v *Lanning* [1959] 1 QB 426 where Diplock J held that in all cases of unintentional trespass to the person the burden of proving negligence lies with the plaintiff. A statement of claim that alleged merely that the defendant shot the plaintiff did not disclose a cause of action. The plaintiff must plead that the defendant shot him either intentionally or negligently, and the burden of proving negligence was the plaintiff's (for criticism see *Salmond and Heuston*, p. 136). This was approved by the Court of Appeal in *Letang* v *Cooper* [1965] 1 QB 232. The plaintiff was sunbathing on a patch of grass where there were parked cars, when the defendant ran over her. The action in negligence was barred by the Limitation Act which specified a three-year time-limit for claims in respect of personal injuries in actions for 'negligence, nuisance or breach of duty'. It was held that these words applied to an action in trespass and therefore the claim was statute-barred. A cause of action was simply a factual situation entitling a person to a remedy, and so an action based on the defendant's carelessness is still an action for negligence, even though it could also be classified as trespass to the person (per Diplock LJ). Lord Denning MR said that actions for personal injuries should no longer be divided into trespass (for direct harm) and case (for indirect harm), but according to the nature of the defendant's conduct. If it was intentional the action was trespass, if unintentional then negligence was appropriate. On this view it would not be possible to commit trespass to the person negligently.

In *Wilson* v *Pringle* [1986] 2 All ER 440 the Court of Appeal has apparently (at pp. 443 and 445) approved Lord Denning's view that where the contact between plaintiff and defendant was unintentional the claim must be brought in negligence. Even if, applying the judgment of Diplock LJ in *Letang* v

Cooper, it is still possible to sue for negligent trespass to the person, in practice there would be virtually no difference between that action and an action in negligence, the burden of proving fault being with the plaintiff in each case. This effectively limits trespass to the person to intentional conduct by the defendant, though it should be noted that intention relates to the defendant's actions, not necessarily the harm that results from his actions (but see *Wasson v Chief Constable of the Royal Ulster Constabulary* [1987] 8 NIJB 34, 55 where the 'unintentional' use of unreasonable force defeated a police officer's plea of self-defence resulting in liability for battery). Thus, A may be liable in trespass to the person for 'accidentally' striking C, having intended to strike B (see para. 12.2).

12.2 ASSAULT AND BATTERY

'An assault is an act which causes another person to apprehend the infliction of immediate, unlawful, force on his person; a battery is the actual infliction of unlawful force on another person' (*Collins v Wilcock* [1984] 3 All ER 374, 377). There may be an assault without a battery. In *Stephens v Myers* (1830) 4 C & P 349 the defendant threatened the plaintiff and moved towards him with a clenched fist, but he was prevented from reaching the plaintiff by someone else. The defendant was liable for assault. The threat must put the plaintiff in reasonable apprehension of an *immediate* battery, and so if the defendant is clearly unable to carry out the threat (e.g., a gesture from a prisoner behind bars) there is no assault (*Thomas v National Union of Mineworkers (South Wales Area)* [1985] 2 All ER 1, 20—violent gestures by picketing miners to working miners in passing vehicles where pickets held back by police, no assault). But pointing a gun at the plaintiff which, unknown to the plaintiff, is unloaded, would produce a reasonable apprehension of a battery and therefore constitutes assault, even though the defendant could not carry out the threat to shoot (*R v St George* (1840) 9 C & P 483, 493; *Blake v Barnard* (1840) 9 C & P 626, which goes the other way, is wrong in principle). Fear is unnecessary. The test is whether the plaintiff reasonably apprehended the infliction of a battery, irrespective of what effect this had on him.

It has been said that threatening words alone, unaccompanied by some act, will not constitute assault, but the authorities are divided on this point (*Meade's Case* (1823) 1 Lew CC 184—not assault; *R v Wilson* [1955] 1 WLR 493—assault; *Clerk and Lindsell,* para. 12–13, and *Salmond and Heuston,* p. 122, favour *Meade* but cf. *Winfield and Jolowicz,* p. 62, and *Fleming,* p. 26). But words accompanying a threatening gesture may indicate that there is no intention to carry out the threat. In *Tuberville v Savage* (1669) 1 Mod 3 the defendant put his hand to his sword, saying 'If it were not assize-time, I would not take such language from you'. This was held not to be an assault. A conditional threat, such as 'I will break your neck if you do not leave' will constitute an assault, at least where there are accompanying gestures and the defendant has no authority to require the plaintiff to leave (*Read v Coker* (1853) 13 CB 850).

There can be a battery without an assault, as where someone is struck from behind or while asleep. The force applied does not have to be personal contact. It can consist of throwing water on the plaintiff (*Pursell* v *Horn* (1838) 8 A & E 602), pulling something from his grasp (*Green* v *Goddard* (1702) 2 Salk 641), pulling a chair from under him (*Hopper* v *Reeve* (1817) 7 Taunt 698), applying a 'tone rinse' to his hair (*Nash* v *Sheen* [1953] CLY 3726), or striking a horse that the plaintiff was riding causing him to be thrown (*Dodwell* v *Burford* (1670) 1 Mod 24). It has even been argued that 'passive smoking' amounts to a battery (McCartney (1988) 138 NLJ 425). But mere passive obstruction of the plaintiff's passage is not a battery, because the tort requires some positive act (*Innes* v *Wylie* (1844) 1 Car & Kir 257).

No one may touch another without his or her consent or some lawful justification (see para. 12.5 for defences). Any contact with the plaintiff, no matter how trivial, is sufficient 'force'. In *Cole* v *Turner* (1704) 6 Mod 149 Holt CJ said that 'the least touching of another in anger is a battery'. This is important because the tort protects the plaintiff not only from physical injury, but also his personal dignity from any form of physical molestation (*Collins* v *Wilcock* [1984] 3 All ER 374). There is no need for any hostile intent, so an unwanted kiss may be a battery.

This is subject to two possible qualifications. First, certain forms of contact are regarded as an unavoidable and generally accepted consequence of social intercourse and therefore not actionable: casual jostling in a busy street or shop; touching someone to engage his attention; a congratulatory slap on the back; all are treated as acceptable if kept within reasonable bounds (*Cole* v *Turner*; *Tuberville* v *Savage*; *Collins* v *Wilcock*). These situations are usually considered to be instances of implied consent, though in *Collins* v *Wilcock* they were regarded as 'falling within a general exception embracing all physical contact which is generally acceptable in the ordinary conduct of daily life'. On the other hand there are limits to what is acceptable, even for trivial contacts. If someone forces his way in 'a rude and inordinate manner' (*Cole* v *Turner*), or persistently touches another for attention in the face of obvious disregard, or acts with some hostile intent, it will be a battery.

The second possible qualification stems from the decision of the Court of Appeal in *Wilson* v *Pringle* [1986] 2 All ER 440 where it was held that 'touching must be proved to be a hostile touching' in order to constitute a battery. On the face of it this would represent a serious and novel restriction on the protection afforded by the tort of battery. Despite Holt CJ's dictum ('the least touching . . . *in anger*'), battery has never been limited to overtly hostile contacts. The surgeon who operates without consent commits a battery although his intention, far from being hostile, is to benefit the patient (see the comment of Wood J in *T* v *T* [1988] 1 All ER 613, 625). The person pushed into a swimming-pool as a joke is surely entitled to maintain battery (*Williams* v *Humphrey*, *The Times*, 20 February 1975, criticised in *Wilson* v *Pringle* for not considering the issue of hostility). The problem turns on what is meant by 'hostile'. It 'cannot be equated with ill-will or malevolence. It cannot be governed by the obvious intention shown in acts like punching, stabbing or shooting. It cannot be solely governed by an expressed intention, although that may be strong evidence. But the element of hostility . . . must be a question of fact' (*Wilson* v *Pringle* [1986] 2 All ER 440, 447–8). Having said what 'hostility' does not mean, the court provided only one example of what it did mean. In *Collins* v *Wilcock* a police officer touched a woman without an intention to do more than restrain her temporarily. This was a hostile contact because the officer was acting unlawfully, having no power to restrain her (cf. *Donnelly* v *Jackman* [1970] 1 WLR 562). In *Wilson* v *Pringle* itself a schoolboy was carrying a bag over his shoulder when another schoolboy pulled at the bag, causing him to fall and suffer an injury to his hip. The defendant argued that this was merely an act of horseplay, and the court held that there was a triable issue as to whether the contact was hostile. This is highly unsatisfactory. The exception for trivial social contact has been effectively extended to the practical joker, provided he can establish as a question of fact that the prank was 'generally acceptable in the ordinary conduct of daily life'. An individual's claim to protection from such molestation should not depend upon whether others regard it as 'unacceptable'. A woman's right to decline unwanted male attention, for example, must not be curtailed by the absence of any hostile intent or the possibility that some people might regard her reaction as fastidious. In *F* v *West Berkshire Health Authority* [1989] 2 All ER 545, 564, Lord Goff doubted whether a touching must be 'hostile' for the purpose of battery: 'A prank that gets out of hand, an over-friendly slap on the back, surgical treatment by a surgeon who mistakenly thinks that the patient has consented to it, all these things may transcend the bounds of lawfulness, without being characterised as hostile. Indeed, the suggested qualification is difficult to reconcile with the principle that any touching of another's body is, in the absence of lawful excuse, capable of amounting to a battery and a trespass'. It is respectfully submitted that this view is correct.

The defendant must have intended to commit the act that constitutes the trespass, but an intention to injure is not necessary (*Wilson* v *Pringle* [1986] 2 All ER 440, 445. This has long been the law, see Trindade (1982) 2 OJLS 211, 219–25). Often he will intend both, but not always. Possibly, recklessness will suffice (Trindade, op. cit.). Moreover, if A, intending to strike B, misses B but accidentally strikes C he is liable in battery to C on the basis of a 'transferred' intention (*James* v *Campbell* (1832) 5 C & P 372; *Livingstone* v *Ministry of Defence* [1984] NI 356, NICA, soldier who fired a baton round at a rioter but missed and struck the plaintiff held to have intentionally applied force to the plaintiff; liable in battery unless the use of force could be justified by a defence).

It is arguable that where a person intends to cause physical harm and does cause that harm then he should be liable in trespass. In *Wilkinson* v *Downton* [1897] 2 QB 57 the defendant told the plaintiff that her husband had been seriously injured in an accident. This was untrue, but was intended as a 'joke'. The plaintiff suffered nervous shock. Wright J held the defendant liable, because he had wilfully done an act calculated to cause physical harm to the plaintiff, i.e., to infringe her legal right to personal safety, and had thereby caused physical harm. Since the defendant's act was obviously intended to produce some effect of the kind that it did cause, an intention to produce the harm was imputed to the defendant, and it was no answer to say more harm was done than was anticipated, 'for that is commonly the case with all wrongs' (approved in *Janvier* v *Sweeney* [1919] 2 KB 316, CA—note that at the time of *Wilkinson* v *Downton* there was no liability in negligence for nervous shock).

The problem with treating this as either an assault or a battery is that the harm is indirect and there is no application, or threat, of force. It could be regarded as a residuary category of trespass to the person or as a separate unclassified tort (*Winfield and Jolowicz*, p. 74) but, whichever view is preferred, the underlying principle that a person is liable for any intentionally inflicted bodily harm is sound. The man who poisons someone's drink, who deliberately infects someone with a contagious disease, who startles someone descending a flight of stairs causing a fall, who prevents a doctor from treating a sick patient—in each case he *ought* to be liable even though the specific requirements of assault or battery are not satisfied. Now that the Court of Appeal has said that the relevant distinction between trespass and negligence is intentional and unintentional conduct (para. 12. 1), it is arguable that it is time to drop the requirement of directness in trespass to the person, at least for intended physical harm. If this is thought to be too revolutionary, the courts would have to rely on a general principle of liability drawn from *Wilkinson* v *Downton*.

It has also been persuasively argued that the intentional infliction of purely mental distress falling short of nervous shock should be an actionable tort (Trindade (1986) 6 OJLS 219; for the distinction between nervous shock and mental distress see para. 2.2.4.3). Indeed, in *Hunter* v *Canary Wharf Ltd* [1997] 2 All ER 426, Lord Hoffmann (at p. 452, *obiter*) could see no reason why the rule in *Wilkinson* v *Downton*, being a species of deliberate harm, had to be restricted by rules in negligence that required plaintiffs to suffer a recognisable psychiatric illness. Also, in both *Burnett* v *George* (1986), [1992] 1 FLR 525 and *Khorasandjian* v *Bush* [1993] 3 WLR 476 the Court of Appeal had held that an injunction could be granted to restrain a defendant from harassing the plaintiff by persistent unwanted telephone calls relying on the principle of *Wilkinson* v *Downton* and *Janvier* v *Sweeney*. In *Burnett* v *George* the injunction was limited to restraining the defendant from doing acts calculated to cause harm in the form of impairment to the plaintiff's health. In *Khorasandjian* v *Bush*, however, the injunction was cast in wider terms to cover conduct that created a risk of future harm to the plaintiff's health. *Janvier* v *Sweeney* was accepted as establishing that verbal threats could be actionable if they caused illness, and to the extent that there were threats to assault the plaintiff made in the course of the defendant's campaign of harassment, they could be restrained by injunction even without consequent illness since they were threats to commit a tort. Furthermore, although there was no medical evidence and it could not be said that the plaintiff was suffering from any physical or psychiatric illness, the plaintiff was under enormous stress and there was 'an obvious risk that the cumulative effect of continued and unrestrained further harassment such as she has undergone would cause such an illness' (per Dillon LJ at p. 483). Following *Janvier* v *Sweeney* the court was entitled to look at the defendant's conduct as a whole and restrain also those aspects of his campaign of harassment which could not strictly be classified as threats to commit the torts of assault or battery (ibid.). The Court of Appeal's decision in *Khorasandjian* v *Bush*, although said to be based on *Wilkinson* v *Downton* and *Janvier* v *Sweeney*, was undoubtedly an extension of the principle established in those cases and, in effect, recognised a new form of damage which has more to do with protecting an individual's interest in privacy than personal security (notwithstanding that the common law had consistently refused to recognise a claim for invasion of privacy: see *Kaye* v *Robertson* [1991] FSR 62; see further Fricker [1992] Fam Law 158 and Brazier [1992] Fam Law 346, both written before *Khorasandjian* v *Bush*; for comment on *Khorasandjian* v *Bush* see Bridgeman and Jones (1994) 14 LS 180; Cooke (1994) 57 MLR 289; Townshend-Smith (1995) 24 Anglo-Am LR 299). Subsequently, in *Burris* v *Azadani* [1995] 4 All ER 802, the Court of Appeal held that the court's power to grant an injunction was not limited to restraining conduct which is in itself tortious or otherwise unlawful. Thus, the court had the power to make an 'exclusion zone' order despite the fact that the conduct to be restrained was not in itself tortious or otherwise unlawful, provided the order was reasonably regarded as necessary for the protection of the plaintiff's legitimate interests from harassment. Sir Thomas Bingham MR also appeared to accept that harassment could be regarded as an independent tort.

The position in relation to harassment was subsequently altered through the combined effect of the Protection from Harassment Act 1997 and the House of Lords' decision in *Hunter* v *Canary Wharf Ltd* [1997] 2 All ER 426 (para. 7.1.4). In *Hunter*, the House of Lords treated *Khorasandjian* v *Bush* as a claim in private nuisance and overruled it because the plaintiff did not have a qualifying proprietary or possessory interest in the land affected (she was a teenager residing with her parents). Their Lordships were satisfied that this would not necessarily leave a harassed plaintiff without a civil remedy, particularly in view of the enactment of a statutory regime to address the problem of stalking and harassment, in the shape of the Protection from Harassment Act 1997 (see Lawson-Cruttenden and Addison, *Guide to the Protection from Harassment Act 1997*, (1997), Blackstone Press). The 1997 Act creates both civil remedies (s. 3(1)) and criminal offences (s. 2(1)) in respect of 'a course of conduct which amounts to harassment' which the defendant 'knows or ought to know amounts to harassment' (s. 1(1)) (for other developments in the criminal law relating to telephone harassment, see *R* v *Ireland* [1997] 3 WLR 534, HL; for comment see Gardner (1998) 114 LQR 33). This is an objective standard. The defendant will be taken to have known that his conduct was harassing 'if a reasonable person in possession of the same information would think the course of conduct amounted to harassment (s. 1(2)). 'Harassment' is not defined in the 1997 Act, though it is stated in s. 7(2) that it 'includes alarming the person or causing the person distress', and 'conduct' includes speech (s. 7(4)). The civil remedies available to a plaintiff are damages and/or injunction. Damages can be awarded for, inter alia, any anxiety caused by the harassment and any resulting financial loss. Unusually, the Act provides that breach of a civil injunction granted for the purpose of restraining the defendant from pursuing harassing conduct is a criminal offence (s. 3(6)). The remedies are available even where the harassment does not cause the plaintiff to fear that violence will be used, effectively codifying *Khorasandjian* v *Bush*. The 1997 Act does not, however, catch a single act of harassment, hence the reference in s. 1(1) to 'a course of conduct'. The harassment must occur at least twice to be actionable. There are defences for conduct pursued for the purpose of preventing or detecting crime; pursued under any enactment or rule of law or to comply with a condition or requirement imposed by any person under any enactment; or for conduct that was reasonable in the particular circumstances (s. 1(3)).

It remains to be seen whether the 1997 Act provides adequate protection for harassed plaintiffs, although it has already been held that the Act was not intended to be used to prevent individuals from exercising a right to protest about issues of public interest and the courts will resist attempts to interpret it widely (*Huntingdon Life Sciences Ltd* v *Curtin, The Times*, 11 December 1997). What is clear is that the House of Lords in *Hunter* anticipate that such plaintiffs ought to seek refuge in the new statutory provisions rather than in any common law developments. It is noteworthy, though, that the overruling of one such development in that case (*Khorasandjian* v *Bush*) was expressly because of its inadequacies as a nuisance action. It was not specifically criticised as a species of *Wilkinson* v *Downton*, which Lord Hoffmann (at p. 452) was content not only to preserve as a general cause of action, but even to treat as an appropriate one for the intended infliction of mental distress falling short of nervous shock. It may still, therefore, be open for a plaintiff to rely on the common law, in the name of *Wilkinson* v *Downton*, in a harassment case, either as a 'second string' to the statutory cause of action, or even as a first port of call in the case of the single act of harassment not covered by the 1997 Act. (Note also that it is possible for numerous obscene telephone calls to different people to be treated as a public nuisance, on account of the cumulative effect on a section of the public: *R* v *Johnson* [1997] 1 WLR 367.)

12.3 CRIMINAL INJURIES

Most cases of assault and battery are also criminal offences. The Criminal Injuries Compensation Scheme, introduced in 1964, provides for State-funded payments to persons who suffer criminal injuries. The scheme has now been placed on a statutory footing by the Criminal Injuries Compensation Act 1995 (the '1995 Act'). Originally, it was wholly administrative in nature, with payments being *ex gratia* and decisions subject to judicial review but not appeal as such. The first attempt to replace it with a statutory scheme (under the Criminal Justice Act 1988, ss. 108–117 and schs 6 and 7) floundered in the face of concern expressed by the Criminal Injuries Compensation Board (which then administered the scheme) that the immediate introduction of a statutory scheme would add to the problem of delays in processing claims. Consequently, that statutory scheme was not brought into force. In the interim, a revised administrative scheme was brought in, to apply to all applications received on or after 1 February 1990 (see *Hepple and Matthews*, pp. 920–7). As the new statutory scheme under the 1995 Act applies to applications received on or after 1 April 1996, the administrative scheme remains in place to deal with outstanding claims made before that date. Given its residual importance, it is still necessary to appreciate the key features of the earlier scheme.

The administrative scheme was open to those who sustained personal injury directly attributable to a 'crime of violence', a term that was not defined. The absence of a definition meant that eligibility was determined on a case by case basis. Though this could result in some anomalous decisions (see *Atiyah*, pp. 257–61), the Court of Appeal seemed to dismiss this problem with the sweeping statement that the Board 'will recognise a crime of violence when they hear about it' (*R v Criminal Injuries Compensation Board, ex parte Warner* [1986] 2 All ER 478). On this basis, they confirmed that arson, poisoning and trespass on a railway all qualified as crimes of violence, and that the scheme also covered injury sustained in the apprehension or attempted apprehension of an offender or the prevention or attempted prevention of an offence. Applications for compensation could be made by the victims themselves, or by a dependant for loss of dependency if the victim died as a result of a criminal injury. It was not necessary for there to have been a criminal conviction of the offender before a claim could be made, but the Board had a discretion to withhold or reduce compensation if the claimant did not take reasonable steps to inform the police of the circumstances of the injury and cooperate in bringing the offender to justice, or if there was a possibility that the offender might benefit from the award. The Board also had a discretion to withhold or reduce an award in the light of the claimant's criminal convictions or unlawful conduct, or his conduct in connection with the injury. Also excluded from the scope of the scheme were: (a) injuries resulting from domestic violence unless the offender has been prosecuted and the claimant has ceased to live in the same household (unless there are good reasons for this); (b) accidental injuries sustained in apprehending an offender or preventing the commission of an offence unless the claimant took an exceptional risk which was justified in all the circumstances; (c) injuries arising from the use of a motor vehicle on a road where the injury would be covered by compulsory insurance or by the Motor Insurers' Bureau (see para. 1.3); (d) minor injuries where the compensation would be less than the minimum award.

Under the administrative scheme compensation awards were assessed on a similar basis to tort damages, save for an earnings limit of one and a half times the gross average industrial earnings, full deduction of all social security benefits and certain pensions accruing as a result of the injury, no allowance for the cost of private medical treatment unless it was essential (cf. tort damages: see paras 15.1.3.1, 15.1.3.2.4) and no allowance for exemplary damages. Consistent with tort damages, the compensation award would normally take the form of a lump sum, though there was provision for seeking further compensation if, since the previous award, the claimant's medical condition had deteriorated as a result of the injury and it would be unjust not to award a further sum. (Any compensation received from the offender through a civil action or by virtue of an order under the Powers of Criminal Courts Act 1973, s. 35 (see below) would be deducted from the criminal injuries award, or if received after the award, the claimant would be liable to repay the Board, where the loss for which he received an award had been reduced.) Significantly, under the guise of a further revision to the administrative scheme, the Home Secretary tried to replace this quasi-tortious basis of assessment with a compensation 'tariff', based on objective loss of amenity levels. Whilst such standardisation might achieve the twin objectives of simplification and cost saving, the proposed tariff system was fiercely criticised, *inter alia*, for providing insufficient levels of payment (Holgate (1995) 15(2) *Litigation* 61), and was declared *ultra vires* by the House of Lords in *R v Secretary of State for the Home Department ex parte Fire Brigades Union* [1995] 2 WLR 1 on the basis that only Parliament could so radically alter the scheme that it had set up in the (albeit unimplemented) Criminal Justice Act 1988.

Under the new statutory scheme the Criminal Injuries Compensation Board is replaced by a Criminal Injuries Compensation Authority, which hears applications for compensation (received on or after 1 April 1996) from those who have sustained 'criminal injuries' (s. 1(1)) or from their dependants if the victim dies. The application is dealt with by a claims officer, whose decision can be subject to review by a more senior officer, with a further right of appeal to the Authority itself. Though there is no formal definition of 'criminal injuries' in the 1995 Act, the scheme that it sets up does provide some guidance, perhaps in order to avoid the sort of difficulties of interpretation that arose under the previous scheme with its undefined reference to a 'crime of violence'. Nonetheless, 'criminal injuries' are defined in fairly broad terms, effectively adopting the broad categories of eligibility formulated under the administrative scheme, rather than the greater precision afforded by the list of offences set out in the unadopted statutory scheme (Criminal Justice Act 1988 s. 109; Duff (1989) 52 MLR 518). So, the scheme is available to those who have sustained personal injury (including any medically recognised psychiatric or psychological injury or disease) in Great Britain directly attributable to a crime of violence (including arson or poisoning), an offence of trespass on the railway, the apprehension or attempted apprehension of an offender or the prevention or attempted prevention of an offence. Injury attributable to a road traffic accident remains outside the scope of the scheme, as does accidental injury sustained in crime prevention or rescue, unless in these latter cases the victim took an exceptional risk. As before, though a conviction is not a precondition of eligibility, applicants may prejudice their awards if they fail to take reasonable steps to inform the police of the circumstances of the injury and cooperate in bringing the offender to justice. Similarly the award can be reduced by reference to the general 'conduct' of applicants before, during or after the incident, and to their general character as evidenced, *inter alia*, by criminal convictions (unless 'spent' by virtue of the Rehabilitation of Offenders Act 1974).

If the new statutory scheme and the administrative scheme seem to share much in the way of basic procedures and eligibility mechanism, the resemblance ends when account is taken of the basis upon which compensation awards are assessed. For, unlike the previous scheme, awards made under the new statutory scheme are not assessed by analogy with tort rules. Instead, compensation is paid by reference to a 'tariff', under which standard awards relate to specific types of injury, with provision for adjustment according to severity but not according to other subjective factors such as age, sex and financial circumstances (Burn (1996) 93(12) *Law Society Gazette* 22; for criticism of the 'tariff' system of compensation, see Duff (1998) 18 OJLS 105). In the light of the House of Lords' decision in *R* v *Secretary of State for the Home Department, ex parte Fire Brigades Union*, the 1995 Act became the only legitimate means of achieving such a radical change. However, the new tariff differs from the one rejected in that case, by providing for payment for loss of earnings and special care for those incapacitated for 28 weeks or more. Only time will tell whether this 'enhanced' tariff (Holgate op. cit.) will prove any more popular than the earlier one and whether the new scheme will prove generally more efficient than the previous administrative scheme.

Reactions to the old scheme varied considerably and it may be that the new statutory scheme will divide opinion along similar lines. On one view it supplements the law of tort by ensuring that funds are available to compensate a person who has undoubtedly been the victim of a tort (*Winfield and Jolowicz,* p. 37). Very few offenders have the resources to satisfy a judgment (perhaps one in a thousand: *Atiyah,* p. 250), and so in most cases the tort remedy is useless. The scheme merely 'guarantees payment' (cf. the Motor Insurers' Bureau, para. 1.3). On the other hand it has been criticised as merely 'selecting yet another group of unfortunates for special treatment' when other, equally deserving victims of misfortune receive little or no compensation (*Atiyah,* p. 253; for discussion of the underlying rationale of the scheme see *Atiyah,* pp. 252–7; Veitch and Miers (1975) 38 MLR 139, 148–52; and Duff [1995] 1 JR 102).

Despite strong criticism (principally by *Atiyah,* ch. 12, who points out some particularly anomalous cases) the scheme has been regarded as a popular success. In 1986–87 some £48 million was paid out, and it has been suggested that the law relating to intentional torts has already been superseded (Veitch and Miers (1975) 38 MLR 139, 152). This is effectively true of cases involving personal injuries, at least where they are serious, because of the likelihood that an offender will be unable to pay damages. Trespass to the person is still important, however, in protecting an individual from molestation and indignity falling short of personal injury, and in particular from the abuse of power by agencies of the State (see especially *Weir,* p. 333; Trindade (1982) 2 OJLS 211, 214–16, though note that most of Trindade's comments about the advantages of tort over criminal injuries compensation assume that the defendant can pay). In *White* v *Metropolitan Police Commissioner, The Times,* 24 April 1982, for example, two plaintiffs were each awarded £20,000 exemplary damages for assault, false imprisonment and malicious prosecution by the police, and in *Taylor* v *Metropolitan Police*

Commissioner, The Times, 6 December 1989, exemplary damages of £70,000 were awarded in an action against the police for false imprisonment and malicious prosecution.

Under the Powers of Criminal Courts Act 1973, ss. 35–8, as amended, where a person is convicted of an offence, the court has a discretion to order him to pay compensation to the victim for any personal injury, loss or damage resulting from the offence (on the meaning of 'personal injury' see *Bond* v *Chief Constable of Kent* [1983] 1 All ER 456). The court must take into account the offender's means, and in the magistrates' court there is a limit of £2,000 on the amount of the order (but no limit in the Crown Court). No award can be made to the dependants of a deceased person except for funeral expenses and bereavement (s. 35(1)(3B) and (3D)). An award may only be made in respect of injury, loss or damage resulting from a road accident if it is in respect of damage to property occurring while it was out of the owner's possession (where the offender is charged under the Theft Act 1968), or if the offender is uninsured in respect of the vehicle and compensation is not payable under the Motor Insurers' Bureau agreement (s. 35(3)). In any event an award will not be made to dependants in relation to a death due to a motor accident. The court also has a power to make an order applying the proceeds of sale not be made to dependants in relation to a death due to a motor accident. The court also has a power to make an order applying the proceeds of sale of property forfeited by the offender for the benefit of the victim (s. 43A, added by Criminal Justice Act 1988, s. 107). Compensation orders are not appropriate in complicated cases (*R* v *Kneeshaw* [1975] 1 QB 57; *R* v *Vivian* [1979] 1 All ER 48) or where the payments will extend over several years (*R* v *Daly* [1974] 1 WLR 133). The vast majority of compensation orders relate to the offences of criminal damage and theft, but they do play a small role in compensating people who have suffered minor injuries as a result of a criminal offence (see Ogden [1985] Crim LR 500).

Finally, it should be noted that summary criminal proceedings for assault or battery may constitute a bar to subsequent civil proceedings (Offences against the Person Act 1861, ss. 42–5). This applies whether there has been a conviction or an acquittal, provided there was a hearing on the merits and the proceedings were commenced by or on behalf of 'the party aggrieved'. The solution to this rule from a plaintiff's point of view is to sue first and prosecute later (North (1966) 29 MLR 16), though in minor cases it might be simpler and cheaper to prosecute and apply for a compensation order (but bearing in mind the different standards of proof in criminal and civil cases).

12.4 FALSE IMPRISONMENT

False imprisonment is 'the unlawful imposition of constraint on another's freedom of movement from a particular place' (*Collins* v *Wilcock* [1984] 3 All ER 374, 377). Imprisonment in the sense of incarceration is not necessary, nor is any use of force. Submitting to the control of a policeman at the defendant's instigation is sufficient (*Warner* v *Riddiford* (1858) 4 CB NS 180). So a person may be imprisoned in an open field if his movement is restrained, e.g., by the defendant pointing a gun and saying 'Do not move'. Similarly, the Ministry of Defence's power to compel service in the armed forces could amount to total restraint and so could constitute false imprisonment if unlawfully exercised (*Prichard* v *Ministry of Defence, The Times,* 27 January 1995). An unlawful arrest constitutes false imprisonment, as does preventing someone from leaving. Where a person, such as a store detective, requests a police officer to take the plaintiff into custody, that person can be liable for false imprisonment if the arrest turns out to be unlawful. The test will be 'whether what [the store detective] did went beyond laying information before police officers for them to take such action as they saw fit and amounted to some direction, or procuring, or direct request, or direct encouragement that they should act by way of arresting . . .' (*Davidson* v *Chief Constable of the North Wales Police* [1994] 2 All ER 597, 604 per Sir Thomas Bingham MR; for comment see Woollard (1995) 3 Tort L Rev 93). Consent is a defence, and so a person who voluntarily accompanies a police officer to the police station is not falsely imprisoned, though it is different if the officer makes it clear that he has no choice (*Alderson* v *Booth* [1969] 2 QB 216).

The restraint must be complete. If the plaintiff could have left, although not by the route that he would have preferred, there is no imprisonment. In *Bird* v *Jones* (1845) 7 QB 742 the plaintiff insisted on his right to use part of the highway that had been cordoned off, but he was prevented from doing so by the defendant. The plaintiff was told that he could go back the way that he had come, but could not go straight on. This was not false imprisonment because it was not a total restraint of his liberty. Thus, if there is a means of escape, then provided it is reasonable to expect the plaintiff to have taken it there will be no false imprisonment. Any escape involving danger is probably unreasonable. In *R* v *Bournewood Community and Mental Health NHS Trust, ex parte L* [1998] 3 All ER 289 a majority of the House of Lords held that a voluntary mental patient in an open, unlocked ward was not in fact detained, even though if he had attempted to leave he would have been prevented from doing so by the medical staff, who would then have taken steps to detain him compulsorily under the Mental Health Act 1983. This was notwithstanding that it is not necessary for a plaintiff to be aware that he is being detained for the purpose of the tort of false imprisonment (see *Meering* v *Grahame-White Aviation Co. Ltd,* below). Lord Goff said (at p. 298) that there must *in fact* be a complete deprivation of, or restraint upon, the plaintiff's liberty, and the deprivation must be actual, rather than potential. A 'restraint upon the plaintiff's liberty which is conditional upon his seeking to exercise his freedom' would not amount to false imprisonment, whereas an 'actual retraint upon his liberty', such as placing a policeman outside the door of a room to stop the plaintiff leaving would amount to false imprisonment (but query why the latter case is not also conditional upon the plaintiff seeking to exercise his freedom—the policeman would have no need to act to restrain the plaintiff if he did not attempt to leave the room). Lord Steyn, dissenting on this point, said that the argument that the patient was free to leave was 'a fairy tale'. The health care professionals had detained him because they intentionally assumed control over him to such a degree (including sedating him with drugs, keeping him under continuous observation, preventing his carers from visiting and resolving to apply for compulsory admission if he physically resisted) as to amount to a complete deprivation of his liberty.

An occupier of premises is entitled to impose reasonable conditions on the manner in which entrants leave the premises. In *Robinson* v *Balmain Ferry Co. Ltd* [1910] AC 295 the defendants operated a ferry, with turnstiles for payment of the fare on only one side of the river. Notices stipulated that a penny must be paid on entering and leaving the wharf. The plaintiff paid to enter, but changed his mind about taking the ferry. He then refused to pay another penny to exit the wharf and the defendants prevented him from leaving. The Privy Council held that this was not false imprisonment. The plaintiff had contracted to leave the wharf by another way (i.e., on the ferry) and, it was said, the payment of a penny was a reasonable condition on his leaving by another route (i.e., by the turnstile; see *Weir*, p. 352, questions 2–6). The facts in *Robinson* v *Balmain Ferry Co. Ltd* were rather unusual. It should not be taken as authority for a wider proposition that there is a general right to detain people to enforce contractual rights. In *Sunbolf* v *Alford* (1838) 3 M & W 248 an innkeeper locked up a customer for not paying the bill. This was false imprisonment. *Robinson* v *Balmain Ferry Co. Ltd* might be distinguished on the basis that restraint was not complete, because the plaintiff could have left the wharf via the ferry, even though this would have involved waiting for it to depart. But it is clearly reasonable in some circumstances to impose conditions as to the point, both in time and place, of exit. So a passenger on a train or a boat or plane cannot demand to get off at an unscheduled stop (*Herd* v *Weardale Steel, Coal & Coke Co. Ltd* [1915] AC 67, 71).

In *Herd* v *Weardale Steel, Coal & Coke Co. Ltd* itself, a miner employed by the defendants refused to carry out what he considered to be dangerous work, and asked to use the lift to be brought to the surface before the end of his shift. The defendants refused and the House of Lords held that this was not false imprisonment because the plaintiff had voluntarily descended the mine on the basis that he would be brought to the surface at the end of his shift, not before. An alternative explanation of the decision is that there was no positive act by the defendants, and that trespass does not lie for a mere omission (because any consequences would be indirect; on the distinction between direct and indirect consequences see *Harnett* v *Bond* [1925] AC 669). It has been argued that both *Robinson* and *Herd* should not be treated as authority for the proposition that the imposition of a reasonable condition may negative false imprisonment. Rather they are cases of consent to the restraint of liberty. Such consent may normally be withdrawn at any time, but in some situations where there is substantial inconvenience in meeting the withdrawal of consent, the consent may be treated as irrevocable for a critical period (Tan (1981) 44 MLR 166). This explains the case of the passenger on a train or a boat, and probably explains *Herd* in part, but it does not deal with the decision in *Robinson*. It may be that both cases are wrong on their facts (ibid. pp. 173–5), but on any view they are unsatisfactory to the extent that they appear to sanction extra-judicial detention for breach of contract.

Does the plaintiff have to know that he has been detained in order to sue for false imprisonment? In *Meering* v *Grahame-White Aviation Co. Ltd* (1920) 122 LT 44 Atkin LJ said that the plaintiff's lack of knowledge was irrelevant, so a person could be falsely imprisoned while he was unconscious or insane or otherwise unaware of his position. This is contrary to a decision of the Court of Exchequer in *Herring* v *Boyle* (1834) 1 Cr M & R 377 which was not cited in *Meering* v *Grahame-White Aviation Co. Ltd.* The view of Atkin LJ has now been approved by the House of Lords in *Murray* v *Ministry of Defence* [1988] 2 All ER 521. A person who is unaware that he has been falsely imprisoned and has suffered no harm will normally receive only nominal damages, but because of the importance attached to individual liberty the detention will be actionable. Thus the kidnappers of a very young baby or a senile millionaire would be liable for false imprisonment (see, however, Williams (1991) 54 MLR 408,411, for criticism of the approach taken in *Murray* v *Ministry of Defence*).

A prisoner who is lawfully detained in prison under Prison Act 1952, s. 12, does not have a 'residual liberty' *vis-à-vis* the governor of the prison since he has no liberty to be in any place other than where the prison regime requires him to be, and therefore he has no liberty of which he can be deprived by the tort of false imprisonment (*Hague* v *Deputy Governor of Parkhurst Prison*; *Weldon* v *Home Office* [1991] 3 All ER 733, HL). Placing a prisoner in a strip cell or segregating him substituted one form of restraint for another and altered the conditions under which he was detained, but did not deprive him of any liberty which he had not already lost when initially confined under the authority of the Prison Act 1952, s. 12 which provides a complete defence to any claim for false imprisonment against the governor or anyone acting on his behalf (ibid.). Similarly, a prison governor is not liable for the tort of false imprisonment where a remand prisoner remains in prison after the expiry of a time limit through the failure of the Crown Prosecution Service to apply for its extension and in the absence of the prisoner's application for bail, nor will an action lie for breach of statutory duty (*Olotu* v *Secretary of State for the Home Department* [1997] 1 All ER 385, CA, para. 9.1.1; cf. *R* v *Governor of Brockhill Prison, ex parte Evans (No. 2)*, *The Times*, 6 July 1998, CA—a prisoner who is detained for additional days because her sentence of imprisonment was wrongly calculated is entitled to damages for false imprisonment, even though the error was due to a judicial decision which changed the basis of the calculation and the governor was not at fault). It was accepted in *Hague* that a prisoner could sue in respect of torts committed against him by fellow prisoners or prison officers acting outside the scope of their authority (including false imprisonment) because the defendant would not have the protection of s. 12. But the mere fact that the conditions under which a prisoner is detained are intolerable and seriously prejudicial to health does not change an otherwise lawful detention into false imprisonment: an alteration in the conditions of confinement does not change the nature of the confinement. Thus, false imprisonment is not a tort committed by degrees. There are two ingredients: the fact of imprisonment and the absence of lawful authority to justify it (per Lord Bridge at p. 743; see also the observations of

Lord Jauncey at pp. 756–7). A prisoner subjected to intolerable conditions while detained would have remedies in public law, and, if he sustained physical injury a remedy in the tort of negligence for breach of a duty of care owed by a gaoler to persons in his custody (see further Fordham [1991] Sing JLS 348). In *H* v *Secretary of State for the Home Department, The Times,* 7 May 1992 the Court of Appeal held that a prisoner who had been segregated from other prisoners under the Prison Rules, allegedly as a result of negligence, could not sue the prison authority in negligence since segregation was expressly authorised by the Prison Rules and could not of itself constitute intolerable conditions. If the treatment complained of fell short of being subjected to intolerable conditions the plaintiff would have a remedy in damages only if he could establish the tort of misfeasance in public office, which would require proof of malice (*Three Rivers District Council* v *Bank of England (No. 3)* [1996] 3 All ER 558; *Bennett* v *Commissioner of Police of the Metropolis* [1995] 1 WLR 488), and it would appear that the prison authorities can be vicariously liable for the tort of misfeasance in public office committed by a prison officer (*Racz* v *Home Office* [1994] 2 WLR 23, HL).

12.5 DEFENCES

Once the plaintiff has proved the direct interference that constitutes trespass, it is for the defendant to justify his action by reference to one of the defences. Necessity and inevitable accident are considered elsewhere (paras 14.4.2 and 14.4.3). Contributory negligence may be a defence in some circumstances (see para. 14.5.1), though it is not a defence to either false imprisonment or battery that the plaintiff has been convicted of an offence for which he was arrested, whether lawfully or unlawfully, by the defendant (*Hill* v *Chief Constable of South Yorkshire Police* [1990] 1 All ER 1046; *Simpson* v *Chief Constable of South Yorkshire Police, The Times,* 7 March 1991). Parents can administer reasonable chastisement to their children and restrain their freedom of movement (see Children and Young Persons Act 1933, s. 1(7)), but parental authority must be exercised for the welfare of the child. It might be thought that this authority lasts as long as the child is a minor, but it is arguable that a parent's authority varies with the child's capacity to determine his own best interests (following *Gillick* v *West Norfolk and Wisbech Area Health Authority* [1985] 3 All ER 402, para. 12.5.1; see also *R* v *Rahman* [1985] Crim LR 596—a parent can falsely imprison his child if he exceeds reasonable parental discipline). Certain statutes also render lawful what would otherwise amount to a trespass (e.g., the Mental Health Act 1983 provides for the compulsory admission to hospital and treatment of certain categories of mentally disordered persons, though the interference with individual liberty that such compulsion involves means that the Act is construed strictly as applying only when the prescribed conditions for detention are satisfied and only in respect of treatment for the patient's mental condition: see *St George's Healthcare NHS Trust* v *S* [1998] 3 All ER 673). Three defences—consent, lawful arrest and self-defence—will be considered in more detail.

12.5.1 Consent

There are many instances where conduct that would otherwise constitute trespass to the person is not actionable because of express or implied consent. It is a matter of some debate whether consent is a true defence in an action for trespass or whether the absence of consent is part and parcel of the tort itself. This issue resolves itself into the question of where the burden of proof lies. Must the plaintiff prove that he did not consent in order to establish his cause of action, or is it sufficient to prove a direct interference, leaving the defendant to assert and prove that the plaintiff consented? It has been held at first instance in this country that the plaintiff has the burden of proof (*Freeman* v *Home Office* [1983] 3 All ER 589, 594–5; cf. *R* v *Brown* [1993] 2 All ER 75, 92 per Lord Jauncey, suggesting that consent is a defence in criminal assault) but the position is more questionable in other Commonwealth jurisdictions (Blay (1987) 61 ALJ 25. Also cf. *Street*, p. 22 putting the burden on the plaintiff, with *Fleming*, p. 79 and *Salmond and Heuston*, p. 471 apparently placing it with the defendant). It remains convenient, however, to consider consent as a defence. The normal rule with other defences such as lawful arrest or self-defence is that the burden of proving the defence rests with the defendant.

Participants in a sport where physical contact is part and parcel of the game impliedly consent to contacts that occur within the rules of the game, and even to certain forms of contact that are not permitted under the rules. But a sportsman does not consent to force which could not reasonably be expected to happen in the course of a game, even in a very tough and physical sport such as rugby (*R* v *Billinghurst* [1978] Crim LR 553—a deliberate punch at a player without the ball). Even if some games degenerate into little more than 'open warfare', it is not *reasonable* to infer consent from the plaintiff's knowledge and continued participation. So in a game of football, deliberate contact with a player who does not have the ball is a battery (*McNamara* v *Duncan* (1979) 26 ALR 584). Similarly, in boxing, where the very object of the sport is to strike the opponent, there would be no implied consent to a deliberate foul punch. (Query why consent affords a defence in a boxing match when it would not do so in the case of a 'prize fight' in respect of similar injuries. See the observations of Lord Mustill in *R* v *Brown* [1993] 2 All ER 75, 108–9.) It is sometimes said that sportsmen 'assume the risk of injury' by their fellow competitors, but it is important to appreciate how this phrase is being used. It does *not* mean that they have assumed the risk of negligence, and therefore it is not an application of the defence of *volenti non fit injuria* (para. 14.1). In *Condon* v *Basi* [1985] 2 All ER 453, for example, a footballer was held liable in negligence for breaking another player's leg in a foul tackle. Consent in sport negatives liability in battery for those contacts that can reasonably be expected to occur in the course of the game, and so competitors 'assume the risk of injury' from such contacts in the absence of negligence. But this is no more than saying that in the absence of a battery there is no liability for non-negligently inflicted injury, and in this sense everyone 'assumes the risk of injury' when liability depends on the proof of negligence. (Consent is sometimes used to justify a lower standard of care in sport, see paras 3.2.2 and 14.1.4.)

It has been said that in 'an ordinary fight with fists' none of the participants would have an action in battery because they would be taken to have consented (*Lane* v *Holloway* [1968] 1 QB 379). The defence of *ex turpi causa* might also apply, para. 14.3. Consent is not a defence to a criminal assault involving actual or grievous bodily harm (*Attorney-General's Reference (No. 6 of 1980)* [1981] QB 715; *R* v *Brown* [1993] 2 All ER 75). In *Murphy* v *Culhane* [1977] QB 94 the plaintiff's husband was killed by the defendant, who subsequently pleaded guilty to manslaughter. It was alleged that this occurred during the course of a criminal affray brought about by the deceased and others who had decided to beat up the defendant. On these assumed facts Lord Denning MR said that the deceased would probably be unable to sue if he 'got more than he bargained for' because either he had 'assumed the risk' or *ex turpi causa*. This does not apply when the plaintiff's conduct was trivial but the defendant gave a 'savage blow out of all proportion to the occasion' (*Lane* v *Holloway*). Similarly, in *Barnes* v *Nayer*, *The Times*, 19 December 1986, in which the defendant killed the plaintiff's wife following a prolonged course of abuse, insult and minor assault by the plaintiff's family, the Court of Appeal held that, though in an appropriate case assumption of risk and *ex turpi causa* could be complete defences to an action for trespass to the person, the disparity between the deceased's behaviour and the defendant's response was so great that the defences must fail. There may be some difficulty in determining just when the parties were engaged in an 'ordinary fight with fists' and which blows are in proportion, but this will be treated as a question of fact. Moreover, many fights which may appear to be 'ordinary' will have been deliberately started by one person, and the other cannot realistically be taken to consent when he is exercising the right of self-defence (para. 12.5.3). It has been said, *obiter*, that where a defence of using reasonable force in the prevention of crime fails because the force is held to be excessive and therefore unreasonable (see para. 12.5.2), then the defendant cannot rely on either assumption of risk or *ex turpi causa* as a defence (*Lynch* v *Ministry of Defence* [1983] NI 216; query whether this applies only where the defendant is a soldier or a police officer).

Another common instance of consent is that of a patient who agrees to a medical examination or operation by a doctor or dentist. In the case of a competent adult patient any medical diagnosis or treatment which involves a direct application of force to the patient performed without the consent of the patient constitutes a battery. The corollary of this is that (subject to statutory exceptions such as compulsory treatment under the Mental Health Act 1983) an adult patient has an absolute right to refuse to consent to treatment, even if the consequence is that she will suffer serious injury or die (*Airedale NHS Trust* v *Bland* [1993] 1 All ER 821, 860, 866, 882, 889, HL). In appropriate circumstances a competent adult patient may be entitled to an injunction restraining a doctor or hospital from carrying out a medical procedure in the future without his express consent (*Re C (adult: refusal of treatment)* [1994] 1 WLR 290; Stern (1994) 110 LQR 541; Roberts (1994) 10 PN 98). In *Re S (adult: refusal of medical treatment)* [1992] 4 All ER 671, Sir Stephen Brown P granted a declaration that it would be lawful to perform a Caesarian section operation on a competent 30-year-old woman who had refused consent to the operation, because it was 'in the vital interests' of the patient and her unborn child. In view of the clear statement of principle by their Lordships in *Airedale NHS Trust v Bland* it is respectfully submitted that the decision in *Re S* is wrong, since there was no legal basis for overriding the decision of the competent patient to refuse surgical intervention (see Stern (1993) 56 MLR 238; de Gama [1993] JSWFL 147; Thomson (1994) 2 Med L Rev 127; Wells [1994] JSWFL 65). Note that a foetus has no legal personality until it is born and cannot, while a foetus, be made a ward of court: *Paton v British Pregnancy Advisory Service* [1978] 2 All ER 987; *C v S* [1987] 1 All ER 1230; *Re F (in utero)* [1988] 2 All ER 193.) Subsequently, in *Re MB (Medical Treatment)* [1997] 2 FLR 426, the Court of Appeal had to decide whether to grant a declaration overriding a patient's refusal to consent to a Caesarian section because of her needle phobia, where the absence of such a procedure might greatly increase the risk of death or brain damage to the foetus. The Court of Appeal were at pains to restate several inter-linking general principles. First, that, notwithstanding the decision of Sir Stephen Brown P in *Re S,* a mentally competent patient had an absolute right to refuse to consent to medical treatment for any reason, rational or irrational, or for no reason at all, even where that decision might lead to his or her death. Secondly, the Court of Appeal confirmed that the only situation in which it was lawful for doctors to intervene was if it was believed that the adult patient lacked the capacity to decide and the treatment was in the patient's best interests. Thirdly, it was stated that a court did not have the jurisdiction to take into account the interests of an unborn child at risk from the refusal of a competent mother to consent to medical intervention. In *Re MB*, the Court of Appeal observed that the decision in *Re S* was out of line with other authorities (particularly *Re T (Adult: Refusal of Treatment)* [1992] 4 All ER 649). It was explained away as having been made under excessive pressure of time, as a result of which the competence of the patient, who was not represented, could not adequately have been considered. Notably, though, having preserved the sanctity of the principle of competent patient autonomy, the Court of Appeal in *Re MB* still managed to authorise surgical intervention in the face of the patient's refusal to consent, because they accepted evidence that, at the critical point, her needle phobia put her in a state of such panic that she was incapable of making a decision and, thus, was incompetent. (See also *St George's Healthcare NHS Trust v S* [1998] 3 All ER 673, CA—no authority to detain a patient under the Mental Health Act 1983 in order to perform a non-consensual Caesarian section.)

In order to be valid the patient's consent must be 'real', but once a patient is informed in broad terms of the nature of the intended procedure and gives consent, that consent is real (*Chatterton v Gerson* [1981] 1 All ER 257, 265). A failure by the doctor to disclose the risks associated with the procedure, which would have allowed the patient to make an informed decision about giving consent, does not invalidate the consent (cf. *volenti non fit injuria,* para. 14.1.3). Any action in respect of a doctor's failure to disclose relevant information must be based in negligence, where the question is not whether the patient had a right to know but whether a reasonable doctor would have acted as the defendant did (*Sidaway* v *Bethlem Royal Hospital Governors* [1985] 1 All ER 643; Teff (1985) 101 LQR 432; see generally Kennedy (1984) 47 MLR 454 and Brazier (1987) 7 Legal Stud 169; cf. Tan (1987) 7 Legal Stud 149). This principle applies to both therapeutic and 'non-therapeutic' treatment (*Gold* v *Haringey Health Authority* [1987] 2 All ER 888), and also where the patient asks general (and possibly specific) questions about risks inherent in the treatment (*Blyth* v *Bloomsbury Area Health Authority* (1987) 5 PN 167; [1993] 4 Med LR 151, CA—notwithstanding dicta to the contrary in *Sidaway*, see Montgomery (1988) 51 MLR 245; cf. the approach of the High Court of Australia in *Rogers* v *Whitaker* (1992) 109 ALR 625 distinguishing *Sidaway* and requiring disclosure of a 1 in 14,000 risk of adverse consequences in response to questions asked by the patient; see Trindade (1993) 109 LQR 352; Jones (1994) 2 Tort L Rev 5; Malcolm (1994) 2 Tort L Rev 81).

Problems can arise with children who may not have the capacity to give a valid consent to treatment. The consent of a minor of 16 or 17 years is as valid as if he were of full age (Family Law Reform Act 1969, s. 8(1)). With children under 16 a child's capacity to consent depends on whether he has sufficient understanding and intelligence to know what is involved in the procedure (*Gillick* v *West Norfolk & Wisbech Area Health Authority* [1985] 3 All ER 402—the difficulty is to know what amounts to 'sufficient understanding' and whether the particularly high level of understanding that the House of Lords appeared to require in *Gillick* applies to all forms of medical treatment, or merely contraceptive advice and treatment: see Jones (1986) 2 PN 41, 43–5). It is generally assumed that where children lack the relevant capacity parental consent is both necessary and sufficient (*Gillick* v *West Norfolk & Wisbech Area Health Authority*; *F* v *West Berkshire Health Authority* [1989] 2 WLR 1025, 1041, CA per Lord Donaldson MR), though the court's inherent wardship jurisdiction may be invoked either to give or withhold consent to treatment, depending upon the court's assessment of the child's best interests (*Re J (A minor) (Wardship: medical treatment)* [1990] 3 All ER 930; *Re B (A minor) (Wardship: sterilisation)* [1987] 2 All ER 206; *Re D (A minor) (Wardship: sterilisation)* [1976] 1 All ER 326). It now appears to be the case that even where a minor is '*Gillick* competent', and therefore has the capacity to give a valid consent to medical treatment, this is not sufficient to enable the minor *to refuse* medical treatment where either the court, exercising its inherent jurisdiction for the protection of minors, authorises treatment or the minor's parent(s) gives a valid consent (*Re R (A minor) (Wardship: medical treatment)* [1991] 4 All ER 177; *Re W (A minor) (medical treatment)* [1992] 4 All ER 627, CA). This is the position with minors of 16 or 17 years as well as minors under 16. Although there could be practical problems if a competent minor refuses to submit to treatment (would the doctors physically restrain her to administer treatment?) the effect of the court order or a valid parental consent would be to protect the doctor from a claim in battery (for comment see Bainham (1992) 108 LQR 194; Douglas (1992) 55 MLR 569;

Mulholland (1993) 9 PN 21; Eekelaar (1993) 109 LQR 182; Bridgeman (1993) 13 LS 69).

With adult patients who need emergency treatment but are unable to consent because they are unconscious it has long been assumed that a doctor would be justified in proceeding on the basis of either a fictional implied consent or the defence of necessity (Skegg (1974) 90 LQR 512). The House of Lords has now confirmed that the doctor is justified by the principle of necessity (*F* v *West Berkshire Health Authority* [1989] 2 All ER 545; *R* v *Bournewood Community and Mental Health NHS Trust, ex parte L* [1998] 3 All ER 289). The test of what is necessary is the 'best interests of the patient' and this is to be determined by the *Bolam* test, i.e., the treatment was necessary if a responsible body of professional opinion agree that it was in the best interests of the patient to have that treatment (*Bolam* v *Friern Hospital Management Committee* [1957] 2 All ER 118, para. 3.2.1). This is a remarkable decision since it gives the medical profession considerable, and arguably unwarrantable, latitude to decide for itself what the limits of this defence should be (see Jones (1989) 5 PN 178; cf. the more cautious approach of Lord Donaldson MR in the Court of Appeal [1989] 2 WLR 1025; and of Wood J in *T* v *T* [1988] 1 All ER 613). On the other hand, Lord Goff said that in a case of temporary unconsciousness the doctor should do no more than is reasonably required in the best interests of the patient, before he recovers consciousness; nor would it be justifiable to proceed contrary to the known wishes of the patient, to the extent that he is rationally capable of forming such a wish (at p. 566). Lord Brandon commented (at p. 551) that in many cases 'it will not only be lawful for doctors, on the ground of necessity, to operate on or give other medical treatment to adult patients disabled from giving their consent: it will also be their common law duty to do so'. An operation or other treatment said his Lordship, would be in the patient's best interests if, but only if, it is carried out to save the patient's life or ensure improvement or prevent deterioration in his physical or mental health.

Where an adult permanently lacks the requisite capacity to give a valid consent there is no equivalent of the wardship jurisdiction by which the court can act on the patient's behalf (*T* v *T*; *F* v *West Berkshire Health Authority*). The same principle of necessity will apply, however, in justifying treatment without consent, but it will be wider in its application covering both emergency and routine medical procedures, provided the 'best interests' test is satisfied. This will extend even to the sterilisation of a mentally handicapped woman. As a matter of good professional practice doctors should seek a declaration from the court that such an operation would be lawful (i.e., in the woman's best interests), but a declaration is not an essential prerequisite to the lawfulness of the operation if a responsible body of medical opinion agree that it was in the patient's best interests (*F* v *West Berkshire Health Authority*, Lord Griffiths dissenting. On the sterilisation of a temporarily unconscious patient see *Murray* v *McMurchy* [1949] 2 DLR 442—it would not have been unreasonable to postpone the operation, it was merely convenient to perform it while the patient was under general anaesthetic, doctor liable in trespass;

cf. *Marshall* v *Curry* [1933] 3 DLR 260). In the case of a permanently
unconscious and insensate patient (i.e., extreme 'persistent vegetative state')
it cannot be said to be in the patient's best interests to continue to receive
medication or nourishment which is futile, and therefore the justification for
continuing treatment under *F* v *West Berkshire Health Authority* does not
apply. Accordingly, it is not unlawful to terminate medical treatment or
nourishment for such a patient, even though it is known, and indeed it is the
intention, that the consequence will be that the patient will die (*Airedale NHS
Trust* v *Bland* [1993] 1 All ER 821, HL). The Law Commission has
recommended that there should be a new jurisdiction and new procedures for
dealing with adult patients who lack the capacity to make their own decisions,
with a statutory definition of incapacity (*Mental Incapacity*, Law Com. No.
231, 1995).

Consent is limited to the act for which permission is given. So, consent to
the application of a permanent wave solution to the plaintiff's hair is not
consent to the application of a tone rinse by a hairdresser (*Nash* v *Sheen*
[1953] CLY 3726), and consent to an operation on the plaintiff's toe does
not authorise spinal fusion (*Schweizer* v *Central Hospital* (1975) 53 DLR (3d)
494; see also *Allan* v *New Mount Sinai Hospital* (1980) 109 DLR (3d)
635—consent to an injection in one arm is not consent to an injection in the
other arm where the patient has specifically refused permission for an
injection in that arm). But the question of what the patient has consented to
will be treated as a question of fact. In *Davis* v *Barking, Havering and
Brentwood Health Authority* [1993] 4 Med LR 85 the plaintiff signed a general
consent form authorising the performance of an operation and the administration of a general anaesthetic, but during the operation the anaesthetist
administered a caudal block (a type of epidural anaesthetic). The plaintiff
alleged that since she had not been informed about the possibility of a caudal
block being performed she had not consented to the procedure (which had
left her with some residual disability). McCullough J held that, looking
compendiously at what the plaintiff had been told about the proposed
operation, including the requirement for a general anaesthetic, she had been
informed in sufficient detail to have consented to the caudal block. There was
no obligation to explain every detail of what was proposed, and whether a
particular aspect was a matter of detail or was in reality a matter sufficiently
separate to call for separate mention was a question of fact and degree. (See
also *Brushett* v *Cowan* (1990) 69 DLR (4th) 743 where consent to a muscle
biopsy was held to cover a bone biopsy on the basis that the plaintiff had
consented to a diagnostic procedure, and in the circumstances this was a
sufficient consent to the bone biopsy.)

Consent must be given freely. If it is obtained under duress it will not be
valid. In *Latter* v *Braddell* (1881) 50 LJ QP 448 it was held that a housemaid
who, at the insistence of her employer, submitted to a medical examination
protesting and sobbing throughout, had consented, even though she mistakenly believed that she had to comply. This was a remarkable decision, even
for the time, and would probably not be followed today (see the dissent of
Lopes J at (1880) 50 LJ CP 166). In *Freeman* v *Home Office* [1983] 3 All ER

589; [1984] 1 All ER 1036, CA, it was accepted that in some circumstances a person's apparent consent might be vitiated by the defendant's exercise of authority over him, without any threat of physical violence. A similar principle applies in relation to a patient's competence validly to refuse consent to medical treatment. In *Re T (Adult: refusal of medical treatment)* [1992] 4 All ER 649 the patient, T, was in urgent need of a blood transfusion having been involved in a car accident and undergone a Caesarian section operation. T's mother, who was a Jehovah's Witness, prevailed upon T, in her weakened physical condition, to refuse consent to a blood transfusion. The Court of Appeal held that T had not been fit to make a genuine decision due to her medical condition and the fact that she had been subjected to the undue influence of her mother which vitiated the decision to refuse a blood transfusion. In the absence of either a valid consent or a valid refusal the doctors acted lawfully, under the principle of *F* v *West Berkshire Health Authority*, in giving the transfusion.

Consent induced by fraud or misrepresentation is not valid. In the criminal law consent is ineffective only if the victim's mistake concerns the real nature of the transaction (e.g., where a man persuades a girl to have sexual intercourse by telling her that it is a medical operation: *R* v *Flattery* (1877) 2 QBD 410). It will be valid if the mistake is as to the consequences of the act (*R* v *Clarence* (1888) 22 QBD 23—no offence when the defendant infected his wife with venereal disease; her consent to sexual intercourse was still valid despite her ignorance of the defendant's infection; *R* v *Linekar* [1995] 3 All ER 69). The same rule appears to be applied in tort (*Clerk and Lindsell,* para. 12–09, citing *Hegarty* v *Shine* (1878) 14 Cox CC 145 where the plaintiff's action against her former lover for infecting her with venereal disease failed because she had consented to the sexual intercourse). Although it is said that fraud or misrepresentation will invalidate a patient's consent to medical treatment (*Chatterton* v *Gerson* [1981] 1 All ER 257, 265) it would appear that the exception is limited to those cases where the fraud or misrepresentation results in the patient being unaware of the nature of the procedure, as opposed to its consequences or associated risks. Thus, in *Sidaway* v *Bethlem Royal Hospital Governors* [1985] 1 All ER 1018, 1026 Sir John Donaldson MR said that:

> It is only if the consent is obtained by fraud or by misrepresentation of the nature of what is to be done that it can be said that an apparent consent is not a true consent. This is the position in the criminal law . . . and the cause of action based on trespass to the person is closely analogous.

The problem with this approach is that if the plaintiff does not consent to *the nature* of what is done the consent is not real in any event, *irrespective of the reason why* (see Tan (1987) 7 LS 149, 156). Conversely, if the patient is aware of the nature of the procedure and consents, the consent is valid for the purpose of the tort of battery (*Chatterton* v *Gerson* above) even if the defendant has misrepresented the risks. This is because, in the context of claims for medical malpractice, the courts have drawn a distinction between the lack of information which concerns the *nature* of the procedure, which gives rise to an action in battery, and a lack of information about the consequences and risks associated with the procedure, where the action must be based in negligence (for criticism of this distinction see Tan (1987) 7 LS 149). Thus, if the patient is aware of the nature of the treatment (but ignorant about the consequent risks) the consent is valid and the defendant's motive, whether in good faith, deliberately misleading or 'fraudulent' cannot change the character of the plaintiff's knowledge and/or ignorance. In *Appleton* v *Garrett* [1996] PIQR P1 a dentist was held liable in trespass to the person for carrying out large-scale, unnecessary dental treatment. In bad faith (and for profit) he deliberately withheld the information that the treatment was unnecessary because he knew that the plaintiffs would not have consented had they known the true position. Dyson J did not specify the nature of the procedure to which the plaintiffs had 'consented', but appears to have taken the view that the consent was invalid because the plaintiffs would not have proceeded had they known the true position (though this, presumably, was also the case in *Hegarty* v *Shine*). The implication to be taken from *Appleton* v *Garrett* is that where medical treatment is not necessary the 'nature' of the procedure is different. Indeed, it is arguable that it ceases to be 'medical treatment', but this means that the patient's consent must go, not simply to the defendant's act (e.g., the drilling of a tooth), but also to the context in which the act takes place, i.e., that the performance of the act is part and parcel of a bona fide decision to provide appropriate medical treatment.

There is no obvious justification for applying the criminal law rule in tort, since it is unduly favourable to the defendant. The consequences of an act are often the crucial factor in the granting of a genuine consent. Except in a dire emergency, no one would consent to major surgery by someone who was not trained to perform it. If the defendant obtained the plaintiff's consent to an operation by misrepresenting his ability to carry it out, it is difficult to see why the plaintiff's consent should not be regarded as vitiated by the misrepresentation, even though there is no mistake as to the nature of the act (i.e., surgery) (though see *R* v *Richardson*, *The Independent*, 3 April 1998, CA—no assault when a dentist gave treatment to patients while suspended from practice by the General Dental Council; consent for the purpose of the criminal law was vitiated only where there was a mistake as to the nature or quality of the act or the identity of the person performing it, not their qualifications or attributes, such as being authorised to provide dental treatment). Similarly, it is arguable that a deliberate lie in response to a specific question from the patient as to the risks of proposed treatment could be taken as evidence of bad faith which might vitiate the patient's consent. This view is supported by observations of Lord Donaldson MR in *Re T (Adult: refusal of medical treatment)* [1992] 4 All ER 649, 663 where, having said that the failure to inform a patient about the risks of treatment went to negligence rather than invalidating consent, his Lordship continued:

> On the other hand, misinforming a patient, whether or not innocently, and the withholding of information which is expressly or impliedly sought by the patient may well vitiate either a consent or a refusal.

It remains to be seen whether this dictum heralds a change of approach to the effect in law of obtaining consent through misrepresentation or fraud.

12.5.2 Lawful arrest

Lawful arrest is not false imprisonment, and in so far as the person carrying out the arrest is entitled to use reasonable force it will not be a battery either. An otherwise lawful arrest will still be lawful, and therefore not amount to false imprisonment, even if made by a police officer in respect of bye-laws subsequently declared void for uncertainty (*Percy* v *Hall* [1996] 4 All ER 524, CA), or if made for a collateral motive (e.g., a desire to prevent further and more serious crime: *R* v *Chalkley* [1998] 2 All ER 15). An arrest occurs 'when a police officer states in terms that he is arresting or when he uses force to restrain the individual concerned. It occurs also when, by words or conduct, he makes it clear that he will, if necessary, use force to prevent the individual from going where he may want to go' (*Hussien* v *Chong Fook Kam* [1970] AC 942, 947 per Lord Devlin). Thus, there is no distinction between detention to the knowledge of the detainee and arrest (*Murray* v *Ministry of Defence* [1988] 2 All ER 521; see Williams (1991) 54 MLR 408 for discussion of the meaning of the term 'arrest'). Under the Police and Criminal Evidence Act 1984 the police have extensive powers of stop and search (ss. 1–3), and to enter premises, search and seize items for use in evidence (ss. 17, 18 and 32). The powers of arrest under the Act are detailed, and it is not possible to give more than a brief outline here.

Lawful arrest may take place in the execution of a warrant, to prevent a breach of the peace, and in the circumstances specified by the Police and Criminal Evidence Act 1984, ss. 24 and 25. (In this paragraph section numbers refer to the Police and Criminal Evidence Act 1984 unless specified. Numerous statutes confer specific powers of arrest, but these are no longer exercisable by police officers, unless specified in sch. 2 or s. 24(2) of the Act (s. 26), although subsequent legislation may grant specific powers of arrest to police officers (see, e.g., Public Order Act 1986 and the Protection from Harassment Act 1997).

At common law, 'every citizen in whose presence a breach of the peace is being, or reasonably appears to be about to be, committed has the right to take reasonable steps to make the person who is breaking or threatening to break the peace refrain from doing so; and those reasonable steps in appropriate cases include detaining him against his will' (*Albert* v *Lavin* [1982] AC 546, 565). A breach of the peace occurs when an assault on an individual is committed or public alarm and excitement is caused (though it has been said that 'public alarm and excitement' is too wide a definition of breach of the peace: *Lewis* v *Chief Constable of Greater Manchester, The Independent*, 23 October 1991). Insults or annoyance are not sufficient. This power (indeed, it is a duty, but of 'imperfect obligation': *Albert* v *Lavin* ibid.) to prevent breaches of the peace ends once the danger has passed. Where an arrest is made on the basis that a breach of the peace is imminent, the defendant's belief that a breach is about to occur must be both honest and based on reasonable grounds (*R* v *Howell* [1981] 3 All ER 383), though due allowance will be made for the circumstances in which he has to make a spur of the moment decision in an emergency (*G* v *Chief Superintendent of Police, Stroud* (1986) 86 Cr App R 92). Where no breach of the peace has occurred in his presence but a constable arrests the plaintiff on the basis that he anticipates a breach will occur, the apprehended breach must be imminent, since the power of arrest in anticipation of a breach of the peace is exceptional. It is not sufficient that the plaintiff has refused to accept the constable's advice to leave the immediate vicinity for a short time, when he was not acting unlawfully at the time (*Foulkes* v *Chief Constable of Merseyside Police* [1998] 3 All ER 705). In the case of an altercation it is irrelevant who started the dispute. The person making the arrest does not have to hold an inquiry or conduct an investigation, but is required to act promptly. Accordingly, it is irrelevant that the person arrested is in fact the victim of an assault by another person (*Kelly* v *Chief Constable of Hampshire, The Independent,* 25 March 1993, CA).

By s. 24(1) an 'arrestable offence' is any offence (a) for which the sentence is fixed by law, or (b) for which on first conviction a person may be sentenced to imprisonment for a term of five years or more, or (c) which is among the specific offences listed in s. 24(2) and (3). Any person may arrest without a warrant anyone who is, or whom he has reasonable grounds for suspecting to be, in the act of committing an arrestable offence (s. 24(4)). Where an arrestable offence has been committed any person may arrest without a warrant anyone who is guilty, or whom he has reasonable grounds for suspecting to be guilty, of the offence (s. 245)). A private individual will not be protected from civil liability by s. 24(5) if in fact no offence has been committed. In *R* v *Self* [1992] 3 All ER 476, 480, CA Garland J said that the power of arrest conferred by s. 24(5) requires 'as a condition precedent an offence committed. If subsequently there is an acquittal of the alleged offence no offence has been committed. The power to arrest is confined to the person guilty of the offence or anyone who the person making the arrest has reasonable grounds for suspecting to be guilty of it. But of course if he is not guilty there can be no valid suspicion . . .'. The effect of this, as Spencer [1992] CLJ 405 points out, is that the private citizen acts at his peril when he effects a 'citizen's arrest' since he has no way of knowing whether ultimately the person arrested will subsequently be convicted or acquitted, even though at the time of the arrest it seemed reasonably, or even abundantly, clear that an arrestable offence had been committed. The law is clearly unsatisfactory here, since it provides 'inadequate protection to the public-spirited citizen who behaves reasonably on the facts as they appeared to him, and permits him to be hit [by the person resisting the unlawful arrest] or sued by someone who, if not actually a criminal, had no more sense than to put on a pantomime of being one' (Spencer, op. cit. p. 406). A police officer has additional powers of arrest beyond those of an ordinary citizen. Where a constable has reasonable grounds for suspecting that an arrestable offence has been committed, he may arrest without a warrant anyone whom he has reasonable grounds for suspecting to be guilty of the offence (s. 24(6)). A constable may also arrest without a warrant anyone who is, or whom he has reasonable grounds for suspecting to be, about to commit an arrestable offence (s. 24(7)).

These provisions substantially re-enact the Criminal Law Act 1967, s. 2, but the 1984 Act grants the police new powers in respect of any offence. Where a constable has reasonable grounds for suspecting that any offence which is not an arrestable offence has been committed or attempted, or is being committed or attempted, he may arrest the relevant person if it appears to him that service of a summons is impracticable or inappropriate because any of the general arrest conditions are satisfied (s. 25(1)). The general arrest conditions include circumstances where the constable has reasonable grounds for doubting that the person has given his correct name and address, or the arrest is necessary to prevent him from causing injury to himself or others, damaging property, committing an offence against public decency or causing an unlawful obstruction of the highway (s. 25(3)).

It is for the person who made the arrest to prove that he had reasonable grounds for his suspicion (*Dallison* v *Caffery* [1965] 1 QB 348; though if, despite reasonable suspicion by the person making the arrest, the plaintiff can prove that at the time of the arrest the arresting officer knew that there was no possibility of a charge being made this would make the arrest unlawful: *Plange* v *Chief Constable of South Humberside Police, The Times,* 23 March 1992). This is not the same as prima facie proof. Suspicion can be based on facts or information that would not be admissible in evidence (*Hussien* v *Chong Fook Kam* [1970] AC 942, 949). Whether reasonable grounds exist is to be determined objectively from the information available to the person making the arrest. It has nothing to do with his subjective state of mind (*Castorina* v *Chief Constable of Surrey* [1988] NLJ Law Rep 180, CA). Detention other than by a valid arrest is unlawful, except in the limited case where a person may be detained short of arrest in order to prevent a breach of the peace (*Albert* v *Lavin*) and in some exceptional circumstances defined by statute. At common law, for the arrest to be valid, the person arrested had to be informed in substance of the real reason for the arrest unless in the circumstances the reason was obvious or it was impossible because he ran away (*Christie* v *Leachinsky* [1947] AC 573; *Abbassy* v *Commissioner of Police of the Metropolis* [1990] 1 All ER 193, a person exercising the power of arrest does not have to give a precise technical definition of the offence provided he informs the arrested person in commonplace language of the nature of the offence for which he is being arrested; note that the common law still applies to arrests for breach of the peace). Now, by s. 28 a person arrested must be informed that he is under arrest and the ground of the arrest at the time of, or as soon as practicable after, the arrest. Where the arrest is by a constable this applies regardless of whether the fact of, or the ground for, the arrest is obvious. These requirements do not apply where it was not reasonably practicable to inform him because he escaped from arrest before the information could be given (s. 28(5)). A failure to inform the arrested person of the grounds for the arrest as soon as it becomes practicable to do so renders the arrest unlawful, but only from the time at which it became practicable to inform him. The failure to inform does not mean that the initial detention becomes retrospectively unlawful (*DPP v Hawkins* [1988] 3 All ER 673). Conversely, an arrest which was initially unlawful due to a failure to give the reasons will become lawful from the point at which reasons are given (*Lewis v Chief Constable of the South Wales Constabulary* [1991] 1 All ER 206, CA—damages only for the period of detention prior to being informed of the reasons for the arrest).

Once the arrest is complete the person arrested must be taken before a magistrate or to a police officer as soon as reasonably possible (*John Lewis & Co. Ltd v Tims* [1952] AC 676—delay by a store detective in order to obtain authority from his superiors to institute a prosecution not unreasonable). However, a police officer can undertake reasonable investigations, such as checking an alibi or taking the person arrested to premises to check for stolen property, before taking him to a police station (*Dallison v Caffery* and s. 30(10)).

Section 117 authorises constables to use reasonable force in the exercise of powers conferred on them by the Act (except where the power may only be exercised with the consent of a person other than a police officer). In addition, by s. 3(1) of the Criminal Law Act 1967 any person may use such force as is reasonable in the prevention of crime, or in effecting or assisting the lawful arrest of offenders or suspected offenders, or of persons unlawfully at large. Unreasonable force will constitute a battery, and this is treated as a question of fact (see *Farrell v Secretary of State for Defence* [1980] 1 All ER 166; Bennett and Rowe (1981) 131 NLJ 991).

12.5.3 Self-defence

A person may use reasonable force to defend himself from attack or unlawful arrest. The force must be the minimum necessary and reasonable in the circumstances, which means that it must be proportionate to the occasion. 'A man cannot justify a maim for every assault; as if A strike B, B cannot justify drawing his sword and cutting off his hand; but it must be such an assault whereby in probability his life may be in danger' (*Cook v Beal* (1697) 1 Ld Raym 176; *Cockcroft v Smith* (1705) 11 Mod 43; *Berntt v Vancouver City* [1997] 4 WWR 505—a riot)). But a person attacked by a prize-fighter does not have to adhere to the Queensberry rules in his defence (*Turner v Metro-Goldwyn-Mayer Pictures Ltd* [1950] 1 All ER 449, 471), and if he is threatened with an assault he does not necessarily have to wait for the other to give the first blow, because then it might be too late (*Chaplain of Gray's Inn Case* (1400) YB 2 Hen 4, fol. 8, pl. 40; *Beckford v R* [1987] 3 All ER 425, 431 PC). This common law right of self-defence overlaps with the power conferred by the Criminal Law Act 1967, s. 3(1), to use reasonable force in the prevention of crime. This removes any doubt about the applicability of the defence where someone goes to the aid of others under attack (see *R v Duffy* [1967] 1 QB 63). Self-defence will be available where the attack is not criminal, e.g., where the attacker lacks *mens rea*, though it has been questioned whether s. 3(1) can be relied upon in this situation (*Street*, p. 83). The criminal law allows a defendant to rely on self-defence where he has made an honest but unreasonable mistake of fact, e.g., he mistakenly believed that he was under attack (*Beckford* v *R*). It is arguable, however, that for the purposes of the law of tort the mistake must be based on reasonable grounds (as was formerly the position in criminal law: *Albert* v *Lavin* [1981] 1 All ER 628; see also *Winfield and Jolowicz*, p. 748).

A similar principle applies to defence of the defendant's property, though the measure of force that is reasonable may be less than in defence of the person (see, e.g., *Collins* v *Renison* (1754) 1 Say 138; cf. *Attorney-General's Reference (No. 2 of 1983)* [1984] QB 456). The occupier of land may use reasonable force to eject, or prevent the entry of, a trespasser, after first requesting him to leave. Possession or the right to possession is essential (*Holmes* v *Bagge* (1853) 1 E & B 782). A person in possession of chattels can use reasonable force to protect them from damage or theft (see, e.g., Animals Act 1971, s. 9, para. 8.3.7; at common law the owner can take reasonable steps to protect animals other than livestock). Again, the force must be proportionate. It is reasonable to mount spikes or broken glass on a wall to deter intruders (unless it is a low wall adjoining the highway, when it would constitute a public nuisance: *Fenna* v *Clare & Co.* [1895] 1 QB 199), but not to set spring guns (*Bird* v *Holbrook* (1828) 4 Bing 628).

12.6 MALICIOUS PROSECUTION

Malicious prosecution is the commonest form of the tort of abuse of legal procedure which is available against persons who deliberately abuse the legal process in order to harm another. It may be combined with a claim for false imprisonment but the differences between the two torts are significant. False imprisonment being an action in trespass, the detention must be a direct result of the defendant's act. The act of a ministerial officer, such as a police officer acting on the defendant's instructions, will not render the detention indirect, but the interposition of an exercise of judicial discretion does (see *Austin* v *Dowling* (1870) LR 5 CP 534, 540 and the test laid down by Sir Thomas Bingham MR in *Davidson* v *Chief Constable of the North Wales Police*, para. 12.4 above. Note, however, that today it is rare for a police officer to take someone into custody in this way. He would normally conduct his own independent investigations, so the private complainant's responsibility for the false imprisonment would cease: Atiyah, *Vicarious Liability*, p. 267). So a person wrongfully arrested and remanded in custody by a magistrate must sue in false imprisonment for the detention up to the time of remand and in malicious prosecution for the period after remand. However, it is much more difficult to establish an action for malicious prosecution. In false imprisonment the plaintiff need only prove the detention and it is then for the defendant to justify it. In malicious prosecution the plaintiff must prove that (a) the defendant initiated the proceedings, (b) the prosecution ended in his favour, (c) there was no reasonable and probable cause for the prosecution, (d) the defendant acted maliciously, and (e) he has suffered damage. This is an onerous burden to discharge, because historically the courts did not want to discourage the bringing of criminal proceedings against suspected offenders. For the purposes of limitation, time does not start to run in an action for malicious prosecution until the plaintiff's acquittal (*Dunlop* v *Commissioners of Customs and Excise*, *The Times*, 17 March 1998, CA).

12.6.1 Initiating proceedings

The defendant need not have conducted the prosecution if he has initiated the proceedings, e.g., by laying an information before a magistrate or signing a charge sheet and agreeing to give evidence. A person who merely reports the facts to the police or a magistrate does not initiate the proceedings, nor does a forensic scientist who prepares a report for the police which results in a prosecution (*Evans* v *London Hospital Medical College* [1981] 1 All ER 715). The House of Lords' decision in *Martin* v *Watson* [1996] 1 AC 74 provides for an exception in cases where such informants have lied. In *Martin* charges that had been brought against the plaintiff solely on the strength of information provided by the defendant had been dropped when it transpired that the defendant had lied. The Court of Appeal [1994] 2 All ER 606 (McGowan LJ dissenting) had dismissed the plaintiff's action for malicious prosecution, because, technically, not having signed the charge sheet, the defendant had not initiated the prosecution. Hobhouse LJ (at p. 632) said that the fact that the defendant had lied was only relevant to her conduct as a 'witness' and could not transform her into a 'prosecutor'. A unanimous House of Lords disagreed and held that a complainant who *falsely* and maliciously gives information to the police can be said to have initiated proceedings for the purposes of the tort. Though the first English authority directly on this point, *Martin* is in line with earlier Commonwealth authorities (e.g., *Watters* v *Pacific Delivery Service Ltd* (1963) 42 DLR (2d) 661, 669 per Munroe J) and with the potential for similar liability for false imprisonment following the Court of Appeal's decision in *Davidson* v *Chief Constable of the North Wales Police* (para. 12.4). However, two aspects of their Lordships' reasoning should ensure that the decision will be kept within tight bounds. First, it was considered significant that the defendant was the only witness, thereby limiting the police's ability to exercise independent discretion in the decision to prosecute (cf. Woollard (1996) 4 Tort L Rev 23, who argues that this reasoning is incomplete, there being no accompanying guidance on 'how far must the discretion of the police officer be fettered by the evidence of the defendant in order to justify a finding that he or she has procured the prosecution?' Woollard also questions their Lordships' fundamental assumption as to the implications of *untrue* evidence on the authorities' ability to exercise a discretion to prosecute: 'if it is the role of the police to weigh the evidence and then proceed at their own discretion, any conclusion reached by a police officer should not be attributed to a particular witness or piece of evidence . . . no one would argue that the provision of *true* evidence acts to fetter discretion . . . the discretion operates regardless of the veracity of the information provided'). Secondly, their Lordships emphasised that the onerous burden of proving that an informant had been both malicious *and* mendacious would sufficiently safeguard the underlying policy that immunity is necessary in order to encourage informing (see Spencer [1996] CLJ 8).

12.6.2 Prosecution ended in the plaintiff's favour

The prosecution must have terminated in the plaintiff's favour, although this does not mean that he must have been acquitted on the merits. It is sufficient if the prosecution has been discontinued (even where discontinuance had been conditional on the plaintiff agreeing to be bound over to keep the peace—*Hourihane* v *Metropolitan Police Commissioner, The Independent,* 18 January 1995, CA), or there was an acquittal on a technical point, or the conviction was quashed on appeal (*Herniman* v *Smith* [1938] AC 305). But if he has been convicted the plaintiff cannot use an action for malicious prosecution to establish his innocence. This is the case even though there is no right of appeal against the conviction and the plaintiff can prove that it was obtained through the prosecutor's fraud (*Basebé* v *Matthews* (1867) LR 2 CP 684; *Everett* v *Ribbands* [1952] 2 QB 198). The courts will not allow a civil action to be used as a retrial of a criminal prosecution.

12.6.3 No reasonable and probable cause

Reasonable and probable cause means an honest belief based on reasonable grounds that the plaintiff was probably guilty of the offence (*Hicks* v *Faulkner* (1878) 8 QBD 167, 171). This does not mean that the defendant must have believed that the plaintiff would probably be convicted. The question is whether there was a case fit to be tried (*Glinski* v *McIver* [1962] AC 726, 766–7). This question is determined by reference to the facts known to, or believed by, the defendant at the time, even though these facts or beliefs subsequently turn out to be incorrect (*Herniman* v *Smith* [1938] AC 305). But the facts believed by the defendant must themselves have furnished reasonable grounds for the prosecution (*Tims* v *John Lewis & Co. Ltd* [1951] 2 KB 459, 472). Thus there are two elements to the issue, namely, was there reasonable and probable cause in fact, and did the prosecutor genuinely believe that the plaintiff was probably guilty? If there was no probable cause in fact the prosecutor's honest belief is not sufficient (*Tempest* v *Snowden* [1952] 1 KB 130, 138).

The burden of proving lack of reasonable and probable cause is the plaintiff's, and this is particularly difficult because it involves proving a negative. Additionally, the question is treated as a matter for the judge rather than the jury, because it is said that juries are too ready to grant a civil action to someone who has been prosecuted and acquitted. The question of the prosecutor's honest belief that proceedings were justified is a jury matter, but if objectively there was reasonable and probable cause it will be very difficult to prove that the prosecutor did not honestly believe that it existed (*Dallison* v *Caffery* [1965] 1 QB 348, 372).

12.6.4 Malice

Malice means some wrongful or improper motive, but motives such as anger or revenge for the harm inflicted by the alleged offence are not improper because the law relies on such motives in bringing offenders to justice (*Brown* v *Hawkes* [1891] 2 QB 718, 722). Malice 'covers not only spite and ill-will but also any motive other than a desire to bring a criminal to justice' (*Glinski* v *McIver* [1962] AC 726 per Lord Devlin). Again, the burden of proof is the plaintiff's. Malice is not itself sufficient to maintain malicious prosecution. If there is reasonable and probable cause the prosecutor will not be liable, no matter how malicious or spiteful his motives (*Glinski* v *McIver*). Conversely, the prosecutor who does not act maliciously is not liable, even in the absence of reasonable and probable cause.

The lack of reasonable and probable cause is not evidence of malice, unless it is based on the absence of honest belief in the plaintiff's guilt (*Turner* v *Ambler* (1847) 10 QB 252) but if there was honest belief then there must be some independent evidence of malice (*Brown* v *Hawkes*). Similarly, malice is not evidence of lack of probable cause, unless the same evidence is sufficient to establish both, e.g., if it is proved that the defendant knew that the plaintiff was innocent.

12.6.5 Damage
In *Savill* v *Roberts* (1698) 12 Mod 208, Holt CJ said that there were three types of damage: (a) damage to the plaintiff's reputation, which depends on the nature of the offence with which he is charged (being charged with an offence punishable by imprisonment is in itself defamatory, even if the plaintiff was not imprisoned: *Wiffen* v *Bailey* [1915] 1 KB 600); (b) damage to the person, such as detention; and (c) damage to property, such as any unrecovered costs of defending the prosecution (*Berry* v *British Transport Commission* [1962] 1 QB 306).

An action in tort will lie for malicious bankruptcy or insolvency proceedings (*Quartz Hill Consolidated Gold Mining Co.* v *Eyre* (1883) 11 QBD 674), but not for bringing other unfounded civil proceedings, no matter how maliciously. This has been explained on the basis that a successful defendant in civil proceedings suffers no damage on recovering his costs, but in practice the costs paid by the unsuccessful party are rarely a full indemnity. Moreover, it is not clear why injury to a person's reputation does not constitute damage, as it does in the case of malicious criminal proceedings.

THIRTEEN
Defamation

The tort of defamation protects a person from untrue imputations which harm his reputation with others. This should be distinguished from an untrue statement which does not damage the plaintiff's reputation but does cause harm, e.g., a statement that a trader has ceased business is not defamatory, but may cause him to lose custom. This is actionable, if at all, under the tort of injurious (or malicious) falsehood in which the plaintiff must prove: (a) that the words are untrue, (b) that the defendant was actuated by malice and (c) that he has suffered actual damage (except where the Defamation Act 1952, s. 3, applies) (*Allason* v *Campbell, The Times*, 8 May 1996). In defamation, if the words are defamatory they are presumed to be untrue unless the defendant proves otherwise, malice is generally not essential, and most forms of defamation are actionable *per se*. A requirement of pleading that the words must be 'maliciously' published is purely formal—the word 'maliciously' is treated as mere verbiage (though express malice will defeat the defences of qualified privilege and fair comment).

Defamation is a peculiar tort. It is one of the few civil actions that are still tried with juries. An action can be brought only in the High Court, and legal aid is not available (although a plaintiff is entitled to bring a claim based on an alternative cause of action, such as malicious falsehood, for which legal aid is available provided that the facts will support such an action, notwithstanding that this has been done with the specific objective of securing legal aid and that the defendant would not be entitled to a jury trial as of right or that the damages recoverable might be insignificant compared to the costs: *Joyce* v *Sengupta* [1993] 1 All ER 897, CA). The law is often highly technical, complicated by rules of evidence and the demarcation between the different functions of judge and jury, and frequently quite arbitrary in its application. Juries sometimes make awards of damages which far exceed the sums that would be awarded in cases of very serious personal injuries, without always distinguishing between grave allegations which might affect a person's livelihood and trivial comments which have merely hurt the plaintiff's vanity or pride (see the comments of the Court of Appeal on this question in *Sutcliffe v Pressdram Ltd* [1990] 1 All ER 269, 281–2, 291–2). The Court of Appeal now has the power to substitute an award of damages instead of ordering a new trial in cases where the damages awarded by a jury are excessive or inadequate (Courts and Legal Services Act 1990, s. 8). In *Rantzen* v *Mirror Group Newspapers* [1993] 4 All ER 975 the Court of Appeal exercised its power under s. 8 to substitute an award of £110,000 for the jury's award of £250,000. They held that in determining whether the award was excessive the test was whether a reasonable jury could have thought that the award was necessary to compensate the plaintiff and to re-establish his reputation, and although juries may be referred to previous cases in which the Court of Appeal has considered the award of damages under s. 8, they should not be referred to jury awards in libel cases or to awards made in personal injury actions. The ability to make comparisons with damages awarded for non-pecuniary losses in personal injury actions might have a salutory effect on libel juries. Indeed, it was, *inter alia*, the absence of such guidance that prompted a later Court of Appeal to describe the jury as 'sheep loosed on an unfenced common, with no shepherd' (*John* v *Mirror Group Newspapers Ltd* [1996] 2 All ER 35, 49 per Sir Thomas Bingham MR; for comment see (1996) 15 CJQ 85). As a result, the Court of Appeal in *John* modified its earlier pronouncements in *Rantzen* and held that, in line with developments in the High Court of Australia (*Carson* v *John Fairfax and Sons Ltd* (1993) 67 ALJR 634), juries in defamation cases could have their attention drawn to conventional personal injury awards. However, at the same time, the court recognised that, logically, there could be no direct correlation between a personal injury and a damaged reputation. Therefore, the purpose of any reference to personal injury awards would be to provide a general check on the reasonableness of a proposed award, rather than a precise comparator or analogy (per Sir Thomas Bingham MR, at p. 54; note the Law Commission's views on this in the context of the corresponding concerns that levels of damages for non-pecuniary personal injury are too *low* in comparison with awards in defamation cases, para. 15.1.3.4). Perhaps in view of this qualification, it may be that the more significant addition to the repertoire of permissible jury guidance made by the Court of Appeal in *John* was in holding that the judge or counsel can refer the jury to what they consider to be an appropriate award and its appropriate bracket, as has become the practice in personal injury cases. Though the Court of Appeal in *John* has effected potentially radical alterations to the role of the jury in the assessment of damages process, other more general anomalies remain. For example, it remains the case that substantial damages may be awarded even when it is proved that the plaintiff did not suffer any loss, e.g., because the person to whom a libel was published disbelieved the statement. Also a defendant in a libel action cannot put before the jury specific figures of money offered to the plaintiff in open pre-trial correspondence to mitigate the damages the jury might award (*Kiam* v *Neil, The Times*, 14 December 1994, CA).

The Faulks Committee suggested that the purpose of the law of defamation was to preserve a balance between the individual's right to protect his reputation and the general right of free speech (*Faulks,* para. 19), but it is questionable whether the present law strikes the correct balance. The crux of the problem is neatly illustrated by *Tolstoy Miloslavsky* v *United Kingdom* (1995) 20 EHRR 442 in which the plaintiff obtained a declaration from the European Court of Human Rights that libel damages of £1.5 million awarded against him by an English jury amounted to a violation of his right to freedom of expression under art. 10 of the European Convention on Human Rights. However, though the UK is a signatory to the Convention, it has not yet formally adopted it as part of its constitutional law. Therefore, strictly, the decision can only be symbolic and the plaintiff's victory pyrrhic. On the other hand, the government has promised legislation to incorporate the provisions of the Convention, and it is significant that the House of Lords drew heavily on a more generalised common law principle of freedom of speech to justify their decision in *Derbyshire County Council* v *Times Newspapers Ltd* [1993] 1 All ER 1011. It remains to be seen, though, whether these developments will herald a new era in which the 'right' to freedom of expression will not only be formally recognised as such, but will also enjoy more positive judicial protection (see Cumberbatch (1994) 45 NILQ 219; Bix and Tomkins (1993) 56 MLR 738; Mullany (1995) 111 LQR 206; Grant and Small (1994) 14 OJLS 287; Loveland (1994) 14 LS 206 and (1997) 26 Anglo-Am LRev 175). A strong indication that that might, indeed, be the case, is *Reynolds* v *Times Newspapers Ltd* (1998) 148 NLJ 1051, in which the Court of Appeal confirmed that, in order to keep faith with article 10, a common law qualified privilege defence should be available to newspapers when making statements about public figures (see para. 13.2.3.1). In *Slim* v *Daily Telegraph Ltd* [1968] 2 QB 157, Diplock LJ described the tort of defamation as artificial and archaic, 'beyond the redemption of the courts' (see also the criticisms of Lord Donaldson MR in *Singh* v *Gillard* [1988] NLJ Law Rep 144; and *Weir,* pp. 558–9; cf. *Hill* v *Church of Scientology of Toronto* (1995) 126 DLR (4th) 129 in which, in approving an award of $1.6 million, the Supreme Court of Canada asserted that the common law could tolerate such awards, Cory J concluding, more generally, that he 'simply [could not] see that the law of defamation is unduly restrictive or inhibiting'). The recommendations of the Faulks Committee would have removed some of the anomalies, but that report continues to gather dust.

The Defamation Act 1996 mainly effects changes to the conduct of defamation cases, rather than a wholesale reform of the substantive law upon which they are based, but it could affect the role of the jury through the new 'fast track' procedure (for general comment on the Defamation Act 1996, see Williams (1997) 5 Tort LRev 206; McK Norrie 1996 SLT 311). This enables the court, alone, to dispose summarily of those cases that are inordinately weak, and provide 'summary relief' in those that are inordinately strong (Defamation Act 1996, ss. 8–10). However, realistically, restricting summary relief to those cases that can be compensated adequately by an award not exceeding £10,000 may limit the practical impact that the fast track provision can have on the role of the jury and its controversial assessment of damages function (Milmo (1996) 146 NLJ 222).

Defamation can be either libel or slander. Libel is defamatory material in permanent form, whereas slander takes a transient form (para. 13.1.4). The importance of this distinction lies in the fact that libel is actionable *per se,* but slander is only actionable on proof of special damage, except for four categories which are actionable *per se.* Apart from this, the requirements are the same. The plaintiff must prove: (a) that the material about which he complains was defamatory, (b) that it referred to him, and (c) that it was published to a third person. Once this has been established the onus shifts to the defendant to prove a defence. It is a defence to prove: (a) that the imputation was true, or (b) that it was made on a privileged occasion, which may be either absolute or qualified privilege, or (c) that it was fair comment on a matter of public interest.

13.1 THE CAUSE OF ACTION

A person's reputation is protected by the tort of defamation during his lifetime. The action does not survive for the benefit of a deceased person's estate. A trading corporation can sue in defamation to protect its commercial reputation (*Metropolitan Saloon Omnibus Co.* v *Hawkins* (1859) 4 H & N 87—imputing insolvency; *South Hetton Coal Co. Ltd* v *North Eastern News Association Ltd* [1894] 1 QB 133—allegation that houses in which the company accommodated employees were in an insanitary condition). Although it was formerly possible for a trade union to bring an action for libel (see *National Union of General and Municipal Workers* v *Gillian* [1946] KB 81) it has been held that s. 2(1) of the Trade Union and Labour Relations Act 1974 (now s. 10 of the Trade Union and Labour Relations (Consolidation) Act 1992), which prevents a trade union from being treated as a body corporate with the result that it is an unincorporated association, deprives a trade union of the necessary legal personality to be defamed (*Electrical, Electronic, Telecommunication & Plumbing Union* v *Times Newspapers Ltd* [1980] QB 585). This is despite the wording of s. 2(1)(c) stating that a trade union shall be capable of suing and being sued in its own name in contract or tort or 'any other cause of action whatsoever'. In *Bognor Regis Urban District Council* v *Campion* [1972] 2 QB 169 it was held that a local authority had a 'governing reputation' which could be protected by an action for defamation. This decision was overruled, however, by the House of Lords in *Derbyshire County Council* v *Times Newspapers Ltd* [1993] 1 All ER 1011, on the ground that the threat of a civil action for defamation would have an inhibiting effect on freedom of speech and it was contrary to the public interest that the organs of government, whether central or local, should have a right to sue for libel (applied in Australia in *Ballina Shire Council* v *Ringland* (1994) 33 NSWLR 680, commented on by Mullany (1995) 111 LQR 206). Lord Keith commented (at p. 1017) that: 'It is of the highest public importance that a democratically elected governmental body, or indeed any governmental body, should be open to uninhibited public criticism'. (Note, however, that criticism of a governmental body such as a local authority which impugns the reputation of an individual or individuals, such as a councillor, could be the subject of a defamation action by the individual notwithstanding its consequences for freedom of speech.) The *Derbyshire* principle has also been employed to deny a political party an action in defamation (*Goldsmith* v *Bhoyrul* [1997] 4 All ER 268).

An employer may be vicariously liable for defamatory statements made by an employee in the course of his employment (*Riddick* v *Thames Board Mills Ltd* [1977] QB 881; the courts tend to take a narrow view of 'the course of employment' for this purpose: Atiyah, *Vicarious Liability* (1967), p. 274). Such a statement may often be made in circumstances where qualified privilege would apply, although malice by the employee will defeat the employer's defence.

13.1.1 What is defamatory?

Defamation consists of the publication of material which reflects on a person's reputation so as to lower the plaintiff in the estimation of right-thinking members of society generally (*Sim* v *Stretch* (1936) 52 TLR 669, 671), or which would tend to cause him to be shunned or avoided. The second limb of this test is necessary to deal with statements that are undoubtedly regarded as defamatory but do not reflect any moral discredit on the plaintiff, such as an imputation of insanity (*Morgan* v *Lingen* (1863) 8 LT (NS) 800) or an allegation that the plaintiff has been raped (*Youssoupoff* v *Metro-Goldwyn-Mayer Pictures Ltd* (1934) 50 TLR 581, 587). The test is objective. It is no defence that the defendant did not intend to defame the plaintiff, nor even that he did not know the circumstances which rendered a statement, apparently innocent on the face of it, defamatory of the plaintiff (though a defendant in such a case may be able to make an 'offer of amends' under ss. 2–4 of the Defamation Act 1996, para. 13.1.2). In *Cassidy* v *Daily Mirror Newspapers Ltd* [1929] 2 KB 331 the defendants announced the engagement of Mr C and Miss X. The plaintiff was Mr C's lawful wife and, though they were not living together, Mr C occasionally stayed with her. The plaintiff alleged that the defendants' report suggested that Mr C was not her husband and that she lived in immoral cohabitation with him. The defendants were found liable and the Court of Appeal upheld the verdict. Russell LJ said that 'Liability for libel does not depend on the intention of the defamer, but on the fact of defamation'. However, the 'fact of defamation' refers to the defamatory meaning of the words, not their effect on the plaintiff's reputation, because it is irrelevant that the statement is not believed to be true by anyone to whom it is published (*Hough* v *London Express Newspaper Ltd* [1940] 2 KB 507, 515; *Morgan* v *Odhams Press Ltd* [1971] 1 WLR 1239).

Vulgar abuse which is spoken in the heat of an argument, and was intended and understood by the people who heard the words as mere insult, is not defamatory (*Parkins* v *Scott* (1862) 1 H & C 153). This will depend on the manner in which the words were spoken. Insult does not reflect on a person's reputation, but the defendant must prove that a reasonable man would not have understood his words as defamatory rather than abuse.

A statement is defamatory if it exposes the plaintiff to ridicule or contempt, even in the absence of an imputation of misconduct. So a humorous caricature can be defamatory (*Dunlop Rubber Co. Ltd* v *Dunlop* [1921] 1 AC 367). In *Berkoff* v *Burchill* [1996] 4 All ER 1008 the plaintiff, an actor and director, complained of a newspaper article in which he was described as 'hideously ugly'. By a majority the Court of Appeal held that these words were capable of being defamatory, since, although they did not impute disgraceful conduct nor lack of skill in his profession, it was open to a jury to conclude that the words gave the impression that the plaintiff was not merely physically unattractive, but actually repulsive. To say that of someone in the public eye was capable of lowering his standing in the estimation of the public and making him an object of ridicule (cf. the dissent of Millett LJ, who pointed out that the words were an attack on the plaintiff's appearance, not his reputation. A decision that it was actionable to describe someone as hideously ugly was an unwarranted restriction on free speech. People must be allowed to poke fun at one another, said his Lordship, without fear of litigation). The statement must lower the plaintiff in the estimation of right-thinking members of society *generally.* Thus it is not defamatory to suggest that the plaintiff informed the police about a criminal offence because right-thinking members of society would regard that as commendable, even if the fellow-members of the plaintiff's golf club might consider it to be an act of disloyalty (*Byrne* v *Deane* [1937] 1 KB 818).

It is the function of the jury to decide whether words are defamatory, but the judge must first determine whether the words are capable of bearing a defamatory meaning in their natural and ordinary sense, or whether they are capable of bearing the innuendo that the plaintiff alleges. The ordinary and natural meaning may include any implication or inference which a reasonable reader guided by general knowledge would draw from the words (*Jones* v *Skelton* [1963] 1 WLR 1362, 1371; *Lewis* v *Daily Telegraph Ltd* [1964] AC 234, 258). The judge must leave the issue to the jury, unless no reasonable man would understand the words in a defamatory sense. This test was stated in *Capital & Counties Bank Ltd* v *Henty & Son* (1882) 7 App Cas 741, though its application to the facts of that case is open to question. After a disagreement with a branch manager of the plaintiffs, the defendants sent a circular to their own customers giving notice that they would not accept payment by cheques drawn on the Capital & Counties Bank. This led to a run on the bank. The plaintiffs alleged that the circular imputed insolvency. After much judicial disagreement the House of Lords held by a majority that the statement was not capable of a defamatory meaning, although clearly many of the bank's customers (some of whom must have been reasonable men) understood the circular to mean that the bank was insolvent (for criticism see *Slim* v *Daily Telegraph Ltd* [1968] 2 QB 157, 187 and cf. *Aspro Travel Ltd* v *Owners Abroad Group plc* [1995] 4 All ER 728, CA—statements that a 'family' company was 'going bust' afforded its directors an action on the basis that such unqualified words were capable of the defamatory meaning that they had permitted the company to trade knowing that it was insolvent and that, being a 'family' company, the words might more easily be understood to refer to them). In *Lewis* v *Daily Telegraph Ltd* [1964] AC 234 it was held that a statement that the Fraud Squad was investigating a company was not capable of meaning that its business was carried on fraudulently. A reasonable man would not infer guilt from the fact of a police inquiry. However, it is the broad impression conveyed by the libel that must be considered. 'Loose talk about suspicion can very easily convey the impression that it is a suspicion that is well founded' (per Lord Devlin). A defendant would have to use careful language to avoid imputing guilt by a statement of suspicion. In *Hartt* v *Newspaper Publishing plc, The Times,* 9 November 1989, Neill LJ said that the hypothetical reasonable reader was not naive but not unduly suspicious. He could read between the lines, and might indulge in a certain amount of loose thinking, but he was not to be treated as someone avid for scandal nor someone who would select one bad meaning where other, non-defamatory meanings were available. In *Mapp* v *News Group Newspapers Ltd* [1998] 2 WLR 260, the Court of Appeal reaffirmed the importance of the distinction between imputations of guilt and statements of reasonable suspicion of guilt, this time in relation to the defendants' article that described the suicide of a policeman who had been ordered to provide information to an inquiry that was investigating allegations of drug dealing and bribery made against eight drugs squad officers. Four of the officers sued the defendants for libel, alleging that the ordinary meaning of the article and its headline ('Drug quiz cop kills himself') was that they were guilty of drug dealing and bribery, and that the policeman had committed suicide because he would otherwise have had to confirm that they were corrupt. The Court of Appeal dismissed the plaintiffs' claim and, having restated the distinction between suspicion and guilt, held that the words complained of were mere statements of suspicion and that the reference to the policeman's suicide did not transform them into imputations of guilt. Moreover, the Court of Appeal stated that, even if the words did impute guilt to at least one of the eight accused officers, they could not impute guilt to all.

Words must be interpreted in their context. The plaintiff cannot select apparently libellous statements if the passage taken as a whole is not defamatory. This principle has been applied in the context of newspaper headlines in *Charleston* v *News Group Newspapers Ltd* [1995] 2 All ER 313. The bizarre facts were that the defendants' *News of the World* newspaper published photographs in which the heads of the plaintiffs, an actor and actress who played the parts of Madge and Harold Bishop ('a respectable married couple' per Lord Bridge at p. 315) in the Australian soap opera *Neighbours*, had been superimposed on to two near naked bodies engaged in sexual intercourse. The photographs were accompanied by a large headline exclaiming 'Strewth! What's Harold up to with our Madge?' and a smaller one announcing 'Porn Shocker for *Neighbours* Stars'. The captions under the photographs and the article itself did, however, make it clear ('in a tone of self-righteous indignation which [contrasted] oddly with the prominence given to the main photographs' ibid. per Lord Bridge at p. 315) that the photographs had been reproduced from a computer game in which the plaintiffs' faces had been used without their knowledge or consent. The plaintiffs alleged that the photographs and headlines were libellous in that their ordinary and natural meaning was that the plaintiffs had posed for pornographic photographs. The House of Lords dismissed their claim and held that potentially defamatory matter in a prominent headline (or a headline and photograph) could not found a claim in libel in isolation from the related text of an article that removed the defamatory imputation. The 'ordinary readers' (per Lord Nicholls at p. 320) would see both, even though a significant minority (the 'limited readers', per Lord Bridge at p. 316) would see only the headline and the photographs (for criticism see Prescott (1995) 58 MLR 752). Lord Nicholls did, however, sound a cautionary note for newspaper proprietors as to the precise content and layout necessary for an article to neutralise the defamatory implication of prominent headlines and photographs. He questioned whether the 'ordinary reader' would notice 'curative words tucked away further down in the article' or '. . . words on a continuation page . . .' (at p. 320).

On the other hand, words which on the face of it are innocent may be defamatory when put into context. In slander, entirely different meanings can be given to the same words by shifts in the tone of voice or changes of emphasis. Entirely innocent material may be so placed that it is possible to infer a defamatory meaning. In *Monson* v *Tussauds Ltd* [1894] 1 QB 671 it was held that a waxwork effigy of the plaintiff placed at the entrance to the 'Chamber of Horrors' was capable of being defamatory (cf. *Wheeler* v *Somerfield* [1966] 2 QB 94).

Words may be defamatory in their natural and ordinary meaning or they may be defamatory only when combined with extrinsic facts known to those to whom the words were published. In the latter case the plaintiff must rely on an innuendo, and he must plead and prove the facts which he alleges renders defamatory, words which are prima facie innocent. For example, in *Tolley* v *J. S. Fry & Sons Ltd* [1931] AC 333 the defendants published an advertisement in which the plaintiff, a famous amateur golfer, endorsed the defendants' brand of chocolate. They had not asked for his permission to do this. The plaintiff alleged that there was a defamatory implication, namely that he had been paid to appear in the advertisement and had thereby prostituted his amateur status. The House of Lords held that the advertisement was capable of bearing a defamatory meaning. Another example of this type of innuendo is the case of *Cassidy* v *Daily Mirror Newspapers Ltd, supra* (see also *Morgan* v *Odhams Press Ltd* [1971] 1 WLR 1239 where the innuendo related not to a defamatory meaning, but the reference to the plaintiff).

The 'true' or 'legal' innuendo should be distinguished from the 'false' or 'popular' innuendo, which is a defamatory implication or inference which can be drawn from the words themselves, without reference to any extrinsic evidence. This is simply a matter of giving the words their natural and ordinary meaning as derived from the context in which they are published. 'The ordinary man does not live in an ivory tower and he is not inhibited by a knowledge of the rules of construction. So he can and does read between the lines in the light of his general knowledge and experience of worldly affairs' (*Lewis* v *Daily Telegraph Ltd* [1964] AC 234, 258 per Lord Reid; see *Faulks*, para. 98, for an example illustrating the distinction between a 'popular' and a 'legal' innuendo). The technical difference between a legal and a popular innuendo is that a legal innuendo constitutes a separate cause of action, additional to any defamatory imputation in the natural and ordinary meaning of the words, and it must be specifically pleaded and proved by the plaintiff, although if the meaning of the words in their ordinary and natural meaning is not clear and explicit the plaintiff must plead the meaning which he alleges to be defamatory (*Allsop* v *Church of England Newspaper Ltd* [1972] 2 QB 161—plaintiff described as 'bent'). Where the plaintiff alleges that some people had knowledge of special facts which rendered the words defamatory he must prove that they were published to such a person (*Fullam* v *Newcastle Chronicle & Journal Ltd* [1977] 3 All ER 32). The extrinsic facts must be known by the person to whom the words are published at the time of publication. Inferences which could be drawn from facts discovered after the publication will not support an innuendo (*Grappelli* v *Derek Block (Holdings) Ltd* [1981] 2 All ER 272; *aliter* where the publication is defamatory on the face of it and the subsequent fact concerns only the plaintiff's identity: *Hayward* v *Thompson* [1982] QB 47).

13.1.2 Reference to the plaintiff
The defamatory statement must refer to the plaintiff, but the reference need not be express, nor is it necessary for any 'key or pointer' in the statement to indicate the plaintiff. Special facts which are known only to certain readers which would identify the plaintiff with the statement are admissible in evidence (*Morgan* v *Odhams Press Ltd* [1971] 1 WLR 1239). The test is whether the ordinary sensible reader, in the light of the special facts, would understand the words as referring to the plaintiff, allowing for the fact that people do not read a newspaper with the same care as a contract (ibid., p. 1245 per Lord Reid). It is irrelevant that no one actually believed the words to be true. Where a defamatory statement does not refer to the plaintiff, he is entitled to rely on a subsequent publication by the defendant identifying the plaintiff with the defamatory words (*Hayward* v *Thompson* [1982] QB 47).

It is also irrelevant, at common law, that the defendant did not intend to refer to the plaintiff. Thus, the defendant is liable for a work of fiction which is reasonably understood to refer to the plaintiff, even if the author did not know of his existence (*E. Hulton & Co.* v *Jones* [1910] AC 20). Similarly, the fact that the words are true of someone else, does not prevent them from being defamatory of the plaintiff if they could reasonably be understood as referring to him. In *Newstead* v *London Express Newspaper Ltd* [1940] 1 KB 377 the defendants reported that 'Harold Newstead, thirty-year-old Camberwell man' had been convicted of bigamy. This was true of a Camberwell barman of that name, but not of the plaintiff, a Camberwell hairdresser. The defendants were liable. This puts the onus on those who make such reports to ensure that they identify the person who is the subject of the report with sufficient particularity to avoid confusion (see *Weir*, pp. 538–40 for comment).

Section 4 of the Defamation Act 1952, applying to both libel and slander, provided a special statutory defence in such cases of 'unintentional defamation', by allowing the defamer to make an 'offer of amends' by way of a suitable correction and apology. If the offer was accepted and duly performed, it barred proceedings for libel or slander by that person against the person making the offer, though not against any other person jointly responsible for that publication. Alternatively, if the offer was not accepted by the party aggrieved, then in any proceedings by him for libel or slander against the person making the offer it would be a defence to prove: (a) that the words were published 'innocently' in relation to the plaintiff; and (b) that the offer was made as soon as practicable after the defendant received notice that they were or might be defamatory of the plaintiff, and had not been withdrawn; and (c) if the publisher was not the author, that the words were written by the author without malice. However, the s. 4 defence fell into disuse, primarily due to the lengths to which a defendant was required to go in order to prove that the words had been published 'innocently'. Section 4(5) defined 'innocently' as meaning either: (a) that the publisher did not intend to publish [the words] of and concerning that other person, and did not know of circumstances by virtue of which they might be understood to refer to him (so potentially covering the circumstances of *E. Hulton & Co.* v *Jones* and *Newstead* v *London Express Newspaper Ltd*); or (b) that the words were not defamatory on the face of them, and the publisher did not know of circumstances by virtue of which they might be understood to be defamatory of that other person (so potentially applying to cases such as *Cassidy* v *Daily Mirror Newspapers Ltd* [1929] 2 KB 331 (see para. 13.1.1)), *and in either case that the publisher exercised all reasonable care in relation to the publication*. In the event, by effectively equating 'innocence' with absence of negligence, s. 4 imposed a burden that few defendants could meet.

The Defamation Act 1996, ss. 2–4, may have breathed new life into the 'unintentional defamation' defence, *inter alia*, by removing the requirement of non-negligent innocence. The section retains the basic shape of the original defence, but makes it available to any person publishing material which he did not know referred to the plaintiff, or did not know was false and defamatory of the plaintiff. Significantly, the burden of proving 'innocence' is reversed, because it is presumed 'until the contrary is shown' that the defendant did not have the relevant knowledge. As before, that person must be willing to offer 'amends', which, in addition to correction and apology, now involves a payment of compensation. If not agreed, the level of compensation will be set by the court, but without a jury, an ostensibly minor amendment which, as Milmo (1995) 145 NLJ 1340, 1341 observes, assumes far greater significance when read in the context of the revised defence as a whole. For, given that the amended defence equates 'innocence' (recast into a subjective rather than an objective framework) with ignorance of both the false *and* the defamatory nature of the statement, the defence will be available to a publisher, such as a newspaper, that deliberately publishes a statement known to be defamatory but believed to be true. In such cases, the newspaper will need to weigh the respective merits of the justification and offer of amends defences because a person who relies on the offer of amends cannot rely on any other defence (s. 4(4); indeed, he cannot make an offer of amends under the Act after serving a defence in defamation proceedings brought by the plaintiff in respect of that publication: s. 2(5)). The dilemma will be whether to trade the former (with its first prize of total victory, but wooden spoon of an uncertain and potentially punitive jury award) for the latter, where the discomfort of capitulation may be mitigated by the relative predictability and stability of the non-jury award. One factor which may encourage defendants to offer amends is that the offer may be relied on in mitigation of damages, presumably where it has been rejected by the plaintiff, whether or not it was relied on as a defence (s. 4(5)).

As a general rule, defamation of a class is not actionable. 'No doubt it is true to say that a class cannot be defamed as a class, nor can an individual be defamed by a general reference to the class to which he belongs' (*Knupffer* v *London Express Newspaper Ltd* [1944] AC 116, 124 per Lord Porter). So the statement that 'all lawyers are thieves' is merely facetious exaggeration which is not actionable by any particular lawyer (*Eastwood* v *Holmes* (1858) 1 F & F 347, 349; *Knupffer* v *London Express Newspaper Ltd* [1944] AC 116, 122). The reason why defamation of a class is not usually actionable is that the words are not published 'of the plaintiff' (*Knupffer* v *London Express Newspaper Ltd* [1944] AC 116, 122). However, if there is something in the words or the circumstances under which they were published which identifies a particular plaintiff or plaintiffs they will be actionable (*Le Fanu* v *Malcolmson* (1848) 1 HL Cas 637; *Orme* v *Associated Newspapers Ltd, The Times,* 4 February 1981—defamatory comments about the Unification Church would reasonably be identified with the leader of the organisation). Similarly, if the reference is to a limited class or group, such as trustees or the members of a firm, so that the words can be taken to refer to every member, they will all be able to sue (*Browne* v *D.C. Thomson & Co.* 1912 SC 359; *Foxcroft* v *Lacey* (1613) Hob 89), as will the directors of a 'family' company (*Aspro Travel Ltd* v *Owners Abroad Group plc* [1995] 4 All ER 728). The size of the class, the generality of the charge and the extravagance of the accusation will be taken into consideration (*Knupffer* v *London Express Newspaper Ltd* [1944] AC 116, 124). Where a defamatory statement referred to one or more but not all members of a class, without identifying which members were referred to, the rule was that none could sue (e.g., 'one of you three is a thief). This rule has been doubted by the Court of Appeal, so that it is now arguable that all can sue on the basis that the finger of suspicion points at each of them (*Farrington* v *Leigh, The Times,* 10 December 1987).

13.1.3 Publication

The defamatory matter must have been communicated to some person other than the plaintiff. The tort protects the plaintiff's reputation in the eyes of others, not his personal feelings of insult (*Powell* v *Gelston* [1916] 2 KB 615). Communication to the defendant's spouse does not constitute publication (*Wennhak* v *Morgan* (1888) 20 QBD 635), but communication to the plaintiff's spouse does (*Wenman* v *Ash* (1853) 13 CB 836). A typist or printer who hands back to the author a defamatory document prepared on the author's instructions does not thereby publish the libel to the author

(*Eglantine Inn Ltd* v *Smith* [1948] NI 29). It would be otherwise if the typist or printer passed the document to someone else.

A person will be liable for any publication which he intends or which he can reasonably anticipate. Thus, leaving documents where they might be read by others, putting letters in the wrong envelope (*Hebditch* v *MacIlwaine* [1894] 2 QB 54, 64), speaking so loudly that others are likely to overhear (*White* v *J. & F. Stone (Lighting & Radio) Ltd* [1939] 2 KB 827, 836), all amount to publication. A letter addressed to a particular person is presumed to be published to the addressee, but in some cases the sender should anticipate that it may be read by someone else, such as a correspondence clerk (*Pullman* v *Walter Hill & Co. Ltd* [1891] 1 QB 524) or, exceptionally, a spouse (*Theaker* v *Richardson* [1962] 1 WLR 151—husband opened letter in error thinking that it was an election address), but not an inquisitive butler (*Huth* v *Huth* [1915] 3 KB 32). The sender can protect himself by marking the correspondence 'private'. It is presumed that postcards or telegrams are published to postal officials or the recipient's family without proof that someone did read them (but not an unsealed letter: *Huth* v *Huth*). However, if there is nothing in the communication which would identify the plaintiff to third parties who might read the postcard, there is no publication to them (*Sadgrove* v *Hole* [1901] 2 KB 1). If unauthorised defamatory matter has been displayed on premises under the defendant's control, he will be liable for failing to remove it, at least where it could be removed without much difficulty or expense, because he is party to the publication (*Byrne* v *Deane* [1937] 1 KB 818, 838—but not where it is very difficult or impossible to remove).

The defendant may be liable for a repetition of defamatory statements where he intends or authorises the repetition (*Parkes* v *Prescott* (1869) LR 4 Ex 169), although he is generally not liable for unauthorised repetition (*Ward* v *Weeks* (1830) 7 Bing 211—unless the person to whom it was published was under a duty to repeat it: *Derry* v *Handley* (1867) 16 LT 263). An unauthorised repetition will normally be treated as a *novus actus interveniens* breaking the chain of causation between the original publication and the damage suffered through the repetition. Nonetheless, in an appropriate case repetition of the sting of the libel by an unauthorised third party may be treated as the natural and probable consequence of the original publication rendering the original publisher liable in respect of the repetition (*Slipper* v *British Broadcasting Corporation* [1991] 1 All ER 165, newspaper reviews of a television broadcast repeating the sting of the libel). This is a question of remoteness of damage, rather than liability, and the issue is whether the repetition was a natural and probable, or foreseeable, consequence, which is a question of fact for the jury.

Where defamatory matter is contained in a book, a journal or a newspaper there will be a series of publications: by the author to the publisher, by the author and publisher jointly to the printer, by the author, publisher and printer jointly to the distributor, and so on. Each repetition is a fresh publication creating a new cause of action (*Duke of Brunswick* v *Harmer* (1849) 14 QBD 185). This applies all the way down the chain of publication, to the bookseller, the librarian, and the newsagent. There is a distinction, however, drawn between those who produced the libel (author, publisher, printer) and those who merely disseminate it. Such a 'mechanical distributor' who disseminates the work in the ordinary way of his business, will be taken not to have published it if he proves: (a) that he did not know that the work contained a libel, (b) that there was nothing in the work or the circumstances in which it came to him or was disseminated by him which ought to have led him to suppose that it contained a libel, and (c) when the work was disseminated by him, it was not by any negligence on his part that he did not know that it contained a libel (*Vizetelly* v *Mudie's Select Library Ltd* [1900] 2 QB 170, 180; *Bottomley* v *F.W. Woolworth & Co. Ltd* (1932) 48 TLR 521). In *Sun Life Assurance Co. of Canada* v *W.H. Smith & Son Ltd* (1934) 150 LT 211, 214, Scrutton LJ suggested that the issue could be reduced to two questions: (a) did the defendant know and (b) ought he to have known (i.e., was he negligent in not knowing) that the work contained defamatory material. In *Vizetelly* v *Mudie's Select Library Ltd* the defendants were liable because they had no procedure for checking for libel the books that they lent and had overlooked the publisher's circular requesting the return of copies of the book in question. The principle is sometimes referred to as 'innocent dissemination', but is more accurately a case of 'no publication' by the defendant. *Faulks*, ch. 11, recommended that the defence should be extended to printers, though in practice printers usually take an indemnity from the publishers (but see *Dering* v *Uris* [1964] 2 QB 669, where printers had paid substantial damages in a settlement, and at the trial of the action against the author the jury awarded damages of one halfpenny). That recommendation has now been taken up in the Defamation Act 1996. Section 1 codifies and modernises the common law principle, by making it available to printers, distributors, sellers, broadcasters of live programmes (such as phone-ins and group discussions) in respect of statements made on the air by persons over whom they have no control, and the operators of a communications system by means of which a defamatory statement is communicated (clearly a reference to the Internet). The section does not apply to the author, editor or publisher (i.e. a commercial publisher whose business is issuing material to the public) of the defamatory statement. However, as Milmo (1996) 146 NLJ 222 and (1995) 145 NLJ 1340, 1341 observes, what the section gives to potential defendants by broadening the ambit of the principle, it may take from them by the subtle alteration that it makes to its chief constituent. Section 1(1) provides that the disseminator's plea of innocence will be defeated by actual knowledge or reasonable foreseeability of a 'defamatory statement', whereas the common law principle that it purports to codify referred to 'libel' (*Vizetelly* v *Mudie's Select Library Ltd*). Strictly, a defamatory statement is a wider and, thus, more foreseeable notion than a libel, which presupposes a defamatory statement *to which there is no defence*, an additional element that increased the extent of knowledge necessary to defeat the plea of innocence at common law. In determining whether the defendant exercised reasonable care the court is directed to have regard to the extent of his responsibility for the content of the statement or the decision to publish it, the nature or circumstances of the publication, and the previous conduct or character of the author, editor or publisher (s. 1(5)).

13.1.4 Libel and slander

A defamatory statement is libel if it is in permanent form such as writing or pictures, or even a waxwork figure (*Monson* v *Tussauds Ltd* [1894] 1 QB 671). It is slander if it takes the form of spoken words, gestures or mimicry. The distinction is that between permanent and transient form (though *Salmond and Heuston,* p. 139, suggests that maybe slander is addressed to the ear, and libel to the eye). Dictating a defamatory letter to a typist is probably slander (*Salmond and Heuston,* p. 154; cf. Hudson (1987) 131 SJ 1236), but when the letter is published to a third party it is libel. Somewhat paradoxically, someone who reads out a libellous letter to a third party commits libel and not slander (*Forrester* v *Tyrrell* (1893) 9 TLR 257 cf. *Salmond and Heuston,* p. 154), though a typist who reads back defamatory matter to the person who dictated it does not publish it (*Eglantine Inn Ltd* v *Smith* [1948] NI 29; cf. *Osborne* v *Thomas Boulter & Son* [1930] 2 KB 226, where the reading back is in the presence of a third party).

Broadcasting for general reception by either radio or television is libel (Broadcasting Act 1990 ss. 166, 201; see also Defamation Act 1952, s. 16; and the public performance of a play is treated as libel (Theatres Act 1968, s. 4, subject to exceptions in s. 7). There is some uncertainty about the status of records and tape recordings. On one view they are in permanent form and therefore libel (*Clerk and Lindsell,* para. 21–06; *Salmond and Heuston,* p. 139), but it can be argued that there is no communication until they are played and this takes the form of speech, which would make it slander (*Winfield and Jolowicz,* pp. 315–16). Films with accompanying sound are libel, at least so far as the visual part is concerned (*Youssoupoff* v *Metro-Goldwyn-Mayer Pictures Ltd* (1934) 50 TLR 581—presumably, video also) but it is not clear whether this is so where the defamatory matter is contained only on the soundtrack.

→   The difference between libel and slander is purely historical in origin (see *Faulks,* para. 86 and app. 6), yet the arbitrary distinctions that have to be drawn can have important consequences for the plaintiff's action. Libel is actionable *per se,* without proof of damage, whereas in slander the plaintiff must prove special damage, except in four types of case. Special damage means the loss of some temporal or material advantage which is either pecuniary or capable of being measured in pecuniary terms (*Chamberlain* v *Boyd* (1883) 11 QBD 407, 415). General damage to the plaintiff's reputation, so that people tend to shun or avoid him is not sufficient (*Roberts* v *Roberts* (1864) 5 B & S 384), but the loss of hospitality, which can be measured in money, is (*Davies* v *Solomon* (1871) LR 7 QB 112; see also *Speight* v *Gosnay* (1891) 60 LJ QB 231—loss of marriage prospects). The damage must not be too remote. It will usually be too remote if it is the result of repetition by others (*Ward* v *Weeks* (1830) 7 Bing 211), unless the defendant authorised or intended the repetition, or it was a natural and probable consequence of the original publication, or the person to whom the original publication was made was under a legal or moral duty to repeat it (*Speight* v *Gosnay* at p. 232; *Slipper* v *British Broadcasting Corporation* [1991] 1 All ER 165).

The four exceptions where slander is actionable *per se* are:

(a)   The imputation of a criminal offence punishable by imprisonment in the first instance, as opposed to the possibility of imprisonment for the non-payment of a fine (*Ormiston* v *Great Western Railway Co.* [1917] 1 KB 598). The suggestion of mere suspicion that the plaintiff has committed such an offence is not sufficient, without proof of special damage (*Simmons* v *Mitchell* (1880) 6 App Cas 156). It is actionable *per se* to say that the plaintiff is 'a convicted person' even though he is not in danger of prosecution, because it would lead people to shun or avoid him (*Gray* v *Jones* (1939) 55 TLR 437).

(b)   The imputation of an existing contagious disease, including veneral disease, leprosy or plague. However, this may be a fixed (and if so, obviously arbitrary) list of diseases (*Clerk and Lindsell*, para. 21–30; cf. *Winfield and Jolowicz*, p. 319). *Clerk and Lindsell* argues, rightly, it is submitted, that an imputation that a person is HIV positive should be actionable *per se*.

(c)   The imputation of unchastity or adultery to any woman or girl (Slander of Women Act 1891).

(d)   An imputation as to the plaintiff's competence or fitness in any office, profession, calling, trade or business. This applies to any trade or profession, no matter how humble, but the plaintiff must carry on the trade or profession at the time of publication. By the Defamation Act 1952, s. 2, it is not necessary for the words to be spoken of the plaintiff in the way of his office, profession, calling, trade or business. This changes the common law position whereby slander which was not connected with the plaintiff's calling was not actionable *per se*, even though the words would tend to injure him in that calling (e.g., an allegation of dishonesty against a solicitor was not actionable *per se* unless it referred to dishonest dealings with his clients: *Hopwood* v *Muirson* [1945] KB 313). It is unclear whether s. 2 also abrogates the common law distinction between offices of profit and offices of honour, whereby the latter were only actionable *per se* where the allegation, if true, would have been a ground for removal from the office. It has been argued that the distinction still applies and that where the office is one of honour, slander is not actionable *per se* unless it imputes dishonesty, lack of integrity or such incompetence as would be a ground for removal from office (*Street*, p. 385, relying on *Robinson* v *Ward* (1958) 108 LJ 491; cf. *Winfield and Jolowicz*, p. 320; *Salmond and Heuston*, p. 189, n. 45).

These differences between libel and slander, and between slanders actionable *per se* and actionable only on proof of special damage, are difficult to justify in principle. The Faulks Committee regarded it as a historical anachronism which could lead to injustice, and recommended the abolition of the distinction (*Faulks*, ch. 2).

13.2   DEFENCES

The defence provided by ss. 2–4 of the Defamation Act 1996 in cases of 'unintentional' defamation, and the defence of 'innocent dissemination' have been mentioned above (paras 13.1.2 and 13.1.3). There is a defence under the Libel Act 1843 available to a newspaper that has published a libel without malice or gross negligence, whereby the defendant may publish a full apology and pay money into court by way of amends. This defence is little used due to substantial procedural disadvantages for the defendant. *Faulks,* para. 373, recommended its repeal. It is also a defence that the plaintiff expressly or impliedly consented to publication of the defamatory matter (*Cookson* v *Harewood* [1932] 2 KB 478n). The defences of truth, absolute and qualified privilege, and fair comment will be considered in more detail.

13.2.1 Truth (or justification)

Once the plaintiff establishes that the imputations against his reputation are defamatory they are presumed to be untrue. It is a complete defence for the defendant to prove that they are true (technically called 'justification'). This applies even where the defendant was actuated by malice. The plaintiff will not be protected from sordid muck-raking about true events, no matter how long in the past they may be. There is an exception to this under s. 8 of the Rehabilitation of Offenders Act 1974 for 'spent convictions'. If the publication by the defendant was malicious (see para. 13.2.5) he cannot rely on the truth about the spent conviction as a defence, the burden of proving malice being the plaintiff's.

There is no duty of care in the tort of negligence to take reasonable care not to injure the plaintiff's reputation by the publication of true statements (*Bell-Booth Group Ltd* v *Attorney-General* [1989] 3 NZLR 148, NZCA). Such a duty would distort the law of defamation and introduce negligence into a field for which it is inappropriate (cf. *Spring* v *Guardian Assurance plc* [1994] 3 All ER 129 where, albeit in the context of an untrue statement, such an argument cut no ice with the House of Lords and did not prevent them holding that an employer owed a duty of care to an employee when providing a reference).

The defendant's honest and reasonable belief that the statement was true is not sufficient, if he cannot prove that it was true. In this sense, mistake is no defence. One consequence of this rule is that the threat of an action for libel can interfere with freedom of speech by deterring publication, since, as Lord Keith commented in *Derbyshire County Council* v *Times Newspapers Ltd* [1993] 1 All ER 1011, 1018: 'Quite often the facts which would justify a defamatory publication are known to be true, but admissible evidence capable of proving those facts is not available'. There is also an element of risk in this defence, because if the defendant's attempt to establish it fails, the jury may take the view that his conduct has aggravated the injury to the plaintiff's reputation and award more in damages. (Note that the revised principle of unintentional defamation under the Defamation Act 1996 may add to the defendants' dilemma in such cases, by enabling them to offer 'amends'. Though amends would have to include the payment of compensation, the fact that, if not agreed, the level of award would be set by the court and not a jury may be enough to make it a viable alternative to justification in cases of evidential uncertainty and fear of jury 'backlash' (see para. 13.1.2 and Milmo (1995) 145 NLJ 1340, 1341).)

It is not necessary to prove the literal truth of a statement if the material facts are proved to be true in substance. The defendant need only prove the facts which justify the 'sting of the charge' (*Edwards* v *Bell* (1824) 1 Bing 403, 409). Allegations which do not affect the plaintiff's reputation will be disregarded. In *Alexander* v *North Eastern Railway Co.* (1865) 6 B & S 340 it was held that a statement that the plaintiff had been convicted of an offence of dishonesty and sentenced to three weeks' imprisonment in default of payment of a fine, could be justified by proof of the conviction and a sentence of two weeks' imprisonment in default of payment.

At common law, where there were several charges the defendant had to prove the substance of each charge in order to rely on the defence. The defendant cannot justify one libel by proving the truth of another distinct libel. Now, by the Defamation Act 1952, s. 5, where a statement contains two or more distinct charges against the plaintiff, a defence of justification will not fail by reason only that the truth of every charge is not proved if the words not proved to be true do not materially injure the plaintiff's reputation having regard to the truth of the remaining charges. However, this defence has been construed narrowly. Section 5 'plainly requires the distinct charges against the plaintiff to be founded on separate words, and these must be contained in the passages of which the plaintiff complains' (*Polly Peck (Holdings) plc* v *Trelford* [1986] 2 All ER 84, 103 per O'Connor LJ). Thus, a plaintiff can bring an action in defamation in respect of one untrue statement which he has selected from a number of other true statements. The defendant *cannot* then rely on the truth of the statements about which the plaintiff has not complained to show that the publication as a whole has not materially injured his reputation (*Speidel* v *Plato Films Ltd* [1961] AC 1090, though this may reduce the amount of damages). This is the position where there are two or more distinct defamatory statements, but the question of whether the statements are distinct is a question of fact and degree. If, in their context, several defamatory statements have a common sting they are not distinct allegations and the defendant may justify the sting by proving the truth of the allegations about which the plaintiff has not complained (*Polly Peck (Holdings) plc* v *Trelford*). The same principle applies to the defence of fair comment.

Faulks, para. 134, recommended that s. 5 be amended so that the defendant should be entitled to rely on the whole publication in assessing the truth of a selected part, thus reversing the effect of *Speidel* v *Plato Films Ltd.* But, in any event, where the plaintiff selects part of a publication alleging that the words are defamatory in their ordinary and natural meaning, and pleads the meaning which he alleges by way of a false innuendo, the defendant is entitled to rely on the whole publication to show that in their context the words bear a different meaning. He may then justify that different meaning even though this involves proving the truth of parts of the publication about which the plaintiff has chosen not to complain (*Polly Peck (Holdings) plc* v *Trelford*).

Where the defendant repeats a defamatory statement made to him, he must prove that the statement was true. He cannot simply rely on the (true) fact that the statement was made to him (*'Truth' (NZ) Ltd* v *Holloway* [1960] 1

WLR 997, PC) or that the statement was made in a document prepared for legal proceedings that are pending (*Stern* v *Piper* [1996] 3 All ER 385, though the defence of privilege may apply to fair and accurate reports of legal proceedings in public). So the person who gives further circulation to an unfounded rumour is as responsible as the person who started it, though he is not prevented from relying on *subsequently* discovered facts to justify it (*Aspro Travel Ltd* v *Owners Abroad Group plc* [1995] 4 All ER 728, CA). Accordingly, a person who publishes a statement to the effect that there are reasonable grounds to suspect the plaintiff of some discreditable conduct will be protected if the occasion was privileged or if he proves that, objectively, there were such reasonable grounds. If the defendant has simply repeated allegations made by others he will either have to call them as witnesses and hope that their evidence as to the reasonableness of the grounds for suspicion is credible, or provide other direct evidence of reasonable grounds (*Shah* v *Standard Chartered Bank, The Times*, 13 May 1998, CA). If the statement carries an innuendo the defendant must prove the truth of the innuendo. It is not sufficient merely to establish the literal truth of the statement. Some doubts have arisen about whether a statement that the plaintiff has been expelled from an organisation or school can be justified by proving the fact of expulsion. In *Cookson* v *Harewood* [1932] 2 KB 478n, 485 Greer LJ said that 'It would be an extraordinary result . . . that if you said that a properly constituted tribunal had found a man guilty of some wrongful act you could be sued for libel unless you could prove that that properly constituted tribunal had rightly decided that he was guilty'. Nonetheless, this was certainly the common law rule with regard to criminal convictions. Proof of the conviction was not proof that the plaintiff had committed the crime, and so the defendant in a defamation action had to prove that the plaintiff was rightly convicted. By the Civil Evidence Act 1968, s. 13 (as amended by the Defamation Act 1996, s. 12), it is provided that where it is relevant in proceedings for defamation, proof that a plaintiff stands convicted of an offence is conclusive evidence that he committed the offence. This does not apply to expulsions, and it is possible that such a statement could support an innuendo that the plaintiff had been expelled for shameful conduct, which might not be justified by proof of the fact of expulsion where there are several possible reasons for expulsion, some of which would not be defamatory (*Salmond and Heuston*, p. 159). Proof that the plaintiff has been acquitted of a criminal charge is not proof of innocence, and so it is still open to a defendant to justify the imputation of an offence (*Loughans* v *Odhams Press Ltd* [1963] CLY 2007). This has not been changed by the Civil Evidence Act 1968.

A defendant seeking to rely on the defence of justification must make clear in the pleadings the meaning of the words which he seeks to justify (*Lucas-Box* v *News Group Newspapers Ltd* [1986] 1 All ER 177).

13.2.2   Absolute privilege

False defamatory statements which are made on a privileged occasion are not actionable. The privilege may be either absolute or qualified. In cases of qualified privilege the defence will be defeated if the plaintiff can prove that the defendant was actuated by malice or that he misused the occasion for an improper purpose. With absolute privilege the defendant is protected no matter how dishonest or malicious his motives. On these occasions the public interest in freedom of speech overrides the individual's claim to protection from false and malicious imputations (*Bottomley* v *Brougham* [1908] 1 KB 584, 587).

Occasions of absolute privilege fall into three broad categories: Parliamentary proceedings, judicial proceedings and official communications.

13.2.2.1 Parliamentary proceedings Statements published during the course of parliamentary proceedings are absolutely privileged (Bill of Rights 1688; *Ex parte Wason* (1869) LR 4 QB 573). This applies to debates, proceedings in committees and the statements of witnesses before committees, but not to statements made by MPs outside Parliament. Where an MP has made a defamatory remark outside Parliament the plaintiff cannot rely on a speech made in Parliament as evidence of the defendant's malice (*Church of Scientology of California* v *Johnson-Smith* [1972] 1 QB 522). The appointment of an MP to, or removal from, a standing committee of the House of Commons forms part of the proceedings of the House and is governed by Parliamentary privilege, as is a letter of complaint written by an MP to the Speaker of the House (*Rost* v *Edwards* [1990] 2 All ER 654). The Register of Members' Interests, however, is a public document and does not fall within the definition of proceedings in Parliament (ibid.). The publication by order of either House of the reports, papers, votes or proceedings of either House is absolutely privileged (Parliamentary Papers Act 1840, s. 1; extracts from such papers have only qualified privilege: s. 3).

In English law, the immunity that Parliamentary privilege affords MPs *qua defendant* does not correspond directly to other principles that might restrict their claims *qua plaintiff* (cf. Australia—defence where defamatory implication contained in 'political discussion or speech' and relates to a 'public officer or a candidate for public office' and defendants can establish that they were neither aware of nor reckless as to its falsity: *Theophanous* v *Herald and Weekly Times Ltd* (1994) 182 CLR 104; subsequently refined and narrowed in *Lange* v *Australian Broadcasting Corporation* (1997) 71 ALJR 818, in which the High Court of Australia held that the defendant in such a case must also act 'reasonably', which meant not only absence of malice but also taking all reasonable steps to obtain and publish a response from the person commented upon—for comment on *Lange* see Chesterman (1998) 6 Tort L Rev 9; Trindade (1998) 114 LQR 1; Twomey (1997) 19 Sydney L Rev 76; America—where a wider version of the defence applies in relation to material defamatory of 'public figures': *The New York Times* v *Sullivan* (1964) 376 US 254; *Curtis Publishing* v *Butts* (1967) 388 US 130; for comment see Cassimatis (1996) 4 Tort L Rev 27 and Loveland (1996) 146 NLJ 148). For a period of time, though, it seemed that the courts' overriding duty to adhere to the principle of Parliamentary privilege itself would, in certain circumstances, indirectly produce that result. In particular, a defamation action brought by an MP was stayed because Parliamentary privilege made it impossible for the defendants to put forward their defence (*Allason* v *Haines* (1995) 145 NLJ 1576—criticism of the plaintiff's performance as an MP in the House of Commons would have involved use of Parliamentary materials to justify it; *Prebble* v *Television New Zealand* [1994] 3 All ER 407, Privy Council; for comment on *Prebble* see Leopold (1995) 15 LS 204). It made no difference that a party (the defendant) wished to use Parliamentary material 'not as a sword but as a shield' (*Prebble* v *Television New Zealand* [1994] 3 All ER 407, 410 per Lord Browne-Wilkinson) as its deployment in either case would be precluded by the Bill of Rights, nor did 'the fact that the maker of the statement is the [plaintiff] . . . affect the question whether [the Bill of Rights] is infringed' (*Prebble* v *Television New Zealand* [1994] 3 All ER 407, 416 per Lord Browne-Wilkinson). The only qualification was that a stay would be ordered only in circumstances where the exclusion of material on the grounds of Parliamentary privilege made it impossible fairly to determine the issue between the parties. As such, the stay was granted in *Allason* because privilege would have deprived the defendants of their only defence, but not in *Prebble* where, despite the exclusion of Parliamentary materials, the defendants were still able to put forward the overwhelming majority of matters upon which they relied in justifying the alleged libel. Therefore, subject to this qualification, this particular consequence of Parliamentary privilege would have the potential to act as a check on an MP's apparent freedom to sue in defamation. However, its impact has been largely nullified by the Defamation Act 1996, s. 13 under which an MP is able to waive Parliamentary privilege and, thus, close the 'loophole' that would otherwise prevent the action (for a review of the earlier conflicting common law on this question see Leopold, op. cit.). The waiver only applies, however, to enable the person waiving privilege to bring proceedings. Section 13(4) preserves the protection from liability as a defendant for words spoken or things done in the course of any proceedings in Parliament, even for the person who has waived the protection under s. 13(1). (See Wilkinson (1997) 60 MLR 388 for comment on s. 13, in the context of the collapse of the libel action brought by Neil Hamilton— then Neil Hamilton MP—against the *Guardian*, as a result of Mr Hamilton's refusal to waive the Parliamentary privilege that, as a result of *Prebble* and *Allason*, had had the effect of staying the proceedings.)

13.2.2.2 Judicial proceedings Statements made in the ordinary course of proceedings before any court or tribunal recognised by law are absolutely privileged (*Dawkins* v *Lord Rokeby* (1875) LR 8 QB 255, 263). This applies to statements made by judges, counsel, witnesses or the parties, in both superior and inferior courts. In relation to witnesses the privilege extends to statements made prior to the issue of proceedings, provided that such a statement was made for the purposes of a possible action and at a time when a possible action was being considered (though the mere fact that a contribution notice had been served did not inevitably mean that judicial proceedings would commence: *Waple* v *Surrey CC* [1998] 1 All ER 624, CA). The privilege also applies to any tribunal exercising an equivalent function, such as a professional disciplinary committee (*Addis* v *Crocker* [1961] 1 QB 11—solicitor, *Leeson* v *General Council of Medical Education* (1889) 43 ChD 366—doctor). It does not apply, however, to administrative proceedings such as a local authority meeting to hear applications for music and dancing licences (*Royal Aquarium & Summer & Winter Garden Society Ltd* v *Parkinson* [1892] 1 QB 431) or licensing justices (*Attwood* v *Chapman* [1914] 3 KB 275) or appeals to the Department of Environment against a planning enforcement notice (*Richards* v *Cresswell, The Times,* 24 April 1987). In *Hasselblad (GB) Ltd* v *Orbinson* [1985] 1 All ER 173 the Court of Appeal held that investigations by the European Commission into anti-competition practices contrary to arts 85 and 86 of the EEC Treaty were administrative rather than judicial proceedings. Nonetheless the court refused to allow a letter of complaint sent to the Commission to be produced in a libel action, because it would be contrary to the public interest, since the Commission should not be frustrated in its duty to enforce compliance with arts 85 and 86 (see *Weir,* p. 546; cf. *Purdew* v *Seress-Smith* [1993] IRLR 77—absolute privilege does not apply to documents or letters written by employers or ex-employees for the purpose of an application for social security benefit, where the position of an adjudication officer is administrative rather than judicial (though qualified privilege would apply). Similarly, the public interest did not require that no action for libel should be allowed in such circumstances; rather the inhibition which a possible action for libel might induce where employers and ex-employees were writing about each other was to be encouraged (cf. *Spring* v *Guardian Assurance Plc* [1994] 3 All ER 129).

The statement does not have to be strictly relevant to the proceedings, but it must have some connection with the case. If a judge or a witness used the occasion to make defamatory comments about issues which were totally unrelated to the proceedings there would be no privilege (*More* v *Weaver* [1928] 2 KB 520, 525; *Seaman* v *Netherclift* (1876) 2 CPD 53). A judge will be liable if he makes defamatory statements in a case over which he has no jurisdiction, but only if he knows of the lack of jurisdiction (*Sirros* v *Moore* [1975] QB 118).

Professional communications between solicitor and client are privileged, and if the communication is made in relation to judicial proceedings the privilege is absolute. It is not clear whether the privilege which attaches to professional communications which are not related to judicial proceedings is absolute or qualified. In *More* v *Weaver* the Court of Appeal held that it was absolute, but in *Minter* v *Priest* [1930] AC 558 the House of Lords expressly left the point open (*Salmond and Heuston,* p. 173 and *Winfield and Jolowicz,* p. 354, regard this as an instance of qualified privilege). The privilege is given a wide and generous ambit of interpretation as long as it is fairly referable to the solicitor and client relationship (*Minter* v *Priest* at p. 568). Thus, discussion about obtaining a loan for a deposit on the purchase of land is within the scope of a solicitor's professional business (ibid.).

By the Defamation Act 1996, s. 14, fair and accurate reports of proceedings in public before a court to which the section applies, if published contemporaneously with such proceedings, are absolutely privileged (see

McCarey v *Associated Newspapers Ltd* [1964] 1 WLR 855). Section 14 applies
to any court in the United Kingdom, including any tribunal or body
exercising the judicial power of the State, the European Court of Justice, the
European Court of Human Rights, and any international criminal tribunal
established by the United Nations or by an international agreement to which
the UK is a party. If the terms of the section are not satisfied, there may be
qualified privilege at common law (para. 13.2.3.3). The publication by the
Lord Chancellor, a designated judge, or the Director General of Fair Trading
of any advice or reasons given by or to him in the exercise of functions under
part II of the Courts and Legal Services Act 1990 (the development of legal
services in England and Wales while maintaining the proper and efficient
administration of justice) is absolutely privileged (Courts and Legal Services
Act 1990, s. 69(2)).

13.2.2.3 Official communications Statements made by an officer of
state to another officer of state in the course of his official duty are absolutely
privileged (*Chatterton* v *Secretary of State for India* [1895] 2 QB 189). This is
said to be based on a rule of public policy that a Minister of the Crown,
including an army officer, should make official communications without the
fear of being sued (*Dawkins* v *Lord Paulet* (1869) LR 5 QB 94, 117). It is not
clear how widely this privilege extends—possibly not to officials below the
rank of Minister (*Szalatnay-Stacho* v *Fink* [1946] 1 All ER 303; see also
Richards v *Naum* [1967] 1 QB 620), and probably not to a Deputy Commissioner of the Metropolitan Police (*Merricks* v *Nott-Bower* [1965] 1 QB 57).
But the fact that a report relates to commercial questions does not prevent it
from being a matter of state (*M. Isaacs & Sons Ltd* v *Cook* [1925] 2 KB 391).

Immunity also attaches to an internal embassy memorandum of a foreign
state. This is based on a different ground of public policy, that by virtue of a
broad concept of international comity an English court should not inquire
into the internal workings of a foreign embassy, particularly when such
documents are regarded as 'inviolable' in international law (*Fayed* v *Al-Tajir*
[1987] 2 All ER 396). The rank of the defendant is irrelevant in this situation;
it is the document itself that is privileged.

Reports of the Parliamentary Commissioner for Administration and of
the Commissioners for Local Administration are absolutely privileged
(Parliamentary Commissioner Act 1967, s. 10(5); Local Government Act
1974, s. 32).

13.2.3 Qualified privilege
According to Lord Atkinson in *Adam* v *Ward* [1917] AC 309, 334, qualified
privilege applies to:

> an occasion where the person who makes a communication has an interest
> or a duty, legal, social, or moral, to make it to the person to whom it is
> made, and the person to whom it is so made has a corresponding interest
> or duty to receive it. This reciprocity is essential.

The rationale for the defence is that in these circumstances:

> the occasion prevents the inference of malice, which the law draws from unauthorised communications. . . . If fairly warranted by any reasonable occasion or exigency, and honestly made, such communications are protected for the common convenience and welfare of society (*Toogood* v *Spyring* (1834) 1 CrM & R 181, 193).

It is for the judge to determine whether the occasion was privileged and whether the communication was made with reference to the privileged occasion. The defendant's mistaken belief that the occasion was privileged is not sufficient to make it so (*Phelps* v *Kemsley* (1942) 168 LT 18, 20; *Davidson* v *Barclays Bank Ltd* [1940] 1 All ER 316). Moreover, the information that is communicated must be related to the occasion which gives rise to the privilege. The defendant cannot use a privileged occasion to make defamatory comments which are unconnected to the purpose of the privilege. It is for the jury to say whether the defendant acted honestly and in good faith. Proof by the plaintiff that the defendant was actuated by express malice removes the privilege (see para. 13.2.5). Similarly, where the range of publication is wider than the occasion warrants, the privilege does not apply. It is sometimes said that the defendant has exceeded his privilege, but this can be misleading. An occasion of privilege between A and B does not necessarily create such an occasion between A and C. 'Excess of privilege' seems to be more a case of 'no privilege' in circumstances where, e.g., A has a duty to communicate to B, but not to C. Confusion will be avoided if it is remembered that it is the occasion of the publication by A to B that is privileged, and not the statement itself.

The defence will be considered under three heads: (a) statements made in pursuance of a duty, (b) statements made for the protection of an interest, and (c) privileged reports.

13.2.3.1 Statements in pursuance of a duty An occasion is privileged if the statement is made pursuant to a legal, social or moral duty incumbent upon the defendant. In itself, this is not sufficient. The person to whom the statement is made must also have an interest or duty to receive the information. Common examples include the giving of a reference about an employee to a prospective employer, and supplying information to the police in response to their questions about a criminal offence. (However, though strictly still available, the defamation claim and the accompanying issue of qualified privilege may become redundant in the case of a referee, in the light of the decision of the House of Lords in *Spring* v *Guardian Assurance plc* [1994] 3 All ER 129, to the effect that in appropriate circumstances, the action against the referee could be framed in negligence. In recognising the existence of a duty of care in negligence in circumstances where the corresponding action in defamation effectively required proof of malice, the House of Lords did not accept that they were thereby encroaching on defamation's proper territory or subverting its influence (concerns that had prevailed in the Court of Appeal [1993] 2 All ER 273; see also *Bell-Booth Group Ltd* v *Attorney-General* [1989] 3 NZLR 148, NZCA para. 13.2.1). Rather, they emphasised that the two torts inhabited entirely separate ground, by protecting different interests via distinct liability mechanisms, and that, in any event, the issue would only arise in those limited instances where there existed the high degree of proximity and foreseeability that had been found in *Spring* (see, especially, Lord Slynn at p. 163).)

In *Watt* v *Longsdon* [1930] 1 KB 130, 147, Scrutton LJ said that:

> Except in the case of communications based on common interest, the principle is that either there must be interest in the recipient and a duty to communicate in the speaker, or an interest to be protected in the speaker and a duty to protect it in the recipient.

The defendant in that case was a director of a company, of which the plaintiff was the overseas managing director. The defendant received information from a foreign manager of the company suggesting that the plaintiff was dishonest and immoral. He wrote back to the foreign manager making defamatory comments about the plaintiff and asking for confirmation of the allegations, but without waiting for this the defendant showed the letter to the chairman of the company, and to the plaintiff's wife, who was an old friend. The statements were untrue. The Court of Appeal held that the defendant's letter to the foreign manager was privileged because they had a common interest in the affairs of the company. The publication to the company chairman was also privileged, because the defendant had a duty as an employee of the company to pass on such information to the chairman. The publication to the plaintiff's wife, however, was not privileged because the defendant had no social or moral duty to inform her about unsubstantiated allegations, even though she might have an interest in hearing about them. It might have been different if the defendant had obtained corroboration or confronted the plaintiff with the allegations beforehand (see also *De Buse* v *McCarthy* [1942] 1 KB 156).

The test for the existence of such a duty is 'Would the great mass of right-minded men in the position of the defendant have considered it their duty under the circumstances to make the communication?' (*Stuart* v *Bell* [1891] 2 QB 341, 350). This must inevitably be a subjective judgment for the judge. All the circumstances will be taken into account, and in particular whether there was a confidential relationship between the defendant and the person to whom he communicated the information, whether the communication was in response to a request for information, and, if it was voluntary, the particular circumstances which might impose a special duty to disclose the information. On these bases, the Court of Appeal in *S* v *London Borough of Newham*, *The Independent*, 26 February 1998, observed that a local authority, while not having a defence of absolute privilege, would be able to claim qualified privilege in an action for defamation brought against it by an employee in respect of information about him sent by the authority to the Department of Health for inclusion on its index of persons unsuitable for work with children.

It is arguable that the contents of an apology attract qualified privilege, on the basis that the publisher of an untrue statement may claim to be under a duty to correct it (*Gatley on Libel and Slander*, 8th ed. (1981) p. 485, para. 1174; see also RSC Ord. 82, r. 5—apology made in open court attracts absolute privilege). However, the first English authority on the point, *Watts v Times Newspapers Ltd* [1996] 1 All ER 152, CA, fell short of providing a generic privilege for apologies and, instead, illustrates that extreme care should be taken not to defame a third party when providing one. The curious facts were that the defendant newspaper had published a defamatory statement suggesting that the plaintiff author had plagiarised another writer's novel when writing a prize-winning work. Inadvertently, the defendant's article was accompanied by a photograph, purportedly of the plaintiff, but in fact of another (entirely unconnected) Mr Watts. In a subsequent edition, the defendant apologised to Mr Watts. At the behest of Mr Watts' solicitors, the apology was detailed and, by virtue of this, had repeated the initial allegation against the plaintiff. The plaintiff commenced libel proceedings in respect of, *inter alia*, the apology. The defendant claimed qualified privilege in respect of the apology, as did Mr Watts' solicitors, who had been joined as third party by the defendant. The Court of Appeal held that the solicitors (and Mr Watts if necessary) were entitled to claim qualified privilege, as the defamatory matter contained in the apology was sufficiently connected to Mr Watts' interest in protecting his reputation and the newspaper's readers' interest in noting that the libel against him had been refuted. However, the court held that the defendant could not simply claim a privilege derivative from that enjoyed by Mr Watts and his solicitors. Rather, the defendants' and third party's claims to privilege called for separate consideration, even though they arose out of the same statement. Accordingly, applying orthodox principles of reciprocal interest, the court held that the defendant did not have a sufficiently direct interest in the provision of the apology, as it was not made to refute an attack on the defendant. As a result, the claim to privilege failed.

Statements made in response to a request for information will usually be privileged, provided the person requesting information has some lawful and reasonable interest in the answer (see, e.g., *Sutherland v British Telecommunications plc, The Times*, 30 January 1989—employers' reply to investigative reporter's request for information as to why plaintiff was dismissed held privileged, since plaintiff had instigated the investigation). In order to be reasonable the questioner's interest in the answer must be relevant to his future conduct, not, e.g., for the satisfaction of his curiosity. Thus, the request by an employer for a reference concerning the character of a prospective employee is intended to guide his decision about whether to engage that person. Similarly, replies to police questions made for the purpose of apprehending offenders are privileged. Replies by trade protection associations to an enquiry by a member about the financial status of customers may, in some circumstances, be privileged (*London Association for Protection of Trade v Greenlands Ltd* [1916] 2 AC 15, 26–7), but probably not if the association is run for profit (*Macintosh v Dun* [1908] AC 390).

A voluntary communication may be privileged, but the courts will tend to look for some relationship between the defendant and the person to whom the information is volunteered, such as a family tie or friendship (see *Todd* v *Hawkins* (1837) 8 C & P 88), or a confidential relationship, such as that between an MP and his constituents (*Beach* v *Freeson* [1972] 1 QB 14) or a host and his guest (*Stuart* v *Bell*). A stranger who volunteers information probably acts on a privileged occasion where the interest of the recipient of the information is particularly strong, e.g., if it is to protect him or his property from danger (see, e.g., *Amann* v *Damm* (1860) 8 CB (NS) 597—defendant believed that the plaintiff had stolen from him, and informed the plaintiff's employer; cf. *Botterill* v *Whytehead* (1879) 41 LT 588).

The person to whom the communication is made must have an interest in receiving the information or a duty to protect the defendant's interest. In *Chapman* v *Ellesmere* [1932] 2 KB 431 the results of an inquiry by the jockey Club into the 'doping' of a racehorse were published in the *Racing Calendar* and *The Times*. The report said that the plaintiff had been 'warned off'. It was held that publication in the *Racing Calendar* was privileged, because the racing public had an interest in this information, but publication in *The Times* was not privileged because the public in general had no such interest (but see now Defamation Act 1996, sch. 1, para. 14, below para. 13.2.3.3.2). Indeed, newspaper defendants have traditionally fared badly when attempting to plead qualified privilege in this way, English courts having regarded it as little more than the sort of general 'public interest' defence that the media demand and to which English law has been antipathetic. It has been said that in some cases communication to the general public may be in the public interest, but it is *not* sufficient that the statement is 'on a matter of public interest believed by the publisher to be true in relation to which he has exercised reasonable care' (*Blackshaw* v *Lord* [1983] 2 All ER 311, 327 per Stephenson LJ). There must be a duty to publish to the public at large and an interest in the public at large to receive the publication. A section of the public is not enough. There is no duty to report to the public where damaging allegations are still under investigation, unless 'the urgency of communicating a warning is so great, or the source of the information so reliable, that publication of suspicion or speculation is justified' (ibid., e.g., danger from suspected terrorists or the distribution of contaminated food or drugs).

There are now significant indications that, notwithstanding traditional judicial resistance to extending common law qualified privilege to newspapers, the tide may yet be turning in the media defendant's favour. In *Tsikata* v *Newspaper Publishing plc* [1997] 1 All ER 655, the Court of Appeal appeared to accept the newspaper defendant's plea that qualified privilege at common law could apply to part of a statement that the plaintiff, a high-ranking Ghanaian government official, had masterminded the assassination of three judges in Ghana (the other part of the statement—a direct report of the Ghanaian judicial inquiry that followed the killings—being covered by statutory qualified privilege under the Defamation Act 1952). It should be noted, though, that the bulk of the Court of Appeal's time in *Tsikata* was taken up with the potential applicability of the statutory qualified privilege defence, and that their Lordships' willingness to afford the defendant the protection of the common law as well could have been as much due to the ease with which the reciprocal public interest/public duty criteria could be met in the unique circumstances of the case (an inquiry into human rights abuse in a Commonwealth country) as to any grand scheme for extending common law qualified privilege for the benefit of media defendants. Much of the doubt has been removed by *Reynolds* v *Times Newspapers Ltd* (1998) 148 NLJ 1051, in which the Court of Appeal confirmed the availability of (but, on the facts, did not allow) a defence of common law qualified privilege for newspaper defendants. The case concerned allegedly defamatory statements published by the defendant newspaper concerning the political crisis in Ireland leading to the resignation of the plaintiff, who was then Taoiseach. The Court of Appeal stated that, in the interests of maintaining a proper balance between the preservation of the right to free speech guaranteed by article 10 of the European Convention for the Protection of Human Rights, and the protection of a public figure's reputation, the defence of common law qualified privilege should be available to a newspaper in respect of a defamatory and factually false publication which was honestly (i.e. not maliciously) made. The Court confirmed, however, that the defence would only be allowed in an individual case if a newspaper could satisfy a three stage test. First, the newspaper had to establish a legal, moral or social duty to the general public to publish the material in question (the 'duty test'). Secondly, it had to be established that the general public had a corresponding interest in receiving the information (the 'interest test'). Thirdly, a defendant has to establish that the nature, status and source of the material and circumstances of its publication are such as to warrant the protection of privilege without malice (the 'circumstantial test'). The media will doubtless welcome the *Reynolds* decision as long overdue judicial acknowledgement of the desirability, in an English law context, of the sort of 'public figure' defence available to the media in other jurisdictions. More caselaw will, however, be required in order to determine the practical availability of the defence and the true nature of a three stage test that does seem somewhat tightly drawn. The first two stages are no more than a reflection of the conventional duty/interest reciprocity central to triggering the defence in other circumstances, while the third stage is an additional, potentially restrictive requirement, likely, in practice, to make a great deal turn on whether newspaper stories are verified and/or come from official sources (the point on which the defendants in *Reynolds* were denied the defence). Moreover, while the Court of Appeal in *Reynolds* suggested that a modern 'human rights' context meant that the first two stages of the test would be more readily held satisfied than formerly, their Lordships also envisaged that consideration of those tests would be restricted to newspaper statements about public figures in their 'public life'.

13.2.3.2 Protection of an interest Qualified privilege attaches to a statement made by the defendant for the protection of a lawful interest. This may be his own interest, a common interest or the public interest. He may protect his own property or his reputation. So an employer may warn employees not to associate with a former employee dismissed for theft (*Somerville* v *Hawkins* (1851) 10 CB 583), and a person whose character is attacked may answer allegations made by the plaintiff with statements which undermine the credibility of the allegations (*Osborne* v *Thomas Boulter & Son* [1930] 2 KB 226). The reply must be relevant to the allegations. The defendant cannot engage in recrimination or trade defamatory comments with the plaintiff. This privilege is analogous to the right of self-defence in trespass to the person (*Turner* v *Metro-Goldwyn-Mayer Pictures Ltd* [1950] 1 All ER 449, 470 per Lord Oaksey).

Cases of common interest arise where both the defendant and the person who receives the communication have a common interest in the subject of the statement. It applies between employees in connection with the business of their employer (*Watt* v *Longsdon* [1930] 1 KB 130). It may also arise between employer and employee. In *Bryanston Finance Ltd* v *De Vries* [1975] QB 703 it was held that where a letter was written to protect the interests of the business there was a common interest between the employer and employee, and so a letter dictated to a secretary in the normal course of business was protected by qualified privilege. Moreover, even where employees have no interest in the communication, this will not defeat a defence of privilege if it is published to them in the ordinary course of business. 'If a business communication is privileged, as being made on a privileged occasion, the privilege covers all the incidents of the transmission and treatment of that communication which are in accordance with the reasonable and usual course of business' (*Edmondson* v *Birch* [1907] 1 KB 371, 382 per Fletcher Moulton LJ). This is a rule of practical common sense, for otherwise the privilege which attaches to the most innocuous transactions, such as supplying an employee's reference, would be defeated. Other examples of common interest include a tenant's complaint to his landlord about the behaviour of a person employed to repair the premises (*Toogood* v *Spyring* (1834) 1 CrM & R 181), and a landlord's complaint to his tenant about the behaviour of lodgers tending to bring the house into disrepute (*Knight* v *Gibbs* (1834) 1 A & E 43). There may also be a common interest between a ratepayer and a local authority councillor in relation to local affairs (*Cutler* v *McPhail* [1962] 2 QB 292; cf. *De Buse* v *McCarthy* [1942] 1 KB 156—ratepayers have no interest in receiving information concerning allegations of dishonesty by council employees while the matter is still under investigation).

Complaints about the conduct of public officials are privileged, since this protects the public interest, but the complaint must be made to the proper authority, i.e., those who have the power to deal with the matter (*Harrison* v *Bush* (1856) 5 E & B 344—an accusation against a magistrate sent to the Home Secretary held privileged even though the correct authority was the Lord Chancellor). Complaint to the general public, e.g., through a newspaper, would be an abuse of the privilege (*Cutler* v *McPhail*; *De Buse* v *McCarthy* — distribution to public libraries). Complaint to an MP about public officials or professional persons will usually be privileged, because he has an interest in the concerns of his constituents and can pass the complaint on to the proper authority (*Beach* v *Freeson* [1972] 1 QB 14).

By the Defamation Act 1952, s. 10, a defamatory statement published by or on behalf of a candidate in a Parliamentary or local government election shall not be deemed to be published on a privileged occasion on the ground that it is material to a question in issue in the election.

13.2.3.3 Privileged reports Fair and accurate reports, by any means, of Parliamentary proceedings have qualified privilege at common law (*Wason v Walter* (1868) LR 4 QB 73), and, by statute, extracts or abstracts of reports, papers, notes or proceedings published by order of Parliament also have qualified privilege (Parliamentary Papers Act 1840, s. 3). This includes publication of such extracts or abstracts by means of a radio or television broadcast (Defamation Act 1952, s. 9(1); Broadcasting Act 1990, sch. 20, para. 1).

Qualified privilege also attaches to fair and accurate reports of judicial proceedings held in public in the United Kingdom. This applies to any court, even if it acts in excess of jurisdiction, and is not limited to contemporaneous or newspaper reports. It does not matter that the proceedings are *ex parte,* or incomplete (*Kimber v Press Association Ltd* [1893] 1 QB 65), but the privilege does not extend to the publication of obscene or blasphemous material, nor to pre-trial reporting of allegations made in court documents that have not been brought into the public arena (*Stern v Piper* [1996] 3 All ER 385, nor where publication has been prohibited by the court. Fair and accurate reports of proceedings in foreign courts are not privileged at common law, unless the public would have a legitimate and proper interest in the subject-matter of the report (*Webb v Times Publishing Co. Ltd* [1960] 2 QB 535—cf. a decision on an important question of commercial law, and a case involving a scandalous affair between private individuals).

By s. 15 of the Defamation Act 1996 the publication of any report or other statement specified in sch. 1 to the Act is subject to qualified privilege. There are two categories: (a) statements privileged without explanation or contradiction; and (b) statements privileged subject to explanation or contradiction. With statements in the second category the defence is not available if it is proved that the defendant has been requested by the plaintiff to publish in a suitable manner a reasonable letter or statement by way of explanation or contradiction, and has refused or neglected to do so. A 'suitable manner' means in the same manner as the publication complained of or in a manner that is adequate and reasonable in the circumstances (s. 15(2); *Khan v Ahmed* [1957] QB 149—a general demand for an apology is not a request within this subsection). Section 15 does not protect the publication of any matter the publication of which is prohibited by law, or of any matter which is not of public concern and the publication of which is not for the public benefit (s. 15(3), (4)—this applies to both categories; 'Public concern' and 'public benefit' are matters for determination by the jury: *Kingshott v Associated Kent Newspapers Ltd* [1991] 2 All ER 99). For example, the publication of irrelevant defamatory comments made at a public meeting will not be protected (e.g., *Kelly v O'Malley* (1889) 6 TLR 62). In all cases under s. 15 the privilege will be defeated by proof of malice.

13.2.3.3.1 Statements privileged without explanation or contradiction (Part I of sch. 1 to the Defamation Act 1996).

Fair and accurate reports of:

(1)   Proceedings in public of a legislature anywhere in the world.

(2)   Proceedings in public before a court anywhere in the world.

(3)   Proceedings in public of a person appointed to hold a public inquiry by a government or legislature anywhere in the world.

(4)   Proceedings in public anywhere in the world of an international organisation or an international conference.

(5)   A fair and accurate copy of or extract from any register or other document required by law to be open to public inspection.

(6)   A notice or advertisement published by or on the authority of a court, or of a judge or officer of a court, anywhere in the world.

(7)   A fair and accurate copy of or extract from matter published by or on the authority of a government or legislature anywhere in the world.

(8)   A fair and accurate copy of or extract from matter published anywhere in the world by an international organisation or an international conference.

13.2.3.3.2   Statements privileged subject to explanation or contradiction   (Part II of sch. 1 to the Defamation Act 1996).

(9)   A fair and accurate copy of or extract from a notice or other matter issued for the information of the public by or on behalf of:

(a)   a legislature in any member State or the European Parliament;

(b)   the government of any member State, or an authority performing governmental functions (including police functions) in a member State, or the European Commission;

(c)   an international organisation or international conference.

The corresponding paragraph contained in the schedule to the Defamation Act 1952 was said to be confined to 'official notices and the like', such as a police message broadcast on television (*Boston* v *W.S. Bagshaw & Sons* [1966] 2 All ER 906), but did not apply to every statement of fact made to a journalist by a government press officer, still less to 'assumption, inference or speculation' (*Blackshaw* v *Lord* [1983] 2 All ER 311).

(10)   A fair and accurate copy of or extract from a document made available in any member State or the European Court of Justice (or any court attached to that court), or by a judge or officer of any such court.

(11)   Fair and accurate reports of proceedings at any public meeting or sitting in the UK of:

(a)   a local authority or local authority committee;

(b)   a justice or justices of the peace acting otherwise than as a court exercising judicial authority;

(c)   a commission, tribunal, committee or person appointed for the purposes of any inquiry by any statutory provision, by Her Majesty or by a Minister of the Crown or a Northern Ireland Department;

(d)   a person appointed by a local authority to hold a local inquiry in pursuance of any statutory provision;

(e)   any other tribunal, board, committee or body constituted by or under, and exercising functions under, any statutory provision.

(12)   A fair and accurate report of proceedings at any public meeting held in a member State, i.e., a meeting bona fide and lawfully held for a lawful purpose and for the furtherance or discussion of a matter of public concern, whether admission to the meeting is general or restricted.

(13)   A fair and accurate report of proceedings at a general meeting of a UK public company; fair and accurate copies or extracts from documents circulated to members of a UK public company on the authority of the board of directors, by the auditors of the company, or by a member of the company in pursuance of a statutory right; and fair and accurate copies or extracts from documents circulated to members of a UK public company relating to the appointment, resignation, retirement or dismissal of directors of the company.

(14)   A fair and accurate report of any finding or decision of any of the following descriptions of association, or of any committee or governing body of such an association, i.e. an association formed in the UK or another member State for the purpose of:

(a)   promoting or encouraging the exercise of or interest in any art, science, religion or learning and empowered by its constitution to exercise control over or adjudicate upon matters of interest or concern to the association, or the actions or conduct of any persons subject to such control or adjudication;

(b)   promoting or safeguarding the interests of any trade, business, industry or profession, or of the persons carrying on or engaged in any trade, business, industry or profession, and empowered by its constitution to exercise control over or adjudicate upon matters connected with that trade, business, industry or profession, or the actions or conduct of those persons;

(c)   promoting or safeguarding the interests of a game, sport or pastime to the playing or exercise of which members of the public are invited or admitted, and empowered by its constitution to exercise control over or adjudicate upon persons connected with or taking part in the game, sport or pastime;

(d)   promoting charitable objects or other objects beneficial to the community, and empowered by its constitution to exercise control over or adjudicate on matters of interest or concern to the association, or the actions or conduct of any person subject to such control or adjudication.

(15)   A fair and accurate report of, or copy of, or extract from any adjudication, report, statement or notice issued by a body, officer or other person designated by order by the Lord Chancellor (for England and Wales and Northern Ireland) or the Secretary of State for Scotland.

13.2.4 Fair comment
The defence of fair comment protects honest expressions of opinion on matters of public interest. It is an important element of freedom of speech

and the courts are careful to preserve its broad scope (*Slim* v *Daily Telegraph Ltd* [1968] 2 QB 157, 170). For the defence to apply it must be a comment on a matter of public interest, it must be a statement of opinion, not fact, and it must be 'fair', which in this context means honest. Proof by the plaintiff that the defendant was actuated by malice will defeat the defence.

Fair comment has occasionally been regarded as a species of qualified privilege, but this does not seem to be correct. Today, they are generally treated as quite distinct defences.

As with the defence of justification, a defendant who seeks to rely on the defence of fair comment must spell out, with sufficient precision to enable the plaintiff to know the case he has to meet, the comment that he claims to be fair comment (*Control Risks Ltd* v *New English Library Ltd* [1989] 3 All ER 577).

13.2.4.1 Matters of public interest The defence is available only for comments on matters of public interest or matters which have been submitted for public criticism. If the subject-matter of the comment does not fall into this category the defendant must rely on truth or privilege. Whether a matter is of public interest is a question to be determined by the judge. This is given a wide classification. 'Whenever a matter is such as to affect people at large, so that they may be legitimately interested in, or concerned at, what is going on; or what may happen to them or to others; then it is a matter of public interest on which everyone is entitled to make fair comment' (*London Artists Ltd* v *Littler* [1969] 2 QB 375, 391 per Lord Denning MR). This includes the behaviour of public figures, such as those in government, public officials and institutions and even some private organisations. Matters submitted for public criticism include such items as books, public exhibitions, theatrical performances, newspapers, and even criticism of another's work may itself be subject to criticism.

13.2.4.2 Comment and fact The defamatory imputation must take the form of a comment and be based on facts which are true. The defence protects a defendant's expression of opinion, not assertions of fact. If the comment amounts to a statement of fact then it must be proved to be true or privileged. The distinction between fact and comment is not always easy to draw. For example, are immorality and sin facts or matters of opinion? (*Winfield and Jolowicz*, p. 346). Where the statement is a mixture of facts and opinion based on the facts, the facts must be proved to be true in substance. This is subject to an exception where the statement of fact is privileged, e.g., a fair and accurate report of a statement made in judicial proceedings can be the subject of fair comment, even though the statement is subsequently proved to be untrue (*Addis* v *Odhams Press Ltd* [1958] 2 QB 275, 285). In these circumstances it is not sufficient for the defendant to establish that the statement upon which he has expressed a fair comment was made on a privileged occasion. He must also prove that his report of the statement was fair and accurate (*Brent Walker Group plc* v *Time Out Ltd* [1991] 2 All ER 753). Additionally, by the Defamation Act 1952, s. 6, a defence of fair comment will not fail 'by reason only that the truth of every allegation of fact is not proved if the expression of opinion is fair comment having regard to such of the facts alleged or referred to in the words complained of as are proved'. But defamatory imputations in the *facts* stated (as opposed to the comment) are actionable unless proved to be true.

Where comment is not based on fact then it will be treated as an assertion of fact and must be proved to be true. The facts must be stated or indicated in such a manner that it is clear upon what facts the comment is based. This does not mean that comment on a book or a play must specify the detailed facts upon which the defendant's opinion is based, but the public must have 'at least the opportunity of ascertaining for themselves the subject-matter on which the comment is founded' (*Kemsley* v *Foot* [1952] AC 345, 356). So where the subject-matter is well known or easily ascertainable the defendant may simply refer to it as the basis of a comment. A sufficient substratum of fact may be impliedly indicated by the comment itself. In *Kemsley* v *Foot* the defendant published an article which was very critical of the conduct of a newspaper which had no connection with the plaintiff, under the heading 'Lower than Kemsley'. It was held that the defence of fair comment was available, because the comment indicated that the relevant facts consisted of the conduct of the Kemsley Press. *Kemsley* v *Foot* is authority for the proposition that if the words complained of by the plaintiff are clearly comment (as opposed to assertions of fact) and the words identify the subject matter (i.e., the facts) commented upon, it is legitimate to look at that extraneous subject matter in order to determine whether the comment is fair. On the other hand, in *Telnikoff* v *Matusevitch* [1991] 4 All ER 817 the House of Lords held that where there was a question of construction as to whether the words were comment or an assertion of fact the court cannot have regard to the wider context of the publication, for example, to documents incorporated in the publication by reference. The subject matter cannot be looked at 'for the purpose of turning what on the face of it is a statement of fact into a comment' (per Lord Keith at p. 824). Thus, where a claim was brought in respect of an allegedly libellous letter published in response to a newspaper article written by the plaintiff, the court could not look at the article, which was the context in which the letter had been written, to determine whether the words complained of were capable of being understood as statements of fact rather than comment (see Sutherland (1992) 55 MLR 278).

13.2.4.3 What is 'fair' comment? To be fair, comment must be based upon true facts which are in existence when the comment is made (*Cohen* v *Daily Telegraph Ltd* [1968] 1 WLR 916). 'To say that you may first libel a man, and then comment upon him is obviously absurd' (*R* v *Carden* (1879) 5 QBD 1, 8 per Cockburn CJ; though see *Addis* v *Odhams Press Ltd* [1958] 2 QB 275, para. 13.2.4.2). But if the facts are true and the defendant is 'an honest man expressing his genuine opinion on a subject of public interest' (*Slim* v *Daily Telegraph Ltd* [1968] 2 QB 157, 170), it is irrelevant that a reasonable man would not hold such an opinion. In *Merivale* v *Carson* (1887) 20 QBD 275, 281, Lord Esher said that the test was 'Would any fair man, however prejudiced he may be, however exaggerated or obstinate his views, have said that which this criticism has said of the work which is criticised?' This is somewhat misleading because it is difficult to see how a 'fair man' could have prejudiced or exaggerated views, and in *Turner* v *Metro-Goldwyn-Mayer Pictures Ltd* [1950] 1 All ER 449 Lord Porter said (at p. 461) that he would adopt this test, but substitute 'honest' for 'fair' in order to avoid the suggestion that the comment must be reasonable. Indeed, the Faulks Committee recommended changing the title of the defence from 'fair comment' to simply 'comment', since in reality it protects comments that, viewed objectively, may be patently unfair (*Faulks,* para. 152). The use of the word 'honest' suggests that the defence of fair comment involves a subjective test, which would require not only that the view expressed be one which an honest man, however prejudiced and obstinate, could hold (objective test), but also that the defendant himself did hold that view (subjective test). In *Telnikoff* v *Matusevitch* [1990] 3 All ER 865 the Court of Appeal held that honesty of belief is not an essential element of the defence which the defendant must prove, a view affirmed by the House of Lords ([1991] 4 All ER 817, 824–5). Once the defendant's comment is considered fair by the objective test, it is presumed to be the honest expression of his view unless the plaintiff pleads and proves express malice. This is essentially a question of who has the burden of proof. It is now clear that the burden of proving malice lies with the plaintiff where the defendant pleads fair comment, as with the defence of qualified privilege.

Comment which is actuated by malice or improper motives will be unfair, but the violence or excess of the criticism does not in itself make the comment unfair. It may be evidence, however, that the defendant is acting maliciously. Moreover, the defendant is not entitled to engage in mere invective or abuse under the guise of criticism (*Turner* v *Metro-Goldwyn-Mayer Pictures Ltd* [1950] 1 All ER 449, 461) or to make personal imputations which are irrelevant to the subject-matter of the comment (*McQuire* v *Western Morning News Co. Ltd* [1903] 2 KB 100, 109). So, whilst it is true that the crank may say what he honestly thinks just as much as the reasonable man who sits on a jury (*Silkin* v *Beaverbrook Newspapers Ltd* [1958] 1 WLR 743, 747), the jury still exercise an element of discretion in determining whether exaggerated, obstinate or prejudiced comments are the defendant's genuine opinion. *Clerk and Lindsell,* para. 21–150, suggests that greater latitude will probably be allowed in dealing with matters of taste and opinion than with matters involving questions of conduct and character.

Where the defendant's comment imputes corrupt, dishonest or wicked motives to the plaintiff the position is different. In *Campbell* v *Spottiswoode* (1863) 3 B & S 769, 776, Cockburn CJ said that a 'man has no right to impute to another, whose conduct may be fairly open to ridicule or disapprobation, base, sordid and wicked motives, unless there is so much ground for the imputation that a jury shall find, not only that he had an honest belief in the truth of his statements, but that his belief was not without foundation'. A requirement that the defendant's belief be 'well-founded' is ambiguous. On one view it suggests that the imputation must be true, so the defence ceases to be fair comment and becomes justification. This is apparently supported by dicta in *Dakhyl* v *Labouchere* [1908] 2 KB 325n, 329 and *Hunt* v *Star Newspaper Co. Ltd* [1908] 2 KB 309, 320 that such an imputation must be 'warranted' by the facts in the sense that it is a reasonable inference from the facts (see also *Salmond and Heuston*, p. 184). However, in *Peter Walker Ltd* v *Hodgson* [1909] 2 KB 239, 253, Buckley LJ said that the defendant would not be liable if the comment was 'in the opinion of the jury warranted by the facts, in the sense that a fair-minded man might upon these facts bona fide hold that opinion'. This test does not require the defendant to establish the truth of the imputation, but it is narrower than the general defence of fair comment because the defendant must show that his opinion was *reasonable* (*Faulks*, para. 164). *Faulks*, para. 169, recommended that neither test was appropriate, and that the normal principles of fair comment should apply to all cases involving expression of opinion.

Where a newspaper publishes a letter which is apparently within the defence of fair comment, the newspaper does not lose the defence simply because it cannot prove that the letter expressed the writer's honest opinion. In *Lyon* v *Daily Telegraph Ltd* [1943] KB 746 the defendants published a letter from a correspondent who had given a false address and possibly a false name also. The defendants had no reason to suspect this, and did not check the name and address. The Court of Appeal held that the defendants did not have to prove that the writer honestly held that opinion in order for them to rely on fair comment, nor was it necessary for a newspaper to verify the names and addresses of all their correspondents. This situation provides an exception to the rule that the comment must be the defendant's genuine opinion. A newspaper or journal may publish letters which express entirely contradictory views, and an editor would hardly be honest if he claimed to adhere to both. Nonetheless, he may still rely on the defence of fair comment. This view is bolstered by the objective test for fairness applied in *Telnikoff* v *Matusevitch* [1991] 4 All ER 817 since if the comment is objectively fair, on the basis that it is a view that any man, however prejudiced and obstinate, could honestly hold, the defendant does not have to prove that he himself did hold that view. The onus shifts to the plaintiff to prove malice.

A comment which is objectively fair, i.e., an expression of opinion which an honest, albeit prejudiced, person could have made, will become unfair if the defendant was actuated by malice (*Thomas* v *Bradbury Agnew & Co. Ltd* [1906] 2 KB 627). Thus, there may be two substantially identical reviews of a play apparently within the scope of the defence, but if one reviewer has a malicious motive he will be unable to rely on the defence, even though there is no substantive difference between the comments made in the reviews (*Faulks*, paras 153–4). Lack of an honest belief in the truth of the comment automatically makes it unfair. But even where the comment represents the defendant's honest opinion, malice in the sense of spite, ill-will or any other indirect or improper motive defeats the defence.

13.2.5 Malice
If the defendant was actuated by malice a defence of fair comment or qualified privilege will fail. In relation to fair comment it covers any indirect

or improper motive which may have actuated the defendant in making the comment, so that as a result the comment is not a genuine expression of his opinion (*Faulks*, para. 157). The test in the context of qualified privilege is very similar. The defendant was malicious if he took improper advantage of the occasion which gave rise to the qualified privilege by making statements which he did not believe to be true, or for the purpose of venting his spite or ill-will towards the plaintiff, or for some other indirect or improper motive (*Faulks*, para. 239; *Horrocks* v *Lowe* [1975] AC 135, 149). As a general rule, if the defendant does not believe the statement to be true he acts maliciously, although there are rare occasions when the defendant may be under a duty to pass on information that he believed to be untrue (*Botterill* v *Whytehead* (1879) 41 LT 588, 590). Where the defendant's statement amounts to a publication of the plaintiff's justifiable attack on the defendant's character, the defendant's 'knowledge' of the facts upon which the plaintiff's comments were based will naturally amount to 'malice' and so defeat a defence of qualified privilege (*Fraser-Armstrong* v *Hadow, The Times*, 21 February 1994, CA, actually decided on the alternative basis that the defendant's knowledge of the justifiable nature of the plaintiff's attack meant that the defence could not arise in the first place). But a defendant who believes the statement to be true does not lose the privilege because he is negligent (*Clark* v *Molyneux* (1877) 3 QBD 237; cf. *Spring* v *Guardian Assurance plc* [1994] 3 All ER 129, HL—duty of care in the tort of negligence in respect of a reference even though corresponding action in defamation would require proof of malice), nor even if his belief is founded on gross unreasoning prejudice (*Horrocks* v *Lowe* [1975] AC 135, 150). It is possible for the defendant to believe in the truth of the statement and yet still act maliciously, by using a privileged occasion for an improper purpose, but the courts will be slow to draw such an inference (ibid.). This can occur where the dominant motive which actuates the defendant is not a desire to perform the relevant duty or to protect the relevant interest, but to give vent to his personal spite or ill-will towards the plaintiff.

The burden of proving malice is the plaintiff's (*Telnikoff* v *Matusevitch* [1991] 4 All ER 817) except in cases of qualified privilege under the Parliamentary Papers Act 1840, s. 3. The publication itself may be evidence of malice, where the language is violently excessive for the occasion, but this is not a necessary inference. The relationship between the parties, before and after the defamatory statement, the defendant's conduct of the litigation and his demeanour in the witness-box may all be evidence of malice. However, his refusal to apologise or withdraw a defence of truth is not evidence of malice because it is consistent with an honest belief in the truth of the statement (*Broadway Approvals Ltd* v *Odhams Press Ltd* [1965] 1 WLR 805; cf. *Simpson* v *Robinson* (1848) 12 QB 511—defendant pleaded truth but did not attempt to prove the defence).

In the case of a joint publication on a privileged occasion the malice of one defendant does not remove the privilege of the other non-malicious defendants. A principal may be vicariously liable for the malice of his agent, but where an agent has an ancillary privilege because the publication by the principal is privileged, the agent's privilege is not destroyed by the principal's malice (*Egger* v *Viscount Chelmsford* [1965] 1 QB 248). It is not clear whether this rule also applies in cases of fair comment, but it is arguable that, in the light of *Lyon* v *Daily Telegraph Ltd* [1943] KB 746, para. 13.2.4.3, it should (see *Faulks*, paras 259–72). The decision in *Telnikoff* v *Matusevitch* appears to provide some support for the view that malice on the part of one defendant, say the writer of a letter to a newspaper, should not defeat a defence of fair comment by another defendant, the newspaper editor, since the objective test means that if the comment is objectively fair it is presumed to be an honest expression of the defendant's opinion unless the plaintiff proves malice. It is difficult to see how proof of malice by, say, the writer renders what is otherwise an objectively fair comment by the editor unfair, unless the editor knew that the writer was actuated by malice (see further Sutherland (1992) 55 MLR 278, 283–4).

FOURTEEN
Defences and limitation

If the plaintiff fails to establish the elements of the tort that he alleges has been committed, his action will fail, and in a sense the defendant's 'defence' has succeeded. The plaintiff loses because he has failed to prove a tort. But even where he succeeds in proving the requirements of a tort, he will still lose if the defendant can rely on a specific defence. As a general rule the burden of proof lies with the defendant when he seeks to rebut liability for a presumptive tort.

Contributory negligence (para. 14.5) is unusual in that it is not a complete defence, but a ground for reducing the plaintiff's damages (though occasionally by 100%). Contribution between tortfeasors (para. 14.6) is not a defence at all, but it is included here because of its similarity to contributory negligence in effectively reducing the sum that a defendant may have to pay (by finding someone else, other than the plaintiff, to blame for the damage). Limitation (para. 14.7) is not strictly a defence either, because it is concerned with the extinction of liability in tort. Its effect, however, is to provide a very good defence in cases where the plaintiff has delayed bringing an action, allowing his claim to become statute barred.

Finally it may be observed that one of the best 'defences' is not usually found in the textbooks. This is the 'judgment proof' defendant, who is uninsured and does not have the resources to satisfy an award of damages (see Davies (1997) 13 PN 72—problems in suing a dissolved company; Pattison [1997] JPIL 264—problems in suing an insolvent defendant). Unless the plaintiff is seeking an injunction it is a profitless exercise to sue a man of straw since, no matter how strong his case, the remedy will be empty and the plaintiff left to meet his own legal costs. Compulsory liability insurance deals with this problem in employment and road accident cases, and the Criminal Injuries Compensation Scheme (para. 12.3) can be seen as serving a similar function for the victims of violent crime. In other areas of tort liability plaintiffs are simply left to rue their experience.

14.1   *VOLENTI NON FIT INJURIA*

Volenti non fit injuria, the plaintiff's voluntary assumption of the risk, is a defence that is in a state of some confusion. This is partly due to a considerable overlap with other conceptual techniques employed to limit or reduce a defendant's liability, such as the exclusion of liability (para. 14.2), contributory negligence (para. 14.5), and the standard of care in negligence. The main problems, however, stem from the indiscriminate use of the word 'consent' in different contexts and for different purposes. *Volenti* is sometimes referred to as 'consent', because it is said that the plaintiff 'consented to run the risk'. But this should be distinguished from consent as a defence to intentional torts such as trespass to the person or to land (where it is called licence; see paras 12.5.1 and 11.3.1). A patient who consents to his doctor performing a surgical operation negatives what would otherwise be a serious battery, but he does not thereby assume the risk of the operation being performed negligently. Consent is sometimes used to justify a different standard of care, at sporting events for example, but here it is being used more as a rationale for a lower standard than as the product of a genuine agreement to run the risk of carelessness by competitors. Occasionally the language of *volenti* is used in circumstances in which it is superfluous. Thus, if the defendant's conduct is not tortious, e.g., if he has not been negligent, it is pointless to speak in terms of the plaintiff assuming the risk (*Smith v Charles Baker & Sons* [1891] AC 325, 366; *Wooldridge v Sumner* [1963] 2 QB 43, 69). A non-negligent motorist who injures a pedestrian is 'not liable' because he is not negligent, not because the pedestrian was *volens* to the risk of non-negligent injury. As a matter of policy the courts impose liability only for negligently inflicted harm on the roads, and so in a sense everyone 'assumes the risk' that he will suffer an injury for which no one is at fault. This is not an application of *volenti* (but see *Titchener v British Railways Board* [1983] 3 All ER 770, 776 and *Slater v Clay Cross Co. Ltd* [1956] 2 QB 264, 271 where this point appears to be overlooked).

Volenti non fit injuria is a voluntary agreement by the plaintiff to absolve the defendant from the legal consequences of an unreasonable risk of harm created by the defendant, where the plaintiff has full knowledge of both the nature and extent of the risk. The defence expresses the concept that an individual should take responsibility for his own actions, although that notion may also be found in other devices which may be employed to prevent a tort claim where the plaintiff is effectively the author of his own misfortune. In *Barrett v Ministry of Defence* [1995] 3 All ER 87 a naval airman died when he fell unconscious and choked to death on his own vomit, having consumed a large amount of extremely cheap alcohol supplied at a Norwegian naval base. The Court of Appeal rejected the suggestion that the defendants owed the deceased a duty of care to prevent him from consuming an excessive amount of alcohol. Beldam LJ (at p. 95) could see:

> . . . no reason why it should not be fair, just and reasonable for the law to leave a responsible adult to assume responsibility for his own actions in

consuming alcoholic drink. No one is better placed to judge the amount that he can safely consume or to exercise control in his own interest as well as the interest of others. To dilute self-responsibility and to blame one adult for another's lack of self-control is neither just nor reasonable . . .

Thus, denying a duty of care in negligence may be just as effective as the *volenti* defence where the court wants to emphasise the individual responsibility of the plaintiff. (The defendants in *Barrett* were held to owe a duty of care on the different basis that after the deceased collapsed the defendants had, by their conduct, assumed responsibility for his care but had been careless in the manner in which they had discharged that responsibility.)

14.1.1 Voluntary
The plaintiff's agreement must be voluntary, which means that he must have a genuine choice.

A man cannot be said to be truly 'willing' unless he is in a position to choose freely, and freedom of choice predicates, not only full knowledge of the circumstances on which the exercise of choice is conditioned, so that he may be able to choose wisely, but the absence from his mind of any feeling of constraint so that nothing shall interfere with the freedom of his will (*Bowater* v *Rowley Regis Corporation* [1944] KB 476, 479 per Scott LJ).

At one time the courts did not place much emphasis on this aspect. An employee who, knowing of the risks of his employment, nonetheless continued in his job was *volens*, though in reality economic pressures meant that he had no true choice about the matter. In *Smith* v *Charles Baker & Sons* [1891] AC 325 the House of Lords recognised this, holding that the plaintiff was not *volens* merely by continuing to work, having already protested to his employer about a dangerous practice. The modern position is that the defence will very rarely be successful in an action by an employee against his employer (*Bowater* v *Rowley Regis Corporation* [1944] KB 476, 480–1 per Goddard LJ, though remember that where the work is inherently dangerous the employer need only take reasonable safety precautions—he does not insure the employee's safety; see further *Johnstone* v *Bloomsbury Health Authority* [1991] 2 All ER 293, 303 where Leggatt LJ said that the employer's duty to exercise reasonable care for the health of employees could not be used to override an express term of the contract of employment as to the number of hours to be worked per week, even if the hours were excessive and injured the plaintiff's health: 'Those who cannot stand the heat should stay out of the kitchen'; query this, however, which in effect amounts to a plea of *volenti*, and cf. the judgment of Stuart-Smith LJ; Browne-Wilkinson V-C would agree with Leggatt LJ if the contract imposed an absolute obligation to work hours which harmed the plaintiff's health, but not where it gave the employer a discretion as to the number of hours: at pp. 304–5; for comment see Dolding and Fawlk (1992) 55 MLR 562; Weir [1991] CLJ 397). Moreover, as a matter of public policy the defence is not available in an action for breach of an employer's statutory duty, except in the limited circumstances specified in *Imperial Chemical Industries Ltd* v *Shatwell* [1965] AC 656 (see para. 5.3.1). The element of compulsion need not come from the defendant, and so an employee who has been instructed by his employer to enter the defendant's premises is not *volens* to the risks he encounters there (*Burnett* v *British Waterways Board* [1973] 2 All ER 631).

In some instances, such as the rescue cases, the plaintiff appears to have faced the risk of injury deliberately. At one time the courts considered that a rescuer had voluntarily assumed the risk of injury in effecting a rescue, but this is no longer accepted as correct (*Haynes* v *Harwood* [1935] 1 KB 146; *Baker* v *T.E. Hopkins & Son Ltd* [1959] 3 All ER 225). This can be justified, if necessary, by saying that the rescuer acted under the compulsion of a legal, social or moral duty and therefore his actions are not truly voluntary. It is simpler to recognise that, if permitted, the *volenti* defence would in effect nullify the courts' recognition of a duty of care owed to rescuers, and this would be self-defeating (see para. 2.2.2), although a rescuer has been held to be contributorily negligent (*Harrison* v *British Railways Board* [1981] 3 All ER 679). If there is no genuine emergency the rescuer might be *volens* (*Cutler* v *United Dairies (London) Ltd* [1933] 2 KB 297).

The potential applicability of *volenti* in the case of a suicide—another ostensibly 'voluntary' act—has caused difficulties. Originally, the Court of Appeal held that where a person of sound mind commits suicide, or injures himself in the attempt, *volenti non fit injuria* would provide a complete defence to an action against hospital or prison authorities in respect of the death or injuries (*Kirkham* v *Chief Constable of the Greater Manchester Police* [1990] 3 All ER 246, 250, 254). In the same case, the Court of Appeal held that where, however, the person's judgment was impaired by mental illness so that he was incapable of coming to a balanced decision, his act would not be regarded as having been truly voluntary and the defence would not apply even though it was a conscious and deliberate act and he was legally sane at the time. As a means of preserving the potential for a *volenti* plea in a suicide case, this distinction would serve its purpose, but it does seem over-technical and, intuitively at least, less suitable than Farquharson LJ's suggestion in *Kirkham* that the defence of *volenti* is inappropriate where the act of the plaintiff relied upon by the defendant to raise the defence is the very act which the defendant was under a duty to prevent. Indeed, subsequently, in *Reeves* v *Commissioner of Police of the Metropolis* [1998] 2 All ER 381, the Court of Appeal adopted that very rationale, in preference to the *Kirkham* distinction, to support their finding that a suicide in custody could not amount to *volenti* even where the suicide was of sound mind (with the plea of *ex turpi causa* failing for the same reason—para. 14.3). This assumes, of course, that the defendant was under a duty of care to prevent a suicide attempt (on which see Jones (1990) 6 PN 107).

14.1.2 Agreement
This is probably one of the most difficult and confused aspects of the defence. Some cases suggest that nothing short of an agreement, whether express or

implied, that the plaintiff will waive any claim against the defendant will suffice (*Nettleship* v *Weston* [1971] 2 QB 691, 701; *Smith* v *Charles Baker &* *Sons* [1891] AC 325, 355). The mere fact that the plaintiff clearly appreciated the risk and was willing to take it is not in itself a basis for inferring such an agreement (*Lynch* v *Ministry of Defence* [1983] NI 216, 237; *Waldick* v *Malcolm* (1991) 83 DLR (4th) 114, Supreme Court of Canada—*volenti* requires not merely knowledge of the physical risk but consent to the legal risk, i.e. a waiver of legal rights that may arise from the harm that is being risked). Indeed, in *Wooldridge* v *Sumner* [1963] 2 QB 43 Diplock LJ went so far as to say (at p. 69) that in the absence of an express contract *volenti* has no application to negligence *simpliciter* (see, however, an explanation of this comment in *Morris* v *Murray* [1990] 3 All ER 801, 805–6, 812–3). Other cases indicate that it applies where the plaintiff merely encounters an existing danger created by the defendant's negligence (*Dann* v *Hamilton* [1939] 1 KB 509, 517; *Titchener* v *British Railways Board* [1983] 3 All ER 770). The latter view is supported by certain statutory provisions such as the Occupiers' Liability Act 1957, s. 2(5), and the Unfair Contract Terms Act 1977, s. 2(3), which assume that *volenti* is available in circumstances not amounting to an agreement, since other subsections deal with the case of agreement between the parties (OLA 1957, s. 2(1), and UCTA 1977, s. 2(1) and (2); see Jaffey [1985] CLJ 87, 93–5).

There is least difficulty in the case of an antecedent agreement between the parties that the defendant will not be liable for a future act of negligence. Where the agreement is express, whether as a contractual term or by notice (as e.g., in *Bennett* v *Tugwell* [1971] 2 QB 267; *Arthur* v *Anker* [1996] RTR 308, CA), then it is operating as an exclusion of liability which is now regulated fairly strictly by statute (see, e.g., *Johnstone* v *Bloomsbury Health Authority* [1991] 2 All ER 293, 301 where the Court of Appeal accepted the possibility that a contractual term which expressly raised the defence of *volenti* might fall within s. 2(1) of the Unfair Contract Terms Act 1977; see para. 14.2). In some circumstances the courts may derive an implied agreement from the parties' conduct that the defendant shall not be liable for future negligence (usually involving vehicle drivers and their passengers, as in the case of extreme inebriation: *Dann* v *Hamilton* and *Morris* v *Murray,* para. 14.1.4; or a criminal escapade: *Ashton* v *Turner* [1981] QB 137). There is an understandable reluctance, however, to conclude that a defendant has been licensed in advance to commit a tort. Moreover, 'if the consent precedes the act of negligence, the plaintiff cannot at that time have full knowledge of the extent as well as the nature of the risk which he will run' (*Wooldridge* v *Sumner* [1963] 2 QB 43, 69 per Diplock LJ). For *volenti* to apply in the case of an antecedent 'agreement', there must at least be some sort of relationship between the parties. A stranger could not be deemed to have agreed to run the risk merely because he knows that the defendant has a propensity to act negligently (see the example of Mellish LJ in *Woodley* v *Metropolitan District Railway Co.* (1877) 2 ExD 384, 394). And even where there is such a relationship, the plaintiff's mere knowledge that the defendant is *likely* to act negligently is not sufficient to imply an agreement (see para. 14.1.4 on drunken or incompetent drivers).

If it is difficult to establish *volenti* from an implied antecedent agreement, it should be virtually impossible to establish where the defendant's negligence has already created a dangerous state of affairs and the plaintiff has simply proceeded to encounter the risk, at least if the defence is based on agreement. As Jaffey [1985] CLJ 87 observes (at p. 91): 'We are clearly in the realm of fiction if a person's conduct in voluntarily taking a known risk is treated as an implied agreement with the person who created the danger'. Certainly, the fact that the plaintiff ran the risk is not itself sufficient to establish an agreement that the defendant should not be liable, where it is reasonable for the plaintiff to do so (see *Clayards v Dethick* (1848) 12 QB 439). Knowledge of a risk is not consent. But where the plaintiff acted unreasonably there is authority for the view that his conduct can amount to *volenti*. The conceptual problem with this approach is that if the plaintiff has acted unreasonably in taking a known risk, why is his conduct not merely contributory negligence? A defendant who takes an unreasonable risk is simply negligent (see para. 3.1.3), so why not a plaintiff? And how is the distinction to be drawn between plaintiffs who are negligent and those who are *volenti*? The distinction is important because *volenti* is a complete defence, whereas damages will be apportioned for contributory negligence. There is a 'serious confusion of thought' in this reasoning (*Atiyah*, p. 54; see generally, Jaffey [1985] CLJ 87, 91–101). Findings of *volenti* in this type of case are not common today, but this should not obscure the fact that the conceptual foundation of the defence is particularly weak here (see Tan (1995) 3 Tort L Rev 208 who proposes an alternative framework for *volenti* based on looser policy notions of whether the plaintiff 'deserves' to be compensated). The very notion of implied consent represents a policy decision about the types of conduct that should defeat a claim in tort. This can be seen from the way in which the requirements of voluntariness and full knowledge of the risk can be either stressed or virtually ignored according to the outcome that the court considers appropriate.

14.1.3 Knowledge

The plaintiff must have knowledge not simply of the existence of a risk, but full knowledge of both its nature and extent (*Osborne v London & North Western Railway Co.* (1888) 21 QBD 220, 223; *Letang v Ottawa Electric Railway Co.* [1926] AC 725, 731; *Wooldridge v Sumner* [1963] 2 QB 43, 69). The test for this is subjective, not objective (*Smith v Austin Lifts Ltd* [1959] 1 WLR 100; *Latchford v Spedeworth International Ltd*, *The Times*, 11 October 1983; cf. *Bennett v Tugwell* [1971] 2 QB 267, 273; see Lowe (1974) 36 MLR 218, 219). In *Morris v Murray* [1990] 3 All ER 801 the Court of Appeal considered the question of whether the plaintiff's intoxication was such that he could be said to be unaware of the nature and extent of the risk of going on a flight with a drunken pilot. Stocker LJ accepted that the test was not objective, rather the question was whether the plaintiff was so intoxicated that he was incapable of appreciating the nature of the risk and did not in fact appreciate it, and so did not consent to it. (Paradoxically, the more in-toxicated the plaintiff is the more likely it is that he was incapable of appreciating the risk, so defeating *the volenti* defence. Thus, constructive knowledge will not suffice. Where the plaintiff did not know, but ought reasonably to have known, of the risk he is not *volens*, though this could be relevant to contributory negligence (*Dixon* v *King* [1975] 2 NZLR 357; *Salmond and Heuston*, p. 477). A strict application of this test combined with insistence on truly voluntary conduct would reduce the *volenti* defence to a residual category of exceptional case, such as deliberate wrongdoing by the plaintiff as in *Imperial Chemical Industries Ltd* v *Shatwell* [1956] AC 656 or *Ashton* v *Turner* [1981] QB 137, para. 14.3. It is, indeed, rare for the defence to succeed today, because the power to apportion responsibility by making a finding of contributory negligence is regarded as a fairer outcome than denying the plaintiff any redress in circumstances where the defendant was in breach of duty (*Nettleship* v *Weston* [1971] 2 QB 691, 701).

It has always been emphasised that knowledge of the risk in itself is not sufficient (though the courts came close to this proposition in 19th-century employers' liability cases). The maxim is *volenti* not *scienti non fit injuria* (*Thomas* v *Quartermaine* (1887) 18 QBD 685, 696; UCTA 1977, s. 2(3); though see the Congenital Disabilities (Civil Liability) Act 1976, s. 1(4), para. 2.2.2, where the parents' knowledge of the risk of disability due to an occurrence prior to conception defeats the child's claim). So knowledge that the defendant is an incompetent driver would not render a passenger in the vehicle *volenti* to his negligent driving (*Nettleship* v *Weston*; *Dann* v *Hamilton* [1939] 1 KB 509, 518). But the plaintiff's knowledge may affect his action in two other ways. In some instances a warning of the danger may be sufficient to discharge the defendant's duty, so that he will not be in breach if the plaintiff knows about the risk (see paras 6.1.3.4 and 6.2.4). Secondly, if the plaintiff knowingly runs a risk, while not necessarily constituting an assumption of the risk, this may be evidence of contributory negligence.

14.1.4 Drunken drivers and sporting events

If the plaintiff accepted a lift in a motor vehicle from a driver who was obviously inebriated, is he taken to have assumed the risk of injury? In *Dann* v *Hamilton* [1939] 1 KB 509, Asquith J held that *volenti* did not apply to this situation, unless the drunkenness was so extreme and so glaring that accepting a lift was equivalent to 'intermeddling with an unexploded bomb or walking on the edge of an unfenced cliff'. This is consistent with the position of a driver who is known to be incompetent. In each case he is not as capable of achieving the standard of the reasonably competent driver, though for different reasons, but the passenger does not consent to the specific act of negligence that causes the injury. *Dann* v *Hamilton* was approved by a majority of the Court of Appeal in *Nettleship* v *Weston* [1971] 2 QB 691, where it was said that the passenger would be guilty of contributory negligence (see *Owens* v *Brimmell* [1977] QB 859—20% reduction; cf. *Donelan* v *Donelan and General Accident Fire and Life Insurance* [1993] PIQR P205—75% reduction where defendant drove plaintiff's car at plaintiff's instigation and plaintiff knew that defendant was an inexperienced driver and drunk; see also *Barrett* v *Ministry of Defence* [1995] 3 All ER 87, CA—airman drank himself unconscious and died due to lack of care by the defendants; two thirds reduction for the deceased's contributory negligence).

In *Morris* v *Murray* [1990] 3 All ER 801 the plaintiff went for a joyride in a light aircraft piloted by the defendant in the knowledge that the defendant was extremely drunk. The aircraft crashed shortly after take-off, killing the defendant and injuring the plaintiff. The Court of Appeal held that the plaintiff was *volens* to the risk because the pilot's drunkenness was so extreme and so glaring that to participate in the flight was to engage in an intrinsically and obviously dangerous occupation (applying the dictum of Asquith J in *Dann* v *Hamilton*): it was equivalent to meddling with an unexploded bomb. The court clearly took the view that accepting a lift with a drunken pilot is inherently more dangerous than with a drunken motorist. Fox LJ said that the 'wild irresponsibility of the venture' was such that the loss should be left where it fell.

The Road Traffic Act 1988, s. 149 (formerly Road Traffic Act 1972, s. 148(3)), seeks to prevent reliance on the *volenti* defence where a passenger sues a vehicle driver in circumstances where, under the Act, insurance is compulsory. It had been argued that, while this negates express agreements such as a notice in the vehicle, it does not apply to cases of implied agreement (Symmons (1973) 123 NLJ 373). Following some judicial disagreement (compare *Gregory* v *Kelly* [1978] RTR 426 with *Ashton* v *Turner* [1981] QB 137) the Court of Appeal has held that the provision prevents a defendant from relying on any form of the *volenti* defence (*Pitts* v *Hunt* [1990] 3 All ER 344, applying the Scottish case of *Winnik* v *Dick* 1984 SLT 185 and disapproving *Ashton* v *Turner* on this point). The Road Traffic Act 1988, s. 149, does not preclude a plea of *ex turpi causa*, however (*Pitts* v *Hunt*, see para. 14.3), and clearly will be irrelevant where the plaintiff was a passenger in a vehicle which is not subject to the Act (as in *Morris* v *Murray* [1990] 3 All ER 801).

In cases involving injury to spectators or competitors at sporting events the courts sometimes speak in terms of assumption of risk. In *Wooldridge* v *Sumner* [1963] 2 QB 43, 68, for example, Diplock LJ said that a 'person attending a game or competition takes the risk of any damage caused to him by any act of a participant done in the course of and for the purposes of the game or competition' (see also *Hall* v *Brooklands Auto Racing Club* [1933] 1 KB 205, 214; *Condon* v *Basi* [1985] 2 All ER 453). This is not an application of *volenti non fit injuria*. It is true that in a sport which necessarily involves some physical contact the players can be taken impliedly to consent to those contacts which occur within the ordinary performance of the game. But this consent negatives what would otherwise be a battery (para. 12.5.1; see, e.g., *Dann* v *Hamilton* [1939] 1 KB 509, 516), it is not consent to negligence by other competitors. For example, in *Smoldon* v *Whitworth* [1997] PIQR P133, 147, a case in which a colts rugby player sued the referee in negligence for failing to control the manner in which the players were scrummaging, the Court of Appeal stated that:

The plaintiff had of course consented to the ordinary incidents of a game of rugby football of the kind in which he was taking part. Given, however, that the rules were framed for the protection of him and other players in the same position, he cannot possibly be said to have consented to a breach of duty on the part of the official whose duty it was to apply the rules and ensure as far as possible that they were observed.

Consent in sport negatives liability in battery for those contacts that can reasonably be expected to occur in the course of the game, and so competitors 'assume the risk of injury' from such contacts in the absence of negligence. But this is no more than saying that in the absence of a battery there is no liability for non-negligently inflicted injury, and in this sense everyone 'assumes the risk of accidental injury' when liability depends on the proof of negligence. Similarly, spectators do not assume the risk of negligence simply by being present at the event. For the purposes of *volenti* the relevant consent 'is not consent to the risk of injury but consent to the lack of reasonable care that may produce that risk' (per Diplock LJ in *Wooldridge* v *Sumner*). Thus, it is one thing to say that spectators, say at a cricket match, 'assume the risk' of injury by a ball struck beyond the boundary, but it is quite another to say that they assume the risk of negligence by the players. (In *Murray* v *Harringay Arena Ltd* [1951] 2 KB 529 a six-year-old spectator was injured by an ice-hockey puck and the occupiers of the arena were held not liable. This cannot be a case of *volenti* because the plaintiff can hardly have appreciated the full extent and nature of the risk.)

Why, then, do the courts speak in terms of assumption of risk in connection with injuries sustained at sporting events? It would appear that this is partly due to the confusion between *volenti* and consent to what otherwise would be a battery, which has already been referred to. But it is also due to an unnecessary misuse of the word 'consent' in order to *justify* a lower measure of the standard of care. In *Hall* v *Brooklands Auto Racing Club* [1933] 1 KB 205 for example, Scrutton LJ said (at p. 214):

> What is reasonable care would depend on the perils which might reasonably be expected to occur, and the extent to which the ordinary spectator might be expected to appreciate and take the risk of such perils.

The conduct that will be sufficient to satisfy the legal standard of reasonable care always varies with the circumstances. The fact that conduct which caused harm occurred in the course of a competitive sport is relevant to whether it was reasonable. So a driver in a race can drive faster and take more risks than would be reasonable if he were driving on the highway (see para. 3.2.2). It is redundant to justify this by reference to a fictional consent by spectators, on the basis that they 'voluntarily' attended the event. People 'voluntarily' go on to the highway, but no one argues that this amounts to 'consent' or an 'assumption of risk' (nor even when they 'voluntarily' go on to someone else's premises, which is a closer analogy). The language of *volenti* simply confuses the real issue here (cf. Jaffey [1985] CLJ 87, 107–8).

14.2 EXCLUDING LIABILITY

It is not uncommon for persons to seek to exclude or limit their liability in tort. This usually takes the form of a contractual provision excluding liability to the other party to the contract, e.g., for 'any damage howsoever caused'. Where such a clause is effective it will normally exclude a concurrent duty in tort, so that a plaintiff will not be able to avoid its consequences by electing to sue in tort rather than contract. Liability may also be excluded by a non-contractual notice, a device which is most frequently encountered in the context of occupiers' liability (see especially paras 6.1.5 and 6.2.6). The element of 'agreement' involved in this defence suggests that it is analogous to the defence of consent or voluntary assumption of risk, but the case of *White* v *Blackmore* [1972] 2 QB 651, where *volenti* failed but an exclusionary notice succeeded as a defence, makes it clear that the two defences are distinct.

The power to exclude liability has been restricted by statute. The most important legislation is the Unfair Contract Terms Act 1977. In relation to 'business liability' (i.e., breach of obligations or duties arising 'from things done or to be done by a person in the course of a business': s. 1(3)(a), see para. 6.1.5), a person cannot exclude or restrict his liability for death or personal injury resulting from negligence (s. 2(1)), and in respect of other loss or damage cannot exclude or restrict liability unless a 'reasonableness' test is satisfied (s. 2(2); see also s. 5 with regard to exclusions operating by reference to consumer 'guarantees'; Coote (1978) 41 MLR 312, 319–22). When determining whether an 'exclusion' or 'restriction' of liability falls within s. 2 of the Act the court will look at the substance and effect of the term rather than its form (*Phillips Products Ltd* v *Hyland* [1987] 2 All ER 620, 626; *Smith* v *Bush* [1989] 2 WLR 790, 809 per Lord Griffiths), so that it is arguable that a contract term which purports to raise the defence of *volenti non fit injuria* is within the Act (*Johnstone* v *Bloomsbury Health Authority* [1991] 2 All ER 293; cf., however, s. 2(3) which appears to assume that exclusion of liability and *volenti* are distinct). In addition, s. 13(1) provides that where the Act prevents the exclusion or restriction of liability it also prevents making enforcement of the liability subject to restrictive or onerous conditions, excluding or restricting any right or remedy or rules of evidence or procedure, or excluding or restricting the relevant obligation or duty. It is now clear that the combined effect of s. 13(1) and s. 2 is that disclaimers of liability in the context of negligent statements are caught by the Act (*Smith* v *Bush* [1989] 2 WLR 790, where an argument that such a disclaimer prevented any duty of care from arising, and so there was no 'liability' to be excluded, was rejected by the House of Lords, see para. 2.2.4.1.3; see also Misrepresentation Act 1967, s. 3). In determining what is 'reasonable' in relation to a non-contractual notice the court must have regard 'to all the circumstances obtaining when the liability arose or (but for the notice) would have arisen' (s. 11(3)). In *Smith* v *Bush* Lord Griffiths listed (at p. 809) a number of factors: Were the parties of equal bargaining power? In the case of advice, would it have been reasonably practicable to obtain the advice from an alternative source taking into account considerations of cost and time? How difficult is the task being undertaken for which liability is being excluded? What are the practical consequences, taking into account the sums of money at stake and the ability of the parties to bear the loss involved, particularly in the light of the existence

of liability insurance? (see also per Lord Templeman at pp. 804–6; and
s. 11(4); Kaye (1989) 52 MLR 841, 846; see further *McCullagh v Lane Fox
and Partners Ltd* [1996] 18 EG 104 and *Omega Trust Co. Ltd v Wright Son &
Pepper* [1997] 18 EG 120, discussed at para. 2.2.4.1.3(h) *Disclaimers*).

The Unfair Contract Terms Act does not prevent the exclusion of duties
in tort which are stricter than a duty to take reasonable care, but there may
be other statutory restrictions. For example, under s. 7 of the Consumer
Protection Act 1987 liability for defective products under Part I of that Act
cannot be excluded. Again, by the Road Traffic Act 1988, s. 149, liability for
personal injury or death to motor vehicle passengers cannot be excluded by
agreement or the *volenti* defence. This applies both to 'business' and private
motorists, though insurance against such liability is compulsory (Road Traffic
Act 1988, ss. 143–145; see also Public Passenger Vehicles Act 1981, s. 29,
preventing the exclusion of a carrier's liability for personal injury to a
passenger in a public service vehicle).

The general policy of the law, then, has been to look unfavourably on the
exclusion of liability, particularly in the case of personal injuries. But in the
realm of damage to property and financial loss, contractual exclusion clauses
may form part of a long-established pattern of commercial risk allocation,
which is reflected in the prices charged for particular goods or services and
the levels of insurance undertaken by the the parties (see, e.g., *Gillespie
Brothers & Co. Ltd v Roy Bowles Transport Ltd* [1973] 1 QB 400, 412). Indeed,
this may even be embodied in international conventions such as the Hague
Rules (see Carriage of Goods by Sea Act 1971). It is a basic rule of the law
of contract that a person who is not a party to the contract is not bound by
and cannot rely on its terms (*Scruttons Ltd v Midland Silicones Ltd* [1962] AC
446). With the rapid expansion of liability in the tort of negligence in recent
years, both in terms of who can maintain an action and the type of (financial)
loss that is actionable, some defendants have found that apparently valid and
reasonable exclusion or limitation clauses might not be effective against third
parties suing in tort. The prospect that tort could be used to undermine
commercial risk allocation has produced two different judicial responses. The
first is to say that the task of fitting contractual obligations into tort actions
is too complex, and so there should be no liability in tort in such a situation
(see, e.g., Lord Brandon of Oakbrook in *Junior Books Ltd v Veitchi Co. Ltd*
[1983] 1 AC 520; Oliver LJ and Sir John Donaldson MR in *Leigh & Sillavan
Ltd v Aliakmon Shipping Co. Ltd* [1985] 2 All ER 44). The alternative is to
allow the provisions of the contract to structure the duty of care owed by the
defendant to the third party (a view preferred in particular by Robert Goff LJ
in *Leigh & Sillavan Ltd v Aliakmon Shipping Co. Ltd* and *Muirhead v Industrial
Tank Specialities Ltd* [1985] 3 All ER 705 and generally more consistent with
the views of Lord Goff in *Henderson v Merrett Syndicates Ltd* [1994] 3 WLR
761, 788 that 'the common law is not antipathetic to concurrent liability'
even though '[t]he result may be untidy').

In *Junior Books Ltd v Veitchi Co. Ltd* the question arose whether defendant
subcontractors could rely on an exclusion clause in their contract with the
main contractors when sued in tort by a building owner. Lord Roskill

conceded that, by analogy with the disclaimer in *Hedley Byrne & Co. Ltd* v *Heller & Partners Ltd* [1964] AC 465, such a clause 'according to the manner in which it was worded might in some circumstances limit the duty of care'. This dictum was subsequently applied in *Southern Water Authority* v *Carey* [1985] 2 All ER 1077 where it was held that a prima facie duty of care owed by subcontractors to a building owner could be negatived by a limitation clause in the main building contract (applying Lord Wilberforce's two-stage test for the duty of care in *Anns* v *Merton London Borough Council* [1978] AC 728, para. 2.1.1). However, in *Leigh & Sillavan Ltd* v *Aliakmon Shipping Co. Ltd* [1986] 2 All ER 145 Lord Brandon of Oakbrook disagreed that the disclaimer used by Heller & Partners Ltd was analogous, because that had operated directly between the plaintiffs and the defendants. His Lordship could not find 'any convincing legal basis for qualifying a duty of care owed by A to B by reference to a contract to which A is, but B is not, a party'. But, with respect, this rather begs the question of what constitutes the legal basis of a duty of care. Since the very *existence* of a duty of care is a policy decision, there is no reason why the nature and extent of the duty should not be qualified by policy considerations, such as the existence of contractual provisions to which the plaintiff is not a party, as Lord Wilberforce's test explicitly recognised.

The more recent trend, at least in 'commercial' as opposed to 'consumer' cases, has been to give effect to the 'contractual structure' by which the parties defined the nature of their relationship (see, e.g., *Greater Nottingham Cooperative Society Ltd* v *Cementation Piling and Foundations Ltd* [1988] 2 All ER 971, para. 2.2.4.2; *Saipem SpA and Conoco (UK) Ltd* v *Dredging VO2 BV and Geosite Surveys Ltd (The 'Volvox Hollandia') (No. 2)* [1993] 2 Lloyd's Rep 315, 322). So if the parties are in a contractual chain with no direct contractual relationship, the possible existence of exempting conditions which might be unenforceable against a plaintiff suing in tort (due to the absence of privity) has been held to be a good reason for denying the existence of a duty of care (*Simaan General Contracting Co.* v *Pilkington Glass Ltd (No. 2)* [1988] 1 All ER 791, 804, 806). On the other hand, the Court of Appeal has also allowed a defendant subcontractor to take the benefit of a clause in a main contract between the main contractor and a building owner which put the risk of loss or damage from fire on the building owner (*Norwich City Council* v *Harvey* [1989] 1 All ER 1180). This was in a case involving physical damage resulting from the subcontractor's negligence, where it was accepted that any 'third party' suffering injury or physical damage to property would have been owed a duty of care. The lack of privity did not prevent the subcontractor from 'relying on the clear basis on which all the parties contracted in relation to damage to the employer's building caused by fire' (at p. 1187). But, it remains to be seen whether this approach can be reconciled with *Scruttons Ltd* v *Midland Silicones Ltd*. It is one thing to say that the contractual structure, including exemption clauses, is such that it is not just and reasonable to impose a duty of care in respect of pure economic loss, given that the parties have chosen not to enter into a direct contractual relationship. It is quite another, however, to dismiss the strictures of privity of contract in order to exclude a duty of care which, in the absence of any contract, would quite clearly have been owed to the plaintiff, when, presumably, the parties have also chosen to 'structure' their relationship so as to avoid direct contractual obligations and immunities. *Norwich City Council* v *Harvey* was applied on similar facts by a majority of the Court of Session, Inner House, in the Scottish case of *British Telecommunications plc* v *James Thomson & Sons (Engineers) Ltd* (1996) 82 BLR 1, though there was a strong dissent by Lord Morison, who pointed out that this approach tends to confuse the effect of the contractual provisions on the contractual rights and obligations of the parties with their effect on the general duty in tort to take reasonable care. His Lordship considered that the strong presumption, in the case of physical damage negligently caused by the defendant, that the *Donoghue* v *Stevenson* duty of care should apply was not displaced by a contract, to which the defendants were not a party, placing the risk of fire damage on the plaintiffs (see, however, Convery 1997 SLT 113).

14.3 ILLEGALITY

The fact that the plaintiff was committing a criminal offence may, in some instances, constitute a defence. This is usually expressed in the Latin maxim *ex turpi causa non oritur actio* (an action cannot be founded on a base cause), or more generally, 'bad people get less' (*Weir*, p. 273). The problem is to determine when the plaintiff's criminal conduct will defeat his claim, since the mere fact that the plaintiff's behaviour is technically wrongful will not be sufficient. There must be some connection between the offence and the plaintiffs damage. So if A and B are proceeding to premises with the intention of committing burglary, and on the way B steals A's watch, A could still sue B in tort. On the other hand if, in the course of opening a safe, B is negligent in handling the explosive and injures A, then A would be caught by the defence (*National Coal Board* v *England* [1954] AC 403, 429, per Lord Asquith). Even where there is a causal connection not all offences will give rise to the defence, and there is no obvious test for deciding which offences are sufficiently *turpis*. In addition, the Court of Appeal has now stated that the defence of *ex turpi causa* is not limited to criminal conduct by the plaintiff but can also apply to immoral conduct (*Kirkham* v *Chief Constable of the Greater Manchester Police* [1990] 3 All ER 246, 251—a suicide, though cf. *Reeves* v *Commissioner of Police of the Metropolis* [1998] 2 All ER 381, para. 14.1.1, in which the Court of Appeal held that neither *volenti* nor *ex turpi causa* was avaialable where suicide was the very act that the defendant was under a duty to prevent; *Euro-Diam Ltd* v *Bathurst* [1988] 2 All ER 23, 28–9 per Kerr LJ, applying the 'affront to public conscience test'; see below). It will be even more difficult to determine which forms of immoral conduct should give rise to the defence.

It has been said that the defence could apply where the plaintiff was involved in a criminal affray and 'got more than he bargained for' (*Murphy* v *Culhane* [1977] QB 94, 98, where the defendant had been convicted of the manslaughter of the plaintiff's husband; see also *Dolson* v *Hughes* (1980) 107

DLR (3d) 343), but not if the plaintiff's conduct was trivial, out of all proportion to the occasion (*Lane* v *Holloway* [1968] 1 QB 379, where the question was whether the plaintiff's damages should be reduced because his assault had provoked the attack. The Court of Appeal said no. The reasoning must apply *a fortiori* to the defence of illegality: *Barnes* v *Nayer, The Times,* 19 December 1986, in which the provocation of prolonged abuse, insult and minor assault were held to be out of all proportion to manslaughter of the plaintiff's wife). The proportionality requirement featured prominently in *Revill* v *Newbery* [1996] 1 All ER 291, a case that attracted extensive coverage in the national media. The 76-year-old defendant was sleeping in a shed on his allotment and, on hearing the plaintiff attempting to break in, poked the barrel of his shotgun through a small hole in the door and pulled the trigger, injuring the plaintiff. The Court of Appeal held that the defendant was in breach of his duty of care to the plaintiff (in firing 'blind' at body level rather than not at all or upwards by way of 'warning shot'—per Neill LJ at p. 299) and could not rely on *ex turpi* because he had employed excessive force out of all proportion to the plaintiff's conduct (though the plaintiff's damages were reduced by two thirds for contributory negligence). On the isolated question of the relationship between the harms posed and suffered by the plaintiff, such a conclusion was unsurprising and in line with the earlier authorities. The real significance of *Revill* is that, for the moment at least, it gives the lie to the earlier notion that the proportionality criterion itself might be applied less rigidly in the case of trespassers engaged in criminal activity. The suggestion that burglars might, thus, be expected to put up with almost anything arose out of cases such as *Cummings* v *Grainger* [1977] 1 All ER 104, 109 (where Lord Denning suggested that *ex turpi* might bar a claim by a burglar bitten by a guard dog) and, in particular, the *obiter* remarks of Lord Denning in *Murphy* v *Culhane* [1977] QB 94, 98 to the effect that *ex turpi* would apply if a burglar was shot by a householder subsequently convicted of his manslaughter (cf. *Bigsharles* v *Merkel* [1973] 1 WWR 324 where the defence did not apply against a burglar of commercial premises who was shot dead, though, as in *Revill*, he was held contributorily negligent (75%)). At the same time, though, it may be naive to conclude that *Revill* has totally removed the potential for such sentiments to reassert their influence on future judicial policy towards trespassers and burglars (see Weir [1996] CLJ 182, 184, who criticises the decision as the 'worst example of the courts' very negative attitude to self-help'). For *Revill* was as notable for revealing a lingering public sympathy for the overzealous, property-protecting defendant and contempt for the trespassing criminal plaintiff, as it was for the force with which the Court of Appeal rejected the proposition that defendant and plaintiff in such circumstances might be above the law and outside of its protection respectively (see especially per Millett LJ at p. 302).

The precise scope of the *ex turpi* principle and the most appropriate methodology through which it might be employed are far from clear, particularly where plaintiff and defendant have been involved in a joint criminal enterprise. Two seemingly distinct approaches have emerged, possibly joined now by a third, which, despite its House of Lords' authority

(*Tinsley* v *Milligan* [1993] 3 All ER 65), may have served more to confuse than clarify. One approach has been to treat the fact of illegality as placing a more or less automatic bar on the plaintiff's compensation claim against his 'partner in crime', by employing it to negate key elements of the tort itself. Applying illegality in such a rigid, 'draconian' (Buckley (1994) 110 LQR 3, 4) fashion is aimed at reducing the amount of judicial discretion otherwise available when it is more traditionally employed as a defence.

In *Ashton* v *Turner* [1981] QB 137 the plaintiff was a passenger in a car driven by the defendant in the course of making their get-away from the scene of a burglary. The car crashed causing the plaintiff serious injuries. Ewbank J held that the courts 'may in certain circumstances not recognise the existence of a duty of care by one participant in a crime to another participant in the same crime, in relation to an act done in connection with the commission of that crime. That law is based on public policy.' Denying the existence of a duty of care may be an effective technique for barring compensation to a criminal where the action is based in negligence (see the Australian cases of *Smith* v *Jenkins* (1970) 44 ALJR 78; *Progress & Properties Ltd* v *Craft* (1976) 51 ALJR 184), but not where the claim is for trespass to the person, where *ex turpi causa* would have to operate as a defence to an otherwise accrued liability (as in *Murphy* v *Culhane*). A variation on the 'automatic bar' theme in the case of a joint criminal enterprise has been to employ the illegality as a means of requiring a much lower standard of care, e.g., in relation to the driving of a get-away car. Not surprisingly the courts have refused to become involved in the distasteful exercise of setting a standard of competence for criminal actions (see, e.g., *Progress & Properties Ltd* v *Craft*). On the other hand, where the criminal is suing a third party who has injured him, such as a policeman, the court will take account of the circumstances of the incident in assessing the standard of care. So the fact that the plaintiff was attempting to escape from the police in a high-speed chase will reflect upon the degree of care that can reasonably be expected from a police driver in hot pursuit (*Marshall* v *Osmond* [1983] QB 1034).

In *Jackson* v *Harrison* (1978) 19 ALR 129 the High Court of Australia held that the plaintiff's action would fail where the illegal nature of the venture in which the parties were engaged was such that it was impossible for the court to determine an appropriate standard of care (see further *Gala* v *Preston* (1991) 100 ALR 29, High Court of Australia). This approach was adopted by a majority of the Court of Appeal in *Pitts* v *Hunt* [1990] 3 All ER 344. The plaintiff was a pillion passenger on a motorcycle ridden by the defendant. To the plaintiff's knowledge the defendant was unlicensed and uninsured. They were both drunk. Encouraged by the plaintiff, the defendant rode the motorcycle in a recklessly dangerous manner and there was a crash in which the defendant was killed and the plaintiff injured. Balcombe and Dillon LJJ held that the circumstances of this joint illegal activity were such that it was impossible to determine a standard of care, and therefore there was no duty of care owed by the defendant to the plaintiff, given that the injuries arose directly *ex turpi causa*, the illegality not being merely incidental. This test, it was said, avoided the difficulties associated with a test based on appeals to the 'public conscience' which must distinguish between cases of serious illegality and minor transgressions, a process which 'would be likely to lead to a graph of illegalities according to moral turpitude' (per Dillon LJ at p. 363) (note also the strong dissent of Ralph Gibson LJ in the Court of Appeal in *Tinsley* v *Milligan* [1992] Ch 310, 344, in which, in the name of deterrence, he rejected any test that might invite *ad hoc* judicial discretion: 'the force of the deterrent effect is in the existence of the known rule and in its stern application').

The other main approach has been to employ *ex turpi* in its traditional role as a defence, expressly allowing for an element of judicial discretion in individual cases. This has recently been given expression in a considerable body of Court of Appeal authority approving a 'public conscience' test formulated by Hutchison J in *Thackwell* v *Barclays Bank plc* [1986] 1 All ER 676 (see *Saunders* v *Edwards* [1987] 2 All ER 651; *Euro-Diam Ltd* v *Bathurst* [1988] 2 All ER 23; *Kirkham* v *Chief Constable of the Greater Manchester Police* [1990] 3 All ER 246; *Howard* v *Shirlstar Container Transport Ltd* [1990] 3 All ER 366). In *Euro-Diam Ltd* v *Bathurst* Kerr LJ (at pp. 28–9) expressed the test in the following terms:

> The *ex turpi causa* defence ultimately rests on a principle of public policy that the courts will not assist a plaintiff who has been guilty of illegal (or immoral) conduct of which the courts should take notice. It applies if, in all the circumstances, it would be an affront to the public conscience to grant the relief which he seeks because the courts would thereby appear to assist or encourage the plaintiff in his illegal conduct or to encourage others in similar acts.

The extent of judicial discretion that such a test might allow is neatly bought out by Nicholls LJ in the Court of Appeal in *Tinsley* v *Milligan* [1992] Ch 310, 319: '[the court has to] weigh or balance the adverse consequences of granting relief against the adverse consequences of refusing relief. The ultimate decision calls for a value judgment'. However, the nature of that 'value judgment' may yet be rendered more impersonal by the majority judgment of McLachlin J in the Supreme Court of Canada in *Hall* v *Hebert* [1993] 4 WWR 113, 126: 'it is not the judge's outrage but a concern for the coherence of the legal system . . . which is operative' (for comment on *Hall* v *Hebert* see McInnes [1993] CLJ 379; Epp (1994) 110 LQR 357; for a general Canadian perspective on illegality see Kostal (1995) 3 Tort L Rev 100). Moreover, in *Kirkham* v *Chief Constable of the Greater Manchester Police* Lloyd LJ observed that on the public policy test the defence is not confined to criminal conduct, and so the court had to consider whether a claim arising directly out of a man's suicide should be barred on the basis that it would affront the public conscience, or as Lloyd LJ preferred to say 'shock the ordinary citizen'. The Court of Appeal concluded that the answer was no and that *ex turpi causa* did not apply to such an action, at least where the suicide was suffering from grave mental instability. The Court of Appeal in *Kirkham* stated that the position might be different (for the purposes of both *volenti* and *ex turpi*), however, where the deceased was 'wholly sane'. Though the Court of Appeal's observation in *Kirkham* in relation to non-criminal acts potentially amounting to *ex turpi* remains authorative, their application of that notion in the context of a suicide is not. In *Reeves* v *Commissioner of Police of the Metropolis* (above and para. 14.1.1) the Court of Appeal held that the defences of *ex turpi* and *volenti* were not appropriate in a case where suicide was the very act that the defendant was under a duty to prevent, whether or not the suicide was of sound mind.

Though no definitive guidance emerged as to which approach ought to be utilised, this line of recent Court of Appeal authority (*supra*, bolstered by the views of the majority in the Supreme Court of Canada in *Hall* v *Hebert, supra*) seemed a strong indication that the public policy test might prevail. Conceptually, too, there appear to be difficulties with the other approach. For example, the 'impossibility' of setting a standard of care, though preferred by the majority in *Pitts* v *Hunt*, cannot be a universal criterion for the *ex turpi causa* defence because the defence can apply to torts other than negligence (and, indeed, in contract), and even in negligence there can be cases where there is really no doubt about what the appropriate standard of care should be. In *Rance* v *Mid-Downs Health Authority* [1991] 1 All ER 801 the plaintiff alleged that as a result of the defendants' negligence a foetal abnormality was not detected during the course of a pregnancy, and therefore she was deprived of the opportunity of having an abortion. Due to the length of the gestation, however, an abortion on the ground of serious foetal handicap would not have been lawful under the Abortion Act 1967 (as it then stood). Brook J held that on the facts there had been no negligence, but that in any event on the ground of public policy the court would not award compensation in circumstances where the plaintiff could not have turned her lost opportunity to value without breaking the law. It could scarcely have been argued in such a case that it was impossible to establish a standard of care for the medical staff.

It is also possible that the two approaches may in fact have a great deal in common. For instance, it is not clear how the court should decide whether it is possible or not to set a standard of care. As *Hepple and Matthews*, p. 401, comment: 'Is the reason for not fixing a standard of care anything other than that to fix a standard of care in these cases would offend the public conscience?' In other words, there may be little difference between these two approaches, and the court may have little more than the degree of moral turpitude associated with the plaintiff's conduct to guide it. In *Pitts* v *Hunt* Balcombe LJ, having said that it was impossible to determine the appropriate standard of care, added that 'if moral turpitude were relevant, here was moral turpitude of a high degree'.

However, being able to reconcile the two approaches in this way may prove cold comfort if the full potential of the House of Lords' decision in *Tinsley* v *Milligan* [1993] 3 All ER 65 to reject them both (albeit in a contractual context) is ever realised. In *Tinsley* v *Milligan* the House of Lords, by majority, allowed the plaintiff to assert his rights against the defendant under a trust of property that had been acquired fraudulently by him. In so doing, the court (self-evidently) rejected any application of a general rule that illegality automatically disqualifies a plaintiff's claim and, at the same time, also firmly rejected the public policy approach, preferring instead a test based on whether the plaintiff has to *rely* on the illegality (see Lord Goff at pp. 79–80). Potentially, this introduces a third approach, effectively side-stepping illegality by the application of technical rules. (On the facts, as the plaintiff did not have to rely on the illegality, his claim to an interest in the property would not be defeated simply because it arose in the course of an illegal transaction.) In the context of the more conventional tort cases, ready analogy may be drawn with the earlier approaches to illegality and their rejection by their Lordships in *Tinsley* v *Milligan*, but not with the narrow property/contractual based test that replaced it. In that sense, the decision may serve only to distort an already confused picture, though it may presage further judicial pronouncements providing the long overdue clarity. (For comment on *Tinsley* v *Milligan* see Stowe (1994) 57 MLR 441; Buckley (1944) 110 LQR 3; Enonchong (1994) 14 OJLS 295.)

Although it is said that *ex turpi causa* is based on public policy, the objectives of that policy are not particularly clear. It can hardly be deterrence because if the criminal law does not deter such conduct it cannot be supposed that the law of tort would have any salutary effect. Indeed, in cases of joint participation in a crime, the defendant criminal actually benefits from the application of the defence to his less fortunate partner (though in *Ashton* v *Turner* the beneficiary was probably the Motor Insurers' Bureau). In *Saunders* v *Edwards* [1987] 2 All ER 651, for example, the defendant was guilty of fraudulent misrepresentation in relation to the value of a flat sold to the plaintiffs, who in turn misrepresented the purchase price to the Inland Revenue in order partially to evade stamp duty. The Court of Appeal refused to apply the defence to the plaintiffs' action in deceit. Kerr LJ commented (at p. 660): 'The moral culpability of the defendant greatly outweighs any on the part of the plaintiffs. He cannot be allowed to keep the fruits of his fraud.' Possibly retribution can justify the defence, but the law of tort is a rather blunt instrument for achieving an aim better left to the law of crime. As Hervey ((1981) 97 LQR 537), points out the plaintiff in *Ashton* v *Turner* was effectively fined £70,000 for the theft of three radios. A third possible justification is that compensating criminals for the consequences of their crimes might bring the law into disrepute (Hervey (1981) 97 LQR 537, 539; *Thackwell* v *Barclays Bank plc* [1986] 1 All ER 676, 687), a view which seems to underpin the 'affront to public conscience' test. This is founded on the notion that people should not profit from their own wrongs (or, at least, the court will not assist someone to do so), although the compensation principle of tort draws a distinction between making people better off than they were, and not leaving them worse off (see, e.g., Gibson (1969) 47 Can Bar Rev 89 who distinguishes between the defence preventing the plaintiff making a *profit* from his illegality, and restoring him to his prior position; this is the distinction between damages in contract and tort).

The Court of Appeal's decision in *Clunis* v *Camden and Islington Health Authority* [1998] 3 All ER 180 is a clear, if perhaps harsh, example of what may yet develop as judicial antipathy to any suggestion that crime (particularly, serious crime) might pay. In *Clunis* the plaintiff, who had a long history of mental illness, had killed a stranger in a vicious unprovoked attack, three months after he had been discharged from the defendant's care. Originally, he was charged with murder, but this was reduced to manslaughter after his plea of diminished responsibility was accepted. Notwithstanding this judicial endorsement of the plaintiff's mental instability, the Court of Appeal considered that public policy, in the shape of the defence of illegality, dictated that he be prevented from relying on his own criminal conduct in order to establish a claim in negligence against the defendant health authority for releasing him prematurely and failing to provide after care (a claim which the Court had decided was not open to the plaintiff anyway, there being no private law action in respect of the defendant's breach of its public duties, under the principles of *X v Bedfordshire CC* [1995] 2 AC 63). Their Lordships held that, in such a case, the illegality defence would be inappropriate only if it could be said that the plaintiff did not know the nature or quality of his act or that it was wrong. Though the acceptance of the plea of diminished responsibility by the criminal court might have indicated that the plaintiff's mental responsibility was significantly impaired, a plea of insanity had been rejected. Their Lordships concluded that the fact that he was, therefore, sufficiently aware as to be liable for his criminal act meant that he met the knowledge threshold beyond which the *ex turpi* defence would apply to bar his claim before the civil courts. This particular rationale is, with respect, a highly superficial attempt by the Court to match the strong policy basis for their decision with a more conventional doctrinal element. It is not doubted that a distinction between insanity and diminished responsibility is technically correct or that it has a role to play in the criminal law, but its employment in *Clunis* as a means of denying the plaintiff a claim seems far less convincing than their Lordships' frank admission that, in the circumstances, they felt constrained by broader notions of public policy to ensure that a particularly violent criminal act could not result in profit for the perpetrator.

The strong moral sentiment that criminality should bar or restrict compensation also finds expression at two other points: first in the assessment of damages, which for the habitual crook are likely to be reduced (*Burns v Edman* [1970] 2 QB 541; but cf. *Meah v McCreamer* [1985] 1 All ER 367 and the apparently inconsistent decision in *Meah v McCreamer (No. 2)* [1986] 1 All ER 943; see para. 4.2.2.2, though note that *Meah*, where illegality was not pleaded, must now be read in the light of the Court of Appeal's decision in *Clunis v Camden and Islington Health Authority*, above); and secondly under the Criminal Injuries Compensation Scheme, which provides that payment may be refused or reduced by the Board in the light of the claimant's criminal convictions or unlawful conduct, or his conduct in connection with the injury. This can apply to convictions or conduct at any time, even after the injury.

The danger of the *ex turpi causa* defence is that it effectively restores the ancient penalty of outlawry, in the civil law, which put a person beyond the protection of the law (Hervey (1981) 97 LQR 537, 541; *Winfield and Jolowicz*, p. 744; note also *Revill v Newbery*, *supra* in which this concern found its fullest expression to date). Moreover, 'public policy' provides no satisfactory criterion for deciding which crimes the defence applies to, or how close the causal connection must be between the offence and the damage. It is generally assumed that the offence must be serious and the causal link strong (see *Thackwell* v *Barclays Bank plc* [1986] 1 All ER 676, 689, and *Clunis* v *Camden and Islington Health Authority*, above—an unprovoked stabbing that resulted in a charge of manslaughter). In *Gala* v *Preston* (1991) 100 ALR 29, 36, Mason CJ commented that it would 'border on the grotesque' for the court to seek to set a standard of care to be exercised by a bank robber for the safety of another bank robber in blowing up a safe during the course of the robbery, but it would be unjust to apply the defence to a passenger in a motor vehicle who momentarily encouraged the driver of the vehicle to commit a minor traffic offence. In the Canadian case of *Tomlinson* v *Harrison* (1972) 24 DLR (3d) 26 Addy J distinguished between common law misdemeanours and indictable offences, and in *Dolson* v *Hughes* (1980) 107 DLR (3d) 343 Taylor J said that the criminal conduct should be of an 'inherently reprehensible nature'. In *Jackson* v *Harrison* (1978) 19 ALR 129 (see especially at pp. 149–50 per Murphy J), for example, the High Court of Australia held that *ex turpi causa* did not apply to a passenger who knew that the driver of the vehicle was disqualified, and in *Weir* v *Wyper* 1992 SLT 579 a passenger who accepted, or even requested, a lift from a driver who she knew did not hold a full driving licence was not caught by the defence, since she was not 'participating in any significant criminal activity'. More significantly in *Farrell* v *Secretary of State for Defence* [1980] 1 All ER 166 the Court of Appeal in Northern Ireland held that the defence did not apply to a person who, intending to commit a robbery, was mistaken for a terrorist and shot dead by a soldier (see Rowe (1981) 131 NLJ 570). Was the plaintiff's conduct in *Ashton* v *Turner* worse than this? (But see also *Tomlinson* v *Harrison*, where the defence was applied to drunken 'joyriders' who crashed in the course of a police chase.)

The dilemma confronting the courts was expressed by Bingham LJ in *Saunders* v *Edwards* [1987] 2 All ER 651, 665–6: 'On the one hand it is unacceptable that any court of law should aid or lend its authority to a party seeking to pursue or enforce an object or agreement which the law prohibits. On the other hand, it is unacceptable that the court should, on the first indication of unlawfulness affecting any aspect of a transaction, draw up its skirts and refuse all assistance to the plaintiff, no matter how serious his loss or how disproportionate his loss to the unlawfulness of his conduct' (see comments to similar affect in *Revill* v *Newbery* [1996] 1 All ER 291, 301 per Evans LJ). Steering a middle course between these two unacceptable positions involves a pragmatic approach, looking at 'all the circumstances' of each case. In *Pitts* v *Hunt* [1990] 3 All ER 344, 355 Beldam LJ observed that if a death other than that of the motor cyclist had occurred it would have amounted to manslaughter. Taking a pragmatic approach the action was barred on grounds of public policy, and, his Lordship added, it was undesirable to go further in an attempt to categorise the degree of seriousness involved in offences which would preclude recovery of compensation.

The defence of *ex turpi causa* can overlap with other defences such as *volenti* and contributory negligence (as in *Ashton* v *Turner*), but since it is based on judicial policy and not the plaintiff's consent, *ex turpi* is not coextensive with *volenti*. This could be important where a statutory provision, such as the Road Traffic Act 1988, s. 149, precludes the use of a *volenti* defence, since the illegality of the plaintiff's conduct might still bar his claim (as in *Pitts* v *Hunt*; see also Road Traffic Act 1988, s. 151(4)). This view can be contrasted with *Lynch* v *Ministry of Defence* [1983] NI 216 where it was held that a soldier or police officer who uses unreasonable force in the prevention of crime or arrest of offenders and who thereby is unable to rely on the defence contained in the Criminal Law Act 1967 s. 3 (see para. 12.5.2), cannot then rely on *ex turpi causa*, because s. 3 replaced the rules of the common law and judicial 'policy' should not usurp parliamentary intention.

14.4 OTHER DEFENCES

Three other pleas may be encountered and therefore warrant brief consideration, although two of them, mistake and inevitable accident, are not of general application.

14.4.1 Mistake
A mistaken belief by the defendant, either of law or fact, is not a general defence. So the defendant's reasonable belief that land belonged to him does not justify trespass, nor does a surgeon's mistaken belief that a patient has consented to an operation; and a mistaken belief in the truth of a statement is not a general defence to defamation. Where, however, the defendant's motive is a condition of liability, mistake may negative liability. Thus a person is not liable in deceit if he honestly believed in the truth of his statement. This will not necessarily provide a defence in negligence, e.g., for negligent misstatement, because the standard of care is set by what a reasonable man would have said, not an honest but unreasonable man. However, if the mistake was such that a reasonable man could have made it, this may indicate that the defendant was not negligent (see also para. 12.5.3 on reasonable mistake of fact and self-defence).

14.4.2 Inevitable accident
An accident may be regarded as inevitable when it was not intended by the defendant and could not have been avoided by the exercise of reasonable care. Where liability depends on fault this is no more than a plea that the defendant was not at fault, and in negligence this is superfluous since the burden of proving fault rests with the plaintiff. Historically the defence applied to actions in trespass, where on proof of the interference it was for the defendant to justify his action. Now, however, liability in trespass depends on proof of the defendant's intention or negligence and the burden of proof is the plaintiff's (*Fowler* v *Lanning* [1959] 1 QB 426; *Letang* v *Cooper* [1965] 1 QB 232; cf. *Salmond and Heuston*, p. 136). Thus, here too inevitable accident amounts to no more than a denial of negligence which it is for the plaintiff to prove (but see *res ipsa loquitur*, para. 3.3.2).

It is not a defence to torts of strict liability since the exercise of reasonable care is not an excuse (but see act of God and act of a stranger, paras 8.1.7.3 and 8.1.7.4).

14.4.3 Necessity

This defence may justify an intentional interference with persons or property where it is necessary to prevent greater damage to the public, a third party or the defendant. It differs from self-defence in that it can apply even though the plaintiff's conduct is entirely innocent or passive (see para. 12.5.3). As *Salmond and Heuston,* p. 467, points out the word necessity 'serves to conceal the fact that the defendant always has a choice between two evils'. The court has to make a value judgment as to whose interests are to be preferred. Where life and limb are at risk then any necessary damage to property will be justified (*Southport Corporation* v *Esso Petroleum Co. Ltd* [1953] 3 WLR 773, 779). Thus a doctor may be justified in performing an operation without consent on an unconscious patient in an emergency (see *F v West Berkshire Health Authority* [1989] 2 All ER 545, para. 12.5.1). But this would not be the case where a competent and conscious adult refused consent to treatment, even if the refusal could lead to serious permanent disability or death (see, e.g., *Malette* v *Shulman* (1990) 67 DLR (4th) 321—blood transfusion administered to an unconscious patient who was a Jehovah's witness who carried a card specifically refusing consent to a blood transfusion; doctor liable in battery even though treatment may have saved the patient's life; cf. *Leigh* v *Gladstone* (1909) 26 TLR 139—defendants not liable for force feeding of prisoner on hunger strike. The decision would probably not be followed today; see Zellick [1976] PL 153). Where an adult permanently lacks the mental capacity to give a valid consent necessity will justify a broader range of treatment, provided it is in the best interests of the patient (*F v West Berkshire Health Authority*; *R v Bournewood Community and Mental Health NHS Trust, ex parte L* [1998] 3 All ER 289).

The defence is limited by the requirement that the defendant must have acted as a reasonable man would have done to avoid a real and imminent danger (*Cope* v *Sharpe* [1912] 1 KB 496, 510, where D was held not liable for trespass to P's land in order to stop the spread of fire, although as it turned out the fire would not have damaged D's property—he had acted reasonably, however, at the time). Where the need to act is brought about by the defendant's own negligence then necessity is not a good defence, and once the issue is raised the defendant 'must show on the whole of the evidence that the necessity arose without negligence on his part' (*Rigby* v *Chief Constable of Northamptonshire* [1985] 2 All ER 985, 994). It follows that necessity can never be a defence to an action in negligence. It might be a defence to an action under *Rylands* v *Fletcher*, at least where the escape was intentional (*Rigby* v *Chief Constable of Northamptonshire*, on the assumption that an intentional escape would not merge the action into one in trespass alone).

The courts have always been cautious about admitting a defence of necessity. In *Southwark London Borough Council* v *Williams* [1971] Ch 734 the Court of Appeal denied the defence to homeless squatters who had occupied a vacant house. Lord Denning MR said (at p. 744) that:

Necessity would open a door which no man could shut . . . The plea would
be an excuse for all sorts of wrongdoing. So the courts must, for the sake
of law and order, take a firm stand. They must refuse to admit the plea of
necessity to the hungry and the homeless: and trust that their distress will
be relieved by the charitable and the good.

Necessity is a complete defence and therefore there is no liability in tort to
compensate for the damage inflicted on the plaintiff. It is unclear whether
there would be any obligation in quasi-contract to make restitution. The
Crown, acting under the royal prerogative is under such an obligation
(*Burmah Oil Co. Ltd* v *Lord Advocate* [1965] AC 75, reversed in effect by the
War Damage Act 1965 where property is destroyed during war). On principle
it seems unreasonable that a private individual or even agencies of the state
(such as the police, as in *Rigby* v *Chief Constable of Northamptonshire*) can
justify the deliberate infliction of harm on an entirely innocent plaintiff while
leaving him to bear the loss. Yet this is what the defence of necessity appears
to do. The decision that the defendant's act was not wrongful and the
question of whether the defendant should compensate for the damage he has
caused are discrete issues, but English law has great difficulty in keeping them
separate (*Weir*, p. 335; *Atiyah*, pp. 158–59). Cf. the American case of *Vincent*
v *Lake Erie Transportation Co.* (1910) 109 Minn 456, 124 NW 221—ship
moored to plaintiff's wharf caused damage to the wharf in a storm. Defendants acted perfectly reasonably in refusing to cast off in the storm, but having
preserved the ship at the expense of the dock were responsible for the damage
(cf. *Romney Marsh* v *Corporation of the Trinity House* (1870) LR 5 Ex 204).

14.5 CONTRIBUTORY NEGLIGENCE

Accidents are not infrequently caused by the conduct of more than one
person. Where the harm is the product of the combination of the fault of
others the plaintiff can sue any one of the joint tortfeasors for the whole
amount of the damage. It is then up to the defendant to claim contribution
from the other tortfeasors for their respective responsibilities under the Civil
Liability (Contribution) Act 1978 (see para. 14.6). Where the harm is
attributable partly to the fault of the defendant and partly to that of the
plaintiff then any award of damages may be reduced by reason of the
plaintiff's contributory negligence.

At common law contributory negligence was a complete defence (*Butterfield* v *Forrester* (1809) 11 East 60). In Admiralty where two ships were at fault
the loss was apportioned equally, but the Maritime Conventions Act 1911,
s. 1, provides for apportionment 'to the degree in which each vessel was in
fault'. In order to avoid some of the harshness of the common law rule, which
applied even though the plaintiff's negligence was slight in comparison to the
defendant's conduct, the courts developed the rule of 'last opportunity'. This
meant, in effect, that the person whose negligence was last in time, and
therefore had the last opportunity to avoid the accident, was treated as the
sole cause of the damage (*Davies* v *Mann* (1842) 10 M & W 546). Moreover,

if but for the defendant's negligence he would have had the last opportunity he was again treated as if he did have the last opportunity and was liable for the full loss (*British Columbia Electric Railway Co. Ltd* v *Loach* [1916] 1 AC 719). The rule was very difficult to apply in cases where the parties' negligence was virtually simultaneous, as for example in road traffic accidents, and it led to a complex body of law in which the courts had to make increasingly fine and arbitrary distinctions about causation.

These problems were largely removed by the Law Reform (Contributory Negligence) Act 1945 which, for the first time, permitted apportionment of the loss for accidents occurring on land. Section 1(1) provides that:

> Where any person suffers damage as the result partly of his own fault and partly of the fault of any other person or persons, a claim in respect of that damage shall not be defeated by reason of the fault of the person suffering the damage, but the damages recoverable in respect thereof shall be reduced to such extent as the court thinks just and equitable having regard to the claimant's share in the responsibility for the damage.

14.5.1 Scope of the Law Reform (Contributory Negligence) Act 1945
By s. 4 of the Law Reform (Contributory Negligence) Act 1945, fault means 'negligence, breach of statutory duty or other act or omission which gives rise to a liability in tort or would, apart from this Act, give rise to the defence of contributory negligence'. Thus the Act extends to actions in nuisance and *Rylands* v *Fletcher,* though it was formerly a matter of some debate whether it applied in actions for trespass to the person (*Murphy* v *Culhane* [1977] QB 94—yes; *Lane* v *Holloway* [1968] 1 QB 379—no. Hudson (1984) 4 Legal Stud 332 reviewed the authorities and concluded that contributory negligence was not a defence to batttery). In *Barnes* v *Nayer, The Times,* 19 December 1986 the Court of Appeal considered that there was no reason why, on appropriate facts, contributory negligence could not be relied on as a defence to battery, although on the facts of the case the defendant's conduct was so out of proportion to the plaintiff's behaviour that it could not be said that the behaviour had contributed to the damage (see para. 12.5.1; see also *Wasson* v *Chief Constable of the Royal Ulster Constabulary* [1987] 8 NIJB 34 where the defence was applied to an action in battery; for general comment see Childs (1993) 44 NILQ 334).

Unsurprisingly, the Act does not apply to an assist a fraudster. Thus, it is not available in an action in deceit, since where the defendant intended that the plaintiff should rely on his statement to the plaintiff's detriment, it is not open to him to argue that the loss could have been avoided if the plaintiff had taken more care to avoid being duped by the defendant (*Alliance and Leicester Building Society* v *Edgestop Ltd* [1994] 2 All ER 38; for criticism see Howarth, *Textbook on Tort,* 1995, p. 661). Similarly, in *Corporacion Nacional del Cobre de Chile* v *Sogemin Metals Ltd* [1997] 1 WLR 1396, it was held that a party who had conspired to bribe the plaintiff's employees could not plead the plaintiff's own lack of diligence as a means of reducing the damages payable.

Although the Act clearly does apply to the tort of negligence there are, in theory, problems with a claim for negligent misstatement. If the plaintiff's conduct in relying on the defendant's statement is so unreasonable as to constitute contributory negligence, it is difficult to see how he could be held to have reasonably placed reliance on the statement for the purpose of establishing liability (*JEB Fasteners Ltd* v *Marks Bloom & Co.* [1981] 3 All ER 289, 297). Logically, if it was reasonable to rely on the statement how can it be negligent to do so? In *Yianni* v *Edwin Evans & Sons* [1982] QB 438 it was held that the defendant surveyors were liable to the plaintiffs who had purchased a property in reliance on a negligent mortgage valuation (a decision approved by the House of Lords in *Smith* v *Bush* [1989] 2 WLR 790, see para. 2.2.4.1.3). Park J considered and rejected a plea of contributory negligence without adverting to this point (cf. *Perry* v *Tendring District Council* (1984) 2 PN 58. Harwood (1987) 50 MLR 588 argues that as a matter of policy contributory negligence should not be a defence in cases involving house purchase in reliance on a negligent survey, an argument now supported by the policy considerations which were held to prevent the exclusion of liability in such cases, in *Smith* v *Bush,* see para. 14.2). In *Edwards* v *Lee, The Independent,* 1 November 1991, Brooke J held that the plaintiff, who had relied on a negligent reference given by a solicitor about a fraudulent client, was contributorily negligent in failing to take greater steps to protect himself. In Canada contributory negligence has been accepted as a defence to an action for negligent misstatement (*Grand Restaurants of Canada Ltd* v *Toronto* (1981) 123 DLR (3d) 349, although this case may be explicable on its own unusual facts: see *Dugdale and Stanton,* para. 21.19; cf. Buckley, *The Modern Law of Negligence,* 2nd ed., 1993, p. 114). A further difficulty in cases of misstatement is that carelessness by the plaintiff may defeat the claim on the basis that the representation did not *cause* the loss, because if the plaintiff had known the true position, which he ought reasonably to have known, then he would not have relied on the defendant's statement. Thus, it was the plaintiff's conduct rather than the defendant's which caused the damage (see, e.g., *Strover* v *Harrington* [1988] 1 All ER 769, 780–1). This reasoning is reminiscent of the 'last opportunity' rule which applied to contributory negligence before 1945.

In *Gran Gelato Ltd* v *Richcliff (Group) Ltd* [1992] 2 WLR 867, Sir Donald Nicholls V-C held that contributory negligence applies to a claim under s. 2(1) of the Misrepresentation Act 1967 in a case where there were concurrent claims under the 1967 Act and the tort of negligent misstatement, on the basis that liability under the Act is 'essentially founded on negligence'. On the other hand, the action under s. 2(1) is based on the fiction that the defendant has been fraudulent unless he proves that he exercised reasonable care, and damages are assessed on the basis of the measure of damages in the tort of deceit (see para. 2.2.4.1.2). This might suggest that, by analogy with deceit, contributory negligence should not be available as a defence to an action under s. 2(1). In any event, having concluded that contributory negligence could be a defence, Sir Donald Nicholls V-C held that it would not be just and equitable to make any reduction in the plaintiff's damages because the defendant intended that the plaintiff should act in reliance on the accuracy of the answers given to inquiries before contract. 'In principle', said his Lordship, 'carelessness in not making other inquiries provides no answer to a claim when the plaintiff has done that which the representor intended he should do'. This approach will tend to reduce the value of the contributory negligence defence in a Misrepresentation Act claim, since it is arguable that in most, if not all, cases where the representation falls within the requirements of s. 2(1) the representor will have intended that the plaintiff act in reliance on the accuracy of the statement.

The extent to which the Act applies to actions in contract has been a matter of some controversy. The Act is open to different interpretations and this has produced conflicting lines of authority (see *Burrows*, pp. 80–7 for the arguments; supporting the view that apportionment under the Act is possible in contract are: *Sayers* v *Harlow Urban District Council* [1958] 1 WLR 623; *Quinn* v *Burch Brothers (Builders) Ltd* [1966] 2 QB 370; *De Meza and Stuart* v *Apple, Van Straten, Shena and Stone* [1974] 1 Lloyd's Rep 508, affd [1975] 1 Lloyd's Rep 498; against this view are: *Sole* v *W. J. Hallt Ltd* [1973] QB 574; *Basildon District Council* v *J. E. Lesser (Properties) Ltd* [1985] 1 All ER 20; *AB Marintrans* v *Comet Shipping Co. Ltd* [1985] 3 All ER 442). The Court of Appeal has now held that in certain types of contractual claim, at least, damages can be apportioned in consequence of the plaintiff's contributory negligence. In *Forsikringsaktieselskapet Vesta* v *Butcher* [1986] 2 All ER 488, 508 Hobhouse J identified three categories:

(a)   where liability does not depend on negligence but arises from breach of a strict contractual duty;

(b)   where liability arises from breach of a contractual obligation which is expressed in terms of exercising reasonable care, but does not correspond to a common law duty of care which would exist independently of the contract;

(c)   where the defendant's negligent breach of contract would have given rise to liability in the tort of negligence independently of the existence of the contract.

Where the defendant's contractual liability was concurrent with an independent tortious liability (category (c)), then, his Lordship concluded, damages could be reduced for the plaintiff's contributory negligence, following the decision of the Court of Appeal in *Sayers* v *Harlow Urban District Council*. The only relevance of the contract in this situation was whether it had varied or redefined the tortious relationship by excluding apportionment. The Court of Appeal upheld this analysis, agreeing that in a category (c) case the Act applies ([1988] 2 All ER 43). It would not be right, said O'Connor LJ, that, in a case of concurrent liability in contract and tort (e.g., employers' liability cases), the plaintiff should be able to avoid the apportionment of damages by pleading his case in contract rather than tort.

Conversely, the plaintiff's fault is irrelevant where the defendant is in breach of a strict contractual obligation (category (a); *Barclays Bank plc* v *Fairclough Building Ltd* [1995] 1 All ER 289, CA; for comment see Hopkins [1995] CLJ 21), unless the plaintiff's conduct is such that the defendant's breach cannot be said to be a *cause* of the loss (see, e.g., *Lambert* v *Lewis*

[1981] 1 All ER 1185 where a retailer sold a defective towing hitch and the buyer continued to use it after it was obviously broken, causing an accident; the dealer was not liable to indemnify the buyer because the accident was caused not by the breach of contract but the buyer's own carelessness). In this situation, of course, the plaintiff's claim fails entirely. More difficult are category (b) cases, or at least the basis of the distinction between category (b) and category (c). *Vesta* v *Butcher* would exclude category (b) cases from the scope of the Law Reform (Contributory Negligence) Act 1945, but it is not clear what is meant by a common law duty of care 'independent of the contract' (see *Dugdale and Stanton,* para. 21.22). For example, though the solicitor/client relationship is now cited as the standard example of concurrent liability, would a solicitor owe a duty of care to a 'client' independently of the existence of a contract? This particular issue has been put beyond doubt by recent cases involving professionals sued by their lender clients in an effort to recover sums lost on borrower default (see Evans (1998) 14 PN 43). In such cases, the courts have recognised that the imprudent lending of an earlier era could amount to contributory negligence (e.g., *Bristol and West Building Society* v *Fancy and Jackson (a firm)* [1997] 4 All ER 582—solicitors; *Platform Home Loans Ltd* v *Oyston Shipways Ltd* (1997) 14 PN 56, CA—valuer; for comment on *Platform Home Loans* see Kenny (1998) 62 Conv 159). Moreover, in *Platform Home Loans Ltd* v *Oyston Shipways Ltd,* the Court of Appeal confirmed that a plaintiff lender's conduct could constitute contributory negligence if it contributed to the overall loss suffered and that it did not have to contribute to the particular item of loss recoverable by the plaintiff. This ended some creative attempts by lenders to limit the potential for a contributory negligence finding, which, for a short period, had met with some success. Most particularly, in *Interallianz Finanz AG* v *Independent Insurance Co. Ltd* [1997] EGCS 91, Thomas J had held that a valuer sued by a lender in respect of a negligent failure to provide a correct valuation could not rely on contributory negligence by the lender which went to credit worthiness or market risk rather than the value of the security itself. Though this inevitably pro-lender approach generated something of a following in some subsequent first instance decisions (e.g., *Coventry Building Society* v *William Martin and Partners* [1997] 48 EG 159; *Britannia Building Society* v *Hallas (t/a Wilds and Griffiths)* [1997] EGCS 117), the Court of Appeal in *Platform Home Loans Ltd* v *Oyston Shipways Ltd* rejected it as an inappropriate superimposition onto the contributory negligence framework of the 'information'/'advice' distinction that had been formulated by the House of Lords in *South Australia Asset Management Corporation* v *York Montague Ltd* [1996] 3 All ER 365 in order to govern the measure of damages issue. (More generally, it may also be relevant that there is no longer a trend away from findings of concurrent liability in contract and tort that might have served to limit the opportunities to apply the Act to contractual claims. For instance, in *Youell* v *Bland Welch & Co Ltd (No 2)* [1990] 2 Lloyd's Rep 431, the Act was applied to a category (c) case involving the concurrent liability of insurance brokers).

In *Tennant Radiant Heat Ltd* v *Warrington Development Corporation* (1988) 11 EG 71, tenants sued their landlord in negligence when the roof of the premises collapsed. The landlord counter-claimed against the tenants in contract for breach of the repairing obligations in the lease. The Law Reform (Contributory Negligence) Act did not apply because the tenants were in breach of a strict covenant which was not itself tortious. The Court of Appeal held that it was possible to apportion the respective claims on a causation basis, by assessing the extent to which the landlord's negligence had caused damage to the tenants' property, and how far the damage to the landlord's building was caused by the breach of covenant. On the facts responsibility was assessed at 90% to the landlord and 10% to the tenants. Thus, the landlord was liable for 90% of the tenants' damage, and the tenants for 10% of the landlord's damage. This amounts to a general common law power to apportion damages, quite distinct from the Act, where there are two contemporaneous causes both of which constitute a breach of a legal duty (whether contractual or tortious). 'Fault', in the sense of contributory negligence, may not be sufficient to invoke this power unless the plaintiff owed a duty to the defendant.

Under the Act, however, it is not necessary that the plaintiff should owe a duty to the defendant. It is sufficient to establish that the plaintiff 'did not in his own interest take reasonable care of himself and contributed, by this want of care, to his own injury' (*Nance* v *British Columbia Electric Railway Co. Ltd* [1951] AC 601, 611 per Viscount Simon). The burden of proving this rests with the defendant (*Owens* v *Brimmell* [1977] QB 859, 864; *Limbrick* v *French* [1993] PIQR P121). The plaintiff's negligence need not have contributed to the accident if it has contributed to the damage caused by the accident, i.e., by adding to the extent of the damage or by failing to avoid or lessen the damage (for discussion of different types of contributory negligence see Gravells (1977) 93 LQR 581). It is on this basis that a passenger in a motor vehicle who does not wear a seat belt will be held contributorily negligent even though the accident was caused entirely by the defendant's negligence. As Lord Denning MR said in *Froom* v *Butcher* [1976] QB 286:

> *The accident* is caused by the bad driving. The *damage* is caused in part by the bad driving of the defendant, and in part by the failure of the plaintiff to wear a seat belt.

(See also *O'Connell* v *Jackson* [1972] 1 QB 270—15% reduction for motor cyclist's failure to wear crash helmet; *Capps* v *Miller* [1989] 2 All ER 333—failure to fasten crash helmet securely is contributory negligence.) The act of accepting a lift in a motor vehicle may be contributory negligence where it is known that the driver has been drinking (*Owens* v *Brimmell*; note *Stewart* v *Pettie* [1994] 1 WWR 372—reduction of 25% for plaintiff passenger failing to wear seatbelt not increased even though plaintiff knew that defendant had been drinking; cf. reduction of 75% in circumstances of *Donelan* v *Donelan and General Accident Fire and Life Insurance*, *supra* para. 14.1.4) or that the car has no footbrake (*Gregory* v *Kelly* [1978] RTR 426).

14.5.2 Causation

The Law Reform (Contributory Negligence) Act 1945 did not resolve all the problems of causation that arise where both plaintiff and defendant have acted negligently. The courts are still prepared to find that in some instances the plaintiff's subsequent negligence constitutes a *novus actus interveniens which* breaks the chain of causation between the defendant's negligence and the damage (see, e.g., *McKew* v *Holland & Hannen & Cubitts (Scotland) Ltd* [1969] 3 All ER 1621, para. 4.2.2.2; for criticism see Millner (1971) 22 NILQ 168, 172 who asks whether 'it is ever justifiable to revert to this spurious causal argument so as to treat one cause alone as being operative'). Moreover, the plaintiff's negligence must have sufficient causative potency to be regarded as a proximate (i.e., effective) cause of the damage, not merely part of the history of events. The point is illustrated by the American case of *Smithwick* v *Hall & Upson Co.* (1890) 59 Conn 261, 21 A 924 (SC Conn) where the plaintiff employee was warned not to go to the east end of a platform on which he was working because it was unsafe. The danger consisted of ice on the platform and the lack of a protective railing. The plaintiff disobeyed his instructions and while standing at the east end of the platform he was knocked down by a wall which collapsed on to him. It was held that his conduct was not a cause of the injury, but merely a condition of its occurrence. If the fall had been the result of slipping on the ice or the absence of a railing the outcome would have been different.

In *Jones* v *Livox Quarries Ltd* [1952] 2 QB 608 the plaintiff, contrary to his employers' express instructions, rode on the back of a 'traxcavator', a tracked quarry vehicle which ran at $2\frac{1}{2}$ m.p.h. A 'dumper' driven by another employee collided with the rear of the traxcavator, crushing the plaintiff. The trial judge said that the plaintiff 'ran the risk of being thrown off and no other risk', but the Court of Appeal upheld a finding of contributory negligence. The Court rejected an argument that the plaintiff's negligence related to the foreseeable risk of falling off, but not the risk of being crushed. 'The man's negligence here was so much mixed up with his injury that it cannot be dismissed as mere history. His dangerous position on the vehicle was one of the causes of his damage' (per Denning LJ). This decision can be justified on the basis that the injury was within the scope of the risk which the plaintiff's conduct had created (*Salmond and Heuston,* p. 494; *Winfield and Jolowicz,* p. 178). This would depend, however, on the danger of crushing being a foreseeable risk. Denning LJ commented that once negligence is proved the consequences do not depend on foreseeability, but on causation. 'Even though the plaintiff did not foresee the possibility of being crushed, nevertheless in the ordinary plain common sense of this business the injury suffered by the plaintiff was due in part to the fact that he chose to ride on the tow bar.' On this approach the plaintiff in *Smithwick* v *Hall & Upson Co.* would be held contributorily negligent, but it is submitted that this view is wrong. It is the plaintiff's *fault* that must contribute to the damage not his *conduct*. The plaintiff's fault in *Smithwick* v *Hall & Upson Co.* was to run the foreseeable risk of slipping from the platform. That did not contribute to the accident that occurred, whereas his conduct (being at that place at the time the wall collapsed) did. But that is true of every person who was ever involved in an accident (see further Fagelson (1979) 42 MLR 646, 655–6). Contributory 'fault' must mean negligence (which involves foreseeability) with respect to the risk that causes the damage, otherwise the plaintiff is penalised for 'faulty' conduct which is essentially coincidental.

On the whole the courts approach the problems of causation pragmatically. They are largely reduced to issues of fact which can be dealt with on an *ad hoc* basis by allowing the discretion of apportionment to smooth out possible inequities. Appeals to 'common sense' are not infrequent. In *Stapley* v *Gypsum Mines Ltd* [1953] AC 663, for example, a miner, S, was killed when the roof of the mine collapsed on him. The foreman had previously instructed him, together with a fellow employee, D, to make the roof safe by bringing it down. They had attempted this without success and so by agreement they resumed their ordinary work. The question before the House of Lords was what caused the death. Was it solely S's fault, or partly D's fault by agreeing to resume ordinary work or failing to call the foreman? Lord Reid said (at p. 681):

> The question must be determined by applying common sense to the facts of each particular case. One may find that as a matter of history several people have been at fault and that if any one of them had acted properly the accident would not have happened, but that does not mean that the accident must be regarded as having been caused by the faults of all of them. One must discriminate between those faults which must be discarded as being too remote and those which must not.

One approach was to ask whether there was 'sufficient separation of time, place or circumstance' between the respective negligence, or whether D's fault was 'so much mixed up with the state of things brought about' by S that on a common-sense view it must be regarded has having contributed to the accident (applying a famous dictum of Viscount Birkenhead LC in *Admiralty Commissioners* v *SS Volute* [1922] 1 AC 129, 144, 145). It was held that D's negligence had contributed to the accident, but that the damages would be reduced by 80% on account of S's negligence.

Although it has been said that the rule of last opportunity is dead (*Jones* v *Livox Quarries Ltd* [1952] 2 QB 608, 615; for rejection of the rule by the Alberta Court of Appeal in a case in which the trial judge had erroneously applied it in order to find the plaintiff 100% contributorily negligent see *Wickberg* v *Patterson* [1997] 4 WWR 591) it must be remembered that causation arguments may indicate that the plaintiff's negligence was the sole cause of the harm, particularly where there is 'sufficient separation of time, place or circumstance' (see *Norris* v *W. Moss & Sons Ltd* [1954] 1 WLR 346; and in the context of breach of statutory duty *Ginty* v *Belmont Building Supplies Ltd* [1959] 1 All ER 414, para. 5.3.1).

14.5.3 Standard of care
'A person is guilty of contributory negligence if he ought reasonably to have foreseen that, if he did not act as a reasonable, prudent man, he might be hurt himself; and in his reckonings he must take into account the possibility of others being careless' (*Jones* v *Livox Quarries Ltd* [1952] 2 QB 608, 615

per Denning LJ). In theory this is meant to be the same standard of care as that applied to defendants. In practice the courts seem to demand less from plaintiffs in the way of prudence than from defendants. This may be partly due to the fact that before 1945 the courts tended to discount comparatively minor carelessness by the plaintiff in order to achieve a substantially fair result. With the power to apportion damages the courts have been more willing to make findings of contributory negligence, but they may also have been influenced by the significant differences in practice between a finding of negligence and a finding of contributory negligence. A finding of negligence usually has the effect of spreading the loss, through insurance (a circumstance which may justify imposing a high objective standard of care on defendant motorists, for example see *Nettleship* v *Weston* [1971] 2 QB 691). Contributory negligence leaves part or all of the loss on the plaintiff personally (*Atiyah*, p. 48—'the only significant group of people who are called upon to pay for the consequences of their negligence are accident victims themselves'; see also *Weir*, p. 260, n. 13).

Nonetheless, the standard of care to be applied to plaintiffs is objective, so the failure to wear a seat belt in a motor vehicle will be regarded as unreasonable and therefore negligent, even though the plaintiff sincerely believed that he would be safer not to wear the belt because of the risk of becoming trapped in an accident (*Froom* v *Butcher* [1976] QB 286, although the Court of Appeal admitted exceptions in the case of an 'unduly fat' man or a pregnant woman, where the belt 'may do more harm than good'; *Condon* v *Condon* [1978] RTR 483—plaintiff had a 'phobia' about wearing a seat belt and becoming trapped, not contributory negligence. The wearing of seat belts in the front and back seats of cars is now compulsory: Road Traffic Act 1988, s. 14, see also s. 15; SI 1991/1255; see *Hepple and Matthews*, p. 368.) Some concessions in the objective test are made, however, for children, the infirm, workmen in an action against their employer, and plaintiffs who were faced with a dilemma or emergency.

14.5.3.1 Children It is usually said that there is no age below which, as a matter of law, a child cannot be guilty of contributory negligence. While strictly speaking this is correct it is difficult to see how in practice a child of two or three years could ever be contributorily negligent. The standard to be applied is 'the degree of care which may reasonably be expected of a person in the plaintiff's situation' (*Lynch* v *Nurdin* (1841) 1 QB 29, 36). In *Gough* v *Thorne* [1966] 3 All ER 398 Lord Denning MR said (at p. 399) that:

A very young child cannot be guilty of contributory negligence. An older child may be; but it depends on the circumstances. A judge should only find a child guilty of contributory negligence if he or she is of such an age as reasonably to be expected to take precautions for his or her own safety.

This is not entirely subjective, for the question is whether an 'ordinary child' of the plaintiff's age could be expected to have done any more than the plaintiff, and an ordinary child is neither a 'paragon of prudence' nor 'scatter-brained' (ibid. p. 400 per Salmon LJ). (Query: what is the position of a 10-year-old with a mental age of 12; or 8?) The Pearson Commission has recommended that in cases of road traffic accidents contributory negligence should not be a defence where the child was under the age of 12 (*Pearson*, vol. 1, para. 1077). But why only in road traffic accidents? In *Gardner* v *Grace* (1858) 1 F & F 359 a 3½-year-old who ran into the road was found not contributorily negligent but in *McKinnell* v *White* 1971 SLT 61 a five-year-old who ran into the road was held contributorily negligent. It may be questioned whether *McKinnell* v *White* was correctly decided.

Where the defendant's negligence consists of putting temptation in a child's path, such that it is foreseeable that the child may injure himself by meddling with a dangerous object or substance, it will be difficult for the defendant to argue that the child's conduct was contributory negligence because that was the very circumstance that the defendant ought to have avoided (*Yachuk* v *Oliver Blais Co. Ltd* [1949] AC 386— nine-year-old supplied with pint of petrol by defendants; no contributory negligence when, in the course of lighting a torch for a game, the petrol exploded).

14.5.3.2 The infirm Since the standard expected of the plaintiff is reasonable care for his own safety it is logical in assessing what is reasonable to make some allowance for his particular circumstances. Thus an elderly pedestrian might be unable to take evasive action from an oncoming vehicle, when a younger, fitter person would, but he will not necessarily be held contributorily negligent (*Daly* v *Liverpool Corporation* [1939] 2 All ER 142). He must exercise such care as is reasonable having regard to his age and physical condition (*Clerk and Lindsell*, para. 3–25; but not, apparently, his mental condition, which must be judged objectively: *Baxter* v *Woolcombers Ltd* (1963) 107 SJ 553). Where the defendant knows or can foresee that a person with a disability may be affected by his conduct then the *defendant* must take additional precautions to allow for the disability (*Haley* v *London Electricity Board* [1965] AC 778—higher duty owed to blind pedestrians). This includes allowing for the disabilities of the 'feeble-minded' (*Latham* v *R. Johnson & Nephew Ltd* [1913] 1 KB 398, 416). The defendant can hardly complain that conduct which he was under an obligation to take precautions against constitutes contributory negligence.

14.5.3.3 Workmen Where an employee is suing his employer for breach of statutory regulations such as those contained in the Factories Acts the courts are less willing to make a finding of contributory negligence. The argument is that safety regulations are often designed to protect employees from the consequences of their own carelessness, and contributory negligence should not be used to undermine the purpose of the statute (*Staveley Iron & Chemical Co. Ltd* v *Jones* [1956] AC 627, 648 per Lord Wright; *Mullard* v *Ben Line Steamers Ltd* [1970] 1 WLR 1414, 1418 per Sachs LJ). In *Carr* v *Mercantile Produce Co. Ltd* [1949] 2 KB 601 Stable J commented (at p. 608) that the Factories Act is not merely for the protection of the careful worker 'but, human nature being what it is, also the careless, the indolent, the inadvertent, the weary, and even, perhaps, in some cases, the disobedient'. The standard of care must reflect the fact that fatigue, constant repetition of the same operation, noise and confusion in the workplace, concentration on the particular task at hand, and familiarity with the risks can dull an employee's sense of danger and cause inattention to his own safety (*Caswell* v *Powell Duffryn Associated Collieries Ltd* [1940] AC 152, 166; see generally, Fagelson (1979) 42 MLR 646). Possibly this relaxed standard applies only to actions for breach of statutory duty and not actions in negligence against employers (*Staveley Iron & Chemical Co. Ltd* v *Jones* [1956] AC 627, 642 per Lord Reid). However, an employer's non-delegable duty with regard to employees' safety requires him to take account of the possibility of carelessness or inadvertence (see, e.g., para. 5.1.4), and, by analogy with statutory duties, it is arguable that a strict application of contributory negligence might allow an employer to avoid his responsibilities.

This does not mean that an employee will never be guilty of contributory negligence, particularly where the factors outlined in *Caswell* v *Powell Duffryn Associated Collieries Ltd* are not present. Indeed, such findings are commonplace, and in some cases the employee's negligence has been treated as the *sole* cause of the damage (*Norris* v *W. Moss & Sons Ltd* [1954] 1 WLR 346—plaintiff's actions described as 'fantastically wrong'; *Rushton* v *Turner Bros Asbestos Co. Ltd* [1960] 1 WLR 96—'crazy'; see also *Ginty* v *Belmont Building Supplies Ltd* [1959] 1 All ER 414, para. 5.3.1; cf. *Stapley* v *Gypsum Mines Ltd* [1953] AC 633, para. 14.5.2, where causation arguments did not prevent apportionment). In *Jayes* v *IMI (Kynoch) Ltd* [1985] ICR 155 the Court of Appeal held that even where there is a breach of statutory duty in circumstances where the statutory intention was to protect the workman from his own folly, there is no principle of law that the workman cannot be 100% contributorily negligent. This tends to undermine the rule of public policy that *volenti non fit injuria* is not a defence to an action for breach of statutory duty by an employee against his employer (see para. 5.3.1), because there is no practical difference in these circumstances between *volenti* and 100% contributory negligence (at least, where *volenti* takes the form of merely encountering a known risk, where the overlap with contributory negligence is most obvious, see para. 14.1.2). In any event, it would seem illogical to speak of *contributory* negligence amounting to *100%*, and in such circumstances it is better to treat the problem as a question of causation—the plaintiff's conduct was the sole *cause*, breaking the chain of causation between the defendant's negligence and the damage. In *Pitts* v *Hunt* [1990] 3 All ER 344 the Court of Appeal held that a finding of 100% contributory negligence was logically unsupportable, though without any reference to *Jayes* v *IMI (Kynoch) Ltd*. Beldam LJ said (at p. 357) that s. 1 of the Law Reform (Contributory Negligence) Act 1945 does not come into operation unless the court is satisfied that there is fault on the part of both parties which has caused damage. It is then expressly provided that the action shall not be defeated by reason of the fault of the person suffering the damage, but a finding that he is entirely responsible for the damage effectively defeats his claim. Thus, *where the Act applies*, i.e., where the fault of both plaintiff and defendant has contributed to the damage, the court must make an apportion-ment, which it will fail to do by assessing the plaintiff's contribution as 100% (see *Wynbergen* v *Hoyts Corporation Pty Ltd* (1997) 149 ALJR 25, in which the High Court of Australia employed this rationale to support their con-clusion that it was not open to the court to make a finding that the plaintiff was 100% contributorily negligent).

14.5.3.4 Emergency Where the plaintiff is faced with an emergency as a result of the defendant's tort and in the agony of the moment has to choose between alternative courses of action, then provided he acted reasonably he will not be guilty of contributory negligence, even though with hindsight he would have been safer if he had opted for the other alternative (*The Bywell Castle* (1879) 4 PD 219). In *Jones* v *Boyce* (1816) 1 Stark 493 the plaintiff was a passenger on a coach and, believing that the coach was about to overturn, he jumped off. The coach did not overturn, but it was held that he was not guilty of contributory negligence because he had acted reasonably in the circumstances (see also *Sayers* v *Harlow Urban District Council* [1958] 1 WLR 623, para. 4.2.2.2—plaintiff trapped in public lavatory may undertake reasonable attempts to escape). 'It was the defendant who created the emergency which led to the accident. It does not lie in his mouth to be minutely critical of the reactive conduct of the plaintiff whose safety he had imperilled by his negligence' (*Neufeld* v *Landry* (1975) 55 DLR (3d) 296, 299, CA of Manitoba, per Freedman CJM). A similar principle also applies to defendants confronted by a dilemma, since this will be one of the circumstances taken into account in deciding whether the conduct fell below that of a reasonable man.

As a general rule, people are entitled to assume that others will act carefully, and so do not have to anticipate their negligence (*Toronto Railway Co.* v *King* [1908] AC 260, 269). But where experience suggests that negligence by others is common, a reasonable man would guard against it (*London Passenger Transport Board* v *Upson* [1949] AC 155, 173—although he is not bound to anticipate folly in all its forms). An employee can normally assume that his employer is not in breach of his statutory duties with respect to safety at work (*Westwood* v *Post Office* [1974] AC 1).

14.5.4 Apportionment
Where the Law Reform (Contributory Negligence) Act 1945 applies the court is directed to reduce the plaintiff's damages 'to such extent as the court thinks just and equitable having regard to the claimant's share in the responsibility for the damage' (s. 1(1)). The court cannot refuse to reduce the award because it is just and equitable to do so (*Boothman* v *British Northrop Ltd* (1972) 13 KIR 112), but where one of the parties is less than 10% responsible no apportionment should be made (*Johnson* v *Tennant Bros Ltd* (1954) unreported, CA; though this rule may be questioned, at least where the plaintiff is in breach of a statutory duty: *Capps* v *Miller* [1989] 2 All ER 333, 340). If there are two accidents and the first contributed causally to the second, there will be a sub-apportionment of that part of the subsequent

damage which is attributable to the first accident (*The Calliope* [1970] P 172).
Where there are two or more defendants in respect of the same accident, the
plaintiff's contributory negligence should be assessed by comparing the
plaintiff's conduct with the totality of the defendants' negligence, not with the
extent to which each defendant's conduct contributed to the damage. Thus
the percentage reduction of the plaintiff's damages will be the same against
each defendant. Any differences in the respective responsibilities of the
defendants should be dealt with in contribution proceedings between the
defendants (para. 14.6) after the issue of contributory negligence between
plaintiff and defendants has been decided (*Fitzgerald* v *Lane* [1988] 2 All ER
961; see McLean [1989] CLJ 14).

How is the 'claimant's share in the responsibility for the damage' to be
assessed? There are two possible tests, causation and culpability. Clearly the
plaintiff's negligence must be causally connected to the damage otherwise the
Act would not apply (para. 14.5.2). But if the plaintiff's conduct is a cause
and the defendant's conduct is also *a* cause it is difficult to see how the
relative causative potency of their actions can be determined without resorting to a simple 50/50 division of responsibility (Fagelson (1979) 42 MLR
646, 657–9; relative causation 'has no necessary connection with anything
that would appeal to the ordinary person as being just and equitable':
Williams (1954) 17 MLR 66, 69; but cf Gravells (1977) 93 LQR 581, 594
et seq.). It is, however, a factor that may be taken into account (*Stapley* v
Gypsum Mines Ltd [1953] AC 663, 682 per Lord Reid; *Davies* v *Swan Motor
Co. (Swansea) Ltd* [1949] 2 KB 291, 326 per Denning LJ). The more
important consideration seems to be culpability, or the comparative blameworthiness of the parties.

Culpability is measured by an objective standard, i.e., deviation from the
standard of conduct of a reasonable man, not by reference to moral fault
(*Westwood* v *Post Office* [1974] AC 1, 16). Relative blameworthiness is not a
particularly satisfactory criterion either, because it can produce quite arbitrary
results. The same conduct by two plaintiffs can lead to different reductions
depending upon the culpability of the respective defendants (see *Atiyah*,
p. 50). Moreover, where the defendant is liable for breach of a strict duty
rather than negligence, his relative blameworthiness could be nil. Not
surprisingly the courts have not followed this reasoning because it would
effectively undermine the purpose of many strict duties which are intended
to protect others from the consequences of their own carelessness (see para.
14.5.3.3). Yet in *Quintas* v *National Smelting Co. Ltd* [1960] 1 All ER 104 the
plaintiff's damages were reduced by 75% at first instance, where the employers were held liable for breach of statutory duty. The Court of Appeal
([1961] 1 All ER 630) held that the defendants were not liable for breach of
statutory duty, but had been negligent and the reduction of the award was
fixed at 50%. This suggests that the nature of the defendant's duty will be
relevant when assessing the degree of responsibility to be attached to his
conduct.

Ultimately, the discretion implicit in a test based on what is 'just and
equitable' allows the court to take an *ad hoc* approach to apportionment,

treating the issue as essentially a question of fact. Where a particular type of accident is common it may be sensible to have guidelines for the appropriate deduction in order to produce both a reasonable level of consistency and certainty (which helps the process of claims settlement). In *Froom v Butcher* [1976] QB 286, for example, the Court of Appeal held that where the plaintiff was injured in a road traffic accident but had not worn a seat belt then the damages should be reduced by 25% if the injury would have been prevented altogether by use of a belt. If the injury would have been less severe, but there would still have been some injury the reduction should be 15%, but if the injuries would have been the same even with the use of a belt there should be no reduction (for a justification of this approach see Gravells (1977) 93 LQR 581, 607–9; see also *Capps v Miller* [1989] 2 All ER 333 applying the same approach to a motor cyclist's failure to wear a crash helmet, though a failure to fasten a helmet that was worn merited a smaller percentage reduction). These figures would apply irrespective of the degree of the defendant's culpability in causing the accident. For this reason also, the fact that the wearing of seat belts is now compulsory should not lead to a change in the percentage reductions (*Capps v Miller*). (Note the comparative effectiveness of the criminal law and the law of tort in 'persuading' people to wear seat belts: *Hepple and Matthews*, p. 368. This must have some implications for the supposed deterrent effect of tort as a means of accident prevention.)

14.6 CONTRIBUTION BETWEEN TORTFEASORS

Where two or more tortfeasors are liable for the *same* damage they will usually be entitled to claim contribution from each other under the Civil Liability (Contribution) Act 1978 (in para. 14.6 section numbers refer to this Act unless otherwise mentioned; see generally, Dugdale (1979) 42 MLR 182). In *Jameson v CEGB* [1997] 4 All ER 38, the Court of Appeal considered the meaning of 'same damage' and held that an employer sued by a deceased employee's dependants under the Fatal Accidents Act 1976 was entitled to claim contribution from another employer which had earlier settled an industrial disease claim brought by the deceased. Even though the settlement sum was relatively small compared to the full value of the claim, the relevant damage for the purpose of the 1978 Act was the alleged wrong causing the injury and death, and not the damages that the deceased could have recovered. The liability of the employers was, therefore, in respect of the 'same damage'. The parties will be 'joint tortfeasors' where they have participated in some common enterprise, where a person has authorised another to commit a tort, and where a master is vicariously liable for the torts of his servants. Where, however, their independent actions coincide to produce the same damage they are 'several concurrent tortfeasors' (e.g., the negligence of two drivers causes a road accident which injures a third party). The only practical consequence of this distinction is that a release from liability granted to a joint tortfeasor will release the others, whereas a release of one several concurrent tortfeasor will not (*Clerk and Lindsell*, para. 4–55; *Jameson v CEGB*, above).

The right to contribution does not operate as a defence to the plaintiff's claim. The plaintiff can sue any one or more of the wrongdoers for the full amount of his loss, although he can only recover the loss once. A judgment against one is not a bar to a subsequent action against the others (s. 3). If the first judgment remains unsatisfied the plaintiff can sue the other tortfeasors, subject to a possible penalty in costs (s. 4). Normally all the persons responsible for the damage will be sued, but if not, it is open to a defendant to join the others to the action in third-party proceedings under RSC Ord. 16. One consequence of this rule is that a defendant who was responsible for say 10% of the loss may have to meet the full claim. Although contribution is not a defence it can be as important as the defence of contributory negligence in reducing the sum that a defendant will have to pay out, especially as he may be entitled to a full indemnity (s. 2(2)).

The Act applies to any type of action and the wrongdoers' liability to the plaintiff need not be based on breach of the same obligation (s. 6(1), cf. contributory negligence, para. 14.5.1). Indeed, there is no rule of law that a party who has been merely negligent cannot be required to make contribution to a party found guilty of fraud, although the discrepancy in their conduct will clearly be relevant when addressing the amount of the contribution, even to the extent of assessing a nil contribution (*K* v *P* (*J, third party*) [1993] 1 All ER 521, where it was held that the common law maxim *ex turpi causa non oritur actio* did not apply as a defence to a claim for contribution under the 1978 Act). Section 2(1) provides that the amount of the contribution shall be 'such as may be found by the court to be just and equitable having regard to the extent of that person's responsibility for the damage in question'. This provides the same basis of apportionment as under the Law Reform (Contributory Negligence) Act 1945, namely causation and blameworthiness, and similar issues are likely to arise (see para. 14.5.4; for a more principled approach in cases of professional negligence based on the relationship between the wrongdoers see Dugdale (1985) 1 PN 11, 13–18). For example, in *Downs* v *Chappell* [1996] 3 All ER 344, 363, a negligent defendant was required to contribute equally with a fraudulent defendant on the basis that the negligence had a greater causative impact. Hobhouse LJ said that: 'It is just and equitable to take into account both the seriousness of the respective parties' faults and their causative relevance. A more serious fault having less causative impact on the plaintiff's damage may represent an equivalent responsibility to a less serious fault which had a greater causative impact'. The court's discretion is limited by s. 2(3) which provides that where the plaintiff's damages would be subject to any limitation (imposed by statute or agreement) or any reduction because of contributory negligence the contribution award should not exceed this amount. In other words a defendant cannot be required to pay more by way of contribution than he would have been liable to pay to the plaintiff.

A settlement before judgment by one tortfeasor, D1, of the plaintiff's claim against him does not remove his right to seek contribution from another tortfeasor, D2 (s. 1(2)). This is 'without regard to whether or not he himself is or ever was liable in respect of the damage, provided, however, that he would have been liable assuming that the factual basis of the claim against him could be established' (s. 1(4)). This changes the situation that arose before the Act whereby D1 could not obtain contribution unless he could *prove* that he was liable to the plaintiff, even though D2 clearly was liable to the plaintiff. That rule discouraged the settlement of claims for fear of prejudicing a contribution claim. The proviso is limited, however, to 'the factual basis of the claim', so s. 1(4) will not apply where the settlement is based on doubts as to the validity in law of the plaintiff's claim against D1 (Dugdale (1979) 42 MLR 182, 184). In this position D1 would probably have to submit to judgment in order to protect his contribution rights.

Contribution may be recovered from 'any other person liable in respect of the same damage' (s. 1(1)). Where, however, D2 has ceased to be liable to P he will nonetheless be subject to a claim for contribution, unless he ceased to be liable by virtue of the expiry of a period of limitation or prescription which extinguished P's right of action against him (s. 1(3)). Most periods of limitation do not extinguish the plaintiff's right but merely bar his remedy. Thus in an ordinary tort action, the fact that D2 would not be liable to P because P's limitation period has expired would not prevent D1 bringing a contribution claim against D2. Similarly, where D2 has settled P's claim against him he may still be liable to make contribution to D1 (*Logan v Uttlesford District Council* (1984) 136 NLJ 541). The limitation period for contribution proceedings under the 1978 Act is two years from the date of judgment or compromise against D1 (Limitation Act, 1980, s. 10). If D2 has been sued by P and held not liable the judgment is conclusive in the contribution proceedings 'as to any issue determined by that judgment' in favour of D2 (s. 1(5)). This creates a possible conflict between s. 1(3) and (5), since if P's action against D2 failed because it was statute-barred by the Limitation Act 1980 then s. 1(5) appears to preclude a contribution claim by D1. Section 1(5) was intended to apply to a determination of D2's liability to P *on the merits*, not where P's action failed on a procedural technicality, but it is questionable whether the wording would permit such an interpretation (*Clerk and Lindsell*, para. 4–61; cf. Balcombe LJ in *Nottingham Health Authority* v *Nottingham City Council* [1988] 1 WLR 903, 906 where, without reference to s. 1(5), it is assumed that a tortfeasor who, being sued to judgment, is found not liable because of a successful limitation plea would still be liable to make contribution). A stay in proceedings or dismissal of an action for want of prosecution, which are procedural not substantive issues, are not covered by s. 1(5) and so do not preclude contribution proceedings (*R. A. Lister & Co. Ltd* v *E. G. Thomson (Shipping) Ltd (No.2)* [1987] 3 All ER 1032, 1039–40).

The Act does not affect an express or implied contractual or other right to indemnity, or an express contractual provision regulating or excluding contribution (s. 7(3); for an example of an implied right to indemnity see *Lister* v *Romford Ice & Cold Storage Co. Ltd* [1957] AC 555, para. 8.4.5). Thus a defendant who is liable to make contribution under the Act may recover this sum from another defendant under an indemnity clause (see, e.g., *Sims v Foster Wheeler Ltd* [1966] 1 WLR 769).

14.7 LIMITATION

There is no limitation period at common law. The rules on limitation are
entirely the creation of statute now consolidated in the Limitation Act 1980
(section numbers in para. 14.7 refer to this Act, unless specified). The basic
rule is that an action in tort cannot be brought more than six years from the
date on which the cause of action accrued (s. 2), though for libel and slander,
and malicious falsehood, the period is one year, with a discretion to allow the
action to proceed notwithstanding the expiry of the one year period (ss. 4A,
32A, as amended by the Defamation Act 1996, s. 5; on the exercise of this
discretion see *Oyston* v *Blaker* [1996] 2 All ER 106). With torts that are
actionable *per se,* such as trespass, the action accrues at the date of the
defendant's act (unless the trespass is continuing, in which case a new action
accrues from day to day). With torts actionable only on proof of damage the
action accrues when the damage occurs, which will usually but not necessarily
be at the same time as the defendant's breach of duty. By contrast, in contract
the action accrues at the date of breach of contract. Thus in cases where the
damage occurs at a time after the breach, the possibility of concurrent liability
in contract and tort may give the plaintiff the advantage of the later
commencement date of the tort limitation period (see, e.g., *Midland Bank
Trust Co. Ltd* v *Hett Stubbs & Kemp* [1979] Ch 384, though in this case it was
held that an *omission* to perform a contractual duty could constitute a
'continuing breach of contract' up to the point at which it was no longer
possible to perform the duty; cf. *Bell* v *Peter Browne & Co.* [1990] 3 All ER
124—solicitors' failure to remedy an initial breach of contract did not give
rise to a 'continuing duty'; see Evans (1991) 7 PN 50).

The rules on limitation periods can be highly technical, complex and
sometimes quite arbitrary in application. The Law Commission is currently
considering options for reform of the law, possibly having a 'core' regime with
a three-year limitation period running from the date of 'discoverability' of the
damage with a 'long-stop' running from the date of the defendant's act or
omission which gives rise to the claim, but with no discretion for the court to
disregard the limitation period (Law Commission Consultation Paper No.
151, *Limitation of Actions*, 1998).

There are currently four circumstances in which special rules of limitation
apply: cases of personal injuries and death, latent damage, concealed fraud,
and persons under a disability (note that some statutes have their own
limitation period, e.g., Carriage by Air Act 1961; Consumer Protection Act
1987, see para. 10.2.7.3).

14.7.1 Personal injuries and death

In actions for personal injuries the basic limitation period is normally three
years from either the date on which the cause of action accrued or the date
of the plaintiff's 'knowledge', whichever is later (s. 11(4)). (For a more
detailed discussion see Jones, *Limitation Periods in Personal Injury Actions*,
Blackstone Press, 1995.) In addition, even if this fixed period has expired the
court has a wide discretion to disregard the time limit and permit the action

to proceed (s. 33). Section 11(1) provides that the three-year period applies to 'any action for damage for negligence, nuisance or breach of duty' where the damages claimed by the plaintiff consist of or include damages in respect of personal injuries. In *Letang* v *Cooper* [1965] 1 QB 232 the Court of Appeal held that these words also applied to an action in trespass to the person, and this was subsequently held to be the position even where the trespass was intentional (*Long* v *Hepworth* [1968] 1 WLR 1299). In *Stubbings* v *Webb* [1993] 1 All ER 322, however, the House of Lords concluded that s. 11 (1) was intended by Parliament to be limited to personal injury resulting from *accidents* caused by negligence, nuisance or breach of a duty of care. Injuries arising from deliberate assault, including indecent assault and rape, were not actions for breach of duty within the meaning of s. 11(1), and were subject to the fixed six-year limitation period under s. 2. Lord Griffiths said that *Letang* v *Cooper* was correctly decided in so far as it held that negligent driving is a cause of action falling within s. 11 (irrespective of whether the cause of action is framed in trespass or negligence), but it was wrong to the extent that it suggested that the words 'breach of duty' had the effect of including within the section all actions in which damages for personal injuries are claimed. One consequence of this is that claims in trespass to the person against a medical practitioner alleging that the doctor failed to obtain consent to a surgical procedure will be subject to the fixed six-year limitation period. Another consequence is that, as in *Stubbings* v *Webb* itself, if the plaintiff suffers psychological trauma as a result of childhood sexual abuse and is thereby unable to bring an action until her later adulthood (i.e., until age 24, the period of her minority, by virtue of s. 28, plus six years), she will be time-barred. The European Court of Human Rights has held that the operation of the Limitation Act 1980 in this manner does not contravene the European Convention on Human Rights (*Stubbings* v *UK* [1997] 1 FLR 105; Mullis (1997) 9 Child and Fam LQ 291). Civil actions for harassment under the Protection from Harassment Act 1997 are subject to a six year limitation period, by virtue of s. 6 of that Act providing that s. 11 of the Limitation Act does not apply (see Limitation Act 1980, s. 9).

In negligence and nuisance the cause of action accrues when the plaintiff sustains actionable damage, irrespective of whether he knows of the damage (*Cartledge* v *E. Jopling & Sons Ltd* [1963] AC 758), but this date is virtually redundant in view of the alternative test of the commencement date. Section 14(1) defines the 'date of knowledge' as references to the date on which he first had knowledge of the following facts:

(a) that the injury was significant; and
(b) that the injury was attributable in whole or in part to the act or omission which is alleged to constitute negligence, nuisance or breach of duty; and
(c) the identity of the defendant; and
(d) if it is alleged that the act or omission was that of a person other than the defendant, the identity of that person and the additional facts supporting the bringing of an action against the defendant.

An injury is 'significant' for the purpose of s. 14(1)(a) if the person whose date of knowledge is in question would reasonably have considered it sufficiently serious to justify proceedings against a defendant who did not dispute liability and was able to satisfy a judgment (s. 14(2)). This makes most injuries significant when measured in terms of their money value. The plaintiff's subjective beliefs and attitudes are irrelevant (*Buck* v *English Electric Co. Ltd* [1977] 1 WLR 806; *McCafferty* v *Metropolitan Police District Receiver* [1977] 1 WLR 1073), though the objective test of what a 'reasonable man' would have known is qualified by what 'a man of the plaintiff's age, with his background, his intelligence and his disabilities' would reasonably have known (*Davis* v *City and Hackney Health Authority* [1991] 2 Med LR 366). His subjective beliefs might be relevant to the exercise of discretion under s. 33. It is the plaintiff's knowledge of *facts* that governs the commencement date. His ignorance that, as a matter of law, the facts would give him a cause of action is irrelevant (s. 14(1)), though again it will be relevant to the court's discretion (*Coad* v *Cornwall and Isles of Scilly Health Authority* [1997] 1 WLR 189; see s. 33(3)(e)). A broad knowledge that the injuries are attributable to the defendant's negligence is sufficient to start time running under s. 14(1)(b), even if the plaintiff does not know the specific acts or omissions that constitute the cause of action (*Wilkinson* v *Ancliff (BLT) Ltd* [1986] 3 All ER 427). In *Nash* v *Eli Lilly & Co.* [1993] 1 WLR 782, 799 the Court of Appeal said that what was required was knowledge of 'the essence of the act or omission to which the injury is attributable'.

The courts have experienced some difficulty in determining what a patient must know about the success or otherwise of medical treatment for the purpose of s. 14(1)(b). On one view, knowledge that an injury was caused by a surgical operation is not knowledge that it was attributable to an act or omission which is alleged to constitute negligence, since an injury following an operation may arise without negligence. Most people would not regard *successful* medical treatment as constituting an *injury*, so that if a patient is informed that surgery was successful she would not even consider that she had been injured, let alone address her mind to the question of which acts or omissions had caused the 'injury'. Thus, the minimum knowledge that a plaintiff would require is knowledge that 'something has gone wrong' with the treatment in order to distinguish those injuries which were unavoidable consequences of the procedure and those which are attributable to the 'act or omission which is alleged to constitute negligence'. On this approach the patient must have knowledge of some act or omission which affected the safety of the operation (*Bentley* v *Bristol & Western Health Authority* [1991] 2 Med LR 359). The contrary view has been adopted by the Court of Appeal, however, on the basis that to require knowledge that something has gone wrong with treatment before the limitation period starts to run is inconsistent with the proviso to s. 14(1)(b) that 'knowledge that any acts or omissions did or did not, as a matter of law, involve negligence . . . or breach of duty is irrelevant' (see *Broadley* v *Guy Clapham & Co.* [1994] 4 All ER 439; *Dobbie* v *Medway Health Authority* [1994] 4 All ER 450). In these cases the Court of Appeal was concerned not to reach a position where the plaintiff could effectively postpone the running of the limitation period by asserting that she did not know that she had a cause of action in law (cf. *Smith* v *West Lancashire Health Authority* [1995] PIQR P514 where the Court of Appeal held that in the case of an omission to operate, a plaintiff cannot know of an omission without knowing what it is that is omitted, and the plaintiff did not know that there had been an omission to operate until he received an expert medical opinion some years later pointing this out). It is certainly arguable that in a medical negligence action the plaintiff needs to know more than simply that the 'injury' was attributable to the treatment or operation. In *Hallam-Eames* v *Merrett Syndicates Ltd* [1996] 7 Med LR 122, 125, which was concerned with the interpretation of the analogous provision in s. 14A of the Limitation Act 1980 in respect of claims for economic loss, Hoffmann LJ commented that:

if all that was necessary was that a plaintiff should have known that the damage was attributable to an act or omission of the defendant, the statute would have said so. Instead, it speaks of the damage being attributable to 'the act or omission which is alleged to constitute negligence.' In other words, the act or omission of which the plaintiff must have knowledge must be that which is causally relevant for the purposes of an allegation of negligence.

The words 'which is alleged to constitute negligence' served to identify the facts of which the plaintiff must have knowledge. It was not sufficient for the plaintiff to know merely that the relevant damage had been caused by *an* act or omission of the defendant:

The plaintiff does not have to know that he has a cause of action or that the defendant's acts can be characterised in law as negligent or as falling short of some standard of professional or other behaviour . . . He must have known the facts which can fairly be described as constituting the negligence of which he complains. It may be that knowledge of such facts will also serve to bring home to him the fact that the defendant has been negligent or at fault. But that in itself is not a reason for saying that he need not have known them. (ibid., at p. 126)

'Knowledge' includes constructive knowledge, though not mere reasonable belief or suspicion (*Wilkinson* v *Ancliff (BLT) Ltd*; *Stephen* v *Riverside Health Authority* [1990] 1 Med LR 261—even a deep-rooted suspicion or conviction on the part of the plaintiff that incompetent treatment had caused her symptoms did not amount to knowledge, when she had been assured by her doctors that the treatment could not have caused the symptoms. See further *Nash* v *Eli Lilly & Co.* [1993] 1 WLR 782, 793–6 for discussion of the distinction between belief and knowledge). Constructive knowledge means knowledge which the person might reasonably have been expected to acquire from facts observable or ascertainable by him, or from facts ascertainable with the help of medical or other appropriate expert advice which it is reasonable for him to seek (s. 14(3)). This is subject to a proviso that he is not fixed with knowledge of a fact ascertainable only with the help of expert advice so long as he has taken all reasonable steps to obtain (and, where appropriate, to act on) that advice. So if the expert fails to discover or disclose a relevant fact, time will not start running (though see *Jones* v *Liverpool Health Authority* [1996] PIQR P251, 266, where Glidewell LJ said that if a plaintiff is informed by a medical expert that he probably does not have a valid claim, and years later he is advised by another medical expert, on the same facts, that he probably does have a valid claim, he cannot claim that he did not have knowledge until he received the later opinion). If the person who gives advice is a solicitor then, to the extent that erroneous advice concerns the law, it will not prevent time running. In *Leadbitter* v *Hodge Finance Ltd* [1982] 2 All ER 167, Bush J accepted that s. 14(3) applied to the expert advice of solicitors in connection with obtaining evidence, but emphasised that the proviso applied to facts which are ascertainable only with the help of expert advice. Where the plaintiff himself could have discovered the information then he is fixed with any knowledge that his solicitors ought to have acquired (*Henderson* v *Temple Pier Co. Ltd* [1998] 3 All ER 324). However, in *Fowell* v *National Coal Board, The Times,* 28 May 1986 the Court of Appeal said that a solicitor was not an expert within the meaning of s. 14(3), which was directed to experts in the sense of expert witnesses. That leaves open the question of whether the plaintiff will be fixed with knowledge of *all* the facts which his solicitors ought reasonably to have discovered, even though he could not have ascertained the information himself (see, e.g., *Simpson* v *Norwest Holst Southern Ltd* [1980] 2 All ER 471, which suggests that he will; see further *Nash* v *Ell Lilly & Co.* [1993] 1 WLR 782, 799–801).

A plaintiff has an indefeasible right to bring an action within the primary three-year limitation period. If that period has expired the court has a discretion to allow the action to proceed if it is equitable to do so, having regard to the degree to which ss. 11 or 12 (i.e., the primary period) prejudice the plaintiff, and the degree to which a decision to exercise the discretion in the plaintiff's favour would prejudice the defendant (s. 33(1)). By s. 33(3) the court must have regard to all the circumstances of the case, and in particular to:

(a) the length of and reasons for the delay on the part of the plaintiff (i.e., delay *after* the limitation period expired, not delay during the limitation period *itself: Donovan* v *Gwentoys Ltd* [1990] 1 All ER 1018; delay during the limitation period can be taken into account as part of 'all the circumstances' under s. 33(3): ibid.);

(b) the extent to which, having regard to the delay, the evidence is likely to be less cogent;

(c) the conduct of the defendant after the cause of action arose;

(d) the duration of any disability (see para. 14.7.4) of the plaintiff arising after the cause of action accrued;

(e) the extent to which the plaintiff acted promptly and reasonably once he knew whether he might have a cause of action against the defendant;

(f)   the steps, if any, taken by the plaintiff to obtain medical, legal or other expert advice and the nature of any such advice.

In *Firman* v *Ellis* [1978] QB 886 the Court of Appeal held that this discretion was unfettered, and not limited to a residual category of exceptional cases, a view approved by the House of Lords in *Thompson* v *Brown Construction (Ebbw Vale) Ltd* [1981] 2 All ER 296. This is subject, however, to *Walkley* v *Precision Forgings Ltd* [1979] 1 WLR 606 where the House distinguished between a plaintiff who had not issued any proceedings within the primary limitation period, who could invoke the discretion, and a plaintiff who had issued a writ within the three-year limit, but had then not proceeded with the action, who could not. A second writ issued out of time would be statute-barred. Where the plaintiff had issued proceedings in time, but had not prosecuted the action, then, it is argued, he is prejudiced not by s. 11 but by his own conduct. However, this argument could be applied with as much force to some plaintiffs who have not issued proceedings within the primary period, but nevertheless are at least permitted to argue that the discretion should be exercised. In *Chappell* v *Cooper* [1980] 2 All ER 463 the Court of Appeal held that *Walkley* v *Precision Forgings Ltd* applies no matter why the plaintiff did not continue the first action, whether for good reasons or bad. *Walkley* v *Precision Forgings Ltd* creates an arbitrary and unjustifiable distinction between categories of plaintiff who are permitted to seek the benefit of s. 33 (Davies (1982) 98 LQR 249, 260–5; Morgan (1982) 1 CJQ 109; Jones (1985) 1 PN 159, 160). *Walkley* does not apply, however, where the first writ is technically invalid, and a second writ is subsequently issued outside the three-year period. The plaintiff in this position can invoke s. 33 (*White* v *Glass, The Times,* 18 February 1989, CA; *Re Workvale Ltd (No. 2)* [1992] 2 All ER 627). Similarly, where a 'protective' writ has been issued within three years of the accident, but the plaintiff did not acquire 'knowledge' within the meaning of s. 14 until a later date, *Walkley* v *Precision Forgings Ltd* is irrelevant if a second writ is issued within three years of the date of knowledge because the plaintiff is within the primary limitation period (*Stephen* v *Riverside Health Authority* [1990] 1 Med LR 261; cf. however, *Nash* v *Eli Lilly & Co.* [1993] 1 WLR 782, 795–6 where the Court of Appeal doubted whether it was possible for a claimant who had taken legal advice and issued proceedings to be held subsequently not then to have had relevant 'knowledge'; cx. *Whitfield* v *North Durham Health Authority* [1995] 6 Med LR 32, 37 stating that the issue of a 'protective writ' by the plaintiff should not be conclusive, by itself, on the question of the plaintiff's knowledge under s. 14). A defendant may also be estopped from relying on the limitation period where the plaintiff has been induced to discontinue the first action by a misrepresentation or improper conduct by the defendant, but an estoppel will not arise merely from an admission of liability and the making of an interim payment (*Deerness* v *John Keeble & Son Ltd* [1983] 2 Lloyd's Rep 260; *Forward* v *Hendricks* [1997] 2 All ER 397).

In some cases the delay in issuing proceedings is attributable to negligence by the plaintiff's solicitors. It could be argued that in this situation the plaintiff will not be prejudiced by refusing to permit his action to proceed, because he could sue his solicitors. But in both *Firman* v *Ellis* and *Thompson* v *Brown Construction (Ebbw Vale) Ltd* it was said that this is merely one of the factors to be considered and is not conclusive against the plaintiff. In practice there are considerable variations in the weight that the courts attach to this particular circumstance, and the inconsistencies make the exercise something of a lottery (see Jones (1985) 1 PN 159; Steiner (1990) 6 PN 183; *Ramsden* v *Lee* [1992] 2 All ER 204; *Hartley* v *Birmingham City District Council* [1992] 2 All ER 213).

Where the victim of a tort has died there are two possible types of action, a claim on behalf of the deceased's estate under the Law Reform (Miscellaneous Provisions) Act 1934 and a claim by the deceased's dependants under the Fatal Accidents Act 1976 (see para. 15.3). Similar limitation rules apply to both actions. If the death occurred before the expiry of the deceased's three-year limitation period, then a new three-year period commences in favour of the personal representative (for the Law Reform Act claim) or the dependants (for the Fatal Accidents Act claim). This period runs from the date of death or the date of knowledge of the personal representative or dependants, whichever date is later (ss. 11(5) and 12(2)). If there is more than one dependant the period runs separately against each of them, but if there is more than one personal representative and their dates of knowledge are different, time runs from the earliest date (ss. 13(1) and 11(7)). In both types of action, if the new limitation period expires, the plaintiff can ask the court to exercise its discretion under s. 33. If the deceased's primary limitation period had expired before he died then in theory there is no claim to survive for the benefit of the estate nor any claim by the dependants. But they can ask the court to exercise the discretion, just as the deceased would have been able to do were he alive, and in doing so the court will have regard to the length of and reasons for delay on the part of the deceased (s. 33(4)).

14.7.2 Latent damage

The objectives of rules on limitation are to protect defendants from stale claims, to encourage plaintiffs to proceed with claims without unreasonable delay, and to provide finality, allowing a person to feel confident, after a certain period of time, that potential claims against him are closed. Two types of case cause particular problems. First, latent damage, where the plaintiff is unaware that damage has occurred, and the cause of action can accrue and become statute-barred before he even knows of his right to sue. This is obviously unfair to the plaintiff, who can hardly be encouraged to prosecute an action expeditiously when he is unaware of its existence. Secondly, cases of 'postponed damage', where the damage arises many years after the defendant's breach of duty, cause difficulties for defendants in terms of maintaining records and obtaining adequate insurance cover. Both types of case tend to frustrate the aims of the law of limitation (see Mullany (1991) 54 MLR 216 and 349 for detailed discussion).

In *Cartledge* v *E. Jopling & Sons Ltd* [1963] AC 758 the plaintiff contracted pneumoconiosis from the inhalation of dust over a long period at his workplace. Damage to his lungs was undetectable for a long time and the plaintiff was unaware of it. The House of Lords held that the cause of action accrued when significant damage to the lungs occurred, and it was irrelevant whether the plaintiff knew of the damage or not. As a result of this decision the law of limitation was changed by statute in cases of personal injuries. The problems of latent damage in cases of property damage and financial loss only became prominent in the 1970s, following the development of liability for defective buildings and the imposition of tortious duties in the context of professional liability, which had previously been regarded as a purely contractual obligation (having different limitation rules).

In the case of defective buildings the first suggestion for the date at which the limitation period should commence was the date of construction (*Dutton v Bognor Regis Urban District Council* [1972] 1 QB 373, 396). But in *Sparham-Souter v Town & Country Developments (Essex) Ltd* [1976] QB 858 the Court of Appeal held that time did not run until the plaintiff discovered the damage or ought reasonably to have discovered it. There was a distinction between damage to the building and damage to the plaintiff, and it was the latter that was relevant to the accrual of the action. The owner of a damaged building did not suffer any loss until the damage became apparent and thereby reduced its market value, since an owner who sold the property before the damage was discoverable would receive the full market price.

The 'reasonable discoverability' test, as it came to be known, was overturned by the ruling of the House of Lords in *Pirelli General Cable Works Ltd v Oscar Faber & Partners* [1983] 2 AC 1 that the action accrued, and the limitation period thereby commenced, when physical damage to the building occurred, irrespective of whether it was discoverable by the plaintiff. A clear distinction was drawn between a defect in a building (e.g., weak foundations) and the physical damage to the building caused by the defect, such as cracking. The defect itself did not constitute damage, except where the building was 'doomed from the start' when the limitation period would run from the date of construction.

Pirelli General Cable Works Ltd v Oscar Faber & Partners raised a number of problems, both practical and theoretical. What was the position where the building suffered progressive deterioration? Was it realistically possible to distinguish clearly between a defect and the damage it caused? How did *Junior Books Ltd v Veitchi Co. Ltd* [1983] 1 AC 520, para. 2.2.4.2.2, where the plaintiff's loss consisted of a *defective* floor, fit into the analysis? When was a building 'doomed from the start'? What about subsequent purchasers of property which had already sustained latent physical damage at the time they acquired it? Under the reasonable discoverability test the action accrued to the person who was the owner at the time when the damage became apparent. After *Pirelli* it accrued to the owner at the time the physical damage occurred. In the absence of an assignment of the cause of action by the vendor to the purchaser it seemed that the purchaser would have no cause of action where the property had already sustained latent damage at the time of purchase, since he had no proprietary interest in the property at the time it suffered the damage (*Perry v Tendring District Council* (1984) 2 PN 58; *Audsley v Leeds City Council, The Times*, 2 June 1988; Jones (1984) 100 LQR 413).

These problems have to a large extent ceased to have any practical relevance following the overruling of *Dutton* v *Bognor Regis Urban District Council* and *Anns* v *Merton London Borough Council* [1978] AC 728 in *Murphy* v *Brentwood District Council* [1990] 2 All ER 908 (see para. 2.2.4.2.2). Where a building is defective due to negligent construction the owner can no longer maintain an action for damage to the building itself nor in respect of removing a dangerous defect which creates a risk of physical injury to persons or other property ('preventive damage'). These forms of damage are treated as pure economic loss which is not recoverable (see para. 2.2.4.2.2). If there is no right of action there can be no issue as to when the action accrued. A dangerous latent defect in a building which caused damage to 'other property' would give rise to an action, but it is unlikely that the damage would be latent, and if such a defect caused personal injuries then the limitation rules for personal injuries would apply. It has now been suggested that both *Pirelli* and *Junior Books* are instances of liability under *Hedley Byrne & Co. Ltd* v *Heller & Partners Ltd* [1964] AC 465 (see, e.g., *Murphy* v *Brentwood District Council* [1990] 2 All ER 908, 919 per Lord Keith, and *D & F Estates Ltd* v *Church Commissioners for England* [1988] 2 All ER 992, 1013 per Lord Oliver), even though neither case was decided on this basis and this interpretation strains the facts somewhat, and indeed tends to undermine the whole basis of the decision in *Pirelli* which was concerned with the occurrence of physical damage not economic loss (see McKendrick (1991) 11 LS 326; O'Dair (1992) 55 MLR 405; Mullany [1993] 1 LMCLQ 34). Nonetheless, if this view comes to be accepted the limitation period would probably run from the date at which the plaintiff acted to his detriment in reliance on the negligent 'advice', rather than the date at which physical damage occurred (although it is arguable that time should run from the date at which the economic loss becomes reasonably discoverable: see McKendrick, op. cit. p. 335; Mullany, op. cit. pp. 43–44). This would bring these cases into line with the approach taken in actions for professional liability.

An exception to the rule that damage to the building itself is irrecoverable applies where the damage can be attributed to a distinct item, such as a defective central heating boiler or a defective electrical installation, incorporated into the structure which malfunctions inflicting positive damage on the building. In these circumstances a negligent manufacturer or electrical contractor could be liable under *Donoghue* v *Stevenson* [1932] AC 562 (see paras 2.2.4.2.2 and 10.1.8), and the limitation period could run from the date of the physical damage (subject to the Latent Damage Act 1986, below). Thus, in *Nitrigin Eireann Teoranta* v *Inco Alloys Ltd* [1992] 1 All ER 854 the defendants manufactured and supplied steel alloy tubing which was used to form part of a primary reformer at the plaintiffs' chemical plant. In 1983 the plaintiffs discovered cracks in the tubing but, despite reasonable investigation, they were unable to ascertain the cause of the cracks. The tubing was repaired. In 1984 the tubing cracked again causing an explosion and damage to the structure of the plant around the tubing, which it was accepted was property other than the tubing. May J held that time ran from the date of the explosion causing physical damage to other property in 1984. The cracking in 1983 consisted of damage to the product itself which, applying *Murphy*, was economic loss that was not actionable. The fact that the plaintiffs were aware in 1983 of the possibility that the tubing was defective did not alter the nature of the cause of action that accrued in 1984; and even if they had been negligent by failing to diagnose the cause of the cracking in 1983 this would not have changed the nature of the cause of action that accrued in 1984 (based on physical damage to 'other property'), though damages might be reduced for contributory negligence.

In cases involving the liability of professionals the limitation period will normally commence when the client acts on the negligent advice by entering into a disadvantageous transaction. In *Forster* v *Oughtred & Co.* [1982] 1 WLR 86 the Court of Appeal held that time ran from the point at which the plaintiff acted on the negligent advice of solicitors by entering into a mortgage to cover her son's debts, not when the subsequent financial loss occurred. This was a 'contingent liability to future loss' (encumbering her property with the mortgage) for which the plaintiff could have sued immediately after having acted on the advice, and it was irrelevant that she was unaware of her right to sue. This approach has been followed in a series of cases involving solicitors (*D. W. Moore & Co. Ltd* v *Ferrier* [1988] 1 All ER 400; *Lee* v *Thompson* (1989) 6 PN 91; *Bell* v *Peter Browne & Co.* [1990] 3 All ER 124), insurance brokers (*Iron Trade Mutual Insurance Co. Ltd* v *J. K. Buckenham Ltd* [1990] 1 All ER 808; *Islander Trucking Ltd* v *Hogg Robinson & Gardner Mountain (Marine) Ltd* [1990] 1 All ER 826; Stanton (1989) 5 PN 158) and surveyors (*Secretary of State for the Environment* v *Essex Goodman & Suggitt* [1986] 2 All ER 69—negligent survey of property actionable when the plaintiff acts in reliance on it by purchasing an interest in the property, not when the defects that ought to have been revealed by the survey cause physical damage). Some types of professional negligence case cannot be analysed in these terms, however, and the action will accrue when the financial loss arises (see, e.g., *Mathew* v *Maughold Life Assurance Co. Ltd* (1984) 1 PN 142, reversed on other grounds (1987) 3 PN 98; *UBAF Ltd* v *European American Banking Corporation* [1984] 2 All ER 226 (though see the comment of *Dugdale and Stanton*, para. 24.24 on this case); *Ross* v *Caunters* [1980] Ch 297, where the disappointed beneficiary's action against the negligent solicitor could not possibly have accrued before the testator's death, when the defective will took effect; *Hopkins* v *Mackenzie* [1995] 6 Med LR 26—plaintiff's action against solicitors who negligently permitted a claim for personal injuries to be struck out for want of prosecution accrued when the action was struck out, not when it became probable or even inevitable that it would be struck out). In *Nykredit Mortgage Bank plc* v *Edward Erdman Group Ltd (No. 2)* [1998] 1 All ER 305 the House of Lords held that in relation to a claim for negligent valuation of property intended as security for a loan, the cause of action accrued on the date that the lender actually suffered a loss attributable to the valuer's breach of duty, which could be before the lender realised the security. In some cases the loss might be suffered immediately on making the loan if the rights he has acquired as a lender are worth less in the open market than they would have been if the security had not been overvalued, though this would be difficult to prove if the borrower was making regular payments of the sums due. On the other hand, the loss will readily be demonstrated if the borrower has defaulted and the security is inadequate to cover the loan (per Lord Hoffmann at pp. 316–7).

The Latent Damage Act 1986 attempted to resolve some of these problems by introducing a special extension of the limitation period in cases of latent damage (other than personal injuries), allowing the plaintiff three years from the date on which he discovered or ought reasonably to have discovered significant damage (see Capper (1987) 3 PN 47). This is subject to a 'longstop' which bars all claims brought more than 15 years from the date of the defendant's negligence. The Act came into force on 18 September 1986, but it does not apply to an action which was already barred or to actions commenced before that date. Section 1 of the Act inserts new ss. 14A and 14B into the Limitation Act 1980. The limitation period is six years from the date on which the cause of action accrued or three years from the 'starting date', whichever expires later (s. 14A(3) and (4)). The 'starting date' is defined in very similar terms to the plaintiff's date of knowledge under s. 14(1) (see para. 14.7.1). It is the earliest date on which the plaintiff (or any person in whom the cause of action was vested before him) first had both a right to bring an action, and knowledge of (a) the material facts about the damage, (b) that the damage was caused by the defendant's negligence, (c) the identity of the defendant, and (d) if the negligence was that of a person other than the defendant, the identity of that person and the facts supporting an action against the defendant (s. 14A(5), (6) and (8)). Material facts are such facts about the damage as would lead a reasonable person who had suffered such damage to consider it sufficiently serious to justify his instituting proceedings for damages against a defendant who did not dispute liability and was able to satisfy a judgment (s. 14A(7); *see Horbury* v *Craig Hall & Rutley* (1991) 7 PN 206—knowledge of defect costing £132 to repair sufficient to set limitation period running, despite subsequent knowledge of much more substantial damage; *Hamlin* v *Edwin Evans* (1996) 80 BLR 85—negligent house survey report gives rise to one single cause action accruing when damage was suffered for the first time, and later, more serious, damage was not relevant). Ignorance of the law will not prevent time running (s. 14A(9)) and the plaintiff will be fixed with constructive knowledge, including the knowledge of experts (s. 14A(10)—see s. 14(3), para. 14.7.1; the same proviso applies). The courts' approach to the interpretation of the plaintiff's 'knowledge' under s. 14A is very similar to that taken to the analogous provisions of s. 14 (see *Spencer-Ward* v *Humberts* [1995] 06 EG 148, CA, and *Hallam-Eames* v *Merrett Syndicates Ltd* [1996] 7 Med LR 122, CA). Thus, the plaintiff must have knowledge of 'the act or omission which is alleged to constitute negligence', i.e., knowledge that the defendant's act or omission was causally relevant for the purpose of an allegation of negligence. It is not sufficient for the plaintiff to know merely that the relevant damage had been caused by *an* act or omission of the defendant (*Hallam-Eames* v *Merrett* per Hoffmann LJ).

Section 14B provides that an action for damages for negligence (other than for personal injuries) shall not be brought more than 15 years from the date

of the act or omission which is alleged to constitute negligence. This overrides
s. 14A, so it is irrelevant that the cause of action has not yet accrued (i.e., no
damage has occurred) or that the starting date has not yet occurred (i.e., the
damage is still latent). Neither s. 14A nor s. 14B apply to cases of deliberate
concealment (para. 14.7.3).

These provisions represented an attempt to find a fairer balance between
the interests of plaintiffs and defendants in cases of latent and postponed
damage. Section 14A is a statutory form of the reasonable discoverability test,
which favours plaintiffs, and was intended to reverse the effect of both *Pirelli
General Cable Works Ltd* v *Oscar Faber & Partners* and *Forster* v *Oughtred &
Co*. The longstop provides some protection for defendants, but arguably it is
too long to be of much practical value. Given the changes in the common law
since the Latent Damage Act 1986 came into force, it will now rarely be
relevant to claims arising from defective buildings. It still has significance,
however, in actions for professional negligence, although here too there are
indications that the Act could be sidestepped. Section 14A(1) provides that
s. 14A applies to 'any action for damages for negligence' other than one to
which s. 11 of the Limitation Act 1980 applies (i.e., other than claims in
respect of personal injuries). In *Iron Trade Mutual Insurance Co. Ltd* v *J. K.
Buckenham Ltd* [1990] 1 All ER 808, 821–3 it was held that these words did
not apply to an action for breach of contract founded on an allegation of
negligent or careless conduct, a view accepted as correct by the Court of
Appeal in *Société Commerciale de Réassurance* v *ERAS (International) Ltd*
(Note) [1992] 2 All ER 82. Since most professional-client relationships are
based on contract the consequence, as Stanton (1989) 5 PN 158, 159
observes, is that a 'sizeable area of professional negligence liability is un-
touched by the latent damage legislation and the mischief against which the
1986 Act was aimed, that of plaintiffs finding their actions time barred before
they could reasonably have discovered that they had suffered damage,
continues to afflict the law'. To the extent that a plaintiff may be able to bring
an action in negligence, based on a concurrent duty of care in tort, this
problem can be avoided (cf. O'Dair (1992) 55 MLR 405,410 suggesting that
s. 14A would not apply in the case of concurrent liability in tort). In
Henderson v *Merrett Syndicates Ltd* [1994] 3 All ER 506, 525 the House of
Lords held that where the defendant owes concurrent duties in contract and
the tort of negligence (which will cover many professional-client relationships) the plaintiff is entitled to pursue the action which will give him a
practical advantage on the question of limitation. If this were not the case the
rather odd consequence would be that a client suing a professional person in
contract would be unable to rely on the latent damage provisions, whereas a
third party suing in tort would have the benefit of the Act. (Note also that a
strict interpretation of the wording of s. 14A(1) would exclude actions for
breach of statutory duty and nuisance from its scope; cf. James (1994) 45
NILQ 301 arguing that it should apply to statutory liability for negligence.)

Pirelli General Cable Works Ltd v *Oscar Faber & Partners* had created a
problem for subsequent purchasers of property that had already sustained
latent physical damage at the time of the purchase, apparently precluding any

claim because the cause of action had already accrued to the previous owner. Section 3(1) of the Latent Damage Act 1986 was intended to deal with this problem by granting a fresh cause of action to the purchaser on the date at which he acquired his interest, provided that the damage had not previously become reasonably discoverable to the owner. For the purpose of s. 14A of the Limitation Act 1980 this fresh cause of action is treated as having accrued at the date on which the original action accrued (presumably the date of physical damage, though note that if *Pirelli General Cable Works Ltd* v *Oscar Faber & Partners* is regarded as an instance of liability under *Hedley Byrne & Co. Ltd* v *Heller & Partners Ltd* (see above) the date of accrual will change to the date on which the previous owner acted in reliance on negligent advice), which allows the subsequent purchaser to rely on the three-year extension running from the date of his knowledge, subject to the longstop. Once again, s. 3 can only be of limited relevance to claims involving defective buildings in view of the decision in *Murphy* v *Brentwood District Council* [1990] 2 All ER 908. For example, a negligent installation of a distinct item of property which causes latent damage to the building itself could fall within the terms of the provision, though in practice this is likely to be rare. Section 3 only applies where the purchaser acquired his interest after the Act came into force, and provided the original cause of action was not already statute-barred (Latent Damage Act 1986, s. 4(3) and (4); on the potentially wider effect of s. 3 see Griew (1986) 136 NLJ 1201).

14.7.3 Deliberate concealment

Where the action is based upon the fraud of the defendant or any fact relevant to the plaintiff's right of action has been deliberately concealed from him by the defendant, the period of limitation does not commence until the plaintiff has discovered the fraud or concealment or could with reasonable diligence have discovered it (s. 32(1)). This is not limited to fraud in a technical sense. The deliberate commission of a breach of duty in circumstances in which it is unlikely to be discovered for some time amounts to deliberate concealment of the facts involved in that breach of duty (s. 32(2)). This applies to the commission of a wrong knowingly or recklessly, but negligence is not sufficient (but see *Kitchen* v *Royal Air Force Association* [1958] 1 WLR 563—failure by solicitors to inform plaintiff of an offer of £100 by potential defendants, because that might reveal their own earlier negligence, constituted deliberate concealment). Active steps to conceal the facts are unnecessary. So a developer who knows that a builder is constructing a house on inadequate foundations is guilty of deliberate concealment, even though he did not encourage the builder (*Applegate* v *Moss* [1971] 1 QB 406). Where a surveyor negligently fails to detect a serious structural fault in a property, and subsequently, on having the symptoms pointed out to him by the purchaser, states that there is 'nothing to worry about', this may constitute deliberate concealment, or alternatively the defendant is estopped from raising the limitation defence (*Westlake* v *Bracknell District Council* (1987) 282 EG 868). At one time it was the view that once the limitation period has commenced, subsequent fraud or concealment would not stop it running (*Tito* v *Waddell* *(No. 2)* [1977] 3 All ER 129, 245). This approach effectively permitted a defendant to reap the fruits of his own unconscionable conduct (subject to the latent damage provisions), and deprived the subsection of much practical substance. But in *Sheldon* v *R.H.M. Outhwaite (Underwriting Agencies) Ltd* [1995] 2 All ER 562 a majority of the House of Lords held that s. 32(1)(b) did postpone the running of the limitation period in every case where there was deliberate concealment by the defendant of facts relevant to the plaintiff's cause of action, regardless of whether the concealment was contemporaneous with or subsequent to the accrual of the cause of action. Thus, subsequent concealment has the effect of bringing s. 32 into play, thereby excluding ss. 2 and 5, and the plaintiff has a full six years from the date of discovery of the concealment in which to bring the action.

14.7.4 Persons under a disability

A person is under a disability while he is an infant or of unsound mind (s. 38(2)). An infant is a person under the age of 18, and a person is of unsound mind if, by reason of mental disorder within the meaning of the Mental Health Act 1983, he is incapable of managing and administering his property and affairs (s. 38(3)). If a person to whom a right of action accrues is under a disability at the date when the action accrued, time does not run until he ceases to be under the disability or dies, whichever occurs first (s. 28(1)). Thus, an infant has an indefeasible right to bring an action for personal injuries at any time before the age of 21 (*Tolley* v *Morris* [1979] 2 All ER 561) and a person of unsound mind has three years from the date he becomes sane. One consequence of this is that for a plaintiff under a permanent disability there is effectively no limitation period. The fact that a defendant may suffer prejudice from a long delay is immaterial. In *Headford* v *Bristol and District Health Authority* [1995] 6 Med LR 1 the defendants sought to overcome this problem by applying to have the plaintiff's action struck out as an abuse of the process of the court. There was an unexplained and unjustified delay of 28 years before proceedings on behalf of the plaintiff, who was under a permanent disability, were commenced. The Court of Appeal concluded that the issue of a first writ, within the time limit permitted by Parliament, was unlikely to be capable of being categorised as an abuse of process. In the absence of a longstop in s. 28(1) of the Limitation Act 1980, there was nothing inherently objectionable in a delay of 28 years (see further Jones (1995) 14 CJQ 258). If the plaintiff was not under a disability when the action accrued, but subsequently becomes of unsound mind this will not prevent time running (although in a personal injuries action this rule can be mitigated by the exercise of the court's discretion: s. 33(3)(d); see also *Kirby* v *Leather* [1965] 2 QB 367—tort causing *immediate* unsoundness of mind, time did not run). However, in cases of latent damage this rule is modified so that if the plaintiff was under a disability when the damage became reasonably discoverable (the 'starting date' under s. 14A(5)) the action may be brought at any time within three years from the date when he ceases to be under a disability or died, whichever occurred first, subject to the 'longstop' prescribed by s. 14B (s. 28A added by the Latent Damage Act 1986, s. 2(1)). Section 28 does not apply to a cause of action which accrues to a subsequent purchaser under s. 3(1) of the Latent Damage Act 1986 (s. 3(3) of that Act).

FIFTEEN
Remedies and death

The two principal remedies available to the victim of a tort are damages to compensate for the harm he has suffered and, where appropriate, an injunction to prevent future harm. Damages is the predominant remedy. Certain forms of self-help, such as abatement of a nuisance or self-defence, can be regarded as remedies, but the courts do not encourage this.

Death in relation to tort requires separate treatment because there are special statutory rules dealing with the death of the plaintiff or defendant which allow an existing action in tort to be continued by or against the estate of the deceased (Law Reform (Miscellaneous Provisions) Act 1934). Similarly, the dependants of a person who has died as a result of the defendant's tortious conduct have a statutory right of action against the tortfeasor for their loss of dependency (Fatal Accidents Act 1976). Although this is a statutory right of action vested in the dependants, it arises only where the deceased person (had he lived) would have had an action in tort against the defendant. Thus the defendant's liability is determined on the basis of whether he has committed a tort, and the Fatal Accidents Act 1976 then confers the action for loss of dependency on the dependants. Essentially, the whole exercise is a question of calculating the dependency, and so it is appropriate to deal with it in a chapter on remedies.

15.1 DAMAGES

The fundamental principle applied to the assessment of an award of damages is that the plaintiff should be fully·compensated for his loss. He is entitled to be restored to the position that he would have been in, had the tort not been committed, in so far as this can be done by the payment of money (*Livingstone v Rawyards Coal Co.* (1880) 5 App Cas 25, 39). There are exceptions to this. Exemplary damages are intended, not to compensate the plaintiff, but to punish the defendant, and represent a windfall to the plaintiff (para. 15.1.1.3). In libel, damages may be awarded even though it is proved that the plaintiff's reputation was not injured, e.g., where the person to whom defamatory matter was published did not believe the statement (see also para. 15.1.3). Nonetheless, the compensatory principle is the norm.

There is usually little difficulty in assessing an appropriate level of compensatory damages in cases of property damage. However, the compensatory principle can be an elusive, if not illusory, objective in cases of personal injury. This is not so much due to the difficulty of placing a monetary value on physical injury itself, as the combination of a rule that damages may be awarded once only, and the inevitable uncertainty involved in predicting what will happen to the plaintiff in the future (further complicated by comparing this to what might have happened if the injury had not occurred). The plaintiff's medical condition may become worse than anticipated at the trial, or it may improve. In the one case he is undercompensated, in the other he is overcompensated. This may be compounded by rules about the deduction from the damages of benefits received as a result of the injuries. Not all benefits are deducted, with the result that a plaintiff can occasionally be financially better off as a result of the accident.

15.1.1 Types of damages

15.1.1.1 Nominal and contemptuous Nominal damages will be awarded where the plaintiff proves that the defendant has committed a tort but the plaintiff has suffered no loss (see, e.g., *Constantine v Imperial Hotels Ltd* [1944] KB 693). The plaintiff receives a small sum of money, in effect, to vindicate his right, e.g., if the defendant has committed a technical trespass to the plaintiff's land. Nominal damages can only be awarded in torts actionable *per se*. Where damage is the gist of the action, as in negligence, the plaintiff must prove actual loss. Where a tort that is actionable *per se* has caused actual loss damages will be awarded to compensate for that loss.

Contemptuous damages consist of the award of a derisory sum, usually the smallest coin of the realm. They are awarded when the court considers that the plaintiff's action, although technically successful, was without merit and should not have been brought. The plaintiff may then be at risk on costs, which are normally awarded to the successful party. The judge has a discretion, however, not to grant the plaintiff costs, or even to order him to pay the defendant's costs. Contemptuous damages are not uncommon in libel actions (see, e.g., *Pamplin v Express Newspapers Ltd (No.2)* [1988] 1 All ER 282).

15.1.1.2 General and special General damage is the damage that is presumed to flow from torts which are actionable *per se*, and so need not be specifically pleaded (e.g., loss of reputation in a libel action). Special damage refers to the damage that the plaintiff must plead and prove as part of his cause of action in torts where damage is the gist of the action (e.g., negligence, nuisance, slander). It is the actual damage which forms the basis of the plaintiff's claim.

There is a second and much more commonly used meaning of the distinction between general damages and special damages. In practice, losses that are capable of being calculated with reasonable accuracy are pleaded as 'special damages'. Inexact or unliquidated losses (although they are not presumed and therefore must be pleaded) are compensated by an award of 'general damages'. For example, in a personal injuries action, accrued expenses such as damaged clothing, medical expenses and loss of earnings to the date of trial are special damages. Pain and suffering and loss of amenity (and prospective loss of earnings) are treated as general damages. This is largely a matter of pleading, but it does have practical significance because different rates of interest apply to special and general damages (see para. 15.1.7).

15.1.1.3 Aggravated and exemplary Where damages are at large, which is where the award is not limited to the pecuniary loss that can be specifically proved (*Rookes* v *Barnard* [1964] AC 1129, 1221; e.g., loss of reputation, injured feelings, pain and suffering or loss of amenity: *Broome* v *Cassell & Co. Ltd* [1972] AC 1027, 1073), the court may take into account the manner in which the tort was committed in assessing damages. If it was such as to injure the plaintiff's proper feelings of dignity and pride then aggravated damages may be awarded, as in *Jolliffe* v *Willmett & Co.* [1971] 1 All ER 478 for an 'insolent and high-handed trespass' by a private investigator. Commission of the tort in a malicious, insulting or oppressive manner may aggravate the plaintiff's injury (*Broome* v *Cassell & Co. Ltd* [1972] AC 1027, 1085 per Lord Reid; for other matters that may support a claim for aggravated damages in a libel action, in particular, see *Sutcliffe* v *Pressdram Ltd* [1990] 1 All ER 269, 288 per Nourse LJ). It is also possible that persistent denial of liability in defence of a civil action, notwithstanding critical comments by the judge of the defendant's evidence in criminal proceedings, could aggravate the plaintiff's damage (*Marks* v *Chief Constable of Greater Manchester Police, The Times, 28* January 1992). Aggravated damages are solely compensatory, but they are higher than would normally be the case to reflect the greater injury to the plaintiff. The Law Commission has recommended that aggravated damages should be renamed 'damages for mental distress' and that it should be made clear that such awards are compensatory. They are not intended to punish the defendant (Law Com. Report No. 247, *Aggravated, Exemplary and Restitutionary Damages*, 1997).

In *Messenger Newspapers Group Ltd* v *National Graphical Association* [1984] IRLR 397, Caulfield J awarded £10,000 aggravated damages to a corporate plaintiff. With respect, this seems to be incorrect. A company has no feelings of dignity or pride which might be injured. It can only suffer economic loss which cannot be aggravated by the insulting or insolent behaviour of the defendant. By contrast, in *Kralj* v *McGrath* [1986] 1 All ER 54, Woolf J held that aggravated damages should not be awarded in an action for negligence against a doctor, even though expert evidence had described the treatment given to the plaintiff as 'horrific', although if the particular procedure increased the plaintiff's actual pain and suffering this would be reflected in a higher award (cf. *Barbara* v *Home Office* (1984) 134 NLJ 888, aggravated, but not exemplary, damages awarded to a remand prisoner who was forcibly injected with a tranquilising drug by prison officers). Woolf J's view was approved by the Court of Appeal in *AB* v *South West Water Services Ltd* [1993] 1 All ER 609. Thus, where the plaintiff suffers personal injuries the measure of compensatory damages will cover all the injuries that have been suffered physically, psychologically and mentally. To the extent that these effects have been exacerbated by distress and anxiety caused by the defendant's conduct, they will be reflected in the ordinary measure of compensatory damages. But anger and indignation aroused by the defendant's conduct is not a proper subject for compensation, since it is neither pain nor suffering (ibid. at pp. 624, 629). Fear and anxiety falling short of physical or mental injury resulting from the manner of the wrong is more appropriately awarded as aggravated damages, rather than as part of the basic compensatory damages (*Gerald* v *Commissioner of Police of the Metropolis, The Times*, 26 June 1998).

In *Appleton* v *Garrett* [1996] PIQR P1 the defendant dentist had carried out large-scale, unnecessary treatment of the plaintiffs in order to increase his income. He deliberately, and in bad faith, withheld from the plaintiffs the information that the treatment was unnecessary because he knew that they would not have consented to the treatment had they known the true position. The defendant was held liable in trespass to the person, and Dyson J took the view that there was contumelious conduct or motive on the part of the defendant, having deliberately caused pain and damage to his patients, taken advantage of their young age, and abused his position of trust. He had 'wilfully damaged teeth on a massive scale'. Dyson J distinguished *AB* v *South West Water Services Ltd* on the basis that, first the tort in that case was a negligently committed nuisance, whereas in *Appleton* v *Garrett* it was a case of trespass to the person. In *AB* v *South West Water* the Court of Appeal appeared to have accepted that indignation aroused by a defendant's conduct can increase the plaintiff's damages in defamation cases because 'injury to the plaintiff's feelings and self-esteem is an important part of the damage for which compensation is awarded'. There was no reason in principle, said his Lordship, why awards of aggravated damages should not be made for feelings of anger or indignation in other causes of action such as trespass to the person, where injury to the feelings is an important part of the damage for which compensation is awarded: 'To say that the law permits recovery of aggravated damages where the relevant conduct has caused injury to feelings, insult, indignity, humiliation and a heightened sense of injury or grievance, but not where it has caused anger or indignation, is very difficult to justify in terms of principle or common sense' (at p. P7). The observations of the Court of Appeal should be understood as being restricted to cases where injury to a plaintiff's feelings and self-esteem are not an important part of the damage for which compensation is awarded. Secondly, and in any event, in addition to feelings of anger and indignation, all the plaintiffs had suffered mental distress and injury to their feelings, as well as a heightened sense of injury or grievance, when they learned that the treatment they had undergone was unnecessary. Assessing the aggravated damages on a 'moderate basis' Dyson J held that they should be assessed at 15% of the sum awarded in each case for general damages for pain, suffering and loss of amenity.

Aggravated damages should be distinguished from exemplary damages, which are punitive in nature (see Ghandhi (1990) 10 LS 182). Exemplary damages are intended to teach the defendant that 'tort does not pay'. They are awarded in addition to compensatory damages, and so the plaintiff receives a windfall over and above his true loss. It has been said that the distinction between aggravated and exemplary damages is that aggravated damages are awarded for conduct that shocks the plaintiff (and therefore constitutes a real loss), and exemplary damages are awarded for conduct that shocks the court.

At one time it was believed that exemplary damages could be awarded in any case where the defendant had behaved outrageously. In *Rookes* v *Barnard* [1964] AC 1129, however, the House of Lords held that, except where specifically authorised by statute, exemplary damages should only be awarded in two categories of case:

(a) Oppressive, arbitrary or unconstitutional action by servants of the government (see, e.g., *Wilkes* v *Wood* (1763) Lofft 1; *Attorney-General of St Christopher* v *Reynolds* [1980] AC 637). This does not apply to private defendants, but 'in the case of the government it is different, for the servants of the government are also the servants of the people and the use of their power must always be subordinate to their duty of service' (per Lord Devlin in *Rookes* v *Barnard* at p. 1226). In *Broome* v *Cassell & Co. Ltd* [1972] AC 1027 the House of Lords made it clear that 'servants of the government' should not be interpreted narrowly, and would include a policeman or local government official, even though they are not servants of the Crown. It is not necessary that an unconstitutional act, such as unlawful arrest by a police officer, should also be oppressive or arbitrary before exemplary damages can be awarded (*Holden* v *Chief Constable of Lancashire* [1986] 3 All ER 836). These are separate categories, but it does not follow that in every case of unlawful arrest by a police officer exemplary damages are appropriate. Possibly there should be some improper use of constitutional or executive power (ibid. at p. 841 per Purchas LJ; see also *Racz* v *Home Office* [1994] 2 WLR 23, HL—claim for exemplary damages included in action against defendants on basis of vicarious liability for misfeasance in public office by prison officers; note also *Lancashire County Council* v *Municipal Mutual Insurance Ltd* [1996] 3 All ER 545 in which the Court of Appeal confirmed that it was not contrary to public policy for defendants to insure against such vicarious liability). A publicly owned utility acting as a monopoly supplier of a necessary commodity does not fall into this category (*AB* v *South West Water Services Ltd* [1993] 1 All ER 609). Although such a body enjoys certain statutory powers and is subject to certain obligations, it does not exercise executive power as an instrument or agent of government.

(b) Where the defendant's conduct has been calculated by him to make a profit for himself which may well exceed the compensation payable. In *Broome* v *Cassell & Co. Ltd*, for example, the defendants published a book, which, before publication, they knew contained defamatory and untrue statements about the plaintiff. Nonetheless, they proceeded with the publication, believing that the profits from sales would exceed any award of damages. The House of Lords upheld an award of £15,000 compensatory damages and £25,000 exemplary damages. In *Rookes v Barnard* [1964] AC 1129 Lord Devlin said (at p. 1227) that 'where a defendant with cynical disregard for a plaintiff's rights has calculated that the money to be made out of his wrongdoing will probably exceed the damages at risk, it is necessary for the law to show that it cannot be broken with impunity'. It is not necessary to show that there has been a precise calculation of profit and loss, because the category extends to cases 'where the defendant is seeking to gain at the expense of the plaintiff some object—perhaps some property which he covets—which either he could not obtain at all or not obtain except at a greater price than he wants to put down'. What is required is knowledge by the defendant that what he proposes to do is against the law or a reckless disregard for whether it is legal or illegal (see *John v Mirror Group Newspapers Ltd* [1996] 2 All ER 35, 57 per Sir Thomas Bingham MR confirming that 'carelessness alone, however extreme, is not enough unless it properly justifies an inference that the publisher had no honest belief in the truth of what he published'), and a decision to proceed because the prospects of material advantage outweigh the prospects of material loss (*Broome v Cassell & Co. Ltd* [1972] AC 1027, 1079, 1130; *John v Mirror Group Newspapers Ltd supra*, at p. 58 per Sir Thomas Bingham MR: 'motivated by mercenary consider-ations'). The defendant may have calculated that the plaintiff would not sue at all, for example, because he was intimidated or could not afford to sue. An attempt by the defendant to conceal the commission of a tort, with the object of limiting the amount of damages payable to the plaintiff, though reprehen-sible, does not fall into this category of conduct (*AB v South West Water Services Ltd* [1993] 1 All ER 609, 623).

In *AB v South West Water Services Ltd* [1993] 1 All ER 609 the Court of Appeal held that, since in *Rookes v Barnard* the House of Lords sought to restrict the availability of exemplary damages, regarding such awards as anomalous, exemplary damages should only be available in torts which were recognised at the time (i.e., before 1964) as grounding a claim for exemplary damages (for comment on *AB v South West Water Services Ltd* see Burrows (1993) 109 LQR 358; Pipe (1994) 57 MLR 91). This 'cause of action test' is in addition to the requirement that the defendant's conduct falls into one of the two categories specified in *Rookes v Barnard*. It followed that there could be no award of exemplary damages in an action for negligence, deceit, or public nuisance (which was the action in issue in *AB v South West Water Services Ltd*), although such an award could be made in a case of private nuisance where there is deliberate and wilful interference with the plaintiff's rights of enjoyment of land where the defendant has calculated that the profit or benefit for him will exceed the damages he may have to pay (per Stuart-Smith LJ at p. 621; for an example of this see *Guppys (Bridport) Ltd v Brookling* (1983) 269 EG 846, 942—harassment by a landlord). One conse-quence of the decision in *AB v South West Water* is that torts which have come into existence since 1964, whether by statute or at common law, cannot be the subject of an award of exemplary damages, at least not without express statutory approval. Thus, there can be no award of exemplary damages in a claim for racial or sexual harassment (*Deane* v *Ealing London Borough Council* [1993] ICR 329), despite an earlier decision of the Court of Appeal apparently supporting an award in these circumstances (*Arora* v *Bradford City Metropolitan Council* [1991] 3 All ER 545). The three types of case in which exemplary damages appear to be awarded most frequently are libel actions (*Faulks*, para. 360, recommended their abolition), actions against the police for assault or false imprisonment (*Hepple and Matthews*, p. 408, n. 2), and actions by tenants against landlords for harassment and unlawful eviction, the cause of action normally being trespass to land and/or trespass to goods (Jones (1984) 4 Lit 55).

Exemplary damages will only be awarded where the compensatory damages are insufficient to punish the defendant. The defendant's means are irrelevant to the assessment of compensatory damages, but they are relevant to the amount of exemplary damages, as is anything which aggravates or mitigates the defendant's conduct (e.g., provocation by the plaintiff. *Lane* v *Holloway* [1968] 1 QB 379). The court has a discretion to take into account any fines imposed on the defendant where he has been convicted of an offence for the same conduct which forms the basis of the action. However, in *Messenger Newspapers Group Ltd* v *National Graphical Association* [1984] IRLR 397, Caulfield J refused to take any account of a £675,000 fine imposed on the defendants for contempt of court in continuing their tortious conduct despite a court order, and awarded exemplary damages of £25,000. The fine, his Lordship stated, was imposed because of the contempt, not because of the tort. But this would also be an argument for ignoring fines imposed for a criminal offence. By way of contrast, in *Archer* v *Brown* [1984] 2 All ER 267, Peter Pain J said that it was a 'basic principle' that a defendant should not be punished twice for the same offence by an award of exemplary damages.

Where there are joint defendants the court should only make one award of exemplary damages, and this should not be more than the sum that would be awarded against any individual defendant. Thus if exemplary damages would not be justified against one of the defendants, no award should be made, no matter how outrageous the behaviour of the other joint defendants. This is because joint defendants are also severally liable to the plaintiff for the full amount of the damages, and it would be wrong that an 'innocent' (or less reprehensible) defendant might have to pay damages which were intended to punish someone else. Similarly, where there are several plaintiffs the court should not make a separate award to each plaintiff, but a single award of exemplary damages which is sufficient to punish the defendant. The award should then be divided amongst the plaintiffs (*Riches* v *News Group Newspapers Ltd* [1985] 2 All ER 845). Where there are a large number of plaintiffs the case will not be suitable for an award of exemplary damages (*AB* v *South West Water Services Ltd* [1993] 1 All ER 609).

Exemplary damages can be criticised on the basis that they confuse the functions of the civil and criminal law, and leave the defendant open to punishment without the safeguards for offenders that are applied by the criminal law (*Rookes* v *Barnard* [1964] AC 1129, 1221, 1227; *Broome* v *Cassell & Co. Ltd* [1972] AC 1027, 1087 per Lord Reid who described exemplary damages as a 'form of palm tree justice'; but cf. Lord Wilberforce at p. 1114; for detailed analysis see Anderson (1992) 11 CJQ 233; and Reed (1996) 15 CJQ 130, who argues for the retention of exemplary damages). However, they were regarded as too firmly embedded in the law to be removed, except by Parliament. *Rookes* v *Barnard* was a conscious attempt to restrict the ambit of exemplary damages, because they were regarded as anomalous, whilst recognising that the two categories in which such damages could be awarded were not necessarily logically defensible.

The amounts awarded as exemplary damages vary considerably, for, though in *Rookes* v *Barnard* it was said that they should be moderate, libel actions and actions against the police for false imprisonment tend to be tried by juries, who are usually more generous and less consistent than judges in assessing damages. In *Thompson* v *Commissioner of Police of the Metropolis* [1997] 2 All ER 762, the Court of Appeal laid down guidelines for juries when awarding exemplary damages against the police. The award was said to be unlikely to be less than £5,000 and might be as much as £25,000 in cases where officers of at least the rank of superintendent had been involved in the misconduct. Significantly, in actions in respect of unlawful eviction, which are usually tried by judge alone, awards of exemplary damages are moderate, ranging from about £500 to £1,000. These sums could probably be justified as aggravated damages (see *Drane* v *Evangelou* [1978] 2 All ER 437).

The Law Commission has considered the question of the future of exemplary damages and emphatically concluded that they should be retained, while being put on a more rational basis (Law Com Report No. 247, *Aggravated, Exemplary and Restitutionary Damages*, 1997). It is proposed that exemplary damages be renamed 'punitive damages' and that a judge, rather than a jury, should determine both whether punitive damages should be awarded and their amount. The Commission proposes that the narrow 'categories' test laid down in *Rookes* v *Barnard* and the cause of action test of *AB* v *South West Water Services Ltd* should be abolished. As the Commission observed: 'there appears to be no sound reason why outrageously wrongful conduct should not attract a punitive award even if it is not committed by a servant of the government' (at para. 5.41). It should be permissible to award punitive damages for any tort or equitable wrong (though not for breach of contract) or for a civil wrong arising under statute (if such an award would be consistent with the policy of the Act) where in committing a wrong, or in conduct subsequent to the wrong, the defendant deliberately and outrageously disregarded the plaintiff's rights. Punitive damages could be awarded in addition to any other remedy, but only if the judge considered that the other remedies available to the court were inadequate to punish the defendant. Moreover, punitive damages should not normally be awarded if at any time before the decision the defendant had been convicted of an offence involving the conduct in question, and the court should also have regard to any other sanctions that have been imposed in relation to the conduct concerned. In assessing the level of damages, the award should not exceed the minimum needed to punish the defendant and should be proportionate to the gravity of the wrongdoing. The defendant's means would be a relevant consideration, but this would include the fruits of any insurance against the risk of liability to pay punitive damages. Liability to pay punitive damages should also be 'several' rather than joint, or joint and several. The Law Commission emphasised that an award of punitive damages should be seen as a remedy of last resort. The proposal to leave such awards to judges is a sensible attempt to achieve a degree of consistency and moderation in awards, together with proportionality to the gravity of the defendant's conduct. Despite the criticism that has been levelled at exemplary damages in the past, the Law Commission's proposal to expand and rationalise liability for punitive damages is welcome. It would bring English law more into line with the law in other Commonwealth jurisdictions, and it recognises both the deterrent (to potential defendants) and symbolic (for plaintiffs) function of the civil law as a means of dealing with egregious behaviour in circumstances where the criminal law may be less than effective.

15.1.2   A single action and the lump sum

A plaintiff can only bring one action in respect of a single wrong. He cannot maintain a second action based on the same facts merely because the damage turns out to be more extensive than was anticipated (*Fetter* v *Beale* (1701) 1 Ld Raym 339, 692; *Bristow* v *Grout*, *The Times*, 9 November 1987, CA). Thus he can recover damages once only, and the cause of action is extinguished by a judgment.

There are some exceptions to this rule. Where a single wrongful act violates two distinct rights the plaintiff can bring separate actions in respect of each right. In *Brunsden* v *Humphrey* (1884) 14 QBD 141 the plaintiff succeeded in an action for damage to his cab caused by the defendant's negligence, and then brought a second action in respect of his injuries sustained in the same accident. It was held that this was a distinct right for which he was entitled to maintain a separate action, although in *Talbot* v *Berkshire County Council* [1994] QB 290, Stuart-Smith LJ said that *Brunsden* v *Humphrey* might have been decided differently if *Henderson* v *Henderson* (1843) 3 Hare 100, applying the doctrine of *res judicata*, had been cited. His Lordship commented that *Henderson* appeared to have escaped attention in the field of personal injury litigation. The rule in *Henderson* v *Henderson* requires the parties to bring their whole case before the court so that all aspects of the case may be finally decided (subject to any appeal) once and for all. In the absence of special circumstances the parties cannot return to court to advance arguments, claims or defences which they could have put forward on the first occasion but failed to raise. It is a rule of public policy based on the desirability that litigation should not drag on indefinitely and that a defendant should not be oppressed by successive actions when one would do (*Barrow* v *Bankside Members Agency Ltd* [1996] 1 WLR 257, 260, per Sir Thomas Bingham MR). In *Talbot* v *Berkshire County Council* the Court of Appeal gave three examples of special circumstances where the rule would not apply:

(a) where the plaintiff was unaware of the existence of the claim;

(b) where an agreement was made between the parties holding the action in abeyance; and

(c) where the plaintiff had not brought his case earlier in reliance on a representation made by the defendant.

In *Barrow* v *Bankside Members Agency Ltd*, the Court of Appeal held that, in the context of the Lloyd's litigation, a plaintiff who, as a member of an 'action group', had successfully prosecuted a claim selected under the management plan as common to that group, could bring a later action against the same defendants in relation to a new issue, because that issue could not have been dealt with in first action. As a general rule, however, *Henderson* v *Henderson* will prevent two actions arising from the same facts from being litigated by the same plaintiff. The fact that the plaintiff will suffer an injustice by not being able to advance his claim is not a special circumstance, otherwise the rule would hardly ever apply, nor is the fact that the defendant or his insurers were aware of the possibility of a separate or more extensive claim (*Talbot* v *Berkshire County Council*). In *Wain* v *F. Sherwood and Sons Transport Ltd*, *The Times*, 16 July 1998, the Court of Appeal held that the rule applied even where the plaintiff had not advanced an earlier claim due the negligence of his lawyer, but due to the advocate's immunity (see para. 2.2.3.1) the plaintiff would have no redress for that negligence. The plaintiff was involved in a road traffic accident and brought an action to recover the cost of damage to his van, but did not include a claim for personal injury. By the time that the first action came to trial, some 18 months after the accident, the plaintiff was suffering from acute backache which his doctor attributed to the accident, but which the plaintiff had not mentioned to his solicitors. On the day of the trial the plaintiff mentioned his back complaint to his counsel, who advised that the action could be adjourned but did not advise that if the pleadings were not amended to include personal injuries any future action might be barred. The plaintiff succeeded in the first action and recovered £450 for damage to his vehicle. Two years later he brought a second action for damages of £100,000 in respect of the back injury. It was held that the fact that the plaintiff had not included a claim for personal injuries in the first action was due to the error of counsel and that the plaintiff would have no remedy in damages for that negligence did not constitute a special circumstance. On that basis, the plaintiff's ignorance of the claim would not constitute a special circumstance; and the prospect, or otherwise, of a remedy against a third party is irrelevant. In the light of *Talbot* v *Berkshire County Council* and *Wain* v *Sherwood and Sons Transport Ltd* it would seem that *Brunsden* v *Humphrey* is not good law.

A second exception to the rule is where there is a continuing injury, such as a continuing nuisance or trespass to land. In trespass, being actionable *per se*, a fresh cause of action arises from day to day, and in nuisance a fresh cause of action arises whenever further damage occurs (*Darley Main Colliery Co.* v *Mitchell* (1886) 11 App Cas 127). In this situation damages can only be awarded for the injury up to the date of the trial. The plaintiff cannot claim for prospective damage, but must bring a new action as and when the damage occurs (subject to the court's power to substitute damages in lieu of an injunction, para. 15.2). Nor can he recover for the reduction in the value of his property which results from the risk of future damage (*West Leigh Colliery Co. Ltd* v *Tunnicliffe & Hampson Ltd* [1908] AC 27; *Midland Bank* v *Bardgrove Property Services* [1992] 37 EG 126, CA).

The final exception is that where a single wrong produces successive and distinct damage, then in torts which are actionable only on proof of damage (as opposed to torts actionable *per se*), a separate and distinct cause of action will accrue (*Mount Albert BC* v *Johnson* [1979] 2 NZLR 234). This is analogous to the position in *Brunsden* v *Humphrey* except that the actions accrue at different points in time, and the damage may be of the same type in the successive actions provided the damage is distinct. Where the second damage is a result of or flows from the first damage then it is not sufficiently distinct to maintain a fresh action.

Damages are assessed once and for all and must be awarded in the form of a lump sum. This applies both to accrued and prospective losses. The court has no power to require the defendant to make periodical payments (*Burke* v *Tower Hamlets Health Authority, The Times,* 10 August 1989). In *Wells* v *Wells* [1998] 3 All ER 481, 502, Lord Steyn said that the court ought to be given the power, of its own motion, to make an award of periodical payments in appropriate cases. Such a power would be consistent with the principle of full compensation for pecuniary loss, but, said his Lordship, this could only be introduced by Parliament. Nor does the court have the power to review the award at a later date if the estimate of loss turns out to be too low or too high. An exception of very limited application was accepted in *Mulholland* v *Mitchell* [1971] AC 666. Where there is evidence of a change of circumstances after the trial but before an appeal, the Court of Appeal will admit the new evidence. New evidence was also admitted by the House of Lords in *Lim Poh Choo* v *Camden & Islington Area Health Authority* [1980] AC 174 to 'mitigate the injustices of a lump sum system'. But, said Lord Scarman (at p. 183) 'it is an unsatisfactory makeshift, and of dubious value in any case where the new facts are themselves in issue'. Generally, once the time-limit for appeal has expired, an appeal out of time on the basis of changed circumstances will not be permitted (see *Norwich & Peterborough Building Society* v *Steed* [1991] 2 All ER 880; *Mallory* v *Butler* [1991] 2 All ER 889).

The lump-sum principle, combined with the rule that damages can be recovered once only, causes serious difficulties in actions for personal injuries, particularly where the medical prognosis is uncertain. The plaintiff's condition may become worse than anticipated or, less commonly, may unexpectedly improve. The court has to assess the amount of damages on the basis of assumptions that may well prove to be incorrect. In *Lim Poh Choo* (at p. 183), Lord Scarman commented that:

> Knowledge of the future being denied to mankind, so much of the award as is to be attributed to future loss and suffering will almost surely be wrong. There is really only one certainty: the future will prove the award to be either too high or too low.

This is most obvious in cases where there is a risk that, as a result of his injuries, the plaintiff may develop a specific medical condition in the future. For example, assume that there are 100 accident victims, each of whom has a 50% chance of developing epilepsy in the future. Under a system providing lump-sum compensation, none of them will receive damages that reflects his true loss. Each would receive a sum which would compensate for the epilepsy, reduced by 50% to allow for the 50% change that it will not develop (these figures are simplified—in fact the reduction would be greater). Statistically, 50 will develop the disease. They are undercompensated because they have received only 50% of the damages that the court considers appropriate compensation for epilepsy. The 50 who do not develop the disease have been compensated for a loss they have not suffered.

There is now a procedure for the award of provisional damages in this type of case (RSC, Ord. 37, rr. 7–10; and see *Hurditch* v *Sheffield Health Authority* [1989] 2 All ER 869). Section 32A of the Supreme Court Act 1981 provides that in personal injury cases where there is a 'chance' that, as a result of the tort, the plaintiff will develop some serious disease or suffer some serious deterioration in his condition, he may be awarded provisional damages assessed on the basis that the disease or deterioration will not occur (so he would receive less than under the lump-sum system at this stage, unless, of course, the serious deterioration would lead to death, in which case he would receive more, prompting the court in *Molinari* v *Ministry of Defence* [1994] PIQR Q33 to note *obiter* that in 'extreme cases' the potential injustice to the defendants of making a provisional damages award may outweigh the potential injustice to the plaintiff of a traditional award and therefore the court might refuse to award provisional damages where the risk of deterioration could lead to a decrease in the plaintiff's loss; for the meaning of 'chance' and 'serious deterioration' see *Willson* v *Ministry of Defence* [1991] 1 All ER 638). If the event subsequently materialises the plaintiff can then make an application for further damages, which will more accurately compensate his loss. There can only be one such application in respect of a disease or type of injury specified in the original action. Thus a general deterioration in the plaintiff's condition or an unforeseen complication is not covered by the procedure. Nor are changes, such as a supervening illness, which are unrelated to the tort. The plaintiff has to prove that the disease or deterioration was causally connected with the original injury. 'Chance' cases should be distinguished from cases where the medical evidence can forecast with a reasonable degree of certainty that the plaintiff's condition will deteriorate causing a reasonably probable degree of disability (e.g., it is possible to predict with reasonable accuracy that over the years arthritis is likely to develop in a damaged joint). In *Willson* v *Ministry of Defence* [1991] 1 All ER 638 it was held that the development of arthritis to the point at which surgery is required, or which requires the plaintiff to change employment, was simply an aspect of the progression of the particular disease and did not fall within the terms of the procedure. Provisional damages are appropriate for cases with 'a clear and severable risk rather than a continuing deterioration, as is the typical osteoarthritic picture' (per Scott Baker J, at p. 644). Nor does the chance that due to a disabling injury the plaintiff may sustain a further injury call for provisional damages, even if the subsequent injury could be severe (ibid.). There must be a clear-cut event which will trigger the entitlement to further compensation, but the risk of serious injury is not to be equated with a serious deterioration in the plaintiff's condition. In these cases damages are assessed on the single lump-sum basis, discounted for the chance that the deterioration or injury will not occur. The difference between 'chance' and 'forecast' cases is only a difference of degree, but in the latter case the medical prognosis is more likely to be correct. A claim for provisional damages cannot include a declaration that the plaintiff's surviving dependants should be entitled to bring a claim under the Fatal Accidents Act 1976 if the plaintiff should subsequently die as a result of a deterioration of his physical condition (*Middleton* v *Elliott Turbomachinery Ltd, Independent,* 16 November 1990, CA; see further, paras 15.1.3.2.3, 15.3.2.1). The Damages Act 1996, s. 3 now permits dependants to claim in respect of losses not compensated by the initial award of damages.

The availability of provisional damages reduces the errors inherent in lump-sum compensation to a limited extent. But the procedure (which came into effect on 1 July 1985) has not had a widespread impact, even in the somewhat limited type of case to which it can be applied if the plaintiff opts to do so. Lewis (1997) 60 MLR 230, 237 describes provisional damages as a 'backwater of personal injury litigation' because they are rarely used. The Pearson Commission recommended a more radical solution to the problem of estimating future losses. They proposed that for future pecuniary loss (which is mainly loss of earnings and/or medical expenses) provision should be made for the award of damages in the form of periodical payments, which would be subject to review at fixed intervals (*Pearson*, vol. 1, para. 573; cf. Law Com No. 56 HC 373, 1973, para. 28 rejecting the introduction of periodical payments). This would solve the problem of 'crystal-ball jurisprudence' because the damages could be varied to match the plaintiff's real pecuniary loss. If his medical condition deteriorated to the extent that he lost his job or had to take a lower-paid job, the periodical payments would be increased. Conversely, if he improved and was able to return to work, the payments would be reduced. This would remove the need for provisional damages, at least for pecuniary losses. It would also overcome the problem of inflation eroding the value of damages for prospective losses (see para. 15.1.3.2.2) because the Commission recommended that payments should be index-linked to average earnings. It is unlikely that such a scheme, which would certainly be more expensive to administer, will be introduced in the foreseeable future (*see Pearson*, vol. 1, ch. 14, for the arguments, and *Atiyah* p. 199 for explanation of the difficulties that insurers have with periodic payments).

An alternative to provisional damages which is currently available, but little used, is a procedure for separate trials on liability and damages, so that the assessment can be made at a later date when the plaintiff's medical prognosis is more certain (RSC, Ord. 33, r. 4). This will only be of value where the plaintiff's medical condition is unstable and needs time to settle. At that stage the court still has to make guesses about future developments. Where liability has been established or admitted the plaintiff could apply for an interim payment, to meet his immediate needs, which is deducted from the final award of damages (RSC, Ord. 29).

A recent development has been the introduction into this country of the North American concept of a 'structured settlement' (for a definition see the Damages Act 1996, s. 5; *Kelly* v *Dawes, The Times* 27 September 1990). This is a private arrangement between the plaintiff and the defendant's liability insurer whereby the normal lump sum payment for future losses is taken in the form of periodic payments. These payments can be varied or 'structured' over a period of time. They can be for a fixed period or until the plaintiff's death, and they can be index-linked. The payments are financed by the purchase of an annuity by the liability insurer with the money that would have been paid to the plaintiff as a lump sum. This annuity is held by the insurer on behalf of the plaintiff, and, as a result of a concession by the Inland Revenue, the payment is not taxable as income in the plaintiff's hands. The insurer is not liable to tax on the annuity either (see Taxes Act 1988, ss. 329A, 329B, added by the Finance Act 1995, s. 142). This substantially increases the value of such an arrangement both to the plaintiff and the insurer, and the possibility of index-linking removes the problem of inflation eroding the lump sum award. Structured settlements are not, however, the same as the Pearson Commission's proposal for periodic payments. They depend upon agreement between the plaintiff and the defendant's insurers; the court has no power to order such an arrangement without the consent of the parties (Damages Act 1996, s. 2). It is still necessary to calculate what the lump sum would be applying the usual principles (with all the drawbacks that this involves) before setting up the structured settlement. The periodic payments are only varied over time in accordance with the terms agreed at the outset. There is no variation to take account of deterioration or improvement in the plaintiff's medical condition or earning capacity, which is a common criticism of the lump sum system of awarding damages. Perhaps the most telling objection to structured settlements is that the advantages to both plaintiff and insurer are at the taxpayer's expense. Since it is well known that those who recover tort compensation for accidental injury are treated very generously compared with other accident victims (see para. 1.5), there can be little justification for enhancing that discrepancy at the expense of taxpayers, many of whom may, themselves, have suffered non-tortious injuries (see, e.g., the comments of Lord Bridge in *Hodgson* v *Trapp* [1988] 3 All ER 870, 876). It would seem that, in any event, structured settlements will be appropriate in only a small minority of personal injuries cases, where there is a substantial claim for future financial loss (for further discussion see Lewis (1988) 15 J of Law and Soc 392; Allen (1988) 104 LQR 448; Lewis (1991) 10 CJQ 212; Allen (1993) 12 CJQ 8; Lewis (1993) 12 CJQ 251, discussing the Law Commission's Consultation Paper, No. 125, on *Structured Settlements and Interim and Provisional Damages* (1992); Allen (1996) 15 CJQ 58 discussing, *inter alia*, the Law Commission's resulting Report, No. 224, 1994; Lewis (1993) 13 OJLS 530; Lewis, *Structured Settlements: The Law and Practice*, Sweet and Maxwell, 1993).

Remedies and death

15.1.3 Personal injuries

In most actions for personal injuries the plaintiff suffers two distinct types of loss—pecuniary and non-pecuniary loss. Pecuniary loss is the damage that is capable of being directly calculated in money terms. The commonest example is loss of earnings, both actual and future, but it includes all other expenses attributable to the tort, such as medical expenses, travelling expenses, the cost of special equipment or of employing someone to carry out domestic duties which the plaintiff is no longer able to perform, or loss of pension rights. Non-pecuniary losses are such immeasurable matters as pain and suffering caused by the injury, and loss of amenity attributable to a disability. Here the principle of restoring the plaintiff to his pre-accident position is inapplicable. No amount of money can restore a lost limb or take away the plaintiff's experience. *Pearson,* para. 360, identified three possible purposes of an award for non-pecuniary loss. First, as a palliative; secondly, to enable the plaintiff to purchase alternative sources of satisfaction to replace those he has lost; and thirdly, to help meet hidden expenses caused by the injury (see also Ogus (1972) 35 MLR 1). The principle applied by the courts to the assessment of non-pecuniary losses is said to be that damages should be 'fair' or 'reasonable'. This is unhelpful, because the very question is what sum would be reasonable. The business of translating this type of injury into money is inevitably arbitrary. As *Atiyah,* p. 139, observes, 'All such damage awards could be multiplied or divided by two overnight and they would be just as defensible or indefensible as they are today'. In practice the courts adopt a tariff or 'going rate' for specific types of injury, which has the effect of suggesting that such losses can be objectively measured. It does at least produce a degree of consistency between plaintiffs with similar injuries, and this provides the basis for negotiation and settlement of claims.

The Pearson Commission found that non-pecuniary loss accounts for more than half of all tort compensation for personal injury, and for a particularly high proportion of small payments. The Commission recommended that no damages should be recoverable for non-pecuniary loss suffered during the first three months after the date of the injury (*Pearson,* vol. 1, para. 388). This would have eliminated many small claims altogether, with a consequent saving of administration costs, and reduced by about 20% the total tort compensation for personal injury (for criticism see *Weir,* p. 642). As with most of the Commission's recommendations, however, this is unlikely to be implemented.

The courts assess damages under several 'heads', but for the purpose of calculating interest there are three broad heads: accrued pecuniary damages; non-pecuniary damages; and loss of future earnings. The House of Lords has stressed, however, that the court should also have regard to the appropriateness of the total award to avoid overlapping of different heads of damages (*Lim Poh Choo* v *Camden & Islington Area Health Authority* [1980] AC 174, 191; though it may be doubted whether there can be any overlap between pecuniary and non-pecuniary losses: ibid. p. 192; *Pearson,* vol. 1, para. 759).

15.1.3.1 Medical and other expenses
The plaintiff is entitled to recover his medical and other similar expenses reasonably incurred. Accrued

expenses will be awarded as part of the special damages, whereas future medical expenses will be estimated and awarded as general damages. The Law Reform (Personal Injuries) Act 1948, s. 2(4), provides that the possibility of avoiding medical expenses or part of them by taking advantage of National Health Service facilities is to be disregarded. So the plaintiff can insist on private medical treatment at the defendant's expense, though where, as commonly happens, the plaintiff has in fact used National Health Service facilities, he cannot recover what he would have paid had he been treated privately. The good sense of this latter rule is obvious enough, but it does not apply to future treatment. The plaintiff can claim for the private cost of future medical care, but he is not required to spend that, or indeed any, part of the damages on medical treatment. The court does not exercise any control over how the plaintiff uses the award of damages (except where he is a minor or of unsound mind). *Pearson*, para. 342, recommended that s. 2(4) should be repealed, and that private medical expenses should be recoverable only if it was reasonable on medical grounds that the plaintiff should incur them. This sensible proposal has not been implemented. If it seems likely that the plaintiff will be unable to receive privately all the treatment that he needs, and will eventually have to enter a NHS hospital, a deduction from the damages will be made to allow for this (*Lim Poh Choo v Camden & Islington Area Health Authority* [1980] AC 174; *Housecroft* v *Burnett* [1986] 1 All ER 332, 342). Indeed, if private medical treatment is not going to be used, for *whatever* reason, the plaintiff is not entitled to claim for an expense that he is not going to incur (*Woodrup* v *Nicol* [1993] PIQR Q104, 114, CA).

Section 5 of the Administration of Justice Act 1982 provides that any saving to the injured person which is attributable to his maintenance wholly or partly at public expense in a hospital, nursing home or other institution shall be set off against any income lost by him as a result of his injuries. A similar proposition had been expressed in *Lim Poh Choo* v *Camden & Islington Area Health Authority,* and since s. 5 is restricted to plaintiffs maintained at public expense, that decision effectively applies the same rule to plaintiffs who make savings in domestic expenditure while being looked after in a private institution.

If the plaintiff has to live in a special institution, such as a nursing home, or receive attendance at home he is entitled to the cost of that, provided that it is reasonably necessary (*Shearman* v *Folland* [1950] 2 KB 43). In *Rialas* v *Mitchell, The Times,* 17 July 1984 the Court of Appeal held that a plaintiff may be entitled to be cared for at home rather than in an institution, even though it was more expensive, provided that it was reasonable in the circumstances. Where the cost of care at home was substantially greater than that of the institution, the burden of proving reasonableness is the plaintiff's. The plaintiff can recover the cost of adapting accommodation to his special needs resulting from a disability, subject to a deduction for the added capital value of the property which would be recoverable on a sale (*Roberts* v *Johnstone* [1988] 3 WLR 1247). If it is not possible to adapt existing accommodation damages will be awarded in respect of the purchase of special accommodation. They will be assessed, not on the basis of the capital cost of the purchase, but by the additional annual cost over the plaintiff's lifetime of providing that accommodation, as compared with ordinary accommodation. The point of this method of assessment is that damages are intended to be compensatory—they should not enhance the capital value of the plaintiff's estate after death. Damages 'are notionally intended to be such as will exhaust the fund, contemporaneously with the termination of the plaintiff's life expectancy' (ibid. at pp. 1257–8).

In *Pritchard* v *J. H. Cobden Ltd* [1987] 1 All ER 300 the Court of Appeal held that, where the plaintiff's injuries lead to the break up of his marriage, the financial consequences of the divorce are not recoverable from the defendant, either on the basis that the loss is too remote or on the ground of public policy. Perhaps surprisingly, the same court subsequently held that the legal costs of the divorce action were recoverable on the particular facts of the case (*Pritchard* v *Cobden Ltd* [1987] 2 FLR 56. See also *Meah* v *McCreamer* [1985] 1 All ER 367 in which the plaintiff received compensation for his own imprisonment, having been convicted of serious offences of violence. He claimed that the crimes were the result of a personality change caused by injuries received in a car accident for which the defendant was responsible; cf. *Meah* v *McCreamer (No. 2)* [1986] 1 All ER 943. For criticism see para. 4.2.2.2.)

Where a non-earner, such as a housewife, is injured she cannot claim for the earnings that she would have lost had she been in paid employment. But a housewife who is deprived of her ability to look after her family suffers a real loss, and will be entitled to compensation, even though other members of the family now perform the tasks that she used to do (*Daly* v *General Steam Navigation Co. Ltd* [1981] 1 WLR 120). The loss will be estimated on the basis of the cost of domestic help, irrespective of whether a housekeeper will be employed, at least for future loss. Past loss will be compensated as general damages if a housekeeper has not been employed. This difference of approach to past and future loss seems illogical (*Burrows,* pp. 195–6). The loss is not necessarily limited to the cost of domestic help because a wife and mother does not work set hours and provides some less tangible services (*Regan* v *Williamson* [1976] 1 WLR 305, a Fatal Accident Act case).

It often happens that a third person, such as a relative or friend, bears part of the cost of the plaintiff's injury, either in the form of direct financial payments or by providing nursing assistance. Sometimes a spouse or close relative may give up paid employment in order to care for the plaintiff. The third party has no direct claim in tort against the defendant, and the question arises whether the plaintiff can recover this cost. At one time it was thought that he could not, unless he was under some legal obligation to pay for the services or repay the financial assistance he had received (though in *Roach* v *Yates* [1938] 1 KB 256 a moral obligation had been regarded as sufficient). It is now clear that the plaintiff can recover the cost of such care. Until recently, the basis for such recovery was the Court of Appeal's decision in *Donnelly* v *Joyce* [1974] QB 454 where it was held that the existence of a legal or moral obligation to reimburse the third party was irrelevant. It was incorrect, said the Court, to think of this as someone else's loss. It was the plaintiff's loss. His loss was the existence of the *need* for nursing services or special equipment, not the expenditure of the money itself. So far as the defendant was concerned, the question from what source the plaintiff's needs had been met, who had paid the money or given the services, or whether the plaintiff was under a legal or moral obligation to repay, were all irrelevant. The measure of the loss is the 'proper and reasonable cost' of supplying those needs. In the case of a relative who has given up paid employment this would be at least the loss of earnings, subject to a ceiling of the commercial rate for supplying those services to the plaintiff (*Housecroft* v *Burnett* [1986] 1 All ER 332). Normally, the full commercial rate will not be applied, unless the relative has given up paid employment, since the commercial rate is inappropriate where a relative acts out of love or a sense of duty (*McCamley* v *Cammell Laird Shipbuilders Ltd* [1990] 1 All ER 854, 857; cf. *Van Gervan* v *Fenton* (1992) 109 ALR 283 where the High Court of Australia held that the reasonable value of a carer's services should be the market cost). In practice the loss will usually be assessed on the basis of the carer's net loss of earnings, even where the commercial rate is higher and the carer is providing 24-hour a day care and had previously been employed five days a week for eight hours a day (*Fitzgerald* v *Ford* [1996] PIQR Q72, CA). The decision in *Donnelly* v *Joyce* was approved by the Pearson Commission, which also accepted that the plaintiff should not be under any duty to account for the damages to the person rendering the services (*Pearson*, vol. 1, paras 343–51: 'In practice, the damages will often compensate for a loss suffered by a family income pool'). While retaining the general rule that the plaintiff can recover for the gratuitous provision of care by a third party and preserving the principles as to quantum, the House of Lords in *Hunt* v *Severs* [1994] 2 All ER 385 have dramatically altered the basis upon which such an award is made. In so doing, they have reverted to the approach suggested by Lord Denning MR in *Cunningham* v *Harrison* [1973] QB 942, 952 that the award reflects the plaintiff's obligation to hold that portion of the damages in trust, to be paid to the person supplying the services. One consequence of shifting the focus from the plaintiff to the third party is that, as in *Hunt* v *Severs* itself, an award could not be made where the services are provided by the defendant tortfeasor. The position is neatly summarised by Lord Bridge (at p. 394):

> By concentrating on the plaintiff's need and the plaintiff's loss as the basis of an award . . ., the reasoning in *Donnelly* diverts attention from the award's central objective of compensating the voluntary carer. Once this is recognised it becomes evident that there can be no ground in public policy or otherwise for requiring the tortfeasor to pay to the plaintiff, in respect of services which he himself has rendered, a sum of money which the plaintiff must then repay to him.

(See also *Hayden* v *Hayden* [1992] 1 WLR 986 where the Court of Appeal held that in a claim under the Fatal Accidents Act 1976 the gratuitous services of the tortfeasor could be taken into account as reducing the plaintiff's loss, and were not a 'benefit' accruing as a result of the death which, under s. 4, would have to be disregarded; for criticism see Kemp (1993) 109 LQR 173. For criticism of *Hunt* v *Severs* see Kemp (1994) 110 LQR 524; Hoyano (1995) 3 Tort L Rev 63; Reed (1995) 15 OJLS 133; Matthews (1994) 13 CJQ 302; Matthews and Lunney (1995) 58 MLR 395.) The Australian High Court has declined to follow *Hunt* v *Severs*, preferring instead the approach of the Court of Appeal in *Donelly* v *Joyce*, while taking a more robust view of the practical realities in such cases, including the insurance position (see *Kars* v *Kars* (1996) 141 ALR 37; Luntz (1997) 113 LQR 201; Degeling (1997) 71 ALJ 882; Vines (1997) 5 Tort L Rev 93).

15.1.3.2 Loss of earnings

15.1.3.2.1 Actual loss It is not usually difficult to calculate the plaintiff's actual loss of earnings from the date of the injury to the date of assessment. This is the net loss, after deducting income tax and social security contributions (*British Transport Commission* v *Gourley* [1956] AC 185; *Cooper* v *Firth Brown Ltd* [1963] 1 WLR 418; for criticism of the principle in *Gourley* see Bishop and Kay (1987) 104 LQR 211; cf. *Burrows*, pp. 133–5). An employee's contributions to a pension scheme are also deducted in calculating his actual loss of earnings (*Dews* v *National Coal Board* [1987] 2 All ER 545; see Anderson (1987) 50 MLR 963). Any loss of pension rights resulting from contributions not being paid is calculated separately from loss of earnings. All forms of earnings, such as perquisites, are included, e.g., the value of the use of a company car. If the plaintiff's rate of pay would have changed in this period, then this is taken into account.

15.1.3.2.2 Prospective loss The calculation of future loss of earnings, however, presents real problems, largely because the court has to engage in the exercise of prophesying both what will happen to the plaintiff in the future and what would have happened if he had not been injured, in order to estimate the difference. The starting-point in this process is to work out the plaintiff's net annual loss of earnings (as at the date of assessment, not the date of the injury: *Cookson* v *Knowles* [1979] AC 556). The loss of earnings may be total, or partial if the plaintiff's injuries are such that he can take a lower-paid job. The net annual loss is known as the 'multiplicand', and will be adjusted to take account of the plaintiff's individual prospects of promotion (*Roach* v *Yates* [1938] 1 KB 256), but no allowance is made for real increases in average earnings generally. This sum is then multiplied by another figure, called the 'multiplier', which is based initially on the number of years that the loss is likely to continue. So a person aged 45, who was expected to continue working until age 65, but can no longer work at all, will suffer a loss of earnings over 20 years. The multipier is then reduced, or 'discounted', to take account of: (a) the uncertainty of the prediction—the plaintiff might have lost his job in any event at some point in the future, e.g., through redundancy or illness; and (b) the fact that the plaintiff receives the money now as a capital sum, instead of in instalments over the rest of his working life (note that no reduction is made for the fact that the plaintiff does not have to earn the money). Thus the plaintiff is compensated on an annuity basis. It is expected that he will invest the award of damages, and use both the income and part of the capital to meet his living expenses over the 20-year period, so that at the end of that time the whole award will be exhausted (of course, part of his living expenses may have included saving for retirement).

The maximum multiplier that used to be applied by the courts was 18, but it was rarely that high. In the past the multipliers used rested on the assumption that a person who invested a capital sum would receive a return of approximately 4.5% after the effects of tax and inflation had been taken into account (*Pearson*, vol. 1, para. 648; see also *Cookson* v *Knowles* [1979] AC 556, 577, per Lord Fraser). It had long been argued that that assumption was unrealistic, with the result that the multipliers were too low and plaintiffs were being under-compensated (see Kemp (1985) 101 LQR 556). To illustrate the difference that the assumed rate of investment return has on the necessary lump sum, take the example given by Lord Lloyd in *Wells* v *Wells* [1998] 3 All ER 481, 485 of a need to provide £10,000 per year over 20 years. Clearly, a sum of £200,000 (20 × £10,000) would be inappropriate because in year 20 the £10,000 would have been earning interest for 19 years. The discount is designed to remove this element of over-compensation: 'The higher the assumed return on capital, net of tax, the lower the lump sum. If one assumes a net return of 5 per cent the discounted figure would be £124,600, instead of £200,000. If one assumes a net return of 3 per cent the figure would be £148,800.' The problem of potential under-compensation of plaintiffs can be exacerbated in periods of high inflation because the value of the return on investment is reduced. The courts refused to make allowance for future inflation eroding the real value of an award. The assumption was that protection from the effects of inflation had to be left to 'sound investment policy', with the plaintiff investing in a spread of equities as well as more secure government stocks. On this basis the capital appreciation of the invested damages was assumed to be sufficient to deal with inflation, provided the investments performed sufficiently well (see *Taylor* v *O'Connor* [1971] AC 115; *Cookson* v *Knowles* [1979] AC 556; and *Lim Poh Choo* v *Camden & Islington Area Health Authority* [1980] AC 174). In *Lim Poh Choo* it was accepted that in an exceptional case some allowance might be made if on the particular facts an assessment which ignored inflation would not result in 'fair compensation'. But, said Lord Scarman, 'the victims of tort who receive a lump-sum award are entitled to no better protection against inflation than others who have to rely on capital for their support'. This statement is inconsistent with the fundamental principle of restoring the plaintiff to his pre-accident position, because if the plaintiff would have had better protection from inflation as an earner, he is worse off as a result of the tort by now being forced to rely on investment income (a point acknowledged by Lords Lloyd and Hutton in *Wells* v *Wells*).

This traditional approach to calculating the multiplier was challenged in three consolidated appeals in the House of Lords (*Wells* v *Wells*; *Thomas* v *Brighton Health Authority*; *Page* v *Sheerness Steel Co. Ltd* [1998] 3 All ER 481, hereafter '*Wells* v *Wells*'). It was argued that the advent of index-linked government securities (ILGS) provided a much fairer solution to the problem of protecting plaintiffs from the effects of inflation (a point first made by Kemp (1985) 101 LQR 556; see also Kemp (1997) 113 LQR 195, commenting on the decision of the Court of Appeal in *Wells* v *Wells*). The purchaser of £100 of ILGS knows that the investment will be worth £100 plus x per cent at the maturity date, where x represents the percentage increase in the retail price index between the date of issue and the date of maturity. The advantage of ILGS from the plaintiff's perspective is that it is virtually a risk-free investment. The same sum invested in equities might produce a much higher return, but might equally produce a significantly lower return. Shares are an inherently volatile investment, particularly in the short term. That volatility creates a serious risk because a plaintiff has to sell part of the investment at regular intervals to meet his income needs (this is the assumption built into the annuity basis of compensation). If the plaintiff has to sell in a period when the stock market is depressed, he will have to realise a larger part of the underlying investment to produce the same sum, and as Lord Lloyd observed, 'the depleted fund may never recover'. The defendants argued that in calculating the lump sum the courts are entitled to assume that the plaintiff will behave prudently, and an investment adviser dealing with large sums of money would always advise investing in a spread of equities and more secure bonds and gilts. But, said Lord Lloyd, what is prudent for an ordinary investor is not necessarily prudent for a plaintiff, because an ordinary investor may be able to take a long-term view and 'ride out' falls in the market until the value of equities has recovered, whereas 'what the prudent plaintiff needs is an investment which will bring him the income he requires without the risks inherent in the equity market'. The plaintiffs argued that they should not have to bear the additional risk associated with being invested in equities for the benefit of the defendants. The House of Lords held that the plaintiffs were entitled to be compensated on the assumption that they would invest in ILGS, a view which had been recommended by the Law Commission (*Structured Settlements and Interim and Provisional Damages*, Law Com. No. 224, 1994, paras 2.25–2.28, which had described the traditional approach of assuming an investment return of 4.5% after inflation as an 'arbitrary presumption').

The average return on ILGS in recent years has been approximately 3%, significantly lower than the assumed return of 4.5% upon which the traditional approach was based (because investment in equities carries a premium for the risk involved). Their Lordships indicated, as a matter of guidance rather than precedent, that the appropriate discount rate should be 3% (different economic circumstances might justify a change to the guide figure in the future). This would require a larger initial lump sum, which is reflected in a higher multiplier. The consequence of this change is that for seriously injured plaintiffs awards of damages will increase significantly. For example, Lord Steyn estimated that the use of a 3% discount rate instead of 4.5% increased the awards by roughly £108,000 in the case of Wells (a 58-year-old nurse), £186,000 in the case of Page (a 28-year old steelworker), and £300,000 in the case Thomas (age 6). The rationale of investing in ILGS is reflected in the 'Ogden Tables', originally produced in 1984 by a joint working party of lawyers and actuaries. The Ogden Tables are regularly relied upon by counsel when valuing claims, and though they have not been formally adopted by the courts, the practice was endorsed in *Wells* v *Wells* (again, a view supported by the Law Commission, *Structured Settlements and Interim and Provisional Damages*, Law Com. No. 224, 1994, para. 2.15). The Damages Act 1996, s. 1, permits the Lord Chancellor to give general guidance on rates of return, though leaving discretion to the courts to apply different rates where appropriate. It seems likely, however, that in the light of the House of Lords' ruling in *Wells* v *Wells* the rate will be fixed at 3% (see Lewis (1997) 60 MLR 230, 234, pointing out that the Lord Chancellor has indicated that he was awaiting the guidance of the House of Lords in these cases).

It is important to note that the House of Lords in *Wells* v *Wells* was not insisting that plaintiffs must in fact invest in ILGS. Except for plaintiffs who fall within the jurisdiction of the Court of Protection, the courts do not exercise a supervisory role, and a plaintiff is normally free to spend the damages award as he sees fit. The point is that in *assessing* the level of compensation, the calculation is not to be made on the assumption that he is obliged to invest in equities.

A similar issue arises in connection with the effect of taxation. The damages award is not itself liable to tax, but the income that is produced by investing the damages is taxable. If the plaintiff receives a very large award it is possible that the income generated will be subject to higher rate (rather than standard rate) taxation with the result that the combined fund of capital and income from which the plaintiff is expected to meet his annual loss may be inadequate in the long term. In *Thomas* v *Wignall* [1987] 1 All ER 1185 the Court of Appeal made a specific increase in the multiplier in order to allow for the incidence of higher rate taxation. This decision was overruled, however, by the House of Lords in *Hodgson* v *Trapp* [1988] 3 All ER 870. It is not permissible, having established the multiplicand and selected a multiplier on the conventional basis, then to increase the multiplier to take account of higher rates of tax. Lord Oliver commented (at p. 879) that the task of assessing future pecuniary loss cannot, by its nature, be a precise science. 'The presence of so many imponderable factors necessarily renders the process a complex and imprecise one and one which is incapable of producing anything better than an approximate result.' Future taxation is just as uncertain as future inflation, and so predicting what might happen to 'future political, economic or fiscal policies requires not the services of an actuary or an accountant but those of a prophet' (at p. 884). Thus there was no justification for singling out taxation for special treatment when it is merely one of the many imponderables that have to be taken into account in the conventional method of assessing damages (for criticism of this aspect of the decision see Anderson (1989) 52 MLR 550; Burrows (1989) 105 LQR 366). It was accepted that there might be very exceptional cases, where it could be proved that justice required it, where special allowance might have to be made for the effects of higher rate tax (a point which was accepted in *Wells* v

Wells—see the speech of Lord Steyn in that case). But as Lord Oliver observed, it is difficult to envisage circumstances in which something so inherently uncertain could be proved to the satisfaction of the court. It might possibly tip the balance in favour of the selection of a higher multiplier as part of the court's assessment of all the uncertain factors that have to be taken into account, but it would not be proper to make a specific addition to the multiplier on account of this one factor. Moreover, when considering the impact of higher rate tax the court must look only at the damages awarded for future loss (whether future earnings or cost of future care) to which the multiplier method is appropriate. It is only the income on that fund which is relevant to the question of higher rate taxation. If, for example, the plaintiff chose to invest the damages awarded for non-pecuniary loss so as to supplement his income, and this put him into a higher tax bracket, that is not a reason for increasing the award for loss of future earnings and future care.

15.1.3.2.3 The lost years   If the plaintiff's life expectancy has been reduced by his injuries, can he claim for the earnings that he would have received in the period between his expected date of death and the date that he would have stopped working but for the accident? In *Oliver* v *Ashman* [1962] 2 QB 210 the Court of Appeal held that losses incurred in these 'lost years' were not recoverable, on the basis that a plaintiff cannot suffer a loss during a period when he will be dead. This rule created a problem for plaintiffs with dependants. Normally, where the victim of a tort dies as a result of his injuries, his dependants will have a claim against the tortfeasor for their loss of financial dependency (para. 15.3.2). This claim arises only where at the date of the death, the victim would have had a right of action against the tortfeasor. If, while still alive, the deceased had sued the tortfeasor to a judgment or settled his claim, then on his death there is no subsisting right of action which would permit the dependants to sue under the Fatal Accidents Act 1976. Thus the rule in *Oliver* v *Ashman* effectively penalised the plaintiff's dependants, since their dependency in the 'lost years' would have been met from the plaintiff's earnings during that period. This consideration led the House of Lords to overrule *Oliver* v *Ashman* in *Pickett* v *British Rail Engineering Ltd* [1980] AC 136. Damages for prospective loss of earnings are now awarded for the whole of the plaintiff's pre-accident life expectancy, subject to a deduction for the money that the plaintiff would have spent on his own (not his dependants') living expenses during the lost years. His own living expenses will not be incurred and therefore they are not a real loss (see *Harris* v *Empress Motors Ltd* [1983] 3 All ER 561 and *Phipps* v *Brooks Dry Cleaning Service Ltd* [1996] PIQR Q100 on the calculation of living expenses).

Though the object of *Pickett* v *British Rail Engineering Ltd* was to prevent dependants losing out, there is no guarantee, of course, that the plaintiff will use the damages to make provision for his dependants in the lost years. Moreover, the plaintiff is still entitled to such an award, even though he has no dependants. It is easier to make such a calculation where the plaintiff has an established pattern of earnings, and in the case of a young single person the award is likely to be modest to take account of the high degree of speculation involved (*Harris* v *Empress Motors Ltd*; *Adsett* v *West* [1983] 2 All ER 985). Exceptionally, a young child may have a claim for loss of earnings in the lost years (*Gammell* v *Wilson* [1982] AC 27, 78), but though in principle this loss is recoverable the speculative nature of the loss will often result in an assessment of nil damages (*Croke* v *Wiseman* [1981] 3 All ER 852; *Connolly* v *Camden & Islington Area Health Authority* [1981] 3 All ER 250; Davies (1982) 45 MLR 333). A more sensible way of dealing with provision for the dependants of a person whose working life expectancy has been reduced, would have been to amend the Fatal Accidents Act 1976 to permit a loss-of-dependency claim even though the deceased has sued the tortfeasor to judgment (see Cane and Harris (1983) 46 MLR 478, 480–1, who also point to the tension between the assessment of damages on the theoretical basis of the plaintiff's 'objective loss' and the competing 'needs-based' approach; for a third approach to this problem see *Burrows*, p. 201).

15.1.3.2.4 Deductions A person who suffers personal injury may receive financial support from a number of sources other than tort damages. The most common source is social security but others include, for example, sick pay, pensions, private insurance and charitable donations. In theory, the compensatory principle of tort should mean that these receipts are deducted in full from the award of damages, since they reduce the plaintiff's 'loss'. There is a number of competing policy factors, however, which may justify non-deduction of these 'collateral benefits'. (For an analysis of the policy issues see Lewis (1998) 18 LS 15; Law Commission Consultation Paper No. 147, *Damages for Personal Injury: Collateral Benefits*, 1997.)

(a) *Social security benefits*. In principle benefits paid by the state, in the form of social security, as a result of the injuries caused by the tortfeasor should be deducted, on the basis that the plaintiff should not be compensated twice for the same loss. By 1988 this was, essentially, the position that had been reached at common law in respect of most benefits (see *Hodgson* v *Trapp* [1988] 3 All ER 870, 876). By statute special rules applied to certain benefits. Under s. 2(1) of the Law Reform (Personal Injuries) Act 1948, half the value of any rights which had accrued or would accrue to the plaintiff in respect of sickness benefit, invalidity benefit, severe disablement allowance, and disablement benefit, for a period of five years after the accident were deducted. The Pearson Commission recommended that there should be no overlap between tort damages and social security payments and that accordingly they should be fully deductible (*Pearson*, vol. 1, para. 482; see also *Atiyah*, pp. 326–30).

The effect of deducting social security benefits from the calculation of damages was that insurers received a 'windfall', in that part of the economic loss which flowed from the tort was not paid for by the tortfeasor/insurer, but was borne by the taxpayer. This was changed by the Social Security Act 1989 (subsequently incorporated into Pt IV of the Social Security Administration Act 1992) which introduced a scheme of 'recoupment' of prescribed social security benefits from tortfeasors/insurers by the state for accidents or injury

occurring on or after 1 January 1989. This system has been further amended by
the Social Security (Recovery of Benefits) Act 1997. Under 'recoupment' the
amount of any 'relevant benefit' paid or likely to be paid to or for the plaintiff
was disregarded in assessing damages in respect of an accident, injury or
disease. Relevant benefits included: attendance allowance; disablement benefit
or pension; family credit; income support; incapacity benefit; mobility allowance; benefits payable under schemes made under the Industrial Injuries and
Diseases (Old Cases) Act 1975; reduced earnings allowance; retirement
allowance; severe disablement allowance; statutory sick pay; unemployment
benefit; disability living allowance; and disability working allowance. (Benefits
which were not prescribed, such as housing benefit, child benefit and widows'
benefit, *inter alia*, continued to be dealt with under the common law rules of
deduction from damages.) The person paying compensation (the 'compensator') in respect of an accident, injury or disease suffered by the 'victim' was
not allowed to make the payment until the Secretary of State had furnished him
with a certificate of the total benefit. The compensator then deducted from the
payment a sum equal to the gross amount of any relevant benefits paid or likely
to be paid to or for the victim during the 'relevant period' in respect of that
accident, injury or disease. That deduction was then paid to the Secretary of
State. Even where the damages were reduced to take account of the plaintiff's
contributory negligence the whole of the 'relevant benefits' had to be deducted.
The 'relevant period' was five years from the date of the accident or injury; or in
the case of a disease, five years from the first claim for a relevant benefit
consequent upon the disease, but a payment of compensation in final discharge
of the plaintiff's claim before the end of the five years brought the 'relevant
period' to an end. After the relevant period the recoupment provisions did not
apply, but under the legislation the relevant benefits were still to be disregarded
in assessing damages and so were not deducted. This produced double recovery
in any case where the plaintiff's entitlement to benefit continued after the
settlement of the damages claim (indirectly encouraging early settlement) and
in any case where the entitlement to benefit exceeded five years (which would
tend to be the more serious cases). Certain compensation payments were
exempted, most notably 'small payments', namely payments under £2,500.

Under these 'recoupment' rules any relevant benefit could be recouped
against the whole award of damages. Thus, a plaintiff's non-pecuniary losses
could be set against benefits received, with the result that in some cases
plaintiffs received no damages at all. In many instances, insurers would make
an offer of settlement under £2,500, which the plaintiff would effectively be
forced to accept because a higher settlement would mean that all the damages
would be recouped. This meant that the plaintiff did not receive an award of
damages that reflected his true loss under normal tort rules, and the Secretary
of State did not recoup any social security benefits either. Again, this resulted
in a 'windfall' to insurers. Moreover, once the level of benefits reached the
point at which it equalled or exceeded the damages, that was the limit of the
compensator's liability to repay to the Secretary of State the benefits paid as
a result of the accident/disease. Thus, recoupment worked more harshly on
plaintiffs than on defendants.

The Social Security (Recovery of Benefits) Act 1997 (the '1997 Act', which applies retrospectively to all settlements made or judgments given on or after 6 October, 1997; the Act is discussed in detail by Dismore [1998] JPIL 14) has changed this system. Benefits are no longer 'recouped'; they are 'recovered' from the compensator. Any 'recoverable benefits' paid to the victim of an accident, injury or disease in the 'relevant period' are recoverable from the compensator. The two most significant changes are that:

(a)   only certain specified benefits are recoverable against specified heads of damages; and

(b)   the compensator is liable to pay to the Secretary of State an amount equal to the total amount of the recoverable benefits, which can exceed the amount that would have been payable as compensation (1997 Act, s. 6).

Schedule 2 of the 1997 Act sets out the heads of damages against which the specified benefits can be recovered. There has been an attempt to relate the benefits to the nature of the loss for which the damages have been awarded. Thus, the following benefits can be recovered only against that part of the award of compensation relating to *loss of earnings* during the relevant period: disability working allowance; disablement pension; incapacity benefit; income support; invalidity pension and allowance; reduced earnings allowance; severe disablement allowance; statutory sick pay (paid before 6 April 1994); unemployability supplement; and jobseeker's allowance. The following benefits are recoverable only against the compensation for the *cost of care* incurred during the relevant period: attendance allowance; care component of disability living allowance; and disablement pension increase. During the passage of the Act through the Committee stage of the House of Lords a government minister said that 'the cost of care' does not include the costs of medical treatment, thus suggesting that recoverable benefits could not be set off against damages in respect of medical expenses. There is, however, no definition of the 'cost of care' in the legislation. Lastly, the following benefits are recoverable only against the compensation for *loss of mobility* during the relevant period: mobility allowance (which ceased to be paid from 6 April 1992); mobility component of disability living allowance.

One consequence of the new system is that, in the absence of agreement between the parties, the courts will now have to specify the amount of the damages attributable to 'earnings lost during the relevant period', the 'cost of care incurred during the relevant period' and 'loss of mobility during the relevant period' (1997 Act, s. 15). The first two heads are normally calculated separately, but compensation for loss of mobility could in theory include pecuniary losses (e.g., walking aids, adaptations to vehicles etc.) and non-pecuniary loss (e.g., loss of amenity from the inability to get around as easily). The intention behind the amendments, however, was that benefits should not be deducted from awards for non-pecuniary loss.

If the amount of recoverable benefit is greater than the amount deductible from the compensation payment, the tortfeasor/insurer is liable to repay the additional amount to the Secretary of State. For example, say the plaintiff has losses of £12,000 in respect of lost earnings, and £10,000 in respect of non-pecuniary pain and suffering, and has received £15,000 in incapacity benefit and £5,000 in respect of disability living allowance (care component) as result of the injuries he received. The plaintiff's compensation for loss of earnings will be reduced to nil, because the incapacity benefit is a benefit listed against loss of earnings and can be set off against the lost earnings element. Neither the balance of £3,000 incapacity benefit (£15,000 minus £12,000) nor the £5,000 disability living allowance (care component) can be deducted from the compensation for pain and suffering. The plaintiff therefore receives £10,000 for pain and suffering. The compensator is liable to pay £20,000 of recoverable benefit to the Department of Social Security. Thus, the compensator pays in total £30,000, of which the plaintiff receives £10,000 and the DSS £20,000. This exceeds the total compensation (£22,000 for loss of earnings and pain and suffering) that would have been payable to the plaintiff in the absence of social security benefits.

The 1997 Act provides that certain compensation payments are exempted payments (sch. 1 and Social Security (Recovery of Benefits) Regulations 1997, reg. 2). These include, *inter alia*: small payments; awards under the Criminal Injuries Compensation Scheme; payments under the Powers of Criminal Courts Act 1973, s. 35; payments made in respect of Fatal Accidents Act 1976 claims; payments under the Vaccine Damage Payments Act 1979; payments under accident insurance policies entered into by the victim before the accident; any redundancy payments taken into account in assessing damages; payments from certain trusts; contractual sums paid by an employer to his employee in respect of a period of incapacity for work; and so much of the payment as is referable to costs. Although the Act provides for small payments to be exempted no figure has been prescribed in Regulations, and there must be some prospect that this will not be done because the small payments limit was used by insurers to drive down offers of settlement under the old recoupment system.

The justification for the recovery of social security benefits is relatively simple to state. The pre-1989 method of deducting benefits meets the compensation principle by reflecting the plaintiff's actual loss. It ignores, however, the consequences for the defendant, or more realistically his insurers, which is that the damages are reduced and he is better off by an amount equivalent to the benefits paid by the State and funded by the taxpayer. Recovery merely puts the loss where it belongs, with the defendant's insurers rather than the taxpayer, reducing public expenditure and contributing to economic efficiency by internalising this cost to the activity generating the risk of injury (see para. 1.4.2). This assumes, however, that there is a clear distinction to be drawn between, on the one hand, taxpayers, and on the other hand those who pay personal injuries compensation through the tort system. Almost 90% of personal injury actions are for road or work accidents (see para. 1.5). Damages are funded by the insurance premiums paid by both private and business motorists and employers. Private motorists will usually also be taxpayers; indeed this activity itself makes a substantial contribution to tax revenue. Business motorists and employers will usually pass on the cost of insurance, in the price of the goods and services they produce, to consumers, the bulk of whom are probably taxpayers. Thus 'savings' to the *taxpayer* may be illusory if this is merely translated into other costs which have to be met by broadly the same group of people. Recovery also involves additional administrative costs which will reduce these savings, although it would seem that the unit cost of administering the system is low (Dismore [1998] JPIL 14, 33 suggests that this is, on average, £10 per case). Moreover, national insurance benefits (such as jobseeker's allowance) are paid for wholly by employees' and employers' contributions to the National Insurance Fund, and it is arguable that the taxpayer should not benefit from recovery of contributory benefits, which are analogous to private insurance purchased by the plaintiff (see below, (b) *Other collateral benefits*).

(b) *Other collateral benefits*. Where the plaintiff has received compensation or pecuniary benefits from another source, other than social security, the question of deduction depends upon the nature and the source of the benefit. Certain receipts are disregarded as 'collateral benefits' (for the arguments used to justify non-deduction of some 'compensating advantages' see *Burrows*, pp. 124–6). The proceeds of a personal accident insurance policy taken out by the plaintiff are ignored, on the basis that otherwise the plaintiff's foresight and thrift would benefit the defendant (by reducing the damages payable) instead of himself (*Bradburn v Great Western Railway* (1874) LR 10 Ex 1; cf. property damage where the plaintiff would be obliged to reimburse the insurer if he recovered tort damages). Gratuitous payments to the plaintiff from charitable motives are not deducted, again on the assumption that the donor intended to benefit the plaintiff rather than the defendant (*Redpath v Belfast & Co. Down Railway* [1947] NI 167), or alternatively, on the basis that the courts do not want to discourage benevolence (*Burrows*, p. 131). This would apply, for example, to payments received from disaster relief funds such as the funds set up after the King's Cross fire, the Bradford Football Club fire, or the Herald of Free Enterprise disaster. By a bare majority the House of Lords held in *Parry v Cleaver* [1970] AC 1 that an occupational disability pension should not be deducted from lost earnings, whether the pension was contributory or non-contributory. The majority took the view that the nature of a pension makes it analogous to private insurance effected by the plaintiff and so within the general principle of *Bradburn v Great Western Railway*. This, however, is highly questionable. Lord Morris of Borth-y-Gest, dissenting, pointed out that in reality there is no difference between receipt of sick pay and receipt of a pension. The true loss of earnings in each case is the difference between what the plaintiff received prior to his injury and what he now receives by virtue of his contract of employment. Moreover, it is no answer to say that he 'earned' his pension entitlement by his own efforts. If he obtains alternative employment the plaintiff must account for his earnings in the new employment in mitigation of his lost earnings, notwithstanding that these receipts were 'earned'. Perhaps surprisingly *Pearson*, vol. 1 para. 520, recommended no change to the rule in *Parry v Cleaver*. In *Smoker v London Fire & Civil Defence Authority* [1991] 2 All ER 449, the House of Lords affirmed that *Parry v Cleaver* was correctly decided, on the basis that pension benefits constitute deferred remuneration in respect of the plaintiff's past work, and the tortfeasor cannot appropriate the fruit of the plaintiff's past service. In *Longden* v *British Coal Corporation* [1998] 1 All ER 289, the plaintiff was unable to work following an accident at work. He was awarded an incapacity pension under his occupational pension scheme which he would continue to receive after his normal retirement age of 60, though it was lower than the pension he would have received had he continued to work to age 60. The defendants sought to deduct the incapacity pension that would be received to age 60 from the plaintiff's claim in respect of loss of pension rights from age 60 (the disability pension payable *after* age 60 was clearly deductible from the sum claimed in respect of lost retirement pension). The House of Lords held that (with the exception of a lump sum received on accepting the disability pension) such payments received before the normal retirement age did not have to be brought into account. Lord Hope said that the plaintiff could not reasonably be expected to set aside the sums received as incapacity pension during the period when he is unable to earn wages because of his disability in order to make good his loss of pension after his normal retirement age. It would be 'unjust if the plaintiff's claim for loss of pension after his normal retirement age were to be extinguished by capitalising sums paid to him before that age as an incapacity pension to assist him during his disability' (at pp. 300–301).

On the other hand it is clear that occupational sick pay will be deducted if paid as a term of the plaintiff's contract of employment (unless there is a contractual obligation to repay the employer on receipt of tort damages: *Browning* v *War Office* [1963] 1 QB 750; though note *Franklin* v *British Railways Board* [1993] IRLR 441, CA—plaintiff's obligation to repay the employer will normally be limited to the sums received net of income tax and national insurance contributions; see also *Berriello* v *Felixstowe Dock & Railway Co.* [1989] 1 WLR 695, payments to plaintiff from Italian state seamen's fund recoverable from him should he obtain damages for loss of earnings, held not deductible). This is the position whether or not the employer has taken out a policy of insurance to cover the contractual commitment to pay sick pay, and irrespective of the fact that the entitlement to sick pay applies to long-term incapacity for work (*Hussain* v *New Taplow Paper Mills Ltd* [1988] 1 All ER 541, HL, distinguishing *Parry* v *Cleaver*). Sick pay is 'a partial substitute for earnings and . . . the very antithesis of a pension, which is payable only after employment ceases' (ibid. at pp. 546–7). However, it is arguable that where there is some direct or indirect link between the benefits received by the plaintiff and wages forgone (e.g. as part of the overall wage structure) then the position will be closer to *Parry* v *Cleaver* in the sense that the plaintiff has, in effect, 'purchased' the benefits himself (see Anderson (1987) 50 MLR 963, 970). Gratuitous payments of sick pay are analogous to charitable payments and so should not be deducted, except where the employer who makes the payments is the defendant in the action (*Hussain* v *New Taplow Paper Mills Ltd* [1987] 1 All ER 417, 428 CA; approved by the House of Lords in *Hunt* v *Severs* [1994] 2 All ER 385, 389–90). In *McCamley* v *Cammell Laird Shipbuilders Ltd* [1990] 1 All ER 854 the Court of Appeal held that the proceeds of an ordinary personal accident policy taken out by an employer for the benefit of employees should not be deducted from an award of damages against the employer, although the plaintiff made no contribution to the premiums. The money was payable as a lump sum, quantified in advance, when it could not be foreseen what damages might have to be paid in the event of an accident. This, said the court, was analogous to an act of benevolence by the employer. it was not a method of meeting the employer's liability to pay sick pay (as in *Hussain* v *New Taplow Paper Mills Ltd*); nor was it equivalent to an *ex gratia* payment by the tortfeasor where the accident had already occurred.

If the plaintiff is made redundant as a result of his injuries, in the sense that his disability makes him a more likely candidate for redundancy, then any redundancy payment received will be deducted (*Colledge* v *Bass Mitchells & Butlers Ltd* [1988] 1 All ER 536). But if he would have been made redundant regardless of the accident the payment will not be deducted (ibid. at p. 540), though this circumstance may be relevant in calculating the compensation for loss of earnings attributable to the tort, since it is now known that he would not have continued in that employment.

15.1.3.2.5 Loss of earning capacity Where a person suffers a permanent disability which affects his ability to earn in the future at the same rate as he earned before his injury, then he may or may not suffer a loss of earnings. His loss of earnings may be total if he is unable to work at all, or partial, if he is able to take a less remunerative job. But in some cases, although his injuries have affected his ability to earn, the plaintiff suffers no loss of earnings because his employer continues to employ him at the same rate of pay. In these circumstances the plaintiff is entitled to damages for his loss of earning capacity, if there is a real risk that he could lose his existing employment, because his capacity to find an equivalent job has been reduced (*Smith* v *Manchester Corporation* (1974) 17 KIR 1; *Moeliker* v *Reyrolle & Co. Ltd* [1977] 1 All ER 9). This involves a two-stage test: (1) was there a substantial or real risk that the plaintiff would lose his present job at some time before the end of his working life? and (2) if so, what is the present value of that future risk? A risk can be real even though it is unlikely, and substantial does not mean that it is likely to happen on the balance of probabilities (*Robson* v *Liverpool City Council* [1993] PIQR Q78, CA). A claim for loss of earning capacity applies most clearly in the case of a young child who has never been employed, where it is obvious that there is no actual loss of earnings (see, e.g., *S* v *Distillers Co. (Biochemicals) Ltd* [1970] 1 WLR 114; *Mitchell* v *Liverpool Area Health Authority, The Times,* 17 June 1985).

There is no real distinction between damages for loss of earning capacity and damages for future loss of earnings (*Pearson*, vol. 1, para. 338; *Foster* v *Tyne & Wear County Council* [1986] 1 All ER 567, 571–2, so s. 2(1) of the Law Reform (Personal Injuries) Act 1948 applies to loss of earning capacity as well as prospective loss of earnings). A reduction in the plaintiff's present earning capacity is ultimately likely to have some impact on his level of future earnings. In practice, awards for loss of earning capacity are more impressionistic and less susceptible to the multiplier method of calculation (though in an appropriate case the multiplier method can be used: *Tait* v *Pearson* [1996] PIQR Q92). The assessment is particularly speculative in the case of children where there may be almost no evidence about what the plaintiff may eventually do for a living. In *Cronin* v *Redbridge London Borough Council, The Times,* 20 May 1987 the Court of Appeal complained that it was an exercise in unsatisfactory guesswork. The solution is to award only moderate sums in this situation, although there is no tariff or conventional award and each case must be considered on its own facts (*Page* v *Enfield and Haringey Area Health Authority, The Times,* 7 November 1986; see Denyer [1997] JPIL 244). In *Foster* v *Tyne & Wear County Council,* for example, an award of £35,000 to an adult plaintiff under this head was upheld.

If the court makes a separate assessment for loss of earning capacity and loss of future earnings, care must be taken to avoid any duplication in the award (*Clarke* v *Rotax Aircraft Equipment Ltd* [1975] 1 WLR 1054).

15.1.3.3 Pain and suffering The plaintiff is entitled to damages for actual and prospective pain and suffering caused by the injury, by a neurosis resulting from the injury, or attributable to any necessary medical treatment. A person who suffers mental anguish because he knows that his life expectancy has been reduced can recover for that anguish (Administration of Justice Act 1982, s. 1(1)(b), restating the common law position; a former head of damages known as 'loss of expectation of life' which was awarded for the fact that the plaintiff's life expectancy had been reduced was abolished by s. 1(1)(a)). Similarly, a person who has been incapacitated and is capable of appreciating his condition will be compensated for the anguish that this creates (*H. West & Son Ltd* v *Shephard* [1964] AC 326). However, where the plaintiff is permanently unconscious or for some other reason is incapable of subjectively experiencing pain, there will be no award for pain and suffering (*Wise* v *Kaye* [1962] 1 QB 638). A plaintiff whose injuries have affected her prospects of marriage is entitled to compensation under this head, which includes the loss of comfort and companionship which marriage might have brought (*Hughes* v *McKeown* [1985] 3 All ER 284).

In cases of psychiatric injury the plaintiff can recover for injury by shock, but not for mere sorrow or grief (*Hinz* v *Berry* [1970] 2 QB 40). However, in *Kralj* v *McGrath* [1986] 1 All ER 54 the plaintiff suffered physical injury as a result of 'horrific treatment' in the course of delivering a baby. She also suffered shock as a result of being told of the baby's injuries and seeing the child for the eight weeks that it survived. No award was made for her grief resulting from the death itself, but some allowance was made for the fact that her grief exacerbated her experience of her own injuries (see also *Kerby* v *Redbridge Health Authority* [1994] PIQR Q1—plaintiff's child survived only three days due to defendants' clinical negligence; no award for her 'dashed hopes' of giving birth to a healthy child). Conversely, if the child had been healthy this would probably have reduced the impact of the plaintiff's injuries, because she would have had the joy of motherhood to console her. (For the circumstances in which damages for 'mental distress' may be awarded, see *Burrows,* pp. 237–41; *Dickinson* v *Jones Alexander & Co.* [1990] Fam Law 137, damages for mental stress and vexation attributable to the defendant solicitors' negligent handling of the plaintiff's matrimonial litigation.)

15.1.3.4 Loss of faculty and amenity The injury itself represents loss of faculty whereas the consequences of the injury on the plaintiff's activities represents loss of amenity, e.g., loss of job satisfaction, loss of leisure activities and hobbies, and loss of family life. It is rarely necessary to distinguish between these heads because the courts usually award a single global sum to cover all the plaintiff's non-pecuniary losses. The courts operate a tariff system—£X for the loss of a leg, £Y for the loss of an arm, £Z for the loss of an eye, and so on (note *Griffiths* v *Williams, The Times,* 24 November 1995, in which the Court of Appeal commented that the circumstances and consequences of rape placed it in a quite different category from personal injury cases in general, and approved an award of £50,000). This is arbitrary, but inevitably so, and no one pretends that such losses can be truly compensated by the payment of money. It is a pragmatic solution which allows for some degree of uniformity between comparable injuries, and facilitates the settlement of claims (see, e.g., *Housecroft* v *Burnett* [1986] 1 All ER 332 where the Court of Appeal set a figure of £75,000 for an 'average' case of tetraplegia with no complications (equivalent to £111,000 in July 1993: *Fitzgerald* v *Ford* [1996] PIQR Q72, Q75)). The tariff is not precisely fixed. There is a band or range of figures for particular injuries which allows the court to take account of subjective factors. Thus an amateur sportsman who loses a leg will probably feel the loss of amenity more keenly than a person whose hobbies are of a more sedentary nature (for examples of awards for different injuries see Kemp and Kemp, *The Quantum of Damages,* revised ed., 1982, or *Current Law).*

An award will be made for loss of amenity, even though the plaintiff is permanently unconscious and cannot appreciate his condition (*Wise* v *Kaye* [1962] 1 QB 638). In *H. West & Son Ltd* v *Shephard* [1964] AC 326, by a bare majority, the House of Lords upheld the Court of Appeal's majority decision in *Wise* v *Kaye.* This treats loss of amenity as, somehow, an 'objective' loss. Lord Morris of Borth-y-Gest said (at p. 349) that:

> The fact of unconsciousness is therefore relevant in respect of and will eliminate those heads or elements of damage which can only exist by being felt or thought or experienced. The fact of unconsciousness does not, however, eliminate the actuality of the deprivations of the ordinary experiences and amenities of life which may be the inevitable result of some physical injury.

It is difficult to see, however, how the 'deprivations of the ordinary experiences and amenities of life' can be actual to someone who cannot experience the deprivation. As Lord Reid, dissenting, said (at p. 341):

there is something unreal in saying that a man who knows and feels nothing should get the same as a man who has to live with and put up with his disabilities, merely because they have sustained comparable physical injuries. It is no more possible to compensate an unconscious man than it is to compensate a dead man.

The 'objective loss' approach fails to address a fundamental question: namely, what is the purpose of an award of damages for non-pecuniary loss? Of the purposes identified by the Pearson Commission (see para. 15.1.3), it is obvious that an unconscious person can neither find solace in an award nor purchase alternative forms of happiness. The third purpose, meeting hidden expenses, is unnecessary if pecuniary losses have been correctly estimated. The Commission took the sensible view that damages for non-pecuniary loss should be awarded only where they can serve some useful purpose, and so should not be recoverable for permanent unconsciousness (*Pearson*, vol. 1, para. 397–8). This proposal has not been implemented, and in *Lim Poh Choo v Camden & Islington Area Health Authority* [1980] AC 174 the House of Lords declined an invitation to reverse *H. West & Son Ltd v Shephard*, preferring to leave the matter to legislative intervention. The Law Commission's Consultation Paper on *Damages for Personal Injury: Non-Pecuniary Loss*, No. 140, 1995, also addressed the issue of the permanently unconscious plaintiff, but made no specific recommendation (paras 4.11–4.22). Generally, the Commission advocated that courts should continue to award damages for non-pecuniary loss (paras 4.5–4.8) and rejected the more subjective Canadian 'functional' approach as an alternative basis of assessment (paras 4.9–4.10). The Commission observed that awards have not kept pace with inflation, at least in serious cases (paras 4.34–4.51; see also Law Commission Report No. 225, *Personal Injury Compensation: How Much is Enough?*, 1994, suggesting that levels of compensation for personal injury are still too low), and are low in comparison with awards made in defamation cases, prompting the suggestion that the jury in defamation cases ought to be referred to the 'tariff' employed in personal injury cases (paras 4.101–4.103) (see *John v Mirror Group Newspapers Ltd* [1996] 2 All ER 35 now providing for some limited reference to the tariff, by way of general guidance).

15.1.4 Damage to property

In the case of damage to property, the basic rule for the measure of damages is again that the plaintiff should be restored to his position before the tort was committed. Where the property has been completely destroyed the measure of the loss is the market value of the property at the time of destruction (*Liesbosch Dredger v SS Edison* [1933] AC 449). Damages are also recoverable for loss of use of the property before it is replaced (*Moore v DER Ltd* [1971] 1 WLR 1476). Damages for loss of use may include the cost of hiring a substitute where it is reasonable to do so (*Martindale v Duncan* [1973] 1 WLR 574; *HL Motorworks Ltd v Alwahbi* [1977] RTR 276—reasonable to hire a Rolls-Royce motor car to replace the plaintiff's Rolls-Royce while it was being repaired; cf. *Ramwade Ltd v Emson & Co. Ltd* (1986) 2 PN 197 CA, where the plaintiffs' claim was against insurance brokers for negligently failing to effect comprehensive insurance on their vehicle. They could not afford to replace the damaged vehicle until judgment against the defendants. Held the cost of hiring a substitute was not recoverable; cx. *Mattocks* v *Mann* [1993] RTR 13, CA—plaintiff entitled to recover hire charges for a replacement vehicle in the period of delay caused by insurers failing to pay the repair costs for her own vehicle, despite her inability to meet the repair costs herself). If the property was used in a business then loss of use includes loss of profit. The value of the property has to be assessed as a 'going concern' at the time of the loss (*Liesbosch Dredger* v *SS Edison*). Of course, if the plaintiff has hired a substitute there should be no loss of profit. Even in the case of non-profit-earning chattels the plaintiff is entitled to claim for loss of use (*The Mediana* [1900] AC 113; cf. *Brandeis Goldschmidt & Co. Ltd* v *Western Transport Ltd* [1981] QB 864, but see the explanation of *Weir*, p. 653). This can be measured by the cost of hiring a substitute, or in the last resort as interest on the capital value of the property (*The Hebridean Coast* [1961] AC 545, 562).

Where property has been damaged, but not destroyed, the measure of damages is the diminution in value, and with damaged chattels this is normally the cost of repair (*The London Corporation* [1935] P 70). It is irrelevant that repairs have not been carried out at the date of the trial (*The Kingsway* [1918] P 344), or that they are never carried out at all (*The York* [1929] P 178, 184–5), or that the plaintiff has not paid for the repairs out of his own pocket (*Jones* v *Stroud District Council* [1986] 1 WLR 1141, 1150–1). But if the repair costs are greater than the value of the property in its undamaged state the plaintiff can only recover the value of the property. He cannot claim the full repair costs (*Darbishire* v *Warran* [1963] 1 WLR 1067), unless the property is unique, so that the standard market value is irrelevant (*O'Grady* v *Westminster Scaffolding Ltd* [1962] 2 Lloyd's Rep 238). If the property is less valuable in its repaired state than it was before the tort, the plaintiff can claim both repair costs and this additional diminution in value (*Payton* v *Brooks* [1974] RTR 169). Loss of use while the property is being repaired is also recoverable, on the basis of the principles stated above.

Where the damaged property consists of land or buildings the same rules apply, except that there is more flexibility in allowing claims for repair costs even though they exceed the diminution in market value. Land is not so readily replaceable as chattels, and is, to some extent, treated in the same manner as a unique chattel. The question depends on the plaintiff's future intentions as to the use of the property and the reasonableness of those intentions. 'If he reasonably intends to sell the property in its damaged state, clearly the diminution of capital value is the true measure of damage. If he reasonably intends to continue to occupy it and to repair the damage, clearly the cost of repairs is the true measure. And there may be in-between situations' (*Dodd Properties (Kent) Ltd* v *Canterbury City Council* [1980] 1 All ER 928, 938 per Donaldson LJ; see also *Perry* v *Sidney Phillips & Son* [1982] 3 All ER 705; *Hollebone* v *Midhurst & Fernhurst Builders Ltd* [1968] 1 Lloyd's Rep 38). Damages may extend to the cost of acquiring new business premises, even where this substantially exceeds the diminution in value of the damaged premises, where obtaining new premises is a reasonable course to adopt in order to mitigate the plaintiff's damage, in the form of loss of profits that would be caused during the period of rebuilding (*Dominion Mosaics & Tile Co. Ltd* v *Trafalgar Trucking Co. Ltd* [1990] 2 All ER 246.

Thus in the case of land, where it is reasonable, the plaintiff may be entitled to the cost of repair even though this is greater than the diminution in value. Moreover, as a general rule, diminution in value is assessed at the date of the tort (*Miliangos* v *George Frank (Textiles) Ltd* [1976] AC 443, 468; cf. *Ward* v *Cannock Chase District Council* [1985] 3 All ER 537, 559, where the facts were somewhat exceptional). But repair costs are assessed at the earliest date at which it is reasonable to carry out the repairs, and it may be reasonable for the plaintiff to defer repairs where this would result in a cash flow deficiency, particularly when the defendants are denying liability and there is dispute as to what work is necessary (*Dodd Properties (Kent) Ltd* v *Canterbury City Council;* Wallace (1980) 96 LQR 341; and more generally, Waddams (1981) 97 LQR 445). The effect of deferring repairs, of course, may be to increase the cost considerably over the initial diminution in value caused by the defendant's tort. As long as this can be categorised as 'commercial prudence' rather than the result of the plaintiff's impecuniosity, it seems that the loss will be recoverable (see para. 4.3.4.2).

15.1.5   Economic loss from misstatements
Where property has negligently been overvalued as a result of which a lender has advanced money to a borrower on the security of the property, if the borrower defaults on the loan the lender may suffer a loss when the property turns out to be worth less than the sum loaned. If, in the time between the negligent valuation and the borrower's default, the property market has fallen can the lender claim this fall in value as damages from the negligent valuer, on the basis that but for the negligent valuation the lender would never have entered into the loan transaction at all and therefore all the losses flowing from the transaction are attributable to the valuer's negligence? In *Banque Bruxelles Lambert SA* v *Eagle Star Insurance Co. Ltd* [1995] 2 All ER 769 the Court of Appeal held that in 'no transaction' cases (i.e., where the lender would not have entered into the transaction had the true valuation been known), as opposed to 'successful transaction' cases (where had the true valuation been known there would still have been a transaction, but on different terms, e.g. lower amount advanced, higher rate of interest etc.), the borrower was entitled to recover the full extent of the loss, including the fall in market value of the property. The House of Lords reversed this decision, however, concluding that the valuer is not responsible for that part of the lender's loss attributable to a fall in the property market (sub. nom. *South Australia Asset Management Corp.* v *York Montague Ltd* [1996] 3 All ER 365; for comment see Stapleton (1997) 113 LQR 1; McLauchlan (1997) 113 LQR 421; Dugdale (1997) 13 PN 94 and (1996) 12 PN 71; Davidson (1997) 13 PN 89; Rogers (1997) 5 Tort L Rev 12; Wightman (1998) 61 MLR 68; Allinson [1998] Conv 57). A valuer who had negligently overvalued property was not responsible for all the consequences of the transaction entered into

in reliance on the valuation, but only for the foreseeable consequences. The correct approach was to ascertain the element of the loss attributable to the inaccuracy of the information, and thus the measure of damages was the difference between the negligent valuation and the correct property valuation at the time of the valuation. The basis for this is that the defendant is not responsible for all the consequences of the events that result from his conduct, but only for those consequences that fall within the scope of his duty of care. Lord Hoffmann drew a distinction (at pp. 372-3) between a duty *to provide information* for the purpose of enabling someone else to decide upon a course of action and a duty to *advise* someone as to what course of action he should take. In the case of advice the adviser must take reasonable care to consider all the potential consequences of that course of conduct, and if he is negligent he will be responsible for all the foreseeable loss which is a consequence of that course of action, but if the duty is only to supply information he must take reasonable care to see that the information is correct, and if he is negligent he will be responsible for all the foreseeable consequences of the information being wrong. The valuer merely provides information as to the value of the property and therefore this limits the scope of the duty of care that has been undertaken. Losses attributable to the fall in the property market did not fall within the scope of the duty and therefore were not caused by the defendants' negligence. In other words, it is crucial to determine what the scope of a defendant's duty is and what loss is attributable to the breach of duty, before assessing the measure of damages which will compensate for that loss. The distinction between 'no transaction' cases and 'successful transaction' cases was rejected by the House of Lords as a principled basis for assessing the loss, although in practice if the lender would in fact have entered into a different (and *ex hypothesi* less disastrous) transaction with the borrower had the valuation been accurate this could produce a different measure of damages from that applicable where the lender would not have entered any transaction had the valuation been accurate.

Though expressly decided in the context of the lender–borrower–valuer cases, there was no reason to suppose that the principles enunciated by the House of Lords in the *South Australia* case might not be applicable to solicitors in similar situations, nor that they might not typically benefit from the principles' potential to 'cap' damages. It is difficult to conceive of many instances where a solicitor's duty would be other than as a provider of information (as to title, valuation and the like) that was important, but nonetheless peripheral, to a lender's decision to lend in the first place. Indeed, this has generally been the case in the flurry of decisions that have had to address attempts by lenders to recover from careless solicitors large losses sustained on borrowers' default (e.g., *Bristol and West Building Society* v *Fancy and Jackson* [1997] 4 All ER 582; *Bristol and West Building Society* v *May, May and Merrimans (No. 2)* [1997] 3 All ER 206; *Bristol and West Building Society* v *Mothew* [1996] 4 All ER 698; for a survey of the cases and analysis of the issues see Sprince (1998) 14 PN 3). Notably, such cases have also provided the courts with the opportunity to apply principles of contributory negligence as a means of recognising that the losses might partially be attributed to some less than fastidious lending practices (see *Platform Home Loans Ltd* v *Oyston Shipways Ltd* (1997) 14 PN 56, para. 14.5.1; Evans (1998) 14 PN 43).

In *South Australia Asset Management Corp.* v *York Montague Ltd* [1996] 3 All ER 365, 373–4, Lord Hoffmann observed that where the defendant has been fraudulent then it would be justifiable to take a different approach and impose the whole risk of loss (which would not have been suffered if the plaintiff had not been fraudulently induced to enter into the transaction) upon the defendant, including falls in the market. This has long been thought to be the correct approach to the assessment of damages in the tort of deceit (see *Doyle* v *Olby (Ironmongers) Ltd* [1969] 2 QB 158; *Swindle* v *Harrison* [1997] 4 All ER 705). The normal method of calculating a loss caused by deceit is the price paid less the real value of the subject of the sale as at the date of the transaction induced by the defendant's deceit. The overriding principle, however, is that the plaintiff is entitled to be fully compensated, and therefore the 'date of transaction' rule does not apply where the misrepresentation continues to operate after the date of acquisition of the asset so as to induce the plaintiff to retain the asset, nor where the plaintiff is 'locked into the property' as a result of the fraud (*Smith New Court Securities Ltd* v *Scrimgeour Vickers (Asset Management) Ltd* [1996] 4 All ER 769, HL). Thus, if the value of the asset falls in the interim, the plaintiff will be entitled to recover the difference between the price paid and the actual value of the asset realised on sale. The plaintiff must prove that the loss was caused by the defendant's wrong, and must mitigate his loss where he is able to do so once he is aware of the fraud (see para. 15.1.6), but, with respect to remoteness of damage, the victim of a fraud is entitled to be compensated for all the actual loss flowing directly from the tort, including consequential loss, even if that loss was not reasonably foreseeable (*ibid.* at pp. 778–9, per Lord Browne-Wilkinson).

15.1.6 Mitigation
The plaintiff has a duty to mitigate the damage that results from the defendant's tort, although he commits no wrong against the defendant if he fails to do so. The plaintiff 'is fully entitled to be as extravagant as he pleases but not at the expense of the defendant' (*Darbishire* v *Warran* [1963] 1 WLR 1067, 1075). If, for example, he loses his job because of an injury, he should look for alternative employment if he is capable of working. If he takes a lower-paid job, he can only recover from the defendant as lost wages the difference between his previous earnings and his present earnings. An injured plaintiff should seek medical attention which will improve his condition, but generally he is not required to undergo a medical procedure where there is a substantial risk of further injury or the outcome is uncertain. The test is 'whether in all the circumstances including particularly the medical advice received, the plaintiff acted reasonably in refusing surgery?' (*Selvanayagam* v *University of the West Indies* [1983] 1 All ER 824, 827; Hudson (1983) 46 MLR 754; and see generally Hudson (1983) 3 Legal Stud 50). The burden of proving that the plaintiff acted unreasonably in failing to mitigate the loss is the defendant's (a dictum to the contrary effect in *Selvanayagam* v

University of the West Indies seems to be incorrect: McGregor (1983) 46 MLR 758; Kemp (1983) 99 LQR 497).

If the plaintiff has acted unreasonably in refusing medical treatment a question arises as to how damages should be assessed where the treatment cannot guarantee an improvement in the plaintiff's condition. In *Janiak* v *Ippolito* (1985) 16 DLR (4th) 1 the mitigating operation which the plaintiff had unreasonably refused to undergo had a 70% chance of success. The Supreme Court of Canada held that, rather than assuming, on the basis of the balance of probabilities, that the operation would succeed, the 30% chance of the operation failing to alleviate the plaintiff's condition should be taken into account in assessing damages for prospective loss of earnings. It is submitted that this is the correct approach and that the chance of the treatment failing to achieve its purpose should be taken into account, notwithstanding that objectively the refusal is considered to be unreasonable, particularly since it may well be this factor which persuades the plaintiff to refuse the treatment. It should not be assumed in the defendant's favour that a particular future event would have occurred as a certainty, whereas plaintiffs normally have their future losses discounted for the chance that particular events might not have occurred (though cf. *McAuley* v *London Transport Executive* [1957] 2 Lloyd's Rep 500, 505 per Jenkins LJ, stating that damages should be assessed as if the plaintiff had undergone the operation and in fact secured the degree of recovery expected from it). Thus, where the plaintiff has reasonably refused to undergo an operation in the short term, but might choose to accept treatment in the future, there will be a discount of the award of damages which reflects the chance both that the plaintiff might have the treatment and that it might be successful; it should not be assumed that there will be an operation and that it will be successful (*Thomas* v *Bath District Health Authority* [1995] PIQR Q19, CA).

Similar principles apply to property damage. So if the plaintiff has an old motor car which is worth £85, he cannot claim repair costs of £180. He can mitigate his loss by purchasing a similar vehicle for £85 (*Darbishire* v *Warran*). The matter has to be approached from the point of view of a practical businessman (but see *Weir*, p. 659). Where the plaintiff is unable, through impecuniosity, to mitigate the damage, the defendant is liable for the full loss (*Clippens Oil Co.* v *Edinburgh & District Water Trustees* [1907] AC 291, 303; *Dodd Properties (Kent) Ltd* v *Canterbury City Council* [1980] 1 All ER 928). This should be distinguished from the situation where the damage itself is the product of the plaintiff's impecuniosity, when it will be treated as too remote (para. 4.3.4.2). However, in practice this distinction may not be easy to draw, nor is its justification particularly clear.

15.1.7 Interest on damages
The court has a discretion to award simple interest on all or any part of the damages, and in the case of damages for personal injuries or death exceeding £200 the court must award interest unless there are special reasons for not doing so (Supreme Court Act 1981, s. 35A). Where the plaintiff has delayed in bringing a claim to trial the court has a discretion to disallow all or part of

a claim for pre-trial interest (*Birkett* v *Hayes* [1982] 2 All ER 710, 717; *Corbett* v *Barking, Havering & Brentwood Health Authority* [1991] 1 All ER 498). In the case of special damages for accrued pecuniary loss, interest will normally be awarded at half the special investment rate on money paid into court, from the date of the accident to the date of trial (*Jefford* v *Gee* [1970] 2 QB 130, 146; *Cookson* v *Knowles* [1979] AC 556; SI 1987/821(L3)). No interest is awarded on future pecuniary loss, such as prospective loss of earnings, because the loss has not yet accrued.

Interest on damages for non-pecuniary loss is awarded at a modest rate, currently 2%, from the date of service of the writ to the date of trial. The reason for this low rate is that a large proportion of nominal interest rates is represented by inflation, and inflation is taken into account when the court assesses damages for non-pecuniary loss by the general up-rating of 'tariffs' (*Wright* v *British Railways Board* [1983] 2 AC 773). Interest at 2% represents an approximate real rate of return for the plaintiff not having the use of his money. (Note that this rate may now be increased to 3% in the light of the decision of the House of Lords in *Wells* v *Wells* [1998] 3 All ER 481, para. 15.1.3.2.2—see the comments of Lord Lloyd on *Wright* v *British Railways Board* at p. 491.) It would seem, however, that personal injury cases are in a special category and interest on damages for non-pecuniary loss will not be awarded in actions for deceit or false imprisonment (*Saunders* v *Edwards* [1987] 2 All ER 651; *Holtham* v *Commissioner of Police of the Metropolis, The Times,* 28 November 1987, CA).

15.2 INJUNCTION

A prohibitory injunction is an order of the court requiring the defendant to cease committing a continuing tort, such as a continuing nuisance or trespass, or restraining the repetition of tortious conduct where it is likely to be repeated. It is negative in nature, in that it requires the defendant not to do something or to cease doing something. A mandatory injunction, on the other hand, requires the defendant to undertake some positive act, such as removing an obstruction that he has caused to the plaintiff's right of way.

An injunction is an equitable remedy (though note that a number of statutes confer a jurisdiction to grant injunctions: see, e.g., Protection from Harassment Act 1997), and as such it is a discretionary remedy. A number of factors will be taken into account in deciding whether to exercise the discretion. An injunction will not be granted where damages would be an adequate remedy, nor, possibly, where the harm to the plaintiff from the tort is trivial (*Armstrong* v *Sheppard & Short Ltd* [1959] 2 QB 384, 396; but *cf. Kelsen* v *Imperial Tobacco Co. Ltd* [1957] 2 QB 334). If it is impossible for the defendant to comply with the order it will not be granted (*Earl of Harrington* v *Derby Corporation* [1905] 1 Ch 205, 220), but the fact that the defendant will be put to considerable trouble and expense does not make it impossible to comply (*Pride of Derby & Derbyshire Angling Association Ltd* v *British Celanese Ltd* [1953] Ch 149). The conduct of the parties may be taken into account. So if the plaintiff acquiesced in the defendant's conduct (*Gaskin* v

Balls (1879) 13 ChD 324) or misled the defendant (*Armstrong* v *Sheppard &*
Short Ltd) an injunction may not be issued. The extent to which the public
interest will be taken into account is unclear (see para. 7.1.7.2), but it is
arguable that where the interference with the plaintiff's rights is substantial
the plaintiff should be entitled to an order (*Leeds Industrial Co-operative Society*
v *Slack* [1924] AC 851, 872).

Mandatory injunctions are not granted so readily as prohibitory injunctions. In *Morris* v *Redland Bricks Ltd* [1970] AC 652 the House of Lords said
that a mandatory injunction would not be granted unless there was a strong
probability that very serious damage to the plaintiff will result if it is withheld.
As with all types of injunction, it will be refused if damages would be a
sufficient remedy. The cost to the defendant of complying with a mandatory
injunction will be taken into account. If it is out of all proportion to the injury
to the plaintiff's rights the injunction will be refused, unless the defendant has
acted wantonly or unreasonably or attempted to steal a march on the plaintiff
(*Daniel* v *Ferguson* [1891] 2 Ch 27). The form of the order must specify
precisely what the defendant has to do to comply with its terms.

In some circumstances the plaintiff may be entitled to a *quia timet*
injunction, which will restrain conduct that is likely to cause substantial
damage before any damage has actually occurred (and thus, in torts which
are not actionable *per se*, before any cause of action has accrued). The
likelihood of substantial damage must be strong, and the damage must be
imminent (*Lemos* v *Kennedy Leigh Development Co. Ltd* (1961) 105 SJ 178; cf.
Hooper v *Rogers* [1975] Ch 43). The likelihood of damage is not, in itself, a
sufficient ground for granting an injunction. The plaintiff must be able to
point to a good cause of action in order to restrain the harm (*Associated*
Newspapers Group plc v *Insert Media Ltd* [1988] 2 All ER 420; though
cf. *Burris* v *Azadani* [1995] 4 All ER 802 where the Court of Appeal held that
there was a power to make an 'exclusion zone' order despite the fact that the
conduct restrained was not in itself tortious or unlawful, provided it was
necessary to protect the plaintiff from harassment).

An interlocutory injunction is a provisional order which may be issued
pending a full trial of the action on the merits of the case. This means that
on an application for an interlocutory injunction the court does not investigate the merits, and provided there is a 'serious question' to be tried the court
will exercise its discretion on the 'balance of convenience' (*American Cy-*
anamid Co. v *Ethicon Ltd* [1975] AC 396, 408; see further *NWL Ltd* v *Woods*
[1979] 1 WLR 1294, 1307; cf. *Francome* v *Mirror Group Newspapers Ltd*
[1984] 2 All ER 408, 413 per Sir John Donaldson MR: 'Our business is
justice not convenience'). In proceedings for libel an interlocutory injunction
will not normally be granted where the defendant intends to rely on the
defence of justification, i.e., he asserts that the defamatory statement is true
(*Bonnard* v *Perryman* [1891] 2 Ch 269; *Fraser* v *Evans* [1969] 1 All ER 8). In
Gulf Oil (GB) Ltd v *Page* [1987] 3 All ER 14, however, the Court of Appeal
held that the same principle did not apply where the plaintiff relied on the
tort of conspiracy, leading to the strange result that in interlocutory proceedings a plaintiff can prevent the publication of an allegedly true statement

when it is made by two or more people jointly, but not where the defendant acts alone. Where an interlocutory injunction is granted the plaintiff will usually be required to give an undertaking to pay damages to the defendant for losses sustained by the defendant as a result of the injunction if, at the hearing on the merits, the plaintiff's action fails.

The court has a discretion to award damages in addition to or in substitution for an injunction (Supreme Court Act 1981, s. 50, re-enacting Chancery Amendment Act 1858 (Lord Cairns's Act), s. 2). This discretion has been narrowly confined and is exercised sparingly, because the courts have been reluctant to allow defendants effectively to purchase compulsorily the plaintiff's rights (see para. 7.1.7.2; Jolowicz [1975] CLJ 224; Wakefield and Ingman [1981] Conv 286). Moreover, damages can never be awarded in lieu of a *quia timet* injunction because there is no existing right of action, merely one threatened in the future (*Midland Bank plc* v *Bardgrove Property Services Ltd* [1992] 37 EG 126).

15.3   DEATH IN RELATION TO TORT

At common law, a person's death extinguished any cause of action that may have existed against him, and any cause of action that the deceased may have had against someone else. Similarly, a person's death did not confer any common law right of action on another person against someone who had caused the death. The latter rule meant that the dependants of a person killed by another's negligence, or even deliberately, could not sue in respect of their loss of support by the deceased. Both of these rules have been changed by legislation. The Law Reform (Miscellaneous Provisions) Act 1934 provides for the survival of actions on the death of one or more of the parties, and the Fatal Accidents Act 1976 (replacing earlier legislation) grants the dependants of a deceased person a cause of action for their lost dependency if the deceased would have had an action in tort in respect of the injuries that caused his death.

15.3.1   Survival of actions

By the Law Reform (Miscellaneous Provisions) Act 1934, s. 1(1), on the death of any person all causes of action (with the exception of defamation) subsisting against or vested in him survive against, or, as the case may be, for the benefit of, his estate. The Act does not create a new cause of action, it simply allows an existing action to be maintained by or against the estate of the deceased person. Section 1(4) provides an exception to the rule that the action must have been subsisting at the date of death. Where, as a result of an act or omission by the deceased, damage has been suffered which would have given rise to a cause of action had he not died before or at the same time as the damage suffered, then it is deemed that the cause of action shall subsist as if he had died after the damage was suffered. The commonest example of the application of s. 1(4) is the case of the negligent motorist who dies in the same accident that causes injury to the plaintiff. The cause of action is deemed to have subsisted before the death, allowing the plaintiff to sue the estate.

An action brought by the estate of a deceased plaintiff is dealt with on the same basis as if the plaintiff were alive. Thus the measure of damages is generally the same as for a living plaintiff. The estate can recover for any expenses incurred or loss of earnings attributable to the tort up to the date of death. Similarly, pain and suffering and loss of amenity up to the date of death (not after) are recoverable, although there will be no award for pain and mental agony in the last few moments before death, which are treated as part of the death itself (*Hicks* v *Chief Constable of South Yorkshire Police* [1992] 2 All ER 65—an action arising out of the Hillsborough stadium disaster in which the deceased was asphyxiated). Exemplary damages are not recoverable, nor are damages for loss of income in respect of any period after the plaintiff's death, i.e., the 'lost years' (s. 1(2)(a)).

Thus lost-years claims are available only to living plaintiffs. This latter provision was introduced by the Administration of Justice Act 1982, s. 4(2), to reverse the effect of *Gammell* v *Wilson* [1982] AC 27. In that case the House of Lords held that a claim for loss of earnings in the lost years, which had been established by *Pickett* v *British Rail Engineering Ltd* [1980] AC 136 for living plaintiffs, survived for the benefit of the estate. The result of this was a substantial increase in damages in certain types of fatal accident case. Where a young plaintiff with no dependants was killed there would be no claim under the Fatal Accidents Act 1976, but the beneficiaries of the estate, usually the parents, would receive a substantial windfall in respect of the deceased's prospective loss of earnings. And where the deceased did have dependants but the beneficiaries of the estate were non-dependants, the estate would receive the loss of earnings in the lost years without affecting the dependants' action for loss of dependency (which, had the deceased lived, would have been met from the earnings in the lost years). The result was that in some cases the defendant was having to pay more in damages than the plaintiff could have earned had the tort not occurred. The amended s. 1(2)(a) of the Law Reform (Miscellaneous Provisions) Act 1934, which applies to deaths after 1982, prevents this form of double recovery, although it does not deal with other aspects of windfall gains to the beneficiaries of the deceased's estate, e.g., damages for pain and suffering and loss of amenity for the period during which the deceased survived the tort (for criticism see Cane and Harris (1983) 46 MLR 478).

Where the death was caused by the act or omission which gives rise to the cause of action, damages are calculated without reference to any loss or gain consequent on the death, except that a sum in respect of funeral expenses may be included (s. 1(2)(c)). So gains to the estate, such as the proceeds of a life insurance policy, and losses, such as the loss of a life interest under a trust, are ignored.

15.3.2 Fatal accidents and loss of dependency
In *Baker* v *Bolton* (1808) 1 Camp 493 it had been asserted that 'in a civil court the death of a human being cannot be complained of as an injury', and this common law rule was confirmed by the House of Lords in *Admiralty Commissioners* v *SS Amerika* [1917] AC 38. The Fatal Accidents Act 1846

first provided a statutory cause of action for the dependants of a deceased person who had been wrongfully killed, and today this action is governed by the Fatal Accidents Act 1976. This gives dependants a cause of action in their own right in respect of their *financial* loss (except where damages are awarded for bereavement), irrespective of any claims on behalf of the estate of the deceased under the Law Reform (Miscellaneous Provisions) Act 1934 (see Waddams (1984) 47 MLR 437 for an argument that the Fatal Accidents Act 1976 should be repealed, leaving provision for dependants to the 1934 Act in combination with claims against the deceased's estate).

15.3.2.1 The action The dependants' action is derivative, in the sense that it can be maintained only if the defendant would have been liable to the deceased (Fatal Accidents Act 1976, s. 1(1); see *Pigney* v *Pointer's Transport Services Ltd* [1957] 1 WLR 1121). Any defences that would have been available against the deceased, such as *volenti non fit injuria* or contributory negligence, can also be relied upon in the dependants' action. If the death was caused partly by the negligence of a dependant, some apportionment will be made in respect of that dependant's claim (*Mulholland* v *McRae* [1961] NI 135), but this does not affect the claims of other, non-negligent, dependants (*Dodds* v *Dodds* [1978] QB 543). If for any reason the deceased could not himself have maintained an action at the moment of his death, the dependants have no cause of action under the Fatal Accidents Act 1976. So where he has sued the defendant to a judgment or settled the claim while still alive, the dependants cannot sue (*Pickett* v *British Rail Engineering Ltd* [1980] AC 136, where the House of Lords assumed that this was correct; for the position where the deceased's action is statute-barred by the Limitation Act 1980, see para. 14.7.1).

15.3.2.2 Dependants The category of dependants who can sue under the Fatal Accidents Act 1976 is specifically defined by s. 1. They include: a spouse, former spouse (including a former spouse who had remarried but later returned to live with her first husband: *Shepherd* v *Post Office, The Times*, 15 June 1995, CA) or 'cohabitee' of the deceased; any parent or other ascendant, any child or other descendant, or any person treated by the deceased as his parent or as his child; and any person who is, or is the issue of, a brother, sister, uncle or aunt of the deceased. A relationship by affinity (marriage) is treated as a relationship by consanguinity (blood), and a relationship by half-blood as a relationship of the whole blood. The stepchild of any person is treated as his child, and an illegitimate person is treated as the legitimate child of his mother and reputed father. A 'cohabitee' is restrictively defined as a person who was living as the husband or wife of the deceased in the same household immediately before the date of the death, and had been so living for at least two years (though see *Pounder* v *London Underground Ltd* [1995] PIQR P217—it is possible for a person to live in more than one household at a time for the purposes of s. 1; and contrast the wider definition of a dependant in the Inheritance (Provision for Family and Dependants) Act 1975, s. 1, as a person 'who immediately before the death of the deceased was being maintained, either wholly or partly, by the deceased'). The action is normally instituted by the personal representative of the deceased's estate on behalf of the dependants, but if an action is not commenced within six months any dependant can sue on behalf of all the dependants (Fatal Accidents Act 1976, s. 2).

15.3.2.3 Damages The damages available under the Fatal Accidents Act 1976 are either damages for bereavement or damages for the dependant's actual and prospective pecuniary loss. If the dependants have in fact incurred funeral expenses they are entitled to be reimbursed.

Damages for bereavement were introduced by the Administration of Justice Act 1982, s. 3, creating a new s. 1A of the Fatal Accidents Act 1976. This is a fixed sum of £7,500 (SI 1990/2575) which will be awarded only to the spouse of the deceased or to the parents of an unmarried minor child (but only the mother of an illegitimate child). Where both parents of a child claim damages for bereavement the award is divided equally. The award does not depend upon proof of pecuniary dependency. There is no inquiry into the extent of the spouse's or parent's grief. The damages constitute a conventional figure, which may be increased by statutory instrument but not by the courts. A claim in respect of bereavement damages does not survive for the benefit of a deceased dependant's estate. In part, damages for bereavement have replaced the conventional common law damages for loss of expectation of life, which were awarded to the deceased person's estate in a fatal accident case. This head of damages was abolished by the Administration of justice Act 1982, s. 1(1)(a). Where young children are killed, damages for bereavement plus funeral expenses will commonly be the only sum payable by the defendant (for criticism of damages for bereavement see *Atiyah*, p. 76).

With reference to the dependants' pecuniary loss, s. 3(1) of the Fatal Accidents Act 1976 provides that such damages may be awarded as are proportioned to the injury resulting from the death to the dependants respectively. This is determined by the 'multiplier' method. The purpose of the award is to provide the dependants with a capital sum which with prudent management will be sufficient to provide material benefits of the same standard and duration as would have been provided for them out of the deceased's earnings had he not been killed (*Mallett* v *McMonagle* [1970] AC 166, 174 per Lord Diplock). The starting-point is the amount of the deceased's wages, less an amount for his own personal and living expenses. This provides a basic figure for estimating the dependency (*Davies* v *Powell Duffryn Associated Collieries Ltd* [1942] AC 601, 617). Then the length of the dependency has to be estimated. This is done by considering the deceased's pre-accident working life expectancy, discounted for the contingency that he might not have lived or continued working that long in any event. The process is similar to that employed in calculating a living plaintiff's prospective loss of earnings (para. 15.1.3.2.2). However, the multiplier has to be modified to take account of the dependant's future prospects. With dependent children the dependency would not normally extend beyond the end of their full-time education. A spouse's life expectancy will be taken into account, and where the dependant has died before the trial, damages will only be awarded for the period of survival after the deceased's death (*Williamson v John I. Thornycroft & Co. Ltd* [1940] 2 KB 658; see *Davies v Taylor* [1974] AC 207 for the position where spouses are separated at the date of death). The multiplier runs from the date of death, rather than the date of assessment as with living plaintiffs, because the multiplier method of calculation is appropriate for periods of uncertainty in the assessment and the uncertainty begins at the date of death (*Graham v Dodds* [1983] 2 All ER 953). This does not mean, however, that where something has happened in the period between the death and the date of assessment which makes the calculation more certain the event should be ignored. The court will not speculate when it knows. Thus, where there is a long delay between the death and the trial, and it is known that the dependant has survived for that period, this may result in a higher multiplier being applied to the calculation of the period of the dependency because the discount to be applied to allow for the uncertainty of the dependant's survival should be lower (*Corbett v Barking, Havering & Brentwood Health Authority* [1991] 1 All ER 498; this does not put a premium on delay in bringing a claim because the plaintiff may be penalised for delay by the court refusing to award interest on the damages: ibid.).

Section 3(3) of the Fatal Accidents Act 1976 provides that in assessing damages payable to a widow in respect of the death of her husband, her prospects of remarriage and even the fact of remarriage are not to be taken into account. This rule was introduced in 1971 in order that the courts would be relieved from having to make what were regarded as distasteful assessments of a widow's prospects of remarriage. It represents a departure, however, from the compensatory principle of damages, particularly where the widow has in fact remarried and is being supported by her new husband. She is compensated for a loss that she has patently not suffered. The rule also produces anomalies, in that the prospects of remarriage of a widower, a former spouse and a 'cohabitee' are taken into account, an exercise which, presumably, is no less distasteful to the courts. Moreover, even a widow's prospects of remarriage may have to be considered in relation to her children's loss of dependency (for alternative proposals see *Pearson*, vol. 1, paras. 409–16; *Atiyah*, pp. 115–16). In assessing a spouse's dependency, account will be taken of the possibility that a married couple would divorce, since what has to be valued is the dependant's expectation of continuing dependency on the deceased had he or she lived (*Owen v Martin* [1992] PIQR Q151, CA). Similarly, by s. 3(4), when the court is assessing the dependency of a cohabitee, the fact that the dependant had no enforceable right to financial support by the deceased must be taken into account. This will be reflected in a lower multiplier.

The dependant must prove a pecuniary loss resulting from the deceased's death, but need not prove that he had received an actual pecuniary advantage from the deceased prior to the death. A reasonable expectation of pecuniary benefit as of right, or otherwise, had the deceased lived will be sufficient (*Franklin v South Eastern Railway Co.* (1858) 3 H & N 211, 213). In *Taff Vale*

Railway Co. v *Jenkins* [1913] AC 1, for example, the deceased was a 16-year-old apprentice dressmaker who had not received any earnings before her death, but her parents established a reasonable likelihood that she would have conferred a pecuniary benefit on them in the future (see also *Kandalla* v *British European Airways Corporation* [1981] QB 158). But with young children the prospect of any pecuniary benefit will normally be too speculative (*Barnett* v *Cohen* [1921] 2 KB 46 1). The benefit must be the product of the relationship between the dependant and the deceased not, for example, due to a contractual obligation (*Malyon* v *Plummer* [1964] 1 QB 330). Where the deceased's earnings were obtained from 'moonlighting', whereby he did not disclose his earnings while drawing social security benefits at the full rate, his widow was not entitled to claim for loss of dependency under the Fatal Accidents Act 1976 (*Hunter* v *Butler, The Times,* 28 December 1995, CA). Such a claim was contrary to public policy because: (1) it assumed that someone who had committed fraud in the past would continue to do so in the future, ignoring the possibilities of repentance or detection; and (2) it treated the proceeds of illegally concealed earnings as a valid head of damages. To support a claim for loss of dependency under s. 3(1) the deceased's income must have been honestly earned or received (ibid. per Waite LJ).

The pecuniary advantage lost by the dependant need not be merely financial. The gratuitous domestic services given by a wife or mother have a monetary value which can be the subject of an award (*Regan* v *Williamson* [1976] 1 WLR 305). This will be assessed, not merely on the basis of the physical tasks that a mother would perform but taking account of the whole of a good mother's care of her family *Hay* v *Hughes* [1975] 1 All ER 257—in other words damages are not necessarily limited to the cost of hiring a housekeeper; see also *Mehmet* v *Perry* [1977] 2 All ER 529, where a father gave up his job to care for the children, and the damages were assessed as his loss of earnings). Conversely, where the deceased mother was unreliable and may not have been available to provide steady parental support had she lived, the dependant child's award should be discounted to allow for the real possibility that the mother would not have stayed with her family (*Stanley* v *Saddique* [1991] 1 All ER 529, in these circumstances the multiplier method of assessment will be inappropriate). When assessing the loss of a mother's services on the basis of the commercial cost of hiring a nanny to look after a child, damages will be reduced to take account of the fact that as a child gets older and becomes more independent he will be less in need of the services of a nanny (*Spittle* v *Bunney* [1988] 3 All ER 1031; see also *Corbett* v *Barking, Havering & Brentwood Health Authority* [1991] 1 All ER 498, 506 where Purchas LJ commented that taking the net wages of a notional nanny as the basis for estimating the loss of a mother's services was a crude and approximate instrument, acceptable only because there is no better method of quantifying the loss). In *K* v *JMP Co. Ltd* [1976] QB 85, where three illegitimate children were claiming in respect of their father's death, part of the award to the children included an element of their mother's financial loss, because this affected the mother's ability to provide for the children, and in this respect it constituted their loss. This may still be important where an unmarried mother does not qualify as a dependant under the Act.

Any benefits which have accrued or will or may accrue to any person from the deceased's estate or otherwise as a result of his death are disregarded (Fatal Accidents Act 1976, s. 4, as substituted by the Administration of Justice Act 1982, s. 3). Thus any insurance money, pension, social security benefits or inheritance from the deceased's estate (including any Law Reform (Miscellaneous Provisions) Act 1934 damages if the deceased survived for a time) are ignored in calculating the dependency. This makes for simplicity, even if in some cases dependants are undoubtedly in a better financial position as a result of the tort (see, e.g., *Pidduck* v *Eastern Scottish Omnibuses Ltd* [1990] 2 All ER 69, widow's allowance payable to plaintiff under the terms of her husband's pension scheme to be disregarded in calculating the loss of dependency, notwithstanding that before the husband's death her dependency was met, indirectly, from the husband's pension). 'Benefits' are not limited to direct pecuniary benefits, and so in assessing a child's loss of dependency following the death of his mother the fact that he will have a better home and receive a higher standard of motherly services from his stepmother than he would have received from his natural mother, had she lived, should be disregarded by virtue of s. 4 (*Stanley* v *Saddique* [1991] 1 All ER 529). In *Hayden* v *Hayden* [1992] 1 WLR 986 the defendant was the father of the infant plaintiff who was claiming in respect of the loss of her mother's services following a fatal car accident, and the defendant had given up work to look after the plaintiff. By a majority, the Court of Appeal held that the father's services were not a *benefit* which had accrued to the plaintiff as a result of the death, and so did not fall to be disregarded under s. 4; rather, they could be taken into account in determining the plaintiff's loss under s. 3(1). This appears to be inconsistent with the approach taken in *Stanley* v *Saddique,* or alternatively with the view taken in *Hay* v *Hughes* that gratuitous services provided by the dependant's grandmother should be disregarded on the basis that the services did not result from the death but the generosity of the grandmother. On the other hand, *Hayden* v *Hayden* appears to be consistent with the approach of the House of Lords in *Hunt* v *Severs* [1994] 2 All ER 385, para. 15.1.3.1 to the question of gratuitous services provided to a plaintiff by the tortfeasor in non-fatal accident cases, in that the cost of the services is not recoverable in damages from the tortfeasor (or, in reality his insurers). Since in practice the award of damages for the cost of caring for the plaintiff in these circumstances would probably fall into the 'family pool of income' the practical consequence of these cases is that it does not make financial sense for the tortfeasor to give up work to look after the plaintiff thereby giving up one source of income and effectively preventing the plaintiff from recovering another source of income (see further Kemp (1993) 109 LQR 173; Leech (1994) 144 NLJ 1438).

It will be recalled that the recovery of social security benefits does not apply to awards of damages under the Fatal Accidents Act 1976 (Social Security (Recovery of Benefits) Regulations 1997, reg. 2(2)(a); see para. 15.1.3.2.4).

Index

Abatement 335–6
  trespass to land and 445, 452
Abortion 538
Accident compensation 21–4
  delay 22
  no-fault 23–4
  social security 21, 23
  see also Compensation; Personal injuries
Accumulation 352–3
Act of God
  private nuisance defence 331
  Rylands v Fletcher defence 359
Advice as negligent statement 102–3
  gratuitous advice 114
Aftermath test 150, 152, 153, 156, 160
Agency 5–6
Aggravated damages 576–8
Airspace, trespass to land and 444–6
Animals
  abnormal characteristics 368–71
  Animals Act 367
  common law liability 366–7
  dangerous species 367–8
  defences 371–2
  dogs
    damage to livestock 373
    guard dogs 369, 370, 371
  keeper 368, 370
  livestock
    damage by dogs 373
    straying 372–3
  non-dangerous species 368–71
  remoteness of damage 374
  scienter action 366, 367
  straying onto highway 374
  vicious propensity to attack 369, 370
  warning notices 372
Appeasement 15–16
Apportionment 555–7

Architects, dangerous premises and 292–7
Arrest
  lawful see Lawful arrest
  unlawful 465
Assault and battery 455–60
  assault without battery 455
  battery without assault 456
  conditional threats 455
  consent no defence 469–70
  hostility 456
  intention 457
  molestation 456
  nervous shock 457–8
  passive smoking 456
  threatening words 455
  touching 456
Audits, reliance upon 104, 106–8

Bailees 389, 396
Barristers, immunity from duty of care
  63–8
Battery see Assault and battery
Bereavement damages 461, 464, 617
Bolam test 183–90, 207, 473
Breach of duty of care 172–200
  learner-drivers 173–4
  proof
    burden of proof 194–6
    res ipsa loquitur 196–200
  reasonable man 173–83
    common or general practice 181–3
    foreseeable harm see Risk
    objective standard 173–6
    unforeseeable harm 176
    see also Reasonable man
  risk see Risk
  special standards see Standards of care
Breach of statutory duty 399–415
  actionable, meaning of 400–1

Breach of statutory duty – *continued*
  causation 414
  class benefits 408–9
  defences 414–15
  intention of parliament 406–7
  particular damage 409–10
  public rights 409–10
  public utilities 410
  remedy
    common law 404–8
    statutory 401–4
  statutory negligence 410–13
  terms of statutory duty 413–14
Bright line rule
  economic loss 140
  nervous shock 160
British Medical Association 24
Builders 132, 143–4, 292–7
  original gone out of business 142
Buildings
  builder and 132, 143–4, 292–7
  complex structure hypothesis 133, 134,
    136–7
  defectively constructed 124
    foundations 128, 141, 142, 294
    insurance 141
    latent damage 126–7, 293, 566–72
  health or safety of occupants test 128,
    132–3
  imminent danger test 132–3, 134, 135
  mitigation of loss 143
  negligent inspection 48–9, 77, 78, 80,
    128, 132, 141–2, 294–5
  preventive damage claims 128, 132, 141
  structural and ancillary elements 137–8
  unfit for habitation 134
  see also Dangerous premises
Burden of proof
  breach of duty of care 194–6
  defective products 425–7, 438
  trespass to the person 454
'But for' test 201, 203–8, 209–10, 211
Bystanders 81, 147, 148, 150, 155, 169

Care *see* Breach of duty of care: Duty of care:
    Standards of care
Carelessness *see* Breach of duty of care
Case (trespass on the case) 10
Causation 201–37
  Bolam test 207
  breach of statutory duty 414
  'but for' test 201, 203–8, 209–10, 211
  common sense 222–3
  contributory negligence 225, 229,
    549–51, 556–7
  defective products 420–1, 437–8
  factual 203–22

Causation – *continued*
  failure to take precautions 211
  foreseeability and 228
  indeterminate part only of loss 212
  intervening acts 226–9
    by child 229
    by plaintiff 232–7
    by third parties 229–32
    classification of 228
    contributory negligence 229, 233
    criminal 231
    duty to prevent intervention 228
    foreseeability of 231–2
    reasonableness of 233
    rescuers 235
    special relationships 228
    suicide 234–5
  in law 222–37
  loss of chance 215–22
  material contribution to damage 212–13
  material increase in risk 210–11, 213–14
  proof of 206, 208–15
    occupational diseases 210–11,
      213–14
  remoteness of damage and 229
  successive sufficient causes 223–6
  vicissitudes argument 225–6
  see also Remoteness of damage
Chance loss 215–22
Charitable payments 601
Child protection agencies 41
Children
  abortion 538
  abuse 85
  allurement and dangerous premises
    267–8, 269–71, 278, 282, 287–8
  congenital defects 21, 58, 59, 170
  consent given by 472–3
  contributory negligence and 552–3
  dangerous premises 276, 287–8
  defendants 192–4
  duty of care to 58–9
  embryo care 58
  failure to supervise 193–4
  Gillick competence 472–3
  intervening act by 229
  limitation periods for 573
  local authorities and 85–6
  trespassers 269–71
  unborn 58, 538
  'wrongful life' action 42–3, 58, 170
Class benefits, breach of statutory duty
    408–9
Collateral benefits 597, 601–3
Collateral negligence 397–8
'Common benefit' defence 331
Common humanity duty 278, 284

Company accounts, reliance on   106–8
Compensation   1–2, 15–16, 20
  no-fault   10–11, 251
  transfer payment   1–2
  see also Accident compensation: Damages
Complex structure hypothesis   133, 134,
    136–7, 428–9
Concurrent liability   4–5, 7–9
Congenital disability   21, 58–9, 170
Consent
  by children   472–3
  Gillick competence   472–3
  induced by fraud or misrepresentation
    475
  not defence to criminal assault   469–70
  Rylands v Fletcher defence   358–9
  sporting contacts   469
  to medical examination or treatment
    470–4
    Gillick competence   472–3
    misrepresentation of risk   475–6
    unconscious patient   473
  to trespass to the person   466, 469–77
  under duress   474–5
Contract
  compared with tort   3–9
  concurrent liability   4–5, 7–9
  contributory negligence and actions in
    contract   545–9
  tortious liability and   4–5, 7–9
Contractual relationship   99–100
'Contractual structure' argument   131
Contribution between tortfeasors   557–9
Contributory negligence   225, 229, 233,
    262–3, 544–57
  actions in contract   545–9
  apportionment   555–7
  breach of statutory duty defence   414
  causation   549–51, 556–7
  culpability   556
  dangerous premises   278
  defective products   421–2, 439
  employers' defence   262–3
  hazardous activities   363
  imprudent borrowing   548
  Law Reform (Contributory Negligence)
    Act 1945   545–9
  negligent misstatement   546
  standards of care   551–5
    children   552–3
    emergency actions   555
    infirm or disabled   553
    workmen or employees   553–5
Criminal act defence   534–42
Criminal injuries   460–4
  bereavement damages   461, 464
  dependency loss   461

Criminal injuries – continued
  see also Criminal Injuries Compensation
    Scheme
Criminal Injuries Compensation Scheme
    12, 21, 24, 42, 225, 540
  administrative scheme   461–2
  payments   600
  statutory scheme   460, 462–3
Culpability   556

Damage
  latent see Latent damage
  mitigation of   247, 610–11
  particular damage   345–6, 409–10
  postponed   566
  private nuisance remedy   333
  remoteness of see Remoteness of damage
  severity of   179
  to property, damages for   606–8
  under Rylands v Fletcher   357–8
Damages   4, 574–612
  aggravated   576–8
  bereavement damages   461, 464, 617
  compensatory principle   574–5
  contemptuous   575
  for damage to property   606–8
    loss of use   606
    repair cost   607–8
  death and   617–20
  dependants' pecuniary loss   617–19
  exemplary   574, 576–82
  general   575–6
  Henderson v Henderson rule   582–3
  interest on   611–12
  joint defendants   580, 582
  joint plaintiffs   580
  lump sum principle   582–7, 588
  multipliers   592–5, 617–18, 619
  nominal   575
  periodical payments   587
  for personal injuries see Personal injuries
  private nuisance remedy   337
  provisional awards   585–6
  remarriage and   618
  single action   582–7
    continuing nuisance   583–4
    successive and distinct damage
      produced   584
  special   575–6, 588
  structural settlement   587
Dangerous premises   264–97
  absentee owners   266
  acceptance of risk   274–5, 288–9
  allurement   267–8, 269–71, 278, 282,
    287–8
  architects   292–7
  builders   292–7

Dangerous premises – *continued*
  children
    allurement   267–8, 269–71, 278, 282,
      287–8
    exclusion of liability   276
  common duty of care   269–74
  common humanity duty   278, 284
  complex structures   428–9
  contributory negligence   278
  defective products   428–9
  duty to non-visitor   282–8
    content of   284–8
  exclusion of liability   275–8, 289–90
  fences, state of   284
  implied licence   266–7
  independent contractors   272–3
    liability of non-occupiers to   290–1
  knowledge of danger   283
  landlords   291–2
  latent damage   293, 566–72
  liability of business   277
  liability of non-occupiers to entrants
    290–7
  liability of occupiers
    to other entrants   278–90
    to visitors   265–78
  necessary entrants   275
  occupiers defined   265–6
  Occupiers' Liability Act   279–90
  persons other than visitors defined
    280–2
  private right of way   280
  prohibition on entrance   275–6
  public right of way   268, 280–1, 282
  Scottish legislation   284–5
  skilled visitors   271–2
  statutory rights of entry   268
  third party entrants bound by contract
    277
  tolerance of repeated entry   267
  trespassers   267–8, 269–71, 276, 285–8
  Unfair Contract Terms Act   277–8
  visitors defined   266–8
  volenti non fit injuria   274–5, 278, 288–9
  warnings   273–4, 288
  see also Buildings
Dangerous things   352
Death   574
  the action   566, 616
  bereavement damages   461, 464
  damages   617–20
  dependants
    category of   616–17
    gratuitous domestic service   619
    losses   617–20
    pecuniary loss   617–19
  limitation periods   560–6

Death – *continued*
  remarriage possibility   618
  survival of actions   614–15
Deceit, duty of care and   90–2, 109
Defamation   26, 485–521
  broadcasting   496, 497, 498
  cause of action   488–99
  of class   495
  communication   495–8
  compensation to re-establish reputation
    486
  corporations   489
  deceased persons   488
  defamatory defined   489–93
  defences   499–519
    actuated by malice   518, 519–21
    fair comment *see* Fair comment defence
    innocently published   493–4
    privilege *see* Privilege
    truth (justification)   500–2
  deterrence   16–18
  employers' vicarious liability   489
  exemplary damages   578–9
  fast track procedure   487
  guilt, imputations and suspicions   491
  humorous caricature   489–90
  innocent dissemination or publication
    493–4, 496–7, 499, 500
  innuendo   490, 492–3, 501
  insult and abuse   489
  libel and slander   498–9
    difference between   488, 498
  malice   9, 114–15, 518, 519–21
  mechanical distributor   497
  negligent statements   114–15
  offer to make amends   494
  proper identification required   493
  publication   495–8
  reference to plaintiff   493–5
  slander
    actionable *per se*   488, 499
    tone of voice and emphasis   492
  suspicions   490–1
  trade unions   488
  unauthorised repetition   496
  unincorporated associations   488
  unintentional   493–4, 499
Defective products   416–41
  assemblers   419
  burden of proof   425–7, 438
  causation   420–1, 437–8
  common law   417–30
  complex structure exception   428–9
  continuing duty   425
  contributory negligence   421–2, 439
  dangerous premises   428–9
  defects   434–6

Defective products – *continued*
  defences   438–41
  defendants   432–3
    extension of range of   418–19
  development risks   439–41
  distributors   419
  drugs   426–7, 430
  European law   430, 440, 441
  importer   433
  intermediate inspection   419–20
  limitation periods   441
  manufacturers' duty   417–18
  misuse of product   435, 437–8
  plaintiffs   432
  producer   432–3
  products   418–19, 432, 433–4
  repairers   419
  side-effects   427
  statutory law   430–41
  strict liability   431
  suppliers   433
  types of loss   427–30, 436–7
  ultimate consumer   418
  warnings   422–4, 436
Defences
  breach of statutory duty   414–15
  contribution between tortfeasors   557–9
  contributory negligence *see* Contributory
    negligence
  damage by animals   371–2
  defamation *see* Defamation, defences
  defective products   438–41
  disclaimers   532–3
  employers' liability   261–3
    contributory negligence   262–3
    volenti non fit injuria   261–2
  ex turpi causa   534–42
  excluding liability   530–4
  fatal accidents   615–16
  illegality of plaintiff's act   534–42
  inevitable accident   542–3
  lawful arrest   477–80
  mistake   542
  necessity   543–4
  private nuisance *see* Nuisance, private
  self-defence   480–1
  self-help   535
  under *Rylands* v *Fletcher see Rylands* v
    Fletcher
  Unfair Contract Terms Act   531–2
  volenti non fit injuria see Volenti non fit
    injuria
  see also individual defences
Defensive practices   17–18, 39–40
  rescues   44
Delay, accident compensation   22
Dependency loss   617–20

Design, negligence in   194
Deterrence   1
  commercial or professional reputation
    16–18
  general deterrence   19
  publicity   18
  undermined by insurance   15, 17
Detrimental reliance   47–8, 49
Development risks   439–41
'Direct consequence' test   238–9
Disabled persons
  contributory negligence and   553
  limitation periods for   573
Disclaimers   112–14, 532–3
Disease
  natural and man-made   21
  occupational   208–11, 213–14
Driving offences
  disability of driver   174–5
  drunken drivers   56, 57
  incapacity to control   175
  L-driver standard of care   173–4, 188
  police chases   175, 536
  riding with drunken drivers   528–9
  seat belt wearing   549
Drugs   426–7, 430
Duty of care   25–171
  breach *see* Breach of duty of care
  control of land or dangerous things   56–7
  control over third parties   55–6
  dangerous premises   269–74
  excluded interests   43–57
  in fact and notional   36
  foreseeability   27, 32–5, 38, 45–6
  inadvertence   25
  just and reasonable   30, 31
  in legal proceedings   61–74
  neighbour principle   26–32, 151
  nervous shock *see* Nervous shock
  omissions *see* omissions
  police officers   68–70
  policy issues   36–43, 77–8
  proximity   28–9, 30, 32–5, 38, 115, 278
  reliance   82
  special relationships   54–5
  standards required *see* Standards of care
  tests for   29–32
  types of defendant   61–87
    barristers and solicitors   63–8
    judges   61–2
    magistrates   61–2
    statutory powers of authorities   70–87
    witnesses   62–3
  types of loss   87–171
    see also Economic loss
  types of plaintiff   57–61
    children   58–9, 85, 170

Duty of care – *continued*
  club members 59
  fellow participant in crime 59
  rescuers 59–61
  trespassers 58
  undertakings, voluntary 110–12
  unforeseeable plaintiff 35–6
  voluntary assumption of responsibility
    110–12, 117–18
  Wilberforce test 29, 30, 31

Easement, interference with 300, 309
Economic efficiency 18–20
Economic loss, acts 123–44
  acquisition of defective item 127–44
  'bright line' rule 140
  complex structure hypothesis 133, 134,
    136–7, 428–9
  contract and tort 140
  contractual structure argument 131
  damage to third parties' property 125–7
    latent damage 126–7
    repair expenses 126–7
    ships charterers 126
  defective buildings 124, 132–3, 140–2
    builder 132
    foundations 128, 141, 142, 294
    imminent danger test 132–3, 134, 135
    latent damage 126–7
    local authority 134–5, 140–3, 293,
      294–5
    'health or safety of occupants' test 128,
      132–3
  latent damage 126–7
  physical injury and 139–40
  preventive damage claims 128, 132, 141,
    428
  product liability for damage to product
    124
  professional liability 124, 125
Economic loss, statements 89–123
  deceit 90–2, 109
  misrepresentation 92
  negligent 88–9, 92–123, 124
    advice 102–3, 114
    causation 108–10
    disclaimers 112–14
    employment references 114–16
    mortgage surveys 105–6, 108, 112–13
    silence 100–2, 112
    social occasions 98–9
    special relationships 92, 93
    voluntary undertaking 110–12
    see also reliance
  reliance 88, 90, 103–8
    audits 104, 106–8
    company accounts 106–8

Economic loss, statements – *continued*
    presumed knowledge 103–5
    reasonable 88, 90, 93, 94–6
    third party 114–23
    valuation reports 105–6, 108, 112–13,
      608–10
Efficiency, economic 18–20
'Eggshell-skull' rule 239, 241, 244–6
  damages assessment 246
  eggshell personality 146, 149, 153, 245
Ejectment 450–1, 452
Embryo care 58
Emergency actions, contributory negligence
  and 555
Employees
  contributory negligence and 553–5
  see also Employers' *and* Vicarious liability
Employers' liability 4–5, 250–63
  common law duties 252–8
  competent staff 252, 253
  contributory negligence 262–3, 553–5
  defences 261–3
    contributory negligence 262–3, 553–5
    volenti non fit injuria 261–2
  health and safety at work 258–61
  industrial injuries scheme 251
  insurance 12
  negligent references 114–16
  pre-employment medical assessment
    116–17
  proper plant and equipment 254–5
  safe place of work 253–4
  safe system of work 255–8
  standard of care 252
  statutory duties 258–61
  see also Vicarious liability
Equitable remedy 3
Escape of dangerous things *see Rylands* v
    Fletcher
Ex turpi causa 59
Ex turpi causa defence 534–42
Exemplary damages 574, 576–82
  Law Commission considerations 581–2
Expectation
  of advantage 3
  loss 3

Fair comment defence
  comment and fact 516–17
  'fair' comment 515–16, 517–19
  malice or improper motives 518, 519–21
  matters of public interest 516
False imprisonment 464–8
  complete restraint 465
  exemplary damages 580
  knowledge of restraint 467
  lawful arrest defence 477–80

False imprisonment – *continued*
  lawfully detained person   467–8
  omission   466
  unlawful arrest   465
Falsehood, injurious or malicious   485
Fatal Accidents Act 1846   615–16
Faulks Committee   486–7, 499, 500, 501,
  518
Fault liability   9–11
  no-fault compensation   10–11, 251
Fire
  common law liability   363–5
  insurance claims   366
  negligence and private nuisance   365
  Rylands v *Fletcher* and   363–5
  statute   365–6
Fire service, public policy immunity   70–2
'Floodgates' principle   88
  nervous shock   151, 159, 166
Foreseeability   27, 32–5, 38, 46
  injury by shock   144–69
  of intervening acts   231–2
  of remoteness of damages   228, 238–9
  unforeseeable plaintiff   35–6
Fraud *see* Deceit
Funeral expenses   464
Future loss   569–70

Gillick competence   472–3
'Good Samaritan' legislation   48
Gratuitous domestic service   619

Harassment   459–60
Harm
  foreseeable *see* Risk
  remoteness of types of   241–3
  unforeseeable   176
Hazardous activities, independent
  contractors   395
Health and safety at work   258–61
'Health or safety of occupants' test   128,
  132–3
Hedley Byrne liability   6, 8, 9, 93–5
Highways   49–50
  duty of care   41
  omissions   49–50, 81
Hunter pronouncements   301–5, 317–20,
  458

Illegality defence   534–42
Inadvertence   17, 25
Independent contractors   533
  dangerous premises   272–3
  hazardous activities   395
  liability of non-occupiers to   290–1
  private nuisance and   322–3
  vicarious liability *see* Vicarious liability

Independent contractors – *continued*
  see also Rylands v *Fletcher*
Industrial injuries scheme   251
Inevitable accident defence   542–3
Infirm persons, contributory negligence and
  553
Injunctions   1, 612–14
  interlocutory   613–14
  mandatory   613
  private nuisance remedy   333–5, 337
  prohibitory   612
  quia timet   613
Injurious falsehood   485
Innuendo   490, 492–3, 501
Insurance
  building insurance   141
  compulsory   12–13
  damage to third parties' property   126
  deterrence undermined   15, 17
  employers' liability insurance   12
  fire   366
  first-party   11, 13–14
  loss distribution   14
  medical accidents   24
  MIB   12, 463, 464
  NHBC scheme   296–7
  no-claims discount   17
  personal accident insurance   601
  role of   11–15
  third party   11–13
Intention   9–10
  trespass to the person   454–5
  see also Recklessness
Interest on damages   611–12
Interlocutory injunctions   613–14
Internalisation of costs   18–19, 306
Intervening acts   57, 59–60
  by child   229
  by plaintiff   232–7
    reasonableness   233
    rescues *see* Rescuers
    suicide   234–5
  by third parties   229–32
  causation   226–9
  classification of   228
  criminal   231
  foreseeability of   231–2

Judges immunity   61–2
Jus tertii remedy   451
Just and reasonable requirement   43
Justice   15–16

Landlords
  dangerous premises and   291–2, 324–6
  private nuisance and
    authorisation of nuisance   324

Landlords – *continued*
  existing nuisance   324–5
  obligation to repair   325–6
  reservation of right to enter   325–6
  vicarious liability   396–7
Latent damage
  contingent liability to future loss   569–70
  dangerous premises   293
  defective premises   566–72
  15 years longstop   570, 571, 573
  limitation periods   566–72
  postponed damage   566
  'reasonable discoverability' test   567, 571
  starting date   570, 573
  to third parties' property   126–7
Law Reform (Contributory Negligence) Act
  1945   545–9
Lawful arrest   477–80
  arrestable offence   478
  grounds for suspicion   479
  reasonable force use   480
'Learned intermediary' rule   423, 424
Learner-drivers, standard of care   173–4,
  188
Legal proceedings, duty of care in   61–74
Liability
  concurrent   4–5, 7–9
  employers' *see* Employers' liability
  fault liability   9–11
  insurance *see* Insurance
  standard of
    private nuisance   336–9
    public nuisance   346–7
  see also Vicarious *and* Strict liability
Limitation period   454, 560–73
  court's discretion   564–5
  death   566
  defective products   441
  deliberate concealment   571, 572–3
  knowledge   562–4
  latent damage *see* Latent damage
  negligence of plaintiff's solicitors   565–6
  personal injuries   560–6
  persons under disability   573
  professional liability   569
Livestock *see* Animals
Local authorities
  children   85–6
  defective buildings and   134–5, 140–3,
    293, 294–5
  negligent inspection   48–9, 77, 78, 80,
    127, 132, 294–5
  planning permission and nuisance
    328–31
Locality rule   310, 332
Losses
  allocation and distribution   1, 20, 349

Losses – *continued*
  expectation loss   3
  'floodgates' principle   88
  of future earnings   3
  mitigation of   247, 610–11
  nervous shock   144–69
  other types of loss   170
  purely financial   4
  trade competition   170
  types of   87–171
  see also Economic loss, acts *and*
    statements: Personal injuries
Lost years   596–7, 615
'Lump sum' principle   582–7, 588

Magistrates, duty of care   61–2
Malice   9, 483–4
  defamation actuated by   518, 519–21
  malicious falsehood   485
  private nuisance and   313–14
  see also Malicious prosecution
Malicious falsehood   42
Malicious prosecution   42, 481–4
  damage type   484
  initiating proceedings   482
  malice defined   483–4
  malicious bankruptcy or insolvency
    proceedings   484
  no reasonable and probable cause   483
  prosecution ended in plaintiff's favour
    483
  see also Malice
Mandatory injunctions   613
Marriage
  loss of prospects by personal injury   604
  remarriage possibility after death of spouse
    618
Medical expenses   588–92
Medical profession
  consent   470–4
    Gillick competence   472–3
    misrepresentation of risk   475–6
    unconscious patient   473
  defensive practices   17–18, 39–40
  medical accident insurance   24
  pre-employment medical assessment
    116–17
  standards of care   183–90
    Bolam test   183–90, 473
Mentally handicapped
  limitation periods for   573
  medical consent given by   473–4
Mesne profits   451
Misrepresentation
  consent induced by   475
  duty of care and   92
Mistake defence   542

Mitigation of loss   247, 610–11
Mortgage surveys   105–6, 108, 112–13
Motor Insurance Bureau (MIB)   12, 463,
    464, 539
Multipliers   592–5, 617–18, 619

National House-Bulding Council insurance
    scheme   296–7
Necessity defence   361, 543–4
Negligence
    breach of duty see Breach of duty of care
    causation see Causation
    collateral   397–8
    contributory see Contributory negligence
    dangerous premises see Dangerous
        premises
    duty of care see Duty of care
    employers' liability see Employers' liability
    fire   365
    objective standard of care   11, 14
    private nuisance and   299, 317, 326, 336
    remoteness of damage see Remoteness of
        damage
    statutory   410–13
    trespass to the person and   454–5
    see also Defective products
Negligent misstatement, contributory
    negligence   546
Negligent statements see Economic loss,
    statements
Neighbour principle   26–32
    nervous shock   151
Nervous shock   87, 144–69, 242–3
    aftermath test   150, 152, 153, 156, 160
    assault and battery   457–8
    bright line rule   160
    bystanders   147, 148, 150, 155, 169
    communication of events   156–7
    distress and anguish   144–5
    eggshell personality   146, 149, 153, 245
    employment relationships   162–4
    false reports of death   164–5
    floodgates   151, 159, 166
    foreseeability of   144–69
    live broadcasts of events   152, 157, 169
    manner in which illness caused   157–68
    negligent statements   164–5
    neighbour principle   151
    ordinary fortitude   148–9, 150, 155,
        168
    personal injury and   604
    post-traumatic stress disorder   159
    primary victim   145, 146, 148, 149, 153,
        162, 165–6, 168
        categories   154
    proximity to accident   148, 150, 156, 169
    reasonable man   148

Nervous shock – continued
    relationship with accident victim   147–8,
        150, 152, 154–6, 167, 169
    remoteness of damage   151, 156, 169
    rescuer   147–8, 149, 151, 153, 154,
        160–2
    ricochet victims   147
    secondary victims   146, 148, 153, 164,
        165–6, 168–9
        duty of care   166–7
    'shocking event'   158–9, 169
NHS indemnity, vicarious liability   380
No-fault compensation   10–11, 251
Non-natural use   350, 353–7
Novus actus interveniens see Intervening acts
Nuisance   1, 26
    conduct/fairness dichotomy   299
    reasonableness and   298
    trespass and   443–4
    see also Nuisance, private and public
Nuisance, private   300–39
    abnormal sensitivity   311, 313
    acts of nature   324, 338–9
    constituents of   305–9
        intangible (amenity) damage   307,
            308–9
        interference with enjoyment of land
            308–9
        interference with servitudes   309
        personal discomfort   307
        physical damage   305–8
    defences
        act of God or third party   331
        coming to nuisance   332
        common benefit   331
        consent   331
        contribution of others   332–3
        ignorance   331
        ineffective   331–3
        prescription   326
        public benefit   332
        statutory authority   326–31
        volenti non fit injuria   331
    definition   300–5
    diminution in value of land   301–2
    discomfort   301, 302, 307
    distinguished from public   340
    duration of interference   311–12
    fire   365
    Hunter pronouncements   301–5, 317–20,
        458
    independent contractors   395–6
    isolated events   311–12
    locality rule   310, 332
    malice   313–14
    natural condition of land   314–17
        prevent or minimize risk   315–16

Nuisance, private – *continued*
  wealth of parties and 315–16
  natural use of land 316–17
  negligence and 299, 317, 326, 336
  persons able to sue 317–21
  persons liable 321–6
    creator of nuisance 321
    landlords 324–6
      authorisation of nuisance 324
      existing nuisance 324–5
      obligation to repair 325–6
      reservation of right to enter 325–6
    occupier of land 321–4
      acts of nature 324, 338–9
      independent contractors 322–3
      persons under his control 322
      predecessors in title 323
      trespassers 323
  planning permission and 328–31
  public benefit 312–13
  reasonable user 355–7
  reasonableness 298, 310
  remedies
    abatement 335–6
    damages 333, 337
    injunctions 333–5, 337
  smell 302
  standard of liability 336–9
    act/activity distinction 338–9
  'state of affairs' 311–12
  tort to land 301–2
  unreasonable user 309–17, 355–7
Nuisance, public 298, 339–47
  convenience 341–3
  dangers to the highway
    on the highway 343–4
    premises adjoining the highway 344–5
  definition 339–40
  distinguished from private 340
  independent contractors and 394–5
  obstruction of the highway 341–3
  particular damage 345–6, 409–10
  personal inconvenience 345–6
  public health 341
  public rights protected 341
  standard of liability 346–7

Occupational disability pension 601
Occupational diseases 208–11, 213–14
Occupiers of dangerous premises
  defined 265–6
  duty to non-visitors 282–8
  duty to other entrants 278–90
  duty to visitors 265–78
Occupiers' Liability Act
  dangerous premises and 279–90
  nuisance and 299–300

Ogden Tables 595
Omissions 43–57
  control of land or dangerous things 56–7
  control over third parties 55–6
  mere-omissions rule 44–7, 48, 75, 80, 82
  negligent statutory regulatory
    agencies 50–3
  non-rescue 44, 48
  pure-omissions rule 45, 47, 87
  special relationships 54–5
  undertakings 47–53

Particular damage
  breach of statutory duty 409–10
  public nuisance 345–6
Passive smoking 456
Pearson Commission 22, 23–4, 209, 251,
    349, 362–3, 553, 587, 588, 591, 606
  animals 366
Personal accident insurance 601
Personal injuries
  damages for 586, 588–606
  delay 22
  economic loss and 139–40
  fast track procedure 22
  leading to marriage breakup 590
  limitation periods 560–6
  loss of earning capacity 603–4
  loss of earnings
    actual loss 592
    collateral benefits 597, 601–3
    lost years 596–7, 615
    multipliers 592–5
    prospective loss 592–6
    redundancy 603
    social security benefits 597–601
    taxation effects 595–6
  loss of expectation of life 604
  loss of faculty and amenity 605–6
  lost years 596–7, 615
  marriage prospects 604
  medical and other expenses 588–92
  multi-track procedure 22
  nervous shock 604
  non-pecuniary loss 588
  pain and suffering 604
  pecuniary loss 588
  personality change 590
  to non-earner 590
  unconsciousness 604, 605, 606
  vaccine damage payments 600
  see also Accident compensation
Plaintiff
  contributory negligence *see* Contributory
    negligence
  duty of care *see* Duty of care, types of
    plaintiff

Personal injuries – *continued*
  Rylands v *Fletcher* and 357, 359
  unforeseeable 35–6
Planning permission, nuisance and 328–31
Police
  immunity from duty of care 68–70
  standard of care of drivers 175
  see also Lawful arrest
Post-traumatic stress disorder *see* Nervous
  shock
Preventive damage claims 128, 132, 141
  defective production 428
Privacy protection 459
Private nuisance *see* Nuisance, private
Privilege
  absolute privilege 502–3, 504–5
  'interest tests' 510
  judicial proceedings 504–6, 513
  newspapers 510–11
  official communications 506
  parliamentary proceedings 503–4
  privileged reports 513–15
    subject to explanation or contradiction
      514–15
    without explanation or contradiction
      513–14
  professional communications 505
  protection of an interest 511–12
  qualified privilege 505, 506–15
  statements in pursuance of duty 507–11
Privity of contract 27, 118, 128
Professional negligence 7–8
  Hedley Byrne liability 94–6
  limitation period 569
Profits à prendre 309
Prohibitory injunctions 612
Proof, burden of *see* Burden of proof
Proof of breach *see* Breach of duty of care,
  proof
Proof of causation *see* Causation
Property damage 606–8
  cost of repair 607–8
  loss of use 606
  negligently overvalued property 608–10
Proximity 28–30, 32–5, 38, 80–2, 115,
  278
Public authorities
  awards against 41
  defective buildings and local authority
    134–5, 140–3, 293, 294–5
  duty of care 70–87
  rescue function 44
  see also Buildings, negligent inspection
Public benefit, private nuisance and 332
Public nuisance *see* Nuisance, public
Public policy, duty of care and 36–43
Public rights of way 268, 280–1, 282

Public services
  policy and operational decisions 77–8
  proximity 80, 81, 82
  public policy immunity 70–2
Public utilities 410
Publicity 18

Quia timet injunctions 613

'Reasonable discoverability' test 567, 571
Reasonable man 32–3, 173–83
  common or general practice 181–3
  foreseeable harm *see* risk
  nervous shock 148
  objective standard 173–6
  risk 176–83
    likelihood of harm 177–9
    magnitude of 177–9
    practicability of precautions 180–1
    severity of damage 179
    social utility of defendant's activity
      179–80
  unforeseeable harm 176
Reasonableness, nuisance and 298, 310
Recklessness 9–10
  see also Intention
Redundancy 603
Referees
  employers, negligent 114–16
  sporting events 191–2
Relationships *see* Special relationships
Reliance 7–8, 82
  acts 129, 130, 131
  audits 104, 106–8
  company accounts 106–8
  detrimental 47–8, 49
  economic loss 88, 90, 93–6, 103–8,
    114–23, 129–31
  presumed knowledge 103–5
  reasonable 88, 90, 93, 94–6
  statements 103–8, 114–23
  third party 114–23
Remarriage, after death of spouse 618
Remedies
  breach of statutory duty
    common law 404–8
    statutory 401–4
  equitable remedy 3
  trespass to land 449–52
  see also individual remedies eg Injunctions
Remoteness of damage 4, 25, 234–49
  animals 374
  causation and 229
  direct consequence test 238–9
  directness 238–9
  eggshell skulls 239, 241, 244–6
  extent of harm 243–6

Remoteness of damage – *continued*
  foreseeability test   229, 238–9
  intentional torts   249
  manner of occurrence   239–41
  nervous shock and   151, 156, 169
  plaintiff's impecuniosity   246–7
  rescuers   241
  Rylands v *Fletcher*   361–2
  the *Wagon Mound*   237, 238–9, 245, 246,
    247–9
  types of harm   241–3
  see also Causation
Repairs
  damage to third parties' property   126–7
  damages for costs   607–8
  defective products   419
  nuisance and   325–6
Reputation   16–18
  compensation to re-establish   486
Res ipsa loquitur
  application   196–8
    carelessness needed   197
    cause unknown   197–8
    control   196–7
    outside interference   196
  effect of   198–200
Rescuers
  duty of care to   59–61
  intervening acts by   235
  nervous shock   147–8, 149, 151, 153,
    154, 162
  non-rescue   44, 48
  professionals   149, 160–4
  public authorities   44
  remoteness of damage to   241
  volenti non fit injuria no defence   525
Restitution   3
Restoration   3
Retribution   15
Right of way
  private   280, 309
    obstruction of   300
  public   268, 280–1, 282
Risk   176–83
  allocation, strict liability as   349
  likelihood of harm   177–9
  magnitude of   177–9
  practicability of precautions   180–1
  severity of damage   179
  social utility of defendant's activity
    179–80
  see also Harm
Rylands v *Fletcher*   331, 341, 349–63
  accumulation   352–3
  benefit to community   353, 354
  dangerous things   352
  defences   358–61

Rylands v *Fletcher* – *continued*
    act of God   359
    act of stranger   359–61, 364, 365
    consent   358–9
    necessity   361
    plaintiff's default   359
    statutory authority   361
  escape, meaning of   353
  future of rule in   362–3
  military use   354
  non-natural use   350, 353–7
  plaintiffs   357, 359
  remoteness of damage   361–2
  types of damage   357–8
  unreasonable user   355

Scienter action   366, 367
Self-defence defence   480–1
Self-sown seeds   352
Servitudes, interference with   309
Settlement, before judgment   558–9
Shipping, economic loss of   126
Shock *see* Nervous shock
Sick pay   602
Silence, as negligent statement   100–2, 112
Slander   488, 498–9
Social loss   1–2
Social security payments
  deduction from damages   14
  recoupment from tortfeasors   597–601
Solicitors
  immunity from duty of care   63–8
  negligence
    limitation period and   565–6
    will drafting   118–22
  professional negligence, limitation period
    569
Special relationships
  contractual relationship   99–100
  intervening acts and   228
  negligent statements   92, 93
  social occasions   98–9
Spectators   190, 529–30
Sporting events
  acceptance of risk   274–5
  consent to sporting contacts   469
  cricket ball damage   312
  referees   191–2
  spectators   190, 529–30
  standards of care   190–2
  volenti non fit injuria and   529–30
Stalking   459–60
Standard of liability
  private nuisance   336–9
  public nuisance   346–7
Standards of care   183–90
  Bolam test   183–90, 473

Standards of care – *continued*
  children as defendants   192–4
  contributory negligence *see* Contributory
      negligence
  design or product faults   194
  employers' liability   252
  medical opinion   185–6, 187
  professional   183–90
      common practice   186–7
      error of judgment   188
      responsible body of opinion   185–8
  skills of speciality   188–90
  sports   190–2
Statutory duties   70–87
  breach *see* Breach of statutory duty
  employers' liability   258–61
  inconsistency between statutory and
      common law duties   83–4
  omissions   50–3
  policy and operational decisions   77–8
  proximity   80, 81
  see also Buildings, negligent inspection
Statutory negligence   410–13
Statutory regulatory agencies, omissions by
      40–1
Stranger, act of stranger defence   359–61,
      364
Strict liability   10, 337, 348–98
  animals *see* Animals
  fire *see* Fire
  loss distribution mechanism   349
  Rylands v *Fletcher see Rylands* v *Fletcher*
Sub-agents   5–6
Subrogation right   14, 126, 391
Subsoil, trespass to land and   444–5
Suicide
  intervening action   234–5
  volenti non fit injuria   525, 537–8

Takeovers, reliance on company accounts
      107–8
Taxation, damages and   595–6
'Thin-skull' rule *see* 'Eggshell-skull' rule
Third parties
  act of stranger defence   359–61, 364
  control over   55–6
  intervening acts   229–32
  see also Insurance: Rescuers
Threats   455
Tort
  concurrent liability   4–5, 7–9
  contract compared with   3–9
  interests protected by   2
  objectives   15–20
      see also individual objectives eg
          Deterrence
  scope of   1–9

Tortfeasors
  more than one   557–9
  settlement before judgment   558–9
Trespass   26
  see also Trespass to land: Trespass to the
      person: Trespassers
Trespass on the case   10
Trespass to land
  abatement   445, 452
  damage   443
  ejectment   450–1, 452
  highways   446
  intention   442–3
  interference, the
      airspace   444–6
      subsoil   444–5
      types of trespass   444
  jus tertii   451
  justification   446–8
  licence   446–7
  mesne profits   451
  nature of action   442–4
  nuisance and   443–4
  persons able to sue   448–9
  possession   448–9
  re-entry   451–2
  remedies   449–52
  rights of entry   447–8
  trespass *ab initio*   448
Trespass to the person   453–84
  assault and battery *see* Assault and battery
  burden of proof   454
  criminal injuries   460–4
      bereavement damages   461, 464
      dependency loss   461
      see also Criminal Injuries Compensation
          Scheme
  defences
      consent *see* Consent
      lawful arrest   477–80
      self-defence   480–1
  false imprisonment   464–8
      complete restraint   465
      knowledge of restraint   467
      lawful arrest defence   477–80
      lawfully detained person   467–8
      unlawful arrest   465
  harassment   459–60
  intentional conduct   454–5
  malicious prosecution
      damage type   484
      initiating proceedings   482
      malice defined   483–4
      no reasonable and probable cause   483
      prosecution ended in plaintiff's favour
          483
  negligence and   454–5

Trespass to the person – *continued*
  privacy protection 459
Trespassers
  children 269–71
  common humanity duty to 278
  damage by animals to 371–2
  dangerous premises 267–8, 269–71,
    276, 285–8
  duty of care to 58
  private nuisance created by 323
  straying livestock 372–3

Unconscious patient, consent 473
Unconscious plaintiff, compensation 604,
    605, 606
Undertakings
  detrimental reliance 47–8, 49
  omissions 47–53
  voluntary, negligent statements and
    110–12
Unfair Contract Terms Act, defences
    531–2
Unfit for habitation 134
Unforeseeable plaintiff, duty of care 35–6
Unincorporated associations 59

Valuation reports 105–6, 108, 112–13,
    608–10
Vicarious liability 349, 374–91
  basis of liability 376
  course of employment 383–91
    criminal acts 388–91
    express prohibition 386–8
    'frolics of his own' 383–4
    implied and ostensible authority
      385–6
    meal breaks 384
    unauthorised lifts to passengers 386–7
  for defamation 489
  fraud of servant 390
  independent contractors 379, 391–8
    bailees 389, 396
    basic rule 391–2
    collateral negligence 397–8
    common law duties 394–7
    hazardous activities 395
    landlords 396–7

Vicarious liability – *continued*
    master and servant relationship 396
    primary liability 392–3
    private nuisance 395–6
    public nuisance 394–5
    statutory duties 393–4
    withdrawal of support 394
  justification for imposition 375–6
  landlords 396–7
  lending a servant 380–2
  master's indemnity 391
  NHS indemnity 380
  servant/employee definition 376–83
    allocation of financial risk 378
    degree of control 377–8
    integration within business 378
    intention of parties 377
  vehicle drivers 382–3
  see also Employers' liability
Vicissitudes argument 225–6
Visitors *see* Dangerous premises
Volenti non fit injuria 523–30
  agreement to waive claim 525–7
  breach of statutory duty 414
  dangerous premises 274–5, 278, 288–9
  drunken drivers 528–9
  employers' defence 261–2
  knowledge of nature and extent 527–8
  private nuisance defence 331
  rescue cases 525
  sporting events 529–30
  suicide 525, 537–8
  voluntary, meaning of 524–5
  see also Contributory negligence
Voluntary assumption of responsibility
    117–18, 124

Wagon Mound, The 237, 238–9, 245, 246,
    247–9, 336
Warning notices
  animals 372
  dangerous premises 273–4, 288
  defective products 422–4, 436
  learned intermediary 423, 424
Wilberforce test 29, 30, 31
Wills, negligence 118–23
'Wrongful life' claims 42–3, 58, 170